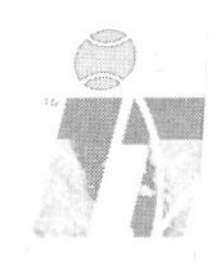

World of Tennis 1998

From the moment 16-year-old Martina Hingis cruised through the field in January to win the Australian Open, her first Grand Slam singles title, it was clear that a new age had dawned. The schoolgirls were on the march. At Wimbledon Russia's shapely Anna Kournikova, barely past her 16th birthday, was the centre of attention as she zoomed to the semi-finals, swept on her emotional way by a shoal of shrieking schoolboys. In between, the French had hailed a new champion in Iva Majoli, almost a pensioner at 19, but too good for Hingis in a magnificent final. At the US Open it was the 17-year-old black American Venus Williams who stole the headlines – and almost the title – when, unseeded, she gate-crashed the final and pushed Hingis to the limit. Not to be outdone, Venus's 16-year-old sister Serena achieved back-to-back wins over Mary Pierce and former world No.1 Monica Seles at the end of the year in Chicago. But it was the tournament wins in Bol and Strasbourg by Germany's Mirjana Lucic that really unnerved the older players. She was only 15.

While Pete Sampras remained firmly in control of the men's Grand Slam scene with wins in Australia and at Wimbledon, there were exciting new champions at the other two venues. In Paris it was noticeable that Gustavo Kuerten was smiling a lot. When he beat three former champions to win the French Open you understood why. Incredibly, this was the 20-year-old Brazilian's first-ever tournament win. In New York it was Australian heart-throb Patrick Rafter who triumphed. His capture of the US Open was the first by an Aussie since John Newcombe's success in 1973.

Yes, the 30th year of open tennis was certainly a colourful one and to mark this milestone *World of Tennis* introduces a 16-page colour section honouring those great players who captured the major honours during that period. In two accompanying features Richard Evans reminds us of the tumultuous events surrounding the introduction of open tennis in 1968 and Ronald Atkin picks out the highlights of the game's evolution since. In other features Peter Bodo reflects upon the reasons behind the phenomenal success of Hingis and John Barrett examines the significance of the building boom that has provided the sport with superb new facilities around the world.

With 32 extra pages, *World of Tennis 1998* gives comprehensive coverage of the great team competitions, the Davis Cup and the Fed Cup, plus details of the two professional Tours for men and women, and news of the events enjoyed by veterans, wheelchair players and juniors. More than 170 players are included in the expanded biographical section with full career details of the top ten men and women in all the major competitions. Lavishly illustrated with pictures from award-winning photographers Tommy Hindley and Michael Cole and others, these 544 pages contain something for everyone who loves tennis and marvels at its continuing growth.

SOMMER

World of Tennis 1998

Celebrating 30 years of Open Tennis

Edited by John Barrett
Compiled by Vicky Humphrys
Biographies by Christine Forrest

CollinsWillow
An Imprint of HarperCollins*Publishers*

Country abbreviations used in this book

AHO	Netherlands Antilles	FIN	Finland	NOR	Norway
ALG	Algeria	FRA	France	NZL	New Zealand
ANT	Antigua and Barbuda	GBR	Great Britain	OMA	Oman
ARG	Argentina	GEO	Georgia	PAC	Pacific Oceania
ARM	Armenia	GER	Germany	PAK	Pakistan
AUS	Australia	GHA	Ghana	PAN	Panama
AUT	Austria	GRE	Greece	PAR	Paraguay
AZE	Azerbaijan	GUA	Guatemala	PER	Peru
BAH	Bahamas	HAI	Haiti	PHI	Philippines
BAN	Bangladesh	HKG	Hong Kong	POL	Poland
BAR	Barbados	HON	Honduras	POR	Portugal
BEL	Belgium	HUN	Hungary	PUR	Puerto Rico
BEN	Benin	INA	Indonesia	QAT	Qatar
BER	Bermuda	IND	India	ROM	Romania
BIH	Bosnia/Herzegovina	IRI	Iran	RSA	South Africa
BLR	Belarus	IRL	Ireland	RUS	Russia
BOL	Bolivia	ISL	Iceland	SEN	Senegal
BOT	Botswana	ISR	Israel	SIN	Singapore
BRA	Brazil	ITA	Italy	SLO	Slovenia
BRN	Bahrain	JAM	Jamaica	SMR	San Marino
BRU	Brunei Darussalam	JOR	Jordan	SRI	Sri Lanka
BUL	Bulgaria	JPN	Japan	SUD	Sudan
CAN	Canada	KAZ	Kazakhstan	SUI	Switzerland
CGO	Congo	KEN	Kenya	SVK	Slovak Republic
CHI	Chile	KGZ	Kyrgyzstan	SWE	Sweden
CHN	People's Rep. of China	KOR	Korea, Republic	SYR	Syria
CIV	Cote d'Ivoire	KSA	Saudi Arabia	TGA	Tonga
CMR	Cameroon	KUW	Kuwait	THA	Thailand
COL	Colombia	LAT	Latvia	TJK	Tajikstan
CRC	Costa Rica	LBA	Libya	TKM	Turkimenistan
CRO	Croatia	LCA	St Lucia	TOG	Togo
CUB	Cuba	LIB	Lebanon	TPE	Chinese Taipei
CYP	Cyprus	LIE	Liechtenstein	TRI	Trinidad and Tobago
CZE	Czech Republic	LTU	Lithuania	TUN	Tunisia
DEN	Denmark	LUX	Luxembourg	TUR	Turkey
DJI	Dijbouti	MAD	Madagascar	UAE	United Arab Emirates
DOM	Dominican Republic	MAR	Morocco	UGA	Uganda
ECA	East Carribean States	MAS	Malaysia	UKR	Ukraine
ECU	Ecuador	MDA	Moldova, Republic	URU	Uruguay
EGY	Egypt	MEX	Mexico	USA	United States
ESA	El Salvador	MKD	Macedonia	UZB	Uzbekistan
ESP	Spain	MLT	Malta	VEN	Venezuela
EST	Estonia	MON	Monaco	YUG	Yugoslavia
ETH	Ethiopia	NED	Netherlands	ZAM	Zambia
FIJ	Fiji	NGR	Nigeria	ZIM	Zimbabwe

Cover photographs: (top) *Martina Hingis*; (below, left to right) *Ken Rosewall, Patrick Rafter, Margaret Court.* (Michael Cole)

Frontispiece: The balloons go up at Roland Garros to commemorate 100 years of women's tennis at the French Championships. (Michael Cole)

This edition published in 1998 by
CollinsWillow
an imprint of HarperCollins*Publishers*
London

A CIP catalogue record for this book is available from the British Library

ISBN 0 00 218824 4

Printed and bound in Great Britain by The Bath Press

Contents

Preface

Even an intelligent young man like Justin Gimelstob had no idea how or why it had happened all those years ago. It was over a light supper together in Hong Kong last year that I told the 20-year-old All-American from UCLA about the origins of open tennis in 1968 – historic events which are fully covered elsewhere in this anniversary volume.

Justin listened open mouthed as I unveiled the shamateur world of which we were all a part, told him about the under-the-counter payments, explained how no-one could travel abroad without the approval of their National Association – and then for only five weeks at a time. He found it difficult to understand why men like Pancho Gonzales, Rod Laver, Ken Rosewall and Tony Trabert, former amateur champions who had turned professional, had been ostracised by The Establishment as they held the ailing pro game together.

When I had finished, Justin looked at me earnestly and said 'We are very lucky today then, aren't we?' It was good that he understood where we have all come from and nice to know that he appreciated his good fortune to be part of an industry that, for the moment at least, is thriving. I have a feeling that Justin will no longer take today's riches for granted. Perhaps he will be moved to persuade his young contemporaries of the need to promote the game more widely at a time when professional tennis is in a life or death struggle with other sports and leisure pursuits for the attention of the public and the media.

These are the issues which dominate discussion among players, agents, administrators, tournament directors, television executives and sports editors. All parties have been wrestling with the need for change and the ATP Tour has bravely proposed for the year 2000 a radically restructured Tour which will unite the men's and women's games at seven leading events alongside the Grand Slams. In addition there will be two other tiers of separate men's and women's tournaments. The current computer points system will still be used for tournament entries but a points race, starting in January each year and ending in November, will decide the world rankings and determine who plays in a combined season-ending Championship.

This initiative is to be applauded because the public will at last understand how the game works. No-one pretends that it will be easy to reconcile the conflicting interests of all the interested parties in producing a final document. During the next two years the Grand Slams, the ITF, the ATP Tour, the WTA Tour, and the tournament directors must all work together on the small print.

The amateur game, by contrast, is thriving in those non-traditional areas where ITF coaching programmes are creating new opportunities. It is in the developed countries where interest is waning – particularly in Germany where the departure of Becker and Stich from the mainstream, plus the temporary disappearance of the injured Steffi Graf from tournaments, has affected the attitudes of TV companies. In the constant fight for air time, tennis is losing out.

The dependence upon star performers is apparent in every market. Pat Rafter captured more than the US Open title last September; he captured the imagination of the Australian public who had been without a Grand Slam champion for 10 years. As a result, people are flocking back to the courts Down Under.

When Gustavo Kuerten went home to Brazil after his French Open triumph, he discovered he was a national hero. Youngsters were rushing to buy the colourful clothing he promotes and dashing out to hit tennis balls in the streets instead of kicking footballs.

It is the same in Britain where they have been waiting even longer for a hero. The sudden successes of Greg Rusedski and Tim Henman in 1997 have already produced results. Sales of tennis equipment are buoyant, more column inches in the national dailies are being devoted to tennis and the TV companies are planning more tennis coverage than ever in 1998.

In the United States there are new initiatives by the USTA, in collaboration with the tennis industry and the teaching professionals, which aim to introduce 800,000 new players to the game over the next five years through an investment of $31 million. It is hoped to increase the number of frequent players in America by 20%. Such dynamic activity, mirrored by equally ambitious plans in other nations, should be effective in maintaining tennis at the forefront of world sport.

It has been a thrilling ride these last 30 years aboard the open tennis roller-coaster. As we soar out of the dip to new heights, let us all remember how lucky we are to be part of a sport that offers opportunities to all members of the family, whether ambitious young professionals or occasional amateurs, from the age of eight to eighty.

This great diversity is reflected within the pages of this 30th edition of *World of Tennis*. With 32 extra pages this year it has been possible to do full justice to all areas of the game. Alongside the Grand Slams, which are the cornerstones of the sport, the great team events – the Davis Cup, the Fed Cup, and now the Hopman Cup – arouse national emotions as no individual competition can. They are all fully reported, as are the two professional tours, plus the international junior game and the fast-expanding worlds of veterans tennis and wheelchair tennis.

I am, as usual, indebted to my colleagues in the press room for their expert contributions and on this anniversary occasion it is perhaps fitting to name them. As well as his customary review of the past year, Ron Atkin has reminded us of the highlights of the 30 years since open tennis began, a story which introduces our new colour section on that same theme.

Richard Evans reflects upon the painful process which led to that momentous decision in 1968 and also covers the extraordinary happenings at last year's French Open.

The scorching weeks at the Australian Open are expertly recalled by Alan Trengove while Bud Collins brings his inimitable yankee flavour to the events at Flushing Meadows.

John Parsons examines the details of another busy ATP Year and remembers the highlights of the Compaq Grand Slam Cup. He also reports on the women's season-ending Chase Championships while the main events of the WTA Tour as a whole are recalled by Barry Wood.

The climactic event of the men's Tour, the ATP Tour Championship, is brought into sharp focus by Barry Flatman, while Henry Wancke covers the two European Cup events.

In a thoughtful piece of analytical writing Peter Bodo reveals how and why the remarkable Martina Hingis goes on winning.

It is a pleasure once again to acknowledge the skills of our two award-winning photographers, Michael Cole and Tommy Hindley, who have provided most of the photographs.

Another vital member of the team is Roger Walker who, for the second year, has brought his design expertise to bear on our pages. The results speak for themselves. Roger's contribution, involving the cheerful acceptance of working through the Christmas period, has been immense.

There are others to thank. At the ITF, Vicky Humphrys has performed heroically in gathering together the myriad facts that populate these pages. Without her attention to detail – and her persuasive powers with colleagues – this volume could not have been produced in the time available.

Once again Christine Forrest has burnt the midnight oil to produce her carefully assembled biographies and I thank her for another painstaking job.

Equally important has been the contribution of the two professional bodies in providing statistics. At the ATP Tour Greg Sharko and Joe Lynch have been particularly helpful as have the entire WTA Tour team headed by Joe Favorito.

Finally I must thank Tom Whiting at Harper Collins for co-ordinating the entire project so that we are able to distribute first copies at the Australian Open. It has not been an easy task.

JOHN BARRETT
January 1998

Foreword

In 1968 tennis recognised the demand for professionalism and embraced the 'Open Era'. *World of Tennis* was published the following year as the *BP Yearbook of World Tennis* to record the happenings of that momentous period. This annual review under John Barrett's editorship has continued to record and highlight the achievements of the sport.

Tennis has come a long way in thirty years. In 1968, Rod Laver – who featured on the first cover of *World of Tennis* – received £2000 for winning Wimbledon. The US Open was still at the West Side Tennis Club in New York and the Australian Open at Kooyong – both grass court venues. In fact, Roland Garros was the only Grand Slam not played on grass. One of the biggest changes is the international reach of tennis. In the absence of official rankings, which did not exist until 1973, a comparison of the men's seedings at Wimbledon underlines the expansion of the game. In 1968, the 16 seeds were from six countries with Australia contributing seven. In 1997, the 16 seeds were from 14 countries with only the USA and Australia having more than one representative.

At the ITF we can take some of the credit for the 'internationalism' of tennis. The ITF Development Programme invests over $4 million per annum in programmes throughout the world. By helping with equipment distribution, the maintenance of facilities and by offering promising youngsters the opportunity of participating in tournaments in other countries through travel grants or places on the ITF Junior teams, the ITF has broadened the base of the tennis pyramid.

New programmes have been a huge success. One such example is the School Tennis Initiative, which was launched in January 1996 with the aim of exposing 6–12 year-olds to tennis through the school curricula, and which now embraces more than 100 nations and more than 500,000 children of that age group.

The International Tennis Federation and its responsibilities have also expanded considerably since the late 1960s. In 1968 there were 91 nations affiliated to the ITF (or ILTF as it was then) compared to the 196 members today. In the same year there were 49 nations competing in the Davis Cup; in 1998 there will be 131 nations participating in a competition which has become the largest annual team event in the world of sport. The Fed Cup has also flourished, growing from 23 nations 30 years ago to 99 in 1998.

Tennis has also come a long way during the last year. In 1997, the ITF Junior Circuit was enhanced by the addition of the Sunshine Cup and the Connolly Continental Cup. The International Wheelchair Tennis Federation became the first independent disabled sports federation to be fully integrated within an international governing body. The ITF has invested in the technical side of the game in order fully to monitor the impact of technical and commercial developments and has set up an equipment testing laboratory.

The ITF staff, which numbered one in 1968, has grown to eighty strong to enable us to administer this expanding game effectively. This has meant we have outgrown our Baron's Court headquarters and will be moving to new premises at the Bank of England Sports Ground in Roehampton, London in the Spring of 1998.

The world of tennis is therefore bigger and hopefully better than it was in 1968 and the *World of Tennis* yearbook has expanded to record this. John Barrett, CollinsWillow and the team here at the ITF have again worked hard to make this publication a definitive work of reference. I hope you find the book informative and useful.

BRIAN TOBIN
President, International Tennis Federation

Australia's Rod Laver, is the only player, man or woman, to win the Grand Slam twice – first as an amateur in 1962, again as a professional in 1969, one year after the introduction of open tennis. The red-headed Queenslander represents all that is best about our sport. Modest in victory, gracious in defeat, he set an example for young players that was eagerly followed by today's world No. 1, Pete Sampras. Despite being unable to compete in the major Championships for his five years as a professional between 1963 and 1967 Laver nevertheless accumulated 11 Grand Slam titles and would surely have won more if open tennis had arrived sooner. (Michael Cole)

Open Tennis – the Painful Birth

Richard Evans

It has been the best of times. And the worst of times? Yes, occasionally that, too, but looking back on thirty years of Open Tennis one can only marvel at what the game has achieved since that day at the West Hants Club in Bournemouth in May, 1968 when Mark Cox made history by becoming the first amateur ever to beat a professional – Pancho Gonzales, no less – in an officially recognized tournament.

It would be difficult for any of today's generation of players to understand what the game was like in that era of no ranking lists, no coaches and cheap hotels. More difficult still would it be to believe what kind of bickering, back-biting and outright confrontation it took to get Cox and Gonzales and their ilk onto the same court, hitting the same ball.

The resistance to the concept of allowing tennis players to compete against each other, regardless of whether or not they were being paid to do so, was nothing short of medieval. The high priests of the Inquisition could barely have stood their ground with more vitriolic fervour than did some of the reactionary amateur officials who brooded in clubhouse bars from Kooyong to Forest Hills, spluttering on about how they were never going to allow those terrible professionals to darken their doors.

The 'terrible professionals' – and worse phrases than that were used – were people like Lew Hoad, Rod Laver, Butch Buchholz, Barry MacKay and a quiet little chap with a sublime backhand called Ken Rosewall. It would have been difficult to find a nicer bunch of villains.

But reason went out of the window when the game's power brokers felt the wind of change threatening their status, their perks and their positions. I think I referred to them in my book *Open Tennis* as blinkered, blazered buffoons but some were worse than that. They represented a class of snob that was clinging desperately to all the unsupportable mores of their generation; the types that tried to run clubs and major amateur sports on the lines of the strictest officers mess where subalterns were barked at and non commissioned officers were never allowed through the door.

It was the kind of age when the Australian LTA, led by 'Big Bill' Edwards – a man irrevocably and vocally opposed to the whole concept of Open Tennis – would not allow its leading players out of the country without its permission and, once it had done so, would then send telegrams to the likes of Fred Stolle, Marty Mulligan, Bob Howe and Bob Hewitt, demanding a full report of their travelling expenses by a certain, imminent date or be faced with a demand to return home. This could happen at any moment of the year. No wonder Mulligan, Hewitt and a few others decided to leave for good.

The whole situation was insufferable, the politics often farcical. The first well supported move for Open Tennis had sprung up in 1960 when Jack Kramer began making an ever greater impact on the amateur game by signing up more and more leading players for his professional troupe. It was the year Britain's Mike Davies, Robert Haillet of France, the Spaniard Andres Gimeno and Kurt Nielsen, the Dane who twice reached the Wimbledon final unseeded, all turned professional.

At the ILTF meeting in Paris, the motion to bring in Open Tennis should have passed. However, three delegates known to favour the motion failed to vote. One was in the toilet, one had fallen asleep and a third was absent arranging the evening's dinner entertainment. Thus the required two-third's majority failed by the narrowest of margins and great players like Gonzales, Pancho Segura, Frank Sedgman, Tony Trabert and their colleagues were denied the chance to parade their talents at the great citadels of the world game for another eight years. For Gonzales it effectively ended his dream of winning Wimbledon and considerably reduced Rosewall's chances.

Nothing happened for a while as the visionaries fell back exhausted. But, by 1966, the forces of change, driven by the realities of the modern world that was turning with increasing interest to sport as a means of high profile entertainment, were at work again. A New Orleans promoter called Dave Dixon started signing players to pro terms and, although he soon bowed out, the Texas oil millionaire Lamar Hunt took over to create World Championship Tennis, an entity that was to become a major presence in the game for the next twenty years.

(Left) *Britain's Mark Cox, whose victories over former US champion Pancho Gonzales* (below left) *and Australia's Wimbledon champion Roy Emerson at Bournemouth in 1968 were the first by an amateur over former professionals.* (Michael Cole)

Even while John Newcombe, who won his first Wimbledon in 1967, Tony Roche, Cliff Drysdale and Nikki Pilic were leaving the amateur ranks to sign with WCT, a former US Davis Cup captain George McCall was picking up some leading members of the disintegrating Kramer tour. The game was being fragmented and those who genuinely feared for its future searched desperately for solutions.

A bold move was needed and when it came, the shock waves echoed around the sporting world. Without warning Wimbledon announced that an eight-man professional tournament would be held following the 1967 Championships as a prelude to an Open Championship in 1968. It was a sinister shot across the bows of the ILTF.

The man who had made the announcement was Herman David, the All England Club's fiery Welsh chairman. Within the confines of the world's most famous tennis club, it was said, his word was law. Of course he had the backing of his committee and, indeed, some enlightened leaders at the LTA a few miles away at Baron's Court. David's rationale was quite simple. His prime interest was to ensure that Wimbledon ran the very best tennis championships in the world and maintained the very highest standard of play. This, he decided, was impossible with so many players being lured away by professional contracts. The present situation, he said was '...a living lie.'

In the boardrooms of national Federations across the globe, the sound of tinkling drinks cabinets could be heard as dumbstruck officials reached for the strongest pick-me-ups they could find. Wimbledon is important and influential today. But in the sixties it far outranked any other tournament in the world. For the players and most of the sporting public Wimbledon WAS tennis. If the All England Club was going to be this radical, how could anyone resist the revolution?

The answer was: not many. But that did not stop several trying. Apart from Bill Edwards, who was fighting a rearguard action against many of his more progressively minded state associations in Australia, there were people like the USLTA stalwart Lawrence Baker who likened it to 'opening the temple to the money changers.' When Judge Robert Kelleher, who, fortuitously, happened to be USLTA President that year, pointed out that the game was already so awash with the hypocrisy of shamateurism that the money changers were already there but simply under cover, Baker shrugged and said, 'Oh, it isn't a perfect world.'

No, indeed. The level of hypocrisy was revealed in an article I wrote for the *London Evening News* in which I quoted the Italian No 1 Nikki Pietrangeli as admitting he had been paid by his Federation President, Giorgio de Stefani, to remain amateur. Obviously without shame, de Stefani then ignored the rich absurdity of his own position by publicly accusing the British LTA of all manner of crimes against the game – the wonderful, furtive 'amateur' game where top players like Roy Emerson and Manolo Santana were routinely being paid up to a $1,000 a week to play in 'amateur' tournaments.

Such criticism from Rome did not rattle the strong nerves at Baron's Court. The nation that had been responsible for creating the modern game of lawn tennis ensured the future prosperity of the sport by taking the Open Tennis crusade to the far corners of the earth. Derek Hardwick and Derek Penman of the LTA can claim to have seized on Herman David's initiative and, with the courageous support of Judge Kelleher, made Open Tennis happen. It was not easy.

First of all, Hardwick and Penman, along with their main ally Eaton Griffiths, had to convince their British colleagues that Open Tennis was the only answer for the future health of the game. With Hardwick lobbying as effectively as ever in the bars and corridors of Queen's Club next door, Penman laid it out in plain language in a speech he gave to the delegates at the LTA's Annual General Meeting on 14 December 1967.

'The first point I would like to make clear is that the main object of this resolution is not that we should have an Open Wimbledon but that we should remove sham and hypocrisy from the game....For too long now we have been governed by a set of amateur rules that are quite unenforceable.'

Penman was referring to the widespread practice of under the counter payments without which, as he put it, players could not live and tournaments could not survive.

The resolution was passed and, almost before the rest of the world had had time to assess the enormity of changes that were being proposed – the elimination of the distinction between amateurs and professionals – Hardwick and Penman set off on a round the world tour designed to drum up support for Britain's position.

After stops in Australia and New Zealand, where they had hardly been garlanded with flowers, the two Dereks arrived out of the clear blue Californian sky in San Diego where the USLTA was holding its AGM at the famous Coronado Hotel.

There Judge Kelleher had been trying to set in the motion the same kind of about turn in traditional thinking that the British had already achieved. He knew, however, that too many of his delegates were too firmly entrenched in their reactionary positions to move as far or as fast. He needed time to lobby and persuade before he laid down the stern resolution he had in mind. The two Dereks had turned up a little too soon for his liking.

'I knew they would be expressing powerful views and I was concerned that some of our delegates might be turned off by that approach,' Kelleher recalled. 'My first reaction was to get them the hell out of there so I hid them in a downtown hotel until I felt the mood was right for them to make an appearance.'

Kelleher's line of attack was more subtle. Knowing that the majority would shy away from the British stance of abolishing all distinctions between amateurs and professionals, he directed his strategy toward the evident incompetence of the ILTF to run the game in an orderly manner.

After being briefed by Hardwick and Penman on the reaction from Down Under, Kelleher rose to tell the meeting that he was laying down a resolution that would empower him to break away from the ILTF if necessary.

'This is not an empty threat,' he told the delegates, 'nor is it merely a vote saying we favour open tournaments....Our resolution directs me to say to the ILTF: "You have failed to promulgate and enforce realistic and practical amateur rules. Therefore the time has come to take away from the ILTF all but small responsibilities..."

This was strong stuff but it worked, largely because Britain was asking them to swallow an even larger pill. After the British resolution was unanimously voted down, Kelleher won an historic victory by getting the main resolution passed by 16 sections to one, a total of 102,064 votes to 9,978.

The scene then shifted to Paris and the offices of the Automobile Club on the Place de la Concorde where the ILTF had convened an emergency meeting. Before it got started Jean Borotra, the great 'Bounding Basque' who was then President of the French Federation swept into the lobby of the Hilton Hotel to have breakfast with Kelleher and his Vice President Alastair Martin. Desperate to find an alternative plan to Britain's frightening idea of making amateurs and professionals merely 'players', Borotra offered a compromise. This entailed creating three categories – 'amateurs' who could compete in open tournaments but could receive no money, 'authorized players' who would be allowed to accept prize money but would remain under the jurisdiction of the national associations, and 'professionals' under contract to professional promoters.

Although the British backed down eventually and accepted Borotra's plan that did not stop Hardwick denouncing the idea in typically forthright terms. 'The authorized player is the quintessence of hypocrisy,' he said. 'It is no cure for shamateurism.'

Hardwick was right. The authorized player was an anachronism at birth and died a couple of years later, having achieved little other than make Tom Okker a little richer by allowing him, as an authorized player, to accept the winner's prize money of $14,000 at Forest Hills in 1968 even though he had lost in the first ever US Open final to Arthur Ashe who was still an amateur.

In return for agreeing to the Borotra formula, the British got what they wanted – a recognition that Open Tennis would become reality and the right to call their own players whatever they wanted. It was a triumph for common sense, hard work and hard bargaining on the part of an enlightened few and the result, following the initial Open event at Bournemouth, was the dawning of a new age.

In Paris that spring, just two months after the final decision had been agreed across town, the tennis world congregated at Roland Garros in a state of relief and happiness. Pros like Gonzales, Segura, Hoad and Rosewall – banned from the very threshold in previous years – wandered around under the chestnut trees being greeted like long lost friends. The sense of well being was palpable. A heavy curtain that had partitioned the game had been pulled back and, like they sang in 'Hair', the rock musical of the year, it let the sunshine in.

Wimbledon 1968 was no less of a celebration. With the pros returning, there were 13 former champions in the field, nine men and four women. The title holder John Newcombe found himself seeded no higher than No 4. This was hardly surprising because Rod Laver was back, returning after a six year absence. On resuming his column in the *Daily Mirror* after a similar absence for the Second World War, the great journalist Cassandra began, 'As I was saying before I was so rudely interrupted...'

Laver felt the same way. Just as disdainful of the passing years, he swept through the new Open field like a king sweeping squatters from his castle. Tony Roche was the last to go but it

The two Dereks – Hardwick (above) *and Penman – who travelled the world to convince the doubters.* (Tommy Hindley & Michael Cole)

did not take Laver long – sixty minutes, in fact – for a final that was a mere exhibition of the popular Queenslander's extravagant skills.

Laver collected just £2,000 for his efforts but it was the start of a trickle of prize money that would turn into a veritable flood. In the thirty years that have elapsed since, no fewer than 219 male players have become millionaires from prize money alone; 41 of them earning a million dollars on court in a single calendar year. For those fighting for change in 1968, these were riches beyond imagining.

Although money should never be the criteria for sporting success, this kind of earning power has kept tennis in the forefront of world sports as the games people play turned into big business. But the cost, emotionally and politically as much as financially, was high. Four years after the advent of Open Tennis, the men players formed the Association of Tennis Professionals with Jack Kramer as their leader. Nine months later they boycotted Wimbledon as the ILTF made a final, fruitless bid to cling on to its fading influence. In 1973 the women followed suit by establishing the Women's Tennis Association. So the power struggles continued through the seventies and eighties until the advent of the newly styled ATP Tour in 1990.

But that is another story...

At 16½ the youngest-ever world No. 1, Martina Hingis ended her spectacular year with three Grand Slam titles – successes that earned her world-wide acclaim. (Tommy Hindley)

The Year in Review

Ronald Atkin

In Britain, the celebrations to baptise the fast-approaching new century have been dubbed The Millennium Experience. The understandable desire of all sporting organisations to flourish a new broom by way of greeting the year 2000 means that a proliferation of Millennium Experiences is guaranteed worldwide, certainly in tennis.

Mark Miles, Chief Executive Officer of the ATP Tour, has already put down a few markers which will, according to his organisation, 'restructure the game and make it easier for fans to follow,' though it has to be said a master plan to halt the drift of these fans away from all but the biggest events in tennis would also be useful.

Miles chose the 1997 ATP Tour World Championships in Hanover to lay out his organisation's Millennium intentions. There will be closer co-operation with the women's game, the sort of thing that this year saw the ATP and WTA's season-ending championships not clashing in the same week for a change. It is planned to have seven Top Tier tournaments – in place of the existing Mercedes Super Nine – 16 Second Tier events and the remainder classed as World Series Open Week tournaments. To guarantee high-quality fields, the proposal is to automatically enter all top players, if eligible, into the Grand Slams and the Top Tiers, and designate the leading men's 50 into four of the Second Tiers. The hope is to make all seven Top Tiers and the season's-end championships a men-and-women occasion, in the manner of Grand Slams. Just like the good old days, in fact, when places like Rome featured men's and women's tennis side by side, rather than in successive weeks as is currently the case.

Since supplanting the Masters in 1990 and moving from Madison Square Garden to Frankfurt, the ATP Tour Championship has been located in Germany, first in Frankfurt and for the past two years in Hanover. From 2000 the show will be taken on the road to a different location each year. 'To bring it to fans around the world' is the official reason, but there is also an implied recognition that with the passing from the scene of Germany's best two players, Boris Becker and Michael Stich, there would be an inevitable diminution of public interest in that country.

The inability of the public to understand the ranking system will also be addressed come the Millennium. The system will change to a calendar year race, in which all players start from 1 January with zero points and take it from there. The ranking of players will be calculated from the four Grand Slams, the seven Top Tiers and the seven best results from other tournaments.

The ATP Tour also promises to continue its calendar-coordination discussions with the ITF about the Davis Cup, to 'work closely' with the Grand Slams on scheduling and to become partners in a season-ending final. This would involve combining the ATP Tour Championships and the Compaq Grand Slam Cup. Such a proposal has to be welcomed as something which would help simplify the demanding and draining end to the calendar year which results in so many players falling victim to assorted injuries caused by playing too much, Pete Sampras being the annual prime example of this.

The Compaq event is already hard at work attempting to incorporate the women into its 16-strong Munich field in the near future, and is again seeking a new date. After seven years of playing the Grand Slam Cup in early December, the organisers moved it this year to late September, only to run into a deadly combination of perfect autumn weather and the Oktoberfest beer carnival which decimated attendances indoors at the Olympiahalle. Mid-October is the new mooted date.

But enough of Things To Come... 1997 provided quite enough drama and trauma for tennis to be coping with; 1997 was the Year of the Swiss Maid, Martina Hingis, who fell off a horse but still managed to come up with three Grand Slams and nine other titles, pocketing just under three and a half million dollars for her efforts; it was the year of a Davis Cup damp squib final as the heavy favourites, the USA, were routed 5–0 by Sweden in Gothenburg after losing Sampras injured in his opening singles rubber; it was the year of an astonishing disappearing act by Andre Agassi, former world number one, who by November could be located only with difficulty through binoculars down at 141 in the rankings; but above all it was another year when Sampras demonstrated his supreme and durable skills at the top of men's tennis and had people starting to praise him as the best player in the game's history.

Sampras finished the year as he started it, at the head of the rankings. He was the one constant in a shifting season which saw new names like Patrick Rafter, Greg Rusedski and Jonas Bjorkman vaulting into the top ten. It was the fifth straight year Sampras had finished as number one, a record matched only by Jimmy Connors from 1974–78.

Sampras celebrated his 200th week as the rankings leader – a total exceeded only by Ivan Lendl (270) and Connors (268) – by winning the ATP Tour Championship title for a fourth time. It was his eighth victory of the year in the 16 tournaments in which he competed. Sampras reached eight finals and won the lot, including two Grand Slams, the Australian Open and Wimbledon, the Compaq Grand Slam Cup and Mercedes Super 9 events in Cincinnati and Paris. He was, of course, suitably recompensed for his efforts, raking in just under six and a half million dollars in prize money.

The ATP Tour, celebrating its 25th anniversary, conducted a poll to nominate the best 25 players over those 25 years and Sampras came out on top, ahead of Bjorn Borg, John McEnroe, Connors and Lendl in that order. He was publicly acclaimed at the Compaq Grand Slam Cup prizegiving, where he became the first player ever to win that trophy twice, as 'the greatest player in the history of the game', to which he smilingly commented, 'I don't know about that.'

Michael Chang, who only lost his grip on the number two spot in the rankings at the last gasp of the season, was another flawless performer in finals, winning all five in which he competed. Elsewhere, however, the scenery was shifting. Tennis players themselves like nothing better than to tell you there has never been greater depth in their game, and the statistics prove them right. All four Grand Slams, for instance, featured an unseeded player and one, Roland Garros, produced an unheralded, unexpected as well as unseeded new champion in Brazil's Gustavo Kuerten.

At the Australian Open, Carlos Moya, the latest addition to the impressive Spanish Armada of players, knocked out defending champion Boris Becker in the first round and Chang in the semi-finals before falling in straight sets to Sampras. At 20 years of age, Moya suddenly found himself in the world's top ten, certainly a high note on which to prepare himself for the six months military service obligatory in his country. However, apart from having his flowing hair shorn to prescribed army length, little changed in Moya's tennis-playing life during the year. Spain was wise enough to let him get on with his real job of promoting the nation's sporting name.

At the French Open, carnage among the seeds was even greater. It was almost as if that capricious upsetter of the climate, El Nino, had decided to scatter tennis form to the winds. Six of the quarter-finalists were unseeded and included Belgium's Filip Dewulf, Morocco's Hicham Arazi, Galo Blanco of Spain, Magnus Norman of Sweden and the young Australian, Rafter, who was to take the US Open by storm. Norman celebrated his 21st birthday by ending Sampras's hopes of a first French title in the third round, but it was Kuerten who caught the eye in Paris. Coming into Roland Garros he had won only two of his nine matches on clay in 1997, had never been past the quarter-final of an ATP Tour event and was ranked 66th. Yet he defeated four of the world's best clay-court specialists, Thomas Muster, Andrei Medvedev, Yevgeny Kafelnikov and then, in the final, Sergi Bruguera to become only the third unseeded French Open champion after Marcel Bernard (1946) and Mats Wilander (1982).

Brazil went wild for its new hero from the beach resort of Florianopolis. A nation whose staple sporting diet has always been soccer saw a 40 per cent rise in the sale of tennis rackets in his home town a week after his triumph and Kuerten-type headbands in the national colours became the new fashion statement.

Sampras restored some sense of order to things by winning Wimbledon for a fourth time – the first American to do so – and marking up his tenth Grand Slam title, only two behind the all-time champion, Roy Emerson, and one in arrears of Borg and Rod Laver. But here, too, there was an unseeded finalist in the shape of Cedric Pioline, the first French player to reach a Wimbledon final since Yvon Petra in 1946. At 44 in the rankings, Pioline was the lowest-ranked Wimbledon finalist since Chris Lewis of New Zealand (91) lost to McEnroe in 1983.

The seismic upheavals continued at Flushing Meadows, with Sampras exiting in the fourth round to Petr Korda and Agassi's comeback bid halted at the same stage by Rafter, who went on to beat Chang in the semi-finals and then overcome yet another unseeded finalist, Greg Rusedski of Britain. Rusedski was the first Briton since Fred Perry in 1936 to get that far at the tournament, but the spotlight in New York was firmly on the bright new Aussie, the first Grand Slam champion from his country since Pat Cash at Wimbledon ten years earlier and the first to

Having narrowly failed to beat Pete Sampras at Wimbledon, the Czech left-hander Petr Korda dismissed the world No. 1 and defending champion from the US Open with a spectacular display of tennis and athleticism. (Michael Cole)

win the US Open since John Newcombe in 1973. That final in New York did wonders for both men. Rafter shot up immediately to number three spot in the rankings, while Rusedski moved to 11 and later broke into the top five, too, another first for a British player.

With the shining exceptions of Sampras and Chang and, to a lesser extent, Jim Courier, US men's tennis was in poor shape in 1997. Surgery to elbow and knee respectively sidelined Todd Martin and MaliVai Washington for much of the year, while Agassi's plummet down the rankings was astonishing. Injury and the distraction of marriage in April to the actress Brooke Shields left Agassi in the undignified position of having to seek points at Challenger tournaments in California and his home town of Las Vegas to lift his ranking.

Other big names passed into the shadows as Michael Stich reached the Wimbledon semi-finals and then abruptly implemented a decision announced earlier that he would be retiring in 1997. It was also Becker's final Wimbledon and, as it turned out, his last Grand Slam, since he missed the US Open because of the death of his manager and close friend, Axel Mayer-Wolden. Becker says he will still play an ocasional tournament but he has stepped off the rankings treadmill and instead taken over as Germany's Davis Cup captain from Nikki Pilic. Guy Forget, one of the heroes of France's Davis Cup triumphs in 1991 and 1996, also decided to make the season his final one.

Goran Ivanisevic, of course, blasted another 1,000 aces, but elsewhere the names were new – Rafter, Rusedski and the exciting Swede, Bjorkman, who won more matches (71) than

Sampras even played in 1997 and who ended the year at fourth in the rankings, having started it at 69. It was Bjorkman who was instrumental in pushing Sweden to their sixth Davis Cup victory. He won the opening singles against Chang in the Gothenburg final against the heavily-favoured Americans and then, after the calf injury which put Sampras out of the running, teamed with Nicklas Kulti to secure the doubles success which gave Sweden a winning margin, a margin they proceeded to extend to a humiliating whitewash.

France, the 1996 Davis Cup champions, had gone out in the first round of the 1997 competition, beaten 4–1 in Australia. But their captain, Yannick Noah, showed what an amazingly versatile fellow he is by taking charge of the French women's team which went on to win the KB Fed Cup for the first time, defeating the Netherlands 4–1 in the final. So, within the space of 12 months, Noah had captained France to victory in the two principal team competitions.

Elsewhere in the women's game, the irrepressible and bouncy Martina Hingis introduced a cheerful note into what was otherwise a rather sombre year. Hingis dominated, just as Sampras had dominated, winning three of the Grand Slams and losing in the final of the other, the French Open, when she ran out of steam following a return to tennis from a knee operation caused by that fall from a horse in April.

Hingis was the youngest winner at the Australian Open, the youngest this century at Wimbledon and was still just short of her 17th birthday when she captured her first US Open title. However, unlike the men's Grand Slams, Hingis defeated experienced opposition in Mary Pierce at the Australian Open and Jana Novotna at Wimbledon. The glorious exception to the rule came in New York, where the unseeded 17-year-old, Venus Williams, galloped into the final only to be summarily halted by the merciless accuracy of Hingis.

The eruption onto the professional scene of the much-heralded Williams, with her beaded hair and punishing ground strokes, helped to boost a tour which had suffered grievously from the absence of its long-time marquee name, Steffi Graf. The German, winner of all six Grand Slams in which she competed during 1995 and 1996, played only in the Australian and French Opens during 1997 and was beaten by the diminutive South African Amanda Coetzer in both. After Melbourne, Graf defaulted before her scheduled final of the Pan Pacific Open in Tokyo against Hingis because of a left knee injury which had been troubling her for some time and spent three and a half months on the sidelines before attempting a comeback at the German Open in Berlin, only to be routed 6–0 6–1 by her nemesis, Coetzer.

On 10 June Graf underwent surgery on the knee and missed the rest of the year. The women's game was lucky indeed to have a ready and talented new number one in Hingis to step into shoes she already seemed eminently capable of filling. The WTA Tour suffered two more body blows when its title sponsor, the computer software company Corel, decided in October not to renew its agreement after 1998 and its Chief Executive Officer, Anne Person Worcester, retired at the end of the year to be replaced by Ric Clarson who brings with him 15 years of marketing, public relations and administrative experience from the PGA Tour.

In Graf's absence, the 29-year-old Jana Novotna struck a blow for the 'oldies' by winning the season's-end Chase Championships at Madison Square Garden but, at 19, Iva Majoli, the French Open champion, was the oldest of the year's female Grand Slam champions. There was also another notable contribution from the Williams family in November when Serena, the 16-year-old sister of Venus and ranked 304 in the world, defeated Mary Pierce and Monica Seles in a Chicago indoor event.

The year was notable, too, for the important improvements brought into operation at Wimbledon and the US Open. Wimbledon opened its new No.1 Court and palatial new Broadcast Centre as part of its ongoing programme for the Millennium – that word again – while the Flushing Meadows scene was dramatically changed by the introduction of the new Arthur Ashe Stadium, a great arena named in honour of a great man. To nobody's surprise, both tournaments announced record crowds thanks to their stunning new facilities. Even the worst weather for years could not stop Wimbledon marking up a bigger attendance. What a contrast Wimbledon's rain was to the heatwave which caused the closure of the main stadium roof at the Australian Open and sparked a debate as fierce as the summer temperatures in Melbourne. Such is the ongoing merit of tennis, rain or shine, as a subject for discussion.

Sadly, the year marked the passing of several important figures in the sport: Wimbledon and US champions, Helen Wills Moody at the age of 92 and Helen Jacobs who was 88; Dr Axel Meyer-Wolden, Chairman of the Compaq Grand Slam Cup and manager of Boris Becker at 56; Pat Hughes, the British Davis Cup player (94) and Basil Hutchins, Chairman of the Wimbledon Lawn Tennis Museum and a vice-president of the All England Club at the age of 70.

Players of the Year

John Barrett

PETE SAMPRAS

With every passing year his stature grows. As a supreme exponent of his art he is approaching perfection. As a collector of major titles he is within reach of the all-time record. As an ambitious but dignified athlete he adds lustre to our sport.

That Pete Sampras does not receive the recognition he deserves is a gross injustice. Nowadays, it seems, champions are expected to be more than majestic match winners. Yet Rod Laver, the man whose gentle genius inspired the young Sampras as he watched tapes of the great man's matches, was not criticised for being undemonstrative. Bjorn Borg was not rejected for concealing his emotions on court. In those years we were content simply to admire greatness.

Yet, few have ever equalled the greatness Sampras showed at the key moments in 1997. His dismemberment of Thomas Muster's game in the semi-finals of the Australian Open was an act of clinical surgery. Sampras had timed his effort to perfection, as Carlos Moya then discovered in the final. It was the same at Wimbledon where Cedric Pioline was Pistol Pete's unfortunate victim in a final of brutal efficiency that, technically, gave the champion more satisfaction than any of his three previous titles there.

Another peak was reached at the year's end when the Grand Slam Cup for the second time and the ATP Tour Championship for the fourth were plundered by the 26-year-old American's powerful racket.

There were failures, too. At the French Open Sampras was once again denied a chance to complete his nap hand of Grand Slam titles. This time it was the young Swede Magnus Norman who exploited the world No.1's impatience. At the US Open Pete's title was snatched from his grasp by an inspired Petr Korda in a match of glorious invention and unbearable tension. It was almost a relief to discover that Sampras was human after all.

Yet as Pete completed his fifth year atop the world rankings, a feat previously achieved only by Jimmy Connors, there was no question about his place in the tennis universe. If, as seems likely, he soon passes Roy Emerson's total of twelve Grand Slam crowns and includes at least one French title among his haul, then we shall all acknowledge that he is the greatest of them all.

PATRICK RAFTER

It is his natural athleticism you notice first. Leaping for smashes, diving for volleys, racing for drop shots, Pat Rafter displays the precision and grace of a stalking panther leaping on his prey. From relative obscurity at the start of the year the 25-year-old Australian serve-and-volley expert leapt from No.62 in the rankings to a year-end No.2 on the back of some outstanding performances. None was more impressive than his run to the semi-finals of the French Open in June (the first Aussie to reach that round since Phil Dent in 1977) and the capture of the US Open in September.

That was the first Grand Slam title for an Australian since the other Pat, Mr Cash, had won at Wimbledon in 1987 and the first in New York since John Newcombe's success 14 years before that.

Yet success has not come easily. When Rafter rose from 301 to 21 in the rankings in 1994, it seemed that Australia had found the new champion they so desperately sought. But a series of career-threatening injuries in 1995 and '96 hampered his progress. They were setbacks that would have daunted a lesser man. It was here that support from his eight brothers and sisters made life easier to bear. Brother Geoff coaxed him back to form on court; brother Stephen managed his business affairs; sisters Teresa, Marie and Louise spoiled him as only sisters can.

Imagine the joy in the Rafter family when Patrick reached seven finals in 1997, winning that all-important one in America, and led Australia to the semi-finals of the Davis Cup. Their faith had been rewarded.

Now the hopes of a nation rest on Pat's broad young shoulders. He will not let them down – either as a player or as a man. Modest in victory, gracious in defeat he is still the same cheerful athlete who was voted the ATP Tour's Newcomer of the Year in 1993. He has come a long way since those days and has proved he can win on any surface. He has certainly won the admiration of his countrymen… and countrywomen. Yes, as his many female admirers will tell you, Patrick Rafter has got everything.

GUSTAVO KUERTEN

Was there ever a more spectacular debut? When the tall and rangy Brazilian Gustavo Kuerten, ranked 66 in the world, beat three former champions on his way to becoming last year's French Open champion it was his first ever tournament success on the main men's Tour. No wonder 'Guga' was smiling! No other Brazilian had ever been further than a quarter-final at one of the four Grand Slams.

With each successive upset – first over the 1995 champion Muster, then the reigning champion Kafelnikov and finally the 1993 and '94 winner Bruguera – the colourful, noisy Brazilian fans grew more and more enthusiastic. Gugamania, as Kuerten cheerfully acknowledged afterwards, was one of his strongest weapons.

Not as powerful, though, as Guga's blazing forehands and lethal down-the-line backhands that blasted holes in enemy defences. All opponents found themselves helpless against the savage onslaught. Winners flowed from Kuerten's racket as fast as the wine from the many celebratory bottles of champagne that were raised to Brazilian lips. For one glorious day in June it was fiesta time in Paris.

Humble in victory, Guga dedicated his win to his coach, Larri Passos, who had become a second father to Gustavo when his own father had died years before while umpiring a junior tennis match. How proud his dad would have been to follow the unfolding saga that had prompted Brazil's Minister of Sport, the famous footballer Pele, to send personal messages of encouragement. The story of Guga's improbable but thoroughly deserved success will inspire hopeful young sportsmen everywhere.

MARTINA HINGIS

In a year of unparalleled success Martina Hingis rewrote the record books. Early in September at the new Arthur Ashe Stadium in New York, just three weeks before her 17th birthday, the Czech-born Swiss Miss claimed her third Grand Slam title of 1997. No-one so young had ever achieved as much.

Already Martina had become the youngest-ever player to be ranked No.1 in the world. She had achieved that feat aged 16 years, 6 months and 1 day when she destroyed Monica Seles in the Lipton final on 30 March during her winning run of 37 matches that brought her six of the twelve titles she would eventually win in 1997. Her first defeat came in the final of the French Open. Fatigue following a long losing women's doubles semi-final the evening before, plus lack of match play, at last caught up with her.

That Martina had played in Paris at all was remarkable. Late in April she had undergone arthroscopic surgery on her left knee which had been injured in a riding accident. Yet with no competition for seven weeks and minimal practice she had resumed her winning ways as if nothing had happened.

That is the measure of this remarkable young woman. Named by her Czech mother, Melanie, after Martina Navratilova and schooled from the first to expect victory, the young Martina goes for her shots with refreshing confidence. Technically she has no blemishes. Able to time the ball with split second precision she takes the ball on the rise and controls the racket face cleverly to project the ball to unusual angles. A good server and a fine natural volleyer, she is as happy at the net as on the baseline. Add to this an uncanny sense of anticipation and a natural match player's ability to find the right shot at the right time and you have some idea of the prodigious nature of her talent.

It was hardly surprising that in the closing stages of her momentous year Martina seemed to run out of mental and physical energy. There was the suspicion that she had played too much. Yet in achieving so much and losing only five times Martina Hingis was outstandingly THE player of the year. For as long as the game is played it is doubtful whether anyone so young will ever match her.

IVA MAJOLI

She describes herself as someone with a lot of energy. She needed plenty in Paris last year. And nerve. For 19-year-old Iva Majoli the situation was normal. It was just another of life's struggles – like trying to get recognition for her talents at home in Zagreb, or trying to adjust to life at Nick Bollettieri's Academy in Florida, where she first went as a 12-year-old.

(Right) *Pete Sampras, supreme at the top of the men's game.* (Stephen Wake)

Martina Hingis reaches new heights with three Grand Slam wins from four finals. (Tommy Hindley)

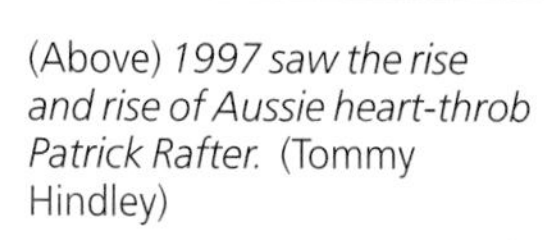

(Above) *1997 saw the rise and rise of Aussie heart-throb Patrick Rafter.* (Tommy Hindley)

(Right) *One of Gustavo Kuerten's killer blows that brought him the French Open title in Paris.* (Michael Cole)

(Above) *Iva Majoli surprises in Paris, while Jana Novotna (right) captures a major title at last.* (Tommy Hindley & Stephen Wake)

In Iva's mind Davenport should not have been leading 7–5 4–0 in their fourth round match at the French Open. It was her own loose shots as much as the American's winners that had produced that scoreline. So, what to do? Hit your way out of trouble, of course, like Monica Seles used to, the player whose game Majoli's so much resembles. And that is just what she did. Reeling off 12 of the next 14 games she turned the match round 5–7 6–4 6–2.

When Iva beat Dragomir in the quarters she was sailing in uncharted Grand Slam waters. A narrow win over Coetzer put her in a Grand Slam final for the first time and a match against the all-conquering Hingis. How would Iva respond? Magnificently, is the answer.

Seldom has the Centre Court at Roland Garros seen such driving. Both young women were going relentlessly for the lines – and often hitting them. The ability to change the pace and direction suddenly and unexpectedly brought Majoli the first set 6–4. Against a dispirited opponent whose long second set bathroom break might have been tactical, Majoli remained rock solid. An eight-game second set brought her the title and the recognition of her peers who had voted her the Most Improved Newcomer back in 1993. In 1977 she was certainly an outstanding Player of the Year.

JANA NOVOTNA

At last. When Jana Novotna scored the winning point to beat Mary Pierce for the Chase Championships last November she leapt high in the air and turned in triumph to her coach, Hana Mandlikova. Novotna was doing much more than win a first major title. Besides cementing her place at No.2 in the world rankings, a new career high, she was laying the ghosts of finals past where mental frailty had been her undoing. At the age of 29 she was also proving the truth of the old adage '...if at first you don't succeed...'

Jana has been trying so hard for so long that even her staunchest supporters were beginning to despair. Would there ever be the chance for this popular athlete to celebrate a major triumph? In the Wimbledon final last year, when she had taken the first set from Hingis, there seemed a real chance of atoning for the 1993 loss to Steffi Graf when Jana had led 4–1 in the final set. But Hingis had raised her game and consigned Jana's dreams to the wish-lists of history. No disgrace there.

That is why the Chase final was so important. When the chips were down Jana did not falter. In fact she flourished. On the crest of an emotional wave after beating Pierce in straight sets, Jana then teamed with Davenport to win the doubles. It was as if the fickle fates were making up for past cruelties.

With three other tournament successes to her name in '97 Novotna was certainly one of the year's best players. Her name deserves to rank with others in the book of champions. If her abundant natural talents are now injected with a large dose of confidence there is even the possibility of a thrilling final chapter.

Major ITF Events

The ITF Year • Davis Cup by NEC • KB Fed Cup
Hopman Cup • ITF Sunshine Cup
ITF Connolly Continental Cup • NEC World Youth Cup
World Junior Tennis • The Junior Spotlight

Yannick Noah, here inspiring his French Fed Cup players during the 1997 final, is the only Fed Cup captain who has also captained winning Davis Cup teams (1991 and 1996). (Paul Zimmer)

Three young players who made their marks in 1997:

(Top) *The American Venus Williams, 17, who reached the US Open final unseeded.* (Stephen Wake)

(Above) *Hicham Arazi of Morocco who spectacularly upset 7th seeded Marcelo Rios in Paris.* (Michael Cole)

(Right) *The precocious Russian, 16-year-old Anna Kournikova , a semi-finalist at Wimbledon.* (Tommy Hindley)

The ITF Year

Wendy Kewley

In 1997, youth took centre-stage in the ITF tennis year as 16-year-old Martina Hingis captured three Grand Slam titles, while Brazil's Gustavo Kuerten, 20, a former member of the ITF Latin American Junior team, emerged as a surprise winner at Roland Garros.

The ITF's junior and development programmes enjoyed unprecedented success in their quest to nurture the champions of tomorrow, with Morocco's Hicham Arazi reaching the quarter-finals in Paris.

The Grand Slams continued to improve their facilities. As part of its plan to take Wimbledon into the 21st century, the All England Club unveiled a spectacular new No. 1 Court and broadcast centre. The new 23,000-seater Arthur Ashe stadium at the US Open formed a stunning focal point to the final Grand Slam of the year where Australia's Patrick Rafter claimed his first Grand Slam title.

Held in mid-September for the first time, the Compaq Grand Slam Cup was tinged with sadness following the premature death of tournament director Dr Axel Meyer-Wolden a month before. On court, Sampras displayed his artistry to lift the mood and title with victory over Rafter in the first Munich final to feature two reigning Grand Slam champions.

The sport's leading team competitions, the Davis Cup by NEC and the KB Fed Cup, continue to embrace more nations every year. The Davis Cup attracted a record 127 countries and was enjoyed by over 400,000 spectators worldwide while a record 98 nations competed in the Fed Cup. After their narrow defeat at the hands of France in last year's Davis Cup Final, Sweden finally brought home the trophy with a 5–0 triumph over USA at Gothenburg, Sweden. In the Fed Cup, the French women won the title for the first time after outplaying the Netherlands 4–1 in front of a capacity crowd at 's-Hertogenbosch, the Netherlands.

In the Hopman Cup, USA defeated South Africa 2–1 in the final. Held in Perth, Australia, this eight-nation mixed-team championship was sanctioned as an international event for the first time by the ITF and attracted record crowds of over 75,000 during the seven days. From 1998 the event will be sponsored by Hyundai.

In 1997, the ITF extended its commitment to developing tennis worldwide. The Grand Slam Development Fund enabled 148 players from 62 countries to participate on ITF junior teams, giving youngsters the chance to gain tournament experience outside their own region under the guidance of an ITF coach. Current ITF team members were extremely successful, capturing seven out of ten junior Grand Slam finals reached in 1997. At Roland Garros, former ITF members reached the final of six out of nine events in the junior and senior categories and had victories in the men's singles and mixed doubles.

Although committed to helping gifted players fulfil their potential on court, the ITF also aims to introduce as many people as possible to the game. The ITF's grass roots campaign also involves the School Tennis Initiative (STI) which has introduced 650,000 children from 79 developing tennis nations to the game since its launch in 1996. The ITF continues to devote $4 million a year to promoting tennis, $2 million of which comes from the Grand Slam Development Fund.

In 1997, the ITF also extended its influence in junior tennis when it added the prestigious 18 & Under international team championships, the ITF Sunshine Cup for boys and the ITF Connolly Continental Cup for girls, to its portfolio of junior team competitions. Held in Florida, both events form the middle leg of three US-based ITF junior world ranking tournaments along with the Orange Bowl and Eddie Herr Junior International.

The Canadian city of Vancouver provided the setting for the 13th NEC World Youth Cup for 16 & Under juniors in September. The Czech Republic won the boys' category and Russia the girls'. In the seventh 14 & Under World Junior Tennis final held in Nagoya, Japan, the South African boys prevailed and Russia again triumphed in the girls' competition.

While a healthy junior game augurs well for the sport's future, players must be able to progress to the senior ranks with ease. To this end, the ITF's Women's Circuit set up the Junior Exempt Project. At the year-end, the top ten girls on the ITF Junior World Ranking are given the chance to select two events on the ITF Women's Circuit Calendar. They are then given a place in the main draw of a tournament, the category depending upon their year-end ranking.

In addition, the ITF Women's Circuit, in association with the Corel WTA Tour, offers the winner or finalist of most $50,000 and $75,000 events a feed-up spot in the main draw of a COREL WTA TOUR Tier III or Tier IV event. The winners or finalists of selected $25,000 events are offered places in the Qualifying Draws of COREL WTA TOUR Tier III or Tier IV events. The programme provides a path through which talented players can better their ranking. After winning the $75,000 ITF Women's Circuit event in Colombia in February, 19-year-old Corina Morariu gained direct entry into the main draw of the Croatian Bol Ladies Open by virtue of the Feed-Up system. Morariu then reached the final in Croatia, pushing her ranking up nearly 40 places to 91 in the world. In 1997, 277 ITF Women's Circuit events were scheduled in 65 countries, offering total prize money of $4,840,000.

The ITF also organised 112 four-week men's Satellite events in nearly 60 countries, providing 448 weeks of professional tennis. A new category of tournaments, single week Futures, will be introduced in 1998 in order to create greater opportunities for aspiring male players.

Tennis is truly a sport for all ages as the popularity of the ITF Veterans competitions demonstrate. The 17th ITF Veteran World Championships and Team Competitions took place in Australia and New Zealand with over 400 players from 25 nations competing in 20 Championship events. Several former Davis Cup and Fed Cup players entered. However, the prize for the oldest competitor in the draw went to Arthur Matthews, who was competing at the tender age of 86. The American teams were dominant on court, retaining five of the events, while their Connolly Cup team defeated France, holders from the previous two years.

The younger age categories for veterans in the Team and Individual Team Competitions were held in South Africa. Eighty-nine teams totalling 286 players from 27 countries participated in the Italia, Dubler, Fred Perry, Young, Margaret Court and Maria Esther Bueno Cups in Johannesburg, Pretoria and Sun City. Three hundred players entered the World Championships during the following week. The competitions attracted many former top players, including Spain's Jairo Velasco, Great Britain's Jeremy Bates and Renata Vojtischeck (nee Tomanova Roth).

To cater for growth, the ITF has launched a new team competition in 1998 for the ladies 70-age category. The trophy will be donated by the USTA and named after Althea Gibson.

Nineteen-ninety-seven proved to be a significant year for wheelchair tennis. It was agreed that the International Wheelchair Tennis Federation (IWTF) would become assimilated into the ITF in the same manner as the other sectors of the game, with its own department and committee. As a result, wheelchair tennis becomes the first disabled sport to be fully governed by its able-bodied counterpart. Wheelchair tennis was also blessed with the exuberant Yannick Noah when France's Davis Cup and Fed Cup captain agreed to become the sport's first patron.

A record 32 nations attended the Action World Team Cup, held in Nottingham, UK, where the top-seeded USA and Netherlands claimed the men's and women's titles, respectively. It was the Americans' ninth success and an impressive 11th for the Dutch women. The year-end NEC Wheelchair Tennis Masters produced several closely fought matches with both finals stretching to three sets. In an all-Dutch women's final, Maaike Smit defeated Monique Kalkman while in the men's draw Germany's Kai Schrameyer defeated Stephen Welch of the USA.

On the administrative side, in June a record 106 of the ITF's 196 member nations travelled to Egypt to attend the AGM where a new Committee of Management was elected. Three new appointments were made: Julia Levering and Harry Marmion of the USTA and Ismail El Shafei of Egypt. Amongst other issues, the AGM discussed the Sydney 2000 Olympic tennis event and decided to retain the current format for the team and individual categories.

A unified ITF/ATP TOUR and WTA TOUR Anti-Doping Program provides standard year-round drug testing and regulatory procedures. Also designed to provide drugs education within the game, the Program has conducted over 1000 random anti-doping tests during the year.

It was also gratifying to witness one of the ITF's most committed sponsors, NEC, extending its title sponsorship of the ITF's flagship competition, the Davis Cup, through to the end of 2001. NEC is also a generous supporter of junior and wheelchair tennis and has agreed to continue its sponsorship in both areas through to 2001. Since 1988, the Japanese electronics and communications company has sponsored the 16 & Under team competition, the World Youth Cup, and in 1992 it helped to establish the NEC International Wheelchair Tennis Tour and the NEC Wheelchair Tennis Ranking System.

Finally, Belgium's Fed Cup captain Steve Martens and Spain's Davis Cup captain Manolo Santana were awarded the Opel/ITF Fair Play Award on behalf of their respective Federations, in recognition of their sportsmanship in both team competitions. The ITF Philippe Chatrier Award, given for outstanding services to the game, went to Chris Evert while, as the best performing male player in the Grand Slams, Pete Sampras was honoured with the Fred Perry Award.

ITF WORLD CHAMPIONS

SINGLES

	Men	***Women***
1978	Bjorn Borg	Chris Evert
1979	Bjorn Borg	Martina Navratilova
1980	Bjorn Borg	Chris Evert
1981	John McEnroe	Chris Evert
1982	Jimmy Connors	Martina Navratilova
1983	John McEnroe	Martina Navratilova
1984	John McEnroe	Martina Navratilova
1985	Ivan Lendl	Martina Navratilova
1986	Ivan Lendl	Martina Navratilova
1987	Ivan Lendl	Steffi Graf
1988	Mats Wilander	Steffi Graf
1989	Boris Becker	Steffi Graf
1990	Ivan Lendl	Steffi Graf
1991	Stefan Edberg	Monica Seles
1992	Jim Courier	Monica Seles
1993	Pete Sampras	Steffi Graf
1994	Pete Sampras	Arantxa Sanchez Vicario
1995	Pete Sampras	Steffi Graf
1996	Pete Sampras	Steffi Graf
1997	Pete Sampras	Martina Hingis

DOUBLES

	Men	***Women***
1996	Todd Woodbridge/Mark Woodforde	Lindsay Davenport/Mary Joe Fernandez
1997	Todd Woodbridge/Mark Woodforde	Lindsay Davenport/Jana Novotna

ITF JUNIOR WORLD CHAMPIONS

Boys' singles

1978 Ivan Lendl (TCH)
1979 Raul Viver (ECU)
1980 Thierry Tulasne (FRA)
1981 Pat Cash (AUS)
1982 Guy Forget (FRA)
1983 Stefan Edberg (SWE)
1984 Mark Kratzmann (AUS)
1985 Claudio Pistolesi (ITA)
1986 Javier Sanchez (ESP)
1987 Jason Stoltenberg (AUS)
1988 Nicolas Pereira (VEN)
1989 Nicklas Kulti (SWE)
1990 Andrea Gaudenzi (ITA)
1991 Thomas Enqvist (SWE)
1992 Brian Dunn (USA)
1993 Marcelo Rios (CHI)
1994 Federico Browne (ARG)
1995 Marian Zabaleta (ARG)
1996 Sebastien Grosjean (FRA)
1997 Arnaud di Pasquale (FRA)

Girls' singles

1978 Hana Mandlikova (TCH)
1979 Mary-Lou Piatek (USA)
1980 Susan Mascarin (USA)
1981 Zina Garrison (USA)
1982 Gretchen Rush (USA)
1983 Pascale Paradis (FRA)
1984 Gabriela Sabatini (ARG)
1985 Laura Garrone (USA)
1986 Patricia Tarabini (ARG)
1987 Natalia Zvereva (URS)
1988 Cristina Tessi (ARG)
1989 Florencia Labat (ARG)
1990 Karina Habsudova (TCH)
1991 Zdenka Malkova (TCH)
1992 Rossana De Los Rios (PAR)
1993 Nino Louarssabichvilli (GEO)
1994 Martina Hingis (SUI)
1995 Anna Kournikova (RUS)
1996 Amelie Mauresmo (FRA)
1997 Cara Black (ZIM)

Boys' doubles

1982 Fernando Perez (MEX)
1983 Mark Kratzman (AUS)
1984 Augustin Moreno (MEX)
1985 Petr Korda (TCH)/ Cyril Suk (TCH)
1986 Tomas Carbonell (ESP)
1987 Jason Stoltenberg (AUS)
1988 David Rikl (TCH)/Tomas Zdrazila (TCH)
1989 Wayne Ferreira (RSA)
1990 Marten Renstroem (SWE)
1991 Karim Alami (MAR)
1992 Enrique Abaroa (MEX)
1993 Steven Downs (NZL)
1994 Benjamin Ellwood (AUS)
1995 Kepler Orellana (VEN)
1996 Sebastien Grosjean (FRA)
1997 Nicolas Massu (CHI)

Girls' doubles

1982 Beth Herr (USA)
1983 Larissa Savchenko (URS)
1984 Mercedes Paz (ARG)
1985 Mariana Perez-Roldan (ARG)/Patricia Tarabini (ARG)
1986 Leila Meskhi (URS)
1987 Natalia Medvedeva (URS)
1988 Jo-Anne Faull (AUS)
1989 Andrea Strnadova (TCH)
1990 Karina Habsudova (TCH)
1991 Eva Martincova (TCH)
1992 Nancy Feber (BEL)/Laurence Courtois (BEL)
1993 Cristina Moros (USA)
1994 Martina Nedelkova (SLK)
1995 Ludmilla Varmuzova (CZE)
1996 Michaela Pastikova (CZE)/Jitka Schonfeldova (CZE)
1997 Cara Black (ZIM)/Irina Selyutina (KAZ)

(Above) *The successful Swedes in Gothenburg celebrate a sixth Davis Cup victory for their country since 1975.* (left to right): *Jonas Bjorkman, Thomas Enqvist, Nicklas Kulti, Magnus Larsson, Carl Axel Hageskog (captain).* (Below) *The US team* (left to right): *Pete Sampras, Todd Martin, Jonathan Stark, Michael Chang and captain Tom Gullikson.* (Paul Zimmer)

Davis Cup by NEC

Wendy Kewley

A year ago Sweden was recovering after a heartbreaking loss to France in the fifth set of the final rubber of one of the greatest Davis Cup Finals ever. But 12 months later the Swedes licked their wounds and bounced back to win the 1997 trophy by dismissing the American team 5–0 in Gothenburg.

Sweden's trump card proved to be the world No. 4 Jonas Bjorkman, one of 19 top-20 players who competed in the 1997 Davis Cup by NEC. The 25-year-old from Vaxjo had played a pivotal role in helping his country to reach their 11th Davis Cup Final, so it was particularly fitting that the title was clinched with a Bjorkman ace in the doubles rubber on the second day. The Swede immediately leapt into partner Nicklas Kulti's arms while the 11,000 capacity crowd roared its approval.

Last year, Bjorkman, then ranked outside the top 50, had been a substitute in the Final but this time he was the man of the match. The moment was also particularly poignant for Kulti as, suffering from severe leg cramps, he had narrowly lost the fifth rubber to France's Arnaud Boetsch in last year's Final. An overjoyed Kulti said, 'This is such a great feeling. Today was perfect.'

The Swedes had opted to play the 1997 Final on an indoor Taraflex court to take advantage of Michael Chang's vulnerability on such a fast surface. The American team was led by the world No. 1 Pete Sampras and No. 3 Michael Chang, so a record 32nd Davis Cup title had seemed within their grasp. But when Chang lost the opening rubber to Bjorkman and Sampras followed by retiring against Larsson because of injury, the omens looked bleak.

With USA 0–2 down overnight, the Americans had to win the doubles to stay in the tie. Yet Todd Martin and Jonathan Stark had played few matches together, so their 6–4 6–4 6–4 defeat at the hands of US Open doubles finalists, Bjorkman and Kulti was no surprise. The Swedes then extended the scoreline on the final day when Bjorkman defeated Stark 6–1 6–1 and Larsson overcame Chang 7–6 6–7 6–4.

The Americans had been hoping to exorcise the ghosts of the 1984 final and the 1994 semi-final when they had also lost to Sweden in Gothenburg, but a disappointed Gullikson conceded, 'You have to play with the cards you're dealt. Certainly, the Swedes were the better team this weekend.'

Sweden, the 1994 champions, had moved into the 1997 final with a 4–1 victory over Italy. In the previous round, Bjorkman had clinched the decisive fifth rubber against South Africa by outlasting Grant Stafford in a five-set marathon. His contribution had been equally vital against a courageous Italian side in Norrkoping, where he took both singles points and then joined Kulti to win the doubles. But it had not been easy. After returning to tennis this year following a lengthy period of injury, Italy's Omar Camporese had been keen to make his mark. In the opening rubber, he produced an inspired performance and stretched Bjorkman to five sets, narrowly failing to pull off a victory. Renzo Furlan went one better, engineering a stirring win over Thomas Enqvist to snatch Italy's solitary point.

In the other semi-final, USA met their traditional Davis Cup rivals, Australia, in the historic setting of Washington DC. The United States had first played Australasia in the 1905 competition and this was the 43rd time that the two most successful Davis Cup nations had clashed. Australia had won the trophy 26 times to USA's 31 but had experienced few moments of glory in recent times, having last lifted the trophy in 1986.

With the world's top three singles players competing – Sampras, Chang and Rafter – tickets had been sold out for several weeks before the tie. Australia's Patrick Rafter had recently risen to No. 3 after winning the US Open. Australia's Davis Cup captain, John Newcombe, also had the benefit of the world's top doubles team, Mark Woodforde and Todd Woodbridge. The match results vindicated the rankings with Chang and Sampras winning two singles each while the Woodies retained the visitors' self-respect by taking Australia's sole point in the doubles. As Sampras remarked afterwards, the occasion was so big that people thought that USA had won the Cup.

Elsewhere in the World Group, a major talking point was the first round defeat of the 1996 champion nation, France, by Australia in the first round. One of the tie's most memorable encounters was Rafter's victory over Cedric Pioline, which France's Davis Cup captain Yannick Noah later cited as the key to the tie. Rafter showed great character in reversing a two-sets deficit to give his country first blood. Afterwards, he said: 'They say you have your best and worst moments in Davis Cup and I'm just glad I've had one of the best moments of my life...'

The second round of the World Group featured an intriguing encounter between Italy and Spain. The Spanish team consisted of world No. 8 Carlos Moya and world No. 12 Albert Costa, prompting Italy's Davis Cup captain Adriano Panatta to remark that his team had a 25% chance of winning the tie. But Camporese started the weekend by picking off Australian Open finalist Moya in a tense five-set contest. Furlan maintained the pressure with another five-set victory over Costa, and when the Italians won the doubles, Panatta's men were through to their second consecutive semi-final. This time, the Italian skipper was more positive, and said, 'We want more respect. It's time to stop calling us little Italy. This is a great Italian team.'

The depth of Davis Cup competition is renowned and with 127 nations participating in 1997, spectators were treated to plenty of drama outside the World Group. Held in September, the World Group Qualifying Round featured 16 nations. The eight winners would earn places in the 1998 World Group while the losers would compete in the 1998 Zonal Group I competition. As with the World Group, the ties involved several leading players including Austria's Thomas Muster, Croatia's Goran Ivanisevic and Chile's Marcelo Rios.

The most surprising result was Belgium's 3–2 defeat of France, confining the 1996 champions to Regional Qualifying in 1998. The French cause was not helped by the No. 1 player, Pioline, having to retire in the second singles. Zimbabwe and Slovak Republic will join the World Group for the first time in 1998. Zimbabwe's Black brothers staged an upset when they imposed a 3–2 defeat on an Austrian team spearheaded by Thomas Muster, while the Slovaks beat the Canadians 4–1 in Montreal.

Gustavo Kuerten delighted his home supporters in Florianopolis by assisting in Brazil's 5–0 victory over New Zealand that ensured Brazil's return to the World Group for a second consecutive year. Boris Becker came to Germany's rescue against Mexico in Essen, winning both his singles to secure his country's World Group status in 1998.

India's tie against Chile in New Delhi produced one of the most action packed weekends of all. The home team eventually came through 3–2 but were severely tested in the process. A natural clay courter, Chile's Rios nevertheless won both his singles matches on the grass. With the tie level, India's Mahesh Bhupathi delighted the home supporters by wiping out a two-set deficit against Gabriel Silberstein in a nail-biting encounter.

The Romania-Russia tie also went to the wire after Andrei Pavel's incredible win over the higher ranked Yevgeny Kafelnikov had levelled proceedings. However Russia emerged unscathed when Alexander Volkov defeated Ion Moldovan in the final rubber.

So in 1998, Belgium, Brazil, Germany, India, Russia, Slovak Republic, Switzerland and Zimbabwe will compete in the World Group leaving Austria, Canada, Chile, France, Korea, Mexico, New Zealand and Romania to compete in the Regional Zone Group I.

In the Euro/African Zone Group I Play-Off, Ukraine and Israel remain in Group I in 1998, while Hungary and Morocco are relegated. In the American Zone Group I Play-Off, Argentina defeated Venezuela 4–1 and compete in Group I, while Venezuela move down to Group II. Uzbekistan defeated the Philippines 5–0 in the Asia/Oceania Zone Group I Play-Off and stay in Group I, while the Philippines are relegated to Group II.

In the Euro/African Zone Group II Final Round, Norway and Finland earned promotion to Group I in 1998. Portugal and Poland remain in Group II. In the American Zone Group II Final Round, Colombia defeated Uruguay 4–1 and are promoted to Group I while Uruguay compete in Group II. In the Asia/Oceania Zone Group II Final Round, Lebanon defeated Iran 4–1 to win promotion to Group I while Iran remain in Group II.

Reflecting on the year, ITF President Brian Tobin said, 'I think 1997 has been a good year for Davis Cup and it has been a good year for player commitment. It's obviously important to us to have the best players playing the Davis Cup competition. This year, we have.'

1997 DAVIS CUP BY NEC

WORLD GROUP

Seeding: USA, Sweden, France, Germany, Czech Republic, Italy, Netherlands, Russia.
FIRST ROUND (7-9 February) – USA d. Brazil 4–1, Ribeirao Preto BRA: M. Washington (USA) d. G. Kuerten (BRA) 3–6 7–6(6) 7–6(3) 6–3; J. Courier (USA) d. F. Meligeni (BRA) 3–6 6–1 6–4 4–6 6–4; G. Kuerten/J. Oncins (BRA) d. A. O'Brien/R. Reneberg (USA) 6–2 6–4 7–5; J. Courier (USA) d. G. Kuerten (BRA) 6–3 6–2 5–7 7–6(11); A. O'Brien (USA) d. F. Meligeni (BRA) 7–5 7–6(4). **Netherlands d. Romania 3–2, Bucharest ROM:** A. Voinea (ROM) d. P. Haarhuis (NED) 4–6 6–1 6–3 6–3; A. Pavel (ROM) d. J. Siemerink (NED) 6–2 6–1 4–6 6–4; J. Eltingh/P. Haarhuis (NED) d. I. Moldovan/R. Sabau (ROM) 7–6(4) 6–4 6–3; J. Siemerink (NED) d. A. Voinea (ROM) 7–6(6) 5–7 6–7(3) 7–6(8) 6–4; P. Haarhuis (NED) d. A. Pavel (ROM) 6–3 6–1 6–2. **Australia d. France 4–1, Sydney AUS:** P. Rafter (AUS) d. C. Pioline (FRA) 3–6 6–7(5) 6–4 7–5 6–4; M. Woodforde (AUS) d. A. Boetsch (FRA) 6–4 6–4 6–3; T. Woodbridge/M. Woodforde (AUS) d. G. Forget/G. Raoux (FRA) 7–6(6) 6–4 6–3; S. Stolle (AUS) d. C. Pioline (FRA) 7–6(3) 6–4; A. Boetsch (FRA) d. P. Rafter (AUS) 4–6 6–4 7–6(5). **Czech Republic d. India 3–2, Pribram IND:** P. Korda (CZE) d. M. Bhupathi (IND) 6–3 6–7(2) 6–1 6–2; L. Paes (IND) d. J. Novak (CZE) 6–2 6–3 6–7(5) 6–3; M. Bhupathi/L. Paes (IND) d. M. Damm/P. Korda (CZE) 7–6(7) 6–3 6–4; P. Korda (CZE) d. L. Paes(IND) 5–7 6–3 6–4 6–1; K. Novak (CZE) d. M. Bhupathi (IND) 6–1 6–4 6–3. **Italy d. Mexico 4–1, Rome ITA:** O. Camporese (ITA) d. A. Hernandez (MEX) 2–6 6–0 6–4 7–5; R. Furlan (ITA) d. L. Herrera (MEX) 3–6 6–1 6–2 6–1; D. Nargiso/S. Pescosolido (ITA) d. A. Hernandez/L. Lavalle (MEX) 6–1 4–6 7–6(7) 6–3; R. Furlan (ITA) d. A. Hernandez (MEX) 6–2 6–3; L. Herrera (MEX) d. O. Camporese (ITA) 2–6 6–3 6–4. **Spain d. Germany 4–1, Mallorca ESP:** C. Moya (ESP) d. M-K. Goellner (GER) 6–4 6–3 6–3; A. Costa (ESP) d. H. Dreekmann (GER) 6–4 6–1 6–4; M-K. Goellner/D. Prinosil (GER) d. A. Corretja/C. Costa (ESP) 6–2 6–2 6–3; C. Moya (ESP) d. H. Dreekmann (GER) 6–4 6–4 7–5; A. Costa (ESP) d. M-K. Goellner (GER) 2–6 7–6(5) 6–1. **South Africa d. Russia 3–1, Durban RSA:** M. Ondruska (RSA) d. A. Chesnokov (RUS) 7–6(2) 6–3 3–6 4–6 7–5; W. Ferreira (RSA) d. A. Cherkasov (RUS) 7–5 6–3 3–6 4–6 8–6; E. Ferreira/G. Stafford (RSA) d. A. Cherkasov/A. Olhovskiy (RUS) 6–2 3–6 6–0 6–2; A. Chesnokov (RUS) d. W. Ferreira (RSA) 6–2 6–7(7) 6–2; M. Ondruska (RSA) vs A. Cherkasov (RUS) not played. **Sweden d. Switzerland 4–1, Lulea SWE:** M. Rosset (SUI) d. M. Larsson (SWE) 7–6(3) 3–6 6–4 4–6 13–11; T. Enqvist (SWE) d. L. Manta (SUI) 7–6(4) 7–6(9) 6–2; N. Kulti/M. Tillstrom (SWE) d. L. Manta/M. Rosset (SUI) 5–7 6–4 6–3 5–7 6–4; T. Enqvist (SWE) d. M. Rosset (SUI) 6–3 6–2 3–6 6–2; M. Larsson (SWE) d. I. Heuberger (SUI) 3–6 6–4 6–2. **SECOND ROUND (4–6 April) – USA d. Netherlands 4–1, Newport Beach USA:** A. Agassi (USA) d. S. Schalken (NED) 7–6(6) 6–4 7–6(2); J. Courier (USA) d. J. Siemerink (NED) 4–6 4–6 6–1 7–6(4) 6–3; J. Eltingh/P. Haarhuis (NED) d. R. Leach/J. Stark (USA) 6–4 6–4 3–6 6–3; A. Agassi (USA) d. J. Siemerink (NED) 3–6 3–6 6–3 6–3 6–3; J. Stark (USA) d. S. Schalken (NED) 6–4 6–0. **Australia d. Czech Republic 5–0, Adelaide AUS:** P. Rafter (AUS) d. M. Damm (CZE) 6–1 7–6(7) 4–6 6–4; M. Philippoussis (AUS) d. D. Rikl (CZE) 6–1 6–4 2–6 6–4; T. Woodbridge/M. Woodforde (AUS) d. M. Damm/D. Rikl (CZE) 4–6 6–1 7–5 6–4; M. Philippoussis (AUS) d. M. Damm (CZE) 6–4 6–2; P. Rafter (AUS) d. D. Rikl (CZE) 7–6(13) 0–6 6–2. **Italy d. Spain 4–1, Pesaro ITA:** O. Camporese (ITA) d. C. Moya (ESP) 6–7(8) 6–7(4) 6–1 6–3 6–3; R. Furlan (ITA) d. A. Costa (ESP) 4–6 6–3 4–6 6–4 6–1; O. Camporese/D. Nargiso (ITA) d. F. Roig/J. Sanchez (ESP) 5–7 7–6(0) 6–2 7–6(5); C. Moya (ESP) d. M. Martelli (ITA) 7–6(5) 4–6 6–3; O. Camporese (ITA) d. A. Costa (ESP) 6–2 3–6 6–4. **Sweden d. South Africa 3–2, Vaxjo SWE:** T. Enqvist (SWE) d. G. Stafford (RSA) 7–5 2–6 6–4 6–1; W. Ferreira (RSA) d. J. Bjorkman (SWE) 6–3 6–4 2–6 7–6(3); J. Bjorkman/N. Kulti (SWE) d. D. Adams/E. Ferreira (RSA) 7–5 2–6 6–4 6–7(6) 6–2; W. Ferreira (RSA) d. T. Enqvist (SWE) 6–4 6–4 6–4; J. Bjorkman (SWE) d. G. Stafford (RSA) 3–6 6–0 3–6 6–2 6–2. **SEMI-FINALS (19–21 September) – USA d. Australia 4–1, Washington USA:** M. Chang (USA) d. P. Rafter (AUS) 6–4 1–6 6–3 6–4; P. Sampras (USA) d. M. Philippoussis (AUS) 6–1 6–2 7–6(5); T. Woodbridge/M. Woodforde (AUS) d. T. Martin/P. Sampras (USA) 3–6 7–6(5) 6–2 6–4; P. Sampras (USA) d. P. Rafter (AUS) 6–7(6) 6–1 6–1 6–4; M. Chang (USA) d. M. Philippoussis (AUS) 7–6(5) 7–6(2). **Sweden d. Italy 4–1, Norrkoping SWE:** J. Bjorkman (SWE) d. O. Camporese (ITA) 6–7(5) 6–3 6–2 3–6 6–3; R. Furlan (ITA) d. T. Enqvist (SWE) 3–6 6–3 6–4 3–6 6–3; J. Bjorkman/N. Kulti (SWE) d. O. Camporese/D. Nargiso (ITA) 6–1 6–1 6–2; J. Bjorkman (SWE) d. R. Furlan (ITA) 4–6 6–4 6–0 6–4; T. Enqvist (SWE) d. O. Camporese (ITA) 6–3 6–7(5) 6–3. **FINAL (28–30 November) – Sweden d. USA 5–0, Gothenburg SWE:** J. Bjorkman (SWE) d. M. Chang (USA) 7–5 1–6 6–3 6–3; M. Larsson (SWE) d. P. Sampras (USA) 3–6 7–6(1) 2–1 ret; J. Bjorkman/N. Kulti (SWE) d. T. Martin/J. Stark (USA) 6–4 6–4 6–4; J. Bjorkman (SWE) d. J. Stark (USA) 6–1 6–1; M. Larsson (SWE) d. M. Chang (USA) 7–6(4) 6–7(6) 6–4.

QUALIFYING ROUND FOR WORLD GROUP (19–21 September) – Zimbabwe d. Austria 3–2, Harare ZIM: B. Black (ZIM) d. G. Schaller (AUT) 6–3 6–2 6–1; T. Muster (AUT) d. W. Black (ZIM) 6–3 6–0 6–4; B. Black/W. Black (ZIM) d. G. Blumauer/G. Mandl (AUT) 7–5 6–4 6–3; T. Muster (AUT) d. B. Black (ZIM) 3–6 6–3 2–6 6–3 6–1; W. Black (ZIM) d. G. Mandl (AUT) 5–7 6–3 6–3 6–0. **Brazil d. New Zealand 5–0, Florianopolis BRA:** G. Kuerten (BRA) d. A. Hunt (NZL) 7–5 6–3 6–2; F. Meligeni (BRA) d. B. Steven (NZL) 6–3 7–5 6–4; G. Kuerten/J. Oncins (BRA) d. A. Hunt/B. Stephen (NZL) 6–0 6–2 6–0; G. Kuerten (BRA) d. B. Steven (NZL) 6–1 6–0; A. Sa (BRA) d. A. Hunt (NZL) 6–2 6–2. **India d. Chile 3–2, Delhi IND:** L. Paes (IND) d. G. Silberstein (CHI) 6–3 6–2 6–2; M. Rios (CHI) d. M. Bhupathi (IND) 6–2 3–6 6–3 6–4; M. Bhupathi/L. Paes (IND) d. M. Rios/N. Massu (CHI) 3–6 6–3 6–4 6–7(3) 6–3; M. Rios (CHI) d. L. Paes (IND) 6–7(5) 6–4 6–0 7–6(3); M. Bhupathi (IND) d. G. Silberstein (CHI) 6–7(4) 4–6 6–4 6–4 6–3. **Belgium d. France 3–2, Gent BEL:** F. Dewulf (BEL) d. F. Santoro (FRA) 6–1 6–3 6–3; J. van Herck (BEL) d. C. Pioline (FRA) 4–6 2–6 7–5 4–1 ret; G. Raoux/F.

Santoro (FRA) d. F. Dewulf/L. Pimek (BEL) 5–7 7–5 7–5 6–1; G. Raoux (FRA) d. F. Dewulf (BEL) 6–3 6–4 7–5; C. van Garsse (BEL) d. L. Roux (FRA) 7–5 6–4 1–6 6–2. **Germany d. Mexico 5–0, Essen GER:** B. Becker (GER) d. L. Herrera (MEX) 7–5 6–2 6–3; M-K. Goellner (GER) d. A. Hernandez (MEX) 7–5 6–3 6–3; M-K. Goellner/J. Knippschild (GER) d. O. Ortiz/D. Roditi (MEX) 7–6(4) 7–6(4) 4–6 6–3; B. Becker (GER) d. A. Hernandez (MEX) 6–4 7–5; J. Knippschild (GER) d. L. Herrera (MEX) 6–2 3–6 6–4. **Russia d. Romania 3–2, Moscow RUS:** A. Volkov (RUS) d. A. Pavel (ROM) 6–3 6–7(5) 6–2 6–4; Y. Kafelnikov (RUS) d. I. Moldovan (ROM) 6–4 7–6(7) 6–4; A. Pavel/G. Trifu (ROM) d. Y. Kafelnikov/A. Olhovskiy (RUS) 6–4 6–4 6–4; A. Pavel (ROM) d. Y. Kafelnikov (RUS) 6–4 3–6 6–4 6–1; A. Volkov (RUS) d. I. Moldovan (ROM) 6–4 6–3 7–5. **Slovak Republic d. Canada 4–1, Montreal CAN:** K. Kucera (SVK) d. D. Nestor (CAN) 6–3 6–3 7–6(0); D. Hrbaty (SVK) d. S. Lareau (CAN) 7–6(7) 4–6 7–6(5) 6–3; G. Connell/D. Nestor (CAN) d. D. Hrbaty/J. Kroslak (SVK) 6–2 6–3 6–4; K. Kucera (SVK) d. S. Lareau (CAN) 5–7 6–2 6–4 6–3; D. Hrbaty (SVK) d. D. Nestor (SVK) 6–4 6–7(3) 6–3. **Switzerland d. Korea 3–2, Locarno SUI:** M. Rosset (SUI) d. H-T. Lee (KOR) 6–3 7–6(2) 7–6(4); I. Heuberger (SUI) d. Y-I. Yoon (KOR) 6–3 6–3 6–4; L. Manta/M. Rosset (SUI) d. H-T. Lee/Y-I. Yoon (KOR) 7–6(5) 7–6(5) 6–4; Y-I. Yoon (KOR) d. L. Manta (SUI) 6–4 6–3; H-T. Lee (KOR) d. I. Heuberger (SUI) 7–5 6–2.
The winners of these eight ties qualified for the World Group for the 1998 competition. The losers remained in, or were relegated to, their respective Group I zones for the 1998 competition.

AMERICAN GROUP I

FIRST ROUND (7–9 February) – Canada d. Bahamas 4–1, Montreal CAN: D. Nestor (CAN) d. R. Smith (BAH) 6–1 6–1 6–2; M. Knowles (BAH) d. S. Lareau (CAN) 6–4 3–6 6–2 5–7 6–1; G. Connell/S. Lareau (CAN) d. M. Knowles/R. Smith (BAH) 6–2 6–7(1) 6–4 6–4; D. Nestor (CAN) d. M. Knowles (BAH) 3–6 7–5 6–4 6–2; S. Lareau (CAN) d. R. Smith (BAH) 6–2 4–6 6–2. **Chile d. Ecuador 4–1, Santiago CHI:** G. Silberstein (CHI) d. N. Lapentti (ECU) 6–2 4–6 1–6 6–3 6–3; M. Rios (CHI) d. L. Morejon (ECU) 6–1 6–3 3–6 6–2; P. Campana/N. Lapentti (ECU) d. O. Bustos/M. Rios (CHI) 4–6 6–4 6–0 6–3; M. Rios (CHI) d. N. Lapentti (ECU) 7–5 6–7(6) 6–3 6–7(6) 8–6; G. Silberstein (CHI) d. L. Morejon (ECU) 7–6(4) 6–2. **SECOND ROUND (4–6 April) – Canada d. Venezuela 5–0, Montreal CAN:** S. Lareau (CAN) d. J. de Armas (VEN) 6–1 6–3 6–2; D. Nestor (CAN) d. J. Szymanski (VEN) 6–2 7–6(5) 6–1; G. Connell/S. Lareau (CAN) d. S. Madden/J. Szymanski (VEN) 6–2 6–1 6–3; S. Lareau (CAN) d. J. Szymanski (VEN) 6–3 7–5; S. le Blanc (CAN) d. J. de Armas (VEN) 2–6 7–6(2) 6–0. **Chile d. Argentina 3–2, Santiago CHI:** M. Rios (CHI) d. J. Frana (ARG) 6–1 6–4 7–6(2); H. Gumy (ARG) d. G. Silberstein (CHI) 6–0 6–4 6–4; M. Rios/G. Silberstein (CHI) d. J. Frana/L. Lobo (ARG) 3–6 7–6(8) 4–6 6–3 6–2; M. Rios (CHI) d. H. Gumy (ARG) 6–4 7–5 6–4; J. Frana (ARG) d. G. Silberstein (CHI) 6–4 6–4.
Canada and Chile qualified for the World Group Qualifying Round.
RELEGATION FIRST ROUND – (11–13 July) – Bahamas d. Venezuela 3–2, Nassau BAH: R. Smith (BAH) d. N. Pereira (VEN) 7–6(4) 6–3 6–4; J. Szymanski (VEN) d. M. Knowles (BAH) 6–3 7–6(4) 6–2; M. Knowles/R. Smith (BAH) d. N. Pereira/J. Szymanski (VEN) 6–3 6–7(4) 7–6(5) 7–5; N. Pereira (VEN) d. M. Knowles (BAH) 5–7 7–5 6–1 7–5; R. Smith (BAH) d. J. Szymanski (VEN) 3–6 1–6 7–6(4) 6–4 6–4. **Ecuador d. Argentina 3–1, Buenos Aires ARG:** L. Morejon (ECU) d. H. Gumy (ARG) 6–1 6–4 5–7 7–5; N. Lapentti (ECU) d. M. Charpentier (ARG) 6–3 6–4 6–3; P. Albano/L. Lobo (ARG) d. G. Carneade/N. Lapentti (ECU) 6–2 6–1 7–6(4); N. Lapentti (ECU) d. H. Gumy (ARG) 6–4 6–4 3–6 0–6 6–3; L. Morejon (ECU) v. M. Charpentier (ARG) not played due to rain. **RELEGATION FINAL – (19–21 September) – Argentina d. Venezuela 4–1, Buenos Aires ARG:** H. Gumy (ARG) d. J. de Armas (VEN) 6–0 6–2 6–1; L. Arnold (ARG) d. J. Szymanski (VEN) 6–4 6–3 7–5; P. Albano/L. Lobo (ARG) d. J. de Armas/J. Szymanski (VEN) 6–1 6–0 6–3; J. Szymanski (VEN) d. L. Lobo (ARG) 6–2 6–2; L. Arnold (ARG) d. J. de Armas (VEN) 6–1 6–2.
Venezuela were relegated to American Group II for the 1998 competition.

ASIA/OCEANIA GROUP I

FIRST ROUND (4–6 February) – China d. Uzbekistan 4–1, Beijing CHN: J-P. Xia (CHN) d. D. Tomashevich (UZB) 6–4 7–6(5) 6–3; O. Ogorodov (UZB) d. B. Pan (CHN) 6–2 6–4 7–5; J-P. Xia/B. Pan (CHN) d. O. Ogorodov/D. Tomashevich (UZB) 7–6(4) 6–3 2–6 6–2; J-P. Xia (CHN) d. O. Ogorodov (UZB) 6–4 4–6 7–6(5) 7–6(7); B. Pan (CHN) d. D. Tomashevich (UZB) 6–4 7–6(3). **Korea d. Japan 3–2, Seoul KOR:** Y-I. Yoon (KOR) d. T. Suzuki (JPN) 1–6 7–5 6–3 6–1; S. Matsuoka (JPN) d. H-T. Lee (KOR) 7–6(5) 6–3 7–6(3); S. Iwabuchi/T. Suzuki (JPN) d. H-T. Lee/Y-I. Yoon (KOR) 6–3 6–4 3–6 4–6 8–6; Y-I. Yoon (KOR) d. S. Matsuoka (JPN) 6–2 6–4 6–3; H-T. Lee (KOR) d. T. Suzuki (JPN) 3–6 6–4 1–6 6–4 6–4. **(7–9 February) – Indonesia d. Philippines 3–2, Manila PHI:** R. Angelo (PHI) d. S. Suwandi (INA) 7–6(8) 7–6(5) 6–3; J. Lizardo (PHI) d. A. Raturandang (INA) 6–4 5–7 7–5 6–2; B. S. Wibowo/Wiryawan (INA) d. M. Misa/P. Tolentino (PHI) 6–1 6–4 6–0; S. Suwandi (INA) d. J. Lizardo (PHI) 6–2 1–6 6–3 5–7 6–2; B. Wiryawan (INA) d. R. Angelo (PHI) 6–3 1–6 4–6 6–1 6–3. **SECOND ROUND (4–6 April) – New Zealand d. Indonesia 5–0, Jakarta INA:** M. Nielsen (NZL) d. S. Suwandi (INA) 7–5 6–3 6–4; A. Hunt (NZL) d. A. Raturandang (INA) 6–3 6–0 6–3; J. Greenhalgh/A. Hunt (NZL) d. S. Wibowo/B. Wiryawan (INA) 6–3 6–4 3–6 6–3; G. Wilson (NZL) d. S. Suwandi (INA) 6–4 7–5; M. Nielsen (NZL) d. A. Raturandang (INA) 6–2 7–5. **Korea d. China, PR 4–1, Beijing, CHN:** H-T. Lee (KOR) d. J-P. Xia (CHN) 6–1 2–6 2–6 7–6(3) 6–1; Y-I. Yoon (KOR) d. B. Pan (CHN) 6–3 6–4 6–2; H-T. Lee/Y-I. Yoon (KOR) d. B. Pan/J-P. Xia (CHN) 6–4 3–6 6–2 6–4; Y-I. Yoon (KOR) d. Y. Zheng (CHN) 6–3 7–5; B. Pan (CHN) d. D-H. Kim (KOR) 7–6(5) 6–4.
Korea and New Zealand qualified for the World Group Qualifying Round.
RELEGATION FIRST ROUND – (11–13 July) – Japan d. Uzbekistan 3–2, Tashkent, UZB: O. Ogorodov (UZB) d. H. Kaneko (JPN) 6–1 7–5 4–6 6–3; G. Motomura (JPN) d. D. Tomashevich (UZB) 6–1 2–6 6–1 6–3; S. Iwabuchi/T. Suzuki (JPN) d. V. Kutsenko/O. Ogorodov (UZB) 6–3 6–4 6–2; O. Ogorodov (UZB) d. G.

Motomura (JPN) 6–2 6–2 6–2; H. Kaneko (JPN) d. D. Tomashevich (UZB) 6–3 4–6 6–1 6–4. **RELEGATION FINAL (19–21 September) – Uzbekistan d. Philippines 5–0, Tashkent UZB:** O. Ogorodov (UZB) d. M. Misa (PHI) 6–3 6–3 6–0; D. Tomashevich (UZB) d. J. Lizardo (PHI) 4–6 6–2 6–2 7–5; O. Ogorodov/D. Tomashevich (UZB) d. R. Angelo/J. Lizardo (PHI) 6–2 6–1 6–3; O. Ogorodov (UZB) d. J. Lizardo (PHI) 6–3 6–4; D. Tomashevich (UZB) d. M. Misa (PHI) 6–1 6–1.
Philippines were relegated to Asia/Oceania Group II for the 1998 competition.

EURO/AFRICAN GROUP I

FIRST ROUND (7–9 February) – Denmark d. Hungary 5–0, Aalborg DEN: F. Fetterlein (DEN) d. J. Krocsko (HUN) 6–4 6–2 7–5; K. Carlsen (DEN) d. A. Savolt (HUN) 6–4 6–4 7–6(3); K. Carlsen/F. Fetterlein (DEN) d. L. Markovits/A. Savolt (HUN) 7–6(4) 7–6(2) 6–4; K. Carlsen (DEN) d. J. Krocsko (HUN) 6–3 6–7(5) 6–3; F. Fetterlein (DEN) d. A. Savolt (HUN) 5–7 6–3 6–4. **Zimbabwe d. Ukraine 5–0, Harare ZIM:** W. Black (ZIM) d. A. Medvedev (UKR) 6–4 6–3 4–6 6–4; B. Black (ZIM) d. A. Rybalko (UKR) 5–7 6–2 7–6(2) 6–3; B. Black/W. Black (ZIM) d. A. Medvedev/D. Poliakov (UKR) 6–7(8) 7–5 4–6 6–1 6–4; B. Black (ZIM) d. D. Yakimenko (UKR) 6–4 6–4; W. Black (ZIM) d. A. Rybalko (UKR) 7–6(3) 6–3. **Croatia d. Morocco 4–1, Osijek CRO:** S. Hirszon (CRO) d. K. Alami (MAR) 6–4 6–1 6–3; G. Ivanisevic (CRO) d. H. Arazi (MAR) 6–2 6–2 6–7(4) 6–2; S. Hirszon/G. Ivanisevic (CRO) d. K. Alami/H. Arazi (MAR) 6–2 6–3 6–3; G. Ivanisevic (CRO) d. K. Alami (MAR) 6–2 7–5; H. Arazi (MAR) d. S. Hirszon (CRO) 6–1 6–4. **SECOND ROUND (4–6 April) – Belgium d. Denmark 3–2, Brussels BEL:** F. Dewulf (BEL) d. K. Carlsen (DEN) 6–4 6–0 6–1; F. Fetterlein (DEN) d. J. van Herck (BEL) 7–6(5) 2–6 6–2 6–1; K. Carlsen/F. Fetterlein (DEN) d. F. Dewulf/L. Pimek (BEL) 6–3 7–5 1–6 6–4; J. van Herck (BEL) d. K. Carlsen (DEN) 6–4 6–1 7–5; F. Dewulf (BEL) d. F. Fetterlein (DEN) 6–0 6–4 3–6 2–6 6–1. **Zimbabwe d. Great Britain 4–1, Crystal Palace GBR:** W. Black (ZIM) d. J. Delgado (GBR) 2–6 6–3 6–1 6–3; A. Richardson (GBR) d. B. Black (ZIM) 3–6 6–4 1–6 6–4 6–4; B. Black/W. Black (ZIM) d. N. Broad/M. Petchey (GBR) 3–6 6–1 6–4 6–7(6) 6–3; B. Black (ZIM) d. J. Delgado (GBR) 6–0 6–0 6–2; W. Black (ZIM) d. A. Richardson (GBR) 6–3 6–7(5) 7–6(2). **Slovak Republic d. Israel 3–1, Bratislava SVK:** D. Hrbaty (SVK) d. E. Ran (ISR) 6–3 4–6 6–3 6–4; K. Kucera (SVK) d. N. Behr (ISR) 6–1 6–3 6–0; N. Behr/E. Erlich (ISR) d. D. Hrbaty/K. Kucera (SVK) 6–4 3–6 6–3 7–6(4); K. Kucera (SVK) d. E. Ran (ISR) 6–2 6–3 6–2; D. Hrbaty (SVK) vs N. Behr (ISR) not played. **Austria d. Croatia 3–2, Graz AUT:** G. Schaller (AUT) d. G. Ivanisevic (CRO) 6–3 6–4 6–7(3) 2–6 3–1 ret; T. Muster (AUT) d. S. Hirszon (CRO) 6–0 6–4 3–6 6–1; S. Hirszon/G. Ivanisevic (CRO) d. T. Muster/U. Plamberger (AUT) 7–5 6–2 6–2; G. Ivanisevic (CRO) d. T. Muster (AUT) 6–7(5) 7–5 6–7(5) 6–2 7–5; G. Schaller (AUT) d. S. Hirszon (CRO) 6–3 6–3 7–5.
Austria, Belgium, Slovak Republic and Zimbabwe qualified for World Group Qualifying Round.
RELEGATION ROUND (11–13 July) – Great Britain d. Ukraine 3–2, Kiev UKR: T. Henman (GBR) d. A. Rybalko (UKR) 3–6 6–4 6–3 4–6 6–4; A. Medvedev (UKR) d. G. Rusedski (GBR) 6–1 6–1 2–6 6–2; T. Henman/G. Rusedski (GBR) d. A. Medvedev/D. Poliakov (UKR) 6–1 6–4 7–6(5); A. Medvedev (UKR) d. T. Henman (GBR) 6–7(5) 6–3 6–4 6–4; G. Rusedski (GBR) d. A. Rybalko (UKR) 7–5 6–3 6–3. **RELEGATION FINAL (19–21 September) – Ukraine d. Hungary 3–2, Budapest HUN:** A. Medvedev (UKR) d. K. Bardoczky (HUN) 6–2 6–2 6–2; A. Savolt (HUN) d. A. Rybalko (UKR) 6–4 6–2 2–6 6–2; A. Medvedev/D. Poliakov (UKR) d. G. Kisgyorgy/A. Savolt (HUN) 6–2 6–3 6–1; A. Medvedev (UKR) d. A. Savolt (HUN) 6–1 6–7(1) 6–3 5–7 6–2; K. Bardoczky (HUN) d. A. Rybalko (UKR) 6–0 6–4. **Israel d. Morocco w/o.**
Hungary and Morocco were relegated to Euro/African Group II for the 1998 competition.

AMERICAN GROUP II

FIRST ROUND (7–9 February) – Peru d. Cuba 3–2, Havana CUB: L. Navarro (CUB) d. A. Aramburu (PER) 6–1 6–4 6–2; A. Venero (PER) d. J. Pino (CUB) 6–4 7–5 5–7 6–3; A. Venero/J. Yzaga (PER) d. L. Navarro/J. Pino (CUB) 6–4 6–4 6–2; J. Pino (CUB) d. J. Yzaga (PER) 4–6 7–6(4) 1–0 def; A. Venero (PER) d. L. Navarro (CUB) 7–6(5) 6–3 6–7(5) 2–6 8–6. **Colombia d. Puerto Rico 3–2, San Juan PUR:** J. Gonzalez (PUR) d. M. Tobon (COL) 6–2 6–2 4–6 6–4; M. Hadad (COL) d. R. Jordan (PUR) 6–4 6–0 5–7 6–2; M. Hadad/M. Tobon (COL) d. E. Fernandez/J. Gonzalez (PUR) 7–6(5) 6–3 6–4; M. Hadad (COL) d. J. Gonzalez (PUR) 6–3 6–2 6–3; R. Jordan (PUR) d. M. Tobon (COL) 6–3 7–6(7). **Paraguay d. Haiti 5–0, Asuncion PAR:** R. Mena (PAR) d. R. Agenor (HAI) 6–4 6–0 6–2; R. Delgado (PAR) d. B. Madsen (HAI) 7–5 6–3 6–1; R. Delgado/R. Mena (PAR) d. R. Agenor/B. Madsen (HAI) 6–2 6–1 3–6 4–6 7–5; R. Delgado (PAR) d. B. Lacombe (HAI) 6–1 6–3; R. Mena (PAR) d. B. Madsen (HAI) 6–2 6–4. **Uruguay d. El Salvador 4–1, San Salvador ESA:** F. Dondo (URU) d. M. Tejada (ESA) 6–1 6–1 6–1; M. Filippini (URU) d. J. Baires (ESA) 6–0 7–5 6–3; F. Dondo/G. Rodriguez (URU) d. J. Mendez/M. Tejada (ESA) 6–3 7–6(4) 6–2; M. Tejada (ESA) d. M. Filippini (URU) 3–1 ret; F. Dondo (URU) d. J. Baires (ESA) 6–3 6–2. **SECOND ROUND (4–6 April) – Colombia d. Peru 5–0, Cali COL:** J. Cortes (COL) d. A. Aramburu (PER) 6–3 7–5 7–5; M. Tobon (COL) d. L. Horna (PER) 6–7(4) 6–4 6–2 6–2; M. Rincon/M. Tobon (COL) d. C. Reano/J. Yzaga (PER) 7–5 6–3 7–6(3); M. Tobon (COL) d. A. Aramburu (PER) 6–4 7–6(3); E. Rincon (COL) d. L. Horna (PER) 4–6 6–4 7–6(6). **Uruguay d. Paraguay 3–2, Asuncion PAR:** R. Delgado (PAR) d. F. Dondo (URU) 3–6 6–2 6–2 7–5; M. Filippini (URU) d. R. Mena (PAR) 6–4 6–4 6–4; M. Filippini/G. Rodriguez (URU) d. R. Delgado/R. Mena (PAR) 3–6 6–3 6–1 6–2; M. Filippini (URU) d. R. Delgado (PAR) 7–5 4–6 7–6(6) 6–2; R. Mena (PAR) d. F. Dondo (URU) 6–3 7–5. **FINAL (19–21 September) – Colombia d. Uruguay 4–1, Bogota COL:** M. Rincon (COL) d. F. Dondo (URU) 5–7 7–6(5) 6–3 6–0; M. Tobon (COL) d. M. Filippini (URU) 7–6(3) 5–7 7–6(5) 6–1; M. Rincon/M. Tobon (COL) d. M. Filippini/G. Rodriguez (URU) 6–2 6–3 6–7(1) 7–5; M. Filippini (URU) d. M. Rincon (COL) 6–2 6–2; P. Moggio (COL) d. F. Dondo (URU) 6–3 6–4.
Colombia were promoted to American Group I for the 1998 competition.

RELEGATION ROUND (4–6 April) – Cuba d. Puerto Rico 4–1, San Juan PUR: J. Pino (CUB) d. H. Nevares (PUR) 6–1 6–1 6–4; L. Navarro (CUB) d. R. Jordan (PUR) 6–4 5–7 6–1 3–6 6–1; L. Navarro/J. Pino (CUB) d. E. Fernandez/R. Jordan (PUR) 3–6 6–4 3–6 6–4 6–4; E. Fernandez (PUR) d. J. Cordova (PUR) 2–6 6–4 6–2; L. Navarro (CUB) d. H. Nevares (PUR) 6–4 6–0. **Haiti d. El Salvador 3–2, San Salvador ESA:** B. Madsen (HAI) d. J. Baires (ESA) 7–5 6–3 6–1; M. Tejada (ESA) d. B. Lacombe (HAI) 7–6(4) 6–3 6–4; B. Lacombe/B. Madsen (HAI) d. J. Mendez/M. Tejada (ESA) 6–2 6–4 7–6(6); B. Madsen (HAI) d. M. Tejada (ESA) 6–2 7–6(4) 6–3; J. Baires (ESA) d. R. Goscinny (HAI) 6–2 6–4.
El Salvador and Puerto Rico were relegated to American Group III for the 1998 competition.

ASIA/OCEANIA GROUP II

FIRST ROUND (14–16 February) – Thailand d. Hong Kong 5–0, Hong Kong HKG: W. Thongkhamchu (THA) d. M. Ferreira (HKG) 6–3 6–2 6–0; W. Samrej (THA) d. M. Tong (HKG) 6–3 5–7 6–2 2–6 6–4; N. Srichaphan/T. Srichaphan (THA) d. M. Ferreira/G. Foster (HKG) 6–1 6–2 6–3; W. Samrej (THA) d. M. Ferreira (HKG) 6–2 6–2; W. Thongkhamchu (THA) d. W. Wong (HKG) 6–3 7–6(2). **(18–20 February) – Lebanon d. Saudi Arabia 5–0, Riyadh KSA:** A. Hamadeh (LIB) d. O. Al-Anazi (KSA) 6–1 6–2 6–4; S. Karam (LIB) d. B. Al-Megayal (KSA) 6–4 6–3 6–4; A. Hamadeh/S. Karam (LIB) d. O. Al-Anazi/B. Al-Megayal (KSA) 6–4 6–1 6–3; A. Hamadesh (LIB) d. B. Al-Megayal (KSA) 6–0 6–1; T. Zahlan (LIB) d. M. Tawfiq (KSA) 7–5 6–3. **(21–23 February) – Chinese Taipei d. Singapore 5–0, Taipei TPE:** Y-H. Lien (TPE) d. C-Y. Chen (SIN) 6–2 6–0 6–0; C-Y. Tsai (TPE) d. K-Y. Ho (SIN) 6–2 6–1 6–4; J-Y. Chiang/Y-H. Lien (TPE) d. K-Y. Ho/Y-Y. Kho (SIN) 6–2 6–3 6–2; C-Y. Tsai (TPE) d. C-Y. Chen (SIN) 6–2 6–2; Y-H. Lien (TPE) d. E-W. Tan (SIN) 6–1 6–0. **Iran d. Pakistan 3–2, Islamabad PAK:** M. Bahrami (IRI) d. O. Rashid (PAK) 6–3 6–4 0–6 6–4; H. Ul-Haq (PAK) d. M-R. Tavakoli (IRI) 7–6(2) 3–6 6–2 6–4; M. Bahrami/R. Raziani (IRI) d. O. Rashid/A. Shafik (PAK) 6–3 7–5 7–6(3); R. Raziani (IRI) d. O. Rashid (PAK) 4–6 6–3 6–2 6–4; H. Ul-Haq (PAK) d. M. Bahrami (IRI) 1–6 6–4 6–2. **SECOND ROUND (4–6 April) – Iran d. Chinese Taipei 4–1, Tehran IRI:** R. Raziani (IRI) d. Y-H. Lien (TPE) 4–6 2–6 7–6(5) 6–4 6–3; M. Bahrami (IRI) d. C-J. Chen (TPE) 7–5 7–6(3) 3–6 6–3; M. Bahrami/R. Raziani (IRI) d. C-J. Chen/Y-H. Lien (TPE) 6–4 7–6(6) 7–6(4); C-J. Chen (TPE) d. R. Raziani (IRI) 2–0 ret; M. Bahrami (IRI) d. C-Y. Tsai (TPE) 6–0 7–6(2). **Lebanon d. Thailand 5–0, Beirut LIB:** H. Zaatini (LIB) d. W. Samrej (THA) 3–6 6–3 6–3 6–2; A. Hamadeh (LIB) d. N. Srichaphan (THA) 7–6(5) 7–5 7–6(4); A. Hamadeh/H. Zaatini (LIB) d. N. Srichaphan/T. Srichaphan (THA) 6–4 3–6 7–6(2) 6–4; A. Hamadeh (LIB) d. W. Samrej (THA) 6–3 3–6 7–6(5); H. Zaatini (LIB) d. T. Srichaphan (THA) 6–4 6–1. **FINAL (19–21 September) –**
Lebanon d. Iran 4–1, Zouk Mihail LIB: A. Hamadeh (LIB) d. R. Nakhai (IRI) 6–3 7–5 6–4; H. Zaatini (LIB) d. M-R. Tavakoli (IRI) 6–2 6–1 6–3; A. Hamadeh/H. Zaatini (LIB) d. R. Nakhai/S. Akhar Taheri (IRI) 6–4 6–4 6–3; H. Zaatini (LIB) d. R. Nakhai (IRI) 7–6(3) 6–3; M-R. Tavakoli (IRI) d. T. Zahlan (LIB) 6–2 6–4.
Lebanon were promoted to American Group I for the 1998 competition.
RELEGATION ROUND (4–6 April) – Pakistan d. Singapore 5–0, Islamabad PAK: O. Rashid (PAK) d. K-Y. Ho (SIN) 6–3 6–0 7–5; H. Ul-Haq (PAK) d. S. Lim (SIN) 6–4 6–2 6–1; O. Rashid/H. Ul-Haq (PAK) d. K-Y. Ho/S. Lim (SIN) 6–3 6–3 6–2; A. Shafik (PAK) d. S. Lim (SIN) 6–1 6–4; N. Sherazi (PAK) d. J. Hui (SIN) 6–1 6–3. **Hong Kong d. Saudi Arabia 4–1, Riyadh KSA:** B. Al-Megayel (KSA) d. W. Wong (HKG) 6–4 7–6(5) 6–3; M. Tong (HKG) d. F. Somali (KSA) 6–2 6–0 6–0; M. Ferreira/M. Tong (HKG) d. T. Al-Ibrahim/B. Al-Megayel (KSA) 6–0 6–1 6–4; M. Tong (HKG) d. B. Al-Megayel (KSA) 7–5 6–2 6–3; W. Wong (HKG) d. M. Tawfiq (KSA) 6–2 6–3.
Saudi Arabia and Singapore were relegated to Asia/Oceania Group III for the 1998 competition.

EURO/AFRICA GROUP II

FIRST ROUND (2–4 May) – **Norway d. Nigeria 5–0, Snaroya NOR:** J-F. Andersen (NOR) d. S. Ladipo (NGR) 6–1 6–0 6–4; C. Ruud (NOR) d. G. Adelekan (NGR) 6–0 6–1 6–0; H. Koll/C. Ruud (NOR) d. G. Adelekan/S. Ladipo (NGR) 6–2 4–6 6–1 7–6(5); C. Ruud (NOR) d. D. Ogu (NGR) 6–0 6–0; T. Heyerdahl (NOR) d. Adelekan (NGR) 7–5 6–3. **Slovenia d. Georgia 3–2, Tbilisi GEO:** I. Bozic (SLO) d. V. Margalitadze (GEO) 6–2 6–3 6–1; V. Gabrichidze (GEO) d. B. Urh (SLO) 6–3 7–5 1–6 3–6 6–4; M. Por/B. Urh (SLO) d. V. Gabrichidze/D. Katcharava (GEO) 7–6(6) 7–5 6–7(2) 6–2; B. Urh (SLO) d. V. Margalitadze (GEO) 6–2 6–2 6–0; V. Gabrichidze (GEO) d. A. Krasevec (SLO) 4–6 7–6(2) 6–2. **Portugal d. Egypt 5–0, Cairo EGY:** N. Marques (POR) d. G. El Deeb (EGY) 6–0 6–4 7–6(5); E. Couto (POR) d. A. Ghoneim (EGY) 2–6 6–4 7–5 6–3; E. Couto/B. Mota (POR) d. A. El Shafei/A. Ghoneim (EGY) 7–5 6–1 6–0; J. Cunha-Silva (POR) d. A. Ghoneim (EGY) 6–4 6–3; E. Couto (POR) d. G. El Deeb (EGY) 6–4 7–5. **Yugoslavia d. Lithuania 3–2, Vilnius LTU:** N. Zimonjic (YUG) d. R. Murashka (LTU) 6–3 6–1 6–3; B. Vujic (YUG) d. E. Cariovas (LTU) 7–6(3) 7–6(4) 6–2; D. Vemic/N. Zimonjic (YUG) d. E. Cariovas/R. Murashka (LTU) 6–4 6–4 6–4; R. Murashka (LTU) d. B. Vujic (YUG) 7–5 6–4; E. Cariovas (LTU) d. V. Pavicevic (YUG) 7–6(5) 4–6 6–3. **Cote d'Ivoire d. Latvia 5–0, Abidjan CIV:** Claude N'Goran (CIV) d. I. Lagzdins (LAT) 6–1 6–2 6–0; Clement N'Goran (CIV) d. R. Sproga (LAT) 6–4 6–0 6–2; Claude N'Goran/Clement N'Goran (CIV) d. I. Lagzdins/R. Sproga (LAT) 6–1 6–2 7–5; I. Lonfo (CIV) d. R. Sproga (LAT) 6–1 6–2; V. Sanon (CIV) d. O. Vaskis (LAT) 6–4 6–4. **Poland d. Ghana 5–0, Poznan POL:** B. Dabrowski (POL) d. Daniel Omaboe (GHA) 6–0 6–2 6–2; F. Aniola (POL) d. F. Ofori (GHA) 6–1 6–3 6–0; B. Dabrowski/B. Kaczorowski (POL) d. N. Dowuona/F. Ofori (GHA) 6–1 6–2 7–6(5); K. Pfeiffer (POL) d. N. Dowuona (GHA) 6–1 6–1; F. Aniola (POL) d. A. Ofori (GHA) 6–1 6–0. **Belarus d. Ireland 4–1, Dublin IRL:** M. Mirnyi (BLR) d. S. Barron (IRL) 6–2 6–3 4–6 6–4; O. Casey (IRL) d. A. Shvec (BLR) 6–2 4–6 6–3 4–6 7–5; M. Mirnyi/V. Voltchkov (BLR) d. S. Barron/T. Hamilton (IRL) 6–4 7–6(5) 6–3; A. Shvec (BLR) d. S. Barron (IRL) 6–1 6–2 7–6(4); M. Mirnyi

(BLR) d. E. Collins (IRL) 7–5 6–3. **Finland d. Greece 3–2, Helsinki FIN:** A. Vasiliadis (GRE) d. T. Ketola (FIN) 6–2 1–6 6–7(6) 6–4 6–4; K. Economidis (GRE) d. K. Tiilikainen (FIN) 6–7(4) 7–5 6–4 6–1; T. Ketola/V. Liukko (FIN) d. K. Economidis/A. Vasiliadis (GRE) 6–3 7–6(6) 6–4; V. Liukko (FIN) d. K. Economidis (GRE) 6–3 6–4 6–4; K. Tiilikainen (FIN) d. A. Vasiliadis (GRE) 6–3 7–6(3) 7–6(3). **SECOND ROUND (11–13 July) – Norway d. Slovenia 4–1, Nova Gorica SLO:** C. Ruud (NOR) d. I. Bozic (SLO) 4–6 6–2 6–4 6–3; J-F. Andersen (NOR) d. B. Trupej (SLO) 4–6 6–4 6–3 6–1; A. Karsevec/M. Por (SLO) d. H. Koll/C. Ruud (NOR) 6–2 6–3 5–7 1–6 6–2; J-F. Andersen (NOR) d. I. Bozic (SLO) 6–3 1–6 6–3 6–2; C. Ruud (NOR) d. B. Trupej (SLO) 6–4 6–4. **Portugal d. Yugoslavia 3–2, Porto POR:** J. Cunha-Silva (POR) d. N. Zimonjic (YUG) 2–6 6–4 6–4 6–4; B. Vujic (YUG) d. E. Couto (POR) 6–3 7–5 5–7 6–2; E. Couto/B. Mota (POR) d. N. Djordjevic/N. Zimonjic (YUG) 6–4 6–4 6–4; B. Vujic (YUG) d. J. Cunha-Silva (POR) 6–4 6–3 3–6 4–6 6–3; E. Couto (POR) d. N. Zimonjic (YUG) 6–7(2) 7–5 7–5 6–3. **Poland d. Cote d'Ivoire 4–1, Bytom POL:** Claude N'Goran (CIV) d. M. Chmela (POL) 6–4 5–7 6–2 6–7(4) 6–4; B. Dabrowski (POL) d. J-C. Nabi (CIV) 7–6(1) 6–1 6–4; B. Dabrowski/M. Gawlowski (POL) d. I. Lonfo/Claude N'Goran (CIV) 6–4 7–6(7) 3–6 6–2; B. Dabrowski (POL) d. Claude N'Goran (CIV) 6–4 6–1 6–0; M. Chmela (POL) d. N. Sangare (CIV) 6–1 6–2. **Finland d. Belarus 3–2, Tampere FIN:** V. Voltchkov (BLR) d. T. Ketola (FIN) 6–3 3–6 7–6(5) 6–1; T. Lenho (FIN) d. A. Shvec (BLR) 7–5 6–1 4–6 4–6 6–3; T. Ketola/V. Liukko (FIN) d. A. Shvec/V. Voltchkov (BLR) 3–6 6–4 6–1 6–1; K. Tiilikainen (FIN) d. A. Shvec (BLR) 6–7(6) 6–1 7–5 6–7(6) 6–0; V. Voltchkov (BLR) d. V. Liukko (FIN) 6–1 4–6 7–5.

FINAL (19–21 September) – Norway d. Portugal 3–2, Porto POR: J. Frode Andersen (NOR) d. N. Marques (POR) 7–5 6–1 1–6 6–3; C. Ruud (NOR) d. E. Couto (POR) 6–1 6–1 6–1; E. Couto/B. Mota (POR) d. H. Koll/C. Ruud (NOR) 6–4 7–6(1) 4–6 6–2; C. Ruud (NOR) d. N. Marques (POR) 7–6(1) 7–6(5) 7–6(2); B. Mota (POR) d. H. Koll (NOR) 6–2 6–3. **Finland d. Poland 3–2, Helsinki FIN:** B. Dabrowski (POL) d. V. Liukko (FIN) 4–6 7–5 7–5 6–1; M. Chmela (POL) d. T. Ketola (FIN) 3–6 6–2 2–6 6–4 6–4; T. Ketola/V. Liukko (FIN) d. M. Chmela/B. Dabrowski (POL) 7–6(4) 6–7(9) 6–0 4–6 6–3; T. Ketola (FIN) d. B. Dabrowski (POL) 7–6(4) 6–1 7–6(4); V. Luikko (FIN) d. M. Chmela (POL) 3–6 3–6 6–4 6–3 6–4.

Finland and Norway were promoted to Euro/African Group I for the 1998 competition.

RELEGATION ROUND (11–13 July) – Georgia d. Nigeria 5–0, Tbilisi GEO: D. Katcharava (GEO) d. G. Adelekan (NGR) 6–1 6–2 6–1; V. Gabrichidze (GEO) d. S. Ladipo (NGR) 6–3 6–2 6–3; V. Gabrichidze/D. Katcharava (GEO) d. G. Adelekan/S. Ladipo (NGR) 6–7(8) 6–3 6–2 7–5; G. Samkaradze (GEO) d. S. Ladipo (NGR) 6–3 ret; V. Gabrichidze (GEO) d. G. Adelekan (NGR) 6–1 6–2. **Egypt d. Lithuania 3–2, Cairo EGY:** R. Murashka (LTU) d. G. El Deeb (EGY) 4–6 6–4 6–2 6–0; A. Ghoneim (EGY) d. E. Cariovas (LTU) 3–6 6–2 7–6(5) 6–4; A. Ghoneim/H. Hemeda (EGY) d. E. Cariovas/R. Murashka (LTU) 7–6(1) 7–6(4) 4–6 7–6(4); R. Murashka (LTU) d. A. Ghoneim (EGY) 6–1 3–6 4–6 6–3 6–3; H. Hemeda (EGY) d. E. Cariovas (LTU) 6–2 7–6(4) 6–7(5) 5–7 11–9. **Latvia d. Ghana 4–1, Jurmala LAT:** G. Dzelde (LAT) d. G. Darkey (GHA) 6–2 6–1 6–1; A. Filimonovs (LAT) d. F. Ofori (GHA) 6–1 6–2 6–2; G. Dzelde/A. Filimonovs (LAT) d. F. Ofori/T. Quaye (GHA) 6–1 6–1 6–0; F. Ofori (GHA) d. G. Dzelde (LAT) 7–6(5) 6–4; A. Filimonovs (LAT) d. G. Darkey (GHA) 6–3 6–2. **Ireland d. Greece 4–1, Dublin IRL:** O. Casey (IRL) d. S. Peppas (GRE) 6–1 6–1 6–0; K. Economidis (GRE) d. S. Barron (IRL) 2–6 2–6 6–3 6–2 6–4; S. Barron/O. Casey (IRL) d. K. Economidis/N. Rovas (GRE) 6–2 6–3 6–2; S. Barron (IRL) d. S. Peppas (GRE) 6–3 6–0 6–1; O. Casey (IRL) d. K. Economidis (GRE) 6–1 6–4.

Ghana, Greece, Lithuania and Nigeria relegated to Euro/African Group III for the 1998 competition.

AMERICAN GROUP III

Southampton, Bermuda 27 April–3 May

GROUP A – Antigua/Barbuda, Barbados, Panama and Trinidad & Tobago

Antigua/Barbuda d. Trinidad & Tobago 3–0: F. Anthony (ANT) d. S. Evelyn (TRI) 6–7(5) 7–5 6–3; P. Williamson (ANT) d. O. Adams (TRI) 7–5 6–2; J. Maginley/P. Williamson (ANT) d. S. Evelyn/I. Grazette (TRI) 6–3 6–2. **Panama d. Barbados 2–1:** J-P. Herrera (PAN) d. J. Betts (BAR) 6–1 6–3; C. Valdez (PAN) d. B. Frost (BAR) 6–3 6–1; J. Betts/B. Frost (BAR) d. J. Gelabert/J. Silva (PAN) 6–7(5) 6–4 6–2. **Antigua/Barbuda d. Barbados 2–1:** J. Betts (BAR) d. F. Anthony (ANT) 6–1 3–6 6–3; P. Williamson (ANT) d. B. Frost (BAR) 6–3 6–4; J. Maginley/P. Williamson (ANT) d. J. Betts/B. Frost (BAR) 6–0 6–4. **Panama d. Trinidad & Tobago 3–0:** J-P. Herrera (PAN) d. S. Evelyn (TRI) 6–1 6–3; C. Valdez (PAN) d. O. Adams (TRI) 7–6(5) 6–1; J. Gelabert/J. Silva (PAN) d. I. Grazette/R. Greaves (TRI) 6–7(1) 7–6(5) 6–4. **Panama d. Antigua/Barbuda 2–1:** J-P. Herrera (PAN) d. F. Anthony (ANT) 6–3 6–4; P. Williamson (ANT) d. C. Valdez (PAN) 6–1 1–6 8–6; J. Gelabert/J-P. Herrera (PAN) d. F. Anthony/J. Maginley (ANT) 6–3 6–4. **Trinidad & Tobago d. Barbados 2–1:** I. Grazette (TRI) d. J. Betts (BAR) 6–1 2–6 6–1; B. Frost (BAR) d. S. Evelyn (TRI) 6–4 7–5; I. Grazette/R. Greaves (TRI) d. C. Smith/D. Williams (BAR) 6–4 4–6 6–2.

GROUP B – Bolivia, Dominican Republic, Guatemala, Jamaica

Guatemala d. Jamaica 2–1: A. Asturias (GUA) d. J. Smith (JAM) 7–6(2) 6–4; D. Chavez-Morales (GUA) d. N. Malcolm (JAM) 6–0 6–3; E. Henry/N. Malcolm (JAM) d. L. Perez-Chete/L. Valencia (GUA) 6–3 3–6 8–6. **Bolivia d. Dominican Republic 2–1:** C. Navarro (BOL) d. S. Camacho (DOM) 2–6 7–6(4) 6–3; R. Vallejo (DOM) d. P. Ugarte (BOL) 6–4 6–2; C. Navarro/P. Ugarte (BOL) d. S. Camacho/R. Vallejo (DOM) 6–7(5) 6–2 6–2. **Dominican Republic d. Guatemala 2–1:** A. Asturias (GUA) d. J. Duenas (DOM) 7–5 6–2; R. Vallejo (DOM) d. D. Chavez-Morales (GUA) 7–5 6–3; S. Camacho/J. Duenas (DOM) d. A. Asturias/L. Perez-Chete (GUA) 7–6(5) 6–4. **Jamaica d. Bolivia 3–0:** J. Smatt (JAM) d. C. Navarro (BOL) 6–2 6–2; J. Smith (JAM) d. P. Ugarte (BOL) 6–4 6–4; E. Henry/N. Malcolm (JAM) d. E. Kohlberg/C. Navarro (BOL) 6–7(5) 6–2 6–2. **Jamaica d. Dominican Republic 2–1:** J. Smatt (JAM) d. J. Duenas (DOM) 6–3 6–4; R. Vallejo (DOM) d. J. Smith (JAM)

7–6(5) 6–4; N. Malcolm/J. Smith (JAM) d. S. Camacho/R. Vallejo (DOM) 6–1 3–6 6–3. **Guatemala d. Bolivia 3–0:** A. Asturias (GUA) d. C. Navarro (BOL) 6–4 6–4; D. Chavez–Morales (GUA) d. P. Ugarte (BOL) 7–5 2–6 7–5; L. Perez-Chete/L. Valencia (GUA) d. E. Kohlberg/C. Navarro (BOL) 6–4 6–1.

Play-offs for 1st–4th positions: Jamaica d. Panama 3–0: J. Smatt (JAM) d. J-P. Herrera (PAN) 6–4 2–6 6–2; J. Smith (JAM) d. C. Valdez (PAN) 5–7 7–5 6–4; E. Henry/N. Malcolm (JAM) d. J. Gelabert/J. Silva (PAN) 6–3 6–3. **Guatemala d. Antigua/Barbuda 2–1:** A. Asturias (GUA) d. F. Anthony (ANT) 6–3 6–1; P. Williamson (ANT) d. D. Chavez-Morales (GUA) 6–3 6–7(2) 6–2; A. Asturias/L. Perez-Chete (GUA) d. J. Maginley/P. Williamson (ANT) 6–3 5–7 6–4. **Dominican Republic d. Trinidad & Tobago 3–0:** S. Camacho (DOM) d. I. Grazette (TRI) 6–4 6–2; R. Vallejo (DOM) d. S. Evelyn (TRI) 6–3 6–3; S. Camacho/J. Duenas (DOM) d. I. Grazette/R. Greaves (TRI) 7–5 6–3. **Bolivia d. Barbados 2–1:** C. Navarro (BOL) d. J. Betts (BAR) 6–3 6–3; P. Ugarte (BOL) d. B. Frost (BAR) 4–6 6–0 6–1; J. Betts/D. Williams (BAR) d. E. Kohlberg/P. Ugarte (BOL) 2–6 6–4 6–3. **Final: Guatemala d. Jamaica 3–0:** A. Asturias (GUA) d. J. Smatt (JAM) 6–0 5–7 6–4; D. Chavez-Morales (GUA) d. J. Smith (JAM) 7–5 6–1; D. Chavez-Morales/L. Perez-Chete (GUA) d. E. Henry/N. Malcolm (JAM) 7–6(4) 6–1. **Play-off for 3rd/4th positions: Antigua/Barbuda d. Panama 2–1:** J-P. Herrera (PAN) d. J. Maginley (ANT) 6–2 6–0; P. Williamson (ANT) d. C. Valdez (PAN) 6–4 6–1; F. Anthony/P. Williamson (ANT) d. J. Gelabert/J-P. Herrera (PAN) 3–6 6–3 6–0.

Play-offs for 5th–8th positions: Dominican Republic d. Trinidad & Tobago 3–0: S. Camacho (DOM) d. I. Grazette (TRI) 6–4 6–2; R. Vallejo (DOM) d. S. Evelyn (TRI) 6–3 6–3; S. Camacho/J. Duenas (DOM) d. I. Grazette/R. Greaves (TRI) 7–5 6–3. **Bolivia d. Barbados 2–1:** C. Navarro (BOL) d. J. Betts (BAR) 6–3 6–3; P. Ugarte (BOL) d. B. Frost (BAR) 4–6 6–0 6–1; J. Betts/D. Williamson (BAR) d. P. Ugarte/E. Kohlberg (BOL) 2–6 6–4 6–3. **Dominican Republic d. Bolivia 2–1:** C. Navarro (BOL) d. J. Duenas (DOM) 2–6 7–5 6–1; R. Vallejo (DOM) d. P. Ugarte (BOL) 5–7 6–4 6–1; S. Camacho/R. Vallejo (DOM) d. C. Navarro/P. Ugarte (BOL) 6–4 6–7(5) 6–4. **Barbados d. Trinidad & Tobago 2–1:** D. Williams (BAR) d. I. Grazette (TRI) 6–4 7–6(4); J. Betts (BAR) d. O. Adams (TRI) 3–5 ret; S. Evelyn/R. Greaves (TRI) d. J. Betts/D. Williams (BAR) 6–2 7–5.

Final Positions: Guatemala 1, Jamaica 2, Antigua/Barbuda 3, Panama 4, Dominican Republic 5, Bolivia 6, Barbados 7, Trinidad & Tobago 8.
Guatemala and Jamaica were promoted to American Group II for the 1998 competition.
Barbados and Trinidad & Tobago were relegated to American Group IV for the 1998 competition.

ASIA/OCEANIA GROUP III

Doha, Qatar 26–30 March

GROUP A – Bangladesh, Bahrain Kazakhstan, Kuwait
Kazakhstan d. Bahrain 2–1: A. Kedriouk (KAZ) d. E. Abdul-Aal (BRN) 7–6(5) 6–4; A. Shehab (BRN) d. I. Chaldounov (KAZ) 6–4 6–2; I. Chaldounov/A. Kedriouk (KAZ) d. E. Abdul-Aal/N. Abdul-Aal (BRN) 7–5 4–6 7–5. **Kuwait d. Bangladesh 3–0:** M. Al-Foudari (KUW) d. H-L. Rahman (BAN) 6–4 6–4; A. Al-Shatti (KUW) d. S. Jamaly (BAN) 6–4 6–3; K. Al-Gharabally/M. Ghareeb (KUW) d. S. Jamaly/H-L. Rahman (BAN) 7–6(1) 6–4. **Kazakhstan d. Bangladesh 3–0:** A. Kedriouk (KAZ) d. H-L. Rahman (BAN) 6–2 6–2; I. Chaldounov (KAZ) d. D. Passia (BAN) 4–6 6–4 6–2; J. Karlov/A. Kedriouk (KAZ) d. S. Jamaly/D. Passia (BAN) 6–2 6–4. **Kuwait d. Bahrain 2–1:** E. Abdul-Aal (BRN) d. M. Ghareeb (KUW) 6–3 6–0; A. Al-Shatti (KUW) d. A. Shehab (BRN) 6–2 6–1; K. Al-Gharabally/A. Al-Shatti (KUW) d. E. Abdul-Aal/N. Abdul-Aal (BRN) 3–6 7–5 6–2. **Kazakhstan d. Kuwait 2–1:** A. Kedriouk (KAZ) d. M. Al-Foudari (KUW) 6–2 6–3; M. Ghareeb (KUW) d. I. Chaldounov (KAZ) 6–1 6–4; I. Chaldounov/A. Kedriouk (KAZ) d. M. Al Foudari/K. Al-Gharabally (KUW) 6–2 6–3. **Bahrain d. Bangladesh 2–1:** S. Shehab (BRN) d. T. Hossain (BAN) 6–3 6–1; D. Passia (BAN) d. A. Shehab (BRN) 6–2 7–6(1); N. Abdul-Aal/ A. Shehab (BRN) d. S. Jamaly/H-L. Rahman (BAN) 6–3 6–3.

GROUP B – Malaysia, Pacific Oceania, Qatar, Sri Lanka
Qatar d. Malaysia 2–1: V. Ortchuan (MAS) d. N. Al-Khulaifi (QAT) 6–2 1–6 6–2; S. Al-Alawi (QAT) d. R. Ramachandran (MAS) 2–6 6–3 6–2; S. Al-Alawi/N. Al-Khulaifi (QAT) d. R. Ramachandran/A-A. Shazali (MAS) 6–2 6–3. **Pacific Oceania d. Sri Lanka 2–1:** R. de Silva (SRI) d. M. Kailahi (POC) 6–3 6–3; L. Tenai (POC) d. J. Wijeyesekera (SRI) 4–6 7–6(2) 6–1; M. Kailahi/L. Tenai (POC) d. R. de Silva/J. Wijeyesekera (SRI) 7–6(4) 3–6 6–3. **Malaysia d. Pacific Oceania 2–1:** V. Ortchuan (MAS) d. M. Kailahi (POC) 6–4 6–3; R. Ramachandran (MAS) d. L. Tenai (POC) 6–0 6–1; M. Kailahi/L. Tenai (POC) d. J. Mulyadi/R. Ramachandran (MAS) 7–6(3) 3–6 6–3. **Qatar d. Sri Lanka 2–1:** N. Al-Khulaifi (QAT) d. R. de Silva (SRI) 6–2 6–7(5) 8–6; S. Al-Alawi (QAT) d. J. Wijeyesekera (SRI) 7–5 6–1; R. de Silva/J. Wijeyesekera (SRI) d. M-A. Al-Saoud/C. Diong (QAT) 6–2 7–5. **Sri Lanka d. Malaysia 3–0:** R. de Silva (SRI) d. V. Ortchuan (MAS) 7–6(1) 6–0; J. Wijeyesekera (SRI) d. R. Ramachandran (MAS) 7–6(6) 5–7 6–4; R. de Silva/J. Wijeyesekera (SRI) d. J. Mulyadi/R. Ramachandran (MAS) 6–3 6–2. **Pacific Oceania d. Qatar 2–1:** M. Kailahi (POC) d. M-A. Al-Saoud (QAT) 4–6 6–2 6–3; S. Al-Alawi (QAT) d. L. Tenai (POC) 6–1 6–2; M. Kailahi/L. Tenai (POC) d. S. Al-Alawi/N. Al-Khulaifi (QAT) 4–6 6–4 6–2.

Play-off's for 1st–4th positions: Pacific Oceania d. Kuwait 2–1: M. Kailahi (POC) d. M. Al-Foudari (KUW) 6–3 6–2; A. Al-Shatti (KUW) d. L. Tenai (POC) 2–6 6–2 6–0; M. Kailahi/L. Tenai (POC) d. K. Al-Gharabally/A. Al-Shatti (KUW) 1–6 6–2 6–2. **Qatar d. Kazakhstan 2–1:** A. Kedriouk (KAZ) d. N. Al-Khulaifi (QAT) 6–2 6–2; S. Al-Alawi (QAT) d. I. Chaldounov (KAZ) 6–0 6–3; S. Al-Alawi/C. Diong (QAT) d. I. Chaldounov/A. Kedriouk (KAZ) 6–2 6–4. **Final: Qatar d. Pacific Oceania 2–1:** M. Kailahi (POC) d. C. Diong (QAT) 7–6(4) ret; S. Al-Alawi (QAT) d. L. Tenai (POC) 6–2 6–3; S. Al-Alawi/N. Al-Khulaifi (QAT) d. M. Kailahi/L. Tenai (POC) 2–6 6–3

6–2. **Play-off for 3rd/4th positions: Kazakhstan d. Kuwait 3–0:** A. Kedriouk (KAZ) d. M. Al-Foudari (KUW) 3–0 ret; I. Chaldounov (KAZ) d. K. Al-Gharabally (KUW) 6–3 0–0 (40–0) ret; I. Chaldounov/A. Kedriouk (KAZ) d. M. Al-Foudari/K. Al-Gharabally (KUW) w/o.

Play-off's for 5th–8th positions: Malaysia d. Bahrain 2–1: E. Abdul-Aal (BRN) d. V. Ortchuan (MAS) 7–5 6–3; R. Ramachandran (MAS) d. A. Shehab (BRN) 6–1 6–0; J. Mulyadi/R. Ramachandran (MAS) d. N. Abdul-Aal/ S. Shehab (BRN) 6–0 6–2. **Sri Lanka d. Bangladesh 2–1:** R. de Silva (SRI) d. D. Passia (BAN) 5–7 6–4 6–1; S. Jamaly (BAN) d. J. Wijeyesekera (SRI) 2–6 6–4 6–2; R de Silva/J. Wijeyesekera (SRI) d. S. Jamaly/D. Passia (BAN) 3–6 6–4 6–4. **Malaysia d. Sri Lanka 3–0:** V. Ortchuan (MAS) d. L. Jayasuriya (SRI) 6–4 7–6(3); R. Ramachandran (MAS) d. R. Razik (SRI) 6–1 6–1; J. Mulyadi/A-A. Shazali (MAS) d. R. de Silva/J. Wijeyesekera (SRI) 4–6 6–4 6–2. **Bahrain d. Bangladesh 2–1:** E. Abdul-Aal (BRN) d. D. Passia (BAN) 6–2 6–1; S. Jamaly (BAN) d. A. Shehab (BRN) 6–1 6–4; N. Abdul-Aal/S. Shehab (BRN) d. S. Jamaly/D. Passia (BAN) 6–2 1–6 6–4.

Final Positions: Qatar 1, Pacific Oceania 2, Kazakhstan 3, Kuwait 4, Malaysia 5, Sri Lanka 6, Bahrain 7, Bangladesh 8.
Qatar and Pacific Oceania were promoted to Asia/Oceania Group II for the 1998 competition.
Bahrain and Bangladesh were relegated to Asia/Oceania Group IV for the 1998 competition.

EURO/AFRICAN GROUP III
ZONE A
Senegal, 22–26 January

GROUP A – Ethiopia, San Marino, Turkey, FYR of Macedonia
FYR of Macedonia d. San Marino 3–0: D. Jovanovski (MKD) d. C. Rosti (SMR) 6–1 2–6 6–3; Z. Sevcenko (MKD) d. D. Vicini (SMR) 6–1 6–3; L. Magdincev/Z. Sevcenko (MKD) d. G. Francini/D. Vicini (SMR) 6–1 7–6(5). **Turkey d. Ethiopia 3–0:** B. Ergun (TUR) d. H. Kidan (ETH) 6–0 6–7(5) 6–3; E. Oral (TUR) d. Y. Setegne (ETH) 6–2 6–3; M. Azkara/A. Karagoz (TUR) d. S. Gabriel/Y. Setegne (ETH) 6–0 6–3. **Turkey d. San Marino 3–0:** B. Ergun (TUR) d. C. Rosti (SMR) 6–4 6–2; E. Oral (TUR) d. D. Vicini (SMR) 6–1 6–4; M. Azkara/A. Karagoz (TUR) d. G. Francini/D. Vicini (SMR) 6–3 6–3. **FYR of Macedonia d. Ethiopia 2–1:** S. Gabriel (ETH) d. D. Jovanovski (MKD) 2–6 6–4 6–0; Z. Sevcenko (MKD) d. Y. Setegne (ETH) 6–0 6–0; L. Magdincev/Z. Sevcenko (MKD) d. S. Gabriel/H. Kidan (ETH) 6–2 6–1. **FYR of Macedonia d. Turkey 2–1:** A. Karagoz (TUR) d. L. Magdincev (MKD) 6–4 6–4; Z. Sevcenko (MKD) d. B. Ergun (TUR) 6–4 6–0; L. Magdincev/Z. Sevcenko (MKD) d. M. Azkara/E. Oral (TUR) 7–5 6–2. **San Marino d. Ethiopia 2–1:** C. Rosti (SMR) d. H. Kidan (ETH) 6–4 6–1; D. Vicini (SMR) d. S. Gabriel (ETH) 6–2 6–4; H. Kidan/Y. Setegne (ETH) d. G. Francini/M. Rosti (SMR) 6–3 7–6(4).

GROUP B – Armenia, Bosnia/Herzegovina, Senegal, Luxembourg.
Senegal d. Armenia 3–0: J. N. Said (SEN) d. A. Aroutiounyan (ARM) 6–3 6–4; Y. Doumbia (SEN) d. D. Babayan (ARM) 6–0 6–0; Y. Doumbia/T. Ly (SEN) d. H. Hakobyan/A. Aroutiounyan (ARM) 6–2 6–3. **Luxembourg d. Bosnia/Herzegovina 2–1:** J. Goudenbour (LUX) d. E. Mustafic (BIH) 6–3 6–3; M. Zahirovic (BIH) d. S. Thoma (LUX) 7–6(11) 6–1; J. Goudenbour/P. Schaul (LUX) d. Mustafic/M. Zahirovic (BIH) 4–6 6–3 6–4. **Senegal d. Bosnia/Herzegovina 3–0:** J. N. Said (SEN) d. H. Basalic (BIH) 7–6(4) 6–3; Y. Doumbia (SEN) d. M. Zahirovic (BIH) 6–1 6–2; Y. Doumbia/T. Ly (SEN) d. H. Basalic/E. Mustafic (BIH) 6–3 6–4. **Luxembourg d. Armenia 3–0:** A. Graimprey (LUX) d. A. Aroutiounyan (ARM) 6–0 6–0; S. Thoma (LUX) d. D. Babayan (ARM) 6–1 6–1; J. Goudenbour/P. Schaul (LUX) d. A. Aroutiounyan/A. Makichian (ARM) 6–2 6–3. **Senegal d. Luxembourg 2–1:** P. Schaul (LUX) d. J. N. Said (SEN) 6–4 6–4; Y. Doumbia (SEN) d. Adrian Graimprey (LUX) 5–7 6–4 6–2; Y. Doumbia/T. Ly (SEN) d. J. Goudenbour/S. Thoma (LUX) 7–6(7) 6–2. **Bosnia/Herzegovina d. Armenia 3–0:** E. Mustafic (BIH) d. A. Aroutiounyan (ARM) 6–3 6–3; M. Zahirovic (BIH) d. D. Babayan (ARM) 6–2 6–1; E. Mustafic/Zahirovic (BIH) d. H. Hakopian/A. Makichian (ARM) 6–4 6–2.

Play-off's for 1st–4th positions: Luxembourg d. FYR of Macedonia 2–1: J. Goudenbour (LUX) d. L. Magdincev (MKD) 6–2 6–3; Z. Sevcenko (MKD) d. S. Thoma (LUX) 6–1 6–4; J. Goudenbour/A. Graimprey (LUX) d. L. Magdincev/Z. Sevcenko (MKD) 7–6(3) 6–7(3) 6–2. **Senegal d. Turkey 2–1:** B. Ergun (TUR) d. Jean Noel Said (SEN) 4–6 6–3 6–3; Y. Doumbia (SEN) d. E. Oral (TUR) 6–2 6–3; Y. Doumbia/T. Ly (SEN) d. B. Ergun/A. Karagoz (TUR) 6–4 6–4.

Final: Luxembourg d. Senegal 2–1: P. Schaul (LUX) d. J. N. Said (SEN) 6–2 6–4; Y. Doumbia (SEN) d. S. Thoma (LUX) 6–2 6–2; J. Goudenbour/A. Graimprey (LUX) d. Y. Doumbia/T. Ly (SEN) 7–6(4) 7–6(5). **Play-off for 3rd–4th positions: Turkey d. FYR of Macedonia 2–1:** M. Azkara (TUR) d. G. Popov (MKD) 6–4 6–1; Z. Sevcenko (MKD) d. B. Ergun (TUR) 6–7(4) 6–2 8–6; M. Azkara/E. Oral (TUR) d. L. Magdincev/Z. Sevcenko (MKD) 6–4 6–2.

Play-off's for 5th–8th positions: San Marino d. Armenia 3–0: C. Rosti (SMR) d. A. Makichyan (ARM) 6–1 6–2; D. Vicini (SMR) d. A. Aroutiounyan (ARM) 5–7 7–5 6–3; G. Francini/C. Rosti (SMR) d. H. Hakobyan/A. Makichyan (ARM) 6–4 6–2. **Bosnia/Herzegovina d. Ethiopia 3–0:** E. Mustafic (BIH) d. Samuel Gabriel (ETH) 6–1 6–2; M. Zahirovic (BIH) d. Y. Setegne (ETH) 2–6 6–3 6–1; H. Basalic/E. Mustafic (BIH) d. H. Kidan/Y. Setegne (ETH) 6–0 6–0.

Final: Bosnia/Herzegovina d. San Marino 3–0: E. Mustafic (BIH) d. C. Rosti (SMR) 7–5 7–5; M. Zahirovic (BIH) d. D. Vicini (SMR) 7–6(3) 7–6(5); H. Basalic/E. Mustafic (BIH) d. G. Francini/D. Vicini (SMR) 6–2 6–0. **Armenia d. Ethiopia 2–1:** A. Aroutiounyan (ARM) d. S. Gabriel (ETH) 6–2 6–1; Y. Setegne (ETH) d. D. Babayan (ARM) 6–4 6–3; A. Aroutiounyan/A. Makichian (ARM) d. S. Gabriel/Y. Setegne (ETH) 6–4 6–2.

Final Positions: Luxembourg 1, Senegal 2, Turkey 3, FYR of Macedonia 4, Bosnia/Herzegovina 5, San Marino 6, Armenia 7, Ethiopia 8.
Luxembourg and Senegal were promoted to Euro/African Group II for the 1998 competition.
Armenia and Ethiopia were relegated to Euro/African Group IV for the 1998 competition.

ZONE B
Plovdiv, Bulgaria 19–25 May

GROUP A – Bulgaria, Estonia, Kenya, Malta.
Bulgaria d. Malta 3–0: I. Keskinov (BUL) d. M. Schembri (MLT) 6–1 6–1; O. Stanoytchev (BUL) d. C. Gatt (MLT) 6–4 6–0; I. Bratanov/I. Traykov (BUL) d. G. Asciak/M. Schembri (MLT) 7–6(8) 6–3. **Estonia d. Kenya 2–1:** A. Luzgin (EST) d. A. Cooper (KEN) 6–2 6–1; P. Wekesa (KEN) d. R. Busch (EST) 6–1 6–2; A. Luzgin/G. Vilms (EST) d. A. Cooper/P. Wekesa (KEN) 6–3 6–4. **Bulgaria d. Estonia 3–0:** I. Keskinov (BUL) d. A. Luzgin (EST) 6–3 6–1; O. Stanoytchev (BUL) d. R. Busch (EST) 6–0 6–2; I. Bratanov/I.Traykov (BUL) d. R. Saluste/G. Vilms (EST) 6–2 6–4. **Kenya d. Malta 2–1:** G. Asciak (MLT) d. N. Oduor (KEN) 6–3 6–4; P. Wekesa (KEN) d. C. Gatt (MLT) 3–6 6–4 6–3; A. Cooper/N. Oduor (KEN) d. G. Asciak/M. Schembri (MLT) 6–4 6–2. **Bulgaria d. Kenya 3–0:** I. Keskinov (BUL) d. N. Oduor (KEN) 6–2 6–4; O. Stanoytchev (BUL) d. A. Cooper (KEN) 6–2 6–1; I. Bratanov/I. Traykov (BUL) d. A. Cooper/N. Oduor (KEN) 6–3 6–2. **Estonia d. Malta 2–1:** A. Luzgin (EST) d. G. Asciak (MLT) 3–6 6–4 6–3; C. Gatt (MLT) d. R. Busch (EST) 6–3 6–3; A. Luzgin/G. Vilms (EST) d. G. Asciak/C. Gatt (MLT) 6–2 6–3.

GROUP B – Algeria, Cameroon, Moldova, Monaco.
Monaco d. Algeria 2–1: C. Bosio (MON) d. M. Mahmoudi (ALG) 6–2 7–6(4); S. Graeff (MON) d. N. Mahmoudi (ALG) 6–4 6–3; N. Hakimi/N. Mahmoudi (ALG) d. C. Boggetti/S. Graeff (MON) 7–6(4) 7–6(6). **Moldova d. Cameroon 3–0:** O. Sinic (MDA) d. A. Mvogo (CMR) 7–5 3–6 7–5; I. Gorban (MDA) d. Y. Auzoux (CMR) 6–3 6–0; I. Gorban/O. Sinic (MDA) d. L. Kemajou/J. Oyebog (CMR) 6–3 6–3. **Moldova d. Algeria 3–0:** O. Sinic (MDA) d. N. Hakimi (ALG) 6–4 6–1; I. Gorban (MDA) d. N. Mahmoudi (ALG) 6–3 6–3; I. Gorban/O. Sinic (MDA) d. N. Hakimi/N. Mahmoudi (ALG) 6–3 6–4. **Monaco d. Cameroon 2–1:** J. Oyebog (CMR) d. C. Bosio (MON) 4–6 6–3 7–5; S. Graeff (MON) d. A. Mvogo (CMR) 6–1 6–2; C. Boggetti/S. Graeff (MON) d. Y. Auzoux/J. Oyebog (CMR) 6–4 3–6 16–14. **Monaco d. Moldova 3–0:** C. Bosio (MON) d. O. Sinic (MDA) 7–5 5–7 6–4; S. Graeff (MON) d. I. Gorban (MDA) 6–4 6–4; C. Boggetti/J. Vincileoni (MON) d. E. Plougarev/M. Savitski (MDA) 6–1 6–1. **Cameroon d. Algeria 2–1:** J. Oyebog (CMR) d. N. Hakimi (ALG) 6–0 6–2; M. Mahmoudi (ALG) d. Y. Auzoux (CMR) 6–0 6–4; L. Kemajou/Oyebog (CMR) d. N. Hakimi/M. Mahmoudi (ALG) 6–1 6–4.

Play-off's for 1st–4th positions: Bulgaria d. Moldova 3–0: I. Keskinov (BUL) d. O. Sinic (MDA) 6–2 6–4; O. Stanoytchev (BUL) d. I. Gorban (MDA) 6–7(6) 6–4 6–3; I. Bratanov/I. Traykov (BUL) d. E. Plougarev/M. Savitski (MDA) 6–1 6–3. **Monaco d. Estonia 3–0:** C. Bosio (MON) d. A. Luzgin (EST) 6–4 6–4; S. Graeff (MON) d. R. Busch (EST) 7–5 6–4; C. Boggetti/J. Vincileoni (MON) d. R. Saluste/G. Vilms (EST) 7–6(5) 7–6(5). **Final: Bulgaria d. Monaco 3–0:** I. Keskinov (BUL) d. C. Bosio (MON) 7–5 6–4; O. Stanoytchev (BUL) d. S. Graeff (MON) 6–3 4–6 6–3; I. Bratanov/I. Traykov (BUL) d. C. Boggetti/S. Graeff (MON) 6–7(6) 6–2 6–1. **Play-off for 3rd–4th positions: Estonia d. Moldova 2–1:** O. Sinic (MDA) d. G. Vilms (EST) 6–1 6–3; R. Busch (EST) d. I. Gorban (MDA) 3–6 6–4 6–1; A. Luzgin/G. Vilms (EST) d. I. Gorban/O. Sinic (MDA) 6–2 6–3.

Play-off's for 5th–8th positions: Malta d. Cameroon 2–1: M. Schembri (MLT) d. J. Oyebog (CMR) 7–6(9) 3–6 6–4; A. Mvogo (CMR) d. C. Gatt (MLT) 6–3 6–3; G. Asciak/M. Schembri (MLT) d. Y. Auzoux/A. Mvogo (CMR) 7–6(4) 6–3. **Kenya d. Algeria 2–1:** M. Mahmoudi (ALG) d. A. Cooper (KEN) 4–6 6–3 6–3; P. Wekesa (KEN) d. N. Mahmoudi (ALG) 6–3 3–6 6–3; A. Cooper/N. Oduor (KEN) d. N. Hakimi/M. Mahmoudi (ALG) 5–7 6–4 6–4. **Final: Kenya d. Malta 2–1:** A. Cooper (KEN) d. G. Asciak (MLT) 6–4 6–2; P. Wekesa (KEN) d. M. Schembri (MLT) 6–3 4–6 6–2; G. Asciak/C. Gatt (MLT) d. A. Cooper/N. Oduor (KEN) w/o. **Play-off for 7th/8th positions: Algeria d. Cameroon 2–1:** A. Mvogo (CMR) d. M. Mahmoudi (ALG) 6–0 0–0 (30–0) ret.; N. Mahmoudi (ALG) d. Y. Auzoux (CMR) 6–0 6–1; N. Hakimi/N. Mahmoudi (ALG) d. Y. Auzoux/A. Mvogo (CMR) 3–6 7–6(7) 6–1.

FINAL POSITIONS: 1st Bulgaria, 2nd Monaco, 3rd Estonia, 4th Moldova, 5th Kenya, 6th Malta, 7th Algeria, 8th Cameroon.
Bulgaria and Monaco were promoted to Euro/African Group II for the 1998 competition.
Algeria and Cameroon were relegated to Euro/African Group IV for the 1998 competition.

AMERICAN GROUP IV
Southampton, Bermuda, 1–3 May
Nations: Bermuda, Costa Rica, OECS.
Bermuda d. Costa Rica 2–1: R. Mallory (BER) d. F. Martinez (CRC) 6–3 7–5; D. Evans (BER) d. F. Camacho (CRC) 2–6 7–6(2) 6–4; M. Echandi/J. Solera (CRC) d. J. Collieson/M. Way (BER) 7–6(2) 3–6 6–4. **Costa Rica**

d. OECS 2–1: G. James (ECA) d. J. Solera (CRC) 6–2 6–4; F. Camacho (CRC) d. V. Lewis (ECA) 0–6 7–5 6–3; M. Echandi/F. Martinez (CRC) d. G. Eugene/G. James (ECA) 7–5 1–3 ret. **Bermuda d. OECS 2–1:** J. Collieson (BER) d. G. Eugene (ECA) 6–2 6–2; V. Lewis (ECA) d. D. Evans (BER) 6–2 6–2; R. Mallory/M. Way (BER) d. G. Eugene/V. Lewis (ECA) 7–5 7–6(4).

Final Positions: Bermuda 1, Costa Rica 2, OECS 3.
Bermuda and Costa Rica were promoted to American Group II for the 1998 competition.

ASIA/OCEANIA GROUP IV

Muscat, Oman 26–30 March

Nations: Brunei, Jordan, Oman, Syria, Tajikistan, United Arab Nations.
Syria d. United Arab Emirates 3–0: R. Bou-Hassoun (SYR) d. M. Nader (UAE) 6–2 6–2; D. Dawoodian (SYR) d. S. Al-Maktoum (UAE) 6–2 6–4; A. Salim/L. Salim (SYR) d. O. Al-Ulama/M. Nader (UAE) 7–5 6–2. **Tajikistan d. Jordan 2–1:** F. Azzouni (JOR) d. S. Makachin (TJK) 6–2 6–2; M. Yakhyaev (TJK) d. A. Al-Hadid (JOR) 6–0 6–0; B. Radjabaliev/M. Yakhyaev (TJK) d. F. Azzouni/G. Hassan-Qadi (JOR) 6–1 6–0. **Oman d. Brunei 2–1:** I. Ibrahim (BRU) d. F. Al-Hashmi (OMA) 6–3 6–1; M. Al-Rawahi (OMA) d. P-C. Chua (BRU) 6–0 6–0; K. Al-Nabhani/M. Al-Rawahi (OMA) d. P-C. Chua/I. Ibrahim (BRU) 4–6 7–5 7–5. **Syria d. Tajikistan 2–1:** R. Bou-Hassoun (SYR) d. S. Makashin (TJK) 6–3 7–5; M. Yakhyaev (TJK) d. D. Dawoodian (SYR) 6–2 6–4; R. Bou-Hassoun/D. Dawoodian (SYR) d. B. Radjabalien/M. Yakhyaev (TJK) 6–3 7–6(5). **United Arab Emirates d. Brunei 2–1:** O. Bahrouzyan (UAE) d. I. Ibrahim (BRU) 6–3 6–2; O. Al-Ulama (UAE) d. P-C. Chua (BRU) 6–2 7–6(3); F. Chin/I. Ibrahim (BRU) d. S. Al-Maktoum/M. Nader (UAE) 6–3 6–4. **Oman d. Jordan 2–1:** F. Azzouni (JOR) d. F. Al-Hashmi (OMA) 6–0 7–5; M. Al-Rawahi (OMA) d. A. Al-Hadid (JOR) 6–1 6–2; K. Al-Nabhani/M. Al-Rawahi (OMA) d. F. Azzouni/G. Hassan-Qadi (JOR) 6–3 6–4. **Tajikistan d. Oman 3–0:** S. Makashin (TJK) d. F. Al-Hashmi (OMA) 6–1 6–0; M. Yakhyaev (TJK) d. M. Al-Rawahi (OMA) 6–0 6–0; B. Radjabalien/M. Yakhyaev (TJK) d. K. Al-Nabhani/M. Al-Rawahi (OMA) 6–3 6–0. **United Arab Emirates d. Jordan 2–1:** O. Bahrouzyan (UAE) d. F. Azzouni (JOR) 7–5 4–6 6–3; O. Al-Ulama (UAE) d. G. Hassan-Qadi (JOR) 6–2 3–6 6–2; T. Al-Quasi/G. Hassan-Qadi (JOR) d. S. Al-Maktoum/M. Nader (UAE) 6–3 6–1. **Syria d. Brunei 3–0:** R. Bou-Hassoun (SYR) d. F. Sulaiman (BRU) 6–0 6–2; D. Dawoodian (SYR) d. F. Chin (BRU) 6–0 6–3; A. Salim/L. Salim (SYR) d. P-C. Chua/I. Ibrahim (BRU) 2–6 6–0 6–3. **Brunei d. Jordan 2–1:** I. Ibrahim (BRU) d. T. Al-Quasi (JOR) 6–2 6–2; F. Azzouni (JOR) d. F. Chin (BRU) 7–5 6–0: P-C. Chua/I. Ibrahim (BRU) d. F. Azzouni/G. Hassan-Qadi (JOR) 6–1 7–5. **Tajikistan d. United Arab Emirates 3–0:** S. Makashin (TJK) d. O. Bahrouzyan (UAE) 6–3 6–4; M. Yakhyaev (TJK) d. O. Al-Ulama (UAE) 6–1 6–1; S. Makashin/M. Yakhyaev (TJK) d. S. Al-Maktoum/M. Nader (UAE) 6–1 6–3. **Syria d. Oman 3–0:** R. Bou-Hassoun (SYR) d. K. Al-Nabhani (OMA) 6–0 6–1; L. Salim (SYR) d. M. Al-Rawahi (OMA) 6–3 7–6(2); A. Salim/L. Salim (SYR) d. F. Al-Hashmi/B. Al-Sharji (OMA) 6–1 6–3. **Syria v Jordan, Tajikistan v Brunei and United Arab Emirates v Oman** not played because of rain.

Final positions: Syria 1, Tajikistan 2, United Arab Emirates 3, Oman 4, Brunei 5, Jordan 6.
Syria and Tajikistan were promoted to Asia/Oceania Group III for the 1998 competition.

EURO/AFRICAN GROUP IV

ZONE A

Gaborone, Botswana 19–23 March

GROUP A – Liechtenstein, Togo, Sudan, Uganda.
Liechtenstein d. Sudan 3–0: J. Tomordy (LIE) d. M. Abdalla (SUD) 6–2 6–3; S. Ritter (LIE) d. A. El Agraa (SUD) 6–2 6–0; H. Birkner/R. Buchel (LIE) d. A. Jeha/A. Jeha (SUD) 6–3 6–3. **Togo d. Uganda 3–0:** K. Apeti (TOG) d. R. Sebbi (UGA) 6–2 6–2; J. Loglo (TOG) d. J. Oduke (UGA) 6–1 6–4; K. Loglo/M. Segbeaya (TOG) d. C. Bagala/R. Sebbi (UGA) 6–1 6–2. **Liechtenstein d. Uganda 3–0:** J. Tomordy (LIE) d. E. Ofuyulu (UGA) 6–2 6–3; S. Ritter (LIE) d. J. Oduke (UGA) 6–3 7–5; H. Birkner/R. Buchel (LIE) d. C. Bagala/R. Sebbi (UGA) 7–6(4) 4–6 10–8. **Togo d. Sudan 3–0:** K. Apeti (TOG) d. M. Abdalla (SUD) 7–5 6–1; J. Loglo (TOG) d. A. El Agraa (SUD) 6–2 6–0; K. Loglo/M. Segbeaya (TOG) d. M. Abdalla/A. Jeha (SUD) 6–1 7–5. **Togo d. Liechtenstein 3–0:** K. Apeti (TOG) d. R. Buchel (LIE) 6–0 6–0; J. Loglo (TOG) d. H. Birkner (LIE) 6–2 6–0; K. Loglo/ M. Segbeaya (TOG) d. H. Birkner/R. Buchel (LIE) 6–4 6–3. **Uganda d. Sudan 2–1:** M. Abdalla (SUD) d. R. Sebbi (UGA) 6–3 6–1; J. Oduke (UGA) d. A. El Agraa (SUD) 6–1 6–2; J. Oduke/R. Sebbi (UGA) d. M. Abdalla/A. El Agraa (SUD) 7–5 6–3.

GROUP B – Botswana, Iceland, Djibouti, Madagascar
Botswana d. Djibouti 3–0: G. Jeftha (BOT) d. O. Mohammed (DJI) 6–0 6–0; P. Molefhe (BOT) d. A. Moussa (DJI) 6–0 6–0; M. Judd/T. Kgosimore (BOT) d. A. Aden/C. Nasser-Saeed (DJI) 6–2 6–1. **Madagascar d. Iceland 3–0:** H. Andrianafetra (MAD) d. E. Sigurgeirsson (ISL) 6–0 6–1; R. Rajoabelina (MAD) d. G. Einarsson (ISL) 6–4 6–4; H. Andrianafetra/D. Radison (MAD) d. S. Palsson/O. Sveinsson (ISL) 6–2 6–0. **Madagascar d. Botswana 2–1:** H. Andrianafetra (MAD) d. G. Jeftha (BOT) 6–2 6–4; P. Molefhe (BOT) d. R. Rajoabelina (MAD) 7–6(5) 7–5; H. Andrianafetra/R. Rajoabelina (MAD) d. T. Kgosimore/P. Molefhe (BOT) 6–1 6–3. **Iceland d. Djibouti 3–0:** E. Sigurgeirsson (ISL) d. A. Aden (DJI) 6–0 6–0; G. Einarsson (ISL) d. C. Nasser-Saeed (DJI) 6–0 6–0; G. Einarsson/S. Palsson (ISL) d. O. Mohammed/A. Moussa (DJI) 6–2 6–1. **Botswana d. Iceland 2–1:** G. Jeftha (BOT) d. E. Sigurgeirsson (ISL) 6–1 6–3; P. Molefhe (BOT) d. G. Einarsson (ISL) 7–6(4) ret; S. Palsson/E. Sigurgeirsson (ISL) d. M. Judd/T. Kgosimore (BOT) 7–6(4) 6–3. **Madagascar d. Djibouti 3–0:** J. Rakotondravelo (MAD) d. A. Aden (DJI) 6–0 6–0; D. Radison (MAD) d. O. Mohammed (DJI) 6–0 6–2; D. Radison/J. Rakotondravelo (MAD) d. A. Moussa/C. Nasser-Saeed (DJI) 6–0 6–0.

Play-off's for 1st–4th positions: Togo d. Botswana 2–1: G. Jeftha (BOT) d. K. Apeti (TOG) 6–3 6–4; J. Loglo (TOG) d. P. Molefhe (BOT) 6–4 7–5; K. Apeti/J. Loglo (TOG) d. M. Judd/T. Kgosimore (BOT) 6–3 6–4. **Madagascar d. Liechtenstein 3–0:** H. Andrianafetra (MAD) d. J. Tomordy (LIE) 6–7(4) 6–1 6–2; R. Rajoabelina (MAD) d. S. Ritter (LIE) 6–4 6–3; D. Radison/J. Rakotondravelo (MAD) d. H. Birkner/R. Buchel (LIE) 6–1 6–1. **Final: Madagascar d. Togo 2–1:** H. Andrianafetra (MAD) d. K. Apeti (TOG) 6–2 6–3; J. Loglo (TOG) d. R. Rajoabelina (MAD) 6–2 6–3; H. Andrianafetra/R. Rajoabelina (MAD) d. K. Apeti/J. Loglo (TOG) 7–5 6–3. **Play-off for 3rd–4th positions: Liechtenstein d. Botswana 2–1:** J. Tomordy (LIE) d. T. Kgosimore (BOT) 7–5 6–3; P. Molefhe (BOT) d. S. Ritter (LIE) 3–6 6–3 6–0; S. Ritter/J. Tomordy (LIE) d. G. Jeftha/M. Judd (BOT) w/o.

Play-off's for 5th–8th positions: Uganda d. Djibouti 3–0: R. Sebbi (UGA) d. A. Aden (DJI) 6–0 6–1; J. Oduke (UGA) d. O. Mohammed (DJI) 6–0 6–0; J. Oduke/R. Sebbi (UGA) d. A. Aden/O. Mohammed (DJI) 6–0 6–1. **Sudan d. Iceland 2–1:** M. Abdalla (SUD) d. S. Palsson (ISL) 6–2 6–4; G. Einarsson (ISL) d. A. El Agraa (SUD) 6–2 5–7 6–3; M. Abdalla/A. Jeha (SUD) d. S. Palsson/E. Sigurgeirsson (ISL) 3–6 6–2 7–5. **Uganda d. Sudan 2–1:** M. Abdalla (SUD) d. R. Sebbi (UGA) 6–3 6–3; J. Oduke (UGA) d. A. El Agraa (SUD) 6–2 6–2; J. Oduke/R. Sebbi (UGA) d. M. Abdalla/A. Jeha (SUD) 6–4 3–6 6–4. **Iceland d. Djibouti 3–0:** E. Sigurgeirsson (ISL) d. A. Aden (DJI) 6–0 6–2; G. Einarsson (ISL) d. O. Mohammed (DJI) 6–3 6–1; G. Einarsson/E. Sigurgeirsson (ISL) d. A. Aden/O. Mohammed (DJI) 6–1 6–1.

Final Positions: Madagascar 1, Togo 2, Liechtenstein 3, Botswana 4, Uganda 5, Sudan 6, Iceland 7, Djibouti 8.
Madagascar and Togo were promoted to Euro/African Group III for the 1998 competition.

ZONE B
Nicosia, Cyprus 19–25 May

Nations: Azerbaijan, Benin, Congo, Cyprus, Tunisia, Zambia.
Cyprus d. Congo 3–0: M. Baghdatis (CYP) d. C. Gnitou (CGO) 6–4 6–0; D. Leondis (CYP) d. A. Bemba (CGO) 6–1 6–1; D. Leondis/N. Neokleous (CYP) d. M. Banguid/C. Gnitou (CGO) 6–2 6–1. **Tunisia d. Benin**

THE WORLD GROUP 1997 (16 nations)

	1st Round 7–9 February	*2nd Round 4–6 April*	*Semi-finals 19–21 September*	*Final 28–30 November*	*Winner*
1	USA				
2	c Brazil	c USA 4–1			
3	NETHERLANDS		c USA 4–1		
4	c Romania	NETHERLANDS 3–2			
5	FRANCE			USA 4–1	
6	c Australia	c Australia 4–1			
7	c CZECH REPUBLIC		Australia 5–0		
8	India	CZECH REP. 3–2			c SWEDEN 5–0
9	Mexico				
10	c ITALY	c ITALY 4–1			
11	c Spain		ITALY 4–1		
10	GERMANY	Spain 4–1			
11	c South Africa			c SWEDEN 4–1	
12	RUSSIA	South Africa 3–1			
13	Switzerland		c SWEDEN 3–2		
14	c SWEDEN	c SWEDEN 4–1			

Seeded nations in capital letters. c = choice of ground

3–0: S. Sidia (TUN) d. A. Gandonou (BEN) 6–1 6–4; O. Jellali (TUN) d. C. Pognon (BEN) 6–1 7–5; O. Jellali/S. Sidia (TUN) d. J-M. da Silva/A. Gandonou (BEN) 6–1 6–2. **Zambia d. Azerbaijan 3–0:** K. Sinkala (ZAM) d. D. Zaraubin (AZE) 6–2 6–0; L. Ndefway (ZAM) d. I. Barisov (AZE) 6–3 6–3; S. Bwalya/L. Chileshe (ZAM) d. R. Eyvazov/D. Zaraubin (AZE) 6–0 1–0 ret. **Cyprus d. Zambia 2–1:** M. Baghdatis (CYP) d. K. Sinkala (ZAM) 6–4 6–4; D. Leondis (CYP) d. L. Ndefway (ZAM) 6–3 6–4; S. Bwalya/L. Ndefway (ZAM) d. D. Leondis/N. Neokleous (CYP) 7–5 6–2. **Tunisia d. Azerbaijan 3–0:** S. Sidia (TUN) d. D. Zaraubin (AZE) 6–1 6–0; O. Jellali (TUN) d. I. Barisov (AZE) 6–2 6–1; O. Jellali/S. Sidia (TUN) d. I. Barisov/D. Zaraubin (AZE) 6–1 6–2. **Benin d. Congo 3–0:** A. Gandonou (BEN) d. M. Banguid (CGO) 6–2 6–0; C. Pognon (BEN) d. C. Gnitou (CGO) 6–3 6–1; J-M. da Silva/A. Gandonou (BEN) d. A. Bemba/C. Gnitou (CGO) 6–4 6–1. **Tunisia d. Congo 3–0:** S. Sidia (TUN) d. P. Madzou (CGO) 6–1 6–1; O. Jellali (TUN) d. M. Banguid (CGO) 6–0 6–1; O. Jellali/S. Sidia (TUN) d. A. Bemba/C. Gnitou (CGO) 6–0 6–1. **Cyprus d. Azerbaijan 3–0:** M. Baghdatis (CYP) d. D. Zaraubin (AZE) 6–1 6–4; D. Leondis (CYP) d. I. Barisov (AZE) 6–2 6–1; D. Leondis/N. Neokleous (CYP) d. I. Barisov/D. Zaraubin (AZE) 6–4 6–4. **Benin d. Zambia 2–1:** A. Gandonou (BEN) d. K. Sinkala (ZAM) 6–4 6–1; C. Pognon (BEN) d. L. Ndefway (ZAM) 6–4 6–2; S. Bwalya/L. Chileshe (ZAM) d. J-M. da Silva/A. Gandonou (BEN) 6–3 7–5. **Cyprus d. Benin 2–1:** M. Baghdatis (CYP) d. A. Gandonou (BEN) 6–3 6–3; C. Pognon (BEN) d. D. Leondis (CYP) 6–4 6–3; D. Leondis/N. Neokleous (CYP) d. J-M. da Silva/A. Gandonou (BEN) 6–3 7–6(6). **Tunisia d. Zambia 2–1:** S. Sidia (TUN) d. S. Bwalya (ZAM) 6–2 7–5; O. Jellali (TUN) d. L. Ndefway (ZAM) 6–1 6–3; S. Bwalya/K. Sinkala (ZAM) d. S. Ben Hadjali/O. Jellali (TUN) 4–6 6–4 6–4. **Azerbaijan d. Congo 2–1:** D. Zaraubin (AZE) d. M. Banguid (CGO) 3–6 6–1 6–0; A. Bemba (CGO) d. I. Barisov (AZE) 6–2 6–1; I. Barisov/D. Zaraubin (AZE) d. M. Banguid/A. Bemba (CGO) 6–2 6–3. **Tunisia d. Cyprus 2–1:** S. Sidia (TUN) d. M. Baghdatis (CYP) 1–6 6–4 6–4; D. Leondis (CYP) d. O. Jellali (TUN) 6–3 6–1; O. Jellali/S. Sidia (TUN) d. D. Leondis/N. Neokleous (CYP) 6–4 6–3. **Zambia d. Congo 3–0:** S. Bwalya (ZAM) d. P. Madzou (CGO) 6–0 6–0: L. Ndefway (ZAM) d. C. Gnitou (CGO) 6–0 6–1; L. Chileshe/ K. Sinkala (ZAM) d. M. Banguid/C. Gnitou (CGO) 6–2 6–4. **Benin d. Azerbaijan 3–0:** A. Gandonou (BEN) d. F. Jafarov (AZE) 6–0 6–0; C. Pognon (BEN) d. D. Zaraubin (AZE) 6–1 6–3; J-M. da Silva/A. Gandonou (BEN) d. I. Barisov/R. Eyvazov (AZE) w/o.

FINAL POSITIONS: Tunisia 1, Cyprus 2, Benin 3, Zambia 4, Azerbaijan 5, Congo 6.
Cyprus and Tunisia were promoted to Euro/African Group III for the 1998 competition.

QUALIFYING ROUND FOR THE WORLD GROUP 1998

Zonal Winners and World Group First Round Losers	*Promoted to World Group in 1998*	
1 AUSTRIA	Zimbabwe	3–2
2 c Zimbabwe		
3 New Zealand	BRAZIL	5–0
4 c BRAZIL		
5 CHILE	India	3–2
6 c India		
7 c Belgium	Belgium	3–2
8 FRANCE		
9 c Germany	Germany	5–0
10 Mexico		
11 Romania	RUSSIA	3–2
12 c RUSSIA		
13 Slovak Republic	Slovak Republic	4–1
14 c Canada		
15 Korea	SWITZERLAND	3–2
16 c SWITZERLAND		

Seeded nations in capital letters.
c = choice of ground.

(Above) *For the first time the French get their hands on the Fed Cup* (left to right): *Yannick Noah (captain), Alexandra Fusai, Nathalie Tauziat, Sandrine Testud, Julie Halard-Decugis, Mary Pierce.*
(Below) *Unfortunately, the Dutch team could not live up to the expectations of their home supporters* (left to right): *Fred Hemmes (captain), Caroline Vis, Manon Bollegraf, Miriam Oremans, Brenda Schultz-McCarthy*. (Paul Zimmer)

KB Fed Cup

Wendy Kewley

Not many people will forget the incredible joy on Yannick Noah's face when France won its first KB Fed Cup title with a 4–1 victory over the Netherlands at the Brabanthallen in 's-Hertogenbosch, the Netherlands.

The occasion was especially significant for Fed Cup team captain Noah as he became the first person to lead a country to titles in both the Davis Cup and Fed Cup competitions. Last year, the former French Open champion had inspired France's Davis Cup team to one of the event's most memorable wins when France defeated Sweden 3–2 in the fifth set of the final rubber at Malmo, Sweden.

US Open quarter-finalist Sandrine Testud continued her successful year when she secured victory for her team by overcoming Miriam Oremans 0–6 6–3 6–3 in the fourth rubber. Noah immediately leapt out of his courtside seat, embraced Testud and declared, 'This is a great moment. It was difficult with such a fast court. I was a little scared in the fourth match. The Dutch really posed some difficult questions for us.' As the magnitude of her win gradually sunk in, Testud gracefully acknowledged Noah's role in the proceedings. 'He really pushed me to give my best. He always believed in me and that is what I needed.'

Later that day, Alexandra Fusai and Nathalie Tauziat extended France's winning margin to 4–1 by defeating the experienced Manon Bollegraf and Caroline Vis. Afterwards, Noah praised his team, saying, 'They made it easy in a way that I didn't have to dig so deep inside to find the right words. They really delivered themselves.'

France and the Netherlands had been severely tested en route to the Final and both survived their semi-finals after capturing the deciding doubles match. The Dutch travelled to Prague to contend with a Czech team fronted by the world No. 2 Jana Novotna. Manon Bollegraf and Miriam Oremans overcame Eva Martincova and Novotna in a tense second tie-break to secure the tie for the Dutch 3–2.

The French had reached the semi-finals every year since 1993 and as they progressed through the rounds, Noah's endless encouragement on court proved crucial. The outcome of the semi-final tie in Nice hung on the final set of the doubles but, spurred on by Noah, Tauziat and Fusai reversed a one set deficit against Belgium's Els Callens and Dominique Van Roost to propel France into a Fed Cup Final at last.

Despite the bitter disappointment at losing what was only its second appearance in a Fed Cup Final, the Netherlands can look back on its performance this year with pride. After winning promotion to World Group I in the 1996 Play-Off Round the Dutch had followed up their success by ousting the 1996 Fed Cup champions, USA, 3–2 at Haarlem in the first round of the 1997 competition. They had enjoyed a dream run, and, as Miriam Oremans summed up, 'We never expected to reach the Final. But once we got there we wanted more, so it was very disappointing to see the French win.'

Following the example of the USA, Germany and Spain's Fed Cup challenge had also ended abruptly in the opening round. All three nations are the only countries to have won the Fed Cup title since 1989, but their fortunes proved less than glorious in 1997. Belgium knocked out 1996 finalists Spain 5–0 at home in Sprimont while Czech Republic completed the trend in Mannheim by defeating a German team without the injured Steffi Graf and Anke Huber. Czech Republic's Jana Novotna was also a late withdrawal through injury but supported her team from the stands, as did Graf and Huber.

One of the most dramatic matches in this year's KB Fed Cup occurred in the first round encounter between France and Japan in Tokyo. With the French leading 2–1, it fell to veteran Fed Cupper Nathalie Tauziat to take her country into the semi-final as she faced the tenacious Naoko Sawamatsu. The match developed into a battle of wills to the pleasure of the fans who became increasingly noisy as the contest stretched to a third set. The crowd was treated to a display of heart-stopping tennis that epitomised the spirit of the Fed Cup before Tauziat eventually edged through 17–15 in the third set.

Former Fed Cup champions Germany, Spain and USA restored their pride by retaining their positions in the 1998 World Group I after coming through their respective World Group I Play-Off Round ties. USA defeated Japan at the Longwood Cricket Club in Chestnut Hill, Massachusetts. Mary Joe Fernandez and Lindsay Davenport won their singles with Davenport claiming the third singles against Japan's Ai Sugiyama to clinch the tie for the Americans. Four-time champion nation Spain fended off Australia, coming through 3–2 at Hope Island, Queensland, Australia. Germany, still minus Steffi Graf, defeated a Croatian team led by Roland Garros champion Iva Majoli in Frankfurt. In the deciding doubles, Anke Huber and Meike Babel came through against Majoli and the highly promising teenager Mirjana Lucic. Switzerland joins Germany, Spain and USA in the World Group I, after the world no 1. Martina Hingis led her country to promotion with a 5–0 victory over Argentina at Zurich. In 1998, Argentina, Australia, Croatia and Japan will compete in World Group II.

In the World Group II Play-Off Round, Russia earned a place for the first time after a 4–1 victory over Korea in Seoul. Italy joined Russia as the top two nations from the Europe/Africa Qualifying Group I and Italy also won a position in the World Group II by defeating Indonesia 5–0 in Jakarta. Slovak Republic and Austria both maintained World Group II status. The Slovaks defeated the Canadians 5–0 in Bratislava while the Austrians overcame a South African team led by Amanda Coetzer 3–2 in Portschach, Austria.

A record 99 nations are set to compete in the 1998 KB Fed Cup with Ghana, Haiti, Iraq and Moldava embracing the largest annual women's team competition for the first time. The players' commitment to Fed Cup has been rewarded by the increasing enthusiasm of the fans. Since revising the format to include two World Groups of eight nations each, TV coverage of the Fed Cup has increased by 400% with the number of spectators soaring from 20,000 to over 100,000 this year.

The 1998 KB Fed Cup promises to be fascinating as the traditional dominance of Germany, Spain and USA comes under threat from up and coming teams. With Martina Hingis at the helm, the Swiss will be tough to beat as they prepare for their first year in World Group I. In World Group II, the newly promoted Russians and the Croatians are also poised to do well next year. Both teams can call on some of the most sensational talents in the women's game. Russia boasts Elena Likhovtseva and the 16-year-old Anna Kournikova, while Croatia can enlist Roland Garros queen Iva Majoli and the 15-year-old Mirjana Lucic.

ITF Fed Cup Executive Director Deborah Jevans points out that one thing is certain, 'The greater number of countries with players ranked in the top ten adds excitement not only to the Fed Cup but to women's tennis as a whole. It is with great anticipation that we look forward to next year's event.'

1997 KB FED CUP

WORLD GROUP I

Seeding: 1 = Spain & USA; 3 = France & Germany

FIRST ROUND (1–2 March) – Netherlands d. USA 3–2, Haarlem, NED: M. Oremans (NED) d. M-J. Fernandez (USA) 6–1 6–4; C. Rubin (USA) d. B. Schultz-McCarthy (NED) 4–6 6–4 6–3; B. Schultz-McCarthy (NED) d. M-J. Fernandez (USA) 1–6 6–4 9–7; M. Oremans (NED) d. C. Rubin (USA) 6–3 6–0; G. Fernandez/K. Po (USA) d. M. Bollegraf/K. Boogert (NED) 6–3 6–2. **Czech Republic d. Germany 3–2, Mannheim, GER:** M. Weingartner (GER) d. L. Richterova (CZE) 3–6 7–5 6–3; A. Gersi (CZE) d. B. Rittner (GER) 6–4 6–2; L. Richterova (CZE) d. B. Rittner (GER) 6–1 6–4; A. Gersi (CZE) d. M. Weingartner (GER) 6–2 6–2; B. Rittner/E. Wagner (GER) d. E. Martincova/L. Richterova (CZE) 7–6(3) 6–2. **France d. Japan 4–1, Tokyo, JPN:** M. Pierce (FRA) d. N. Sawamatsu (JPN) 6–0 7–6(4); N. Tauziat (FRA) d. A. Sugiyama (JPN) 4–6 7–5 6–4; A. Sugiyama (JPN) d. M. Pierce (FRA) 7–5 6–7(7) 6–4; N. Tauziat (FRA) d. N. Sawamatsu (JPN) 7–5 4–6 17–15. A. Fusai/A-G. Sidot (FRA) d. N. Kijimuta/K. Nagatsuka (JPN) 7–5 6–4. **Belgium d. Spain 5–0, Sprimont, BEL:** E. Callens (BEL) d. A. Sanchez Vicario (ESP) 6–3 7–6(4); S. Appelmans (BEL) d. M. L. Serna (ESP) 6–1 4–6 6–3; S. Appelmans (BEL) d. A. Sanchez Vicario (ESP) 6–3 2–6 8–6; E. Callens (BEL) d M. L. Serna (ESP) 6–1 6–3; E. Callens/N. Feber (BEL) d. G. Leon-Garcia/V. Ruano-Pascual (ESP) 5–7 6–2 6–2.

SEMI-FINALS (12–13 July) – Netherlands d. Czech Republic 3–2, Prague, CZE: B. Schultz-McCarthy (NED) d. S. Kleinova (CZE) 6–1 7–6(5); J. Novotna (CZE) d. M. Oremans (NED) 6–3 6–0; J. Novotna (CZE) d. B. Schultz-McCarthy (NED) 7–6(3) 6–3; M. Oremans (NED) d. A. Gersi (CZE) 1–6 6–2 9–7; M. Bollegraf/M. Oremans (NED) d. E. Martincova/J. Novotna (CZE) 6–4 7–6(5). **France d. Belgium 3–2, Nice, FRA:** A. Fusai (FRA) d. S. Appelmans (BEL) 6–7(1) 6–3 6–1; D. van Roost (BEL) d. S. Testud (FRA) 4–6 7–5 6–4; S. Testud (FRA) d. S. Appelmans (BEL) 6–2 6–4; D. van Roost (BEL) d. A. Fusai (FRA) 6–3 6–3; A. Fusai/N. Tauziat (FRA) d. E. Callens/D. van Roost (BEL) 3–6 6–2 7—5.

FINAL (4–5 October) – France d. Netherlands 4–1, Den Bosch, NED: S. Testud (FRA) d. B. Schultz-

McCarthy (NED) 6–4 4–6 6–3; M. Pierce (FRA) d. M. Oremans (NED) 6–4 6–1; B. Schultz-McCarthy (NED) d. M. Pierce (FRA) 4–6 6–3 6–4; S. Testud (FRA) d. M. Oremans (NED) 0–6 6–3 6–3; A. Fusai/N. Tauziat (FRA) d. M. Bollegraf/C. Vis (NED) 6–3 6–4.

WORLD GROUP I PLAY OFFS (12–13 July) – USA d. Japan 5–0, Boston, USA: M. J. Fernandez (USA) d. A. Sugiyama (JPN) 4–6 6–2 6–2; L. Davenport (USA) d. N. Sawamatsu (JPN) 6–1 6–3; L. Davenport (USA) d. A. Sugiyama (JPN) 6–4 7–6(1); K. Po (USA) d. N.o Sawamatsu (JPN) 6–2 6–4; L. Davenport/L. Raymond (USA) d. N. Kijimuta/N. Miyagi (JPN) 6–4 6–4. **Switzerland d. Argentina 5–0, Zurich, SUI:** M. Hingis (SUI) d. M. J. Gaidano (ARG) 6–1 6–2; P. Schnyder (SUI) d. F. Labat (ARG) 3–6 7–5 10–8; M. Hingis(SUI) d. F. Labat (ARG) 6–2 6–1; P. Schnyder (SUI) d. M. J. Gaidano (ARG) 6–1 6–0; E. Gagliardi/M. Hingis (SUI) d. L. Montalvo M./Paz (ARG) 6–3 6–4. **Spain d. Australia 3–2, Hope Island, AUS:** A. Sanchez Vicario (ESP) d. R. McQuillan (AUS) 6–2 6–1; A. Ellwood (AUS) d. M. L. Serna (ESP) 6–4 6–2; A. Sanchez Vicario (ESP) d. A. Ellwood (AUS) 6–2 6–0; M. L. Serna (ESP) d. R. McQuillan (AUS) 6–1 6–3; K-A. Guse/K. Kunce (AUS) d. M. A. Sanchez Lorenzo/C. Torrens-Valero (ESP) 6–2 6–4. **Germany d. Croatia 3–2, Frankfurt, GER:** I. Majoli (CRO) d. M. Babel (GER) 6–2 6–3; A. Huber (GER) d. M. Lucic (CRO) 6–2 6–2; A. Huber (GER) d. I. Majoli (CRO) 6–7(4) 6–2 6–0; M. Lucic (CRO) d. M. Babel (GER) 6–4 6–1; M. Babel/A. Huber (GER) d. M. Lucic /I. Majoli (CRO) 7–6(4) 6–7(4) 6–1.

USA, Switzerland, Spain and Germany qualified for World Group I for the 1998 competition.
Japan, Argentina, Australia and Croatia remained in, or were relegated to World Group II for the 1998 competition.

WORLD GROUP II

Seeding: 1 = Austria & South Africa; 3 = Argentina & Slovak Republic
FIRST ROUND (1–2 March) – Croatia d. Austria 4–1, Zagreb, CRO: I. Majoli (CRO) d. B. Schett (AUT) 7–5 4–6 6–2; M. Lucic (CRO) d. J. Wiesner (AUT) 7–5 6–1; J. Wiesner (AUT) d. I. Majoli (CRO) 6–4 6–4; M. Lucic (CRO) d. B. Schett (AUT) 6–2 5–7 7–5; M. Lucic/M. Muric (CRO) d. K. Kschwendt/M. Maruska (AUT) 6–4 6–3. **Switzerland d. Slovak Republic 3–2, Kosice, SVK:** M. Hingis (SUI) d. K. Studenikova (SVK) 6–1 6–3; K. Habsudova (SVK) d. P. Schnyder (SUI) 7–5 6–1; M. Hingis (SUI) d. K. Habsudova (SVK) 6–2 6–0; H. Nagyova (SVK) d. P. Schnyder (SUI) 6–3 6–1; M. Hingis/P. Schnyder (SUI) d. K. Habsudova/R. Zrubakova (SVK) 6–0 6–1. **Argentina d. Korea Rep 4–1, Seoul, KOR:** S-H. Park (KOR) d. M. Diaz-Oliva (ARG) 6–3 6–1; F. Labat (ARG) d. Y-J. Choi (KOR) 6–1 6–2; F. Labat (ARG) d. S-H. Park (KOR) 6–4 6–1; M. Diaz-Oliva (ARG) d. E-H. Kim (KOR) 4–6 6–3 6–1; L. Montalvo/M. Paz (ARG) d. E-H. Kim/S-H. Park (KOR) 6–7(3) 6–4 7–6(2). **Australia d. South Africa 3–2, Durban, RSA:** A. Ellwood (AUS) d. J. Kruger (RSA) 6–4 6–3; R. McQuillan (AUS) d. A. Coetzer (RSA) 6–3 7–6(10); A. Coetzer (RSA) d. A. Ellwood (AUS)1–6 6–1 6–0; R. McQuillan (AUS) d. J. Kruger (RSA) 7–5 6–4; M. de Swardt/R. Nideffer (RSA) d. K-A. Guse/K. Radford (AUS) 6–3 7–5.

WORLD GROUP II PLAY-OFFS (12–13 July) – Russia d. Korea 4–1, Seoul, KOR Rep: E. Makarova (RUS) d. S-H. Park (KOR) 6–4 4–6 6–1; T. Panova (RUS) d. E-H. Kim (KOR) 6–3 6–4; T. Panova (RUS) d. S-H. Park (KOR) 4–6 6–1 6–1; E. Makarova (RUS) d. E-H. Kim (KOR) 7–6(7) 6–3; Y-J. Cho/Y-J. Choi (KOR) d. E. Koulikovskaya/E. Syssoeva (RUS) 6–1 6–3. **Italy d. Indonesia 5–0, Jakarta, INA:** S. Farina (ITA) d. W. Sawondari (INA) 6–2 6–4; F. Perfetti (ITA) d. W. Prakusya (INA) 6–3 6–7(6) 6–1; S. Farina (ITA) d. W. Prakusya (INA) 6–1 6–4; F. Perfetti (ITA) d. W. Sawondari (INA) 6–4 6–1; F. Lubiani/G. Pizzichini (ITA) d. L. Andriyani/E. Sulistyowati (INA) 6–1 6–2. **Slovak Republic d. Canada 5–0, Bratislava, SVK:** K. Habsudova (SVK) d. R. Simpson (CAN) 6–3 6–4; H. Nagyova (SVK) d. P. Hy-Boulais (CAN) 6–4 6–3; K. Habsudova (SVK) d. P. Hy-Boulais (CAN) 6–2 7–6(6); H. Nagyova (SVK) d. R. Simpson (CAN) 6–0 7–6(6); K. Habsudova/K. Studenikova (SVK) d S. Jeyaseelan/R. Simpson (CAN) 4–6 2–0 ret. **Austria d. South Africa 3–2, Portschach, AUT:** B. Paulus (AUT) d. J. Kruger (RSA) 6–4 6–4; A. Coetzer (RSA) d. B. Schett (AUT) 6–1 7–6(5); A. Coetzer (RSA) d. B. Paulus (AUT) 6–2 6–0; B. Schett (AUT) d. J. Kruger (RSA) 4–6 6–4 6–2; B. Schett/J. Wiesner (AUT) d. A. Coetzer/J. Steck (RSA) 6–1 6–4.

Russia, Italy, Slovak Republic and Austria qualified for World Group II for the 1998 competition.
Korea Republic, Indonesia, Canada and South Africa remained in, or were relegated to Zonal Qualifying Group I for the 1998 competition.

AMERICAS GROUP I

Bogota, Colombia, 28 April – 4 May

GROUP A: Brazil, Canada, Ecuador, Mexico
Round Robin: Brazil d. Mexico 2–1: E. Maia (BRA) d. L. Becerra (MEX) 6–0 6–4; K. Palme (MEX) d. V. Menga (BRA) 6–2 6–1; V. Menga/L. Tella (BRA) d. L. Becerra/G. Velez (MEX) 6–4 6–0. **Canada d. Ecuador 3–0:** S. Jeyaseelan (CAN) d. C. Jairala (ECU) 6–4 6–2; R. Simpson (CAN) d. M. D. Campana (ECU) 6–1 6–7(7) 6–1; P. Hy-Boulais/R. Simpson (CAN) d. C. Jairala/N. Niemes (ECU) 6–2 6–0. **Canada d. Brazil 3–0:** R. Simpson (CAN) d. E. Maia (BRA) 6–2 6–0; P. Hy-Boulais (CAN) d. V. Menga (BRA) 6–2 3–6 6–4; S. Jeyaseelan/R. Simpson (CAN) d. V. Menga/L. Tella (BRA) 6–1 7–5. **Ecuador d. Mexico 2–1:** K. Palme (MEX) d. A. Guzman (ECU) 6–1 7–6(4) 6–1; M. D. Campana (ECU) d. A. Gavaldon (MEX) 6–1 6–1; M. D.

Campana/N. Niemes (ECU) d. L. Becerra/G. Velez (MEX) 6–2 3–6 6–2. **Canada d. Mexico 3–0:** R. Simpson (CAN) d. K. Palme (MEX) 6–3 6–3; P. Hy-Boulais (CAN) d. A. Gavaldon (MEX) 7–6(1) 7–5; P. Hy-Boulais/S. Jeyaseelan (CAN) d. L. Becerra/K. Palme (MEX) 6–4 6–1. **Brazil d. Ecuador 3–0:** E. Maia (BRA) d. C. Jairala (ECU) 6–2 6–2; V. Menga (BRA) d M. D. Campana (ECU) 6–3 6–2; J. Cortes/V. Menga (BRA) d. A. Guzman/N. Niemes (ECU) 7–5 6–0.
Final Positions: Canada 1, Brazil 2, Ecuador 3, Mexico 4.

GROUP B: Chile, Columbia, Peru, Puerto Rico, Venezuela
Round Robin: Chile d. Venezuela 2–1: B. Castro (CHI) d. M. Salinas (VEN) 6–3 6–2; P. Cabezas (CHI) d. M. A. Vento (VEN) 6–1 6–1; P. Stephen/M. A. Vento (VEN) d. B. Castro/M. A. Quezada (CHI) 6–4 7–5. **Peru d. Puerto Rico 2–1:** C. Rodriguez (PER) d. V. Castelvi (PUR) 6–3 6–2; M. Toro (PUR) d. N. Vallejo (PER) 3–6 6–2 7–5; C. Rodriguez/S. Vargas (PER) d. J. Bauza/E. Viqueira (PUR) 5–7 6–2 6–3. **Colombia d. Venezuela 3–0:** C. Giraldo (COL) d. P. Stephen (VEN) 6–0 6–1; F. Zuluaga (COL) d. M. A. Vento (VEN) 5–7 6–3 6–4; C. Giraldo/F. Zuluaga (COL) d. P. Stephen/M. A. Vento (VEN) 6–3 6–4. **Chile d. Puerto Rico 3–0:** B. Castro (CHI) d. V. Castelvi (PUR) 6–2 6–2; P. Cabezas (CHI) d. M. Toro (PUR) 4–6 6–3 6–4; B. Castro/M. A. Quezada (CHI) d. J. Bauza/E. Viqueira (PUR) 6–4 6–2. **Colombia d. Peru 3–0:** C. Giraldo (COL) d. C. Rodriguez (PER) 6–1 6–1; F. Zuluaga (COL) d. N. Vallejo (PER) 6–2 6–0; C. Giraldo/F. Zuluaga (COL) d. C. Rodriguez/S. Vargas (PER) 6–3 6–1; **Puerto Rico d. Venezuela 2–1:** V. Castelvi (PUR) d. M. Salinas (VEN) 7–6(5) 6–0; M. A. Vento (VEN) d. M. Toro (PUR) 6–3 6–2; M. Toro/E. Viqueira (PUR) d. P. Stephen/M. A. Vento (VEN) 6–4 7–5. **Columbia d. Puerto Rico 3–0:** C. Giraldo (COL) d. V. Castelvi (PUR) 6–2 7–6(8); F. Zuluaga (COL) d. M. Toro (PUR) 6–1 6–0; C. Giraldo/F. Zuluaga (COL) d. M. Toro/E. Viqueira (PUR) 6–2 6–2. **Peru d. Chile 2–1:** A. Quezada (CHI) d. C. Rodriguez 7–5 6–2; N. Vallejo (PER) d. P. Cabezas (CHI) 7–6(4) 0–1 ret; C. Rodriguez/S. Vargas (PER) d. P. Cabezas/A. Quezada (CHI) w/o. Chile withdrew because of illness. **Colombia d. Chile 3–0 w/o. Venezuela d. Peru 2–1:** M. Salinas (VEN) d. S. Vargas (PER) 6–1 7–6(2); M. A. Vento (VEN) d. N. Vallejo (PER) 6–1 6–1; C. Rodriguez/S. Vargas (PER) d. M. Salinas/P. Stephen (VEN) 4–6 6–2 6–3.
Final Positions: Colombia 1, Chile 2, Peru 3, Venezuela 4, Puerto Rico 5.

(Chile did not play semi-finals due to team illness and withdrawal from the competition).

SEMI-FINALS: Canada d. Peru 3–0: R. Simpson (CAN) d. C. Rodriguez (PER) 6–0 6–2; P. Hy-Boulais (CAN) d. N. Vallejo (PER) 6–1 6–1; S. Jeyaseelan/R. Simpson (CAN) d. C. Rodriguez/N. Vallejo (PER) 6–0 6–4. **Colombia d. Brazil 3–0:** C. Giraldo (COL) d. E. Maia (BRA) 7–5 4–6 7–5; F. Zuluaga (COL) d V. Menga (BRA) 6–1 6–3; C. Giraldo/F. Zuluaga (COL) d. J. Cortes/L. Tella (BRA) 6–2 6–1.

FINAL: Canada d. Colombia 2–1: R. Simpson (CAN) d. C. Giraldo (COL) 6–2 7–5; F. Zuluaga (COL) d. P. Hy-Boulais (CAN) 6–3 6–1; S. Jeyaseelan/R. Simpson (CAN) d. C. Giraldo/F. Zuluaga (COL) 6–1 7–5.

Canada qualified for the World Group II play-offs.
Mexico and Puerto Rico were relegated to Americas II for the 1998 competition.

ASIA/OCEANIA GROUP I

Wellington Renouf Centre, New Zealand, 10–15 March

GROUP A: Chinese Taipei, India, Indonesia, New Zealand
Round Robin: Chinese Taipei d. India 3–0: J. Huang (TPE) d. J. Parekh (IND) 6–4 6–2; S-T. Wang (TPE) d. A. Ponnappa (IND) 6–1 6–1; H-L. Hsu/S-T. Wang (TPE) d. J. Parekh/A. Ponnappa (IND) 6–0 6–1. **Indonesia d. New Zealand 2–1:** W. Prakusya (INA) d. R. Hudson (NZL) 6–1 7–6(9); Y. Basuki (INA) d. G. McManus (NZL) 6–1 6–0; L. Baker/S. Stephens (NZL) d. M. Chernovita/E. Sulistyowati (INA) 6–2 7–6(4). **Chinese Taipei d. New Zealand 2–1:** T-T. Weng (TPE) d. R. Hudson (NZL) 7–6(4) 1–6 6–3; S-T. Wang (TPE) d. G. McManus (NZL) 6–0 6–1; L. Baker/S. Stephens (NZL) d. H-L. Hsu/S-T. Wang (TPE) 7–5 3–6 7–5. **Indonesia d. India 3–0:** W. Prakusya (INA) d. J. Parekh (IND) 6–1 6–3; Y. Basuki (INA) d. A. Ponnappa (IND) 6–1 6–0; M. Chernovita/E. Sulistyowati (INA) d. U. Khan/J. Parekh (IND) 6–1 6–2. **Indonesia d. Chinese Taipei 2–1:** W. Prakusya (INA) d. J. Huang (TPE) 4–6 6–1 6–2; S-T. Wang (TPE) d. M. Chernovita (INA) 6–0 6–0; Y. Basuki/W. Prakusya (INA) d. S-T. Wang/T-T. Weng (TPE) 6–2 6–2. **New Zealand d. India 2–1:** U. Khan (IND) d. R. Hudson (NZL) 6–2 6–3; G. McManus (NZL) d. A. Ponnappa (IND) 6–3 6–3; L. Baker/S. Stephens (NZL) d. J. Parekh/A. Ponnappa (IND) 6–2 6–2.
Final Positions: Indonesia 1, Chinese Taipei 2, New Zealand 3, India 4.

GROUP B: China PR, Hong Kong, Kazakhstan, Thailand
Round Robin: Hong Kong d. Thailand 3–0: K. P. Tong (HKG) d. P. Suksamran (THA) 6–2 6–2; M. Tang (HKG) d. S. Duangchan (THA) 6–2 6–2; L. Howes/N. Lin (HKG) d. S. Duangchan/P. Suksamran (THA) 4–6 6–4 6–2. **China PR d. Kazakhstan 3–0:** Y. Wen (CHN) d. T. Babina (KAZ) 6–2 4–6 6–3; J. Q. Yi (CHN) d. A. Velts (KAZ) 6–2 6–1; Y. Chen/J. Q. Yi (CHN) d. T. Babina/A. Velts (KAZ) 6–2 6–1. **China PR d. Hong Kong 2–1:** K. P. Tong (HKG) d. Y. Chen (CHI) 6–1 6–3; J. Q. Yi (CHI) d. M. Tang (HKG) 6–3 1–6 7–5; Y. Chen/J. Q. Yi (CHI) d. M. Tang/K. P. Tong (HKG) 7–6 6–4. **Thailand d. Kazakhstan 2–1:** T. Babina (KAZ) d. B. Boontemleaw (THA) 7–5 6–0; S. Duangchan (THA) d. A. Velts (KAZ) 6–1 6–1; S. Duangchan/P. Suksamran (THA) d. T. Babina/A. Velts (KAZ) 7–6(3) 6–4. **Hong Kong d. Kazakhstan 2–1:** T. Babina (KAZ) d. K. P. Tong (HKG) 6–3 3–6 6–4; M. Tang (HKG) d. A. Velts (KAZ) 6–0 6–1; L. Howes/M. Tang (HKG) d. T. Babina/A. Velts (KAZ) 6–3

1–6 6–3. **China PR d. Thailand 3–0:** Y. Wen (CHN) d. B. Boontemleaw (THA) 6–0 6–0; J. Q. Yi (CHN) d. P. Suksamran (THA) 6–1 6–0; L. Chen/Y. Chen (CHN) d. B. Boontemleaw/P. Suksamran (THA) 6–2 6–4.
Final Positions: China PR 1, Hong Kong 2, Thailand 3, Kazakhstan 4
SEMI-FINALS: Indonesia d. Hong Kong 3–0: W. Prakusya (INA) d. K. P. Tong (HKG) 6–4 6–2; Y. Basuki (INA) d. M. Tang (HKG) 6–1 6–0; M. Chernovita/E. Sulistyowati (INA) d. L. Howes/N. Lin (HKG) 6–3 6–2. **Chinese Taipei d. China PR 2–1:** J. Q. Yi (CHN) d. T-T. Wen (TPE) 6–1 6–1; S-T. Wang (TPE) d. L. Chen (CHN) 6–0 6–1; H-L. Hsu/S-T. Wang (TPE) d. L. Chen/J. Q. Yi (CHN) 4–6 6–4 6–3.

FINAL: Indonesia d. Chinese Taipei 3–0: W. Prakusya (INA) d. J. Huang (TPE) 6–2 6–4; Y. Basuki (INA) d. S-T. Wang (TPE) 3–6 7–6(0) 6–3; W. Prakusya/I. Sulistyowati (INA) d. H-L. Hsu d. J. Huang (TPE) 6–3 6–2.

PLAY-OFFS: New Zealand d. Kazakhstan 3–0: R. Hudson (NZL) d. T. Babina (KAZ) 6–2 6–3; G. McManus (NZL) d. A. Velts (KAZ) 6–3 6–4; L. Baker/S. Stephens (NZL) d. T. Babina/A. Velts (KAZ) 6–2 6–3. **Thailand d. India 2–1:** U. Khan (IND) d. P. Suksamran (THA) 6–7(5) 6–3 6–1; S. Duangchan (THA) d. A. Ponnappa (IND) 6–3 6–3; S. Duangchan/P. Suksamran (THA) d. J. Parekh/A. Ponnappa (IND) 2–6 6–3 6–2. **China PR d. Hong Kong 3–0:** J. Q. Yi (CHN) d. N. Lin (HKG) 6–1 6–2; L. Chen (CHN) d. L. Howes (HKG) 6–2 6–0; Y. Chen/Y. Wen (CHN) d. L. Howes/N. Lin (HKG) 6–3 6–2. **New Zealand d. Thailand 3–0:** L. Baker (NZL) d. B. Boontemleaw (THA) 6–0 6–0; G. McManus (NZL) d. P. Suksamran (THA) 6–3 6–1; L. Baker/R. Hudson (NZL) d. B. Boontemleaw/P. Suksamran (THA) 6–1 6–1. **India d. Kazakhstan w/o.**
Final Positions: Indonesia 1, Chinese Taipei 2, China PR 3, Hong Kong 4, New Zealand 5, Thailand 6, India 7, Kazakhstan 8.

Indonesia qualified for the World Group II play-offs.
India and Kazakhstan relegated to Asia/Oceania Group II for the 1998 competition.

EUROPE/AFRICA GROUP I
Circolo Tennis Bari, Italy, 22–26 April

GROUP A: Bulgaria, Greece, Russia
Round Robin: Russia d. Greece 3–0: A. Kournikova (RUS) d. C. Zachariadou (GRE) 6–3 6–4; E. Likhovtseva (RUS) d. C. Papadaki (GRE) 6–3 6–1; A. Kournikova/E. Likhovtseva (RUS) d. C. Papadaki/C. Zachariadou (GRE) 7–5 6–1. **Russia d. Bulgaria 2–1:** D. Topalova (BUL) d. E. Makarova (RUS) 4–6 7–6(5) 6–3; E. Likhovtseva (RUS) d. G. Dimitrova (BUL) 6–1 6–3; A. Kournikova/E. Likhovtseva (RUS) d. T. Nedeva/D. Topalova (BUL) 6–2 6–7(7) 6–0. **Greece d. Bulgaria 2–1:** D. Topalova (BUL) d. C. Zachariadou (GRE) 7–6(4) 6–4; C. Papadaki (GRE) d. G. Dimitrova (BUL) 2–6 6–3 6–4; C. Papadaki/C. Zachariadou (GRE) d. T. Nedeva/D. Topalova (BUL) 6–2 6–1.
Final Positions: Russia 1, Greece 2, Bulgaria 3.

GROUP B: Italy, Romania, Sweden, Ukraine
Round Robin: Italy d. Romania 2–1: A. Tecsor (ROM) d. G. Pizzichini (ITA) 6–2 6–2; S. Farina (ITA) d. R. Sandu (ROM) 3–6 7–6(6) 6–3; G. Casoni/S. Farina (ITA) d. A. Pirsu/R. Sandu (ROM) 6–3 6–1. **Sweden d. Ukraine 2–1:** A-K. Svensson (SWE) d. N. Nemchinova (UKR) 6–4 6–1; T. Kovalchuk (UKR) d. M. Strandlund (SWE) 2–6 6–4 6–2; M. Strandlund/A-K. Svensson (SWE) d. T. Kovalchuk/N. Nemchinova (UKR) 6–3 6–4. **Italy d. Ukraine 3–0:** F. Lubiani (ITA) d. N. Nemchinova (UKR) 6–2 6–2; S. Farina (ITA) d. T. Kovalchuk (UKR) 6–2 6–4; G. Casoni/G. Pizzichini (ITA) d. T. Kovalchuk/N. Nemchinova (UKR) 6–0 6–3. **Sweden d. Romania 3–0:** A-K. Svensson (SWE) d. A. Tecsor (ROM) 6–1 7–6(5); M. Strandlund (SWE) d. R. Sandu (ROM) 7–5 1–6 6–3; S. Finer/A. Lindstedt (SWE) d. R. Sandu/A. Tecsor (ROM) 6–4 6–2. **Italy d. Sweden 3–0:** G. Pizzichini (ITA) d. A-K. Svensson (SWE) 6–7(7) 6–2 6–1; S. Farina (ITA) d. M. Strandlund (SWE) 6–7(5) 6–1 6–1; G. Casoni/F. Lubiani (ITA) d. S. Finer/A. Lindstedt (SWE) 6–2 7–6(5). **Romania d. Ukraine 3–0:** A. Tecsor (ROM) d. N. Nemchinova (UKR) 6–4 6–3; R. Sandu (ROM) d. T. Kovalchuk (UKR) 6–1 6–2; A. Pirsu/A. Tecsor (ROM) d. A. Ponomarenko/E. Zhirnova (UKR) 4–6 7–5 6–2.
Final Positions: Italy 1, Sweden 2, Romania 3, Ukraine 4.

GROUP C: Belarus, Finland, Hungary, Poland
Round Robin: Belarus d. Finland 3–0: O. Barabanschikova (BLR) d. H-K. Aalto (FIN) 6–2 6–3; N. Zvereva (BLR) d. N. Dahlman (FIN) 6–1 2–6 6–3; O. Barabanschikova/N. Zvereva (BLR) d. L. Jansson/K. Lampinen (FIN) 6–1 6–2. **Hungary d. Poland 3–0:** A-M. Foldenyi (HUN) d. K. Teodorowicz (POL) 6–0 6–1; K. Marosi (HUN) d. K. Straczy (POL) 5–7 6–3 6–4; K. Marosi/R. Vidats (HUN) d. K. Straczy/K. Teodorowicz (POL) 7–5 6–2. **Belarus d. Poland 3–0:** O. Barabanschikova (BLR) d. M. Starosta (POL) 6–1 6–0; N. Zvereva (BLR) d. K. Straczy (POL) 4–6 6–3 6–1; T. Ignatieva/T. Poutchek (BLR) d. M. Starosta/K. Teodorwicz (POL) 6–1 6–1. **Hungary d. Finland 3–0:** A-M. Foldenyi (HUN) d. H-K. Aalto (FIN) 6–4 6–0; R. Vidats (HUN) d. N. Dahlman (FIN) 6–2 6–1; K. Marosi/R. Vidats (HUN) d. L. Jansson/K. Lampinen (FIN) 7–5 6–4. **Belarus d. Hungary 2–1:** A-M. Foldenyi (HUN) d. O. Barabanschikova (BLR) 6–3 7–5; N. Zvereva (BLR) d. K. Marosi (HUN) 7–6(5) 3–6 6–3; O. Barabanschikova/N. Zvereva (BLR) d. K. Marosi/R. Vidats (HUN) 4–6 6–1 6–2. **Poland d. Finland 3–0:** K. Teodorowicz (POL) d. H-K. Aalto (FIN) 3–6 6–4 7–5; K. Straczy (POL) d. N. Dahlman (FIN) 6–2 6–3; K. Straczy/K. Teodorowicz (POL) d. L. Jansson/K. Lampinen (FIN) 6–4 6–4.
Final Positions: Belarus 1, Hungary 2, Poland 3, Finland 4.

GROUP D: Georgia, Israel, Latvia, Slovenia
Round Robin: Slovenia d. Latvia 3–0: T. Krizan (SLO) d. A. Barinova (LAT) 6–4 6–1; B. Mulej (SLO) d. L.

Neiland (LAT) 6–2 6–0; T. Krizan/K. Srebotnik (SLO) d. A. Barinova/A. Blumberga (LAT) 6–4 6–2. **Israel d. Georgia 3–0:** H. Rosen (ISR) d. S. Managadze (GEO) 6–3 6–1; A. Smashnova (ISR) d. N. Louarsabishvili (GEO) 6–4 6–4; T. Obziler/H. Rosen (ISR) d. I. Kakoulia/N. Louarsabishvili (GEO) 6–2 6–0. **Slovenia d. Georgia 3–0:** T. Krizan (SLO) d. S. Managadze (GEO) 6–4 6–1; B. Mulej (SLO) d. N. Louarsabishvili (GEO) 6–4 6–1; T. Krizan/B. Mulej (SLO) d. I. Kakoulia/N. Louarsabishvili (GEO) 6–1 6–2. **Israel d. Latvia 2–1:** H. Rosen (ISR) d. A. Blumberga (LAT) 6–1 1–6 6–2; A. Smashnova (ISR) d. A. Barinova (LAT) 6–4 6–2; A. Blumberga/L. Neiland (LAT) d. N. Cahana/T. Obziler (ISR) 6–2 6–3. **Slovenia d. Israel 3–0:** T. Krizan (SLO) d. H. Rosen (ISR) 7–6(4) 6–3; B. Mulej (SLO) d. A. Smashnova (ISR) 7–5 5–7 8–6; T. Krizan/K. Srebotnik (SLO) d. N. Cahana/T. Obziler (ISR) 6–3 6–0. **Latvia d. Georgia 3–0:** A. Blumberga (LAT) d. S. Managadze (GEO) 6–3 6–3; L. Neiland (LAT) d. N. Louarsabishvili (GEO) 6–1 6–2; A. Barinova/L. Neiland (LAT) d. N. Louarsabishvili/S. Managadze (GEO) 6–4 6–4. **Final Positions: Slovenia 1, Israel 2, Latvia 3, Georgia 4.**

Qualifying Round: Russia d. Israel 2–1: H. Rosen (ISR) d. A. Kournikova (RUS) 6–1 7–6(3); E. Likhovtseva (RUS) d. A. Smashnova (ISR) 6–4 6–0; A. Kournikova/E. Likhovtseva (RUS) d. T. Obziler/H. Rosen (ISR) 7–6(1) 3–6 7–5. **Italy d. Greece 3–0:** G. Pizzichini (ITA) d. C. Zachariadou (GRE) 6–0 6–3; S. Farina (ITA) d. C. Papadaki (GRE) 2–6 6–3 9–7; G. Casoni/F. Lubiani (ITA) d. C. Papadaki/C. Zachariadou (GRE) 6–4 7–5. **Belarus d. Sweden 2–1:** O. Barabanschikova (BLR) d. A-K. Svensson (SWE) 7–5 6–3; N. Zvereva (BLR) d. M. Strandlund (SWE) 6–4 6–3; S. Finer/A. Lindstedt (SWE) d. T. Ignatieva/T. Poutchek (BLR) 6–4 2–6 7–5. **Hungary d. Slovenia 2–1:** A-M. Foldenyi (HUN) d. T. Krizan (SLO) 6–4 6–4; K. Marosi (HUN) d. B. Mulej (SLO) 6–1 6–4; T. Krizan/K. Srebotnik (SLO) d. A-M. Foldenyi/K. Marosi (HUN) 6–1 6–2.

PLAY-OFFS: Italy d. Hungary 2–1: A-M. Foldenyi (HUN) d. F. Lubiani (ITA) 7–5 7–5; G. Pizzichini (ITA) d. K. Marosi (HUN) 6–4 6–1; G. Casoni/G. Pizzichini (ITA) d. A-M. Foldenyi/K. Marosi (HUN) 6–3 6–3. **Russia d. Belarus 3–0:** E. Makarova (RUS) d. O. Barabanschikova (BLR) 6–2 6–4; E. Likhovtseva (RUS) d. N. Zvereva (BLR) 6–4 7–6(1); E. Likhovtseva/A. Kournikova (RUS) d. O. Barabanschikova/T. Poutchek 6–3 7–5.

Italy and Russia qualified for the World Group II play-offs.
Bulgaria, Finland, Georgia and Ukraine were relegated to Europe/Africa Group II for the 1998 competition.

AMERICAS GROUP II

Casa de Campo, Dominican Republic, 12–18 May

GROUP A: Bahamas, Barbados, Dominican Republic, Guatemala, Panama, Paraguay, Trinidad & Tobago

Round Robin: Guatemala d. Barbados 2–1: L. Lopez (GUA) d. K. Hunte (BAR) 6–4 7–5; F. de Maria Urrea (GUA) d. J. Carter (BAR) 6–1 6–3; T. A. Greaves/R. Lesaldo (BAR) d. L. Lopez/F. de Maria Urrea (GUA) 6–4 7–5. **Paraguay d. Panama 3–0:** L. Bernal (PAR) d. A. Espinosa (PAN) 6–1 6–3; L. Schaerer (PAR) d. L. Porras (PAN) 6–2 6–1; L. Bernal/V. Rolon (PAR) d. A. Espinosa/L. Porras (PAN) 6–0 6–4. **Trinidad & Tobago d. Bahamas 3–0:** A. Rose (TRI) d. C. A. Aston (BAH) 6–0 6–1; E. Gibson (TRI) d. K. Cartwright (BAH) 6–2 6–1; E. Gibson/A. Rose (TRI) d. C. A. Aston/S. Greene (BAH) 6–1 6–2. **Dominican Republic d. Panama 3–0:** M. Sanchez (DOM) d. A. Espinosa (PAN) 6–3 6–4; J. Schad (DOM) d. L. Porras (PAN) 7–5 6–1; G. Cepeda/M. Pimentel (DOM) d. A. Espinosa/L. Porras (PAN) 6–4 7–5. **Guatemala d. Bahamas 2–1:** L. Lopez (GUA) d. S. Greene (BAH) 6–1 6–3; K. Cartwright (BAH) d. F. de Maria Urrea (GUA) 7–5 6–2; L. Lopez/F. de Maria Urrea (GUA) d. K. Cartwright/S. Greene (BAH) 3–6 6–0 6–2. **Paraguay d. Barbados 3–0:** V. Rolon (PAR) d. R. le Saldo (BAR) 6–0 6–1; L. Schaerer (PAR) d. K. Hunte (BAR) 6–2 6–0; L. Bernal/V. Rolon (PAR) d. T. A. Greaves/R. le Saldo (BAR) 6–0 6–1. **Dominican Republic d. Trinidad & Tobago 2–1:** M. Sanchez (DOM) d. A. Rose (TRI) 6–3 4–6 6–1; J. Schad (DOM) d. E. Gibson (TRI) 7–6(4) 6–4; E. Gibson/A. Rose (TRI) d. G. Cepeda/M. Pimentel (DOM) 6–3 6–2; **Panama d. Barbados 3–0:** A. Espinosa (PAN) d. K. Hunte (BAR) 6–1 6–3; L. Porras (PAN) d. J. Carter (BAR) 1–6 6–2 6–4; A. Espinosa/L. Porras (PAN) d. T. A. Greaves/R. le Saldo (BAR) 6–4 6–4. **Paraguay d. Bahamas 3–0:** L. Bernal (PAR) d. S. Greene (BAH) 6–2 6–1; L. Schaerer (PAR) d. K. Cartwright (BAH) 6–0 6–2; L. Bernal/V. Rolon (PAR) d. C. A. Aston/K. Cartwright (BAH) 6–1 7–5. **Dominican Republic d. Barbados 3–0:** M. Sanchez (DOM) d. K. Hunte (BAR) 6–0 6–3; J. Schad (DOM) d. J. Carter (BAR) 6–1 6–0; G. Cepeda/M. Pimentel (DOM) d. T. A. Greaves/R. le Saldo (BAR) 3–6 7–5 6–1. **Panama d. Bahamas 2–1:** A. Espinosa (PAN) d. C. A. Aston (BAH) 6–2 6–1; K. Cartwright (BAH) d. L. Porras (PAN) 7–6(2) 6–2; A. Espinosa/L. Porras (PAN) d. C. A. Aston/K. Cartwright (BAH) 4–6 6–2 6–4. **Trinidad & Tobago d. Guatemala 3–0:** A. Rose (TRI) d. L. Lopez (GUA) 6–0 6–2; E. Gibson (TRI) d. F. de Maria Urrea (GUA) 6–1 6–2; E. Gibson/A. Rose (TRI) d. L. Lopez/F. de Maria Urrea (GUA) 6–1 6–2. **Bahamas d. Barbados 2–1:** K. Hunte (BAR) d. S. Greene (BAH) 6–2 2–6 6–2; K. Cartwright (BAH) d. J. Carter (BAR) 6–1 6–3; C. A. Aston/K. Cartwright (BAH) d. J. Carter/T. A. Greaves (BAR) 6–7(8) 7–6(1) 6–4. **Dominican Republic d. Guatemala 3–0:** M. Sanchez (DOM) d. L. Lopez (GUA) 6–2 6–1; J. Schad (DOM) d. F. de Maria Urrea (GUA) 6–0 6–2; M. Pimentel/J. Schad (DOM) d. M. F. Carrillo/L. Lopez (GUA) 6–0 4–6 6–1. **Paraguay d. Trinidad & Tobago 3–0:** L. Bernal (PAR) d. A. Rose (TRI) 6–7(3) 6–3 6–3; L. Schaerer (PAR) d. E. Gibson (TRI) 6–3 6–4; V. Rolon/L. Schaerer (PAR) d. E. Gibson/A. Rose (TRI) 6–4 3–6 6–3. **Dominican Republic d. Bahamas 3–0:** M. Sanchez (DOM) d. C. A. Aston (BAH) 6–2 6–1; J. Schad (DOM) d. K. Cartwright (BAH) 6–1 6–1; G. Cepeda/M. Pimentel (DOM) d. C. A. Aston/S. Greene (BAH) 6–1 7–5. **Paraguay d. Guatemala 3–0:** V. Rolon (PAR) d. M. F. Carrillo (GUA) 6–2 6–1; L. Schaerer (PAR) d. L. Lopez (GUA) 6–0 6–0; L. Bernal/L. Schaerer (PAR) d. L. Lopez/F. de Maria Urrea (GUA) 6–0 6–0. **Trinidad & Tobago d. Panama 3–0:** A. Rose (TRI) d. A. Espinosa (PAN) 7–5 6–0; E. Gibson (TRI) d. L. Porras (PAN) 6–1 6–1; E. Gibson/A. Rose (TRI) d. A. Espinosa/L. Porras (PAN) 7–5 6–4. **Panama d. Guatemala 2–1:** A. Espinosa (PAN) d. L. Lopez (GUA) 7–5 2–6 6–4; F. de Maria

Urrea (GUA) d. L. Porras (PAN) 6–3 6–1; A. Espinosa/L. Porras (PAN) d. L. Lopez/F. de Maria Urrea (PAN) 6–1 6–4. **Paraguay d. Dominican Republic 2–1:** L. Bernal (PAR) d. M. Sanchez (DOM) 6–2 7–6(4); L. Schaerer (PAR) d. J. Schad (DOM) 6–3 6–1; M. Sanchez/J. Schad (DOM) d. L. Bernal/V. Rolon (PAR) 6–3 7–5. **Trinidad & Tobago d. Barbados 2–1:** R. le Saldo (BAR) d. N. Kelly (TRI) 6–4 6–4; A. Rose (TRI) d. J. Carter (BAR) 6–2 6–0; E. Gibson/A. Rose (TRI) d. T. A. Greaves/R. le Saldo (BAR) 6–1 6–0.
Final Positions: Paraguay 1, Dominican Republic 2, Trinidad & Tobago 3, Panama 4, Guatemala 5, Bahamas 6, Barbados 7.

GROUP B: Antigua & Barbuda, Bermuda, Bolivia, Costa Rica, Cuba, El Salvador, Jamaica, Uruguay
Round Robin: Bolivia d. Costa Rica 2–1: M. Poveda (BOL) d. M. Golfin (CRC) 7–5 6–1; P. Umana (CRC) d. C. Jimenez (BOL) 6–3 6–3; A. Claure/M. Poveda (BOL) d. M. Leiva/P. Umana (CRC) 6–3 6–2. **Cuba d. Bermuda 3–0:** Y. Ford Guerra (CUB) d. K. Simmons (BER) 6–2 6–3; Y. Montesino (CUB) d. D. Darrell (BER) 6–0 6–0; Y. Ford Guerra/Y. Montesino (CUB) d. K. Holland/D. Paynter (BER) 6–1 6–1. **El Salvador d. Antigua & Barbuda 3–0:** C. Molins (ESA) d. N. Williams (ANT) 6–1 6–3; A. Falkenberg (ESA) d. W. Brown (ANT) 6–1 6–2; A. Falkenberg/C. Molins (ESA) d. F. Harvey/N Williams (ANT) 6–2 6–0. **Uruguay d. Jamaica 3–0:** N. Duxin (URU) d. C. Walter (JAM) 6–4 6–4; E. Juricich (URU) d. S. Hanna (JAM) 6–0 6–1; N. Duxin/E. Juricich (URU) d. A. Samara/C. Walter (JAM) 6–2 6–3. **Bolivia d. Bermuda 3–0:** A. Claure (BOL) d. D. Paynter (BER) 6–1 7–6(3); C. Jimenez (BOL) d. D. Darrell (BER) 6–2 6–1; A. Claure/M. Poveda (BOL) d. K. Holland/K. Simmons (BER) 6–2 6–0. **Cuba d. El Salvador 3–0:** Y. Ford Guerra (CUB) d. A. Falkenberg (ESA) 6–3 6–4; Y. Montesino (CUB) d. I. Gonzalez (ESA) 6–2 6–1; Y. Cordova/Y. Montesino (CUB) d. A. Falkenberg/C. Molins (ESA) 6–3 7–5. **Jamaica d. Costa Rica 3–0:** A. Samara (JAM) d. M. Golfin (CRC) 7–6(5) 6–2; S. Hanna (JAM) d. P. Umana (CRC) 6–2 5–7 6–2; K. Richards/C. Walter (JAM) d. P. Almeida/M. Leiva (CRC) 7–6(7) 6–3. **Uruguay d. Antigua & Barbuda 3–0:** D. Oliveira (URU) d. N. Williams (ANT) 6–0 6–0; E. Juricich (URU) d. W. Brown (ANT) 6–0 6–0; N. Duxin/D. Oliveira (URU) d. W. Brown/F. Harvey (ANT) 6–2 6–1. **Cuba d. Antigua & Barbuda 3–0:** Y. Cordova (CUB) d. N. Williams (ANT) 6–0 6–0; Y. Montesino (CUB) d. W. Brown (ANT) 6–1 6–0; Y. Cordova/Y. Ford Guerra (CUB) d. W. Brown/N. Williams (ANT) 6–3 6–0. **Bolivia d. El Salvador 2–1:** M. Poveda (BOL) d. A. Falkenberg (ESA) 2–6 6–2 6–1; I. Gonzalez (ESA) d. C. Jimenez (BOL) 6–3 6–2; A. Claure/M. Poveda (BOL) d. A. Falkenberg/C. Molins (ESA) 6–2 6–4. **Jamaica d. Bermuda 3–0:** A. Samara (JAM) d. K. Simmons (BER) 6–3 6–0; K. Richards (JAM) d. D. Darrell (BER) 2–6 6–0 6–1; S. Hanna/C. Walter (JAM) d. K. Holland/D. Paynter (BER) 6–2 6–1. **Uruguay d. Costa Rica 3–0:** N. Duxin (URU) d. M. Golfin (CRC) 6–1 6–2; E. Juricich (URU) d. P. Umana (CRC) 6–4 6–3; C. Guillenea/D. Oliveira (URU) d. M. Leiva/P. Umana (CRC) 6–2 6–1. **Jamaica d. El Salvador 3–0:** K. Richards (JAM) d. A. Falkenberg (ESA) 4–6 6–1 9–7; S. Hanna (JAM) d. I. Gonzalez (ESA) 6–3 2–6 6–1; A. Samara/C. Walter (JAM) d. I. Gonzalez/C. Molins (ESA) 6–3 6–4. **Bolivia d. Antigua & Barbuda 3–0:** A. Claure (BOL) d. N. Williams (ANT) 6–0 6–0; C. Herbas (BOL) d. W. Brown (ANT) 6–1 6–1; A. Claure/C. Herbas (BOL) d. F. Harvey/N. Williams (ANT) 6–0 6–0. **Costa Rica d. Bermuda 3–0:** M. Golfin (CRC) d. D. Paynter (BER) 6–0 6–1; P. Umana (CRC) d. K. Simmons (BER) 6–1 6–1; P. Almeida/M. Leiva (CRC) d. K. Holland/K. Simmons (BER) 3–6 6–4 6–2. **Uruguay d. Cuba 2–1:** N. Duxin (URU) d. Y. Ford Guerra (CUB) 6–7(5) 7–5 6–3; Y. Montesino (CUB) d. E. Juricich (URU) 4–6 7–6(5) 6–2; N. Duxin/E. Juricich (URU) d. Y. Cordova/Y. Montesino (CUB) 6–1 7–6(4). **Cuba d. Bolivia 2–1:** Y. Ford Guerra (CUB) d. C. Herbas (BOL) 6–3 4–6 6–2; M. Poveda (BOL) d. Y. Montesino (CUB) 3–6 6–2 6–0; Y. Cordova/Y. Montesino (CUB) d. A. Claure/M. Poveda (BOL) 6–0 6–1. **Costa Rica d. El Salvador 2–1:** M. Golfin (CRC) d. A. Falkenberg (ESA) 6–3 6–0; I. Gonzalez (ESA) d. P. Umana (CRC) 6–4 6–2; M. Golfin/P. Umana (CRC) d. A. Falkenberg/I. Gonzalez (ESA) 5–7 6–1 6–3. **Jamaica d. Antigua & Barbuda 3–0:** C. Walter (JAM) d. T. D. Moore (ANT) 6–0 6–0; S. Hanna (JAM) d. W. Brown (ANT) 6–0 6–1; S. Hanna/A. Samara (JAM) d. W. Brown/F. Harvey (ANT) 6–0 6–2. **Uruguay d. Bermuda 3–0:** N. Duxin (URU) d. K. Holland (BER) 6–0 6–0; E. Juricich (URU) d. D. Darrell (BER) 6–1 6–1; C. Guillenea/D. Oliveira (URU) d. D. Paynter/K. Simmons (BER) 6–1 6–0. **Costa Rica d. Antigua & Barbuda 3–0:** P. Almeida (CRC) d. N. Williams (ANT) 6–1 6–1; M. Golfin (CRC) d. W. Brown (ANT) 6–0 6–0; P. Almeida/M. Leiva (CRC) d. F. Harvey/N. Williams (ANT) 6–3 6–0. **El Salvador d. Bermuda 3–0:** A. Falkenberg (ESA) d. K. Simmons (BER) 3–6 6–3 6–0; I. Gonzalez (ESA) d. D. Darrell (BER) 6–2 6–2; I. Gonzalez/C. Molins (ESA) d. D. Darrell/K. Holland (BER) 6–3 6–2. **Cuba d. Jamaica 2–1:** A. Samara (JAM) d. Y. Ford Guerra (CUB) 7–5 7–5; Y. Cordova (CUB) d. S. Hanna (JAM) 7–6(2) 6–1; Y. Cordova/Y. Montesino (CUB) d. S. Hanna/C. Walter (JAM) 6–3 1–6 6–2. **Uruguay d. Bolivia 2–1:** C. Herbas (BOL) d. N. Duxin (URU) 3–6 7–6(9) 8–6; E. Juricich (URU) d. M. Poveda (BOL) 6–0 6–3; C. Guillenea/E. Juricich (URU) d. C. Jimenez/M. Poveda (BOL) 7–5 6–1. **Bermuda d. Antigua & Barbuda 3–0:** D. Darrell (BER) d. N. Williams (ANT) 6–3 6–0; K. Simmons (BER) d. F. Harvey (ANT) 6–4 6–0; D. Darrell/K. Holland (BER) d. F. Harvey/N. Williams (ANT) 6–1 6–1. **Cuba d. Costa Rica 3–0:** Y. Ford Guerra (CUB) d. M. Leiva (CRC) 6–4 6–2; Y. Cordova (CUB) d. P. Umana (CRC) 6–4 6–4; Y. Ford Guerra/Y. Montesino (CUB) d. M. Golfin/P. Umana (CRC) 6–2 6–1. **Jamaica d. Bolivia 2–1:** K. Richards (JAM) d. C. Herbas (BOL) 2–6 6–0 6–2; S. Hanna (JAM) d. M. Poveda (BOL) 6–4 6–2; A. Claure/M. Poveda (BOL) d. S. Hanna/C. Walter (JAM) 2–6 7–6(8) 6–4. **Uruguay d. El Salvador 3–0:** D. Oliveira (URU) d. A. Falkenberg (ESA) 6–3 6–0; E. Juricich (URU) d. I. Gonzalez (ESA) 6–1 6–1; E. Juricich/D. Oliveira (URU) d. A. Falkenberg/C. Molins (ESA) 6–0 7–6.
Final Positions: Uruguay 1, Cuba 2, Jamaica 3, Bolivia 4, Costa Rica 5, El Salvador 6, Bermuda 7, Antigua & Barbuda 8.

Paraguay and Uruguay were promoted to Americas Group I for the 1998 competition.

ASIA/OCEANIA GROUP II

Wellington Renouf Centre, New Zealand, 10–15 March

GROUP A: Malaysia, Singapore, Sri Lanka, Uzbekistan
Round Robin: Singapore d. Sri Lanka 3–0: J-L. Leong (SIN) d. A. Rajiyah (SRI) 6–0 6–4; R-J. Wong (SIN) d. S. Wickramahewa (SRI) 6–2 6–1; J-L. Leong/R-J. Wong (SIN) d. S. Perera/S. Wickramahewa (SRI) 6–4 6–2. **Malaysia d. Uzbekistan 2–1:** I. Yarikova (UZB) d. L. Y. Tan (MAS) 6–1 6–1; C. B. Khoo (MAS) d. N. Nikitina (UZB) 2–6 6–0 6–4; C. B. Khoo/L. Y. Tan (MAS) d. I. Tulyaganova/O. Yarikova (UZB) 6–0 7–5. **Singapore d. Malaysia 2–1:** L. Y. Tan (MAS) d. J-L. Leong (SIN) 6–1 6–4; R-J. Wong (SIN) d. C. B. Khoo (MAS) 6–4 6–4; J-L. Leong/R-J. Wong (SIN) d. C. B. Khoo/L. Y. Tan (MAS) 2–6 6–0 6–3. **Uzbekistan d. Sri Lanka 3–0:** I. Yarikova (UZB) d. A. Rajiyah (SRI) 6–2 6–3; I. Tulyaganova (UZB) d. S. Wickramahewa (SRI) 6–2 6–2; N. Nikitina/I. Yarikova (UZB) d. S. Perera/S. Wickramahewa (SRI) 6–0 6–0. **Malaysia d. Sri Lanka 3–0:** L. Y. Tan (MAS) d. A. Rajiyah (SRI) 6–2 6–1; C. B. Khoo (MAS) d. S. Wickramahewa (SRI) 6–1 6–1; C. B. Khoo/L. Y. Tan (MAS) d. D. de Silva/S. Perera (SRI) 6–0 6–0. **Uzbekistan d. Singapore 3–0:** I. Yarikova (UZB) d. J-L. Leong (SIN) 7–5 6–3; N. Nikitina (UZB) d. R-J. Wong (SIN) 6–4 6–1; N. Nikitina/I. Yarikova (UZB) d. J-L. Leong/R-J. Wong (SIN) 6–2 6–2.
Final Positions in Group A: Uzbekistan 1, Malaysia 2, Singapore 3, Sri Lanka 4

GROUP B: Pacific Oceania, Pakistan, Philippines, Syria
Round Robin: Pacific Oceania d. Syria 3–0: S. Wichman (PAC) d. F. Dayoub (SYR) 7–6(5) 4–6 6–4; T. So'onalole (PAC) d. S. Tawil (SYR) 6–2 6–0; T. So'onalole/S. Wichman (PAC) d. F. Dayoub/S. Tawil (SYR) 6–2 6–1. **Philippines d. Pakistan 3–0:** J. Saret (PHI) d. M. Chishtie (PAK) 6–0 6–1; M. Jacutin (PHI) d. N. Waseem (PAK) 6–0 6–0; P. Floro/J. Saret (PHI) d. S. Haider/N. Waseem (PAK) 6–0 6–0. **Syria d. Pakistan 3–0:** F. Dayoub (SYR) d. M. Chishtie (PAK) 4–6 6–2 6–2; S. Tawil (SYR) d. N. Waseem (PAK) 7–5 6–3; F. Dayoub/S. Tawil (SYR) d. N. Ehtsham/N. Waseem (PAK) 6–0 6–4. **Philippines d. Pacific Oceania 2–1:** J. Saret (PHI) d. V. Tere (PAC) 6–1 6–1; T. So'onalole (PAC) d. M. Jacutin (PHI) 6–3 7–5; P. Floro/J. Saret (PHI) d. T. So'onalole/V. Tere (PAC) 6–4 6–4. **Pacific Oceania d. Pakistan 2–1:** M. Chishtie (PAK) d. S. Wichman (PAC) 5–6 ret; T. So'onalole (PAC) d. N. Waseem (PAK) 6–4 6–4; T. So'onalole/A. Thaggard (PAC) d. N. Ehtsham/N. Waseem (PAK) 6–1 6–3. **Philippines d. Syria 3–0:** J. Saret (PHI) d. F. Dayoub (SYR) 6–1 6–1; M. Jacutin (PHI) d. S. Tawil (SYR) 6–3 6–3; P. Floro/J. Saret (PHI) d. S. Tawil/S. Tinawi (SYR) 6–1 6–0.
Final Positions in Group B: Philippines 1, Pacific Oceania 2, Syria 3, Pakistan 4

SEMI-FINALS: Uzbekistan d. Pacific Oceania 2–1: I. Yarikova (UZB) d. A. Thaggard (PAC) 6–0 6–3; T. So'onalole (PAC) d. N. Nikitina (UZB) 3–6 7–6(3) 6–1; N. Nikitina/I. Yarikova (UZB) d. T. So'onalole/A. Thaggard (PAC) 6–4 7–5. **Philippines d. Malaysia 2–1:** J. Saret (PHI) d. L. Y. Tan (MAS) 7–5 6–2; M. Jacutin (PHI) d. C. B. Khoo (MAS) 6–1 4–6 6–4; S-S. Liew/L. Y. Tan (MAS) d. P. Floro/J. Saret (PHI) 6–7(6) 6–2 6–3.

FINAL: Philippines d. Uzbekistan w/o.

PLAY-OFFS: Singapore d. Pakistan 3–0: J-L. Leong (SIN) d. M. Chishtie (PAK) 6–3 6–1; R-J. Wong (SIN) d. N. Waseem (PAK) 6–1 6–1; I-J. Chew/J-L. Leong (SIN) d. M. Chishtie/N. Waseem (PAK) 7–5 2–6 6–2. **Syria d. Sri Lanka 2–1:** A. Rajiyah (SRI) d. F. Dayoub (SYR) 6–3 6–3; S. Tawil (SYR) d. S. Wickramahewa (SRI) 6–4 6–4; F. Dayoub/S. Tawil (SYR) d. S. Perera/S. Wickramahewa (SRI) 7–5 6–3. **Malaysia d. Pacific Oceania 2–1:** S. S. Liew (MAS) d. A. Thaggard (PAC) 6–3 6–2: T. So'onalole (PAC) d. C. B. Khoo (MAS) 6–3 3–6 6–3; C. B. Khoo/L. Y. Tan (MAS) d. T. So'onalole/V. Tere (PAC) 6–4 6–2. **Singapore d. Syria 3–0:** J-L. Leong (SIN) d. F. Dayoub (SYR) 6–2 6–4; R-J. Wong (SIN) d. S. Tawil (SYR) 6–2 6–3; I-J. Chew/R-J. Wong (SIN) d. F. Dayoub/S. Tinawi (SYR) 6–1 6–0. **Pakistan d. Sri Lanka 2–1:** M. Chishtie (PAK) d. S. Pereira (SRI) 7–5 6–4; S. Wickramahewa (SRI) d. N. Waseem (PAK) 6–4 6–4; M. Chishtie/N. Waseem (PAK) d. S. Pereira/S. Wickramahewa (SRI) 6–3 6–2.
Final Positions: Philippines 1, Uzbekistan 2, Malaysia 3, Pacific Oceania 4, Singapore 5, Syria 6, Pakistan 7, Sri Lanka 8.

Philippines and Uzbekistan promoted to Asia/Oceania Group I for the 1998 competition.

EUROPE/AFRICA GROUP II

Club Ali Bey, Antalya, Turkey, 5–11 May

GROUP A: Armenia, Denmark, Estonia, Egypt, Great Britain, Lithuania
Great Britain d. Lithuania 3–0: J. Pullin (GBR) d. I. Kastanauskaite (LTU) 6–0 6–0; S. Smith (GBR) d. G. Misiurova (LTU) 6–0 6–0; C. Wood/L. Woodroffe (GBR) d. V. Martinkute/G. Misiurova (LTU) 6–1 6–1. **Estonia d. Egypt 3–0:** L. Suurvarik (EST) d. Y. Attia-Abdalla (EGY) 6–2 6–3; H. Laupa (EST) d. M. El Wany (EGY) 6–4 6–7(3) 6–3; H. Lill/L. Suurvarik (EST) d. Y. Attia-Abdalla/M. El Wany (EGY) 6–1 4–6 6–0. **Denmark d. Armenia 3–0:** E. Dyrberg (DEN) d. A. Khalatian (ARM) 7–5 6–0; S. Albinus (DEN) d. S. Saringulian (ARM) 6–2 6–2; M. Iversen/M. Rasmussen (DEN) d. A. Khalatian/S. Saringulian (ARM) 6–1 6–4. **Great Britain d. Egypt 3–0:** J. Pullin (GBR) d. Y. Attia-Abdalla (EGY) 6–1 6–1; S. Smith (GBR) d. M. El Wany (EGY) 6–1 6–1; C. Wood/L. Woodroffe (GBR) d. Y. Attia-Abdalla/M. El Wany (EGY) 6–1 6–0. **Denmark d. Estonia 3–0:** E. Dyrberg (DEN) d. H. Holter (EST) 2–6 6–4 6–0; S. Albinus (DEN) d. H. Lill (EST) 6–3 7–5; S. Albinus/E. Dyrberg (DEN) d. H. Laupa/L. Suurvarik (EST) 6–1 6–1. **Armenia d. Lithuania 3–0:** A. Khalatian (ARM) d. I. Kastanauskaite (LTU) 6–2 6–0; S. Saringulian (ARM) d. G. Misiurova (LTU) 6–2 6–3; A. Khalatian/S.

Saringulian (ARM) d. V. Martinkute/G. Misiurova (LTU) 6–0 6–1. **Great Britain d. Estonia 3–0:** C. Wood (GBR) d. L. Suurvarik (EST) 6–3 6–0; S. Smith (GBR) d. H. Holter (EST) 6–3 6–4; Julie Pullin/L. Woodroffe (GBR) d. H. Holter/L. Suurvarik (EST) 6–0 6–1. **Armenia d. Egypt 3–0:** A. Khalatian (ARM) d. Y. Attia-Abdalla (EGY) 6–3 6–0; S. Saringulian (ARM) d. M. El Wany (EGY) 6–3 6–2; A. Khalatian/N. Santrosian (ARM) d. Y. Attia-Abdalla/M. El Wany (EGY) 6–1 6–1. **Denmark d. Lithuania 3–0:** E. Dyrberg (DEN) d. I. Kastanauskaite (LTU) 6–1 6–0; S. Albinus (DEN) d. G. Misiurova (LTU) 6–2 7–5; E. Dyrberg/M. Iversen (DEN) d. V. Martinkute/G. Misiurova (LTU) 6–3 6–1. **Great Britain d. Armenia 3–0:** C. Wood (GBR) d. A. Khalatian (ARM) 6–1 6–2; S. Smith (GBR) d. S. Saringulian (ARM) 6–0 6–3; C. Wood/L. Woodroffe (GBR) d. N. Santrosian/S. Saringulian (ARM) 6–2 6–3. **Denmark d. Egypt 3–0:** E. Dyrberg (DEN) d. I. El Tawil (EGY) 6–2 6–1; S. Albinus (DEN) d. D. El Shaikh (EGY) 6–3 6–3; M. Iversen/M. Rasmussen (DEN) d. Y. Attia-Abdalla/M. El Wany (EGY) 6–3 6–1. **Estonia d. Lithuania 3–0:** L. Suurvarik (EST) d. V. Martinkute (LTU) 6–0 6–0; H. Lill (EST) d. G. Misiurova (LTU) 6–3 7–6(3); H. Holter/H. Laupa (EST) d. V. Martinkute/I. Kastanauskaite (LTU) 6–2 6–0. **Great Britain d. Denmark 2–1:** E. Dyrberg (DEN) d. C. Wood (GBR) 6–3 4–6 6–3; S. Smith (GBR) d. S. Albinus (DEN) 4–6 6–4 6–2; J. Pullin/L. Woodroffe (GBR) d. S. Albinus/E. Dyrberg (DEN) 6–4 6–2. **Lithuania d. Egypt 3–0:** I. Kastanauskaite (LTU) d. D. El Sheikh (EGY) 7–6(9) 6–1; G. Misiurova (LTU) d. M. El Wany (EGY) 7–5 6–3; V. Martinkute/G. Misiurova (LTU) d. Y. Attia-Abdalla/M. El Wany (EGY) 6–3 7–5. **Estonia d. Armenia 2–1:** L. Suurvarik (EST) d. A. Khalatian (ARM) 6–3 6–1; H. Holter (EST) d. S. Saringulian (ARM) 6–3 6–4; A. Khalatian/S. Saringulian (ARM) d. H. Laupa/H. Lill (EST) 6–3 6–2.

Final Positions: Great Britain 1, Denmark 2, Estonia 3, Armenia 4, Lithuania 5, Egypt 6.

GROUP B: Algeria, Cameroon, Iceland, Ireland, Tunisia, Yugoslavia

Round Robin: Yugoslavia d. Algeria 3–0: S. Nacuk (YUG) d. L. Hameurlaine (ALG) 6–0 6–1; D. Zaric (YUG) d. O. Bouchabou (ALG) 6–0 6–1; D. Zaric/L. Nanusevic (YUG) d. L. Hameurlaine/S. Takourabet (ALG) 6–3 6–3. **Cameroon d. Iceland 2–1:** C. Njeuma (CMR) d. I. Staub (ISL) 1–6 7–6(5) 6–2; N. Sienkob (CMR) d. S. Stefansdottir (ISL) 6–3 6–3; I. Staub/S. Stefansdottir (ISL) d. A. Belibi/N. Sienkob (CMR) 6–3 2–6 7–5. **Ireland d. Tunisia 2–1:** K. Nugent (IRL) d. I. Zouabi (TUN) 6–1 6–0; S. Sfar (TUN) d. G. Nidland (IRL) 6–2 6–0; G. Nidland/K. Nugent (IRL) d. S. Sfar/I. Zouabi (TUN) 6–4 6–4. **Yugoslavia d. Iceland 3–0:** L. Nanusevic (YUG) d. I. Staub (ISL) 6–2 6–0; D. Zaric (YUG) d. S. Stefansdottir (ISL) 6–2 6–2; D. Zaric/L. Nanusevic (YUG) d. J. Jonsdottir/S. Stefansdottir (ISL) 6–0 6–2. **Tunisia d. Cameroon 3–0:** I. Zouabi (TUN) d. A. Belibi (CMR) 6–2 6–0; S. Sfar (TUN) d. N. Sienkob (CMR) 6–0 6–1; S. Sfar/A. Ferjani (TUN) d. C. Njeuma/N. Sienkob (CMR) 6–0 7–5. **Ireland. d. Algeria 2–1:** L. Hameurlaine (ALG) d. Z. Wolseley (IRL) 6–0 6–1; G. Nidland (IRL) d. O. Bouchabou (ALG) 6–0 6–2; G. Nidland/K. Nugent (IRL) d. O. Bouchabou/L. Hameurlaine (ALG) 6–1 6–1. **Yugoslavia d. Cameroon 3–0:** D. Zaric (YUG) d. C. Njeuma (CMR) 7–6(3) 6–4; S. Nacuk (YUG) d. N. Sienkob (CMR) 6–0 6–0; D. Zaric/L. Nanusevic (YUG) d. C. Njeuma/N. Sienkob (CMR) 6–3 6–3. **Ireland d. Iceland 3–0:** Z. Wolseley (IRL) d. J. Jonsdottir (ISL) 6–1 6–0; G. Nidland (IRL) d. I. Staub (ISL) 6–0 6–0; G. Nidland/Z. Wolseley (IRL) d. I. Staub/S. Stefansdottir (ISL) 6–1 6–2. **Tunisia d. Algeria 2–1:** L. Hameurlaine (ALG) d. I. Zouabi (TUN) 6–3 6–2; S. Sfar (TUN) d. O. Bouchabou (ALG) 6–1 6–0; S. Sfar/I. Zouabi (TUN) d. O. Bouchabou/L. Hameurlaine (ALG) 6–1 5–7 6–0. **Yugoslavia d. Ireland 3–0:** S. Nacuk (YUG) d. K. Nugent (IRL) 6–2 6–4; D. Zaric (YUG) d. G. Nidland (IRL) 6–2 6–2; L. Nanusevic/D. Zaric (YUG) d. K. Nugent/L. O'Halloran (IRL) 6–3 6–4. **Tunisia d. Iceland 3–0:** I. Zouabi (TUN) d. I. Staub (ISL) 6–4 7–6(5); S. Sfar (TUN) d. S. Stefansdottir (ISL) 6–0 6–0; S. Sfar/A. Ferjani (TUN) d. I. Staub/S. Stefansdottir (ISL) 6–2 6–4. **Algeria d. Cameroon 3–0:** S. Takourabet (ALG) d. C. Njeuma (CMR) 6–4 6–1; L. Hameurlaine (ALG) d. N. Sienkob (CMR) 6–4 6–2; L. Hameurlaine/S. Takourabet (ALG) d. C. Njeuma/N. Sienkob (CMR) 4–6 6–1 6–0. **Ireland d. Cameroon 3–0:** Z. Wolseley (IRL) d. C. Njeuma (CMR) 3–6 6–1 6–3; G. Nidland (IRL) d. N. Sienkob (CMR) 6–2 6–0; G. Niland/Z. Wolseley (IRL) d. C. Njeuma/N. Sienkob (CMR) 7–6(2) 6–0. **Yugoslavia d. Tunisia 3–0:** S. Nacuk (YUG) d. I. Zouabi (TUN) 6–2 6–2; D. Zaric (YUG) d. S. Sfar (TUN) 4–6 6–3 6–4; D. Zaric/L. Nanusevic (YUG) d. A. Ferjani/I. Zouabi (TUN) 6–1 6–3. **Algeria d. Iceland 3–0:** S. Takourabet (ALG) d. I. Staub (ISL) 7–6(7) 6–2; L. Hameurlaine (ALG) d. S. Stefansdottir (ISL) 6–2 6–3; L. Hameurlaine/S. Takourabet (ALG) d. I. Staub/S. Stefansdottir (ISL) 6–1 6–0.

Final Positions: Yugoslavia 1, Ireland 2, Tunisia 3, Algeria 4, Cameroon 5, Iceland 6.

GROUP C: Bosnia Herzegovina, Ethiopia, Norway, Portugal, San Marino, Turkey

Portugal d. Ethiopia 3–0: A. Gaspar (POR) d. M. Temesgen (ETH) 6–0 6–0; J. Pedroso (POR) d. S. Gebreail (ETH) 6–1 6–0; A. Nogueira/J. Pedroso (POR) d. S. Gebreail/T. Kifle (ETH) 6–0 6–0. **Bosnia Herzegovina d. Norway 2–1:** E. Fazlic (BIH) d. L. Ullring (NOR) 3–6 6–2 6–2; M. Jugic (BIH) d. T. Samara (NOR) 6–2 6–4; T. Samara/L. Ullring (NOR) d. M. Bajrambasic/E. Fazlic (BIH) 6–4 6–4. **Turkey d. San Marino 2–1:** I-D. Aksit (TUR) d. L. Gatti (SMR) 6–0 6–0; F. Guardigli (SMR) d. G. Gultekin (TUR) 2–6 7–6(6) 6–4; I-D. Aksit/G. Gultekin (TUR) d. L. Gatti/F. Guardigli (SMR) 6–1 6–2. **Portugal d. Norway 3–0:** A. Gaspar (POR) d. L. Ullring (NOR) 6–3 6–0; S. Prazeres (POR) d. T. Samara (NOR) 6–2 6–2; A Nogueira/J. Pedroso (POR) d. L. Ullring/T. Samara (NOR) 7–5 6–3. **Turkey d. Bosnia Herzegovina 2–1:** I-D. Aksit (TUR) d. E. Fazlic (BIH) 6–4 6–1; M. Jugic (BIH) d. G. Gultekin (TUR) 6–4 5–7 6–3; I-D. Aksit/G. Gultekin (TUR) d. E. Fazlic/M. Jugic (BIH) 6–3 6–2. **San Marino d. Ethiopia 3–0:** L. Gatti (SMR) d. T. Kifle (ETH) 6–0 6–0; F. Guardigli (SMR) d. S. Gebreail (ETH) 6–0 6–1; L. Gatti/F. Guardigli (SMR) d. S. Gebreail/M. Temesgen (ETH) 6–0 6–0. **Portugal d. Bosnia Herzegovina 3–0:** A Gaspar (POR) d. E. Fazlic (BIH) 7–5 7–6(7); S. Prazeres (POR) d. M. Jugic (BIH) 6–1 6–0; J Pedroso/S Prazeres (POR) d. M. Bajrambasic/H. Delic (BIH) 6–2 6–2. **Norway d. San Marino 2–1:** L. Ullring (NOR) d. L. Gatti (SMR) 6–1 6–0; F. Guardigli (SMR) d. T. Samara (NOR) 2–6 7–6(5) 6–2; M. Bakken/T. Samara (NOR) d. L. Gatti/F. Guardigli (SMR) 6–3 6–3. **Turkey d. Ethiopia 3–0:** S. Penciu-Elpeze (TUR) d. T. Kifle (ETH)

6–0 6–0; G. Gultekin (TUR) d. S. Gebreail (ETH) 6–0 6–0; S. Ozlu/S. Penciu-Elpeze (TUR) d. S. Gebreail/T. Kifle (ETH) 6–0 6–1. **Portugal d. San Marino 3–0:** A. Gaspar (POR) d. L. Gatti (SMR) 6–0 6–2; S. Prazeres (POR) d. F. Guardigli (SMR) 6–3 1–6 6–3; A. Nogueira/J. Pedroso (POR) d. L. Gatti/F. Guardigli (SMR) 6–1 4–6 6–3. **Turkey d. Norway 2–1:** L. Ullring (NOR) d. I-D. Aksit (TUR) 6–4 4–6 6–3; G. Gultekin (TUR) d. T. Samara (NOR) 7–6(4) 6–3; I-D. Aksit/G. Gultekin (TUR) d. M. Bakken/T. Samara (NOR) 6–3 6–2. **Bosnia Herzegovina d. Ethiopia 3–0:** H. Delic (BIH) d. M. Temesgen (ETH) 6–0 6–0; M. Jugic (BIH) d. S. Gebreail (ETH) 6–1 6–0; M. Bajrambasic/H. Delic (BIH) d. S. Gebreail/T. Kifle (ETH) 6–1 6–0. **Bosnia Herzegovina d. San Marino 2–1:** E. Fazlic (BIH) d. L.Gatti (SMR) 6–0 6–0; F. Guardigli (SMR) d. M. Jugic (BIH) 6–2 6–3; E. Fazlic/M. Jugic (BIH) d. L. Gatti/F. Guardigli (SMR) 6–2 6–2. **Norway d. Ethiopia 2–1:** M. Bakken (NOR) d. M. Temesgen (ETH) 6–0 6–0; L. Ullring (NOR) d. S. Gebreail (ETH) 6–0 6–0; Doubles not played due to injury to Norway players. **Portugal d. Turkey 3–0:** A. Gaspar (POR) d. I-D. Aksit (TUR) 1–6 6–3 6–0; S. Prazeres (POR) d. G. Gultekin (TUR) 6–3 6–4; Doubles – walkover to Portugal.
Final Positions: Portugal 1, Turkey 2, Bosnia Herzegovina 3, Norway 4, San Marino 5, Ethiopia 6.

GROUP D: Botswana, Cyprus, Liechtenstein, Luxembourg, FYR Macedonia, Madagascar, Malta
Madagascar d. Malta 2–1: N. Randriantefy (MAD) d. L. Camenzuli (MLT) 6–3 6–0; D. Randriantefy (MAD) d. S. Wetz (MLT) 6–2 6–1; H. Asciak/L. Camenzuli (MLT) d. A. Rafolomanantsiatosika/F. Rasoarilalao (MAD) 6–2 6–3. **Liechtenstein d. Cyprus 2–1:** F. Gmeiner (LIE) d. E. Constanta (CYP) 1–6 6–0 6–4; D. Nicolatou (CYP) d. C. Vogt (LIE) 6–1 6–0; F. Gmeiner/J. Niedhardt (LIE) d. D. Nicolatou/E. Papanicolaou (CYP) 6–4 7–6(1). **Luxembourg d. Botswana 2–1:** A. Scholer (LUX) d. G. Seleka (BOT) 6–0 6–0; F. Thill (LUX) d. K. Makgale (BOT) 6–1 6–0; K. Makgale/G. Seleka (BOT) d. R. Moyen/F. Thill (LUX) 1–6 6–4 6–3. **Madagascar d. Cyprus 3–0:** N. Randriantefy (MAD) d. E. Constanta (CYP) 6–1 6–0; D. Randriantefy (MAD) d. D. Nicolatou (CYP) 6–0 6–2; A. Rafolomanantsiatosika/D. Randriantefy (MAD) d. D. Nicolatou/E. Papanicolaou (CYP) 6–2 6–0. **Malta d. Liechtenstein 3–0:** H. Asciak (MLT) d. F. Gmeiner (LIE) 6–0 6–1; L. Camenzuli (MLT) d. C. Vogt (LIE) 7–5 6–1; H. Asciak/L. Camenzuli (LIE) d. F. Gmeiner/J. Niedhardt (LIE) 6–0 6–0. **FYR Macedonia d. Botswana 3–0:** E. Manevska (MKD) d. G. Seleka (BOT) 6–4 6–0; B. Trpeska (MKD) d. K. Makgale (BOT) 6–0 6–1; B. Trpeska/Z. Videnova (MKD) d. K. Makgale/G. Seleka (BOT) 7–5 6–3. **Malta d. Luxembourg 2–1:** H. Asciak (MLT) d. F. Thill (LUX) 6–3 6–3; R. Moyen (LUX) d. L. Camenzuli (MLT) 6–2 7–5; H. Asciak/L. Camenzuli (MLT) d. R. Moyen/A. Scholer (LUX) 6–3 6–1. **Liechtenstein d. Botswana 3–0:** F. Gmeiner (LIE) d. G. Seleka (BOT) 6–2 6–0; C. Vogt (LIE) d. K. Makgale (BOT) 7–5 7–5; F. Gmeiner/J. Niedhardt (LIE) d. K. Makgale/G. Seleka (BOT) 6–7 6–1 6–3. **FYR Macedonia d. Cyprus 3–0:** Z. Videnova (MKD) d. E. Constanta (CYP) 6–2 6–0; B. Trpeska (MKD) d. D. Nicolatou (CYP) 7–6(4) 6–4; B. Trpeska/Z. Videnova (MKD) d. D. Nicolatou/E. Papanicolaou (CYP) 6–2 6–2. **Malta d. Cyprus 3–0:** H. Asciak (MLT) d. E. Papanicolaou (CYP) 6–3 6–2; L. Camenzuli (MLT) d. D. Nicolatou (CYP) 6–0 6–2; H. Asciak/L. Camenzuli (MLT) d. E. Constanta/D. Nicolatou (CYP) 6–0 6–0. **Madagascar d. Liechtenstein 3–0:** N. Randriantefy (MAD) d. F. Gmeiner (LIE) 6–1 6–1; D. Randriantefy (MAD) d. C. Vogt (LIE) 6–0 6–0; N. Randriantefy/F. Rasoarilalao (MAD) d. F. Gmeiner/J. Niedhardt (LIE) 6–1 6–3. **Luxembourg d. FYR Macedonia 3–0:** F. Thill (LUX) d. Z. Videnova (MKD) 6–1 6–1; R. Moyen (LUX) d. B. Trpeska (MKD) 6–3 6–1; F. Thill/A. Scholer (LUX) d. B. Trpeska/Z. Videnova (MKD) 6–0 6–1. **Malta d. Botswana 3–0:** L. Camenzuli (MLT) d. G. Seleka (BOT) 6–1 6–0; S. Wetz (MLT) d. K. Makgale (BOT) 6–2 6–3; H. Asciak/C. Gatt (MLT) d. N. Coyne/O. Leepile (BOT) 6–0 6–0. **Madagascar d. Luxembourg 2–1:** N. Randriantefy (MAD) d. F. Thill (LUX) 3–6 6–1 6–1; D. Randriantefy (MAD) d. R. Moyen (LUX) 6–1 6–1; A. Scholer/F. Thill (LUX) d. A. Rafolomanantsiatosika/N. Randriantefy (MAD) 7–6(4) 6–4. **FYR Macedonia d. Liechtenstein 3–0:** Z. Videnova (MKD) d. F. Gmeiner (LIE) 6–1 6–2; B. Trpeska (MKD) d. C. Vogt (LIE) 6–0 6–1; B. Trpeska/Z. Videnova (MKD) d. F. Gmeiner/J. Niedhardt (LIE) 6–2 6–1. **Luxembourg d. Liechtenstein 3–0:** A. Scholer (LUX) d. F. Gmeiner (LIE) 6–1 6–0; R. Moyen (LUX) d. J. Niedhardt (LIE) 6–1 6–1; A. Scholer/F. Thill (LUX) d. F. Gmeiner/J. Niedhardt (LIE) 6–1 6–0. **Madagascar d. FYR Macedonia 3–0:** N. Randriantefy (MAD) d. Z. Videnova (MKD) 6–2 6–2; D. Randriantefy (MAD) d. B. Trpeska (MKD) 6–1 6–0; D. Randriantefy/F. Rasoarilalao (MAD) d. B. Trpeska/Z. Videnova (MKD) 6–4 6–1. **Botswana d. Cyprus 2–1:** G. Seleka (BOT) d. E. Constanta (CYP) 3–6 6–1 6–4; D. Nicolatou (CYP) d. K. Makgale (BOT) 6–3 6–0; K. Makgale/G. Seleka (BOT) d. D. Nicolatou/E. Papanicolaou (CYP) 7–6(7) 6–4. **Luxembourg d. Cyprus 3–0:** F. Thill (LUX) d. E. Constanta (CYP) 6–1 6–0; R. Moyen (LUX) d. D. Nicolatou (CYP) 6–0 6–0; A. Scholer/F. Thill (LUX) d. E. Constanta/D. Nicolatou (CYP) w/o. **Madagascar d. Botswana 3–0:** A. Rafolomanantsiatosika (MAD) d. N. Coyne (BOT) 6–1 6–2; D. Randriantefy (MAD) d. O. Leepile (BOT) 6–0 6–0; A. Rafolomanantsiatosika/F. Rasoarilalao (MAD) d. K. Makgale/G. Seleka (BOT) 6–3 6–7(5) 3–2 ret. **Malta d. FYR Macedonia 3-0:** H. Asciak (MLT) d. Z. Videnova (MKD) 7–6(1) 7–5; L. Camenzuli (MLT) d. B. Trpeska (MKD) 6–3 6–2; Doubles – walkover to Malta.
Final Positions: Madagascar 1, Malta 2, Luxembourg 3, FYR Macedonia 4, Liechtenstein 5, Botswana 6, Cyprus 7.

Great Britain, Yugoslavia, Portugal and Madagascar were promoted to Euro/Africa Group I for the 1998 competition.

Hopman Cup

Edward Johnson

It was one of those improbable but glorious moments that make international sport such a compelling spectacle. 'Game, set and match to the United States' shouted the umpire, struggling to make himself heard above the applause from the packed stands of Perth's Burswood Dome. The atmosphere was electrifying as the fans stood to applaud the American heroine Chanda Rubin and her tall partner Justin Gimelstob. The smiling couple were hugging each other with joy out on Centre Court having just beaten Wayne Ferreira and Amanda Coetzer 3–6 6–2 7–5.

The impossible had happened. Unseeded and unfancied, the United States had just completed a 2–1 win against South Africa to capture the $800,000 Hopman Cup for the first time with its first prize of $176,000. Fittingly, this was its first year as the ITF's official Mixed Team Championship.

No-one could believe it, least of all Gimelstob. The 19-year-old from Key Biscayne had been sunning himself on a Florida Beach when the call had come asking him to replace Richey Reneberg whose wife was expecting some problems with her pregnancy.

A long plane-hop later the former US junior champion and All American from UCLA, who had ended 1996 ranked a lowly 155, found himself up against some classy opposition. Unfazed by losses to Guy Forget and Goran Ivanisevic he had teamed with Rubin to bring home the vital mixed doubles point that had accounted for France and Croatia respectively.

Then against Australia in the last tie of the 'A' Group the gangling Gimelstob had played the match of his life. His thrilling 7–6 4–6 7–6 win over Mark Philippoussis, a full-blooded heavy hitting affair that had roused the home crowd to a frenzy of support for Philippoussis, had ensured the United States a place in the final of this eight nation round-robin competition played in two groups of four.

The real American star, though, was Rubin. Making a welcome return to action after an injury-plagued year, the 19-year-old from Lafayette, Louisiana was unbeaten in singles and performed heroically alongside Gimelstob in mixed doubles. Their only loss was the dead rubber against Australia.

Looking at Rubin's wins, 6–4 6–1 against Mary Pierce, 6–3 3–6 7–6 against Iva Majoli, 7–5 6–0 over Nicole Bradtke and 7–5 6–2 against Amanda Coetzer, it was clear that the American had put the troubles of 1996 behind her.

Most people thought that Switzerland, with Martina Hingis and Marc Rosset, would win the 'B' Group. They probably would have done if Rosset could have avoided the jinx that seems to follow him in Perth. In the previous year's final he had been forced to retire after slamming his fist into a courtside banner during the deciding doubles against the Croatians, Ivanisevic and Majoli.

This time it was a freak injury to his back that forced Rosset to pull out on Day 4. Leading 6–0 2–0 against Ferreira he had fallen awkwardly after colliding with a ball-girl. This was cruel luck for Switzerland because Hingis had looked magnificent in beating Coetzer 6–1 6–2.

The heroine of America's first Hopman Cup win was Chanda Rubin, happily restored to full fitness (Michael Cole)

South Africa had already beaten Germany, but so had Romania. Thus the meeting between these two nations on Day 6 was decisive. When Irina Spirlea beat Coetzer an upset seemed to be on the cards but Ferreira held firm to beat Adrian Voinea in two tie-break sets and then teamed with Coetzer to win the mixed 4–6 6–1 6–4.

With record crowds of 75,070 during the week, an improvement of 2,000 over the previous figure, Tournament Director Paul McNamee was understandably delighted. Even the disappointing late withdrawal of Steffi Graf from the German team (she was replaced at short notice by Petra Begerow) did not deter them. 'The fans here in Western Australia were superb,' he said. 'We are delighted the crowd record was broken...it shows the event is attracting great and growing support.'

HOPMAN CUP 1997

BURSWOOD RESORT, PERTH, 26 DECEMBER 1996 – 4 JANUARY 1997

Round Robin results

Group A

1. USA: d. France 2–1: C. Rubin d. M. Pierce 6–4 6–1; J. Gimelstob lost to G. Forget 2–6 6–3 6–3; Gimelstob/Rubin d. Forget/Pierce 3–6 6–3 6–2. **d. Croatia 2–1:** C. Rubin d. I. Majoli 6–3 3–6 7–6; G. Ivanisevic d. J. Gimelstob 7–6 4–6 7–5; Gimelstob/Rubin d. Ivanisevic/Majoli 3–6 6–3 7–6. **d. Australia 2–1:** C. Rubin d. N. Bradtke 7–5 6–0; Gimelstob d. Philippoussis 7–6 4–6 7–6; Gimelstob/Rubin lost to Philippoussis/Bradtke 6–3 7–5.

2. CROATIA: d. Australia 2–1: I. Majoli d. N. Bradtke 6–4 6–3; G. Ivanisevic lost to M. Philippoussis 6–2 6–3; Ivanisevic/Majoli d. Philippoussis/Bradtke 7–5 7–5. **d. France 3–0:** I. Majoli d. M. Pierce 6–3 6–4; G. Ivanisevic lost to G. Forget def.; Ivanisevic/Majoli d. Forget/Pierce def.

3. AUSTRALIA: d. France 2–1: M. Pierce d. N. Bradtke 7–6 6–1; M. Philippoussis d. G. Forget 7–6 6–2; Philippoussis/Bradtke d. Forget/Pierce 7–6 7–6.

4. FRANCE

Group B

1. SOUTH AFRICA: d. Germany 3–0: A. Coetzer d. P. Begerow 6–0 7–5; W. Ferreira d. B. Karbacher 6–4 6–4; Ferreira/Coetzer d. Karbacker/Begerow 6–3 6–4. **d. Switzerland 2–1:** A.Coetzer lost to M. Hingis 6–1 6–2; W. Ferreira d. M. Rosset def.; Ferreira/Coetzer d. Rosset/Hingis def. **d. Romania 2–1:** A.Coetzer lost to I.Spirlea 5–7 6–4 6–1; W. Ferreira d. A. Voinea 7–6 7–6; Ferreira/Coetzer d. Voinea/Spirlea 4–6 6–1 6–4.

2.SWITZERLAND: d. Romania 2–1: M. Hingis d. I. Spirlea 7–5 6–2; A. Voinea d. M. Rosset def.; Rosset/Hingis d. Voinea/Spirlea 3–6 7–5 6–3. **d. Germany 3–0:** M. Hingis d. P. Begerow 6–1 6–1; M. Rosset d. B. Karacher 7–6 7–6; Rosset/Hingis d. Karbacher/Begerow 7–5 6–1.

3. ROMANIA: d. Germany 3–0: I. Spirlea d. P. Begerow 6–1 6–3; A. Voinea d. B. Karbacher 2–6 7–6 6–2; Voinea/Spirlea d. Karbacher/Begerow 6–1 6–1.

4. GERMANY

FINAL: USA d. SOUTH AFRICA 2–1: Rubin d. Coetzer 7–5 6–2; Gimelstob lost to Ferreira 6–4 7–6; Gimelstob/Rubin d. Ferreira/Coetzer 3–6 6–2 7–5.

Called in as a late replacement, Justin Gimelstob played a full part alongside Chanda Rubin in helping the United States to their first Hopman Cup win. (Stephen Wake)

ITF Youth Cups

Jackie Nesbitt

Sunshine Cup & Connolly Continental Cup

It was a slow start to the week as far as the Florida weather was concerned, but the tennis played by the boys in the ITF Sunshine Cup and the girls in the Connolly Continental Cup (named in 1976 after the former great Maureen 'Little Mo' Connolly Brinker), sparkled from the very first day.

With most of the world's best 18 & Under juniors present, including two in the running for world singles titles, anticipation was high. Indeed past participants have included the likes of McEnroe, Borg, Graf and Evert – names that conjure up fabulous memories.

The French girls, led by US Open runner-up Kildine Chevalier just clinched the final 8th seeding spot, but failed to start in the right gear as they crashed out to Columbia in the only opening round upset.

There were, in fact, remarkably few seeding upsets early on with only Belgium and Japan disturbing the smooth order in the second round.

Kim Clijsters, still only 14 years of age, was outstanding for Belgium as they ousted 5th seeded Belarus. Clijsters' three-set victory over the highly rated Tatiana Poutchek was as impressive as it was unexpected. Much credit was also due to her compatriot, Delphine Troch, for getting Belgium off to a perfect start with a victory over Nadzeya Astrouskaya, one of the best 16 & Under Europeans.

Perhaps more surprising was the nature of Japan's victory over the 3rd seeds, Slovak Republic. All three members of the Slovak team came with strong reputations. Andrea Sebova, their No.1, was expected to finish the year in the top ten girls' singles ranking and when she lost to Rika Fujiwara in the top singles the alarm bells started ringing, albeit quietly. However, when the Slovaks dropped the first set of the deciding doubles panic really set in. Although they dominated the second set against Fujiwara and Remi Uda, the Japanese pair held on for a thrilling 7–5 third set victory.

Both Belgium and Japan saw their hopes for glory end in the quarter-finals. Fourth seeded Spain made heavy going against Belgium in the singles but wrapped up both rubbers in three sets. Japan could make no impression on 6th seeded Russia but that was hardly surprising when you consider they were up against the likes of Elena Dementieva and Anastassia Myskina, ranked only 2 and 3 in the Russian team, who had been responsible for winning the 1997 NEC World Youth Cup back in September!

For the locals it was disappointing to see the United States, seeded No.2, lose in the quarter-finals. Samantha Reeves, the highest WTA ranked player in the competition at 172, kept the flag flying with a top singles win over Jelena Kostanic. The Europeans do tend to play good doubles, however, as the US learnt to their cost, crashing out in the deciding rubber.

Both semi-finals were tough battles. For Slovenia Tina Pisnik ground out a three-set win over Spain's Paula Garcia, which was just as well for the number one seeds, because team-mate Katarina Srebotnik was defeated in the top rubber by Lourdes Dominguez. Fortunately for Slovenia Pisnik and Srebotnik form a formidable doubles team. Despite dropping the first set they eventually ran out comfortable winners of the decider.

In the other semi-final Russia, too, needed the doubles to survive. After a close battle they justified their seeding position, one place ahead of Croatia, who had had a tough passage to the semis, including an amazing 13–11 third set deciding doubles against Argentina in the second round. Although Croatia's Jelena Kostanic managed to pull off a great three-set win over Russia's Ekaterina Syssoeva in the top singles, she was unable to sustain the effort in the doubles as she and Ivana Visic lost a close three-setter to Dementieva and Syssoeva.

The final itself, Slovenia against Russia, was notable not just for the fine tennis, but also for bringing out the best in the top seeds. Pisnik raced to a 5–0 lead in the opening set and appeared on course to rout Dementieva in the opening rubber. Although the Russian eventually overcame her nerves and performed creditably she was beaten 6–3 7–5.

In the top singles, Srebotnik got off to another slow start against Russia's Syssoeva, dropping the first set. Rather more in keeping with the form expected of a player challenging for the world singles crown, Srebotnik finally came good, taking the next two sets and the title for Slovenia.

If the girls were models of decorum throughout the week, the boys made sure there were plenty of fireworks on court to keep the spectators on their toes.

Third seeded Spain were not overly delighted to be drawn against old rivals Italy in the opening round, but the organisers were rubbing their hands in glee. Spain have a terrific record in ITF junior team competitions and it appeared to be business as usual when their No.2 Pedro Canovas won his opening singles against Filippo Volandri.

Federico Luzzi, who had helped Italy to the World Junior Tennis title in 1994, had a great win over Feliciano Lopez to level matters. The deciding doubles was extremely tense but at one set apiece Luzzi moved up a gear to orchestrate a 6–0 final set that ousted the seeds.

All the other seeds successfully negotiated the opening round although Great Britain, seeded 4, found Israel led by Kobi Ziv a real handful.

Despite being led by world No.4 Luis Horna, it was not felt that Peru had sufficient strength in depth to deserve being seeded. When Horna was surprisingly defeated by Morocco's Karim Benmansour that decision seemed correct. But unheralded Ivan Miranda saved his team-mates' blushes, winning his singles and combining with Horna to take the doubles.

It was Miranda again who deserved a great deal of credit for Peru's second round victory, this time over 8th seeds, Slovak Republic, by winning the opening rubber against Frantisek Babej. This made life easier for Horna who completed a good day by partnering brother Marco to victory in the doubles.

Great Britain again found life hard, this time against the Netherlands, relying on their strong doubles pairing of Simon Dickson and David Sherwood to see them through the quarters.

Unquestionably the most exciting tie of the competition was the France versus Argentina quarter-final. Guillermo Coria has proved his talent in the past leading Argentina to the World Junior Tennis title in 1996. He was not, however, expected to have enough firepower to overcome French No. 2 Julien Jeanpierre, ranked No.5 in the world among the Under-18s. But overcome him he did, in a three-set match of the highest quality. It was fortunate for France that they could call out an even bigger gun for the top singles. Arnaud di Pasquale, the soon to be crowned boys singles World Champion, duly delivered a win against Edgardo Massa.

The combination of two great singles players does not always work for doubles and France looked out of the competition when di Pasquale and Jeanpierre trailed Massa and David Nalbandian by a set and 2–5. But di Pasquale truly rose to the occasion and turned around a match that literally had the crowd jumping out of their seats during points in the closing stages.

Italy's run finally came to an end at the hands of 5th seeded Russia and Miranda and Horna could not guide Peru past rivals Chile, the second seeds, who fielded boys' doubles champion Nicolas Massu as their No.1 singles player.

The last quarter-finals saw the demise of the British boys who finally ran out of steam against the efficient German team, seeded six.

Little mention has been made of Germany, but they were moving through the draw with ominous ease. Their semi-final against No.2 seeds Chile was even going into the doubles, Massu demolishing Bjorn Phau to make up for a loss by team-mate Fernando Gonzalez at the hands of Tomas Zivnicek.

With Massu in their doubles line-up the 2nd seeds were hopeful of a place in the final, but Germany brought in Thomas Messmer, himself a 1995 World Youth Cup winner, and the South Americans found themselves in a tremendous scrap. And the winners were... Germany, 4–6 7–6 8–6 victors in another fabulous tie that kept a large crowd thoroughly entertained.

Joining Germany in the final were the top seeds France who overwhelmed Russia in the other semi-final, winning both singles rubbers. Germany's Zivnicek excelled himself in taking Jeanpierre to three sets in a great opening rubber but could not hold on for a win. The writing was on the wall when di Pasquale took the opening set of the top singles 6–0 against Bjorn Phau, so all credit was due to the German for pushing the French No.1 to a tie break, even if he didn't manage to capture the second set.

If the girls champions were elegantly presentable for their closing ceremony the boys were less so – perhaps because the entire team had ended up in the swimming pool in celebration. How wonderful it is to be young and on top of the world!

Congratulations are due to the Russian boys who took the bronze medals with a victory over Chile, and to the girls of Spain who fought hard to defeat Croatia for third place.

ITF SUNSHINE CUP 1997
Boys' 18 & Under International Team Championship
32 nations competed. Event played in Delray Beach, Florida, USA, 15–20 December.
Quarter-finals: France d. Argentina 2–1; Russia d. Italy 3–0; Germany d. Great Britain 2–1; Chile d. Peru 3–0. **Semi-finals:** France d. Russia 2–1; Germany d. Chile 2–1.
Final: France d. Germany 2–1 (J. Jeanpierre d. T. Zivnicek 6–4 6–7(5) 6–4; A. Di Pasquale d. B. Phau 6–0 7–6 (3); Doubles Germany w/o).

ITF CONNOLLY CONTINENTAL CUP 1997
Girls' 18 & Under International Team Championship
31 nations competed. Event played in Delray Beach, Florida, USA, 15–20 December.
Quarter-finals: Slovenia d. Great Britain 3–0; Spain d. Belgium 2–1; Russia d. Japan 3–0; Croatia d. USA 2–1. **Semi-finals:** Slovenia d. Spain 2–1; Russia d. Croatia 2–1.
Final: Slovenia d. Russia 2–1 (T. Pisnik d. E. Dementieva 6–3 7–5; K. Srebotnik d. E. Syssoeva 3–6 6–4 6–3; M. Matevzic/T. Pisnik lost to E. Dementieva/A. Myskina 4–6 1–6).

NEC World Youth Cup

The increasingly high standard of play throughout the world is beginning to threaten the position of seeds at junior team competitions. This was particularly apparent at the 13th NEC World Youth Cup Final staged at the Burnaby Tennis Club in Vancouver, Canada.

Opening day shocks in the boys' 16 team event saw the early departure of 6th seeded France, 4th seeded Italy and most surprisingly of all an Argentine side that had won the 14 & Under World Junior Tennis Final in 1996 and were seeded 3 in Vancouver.

The Canadian boys were suitably ambitious for the first Final to take place on their home soil and wrapped up victory over France following the two singles rubbers. Much was expected of the Italian boys, but they proved no match for a South African team brought up on hard courts, failing to register a set in three rubbers. Argentina's match against Venezuela was probably the finest tie of the boys' event. David Nalbandian got the 3rd seeds off to a good start with an emphatic 6–1 6–2 victory over Ezequiel Nastari, only to watch team mate Guillermo Coria lose a match of the highest standard to the equally talented Jose De Armas, 6–4 7–6. The deciding doubles, De Armas and Nastari versus Edgardo Massa and Nalbandian, went one way then the other, and was watched and enjoyed by many of the other teams. The 6–7 7–6 6–4 scoreline in favour of Venezuela may give some hint of the excitement generated in this deciding match.

The girls' event brought some respite for the seeding committee, with only one seeded team failing to negotiate the first round. Spain, seeded 4, had a tough time against New Zealand, for whom Leanne Baker was outstanding. Defeating Spanish no. 1 Lourdes Dominguez 7–5 6–4 in the top singles rubber, Baker just failed to carry Suzanne Wright to victory in the deciding doubles, losing out to Dominguez and Marta Marrero 6–1 3–6 6–4. Seventh seeded South Africa were not so fortunate, missing a relatively easy smash which would have given them the opening set of the deciding doubles against Italy, who were happy to accept a 2–1 win.

Further devastation to the draw occurred in both events in the second round. Lleyton Hewitt had led Australia boys to the final in 1996, but any title hopes held by the top seeds were dispelled by 8th seeded Czech Republic. With Australia expected to field a very strong doubles pair it was essential for the Czechs that Ladislav Chramosta followed up the win achieved by Jaroslav Levinsky over Glen Bertram in the opening singles. In fact the Czech boy proved to be very much up to the task, posting a fine 2–6 7–5 6–2 victory over Hewitt, the highest ranked player in the competition.

Venezuela ended Canada's hopes with two straight sets singles wins and Great Britain boys, seeded 5, progressed against South Africa, although they did need a deciding doubles to do so. Second seeded Spain could not feel at all hard done by following their 3–0 defeat at the hands of USA boys, because all three rubbers were very one sided affairs in favour of the 7th seeds.

Not to be outdone, the top rated girls teams all had a torrid time in the second round. USA's Melissa Middleton, world ranked 4 at 18 & Under, had been disappointed by her performance at the US Open junior championships the previous week and the nature of her 6–1 6–3 defeat at the hands of Italy's Laura Dell'Angelo saw no improvement in her form. Italy were only level

ITF Vice President, Eiichi Kawatei of Japan, with the Russian girls and their captain who won the 1997 NEC World Youth Cup. (ITF)

at 1–1 following the singles, however, and it still needed a fine doubles win by Dell'Angelo and Flavia Pennetta over Ansley Cargill and Laura Granville to oust the top seeds.

With 4th seeded Spain well beaten by 5th seeded France and 3rd seeded Argentina easily dismissed by 6th seeded Russia, it was left to Australia, captained by former French Open champion Lesley Bowrey (nee Turner), to keep the flag flying for the No.2 seeds. Their tie against Slovenia was an interesting tussle not least because, as defending champions, the Slovenes had expected to be seeded far higher than eighth. When Tina Hergold took the opening rubber for Slovenia 7–5 7–6 over Alicia Molik it appeared that they might have a valid point. However, the loss of their original No. 1 Tina Pisnik due to injury resulted in a costly team adjustment. Tina Hojnik went down to Australia's Rochelle Rosenfield who then partnered Molik to a deciding doubles win.

The last time Russia's Elena Dementieva faced Rochelle Rosenfield, at the US Open, the Australian had posted an emphatic 6–0 6–3 win. Playing for your country can also have a positive effect on concentration and it was Dementieva who was to post an equally comprehensive 6–4 6–0 win to level matters against Australia in the first of the girls' semi-finals. The Australians were confident of winning the deciding doubles, but surprisingly it was the sixth seeded Russians who progressed to the final to meet fifth seeded France who had put an end to Italy's great run.

The first rubber of the final was to prove crucial. Myskina soaked up everything the talented, but as yet undisciplined, French No.2 Samantha Schoeffel could throw at her to emerge a 6–3 2–6 8–6 winner. Dementieva started her match against Stephanie Rizzi in relaxed mood seemingly hitting winners at will. To her credit the young French No.1 fought back well to take the second set and was somewhat unlucky not to take the tie to a deciding doubles. Dementieva it was, however, who held on for a 6–2 4–6 6–4 win and after two previous runner-up finishes, Russia finally claimed the girls' trophy.

The Czech Republic's Levinsky and Chramosta were both playing themselves into top form and their 3–0 defeat of Great Britain in the first of the boys' semi-finals was quite clinical. Venezuela on the other hand had another tough battle against USA and once again needed an exciting 6–4 6–7 7–5 doubles win by De Armas and Nastari, this time over Scott Lipsky and David Martin, to progress to the final. With both finals forced indoors due to constant rain, the faster surface did little for Nastari's hopes against Levinsky who strolled to a 6–0 6–2 win for the Czechs. De Armas was perhaps a little guilty of playing too much to the crowd in the top singles rubber, letting slip a 5–2 first set lead against Chramosta to lose the match 7–6 6–2, but his efforts throughout the week had otherwise been very commendable. While the Czech team were naturally delighted with their title triumph the team's decision to dye their hair blond may be a celebration gesture that will not catch on!

NEC WORLD YOUTH CUP 1997
ITF Team Championships for 16 & Under
92 nations competed, 90 taking part in the boys' event and 68 in the girls' event. Final stages took place in Vancouver, Canada, 10–14 September.

FINAL POSITIONS – BOYS: Champion nation: Czech Republic; Runners-up: Venezuela; 3rd: Great Britain; 4th: USA; 5th equal: Australia, Spain; 7th: South Africa; 8th: Canada; 9th equal: Italy, France; 11th equal: Chile, Denmark; 13th equal: Japan, Argentina; 15th: China; 16th: Chinese Taipei; **GIRLS:** Champion nation: Russia; Runners-up: France; 3rd: Australia; 4th: Italy; 5th: USA; 6th: Slovenia; 7th equal: Spain, Argentina; 9th: Croatia; 10th: South Africa; 11th: Brazil; 12th: Canada; 13th: Japan; 14th: New Zealand; 15th: Uzbekistan; 16th: Uruguay.
BOYS' CHAMPIONSHIP – Semi-finals: Czech Republic d. Great Britain 3–0 (J. Levinsky d. A. Mackin 6–4 6–3; L. Chramosta d. S. Dickson 6–2 6–4; L. Chramosta/J. Levinsky d. S. Dickson/M. Hilton 6–4 6–2). **Venezuela d. USA 2–1:** (E. Nastari lost to S. Lipsky 5–7 2–6; J. De Armas d. D. Martin 7–6(1) 6–3; J. De Armas/E. Nastari d. S. Lipsky/D. Martin 6–4 6–7(2) 7–5). **3rd place play-off: Great Britain d. USA 2–0:** (M. Hilton d. L. Joseph 6–1 6–4; S. Dickson d. D. Martin 3–6 6–3 6–4). **Final: Czech Republic d. Venezuela 2–0:** (J. Levinsky d. E. Nastari 6–0 6–2; L. Chramosta d. J. De Armas 7–6(2) 6–2).
GIRLS' CHAMPIONSHIP – Semi-finals: France d. Italy 3–0: (S. Schoeffel d. N. Vierin 6–3 6–2; S. Rizzi d. L. Dell'Angelo 6–1 7–5; L. Sanchez/S. Schoeffel d. L. Dell'Angelo/F. Pennetta 4–6 6–1 6–2). **Russia d. Australia 2–1:** (A. Myskina lost to A. Molik 7–6(4) 4–6 1–6; E. Dementieva d. R. Rosenfield 6–4 6–0; E. Dementieva/A. Myskina d. A. Molik/R. Rosenfield 6–4 6–0). **3rd place play-off: Australia d. Italy 2–0:** (J. Dokic d. N. Vierin 6–0 7–5; A. Molik d. F. Pennetta 6–4 6–4). **Final: Russia d. France 2–0:** (A. Myskina d. S. Schoeffel 6–3 2–6 8–6; E. Dementieva d. S. Rizzi 6–2 4–6 6–4).

World Junior Tennis

Never mind the heat often faced at the Australian Open or the humidity of New York, finalists from 23 nations gathered in Nagoya, Japan to battle over five days in temperatures hitting 35 degrees for the chance to put their country's name on the ITF's World Junior Tennis trophy.

With 60–70 per cent humidity each day, the playing conditions at the Higashiyama Tennis Centre were quite extreme, in stark contrast to the rain-hit final of the previous year. To their credit the players displayed an approach that would have been worthy of professionals – except that these competitors were all aged 14 or under.

The boys' event produced a couple of interesting first round match-ups. The host nation Japan faced 6th seeded USA and despite dropping the opening rubber, still ended up level going into the doubles when US No.1, Ryan Redondo, was forced to concede the top singles rubber due to heat exhaustion. The US team suffered badly throughout the week as a result of the tough conditions, but on this occasion they were able to pull off a doubles win.

Yen-Hsun Lu was in great form for Chinese Taipei as they reversed their regional qualifying event defeat by Korea to oust the 8th seeds 2–1, but the most notable upset saw the demise of 3rd seeded Germany at the hands of Russia. The 3–0 scoreline does not do justice to a terrific match in which both Dmitri Sitak and Filipp Moukhometov won their singles rubbers 7–5 in the third set.

Germany fared no better in the girls' event where they were defeated 2–1 by Austria. Led by the tall, elegant Bettina Resch, the Austrian side had been disappointed to miss out on a seeded position, but felt much happier after ousting the 4th seeds.

In the only other first round upset, Beti Sekulovski and Jaslyn Hewitt both demonstrated a notable lack of experience in letting slip singles matches they looked poised to win, as the Australian 5th seeds crashed out to USA in a nonetheless entertaining tie.

The top seeded French boys, the champions of Europe, had not looked comfortable in their opening round 2–1 victory over Canada and it was not such a surprise to see them well beaten in the quarters by 7th seeded South Africa. In another quarter-final match-up, USA's No.2

(Above) *Dirk Stegmann of South Africa and* (right) *Elena Bovina of Russia who led their teams to success against, respectively, the Czech Republic and the Slovak Republic in Nagoya.* (ITF)

Samuel Warburg, fell victim to the heat in his opening rubber and was forced to retire against Russia's Dmitri Sitak. Although compatriot Ryan Redondo completed his match against Filipp Moukhometov, the exacting nature of his 2–6 7–5 3–6 defeat was such that USA were unable to field a doubles pairing and the No. 6 seeds bowed out 3–0 to the European side.

In the bottom half of the draw, matches went more to plan with 2nd seeded Czech Republic defeating Chinese Taipei, although the 3–0 scoreline was not as comfortable as it appeared. Spain's No.1, Carlos Cuadrado, was totally overwhelmed by Argentine Luciano Vitullo, but made amends in the doubles as the 4th seeds eased past the 5th seeds 2–1 in the last quarter-final.

The girl's quarters were relatively uneventful. Belgium's Kim Clijsters was to remain undefeated in the top singles position all week and her 6–3 6–1 victory over Slovak Republic's Martina Babakova was very impressive. With Babakova and Daniela Hantuchova forming a strong doubles pair, however, the top seeds and reigning champions recorded a 2–1 victory.

Second seeded Russia also advanced at the expense of No. 7 seeds Mexico, but did not have an easy time. The opening rubber between Melissa Torres and Lina Krasnoroutskaia was an outstanding match, which ended with a draining 7–5 third set victory for the Russian that left both girls in tears.

In the remaining quarters, 3rd seeded Croatia, led by Jelena Pandzic, split the singles rubbers with USA, but were comprehensive winners in the doubles. Austria embarked on yet another marathon against 6th seeded Argentina, but on this occasion lost a close deciding doubles tie.

In both the boys' and girls' semi-finals the favourites prevailed. Russia's Dmitri Sitak had a fine 3–6 6–3 6–3 victory over Andrew Anderson, but his efforts left him unable to play the deciding doubles, which was won by South Africa to take them to the final. In the other semi-final Czech Republic's Jan Masik outlasted Spain's Carlos Cuardrado, winning 6–7 7–6 6–2. Combined with Michal Kokta's earlier straight sets win over Acayamo Medina the second seeds had an unassailable lead.

In the girls' event a repeat of the 1996 final was realised when Croatia's Jelena Pandzic was unable to make an impression against Slovak Republic's Martina Babakova, as the top seeds advanced 3–0. Russia also managed a 3–0 result over Argentina, although Maria Emilia Salerni made Russian No.1 Elena Bovina work very hard for her 4–6 6–3 6–4 top singles victory.

Both finals, it must be said, were somewhat disappointing. For Russia Krasnoroutskaia was as dependable as ever, despite a number of earlier taxing rubbers, as she defeated Hantuchova 6–2 6–4. Slovak Republic's Babakova could make no impression against the tall and very hard hitting Bovina and was also well beaten 6–4 6–1 in the top singles.

Although the doubles went to Slovak Republic, the trophy changed hands, with the Russian girls gaining revenge for their defeat both in the 1996 final and also in the European qualifying stages earlier this year.

The boys' final was also decided after the two singles rubbers. Anderson got the South African underdogs off to a good start with a 7–5 6–4 victory over Czech Michal Kokta. Dirk Stegmann, who had proved himself to be the outstanding player of the tournament, followed this with a commanding 6–3 6–0 victory over Jan Masik and clinched the title for South Africa for the first time in the competition's history.

A good week for Russia was completed when their boys' team defeated Spain 3–0 in the play-off for third place. In the girls' event, Argentina were deserved winners of the bronze medals following a 3–0 defeat of Croatia.

Once again, the final day was graciously attended by His Royal Highness, Prince Takamodo, who presented the ITF trophies to the two champion nations.

WORLD JUNIOR TENNIS 1997
ITF Team Championships for 14 & Under

81 nations competed, 77 taking part in the boys' event and 68 in the girls' event. Final stages took place in Nagoya, Japan, 20–24 August.

FINAL POSITIONS – BOYS: Champion nation: South Africa; Runners-up: Czech Republic; 3rd: Russia; 4th: Spain; 5th: Argentina; 6th: USA; 7th: France; 8th: Chinese Taipei; 9th: Germany; 10th: Italy; 11th: Australia; 12th: Korea; 13th: Canada; 14th: Brazil; 15th: Ecuador; 16th: Japan. **GIRLS:** Champion nation: Russia; Runners-up: Slovak Republic; 3rd: Argentina; 4th: Croatia; 5th: Belgium; 6th: Austria; 7th: USA; 8th: Mexico; 9th: Germany; 10th: Australia; 11th: Indonesia; 12th: Brazil; 13th: Japan; 14th: South Africa; 15th: Chinese Taipei; 16th: Uruguay.

BOYS' CHAMPIONSHIP – Semi-finals: South Africa d. Russia 2–1 (A. Anderson lost to D. Sitak 6–3 3–6 3–6; D. Stegmann d. F. Moukhometov 6–1 6–4; A. Anderson/D. Stegmann d. F. Moukhometov/V. Portnov 6–2 6–0). **Czech Republic d. Spain 2–1** (M. Kokta d. A. Medina 7–5 6–1; J. Masik d. C. Cuadrado 6–7(2) 7–6(8) 6–2; D. Karol/M. Kokta lost to A. Medina/R. Merchan 1–6 1–6). **3rd place play-off: Russia d. Spain 3–0** (D. Sitak d. R. Merchan 6–4 6–4; F. Moukhometov d. C. Cuadrado 6–3 3–6 6–3; F. Moukhometov/V. Portnov d. C. Cuadrado/A. Medina 3–6 6–4 6–4). **Final: South Africa d. Czech Republic 2–1** (A. Anderson d. M. Kokta 7–5 6–4; D. Stegmann d. J. Masik 6–3 6–0; A. Anderson/R. Blair lost to D. Karol/J. Masik 1–6 0–6).

GIRLS' CHAMPIONSHIP – Semi-finals: Slovak Republic d. Croatia 3–0 (D. Hantuchova d. A. Margetic 6–1 6–3; M. Babakova d. J. Pandzic 6–3 6–2; M Babakova/D. Hantuchova d. I. Abramovic/A. Margetic 6–3 6–2). **Russia d. Argentina 3–0** (L. Krasnoroutskaia d. E. Chialvo 6–1 6–2; E. Bovina d. M. Salerni 4–6 6–3 6–4; G. Fokina/L. Krasnoroutskaia d. E. Chialvo/G. Dulko 6–2 6–4). **3rd place play-off: Argentina d. Croatia 3–0** (E. Chialvo d. A. Margetic 7–6(2) 6–0; M. Salerni d. J. Pandzic 6–1 6–4; G. Dulko/M. Salerni d. I. Abramovic/ A. Margetic 6–2 6–1). **Final: Russia d. Slovak Republic 2–1** (L. Krasnoroutskaia d. D. Hantuchova 6–2 6–4; E. Bovina d. M. Babakova 6–4 6–1; G. Fokina/L. Krasnoroutskaia lost to D. Hantuchova/L. Kurhajcova 2–6 6–2 2–6).

(Above) *The 15-year-old Croatian, Mirjana Lucic, too young to play at Wimbledon, was accepted into the main draw at the US Open where she reached the third round and took a set from the No. 3 seed Jana Novotna.* (Clive Brunskill)

South Africa's Westley Whitehouse, who won the junior title at Wimbledon with a straight sets victory over Daniel Elsner of Germany. (Brian Mackness)

The Junior Spotlight

Wendy Kewley

Should aspiring tennis player Westley Whitehouse fail to make the grade on the professional circuit, the 18-year-old South African can always fall back on his psychic talents. As a ten-year-old, he concocted the following headline and pinned it on his bedroom wall: 'Whitehouse wins junior Wimbledon in straight sets.' Sure enough, his prediction came true this year when he captured his first junior Grand Slam at the All England Club. This fairy tale story was fittingly reproduced in several newspapers after Wimbledon, providing welcome press coverage for the juniors.

In 1997, the ITF made a concerted effort to bring the junior game into the public eye by offering a dedicated media service at Roland Garros, Wimbledon and the US Open for the first time. Visitors to the four Grand Slam Championships are always impressed by the high standard of junior play on the outside courts. Stefan Edberg, John McEnroe, Ivan Lendl and Gabriela Sabatini all made their marks as junior Grand Slam champions before achieving greater things in the senior game.

While Sampras and Hingis dominated the tennis pages this year, there were plenty of original stories lurking in the junior game. The absorbing rivalry between Westley Whitehouse and Germany's Daniel Elsner was much discussed. They met in three Grand Slams with the South African eventually carving a 2–1 edge over the German. The boys' game appeared to be a two-horse race, so it was particularly exciting to witness Arnaud di Pasquale's dramatic push up the rankings at the eleventh hour. In April, the French teenager had taken the Japan Open title and then consolidated his progress by overcoming Whitehouse in a three-set tussle at the US Championships later in the year.

The strength of African junior tennis was also underlined, particularly at Wimbledon where Whitehouse lifted the boys' singles trophy and Zimbabwe's Cara Black won the girls' title. Her brothers Byron and Wayne secured Zimbabwe's first ever position in the Davis Cup World Group this year, so Black junior had a difficult act to follow. However, Cara was equally impressive, reaching three Grand Slam finals in 1997. After missing the Australian Open, she made up for lost time by reaching the French Championships final and then winning at Wimbledon and the US Championships. A member of the ITF International Touring Team, Black also displayed her prowess on the doubles court, where she and Kazakhstan's Irina Selyutina won the girls' doubles at the French Open and Wimbledon.

The ITF junior media service was extremely successful at Roland Garros, Wimbledon and the US Open. In Paris, an ITF press officer was on site and 300 junior media guides were produced providing biographies of the top 20 players. Mitzi Ingram Evans, ITF Junior Co-ordinator and Grand Slam press officer, recalls, 'Everybody thought the media guide was great. USA Network used to get on court and interview the juniors every day and they sounded totally authoritative because they'd obviously looked at the guide.'

About 50 interviews were conducted with junior players at the three Grand Slams. Ingram Evans says, 'At the Australian Open, the British boys Sherwood and Trotman reached the doubles final and the British press wanted to talk to them. I thought that the boys were going to be interviewed in a corridor, but they were taken to a formal interview room which must have been a bit of a shock. All the players could have found the interview experience fairly daunting, but they seemed to cope extremely well.'

While the ITF is keen to increase the profile of junior tennis with the media and public, it also recognises that the gap between the junior and senior circuits can be difficult to surmount. To combat this, the Junior Exempt Project was launched at the end of 1996 to enable the top ten girls in the year-end singles rankings to earn two main draw positions in designated ITF Women's Circuit tournaments.

The new scheme was highly successful in 1997 with three out of the top ten junior girls using their Junior Exempt positions to reach the finals of ITF Women's Circuit events. In July, 15-year-old Mirjana Lucic delighted her home crowds by capturing the $75,000 tournament in Makarska when she defeated Austria's Sandra Dopfer 6–1 6–4 in the final. Her outstanding promise was further confirmed at the US Open where she fought tenaciously against third round opponent Jana Novotna before succumbing in three sets. In September, the 1996 ITF Junior World Champion, Amelie Mauresmo, took full advantage of her Junior Exempt place at the $50,000 event in Thessaloniki, Greece. The French girl won the title with a comprehensive 6–0 6–0 demolition of Spain's Eva Bes. Samantha Reeves of the USA also reached the final of the $25,000 ITF Women's Circuit event at Newport Beach, but was pipped to the title by Sandra Cacic.

The graceful Olga Barabanschikova of Belarus is also a name to watch after she reached the semi-finals at the $50,000 event in Southampton during October, before retiring through injury. Half of the top 10 girls in the 1996 junior rankings have reached the top 200 in the women's rankings. As 1997 draws to a close, Lucic and Barabanschikova, are just outside the top-50 and seem poised to go further on the senior tour in 1998. In contrast, the top 10 boys in the 1996 junior rankings enjoyed less success in 1997, with France's Sebastien Grosjean currently the only player to rank amongst the world's top 200 men at the end of the year.

Junior tennis was guaranteed further media coverage when, last April, the United States Tennis Association (USTA) launched a colour magazine aimed at 8–18-year-olds. *Topspin* is the only national magazine for tennis juniors and the USTA plans to publish four issues a year. The ITF is also unveiling *Tennis Stuff*, designed to give juniors a better appreciation of the ITF's role in the game. The first issue will coincide with the 1998 Australian Open and will include interviews with top junior players and news from major junior tournaments as well as advice on health and fitness.

Media coverage is vital in highlighting the junior game, but its growth is also determined by the number of competitive opportunities available. To this end, the ITF extended its portfolio of junior team competitions in 1997 to include the 18 & Under Sunshine Cup for boys and the 18 & Under Continental Players' Cup for girls. These events complement the 14 & Under World Junior Tennis and the 16 & Under NEC World Youth Cup international team competitions. Past participants of the Sunshine Cup and the Continental Players' Cup have included Boris Becker, Bjorn Borg, Michael Chang, Steffi Graf, John McEnroe and Ivan Lendl. With this in mind, who knows what the future holds for the likes of Westley Whitehouse, Cara Black or Daniel Elsner.

Grand Slam Championships

Australian Open Championships
French Open Championships
The Championships – Wimbledon
US Open Championships
Compaq Grand Slam Cup

In a sensational upset Croatia's Iva Majoli defeated the new world No. 1, Martina Hingis, to win her first Grand Slam title in Paris. (Michael Cole)

By winning the Australian Open 16-year-old Martina Hingis of Switzerland becomes the youngest Grand Slam winner this century. (Tommy Hindley)

Australian Open Championships

Alan Trengrove

The first Grand Slam Championship of the year provided a preview of a new era. Martina Hingis, the refreshingly natural yet surprisingly mature Swiss teenager, became this century's youngest winner of a Grand Slam singles title when she swept aside Mary Pierce in the women's final. She was all of 16 years, three months and 26 days when she achieved the feat. Spain's unseeded Carlos Moya, 20, threatened a changing of the guard in men's tennis as well as he defeated Boris Becker and Michael Chang, among others, on his way to the men's final. But Pete Sampras was in too determined a mood to yield supremacy, and Moya will have to wait for his day of Grand Slam glory, which will surely come.

Public enthusiasm for the tournament soared to a new level, with a record attendance of 391,504 despite three successive days of scorching heat that emptied stands. The big crowds were especially remarkable in view of the withdrawal of Monica Seles, Jana Novotna, Andre Agassi, Richard Krajicek, Yevgeny Kafelnikov and local heroes Mark Philippoussis and Jason Stoltenberg, and the loss of Becker in the first round.

Although Sampras was in superb form in winning his second Australian title, the tournament will be best remembered for the exploits and huge popularity of Moya, the growing authority of Hingis, who didn't drop a set, the defeat of world champion Steffi Graf by Amanda Coetzer in the fourth round, and the mini-heatwave that led to controversy when referee Peter Bellenger decided to shut out the fierce sunshine by closing Melbourne Park's moveable roof.

Heat always has been a potential factor in the Australian championships. Oldtimers used to play the best of five advantage sets on extremely hot days without the benefit of chairs and brollies at changeovers. But up to 1988, the tournament was played on grass courts, the kindest of all court surfaces in hot weather. Now it is staged on Rebound Ace, a rubberised cement composition that retains and reflects heat mercilessly. On a day of 40°C, the temperature on court can be as high as 55°C or 131°F.

Bellenger ordered the roof shut for the start of play on the second Tuesday after two searing days, in which several of the top seeds, including Graf, wilted and were eliminated, and newspapers carried warnings of a possible risk to players' lives. He was empowered to do so by tournament policy once the quarter-final stage had been reached and all singles matches were scheduled for centre court, and if the 9 am weather forecast was for 38°C or higher. These conditions existed that day when ash from distant bushfires was dropping on the courts.

Even so, some players strongly disapproved of Bellenger's decision – the first ever taken because of excessive heat – claiming the integrity of the championship was damaged. Felix Mantilla, who played Moya on centre court that day, said later he had filled himself with liquid and warmed-up with the roof open, only to be told at the last minute that the roof would be closed. He was beaten and said he felt disoriented playing under lights and with the temperature controlled at 25°C. A group of players, including Sampras, Chang, Thomas Muster, Goran Ivanisevic and Mantilla, signed a strongly worded letter of protest to tournament director Paul McNamee, who said after the tournament that the policy on heat would be reviewed.

McNamee had already spent some uncomfortable moments earlier in the tournament fending off a barrage of complaints from players that the Slazenger balls, made in the Philippines, were softer than usual. Becker suspected that the balls were responsible for a spate of arm and wrist injuries, and he and other big servers hinted at a plot to counter the dominance of the serve and slow up play. McNamee, however, said that tests showed the balls were no different than in the previous year, when there were no complaints. He assured players there was no 'secret agenda'. But in this matter, too, he promised a review before the next Open.

Whatever the character of the balls, it was more Moya's clever mixture of pace and spin that accounted for his five-set defeat of the defending champion. Many had expected a Sampras-Becker final following the German's strong form at the end of 1996, but he had the toughest of draws, having lost to Moya at the Paris Indoor. What's more, Moya had reached the final of the Sydney International two days earlier and was in fine form.

Playing in only his fifth Grand Slam championship, Moya was part of a 16-player Armada that set out to show the world that Spaniards can excel on surfaces other than clay, and more particularly on cement. Spanish men have been conspicuous by their absence at the Australian Open in recent years, but following their 1997 performances Down Under, when Moya and Albert Costa met in a semi-final in Sydney, and then, with Mantilla, formed three of the quarter-finalists in Melbourne, they are likely to be regular visitors. After ousting Becker, Moya beat some handy hardcourt players in Patrick McEnroe and Jonas Bjorkman, not to mention the tenacious Chang, while Costa got the better of Patrick Rafter and Wayne Ferreira before taking Sampras to five sets.

With Becker out of the way, the Norman Brookes Cup always seemed destined to finish up in Sampras's hands for a second time. The great American had grim memories of his previous two campaigns in Melbourne, where in 1995 his coach, the late Tim Gullikson, fell gravely ill and an emotionally drained Sampras lost to Agassi in the final, and where in 1996 he was ambushed in the third round by Philippoussis. This time he had something to prove, and the energy and form to do so. He made Mark Woodforde pay for the Philippoussis defeat, thrashing the 1996 semi-finalist 6–1 6–0 6–1 in a night match before a stunned crowd. He paced himself through long, difficult matches against Slovakian newcomer Dominik Hrbaty and Costa, and lifted his game to beat both Ivanisevic and Muster in straight sets.

In the final, he simply outgunned Moya, who was denied the opportunity to reproduce his sparkling form of the earlier rounds. Sampras was the complete champion, winning 82 percent of the points on his first serve, attacking more persistently and effectively than the Spaniard, and also outclassing him from the back of the court. The 6–2 6–3 6–3 scoreline accurately reflected the margin between them.

Overall, there were not many outstanding men's matches, the best perhaps being the tussle between Thomas Enqvist and Marcelo Rios, which the gifted Chilean won in five sets. Muster partly answered those critics (and certainly Jim Courier) who charged him with being too much of a clay-court specialist by beating Courier in a torrid four sets that broke the American's seven-match streak against him. As an encore, Muster bundled out an erratic Ivanisevic in straight sets. Tim Henman, the champion in Sydney, was brought back to earth with a third-round, straight-sets hiding by Chang, who was highly concentrated, pumped, and ruthlessly efficient as he took advantage of the Englishman's errors.

In the women's singles, Hingis, the fourth seed, charmed Australia with her insouciance. Nearly always relaxed and having fun, she spent some of her free time by going shopping or to the theatre with her mother, roller-blading along the River Yarra and horse-riding. She even got a laugh out of being tossed by a filly named Magic Girl. On court, though, she played with all the aplomb, coolness and precision that we used to associate with Chris Evert.

After saving three break-points in the first game of the final, she was always in command, defeating Pierce, the 1995 champion, 6–2 6–2 in 59 minutes. She was the first Swiss to win the title and surpassed the record of Seles, who was aged 17 and one month when she defeated Novotna in the 1991 final. For good measure, she won the doubles title with Natasha Zvereva, becoming the first player to win both titles since her namesake Martina Navratilova in 1985.

The only time Hingis became tense during the fortnight was in her fourth-round match with Romania's Ruxandra Dragomir. She had just seen Graf, Conchita Martinez and Lindsay Davenport succumb in the heat, and knew that earlier second seed Arantxa Sanchez Vicario had been removed by Dominique van Roost of Belgium. 'I was just so nervous,' she said later. 'I was the last of the top-seeded players out there. I knew there was a big chance.' Dragomir was the only player to take Hingis into a tiebreak, but in the second set she, too, wavered, as all of Hingis's opponents eventually did.

Against everyone, the youngster thought and reacted quickly, invariably playing the right shot at the right time. She was as adept at making sharply angled winners, as in hitting neat volleys and hard smashes. 'She has the experience of a 24-year-old,' said first-round victim Barbara Rittner.

Graf, a four-time champion, was beaten by Coetzer when the temperature approached 40°C. The little South African had trained in the Florida sun and been well prepared by Australian fitness expert Gavin Hopper to repeat her win over Graf at the '95 Canadian Open. Trading hard-hit groundstrokes, she exploited the German's tendency to make unforced errors, and, after winning the first set 6–2, recovered from a 0–4 deficit in the second set to win that 7–5.

Graf was so affected by the heat that, towards the end, she moved uncharacteristically slowly between points and was several times attended by a trainer, who applied ice-packs to her thighs and neck. Unbeknown to most, she had been taking medication for an infected toe, and this probably added to her distress. For the first time in her career Steffi was unable to give a press conference. She received hydration treatment while her vital signs were monitored, and accepted medical advice to return to her apartment and delay leaving Melbourne until she'd fully recovered. She sent a message to the press in which she congratulated Coetzer.

Graf's defeat was the biggest bombshell of a day of sensations, for also eliminated that day were third seed Martinez, fifth seed Anke Huber, and seventh seed Davenport. 'It's a joke,' Martinez said of the oven-like conditions after losing to Sabine Appelmans, who herself had to be connected to a saline drip in the first-aid room. Huber lost to Pierce before the heat became too oppressive, although Davenport, playing at the same time, was near collapse after losing to Kimberley Po.

One who apparently thrived on the heat was Van Roost (nee Monami), who followed up her defeat of Sanchez Vicario with an equally brave win over 15th seed Chanda Rubin. She thus joined her compatriot Appelmans in the quarter-finals, the first time two Belgian women had advanced so far in a Grand Slam tournament.

The crowds loved Van Roost's go-for-broke style, but she was handicapped by a number of injuries and finally had to retire against Mary Joe Fernandez. Appelmans, meanwhile, lost to Pierce after having held what seemed a commanding lead. In the semi-finals, Fernandez was no match for a super-confident Hingis, and Pierce mastered her sometimes brittle nerves in outhitting Coetzer.

Making light of the torrid heat, Carlos Moya of Spain surpised and delighted his growing army of fans by reaching the final of the Australian Open, unseeded. (Tommy Hindley)

MEN'S SINGLES

Holder: B. Becker (GER)

FIRST ROUND

1 **P. SAMPRAS** (USA) (1)
2 D. Pescariu (ROM) (Q)
3 A. Voinea (ROM)
4 H. Dreekmann (GER)
5 M. Woodforde (AUS)
6 M. Tebbutt (AUS) (W)
7 H. Gumy (ARG)
8 O Stanoytchev (BUL)
9 S. Stolle (AUS)
10 D. Hrbaty (SVK)
11 N. Kulti (SWE)
12 K. Alami (MAR)
13 T. Carbonell (ESP)
14 D. Vacek (CZE)
15 T. Larkham (AUS)
16 **A. BERASATEGUI** (ESP) (16)
17 **A. COSTA** (ESP) (10)
18 P. Rafter (AUS)
19 J. Kroslak (SVK)
20 A. Gaudenzi (ITA)
21 A. Radulescu (GER)
22 S. Draper (AUS)
23 F. Dewulf (BEL)
24 F. Wibier (NED) (Q)
25 P. Tramacchi (AUS) (W)
26 J. Van Herck (BEL)
27 A. Cherkasov (RUS) (Q)
28 R. Furlan (ITA)
29 P. Cash (AUS) (W)
30 J. Frana (ARG)
31 C. Costa (ESP)
32 **W. FERREIRA** (RSA) (8)
33 **G. IVANISEVIC** (CRO) (3)
34 B. Elwood (AUS) (W)
35 P. Haarhuis (NED)
36 K. Kucera (SVK)
37 L. Jonsson (SWE) (Q)
38 J. Novak (CZE)
39 C. Woodruff (USA)
40 M. Norman (SWE)
41 M. Tillstrom (SWE)
42 G. Kuerten (BRZ)
43 A. Chesnokov (RUS)
44 N. Godwin (RSA)
45 L. Paes (IND) (W)
46 J. Crabb (AUS) (W)
47 C. Ruud (NOR)
48 **J. SIEMERINK** (NED) (13)
49 **J. COURIER** (USA) (11)
50 S. Schalken (NED)
51 G. Forget (FRA)
52 S. Dosedel (CZE)
53 M. Rosset (SUI)
54 J. Sanchez (ESP)
55 J. Tarango (USA)
56 B. Shelton (USA) (Q)
57 J.-P. Fleurian (FRA)
58 H. Arazi (MAR)
59 J. Knippschild (GER)
60 S. Lareau (CAN)
61 J. Burillo (ESP)
62 G. Stafford (RSA)
63 G. Grant (USA)
64 **T. MUSTER** (AUT) (5)

SECOND ROUND

SAMPRAS (1) 6–2 6–4 6–2
Voinea 6–2 6–1 4–6 6–4
Woodforde 6–4 6–4 7–5
Gumy 6–4 6–4 6–4
Hrbaty 1–6 7–5 7–5 6–7 6–1
Kulti 6–4 6–2 6–4
Carbonell 6–2 7–6 7–5
BERASATEGUI (16) 6–1 6–2 6–4
COSTA (10) 7–5 6–2 7–5
Kroslak 4–6 6–4 6–2 6–2
Draper 6–2 6–4 6–7 6–3
Dewulf 6–4 6–2 7–5
Tramacchi (W) 6–7 6–3 6–4 3–2 Ret.'d.
Furlan 6–4 4–6 6–3 6–4
Frana 6–4 6–4 6–3
FERREIRA (8) 6–3 6–2 6–2
IVANISEVIC (3) 6–2 7–5 6–3
Kucera 6–1 3–6 6–3 4–6 6–4
Novak 6–3 6–3 6–2
Woodruff 6–4 6–1 6–1
Kuerten 7–5 7–6 3–6 6–4
Godwin 6–1 6–3 3–6 6–1
Paes (W) 6–4 6–3 6–4
Ruud 3–6 4–6 7–5 6–2 10–8
COURIER (11) 6–7 6–3 4–6 6–1 8–6
Dosedel 6–2 3–6 6–3 6–4
Rosset 6–4 7–6 6–1
Tarango 2–6 7–6 7–6 6–2
Fleurian 7–5 6–0 6–3
Knippschild 6–2 6–7 7–6 6–3
Stafford 6–0 6–1 3–0 Ret'd.
MUSTER (5) 6–3 6–4 6–2

THIRD ROUND

SAMPRAS (1) 3–6 6–2 6–3 6–2
Woodforde 6–0 6–1 7–5
Hrbaty 6–2 6–1 6–2
BERASATEGUI (16) 6–3 7–5 6–4
COSTA (10) 6–1 7–6 7–6
Draper 7–6 7–5 6–0
Furlan 7–6 6–7 6–2 7–6
FERREIRA (8) 6–3 3–6 6–2 6–1
IVANISEVIC (3) 6–4 6–2 6–2
Woodruff 6–2 7–6 6–2
Godwin 6–7 6–0 6–1 6–0
Ruud 6–2 6–2 6–2
COURIER (11) 4–6 6–2 3–6 6–4 6–4
Tarango 6–4 6–1 6–1
Knippschild 6–2 7–6 7–5
MUSTER (5) 6–3 6–2 6–2

FOURTH ROUND

SAMPRAS (1) 6–1 6–0 6–1
Hrbaty 6–3 7–6 6–7 2–0 Reg'd.
COSTA (10) 6–4 6–2 7–5
FERREIRA (8) 6–4 6–4 6–7 6–1
IVANISEVIC (3) 6–3 6–7 6–3 6–1
Ruud 7–6 6–7 6–2 7–6
COURIER (11) 6–1 7–6 6–3
MUSTER (5) 6–4 7–6 6–3

QUARTER-FINALS

SAMPRAS (1) 6–7 6–3 6–4 3–6 6–4
COSTA (10) 6–3 6–2 3–2 Ret'd.
IVANISEVIC (3) 4–6 6–2 6–7 6–3 6–3
MUSTER (5) 6–2 3–6 7–6 6–3

SEMI-FINALS

SAMPRAS (1) 6–3 6–7 6–1 3–6 6–2
MUSTER (5) 6–4 6–2 6–3

FINAL

SAMPRAS (1) 6–1 7–6 6–3

6–2 6–3 6–3

65 **B. BECKER** (GER) (6)
66 C. Moya (ESP)
67 P. McEnroe (USA)
68 A. Olhovskiy (RUS)
69 T. Johansson (SWE)
70 M. Damm (CZE)
71 B. Karbacher (GER)
72 M.A. Gorriz (ESP)
73 M. Goellner (GER)
74 K. Carlsen (DEN)
75 B. Ulihrach (CZE)
76 J. Bjorkman (SWE)
77 K. Braasch (GER) (Q)
78 A. O'Brien (USA)
79 G. Doyle (AUS) (W)
80 **M. GUSTAFSSON** (SWE) (12)
81 **F. MANTILLA** (ESP) (14)
82 G. Rusedski (GBR)
83 D. Prinosil (GER)
84 F. Meligeni (BRA)
85 A. Boetsch (FRA)
86 D. Caldwell (USA) (Q)
87 L. Roux (FRA)
88 J. Stark (USA)
89 M. Knowles (BAH) (L)
90 T. Woodbridge (AUS)
91 S. Simian (FRA)
92 G. Blanco (ESP)
93 S. Sargsian (ARM)
94 M. Ondruska (RSA)
95 J. Eltingh (NED) (Q)
96 M. Washington (USA)
97 **T. ENQVIST** (SWE) (7)
98 N. Pereira (VEN)
99 B. Steven (NZL)
100 R. Fromberg (AUS)
101 L. Hewitt (AUS) (Q)
102 S. Bruguera (ESP)
103 M. Larsson (SWE)
104 J.A. Viloca (ESP)
105 A. Reichel (USA) (Q)
106 G. Schaller (AUT)
107 T. Mitchell (AUS) (Q)
108 A. Corretja (ESP)
109 M. Joyce (USA)
110 R. Carretero (ESP)
111 P. Korda (CZE)
112 **M. RIOS** (CHI) (9)
113 **M. STICH** (GER) (15)
114 P. Fredriksson (SWE)
115 T. Champion (FRA)
116 A. Medvedev (UKR)
117 J. Gimelstob (USA) (Q)
118 E. Ran (ISR) (Q)
119 D. Van Scheppingen (NED)
120 B. Black (ZIM)
121 G. Raoux (FRA)
122 D. Nestor (CAN)
123 A. Pavel (ROM) (L)
124 T. Henman (GBR)
125 R. Reneberg (USA)
126 O. Burrieza (ESP) (Q)
127 K. Goossens (BEL) (L)
128 **M. CHANG** (USA) (2)

Moya 5–7 7–6 3–6 6–1 6–4
McEnroe 7–6 6–2 6–4
Johansson 6–4 6–2 3–6 6–7 6–2
Karbacher 6–4 7–6 1–6 6–3
Goellner 6–4 6–1 6–7 6–4
Bjorkman 1–6 6–1 6–4 6–2
Braasch (Q) 3–6 6–3 6–4 7–5
GUSTAFSSON (12) 6–7 6–3 7–5 6–1
MANTILLA (14) 6–4 5–7 7–5 6–2
Meligeni 5–7 1–6 6–1 7–5 9–7
Boetsch 6–0 6–0 6–2
Roux 1–6 4–6 7–6 6–2 13–11
Woodbridge 6–4 6–2 6–1
Simian 6–4 6–2 6–4
Sargsian 7–6 7–5 4–6 6–2
Washington 6–3 6–7 6–3 6–2
ENQVIST (7) 6–1 6–2 6–4
Fromberg 4–6 2–6 7–5 6–3 6–1
Bruguera 6–3 6–4 6–3
Larsson 6–3 6–3 7–6
Schaller 6–4 6–3 6–2
Corretja 7–6 6–0 6–2
Joyce 6–1 7–6 6–1
RIOS (9) 7–6 6–3 6–3
STICH (15) 6–3 6–2 6–2
Medvedev 7–5 6–2 6–2
Ran (Q) 6–3 7–6 3–6 6–4
Van Scheppingen 7–6 7–6 6–4
Raoux 7–6 6–2 6–2
Henman 7–5 6–4 6–2
Reneberg 2–2 Ret'd.
CHANG (2) 6–0 6–3 6–1

Moya 3–6 6–0 6–3 6–1
Karbacher 6–3 6–2 7–6
Bjorkman 6–4 3–6 6–4 6–1
Braasch (Q) 3–6 7–6 6–4 6–4
MANTILLA (14) 6–2 6–4 6–1
Boetsch 6–4 6–4 6–1
Woodbridge 6–3 6–3 7–6
Washington 6–1 6–0 6–2
ENQVIST (7) 6–4 6–4 7–5
Bruguera 4–6 6–3 6–4 7–6
Schaller 4–6 6–3 6–3 4–6 6–3
RIOS (9) 6–0 6–4 6–2
Medvedev 4–6 6–1 6–2 4–6 9–7
Van Scheppingen 6–2 6–2 6–2
Henman 6–3 6–3 6–4
CHANG (2) 6–3 7–5 6–1

Moya 6–2 6–2 6–2
Bjorkman 6–4 7–6 6–3
MANTILLA (14) 6–3 1–6 7–6 6–4
Washington 4–6 6–2 6–3 6–1
ENQVIST (7) 7–6 7–5 6–2
RIOS (9) 4–6 7–6 6–1 6–1
Medvedev 6–1 6–1 6–1
CHANG (2) 6–1 7–6 6–3

Moya 6–3 1–6 3–6 6–2 6–4
MANTILLA (14) 7–5 6–2 6–1
RIOS (9) 4–6 6–4 7–6 6–7 6–3
CHANG (2) 4–6 6–2 6–2 6–1

Moya 7–5 6–2 6–7 6–2
CHANG (2) 7–5 6–1 6–4

Moya 7–5 6–2 6–4

SAMPRAS (

Capital letters denote seeded players. Numbers following player's name gives seeding order (Q) – Qualifier, (W) – Wild Card, (L) – Lucky Loser

WOMEN'S SINGLES

Holder: M. Seles (USA)

FIRST ROUND

1 **S. GRAF** (GER) (1)
2 J. Husarova (SVK)
3 E. Dominikovic (AUS) (W)
4 L. Neiland (LAT)
5 I. Gorrochategui (ARG)
6 B. Stewart (AUS) (W)
7 E. Callens (BEL)
8 G. Fernandez (USA)
9 L. Lee (USA)
10 B. Mulej (SLO)
11 M.L. Serna (ESP) (Q)
12 M. Saeki (JPN)
13 J. Kandarr (GER)
14 K. Nagatsuka (JPN)
15 A. Kournikova (RUS)
16 **A. COETZER** (RSA) (12)
17 **B. SCHULTZ-McCARTHY** (NED) (10)
18 S.-H. Park (KOR)
19 R. Hiraki (JPN)
20 L. Richterova (CZE)
21 G. Leon-Sarcia (ESP)
22 K. Po (USA)
23 C. Cristea (ROM)
24 A. Sugiyama (JPN)
25 J. Taylor (AUS) (W)
26 M.A. Sanchez-Orenzo (ESP)
27 T. Tanasugarn (THA)
28 E. Makarova (RUS)
29 K. Studenikova (SVK)
30 F. Perfetti (ITA)
31 N. Dechy (FRA)
32 **L. DAVENPORT** (USA) (7)
33 **C. MARTINEZ** (ESP) (3)
34 M. Oremans (NED)
35 S. Dopfer (AUT)
36 A. Gersi (CZE)
37 A. Carlsson (SWE)
38 P. Langrova (CZE)
39 P. Hy-Boulais (CAN)
40 A. Dechaume-Balleret (FRA)
41 N. Arendt (USA)
42 K. Boogert (NED)
43 R. Grande (ITA)
44 A. Montolio (ESP)
45 A. Grossman (USA)
46 A. Miller (USA)
47 H. Sukova (CZE)
48 **S. APPELMANS** (BEL) (16)
49 **E. LIKHOVTSEVA** (RUS) (13)
50 M. Pierce (FRA)
51 L. Chen (CHN) (W)
52 N. Medvedeva (UKR)
53 M. Kochta (GER) (Q)
54 M. Werdel-Witmeyer (USA)
55 A. Ellwood (AUS) (W)
56 L. McNeil (USA)
57 N. Zvereva (BLR)
58 N. Feber (BEL)
59 S. Cacic (USA)
60 W. Probst (GER)
61 F. Lubiani (ITA)
62 R. McQuillan (AUS) (W)
63 A. Frazier (USA)
64 **A. HUBER** (GER) (5)

SECOND ROUND

GRAF (1) 5–1 Ret'd.
Neiland 6–2 6–7 6–0
Gorrochategui 6–2 6–1
Fernandez 6–3 6–4
Lee 2–6 6–3 6–2
Serna (Q) 6–3 6–7 7–5
Kandarr 6–3 3–6 6–3
COETZER (12) 6–2 6–2
SCHULTZ-McCARTHY (10) 6–2 2–6 6–2
Hiraki 6–4 2–6 6–4
Po 4–6 7–6 6–2
Sugiyama 7–6 6–4
Taylor (W) 7–5 4–6 7–6
Tanasugarn 6–3 1–6 6–4
Perfetti 6–4 7–6
DAVENPORT (7) 4–6 6–1 6–1
MARTINEZ (3) 6–0 6–2
Gersi 7–6 6–2
Carlsson 6–3 6–2
Hy-Boulais 6–0 2–6 6–4
Boogert 3–6 6–3 6–4
Grande 6–2 6–4
Grossman 7–5 6–2
APPELMANS (16) 6–2 6–2
Pierce 3–6 6–2 6–4
Medvedeva 6–2 3–6 6–3
Kochta (Q) 4–6 7–6 6–0
Ellwood (W) 6–3 6–2
Zvereva 7–6 6–1
Probst 6–4 2–6 7–5
Lubiani 6–2 7–6
HUBER (5) 0–6 6–2 7–5

THIRD ROUND

GRAF (1) 7–5 6–2
Gorrochategui 7–5 7–6
Serna (Q) 7–5 7–6
COETZER (12) 6–2 7–6
Hiraki 0–6 6–1 6–4
Po 6–0 4–6 6–3
Tanasugarn 6–4 6–3
DAVENPORT (7) 6–2 7–5
MARTINEZ (3) 6–2 7–6
Carlsson 2–6 6–3 6–0
Boogert 6–3 7–5
APPELMANS (16) 6–4 6–1
Pierce 6–2 6–2
Kochta (Q) 6–0 4–6 6–1
Zvereva 7–6 6–3
HUBER (5) 4–6 6–2 6–0

FOURTH ROUND

GRAF (1) 7–5 6–3
COETZER (12) 6–3 6–2
Po 6–2 6–2
DAVENPORT (7) 6–1 6–0
MARTINEZ (3) 6–0 6–1
APPELMANS (16) 6–3 3–0 Ret'd.
Pierce 6–0 6–2
HUBER (5) 7–5 6–0

QUARTER-FINALS

COETZER (12) 6–2 7–5
Po 7–6 6–4
APPELMANS (16) 2–6 7–5 6–1
Pierce 6–2 6–3

SEMI-FINALS

COETZER (12) 6–4 6–1
Pierce 1–6 6–4 6–4

FINAL

Pierce 7–5 6–1

6–2 6–2

65 **I. SPIRLEA** (ROM) (8)
66 N. Kumuta (JPN)
67 J. Kruger (RSA)
68 D. Randriantefy (MAD)
69 P. Suarez (ARG)
70 K. Kschwendt (AUT)
71 A. Olsza (POL)
72 S. Farina (ITA)
73 J. Capriati (USA)
74 J. Watanabe (USA)
75 S.-T. Wang (TPE)
76 L. Wild (USA)
77 C. Morariu (USA)
78 N. Bradtke (AUS)
79 S. Talaja (CRO)
80 **K. HABSUDOVA** (SVK) (9)
81 **J. WIESNER** (AUT) (11)
82 R. Dragomir (ROM)
83 V. Ruano-Pascual (ESP)
84 C. Torrens-Valero (ESP)
85 S. Hack (GER)
86 N. Van Lottum (FRA) (L)
87 P. Begerow (GER)
88 K. Brandi (USA) (Q)
89 G. Helgeson-Nielsen (USA)
90 A. Fusai (FRA)
91 B. Schett (AUT)
92 N. Miyagi (JPN)
93 S. Drake-Brockman (AUS) (W)
94 L. Raymond (USA)
95 B. Rittner (GER)
96 **M. HINGIS** (SUI) (4)
97 **I. MAJOLI** (CRO) (6)
98 P. Schnyder (SUI)
99 K. Radford (AUS) (W)
100 M. Endo (JPN)
101 M. Tu (USA) (Q)
102 L. Cenkova (CZE)
103 M. Grzybowska (POL) (Q)
104 S. Pitkowski (FRA)
105 F. Labat (ARG)
106 A. Kremer (LUX)
107 H. Nagyova (SVK)
108 E. Gagliardi (MON)
109 Y. Basuki (INA)
110 N. Sawamatsu (JPN)
111 L. Golarsa (ITA) (Q)
112 **M.J. FERNANDEZ** (USA) (14)
113 **C. RUBIN** (USA) (15)
114 R. Zrubakova (SVK)
115 S. Testud (FRA)
116 E. Wagner (GER)
117 S. Kleinova (CZE) (L)
118 T. Whitlinger-Jones (USA)
119 A.-G. Sidot (FRA)
120 T. Jecmenica (YUG)
121 K. Adams (USA)
122 Y. Yoshida (JPN) (Q)
123 B. Fulco-Villella (ARG)
124 D. Van Roost (BEL)
125 D. Chladkova (CZE)
126 S. de Ville (BEL)
127 G. Pizzichini (ITA)
128 **A. SANCHEZ VICARIO** (ESP) (2)

SPIRLEA (8) 6–2 6–4
Kruger 6–3 2–6 6–2
Suarez 7–6 6–3
Farina 6–3 6–2
Watanabe 6–2 3–6 6–4
Wang 6–3 6–1
Bradtke 6–3 6–2
HABSUDOVA (9) 6–1 6–2
Dragomir 4–6 6–3 10–8
Ruano-Pascual 6–0 3–6 6–3
Van Lottum (L) 4–6 6–3 6–2
Brandi (Q) 6–1 6–1
Fusai 6–2 6–2
Schett 7–6 7–6
Raymond 6–2 6–2
HINGIS (4) 6–1 7–5
Schnyder 7–5 6–1
Endo 7–5 6–1
Tu (Q) 3–6 6–2 6–3
Grzybowska (Q) 4–6 6–3 6–1
Labat 7–5 4–6 6–2
Nagyova 6–3 7–6
Basuki 6–3 4–1 Ret'd.
FERNANDEZ (14) 6–2 4–6 6–2
RUBIN (15) 7–6 6–3
Testud 6–3 6–1
Kleinova 7–6 6–1
Sidot 5–7 7–5 6–4
Yoshida (Q) 7–5 6–3
Van Roost 6–0 6–3
de Ville 6–3 6–7 8–6
SANCHEZ VICARIO (2) 6–4 6–4

SPIRLEA (8) 6–1 6–1
Farina 6–4 6–1
Wang 7–5 6–3
HABSUDOVA (9) 6–3 6–3
Dragomir 7–6 6–1
Brandi (Q) 6–0 1–6 6–4
Schett 2–6 7–5 7–5
HINGIS (4) 6–4 6–2
Schnyder 6–0 6–4
Grzybowska (Q) 6–4 6–7 6–1
Nagyova 6–3 6–2
FERNANDEZ (14) 7–5 6–4
RUBIN (15) 6–2 6–1
Kleinova 6–4 4–6 8–6
Van Roost 4–6 7–5 6–3
SANCHEZ VICARIO (2) 1–0 Ret'd.

SPIRLEA (8) 6–1 6–3
HABSUDOVA (9) 6–3 7–6
Dragomir 6–1 6–1
HINGIS (4) 6–2 6–1
Schnyder 7–6 6–1
FERNANDEZ (14) 6–2 6–1
RUBIN (15) 6–1 6–3
Van Roost 1–6 6–4 8–6

SPIRLEA (8) 6–4 6–4
HINGIS (4) 7–6 6–1
FERNANDEZ (14) 4–6 6–4 6–1
Van Roost 7–5 6–4

HINGIS (4) 7–5 6–2
FERNANDEZ (14) 7–5 4–0 Ret'd.

HINGIS (4) 6–1 6–3

HINGIS

Capital letters denote seeded players. Numbers following player's name gives seeding order (Q) – Qualifier, (W) – Wild Card, (L) – Lucky Loser

MEN'S DOUBLES

Holders: Edberg (SWE)/Korda (CZE)

FIRST ROUND

1 **WOODBRIDGE/WOODFORDE** (1)
2 A. Kratzmann/Tebbutt
3 Flach/Middleton
4 C. Ferreira/Koves
5 Johnson/Montana
6 Ekerot/Tarango
7 Davids/Schalken
8 **NOVAK/SUK** (15)
9 **DAMM/OLHOVSKIY** (10)
10 Hansen-Dent/Macphie
11 Djordjevic/Kitinov
12 Fleurian/Pereira
13 Grant/Smith
14 Bergh/Van Emburgh
15 Crabb/T. Larkham (W)
16 **GRABB/RENEBERG** (8)
17 **E. FERREIRA/GALBRAITH** (4)
18 Dosedel/Vizner
19 McEnroe/Stolle
20 Ivanisevic/Rosset
21 Thorne/Waite
22 Ellwood/Tramacchi (W)
23 Noteboom/Wibier
24 **ADAMS/OOSTING** (13)
25 **LEACH/STARK** (11)
26 Mitchell/Silcock (W)
27 Petchey/Richardson
28 Frana/Shelton
29 Jones/Melville
30 Carbonell/Corretja
31 Behrens/Cannon
32 **BJORKMAN/KULTI** (6)
33 **KNOWLES/NESTOR** (5)
34 Eagle/Florent
35 Henman/Siemerink
36 Draper/Steven (W)
37 Arthurs/Ireland
38 Brandi/Messori
39 Fitzgerald/Rafter (W)
40 **LOBO/SANCHEZ** (12)
41 Kuerten/Meligeni (L)
42 Goellner/Prinosil
43 Belobrajdic/Doyle (W)
44 Kinnear/Woodruff
45 Braasch/Knippschild
46 Ondruska/Stafford
47 Barnard/Randall
48 **ELTINGH/HAARHUIS** (3)
49 **LAREAU/O'BRIEN** (7)
50 Haygarth/Mirnyi
51 Davis/MacPherson
52 Gaudenzi/Nargiso
53 de Jager/Van Rensburg
54 Kempers/Nijssen
55 Albano/Nyborg
56 **PIMEK/TALBOT** (9)
57 **BROAD/NORVAL** (16)
58 Keil/Leblanc
59 Bhupathi/Paes
60 Cash/Korda
61 Holmes/Painter (W)
62 Muller/Ullyett
63 L. Jensen/M. Jensen
64 **B. BLACK/CONNELL** (2)

SECOND ROUND

WOODBRIDGE/WOODFORDE (1) 6–3 7–6
Flach/Middleton 6–3 6–4
Johnson/Montana 7–6 6–7 11–9
NOVAK/SUK (15) 7–5 4–6 6–4
DAMM/OLHOVSKIY (10) 1–6 6–3 6–4
Djordjevik/Kitinov 6–3 7–5
Grant/Smith 6–3 6–4
GRABB/RENEBERG (8) 6–4 6–2
E. FERREIRA/GALBRAITH (4) 6–3 6–0
McEnroe/Stolle 6–3 6–7 6–1
Thorne/Waite 7–6 4–6 6–4
Noteboom/Wibier 7–6 6–3
LEACH/STARK (11) 6–0 6–4
Petchey/Richardson 6–2 6–4
Jones/Melville 3–6 6–4 6–4
BJORKMAN/KULTI (6) 6–4 6–3
KNOWLES/NESTOR (5) 6–4 6–3
Draper/Steven (W) 6–3 6–4
Arthurs/Ireland 6–3 3–6 29–27
LOBO/SANCHEZ (12) 7–5 5–7 6–4
Goellner/Prinosil 6–3 6–4
Kinnear/Woodruff 7–6 6–3
Ondruska/Stafford 6–1 7–5
ELTINGH/HAARHUIS (3) 7–6 7–6
LAREAU/O'BRIEN (7) 4–6 6–3 6–0
Davis/MacPherson 6–1 6–4
Kempers/Nijssen 4–6 6–3 6–4
Albano/Nyborg 7–5 6–4
BROAD/NORVAL (16) 7–5 6–3
Cash/Korda 6–3 6–2
Muller/Ullyett 6–3 3–6 6–1
B. BLACK/CONNELL (2) 6–0 6–4

THIRD ROUND

WOODBRIDGE/WOODFORDE (1) 6–0 3–6 6–1
Johnson/Montana 6–4 7–6
DAMM/OLHOVSKIY (10) 6–4 6–4
GRABB/RENEBERG (8) 6–4 7–6
E. FERREIRA/GALBRAITH (4) 7–5 6–4
Noteboom/Wibier 4–6 6–4 6–2
LEACH/STARK (11) 6–3 6–4
BJORKMAN/KULTI (6) 2–0 Ret'd.
KNOWLES/NESTOR (5) 7–6 7–6
LOBO/SANCHEZ (12) 6–2 6–0
Kinnear/Woodruff w/o
ELTINGH/HAARHUIS (3) 6–3 6–4
LAREAU/O'BRIEN (7) 6–4 6–2
Kempers/Nijssen 6–2 1–6 6–1
BROAD/NORVAL (16) 6–7 7–6 6–3
B. BLACK/CONNELL (2) 7–5 6–2

QUARTER-FINALS

WOODBRIDGE/WOODFORDE (1) 6–1 6–1
DAMM/OLHOVSKIY (10) 5–7 6–4 6–3
E. FERREIRA/GALBRAITH (4) 6–3 6–4
LEACH/STARK (11) 6–3 6–7 6–1
KNOWLES/NESTOR (5) 6–4 6–3
ELTINGH/HAARHUIS (3) 6–0 6–4
LAREAU/O'BRIEN (7) 6–3 6–0
BROAD/NORVAL (16) 4–6 6–3 6–4

SEMI-FINALS

WOODBRIDGE/WOODFORDE (1) 6–3 6–3 6–3
LEACH/STARK (11) 7–5 2–6 6–4 7–6
ELTINGH/HAARHUIS (3) 6–3 1–6 6–2 2–6 6–3
LAREAU/O'BRIEN (7) 3–6 6–3 6–4 7–5

FINAL

WOODBRIDGE/WOODFORDE (1) 6–3 7–6 5–7 6–1
LAREAU/O'BRIEN (7) 4–6 6–2 6–4 5–7 6–2

WOODBRIDGE (AUS)/**WOODFORD** (AUS) 4–6 7–5 7–5 6–3

Capital letters denote seeded players. Numbers following player's name gives seeding order (Q) – Qualifier, (W) – Wild Card, (L) – Lucky Loser

WOMEN'S DOUBLES

Holders: Rubin (USA)/Sanchez Vicario (ESP)

FIRST ROUND

1 **G. FERNANDEZ/SANCHEZ VICARIO** (1)
2 Coetzer/Pierce (W)
3 Capriati/Majoli
4 Lake/Pleming
5 Ellwood/Pratt
6 Cenkova/Krajcovicova
7 Graham/Radford
8 **BOOGERT/SPIRLEA** (10)
9 **DECHAUME-BALLERET/TESTUD** (15)
10 Noorlander/Vildova
11 Huber/Rittner
12 Barclay/Guse
13 Cristea/Jecmenica
14 Lee/Nagyova (L)
15 Drake-Brockman/Musgrave
16 **ARENDT/BOLLEGRAF** (5)
17 **HINGIS/ZVEREVA** (4)
18 Nagatsuka/Richterova
19 Lettiere/Pizzichini
20 Gorrochategui/Montolio
21 Dragomir/Farina
22 Shriver/Smylie
23 Carlsson/Studenikova
24 **FRAZIER/PO** (11)
25 **APPELMANS/OREMANS** (14)
26 Csurgo/Papadak
27 Limmer/McShea (W)
28 Ruano-Pascual/Suarez
29 Martincova/Wagner
30 Bradtke/McQuillan
31 Kournikova/Likhovtseva
32 **RUBIN/SCHULTZ-McCARTHY** (8)
33 **ADAMS/M. FERNANDEZ** (6)
34 Makarova/Medvedeva
35 Krizan/Van Lottum
36 Habsudova/Zrubakova
37 Kschwendt/Schett
38 Hy-Boulais/Morariu
39 Martinek/Schneider
40 **MARTINEZ/TARABINI** (12)
41 **BASUKI/VIS** (9)
42 Grzybowska/Olsza
43 Park/Wang
44 Jeyaseelan/Simpson
45 Saeki/Yoshida
46 Nemeckova/Langrova
47 Grande/Sugiyama
48 **DAVENPORT/RAYMOND** (3)
49 **McNEIL/WILD** (7)
50 Hiraki/Labat
51 Freye/Meier
52 Kroupova/Melicharova
53 Golarsa/Sidot
54 de Lone/Wood
55 Feber/Grossman
56 **KIJIMUTA/MIYAGI** (13)
57 **FUSAI/PAZ** (16)
58 D. Jones/Tanasugarn
59 Krivencheva/Perfetti
60 Probst/Schnyder
61 Werdel-Witmeyer/Whitlinger-Jones
62 Callens/Helgeson-Nielsen
63 Hakami/Pitkowski
64 **NEILAND/SUKOVA** (2)

SECOND ROUND

G. FERNANDEZ/SANCHEZ VICARIO (1) 6–3 6–2
Capriati/Majoli 6–7 6–1 6–4
Ellwood/Pratt 6–1 6–0
Graham/Radford 6–2 2–6 6–4
Noorlander/Vildova 7–6 1–6 6–4
Huber/Rittner 6–1 4–6 6–3
Lee/Nagyova (L) 6–4 4–6 6–3
ARENDT/BOLLEGRAF (5) 6–1 6–2
HINGIS/ZVEREVA (4) 6–1 6–1
Gorrochategui/Montolio 6–4 2–6 7–5
Dragomir/Farina 6–4 6–2
FRAZIER/PO (11) 6–2 6–2
APPELMANS/OREMANS (14) 6–1 6–3
Ruano-Pascual/Suarez 6–2 6–1
Bradtke/McQuillan 6–3 4–6 6–3
RUBIN/SCHULTZ-McCARTHY (8) 6–2 6–3
ADAMS/M. FERNANDEZ (6) 6–2 6–2
Habsudova/Zrubakova 6–0 6–3
Hy-Boulais/Morariu 6–4 6–1
MARTINEZ/TARABINI (12) 6–1 6–3
BASUKI/VIS (9) 6–2 6–3
Park/Wang 7–5 6–2
Nemeckova/Langrova 6–4 0–6 6–4
DAVENPORT/RAYMOND (3) 6–3 7–6
McNEIL/WILD (7) 6–3 6–1
Kroupova/Melicharova 6–2 6–3
de Lone/Wood 6–3 7–6
KIJIMUTA/MIYAGI (13) 7–5 6–1
FUSAI/PAZ (16) 6–2 6–4
Krivencheva/Perfetti 6–3 6–4
Callens/Helgeson-Nielsen 6–2 6–0
NEILAND/SUKOVA (2) 6–1 6–3

THIRD ROUND

G. FERNANDEZ/SANCHEZ VICARIO (1) 6–3 7–6
Graham/Radford 6–1 6–3
Huber/Rittner 6–0 7–6
ARENDT/BOLLEGRAF (5) 6–3 6–3
HINGIS/ZVEREVA (4) 6–0 6–1
Dragomir/Farina 6–4 4–6 6–2
Ruano-Pascual/Suarez 1–6 7–5 6–4
RUBIN/SCHULTZ-McCARTHY (8) 6–4 6–2
Habsudova/Zrubakova 7–6 6–4
MARTINEZ/TARABINI (12) 6–1 7–6
Park/Wang 7–6 7–6
DAVENPORT/RAYMOND (3) 6–3 6–4
McNEIL/WILD (7) 6–3 6–1
KIJIMUTA/MIYAGI (13) 6–3 7–5
Krivencheva/Perfetti 3–6 6–3 6–4
NEILAND/SUKOVA (2) 6–2 6–2

QUARTER-FINALS

G. FERNANDEZ/SANCHEZ VICARIO (1) 6–4 6–3
ARENDT/BOLLEGRAF (5) 6–2 6–4
HINGIS/ZVEREVA (4) 6–2 6–1
Ruano-Pascual/Suarez 6–7 6–1 6–4
MARTINEZ/TARABINI (12) 6–3 6–4
DAVENPORT/RAYMOND (3) 7–6 6–0
KIJIMUTA/MIYAGI (13) 6–4 6–2
NEILAND/SUKOVA (2) 7–5 6–3

SEMI-FINALS

G. FERNANDEZ/SANCHEZ VICARIO (1) 6–4 7–5
HINGIS/ZVEREVA (4) 6–3 6–2
DAVENPORT/RAYMOND (3) 6–4 7–6
NEILAND/SUKOVA (2) 6–2 6–3

FINAL

HINGIS/ZVEREVA (4) 6–3 5–7 6–2
DAVENPORT/RAYMOND (3) 7–5 6–3

HINGIS (SUI)/**ZVEREVA** (BLR) (4) 6–2 6–2

Capital letters denote seeded players. Numbers following player's name gives seeding order (Q) – Qualifier, (W) – Wild Card, (L) – Lucky Loser

MIXED DOUBLES

Holders: Woodforde (AUS)/Neiland (LAT)

FIRST ROUND	SECOND ROUND	QUARTER-FINALS	SEMI-FINALS	FINAL
1 **CONNELL/DAVENPORT** (1)	**CONNELL/DAVENPORT** (1) 6–2 7–5	Johnson/Spirlea 7–6 4–6 6–4	MacPhie/McNeil w/o	**LEACH/BOLLEGRAF** (3) 7–6 6–1
2 Olhovskiy/Likhovtseva				
3 Montana/Lettiere (L)	Johnson/Spirlea 7–5 6–0			
4 Johnson/Spirlea				
5 Florent/G. Fernandez	Florent/G. Fernandez 6–7 6–2 7–6	MacPhie/McNeil 6–4 6–3		
6 Albano/Tarabini				
7 MacPhie/McNeil	MacPhie/McNeil 6–2 6–1			
8 **PIMEK/ADAMS** (5)				
9 **LEACH/BOLLEGRAF** (3)	**LEACH/BOLLEGRAF** (3) 7–6 7–5	**LEACH/BOLLEGRAF** (3) 6–2 6–3	**LEACH/BOLLEGRAF** (3) 3–6 6–3 6–4	
10 Adams/Fusai				
11 Davids/Oremans	Davids/Oremans 7–5 6–4			
12 Van Rensburg/Arendt				
13 Cash/Capriati (W)	Cash/Capriati (W) 6–0 7–5	Eltingh/Medvedeva 6–3 6–2		
14 MacPherson/McQuillan				
15 Eltingh/Medvedeva	Eltingh/Medvedeva 6–1 6–4			
16 **OOSTING/BOOGERT** (8)				
17 A. Kratzmann/Wild (L)	Bradtke/Eagle (W) 6–2 4–6 6–2	Bradtke/Eagle (W) 6–3 6–0	de Jager/Neiland 6–4 2–6 6–4	de Jager/Neiland 6–4 6–3
18 Bradtke/Eagle (W)				
19 Grabb/Dechaume-Balleret	Grabb/Dechaume-Balleret 7–5 6–0			
20 Lobo/Golarsa				
21 de Jager/Neiland	de Jager/Neiland 6–1 6–4	de Jager/Neiland 6–3 7–6		
22 Barnard/Basuki				
23 Draper/Smylie (W)	**SUK/SUKOVA** (4) 6–4 6–1			
24 **SUK/SUKOVA** (4)				
25 **TALBOT/VIS** (6)	Waite/Po 6–3 6–1	Knowles/Kournikova 6–7 6–4 6–0	Knowles/Kournikova 6–4 7–6	
26 Waite/Po				
27 Kinnear/Miyagi	Knowles/Kournikova 6–3 6–2			
28 Knowles/Kournikova				
29 Norval/Guse	Norval/Guse 6–4 5–7 7–5	**GALBRAITH/RAYMOND** (2) 6–1 6–0		
30 Nyborg/Graham				
31 Nestor/Simpson	**GALBRAITH/RAYMOND** (2) 6–3 6–2			
32 **GALBRAITH/RAYMOND** (2)				

LEACH (USA)/**BOLLEGRAF** (NED) (3)
6–3 6–7 7–5

Capital letters denote seeded players. Numbers following player's name gives seeding order (Q) – Qualifier, (W) – Wild Card, (L) – Lucky Loser

While Hingis went on to seize her destiny, there was lingering sadness for Jennifer Capriati, the onetime teenage prodigy who had lost to Hingis in the Sydney final. Capriati appeared set to enjoy another important stage of her rehabilitation, but on a windy day was outsteadied by fellow-American Jolene Watanabe in the first round. Russia's blossoming Anna Kournikova was unlucky to draw Coetzer in her first Australian Open match, but Patty Schnyder, 18, reinforced Switzerland's emergence as a major power in women's tennis by beating sixth seed Iva Majoli and making the fourth round.

For Australia there were no such happy omens. In this, Nicole Bradtke's 12th and almost certainly last Open, she bowed out in the second round to Karina Habsudova. She has no obvious successor among the young Australians trying to make their way in the game.

With no local players surviving the second round of the women's singles or the third round of the men's, the '97 Open might indeed have ended on a sombre note for Australian fans but for Todd Woodbridge and Mark Woodforde again salvaging national pride by winning their third successive Grand Slam crown, their eighth in all. They defeated in the final the North American team of Alex O'Brien and Sebastian Lareau. The Woodies, statistically, are now the most successful duo in the history of Open tennis, and richly deserved the Order of Australia Medals that they received during the tournament on Australia Day, 26 January.

JUNIOR EVENTS

BOYS' SINGLES – Final: Daniel Elsner (GER) (1) d. Westley Whitehouse (RSA) (14) 7–6 6–2
GIRLS' SINGLES – Final: Mirjana Lucic (CRO) (1) d. Marlene Weingartner (2) 6–2 6–2.
BOY'S DOUBLES – Final: David Sherwood (GBR)/James Trotman (GBR) (2) d. Jaco van der Westhuizen (RSA)/Westley Whitehouse (RSA) 7–6 6–3.
GIRLS' DOUBLES – Final: Mirjana Lucic (CRO)/Jasmin Wohr (GER) (6) d. Yoon-Jeong Cho (KOR) /Shi-Ho Hisamatsu (JPN) 6–2 6–2.
LEGENDS' DOUBLES – Final: Peter McNamara/Fred Stolle d. Mark Edmondson/Ken Rosewall 6–4 6–4

FORD AUSTRALIAN OPEN CHAMPIONSHIPS 1997
PRIZE MONEY – AUS $9,450,000

MEN'S SINGLES – Winner $585,000. Runner-up $292,500. Semi-finalists $146,000. Quarter-finalists $75,000. Fourth-round losers $40,000. Third-round losers $23,000. Second-round losers $14,000. First-round losers $9,000.
Total: $3,181,500

WOMEN'S SINGLES – Winner $542,000. Runner-up $271,000. Semi-finalists $135,000. Quarter-finalists $70,000. Fourth-round losers $37,000. Third-round losers $21,500. Second-round losers $13,000. First-round losers $8,200.
Total: $2,943,800

MEN'S DOUBLES (per team) – Winner $244,000. Runner-up $122,000. Semi-finalists $60,000. Quarter-finalists $30,000. Third-round losers $17,000. Second-round losers $9,400. First-round losers $5,200
Total: $1,058,800

WOMEN'S DOUBLES (per team) – Winners $225,000. Runners-up $112,500. Semi-finalists $56,000. Quarter-finalists $28,000. Third-round losers $15,700. Second-round losers $8,500.
First-round losers $4,900.
Total: $979,900

MIXED DOUBLES (per team) – Winners $92,000. Runners-up $46,000. Semi-finalists $23,000. Quarter-finalists $10,700. Second-round losers $5,400. First-round losers $2,600.
Total: $311,600

LEGENDS' DOUBLES (per player) – Winners (2) $10,000. Runners-up (2) $8,500. Other players (8) $7,500.
Reserves (2) $2,500
Total: $102,000

MEN'S QUALIFYING (128 DRAW)
Losers in round of 32 – $5,800
Losers in round of 64 – $3,000
Losers in round of 128 – $1,550
Total:$288,000

WOMEN'S QUALIFYING (64 DRAW)
Losers in round of 16 – $5,400
Losers in round of 32 – $2,900
Losers in round of 128 – $1,400
Total:$134,400

Plus per diem allowances of $450,000 (estimated)

'Gugamania' broke out in Paris when the ever-smiling Brazilian newcomer, Gustavo Kuerten, won the French Open. Incredibly, this was 'Guga's' first ever tournament win on the Tour.
(Michael Cole)

65 **R. KRAJICEK** (NED) (6)
66 S. Draper (AUS)
67 B. Ulihrach (CZE)
68 N. Kiefer (GER)
69 P. Fredriksson (SWE)
70 F. Fontang (FRA) (W)
71 A. Gaudenzi (ITA)
72 P. Rafter (AUS)
73 M. Woodforde (AUS)
74 J. Sanchez (ESP)
75 D. Nestor (CAN)
76 A. Volkov (RUS)
77 A. Pavel (ROM)
78 A. O'Brien (USA)
79 A. Voinea (ROM)
80 **A. COSTA** (ESP) (11)
81 **W. FERREIRA** (RSA) (13)
82 M. Tillstrom (SWE)
83 E. Alvarez (ESP)
84 R. Carretero (ESP)
85 D. Flach (USA)
86 C. Costa (ESP)
87 J. Burillo (ESP) (Q)
88 P. Korda (CZE)
89 D. Vacek (CZE)
90 C. Woodruff (USA)
91 F. Fetterlein (DEN) (L)
92 N. Lapentti (ECU) (Q)
93 N. Godwin (RSA)
94 G. Blanco (ESP)
95 M. Gustafsson (SWE)
96 **G. IVANISEVIC** (CRO) (4)
97 **M. RIOS** (CHI) (7)
98 W. Black (ZIM) (Q)
99 F. Squillari (ARG)
100 B. Black (ZIM)
101 A. Boetsch (FRA)
102 K. Kucera (SVK)
103 M. Ondruska (RSA)
104 M. Pastura (ARG) (Q)
105 K. Carlsen (DEN)
106 T. Woodbridge (AUS)
107 H. Dreekmann (GER)
108 H. Arazi (MAR)
109 J. Courier (USA)
110 M. Larsson (SWE)
111 R. Fromberg (AUS)
112 **F. MANTILLA** (ESP) (10)
113 **S. BRUGUERA** (ESP) (16)
114 J. Van Herck (BEL)
115 P. Haarhuis (NED)
116 D. Van Scheppingen (NED)
117 S. Sargsian (ARM)
118 D. Norman (BEL) (Q)
119 S. Stolle (AUS)
120 R. Furlan (ITA)
121 J. Krocsko (HUN) (L)
122 J. Kroslak (SVK)
123 G. Schaller (AUT)
124 S. Simian (FRA)
125 A. Clement (FRA) (W)
126 J. Golmard (FRA)
127 R. Gilbert (FRA) (Q)
128 **M. CHANG** (USA) (2)

KRAJICEK (6) 7–6 6–2 6–1
Ulihrach 6–3 6–3 6–3
Fontang (W) 6–3 6–7 6–0 4–6 6–2
Rafter 3–6 7–6 6–3 6–4
Woodforde 5–7 7–6 6–7 6–4 8–6
Volkov 6–1 6–1 3–6 6–2
Pavel 6–4 7–5 6–0
COSTA (11) 6–4 7–5 6–4
FERREIRA (13) 6–7 7–6 6–7 6–3 6–1
Carretero 5–7 7–6 6–3 7–5
Costa 6–4 6–0 6–1
Korda 6–4 6–0 7–6
Woodruff 6–4 6–2 6–3
Lapentti (Q) 6–4 6–1 6–2
Blanco 6–3 6–2 1–6 7–5
Gustafsson 4–6 6–3 7–6 6–3
RIOS (7) 6–4 5–7 4–6 6–2 6–1
Black 1–6 6–3 6–3 6–3
Boetsch 6–1 6–1 6–4
Ondruska 7–6 6–2 6–1
Woodbridge 7–6 4–6 6–4 6–0
Arazi 6–3 6–4 6–2
Larsson 6–1 6–2 4–6 1–6 6–4
MANTILLA (10) 6–3 6–2 6–2
BRUGUERA (16) 6–3 0–6 6–2 6–0
Van Scheppingen 6–2 6–4 5–7 6–4
Norman (Q) 6–2 7–5 6–3
Stolle 7–5 6–1 4–6 6–3
Krocso (L) 7–5 6–3 4–6 7–6
Simian 2–6 6–4 4–6 6–4 6–2
Golmard 6–1 6–2 6–3
CHANG (2) 6–2 6–3 6–2

KRAJICEK (6) 6–2 3–6 6–2 6–3
Rafter 6–3 6–4 6–3
Woodforde 7–6 6–3 7–5
COSTA (11) 6–1 4–6 0–6 6–3 6–4
FERREIRA (13) 7–6 4–6 6–1 2–6 6–4
Korda 6–3 7–5 6–4
Woodruff 6–4 5–7 3–6 6–4 6–1
Blanco 6–4 4–6 6–4 7–6
RIOS (7) 6–7 6–7 6–4 7–6 6–0
Boetsch 6–3 6–2 6–1
Arazi 6–4 7–5 6–2
Larsson 6–2 6–4 3–6 6–3
BRUGUERA (16) 6–2 6–3 6–3
Norman (Q) 5–7 6–4 7–6 6–3
Simian 6–3 6–3 7–6
CHANG (2) 6–2 6–3 3–6 6–2

Rafter 6–3 4–6 6–4 6–2
Woodforde 6–4 7–6 6–3
Korda w/o
Blanco 7–6 6–3 7–6
RIOS (7) 7–6 6–3 6–4
Arazi 6–2 6–3 7–5
BRUGUERA (16) 6–3 6–1 6–3
CHANG (2) 6–1 5–2 Ab

Rafter 6–2 5–7 6–1 6–2
Blanco 1–6 6–1 7–5 6–4
Arazi 6–2 6–1 5–7 7–6
BRUGUERA (16) 3–6 6–4 6–3 6–4

Rafter 6–3 7–6 6–3
BRUGUERA (16) 4–6 6–3 6–2 6–2

BRUGUERA (16) 6–7 6–1 7–5 7–6

Kuerten

Capital letters denote seeded players. Numbers following player's name gives seeding order (Q) – Qualifier, (W) – Wild Card, (L) – Lucky Loser

WOMEN'S SINGLES

Holder: Graf (GER)

FIRST ROUND

1 **M. HINGIS** (SUI) (1)
2 H. Nagyova (SVK)
3 S. Cacic (USA) (Q)
4 G. Pizzichini (ITA)
5 R. Zrubakova (SVK)
6 A. Kournikova (RUS)
7 M. Endo (JPN)
8 S. Cecchini (ITA)
9 S. Farina (ITA)
10 J. Wiesner (AUT)
11 M. Grzybowska (POL)
12 P. Begerow (GER)
13 S.-T. Wang (TPE)
14 S. De Ville (BEL)
15 T. Whitlinger-Jones (USA)
16 **B. PAULUS** (AUT) (16)
17 **B. SCHULTZ-McCARTHY** (NED) (14)
18 L. Cenkova (CZE)
19 F. Labat (ARG)
20 K. Boogert (NED)
21 M. Lamarre (FRA) (W)
22 B. Schett (AUT)
23 M. Tu (USA)
24 N. Zvereva (BLR)
25 B. Rittner (GER)
26 D. Van Roost (BEL)
27 E. Gagliardi (SUI)
28 K. Brandi (USA)
29 E. Wagner (GER)
30 A. Sugiyama (JPN)
31 K. Jagieniak (FRA) (W)
32 **A. SANCHEZ VICARIO** (ESP) (6)
33 **M. SELES** (USA) (3)
34 M. Saeki (JPN)
35 S. Pitkowski (FRA)
36 F. Lubiani (ITA)
37 N. Sawamatsu (JPN)
38 V. Williams (USA)
39 N. Tauziat (FRA)
40 R. Simpson (CAN)
41 S. Testud (FRA)
42 S.-H. Park (KOR) (Q)
43 W. Probst (GER)
44 C. Cristea (ROM)
45 P. Hy-Boulais (CAN)
46 N. Dechy (FRA)
47 T. Panova (RUS)
48 **M. PIERCE** (FRA) (10)
49 **M.J. FERNANDEZ** (USA) (12)
50 L. McNeil (USA)
51 A. Glass (GER)
52 E. Callens (BEL)
53 M. Oremans (NED)
54 L. Ghirard-Rubbi (FRA) (W)
55 N. Miyagi (JPN)
56 F. Perfetti (ITA)
57 M. Maleeva (BUL)
58 L. Raymond (USA)
59 L. Courtois (BEL)
60 T. Tanasugarn (THA)
61 Y. Yoshida (JPN)
62 R. McQuillan (AUS)
63 K. Po (USA)
64 **A. HUBER** (GER) (8)

SECOND ROUND

HINGIS (1) 6–0 6–2
Pizzichini 7–6 7–5
Kournikova 6–3 6–2
Cecchini 7–6 7–6
Farina 6–2 1–6 6–0
Begerow 3–6 6–3 6–4
Wang 6–3 7–5
PAULUS (16) 6–0 6–1
SCHULTZ-McCARTHY (14) 6–3 7–5
Labat 7–5 6–0
Lamarre (W) 6–1 0–0 Ab
Zvereva 6–3 3–6 6–4
Van Roost 3–0 Ab
Gagliardi 6–3 6–4
Sugiyama 5–7 6–4 6–1
SANCHEZ VICARIO (6) 6–0 6–2
SELES (3) 6–0 6–3
Pitkowski 7–6 6–2
Williams 6–2 6–7 7–5
Tauziat 6–3 6–2
Testud 6–0 6–4
Cristea 6–3 6–4
Hy-Boulais 6–7 6–4 11–9
PIERCE (10) 6–2 4–6 6–4
FERNANDEZ (12) 6–2 6–3
Glass 6–3 4–6 6–2
Ghirard-Rubbi (W) 2–6 6–2 6–3
Perfetti 7–6 2–6 6–0
Raymond 4–6 7–5 6–3
Tanasugarn 7–6 6–4
Yoshida 6–2 6–4
Po 6–3 4–6 6–3

THIRD ROUND

HINGIS (1) 3–6 6–4 6–1
Kournikova 6–2 6–2
Farina 6–4 6–2
PAULUS (16) 6–2 6–2
SCHULTZ-McCARTHY (14) 4–6 7–6 6–4
Zvereva 6–4 7–5
Van Roost 6–2 6–0
SANCHEZ VICARIO (6) 6–3 6–1
SELES (3) 6–3 7–5
Tauziat 5–7 6–3 7–5
Testud 6–0 6–4
PIERCE (10) 6–1 6–3
FERNANDEZ (12) 6–1 6–0
Perfetti 6–4 6–1
Raymond 6–1 6–1
Po 6–3 6–0

FOURTH ROUND

HINGIS (1) 6–1 6–3
PAULUS (16) 6–4 6–1
Zvereva 7–6 6–4
SANCHEZ VICARIO (6) 6–0 6–3
SELES (3) 6–0 6–1
PIERCE (10) 6–1 6–3
FERNANDEZ (12) 6–3 7–6
Raymond 6–4 2–6 6–1

QUARTER-FINALS

HINGIS (1) 6–3 0–6 6–0
SANCHEZ VICARIO (6) 6–4 6–2
SELES (3) 6–4 7–5
FERNANDEZ (12) 6–7 6–2 6–2

SEMI-FINALS

HINGIS (1) 6–2 6–2
SELES (3) 3–6 6–2 7–5

FINAL

HINGIS (1) 6–7 7–5 6–4

6–4 6–2

65 **L. DAVENPORT** (USA) (5)
66 J. Kruger (RSA) (Q)
67 E. Makarova (RUS)
68 A. Dechaume-Balleret (FRA)
69 M. Maruska (AUT)
70 P. Schnyder (SUI)
71 K. Studenikova (SVK)
72 P. Langrova (CZE)
73 A.-G. Sidot (FRA)
74 L. Neiland (LAT)
75 A. Gersi (CZE)
76 A. Grossman (USA)
77 L. Richterova (CZE)
78 A. Fusai (FRA)
79 S. Kleinova (CZE)
80 **I. MAJOLI** (CRO) (9)
81 **K. HABSUDOVA** (SVK) (15)
82 O. Barabanschikova (BLR)
83 L. Nemeckova (CZE)
84 E. Likhovtseva (RUS)
85 Y. Basuki (INA)
86 A. Carlsson (SWE)
87 R. Dragomir (ROM)
88 S. Jeyaseelan (CAN) (Q)
89 R. Hiraki (JPN)
90 N. Arendt (USA)
91 L. Golarsa (ITA) (Q)
92 N. Van Lottum (FRA)
93 J. Kandarr (GER)
94 G. Leon-Garcia (ESP)
95 C. Torrens-Valero (ESP)
96 **J. NOVOTNA** (CZE) (4)
97 **C. MARTINEZ** (ESP) (7)
98 E. Loit (FRA) (W)
99 C. Rubin (USA)
100 M. Diaz-Oliva (ARG)
101 C. Dhenin (FRA) (W)
102 S. Appelmans (BEL)
103 S. Talaja (CRO)
104 M. Kochta (GER) (Q)
105 M. Babel (GER)
106 E. Curutchet (FRA) (Q)
107 S. Dopfer (AUT)
108 H. Sukova (CZE)
109 D. Chladkova (CZE)
110 A. Frazier (USA)
111 R. Grande (ITA)
112 **A. COETZER** (RSA) (11)
113 **I. SPIRLEA** (ROM) (13)
114 J. Lee (USA) (Q)
115 A. Olsza (POL)
116 I. Gorrochategui (ARG)
117 A. Montolio (ESP)
118 V. Ruano-Pascual (ESP)
119 A. Ellwood (AUS)
120 A. Cocheteux (FRA) (W)
121 N. Kijimuta (JPN)
122 L. Andretto (FRA) (W)
123 M. Serna (ESP)
124 L. Wild (USA)
125 A. Mauresmo (FRA) (W)
126 J. Watanabe (USA)
127 P. Suarez (ARG)
128 **S. GRAF** (GER) (2)

DAVENPORT (5) 6–2 6–3
Makarova 6–4 6–2
Schnyder 6–3 6–3
Studenikova 6–2 6–2
Neiland 6–2 7–5
Grossman 6–3 6–0
Fusai 7–5 3–0 Ab
MAJOLI (9) 7–5 6–4
HABSUDOVA (15) 6–3 6–3
Likhovtseva 6–4 6–3
Basuki 6–4 4–6 6–1
Dragomir 6–3 6–2
Arendt 6–2 6–1
Golarsa (Q) 4–6 7–5 12–10
Kandarr 7–6 6–3
NOVOTNA (4) 6–3 6–2
MARTINEZ (7) 4–6 6–2 6–3
Rubin 7–6 7–5
Dhenin (W) 6–7 6–2 6–1
Talaja 7–5 6–3
Babel 1–6 6–4 6–2
Sukova 6–3 6–4
Frazier 6–4 6–0
COETZER (11) 6–4 6–0
SPIRLEA (13) 6–1 6–0
Gorrochategui 6–3 6–3
Ruano-Pascual 6–0 6–0
Cocheteux (W) 6–2 3–6 6–3
Kijimuta 6–3 6–3
Serna 7–6 6–0
Mauresmo (W) 6–3 6–4
GRAF (2) 6–1 6–4

DAVENPORT (5) 6–1 6–1
Schnyder 6–0 2–0 Ret'd.
Grossman 6–4 6–4
MAJOLI (9) 6–2 6–3
HABSUDOVA (15) 6–2 6–2
Dragomir 7–5 4–6 8–6
Arendt 6–2 6–2
NOVOTNA (4) 6–4 6–0
MARTINEZ (7) 6–3 6–0
Dhenin (W) 6–2 7–5
Babel 4–6 6–4 12–10
COETZER (11) 7–6 6–4
SPIRLEA (13) 6–4 4–6 6–2
Ruano-Pascual 6–4 6–2
Serna 3–6 6–4 6–2
GRAF (2) 6–3 6–3

DAVENPORT (5) 4–6 6–3 9–7
MAJOLI (9) 6–1 4–6 6–1
Dragomir 6–3 6–2
Arendt 3–6 6–4 6–4
MARTINEZ (7) 6–2 6–1
COETZER (11) 6–4 6–2
SPIRLEA (13) 6–1 6–1
GRAF (2) 7–6 6–1

MAJOLI (9) 5–7 6–4 6–2
Dragomir 6–1 6–1
COETZER (11) 6–7 6–4 6–3
GRAF (2) 6–7 6–2 6–2

MAJOLI (9) 6–3 5–7 6–2
COETZER (11) 6–1 6–4

MAJOLI (9) 6–3 4–6 7–5

MAJOLI (

Capital letters denote seeded players. Numbers following player's name gives seeding order (Q) – Qualifier, (W) – Wild Card, (L) – Lucky Loser

MEN'S DOUBLES

Holders: Kafelnikov (RUS)/Vacek (CZE)

FIRST ROUND

1 **WOODBRIDGE/WOODFORDE** (1)
2 Bachelot/Perlant (W)
3 Arthurs/Kratzmann
4 Mirnyi/Ullyett
5 Haygarth/Middleton
6 Davis/Van Rensburg
7 Korda/Salzenstein
8 **PIMEK/TALBOT** (15)
9 **BJORKMAN/KULTI** (9)
10 Grosjean/Mutis (W)
11 Marques/Vanhoudt
12 Kempers/Oosting
13 Kuerten/Meligeni
14 Pereira/Tarango
15 Marx/Morel
16 **LEACH/STARK** (7)
17 **KNOWLES/NESTOR** (3)
18 Barnard/de Jager
19 Carbonell/Roig
20 Sanchez/Wibier
21 Bhupathi/Paes
22 Randall/Waite
23 Groen/Siemerink
24 **JOHNSON/MONTANA** (14)
25 **DAMM/OLHOVSKIY** (11)
26 Hirszon/Ivanisevic
27 Albano/Nyborg
28 Delaitre/Santoro
29 Djordjevic/Flach
30 Arnold/Orsanic
31 Petchey/Rikl
32 **LAREAU/O'BRIEN** (5)
33 **E. FERREIRA/GALBRAITH** (6)
34 Kitinov/Van Emburgh
35 Davids/Schalken
36 Braasch/Knippschild
37 L. Jensen/M. Jensen
38 Keil/Woodruff
39 Couto/Mota
40 **STOLLE/SUK** (12)
41 **BROAD/NORVAL** (13)
42 B. Black/Gimelstob
43 Kinnear/Vizner
44 W. Black/Grabb
45 Nijssen/Noteboom
46 Boetsch/Rosset (W)
47 Bergh/Ekerot
48 **KAFELNIKOV/VACEK** (4)
49 **LOBO/SANCHEZ** (8)
50 Ondruska/Stafford
51 Clement/Escude (W)
52 Eagle/Florent
53 Gilbert/Raoux (W)
54 Fleurian/Simian (W)
55 MacPhie/Muller
56 **PHILIPPOUSSIS/RAFTER** (10)
57 **KRONEMANN/MACPHERSON** (16)
58 Frana/Lapentti
59 Brandi/Messori
60 Jones/Melville
61 Kilderry/Tebbutt
62 Cash/Reneberg
63 Adams/W. Ferreira
64 **ELTINGH/HAARHUIS** (2)

SECOND ROUND

WOODBRIDGE/WOODFORDE (1) 6–2 6–1
Arthurs/Kratzmann 6–3 7–6
Davis/Van Rensburg 6–1 7–6
Korda/Salzenstein 7–5 6–0
BJORKMAN/KULTI (9) 6–1 6–4
Kempers/Oosting 6–4 6–2
Kuerten/Meligeni 6–1 4–6 8–6
LEACH/STARK (7) 7–5 6–3
KNOWLES/NESTOR (3) 6–3 7–6
Carbonell/Roig 6–3 6–4
Bhupathi/Paes 6–2 6–2
Groen/Siemerink 2–6 7–6 6–4
DAMM/OLHOVSKIY (11) 6–4 4–6 6–1
Delaitre/Santoro 3–6 7–6 6–4
Arnold/Orsanic 6–2 6–1
LAREAU/O'BRIEN (5) 6–4 7–6
E. FERREIRA/GALBRAITH (6) 6–3 6–2
Braasch/Knippschild 5–7 6–4 9–7
L. Jensen/M. Jensen 6–3 6–4
Couto/Mota 6–2 6–7 6–2
BROAD/NORVAL (13) 6–3 6–2
W. Black/Grabb 6–3 7–6
Nijssen/Noteboom 6–4 6–2
KAFELNIKOV/VACEK (4) 6–1 5–7 6–3
LOBO/SANCHEZ (8) 6–3 4–6 6–3
Eagle/Florent 4–6 6–4 6–2
Fleurian/Simian 5–7 6–4 6–1
PHILIPPOUSSIS/RAFTER (10) 6–7 7–6 8–6
KRONEMANN/MACPHERSON (16) 4–6 7–6 6–3
Brandi/Messori 6–4 7–5
Cash/Reneberg 5–7 7–5 6–3
ELTINGH/HAARHUIS (2) 6–4 4–6 6–1

THIRD ROUND

WOODBRIDGE/WOODFORDE (1) 7–6 6–3
Korda/Salzenstein 6–4 7–6
Kempers/Oosting 6–3 1–6 6–3
LEACH/STARK (7) 6–3 6–3
Carbonell/Roig 7–6 6–1
Groen/Siemerink 6–7 7–6 6–3
Delaitre/Santoro 6–1 3–6 6–3
Arnold/Orsanic 7–6 4–6 6–1
Braasch/Knippschild 6–4 3–6 10–8
L. Jensen/M. Jensen 4–6 6–4 11–9
W. Black/Grabb 7–6 2–6 10–8
KAFELNIKOV/VACEK (4) 6–1 6–4
Eagle/Florent 6–2 7–6
PHILIPPOUSSIS/RAFTER (10) 5–7 6–3 6–4
Brandi/Messori 7–5 6–4
ELTINGH/HAARHUIS (2) 3–6 6–1 6–4

QUARTER-FINALS

WOODBRIDGE/WOODFORDE (1) 2–6 6–3 9–7
LEACH/STARK (7) 6–3 6–7 6–2
Carbonell/Roig 3–6 6–3 6–2
Arnold/Orsanic 7–6 6–1
Braasch/Knippschild 6–4 7–6
KAFELNIKOV/VACEK (4) 6–4 7–6
Eagle/Florent 6–2 6–7 6–3
ELTINGH/HAARHUIS (2) 6–3 6–3

SEMI-FINALS

WOODBRIDGE/WOODFORDE (1) 6–2 7–6
Arnold/Orsanic 4–6 6–4 6–4
KAFELNIKOV/VACEK (4) 4–6 7–6 6–3
ELTINGH/HAARHUIS (2) 6–7 6–4 6–2

FINAL

WOODBRIDGE/WOODFORDE (1) 4–6 6–4 6–3
KAFELNIKOV/VACEK (4) 7–6 7–6

KAFELNIKOV (RUS)/**VACEK** (CZE) (4) 7–6 4–6 6–3

Capital letters denote seeded players. Numbers following player's name gives seeding order (Q) – Qualifier, (W) – Wild Card, (L) – Lucky Loser

WOMEN'S DOUBLES

Holders: Davenport (USA)/M.J. Fernandez (USA)

FIRST ROUND

1 **G. FERNANDEZ/ZVERERA** (1)
2 Grossman/Habsudova
3 Graham/Kunce
4 Curutchet/Georges (W)
5 A. Barna/A. Barna
6 Nagyova/Schnyder
7 Rubin/Schultz-McCarthy
8 **APPELMANS/OREMANS** (12)
9 **DRAGOMIR/MAJOLI** (16)
10 Rittner/Van Roost
11 Elwood/McQuillan
12 Probst/Sugiyama
13 Loit/Mauresmo (W)
14 de Swardt/Temesvari
15 Freye/Noorlander
16 **ARENDT/BOLLEGRAF** (6)
17 **HINGIS/SANCHEZ VICARIO** (3)
18 Grande/Guse
19 Dhenin/Pitkowski
20 Feber/Hy-Boulais
21 Cristea/Ruano-Pascual
22 Farina/Pizzichini
23 Grzybowska/Olsza
24 **BOOGERT/SPIRLEA** (14)
25 **ADAMS/MCNEIL** (9)
26 Krizan/Van Lottum
27 Langrova/Nemeckova
28 Paz/Simpson
29 Gorrochategui/Wild
30 Meier/Schwarz
31 Lugina/Wagner
32 **BASUKI/VIS** (7)
33 **M.J. FERNANDEZ/RAYMOND** (5)
34 Morariu/Sidot
35 Saeki/Yoshida
36 Krivencheva/Makarova
37 Callens/Helgeson-Nielsen
38 Montalvo/Suarez
39 D. Jones/Tanasugarn
40 **FRAZIER/PO** (13)
41 **KIJIMUTA/MIYAGI** (11)
42 Bobkova/Melicharova
43 Csurgo/Horn
44 Berger/Jagieniak (W)
45 Muric/Whitlinger-Jones
46 de Lone/Zrubakova
47 Barclay/Wood
48 **NEILAND/SUKOVA** (4)
49 **FUSAI/TAUZIAT** (8)
50 Park/Wang
51 Dechy/Ghirardi-Rubbi (W)
52 Hiraki/Labat
53 Babel/Golarsa
54 Nideffer/Rinaldi-Stunkel
55 Martincova/Vildova
56 **KOURNIKOVA/LIKHOVTSEVA** (15)
57 **MARTINEZ/TARABINI** (10)
58 Dechaume-Balleret/Testud
59 Coetzer/Pierce
60 Jeyaseelan/Lee
61 Carlsson/Perfetti
62 Huber/Seles
63 Pleming/Pratt
64 **DAVENPORT/NOVOTNA** (2)

SECOND ROUND

G. FERNANDEZ/ZVERERA (1) 6–0 6–0
Curutchet/Georges (W) 3–6 7–6 6–1
Nagyova/Schnyder 6–2 7–5
Rubin/Schultz-McCarthy 2–6 7–5 6–3
DRAGOMIR/MAJOLI (16) 6–4 6–2
Probst/Sugiyama 6–3 6–1
Loit/Mauresmo (W) 6–3 6–4
ARENDT/BOLLEGRAF (6) 6–1 6–0
HINGIS/SANCHEZ VICARIO (3) 6–3 7–6
Feber/Hy-Boulais 6–4 6–2
Farina/Pizzichini 6–3 3–6 7–5
BOOGERT/SPIRLEA (14) 6–1 6–4
ADAMS/MCNEIL (9) 4–6 6–2 6–4
Paz/Simpson 6–3 6–2
Gorrochategui/Wild 6–3 6–1
BASUKI/VIS (7) 6–3 6–2
M.J. FERNANDEZ/RAYMOND (5) 6–1 6–3
Saeki/Yoshida 7–6 6–3
Callens/Helgeson-Nielsen 7–5 1–6 6–2
FRAZIER/PO (13) 3–6 6–4 6–4
KIJIMUTA/MIYAGI (11) 6–3 6–1
Csurgo/Horn 6–2 6–3
deLone/Zrubakova 6–2 4–6 6–3
NEILAND/SUKOVA (4) 6–2 6–3
FUSAI/TAUZIAT (8) 6–3 6–4
Hiraki/Labat 6–4 6–4
Babel/Golarsa 6–0 6–2
KOURNIKOVA/LIKHOVTSEVA (15) 4–6 6–1 6–4
MARTINEZ/TARABINI (10) 6–3 6–3
Coetzer/Pierce 6–4 6–4
Huber/Seles 6–4 7–5
DAVENPORT/NOVOTNA (2) 6–0 6–1

THIRD ROUND

G. FERNANDEZ/ZVERERA (1) 6–1 6–3
Nagyova/Schnyder 6–1 6–2
DRAGOMIR/MAJOLI (16) 5–7 6–4 6–2
ARENDT/BOLLEGRAF (6) 3–6 6–3 9–7
HINGIS/SANCHEZ VICARIO (3) 6–4 6–0
Farina/Pizzichini 7–5 1–6 6–2
Paz/Simpson 6–4 6–3
BASUKI/VIS (7) 6–3 6–3
M.J. FERNANDEZ/RAYMOND (5) 6–1 6–2
Callens/Helgeson-Nielsen 7–6 6–1
KIJIMUTA/MIYAGI (11) 6–3 6–3
NEILAND/SUKOVA (4) 6–4 6–1
FUSAI/TAUZIAT (8) 6–4 6–3
KOURNIKOVA/LIKHOVTSEVA (15) 8–6 6–1
MARTINEZ/TARABINI (10) w/o
DAVENPORT/NOVOTNA (2) 7–5 7–6

QUARTER-FINALS

G. FERNANDEZ/ZVERERA (1) 6–4 6–2
ARENDT/BOLLEGRAF (6) 5–7 6–4 7–5
HINGIS/SANCHEZ VICARIO (3) 6–4 6–1
BASUKI/VIS (7) 6–4 3–6 6–3
M.J. FERNANDEZ/RAYMOND (5) 4–6 6–3 6–4
NEILAND/SUKOVA (4) 6–1 6–2
FUSAI/TAUZIAT (8) 6–3 6–4
MARTINEZ/TARABINI (10) 5–7 6–4 6–4

SEMI-FINALS

G. FERNANDEZ/ZVERERA (1) 7–6 1–6 6–1
HINGIS/SANCHEZ VICARIO (3) 7–6 7–5
M.J. FERNANDEZ/RAYMOND (5) 6–2 6–3
FUSAI/TAUZIAT (8) 6–2 6–4

FINAL

G. FERNANDEZ/ZVERERA (1) 3–6 7–6 10–8
M.J. FERNANDEZ/RAYMOND (5) 3–6 6–4 6–1

G. FERNANDEZ (USA)/**ZVERERA** (BLR) (1) 6–2 6–3

Capital letters denote seeded players. Numbers following player's name gives seeding order (Q) – Qualifier, (W) – Wild Card, (L) – Lucky Loser

MIXED DOUBLES

Holders: Frana (ARG)/Tarabini (ARG)

FIRST ROUND

1 **GALBRAITH/RAYMOND** (1)
2 bye/
3 Kilderry/Testud
4 Gilbert/Quentrec-Eagle (W)
5 Kronemann/Rinaldi-Stunkel
6 Muller/Van Lottum
7 bye/
8 **OOSTING/BOOGERT** (11)
9 **JOHNSON/SPIRLEA** (10)
10 bye/
11 Keil/Adams
12 Frana/Tarabini
13 MacPherson/McQuillan
14 Kempers/Jeyaseelan
15 bye/
16 **TALBOT/VIS** (5)
17 **LEACH/BOLLEGRAF** (3)
18 bye/
19 Fleurian/Dechaume-Balleret
20 Roux/Sidot (W)
21 Messori/Vildova
22 Van Emburgh/Miyagi
23 bye/
24 **ALBANO/PAZ** (15)
25 **TARANGO/LIKHOVTSEVA** (14)
26 bye/
27 Paes/Dragomir
28 Grabb/Simpson
29 Nyborg/Krizan
30 Nijssen/Basuki
31 bye/
32 **NORVAL/SCHULTZ-McCARTHY** (7)
33 **E. FERREIRA/GRAHAM** (8)
34 bye/
35 Arnold/Montalvo
36 Waite/Helgeson-Nielsen
37 Broad/Pleming
38 Florent/Ellwood
39 bye/
40 **DAVIDS/OREMANS** (13)
41 **PIMEK/GRANDE** (12)
42 bye/
43 Eagle/Wood
44 Middleton/McNeil
45 Bahrami/Sanchez Vicario (W)
46 Bergh/Po
47 bye/
48 **SUK/SUKOVA** (4)
49 **ADAMS/FUSAI** (6)
50 bye/
51 Delaitre/Lamarre (W)
52 Groen/Wagner
53 Davis/Kunce
54 Grosjean/Mauresmo (W)
55 bye/
56 **BHUPATHI/HIRAKI** (16)
57 **KNOWLES/KOURNIKOVA** (9)
58 bye/
59 Kratzmann/Labat
60 L. Jensen/Arendt
61 Stafford/de Swardt
62 Braasch/Rittner
63 bye/
64 **OLHOVSKIY/NEILAND** (2)

SECOND ROUND

GALBRAITH/RAYMOND (1)
Gilbert/Quentrec-Eagle (W) 6–3 6–4
Kronemann/Rinaldi-Stunkel 6–3 7–5
OOSTING/BOOGERT (11)
JOHNSON/SPIRLEA (10)
Frana/Tarabini 6–4 6–1
MacPherson/McQuillan 3–6 6–4 6–2
TALBOT/VIS (5)
LEACH/BOLLEGRAF (3)
Fleurian/Dechaume-Balleret 7–6 6–4
Messori/Vildova 6–3 6–2
ALBANO/PAZ (15)
TARANGO/LIKHOVTSEVA (14)
Paes/Dragomir 6–2 6–0
Nijssen/Basuki 6–3 6–2
NORVAL/SCHULTZ-McCARTHY (7)
E. FERREIRA/GRAHAM (8)
Arnold/Montalvo 7–5 6–4
Broad/Pleming 6–2 6–4
DAVIDS/OREMANS (13)
PIMEK/GRANDE (12)
Middleton/McNeil 6–3 7–5
Bergh/Po 6–1 6–3
SUK/SUKOVA (4)
ADAMS/FUSAI (6)
Delaitre/Lamarre (W) 6–2 6–3
Davis/Kunce 6–7 6–4 6–3
BHUPATHI/HIRAKI (16)
KNOWLES/KOURNIKOVA (9)
Kratzmann/Labat 3–6 7–6 8–6
Braasch/Rittner 6–2 6–4
OLHOVSKIY/NEILAND (2)

THIRD ROUND

GALBRAITH/RAYMOND (1) 4–6 6–2 6–3
Kronemann/Rinaldi-Stunkel 4–6 6–3 6–4
Frana/Tarabini 7–6 6–3
MacPherson/McQuillan 6–4 7–5
LEACH/BOLLEGRAF (3) 6–7 6–3 6–2
ALBANO/PAZ (15) 6–3 7–5
Paes/Dragomir 7–6 6–4
NORVAL/SCHULTZ-McCARTHY (7) 6–3 7–5
E. FERREIRA/GRAHAM (8) 6–4 6–4
DAVIDS/OREMANS (13) 6–4 4–6 6–4
PIMEK/GRANDE (12) 4–6 6–2 6–4
SUK/SUKOVA (4) 6–3 4–6 6–2
ADAMS/FUSAI (6) 7–5 6–2
BHUPATHI/HIRAKI (16) 2–6 6–2 9–7
KNOWLES/KOURNIKOVA (9) 4–6 6–3 9–7
Braasch/Rittner 6–3 7–6

QUARTER-FINALS

GALBRAITH/RAYMOND (1) 6–3 6–3
MacPherson/McQuillan 6–2 7–5
LEACH/BOLLEGRAF (3) 6–2 3–6 6–3
NORVAL/SCHULTZ-McCARTHY (7) w/o
DAVIDS/OREMANS (13) 6–4 6–3
SUK/SUKOVA (4) 4–6 6–1 6–1
BHUPATHI/HIRAKI (16) 3–6 7–6 6–4
KNOWLES/KOURNIKOVA (9) 6–4 1–6 7–5

SEMI-FINALS

GALBRAITH/RAYMOND (1) 6–3 6–4
LEACH/BOLLEGRAF (3) 6–2 6–4
SUK/SUKOVA (4) 6–2 6–3
BHUPATHI/HIRAKI (16) 7–5 6–0

FINAL

GALBRAITH/RAYMOND (1) 4–6 6–2 6–3
BHUPATHI/HIRAKI (16) 6–4 6–4

BHUPATHI (IND)/**HIRAKI** (JPN) (16) 6–4 6–1

Capital letters denote seeded players. Numbers following player's name gives seeding order (Q) – Qualifier, (W) – Wild Card, (L) – Lucky Loser

had little left to offer in the final. Majoli deservedly became, at No. 9, the lowest seed to win at Roland Garros since Britain's Peggy Scriven in 1933.

In the doubles Fernandez and Zvereva, re-united after a year's separation, won their 13th Grand Slam title with a 6–2 6–3 victory over Mary Joe Fernandez and Lisa Raymond.

So ended a meeting of memorable upsets which had been witnessed by record crowds of 364,907, an increase of some 1,500 over the previous year's total.

JUNIOR EVENTS

BOYS' SINGLES – Final: Daniel Elsner (GER) (1) d. Luis Horna (PER)(2) 6–4 6–4
GIRLS' SINGLES – Final: Justine Henin (BEL) d. Clara Black (ZIM) 4–6 6–4 6–4
BOYS' DOUBLES – Final: Jose de Armas (VEN)/Luis Horna (PER) d. Arnaud di Pasquale (FRA)/Julien Jeanpierre (FRA) 6–4 2–6 7–5
GIRLS' DOUBLES – Final: Clara Black (ZIM)/Irina Selyutina (KAZ) (1) d. Maia Matevzic (SLO)/Katerina Srebotnik (SLO) (2) 6–0 5–7 7–5

FRENCH OPEN CHAMPIONSHIPS
PRIZE MONEY – 56,985,800FF

MEN – Total: 28,408,400

MEN'S SINGLES – Winner 3,668,000. Runner-up 1,834,000. Semi-finalists 917,000. Quarter-finalists 483,500. Fourth-round losers 259,000. Third-round losers 150,000. Second-round losers 91,700. First-round losers 55,250.
Total: 20,212,400

MEN'S DOUBLES (per team) – Winners 1,508,000. Runners-up 754,000. Semi-finalists 377,000. Quarter-finalists 191,800. Third-round losers 109,400. Second-round losers 54,700. First-round losers 37,200.
Total: 6,724,000

MEN'S QUALIFYING (each) – 16 x Third-round losers 30,000. 32 x Second-round losers 15,000. 64 x First-round losers 8,000.
Total: 1,472,000

WOMEN – Total: 23,396,200

WOMEN'S SINGLES – Winner 3,450,000. Runner-up 1,725,000. Semi-finalists 862,500. Quarter-finalists 431,250. Fourth-round losers 221,000. Third-round losers 123,800. Second-round losers 74,400. First-round losers 45,700.
Total: 17,666,600

WOMEN'S DOUBLES (per team) – Winners 1,182,400. Runners-up 591,200. Semi-finalists 295,500. Quarter-finalists 150,200. Third-round losers 76,500. Second-round losers 40,700. First-round losers 23,900.
Total: 4,993,600

WOMEN'S QUALIFYING (each) – 8 x Third-round losers 30,000. 16 x Second-round losers 15,000. 32 x First-round losers 8,000.
Total: 736,000

MIXED DOUBLES (per team) – Winners 330,000. Runners-up 198,000. Semi-finalists 118,500. Quarter-finalists 72,500. Second-round losers 39,300. First-round losers 17,300.
Total: 1,646,200

Per Diem allowances (estimated total): 3,445,000F

Re-imposing his authority (which had been rudely interrupted by Richard Krajicek in 1996), Pete Sampras claimed his fourth Wimbledon title in five years. (Tommy Hindley)

The Championships – Wimbledon

John Barrett

It was a fortnight of fabulous firsts: a first look at Wimbledon's three new courts – numbers 1, 18 and 19; the first year of the new Broadcast Centre; the first use of the terraced picnic area; a first singles success for the teenage Swiss miss, Martina Hingis; a double first for the two first seeds – Hingis and Pete Sampras; plus a first doubles five-timer this century for the Woodies – Australia's Todd Woodbridge and Mark Woodforde...oh yes, and a not so fabulous first week of relentless rain.

That the 111th Championship meeting splashed to completion on time was something of a miracle. After the wettest first five days in the tournament's history (only 94 matches were completed instead of the normal 300), the men's doubles was reduced to the best of three sets until the quarter-finals and the boys' and girls' doubles fields halved to 16 pairs. Only two matches were completed on the first Wednesday and none at all on the Thursday and Friday – another dismal record for three consecutive days that tested the patience of players, spectators and Championship Referee Alan Mills to the limit. It was no surprise when, for the second time in seven years, play was scheduled on the middle Sunday with matches on the succeeding days commencing at 11.00 am. Before play began on the first day the new No.1 Court witnessed a parade of 10 of Wimbledon's greatest former champions, all of whom had won the singles at least three times. Accompanied by the Central Band of the Royal Air Force playing 'Purple & Green' they marched on with a team of Wimbledon ballboys and ballgirls carrying the flags of the 58 nations represented in the Championships.

It was a moving occasion as the crowd applauded Louise Brough (4 wins), Rod Laver (4), Margaret Court (3), Billie Jean King (6), John Newcombe (3), Chris Evert (3), Martina Navratilova (9), John McEnroe (3), Boris Becker (3) and Pete Sampras (3) who each came forward to receive a suitably engraved silver salver from the All England Club's President, His Royal Highness the Duke of Kent, who then declared the court open.

He was only just in time. Within 15 minutes the first rain of the Championships fell, interrupting the warm-up of Britain's Tim Henman, the No.14 seed, who had been given the honour of playing the first match in the new 11,500 seat stadium against the Canadian left-hander, Daniel Nestor.

Henman's straight sets victory was the prelude to another splendid run to the quarter-finals. As Greg Rusedski fought through to join him there – a career-best Grand Slam performance this for the Canadian-born left-hander – national enthusiasm ran riot. For the first time since 1961, when Bobby Wilson and Mike Sangster had achieved this feat, two British men were in the last eight and it seemed that fate had decreed they should meet in the semi-finals.

Rusedski had played brilliantly on day two to complete a straight sets win on Centre Court against Australia's No.7 seed Mark Philippoussis, the man whose tremendous serve had earned him the nickname 'Scud'. Over the two days Rusedski's own explosive delivery, equally fast and spiced with left-handed spin, had been superior.

Not until Saturday did Rusedski return to court – this time on No.1 – to play America's Jonathan Stark who had been good enough to beat Jim Courier in the first round twelve months earlier. Rusedski's emotion-packed recovery from two sets to love down to win 11–9 in the fifth set as darkness was falling was the stuff of legend. This was a raging battle between two men who refused to submit. Each served 36 aces and Rusedski's delay after an anguished outburst against a line decision at 4–5 0–30 in the opening set had earned him a time warning. 'Why do you do this to me?' he cried, his face contorted in frustration. Afterwards he recognised that fate was impartial. 'Sometimes the calls go with you, sometimes not,' he said, 'but it's better to get the emotion out of you'.

This was the first of many thrilling encounters in the new stadium that was already receiving praise from competitors and spectators alike for the firm playing surface and the comfort of the seats. Sadly, the Centre Court did not perform to its usual high standard. Wearing much more quickly than usual it looked patchy early in the second week and produced the odd bad bounce.

The wildly partisan behaviour of the noisy middle Sunday crowd in the famous arena was something of an embarrassment during the climax of Henman's thrilling 3 hour 58 minute battle against 63rd ranked Paul Haarhuis of Holland. Drunk with success as Henman fought off two match points to win the towering fifth set in the 26th game, the 13,000 crowd, most of whom had queued all night, erupted to become a swaying sea of flag-waving, arm-flailing patriots. Throughout this compelling encounter they had chanted 'Hen-man, Hen-man, Hen-man' – often applauding the 31-year-old Dutchman's mistakes – for all the world like a football crowd at Stamford Bridge exulting in an unexpected Chelsea win in the European Cup.

Henman admitted that the fervent support had played a large part in his win. 'The atmosphere created by the crowd was something I've never experienced before. It was at a totally different level to last year when I beat Kafelnikov,' said Henman. 'That's as good as it gets in tennis.' Good for the player perhaps but, at this level of insensitive intensity, bad for the sport.

While Henman was beating Haarhuis, Rusedski was pounding down unplayable serves to eliminate another Briton, the newest Davis Cup recruit, Andrew Richardson. Meanwhile on Court 7 Mark Petchey was completing an excellent win against the young German Tommy Haas to become the fourth British man in the third round, the first time there had been as many since open tennis arrived in 1968. Improbably, there were more Britons than Americans left at this stage. With only 14 men in the original draw, three of them qualifiers, American representation was the thinnest it has been since 1953 when 11 had competed. The first round losses of Michael Chang (5) and Jim Courier, whose match against Michael Stich had thrilled the first day crowd on Court No.1 – plus nine others, left only Sampras, Alex O'Brien and Richey Reneberg to fly the Stars and Stripes.

On the second Tuesday Reneberg became Rusedski's next victim on Court No.1 while on Centre Court Henman took on defending champion Richard Krajicek. The Dutchman had been controversially left out of the original seedings last year but this time was in at No.4. The atmosphere was only marginally more respectable than it had been for Henman's battle with Haarhuis. At 8.39 pm, with Henman leading 7–6 6–7 7–6, failing light forced a halt. On the morrow, playing with rare authority, the British No.1 coolly won the fourth set 6–4 after an anxious Krajicek had missed crucial volleys on his serve in the fifth game.

In the quarter-finals, played a day later than usual on the second Thursday, five of the men were unseeded – as in 1996, the first time so many had intruded. There were also three Germans among the elite eight for the first time at any Grand Slam in the open era – Stich, Becker and Nicolas Kiefer, one of Becker's first selections for his new Mercedes Benz squad, whose four sets victory over No.3 seed Yevgeny Kafelnikov had already stamped him as a man of the future.

Becker himself figured in the dream match of the round. His much anticipated meeting against Sampras who had won 10 of their 17 previous meetings fully lived up to our expectations. The 29-year-old German was running hot. He had been elevated to eighth seed despite a ranking of 18 on the strength of his amazing Wimbledon record – three wins from seven finals plus two semi-final finishes in 13 challenges.

Becker had not conceded a set in beating Gorriz, Johansson, Petchey and Rios. Sampras, by contrast, had got himself into trouble against the mercurial Czech Petr Korda. After winning the first two sets Sampras had dropped the next two and had survived only narrowly in a ten game final set.

On the day Sampras was cool and focused, playing in the form that had made him invincible at Wimbledon between 1993 and 1995. Despite a purple patch from Becker that won him the second set, the American, four years younger and marginally faster, won going away 6–1 6–7 6–1 6–4. As Becker left Centre Court to a standing ovation he turned, paused as the memories flooded over him and gave one last wave to the delighted crowd. In that moment you knew that he would never be back. The boy of 17 who had been the youngest-ever champion in 1985 had been through a lifetime of emotions in the 12 years since. He knew he had run his course. Later in the day Becker announced his retirement from The Championships.

'I feel it's the right moment for me,' he said. 'I feel very relieved. I've come to the end of the road with my head held high. I always wanted to go out on top and that's where I feel I am right now.' A glorious chapter of Wimbledon history had ended.

The first meeting between four-time doubles champion Todd Woodbridge and the 20-year-old Kiefer, ranked 88, two of the five unseeded men in the last eight, was a contest of promise versus experience. It was no surprise that Woodbridge, 41 places higher in the rankings, should have won. But over the course of four sets it was easy to see why Becker had picked the talented Kiefer to be among the first intake of his new squad.

Australia's popular 'Woodies', Todd Woodbridge and Mark Woodforde won a fifth consecutive Wimbledon doubles title together to put themselves among the greatest doubles pairs of all time. (Michael Cole)

In the lower half British hopes, sky high as the result of intense media hype, were dashed on the rocks of talent and experience. Stich, the 1991 champion and a finalist at the US Open three years later, made light of the shoulder condition that had caused him to announce that he would retire at the end of 1997. The 28-year-old German was simply too good in all departments for an off-form Henman. The expectant crowd on Court No.1 was never given anything to cheer. If Henman had served at his best he might have gone close. He didn't and Stich was therefore given no problems as he sailed through to the semi-finals 6–3 6–2 6–4.

There he met Cedric Pioline, ranked 44, who had been too efficient on return of serve for a below par Rusedski. The unseeded Frenchman, a US Open finalist in 1993, had confirmed his ability on grass by beating Wayne Ferreira, South Africa's No.15 seed, and Brett Steven. The unseeded New Zealander had emerged from the bottom quarter where No.2 seed Goran Ivanisevic had lost 14–12 in the final set to Magnus Norman in the second round and had then stormed off without attending the obligatory press conference, thus incurring an automatic fine.

Sadly, Rusedski looked flat and tired. On another day of early starts there were few spectators on No.1 Court to see the British left-hander take the second set. He was also much too and brittle against an opponent who served well and displayed exquisite volleying skills as he moved ahead 6–4 4–6 6–4 6–3.

Not since 1967 had there been three unseeded semi-finalists (if you allow that in 1996 Krajicek was, after all, a seed). As in that last year of amateur tennis when John Newcombe had ultimately prevailed, the lone seed won the title. Sampras swept aside Woodbridge 6–2 6–1 7–6 and was equally severe in the final against Pioline. His 6–4 6–2 6–4 victory brought him a prize of £415,000 and revealed the gulf that separates the current world No.1 from his challengers. If the Frenchman could have returned serve as he had done against Stich in a glorious semi-final, then there might have been an outside chance of victory.

That semi-final, won by Pioline 6–7 6–2 6–1 5–7 6–4, was the match of the Championships, full of passion and furious commitment from two all-court players whose piercing service returns were matched by first volleys of the highest class. The battle raged for almost three hours, three glorious hours of cut and thrust that had the crowd fully involved until the last ball. 'I'm so happy,' said the winner, who became the first French finalist since the 1946 champion Yvon Petra. 'I was so nervous in the fifth...I've lost some long matches like that one... and I'm so tired...all I want to do is to go back to the hotel and sleep.'

'The atmosphere was fantastic,' said Stich. '...our bodies were on court but our minds were floating. Matches like this are very rare and I was very happy to be part of this one.' It was a fitting end to the 1991 champion's Wimbledon career.

In a one-sided final that lasted a bare 94 minutes Sampras served 17 aces bringing his tournament total to 119. That part of his game was rock solid, as it had been all fortnight. Only twice in 24 sets was he broken. 'It was the shot that won me the tournament,' he agreed afterwards, '...but in order to win here you need to return and that was also a great shot I was hitting...and I was passing quite well...but this is the best I've ever served in my career.'

Add to that his concentration, plus his speed of movement and reflex that enabled him to execute so many crushing volleys – all timed to perfection as he sped effortlessly into position – and you begin to understand the measure of his superiority. This fourth title was a 10th Grand Slam success for Sampras and brought him level with fellow American Bill Tilden in the all-time list of winners. Only his boyhood idol Laver and Bjorn Borg with 11 each, and Roy Emerson with 12, have won more. Sampras is fully aware of the game's history and has often said he would like to be remembered for the number of major titles he accumulates. Aged 25 and playing as well as he is there seems no reason why he cannot become the most successful collector of Grand Slam titles in the game's history.

The women's event suffered from the late withdrawal of defending champion and seven-time winner Steffi Graf. The popular German had celebrated her 28th birthday on 14 June in a hospital bed following surgery on her right knee. During 29 years of open tennis only three other champions had failed to defend their titles – Billie Jean King in 1976, Ann Jones in 1970 and Evonne Goolagong Cawley in 1981.

Instead of harming The Championships, Graf's absence seemed to inspire a group of exciting young players to rise to the challenge. For the first time in the open era four teenagers reached the last eight. None was more impressive than the 16-year-old world No.1 and eventual champion Martina Hingis. Ever since she became the youngest-ever Wimbledon winner in 1996 when, aged 15 years 282 days, she had won the doubles title with Helena Sukova, this remarkable Swiss teenager has been setting new records. 'That was the moment when I realised I could beat the great players,' she had said.

This year she has been proving it. A first Grand Slam title in Australia, following a win in Sydney, was part of a six tournament streak that had brought her 31 match wins by the first week in April. Two weeks later, on 21 April, she was involved in a riding accident that required arthroscopic surgery on an injured left knee and forced her to miss tournaments in Rome and Berlin. Going into the French Open with no competition for seven weeks Hingis had done well to reach the final where Iva Majoli had ended her winning streak at 37.

Majoli (4), one of four seeded players to reach the quarter-finals, was rather lucky to be there since she had been match point down to Britain's Karen Cross in the third round. Her opponent, the precociously talented 16-year-old Russian, Anna Kournikova, a Wimbledon newcomer, had also survived dangerously. In her second round match against Barbara Rittner of Germany she had saved two match points at 3–5 in the second set. Buoyed by that success she had then knocked out another German, 7th seeded Anke Huber in the third round.

Dressed provocatively against Majoli and christened 'Lolita' by the media, Kournikova was the focus of attention as she blasted aside the new French champion 7–6 6–4 with a display of fierce driving that was remarkable for its maturity.

Kournikova's prize was a semi-final against Hingis whose 6–3 6–2 destruction of the unseeded Czech 18-year-old Denisa Chladkova, a friend from junior days in Czechoslovakia, meant that the world No.1 had conceded a miserly 25 games in five matches.

Despite some entertaining rallies played at breakneck pace, Kournikova could not match Hingis's consistency and went down 6–3 6–2. Nine months younger than Hingis, Kournikova is light years behind in poise and professionalism. Thus Hingis had moved into her third consecutive Grand Slam final.

In the lower half the No.3 seed, 28-year-old Jana Novotna of the Czech Republic, emerged to her third Wimbledon semi-final with a 6–3 6–3 win against Yayuk Basuki. The 26th ranked Indonesian had reached the fourth round four times before but this was her first taste of a Grand Slam quarter-final. The difference in experience and ability on fast grass was all too apparent.

Novotna's semi-final opponent was Arantxa Sanchez Vicario, the finalist of the previous two years, who had dropped only 20 games in five matches. In the quarter-final the Spaniard had scored a 6–2 7–5 win over the 29-year-old Frenchwoman, Nathalie Tauziat, whose presence there was somewhat fortunate since she had survived a match point against compatriot Sandrine Testud in the previous round. How different it all might have been if No.2 seed Monica Seles had converted the match point she had held against Testud in round three!

Novotna handled the pressure of a semi-final rather better than Sanchez Vicario who looked slightly nervous as she went down 6–4 6–2. Did this mean that Novotna had forgotten the trauma of that notorious 4–1 lead in the third set of her final against Graf in 1993?

It appeared she had as she volleyed her way into a 4–0 lead against Hingis and pocketed the opening set 6–2 in 22 minutes, despite an abdominal muscle pull sustained in her semi-final. But the unflappable Hingis merely tightened her game. Taking her passing shots noticeably earlier she began too find gaps down the lines.

One break of serve in the sixth game brought her level and after recovering from 0–2 in the final set she sailed imperiously to a 2–6 6–3 6–3 victory on a tide of perfectly placed drives and crisply hit volley winners that left Novotna groping at thin air. 'It's like a dream come true,' said the young champion. 'There was a great atmosphere out there...maybe tomorrow I'll realise I won this tournament...but it was great.'

This second Grand Slam success, planned and plotted with painstaking care by her mother and coach, Melanie, had taken an hour and 50 minutes and had netted the new champion £373,500. After just two and a half years on the Tour her on-court earnings were already approaching the $4 million mark and there seemed no reason why she would not one day surpass the record total of $20.3 million amassed by the great champion after whom her mother had consciously named her, Martina Navratilova.

Woodbridge and Woodforde achieved a personal goal by equalling the record of five consecutive doubles titles set by the famous Doherty brothers, Laurie and Reggie, between 1897 and 1901. They were too solid in the many crises of a hotly disputed final against the Dutchmen Jacco Eltingh and Paul Haarhuis, winning 7–6 7–6 5–7 6–3. Down 2–4 in the first set the Woodies won it on a tie-break 7 points to 4. Down three sets points in the second tie-break they won that one 9–7. At 5–3 40–0 on Woodbridge's serve and then at advantage they squandered four Championship points and lost the set 7–5. 'At the Olympics we had a 40–0 game against them as well and the same thing happened,' remembered Woodbridge. 'We lost the serve and went on to win 16–14 ... that was going through my mind...it made me nervous.'

The women's doubles title went to top seeds Gigi Fernandez and Natasha Zvereva, 7–6 6–4 winners over America's Nicole Arendt and Manon Bollegraf of Holland who were playing in their first Grand Slam final. This fourth win in six years, coming on top of a fifth French win during the same period, was especially pleasing for a pair who had re-united in the spring after deciding to part last year.

Cyril Suk and his sister Helena Sukova, seeded four, retained their mixed title with a 4–6 6–3 6–4 victory over the No.3 seeds Andrei Olhovskiy of Russia and his Latvian partner Larisa Neiland – another first for a brother and sister combination.

Despite the appalling weather 436,531 spectators attended the meeting, a tournament record. Even without the 31,204 who attended on the middle Sunday, the total was within 6,000 of the previous record of 411,270 in 1988 when play was carried over to a third Monday.

MEN'S SINGLES

Holder: R. Krajicek (NED)

FIRST ROUND

1 **P. SAMPRAS** (USA) (1)
2 M. Tillstrom (SWE)
3 H. Dreekmann (GER)
4 P. Fredriksson (SWE)
5 D.E. Sapsford (GBR) (W)
6 N. Pereira (VEN) (L)
7 B. Black (ZIM)
8 P. Cash (AUS) (Q)
9 H. Holm (SWE)
10 A. O'Brien (USA)
11 N. Godwin (RSA)
12 H.J. Davids (NED) (Q)
13 M. Rosset (SUI)
14 K. Kucera (SVK)
15 M. Filippini (URU)
16 **P. KORDA** (CZE) (16)
17 **M. RIOS** (CHI) (9)
18 M. Bhupathi (IND) (Q)
19 D. Van Scheppingen (NED)
20 R. Fromberg (AUS)
21 O. Stanoytchev (BUL)
22 J. Van Lottum (NED) (Q)
23 J. Siemerink (NED)
24 R. Furlan (ITA)
25 C. Ruud (NOR)
26 T. Haas (GER)
27 M.R.J. Petchey (GBR) (W)
28 J. Kroslak (SVK)
29 D. Hrbaty (SVK)
30 T. Johansson (SWE)
31 M. Gorriz (ESP)
32 **B. BECKER** (GER) (8)
33 **Y. KAFELNIKOV** (RUS) (3)
34 J. Marin (ESP)
35 M. Tebbutt (AUS) (Q)
36 J. Sanchez (ESP)
37 N. Kulti (SWE)
38 M. Sinner (GER)
39 O. Burrieza (ESP) (Q)
40 J. Stoltenberg (AUS)
41 J. Salzenstein (USA) (Q)
42 P. Baur (GER) (Q)
43 A. Volkov (RUS)
44 N. Kiefer (GER)
45 S. Sargsian (ARM)
46 J. Van Herck (BEL)
47 F. Santoro (FRA)
48 **A. MEDVEDEV** (UKR) (13)
49 **P. RAFTER** (AUS) (12)
50 G. Stafford (RSA)
51 W. McGuire (USA) (Q)
52 J. Knippschild (GER)
53 C. Van Garsse (BEL) (Q)
54 N. Weal (GBR) (W)
55 M. Gustafsson (SWE)
56 V. Spadea (USA)
57 A. Voinea (ROM)
58 A. Radulescu (GER)
59 M. Martelli (ITA)
60 B. Karbacher (GER)
61 S. Schalken (NED)
62 M. Ondruska (RSA)
63 T.A. Woodbridge (AUS)
64 **M. CHANG** (USA) (5)

SECOND ROUND

SAMPRAS (1) 6–4 6–4 6–2
Dreekmann 6–3 6–4 6–3
Sapsford (W) 3–6 6–2 7–6 6–3
Black 3–6 7–6 6–4 6–4
O'Brien 7–6 6–4 7–6
Godwin 7–5 7–6 6–3
Rosset 7–6 6–2 6–3
KORDA (16) 4–6 7–6 6–1 6–4
RIOS (9) 6–4 6–4 6–3
Van Scheppingen 5–7 6–4 3–6 6–1 6–4
Van Lottum (Q) 3–6 2–6 6–3 6–1 6–3
Furlan 6–7 6–7 6–4 6–4 6–4
Haas 6–2 6–1 6–2
Petchey (W) 6–1 6–2 6–1
Johansson 7–5 6–3 6–1
BECKER (8) 6–3 6–2 6–3
KAFELNIKOV (3) 6–4 6–2 6–0
Sanchez 3–6 4–6 6–4 7–5 14–12
Kulti 7–6 6–2 6–3
Stoltenberg 6–3 6–4 6–3
Baur (Q) 7–6 3–6 3–6 6–4 9–7
Kiefer 6–4 6–4 6–2
Sargsian 7–6 6–2 6–4
MEDVEDEV (13) 6–2 6–3 6–4
RAFTER (12) 2–6 4–6 6–3 6–2 6–2
Knippschild 6–4 6–4 6–4
Van Garsse (Q) 6–1 7–6 7–6
Gustafsson 6–2 6–1 6–1
Radulescu 7–6 3–6 6–1 3–6 6–4
Martelli 6–4 6–3 6–1
Ondruska 3–6 7–5 6–0 0–1 Ret'd.
Woodbridge 7–6 3–6 6–2 3–6 8–6

THIRD ROUND

SAMPRAS (1) 7–6 7–5 7–5
Black 6–2 7–5 6–2
O'Brien 6–3 6–3 6–7 7–6
KORDA (16) 6–3 6–0 7–6
RIOS (9) 6–2 6–3 6–7 7–6
Van Lottum (Q) 6–3 6–3 6–3
Petchey (W) 7–6 6–4 6–2
BECKER (8) 6–1 6–4 6–4
KAFELNIKOV (3) 6–2 4–6 6–3 6–4
Stoltenberg 6–2 3–6 6–2 6–3
Kiefer 7–5 7–6 6–1
MEDVEDEV (13) 6–1 6–4 7–5
RAFTER (12) 6–3 4–6 6–3 6–0
Van Garsse (Q) 6–4 6–4 6–1
Radulescu 6–3 7–5 6–4
Woodbridge 7–5 6–1 7–6

FOURTH ROUND

SAMPRAS (1) 6–1 6–2 6–2
KORDA (16) 6–3 4–6 6–3 6–7 6–4
RIOS (9) 7–6 6–3 6–7 6–4
BECKER (8) 6–3 6–3 6–2
KAFELNIKOV (3) 6–3 7–6 4–6 6–3
Kiefer 6–4 6–2 6–7 6–4
RAFTER (12) 7–5 6–4 4–6 6–3
Woodbridge 6–4 6–4 6–4

QUARTER-FINALS

SAMPRAS (1) 6–4 6–3 6–7 6–7 6–4
BECKER (8) 6–2 6–2 7–6
Kiefer 6–2 7–5 2–6 6–1
Woodbridge 6–7 6–4 7–6 6–3

SEMI-FINALS

SAMPRAS (1) 6–1 6–7 6–1 6–4
Woodbridge 7–6 2–6 6–0 6–4

FINAL

SAMPRAS (1) 6–2 6–1 7–6

6–4 6–2 6–4

65 **J. BJORKMAN** (SWE) (17)
66 C. Wilkinson (GBR) (W)
67 M. Woodforde (AUS)
68 L. Paes (IND)
69 A. Clement (FRA) (Q)
70 L. Milligan (GBR) (W)
71 N. Marques (POR)
72 M. Lee (GBR) (W)
73 K. Carlsen (DEN)
74 E. Alvarez (ESP)
75 S. Stolle (AUS)
76 C. Woodruff (USA)
77 M. Stich (GER)
78 J. Courier (USA)
79 J. Gimelstob (USA)
80 **G. KUERTEN** (BRA) (11)
81 **T. HENMAN** (GBR) (14)
82 D. Nestor (CAN)
83 J. Delgado (GBR) (W)
84 J. Golmard (FRA)
85 S. Dosedel (CZE)
86 T. Larkham (AUS) (Q)
87 S. Lareau (CAN)
88 P. Haarhuis (NED)
89 N. Lapentti (ECU)
90 F. Clavet (ESP)
91 D. Rikl (CZE) (Q)
92 D. Vacek (CZE)
93 A. Pavel (ROM)
94 F. Dewulf (BEL)
95 M. Craca (GER)
96 **R. KRAJICEK** (NED) (4)
97 **M. PHILIPPOUSSIS** (AUS) (7)
98 G. Rusedski (GBR)
99 S. Huet (FRA) (L)
100 J. Stark (USA)
101 A.L. Richardson (GBR) (W)
102 S. Duran (ESP) (Q)
103 J. Viloca (ESP)
104 M. Goellner (GER)
105 B. Ellwood (AUS) (L)
106 D. Flach (USA)
107 G. Raoux (FRA)
108 A. Boetsch (FRA)
109 H. Arazi (MAR)
110 R.A. Reneberg (USA)
111 S. Bryan (USA) (L)
112 **C. MOYA** (ESP) (10)
113 **W. FERREIRA** (RSA) (15)
114 S. Draper (AUS)
115 J. Tarango (USA)
116 R. Gilbert (FRA) (Q)
117 J. Frana (ARG)
118 M. Damm (CZE)
119 M. Charpentier (ARG)
120 C. Pioline (FRA)
121 F. Fetterlein (DEN)
122 J. Novak (CZE)
123 L. Roux (FRA)
124 B. Steven (NZL)
125 M. Norman (SWE)
126 L.E. Herrera (MEX) (Q)
127 D. Pescariu (ROM)
128 **G. IVANISEVIC** (CRO) (2)

Wilkinson (W) 7–6 0–6 5–7 6–3 6–4
Woodforde 6–3 7–5 6–4
Clement (Q) 2–6 7–6 7–5 6–2
Lee (W) 7–5 6–3 6–3
Alvarez 6–7 3–6 6–4 6–1 6–2
Stolle 6–2 6–2 6–4
Stich 7–6 7–5 7–6
Gimelstob 6–3 6–4 4–6 1–6 6–4
HENMAN (14) 7–6 6–1 6–4
Golmard 6–4 6–2 6–7 6–2
Larkham (Q) 6–7 6–3 6–4 7–5
Haarhuis 6–1 6–2 7–6
Clavet 7–5 6–1 6–3
Rikl (Q) 6–1 6–3 6–3
Pavel 6–1 4–6 2–6 6–2 6–3
KRAJICEK (4) 7–6 6–2 6–4
Rusedski 7–6 7–6 6–3
Stark 7–6 6–7 6–3 2–6 6–3
Richardson (W) 7–6 6–3 6–3
Viloca 7–5 4–6 7–6 7–6
Flach 6–1 7–6 3–6 6–4
Raoux 6–3 6–4 6–1
Reneberg 7–6 6–4 7–6
MOYA (10) 7–6 6–3 4–6 6–2
FERREIRA (15) 6–7 3–6 6–4 6–0 7–5
Gilbert (Q) 3–6 7–5 7–6 6–4
Frana 6–7 6–4 6–3 6–2
Pioline 5–7 6–3 7–5 6–2
Fetterlein 4–6 3–6 6–4 7–6 6–4
Steven 6–2 6–2 7–6
Norman 7–6 6–1 6–4
IVANISEVIC (2) 6–1 6–3 6–3

Woodforde 5–7 5–7 6–2 6–4 6–1
Clement (Q) 4–6 6–2 6–3 6–4
Stolle 6–4 6–4 6–4
Stich 7–5 6–1 6–1
HENMAN (14) 7–6 6–3 6–3
Haarhuis 3–6 6–3 6–1 6–2
Rikl (Q) 6–4 7–6 6–4
KRAJICEK (4) 3–6 6–4 6–7 6–3 6–3
Rusedski 4–6 6–7 6–4 6–3 11–9
Richardson (W) 6–3 3–6 6–4 2–6 6–2
Raoux 6–3 6–7 6–3 6–1
Reneberg 6–4 6–3 6–3
FERREIRA (15) 7–6 4–6 6–3 3–6 9–7
Pioline w/o
Steven 4–6 7–5 6–3 6–2
Norman 6–3 2–6 7–6 4–6 14–12

Woodforde 6–2 6–3 6–3
Stich 6–3 6–7 6–2 7–6
HENMAN (14) 6–7 6–3 6–2 4–6 14–12
KRAJICEK (4) 6–4 6–3 7–5
Rusedski 6–3 6–4 6–4
Reneberg 7–5 6–7 7–6 6–3
Pioline 6–4 6–3 6–3
Steven 6–7 6–2 6–3 6–1

Stich 6–4 6–7 6–3 7–5
HENMAN (14) 7–6 6–7 7–6 6–4
Rusedski 7–6 6–4 7–6
Pioline 3–6 6–3 6–4 7–5

Stich 6–3 6–2 6–4
Pioline 6–4 4–6 6–4 6–3

Pioline 6–7 6–2 6–1 5–7 6–4

SAMPRAS (

Capital letters denote seeded players. Numbers following player's name gives seeding order (Q) – Qualifier, (W) – Wild Card, (L) – Lucky Loser

WOMEN'S SINGLES

Holder: S. Graf (GER)

FIRST ROUND	SECOND ROUND	THIRD ROUND	FOURTH ROUND	QUARTER-FINALS	SEMI-FINALS	FINAL
1 **M. HINGIS** (SUI) (1)	**HINGIS** (1)					
2 A.L. Kremer (LUX) (Q)	6–4 6–4	**HINGIS** (1)				
3 P. Begerow (GER)	Barabanschikova	6–2 6–2				
4 O. Barabanschikova (BLR)	6–3 6–3		**HINGIS** (1)			
5 E. Martincova (CZE)	Raymond		6–1 6–3			
6 L.M. Raymond (USA)	6–4 6–2	Arendt				
7 N.J. Arendt (USA)	Arendt	1–6 6–4 6–3				
8 P. Langrova (CZE)	6–2 6–0			**HINGIS** (1)		
9 L. Golarsa (ITA) (Q)	Golarsa (Q)			6–1 6–3		
10 A. Dechaume-Balleret (FRA)	6–1 4–6 6–3	Appelmans				
11 S. Appelmans (BEL)	Appelmans	6–2 6–0				
12 R. Simpson (CAN)	6–2 3–6 6–0		Appelmans			
13 S. Cacic (USA)	Frazier		6–2 6–3			
14 A. Frazier (USA)	7–5 6–4	**SCHULTZ-McCARTHY** (14)				
15 S. Farina (ITA)	**SCHULTZ-McCARTHY** (14)	7–6 6–3				
16 **B. SCHULTZ-McCARTHY** (NED) (14)	5–6 6–3 6–2				**HINGIS** (1)	
17 **R. DRAGOMIR** (ROM) (15)	Glass				6–3 6–2	
18 A. Glass (GER)	5–7 6–2 10–8	Vento (Q)				
19 A. Ellwood (AUS)	Vento (Q)	2–1 Ret'd.				
20 M.A. Vento (VEN) (Q)	7–5 6–1		Vento (Q)			
21 G. Helgeson-Nielsen (USA)	Helgeson-Nielsen		6–2 7–5			
22 L.A. Ahl (GBR) (W)	6–2 6–4	Maleeva				
23 M. Maleeva (BUL)	Maleeva	7–5 7–5				
24 J.M. Pullin (GBR) (W)	6–1 6–3			Chladkova		
25 K. Studenikova (SVK)	Pratt (Q)			6–1 6–3		
26 N.J. Pratt (AUS) (Q)	6–3 4–6 6–3	Zrubakova				
27 R. Zrubakova (SVK)	Zrubakova	6–4 7–5				
28 N. Feber (BEL) (Q)	6–1 7–5		Chladkova			
29 D. Chladkova (CZE)	Chladkova		6–7 6–3 8–6			
30 S. Kleinova (CZE)	7–6 6–4	Chladkova				
31 T.S. Jones (USA)	**DAVENPORT** (5)	7–5 6–2				
32 **L.A. DAVENPORT** (USA) (5)	5–7 6–2 6–2					**HINGIS** (1)
33 **I. MAJOLI** (CRO) (4)	**MAJOLI** (4)					6–3 6–2
34 M. Diaz-Oliva (ARG)	2–6 6–0 6–3	**MAJOLI** (4)				
35 M. Maruska (AUT)	Maruska	6–3 6–3				
36 A. Gersi (CZE)	7–6 6–4		**MAJOLI** (4)			
37 K.M. Cross (GBR) (Q)	Cross (Q)		4–6 7–6 6–4			
38 L.M. Wild (USA)	6–4 6–2	Cross (Q)				
39 F. Perfetti (ITA)	Sanchez-Lorenzo	6–4 6–0				
40 M. Sanchez-Lorenzo (ESP)	6–4 6–4			**MAJOLI** (4)		
41 G. Fernandez (USA) (W)	Fernandez (W)			6–7 6–1 9–7		
42 M. Oremans (NED)	7–6 6–3	Fernandez (W)				
43 N. Dechy (FRA)	Dechy	6–3 4–6 6–3				
44 L. Courtois (BEL)	6–7 6–1 6–2		**SPIRLEA** (12)			
45 E. Makarova (RUS)	Makarova		6–3 6–1			
46 T. Panova (RUS)	6–4 4–6 6–3	**SPIRLEA** (12)				
47 H. Nagyova (SVK)	**SPIRLEA** (12)	4–6 6–1 10–8				
48 **I. SPIRLEA** (ROM) (12)	6–1 6–0				Kournikova	
49 **C. MARTINEZ** (ESP) (10)	**MARTINEZ** (10)				7–6 6–4	
50 K. Habsudova (SVK)	6–1 6–2	**MARTINEZ** (10)				
51 Y. Yoshida (JPN)	Yoshida	6–0 6–0				
52 R. Hiraki (JPN)	6–2 6–3		Sukova			
53 H. Sukova (CZE)	Sukova		6–4 6–2			
54 S.-A. Siddall (GBR) (W)	7–6 6–1	Sukova				
55 S. Wang (TPE)	Wang	6–0 6–3				
56 L.M. McNeil (USA)	6–1 2–6 7–5			Kournikova		
57 C. Rubin (USA)	Kournikova			2–6 6–2 6–3		
58 A. Kournikova (RUS)	6–1 6–1	Kournikova				
59 A.-G. Sidot (FRA)	Rittner	4–6 7–6 6–3				
60 B. Rittner (GER)	7–6 6–4		Kournikova			
61 J. Kruger (RSA)	Kruger		3–6 6–4 6–4			
62 S. de Ville (BEL)	7–6 6–3	**HUBER** (7)				
63 H. Inoue (JPN) (Q)	**HUBER** (7)	6–2 6–0				
64 **A. HUBER** (GER) (7)	6–3 6–3					

2–6 6–3 6–3

65 **A.J. COETZER** (RSA) (6)
66 A. Fusai (FRA)
67 M. Saeki (JPN)
68 P. Hy-Boulais (CAN)
69 V. Williams (USA)
70 M. Grzybowska (POL)
71 B. Schett (AUT)
72 A. Carlsson (SWE)
73 A. Sugiyama (JPN)
74 Y. Basuki (INA)
75 M. Tu (USA)
76 I. Gorrochategui (ARG)
77 L. Neiland (LAT)
78 N. Kijimuta (JPN)
79 K. Boogert (NED)
80 **B. PAULUS** (AUT) (16)
81 **M.J. FERNANDEZ** (USA) (11)
82 N. Van Lottum (FRA)
83 A. Olsza (POL)
84 L. Nemeckova (CZE)
85 N. Sawamatsu (JPN)
86 S. Smith (GBR) (W)
87 L. Richterova (CZE)
88 T. Tanasugarn (THA)
89 M. Endo (JPN)
90 G. Leon-Garcia (ESP)
91 C. Torrens-Valero (ESP)
92 G. Pizzichini (ITA)
93 N. Zvereva (BLR)
94 E. Likhovtseva (RUS)
95 W. Probst (GER)
96 **J. NOVOTNA** (CZE) (3)
97 **A. SANCHEZ VICARIO** (ESP) (8)
98 C.J. Wood (GBR) (W)
99 E. Gagliardi (SUI)
100 C. Cristea (ROM)
101 F. Labat (ARG)
102 R. Grande (ITA)
103 E.S.H. Callens (BEL)
104 P. Suarez (ARG)
105 F. Lubiani (ITA)
106 S. Pitkowski (FRA)
107 J. Watanabe (USA)
108 M. Serna (ESP)
109 V. Ruano-Pascual (ESP)
110 S. Dopfer (AUT)
111 D. Van Roost (BEL)
112 **M. PIERCE** (FRA) (9)
113 **K. PO** (USA) (13)
114 K.-A. Guse (AUS)
115 N. Tauziat (FRA)
116 N. Miyagi (JPN) (L)
117 L.A. Woodroffe (GBR) (W)
118 P. Schnyder (SUI)
119 J.K. Wiesner (AUT)
120 J. Kandarr (GER)
121 C. Morariu (USA)
122 C. Taylor (GBR) (W)
123 M. Schnitzer (GER) (Q)
124 S. Testud (FRA)
125 A. Grossman (USA)
126 K. Brandi (USA)
127 R.McQuillan (AUS)
128 **M. SELES** (USA) (2)

COETZER (6) 7–6 6–1
Hy-Boulais 6–2 1–6 6–2
Grzybowska 4–6 6–2 6–4
Schett 2–6 6–3 6–0
Basuki 6–3 6–0
Gorrochategui 6–0 6–3
Kijimuta 7–5 6–2
PAULUS (16) 6–3 1–6 6–3
FERNANDEZ (11) 6–2 6–2
Olsza 3–6 6–1 6–2
Sawamatsu 6–1 6–3
Tanasugarn 6–3 6–1
Leon-Garcia 6–3 6–3
Torrens-Valero 1–6 6–3 6–4
Likhovtseva 6–2 6–2
NOVOTNA (3) 6–4 4–6 6–0
SANCHEZ VICARIO (8) 6–0 6–0
Gagliardi 3–6 7–5 6–1
Labat 6–4 6–4
Callens 6–4 6–2
Pitkowski 6–3 4–6 6–1
Serna 6–3 6–1
Ruano-Pascual 6–2 6–2
PIERCE (9) 6–3 6–4
Guse 3–6 7–5 6–2
Tauziat 6–3 6–4
Woodroffe (W) 6–4 6–4
Wiesner 7–5 6–2
Morariu 6–2 6–1
Testud 6–3 6–0
Brandi 6–2 7–6
SELES (2) 6–0 6–2

Hy-Boulais 6–2 6–1
Grzybowska 4–6 6–3 6–2
Basuki 6–2 6–0
Kijimuta 5–7 6–3 6–3
FERNANDEZ (11) 6–4 6–0
Tanasugarn 6–2 6–2
Leon-Garcia 3–6 6–2 6–3
NOVOTNA (3) 6–1 4–6 6–4
SANCHEZ VICARIO (8) 6–4 6–2
Labat 6–2 6–3
Serna 6–2 6–0
PIERCE (9) 6–0 2–6 6–3
Tauziat 6–0 6–3
Wiesner 6–2 6–3
Testud 6–7 6–3 6–1
SELES (2) 5–7 6–3 6–3

Hy-Boulais 6–4 6–1
Basuki 6–3 6–2
FERNANDEZ (11) 6–2 6–4
NOVOTNA (3) 6–4 6–2
SANCHEZ VICARIO (8) 6–1 6–2
PIERCE (9) 6–4 6–3
Tauziat 3–6 6–3 6–2
Testud 0–6 6–4 8–6

Basuki 6–0 7–6
NOVOTNA (3) 5–7 6–4 7–5
SANCHEZ VICARIO (8) 6–1 6–3
Tauziat 4–6 7–5 12–10

NOVOTNA (3) 6–3 6–3
SANCHEZ VICARIO (8) 6–2 7–5

NOVOTNA (3) 6–4 6–2

HINGIS (S

Capital letters denote seeded players. Numbers following player's name gives seeding order (Q) – Qualifier, (W) – Wild Card, (L) – Lucky Loser

MEN'S DOUBLES

Holders: Woodbridge (AUS)/Woodforde (AUS)

FIRST ROUND

1 **WOODBRIDGE/WOODFORDE** (1)
2 Pereira/Van Rensburg
3 MacPhie/Muller
4 Petchey/Richardson (W)
5 Berg/Ekerot
6 Knippschild/Tarango
7 Nyborg/Orsanic
8 **CONNELL/DAVIS** (15)
9 **BJORKMAN/KULTI** (9)
10 Siemerink/Stoltenberg (W)
11 B. Black/Gimelstob
12 Jones/Melville
13 Kinnear/Kitinov
14 Baur/Goellner
15 Fleurian/Forget
16 **LEACH/STARK** (8)
17 **KAFELNIKOV/VACEK** (3)
18 E. Sanchez/Santoro
19 Lavergne/Simian (L)
20 W. Black/Grabb
21 Cunha-Silva/Marques
22 Albano/Dosedel
23 Behrens/Haggard (L)
24 **PIMEK/TALBOT** (14)
25 **JOHNSON/MONTANA** (12)
26 Cash/Reneberg
27 de Jager/Nijssen
28 Sapsford/Wilkinson (W)
29 Novak/Rikl
30 Keil/Salzenstein
31 Noteboom/Wibier
32 **LAREAU/O'BRIEN** (5)
33 **E. FERREIRA/GALBRAITH** (6)
34 Middleton/Woodruff
35 Delgado/Foster (W)
36 Olhovskiy/Steven
37 Bhupathi/Paes
38 Brandi/Messori
39 Ellwood/Tramacchi (Q)
40 **BROAD/NORVAL** (11)
41 **DAMM/VIZNER** (13)
42 Adams/Barnard
43 Cowan/Weal (W)
44 Couto/Mota
45 Haygarth/Van Emburgh
46 Delaitre/Raoux
47 Kempers/Oosting
48 **KNOWLES/NESTOR** (4)
49 **PHILIPPOUSSIS/RAFTER** (7)
50 L.B. Jensen/M. Jensen
51 Lee/Trotman (W)
52 H. Holm/N. Holm (L)
53 Koenig/Rueb (Q)
54 Kronemann/Macpherson
55 Dilucia/Smith (Q)
56 **STOLLE/SUK** (10)
57 **EAGLE/FLORENT** (16)
58 Randall/Waite
59 Arthurs/Kratzmann
60 Groen/Hirszon
61 Mirnyi/Ullyet
62 Ondruska/Stafford
63 Kilderry/Tebbutt
64 **ELTINGH/HAARHUIS** (2)

SECOND ROUND

WOODBRIDGE/WOODFORDE (1) 6–1 6–4
MacPhie/Muller 7–6 6–3
Knippschild/Tarango 6–4 7–5
CONNELL/DAVIS (15) 7–5 5–7 6–3
BJORKMAN/KULTI (9) 7–6 6–3
B. Black/Gimelstob 6–4 5–7 6–2
Kinnear/Kitinov 7–6 6–7 14–12
LEACH/STARK (8) 6–4 6–3
Sanchez/Santoro 6–2 7–6
W. Black/Grabb 6–1 6–4
Albano/Dosedel 6–7 6–3 7–5
Behrens/Haggard (L) 4–6 6–3 14–12
JOHNSON/MONTANA (12) 3–6 6–3 6–4
De Jager/Nijssen 7–6 6–4
Novak/Rikl 7–5 6–4
Noteboom/Wibier 7–6 3–6 6–4
E. FERREIRA/GALBRAITH (6) 6–4 6–4
Olhovskiy/Steven 4–6 7–6 6–1
Brandi/Messori 6–4 3–6 6–3
BROAD/NORVAL (11) 6–4 5–7 9–7
DAMM/VIZNER (13) 7–6 6–4
Couto/Mota 6–4 7–6
Haygarth/Van Emburgh 7–6 6–2
KNOWLES/NESTOR (4) 6–3 6–4
PHILIPPOUSSIS/RAFTER (7) 4–6 6–3 6–4
H. Holm/N. Holm (L) 6–4 3–6 6–3
Kronemann/Macpherson 6–1 6–4
STOLLE/SUK (10) 6–0 3–6 6–4
Randall/Waite 7–6 6–2
Groen/Hirszon 7–6 6–4
Ondruska/Stafford 6–3 6–4
ELTINGH/HAARHUIS (2) 7–6 7–6

THIRD ROUND

WOODBRIDGE/WOODFORDE (1) 6–4 6–2
Knippschild/Tarango 6–4 6–7 6–3
BJORKMAN/KULTI (9) 6–2 6–1
LEACH/STARK (8) 6–3 7–6
W. Black/Grabb 7–5 6–4
Behrens/Haggard (L) 7–6 6–7 6–4
JOHNSON/MONTANA (12) 6–2 6–7 6–2
Noteboom/Wibier 6–3 3–6 7–5
E. FERREIRA/GALBRAITH (6) 6–3 6–3
BROAD/NORVAL (11) 7–6 6–1
DAMM/VIZNER (13) 6–4 7–6
KNOWLES/NESTOR (4) 5–7 6–1 6–4
PHILIPPOUSSIS/RAFTER (7) 6–3 6–4
STOLLE/SUK (10) 6–3 6–4
Groen/Hirszon 6–7 6–4 6–2
ELTINGH/HAARHUIS (2) 6–4 6–3

QUARTER-FINALS

WOODBRIDGE/WOODFORDE (1) 7–5 6–4
BJORKMAN/KULTI (9) 6–2 3–6 6–3
W. Black/Grabb 7–5 6–1
JOHNSON/MONTANA (12) 6–4 6–4
BROAD/NORVAL (11) 7–6 7–6
DAMM/VIZNER (13) 6–4 6–4
PHILIPPOUSSIS/RAFTER (7) 6–4 7–6
ELTINGH/HAARHUIS (2) 7–6 6–4

SEMI-FINALS

WOODBRIDGE/WOODFORDE (1) 2–6 6–2 6–3 6–4
W. Black/Grabb 6–4 6–1 6–2
DAMM/VIZNER (13) 4–6 4–6 7–6 6–4 6–4
ELTINGH/HAARHUIS (2) 4–6 7–6 3–6 6–3 10–8

FINAL

WOODBRIDGE/WOODFORDE (1) 7–6 6–4 3–6 6–3
ELTINGH/HAARHUIS (2) 6–2 6–2 6–4

WOODBRIDGE (AUS)/**WOODFORDE** (AUS) (1) 7–6 7–6 5–7 6–3

Capital letters denote seeded players. Numbers following player's name gives seeding order (Q) – Qualifier, (W) – Wild Card, (L) – Lucky Loser

WOMEN'S DOUBLES

Holders: Hingis (SUI)/Sukova (CZE)

FIRST ROUND

1 **G. FERNANDEZ/ZVEREVA** (1)
2 Barabanschikova/Smith (W)
3 Freye/Noorlander
4 Hy-Boulais/Studenikova
5 Barclay/Wood
6 Farina/Schett
7 Puilin/Woodroffe (W)
8 **BOOGERT/SPIRLEA** (16)
9 **ADAMS/McNEIL** (9)
10 Ruano-Pasqual/Suarez
11 Rittner/Van Roost
12 Ellwood/McQuillan
13 Cristea/Grzybowska
14 Carlsson/Perfetti
15 de Swardt/Horn
16 **M.J. FERNANDEZ/RAYMOND** (5)
17 **DAVENPORT/NOVOTNA** (3)
18 Krizan/Van Lottum
19 Graham/Kunce
20 Lutrova/Wood (L)
21 Siddall/Wainwright (W)
22 Langrova/Zrubakova
23 Paz/Sidot
24 **FUSAI/GRANDE** (13)
25 **APPELMANS/OREMANS** (12)
26 Dragomir/Majoli
27 Jones/Tanasugam
28 Dechaume-Balleret/Testud
29 Garrone/Pizzichini
30 Grossman/Habsudova
31 Jeyaseelan/Simpson
32 **BASUKI/VIS** (8)
33 **MARTINEZ/TARABINI** (7)
34 Callens/Helgeson-Nielsen
35 Nideffer/Rinaldi-Stunkel
36 Huber/Seles
37 Brioukhovets/Tatarkova (Q)
38 T. Jones/Muric
39 Hiraki/Labat
40 **FRAZIER/PO** (14)
41 **TAUZIAT/WILD** (10)
42 Coetzer/Pierce
43 Lee/Olsza
44 Golarsa/Schnyder
45 Meier/Nemeckova
46 Lugina/Wagner
47 Montalvo/Nagyova
48 **NEILAND/SUKOVA** (4)
49 **ARENDT/BOLLEGRAF** (6)
50 Taylor/Ward (W)
51 Park/Wang
52 Lake/Pleming (Q)
53 Shriver/Smylie
54 Kournikova/Likhovtseva
55 Csurgo/Schneider
56 **KIJIMUTA/MIYAGI** (11)
57 **RUBIN/SCHULTZ-McCARTHY** (15)
58 Probst/Sugiyama
59 Saeki/Yoshida
60 de Lone/Pratt
61 Bobkova/Melicharova
62 Guse/Morariu
63 Martincova/Vildova
64 **HINGIS/SANCHEZ VICARIO** (2)

SECOND ROUND

G. FERNANDEZ/ZVEREVA (1) 6–2 6–2
Freye/Noorlander 7–6 4–6 6–2
Barclay/Wood 6–4 6–3
BOOGERT/SPIRLEA (16) 6–3 6–2
ADAMS/McNEIL (9) 7–6 6–3
Rittner/Van Roost 4–6 6–1 6–1
Cristea/Grzybowska 7–5 6–3
M.J. FERNANDEZ/RAYMOND (5) 6–2 6–1
DAVENPORT/NOVOTNA (3) 6–0 6–2
Graham/Kunce 6–4 6–1
Siddall/Wainwright (W) 6–3 6–2
FUSAI/GRANDE (13) 6–3 6–0
APPELMANS/OREMANS (12) w/o
Dechaume-Balleret/Testud 6–2 7–6
Garrone/Pizzichini 6–2 6–4
BASUKI/VIS (8) 6–4 6–2
Callens/Helgeson-Nielsen 6–4 7–5
Huber/Seles 7–5 6–3
T. Jones/Muric 6–3 6–1
FRAZIER/PO (14) 7–5 6–3
TAUZIAT/WILD (10) 6–1 1–6 10–8
Golarsa/Schnyder 7–5 6–3
Lugina/Wagner 6–4 4–6 6–4
NEILAND/SUKOVA (4) 3–6 6–1 6–4
ARENDT/BOLLEGRAF (6) 6–4 6–4
Park/Wang 6–4 6–4
Kournikova/Likhovtseva 3–6 7–5 9–7
KIJIMUTA/MIYAGI (11) 6–4 6–3
RUBIN/SCHULTZ-McCARTHY (15) 6–1 7–5
Saeki/Yoshida 6–7 7–5 6–4
Guse/Morariu 6–7 7–6 6–1
HINGIS/SANCHEZ VICARIO (2) 6–2 6–3

THIRD ROUND

G. FERNANDEZ/ZVEREVA (1) 6–0 6–2
Barclay/Wood 4–6 7–6 6–4
ADAMS/McNEIL (9) 6–3 1–6 6–4
M.J. FERNANDEZ/RAYMOND (5) 6–3 6–0
DAVENPORT/NOVOTNA (3) 6–1 6–2
FUSAI/GRANDE (13) 6–3 6–4
APPELMANS/OREMANS (12) 6–4 6–3
BASUKI/VIS (8) 5–7 6–4 6–2
Callens/Helgeson-Nielsen 6–2 6–4
FRAZIER/PO (14) 6–2 6–3
TAUZIAT/WILD (10) 6–7 7–6 6–3
NEILAND/SUKOVA (4) 6–3 6–2
ARENDT/BOLLEGRAF (6) 6–2 6–0
KIJIMUTA/MIYAGI (11) 4–6 6–2 7–5
RUBIN/SCHULTZ-McCARTHY (15) 7–6 6–3
HINGIS/SANCHEZ VICARIO (2) 6–3 6–3

QUARTER-FINALS

G. FERNANDEZ/ZVEREVA (1) 7–5 7–5
M.J. FERNANDEZ/RAYMOND (5) 6–1 7–6
DAVENPORT/NOVOTNA (3) 6–1 6–1
APPELMANS/OREMANS (12) 7–5 6–1
Callens/Helgeson-Nielsen 7–6 6–3
NEILAND/SUKOVA (4) 6–4 6–4
ARENDT/BOLLEGRAF (6) 6–2 3–6 6–1
HINGIS/SANCHEZ VICARIO (2) 7–6 6–7 13–11

SEMI-FINALS

G. FERNANDEZ/ZVEREVA (1) 5–7 6–4 6–4
APPELMANS/OREMANS (12) w/o
NEILAND/SUKOVA (4) 6–4 6–4
ARENDT/BOLLEGRAF (6) 6–4 5–7 6–2

FINAL

G. FERNANDEZ/ZVEREVA (1) 6–1 6–2
ARENDT/BOLLEGRAF (6) 6–2 3–6 6–1

G. FERNANDEZ (USA)/**ZVEREVA** (BLR) (1) 7–6 6–4

Capital letters denote seeded players. Numbers following player's name gives seeding order (Q) – Qualifier, (W) – Wild Card, (L) – Lucky Loser

MIXED DOUBLES

Holders: Suk (CZE)/Sukova (CZE)

FIRST ROUND

1 **CONNELL/DAVENPORT** (1)
2 Kempers/Van Lottum
3 Waite/Muric
4 Orsanic/Labat
5 Noteboom/Jeyaseelan
6 Middleton/McNeil
7 Mirnyi/Likhovtseva
8 **EAGLE/VIS** (9)
9 **BHUPATHI/HIRAKI** (15)
10 Van Rensburg/Williams (W)
11 Messori/Perfetti
12 Davis/Tarabini
13 Petchey/Wood (W)
14 Sanchez/Sanchez Vicario
15 Smith/Frazier
16 **LEACH/BOLLEGRAF** (5)
17 **SUK/SUKOVA** (4)
18 Kronemann/Rinaldi-Stunkel
19 M. Jensen/Schultz-McCarthy
20 Gimelstob/Rubin
21 Norval/Horn
22 Kinnear/Miyagi
23 Florent/Barclay
24 **L.B. JENSEN/ADAMS** (13)
25 **PIMEK/APPELMANS** (11)
26 Nijssen/Basuki
27 Keil/Helgeson-Nielsen
28 Kilderry/Testud
29 Raoux/Golarsa
30 Talbot/Van Roost
31 Ullyett/Nideffer
32 **ADAMS/FUSAI** (7)
33 **KNOWLES/KOURNIKOVA** (8)
34 Melville/Pratt
35 Wilkinson/Smith (W)
36 Paes/Dragomir
37 Barnard/Boogert
38 Van Emburgh/Melicharovoa
39 Macpherson/McQuillan
40 **O'BRIEN/MORARIU** (16)
41 **ALBANO/PAZ** (14)
42 A. Kratzmann/Guse
43 Arthurs/Krizan
44 Kitinov/Olsza
45 Bergh/Hy-Boulais
46 Nyborg/Carlsson
47 Ekerot/Pleming
48 **OLHOVSKIY/NEILAND** (3)
49 **STOLLE/M.J. FERNANDEZ** (6)
50 Brandi/Dechaume-Balleret
51 Broad/de Swardt
52 Randall/D. Jones
53 Groen/Vildova
54 Sapsford/Siddall (W)
55 Davids/Oremans
56 **JOHNSON/WILD** (10)
57 **GRABB/GRAHAM** (12)
58 Braasch/Rittner
59 K. Jones/Kunce
60 Haygarth/T.S. Jones
61 Hand/Lake
62 de Jager/Hingis
63 W. Black/Grossman
64 **GALBRAITH/RAYMOND** (2)

SECOND ROUND

CONNELL/DAVENPORT (1) 4–6 6–2 6–2
Orsanic/Labat 6–4 7–6
Middleton/McNeil 7–6 7–5
Mirnyi/Likhovtseva 7–6 6–4
BHUPATHI/HIRAKI (15) 6–7 6–3 6–2
Messori/Perfetti 6–4 6–4
Petchey/Wood (W) 4–6 Ret'd.
LEACH/BOLLEGRAF (5) 6–1 2–6 6–2
SUK/SUKOVA (4) 6–1 7–5
Gimelstob/Rubin 7–5 6–7 6–1
Kinnear/Miyagi 7–6 6–3
L.B. JENSEN/ADAMS (13) 6–7 6–1 13–11
Nijssen/Basuki 7–5 4–6 6–1
Keil/Helgeson-Nielsen 4–6 6–0 6–3
Raoux/Golarsa 6–3 7–6
ADAMS/FUSAI (7) 6–7 6–4 6–2
KNOWLES/KOURNIKOVA (8) 6–4 7–5
Paes/Dragomir 4–6 6–3 6–1
Barnard/Boogert 6–2 7–6
O'BRIEN/MORARIU (16) 6–7 7–6 13–11
ALBANO/PAZ (14) 6–2 6–4
Arthurs/Krizan 7–5 1–6 11–9
Nyborg/Carlsson 7–5 5–7 6–4
OLHOVSKIY/NEILAND (3) 7–6 6–1
STOLLE/M.J. FERNANDEZ (6) 7–6 3–6 7–5
Broad/de Swardt 7–5 6–4
Sapsford/Siddall (W) 7–5 7–5
JOHNSON/WILD (10) 6–3 6–4
Braasch/Rittner 4–6 7–5 15–13
K. Jones/Kunce 6–4 6–3
de Jager/Hingis 6–1 6–3
GALBRAITH/RAYMOND (2) 4–6 6–3 7–5

THIRD ROUND

CONNELL/DAVENPORT (1) 6–3 6–3
Middleton/McNeil 7–6 6–4
BHUPATHI/HIRAKI (15) 3–6 7–5 6–3
LEACH/BOLLEGRAF (5) 7–6 6–3
SUK/SUKOVA (4) 7–6 6–1
Kinnear/Miyagi 7–5 6–4
Nijssen/Basuki 6–3 6–4
ADAMS/FUSAI (7) 6–3 6–4
Paes/Dragomir w/o
Barnard/Boogert 2–6 6–4 6–3
Arthurs/Krizan 6–4 6–2
OLHOVSKIY/NEILAND (3) 7–5 6–3
Broad/de Swardt 6–3 3–6 6–3
Sapsford/Siddall (W) 6–2 6–3
Braasch/Rittner 6–2 5–7 6–4
de Jager/Hingis 6–4 0–6 10–8

QUARTER-FINALS

CONNELL/DAVENPORT (1) 4–6 7–6 6–4
LEACH/BOLLEGRAF (5) 6–3 5–7 6–4
SUK/SUKOVA (4) 6–2 7–5
Nijssen/Basuki 6–4 7–5
Paes/Dragomir 5–7 6–3 6–4
OLHOVSKIY/NEILAND (3) 6–2 7–6
Broad/de Swardt 7–5 6–3
de Jager/Hingis 6–4 6–3

SEMI-FINALS

CONNELL/DAVENPORT (1) 6–4 6–4
SUK/SUKOVA (4) 6–1 0–6 6–4
OLHOVSKIY/NEILAND (3) 6–3 7–6
Broad/de Swardt 5–7 6–3 6–4

FINAL

SUK/SUKOVA (4) 3–6 6–2 6–3
OLHOVSKIY/NEILAND (3) 7–6 4–6 6–3

SUK (CZE)/**SUKOVA** (CZE) (4) 4–6 6–3 6–4

Capital letters denote seeded players. Numbers following player's name gives seeding order (Q) – Qualifier, (W) – Wild Card, (L) – Lucky Loser

JUNIOR EVENTS

BOYS' SINGLES – Final: Westley Whitehouse (RSA) (5) d. Daniel Elsner (GER) 6–3 7–6.
GIRLS' SINGLES – Final: Cara Black (ZIM) (3) d. Aubrie Rippner (USA) (6) 6–3 7–5.
BOYS' DOUBLES – Final: Luis Horna (PER)/N Massu (CHI) (1) d. Jaco van de Westhuizen (RSA)/Westley Whitehouse (RSA) (2) 6–4 6–2.
GIRLS' DOUBLES – Final: Cara Black (ZIM)/Irina Selyutina (KAZ) (1) d. Maja Matevzic (SLO) /Katarina Srebotnik (SLO) (3) 3–6 7–5 6–3.

SENIOR EVENTS

35 AND OVER GENTLEMEN'S INVITATION DOUBLES (Round robin in 4 groups of 4 with knock-out sf and f) – Final: Jeremy Bates (GBR)/Ramesh Krishnan (IND) d. Kevin Curren (USA)/Johan Kriek (USA) 6–4 6–4
35 AND OVER LADIES' INVITATION DOUBLES(Round robin in 2 groups of 4 with knock-out final) – Final: Jo Durie (GBR)/Anne Smith (USA) d. Wendy Turnbull (AUS)/Virginia Wade (GBR) 6–2 6–1
45 AND OVER GENTLEMEN'S INVITATION DOUBLES(Knock-out for 16 prs.) – Final: Jaime Fillol (CHI)/ Dick Stockton (USA) d. Owen Davidson (AUS)/Cliff Drysdale (RSA) 6–1 6–2

THE CHAMPIONSHIPS
TOTAL PRIZE MONEY – £6,884,952

MEN'S SINGLES – Winner £415,000. Runner-up £207,500. Semi-finalists £103.750. Quarter-finalists £53,925. Fourth-round losers £29,050. Third-round losers £16,810. Second-round losers £10,165. First-round losers £6,225.
Total: £2,270,740

WOMEN'S SINGLES – Winner £373,500. Runner-up £186,750. Semi-finalists £88,350. Quarter-finalists £45,825. Fourth-round losers £24,000. Third-round losers £13,025. Second-round losers £7,880. First-round losers £4,825.
Total: £1,881,610

MEN'S DOUBLES (per pair) – Winners £170,030. Runners-up £85,010. Semi-finalists £43,620. Quarter-finalists £22,650 Third-round losers £12,070. Second-round losers £6,550. First-round losers £3,830.
Total: £756,800

WOMEN'S DOUBLES (per pair) – Winners £147,010. Runners-up £73,270. Semi-finalists £34,900. Quarter-finalists £18,210. Third-round losers £9,050. Second-round losers £4,930. First-round losers £2,780.
Total: £603,160

MIXED DOUBLES (per pair) – Winners £72,200. Runners-up £36,100. Semi-finalists £18,060. Quarter-finalists £8,310. Third-round losers £4,150. Second-round losers £2,060. First-round losers £940.
Total: £273,900

35 AND OVER MEN'S INVITATION DOUBLES (per pair) – Winners £14,000. Runners-up £11,000. Semi-finalists £8,650. Second place in each group £6,950. Third place in each group £6,350. Fourth place in each group £5,800.
Total: £118,700

45 AND OVER MEN'S INVITATION DOUBLES (per pair) – Winners £11,000. Runners-up £8,750. Semi-finalists £7,000. Second round losers £5,750. First round losers £5,000.
Total: £96,750

35 AND OVER WOMEN'S INVITATION DOUBLES (per pair) – Winners £10,000. Runners-up £7,500. Second place in each group £5,750. Third place in each group £5,250. Fourth place in each group £4,500.
Total: £48,500

QUALIFYING – MEN (each): 16 x Third-round losers £3,925. 32 x Second-round losers £1,976.. 64 x First-round losers £988.
Total £189,696

QUALIFYING – WOMEN (each): 8 x Third-round losers £3,064. 16 x Second-round losers £1,532. 32 x First-round losers £766.
Total: £73,536

Per Diem allowances (estimated): £571,560

It was the fulfilment of a dream for Australia's Patrick Rafter when he won his first Grand Slam title at the US Open. (Stephen Wake)

US Open Championships

Bud Collins

Newness, novelty and, yes, nostalgia were the themes at a rehabilitated Flushing Meadow where tennis attendance records were set and such favourites as world Nos. 1 and 2, Pete Sampras and Monica Seles, suffered setbacks, failing to arrive at finals they'd inhabited the two previous years.

Centrepiece of the attractive $300 million transformation of the US Open locale is 22,547 seat Arthur Ashe Stadium, the world's largest tennis pen. Though too large for the kind of up-closer centre court viewing afforded by the other three major championships, it does have sight lines superior to Louis Armstrong Stadium (now the secondary enclosure), and more comfortable seating and amenities for the customers. Moreover the brick-walled outer court arenas are the best of their kind in the game. Two broad plazas leading to them created a joyful atmosphere, a blend of Italian piazzas and French sidewalk cafes.

The newly minted complex, along with the heartfelt dedicatory parade of US champions, made the $11,821,890 Open a splendid affair. Led by the venerable Don Budge, 82, marking the 60th anniversary of his final round triumph over Gottfried von Cramm, and Pauline Betz Addie, 78, a winner 55 years previously over Louise Brough Clapp (also present), the cavalcade included 37 of 47 living singles champs. Jack Kramer, Tony Trabert, Frank Sedgman, Rod Laver, Roy Emerson, Ken Rosewall, John Newcombe, John McEnroe, Ivan Lendl, Maria Bueno, Billie Jean King, Chris Evert, Tracy Austin and Martina Navratilova were all there, along with two contemporaries absent from the '97 draw, injured defender Steffi Graf, and fellow German Boris Becker, withdrawn from the major scene.

The excitement just kept on going. Although Ashe Stadium was never completely filled (21,566 attended the dual singles finals Sunday), fine weather and the compelling tournament were factors in the fortnight's crowds totalling 559,544 for 25 sessions, an increase of 25,270 over the previous record, set in 1996.

For novelty and newness nobody came close to 17-year-old Venus Starr Williams. As rare as her hair – hundreds of red, white and blue beads embellished Venus's cornrow braids – she was that practically unheard of breaker-through: a rookie going all the way to the final the first time around. As the lowest regarded finalist ever (No. 66 on the computer), she captivated Flushing and made the Open her tournament in innumerable eyes.

She wasn't alone. No Swiss had ever won the US Open. Unsurprisingly No. 1 Martina Hingis did, 6–0 6–4, over Williams. At 16 years 11 months Martina is the second youngest champ, behind Austin (16–8 in 1979), and just ahead of Maureen Connolly (13 days older at 16–11 in 1951).

No Australian had won for nearly a quarter-century, and no Englishman for 61 years. Bounding Queenslander Patrick Rafter did. Despite being a very-long-shot ranked at No. 14 and seeded 13th, he spoiled the longer-shot revery of high-velocity serving lefty Greg Rusedski, the born-again Brit, 6–3 6–2 4–6 7–5. As 10th in the brilliant line of Australian rulers of the USA who have accounted for 16 titles, beginning with Frank Sedgman in 1951, Pat followed his Davis Cup captain, John Newcombe, monarch in 1973.

Yevgeny Kafelnikov became the only Russian male to win a US title, bonding with Czech Daniel Vacek for a 7–6 (8–6) 6–3, decision over Swedes Jonas Bjorkman and Nicklas Kulti. Incredibly the Australian 'Woodies,' 1995–96 champs Mark Woodforde and Todd Woodbridge, were dumped in the first round by the Dutchmen Menno Oosting and Tom Kempers, 6–4 3–6 6–1.

Jana Novotna, with her 12th major doubles title, joined Lindsay Davenport in a Czech-American coalition to beat three-time champs Gigi Fernandez and Natasha Zvereva, 6–3 6–4.

Netherlands and the US split the mixed as Manon Bollegraf and lefty Rick Leach beat Argentines Mercedes Paz and Pablo Albano, 3–6 7–5 7–6 (7–3), Leach taking his seventh major in doubles.

Rusedski, ranked No. 20 and celebrant of his 24th birthday in a 6–1 3–6 3–6 6–3 7–5 comeback semis victory over Sweden's No. 17 Jonas Bjorkman, also unseeded, hoped vainly to emu-

A delighted Greg Rusedski reaches the final of the US Open unseeded with a blistering display of power tennis – the first Briton to do as well in New York since Fred Perry. (Stephen Wake)

late 1936 victor Fred Perry in flying the Union Jack victoriously. At least he beat a Wimbledon champ (Richard Krajicek) in the quarters, the first Brit to make it that far since John Lloyd in 1984. He also blowtorched an Open and world record 143 mph serve against Rafter and was the ninth non-seeded finalist in the 70 years since such favouritism began in the US.

When 25-year-old Rafter, winner of but one other career title, and loser of five previous finals during the season, shut down floundering ex-champ Andre Agassi (fallen to No. 63) in the fourth round, 6–3 7–6 (7–4) 4–6 6–3, he served notice that a serve-and-volleying daredevil could go all the way.

Especially since the tournament had been fiercely jiggled the day before by Petr Korda to become Sampras-free. Seeded 15th, the mercurial Czech lefty flashed astoundingly unanswerable backhands, turning sorcerer-for-a-day to make Sampras (and his 17 match Flushing streak) disappear, 6–7 (4–7) 7–5 7–6 (7–2) 3–6, 7–6 (7–3) in a tense struggle thrice interrupted by rain. Abruptly the Open was an absorbingly disorderly drama from which any extra might step forward in the lead.

Sampras seemed to have righted himself in the fifth, going up 3–0, then 3–1. His serve (24 aces to Korda's 15) was humming, but he lost it to 3–2 carelessly – 'the key game', he lamented afterwards. Even though Korda caught up, Pete edged within two points of victory at 5–6, 30-all, only to whack two short forehands puzzlingly into the net.

Korda, so tough and electrifying for 3 hours 36 minutes, failed to capitalize on that splendid performance, tarnishing his reputation by playing a listless quarter-final against Bjorkman. Defaulting after losing two sets, he complained lamely of 'a cold.'

Sampras's demise was the acme of rampant form-busting throughout the men's field. Most of the somebodies were gone after the third round. Of the first 11 seeds only Sampras, Michael Chang (2), Sergi Bruguera (7) and Marcelo Rios (10) could be found among the last 16. Old Unreliable Goran Ivanisevic (4) started the backward parade, tripped up by 91st ranked Romanian Dinu Pescariu in the opening round. He was accompanied by usually reliable Thomas Muster (5), beaten by Tim Henman, ranked 21. Soon after, 3rd seed Kafelnikov had been slickered by the elder, Mark Woodforde, ranked 43 and days short of his 32nd birthday, and French champ Gustavo Kuerten (9) was mowed down by Bjorkman's impressive volleying. A pulled thigh muscle removed 6th seeded Alex Corretja, who had come within a stroke of beating Sampras a year earlier.

With Sampras gone, Chang, the 1996 runner-up, became the favourite. Although the opportunity for a major title looked better than at any time since his flabbergasting French triumph in 1989, two tremendous 5-set struggles prior to the semis may have softened him up for his ravaging by Rafter, 6–3 6–3 6–4, during which the Aussie was inviolable through eight break points.

Seldom has Chang's Wall of China will been tested more severely – and prevailed – than in his fourth rounder, a rebounding 6–3 0–6 5–7 7–5 6–1, decision over Wimbledon finalist Cedric Pioline. Pioline served for the match in the fourth at 5–3, but Michael wouldn't flinch, countering to win 11 of the last 12 games, leaving Pioline in an exhausted, cramping heap.

Next came the gifted Chilean lefty Marcelo Rios in perhaps the most eye-catching encounter of the Open, a feast of shotmaking and enthralling court covering that went to Chang in a closing three-game surge, 7–5 6–2 4–6 4–6 6–3. Michael was in his third US semi, but Rafter would make it unbearable.

In the final Pat kept his foot on the gas, quicker to the net than Rusedski, surer with his low backhand returns and sharper in volleying. Rusedski stalled him in the third and, although down 1–3 in the fourth, Greg fought to 2–3 through four break points and capsized Rafter in the next game. He served ahead, 5–4 and chances of an ultimate set showdown looked good. However, Rafter regained purpose – and his returning and volleying touch – to run nine points, seizing 12 of the remaining 13.

Among the women, high-rising Venus, towering over her foes at 6-feet-2 (the tallest American female to grace a major final), put down five opponents rated above her in becoming only the second unseeded finalist. She beat Spaniard Gala Leon Garcia (64), German Anke Huber (8), South African Joanette Kruger (45), French Sandrine Testud (17) and Romanian Irina Spirlea (12). Her non-seeded predecessor as finalist, Darlene Hard, the loser to Althea Gibson in 1958, was, however, No. 4 in the US at the time. Williams is the fifth teen this century to make the final in her debut, following champ May Sutton, 17 in 1904, and 16-year-old runners-up Helen Wills, 1922, Brit Betty Nuthall, 1927, and Pam Shriver, 1978.

Testud, a determined groundstroker, removed Croatia's French Open champ, 4th ranked Iva Majoli, in the second round, 6–4 2–6 6–1. Aussie Rachel McQuillan, No. 100, scored the most resounding upset numerically, a 6–2 7–5 success, when she ran off the last six games in a third round dusting of 7th rated Conchita Martinez, the ex-Wimbledon champ who had been a 1995–96 semi-finalist.

However, considering that highly inexperienced Venus came in with a losing career record as a pro (15–18; 1–2 in majors), had never gone beyond the quarters in 18 tournaments and underwent little junior competition, the magnitude of her accomplishment truly astonishes. Learning on the job, aloof and composed all the way, she showed remarkable athleticism and competitive fire in her masterpiece: the 7–6 (7–5) 4–6 7–6 (9–7) stadium-rocking semi-final triumph over 11th seeded Spirlea in which both cancelled match points.

Nervelessly Venus ducked two from 4–6 during the excruciating 11 minute overtime. Her two-fisted backhand down the line took Spirlea's serving point. Venus then went to 7–6 on a heavily sliced low backhand from virtually a kneeling position, plus a big forehand.

Spirlea had devastated 2nd seed Seles in their thrilling quarter-final, 6–7 (5–7) 7–6 (10–8) 6–3 with barrages of explosive forehands (37 winners), slipping a match point in the second set breaker with an attacking forehand and volley. Now, against Williams, it was her turn to rescue another, to 7–7, with one last forehand blast. There her resolve melted before Williams with two errors.

Hingis, conceding only 28 games and no sets, was the most dominant champ since Seles (27 games) in 1992. In the greenest final in major annals – 33 years between them – Martina was her most cheerful self in subjecting Williams to a 62-minute ordeal. Quick and unerring in finding the openings, she committed a miserly 15 unforced errors and received 38 from oft-erring Venus. Williams had opened her 40th professional start by serving to 40–15 before the diminutive Swiss Alp avalanched her for a 22 minute bagel. Martina lost serve to 4–4 in the second, and the next two points, but quickly righted herself to grab eight of the last 11.

Having lost only the French final to Majoli, Hingis completed the Big Four with a 27–1 match tally, tying 1988 Grand Slammer Steffi Graf (27–0) for most major wins in a season, one ahead of 1969 Grand Slammer Rod Laver (26–0). Youngest to capture three majors in a season, Martina is just the eighth to make the four finals within a calendar year, following Aussie Jack Crawford (1933), Americans Budge (1938) and Connolly (1953), Aussies Lew Hoad (1956), Laver (1962–69) and Margaret Court (1970) plus Graf (1988).

MEN'S SINGLES

Holder: P. Sampras (USA)

FIRST ROUND

1 **P. SAMPRAS** (USA) (1)
2 T. Larkham (AUS) (Q)
3 P. Baur (GER) (Q)
4 J. Oncins (BRA) (Q)
5 R. Fromberg (AUS)
6 P. McEnroe (USA)
7 A. Radulescu (GER)
8 O. Ogorodov (UZB) (Q)
9 J.A. Viloca (ESP)
10 B. Steven (NZL)
11 T. Ho (USA) (Q)
12 M. Damm (CZE)
13 M. Martelli (ITA)
14 H. Dreekmann (GER)
15 V. Spadea (USA)
16 **P. KORDA** (CZE) (15)
17 **G. KUERTEN** (BRA) (9)
18 G. Grant (USA) (Q)
19 D. Van Scheppingen (NED)
20 S. Schalken (NED)
21 F. Clavet (ESP)
22 J. Bjorkman (SWE)
23 T. Martin (USA)
24 J. Courier (USA)
25 J. Novak (CZE)
26 D. Sanguinetti (ITA)
27 J.-M. Gambill (USA) (W)
28 S. Draper (AUS)
29 D. Prinosil (GER)
30 J. Tarango (USA)
31 G. Raoux (FRA)
32 **C. MOYA** (ESP) (8)
33 **G. IVANISEVIC** (CRO) (4)
34 D. Pescariu (ROM)
35 J. Knippschild (GER)
36 S. Dosedel (CZE)
37 F. Santoro (FRA)
38 M. Ondruska (RSA)
39 G. Rusedski (GBR)
40 D. Wheaton (USA) (W)
41 L. Tieleman (ITA) (Q)
42 D. Vacek (CZE)
43 M. Sell (USA) (Q)
44 C. Mamiit (USA) (W)
45 J. Golmard (FRA)
46 H. Arazi (MAR)
47 K. Alami (MAR)
48 **M. PHILIPPOUSSIS** (AUS) (14)
49 **F. MANTILLA** (ESP) (12)
50 J. Stoltenberg (AUS)
51 J. Sanchez (ESP)
52 A. Portas (ESP)
53 J. Van Lottum (NED) (Q)
54 R. Reneberg (USA)
55 J. Van Herck (BEL)
56 F. Dewulf (BEL)
57 M. Filippini (URU)
58 A. O'Brien (USA)
59 W. Black (ZIM) (Q)
60 R. Krajicek (NED)
61 R. Rake (USA) (W)
62 B. Ulihrach (CZE)
63 M. Rosset (SUI)
64 **A. CORRETJA** (ESP) (6)

SECOND ROUND

SAMPRAS (1) 6–3 6–1 6–3
Baur (Q) 4–6 3–6 6–4 6–3 6–3
Fromberg 6–2 6–2 6–7 6–3
Radulescu 3–6 6–4 7–6 6–1
Steven 4–6 6–2 6–1 6–2
Damm 6–3 6–4 6–7 6–4
Martelli 6–1 7–6 6–3
KORDA (15) 2–6 7–5 7–6 6–4
KUERTEN (9) 6–4 3–6 6–7 6–2 6–3
Schalken 6–4 6–3 6–4
Bjorkman 6–2 6–4 6–4
Martin 3–6 6–3 6–4 6–2
Novak 5–7 6–2 7–6 6–2
Draper 6–4 6–3 7–6
Tarango 6–4 6–2 7–6
Raoux 6–4 7–6 6–2
Pescariu 4–6 7–6 6–1 7–6
Knippschild 7–5 5–7 6–4 6–7 6–4
Ondruska 5–7 6–4 4–6 6–2 6–3
Rusedski 6–2 6–3 6–3
Vacek 4–6 6–4 1–6 6–3 6–2
Sell (Q) 6–3 3–6 6–4 7–5
Golmard 6–4 1–6 7–6 4–6 7–5
PHILIPPOUSSIS (14) 6–3 6–4 3–6 6–4
MANTILLA (12) 7–6 6–3 6–2
Sanchez 7–5 6–2 7–5
Van Lottum (Q) 6–1 6–4 2–6 6–4
Van Herck 6–4 4–6 7–6 7–6
Filippini 6–2 6–4 6–4
Krajicek 6–4 6–2 6–2
Ulihrach 6–2 6–3 6–2
CORRETJA (6) 4–6 6–3 6–2 6–2

THIRD ROUND

SAMPRAS (1) 7–6 6–4 6–3
Radulescu 3–6 6–4 6–3 3–6 6–4
Damm 6–4 6–4 3–6 7–6
KORDA (15) 6–3 7–6 7–6
KUERTEN (9) 6–4 6–4 6–2
Bjorkman 7–5 6–4 6–2
Draper 7–5 7–6 3–6 6–3
Tarango 6–4 6–7 6–7 6–2 6–4
Knippschild 6–3 7–5 6–1
Rusedski 7–6 6–4 6–1
Vacek 4–6 7–6 6–1 6–2
PHILIPPOUSSIS (14) 7–6 6–2 1–0 Ret'd.
MANTILLA (12) 7–5 6–4 6–2
Van Lottum (Q) 6–3 6–4 6–4
Krajicek 7–6 6–2 7–5
CORRETJA (6) 7–5 6–4 3–6 6–4

FOURTH ROUND

SAMPRAS (1) 6–3 6–4 6–4
KORDA (15) 4–6 6–3 6–4 7–5
Bjorkman 6–3 6–1 7–5
Draper 7–6 3–6 2–6 6–4 6–4
Rusedski 7–6 6–3 6–1
Vacek 7–6 7–5 6–2
MANTILLA (12) 6–7 6–2 4–6 7–6 6–2
Krajicek w/o

QUARTER-FINALS

KORDA (15) 6–7 7–5 7–6 3–6 7–6
Bjorkman 6–3 6–3 1–6 7–6
Rusedski 7–6 6–2 6–2
Krajicek 7–5 6–3 6–4

SEMI-FINALS

Bjorkman 7–6 6–2 1–0 Ret'd.
Rusedski 7–6 6–2 6–2

FINAL

Rusedski 6–1 3–6 3–6 6–3 7–5

6–3 6–2 4–6 7–5

First round

65 **T. MUSTER** (AUT) (5)
66 T. Henman (GBR)
67 A. Berassategui (ESP)
68 W. Ferreira (RSA)
69 J. Gimelstob (USA)
70 D. Nestor (CAN) (Q)
71 J. Stark (USA)
72 M. Gustafsson (SWE)
73 C. Ruud (NOR)
74 M.-K. Goeliner (GER)
75 F. Meligeni (BRA)
76 J. Szymanski (VEN) (Q)
77 J. Siemerink (NED)
78 M. Larsson (SWE)
79 M. Joyce (USA) (W)
80 N. Escude (FRA) (L)
81 **P. RAFTER** (AUS) (13)
82 A. Medvedev (UKR)
83 K. Kucera (SLO)
84 M. Norman (SWE)
85 P. Haarhuis (NED)
86 G. Blanco (ESP)
87 G. Schaller (AUT)
88 L. Roux (FRA)
89 R. Furlan (ITA)
90 A. Voinea (ROM)
91 S. Campbell (USA) (W)
92 A. Agassi (USA)
93 M. Woodforde (AUS)
94 B. Black (ZIM)
95 C. Caratti (ITA) (Q)
96 **Y. KAFEINIKOV** (RUS) (3)
97 **S. BRUGUERA** (ESP) (7)
98 M. Tebbutt (AUS) (Q)
99 G. Stafford (RSA)
100 E. Alvarez (ESP)
101 H. Gumy (ARG)
102 D. Hrbaty (SLO)
103 T. Woodbridge (AUS)
104 J.A. Marin (ESP)
105 J. Kroslak (SLO)
106 A. Volkov (RUS)
107 T. Haas (GER)
108 O. Gross (GER)
109 K. Carlsen (DEN)
110 T. Ketola (FIN) (Q)
111 L. Smith (AUS) (W)
112 **M. RIOS** (CHI) (10)
113 **A. COSTA** (ESP) (16)
114 A. Boetsch (FRA)
115 C. Costa (ESP)
116 L. Paes (IND)
117 C. Pioline (FRA)
118 P. Wessels (NED) (Q)
119 A. Pavel (ROM)
120 N. Lapentti (ECU)
121 J. Alomso (ESP)
122 S. Sargsian (ARM)
123 T. Johansson (SWE)
124 C. Woodruff (USA)
125 J. Salzenstein (USA) (W)
126 M. Tilstrom (SWE)
127 P. Fredriksson (SWE)
128 **M. CHANG** (USA) (2)

Second round

Henman 6–3 7–6 4–6 6–4
Ferreira 6–7 2–6 6–3 6–1 6–3
Gimelstob 7–6 6–7 6–3 6–2
Gustafsson 6–3 6–2 7–5
Ruud 6–4 4–6 1–6 6–4 6–3
Meligeni 6–2 6–2 6–1
Larsson 6–4 6–2 6–3
Escude (L) 7–6 4–6 6–3 6–1
RAFTER (13) 6–3 6–4 7–5
Norman 6–7 6–4 6–2 6–3
Haarhuis 7–6 6–0 6–7 6–7 6–3
Roux 4–6 0–6 6–3 6–2 6–1
Voinea 6–7 7–6 6–4 6–7 6–3
Agassi 6–1 6–1 4–6 6–3
Woodforde 7–6 6–3 6–2
KAFEINIKOV (3) 6–2 6–4 7–6
BRUGUERA (7) 3–6 4–6 6–3 6–2 6–2
Stafford 6–4 6–2 6–2
Gumy 6–7 6–3 6–7 6–3 6–2
Woodbridge 7–6 6–3 4–6 6–1
Kroslak 3–6 7–6 6–0 6–1
Haas 6–3 6–4 2–6 6–4
Carlsen 6–2 6–3 6–1
RIOS (10) 6–1 6–1 6–4
Boetsch 6–2 6–4 6–4
Paes 6–1 7–5 6–4
Pioline 6–4 6–2 6–2
Lapentti 6–4 5–0 Ret'd.
Sargsian 2–6 0–6 6–0 6–4 6–4
Woodruff 6–3 6–0 3–6 6–0
Salzenstein (W) 6–4 1–6 7–6 7–5
CHANG (2) 6–3 6–4 6–2

Third round

Ferreira 6–3 6–2 6–4
Gimelstob 6–3 3–6 7–6 4–6 6–1
Meligeni 6–3 6–4 6–3
Larsson 6–4 6–2 7–6
RAFTER (13) 6–2 6–1 6–2
Roux 7–6 6–3 6–7 6–7 6–4
Agassi 6–0 6–2 6–2
Woodforde 6–3 6–4 7–6
BRUGUERA (7) 6–4 6–2 7–6
Gumy 7–5 6–4 6–2
Haas 6–4 6–1 6–2
RIOS (10) 6–4 5–7 3–6 6–1 7–6
Paes 6–4 6–0 2–1 Ret'd.
Pioline 6–0 6–4 6–2
Sargsian w/o
CHANG (2) 4–6 6–2 6–3 6–4

Fourth round

Ferreira 5–7 7–6 6–3 6–0
Larsson 6–2 6–4 6–3
RAFTER (13) 6–1 6–1 6–2
Agassi 6–2 6–2 6–4
BRUGUERA (7) 6–1 6–4 5–7 3–6 6–4
RIOS (10) 6–4 3–6 6–3 1–6 6–1
Pioline 3–6 7–6 1–6 6–3 6–4
CHANG (2) 6–1 6–3 7–5

Quarter-finals

Larsson 6–3 7–6 6–3
RAFTER (13) 6–3 7–6 4–6 6–3
RIOS (10) 7–5 6–2 6–4
CHANG (2) 6–3 0–6 5–7 7–5 6–1

Semi-finals

RAFTER (13) 7–6 6–4 6–2
CHANG (2) 7–5 6–2 4–6 4–6 6–3

Final

RAFTER (13) 6–3 6–3 6–4

RAFTER (AUS

Capital letters denote seeded players. Numbers following player's name gives seeding order (Q) – Qualifier, (W) – Wild Card, (L) – Lucky Loser

WOMEN'S SINGLES

Holder: S. Graf (GER)

FIRST ROUND	SECOND ROUND	THIRD ROUND	FOURTH ROUND	QUARTER-FINALS	SEMI-FINALS	FINAL
1 **M. HINGIS** (SUI) (1)	**HINGIS** (1) 6–0 6–1	**HINGIS** (1) 6–1 6–2	**HINGIS** (1) 7–5 6–2	**HINGIS** (1) 6–0 6–2	**HINGIS** (1) 6–3 6–2	**HINGIS** (1) 6–3 6–2
2 T. Jones (USA)						
3 D. Chadkova (CZE)	Chadkova 6–1 1–6 6–1					
4 H. Sukova (CZE)						
5 P. Langrova (CZE)	Likhovtseva 7–5 6–4	Likhovtseva 7–5 6–1				
6 E. Likhovtseva (RUS)						
7 J. Kandarr (GER)	Richterova (Q) 6–1 6–1					
8 L. Richterova (CZE) (Q)						
9 A. Gavaldon (MEX) (Q)	Labat 6–2 6–1	Labat 6–1 6–1	Labat 4–6 7–6 6–1			
10 F. Labat (ARG)						
11 F. Li (CHN) (Q)	Lubiani 6–4 3–6 6–2					
12 F. Lubiani (ITA)						
13 L. Golarsa (ITA)	Barabanschikova 6–3 6–3	Barabanschikova 6–3 6–3				
14 O. Barabanschikova (BLR)						
15 A. Carlsson (SWE)	**SCHULTZ-McCARTHY** (13) 6–7 6–3 6–4					
16 **B. SCHULTZ-McCARTHY** (NED) (13)						
17 **A. SANCHEZ VICARO** (ESP) (10)	**SANCHEZ VICARO** (10) 6–2 6–4	**SANCHEZ VICARO** (10) 6–2 5–7 6–2	**SANCHEZ VICARO** (10) 6–2 6–1	**SANCHEZ VICARO** (10) 6–1 6–2		
18 K.-A. Guse (AUS)						
19 J. Watanabe (USA)	Tu 6–4 7–5					
20 M. Tu (USA)						
21 I. Gorrochategui (ARG)	Miyagi 6–2 7–5	Fusai 6–3 3–6 6–4				
22 N. Miyagi (JPN)						
23 A. Fusai (FRA)	Fusai 6–1 6–1					
24 E. Gagliardi (SUI)						
25 R. Hiraki (JPN)	Hiraki 6–4 4–6 6–2	McQuillan 6–0 6–2	McQuillan 6–2 7–5			
26 M. Diaz-Oliva (ARG)						
27 R. McQuillan (AUS)	McQuillan 4–6 7–5 6–4					
28 C. Torrens-Valero (ESP)						
29 S. Smith (GBR) (Q)	Smith (Q) 6–3 6–1	**MARTINEZ** (7) 6–1 6–0				
30 N. Pratt (AUS) (Q)						
31 J. Capriati (USA)	**MARTINEZ** (7) 6–1 6–2					
32 **C. MARTINEZ** (ESP) (7)						
33 **J. NOVOTNA** (CZE) (3)	**NOVOTNA** (3) 6–0 6–4	**NOVOTNA** (3) 6–4 6–2	**NOVOTNA** (3) 6–2 6–7 6–3	**NOVOTNA** (3) 7–5 6–4	**DAVENPORT** (6) 6–2 4–6 7–6	
34 V. Ruano-Pascual (ESP)						
35 Y. Basuki (INA)	Basuki 6–3 6–4					
36 N. Van Lottum (FRA)						
37 A. Rippner (USA) (W)	Rippner (W) 6–2 6–2	Lucic 6–0 6–1				
38 N. Medvedeva (UKR)						
39 S. Kleinova (CZE)	Lucic 6–0 6–3					
40 M. Lucic (CRO)						
41 S. Dopfer (AUT)	Suarez 6–3 3–6 7–6	Suarez 4–6 7–5 6–4	**FERNANDEZ** (12) 6–1 6–2			
42 P. Suarez (ARG)						
43 J. Trail (USA) (W)	Trail (W) 7–6 6–2					
44 A. Gersi (CZE)						
45 S. Cacic (USA)	Grande 6–2 6–1	**FERNANDEZ** (12) 4–6 6–2 6–2				
46 R. Grande (ITA)						
47 N. Kijimuta (JPN)	**FERNANDEZ** (12) 6–2 6–3					
48 **M.J. FERNANDEZ** (USA) (12)						
49 **K. PO** (USA) (16)	**PO** (16) 6–4 6–1	**PO** (16) 6–3 4–6 7–5	Serna 6–4 6–3	**DAVENPORT** (6) 6–0 6–3		
50 E. Martincova (CZE)						
51 M. Maruska (AUT)	Schett 6–1 6–0					
52 B. Schett (AUT)						
53 M. Serna (ESP)	Serna 6–4 1–6 6–3	Serna 6–4 6–4				
54 M. Grzybowska (POL)						
55 P. Begerow (GER)	Dechy (Q) 6–3 6–1					
56 N. Dechy (FRA) (Q)						
57 P. Schnyder (SUI)	Schnyder 6–2 6–2	Schnyder 4–6 6–2 6–4	**DAVENPORT** (6) 1–6 6–1 6–4			
58 D. Van Roost (BEL)						
59 K. Brandi (USA)	Yoshida 6–7 6–1 6–4					
60 Y. Yoshida (JPN)						
61 W. Probst (GER)	Probst 6–1 5–7 6–3	**DAVENPORT** (6) 6–2 6–3				
62 L. Lee (USA) (W)						
63 L. McNeil (USA) (W)	**DAVENPORT** (6) 6–2 7–6					
64 **L. DAVENPORT** (USA) (6)						

6–0 6–4

65 **A. HUBER** (GER) (8)
66 G. Pizzichini (ITA)
67 J. Lee (USA)
68 M. Saeki (JPN)
69 L. Neiland (LAT)
70 V. Williams (USA)
71 G. Leon-Garcia (ESP)
72 A. Miller (USA)
73 C. Rubin (USA)
74 T. Tanasugarn (THA)
75 M.A. Vento (VEN)
76 A. Glass (GER)
77 H. Nagyova (SLO)
78 A. Olsza (POL)
79 J. Kruger (RSA)
80 **B. PAULUS** (AUT) (14)
81 **R. DRAGOMIR** (ROM) (15)
82 L. Raymond (USA)
83 M. Maleeva (BUL)
84 P. Stojanova (BUL) (Q)
85 N. Tauziat (FRA)
86 K. Habsudova (SLO)
87 A. Grossman (USA)
88 A. Sugiyama (JPN)
89 P. Hy-Boulais (CAN)
90 M. Kochta (GER)
91 K. Studenikova (SLO)
92 E. Wagner (GER)
93 M.A. Sanchez Lorenzo (ESP)
94 S. Testud (FRA)
95 C. Cristea (ROM)
96 **I. MAJOLI** (CRO) (4)
97 **A. COETZER** (RSA) (5)
98 N. Arendt (USA)
99 A.-G. Sidot (FRA)
100 A. Dechaume-Balleret (FRA)
101 S. Pitkowski (FRA)
102 R. Simpson (CAN)
103 E. Callens (BEL)
104 F. Perfetti (ITA)
105 C. Morariu (USA)
106 A. Ellwood (AUS)
107 B. Rittner (GER)
108 L. Osterloh (USA) (W)
109 A. Kournikova (RUS)
110 S. Appelmans (BEL)
111 A. Frazier (USA)
112 **I. SPIRLEA** (ROM) (11)
113 **M. PIERCE** (FRA) (9)
114 G. Fernandez (USA) (W)
115 S. Farina (ITA)
116 L. Wild (USA)
117 N. Sawamalsu (JPN)
118 E. de Lone (USA) (W)
119 R. Zrubakova (SLO)
120 N. Zvereva (BLR)
121 T. Panova (RUS)
122 M. Babel (GER)
123 E. Makarova (RUS)
124 M. Oremans (NED)
125 T. Snyder (USA) (W)
126 O. Lugina (UKR) (Q)
127 K. Boogert (NED)
128 **M. SELES** (USA) (2)

HUBER (8) 6–2 6–2
Lee 6–3 6–7 6–3
Williams 5–7 6–0 6–1
Leon-Garcia 4–6 6–2 6–3
Tanasugarn 6–4 6–0
Vento 1–6 7–6 6–2
Nagyova 6–3 6–0
Kruger 6–1 6–7 6–1
Raymond 6–2 3–6 6–3
Maleeva 6–2 6–3
Habsudova 7–5 7–6
Sugiyama 6–7 7–5 6–2
Hy-Boulais 6–2 6–1
Wagner 6–2 6–3
Testud 6–3 6–3
MAJOLI (4) 6–3 6–2
COETZER (5) 6–3 6–2
Dechaume-Balleret 6–3 3–6 6–3
Pitkowski 6–1 4–6 7–6
Perfetti 6–3 6–4
Morariu 7–6 7–6
Osterloh (W) 6–3 1–6 6–3
Kournikova 6–2 6–0
SPIRLEA (11) 6–1 6–1
PIERCE (9) 6–1 6–2
Farina 6–4 6–7 6–4
Sawamalsu 6–4 6–3
Zvereva 6–1 7–5
Babel 6–4 6–1
Oremans 3–6 6–4 6–4
Snyder (W) 6–0 7–6
SELES (2) 6–1 6–2

HUBER (8) 6–2 6–1
Williams 6–0 6–1
Tanasugarn 6–4 6–3
Kruger 6–4 7–6
Maleeva 3–6 6–2 6–4
Habsudova 5–7 6–3 7–5
Wagner 6–3 0–6 7–6
Testud 6–4 2–6 6–1
COETZER (5) 6–1 6–1
Perfetti 6–4 6–3
Osterloh (W) 6–7 6–1 3–0 Ret'd.
SPIRLEA (11) 6–1 3–6 6–3
PIERCE (9) 6–2 3–0 Ret'd.
Zvereva 6–4 3–6 6–3
Oremans 7–5 6–1
SELES (2) 6–2 6–3

Williams 6–3 6–4
Kruger 6–7 7–5 6–4
Habsudova 0–6 7–5 6–1
Testud 6–1 6–3
COETZER (5) 6–2 7–5
SPIRLEA (11) 6–2 7–5
PIERCE (9) 7–6 6–1
SELES (2) 6–1 6–1

Williams 6–2 6–3
Testud 6–3 4–6 7–6
SPIRLEA (11) 7–6 6–4
SELES (2) 1–6 6–2 6–2

Williams 7–5 7–5
SPIRLEA (11) 6–7 7–6 6–3

Williams 7–6 4–6 7–6

HINGIS

Capital letters denote seeded players. Numbers following player's name gives seeding order (Q) – Qualifier, (W) – Wild Card, (L) – Lucky Loser

MEN'S DOUBLES

Holders: Woodbridge (AUS)/Woodforde (AUS)

FIRST ROUND

1 **WOODBRIDGE/WOODFORDE** (1)
2 Kempers/Oosting
3 W. Black/Grabb
4 Ekerot/Tebbutt
5 Albano/Corretja
6 Coupe/Djordjevic
7 Cash/A. Kratzmann
8 **CONNELL/NESTOR** (15)
9 **LEACH/STARK** (9)
10 Ivanisevic/Suk
11 Middleton/Pereira
12 Davids/Knippschild
13 Schalken/Siemerink
14 Sell/Witt (W)
15 Pimek/Talbot
16 **DAMM/OLHOVSKIY** (7)
17 **LAREAU/O'BRIEN** (3)
18 Mirnyi/Ullyett
19 Godwin/Muller
20 Novak/Riki
21 Ondruska/Stafford
22 Gimelstob/Woodruff (W)
23 Grant/Merklein
24 **KRONEMANN/MACPHERSON** (14)
25 **BJORKMAN/KULTI** (11)
26 B. Bryan/M. Bryan (W)
27 Hawk/Overholser (W)
28 Barnard/Nijssen
29 Davis/Jones
30 Pescariu/Sanguinetti (Q)
31 Korda/Reneberg
32 **PHILIPPOUSSIS/RAFTER** (5)
33 **LOBO/SANCHEZ** (6)
34 Groen/Prinosil
35 Randall/Waite
36 Spadea/Taino (W)
37 Haygarth/Van Emberg
38 MacPhie/Salzenstein
39 de Jager/Koenig (Q)
40 **BROAD/NORVAL** (12)
41 **JOHNSON/MONTANA** (13)
42 Eagle/Florent
43 L. Jensen/M. Jensen
44 Nyborg/Sargisian
45 Fredriksson/Van Houdt
46 Smith/Tramacchi (Q)
47 Ortiz/Sa (Q)
48 **KAFELNIKOV/VACEK** (4)
49 **E. FERREIRA/GALBRAITH** (8)
50 Behrens/McEnroe
51 Brandi/Messori
52 Raoux/Tarango
53 Braasch/Shelton
54 Kilderry/Lapentti
55 Arthurs/Kitinov
56 **BHUPATHI/PAES** (10)
57 **DELAITRE/SANTORO** (16)
58 Berasategui/Roditi
59 Noteboom/Wibier
60 Blenkiron/Smith (W)
61 Adams/W. Ferreira
62 Kuerten/Meligeni
63 B. Black/Steven
64 **ELTINGH/HAARHUIS** (2)

SECOND ROUND

Kempers/Oosting 6–4 3–6 6–1
W. Black/Grabb 3–6 6–2 6–3
Albano/Corretja 7–5 6–4
CONNELL/NESTOR (15) 6–3 7–6
Ivanisevic/Suk 6–4 7–5
Davids/Knippschild 6–3 7–6
Sell/Witt (W) 6–7 7–6 7–6
DAMM/OLHOVSKIY (7) 4–6 6–3 7–6
LAREAU/O'BRIEN (3) 7–5 7–6
Novak/Riki 7–5 7–6
Gimelstob/Woodruff (W) 5–7 7–6 6–4
KRONEMANN/MACPHERSON (14) 2–6 7–6 7–5
BJORKMAN/KULTI (11) 6–4 6–3
Hawk/Overholser (W) 7–5 7–6
Pescariu/Sanguinetti (Q) 6–1 6–3
PHILIPPOUSSIS/RAFTER (5) 7–6 7–6
LOBO/SANCHEZ (6) 4–6 7–6 7–6
Randall/Waite 6–2 6–4
MacPhie/Salzenstein 7–6 6–3
de Jager/Koenig (Q) 2–6 7–6 6–3
JOHNSON/MONTANA (13) 6–4 6–4
Nyborg/Sargisian 7–6 6–7 6–4
Fredriksson/Van Houdt 6–4 2–6 6–3
KAFELNIKOV/VACEK (4) 6–3 6–2
Behrens/McEnroe 7–6 4–6 7–5
Raoux/Tarango 7–6 6–4
Kilderry/Lapentti 4–6 7–6 6–4
BHUPATHI/PAES (10) 6–4 6–4
Berasategui/Roditi 6–7 6–3 6–3
Noteboom/Wibier 2–6 7–5 6–2
Adams/W. Ferreira 4–6 7–5 6–3
ELTINGH/HAARHUIS (2) 7–6 7–6

THIRD ROUND

W. Black/Grabb 5–7 6–4 7–6
CONNELL/NESTOR (15) w/o
Ivanisevic/Suk 4–6 6–4 6–3
DAMM/OLHOVSKIY (7) 7–5 3–6 7–6
Novak/Riki 6–4 7–6
KRONEMANN/MACPHERSON (14) w/o
BJORKMAN/KULTI (11) 6–2 6–1
PHILIPPOUSSIS/RAFTER (5) 6–2 6–4
Randall/Waite 6–3 7–6
de Jager/Koenig (Q) 7–5 7–6
JOHNSON/MONTANA (13) 2–6 7–6 6–4
KAFELNIKOV/VACEK (4) 4–6 6–2 6–1
Raoux/Tarango 6–3 6–7 7–6
BHUPATHI/PAES (10) 6–7 6–3 7–6
Berasategui/Roditi 6–4 6–3
Adams/W. Ferreira 6–4 7–6

QUARTER-FINALS

W. Black/Grabb 7–6 6–1
Ivanisevic/Suk 6–4 6–2
Novak/Riki 6–4 7–5
BJORKMAN/KULTI (11) 6–2 6–4
de Jager/Koenig (Q) 6–2 3–6 6–2
KAFELNIKOV/VACEK (4) 1–6 6–3 6–4
BHUPATHI/PAES (10) 4–6 6–4 7–6
Adams/W. Ferreira 6–3 6–3

SEMI-FINALS

W. Black/Grabb 7–6 6–3
BJORKMAN/KULTI (11) 7–6 3–6 6–4
KAFELNIKOV/VACEK (4) 7–5 7–5
BHUPATHI/PAES (10) 6–4 7–6

FINAL

BJORKMAN/KULTI (11) 7–5 7–6
KAFELNIKOV/VACEK (4) 7–6 7–6

KAFELNIKOV (RUS)/**VACEK** (CZE) (4) 7–6 6–3

Capital letters denote seeded players. Numbers following player's name gives seeding order (Q) – Qualifier, (W) – Wild Card, (L) – Lucky Loser

WOMEN'S DOUBLES

Holders: G. Fernandez (USA)/Zvereva (BLR)

FIRST ROUND

1 **G. FERNANDEZ/ZVEREVA** (1)
2 Pullin/Woodroffe
3 Probst/Sugiyama
4 Richterova/Stojanova (Q)
5 Hetherington/Rinaldi-Stunkel
6 S. Williams/V. Williams (W)
7 Nemeckova/Noorlander
8 **RAYMOND/STUBBS** (10)
9 **M.J. FERNANDEZ/HUBER** (12)
10 Lugina/Wagner
11 Olsza/Studenikova
12 Ruano-Pascual/Suarez
13 Rubin/Schultz-McCarthy
14 Jeyaseelan/Simpson
15 Buth/Nickitas (W)
16 **FUSAI/TAUZIAT** (7)
17 **ARENDT/BOLLEGRAF** (4)
18 Morariu/Muric
19 Park/Tanasugarn
20 Barclay/Wood
21 Cristea/Grzybowska
22 Freye/Van Lottum
23 Melicharova/Vildova
24 **FRAZIER/PO** (13)
25 **DRAGOMIR/MAJOLI** (16)
26 Schett/Siddall
27 Garrone/Pizzichini
28 Medvedeva/Tatarkova
29 Guse/McQuillan
30 Irvin/Stevenson (W)
31 Callens/Helgeson-Nielsen
32 **NEILAND/SUKOVA** (5)
33 **BASUKI/VIS** (6)
34 Carlsson/Hy-Boulais
35 Grossman/Habsudova
36 McShea/Wainwright (Q)
37 J. Lee/L. Lee
38 Montalvo/Pleming
39 Ellwood/Kunce
40 **APPELMANS/OREMANS** (11)
41 **KIJIMUTA/MIYAGI** (9)
42 Grande/Wild
43 Hiraki/Sidot
44 D. Jones/T. Jones
45 Rittner/Van Roost
46 Dechaume-Balleret/Testud
47 Garrison/McNeil (W)
48 **DAVENPORT/NOVOTNA** (3)
49 **MARTINEZ/TARABINI** (8)
50 Moros/Scott (Q)
51 de Swardt/Graham
52 Langrova/Zrubakova
53 Labat/Paz
54 Lettiere/Tu
55 Saeki/Yoshida
56 **ADAMS/BOOGERT** (14)
57 **KOURNIKOVA/LIKHOVTSEVA** (15)
58 Miller/Steven (Q)
59 Krizan/Martincova
60 Babel/Golarsa
61 Nagyova/Schnyder
62 Coetzer/Pierce
63 Gorrochategui/Spirlea
64 **HINGIS/SANCHEZ VICARIO** (2)

SECOND ROUND

G. FERNANDEZ/ZVEREVA (1) 6–4 6–4
Probst/Sugiyama 6–1 6–3
Hetherington/Rinaldi-Stunkel 6–4 7–5
RAYMOND/STUBBS (10) 6–1 6–2
M.J. FERNANDEZ/HUBER (12) 6–1 6–3
Ruano-Pascual/Suarez 6–1 7–5
Jeyaseelan/Simpson 6–1 7–5
FUSAI/TAUZIAT (7) 6–7 6–3 6–2
ARENDT/BOLLEGRAF (4) 6–4 6–4
Park/Tanasugarn 7–6 6–4
Cristea/Grzybowska 6–2 6–4
FRAZIER/PO (13) 6–0 6–3
DRAGOMIR/MAJOLI (16) 6–4 7–5
Medvedeva/Tatarkova 6–4 6–4
Guse/McQuillan 6–1 6–4
NEILAND/SUKOVA (5) 6–3 7–5
BASUKI/VIS (6) 2–6 6–3 6–1
McShea/Wainwright (Q) 6–3 6–2
Montalvo/Pleming 6–3 7–5
Ellwood/Kunce 6–2 6–2
KIJIMUTA/MIYAGI (9) 6–3 6–3
Hiraki/Sidot 6–1 6–4
Dechaume-Balleret/Testud 7–6 7–5
DAVENPORT/NOVOTNA (3) 6–2 4–6 6–3
MARTINEZ/TARABINI (8) 6–2 6–3
de Swardt/Graham 6–1 6–3
Labat/Paz 6–1 6–3
ADAMS/BOOGERT (14) 6–2 7–5
KOURNIKOVA/LIKHOVTSEVA (15) 6–2 6–7 6–4
Babel/Golarsa 7–5 6–4
Coetzer/Pierce 6–0 6–1
HINGIS/SANCHEZ VICARIO (2) 6–3 6–1

THIRD ROUND

G. FERNANDEZ/ZVEREVA (1) 6–1 6–4
RAYMOND/STUBBS (10) 6–1 5–7 6–3
M.J. FERNANDEZ/HUBER (12) 6–2 6–4
FUSAI/TAUZIAT (7) 7–6 6–2
ARENDT/BOLLEGRAF (4) 7–6 6–4
FRAZIER/PO (13) 6–4 7–5
DRAGOMIR/MAJOLI (16) 6–2 4–6 6–4
NEILAND/SUKOVA (5) 6–4 6–4
BASUKI/VIS (6) 6–2 7–6
Ellwood/Kunce 6–4 6–1
KIJIMUTA/MIYAGI (9) 2–1 Ret'd.
DAVENPORT/NOVOTNA (3) 7–6 6–2
MARTINEZ/TARABINI (8) 7–6 4–6 6–4
ADAMS/BOOGERT (14) 6–2 6–3
KOURNIKOVA/LIKHOVTSEVA (15) 5–7 6–3 6–3
HINGIS/SANCHEZ VICARIO (2) 6–4 6–2

QUARTER-FINALS

G. FERNANDEZ/ZVEREVA (1) 6–3 6–4
FUSAI/TAUZIAT (7) 4–6 6–3 6–1
ARENDT/BOLLEGRAF (4) 6–4 6–2
DRAGOMIR/MAJOLI (16) 6–2 Ret'd.
BASUKI/VIS (6) 6–0 6–4
DAVENPORT/NOVOTNA (3) 6–7 6–2 6–2
MARTINEZ/TARABINI (8) 6–4 6–7 6–4
HINGIS/SANCHEZ VICARIO (2) 6–4 6–4

SEMI-FINALS

G. FERNANDEZ/ZVEREVA (1) 4–6 6–2 6–2
ARENDT/BOLLEGRAF (4) 6–3 3–6 6–4
DAVENPORT/NOVOTNA (3) 6–3 7–5
HINGIS/SANCHEZ VICARIO (2) 4–0 Ret'd.

FINAL

G. FERNANDEZ/ZVEREVA (1) 3–6 7–6 6–2
DAVENPORT/NOVOTNA (3) 6–4 6–3

DAVENPORT (USA)/**NOVOTNA** (CZE) (3) 6–3 6–4

Capital letters denote seeded players. Numbers following player's name gives seeding order (Q) – Qualifier, (W) – Wild Card, (L) – Lucky Loser

MIXED DOUBLES

Holders: Galbraith (USA)/Raymond (USA)

FIRST ROUND	SECOND ROUND	QUARTER-FINALS	SEMI-FINALS	FINAL	
1 **GALBRAITH/RAYMOND** (1)	**GALBRAITH/RAYMOND** (1) 7–5 4–6 6–3	**GALBRAITH/RAYMOND** (1) 6–3 4–6 6–3	**GALBRAITH/RAYMOND** (1) 7–5 6–3	Albano/Paz 6–4 7–6	**LEACH (USA)/BOLLEGRAF (NED) (5)** 3–6 7–5 7–6
2 Lobo/Gorrochategui					
3 Johnson/Boogert	Kitinov/Miyagi 7–6 6–2				
4 Kitinov/Miyagi					
5 Middleton/McNeil	Tarango/Likhovtseva 7–6 6–2	Tarango/Likhovtseva 6–3 5–7 6–2			
6 Tarango/Likhovtseva					
7 Davids/Oremans	**OOSTING/BASUKI** (7) 3–6 6–3 7–5				
8 **OOSTING/BASUKI** (7)					
9 **OLHOVSKIY/NEILAND** (3)	**OLHOVSKIY/NEILAND** (3) 6–0 7–6	**OLHOVSKIY/NEILAND** (3) 6–3 6–3	Albano/Paz w/o		
10 Bryan/Osterloh					
11 Philippoussis/Kournikova	Philippoussis/Kournikova 6–4 6–3				
12 Grabb/Graham					
13 Albano/Paz	Albano/Paz 6–3 6–4	Albano/Paz 7–6 6–3			
14 Broad/Wild					
15 Eagle/Huber	**SUK/SUKOVA** (6) 4–1 Ret'd.				
16 **SUK/SUKOVA** (6)					
17 **LEACH/BOLLEGRAF** (5)	**LEACH/BOLLEGRAF** (5) 6–4 6–4	**LEACH/BOLLEGRAF** (5) 6–3 6–3	**LEACH/BOLLEGRAF** (5) 7–5 6–3	**LEACH/BOLLEGRAF** (5) 6–3 6–4	
18 Kronemann/Frazier					
19 Macpherson/Guse	Macpherson/Guse 6–4 2–6 7–6				
20 Paes/Dragomir					
21 Wibier/Vis	Waite/Po 6–1 7–5	**NESTOR/TAUZIAT** (4) 6–2 4–6 6–3			
22 Waite/Po					
23 M. Jensen/R. Jensen	**NESTOR/TAUZIAT** (4) 6–2 7–6				
24 **NESTOR/TAUZIAT** (4)					
25 **BHUPATHI/HIRAKI** (8)	Florent/Adams 6–4 2–6 6–2	L. Jensen/Schultz-McCarthy 7–6 6–2	L. Jensen/Schultz-McCarthy 7–6 6–4		
26 Florent/Adams					
27 Talbot/Stubbs	L. Jensen/Schultz-McCarthy 6–4 6–3				
28 L. Jensen/Schultz-McCarthy					
29 Pimek/Tarabini	Norval/Callens 6–2 6–3	**E. FERREIRA/G. FERNANDEZ** (2) 7–6 6–2			
30 Norval/Callens					
31 Gimelstob/Rubin	**E. FERREIRA/G. FERNANDEZ** (2) 6–3 6–4				
32 **E. FERREIRA/G. FERNANDEZ** (2)					

Capital letters denote seeded players. Numbers following player's name gives seeding order (Q) – Qualifier, (W) – Wild Card, (L) – Lucky Loser

Although Martina lost serve to start both sets in her 6–2 6–4 semi-final success against 6th seeded Davenport, the match was otherwise uneventful. But Lindsay's wind-tormented 6–2 4–6 7–6 (7–5) quarter-final win over 3rd seeded Novotna was a suspenseful screamer that Jana surrendered by failing to cash two match points. Serving for it at 5–4 she saw an apparent winning backhand gusted barely wide. At 6–5 the match point was wrenched away by Lindsay's roaring forehand. In the breaker Novotna had 5–4 with serve but Davenport crashed winners on two of the last three points.

Novotna had firmed up late but impressively in the third round, winning the last five games to chase the other marvellous rookie, 15-year-old Croatian wild card Mirjana Lucic, 6–2 6–7 (3–7) 6–3.

The Aussie-Swiss double paid each champion $650,000. A 20-year-old Thai, Tamarine Tanasugarn, had struck the first ball, lost the first point with a wayward backhand, but won the first match in the freshly risen amphitheatre, 6–4 6–0, over American Chanda Rubin. Rafter had volleyed the last point of the first annual recital in 'Arthur's Gulch' to crown himself as the king of Queens (and the rest of the country). And from one of his provinces an unknown 16-year-old out of Possum Trot, Kentucky, No. 897 wild card Jacqueline Trail, won a round.

Presumably that made the possums as happy as the majority of the thousands who came rushing to Flushing to launch a new American era in the 30th year of Open tennis.

JUNIOR EVENTS

BOYS' SINGLES – Final: Arnaud di Pasquale (FRA) (4) d. Westley Whitehouse (RSA) (3) 6–7 6–4 6–1
GIRLS' SINGLES – Final: Cara Black (ZIM) (1) d. Kildine Chevalier (FRA) 6–7 6–1 6–3
BOYS' DOUBLES – Final: Fernando Gonzalez (CHI)/Nicolas Massu (CHI) (1) d. Jean-Rene Lisnard (FRA)/ Michael Llodra (FRA) 6–4 6–4
GIRLS' DOUBLES – Final: Marissa Irvin (USA)/Alexandra Stevenson (USA) (6) d. Cara Black (ZIM)/Irina Selyutina (KAZ) (1) 6–2 7–6

SENIOR EVENTS

MEN'S 35s DOUBLES MASTERS (Round robin in two groups of 4) – Final: Johan Kriek (USA)/John Lloyd (GBR) d. Gene Mayer (USA)/Hank Pfister (USA) 7–6 6–2
MEN'S 45s DOUBLES MASTERS (Round robin in four groups of 4) – Final: Brian Gottfried (USA)/ Alexander Mayer (USA) d. Bob Lutz (USA)/Stan Smith (USA) 7–6 6–1
WOMEN'S DOUBLES MASTERS (Round robin in two groups of 4) – Final: Wendy Overton (USA)/Anne Smith (USA) d. Terry Holladay (USA)/ Olga Morozova (RUS) 6–3 3–6 7–6
MIXED DOUBLES MASTERS (Eight teams, knock-out) – Final: Sherwood Stewart (USA)/Jo Durie (GBR) d. Dick Stockton (USA)/Rosie Casals (USA) 7–6 7–6

1997 US OPEN CHAMPIONSHIPS
PRIZE MONEY – Total $11,821,890

MEN'S AND WOMEN'S SINGLES – Winner $650,000. Runner-up $350,000. Semi-finalists $175,000. Quarter-finalists $90,000. Fourth-round losers $45,000. Third-round losers $25,000. Second-round losers $15,000. First-round losers $10,000.
Totals: MEN $3,590,000; WOMEN $3,590,000.

MEN'S AND WOMEN'S DOUBLES – 64 draws (per pair) – Winners $300,000. Runners-up $150,000. Semi-finalists $75,000. Quarter-finalists $32,500. Third-round losers $16,000. Second-round losers $10,000. First-round losers $6,000.
Totals: MEN $1,210,000; WOMEN $1,210,000.

MIXED DOUBLES – 32 draw (per pair) – Winners $100,000. Runners-up $50,000. Semi-finalists $25,000. Quarter-finalists $12,500. Second-round losers $6,000. First-round losers $3,000.
Total: $346,000

QUALIFYING COMPETITIONS – $456,000
MEN – 128 draw (each): 16 x Third-round losers $6,000. 32 x Second-round losers $4,000. 64 x First-round losers $2,000.
Total: $352,000
WOMEN – 64 draw (each): 8 x Third-round losers $6,000. 16 x Second-round losers $4,000. 32 x First-round losers $2,000.
Total $176,000

Total for doubles qualifying – $40,000
Total for senior events – $400,000
Total for per diem allowances and other fees – $907,890

Pete Sampras, the only man to have won the Compaq Grand Slam Cup twice, has banked a cool $7,393,750 from that event alone among his astronomical on-court career earnings of $32,060,658. (Stephen Wake)

Compaq Grand Slam Cup

John Parsons

In many ways this was the year in which the Compaq Grand Slam Cup dismissed all doubts about its credibility – despite what its ingrained critics would have you believe.

While the all too evident drop in attendances was a matter for some concern, the fierceness of the competition and the quality of the tennis made this a hugely successful tournament. That fans who had purchased seats decided to stay away could be explained by the clash with Munich's annual Oktoberfest during a spell of glorious sunny weather.

For the first time since the event was conceived in 1990, the final was fought out between two reigning Grand Slam champions. The manner in which Pete Sampras, holder of both the Australian and Wimbledon titles, beat Patrick Rafter, the recently crowned US Open champion, 6–2 6–4 7–5 was the sort of handsome performance befitting the world number one.

This was the second successive Sunday that Rafter, recently installed in a career best third place in the rankings, had lost to the American. The previous week it had been in the semi-finals of the Davis Cup in Washington when Rafter at least took the first set. This time, though, Sampras's overwhelming mastery – he dropped only eight points in his 15 service games – would probably have been just as clear cut even if Rafter had not played such an exhausting semi-final against Petr Korda the day before. In that epic contest, which lasted 4 hours 16 minutes, Rafter, whose personality on court was winning him almost as many admirers as his refreshingly positive tennis, had to save three match points in the fourth set and then missed three of his own in the fifth before winning 7–5 3–6 6–7 7–6 9–7.

Rafter, who had earlier dismissed a fading Thomas Muster 6–2 6–3 and then Marcelo Rios from Chile 6–1 7–6, was clearly enjoying his new found situation so close to the top of the tennis tree after his success at Flushing Meadows. There were many in Munich ready to nominate him as the likely successor to Sampras as world number one, though none of them – and certainly not Rafter – was suggesting that the passing of the crown was imminent. On the other hand, Rafter's style of play indicated that the wait would be worthwhile.

Whatever the lack of commitment there might have been in some matches in previous years, that was certainly not the case this time. While it was disappointing that first Filip Dewulf against Cedric Pioline and then Gustavo Kuerten against Korda, had to default through injuries in first round matches, no-one who saw the extent to which their respective ankles ballooned after two nasty falls, could have doubted the legitimacy of such problems.

Furthermore Korda, the 1993 winner, who had been severely lambasted for apparently giving up so tamely against Jonas Bjorkman at the US Open while suffering from a heavy cold, fought with great tenacity and willpower in that thrilling semi-final. His returning in the third set, especially, was spectacular and it looked as if the balance had swung his way when he won the opening point of the tie-break with a scintillating backhand return and then hit four aces as Rafter looked as if he might crumble. Instead the Australian held on even more doggedly, saving two break points in the sixth game of the fourth set and another in the eighth – all with aces.

It was the same when Korda held three match points at 6–5 in the fourth. The Czech left-hander was effectively stunned into errors by the sheer refusal of his opponent to submit. Rafter's victory, with his $250,000 bonus for winning in New York, meant that he would be going home to his tax refuge in Bermuda with at least $1 million.

For his part, Sampras had looked a shade rusty as he dropped a set to the persistent, rather than totally persuasive Felix Mantilla, before beating the Spaniard 6–4 3–6 6–2 and he was still not totally at ease during his 7–6 6–4 victory over Sweden's Bjorkman. Atlantic hopping, as Sampras called it, can take it out of you, even on Concorde.

The first set tie-break was the crunch. Sampras led 4 points to 1 but Bjorkman, with double-handed backhand returns and then a net cord coming to the rescue, levelled at 5–5. In an extraordinary climax to the match, Bjorkman double faulted to present the American with set point at 6–5 only for Sampras to overhit a backhand. A winning service gave Sampras a second set point on which another Bjorkman double fault, this time another cruel net cord, was decisive.

It was again a double fault that gave Sampras the one break he needed in the second set.

Bjorkman will no doubt always insist he was unlucky, especially in the tie-break but it was more a case of his luck running out. For when he was serving at 0–30, 5–6 in the first set, television showed that another of those elegant Sampras backhand volleys which was called out, had clearly been in. Not only would Sampras, in all probability, have then taken the set without need of a nail-biting tie-break but he would also have started serving in the second set. On the other hand the match might not have been so compelling.

So to the contribution by Greg Rusedski, the first British player to qualify for the tournament on merit, rather than as a reserve for absentees, who this time were Michael Chang, Carlos Moya and the injured Richard Krajicek. In what at times was an agonisingly close affair, mainly because both players were so erratic, the British number one increased his guaranteed prize money from $100,000 to $250,000 when, thanks almost entirely to the under-pinning provided by 20 aces, he edged past Todd Woodbridge 4–6 6–1 7–5.

Woodbridge had raced to 4–0 in the first set, playing superbly. By the end, however, he had also hit a disastrous 14 double faults. But Rusedski missed three break points when Woodbridge was 0–40 in the first game of the final set and then had to volley and ace his way out of two self-inflicted break points in the seventh game and two more when serving for the match. It was that kind of occasion.

'It's hard not to think about the $250,000 at stake when you start serving in the last game of a match like this but fortunately I managed to serve it out,' said Rusedski. There was plenty of time for more thought during the two clear days he had to wait before tackling Yevgeny Kafelnikov, the Russian who had trounced him the only other time they had met.

The first set went to a tie-break after Rusedski had saved two set points in the tenth game. The British No.1 had won his previous seven tie-breaks but lost this one 7–5 after his fifth double fault had put him 2–4 down. Once again, though, Rusedski responded with courage after a wild overhead which flew yards out of court left him 15–40 in the opening game of the second set. Two aces, the second of them needing an over-rule to confirm its validity, provided not only that moment's salvation but also the inspiration for Rusedski to turn things round. He made it 3–0 with a world record 143mph 15th ace, one of 23 he delivered in the course of a rousing 6–7 6–3 6–1 win. It also transpired that this was his first match being assisted, albeit only in pre-match telephone calls at this stage, by his new coach, Tony Pickard.

Although Sampras eventually stemmed the tide of aces, Rusedski was looking altogether a more complete player as he went down 3–6 7–6 7–6 6–2 in the semi-finals. Some of his first volleys had Sampras raising his bushy eyebrows and his backhand returns and passes were also causing embarrassment. It was another tremendously spirited and challenging effort. 'For two sets that was probably the best anyone has served against me,' said Sampras. 'I was just happy that he eventually gave me a couple of second serves which gave me the chance to strike back and from then I felt I returned too well for him.'

As to the future of the event, opinion is still divided between those who argue that it should combine with the ATP Tour Championships and those who feel that the present concept is valid. I take the latter view and believe it should be extended and made a true reflection of the Grand Slam year by incorporating the women and, indeed, also the juniors. That would highlight the way the event also produces $2 million each year for the International Tennis Federation to plough back into junior development which in turn helps produce future Grand Slam winners.

One other thing. A date change was absolutely necessary but this was not the right one. Ideally the Grand Slam Cup should take place a little later, in mid-October. This would give a little more build-up time after the US Open and would separate it both from the semi-finals of the Davis Cup... and that marvellous but so distracting Munich beer festival!

COMPAQ GRAND SLAM CUP 1997

Olympiahall, Munich, 23–28 September

Prize money $6 million (Winner $1,500,000; Runner-up $750,000; Semi-finalists $425,000; Quarter-finalists $250,000; First round $100,000; Alternates $50,000) Note: A bonus of $250,000 is paid to the winner of each Grand Slam who participates.

First round: P. Sampras (1) d. F. Mantilla 6–4 3–6 6–2; J. Bjorkman (8) d. B. Becker (WC) 6–3 6–2; G. Rusedski (4) d. T. Woodbridge 4–6 6–1 7–5; Y. Kafelnikov d. S. Bruguera (5) 6–4 6–3; C. Pioline (6) d. F. Dewulf 7–6 2–2 ret; P. Korda d. G. Kuerten (3) 6–3 5–3 ret; M. Rios (7) d. M. Woodforde (A) 6–7 6–3 6–1; P. Rafter (2) d. T. Muster 6–2 6–3. ***Quarter-finals:*** Sampras (1) d. Bjorkman (8) 7–6 6–4; Rusedski (4) d. Kafelnikov 6–7 6–3 6–1; Korda d. Pioline (6) 7–5 6–3; Rafter (2) d. Rios (7) 6–1 7–6. ***Semi-finals:*** Sampras (1) d. Rusedski (4) 3–6 7–6 7–6 6–2; Rafter (2) d. Korda 7–5 3–6 6–7 7–6 9–7. ***Final:*** Sampras (1) d. Rafter (2) 6–2 6–4 7–5.

COMPAQ GRAND SLAM CUP RESULTS 1990–96 – Olympiahalle, Munich

1990 (11–16 Dec) **Prize Money $6 million** (Winner $2,000,000; Runner-up $1,000,000; Semi-finalists $450,000; Quarter-finalists $300,000; First Round $100,000; Alternates $50,000.) **First round:** M. Chang d. S. Edberg(1) 6–4 4–6 7–5; H. Leconte d. T. Muster(7) 6–3 6–4; P. Sampras(4) d. A. Cherkasov 5–7 6–2 7–5; G. Ivanisevic(5) d. K. Curren 7–6 7–6; B. Gilbert d. J. Svensson(6) 2–6 6–3 6–4; A. Krickstein d. A. Gomez(3) 6–3 6–4; D. Wheaton(8) d. Y. Noah 7–6 6–7 6–3; I. Lendl(2) d. C. Bergstrom 6–4 6–0. **Quarter-finals:** Chang d. Leconte 7–6 6–3; Sampras(4) d. Ivanisevic(5) 7–6 6–7 8–6; Gilbert d. Krickstein 6–7 6–4 6–3; Wheaton(8) d. Lendl(2) 6–2 7–6. **Semi-finals:** Sampras(4) d. Chang 6–3 6–4 6–4; Gilbert d. Wheaton(8) 6–3 3–6 7–6 2–6 6–4. **Final:** Sampras(4) d. Gilbert 6–3 6–4 6–2.

1991 (10–15 Dec) **Prize Money $6 million** (Winner $2,000,000; Runner-up $1,000,000; Semi-finalists $450,000; Quarter-finalists $300,000; First Round $100,000; Alternates $50,000.) **First round:** T. Woodbridge (ALT) d. A. Krickstein 6–3 6–3; D. Wheaton(7) d. P. Haarhuis, 1–6 6–3 6–2; M. Stich(3) d. G. Prpic 6–4 6–3; G. Forget(5) d. J. Yzaga 6–3 6–3; J. Hlasek d. J. Connors(6) 0–6 6–4 6–4; I. Lendl(4) d. C. Caratti 6–4 6–1; P. McEnroe(8) d. T. Champion 4–6 6–1 6–4; M. Chang d. J. Courier(2) 6–4 6–2. **Quarter-finals:** Wheaton(7) d. Woodbridge 6–4 7–6; Stich(3) d. Forget(5) 7–6 6–4; Lendl(4) d. Hlasek 7–6 6–3; Chang d. McEnroe 6–2 6–4. **Semi-finals:** Wheaton(7) d. Stich(3) 7–6 7–6 7–6; Chang d. Lendl(4) 2–6 4–6 6–4 7–6 9–7. **Final:** Wheaton(7) d. Chang 7–5 6–2 6–4.

1992 (8–13 Dec) **Prize Money $6 million** (Winner $2,000,000; Runner-up $1,000,000; Semi-finalists $450,000 Quarter-finalists $300,000; First Round $100,000; Alternates $50,000.) **First round:** M. Stich d. S. Edberg(1) 7–6 6–7 8–6; R. Krajicek(8) d. E. Sanchez 6–3 6–2; P. Sampras(3) d. A. Volkov 6–3 6–4; H. Leconte d. W. Ferreira(5) 3–6 6–3 6–0; P. McEnroe(6) d N. Kulti 6–1 6–4 G. Ivanisevic(4) d. G. Forget 7–5 6–4; P. Korda(7) d. W. Masur 2–6 7–5 6–4 M. Chang d. A. Agassi(2) 6–4 6–2. **Quarter-finals:** Stich d. Krajicek(8) 7–6 7–5; Sampras(3) d. Leconte 7–6 6–4; Ivanisevic(4) d. McEnroe(6) 3–6– 6–4 6–2; Chang d. Korda(7); **Semi-finals:** Stich d. Sampras(3) 7–6 7–6 3–6 7–6; Chang d. Ivanisevic(4). **Final:** Stich d. Chang 6–7 6–2 6–4 3–6 6–3.

1993 (7–12 Dec) **Prize Money $6 million** (Winner $1,625,000; Runner-up $812,500; Semi-finalists $431,250; Quarter-finalists $262,500; First round $100,000; Alternates $50,000) (Note: A bonus of $250,000 is paid to the winner of each Grand Slam Championship who participates.) **First round:** P. Sampras(1) d. T. Muster 6–3 6–1; M. Chang d. W. Masur(8) 6–2 4–6 7–5; S. Bruguera(3) d. M. Larsson 6–3 6–4; P. Korda d. A. Volkov 6–2 6–3; M. Stich(5) d. M. Washington 6–3 6–1; B.Steven(ALT) d. C. Pioline(4) 6–4 7–6(9–7); W. Ferreira d. B. Becker(7) 7–5 6–4; S. Edberg(2) d. T. Martin 6–3 6–2. **Quarter-finals:** Sampras(1) d. Chang 7–6(9–7) 6–3; Korda d. Sergi Bruguera(3) 4–6 6–0 6–4; Stich(5) d. Steven 5–7 6–4 6–4; Edberg(2) d. Ferreira 6–7(7–5) 6–1 6–0. **Semi-finals:** Korda d. Sampras(1) 3–6 7–6(7–3) 3–6 7–6(12–10) 13–11; Stich(5) d. Edberg(2) 2–6 3–6 6–3 6–3 6–l. **Final:** Korda d. Stich(5) 2–6 6–4 7–6 2–6 11–9.

1994 (6–11 Dec) **Prize money $6 million** (Winner $1,500,000; Runner-up $750,000; Semi-finalists $425,000; Quarter-finalists $250,000; First round $100,000; Alternates $50,000.) (Note: A bonus of $250,000 is paid to the winner of each Grand Slam Championship who participates.) **First round:** P. Sampras(1) d. J. Yzaga 6–2 6–4; M. Chang(8) d. A. Berasategui 6–1 7–5; B. Becker(3) d. W. Ferreira 5–7 6–4 6–3; G. Ivanisevic(6) d. J. Bjorkman 6–4 6–2; T. Martin(5) d. K. Novacek 7–6 6–4; S. Bruguera(4) d. A. Medvedev 5–7 6–4 6–0; M. Larsson d. S. Edberg(7) 6–4 6–7 8–6; A. Agassi(2) d. T. Muster. **Quarter-finals:** Sampras(1) d. Chang(8) 6–4 6–3; Ivanisevic(6) d. Becker(3) 6–4 6–1; Martin(5) d. Bruguera(4) 7–6 6–4; Larsson d. Agassi(2) 6–3 1–6 6–0. **Semi-finals:** Sampras(1) d. Ivanisevic(6) 5–7 6–3 6–4 6–7(5) 10–8; Larsson d. Martin(5) 6–4 6–1 6–1; **Final:** Larsson d. Sampras(1) 7–6 4–6 7–6 6–4.

1995 (5–10 Dec) **Prize money $6 million** (Winner $1,625,000; Runner-up $812,500; Semi-finalists $431,250; Quarter-finalists $262,500; First round $100,000; Alternates $50,000.) (Note: A bonus of $250,000 is paid to the winner of each Grand Slam who participates). **First round:** P. Sampras(1) d P. McEnroe 6–1 7–6; G. Ivanisevic(8) d P. Korda 7–6 6–3; J. Eltingh d M. Chang(4) 7–6 6–3; Y. Kafelnikov(6) d R.Furlan 6–4 6–1; B. Black d T. Muster(5) 7–6 2–6 6–1; B. Becker(3) d C. Pioline 6–1 6–7 9–7; A. Medvedev(10) d A. Krickstein 6–2 7–6; T. Martin(9) d S. Bruguera 7–6 6–4. **Quarter-finals:** Ivanisevic(8) d Sampras(1) injured; Kafelnikov(6) d Eltingh 3–6 6–3 6–2; Becker(3) d Black 7–6 6–1; Martin(9) d Medvedev(10) 6–3 1–6 4–0 ret. **Semi-finals:** Ivanisevic(8) d Kafelnikov(6) 7–6 4–6 6–3 6–4; Martin(9) d Becker(3) 5–7 6–3 6–4; **Final:** Ivanisevic(8) d Martin(9) 7–6 6–3 6–4.

1996 (3–8 Dec) **Prize money $6 million** (Winner $1,625; Runner-up $812,500; Semi-finalists $431,250; Quarter-finalists $262,500; First round $100,000; Alternates $50,000.) (Note: A bonus of $250,000 is paid to the winner of each Grand Slam who participates.) **First round:** T. Henman(ALT) d M.Stich(11) 6–3 6–3; M.Washington d R.Krajicek(7) 6–1 6–2; B.Becker(4) d J.Stoltenberg 6–3 6–3; J.Hlasek d C.Pioline(10) 2–6 6–3 6–4; J.Courier d M.Rosset(9) 7–5 6–2; Y.Kafelnikov(3) d A.Corretja 6–4 7–6; Woodforde d Agassi(8) 6–3 6–4; Ivanisevic(2) d Tillstrom 6–4 6–2. **Quarter-finals:** Henman d Washington 7–6 6–3; Becker(4) d J.Hlasek 6–4 6–1; Kafelnikov(3) d Courier 2–6 6–4 8–6; Ivanisevic(2) d Woodfrode 6–4 6–4. **Semi-finals:** Becker(4) d Henman 7–6 6–3 6–1; Ivanisevic(2) d Kafelnikov(3) 6–7 2–6 6–3 6–2 6–4. **Final:** Becker(4) d Ivanisevic(2) 6–3 6–4 6–4.

COMPAQ GRAND SLAM CUP PRIZE MONEY

During the eight years of its existence the Compaq Grand Slam Cup has offered a total of $48 million in prize money, as well as contributing $16 million to the ITF's Grand Slam Development Fund. None of the seventy-two players who have benefitted has taken part every year. The 1990 and 1997 champion, Pete Sampras, has been the most successful financially by virtue of also reaching the semi-finals in 1992 and 1993, the final in 1994 and the second round in 1995 when injury forced his retirement. From 1993 onwards the winner of each of the Grand Slam titles was awarded a bonus of $250,000 which reduced the on-site prize money to $5 million. If any player eligible for a bonus does not take part his $250,000 is added to the general prize fund. This occurred in 1993 when Jim Courier (the Australian Open champion) did not compete. The same action was taken in 1995 when injury prevented the Australian Open champion, Andre Agassi, from taking part and again in 1996 when Sampras, the US Open champion, was injured and could not take up his place. (*Figures in US Dollars.*)

	NAME	*1990*	*1991*	*1992*	*1993*	*1994*	*1995*	*1996*	*1997*	*TOTAL*
1	Sampras P.	2,000,000	—	450,000	931,250 *	1,250,000 *	762,500 *	—	2,000,000	7,393,750
2	Ivanisevic G.	300,000	—	450,000	—	425,000	1,625,000	812,500	—	3,612,500
3	Stich M.	450,000	2,000,000	812,500	—	—	100,000	—	—	3,362,500
4	Chang M.	450,000	1,000,000	1,000,000	262,500	250,000	100,000	—	—	3,062,500
5	Becker B.	—	—	—	100,000	250,000	431,250	1,875,000 **	100,000	2,756,250
6	Wheaton D.	450,000	2,000,000	50,000 ***	—	—	50,000 ***	—	—	2,550,000
7	Korda P.	—	—	300,000	1,625,000	—	100,000	—	425,000	2,450,000
8	Larsson M.	—	—	—	100,000	1,500,000	—	—	—	1,600,000
9	Martin T.	—	—	—	100,000	425,000	812,500	—	—	1,337,500
10	Kafelnikov Y.	—	—	—	—	50,000 ***	431,250	681,250 **	—	1,412,500
11	Bruguera S.	—	—	—	512,500 **	500,000 **	100,000	—	100,000	1,212,500
12	Gilbert B.	1,000,000	—	—	—	—	—	—	—	1,000,000
13	Rafter P.	—	—	—	—	—	—	—	1,000,000	1,000,000
14	Lendl I.	300,000	450,000	—	—	—	—	—	—	750,000
15	Muster T.	100,000	—	—	100,000	100,000	350,000 **	—	100,000	750,000
16	Edberg S.	100,000	—	100,000	431,250	100,000	—	—	—	731,250
17	Agassi A.	—	—	100,000	—	500,000 **	—	100,000	—	700,000
18	Krajicek R.	—	—	300,000	—	—	—	350,000 **	—	650,000
19	Leconte H.	300,000	—	300,000	—	—	—	—	—	600,000
20	Hlasek J.	—	300,000	—	—	—	—	—	262,500	562,500
21	Pioline C.	—	—	—	100,000	—	100,000	100,000	250,000	550,000
22	Krickstein A.	300,000	100,000	—	—	—	100,000	—	—	500,000
23	Ferreira W.	—	—	100,000	262,500	100,000	—	—	—	462,500
24	Henman T.	—	—	—	—	—	—	431,250	—	431,250
25	Rusedski G.	—	—	—	—	—	—	—	425,000	425,000
26	Forget G.	—	300,000	100,000	—	—	—	—	—	400,000
27	McEnroe P.	—	300,000	—	—	—	100,000	—	—	400,000
28	Wooodbridge T.	—	300,000	—	—	—	—	—	100,000	400,000
29	Medvedev A.	—	—	—	—	100,000	262,500	—	—	362,500
30	Courier J.	—	100,000	—	—	—	—	262,500	—	362,500

31	Washington M.	—	—	—	100,000	—	—	262,500	—	362,500
32	Woodforde M.	—	—	—	—	—	—	262,500	100,000	362,500
33	Bjorkman J.	—	—	—	—	100,000	—	—	250,000	350,000
34	Kuerten G.	—	—	—	—	—	—	—	350,000	350,000
35	McEnroe J.	—	—	300,000	—	—	—	—	—	300,000
36	Steven B.	—	—	—	262,500	—	—	—	—	262,500
37	Eltingh J.	—	—	—	—	—	262,500	—	—	262,500
38	Black B.	—	—	—	—	—	262,500	—	—	262,500
39	Rios M.	—	—	—	—	—	—	—	250,000	250,000
40	Novacek K.	50,000 ***	—	—	50,000 ***	100,000	—	—	—	200,000
41	Yzaga J.	—	100,000	—	—	100,000	—	—	—	200,000
42	Masur W.	—	—	100,000	100,000	—	—	—	—	200,000
43	Volkov A.	—	—	100,000	100,000	—	—	—	—	200,000
44	Champion T.	50,000 ***	100,000	—	—	—	—	—	—	150,000
45	Furlan R.	—	—	—	—	—	100,000	50,000 ***	—	150,000
46	Cherkasov A.	100,000	—	—	—	—	—	—	—	100,000
47	Curren K.	100,000	—	—	—	—	—	—	—	100,000
48	Svensson J.	100,000	—	—	—	—	—	—	—	100,000
49	Noah Y.	100,000	—	—	—	—	—	—	—	100,000
50	Gomez A.	100,000	—	—	—	—	—	—	—	100,000
51	Bergstrom C.	100,000	—	—	—	—	—	—	—	100,000
52	Haarhuis P.	—	100,000	—	—	—	—	—	—	100,000
53	Prpic G.	—	100,000	—	—	—	—	—	—	100,000
54	Connors J.	—	100,000	—	—	—	—	—	—	100,000
55	Caratti C.	—	100,000	—	—	—	—	—	—	100,000
56	Sanchez E.	—	—	100,000	—	—	—	—	—	100,000
57	Kulti N.	—	—	100,000	—	—	—	—	—	100,000
58	Berasategui A.	—	—	—	—	100,000	—	—	—	100,000
59	Stoltenberg J.	—	—	—	—	—	—	100,000	—	100,000
60	Rosset M.	—	—	—	—	—	—	100,000	—	100,000
61	Corretja A.	—	—	—	—	—	—	100,000	—	100,000
62	Tillstrom M.	—	—	—	—	—	—	100,000	—	100,000
63	Mantilla F.	—	—	—	—	—	—	—	100,000	100,000
64	Dewulf F.	—	—	—	—	—	—	—	100,000	100,000
65	Sanchez J.	—	50,000 ***	—	—	—	—	—	—	50,000
66	Boetsch A.	—	50,000 ***	—	—	—	—	—	—	50,000
67	Mansdorf A.	—	—	50,000 ***	—	—	—	—	—	50,000
68	Costa C.	—	—	—	50,000 ***	—	—	—	—	50,000
69	Frana J.	—	—	—	—	50,000 ***	—	—	—	50,000
70	Voinea A.	—	—	—	—	—	50,000 ***	—	—	50,000
71	Karbacher B.	—	—	—	—	—	—	50,000 ***	—	50,000
72	Norman M.	—	—	—	—	—	—	—	50,000 ***	50,000

* Includes $500,000 bonus ** Includes $250,000 bonus *** Alternates

GREATEST GRAND SLAM SINGLES WINNERS

Below are lists of all those players who have won five or more singles titles at the four Grand Slam Championships in Australia, France, Great Britain and the United States, the cornerstones of the sport. Listed separately are their combined doubles and mixed doubles totals at the four events to give a final overall total of Grand Slam titles won.

It is interesting that no men have totally dominated the sport during their playing spans like several of their female counterparts. That is partly because there has always been a greater strength in depth among the men and partly because from the late 1930s to the arrival of open tennis in 1968 most of the top amateur men turned professional and could not participate in the great Championships. One can only speculate how many more titles Rod Laver, for instance, might have won if he had not been barred from the Grand Slams from 1963 to 1967.

Four of the top men in the overall list are Australians who lived in an age when all the top men played doubles and many played mixed doubles too. That is not the case today. The totals for Lendl, Sampras and Becker contain only singles victories.

Furthermore, all the players in the lists who won their titles at Wimbledon, the US Championships and the Australian Championships before 1975 won them on grass courts. In 1975 the US Open became a clay court event for three years before switching to its present hard court surface, while the Australian Open changed to another type of hard court in 1988.

In comparing players of different eras it must always be remembered that before 1939 inter-continental travel meant a sea voyage. Thus only a handful of players crossed the Atlantic each year and fewer still ventured to Australia. In considering the overall totals, also remember that the opportunities for competition were fewer in the early years. Although Wimbledon's 1877 meeting was the world's first tennis tournament, there was no ladies' doubles or mixed doubles at the All England Lawn Tennis and Croquet Club until 1913. Furthermore, the Australian men's Championship began in 1906 and the women's in 1922 while the French Championships were open only to national players until 1924. Accordingly their international records do not begin until 1925.

	MEN	TOTAL SING	AUS	FRA	WIM	USA	Dbls	Mxd	TOTAL
1	Roy Emerson (1961–67)	12	6	2	2	2	16	0	28 (1)
=2	Rod Laver (1960–69)	11	3	2	4	2	6	3	20 (5)
	Bjorn Borg (1974–81)	11	0	6	5	0	0	0	11
=4	William Tilden (1920–30)	10	0	0	3	7	6	5	21 (4)
	Pete Sampras (1990–97)	10	2	0	4	4	0	0	10
=6	Fred Perry (1933–36)	8	1	1	3	3	2	4	14
	Ken Rosewall (1953–72)	8	4	2	0	2	9	1	18
	Jimmy Connors (1974–83)	8	1	0	2	5	3	0	11
	Ivan Lendl (1984–90)	8	2	3	0	3	0	0	8
=10	Richard Sears (1881–87)	7	0	0	0	7	6	0	13
	William Renshaw (1882–86)	7	0	0	7	0	5	0	12
	William Larned (1901–1911)	7	0	0	0	7	0	0	7
	Rene Lacoste (1925–28)	7	0	3	2	2	3	0	10
	Henri Cochet (1926–32)	7	0	4	2	1	5	3	15
	John Newcombe (1967–75)	7	2	0	3	2	17	2	26 (2)
	John McEnroe (1979–84)	7	0	0	3	4	9	1	17
	Mats Wilander (1982–88)	7	3	3	0	1	1	0	8
=18	Laurence Doherty (1902–06)	6	0	0	5	1	10	0	16
	Anthony Wilding (1906–1913)	6	2	0	4	0	5	0	11
	Don Budge (1937–38)	6	1	1	2	2	4	4	14
	Jack Crawford (1931–35)	6	4	1	1	0	6	5	17
	Stefan Edberg (1985–92)	6	2	0	2	2	2	0	8
	Boris Becker (1985–96)	6	2	0	3	1	0	0	6
=24	Frank Sedgman (1949–52)	5	2	0	1	2	9	8	22 (3)
	Tony Trabert (1953–55)	5	0	2	1	2	5	0	10

WOMEN		TOTAL SING	AUS	FRA	WIM	USA	Dbls	Mxd	TOTAL
1	Margaret Court (1960–75)	24	11	5	3	5	19	19	62 (1)
2	Steffi Graf (1987–1996)	21	4	5	7	5	1	0	22
3	Helen Wills Moody (1923–38)	19	0	4	8	7	9	3	31 (5)
=4	Martina Navratilova (1974–95)	18	3	2	9	4	31	7	56 (2)
	Chris Evert (1974–89)	18	2	7	3	6	3	0	21
6	Billie Jean King (1961–1981)	12	1	1	6	4	16	11	39 (3)
=7	Maureen Connolly (1951–54)	9	1	2	3	3	2	1	12
	Monica Seles (1990–96)	9	4	3	0	2	0	0	9
=9	Molla Bjurstedt Mallory (1915–1922)	8	0	0	0	8	2	3	13
	Suzanne Lenglen (1919–1926)	8	0	2	6	0	8	5	21
=11	Dorothea Lambert Chambers (1903–14)	7	0	0	7	0	0	0	7
	Maria Bueno (1958–68)	7	0	0	3	4	12	1	20
	Evonne Goolagong (1971–80)	7	4	1	2	0	6	1	14
=14	Blanche Bingley Hillyard (1889–1900)	6	0	0	6	0	0	0	6
	Nancy Wynne–Bolton (1936–52)	6	6	0	0	0	10	4	20
	Louise Brough (1942–57)	6	1	0	4	1	17	7	30
	Margaret Osborne DuPont (1941–60)	6	0	2	1	3	16	7	29
	Doris Hart (1950–55)	6	1	2	1	2	14	15	35 (4)
=19	Lottie Dod (1887–93)	5	0	0	5	0	0	0	5
	Charlotte Cooper Sterry (1895–1908)	5	0	0	5	0	0	0	5
	Daphne Akhurst (1924–30)	5	5	0	0	0	5	4	14
	Helen Jacobs (1932–36)	5	0	0	1	4	3	1	9
	Alice Marble (1936–39)	5	0	0	1	4	6	7	18
	Pauline Betz (1942–46)	5	0	0	1	4	0	1	6
	Althea Gibson (1956–58)	5	0	1	2	2	5	1	11
	Doubles titles only:								
	Elizabeth Ryan (1914–34)	0	0	0	0	0	17	9	26

GRAND SLAM WINNERS IN THE OPEN ERA

The first figure in brackets after a player's name denotes the number of titles won at that Championship, the second figure denotes the total number of Grand Slam titles won. Several of the players winning titles in the early years of open tennis had already won some as amateurs.

YEAR	AUSTRALIAN 1968–77 Jan 1977–85 Dec 1987 Jan	FRENCH May/Jun	WIMBLEDON Jun/Jul	US OPEN Aug/Sep
1968	**(Last Amateur)**	**(First OPEN)**		
	Bowrey (1,1)	Rosewall (2,5)	Laver (3,7)	Ashe (1,1)
	King (1,4)	Richey (1,2)	King (3,5)	Wade (1,1)
1969	**Laver (2,8)**	**Laver (2,9)**	**Laver (4,10)**	**Laver (2,11)GS**
	Court (8,14)	Court (3,15)	Jones (1,3)	Court (3,16)
1970	Ashe (1,2)	Kodes (1,1)	Newcombe (2,3)	Rosewall (2,6)
	Court (9,17)	**Court (4,18)**	**Court (3,19)**	**Court (4,20)GS**
1971	Rosewall (3,7)	Kodes (2,2)	Newcombe (3,4)	Smith (1,1)
	Court (10,21)	Goolagong(1,1)	Goolagong (1,2)	King (2,6)
1972	Rosewall (4,8)	Gimeno (1,1)	Smith (1,2)	Nastase (1,1)
	Wade (1,2)	King (1,7)	King (4,8)	King (3,9)
1973	Newcombe (1,5)	Nastase (1,2)	Kodes (1,3)	Newcombe (1,6)
	Court (11,22)	Court (5,23)	King (5,10)	Court (5,24)

The greatest of all Grand Slam winners is Australia's Margaret Court whose total of 62 singles, doubles and mixed titles will surely never be equalled. (Michael Cole)

YEAR	AUSTRALIAN	FRENCH	WIMBLEDON	US OPEN
1974	Connors (1,1) Goolagong (1,3)	Borg (1,1) Evert (1,1)	Connors (1,2) Evert (1,2)	Connors (1,3) King (4,11)
1975	Newcombe (2,7) Goolagong (2,4)	Borg (2,2) Evert (2,3)	Ashe (1,3) King (6,12)	Orantes (1,1) Evert (1,4)
1976	Edmondson (1,1) Cawley (3,5)	Panatta (1,1) Barker (1,1)	Borg (1,3) Evert (2,5)	Connors (2,4) Evert (2,6)
1977 Jan Dec Jan Dec	Tanner (1,1) Gerulaitis (1,1) Reid (1) Cawley (4,6)	Vilas (1,1) Jausovec (1,1)	Borg (2,4) Wade (1,3)	Vilas (1,2) Evert (3,7)
1978 Dec	Vilas (1,3) O'Neil (1,1)	Borg (3,5) Ruzici (1,1)	Borg (3,6) Navratilova (1,1)	Connors (3,5) Evert (4,8)
1979 Dec	Vilas (2,4) Jordan (1,1)	Borg (4,7) Evert Lloyd (3,9)	Borg (4,8) Navratilova (2,2)	McEnroe (1,1) Austin (1,1)
1980 Dec	Teacher (1,1) Mandlikova (1,1)	Borg (5,9) Evert Lloyd (4,10)	Borg (5,10) Cawley (2,7)	McEnroe (2,2) Evert Lloyd (5,11)
1981 Dec	Kriek (1,1) Navratilova (1,3)	Borg (6,11) Mandlikova (1,2)	McEnroe (1,3) Evert Lloyd (3,12)	McEnroe (3,4) Austin (2,2)
1982 Dec	Kriek (2,2) Evert Lloyd (1,13)	Wilander (1,1) Navratilova (1,4)	Connors (2,6) Navratilova (3,5)	Connors (4,7) Evert Lloyd (6,14)
1983 Dec	Wilander (1,2) Navratilova (2,6)	Noah (1,1) Evert Lloyd (4,15)	McEnroe (2,5) Navratilova (4,7)	Connors (5,8) Navratilova (1,8)
1984 Dec	Wilander (2,3) Evert Lloyd (2,16)	Lendl (1,1) Navratilova (2,9)	McEnroe (3,6) Navratilova (5,10)	McEnroe (4,7) Navratilova (2,11)
1985 Dec	Edberg (1,1) Navratilova (3,12)	Wilander (2,4) Evert Lloyd (5,17)	Becker (1,1) Navratilova (6,13)	Lendl (1,2) Mandlikova (1,3)
1986	Not Held	Lendl (2,3) Evert Lloyd (6,18)	Becker (2,2) Navratilova (7,14)	Lendl (2,4) Navratilova (3,15)
1987 Jan	Edberg (2,2) Mandlikova (2,4)	Lendl (3,5) Graf (1,1)	Cash (1,1) Navratilova (8,16)	Lendl (3,6) Navratilova (4,17)
1988	Wilander (3,5) **Graf (1,2)**	Wilander (3,6) **Graf (2,3)**	Edberg (1,3) **Graf (1,4)**	Wilander (1,7) **Graf (1,5) GS**
1989	Lendl (1,7) Graf (2,6)	Chang (1,1) Sanchez Vicario (1,1)	Becker (3,3) Graf (2,7)	Becker (1,4) Graf (2,8)
1990	Lendl (2,8) Graf (3,9)	Gomez (1,1) Seles (1,1)	Edberg (2,4) Navratilova (9,18)	Sampras (1,1) Sabatini (1)
1991	Becker (1,5) Seles (1,2)	Courier (1,1) Seles (2,3)	Stich (1) Graf (3,10)	Edberg (1,5) Seles (1,4)
1992	Courier (1,2) Seles (2,5)	Courier (2,3) Seles (3,6)	Agassi (1,1) Graf (4,11)	Edberg (2,6) Seles (2,7)
1993	Courier (2,4) Seles (3,8)	Bruguera (1,1) Graf (3,12)	Sampras (1,2) Graf (5,13)	Sampras (2,3) Graf (3,14)
1994	Sampras (1,4) Graf (4,15)	Bruguera (2,2) Sanchez Vicario (2,2)	Sampras (2,5) Martinez (1,1)	Agassi (1,2) Sanchez Vicario (1,3)
1995	Agassi (1,3) Pierce (1,1)	Muster (1,1) Graf (4,16)	Sampras (3,6) Graf (6,17)	Sampras (3,7) Graf (4,18)
1996	Becker (2,6) Seles (4,9)	Kafelnikov (1,1) Graf (5,19)	Krajicek (1,1) Graf (7,20)	Sampras (4,8) Graf (5,21)
1997	Sampras (2,9) Hingis (1,1)	Kuerten (1,1) Majoli (1,1)	Sampras (4,10) Hingis (1,2)	Rafter (1,1) Hingis (1,3)

(Above) Wimbledon's new No. 1 Court (top right of picture) was opened by the All England Club's President, His Royal Highness The Duke of Kent at a ceremony attended by 10 of the 14 living champions who have each won the singles title at least three times. (Below, left to right) Pete Sampras (1993, '94, '95), Boris Becker (1985, '86, '89), John McEnroe (1981, '83, '84), Martina Navratilova (1978, '79, '82–87, '90), Chris Evert (1974, '76, '81), John Curry (AELTC Chairman), The Duke of Kent, Sir Geoffrey Cass (President, LTA), Christopher Gorringe (AELTC Chief Executive), John Newcombe (1967, '70, '71), Billie Jean King (1966–68, '72, '73, '75), Margaret Court (1963, '65 '70), Rod Laver (1961, '62, '68, '69), Louise Brough (1948–50, '55). (Tommy Hindley)

Building for the Future

John Barrett

Darwin was right. In the evolutionary world of professional sport, as in all areas of commercial life, only the fittest survive. To their credit, the four Grand Slam Championships have recognised this fact. Indeed, the massive investment in infrastructure over the past decade has displayed a reassuring faith in the future.

In 1988 Tennis Australia unveiled their A$105 million state-of-the-art National Tennis Centre in Flinders Park whose centre court, with its sliding roof, became Melbourne's Entertainment Centre out of season. In 1996 the size of the complex was doubled by expanding across the Flinders Park railway sidings. A new show court, a Conference Centre and a paved piazza with giant TV screen were added at a cost of A$23 million to transform the enjoyment level for spectators. The fans, 84% of whom are inter-state or overseas visitors, responded positively. In 1997 – the last year of Ford's title sponsorship – crowds totalling 391,504 attended the Championships, a record.

Modernisation on this scale could not have been achieved without the help of State funds. For Victoria this has proved to be a good investment. The return to the community – more than $100 million annually – is massive. No less important is Melbourne's international image. With a TV audience of some 600 million households in 150 countries, many of which receive more than 100 hours of free-to-air live coverage, the Open is Australia's largest sporting event. With such world-wide publicity it was inevitable that the politicians would insist that the name of the venue should be changed from Flinders Park to Melbourne Park. I feel sorry for poor old Matthew Flinders. I wonder if he would have bothered to circumnavigate Australia if he'd known how ungrateful future generations would be.

In 1995 the French Tennis Federation invested FF240 million at the Stade Roland Garros in Paris when the adjacent football field was annexed to allow construction of the 10,000 seat Stade Suzanne Lenglen, with its superb new player accommodation, and a re-positioning of the outside courts that provided more room for visitors. All this at a site that had already set new standards when a circular No.1 Court had been added and the old Centre Court, built in 1926, modernised. Journalists marvelled at the space age press centre where monitors on every desk allowed them to follow matches on all the show courts and listen to every interview. It was rumoured that some writers never left their desks for a fortnight!

Five years ago Wimbledon announced an ambitious Long Term Plan, to be tackled in three stages, which would completely transform the site in Church Road at a guestimated cost of £100 million (the All England Club never did reveal the actual figure). Last year, despite the wettest first week in living memory, there was universal acclaim when Stage One was unveiled. The centrepiece was a new No.1

(Above) *The world's largest tennis stadium, a giant 22,547 seater bowl named after former US Open champion Arthur Ashe was unveiled at Flushing Meadows.* (Stephen Wake)
(Top right) *An expansion programme at Melbourne Park, completed in time for the 1996 Australian Open, provided much needed extra space for spectators.* (Tommy Hindley)
(Right) *The Suzanne Lenglen court at Roland Garros was combined with a re-alignment of all the outside courts to improve conditions for visitors at the French Open.* (Tommy Hindley)

Court complex in Aorangi Park. With its 11,500 seats, four public restaurants, a massive shop, a debenture holders lounge, LTA and ITF offices, plus a terraced picnic area with large TV screen, life was much more comfortable for the fans – provided they were carrying umbrellas!

Equally impressive was the new Broadcast Centre which provided indoor studio and production facilities for the BBC and 40 overseas TV and radio companies. From the comfort of custom built sets they carried news of the 111th Championships to more than 167 countries and a potential audience of approximately one billion fans around the world. This was the first time at any outdoor sporting event that permanent facilities had been provided for broadcasters on such a scale. Stage Two, which will provide a huge new facilities building for the media, the players and the members, is already under construction and will be ready for the 2000 Championships.

Equally momentous last year was the opening of the new complex at Flushing Meadows. The scale of the US Tennis Association's redevelopment is breathtaking – literally so if you choose to walk to the top of the massive new Arthur Ashe stadium instead of taking one of several lifts or escalators. This giant arena dominates a site that has grown from 21.6 acres to the present 46.5 acres.

The beautifully designed Centre Court at Crandon Park, Key Biscayne, Florida, gives the Lipton tournament a taste of sub-tropical splendour with its palm trees and comfortable entertainment boxes. (Michael Cole)

The new public entrance to the ground has cleverly been sited to take advantage of the old World's Fair globe with its spectacular fountain. As you pass through the gate and approach the new Stadium you find yourself in a huge piazza which contains several large self-contained booths selling merchandise and refreshments. The old food village has been massively enlarged to provide an attractive outdoor restaurant area – more Poughkeepsie than Paris it is true, but a welcome improvement nonetheless – and along the perimeter of the site are ranged the new match courts, each well provided with bleachers.

Dominating the whole scene is the Stadium itself. With nearly 23,000 seats, a tier of luxurious glass fronted boxes for corporate hospitality and other pricey outdoor boxes, the new structure is the largest of its kind in the world though spectators in the top rows found it difficult to recognise the ants crawling about on the court below. On one of the pre-tournament practice days Andre Agassi made an ascent to the summit, looked down at the two players hitting balls on the court below and remarked 'I can't tell which is Rosset and which is Chang!'

The total cost of the re-development, which incorporates 48 courts (19 match, 20 practice, 9 indoor), plus a well appointed new media centre and numerous restaurants and offices within the main stadium, was $234 million.

As in Melbourne, the fans turned out in record numbers in Paris (364,907), Wimbledon (436,531) and New York (559,544). The same has been true at other stops on the tennis roundabout where far-sighted committees have improved facilities. At the Lipton tournament in Key Biscayne, where Butch Buchholz and Dade County have between them created one of the world's most attractive centre courts in a colourful, semi-tropical setting, the 1997 event attracted record crowds.

Equally, at Halle in Germany, the enterprising industrialist Gerry Weber has pulled out all the promotional stops at his pre-Wimbledon grass court tournament where the crowds have flocked to the ground in record numbers. A retractable roof on the new centre court maintains continuity of play while the court itself, grown afresh each year on site, is lifted in sections and transferred to the arena on pallets. Even Darwin would have been impressed by that.

ATP Tour

ATP Tour Year • Points Explanation and Allocation • ATP Tour Tournaments – Mercedes Super 9, Championship and World Series • ATP Tour World Championship

Despite enjoying a tremendous year that produced five tournament wins, Michael Chang was again left empty-handed at the Grand Slams. (Stephen Wake)

Two men who shot to prominence in 1997:

(Above) *Carlos Moya of Spain, a finalist at the Australian Open finished the year at No.7 after reaching a career-high of five in September.* (Tommy Hindley)

(Left) *Greg Rusedski, the first Briton to reach the US Open final in New York since Fred Perry (who won the title in 1936), won two Tour titles in Nottingham and Basle.* (Tommy Hindley)

ATP Tour Year

John Parsons

The final stretch on the road to Hanover, the eleven month journey spanning 79 tournaments in 33 countries, was the most crowded in the history of the ATP Championships or the Masters which preceded it. When the final week of the Tour began, only four players had secured places for the end-of-the-year showpiece climax in Germany and there were ten others who, mathematically at least, were still in contention for the other four spots.

When Yevgeny Kafelnikov, by winning in Moscow, secured his place and then Sergi Bruguera discovered, late on the night before the draw, that he would be playing because Marcelo Rios had lost his final in Santiago, it was the first time since 1992 that even one player had qualified at such a late stage, let alone two.

One natural conclusion to be drawn from this was that the strength in depth at the top of the men's game had never been greater. Without wishing to detract from those who contributed to the exciting countdown to Hanover in the final month of the Tour, it was probably too soon to accept the evidence at face value.

In many ways it was a year of change. Some familiar top ten figures, most obviously Boris Becker, were starting to fade from the scene and new contenders, led by Australian Pat Rafter, were beginning to stake their claims for elite status. Rafter, the US Open champion, was one of four newcomers in Hanover. The others were Jonas Bjorkman of Sweden, Britain's Greg Rusedski and the Spaniard Carlos Moya. Apart from Becker, those who missed out from the previous year were Goran Ivanisevic and Richard Krajicek, both injured in the final stages of the race, Andre Agassi and Thomas Muster, although the latter did come in as alternate when Rusedski's hamstring injury forced him to default from his final round-robin match against Moya.

At least Agassi (who was also absent in 1995 through injury) was in the news during the week of Hanover. He was competing in a Challenger tournament in his native Las Vegas, the first step in what he hoped would be the full rehabilitation of his enthusiasm, as well as his form in 1998. Having played only a handful of tournaments during the year, the American who had started 1997 ranked eight, had by then slid to 141. He climbed back to 122 but his aggregate drop of 114 places was still one of the greatest for any player who had been in the top 50 the year before. MaliVai Washington fell even further, from 20 to 256. That was because an injury had prevented him from playing since April. Similarly Todd Martin's decline from 12th in 1996 to 81, could be explained by the months he spent recuperating from surgery on his arm.

Moya had given notice during the Australian Open, where he beat Becker, fellow Spaniard Felix Mantilla and then Michael Chang to reach the final, that he was poised to become the next Spanish player to surge into the limelight. The breakthroughs made by Bjorkman and Rusedski were much more unexpected. Bjorkman, 25, had started the year ranked 69. Despite possessing one of the finest double-handed backhands in the business he did not begin to attract serious interest until after a first round defeat at Wimbledon against Britain's lowly ranked Chris Wilkinson. That earned him attention for all the wrong reasons.

In a sense, though, it was the prod he needed. Victory over Moya in the final at Indianapolis and a place in the US Open semi-finals, provided the adrenalin, as well as the springboard of inspiration. In a year when there were chances for so many to make a mark, he was one of them.

The man who beat Bjorkman at Flushing Meadows was Britain's Canadian-born Rusedski. Starting the year ranked 48th he had slipped out of the top 50 when a wrist injury effectively prevented him playing between February and April. He then spent the next eight months excitingly breaking one modern British record after another.

During the US Open he became the first Briton to reach the final of a Grand Slam tournament since John Lloyd 20 years earlier in Australia and the first in New York since Fred Perry in 1936. He also reached 11th in the rankings, the highest for any British player since rankings began in 1973. One week later, appropriately enough in England, he reached the semi-finals in Bournemouth and broke into the top ten. Then in Vienna, by beating British rival Tim Henman, who was also heading for a year-ending career best 17th place, Rusedski soared to fourth place, which he held until first Bjorkman and then Kafelnikov overtook him during the closing fortnight.

Until 1997, Rusedski had been rated as little more than a raw-boned, supremely ambitious big server. During the year, as his results demonstrated, he added much more to his all-round game while losing nothing from the serve. Indeed, although the 142.3 mph delivery by Australia's Mark Philippoussis in Dusseldorf held the record for several months, the London-based left-hander responded with a 143 mph serve during the US Open. This was the fastest recorded during the year.

It was the second consecutive year that had Rusedski finished first in the year-ending fastest serving table although one has to remember that in most tournaments timing is only available for centre court matches – and even then not all of them. Julian Alonso of Spain became the third modern player to reach the 140mph mark with one serve in the last tournament of the year in Santiago.

Amid the joy in Australia, Sweden, Britain and Spain, over their new men in the top ten, one thing remained brilliantly constant – the reign by Pete Sampras as the undisputed best player in the world. As in the previous year, the 26-year-old American, who had a 13–1 record against other top ten players, was already secure in the knowledge that whatever happened in Hanover he could not be overtaken in the rankings, even before the first round-robin match was played there. Rafter, the only possible rival to overtake him (if he had won Hanover) lost that chance by losing to Bjorkman in the semi-finals in Stockholm.

So Sampras, who had held the top ranking continuously since 15 April 1996, was declared the year-ending No. 1 ranked player for a fifth consecutive year, equalling the record set by Jimmy Connors (1974–78). Whatever momentary concern there might have been about the authenticity of Sampras's status when he was beaten in his opening round-robin match in Hanover by Carlos Moya of Spain, was first calmed and then gloriously cast aside. Like a true champion he picked up his form, match by match, against Greg Rusedski, Rafter, Bjorkman and then most emphatically of all, against Kafelnikov, to win the title for the fourth time in seven years.

On the day of the final it was also announced that in a poll conducted to celebrate the 25th anniversary of the ATP Tour among 100 current and past players, tournament directors and leading members of the tennis media, Sampras had come out on top as the best player on the tour in that time. (The honour would probably have gone to Rod Laver had it covered the whole period of Open tennis.) Sampras earned 26 of the first-place votes, nine more than Bjorn Borg, who finished second, ahead of John McEnroe and Jimmy Connors.

Becker, who finished sixth, spoke for the majority, surely, when he said 'I had an opportunity in the last 12 years to play almost everybody, including Borg, Lendl and McEnroe and he (Sampras) has such a combination of talents. He has the power of today's game with the finesse of the old game. He prepares for his year so well and his record speaks for itself.'

That record in 1997 included winning eight titles, three more than Chang and Mantilla. Sampras's successes were evenly spread throughout the year, beginning with the Australia Open. At Wimbledon, where his quarter-final defeat of Becker signalled the moment for the German to announce his retirement from the Grand Slams, he won the title for a fourth time in five years and moved to joint fourth place with Bill Tilden, in the list of men's all-time Grand Slam tournament winners, one behind Laver and Borg and two behind the leader, Roy Emerson.

Significantly Chang, who won the first Super Nine tournament of the year at Indian Wells in early March, had the last of his successes in July. Thus it was not entirely surprising when Rafter stole the world number two ranking from him in the last week of the reckoning. Mantilla's quintet of titles was, predictably, registered entiely on clay. Next on the honours board came seven players who won three titles each: Bjorkman, Alex Corretja, Jim Courier, Ivanisevic, Krajicek, Philiippoussis and Kafelnikov.

For a fourth consecutive year no-one won titles on four different surfaces but the number winning on three rose from one in 1996 to four. Sampras naturally did best and with five titles on hard courts, two on carpet and Wimbledon on grass at the top of his list, he alone won more than one event on more than one surface. The others, all with one singles title on three surfaces, were Kafelnikov, Krajicek and Philippoussis.

Even so, one of the trends in recent years towards fewer players winning more than one event, was reversed. In 1997 there were 17 who won two or more tournaments, compared with only 13 the previous year and 14 in 1995, while the division of honours in the Super Nine events, where competition is obviously the strongest, was generously spread. Indeed until Sampras, who also won Cincinnati in mid-summer, came through a star-studded field at the Paris Indoor tournament in Bercy in October, the eight Super Nine tournaments had produced eight different winners.

Such were the great strides made by Bjorkman during the year that if he had won the Championships in Hanover, instead of losing in the semi-finals, he would have finished second in the end-of-the year world rankings. He was also one of 12 first-time winners on the tour, making his title breakthrough in Auckland in January, continuing it in Indianapolis in August and rounding off his tournament year ideally. First he had a victory in front of his home crowd in Stockholm and then gave Sweden a winning start in their runaway Davis Cup success against the Americans after Sampras had been injured in his opening rubber.

Fellow Swede, Thomas Johansson and Britain's Tim Henman were other first-time winners and both went on to claim a second title as well. Johansson was suddenly spectacularly successful, in that he won in successive weeks in Copenhagen and St Peterburg. Henman, in a year when the exciting race between him and Rusedski to be the highest ranked British player benefitted them both, had his successes in Sydney in January and Tashkent in September.

Of the other first-time title winners, the most memorable victory was clearly that of Brazil's Gustavo Kuerten, ranked 66 at the time, who came through to win the French Open in June. Hicham Arazi (Casablanca), Mikael Tillstrom (Chennai), Magnus Norman (Bastad), Sargis Sargsian (Newport), Chris Woodruff (Montreal), Nicolas Kiefer (Toulouse), Fabrice Santoro (Lyon) – in his seventh year on the Tour – and Julian Alonso (Santiago), completed the first time list.

For the record, the oldest tournament winner in the year was Sweden's Magnus Larsson, 30 years 9 months when he won in Singapore. The youngest was Nicolas Kiefer, a protege of Boris Becker, who was only two months past his 20th birthday when he won in Toulouse.

Whatever disappointment Sampras felt at once again failing to show either the form or, more significantly, the belief he needs if he is ever to win the French Open (he succumbed surprisingly to Magnus Norman in the fourth round), was probably not so great as his fourth round defeat by Petr Korda at the US Open in September. However, he finished the year in great style, with victories in the Compaq Grand Slam Cup, the Paris Indoor and then Hanover, before calamity struck in Gothenburg.

It was the second year in succession that Sampras won eight tournaments. Thomas Muster, who, through his total mastery on clay at the time, had won 12 in 1996, collected only two titles in the year. That put him at eleventh equal, with six others in the list of champions, which honoured 44 different winners from 21 countries, compared with 47 from 21 countries in 1966.

The most significant statistic in this table was the continuing decline of American players in men's tennis. They retained first place as the country winning the most titles, but only just. Thanks principally to Sampras, who won almost half their total, they scored 17, three less than in 1996 and another new low for them. On the other hand, Spain's growing influence which saw them climb to second place with 12 titles a year earlier, was handsomely maintained as they increased their tally to 15, followed by Sweden with nine, also three more than in 1996. With Becker not winning a title for the first time in 13 years, Germany suffered the biggest decline, dropping from eight titles to one.

Encouragingly for them, Germany finished the year with nine players ranked among the top 100, two more than the previous year. Perhaps their belief that a new wave of potential German champions is on its way will be justified.

Meanwhile there is no stopping the Spanish conveyor belt. At the end of the ATP Year there were a record 16 Spaniards in the top 100, also two more than in 1996. That increased the gap to six between them and their nearest rivals, still the US, whose total dropped from 12 to 10. Behind Spain, the US and Germany came Australia and Sweden both with eight, France with seven and the Czech Republic with six. Probably nowhere was there greater delight that in Armenia where, thanks to Sargis Sargsian, they produced a top 100 player for the first time.

Players moving up at least 100 places into the top 100, were led by Frenchman, Nicolas Escude, who started the year ranked 406 and finished it at 93, a rise of 313 places. He was followed by Alonso of Spain, who climbed from 289 to 36, an improvement of 253 places. Davide Sanguinetti of Italy rose from 283 to 92, Wayne Black from 254 to 97 and Tommy Haas from 196 to 41. Higher up the ladder, the improvements of 95 places from 127 to 32 by Nicolas Kiefer and the resurgence of Fabrice Santoro as he rose from 118 to 29, were just as impressive and, in Kiefer's case, more significant.

Other statistical gems unearthed by Greg Sharko of the ATP Tour, included the fact that Krajicek, although losing a tie-break set in Rosmalen, was the only player to win a title during the year without losing his serve. The Dutchman also, incidentally, had fewer first round losses in 1997 than anyone – just two in 22 tournaments. And in the 79 tournaments, the top seed won the title 23 times.

The shortest final consisted of 15 games, a total that was registered twice, first by Todd Woodbridge when he beat fellow Australian, Scott Draper 6–2, 6–1 in Adelaide and then by Julian Alonso as he defeated Marcelo Rios by the same score in Santiago. In time the shortest final was Goran Ivanisevic's win over Sergi Bruguera in Milan which lasted a mere 47 minutes. The 3 hours 23 minutes it took Slava Dosedel to outlast Carlos Moya in Spain was the longest. The Vienna final, in which Ivanisevic recovered to beat Greg Rusedski 3–6 6–7 7–6 6–3 6–2, was the longest in games.

The Croatian was also one of three players who won singles and doubles titles at the same event. His success came in Zagreb where he won the doubles with Sasa Hirszon. Thomas Enqvist completed his double in Marseille where he was partnered by Magnus Larsson and Mark Philippoussis followed up his singles victory at Queen's Club by winning the doubles with Pat Rafter. Not one of that trio, though, played enough doubles to qualify for the World Doubles Championships in Hartford, Connecticut, where once again the favourites going into the final were the Woodies – Todd Woodbridge and Mark Woodforde. The popular Australians were making their seventh consecutive appearance, a record surpassed only by Spaniards, Sergio Casal and Emilio Sanchez, who qualified eight times between 1985–93. The Woodies, who had won the Australian Open in January and then a record fifth consecutive Wimbledon in July, had already clinched their third year in a row at the top of year-ending doubles team rankings. But the defending champions, whose form had been slipping, knew that nothing could be taken for granted. That was borne out in the round-robin section when, even after beating Don Johnson and Francisco Montana and then Rick Leach and Jonathan Stark, they still needed a set against Sebastien Lareau and Alex O'Brien if they were to reach the semi-finals. They were beaten 7–6 7–5.

Curiously enough the title eventually went to Rick Leach and Jonathan Stark, both accomplished doubles players but a pair without a tournament win in '97, had lost in the round-robin to Woodforde and Woodbridge and who, as far back as August, had decided that in 1998 they would go their separate ways, with different partners. 'It's probably not the smartest business move but I didn't realise we'd play so well and thought this could be my last year,' said Leach, 32, who had qualified for the seventh time in ten years, with his fifth different partner.

They were 0–5 in finals for the year going into the tournament but in the semi-finals really began to find their best form as they upset former champions, Jacco Eltingh and Paul Haarhuis 6–3 6–4. Their opponents for the final were Mahesh Bhupathi and Leander Paes, the first Indians to attract attention at such a level since the heyday of the Amritraj brothers. They also lost one of their round-robin matches, against Eltingh and Haarhuis and then edged past Lareau and O'Brien 6–1 2–6 7–6 in the semi-finals.

Although Leach was broken in the third game of the final, he and Stark broke Bhupathi to make it 3–3. From there they took control by breaking the Paes serve and went on to win 6–3 6–4 7–6. Stark, who then had to fly off the join the United States Davis Cup team for the final in Sweden, saved one break point when serving for the first set but thereafter he and Leach did not face another break point in the match.

POINTS EXPLANATION

The tables opposite show the ranking points to be won at the four Grand Slam Championships and all tournaments on the ATP Tour – including Challengers with minimum prize money of $50,000. A player's ranking alone decides whether or not he is accepted directly into the main draw or the qualifying event at all Tour tournaments.

Identical points are awarded for singles and doubles. No points are awarded until a player has completed a match. Anyone who reaches the second round via a bye and then loses is considered to have lost in the first round and receives one point, but he does receive second round prize money. There are additional 'Bonus Points' awarded for beating players ranked between 1 and 200 in singles, or a team ranked between 2 and 400 in doubles. In addition to the points won in any tournament, a player or doubles team winning a place in the main draw via qualifying also receives half the points awarded to the second round loser in that tournament. Lucky Losers receive no qualifying points.

POINTS ALLOCATION

Category	Total Prize Money (All US$)	W	F	S	Q	16	32	64	128
Grand Slams (averaged)	4.75 Million	750	537	325	163	82	41	20	*
Mercedes Super Nine (averaged)	2.25 Million	370	265	160	80	40	20	10	1
Championship Series	1.500 Million	320	228	135	68	34	17	1	–
	1.375 Million	310	220	130	65	33	17	1	–
	1.250 Million	300	213	125	63	32	16	1	–
	1.125 Million	290	205	120	60	30	15	1	–
	1.000 Million	280	198	115	58	29	15	1	–
	875,000	270	190	110	55	28	14	1	–
	750,000	260	183	105	53	27	14	1	–
	625,000	250	175	100	50	25	13	1	–
World Series	1.375 Million	250	183	115	58	29	15	1	
	1.250 Million	240	175	110	55	28	14	1	
	1.125 Million	230	168	105	53	27	14	1	
	1.000 Million	220	160	100	50	25	13	1	
	875,000	210	153	95	48	24	12	1	–
	750,000	200	145	90	45	23	12	1	–
	625,000	190	138	85	43	22	11	1	–
	550,000	180	130	80	40	20	10	1	–
	475,000	170	123	75	38	19	10	1	–
	400,000	160	115	70	35	18	9	1	–
	325,000	150	108	65	33	17	1	–	–
	250,000	140	100	60	30	15	1	–	–
	175,000	130	93	55	28	14	1	–	–
Challenger Series	** 125,000+H	100	73	45	23	12	1		
	125,000	90	65	40	20	10	1	–	–
	100,000	80	58	35	18	9	1	–	–
	75,000	70	50	30	15	8	1	–	–
	37,500+H	65	47	28	14	7	1		
	50,000	60	43	25	13	7	1	–	–

* To be determined

** Any Challenger providing hospitality will receive the points of the next highest prize money level. $25,000+H receive points shown at $50,000. Monies shown are on-site prize amounts.

BONUS POINTS

Double for all Grand Slam matches and best-of-five matches at Super Nine tournaments. No points for a walk-over.

Singles

Ranking	Bonus Points
1	50
2–5	45
6–10	36
11–20	24
21–30	18
31–50	12
51–75	6
76–100	3
101–150	2
151–200	1

Doubles

Team Ranking	Team Bonus Points
2–3	50
4–10	45
11–20	36
21–40	24
41–60	18
61–100	12
101–150	6
151–200	3
201–300	2
301–400	1

GRAND SLAM CHAMPIONSHIPS AND ATP TOUR 1997

DATE	*VENUE*	*SURFACE*	*SINGLES FINAL*	*DOUBLES WINNERS*
30 Dec–5 Jan	Adelaide	Hard	T. Woodbridge d. S. Draper 6–2 6–1	Rafter/Shelton
30 Dec–5 Jan	Doha	Hard	J. Courier d. T. Henman 7–5 6-7 6–2	Eltingh/Haarhuis
6–12 Jan	Auckland	Hard	J. Bjorkman d. K. Carlsen 7–6 6–0	E. Ferreira/Galbraith
6–12 Jan	Sydney	Hard	T. Henman d. C. Moya 6–3 6–1	Lobo/J. Sanchez
13–26 Jan	**Ford Australian Open**	**Hard**	**P. Sampras d. C. Moya 6–2 6–3 6–3**	**Woodbridge/ Woodforde**
27 Jan–2 Feb	Shanghai	Carpet	J. Kroslak d. A. Volkov 6–2 7–6	Mirnyi/Ullyett
27 Jan–2 Feb	Zagreb	Carpet	G. Ivanisevic d. G. Rusedski 7–6 4–6 7–6	Hirszon/Ivanisevic
10–16 Feb	Dubai	Hard	T. Muster d. G. Ivanisevic 7–5 7–6	Groen/Ivanisevic
10–16 Feb	San Jose, CA	Hard	P. Sampras d. G. Rusedski 3–6 5–0 ret	MacPhie/Muller
11–16 Feb	Marseilles	Carpet	T. Enqvist d. M. Rios 6–4 1–0 ret	Enqvist/Larsson
17–23 Feb	Antwerp	Carpet	M. Rosset d. T. Henman 6–2 7–5 6–4	Adams/ Delaitre
17–23 Feb	Memphis, TN	Hard	M. Chang d. T. Woodbridge 6–3 6–4	E. Ferreira/Galbraith
24 Feb–2 Mar	Milan	Carpet	G. Ivanisevic d. S. Bruguera 6–2 6–2	Albano/Nyborg
24 Feb–2 Mar	Philadelphia, PA	Carpet	P. Sampras d. P. Rafter 5–7 7–6 6–3	Lareau/O'Brien
3–9 Mar	Rotterdam	Carpet	R. Krajicek d. D. Vacek 7–6 7–6	Eltingh/Haarhuis
3–9 Mar	Scottsdale, AZ	Hard	M. Philippoussis d. R. Reneberg 6–4 7–6	Lobo/J. Sanchez
10–16 Mar	Indian Wells, CA	Hard	M. Chang d. B. Ulihrach 4–6 6–3 6–4 6–3	Knowles/Nestor
10–16 Mar	Copenhagen	Carpet	T. Johansson d. M. Damm 6–4 3–6 6–2	Olhovskiy/Steven
17–23 Mar	St. Petersburg	Carpet	T. Johansson d. R. Furlan 6–3 6–4	Olhovskiy/Steven
20–30 Mar	Key Biscayne, FL	Hard	T. Muster d. S. Bruguera 7–6 6–3 6–1	Woodbridge/ Woodforde
24–30 Mar	Casablanca	Clay	H. Arazi d. F. Squillari 3–6 6–1 6–2	Cunha-Silva/ Marques
7–13 Apr	Estoril	Clay	A. Corretja d. F. Clavet 6–3 7–5	Kuerten/Meligeni
7-13 Apr	Hong Kong	Hard	M. Chang d. P. Rafter 6–3 6–3	Damm/Vacek
7–13 Apr	Madras	Hard	M. Tillstrom d. A. Radulescu 6–4 4–6 7–5	Bhupathi/Paes
14–20 Apr	Barcelona	Clay	A. Costa d. A. Portas 7–5 6–4 6–4	Berasategui/Burillo
14–20 Apr	Tokyo, Japan Open	Hard	R. Krajicek d. L. Roux 6–2 3–6 6–1	Damm/Vacek
21–27 Apr	Monte Carlo	Clay	M. Rios d. A. Corretja 6–4 6–3 6–3	Johnson/Montana
21–27 Apr	Orlando, FL	Clay	M. Chang d. G. Stafford 4–6 6–2 6–1	Merklein/Spadea
28 Apr–4 May	Atlanta, GA	Clay	M. Filippini d. J. Stoltenberg 7–6 6–4	Bjorkman/Kulti
28 Apr–4 May	Munich	Clay	M. Philippoussis d. A. Corretja 7–6 1–6 6–4	Albano/Corretja
28 Apr–4 May	Prague	Clay	C. Pioline d. B. Ulihrach 6–2 5–7 7–6	Bhupathi/Paes
5–11 May	Hamburg	Clay	A. Medvedev d. F. Mantilla 6–0 6–4 6–2	Lobo/J. Sanchez
5–11 May	Coral Springs, FL	Clay	J. Stoltenberg d. J. Bjorkman 6–0 2–6 7–5	Randall/van Emburgh
12–18 May	Rome	Clay	A. Corretja d. M. Rios 7–5 7–5 6–3	Knowles/Nestor
19–24 May	St. Polten	Clay	M. Filippini d. P. Rafter 7–6 6–2	Jones/Melville
26 May–8 Jun	**French Open**	**Clay**	**G. Kuerten d. S. Bruguera 6–3 6–4 6–2**	**Kafelnikov/Vacek**
9–15 Jun	Halle	Grass	Y. Kafelnikov d. P. Korda 7–6 6–7 7–6	Braasch/Stich
9–15 Jun	London, Queen's	Grass	M. Philippoussis d. G. Ivanisevic 7–5 6–3	Philippoussis/Rafter
9–15 Jun	Bologna	Clay	F. Mantilla d. G. Kuerten 4–6 6–2 6–1	Kuerten/Meligeni
16–21 Jun	Nottingham	Grass	G. Rusedski d. K. Kucera 6–4 7–5	E. Ferreira/Galbraith
16–22 Jun	Rosmalen	Grass	R. Krajicek d. G. Raoux 6–4 7–6	Eltingh/Haarhuis
23 Jun–6 Jul	**Wimbledon**	**Grass**	**P. Sampras d. C. Pioline 6–4 6–2 6–4**	**Woodbridge/ Woodforde**
7–13 Jul	Gstaad	Clay	F. Mantilla d. J. Viloca 6–1 6–4 6–4	Kafelnikov/Vacek
7–13 Jul	Bastad	Clay	M. Norman d. J. Marin 7–5 6–2	Kulti/Tillstrom
7–13 Jul	Newport	Grass	S. Sargsian d. B. Steven 7–6 4–6 7–5	Gimelstob/Steven
14–20 Jul	Stuttgart	Clay	A. Corretja d. K. Kucera 6–2 7–5	Kuerten/Meligeni
14–20 Jul	Washington DC	Hard	M. Chang d. P. Korda 5–7 6–2 6–1	L. Jensen/M. Jensen
21–27 Jul	Kitzbuhel	Clay	F. Dewulf d. J. Alonso-Pintor 7–6 6–4 6–1	Arthurs/Fromberg
21–27 Jul	Umag	Clay	F. Mantilla d. S. Bruguera 6–3 7–5	Pescariu/Sanguinetti
21–27 Jul	Los Angeles	Hard	J. Courier d. T. Enqvist 6–4 6–4	Lareau/O'Brien
28 Jul–3 Aug	Montreal	Hard	C. Woodruff d. G. Kuerten 7–5 4–6 6–3	Bhupathi/Paes
28 Jul–3 Aug	Amsterdam	Clay	C. Dosedel d. C. Moya 7–6 6–7 7-6 6–2	Kilderry/Lapentti
4–10 Aug	Cincinnati	Hard	P. Sampras d. T. Muster 6–3 6–4	Woodbridge/ Woodforde
4–10 Aug	San Marino	Clay	F. Mantilla d. M. Gustafsson 6–4 6–1	Brandi/Messori
11–17 Aug	Indianapolis	Hard	J. Bjorkman d. C. Moya 6–3 7–6	Tebbutt/Tillstrom
11–17 Aug	New Haven	Hard	Y. Kafelnikov d. P. Rafter 7–6 6–4	Bhupathi/Paes
18–24 Aug	Boston	Hard	S. Schalken d. M. Rios 7–5 6–3	Eltingh/Haarhuis
18–24 Aug	Long Island	Hard	C. Moya d. P. Rafter 6–4 7–6	Ondruska/Prinosil
25 Aug–7 Sep	**US Open**	**Hard**	**P. Rafter d. G. Rusedski 6–3 6–2 4–6 7–5**	**Kafelnikov/Vacek**

A year of near misses for Australia's Mark Philippoussis, whose only title came on grass at Queen's Club. (Stephen Wake)

DATE	*VENUE*	*SURFACE*	*SINGLES FINAL*	*DOUBLES WINNERS*
8–14 Sept	Tashkent	Hard	T. Henman d. M. Rosset 7–6 6–4	Santopadre/Spadea
8–14 Sept	Bournemouth	Clay	F. Mantilla d. C. Moya 6–2 6–2	Kinnear/Kitinov
8–14 Sept	Marbella	Clay	A. Costa d. A. Berasategui 6–3 6–2	Alami/Alonso-Pintor
22–28 Sept	Compaq GS Cup	Carpet	P. Sampras d. P. Rafter 6–2 6–4 7–5	—
22–28 Sept	Bucharest	Clay	R. Fromberg d. A. Gaudenzi 6–1 7–6	Lobo/J. Sanchez
22–28 Sept	Toulouse	Hard	N. Kiefer d. M. Philippoussis 7–5 5–7 6–4	Eltingh/Haarhuis
29 Sept–5 Oct	Basle	Hard	G. Rusedski d. M. Philippoussis 6–3 7–6 7–6	Henman/Rosset
29 Sept–5 Oct	Beijing	Clay	J. Courier d. M. Gustafsson 7–6 3–6 6–3	Bhupathi/Paes
29 Sept–5 Oct	Palermo	Clay	A. Berasategui d. D. Hrbaty 6–4 6–2	Kratzmann/Pimek
6–12 Oct	Vienna	Carpet	G. Ivanisevic d. G. Rusedski 3–6 6–7 7–6 6–2 6–3	E. Ferreira/Galbraith
6–12 Oct	Singapore	Carpet	M. Gustafsson d. N. Kiefer 4–6 6–3 6–3	Bhupathi/Paes
13–19 Oct	Lyon	Carpet	F. Santoro d. T. Haas 6–4 6–4	E. Ferreira/Galbraith
13–19 Oct	Ostrava	Carpet	K. Kucera d. M. Norman 6–2 ret	Novak/Rikl
20–26 Oct	Stuttgart	Carpet	P. Korda d. R. Krajicek 7–6 6–2 6–4	Woodbridge/ Woodforde
20–26 Oct	Mexico City	Clay	F. Clavet d. J. Viloca 6–4 7–6	Lapentti/Orsanic
27 Oct–2 Nov	Paris	Carpet	P. Sampras d. J. Bjorkman 6–3 4–6 6–3 6–1	Eltingh/Haarhuis
27 Oct–2 Nov	Bogota	Clay	F. Clavet d. N. Lapentti 6–3 6–3	Lobo/Meligeni
3–9 Nov	Moscow	Carpet	Y. Kafelnikov d. P. Korda 7–6 6–4	Damm/Suk
3–9 Nov	Stockholm	Carpet	J. Bjorkman d. J. Siemerink 3–6 7–6 6–2 6–4	Goellner/Reneberg
3–9 Nov	Santiago	Clay	J. Alonso-Pintor d. M. Rios 6–2 6–1	Davids/Kratzmann
10–16 Nov	Hanover, ATP Chp.	Carpet	P. Sampras d. Y. Kafelnikov 6–3 6–2 6–2	—
19–23 Nov	Hartford, ATP Dbls.	Carpet	—	Leach/Stark
28–30 Nov	**Davis Cup by NEC Final**	**Carpet**	**Sweden d. USA 5–0**	

PLAYER NATIONALITIES AND BIRTHDAYS (MEN)

The following players have competed in the 1997 Grand Slam Championships, the ATP Tour and Davis Cup ties. (Birthdays dd-mm-yy.)

Surname / Forename	*Nation*	*DOB*
ADAMS, David	(RSA)	05-01-70
AERTS, Nelson	(BRA)	25-04-63
AGASSI, Andre	(USA)	29-04-70
AL-ALAWI, Sultan-Khalfan	(QAT)	16-03-77
ALAMI, Karim	(MAR)	24-05-73
ALBANO, Pablo	(ARG)	11-04-67
ALONSO-PINTOR, Julian	(ESP)	02-08-77
ALVAREZ, Emilio	(ESP)	15-11-72
ANCIC, Ivica	(CRO)	29-10-79
ANDERSEN, Thomas	(DEN)	11-03-72
ANDERSSON, Henrik	(SWE)	01-05-77
APELL, Jan	(SWE)	04-11-69
ARAZI, Hicham	(MAR)	19-10-73
ARNOLD, Lucas	(ARG)	12-10-74
ARNOLD, Milton	(USA)	15-07-74
ARRIENS, Carsten	(GER)	11-04-69
ARTHURS, Wayne	(AUS)	18-03-71
BACHELOT, Jean-Francois	(FRA)	11-06-77
BALCELLS, Joan	(ESP)	20-06-75
BALE, Lan	(RSA)	07-09-69
BARNARD, Marius	(RSA)	20-01-69
BARON, Ivan	(USA)	12-11-72
BARTHEZ, Lionel	(FRA)	18-05-67
BAUR, Patrick	(GER)	03-05-65
BEARDSLEY, John	(USA)	08-11-75
BECKER, Boris	(GER)	22-11-67
BEHR, Noam	(ISR)	13-10-75
BEHREND, Tomas	(GER)	12-12-74
BEHRENS, Wilhelm 'Bill'	(USA)	26-06-70
BELOBRAJDIC, Allen	(AUS)	18-09-76
BELOV, Alexei	(RUS)	19-05-72
BERASATEGUI, Alberto	(ESP)	28-06-73
BERGH, Fredrik	(SWE)	22-04-75
BERGH, Rikard	(SWE)	14-06-66
BHUPATHI, Mahesh	(IND)	07-06-74
BJORKMAN, Jonas	(SWE)	23-03-72
BLACK, Byron	(ZIM)	06-10-69
BLACK, Wayne	(ZIM)	14-11-73
BLAKE, Ryan	(USA)	04-02-66
BLANCO, Galo	(ESP)	08-10-76
BLENKIRON, Tim	(AUS)	26-11-75
BLUMAUER, Georg	(AUT)	16-07-74
BOETSCH, Arnaud	(FRA)	01-04-69
BOK, Martijn	(NED)	08-03-73
BOWEN, Devin	(USA)	18-05-72
BRAASCH, Karsten	(GER)	14-07-67
BRANDI, Cristian	(ITA)	10-06-70
BROAD, Neil	(RSA)	20-11-66
BRUGUERA, Sergio 'Sergi'	(ESP)	16-01-71
BRUNO, Nicola	(ITA)	26-01-71
BRYAN, Mike	(USA)	29-04-78
BRYAN, Robert 'Bob'	(USA)	29-04-78
BRYAN, Steven 'Steve'	(USA)	10-08-70
BUCHMAYER, Thomas	(AUT)	14-02-71
BURGSMULLER, Lars	(GER)	06-12-75
BURILLO, Jordi	(ESP)	07-12-72
BURRIEZA, Oscar	(ESP)	22-07-75
CABALLERO, David	(ESP)	14-11-74
CABELLO, Francisco	(ARG)	06-12-72
CALDWELL, David	(USA)	13-06-74
CAMPBELL, Steve	(USA)	22-10-70
CAMPORESE, Omar	(ITA)	08-05-68
CANAS, Guillermo	(ARG)	25-11-77
CANNON, Shelby	(USA)	19-08-66
CANTWELL, Danny	(USA)	01-12-69
CARATTI, Cristiano	(ITA)	24-05-70
CARBONELL, Tomas	(ESP)	07-08-68
CARLSEN, Kenneth	(DEN)	17-04-73
CARRAZ, Gregory	(FRA)	09-04-75
CARRETERO, Roberto	(ESP)	30-08-75
CASAL, Sergio	(ESP)	08-09-62
CASH, Patrick 'Pat'	(AUS)	27-05-65
CHAMPION, Thierry	(FRA)	31-08-66
CHANG, Albert	(CAN)	27-02-71
CHANG, Carl	(USA)	13-02-69
CHANG, Michael	(USA)	22-02-72
CHARPENTIER, Marcelo	(ARG)	11-07-73
CHAUVIN, Julien	(FRA)	17-04-75
CHERKASOV, Andrei	(RUS)	04-07-70
CHESNOKOV, Andrei	(RUS)	02-02-66
CLARK, Chad	(USA)	28-10-73
CLAVET, Francisco	(ESP)	24-10-68
CLEMENT, Arnaud	(FRA)	17-12-77
COETZEE, Jeff	(RSA)	25-04-77
COMMANDEUR, Malte	(GER)	09-02-78
CONDE, Jose-Antonio	(ESP)	11-03-70
CONNELL, Grant	(CAN)	17-11-65
CORDISH, Reed	(USA)	19-06-74
CORRETJA, Alex	(ESP)	11-04-74
COSAC, Gheorghe 'George'	(ROM)	26-01-68
COSTA, Albert	(ESP)	25-06-75
COSTA, Carlos	(ESP)	22-04-68
COUPE, Brandon	(USA)	11-04-72
COURIER, James 'Jim'	(USA)	17-08-70
COUTO, Emanuel	(POR)	06-08-73
COWAN, Barry 'Baz'	(GBR)	25-08-74
CRABB, Jaymon	(AUS)	06-03-78
CRACA, Marcello	(GER)	27-10-74
CUNHA-SILVA, Joao	(POR)	27-11-67
DAMM, Martin	(CZE)	01-08-72
DAVIDS, Hendrik-Jan	(NED)	30-01-69
DAVIS, Scott	(USA)	27-08-62
DE JAGER, John-Laffnie	(RSA)	17-03-73
DELAITRE, Olivier	(FRA)	01-06-67
DELGADO, James 'Jamie'	(GBR)	21-03-77
DELGADO, Ramon	(PAR)	14-11-76
DEREPASKO, Artem	(RUS)	26-01-79
DEWULF, Filip	(BEL)	15-03-72
DI LUCIA, David 'Dave'	(USA)	15-01-70
DIAZ, Jacobo	(ESP)	11-07-76
DIER, Dirk	(GER)	16-02-72
DJORDJEVIC, Nebojsa	(YUG)	24-04-73
DOSEDEL, Ctislav 'Slava'	(CZE)	14-08-70
DOWNS, Steven	(NZL)	08-09-75
DOYLE, Grant	(AUS)	09-01-74
DRAPER, Scott	(AUS)	05-06-74

Surname / Forename	*Nation*	*DOB*
DREEKMANN, Hendrik	(GER)	29-01-75
DUMANIC, Josip 'Jozo'	(CRO)	12-12-74
DURAN, Sergi	(ESP)	23-06-76
DZELDE, Girts	(LAT)	16-07-63
EAGLE, Joshua 'Josh'	(AUS)	10-05-73
EKEROT, David	(SWE)	01-02-70
EL AAREJ, Mounir	(MAR)	16-06-77
EL AYNAOUI, Younes	(MAR)	12-09-71
EL SAWY, Tamer	(EGY)	11-02-72
ELLWOOD, Ben	(AUS)	12-03-76
ELSNER, Daniel	(GER)	04-01-79
ELTINGH, Jacco	(NED)	29-08-70
ENQVIST, Thomas	(SWE)	13-03-74
ERLICH, Eyal	(ISR)	01-01-77
ESCHAUER, Werner	(AUT)	26-04-74
ESCUDE, Nicolas	(FRA)	03-04-76
ETLIS, Gaston	(ARG)	04-11-74
FERNANDEZ, Ruben	(ESP)	12-01-78
FERREIRA, Clinton	(RSA)	05-07-68
FERREIRA, Ellis	(RSA)	19-02-70
FERREIRA, Wayne	(RSA)	15-09-71
FETTERLEIN, Frederik	(DEN)	11-07-70
FIALA, Daniel 'Danie'	(CZE)	24-06-72
FILIPPINI, Marcelo	(URU)	04-08-67
FITZGERALD, John	(AUS)	28-12-60
FLACH, Doug	(USA)	10-08-70
FLEURIAN, Jean-Philippe	(FRA)	11-09-65
FLORENT, Andrew	(AUS)	24-10-70
FONTANG, Frederic	(FRA)	18-03-70
FORGET, Guy	(FRA)	04-01-65
FOSTER, Andrew	(GBR)	16-03-72
FRAGOSO, Bruno	(POR)	23-11-72
FRANA, Javier	(ARG)	25-12-66
FREDRIKSSON, Patrik	(SWE)	16-05-73
FROMBERG, Richard	(AUS)	28-04-70
FRONTERA, Jose	(PUR)	31-01-71
FURLAN, Renzo	(ITA)	17-05-70
FURMANSKI, Damian	(ARG)	05-10-75
GALBRAITH, Patrick	(USA)	16-04-67
GAMBILL, Jan-Michael	(USA)	03-06-77
GAMONAL, Hermes	(CHI)	31-05-77
GANIEV, Timur	(UZB)	24-10-75
GAUDENZI, Andrea	(ITA)	30-07-73
GAUTHIER, Pier	(FRA)	20-04-72
GILBERT, Bradley 'Brad'	(USA)	09-08-61
GILBERT, Rodolphe	(FRA)	12-12-68
GIMELSTOB, Justin	(USA)	26-01-77
GODWIN, Neville	(RSA)	31-01-75
GOELLNER, Marc	(GER)	22-09-70
GOLDSTEIN, Paul	(USA)	04-08-76
GOLMARD, Jerome	(FRA)	09-09-73
GOMEZ-BARRIO, Sergio	(ESP)	16-10-70
GONCALVES, Vasco	(POR)	22-01-74
GOOSSENS, Kris	(BEL)	20-02-74
GORRIZ, Marcos-Aurelio	(ESP)	04-03-64
GRABB, James 'Jim'	(USA)	14-04-64
GRANT, Geoffrey 'Geoff'	(USA)	16-01-70
GREENHALGH, James	(NZL)	19-02-75
GROEN, Sander	(NED)	16-06-68
GROSJEAN, Sebastien	(FRA)	29-05-78
GROSS, Oliver	(GER)	17-06-73
GROSSI, Elia	(ITA)	03-06-74
GUMY, Hernan	(ARG)	05-03-72
GUSTAFSSON, Magnus	(SWE)	03-01-67
HAARHUIS, Paul	(NED)	19-02-66

Surname / Forename	*Nation*	*DOB*
HAAS, Thomas 'Tommy'	(GER)	03-04-78
HAGGARD, Christopher 'Chris'	(RSA)	28-04-71
HANAK, Rene	(CZE)	04-05-73
HANQUEZ, Jerome	(FRA)	11-03-74
HANSEN-DENT, Brett	(USA)	02-07-72
HAWK, Brandon	(USA)	03-09-79
HAYGARTH, Brent	(RSA)	27-12-67
HEDE, Johan	(SWE)	10-07-74
HENMAN, Tim	(GBR)	06-09-74
HERNANDEZ, Alejandro 'Alex'	(MEX)	01-10-77
HERRERA, Luis-Enrique	(MEX)	27-08-71
HEUBERGER, Ivo	(SUI)	19-02-76
HEWITT, Lleyton	(AUS)	24-02-81
HILPERT, Marcus	(GER)	01-07-71
HIPFL, Markus	(AUT)	26-04-78
HIRSZON, Sasa	(CRO)	14-07-72
HO, Thomas 'Tommy'	(USA)	17-06-73
HOLM, Henrik	(SWE)	22-08-68
HOLM, Nils	(SWE)	30-10-69
HOLMES, James 'Jamie'	(AUS)	04-05-73
HOOD, Mariano	(ARG)	14-08-73
HRBATY, Dominik	(SVK)	04-01-78
HUET, Stephane	(FRA)	25-04-71
HUMPHRIES, Scott	(USA)	26-05-76
HUNING, Mathias	(GER)	25-06-69
HUNT, Alistair	(NZL)	11-11-72
HUTHMANN-MANOLA, Marcelo	(GER)	22-01-74
ILOWSKI, Jakub	(POL)	15-09-80
IRELAND, Jon	(AUS)	26-09-67
ISHII, Hiroki	(JPN)	27-07-71
IVANISEVIC, Goran	(CRO)	13-09-71
IVANOV, Anton	(UZB)	18-01-70
IVANOV-SMOLENSKY, Kerill	(RUS)	19-01-81
IWABUCHI, Satoshi	(JPN)	07-10-75
JABALI, Roberto	(BRA)	16-05-70
JENSEN, Luke	(USA)	18-06-66
JENSEN, Murphy	(USA)	30-10-68
JOHANSSON, Thomas	(SWE)	24-03-75
JOHNSON, Donald	(USA)	09-09-68
JONES, Kelly	(USA)	31-05-64
JONSSON, Fredrik	(SWE)	28-03-77
JONSSON, Lars	(SWE)	27-06-70
JOYCE, Michael	(USA)	01-02-73
KAFELNIKOV, Yevgeny	(RUS)	18-02-74
KANEKO, Hideki	(JPN)	06-03-74
KARBACHER, Bernd	(GER)	03-04-68
KARLOVIC, Ivo	(CRO)	28-02-79
KEIL, Mark	(USA)	03-06-67
KEMPERS, Tom	(NED)	01-06-69
KEMPES, Edwin 'Ed'	(NED)	23-06-76
KETOLA, Tuomas	(FIN)	21-02-75
KHANKODJAEV, Timur	(UZB)	29-06-75
KIEFER, Nicolas	(GER)	05-07-77
KILDERRY, Paul	(AUS)	11-04-73
KIM, Alex	(USA)	20-12-78
KIM, Kevin	(USA)	26-07-78
KINNEAR, Kent	(USA)	30-11-66
KIRTANE, Nitin	(IND)	04-03-74
KIRTANE, Sandeep	(IND)	27-10-73
KITINOV, Aleksandar	(MKD)	13-01-71
KNIPPSCHILD, Jens	(GER)	15-02-75
KNOWLES, Mark	(BAH)	04-09-71
KOENIG, Robbie	(RSA)	05-07-71
KOKAVEC, Robert 'Bobby'	(CAN)	17-05-76

Surname / Forename	*Nation*	*DOB*
KOKURIN, Anton	(UZB)	16-04-80
KORDA, Petr	(CZE)	23-01-68
KOUBEK, Stefan	(AUT)	02-01-77
KOVES, Gabor	(HUN)	01-07-70
KRAJAN, Zeljko	(CRO)	03-02-79
KRAJICEK, Richard	(NED)	06-12-71
KRALERT, Petr	(CZE)	20-10-79
KRATZMANN, Andrew	(AUS)	03-11-71
KRISTIANSSON, Ola	(SWE)	23-09-71
KROCSKO, Jozsef	(HUN)	20-04-68
KRONEMANN, Trevor	(USA)	03-09-68
KROSLAK, Jan	(SVK)	17-10-74
KUCERA, Karol	(SVK)	04-03-74
KUERTEN, Gustavo	(BRA)	10-09-76
KUHNEN, Patrik	(GER)	11-02-66
KULTI, Nicklas	(SWE)	22-04-71
KUTSENKO, Vadim	(UZB)	16-03-77
LANGVARDT, Patrik	(DEN)	06-12-71
LAPENTTI, Nicolas	(ECU)	13-08-76
LAREAU, Sebastien	(CAN)	27-04-73
LARKHAM, Todd	(AUS)	13-10-74
LARSEN, Thomas	(DEN)	15-07-75
LARSSON, Magnus	(SWE)	25-03-70
LAVALLE, Leonardo	(MEX)	14-07-67
LAVERGNE, Regis	(FRA)	28-01-74
LE BLANC, Sebastien	(CAN)	27-12-73
LEACH, Richard 'Rick'	(USA)	28-12-64
LECONTE, Henri	(FRA)	04-07-63
LEE, Martin	(GBR)	13-01-78
LJUBICIC, Ivan	(CRO)	19-03-79
LOBO, Luis	(ARG)	09-11-70
LOOMIS, Jeremy	(USA)	17-09-70
LOPEZ, German	(ESP)	29-12-71
LOPEZ-MORON, Alex	(ESP)	28-11-70
LOZANO, Diego	(ESP)	21-05-73
LU, Ling	(CHN)	18-01-74
LUXA, Petr	(CZE)	03-03-72
MACLAGAN, Miles	(GBR)	23-09-74
MACPHERSON, David	(AUS)	03-07-67
MACPHIE, Brian	(USA)	11-05-72
MADSEN, Bertrand	(HAI)	18-05-72
MAGGI, Fabio	(ITA)	30-01-75
MAKHKAMOV, Abdul-Hamid	(UZB)	19-04-76
MAMIIT, Cecil	(USA)	27-06-76
MANDL, Gerald	(AUT)	12-11-70
MANTA, Lorenzo	(SUI)	16-09-74
MANTILLA, Felix	(ESP)	23-09-74
MARIN, Juan-Antonio	(ESP)	02-03-75
MARKOVITS, Laszlo	(HUN)	04-04-70
MARQUES, Nuno	(POR)	09-04-70
MARTELLI, Marzio	(ITA)	14-12-71
MARTIN, Alberto	(ESP)	20-08-78
MARTIN, Todd	(USA)	08-07-70
MARTINEZ, Bernardo	(MEX)	21-08-72
MARTINEZ, Carlos	(ESP)	05-09-74
MARTINEZ, Oscar	(ESP)	09-03-74
MARX, Guillaume	(FRA)	24-05-72
MASSU, Nicolas	(CHI)	10-11-79
MATSUOKA, Shuzo	(JPN)	06-11-67
MAZUR, Dimitri	(UZB)	08-09-79
McENROE, Patrick	(USA)	01-07-66
McGUIRE, Wade	(USA)	19-08-69
MEDVEDEV, Andrei	(UKR)	31-08-74
MELIGENI, Fernando	(BRA)	12-04-71
MELVILLE, Scott	(USA)	04-08-66

Surname / Forename	*Nation*	*DOB*
MENESCHINCHERI, Marco	(ITA)	25-04-72
MERINOV, Andrei	(LAT)	23-06-71
MERKLEIN, Mark	(USA)	28-06-72
MESSORI, Filippo	(ITA)	12-11-73
MICHIBATA, Glenn	(CAN)	13-06-62
MIDDLETON, Todd 'T.J.'	(USA)	02-05-68
MILLIGAN, Luke	(GBR)	06-08-76
MIRNYI, Maxim 'Max'	(BLR)	06-07-77
MITCHELL, Toby	(AUS)	20-08-76
MOGGIO, Philippe	(COL)	23-03-73
MOLDOVAN, Ion	(ROM)	17-01-78
MONTANA, Francisco	(USA)	05-11-69
MORDEGAN, Federico	(ITA)	01-02-70
MOREJON, Luis	(ECU)	28-03-73
MOREL, Olivier	(FRA)	03-08-72
MOTA, Bernardo	(POR)	14-06-71
MOTEVASSEL, Oren	(USA)	26-08-67
MOTOMURA, Gouichi	(JPN)	25-12-73
MOYA, Carlos	(ESP)	27-08-76
MULLER, Gary	(RSA)	27-12-64
MUNOZ-HERNANDEZ, Joaquin Jr.	(ESP)	04-01-75
MUSA, Daniele	(ITA)	10-09-72
MUSIL, Adolf	(CZE)	10-02-74
MUSTER, Thomas	(AUT)	02-10-67
MUTIS, Olivier	(FRA)	02-02-78
NAINKIN, David	(RSA)	20-09-70
NARGISO, Diego	(ITA)	15-03-70
NARLA, Susheel	(IND)	07-12-76
NATEKAR, Gaurav	(IND)	04-04-72
NAVARRO, Salvador	(ESP)	08-01-77
NEEFS, Wim	(BEL)	08-03-76
NEMECEK, Libor	(CZE)	26-10-68
NESTOR, Daniel	(CAN)	04-09-72
N'GORAN, Clement-N'dri	(CIV)	07-08-69
NICOLAS, Eduardo	(ESP)	22-09-72
NIEMEYER, Frederic	(CAN)	24-04-76
NIJSSEN, Tom	(NED)	01-10-64
NORMAN, Dick	(BEL)	01-03-71
NORMAN, Magnus	(SWE)	30-05-76
NORVAL, Pieter 'Piet'	(RSA)	07-04-70
NOTEBOOM, Stephen	(NED)	31-07-69
NOVAK, Jiri	(CZE)	22-03-75
NYBORG, Peter	(SWE)	12-12-69
NYDAHL, Tomas	(SWE)	21-03-68
O'BRIEN, Alex	(USA)	07-03-70
OGORODOV, Oleg	(UZB)	16-07-72
OLHOVSKIY, Andrei	(RUS)	15-04-66
ONCINS, Jaime	(BRA)	16-06-70
ONDRUSKA, Marcos	(RSA)	18-12-72
ONODA, Michihisa	(JPN)	31-01-78
OOSTING, Menno	(NED)	17-05-64
ORESIC, Goran	(CRO)	28-04-75
ORSANIC, Daniel	(ARG)	11-06-68
ORTIZ, Oscar	(MEX)	09-05-73
OSORIO, Marco-Aurelio	(MEX)	01-04-72
OVERHOLSER, Nathan	(USA)	23-06-79
PAES, Leander	(IND)	17-06-73
PAINTER, Andrew	(AUS)	18-07-75
PALMER, Jared	(USA)	02-07-71
PAN, Bing	(CHN)	13-02-70
PAPP, Zoltan	(HUN)	14-09-79
PARMAR, Arvind	(GBR)	22-03-78
PASTEL, Jonathan	(USA)	15-08-76
PASTURA, Miguel	(ARG)	27-05-73

A dream year for French Open semi-finalist Filip Dewulf, the first Belgian to reach that stage at a Grand Slam. He went on to win his first tour title at Kitzbuhel. (Michael Cole)

Surname / Forename	*Nation*	*DOB*
PATE, David	(USA)	16-04-62
PAVEL, Andrei	(ROM)	27-01-74
PEREIRA, Nicolas	(VEN)	29-09-70
PERLANT, Jean-Baptiste	(FRA)	22-02-77
PESCARIU, Dinu	(ROM)	12-04-74
PESCOSOLIDO, Stefano	(ITA)	13-06-71
PEST, Valentino	(GER)	12-09-76
PETCHEY, Mark	(GBR)	01-08-70
PHAU, Bjorn	(GER)	04-10-79
PHILIPPOUSSIS, Mark	(AUS)	07-11-76
PHILLIPS, Trey	(USA)	27-06-73
PIMEK, Libor	(BEL)	03-08-63
PIOLINE, Cedric	(FRA)	15-06-69
PLAMBERGER, Udo	(AUT)	01-01-71
PORTAS, Albert	(ESP)	15-11-73
POZZI, Gianluca	(ITA)	17-06-65
PRIETO, Sebastian	(ARG)	19-05-75
PRINOSIL, David	(GER)	09-03-73
PUERTA, Mariano	(ARG)	19-09-78
RADULESCU, Alexandru 'Alex'	(GER)	07-12-74
RAFTER, Patrick 'Pat'	(AUS)	28-12-72
RAKE, Rodolfo 'Rudy'	(PER)	13-07-79
RAN, Eyal	(ISR)	21-11-72
RANDALL, Dave	(USA)	08-05-67

Surname / Forename	*Nation*	*DOB*
RAOUX, Guillaume	(FRA)	14-02-70
RASBERGER, Emanuel	(CRO)	03-06-72
REHMANN, Lars	(GER)	21-05-75
REICHEL, Alexander 'Alex'	(USA)	09-03-71
RENEBERG, Richard 'Richey'	(USA)	05-10-65
RHARNIT, Larbi	(MAR)	18-04-76
RICHARDSON, Andrew	(GBR)	14-03-74
RIKL, David	(CZE)	27-02-71
RINCON, Eduardo	(COL)	22-03-76
RINCON, Mario	(COL)	13-12-67
RIOS, Marcelo	(CHI)	26-12-75
RIZO, Ricardo	(MEX)	25-07-79
ROBERMAN, Alex	(USA)	17-04-75
ROBICHAUD, Jocelyn	(CAN)	08-04-78
RODITI, David	(MEX)	30-11-73
RODRIGUEZ, Martin	(ARG)	18-12-69
ROIG, Francisco	(ESP)	01-04-68
ROSNER, Paul	(RSA)	11-12-72
ROSSET, Marc	(SUI)	07-11-70
ROUX, Lionel	(FRA)	12-04-73
RUAH, Maurice	(VEN)	19-02-71
RUEB, Andrew 'Andy'	(USA)	18-11-72
RUIZ, Francisco	(CHI)	17-02-73
RUSEDSKI, Gregory 'Greg'	(GBR)	06-09-73

Surname / Forename	*Nation*	*DOB*
RUUD, Christian	(NOR)	24-08-72
RYBALKO, Andrei	(UKR)	05-06-72
SA, Andre	(BRA)	06-05-77
SABAU, Razvan	(ROM)	18-06-77
SACEANU, Christian	(GER)	08-07-68
SAFIN, Marat	(RUS)	27-01-80
SALVADOR, David	(ESP)	20-10-73
SALZENSTEIN, Jeff	(USA)	14-10-73
SAMPRAS, Peter 'Pete'	(USA)	12-08-71
SANCHEZ, David	(ESP)	20-04-78
SANCHEZ, Emilio	(ESP)	29-05-65
SANCHEZ, Fernando	(ESP)	17-06-77
SANCHEZ, Javier	(ESP)	01-02-68
SANCHEZ, Mariano	(MEX)	03-07-78
SANGUINETTI, Davide	(ITA)	25-08-72
SANTOPADRE, Vincenzo	(ITA)	11-08-71
SANTORO, Fabrice	(FRA)	09-12-72
SAPSFORD, Danny	(GBR)	03-04-69
SARGSIAN, Sargius	(ARM)	03-06-73
SARIC, Igor	(CRO)	04-07-67
SARSTRAND, Marcus	(SWE)	24-07-78
SCALA, Davide	(ITA)	02-01-72
SCHALKEN, Sjeng	(NED)	08-09-76
SCHALLER, Gilbert	(AUT)	17-03-69
SCHIESSLING, Thomas	(AUT)	01-11-74
SCHMIDT, John	(USA)	25-01-66
SCHNALL, Larry	(USA)	
SCHRANZ, Wolfgang	(AUT)	18-03-76
SCHUTTLER, Rainer	(GER)	25-04-76
SEKULOV, James	(AUS)	13-10-76
SELL, Michael 'Mike'	(USA)	23-08-72
SHELTON, Bryan	(USA)	22-12-65
SHIMADA, Thomas 'Tommy'	(JPN)	10-02-75
SHYJAN, Michael 'Mike'	(USA)	29-10-69
SIEMERINK, Jan	(NED)	14-04-70
SILBERSTEIN, Gabriel	(CHI)	17-10-74
SILCOCK, Grant	(AUS)	21-05-75
SIMIAN, Stephane	(FRA)	08-06-67
SINNER, Martin	(GER)	07-02-68
SKOCH, David	(CZE)	06-11-76
SLUITER, Raemon	(NED)	13-04-78
SMITH, Luke	(AUS)	25-10-76
SMITH, Roger	(BAH)	20-01-64
SOLVES, Gerard	(FRA)	07-04-68
SPADEA, Vincent 'Vince'	(USA)	19-07-74
SPRENGELMEYER, Mitch	(USA)	09-01-75
SQUILLARI, Franco	(ARG)	22-08-75
SRICHAPHAN, Paradorn	(THA)	14-06-79
STAFFORD, Grant	(RSA)	27-05-71
STANOYTCHEV, Orlin	(BUL)	24-09-71
STARK, Jonathan	(USA)	03-04-71
STAUDER, Franz	(GER)	28-05-77
STEPANEK, Radek	(CZE)	27-11-78
STEVEN, Brett	(NZL)	27-04-69
STICH, Michael	(GER)	18-10-68
STOLIAROV, Andrei	(RUS)	09-01-77
STOLLE, Sandon	(AUS)	13-07-70
STOLTENBERG, Jason	(AUS)	04-04-70
STRENGBERGER, Thomas	(AUT)	05-10-75
SUK, Cyril	(CZE)	29-01-67
SUZUKI, Takao	(JPN)	20-09-76
SZYMANSKI, Jimmy 'Jimy'	(VEN)	15-09-75
TABARA, Michael	(CZE)	11-08-79
TAHIRI, Mehdi	(MAR)	28-07-77
TAINO, Eric	(USA)	18-03-75
TAKADA, Mitsuru	(JPN)	26-09-69
TALBOT, Byron	(RSA)	15-09-64
TARANGO, Jeffrey 'Jeff'	(USA)	20-11-68
TCHELYCHEV, Igor	(RUS)	07-07-76
TEBBUTT, Michael	(AUS)	22-12-70
THOMANN, Nicolas	(FRA)	29-11-72
THOMS, Arne	(GER)	01-01-71
THORNE, Kenny	(USA)	24-01-66
TIELEMAN, Laurence	(ITA)	14-11-72
TILLSTROM, Mikael	(SWE)	05-03-72
TIMFJORD, Niklas	(SWE)	18-03-77
TOBON, Miguel	(COL)	22-06-68
TOMASHEVICH, Dmitri	(UZB)	06-03-74
TONG, Man-Chung 'Melvin'	(HKG)	19-02-75
TRAMACCHI, Peter	(AUS)	08-11-70
TRIFU, Gabriel	(ROM)	14-04-75
TRIMMEL, Clemens	(AUT)	08-06-78
TROTMAN, James	(GBR)	16-02-79
TSUJINO, Ryuso	(JPN)	24-02-69
TUDOR, Mario	(CRO)	13-07-78
ULIHRACH, Bohdan	(CZE)	23-02-75
ULLYETT, Kevin	(RSA)	23-05-72
VACEK, Daniel	(CZE)	01-04-71
VALERI, Massimo	(ITA)	13-03-72
VAN EMBURGH, Gregory 'Greg'	(USA)	10-05-66
VAN GARSSE, Christophe	(BEL)	21-06-74
VAN HERCK, Johan	(BEL)	24-05-74
VAN HOUDT, Tom	(BEL)	28-07-72
VAN LOTTUM, John	(NED)	10-04-76
VAN RENSBURG, Christo	(RSA)	23-10-62
VAN SCHEPPINGEN, Dennis	(NED)	05-07-75
VASEK, Radomir	(CZE)	23-09-72
VERKERK, Martin	(NED)	10-10-78
VICENTE, Fernando	(ESP)	08-03-77
VILOCA, Joan-Albert	(ESP)	17-01-73
VIZNER, Pavel	(CZE)	15-07-70
VOINEA, Adrian	(ROM)	06-08-74
VOLKOV, Alexander	(RUS)	03-03-67
VOLTCHKOV, Vladimir 'Vlad'	(BLR)	07-04-78
WAHLGREN, Lars-Anders	(SWE)	24-08-66
WAITE, Jack	(USA)	01-05-69
WASHINGTON, MaliVai	(USA)	20-06-69
WASHINGTON, Mashiska	(USA)	19-12-74
WASSEN, Rogier	(NED)	09-08-76
WEAL, Nicholas 'Nick'	(GBR)	04-09-73
WEIDENFELD, Raviv	(ISR)	12-10-70
WEINER, Glenn	(USA)	27-04-76
WELGREEN, Nir	(ISR)	17-12-76
WESSELS, Peter	(NED)	07-05-78
WHEATON, David	(USA)	02-06-69
WIBIER, Fernon	(NED)	25-02-71
WILKINSON, Chris	(GBR)	05-01-70
WILSON, Glenn	(NZL)	17-08-67
WILTSCHNIG, Herbert	(AUT)	21-11-75
WINNINK, Joost	(NED)	30-06-71
WITT, David	(USA)	02-06-73
WOLTERS, Ryan	(USA)	01-02-77
WOODBRIDGE, Todd	(AUS)	02-04-71
WOODFORDE, Mark	(AUS)	23-09-65
WOODRUFF, Chris	(USA)	02-01-73
XIA, Jia-Ping	(CHN)	01-03-69
YAMAMOTO, Yasufumi	(JPN)	03-05-71
ZABALETA, Mariano	(ARG)	28-02-78
ZDRAZILA, Tomas	(CZE)	24-06-70
ZINGMAN, Andres	(ARG)	16-06-74

Mercedes Super 9 Tournaments

NEWSWEEK CHAMPIONS CUP ($2,050,000)

INDIAN WELLS, 10–16 MARCH

MEN'S SINGLES – 1st round: P. Sampras (1) bye; B. Ulihrach d. H. Gumy 4–6 6–1 6–0; J. Sanchez d. R. Reneberg 6–4 5–7 6–4; F. Clavet d. J. Courier (16) 6–4 4–6 6–4; B. Black d. A. Costa (9) 6–2 6–2; A. O'Brien d. S. Bruguera 6–4 6–4; G. Kuerten (Q) d. M. Woodforde 6–4 7–6; W. Ferreira (7) bye; G. Ivanisevic (4) bye; J. Stark (WC) d. C. Ruud 7–6 6–2; N. Kulti (Q) d. A. Medvedev 6–4 6–4; A. Berasategui (14) d. S. Lareau (Q) 7–6 7–6; J. Tarango (Q) d. M. Tillstrom (LL) 6–3 6–3; J. Bjorkman d. A. Gaudenzi 6–1 6–3; C. Woodruff d. J. Gimelstob (WC) 6–4 6–7 6–3; T. Enqvist (6) bye; M. Rios (5) bye; M. Larsson (WC) d. V. Spadea 6–4 6–3; C. Pioline d. J. Stoltenberg 6–4 6–4; S. Stolle d. F. Mantilla (12) 0–6 6–3 6–3; M. Rosset (13) d. M. Zabaleta (WC) 6–3 7–5; H. Dreekmann d. P. Rafter 7–6 6–3; S. Schalken (Q) d. L. Paes (Q) 7–6 6–2; M. Chang (3) bye; C. Moya (8) bye; J. Novak (WC) d. M-K. Goellner 5–7 6–4 6–2; T. Woodbridge (WC) d. D. Hrbaty 7–5 5–7 6–2; M. Philippoussis d. A. Agassi (10) 7–6 7–6; A. Corretja (15) d. F. Meligeni (Q) 6–3 6–3; C. Dosedel d. P. Haarhuis 6–7 6–2 6–1; A. Voinea d. G. Forget 4–6 4–2 ret; Muster (2) bye.
2nd round: Ulihrach d. Sampras (1) 7–6 7–5; Clavet d. Sanchez 6–4 4–6 7–6; Black d. O'Brien 3–6 6–1 7–6; Kuerten (Q) d. Ferreira (7) 7–6 1–6 6–3; Stark (WC) d. Ivanisevic (4) 7–5 6–3; Berasategui (14) d. Kulti (Q) 6–3 6–7 6–3; Bjorkman d. Tarango (Q) 6–4 6–2; Woodruff d. Enqvist (6) 6–4 6–4; Larsson (WC) d. Rios (5) 6–3 5–7 7–6; Pioline d. Stolle 6–4 6–4; Rosset (13) d. Dreekmann 3–6 6–3 7–6; Chang (3) d. Schalken (Q) 6–4 6–3; Moya (8) d. Novak (WC) 6–4 6–2; Philippoussis d. Woodbridge (WC) 7–6 7–6; C. Dosedel d. A. Corretja (15) 6–4 4–1 ret; T. Muster (2) d. A. Voinea 6–2 6–4.
3rd round: Ulihrach d. Clavet 7–5 7–6; Black d. Kuerten (Q) 6–3 6–3; Berasategui (14) d. Stark (WC) 7–6 6–3; Bjorkman d. Woodruff 2–6 7–5 6–1; Pioline d. Larsson (WC) 6–7 6–2 6–4; Chang (3) d. Rosset (13) 6–2 7–5; Philippoussis d. Moya (8) 6–4 6–3; Muster (2) d. Dosedel 6–4 6–4.
Quarter-finals: Ulihrach d. Black 6–4 6–2; Bjorkman d. Berasategui (14) 6–2 6–3; Chang (3) d. Pioline 6–3 6–2; Muster (2) d. Philippoussis 6–3 7–6.
Semi-finals: Ulihrach d. Bjorkman 6–3 6–2; Chang (3) d. Muster (2) 6–1 7–6.
Final: Chang (3) d. Ulihrach 4–6 6–3 6–4 6–3.
MEN'S DOUBLES – Final: Knowles/Nestor (6) d. Philippoussis/Rafter 7–6 4–6 7–5.

THE LIPTON CHAMPIONSHIPS ($2,450,000)

KEY BISCAYNE, 20–30 MARCH

MEN'S SINGLES – 1st round: P. Sampras (1) bye; A. Voinea d. M. Zabaleta 5–7 7–5 6–6 def; N. Kiefer (WC) d. D. van Scheppingen 6–2 5–7 7–6; F. Clavet (31) bye; J. Siemerink (17) bye; M. Larsson d. P. Haarhuis 7–5 0–6 7–5; C. Dosedel d. D. Flach (Q) 7–6 2–6 6–2; M. Rosset (15) bye; L. Arnold (LL) bye; H. Dreekmann d. M. Filippini 6–4 6–4; G. Kuerten d. M. Joyce 6–1 4–6 6–3; B. Ulihrach (23) bye; T. Woodbridge (26) bye; M. Tillstrom d. L. Roux 7–6 6–1; M. Charpentier (Q) d. J. Gimelstob (WC) 7–6 3–6 6–4; C. Moya (7) bye; M. Chang (3) bye; M. Merklein (Q) d. N. Godwin 2–6 6–4 6–4; J. Stoltenberg d. J. Grabb (Q) 6–3 6–2; S. Bruguera (30) bye; R. Reneberg (19) bye; G. Etlis (Q) d. G. Blanco 6–4 6–4; J. Alonso-Pintor (Q) d. S. Bryan (Q) 6–4 6–0; T. Henman (14) bye; A. Costa (11) bye; F. de Wulf (WC) d. A. Hernandez (Q) 7–6 6–1; A. Medvedev d. C. Ruud 6–4 6–4; P. Korda (21) bye; C. Pioline (28) bye; N. Kulti d. M. Ondruska (WC) 6–0 6–2; D. Nestor (WC) d. J. Stark 6–3 0–6 6–3; T. Enqvist (6) bye; R. Krajicek (5) bye; H. Gumy d. P. Rafter 6–4 6–4; F. Meligeni d. M-K. Goellner 4–6 6–2 6–3; A. Boetsch (27) bye; J. Courier (22) bye; S. Stolle d. M. Gorriz 6–0 6–7 7–5; S. Draper d. S. Schalken 6–3 7–6; A. Agassi (12) bye; F. Mantilla (13) bye; D. Hrbaty d. T. Champion 6–7 7–5 6–3; C. Woodruff d. A. Radulescu 6–4 6–4; N. Lapentti (LL) bye; A. O'Brien (29) bye; V. Spadea d. J. Frana (Q) 4–6 6–3 6–4; B. Black d. A. Gaudenzi 6–2 6–3; G. Ivanisevic (4) bye; M. Rios (8) bye; J. Tarango d. S. Sargsian 6–2 7–5; J. Salzenstein (Q) d. J. van Herck 6–7 6–3 6–4; J. Bjorkman (25) bye; M. Philippoussis (24) bye; M. Damm d. C. Costa 6–1 5–7 6–4; J. Novak d. J. Viloca 6–0 6–3; W. Ferreira (9) bye; A. Berasategui (16) bye; S. Lareau (Q) d. M. Woodforde 6–2 6–4; J. Golmard (Q) d. G. Raoux 6–2 6–3; A. Corretja (18) bye; J. Sanchez (32) bye; T. Haas (WC) d. G. Forget 7–6 7–5; G. Stafford d. L. Paes 7–6 7–6; T. Muster (2) bye.
2nd round: Sampras (1) d. Voinea 6–2 6–0; Clavet (31) d. Kiefer (WC) 6–2 6–3; Larsson d. Siemerink (17) 6–1 6–3; Dosedel d. Rosset (15) 5–7 6–2 7–5; Dreekmann d. Arnold (LL) 6–1 6–1; Kuerten d. Ulihrach (23) 7–6 6–3; Tillstrom d. Woodbridge (26) 7–6 5–7 6–4; Moya (7) d. Charpentier (Q) 7–6 6–4; Chang (3) d. Merklein (Q) 6–3 7–6; Bruguera (30) d. Stoltenberg 6–3 3–6 7–5; Etlis (Q) d. Reneberg (19) 6–4 ret; Alonso-Pintor (Q) d. Henman (14) 6–7 6–2 6–3; A. Costa (11) d. de Wulf (WC) 6–3 6–2; Medvedev d. Korda (21) 6–2 6–7 7–6; Kulti d. Pioline (28) 2–6 6–4 7–6; Nestor (WC) d. Enqvist (6) 7–6 6–3; Krajicek (5) d. Gumy 7–5 7–6; Boetsch (27) d. Meligeni 6–4 6–3; Courier (22) d. Stolle 6–2 6–2; Draper d. Agassi (12) 7–6 6–1; Hrbaty d. Mantilla (13) 6–4 6–4; Woodruff d. Lapentti (LL) 6–3 6–3; Spadea d. O'Brien (29) 7–6 7–5; Ivanisevic (4) d. Black 6–3 6–3; Rios (8) d. Tarango 7–5 6–2; Bjorkman (25) d. Salzenstein (Q) 6–2 6–3; Philippoussis (24) d. Damm 7–5 7–6; Ferreira (9) d. Novak 6–4 6–2; Lareau (Q) d. Berasategui (16) 6–2 7–6; Corretja (18) d.

Golmard (Q) 7–5 6–3; Haas (WC) d. Sanchez (32) 4–6 6–2 6–1; Muster (2) d. Stafford 6–4 2–6 6–1.
3rd round: Sampras (1) d. Clavet (31) 6–3 7–6; Larsson d. Dosedel 5–7 7–5 6–3; Dreekmann d. Kuerten 7–6 3–6 7–6; Tillstrom d. Moya (7) 6–4 3–6 6–3; Bruguera (30) d. Chang (3) 6–4 6–3; Etlis (Q) d. Alonso-Pintor (Q) 7–6 7–6; Medvedev d. A. Costa (11) 6–3 3–6 7–6; Kulti d. Nestor (WC) 6–4 7–5; Krajicek (5) d. Boetsch (27) 6–3 7–5; Courier (22) d. Draper 4–6 6–1 6–4; Hrbaty d. Woodruff 6–3 6–2; Ivanisevic (4) d. Spadea 3–6 7–6 6–4; Bjorkman (25) d. Rios (8) 6–3 3–6 6–1; Philippoussis (24) d. Ferreira (9) 6–3 6–3; Corretja (18) d. Lareau (Q) 6–1 7–5; Muster (2) d. Haas (WC) 6–1 6–2.
4th round: Sampras (1) d. Larsson 6–2 6–0; Dreekmann d. Tillstrom 6–3 6–4; Bruguera (30) d. Etlis (Q) 7–6 6–4; Medvedev d. Kulti 4–6 6–3 7–5; Courier (22) d. Krajicek (5) 7–6 6–4; Ivanisevic (4) d. Hrbaty 6–4 6–4; Bjorkman (25) d. Philippoussis (24) 6–3 6–4; Muster (2) d. Corretja (18) 6–4 6–4.
Quarter-finals: Sampras (1) d. Dreekmann w/o; Bruguera (30) d. Medvedev 6–0 6–3; Courier (22) d. Ivanisevic (4) 6–2 7–6; Muster (2) d. Bjorkman (25) 7–5 6–2.
Semi-finals: Bruguera (30) d. Sampras (1) 5–7 7–6 6–4; Muster (2) d. Courier (22) 6–3 6–4.
Final: Muster (2) d. Bruguera (30) 7–6 6–3 6–1.
MEN'S DOUBLES – Final: Woodbridge/Woodforde (1) d. Knowles/Nestor (5) 7–6 7–6.

MONTE CARLO OPEN ($2,050,000)

MONTE CARLO, 21–27 APRIL
MEN'S SINGLES – 1st Round: P. Sampras (WC) (1) bye; M. Larsson d. H. Arazi 6–3 6–3; D. Vacek d. M. Tillstrom 6–1 6–3; M. Rosset (15) d. R. Carretero 7–6 6–0; A. Costa (10) d. J. Bjorkman 6–4 6–0; C. Dosedel d. G. Kuerten (Q) 6–1 3–6 6–1; A. Gaudenzi (WC) d. L. Roux 6–1 6–2; M. Rios (7) bye; R. Krajicek (4) bye; M. Stich d. M. Woodforde 3–6 7–5 7–5; M. Philippoussis d. H. Gumy 6–1 7–6; J. Courier (13) d. D. Hrbaty 6–7 7–5 6–4; F. Mantilla (11) d. M. Damm 6–1 6–1; A. Medvedev d. N. Kulti (WC) 4–6 6–2 6–3; F. Clavet d. T. Johansson 6–1 6–2; C. Moya (6) bye; T. Enqvist (5) bye; B. Ulihrach d. M. Gustafsson 7–6 6–2; C. Pioline d. O. Camporese (WC) 6–3 6–4; A. Corretja (12) d. N. Marques (Q) 6–0 6–0; A. Berasategui (14) d. P. Haarhuis 6–3 7–5; E. Alvarez (Q) d. K. Alami 6–3 3–6 6–0; C. Ruud d. S. Schalken 6–4 6–2; Y. Kafelnikov (3) bye; W. Ferreira (8) bye; C. Costa (Q) d. K. Kucera 6–3 5–7 6–3; A. Boetsch d. D. Sanguinetti (Q) 6–2 6–7 6–4; R. Furlan d. B. Becker (9) 1–6 6–3 7–6; S. Bruguera (16) d. J. Sanchez 6–4 6–1; J. Siemerink d. A. Merinov (Q) 7–6 6–3; F. Santoro (WC) d. F. Roig (Q) 6–4 6–1; T. Muster (2) bye.
2nd round: Larsson d. Sampras (WC) (1) 3–6 6–2 6–3; Vacek d. Rosset (15) 7–6 6–1; A. Costa (10) d. Dosedel 6–3 6–3; Rios (7) d. Gaudenzi (WC) 6–2 6–2; Krajicek (4) d. Stich 6–3 6–0; Philippoussis d. Courier (13) 7–5 7–5; Medvedev d. Mantilla (11) 6–2 6–4; Moya (6) d. Clavet 6–1 4–6 6–1; Ulihrach d. Enqvist (5) 7–5 4–6 6–3; Corretja (12) d. Pioline 6–4 6–3; Alvarez (Q) d. Berasategui (14) 6–3 3–6 6–4; Ruud d. Kafelnikov (3) 6–4 2–6 6–4; C. Costa (Q) d. Ferreira (8) 6–4 7–6; Boetsch d. Furlan 3–6 6–4 6–2; Bruguera (16) d. Siemerink 6–4 6–4; Santoro (WC) d. T. Muster (2) 6–2 7–6.
3rd round: Larsson d. Vacek 7–5 6–0; Rios (7) d. A. Costa (10) 7–6 6–4; Krajicek (4) d. Philippoussis 6–3 6–2; Moya (6) d. Medvedev 6–4 7–6; Corretja (12) d. Ulihrach 4–6 7–6 6–0; Ruud d. Alvarez (Q) 5–7 7–6 6–1; C. Costa (Q) d. Boetsch 6–4 7–5; Santoro (WC) d. S. Bruguera (16) 3–6 7–5 6–1.
Quarter-finals: Rios (7) d. Larsson 6–2 6–1; Moya (6) d. Krajicek (4) 1–6 6–2 6–4; Corretja (12) d. Ruud 6–2 6–0; Santoro (WC) d. C. Costa (Q) 6–3 7–5.
Semi-finals: Rios (7) d. Moya (6) 6–4 7–6; Corretja (12) d. Santoro (WC) 6–4 6–4.
Final: Rios (7) d. Corretja (12) 6–4 6–3 6–3.
MEN'S DOUBLES – Final: Johnson/Montana d. Eltingh/Haarhuis (1) 7–6 2–6 7–6.

GERMAN OPEN ($2,050,000)

HAMBURG, 5–11 MAY
MEN'S SINGLES – 1st Round: T. Muster (1) bye; A. Radulescu d. T. Nydahl (Q) 4–6 7–6 7–5; M. Craca (WC) d. M-K. Goellner 6–4 6–3; H. Arazi d. J. Siemerink (15) 6–4 6–2; F. Mantilla (10) d. M. Larsson 6–7 6–4 6–3; R. Carretero d. J. Knippschild (WC) 4–6 6–3 6–3; N. Kiefer (WC) d. M. Martelli (Q) 4–6 7–6 6–2; B. Becker (8) bye; C. Moya (4) bye; T. Haas (WC) d. D. Hrbaty 7–6 6–3; C. Costa (LL) d. D. Elsner (WC) 6–4 6–4; O. Gross (LL) d. K. Alami 6–4 6–4; A. Berasategui (11) d. A. Boetsch 6–2 6–4; M. Gustafsson d. C. Pioline 6–4 1–6 6–3; C. Ruud d. M. Tillstrom 6–1 4–6 6–3; M. Rios (5) bye; W. Ferreira (6) bye; A. Martin (Q) d. F. de Wulf (Q) 3–6 7–6 7–6; J. Tarango d. H. Gumy 6–3 6–1; S. Bruguera (12) d. S. Draper 6–0 6–4; J. Diaz (Q) d. M. Rosset (13) 6–4 6–2; P. Haarhuis d. H. Dreekmann 6–4 6–4; A. Medvedev d. M. Knowles (Q) 7–5 4–6 6–0; R. Krajicek (3) bye; A. Costa (7) bye; S. Schalken d. J. Sanchez 6–4 6–2; F. Clavet d. M. Gorriz (Q) 7–5 6–4; A. Corretja (9) d. D. Prinosil 6–1 6–3; M. Stich (16) d. K. Kucera 6–4 6–4; C. Dosedel d. R. Furlan 7–6 6–2; R. Fromberg d. G. Kuerten 7–6 6–3; Y. Kafelnikov (2) bye.
2nd round: Muster (1) d. Radulescu 6–2 6–2; Arazi d. Craca (WC) 7–6 7–5; Mantilla (10) d. Carretero 6–1 6–1; Becker (8) d. Kiefer (WC) 7–5 6–2; Haas (WC) d. Moya (4) 6–4 6–1; Gross (LL) d. C. Costa (LL) 6–3 6–1; Berasategui (11) d. Gustafsson 6–1 6–1; Rios (5) d. Ruud 6–1 7–5; Ferreira (6) d. Martin (Q) 3–6 7–5 7–5; Bruguera (12) d. Tarango 4–6 6–3 6–2; Diaz (Q) d. Haarhuis 6–2 3–6 7–5; Medvedev d. Krajicek (3) 6–1 6–1; A. Costa (7) d. Schalken 6–3 7–6; Corretja (9) d. Clavet 3–6 6–4 7–5; Dosedel d. Stich (16) 7–6 6–2; Kafelnikov (2) d. Fromberg 7–6 7–6.
3rd round: Arazi d. Muster (1) 6–1 6–2; Mantilla (10) d. Becker (8) 7–6 6–2; Haas (WC) d. Gross (LL) 5–7 7–5 6–3; Berasategui (11) d. Rios (5) 6–4 6–1; Bruguera (12) d. Ferreira (6) 6–1 6–3; Medvedev d. Diaz (Q) 6–3 6–3; A. Costa (7) d. Corretja (9) 6–3 6–4; Kafelnikov (2) d. Dosedel 6–2 6–1.

Quarter-finals: Mantilla (10) d. Arazi 4–6 7–6 6–4; Haas (WC) d. Berasategui (11) 2–6 6–2 6–3; Medvedev d. Bruguera (12) 6–4 7–6; Kafelnikov (2) d. A. Costa (7) 6–3 6–0.
Semi-finals: Mantilla (10) d. Haas (WC) 4–6 6–3 6–4; Medvedev d. Kafelnikov (2) 6–3 6–1.
Final: Medvedev d. Mantilla (10) 6–0 6–4 6–2.
MEN'S DOUBLES – Final: Lobo/Sanchez (7) d. Broad/Norval (8) 6–3 7–6.

CAMPIONATI INTERNAZIONALI D'ITALIE ($2,050,000)

ROME, 12–18 MAY
MEN'S SINGLES – 1st round: J. Courier d. P. Sampras (1) 7–6 6–4; A. Portas (Q) d. G. Rusedski 7–6 7–6; E. Alvarez (Q) d. F. Clavet 4–6 6–3 6–3; M. Rosset (15) d. J. Golmard (Q) 7–5 6–4; M. Larsson d. W. Ferreira (9) 4–6 7–5 7–6; T. Johansson d. D. Sanguinetti (Q) 5–7 6–3 6–2; F. Santoro (Q) d. R. Furlan 6–4 6–1; M. Rios (7) d. O. Camporese (WC) 6–3 7–5; Y. Kafelnikov (4) d. J. Sanchez 7–5 7–6; P. Haarhuis d. T. Woodbridge 7–6 6–1; A. Berasategui d. D. Vacek 6–3 6–4; P. Rafter d. F. Mantilla (13) 6–1 3–6 6–4; A. Costa (11) d. A. Radulescu 7–5 6–2; J. Siemerink d. J. Tarango 7–5 6–3; M-K. Goellner d. J. Stark 7–6 6–4; R. Krajicek (5) d. D. Nargiso (WC) 7–5 6–3; G. Ivanisevic (6) d. M. Woodforde 6–2 6–7 6–4; C. Ruud d. F. Fetterlein (Q) 6–4 7–5; C. Pioline d. B. Black 6–4 6–3; B. Becker (12) d. A. Gaudenzi (WC) 7–6 6–2; T. Henman (14) d. R. Carretero 4–6 7–5 2–0 ret; D. Scala (Q) d. D. Musa (Q) 6–4 6–7 7–6; S. Draper d. A. Medvedev 7–5 6–3; T. Muster (3) d. M. Martelli (WC) 6–3 6–2; C. Moya (8) d. S. Pescosolido (WC) 6–4 6–4; T. Haas d. M. Gustafsson 3–6 6–4 7–5; A. Boetsch d. A. O'Brien 7–6 6–4; A. Corretja (10) d. H. Arazi 6–0 6–3; K. Alami d. M. Philippoussis (16) 6–2 6–0; C. Woodruff d. D. Prinosil 6–3 6–2; S. Bruguera d. S. Stolle 6–1 6–4; H. Gumy d. M. Chang (2) 6–3 6–2.
2nd round: Courier d. Portas (Q) 7–6 6–2; Rosset (15) d. Alvarez (Q) 7–5 6–7 6–3; Larsson d. Johansson 7–6 6–3; Rios (7) d. Santoro (Q) 6–2 6–2; Kafelnikov (4) d. Haarhuis 7–6 3–6 6–3; Berasategui d. Rafter 3–6 6–4 7–5; Costa (11) d. Siemerink 6–4 6–2; Goellner d. Krajicek (5) 7–6 7–6; Ivanisevic (6) d. Ruud 6–2 6–2; Becker (12) d. Pioline 6–4 7–5; Scala (Q) d. Henman (14) 1–6 6–3 6–4; Draper d. Muster (3) 7–6 5–7 7–5; Moya (8) d. Haas 6–4 6–2; Corretja (10) d. Boetsch 6–2 6–3; Alami d. Woodruff 6–0 6–4; Bruguera d. Gumy 6–1 6–4.
3rd round: Courier d. Rosset (15) 7–6 6–3; Rios (7) d. Larsson 4–6 7–5 6–4; Berasategui d. Kafelnikov (4) 6–3 6–2; Goellner d. Costa (11) 6–4 3–6 6–4; Ivanisevic (6) d. Becker (12) 7–6 6–3; Draper d. Scala (Q) 7–5 6–2; Corretja (10) d. Moya (8) 6–4 6–4; Alami d. Bruguera 3–6 6–2 7–5.
Quarter-finals: Rios (7) d. Courier 6–3 3–6 7–6; Berasategui d. Goellner 7–5 7–5; Ivanisevic (6) d. Draper 6–4 6–4; Corretja (10) d. Alami 4–6 7–5 6–3.
Semi-finals: Rios (7) d. Berasategui 6–3 3–6 6–1; Corretja (10) d. Ivanisevic (6) 7–6 7–6.
Final: Corretja (10) d. Rios (7) 7–5 7–5 6–3.
MEN'S DOUBLES – Final: Knowles/Nestor (3) d. Black/O'Brien (5) 6–3 4–6 7–5.

DU MAURIER OPEN ($2,050,000)

MONTREAL, 28 JULY–3 AUGUST
MEN'S SINGLES – 1st round: M. Chang (1) bye; S. Stolle d. S. Lareau 6–1 7–5; M. Ondruska d. G. Stafford 4–6 7–5 6–2; A. O'Brien (15) d. A. Boetsch 6–1 6–2; J. Gimelstob d. P. Korda (9) 6–4 6–4; S. Draper d. T. Champion 4–6 6–1 6–2; N. Godwin d. B. Black 7–6 4–6 6–4; R. Krajicek (8) bye; T. Muster (3) bye; J. Salzenstein (Q) d. W. McGuire (Q) 6–4 6–2; G. Grant d. E. Ran 7–6 7–6; F. Santoro d. J. Courier (14) 7–5 4–6 6–4; P. Rafter (11) d. O. Delaitre 6–4 6–1; M. Tebbutt (Q) d. F. Niemeyer (WC) 7–6 6–3; J. Stark d. S. Sargsian 6–7 6–3 6–3; G. Kuerten (WC) (6) bye; T. Enqvist (5) bye; T. Haas d. D. Nestor 5–7 6–4 6–4; D. Flach d. J. Golmard 7–6 6–4; J. Bjorkman (12) d. R. Kokavec (WC) 6–3 6–2; W. Ferreira (13) d. D. Vacek 7–6 6–1; C. Caratti (Q) d. M. Damm 6–3 6–1; V. Spadea d. L. Roux 3–6 6–3 6–1; Y. Kafelnikov (4) bye; M. Philippoussis (7) bye; S. Campbell (Q) d. C. Mamiit (Q) 6–1 4–6 7–5; G. Raoux d. P. Gauthier (Q) 6–3 7–6; S. le Blanc (WC) d. T. Henman (10) 7–6 3–6 6–4; J. Siemerink (16) d. L. Paes 6–3 6–4; C. Woodruff d. J. Robichaud (WC) 7–6 6–3; B. Steven d. F. Fetterlein 6–2 6–0; G. Ivanisevic (2) bye.
2nd round: Chang (1) d. Stolle 6–1 1–0 ret; O'Brien (15) d. Ondruska 6–4 7–6; Gimelstob d. Draper 6–3 6–1; Krajicek (8) d. Godwin 7–6 6–1; Muster (3) d. Salzenstein (Q) 4–6 7–6 6–3; Santoro d. Grant 6–2 6–1; Tebbutt (Q) d. Rafter (11) 6–7 6–4 6–4; Kuerten (WC) (6) d. Stark 6–2 6–4; Enqvist (5) d. Haas 6–7 6–4 6–4; Bjorkman (12) d. Flach 5–7 6–3 7–5; Ferreira (13) d. Caratti (Q) 6–1 6–2; Kafelnikov (4) d. Spadea 4–6 6–3 7–6; Philippoussis (7) d. Campbell (Q) 6–2 6–4; Raoux d. le Blanc (WC) 6–1 6–4; Woodruff d. Siemerink (16) 6–7 7–5 7–6; Ivanisevic (2) d. Steven 6–3 6–7 6–4.
3rd round: Chang (1) d. O'Brien (15) 4–6 6–2 6–3; Krajicek (8) d. Gimelstob 6–2 6–4; Santoro d. Muster (3) 6–2 2–6 6–4; Kuerten (WC) (6) d. Tebbutt (Q) 5–7 6–4 6–4; Enqvist (5) d. Bjorkman (12) 6–3 6–2; Kafelnikov (4) d. Ferreira (13) 7–5 6–3; Philippoussis (7) d. Raoux 7–5 6–3; Woodruff d. Ivanisevic (2) 7–6 6–2.
Quarter-finals: Chang (1) d. Krajicek (8) 7–6 6–4; Kuerten (WC) (6) d. Santoro 6–3 7–6; Kafelnikov (4) d. Enqvist (5) 7–5 6–7 6–1; Woodruff d. Philippoussis (7) 6–4 6–4.
Semi-finals: Kuerten (WC) (6) d. Chang (1) 6–3 6–1; Woodruff d. Kafelnikov (4) 5–7 7–5 6–3.
Final: Woodruff d. Kuerten (WC) (6) 7–5 4–6 6–3.
MEN'S DOUBLES – Final: Bhupathi/Paes d. Lareau/O'Brien (3) 7–6 6–3.

GREAT AMERICAN INSURANCE ATP CHAMPIONSHIPS ($2,050,000)

CINCINNATI, 4–10 AUGUST
MEN'S SINGLES – 1st round: P. Sampras (1) bye; J. Gimelstob (WC) d. B. Black 6–3 6–4; D. Wheaton (Q) d. D. Vacek 7–6 6–2; P. Rafter (16) d. M. Larsson 5–7 6–4 7–5; M. Rios (9) d. J. Bjorkman 6–3 7–5; T. Johansson

d. K. Ullyett (Q) 6–4 3–6 6–2; C. Woodruff d. S. Sargsian 6–2 6–4; Y. Kafelnikov (7) bye; A. Corretja (4) bye; J. Stark d. G. Rusedski 1–6 6–3 7–6; T. Haas d. G. Stafford 6–4 4–6 6–4; A. Costa (14) d. J. Courier 4–6 7–6 6–3; S. Schalken d. M. Philippoussis (11) 7–6 6–3; J. Novak d. M-K. Goellner 7–5 7–6; S. Draper d. R. Reneberg 1–6 7–6 6–4; S. Bruguera (6) bye; T. Muster (5) bye; F. Santoro d. P. McEnroe (WC) 6–0 6–4; M. Damm d. G. Raoux 6–3 7–6; R. Krajicek (12) d. C. Pioline 6–3 6–4; P. Korda (13) d. M. Tillstrom 7–6 6–1; J. Siemerink d. B. Steven (Q) 7–6 7–6; D. Nestor (Q) d. A. O'Brien 6–2 6–1; G. Ivanisevic (3) bye; T. Enqvist (8) bye; V. Spadea (Q) d. J. Golmard (Q) 6–2 6–1; T. Woodbridge d. J. Stoltenberg 3–6 7–6 6–3; G. Kuerten (10) d. A. Agassi 6–3 6–1; A. Medvedev d. T. Henman (15) 6–3 6–3; M. Woodforde d. O. Delaitre (Q) 6–2 3–6 6–0; W. Ferreira d. A. Boetsch 6–3 6–4; M. Chang (2) bye.

2nd round: Sampras (1) d. Gimelstob (WC) 6–2 6–4; Rafter (16) d. Wheaton (Q) 3–6 6–3 6–2; Rios (9) d. Johansson 6–3 6–2; Kafelnikov (7) d. Woodruff 7–6 7–6; Corretja (4) d. Stark 7–6 6–4; Costa (14) d. Haas 6–3 6–4; Novak d. Schalken 6–3 6–2; Bruguera (6) d. Draper 7–6 6–2; Muster (5) d. Santoro 6–3 5–7 6–4; Damm d. Krajicek (12) 6–4 7–6; Siemerink d. Korda (13) 7–5 1–6 6–1; Ivanisevic (3) d. Nestor (Q) 4–6 7–5 7–6; Spadea (Q) d. Enqvist (8) 6–7 6–3 6–3; Kuerten (10) d. Woodbridge 3–6 6–1 6–4; Medvedev d. Woodforde 6–4 1–6 7–6; Chang (2) d. Ferreira 6–7 6–1 6–2.

3rd round: Sampras (1) d. Rafter (16) 7–6 6–4; Kafelnikov (7) d. Rios (9) 7–5 6–2; Costa (14) d. Corretja (4) 6–1 7–6; Bruguera (6) d. Novak 7–6 6–3; Muster (5) d. Damm 6–3 3–6 7–5; Siemerink d. Ivanisevic (3) 6–4 6–4; Kuerten (10) d. Spadea (Q) 6–7 6–3 6–4; Chang (2) d. Medvedev 3–6 6–1 6–4.

Quarter-finals: Sampras (1) d. Kafelnikov (7) 6–2 6–2; Costa (14) d. Bruguera (6) 4–6 6–3 5–2 ret; Muster (5) d. Siemerink 6–7 7–6 7–6; Chang (2) d. Kuerten (10) 6–1 6–2.

Semi-finals: Sampras (1) d. Costa (14) 6–3 6–4; Muster (5) d. Chang (2) 6–3 4–6 7–6.

Final: Sampras (1) d. Muster (5) 6–3 6–4.

MEN'S DOUBLES – Final: Woodbridge/Woodforde (1) d. Philippoussis/Rafter (7) 7–6 4–6 6–4.

EUROCARD OPEN ($2,050,000)

STUTTGART, 20–26 OCTOBER

MEN'S SINGLES – 1st round: P. Sampras (1) bye; M. Gustafsson d. A. Portas 6–1 6–1; B. Becker d. M-K. Goellner 6–2 6–4; R. Krajicek (16) bye; A. Corretja (10) bye; M. Larsson d. T. Woodbridge 6–2 6–3; F. Santoro d. M. Philippoussis 7–6 6–1; S. Bruguera (8) bye; G. Ivanisevic (4) bye; T. Henman d. T. Haas (WC) 7–5 3–6 6–4; J. Siemerink d. S. Schalken (Q) 6–4 6–2; J. Bjorkman (13) bye; T. Muster (12) bye; P. Haarhuis (Q) d. F. Dewulf 4–6 6–1 6–3; N. Kiefer (WC) d. T. Johansson 6–3 3–6 6–1; G. Rusedski (5) bye; C. Moya (6) bye; T. Martin (LL) d. A. Agassi 6–4 6–4; H. Arazi (WC) d. A. O'Brien (Q) 6–3 2–6 6–3; G. Kuerten (11) bye; F. Mantilla (14) bye; D. Prinosil (Q) d. M. Rosset 5–7 6–4 6–2; T. Enqvist d. A. Berasategui 6–1 6–4; P. Rafter (3) bye; Y. Kafelnikov (7) bye; A. Medvedev d. P. Cash (Q) 6–2 6–0; K. Kucera d. M. Woodforde 4–6 6–4 7–6; M. Rios (9) bye; P. Korda (15) bye; C. Woodruff d. B. Ulihrach 6–3 0–1 ret; C. Pioline d. J. Tarango (Q) 7–5 4–6 6–4; M. Chang (2) bye.

2nd round: Sampras (1) d. Gustafsson 6–3 6–4; Krajicek (16) d. Becker 7–6 6–4; Larsson d. Corretja (10) 6–2 7–6; Santoro d. Bruguera (8) 7–5 7–6; Henman d. Ivanisevic (4) 6–3 2–0 ret; Bjorkman (13) d. Siemerink 6–3 6–4; Haarhuis (Q) d. Muster (12) 6–2 6–7 6–2; Kiefer (WC) d. Rusedski (5) 5–7 6–2 6–4; Martin (LL) d. Moya (6) 6–3 7–6; Kuerten (11) d. Arazi (WC) 6–3 6–7 6–3; Prinosil (Q) d. Mantilla (14) 7–5 6–4; Rafter (3) d. Enqvist w/o; Kafelnikov (7) d. Medvedev 6–0 2–6 6–4; Rios (9) d. Kucera 6–7 6–4 6–4; Korda (15) d. Woodruff 6–3 6–3; Pioline d. Chang (2) 7–5 1–6 6–4.

3rd round: Krajicek (16) d. Sampras (1) 6–4 6–4; Larsson d. Santoro 6–3 7–5; Bjorkman (13) d. Henman 6–2 3–6 6–3; Kiefer (WC) d. Haarhuis (Q) 6–7 7–6 7–5; Martin (LL) d. Kuerten (11) 6–3 6–4; Rafter (3) d. Prinosil (Q) 3–6 6–2 6–1; Rios (9) d. Kafelnikov (7) 7–6 6–3; Korda (15) d. Pioline 6–3 ret.

Quarter-finals: Krajicek (16) d. Larsson 6–2 7–5; Bjorkman (13) d. Kiefer (WC) 6–4 6–2; Rafter (3) d. Martin (LL) 4–6 7–6 6–4; Korda (15) d. Rios (9) 6–3 6–4.

Semi-finals: Krajicek (16) d. Bjorkman (13) 6–4 3–6 6–3; Korda (15) d. Rafter (3) 6–4 7–6.

Final: Korda (15) d. Krajicek (16) 7–6 6–2 6–4.

MEN'S DOUBLES – Final: Woodbridge/Woodforde (1) d. Leach/Stark (6) 6–3 6–3.

12eme OPEN DE PARIS ($2,300,000)

PARIS, 27 OCTOBER–2 NOVEMBER

MEN'S SINGLES – 1st round: P. Sampras (1) bye; B. Becker d. M. Woodforde 6–2 6–4; A. Clement (WC) d. M. Rosset 5–7 6–2 6–4; P. Korda (16) bye; A. Corretja (10) bye; T. Henman d. H. Arazi 6–1 6–0; M. Norman d. C. Woodruff 6–4 7–6; T. Muster (8) bye; G. Rusedski (4) bye; J. Siemerink d. T. Martin 4–6 7–6 6–2; B. Ulihrach d. J. Courier 7–6 6–1; F. Mantilla (13) bye; G. Kuerten (11) bye; N. Escude (WC) d. A. Berasategui 6–4 6–1; D. Vacek (Q) d. J. Tarango (Q) 4–6 7–6 6–1; Y. Kafelnikov (5) bye; C. Moya (6) bye; T. Woodbridge d. M. Tillstrom (Q) 6–3 6–3; T. Johansson d. S. Schalken (Q) 6–4 6–7 6–3; J. Bjorkman (12) bye; R. Krajicek (14) bye; F. Santoro d. M. Larsson 0–6 6–4 7–6; C. Pioline d. L. Roux (WC) 6–2 6–4; P. Rafter (3) bye; S. Bruguera (7) bye; M-K. Goellner d. A. Portas 6–3 5–7 6–3; G. Raoux (WC) d. F. Dewulf 7–5 6–3; M. Rios (9) bye; T. Enqvist (15) bye; D. Prinosil (Q) d. S. Sargsian (Q) 4–6 6–3 7–6; M. Gustafsson d. M. Damm 7–6 5–7 6–4; M. Chang (2) bye.

2nd round: Sampras (1) d. Becker 7–6 3–6 6–3; Korda (16) d. Clement (WC) 6–4 6–4; Corretja (10) d. Henman 6–3 7–5; Muster (8) d. Norman 6–3 7–6; Rusedski (4) d. Siemerink 6–4 6–3; Ulihrach d. Mantilla (13) 7–6 5–7 7–6; Escude (WC) d. Kuerten (11) 7–6 6–3; Kafelnikov (5) d. Vacek (Q) 6–1 6–2; Woodbridge d.

After his most successful year since turning pro in 1991, Jonas Bjorkman led Sweden to victory in the Davis Cup Final against the Americans and ended at No.4 in the rankings. He was already assuming the mantle of leadership passed on by the retired Swedish No. 1, Stefan Edberg. (Michael Cole)

Moya (6) 7–6 6–2; Bjorkman (12) d. Johansson 6–3 6–7 7–6; Krajicek (14) d. Santoro 6–3 6–4; Rafter (3) d. Pioline 6–7 7–6 6–1; Bruguera (7) d. Goellner 6–3 7–6; Raoux (WC) d. Rios (9) 7–6 3–6 7–5; Enqvist (15) d. Prinosil (Q) 7–5 6–1; Gustafsson d. Chang (2) 6–3 6–2.
3rd round: Sampras (1) d. Korda (16) 4–6 7–6 6–4; Muster (8) d. Corretja (10) 7–5 6–4; Rusedski (4) d. Ulihrach 7–5 6–3; Kafelnikov (5) d. Escude (WC) 6–3 6–4; Bjorkman (12) d. Woodbridge 7–6 7–5; Krajicek (14) d. Rafter (3) 7–5 6–2; Raoux (WC) d. Bruguera (7) 6–4 3–6 7–5; Enqvist (15) d. Gustafsson 6–1 6–4.
Quarter-finals: Sampras (1) d. Muster (8) 6–1 4–6 6–2; Kafelnikov (5) d. Rusedski (4) 6–4 3–6 6–3; Bjorkman (12) d. Krajicek (14) 6–4 0–1 ret; Enqvist (15) d. Raoux (WC) 7–5 6–2.
Semi-finals: Sampras (1) d. Kafelnikov (5) 7–6 6–3; Bjorkman (12) d. Enqvist (15) 7–6 7–5.
Final: Sampras (1) d. Bjorkman (12) 6–3 4–6 6–3 6–1.
MEN'S DOUBLES – Final: Eltingh/Haarhuis (2) d. Leach/Stark (6) 6–2 7–6.

Championship Series

EUROPEAN COMMUNITY CHAMPIONSHIP ($875,000)

ANTWERP, 17–23 FEBRUARY

MEN'S SINGLES – 1st round: F. de Wulf (LL) d. G. Forget 6–4 5–7 6–4; C. Pioline d. J. Courier 6–0 6–2; M. Rosset d. A. Medvedev 7–6 6–2; N. Kiefer (Q) d. J. Siemerink (8) 3–6 6–4 7–5; P. Korda d. D. van Scheppingen (LL) 6–3 6–2; J. Sanchez d. H. Dreekmann 6–4 6–2; D. Norman (Q) d. B. Ulihrach 5–2 ret; F. Mantilla (5) d. B. Karbacher 6–2 6–1; T. Henman (6) d. S. Bruguera (WC) 6–3 4–6 6–4; M. Tillstrom d. H. Gumy 4–6 6–1 6–4; J. van Herck (WC) d. A. Boetsch 6–2 6–4; F. Clavet d. T. Enqvist (3) 4–6 7–6 6–3; M-K. Goellner d. M. Stich (7) 7–6 6–4; C. van Garsse (Q) d. R. Furlan 7–5 6–3; M. Damm d. M. Sinner (Q) 6–7 6–4 6–3; M. Rios (2) d. A. Voinea 6–1 6–4.

2nd round: de Wulf (LL) d. Pioline 7–6 6–4; Rosset d. Kiefer (Q) 3–6 6–3 6–1; Korda d. Sanchez 6–3 6–3; Norman (Q) d. Mantilla (5) 6–3 1–6 7–6; Henman (6) d. Tillstrom 6–2 6–3; Clavet d. van Herck (WC) 3–6 6–3 6–3; Goellner d. van Garsse (Q) 6–3 6–4; Damm d. Rios (2) 4–6 7–5 7–6.

Quarter-finals: Rosset d. de Wulf (LL) 4–6 6–1 6–4; Korda d. Norman (Q) 6–3 6–4; Henman (6) d. Clavet 7–6 6–4; Goellner d. Damm 3–1 ret.

Semi-finals: Rosset d. Korda 7–6 6–3; Henman (6) d. Goellner 6–4 6–4.

Final: Rosset d. Henman (6) 6–2 7–5 6–4.

MEN'S DOUBLES – Final: Adams/Delaitre d. Stolle/Suk 3–6 6–2 6–1.

KROGER ST. JUDE ($700,000)

MEMPHIS, 17–23 FEBRUARY

MEN'S SINGLES – 1st round: M. Chang (1) bye; P. Rafter d. G. Stafford 6–4 6–3; J. Eltingh (WC) d. J. Gambill (Q) 6–3 6–3; K. Carlsen (15) bye; A. O'Brien (9) bye; S. Sargsian d. J. Stark 6–7 7–6 6–4; J. Viloca d. S. Schalken 6–4 4–6 6–0; R. Reneberg (7) bye; T. Martin (3) bye; B. Shelton (Q) d. S. Bryan (Q) 5–7 7–6 6–4; G. Raoux d. T. Johansson 6–4 6–4; M. Woodforde (14) bye; N. Lapentti (LL) bye; B. Steven d. M. Ondruska 6–3 6–4; A. Radulescu d. M. Joyce 7–5 4–6 6–0; J. Stoltenberg (6) bye; P. Haarhuis (5) bye; J. Gimelstob (Q) d. J. Grabb (Q) 4–6 6–3 7–6; S. Draper d. L. Jensen (WC) 7–6 7–5; C. Woodruff (12) bye; J. Bjorkman (13) bye; R. Fromberg d. P. McEnroe (WC) 7–6 6–3; J. Frana d. M. Filippini 6–4 6–4; M. Washington (4) bye; T. Woodbridge (8) bye; S. Lareau d. J. Hede (Q) 2–6 6–3 7–5; M. Norman d. T. Carbonell 7–5 3–6 6–3; M. Philippoussis (10) bye; V. Spadea (16) bye; J. Tarango d. G. Blanco 6–2 6–3; G. Kuerten d. B. Black 6–2 6–7 7–6; A. Agassi (WC) (2) bye.

2nd round: Chang (1) d. Rafter 6–2 6–4; Carlsen (15) d. Eltingh (WC) 7–6 6–3; Sargsian d. O'Brien (9) 6–4 6–4; Reneberg (7) d. Viloca 6–3 6–2; Martin (3) d. Shelton (Q) 6–4 6–4; Raoux d. Woodforde (14) 7–5 5–7 6–4; Steven d. Lapentti (LL) 7–6 6–4; Radulescu d. Stoltenberg (6) 6–3 6–2; Haarhuis (5) d. Gimelstob (Q) 6–4 6–3; Woodruff (12) d. Draper 4–6 6–2 6–1; Bjorkman (13) d. Fromberg 6–4 6–3; Frana d. Washington (4) 7–6 6–3; Woodbridge (8) d. Lareau 6–4 7–6; Norman d. Philippoussis (10) 6–4 7–5; Tarango d. Spadea (16) 6–3 6–4; Kuerten d. Agassi (WC) (2) 6–2 6–4.

3rd round: Chang (1) d. Carlsen (15) 6–7 6–2 6–0; Reneberg (7) d. Sargsian 6–2 2–6 6–3; Martin (3) d. Raoux 6–4 6–7 7–6; Steven d. Radulescu 7–6 6–4; Haarhuis (5) d. Woodruff (12) 6–4 6–4; Bjorkman (13) d. Frana 6–0 6–4; Woodbridge (8) d. Norman 7–5 6–3; Tarango d. Kuerten 7–6 7–6.

Quarter-finals: Chang (1) d. Reneberg (7) 7–6 6–4; Martin (3) d. Steven 6–4 7–6; Bjorkman (13) d. Haarhuis (5) 6–3 6–4; Woodbridge (8) d. Tarango 6–3 6–1.

Semi-finals: Chang (1) d. Martin (3) 3–6 6–4 6–4; Woodbridge (8) d. Bjorkman (13) 6–1 7–5.

Final: Chang (1) d. Woodbridge (8) 6–3 6–4.

MEN'S DOUBLES – Final: E. Ferreira/Galbraith (4) d. Leach/Stark (7) 6–3 3–6 6–1.

ITALIAN INDOORS ($689,250)

MILAN, 24 FEBRUARY–2 MARCH

MEN'S SINGLES – 1st round: G. Ivanisevic (1) d. A. Olhovskiy (Q) 7–6 6–7 6–2; C. Pioline d. O. Camporese (WC) 4–6 6–4 6–1; D. Vacek d. F. Wibier (LL) 6–3 7–6; B. Ulihrach d. A. Corretja (8) 7–5 6–0; T. Henman (4) d. A. Voinea 6–1 6–2; P. Korda d. A. Medvedev 6–3 6–3; M. Philippoussis (WC) d. D. Musa (Q) 6–1 6–3; D. Prinosil d. M. Stich (5) 5–7 6–4 6–2; A. Berasategui (6) d. A. Gaudenzi 6–3 6–4; K. Kucera d. C. Caratti (Q) 6–4 6–2; M. Martelli (LL) d. M-K. Goellner 2–6 6–4 6–4; N. Kiefer (Q) d. G. Forget 6–1 6–4; M. Rosset (7) d. F. Clavet 6–4 6–2; A. Boetsch d. K. Alami 6–2 6–2; J. Sanchez d. C. Costa 4–6 6–3 6–2; S. Bruguera (WC) d. R. Krajicek (2) 4–6 7–6 7–6.

2nd round: Ivanisevic (1) d. Pioline 7–6 7–6; Vacek d. Ulihrach 7–6 6–3; Korda d. Henman (4) 6–4 6–4; Prinosil d. Philippoussis (WC) 6–7 6–2 6–3; Kucera d. Berasategui (6) 7–6 6–2; Kiefer (Q) d. Martelli (LL) 6–3 6–4; Boetsch d. Rosset (7) 3–6 7–6 6–4; Bruguera (WC) d. Sanchez 6–4 6–0.

Quarter-finals: Ivanisevic (1) d. Vacek 6–3 6–7 6–4; Prinosil d. Korda 4–6 7–6 6–3; Kiefer (Q) d. Kucera 2–6 6–3 6–4; Bruguera (WC) d. Boetsch 6–3 5–7 7–6.
Semi-finals: Ivanisevic (1) d. Prinosil 6–0 7–6; Bruguera (WC) d. Kiefer (Q) 6–3 6–4.
Final: Ivanisevic (1) d. Bruguera (WC) 6–2 6–2.
MEN'S DOUBLES – Final: Albano/Nyborg d. Adams/Olhovskiy (3) 6–4 7–6.

ADVANTA CHAMPIONSHIPS ($589,250)

PHILADELPHIA, 24 FEBRUARY–2 MARCH
MEN'S SINGLES – 1st round: P. Sampras (1) d. M. Filippini 6–4 6–1; J. Bjorkman d. P. Cash (WC) 6–4 6–0; D. Flach (Q) d. S. Lareau (Q) 6–4 6–3; T. Johansson d. G. Rusedski (8) 6–4 6–2; P. Haarhuis (3) d. J. Novak 6–4 1–6 6–3; J. Stark d. P. McEnroe (WC) 7–6 7–6; K. Carlsen d. T. Carbonell 4–6 6–4 6–2; S. Schalken (Q) d. J. Stoltenberg (5) 6–2 6–4; T. Woodbridge (6) d. A. Chesnokov 6–3 1–0 ret; B. Black d. R. Fromberg (Q) 6–4 6–3; P. Rafter d. M. Woodforde 6–2 6–2; J. Gimelstob (WC) d. M. Joyce (LL) 6–0 6–3; J. Viloca d. A. O'Brien (7) 6–2 3–6 6–3; S. Stolle d. V. Spadea 7–6 5–7 6–1; G. Stafford d. A. Radulescu 6–4 6–3; J. Courier (2) d. G. Raoux 6–3 7–6.
2nd round: Sampras (1) d. Bjorkman 7–5 7–6; Flach (Q) d. Johansson 6–3 0–6 7–6; Stark d. Haarhuis (3) 6–3 6–4; Schalken (Q) d. Carlsen 7–6 4–6 6–3; Black d. Woodbridge (6) 6–2 6–0; Rafter d. Gimelstob (WC) 6–3 5–7 7–5; Stolle d. Viloca 4–6 6–3 6–4; Stafford d. Courier (2) 6–3 5–7 6–2.
Quarter-finals: Sampras (1) d. Flach (Q) 6–4 6–2; Schalken (Q) d. Stark 6–2 6–4; Rafter d. Black 6–3 1–6 6–1; Stafford d. Stolle 6–4 6–2.
Semi-finals: Sampras (1) d. Schalken (Q) 3–6 7–5 6–3; Rafter d. Stafford 6–3 6–4.
Final: Sampras (1) d. Rafter 5–7 7–6 6–3.
MEN'S DOUBLES – Final: Lareau/O'Brien d. E. Ferreira/Galbraith (4) 6–3 6–3.

JAPAN OPEN ($935,000)

TOKYO, 14–20 APRIL
MEN'S SINGLES – 1st round: R. Krajicek (1) bye; N. Godwin d. A. Pavel 6–4 6–4; J. Gimelstob d. F. Wibier 6–4 7–6; M. Norman (10) d. L. Paes 7–6 6–1; J. Stark (15) d. O. Stanoytchev 6–3 3–6 6–1; F. Fetterlein d. G. Motomura 3–6 6–4 6–3; J. Golmard d. D. Flach 6–2 6–4; D. Prinosil (8) bye; T. Woodbridge (4) bye; R. Sabau d. T. Shimada (WC) 6–2 6–2; T. Suzuki (WC) d. A. Thoms 6–4 6–2; J. Tarango (14) d. J. Winnink (Q) 6–3 6–2; M. Tillstrom (12) d. K. Ullyett 7–6 2–6 7–5; H. Holm d. M. Joyce 4–6 6–3 7–5; E. Ran d. L. Jonsson 6–3 6–2; P. Rafter (6) bye; T. Johansson (5) bye; D. Nestor d. D. Skoch 6–1 6–7 6–3; H. Kaneko (WC) d. T. El Sawy 6–1 6–1; S. Matsuoka d. A. Radulescu (11) 7–6 6–7 6–4; M. Woodforde (13) d. S. Iwabuchi (WC) 6–1 6–3; M. Sinner d. A. Olhovskiy 6–3 6–4; A. Richardson (Q) d. T. Nydahl 3–6 6–2 6–4; M. Rosset (3) bye; M. Damm (7) bye; O. Delaitre (Q) d. R. Smith (Q) 6–7 6–3 6–3; C. Arriens (Q) d. Y. Yamamoto (WC) 6–2 7–5; A. Cherkasov d. D. Vacek (9) 6–3 7–6; L. Roux (16) d. D. Adams (Q) 6–1 6–4; J. Fleurian d. J. Grabb (Q) 6–3 6–2; S. Lareau d. S. Simian 6–3 6–2; B. Becker (2) bye.
2nd round: Krajicek (1) d. Godwin 6–3 6–4; Norman (10) d. Gimelstob 6–4 6–2; Stark (15) d. Fetterlein 4–6 6–3 7–5; Prinosil (8) d. Golmard 7–5 6–1; Woodbridge (4) d. Sabau 6–3 6–4; Tarango (14) d. Suzuki (WC) 6–3 6–2; Holm d. Tillstrom (12) 4–6 6–3 6–3; Rafter (6) d. Ran 6–0 6–4; Johansson (5) d. Nestor 6–4 6–4; Matsuoka d. Kaneko (WC) 7–5 6–1; Woodforde (13) d. Sinner 6–1 6–4; Rosset (3) d. Richardson (Q) 7–6 2–6 6–2; Damm (7) d. Delaitre (Q) 7–5 4–6 6–4; Cherkasov d. Arriens (Q) 6–1 4–6 7–5; Roux (16) d. Fleurian 7–6 6–4; Becker (2) d. Lareau 6–2 4–6 6–2.
3rd round: Krajicek (1) d. Norman (10) 7–5 6–0; Prinosil (8) d. Stark (15) 6–7 7–6 7–5; Woodbridge (4) d. Tarango (14) 7–5 6–2; Rafter (6) d. Holm 6–1 6–2; Johansson (5) d. Matsuoka 6–2 6–2; Woodforde (13) d. Rosset (3) 6–2 6–3; Damm (7) d. Cherkasov 7–6 7–5; Roux (16) d. Becker (2) 4–6 6–3 6–1.
Quarter-finals: Krajicek (1) d. Prinosil (8) 6–4 6–3; Rafter (6) d. Woodbridge (4) 6–4 7–6; Johansson (5) d. Woodforde (13) 6–3 6–4; Roux (16) d. Damm (7) 6–3 6–1.
Semi-finals: Krajicek (1) d. Rafter (6) 7–6 6–3; Roux (16) d. Johansson (5) 4–6 7–5 6–3.
Final: Krajicek (1) d. Roux (16) 6–2 3–6 6–1.
MEN'S DOUBLES – Final: Damm/Vacek (4) d. Gimelstob/Rafter (7) 2–6 6–2 7–6.

OPEN SEAT – GODO '97 ($825,000)

BARCELONA, 14–21 APRIL
MEN'S SINGLES – 1st round: T. Muster (1) bye; R. Furlan d. J. Diaz (Q) 6–7 6–3 7–5; M. Filippini d. A. Gaudenzi 4–6 6–4 6–3; C. Pioline (16) d. H. Gumy 7–6 6–3; M-K. Goellner d. S. Bruguera (10) 6–4 2–6 6–2; G. Lopez (Q) d. D. Salvador (Q) 6–4 6–1; J. Viloca d. K. Carlsen 6–3 6–0; A. Costa (7) bye; C. Moya (4) bye; F. Clavet d. T. Carbonell 6–3 1–6 6–4; H. Arazi d. M. Gorriz (Q) 6–3 6–4; J. Alonso-Pintor (WC) d. M. Gustafsson (14) 7–6 3–6 6–3; A. Medvedev d. A. Corretja (11) 7–5 2–6 6–4; C. Costa d. S. Schalken 6–2 6–1; A. Martin (WC) d. A. Voinea 6–1 6–1; W. Ferreira (6) bye; M. Rios (5) bye; A. Portas (Q) d. G. Kuerten 6–2 6–1; J. Burillo d. E. Sanchez (WC) 6–3 6–0; F. Vincente (WC) d. J. Siemerink (12) 6–4 6–3; C. Ruud d. B. Ulihrach (13) 6–3 6–4; D. Johnson (Q) d. R. Carretero 7–6 3–6 6–3; K. Alami d. G. Blanco 6–4 6–4; G. Ivanisevic (3) bye; F. Mantilla (8) bye; F. Roig d. A. Lopez-Moron (Q) 7–6 6–4; R. Fromberg d. S. Draper 7–6 6–3; A. Berasategui (9) d. J. Sanchez 6–1 6–2; G. Schaller d. M. Stich (15) 6–2 6–2; F. Meligeni d. K. Kucera 7–5 6–0; M. Larsson d. D. Hrbaty 7–5 6–4; Y. Kafelnikov (2) bye.
2nd round: Muster (1) d. Furlan 5–7 6–4 6–4; Pioline (16) d. Filippini 6–2 6–4; Goellner d. Lopez (Q) 6–7 6–4

7–6; A. Costa (7) d. Viloca 6–4 6–3; Moya (4) d. Clavet 6–4 6–4; Arazi d. Alonso-Pintor (WC) 6–3 4–6 6–3; Medvedev d. C. Costa 6–2 6–0; Martin (WC) d. Ferreira (6) 4–6 6–2 7–5; Portas (Q) d. Rios (5) 7–5 7–6; Vicente (WC) d. Burillo 6–4 6–2; Ruud d. Johnson (Q) 6–4 7–6; Alami d. Ivanisevic (3) bye; 6–2 6–3; Mantilla (8) d. Roig 6–4 6–0; Berasategui (9) d. Fromberg 6–4 6–3; Meligeni d. Schaller 7–5 6–2; Larsson d. Kafelnikov (2) 3–6 6–2 6–3.
3rd round: Pioline (16) d. Muster (1) 7–6 6–4; A. Costa (7) d. Goellner w/o; Moya (4) d. Arazi 7–5 4–6 6–1; Medvedev d. Martin (WC) 6–4 6–2; Portas (Q) d. Vicente (WC) 7–5 3–6 6–1; Alami d. Ruud 6–3 6–2; Berasategui (9) d. Mantilla (8) 7–6 6–1; Meligeni d. Larsson 6–3 7–5.
Quarter-finals: A. Costa (7) d. Pioline (16) 6–4 6–2; Moya (4) d. Medvedev 6–4 6–2; Portas (Q) d. Alami 6–2 7–5; Berasategui (9) d. Meligeni 6–2 7–5.
Semi-finals: A. Costa (7) d. Moya (4) 7–6 7–5; Portas (Q) d. Berasategui (9) 6–3 7–5.
Final: A. Costa (7) d. Portas (Q) 7–5 6–4 6–4.
MEN'S DOUBLES – Final: Berasategui/Burillo (WC) d. Albano/Corretja 6–3 7–5.

1997 MERCEDES CUP ($915,000)

STUTTGART, 14–20 JULY

MEN'S SINGLES – 1st round: T. Muster (1) bye; A. Portas d. C. Ruud 5–7 6–0 7–6; H. Gumy d. O. Stanoytchev (Q) 6–3 2–6 6–2; B. Ulihrach (15) bye; F. Mantilla (10) bye; F. Meligeni (Q) d. A. Radulescu 6–1 6–3; J. Knippschild (WC) d. M. Damm 6–3 4–6 6–4; G. Kuerten (8) bye; S. Bruguera (4) bye; F. Dewulf (WC) d. B. Karbacher (Q) 6–4 1–0 ret; M. Sinner (Q) d. T. Johansson 6–7 7–6 7–5; W. Ferreira (14) bye; A. Medvedev (11) bye; K. Kucera d. N. Kiefer (WC) 1–2 ret; J. Sanchez d. M. Norman 6–3 7–6; M. Rios (5) bye; C. Moya (6) bye; G. Blanco (LL) d. H. Arazi 7–5 7–6; F. Vicente (Q) d. R. Furlan 6–3 6–4; A. Berasategui (12) bye; G. Rusedski (13) bye; M. Larsson d. D. Elsner (WC) 6–3 6–4; M-K. Goellner d. R. Reneberg 4–6 7–5 1–0 ret; A. Corretja (3) bye; B. Becker (7) bye; K. Alami d. J. Novak 7–6 4–6 7–5; C. Dosedel (Q) d. D. Hrbaty 7–6 6–2; A. Costa (9) bye; M. Rosset (16) bye; F. Clavet d. M. Gustafsson 6–3 1–6 6–1; F. Santoro d. M. Filippini 7–6 6–3; Y. Kafelnikov (2) bye.
2nd round: Portas d. Muster (1) 6–4 7–5; Gumy d. Ulihrach (15) 7–5 6–2; Mantilla (10) d. Meligeni (Q) 6–4 6–4; Kuerten (8) d. Knippschild (WC) 6–7 6–4 6–4; Bruguera (4) d. Dewulf (WC) 7–6 3–6 6–1; Ferreira (14) d. Sinner (Q) 3–6 6–0 6–4; Kucera d. Medvedev (11) 6–2 6–4; Rios (5) d. Sanchez 6–2 6–3; Blanco (LL) d. Moya (6) 4–6 7–6 7–5; Berasategui (12) d. Vicente (Q) 6–4 6–2; Larsson d. Rusedski (13) 7–6 6–7 6–4; Corretja (3) d. Goellner 7–5 6–1; Becker (7) d. Alami 7–6 7–6; Costa (9) d. Dosedel (Q) 6–3 7–5; Clavet d. Rosset (16) 7–5 6–1; Kafelnikov (2) d. Santoro 2–6 6–3 6–4.
3rd round: Portas d. Gumy 3–6 6–2 7–6; Mantilla (10) d. Kuerten (8) 4–1 ret; Bruguera (4) d. Ferreira (14) 1–6 6–3 7–5; Kucera d. Rios (5) 6–4 6–4; Berasategui (12) d. Blanco (LL) 7–5 7–5; Corretja (3) d. Larsson 7–6 6–4; Costa (9) d. Becker (7) w/o; Kafelnikov (2) d. Clavet 4–6 6–3 6–2.
Quarter-finals: Portas d. Mantilla (10) 6–2 6–4; Kucera d. Bruguera (4) 6–3 2–6 7–5; Corretja (3) d. Berasategui (12) 6–4 6–4; Costa (9) d. Kafelnikov (2) 6–4 6–4.
Semi-finals: Kucera d. Portas 6–4 6–3; Corretja (3) d. Costa (9) 6–4 6–4.
Final: Corretja (3) d. Kucera 6–2 7–5.
MEN'S DOUBLES – Final: Kuerten/Meligeni d. Johnson/Montana (6) 6–4 6–4.

LEGG MASON TENNIS CLASSIC ($550,000)

WASHINGTON, 14–20 JULY

MEN'S SINGLES – 1st round: M. Chang (1) bye; L. Herrera (Q) d. J. Grabb 1–6 6–1 7–5; M. Joyce d. S. Bryan 6–1 6–4; N. Godwin (15) d. G. Etlis 4–6 6–4 6–4; S. Campbell d. S. Sargsian (10) 6–4 6–3; B. Ellwood d. M. Knowles 5–4 ret; G. Solves d. T. Ho 3–6 6–3 6–1; S. Draper (7) bye; A. Agassi (3) bye; D. Flach d. C. Caratti 6–2 6–2; M. Hilpert (Q) d. R. Cordish (Q) 2–6 6–3 6–2; R. Schuttler d. J. Gimelstob (13) 6–3 6–3; B. Steven (11) d. L. Jensen (Q) 7–6 6–3; A. Merinov d. E. Ran 6–7 7–6 6–4; L. Smith (WC) d. M. Bhupathi (Q) 7–6 7–6; L. Roux (6) bye; J. Stoltenberg (5) bye; A. Cherkasov d. O. Motevassel 6–3 6–7 2–1 ret; D. Wheaton (Q) d. R. Jabali 2–6 6–3 6–3; M. Martelli (12) d. I. Ljubicic (WC) 7–6 7–5; V. Spadea (14) d. S. Simian 2–6 6–1 6–1; B. Shelton d. A. Kim (WC) 7–6 6–3; M. Tebbutt (Q) d. N. Pereira 6–2 6–4; C. Woodruff (4) bye; T. Haas (8) bye; M. Merklein d. J. Salzenstein 4–6 6–1 6–3; G. Pozzi d. G. Grant 6–1 6–4; K. Carlsen (9) d. C. Mamiit 7–6 6–3; F. Wibier (16) d. M. Mirnyi (WC) 7–6 7–6; D. Scala d. P. McEnroe (WC) 6–1 4–6 7–5; D. Nainkin d. K. Ullyett 6–3 0–6 7–5; P. Korda (2) bye.
2nd round: Chang (1) d. Herrera (Q) 6–3 6–7 7–6; Joyce d. Godwin (15) 7–6 7–6; Campbell d. Ellwood 6–4 4–6 6–3; Draper (7) d. Solves 7–5 6–1; Flach d. Agassi (3) 2–6 6–4 6–4; Schuttler d. Hilpert (Q) 7–5 6–2; Steven (11) d. Merinov 6–0 6–1; Smith (WC) d. Roux (6) 6–3 6–3; Stoltenberg (5) d. Cherkasov 6–2 6–3; Wheaton (Q) d. Martelli (12) 7–6 6–1; Spadea (14) d. Shelton 6–4 6–4; Tebbutt (Q) d. Woodruff (4) 6–3 6–3; Haas (8) d. Merklein 6–4 2–6 6–3; Carlsen (9) d. Pozzi 6–2 6–0; Wibier (16) d. Scala 7–6 6–4; Korda (2) d. Nainkin 6–4 6–2.
3rd round: Chang (1) d. Joyce 4–6 6–1 6–2; Draper (7) d. Campbell 6–3 7–6; Schuttler d. Flach 4–6 6–2 7–6; Steven (11) d. Smith (WC) 7–6 6–2; Wheaton (Q) d. Stoltenberg (5) 3–6 7–6 7–6; Spadea (14) d. Tebbutt (Q) 5–7 7–6 6–3; Haas (8) d. Carlsen (9) 6–7 6–4 6–4; Korda (2) d. Wibier (16) 6–4 6–4.
Quarter-finals: Chang (1) d. Draper (7) 6–2 6–3; Steven (11) d. Schuttler 6–3 6–3; Wheaton (Q) d. Spadea (14) 6–3 4–6 6–2; Korda (2) d. Haas (8) 6–7 6–4 6–4.
Semi-finals: Chang (1) d. Steven (11) 6–2 7–6; Korda (2) d. Wheaton (Q) 6–2 6–3.

Final: Chang (1) d. Korda (2) 5–7 6–2 6–1.
MEN'S DOUBLES – Final: L. Jensen/M. Jensen (3) d. Godwin/Wibier 6–4 6–4.

RCA CHAMPIONSHIPS ($915,000)

INDIANAPOLIS, 11–17 AUGUST
MEN'S SINGLES – 1st round: P. Sampras (1) bye; J. Eagle (Q) d. J. Stark 7–6 6–3; F. Santoro d. S. Draper 6–3 6–4; M. Larsson (16) d. D. Nestor 6–4 6–1; W. Ferreira (10) d. M. Tebbutt (Q) 6–4 6–3; E. Ran d. K. Kinnear (WC) 7–6 6–7 3–0 ret; G. Stafford d. A. Radulescu 6–4 7–5; C. Pioline (8) bye; T. Enqvist (4) bye; R. Weidenfeld (Q) d. N. Godwin 3–6 6–4 6–3; J. Novak d. M. Tillstrom 6–4 6–7 6–1; B. Ulihrach (13) d. D. Flach 6–4 7–5; R. Fromberg d. A. Berasategui (11) 5–7 7–6 6–1; M. Merklein (WC) d. T. Haas 3–6 6–1 6–3; S. Campbell (WC) d. B. Karbacher 6–4 4–6 6–2; C. Moya (5) bye; M. Rios (6) bye; T. Champion d. M. Bryan (Q) 6–4 5–7 6–2; M. Woodforde d. J. van Herck (Q) 6–1 6–2; C. Woodruff (12) d. J. Gimelstob 3–6 6–4 6–1; A. Agassi (14) d. D. Sanguinetti 6–2 4–6 6–4; O. Delaitre d. D. Norman 6–4 6–2; A. Boetsch d. R. Reneberg 6–2 6–4; A. Corretja (3) bye; T. Woodbridge (7) bye; M. Damm d. J. Golmard 6–1 6–1; L. Roux d. R. Sabau 6–1 6–2; J. Bjorkman (9) d. L. Smith (WC) 6–2 7–6; G. Weiner (WC) d. T. Johansson (15) 6–7 7–5 6–4; T. Ho (Q) d. S. Bryan (Q) 6–3 6–3; J. Stoltenberg d. M. Ondruska 6–2 7–6; G. Ivanisevic (2) bye.
2nd round: Sampras (1) d. Eagle (Q) 6–3 7–5; Larsson (16) d. Santoro 6–3 6–2; Ferreira (10) d. Ran 6–2 6–3; Stafford d. Pioline (8) 2–6 6–4 6–4; Enqvist (4) d. Weidenfeld (Q) 6–3 6–0; Novak d. Ulihrach (13) 6–2 6–2; Fromberg d. Merklein (WC) 6–3 7–6; Moya (5) d. Campbell (WC) 7–6 5–7 7–6; Rios (6) d. Champion 3–6 6–2 6–3; Woodforde d. Woodruff (12) 6–3 6–3; Agassi (14) d. Delaitre 7–6 6–1; Corretja (3) d. Boetsch 6–2 6–7 6–2; Woodbridge (7) d. Damm 6–7 7–5 7–5; Bjorkman (9) d. Roux 6–3 6–3; Ho (Q) d. G. Weiner (WC) 3–6 7–6 6–3; Stoltenberg d. Ivanisevic (2) 6–7 7–5 6–4.
3rd round: Larsson (16) d. Sampras (1) 7–6 4–6 7–6; Ferreira (10) d. Stafford 6–4 7–6; Novak d. Enqvist (4) 7–5 3–6 6–3; Moya (5) d. Fromberg 6–2 6–4; Woodforde d. Rios (6) 7–6 6–4; Agassi (14) d. Corretja (3) 7–5 6–1; Bjorkman (9) d. Woodbridge (7) 6–2 7–5; Ho (Q) d. Stoltenberg 6–4 6–3.
Quarter-finals: Ferreira (10) d. Larsson (16) 3–6 6–3 7–6; Moya (5) d. Novak 6–3 7–5; Woodforde d. Agassi (14) 6–3 5–7 6–3; Bjorkman (9) d. Ho (Q) 5–7 6–4 7–5.
Semi-finals: Moya (5) d. Ferreira (10) 6–4 6–2; Bjorkman (9) d. Woodforde 6–0 6–2.
Final: Bjorkman (9) d. Moya (5) 6–3 7–6.
MEN'S DOUBLES – Final: Tebbutt/Tillstrom (Q) d. Bjorkman/Kulti (4) 6–3 6–2.

PILOT PEN INTERNATIONAL ($915,000)

NEW HAVEN, 11–17 AUGUST
MEN'S SINGLES – 1st round: Y. Kafelnikov (1) bye; C. Mamiit (Q) d. F. Wibier 6–2 7–5; C. Dosedel d. B. MacPhie (WC) 6–1 4–6 6–1; V. Spadea d. K. Kucera (15) 6–3 6–2; B. Steven d. J. Courier (10) 6–2 6–2; D. Pescariu d. A. Hernandez (Q) 6–1 0–6 6–4; D. Vacek d. D. Prinosil 6–2 6–4; T. Henman (7) bye; M. Philippoussis (3) bye; D. Wheaton d. L. Paes 6–3 6–7 6–3; M-K. Goellner d. P. McEnroe 7–6 6–1; A. O'Brien (14) d. I. Ljubicic (WC) 6–3 6–1; P. Haarhuis d. M. Norman (12) 6–3 6–2; J. Sanchez d. M. Bhupathi (Q) 6–2 6–7 7–5; J. Gambill (WC) d. F. Dewulf 7–6 7–5; P. Korda (5) bye; A. Costa (6) bye; W. Black (Q) d. O. Stanoytchev 6–4 6–1; J. Salzenstein (WC) d. D. Caldwell (Q) 6–2 6–4; G. Rusedski (11) d. P. Wessels (Q) 6–3 6–2; S. Sargsian d. M. Rosset (13) 4–6 6–1 6–3; K. Carlsen d. H. Gumy 2–6 6–4 6–2; N. Lapentti d. S. Schalken 6–1 ret; R. Krajicek (4) bye; P. Rafter (8) bye; M. Martelli d. J. Oncins 7–6 6–4; F. Meligeni d. J. Tarango 7–6 7–6; A. Medvedev (9) d. N. Welgreen (Q) 6–3 6–3; J. Siemerink (16) d. O. Ogorodov 7–6 4–6 6–1; F. Clavet (WC) d. S. Lareau 6–3 6–1; B. Black d. R. Furlan 6–1 6–2; S. Bruguera (2) bye.
2nd round: Kafelnikov (1) d. Mamiit (Q) 5–7 6–1 6–3; Dosedel d. Spadea 7–5 3–6 6–3; Steven d. Pescariu 6–4 0–6 6–3; Henman (7) d. Vacek 4–6 7–6 6–4; Wheaton d. Philippoussis (3) 6–7 6–3 6–4; Goellner d. O'Brien (14) 7–5 6–3; Sanchez d. Haarhuis 3–6 6–3 6–3; Korda (5) d. Gambill (WC) 6–3 6–3; Costa (6) d. W. Black (Q) 6–1 6–1; Rusedski (11) d. Salzenstein (WC) 6–4 6–0; Carlsen d. Sargsian 6–4 6–7 6–1; Krajicek (4) d. Lapentti 6–4 6–3; Rafter (8) d. Martelli 6–3 6–4; Medvedev (9) d. Meligeni 7–6 6–2; Clavet (WC) d. Siemerink (16) 1–6 6–3 7–6; Bruguera (2) d. B. Black 6–3 6–2.
3rd round: Kafelnikov (1) d. Dosedel 6–2 6–3; Henman (7) d. Steven 6–4 6–4; Wheaton d. Goellner 7–6 6–4; Korda (5) d. Sanchez 6–2 6–4; Rusedski (11) d. Costa (6) 6–3 7–6; Krajicek (4) d. Carlsen 7–6 6–2; Rafter (8) d. Medvedev (9) 6–3 2–6 6–4; Bruguera (2) d. Clavet (WC) 6–4 7–6.
Quarter-finals: Kafelnikov (1) d. Henman (7) 5–7 6–3 6–4; Korda (5) d. Wheaton 4–6 7–6 6–4; Rusedski (11) d. Krajicek (4) 7–6 3–6 6–3; Rafter (8) d. Bruguera (2) 7–5 2–6 6–2.
Semi-finals: Kafelnikov (1) d. Korda (5) 6–4 7–6; Rafter (8) d. Rusedski (11) 7–5 4–6 6–3.
Final: Kafelnikov (1) d. Rafter (8) 7–6 6–4.
MEN'S DOUBLES – Final: Bhupathi/Paes (6) d. Lareau/O'Brien (3) 6–4 6–7 6–2.

CA TENNIS TROPHY ($675,000)

VIENNA, 6–12 OCTOBER
MEN'S SINGLES – Ist round: K. Kucera d. Y. Kafelnikov (1) 6–4 7–5; T. Haas (WC) d. A. Boetsch 6–3 6–2; J. Apell (Q) d. J. Siemerink 6–2 6–4; T. Henman d. F. Mantilla (7) 6–4 4–6 6–4; G. Rusedski (4) d. A. Medvedev 7–6 6–4; M. Norman d. D. Prinosil (Q) 6–2 7–6; T. Martin (WC) d. J. Sanchez 6–2 6–2; T. Muster (6) d. H. Arazi 6–2 6–2; G. Kuerten (5) d. A. Costa 7–5 3–6 7–6; B. Ulihrach d. S. Schalken (Q) 6–2 6–2; C. Woodruff d. M. Philippoussis 6–4 6–4; G. Ivanisevic (3) d. F. Fetterlein (LL) 6–3 4–6 6–3; T. Enqvist (8) d. M. Rosset 6–4 4–0

A return to the top ten for Sergi Bruguera of Spain, who narrowly failed to win a third French Open title when he was upset by surprise finalist, Gustavo Kuerten. (Tommy Hindley)

ret; M. Larsson d. M-K. Goellner 2–6 7–6 7-6; R. Krajicek d. F. Dewulf 6–2 6–4; A. Clement (Q) d. S. Bruguera (2) 6–2 7–6.
2nd round: Kucera d. Haas (WC) 6–1 6–3; Henman d. Apell (Q) 6–3 6–3; Rusedski (4) d. Norman 6–4 6–2; Martin (WC) d. Muster (6) 6–4 3–6 6–4; Ulihrach d. Kuerten (5) 6-4 6–4; Ivanisevic (3) d. Woodruff 6–4 7–6; Larsson d. Enqvist (8) 7–5 6–4; Krajicek d. Clement (Q) 3–6 6–4 6–2.
Quarter-finals: Henman d. Kucera 6–4 6–l; Rusedski (4) d. Martin (WC) 6–l 6–7 6–3; Ivanisevic (3) d. Ulihrach 7–6 3–6 6–3; Krajicek d. Larsson 6–4 6–4.
Semi-finals: Rusedski (4) d. Henman 6–4 6–4; Ivanisevic (3) d. Krajicek 5–7 6–4 7–6.
Final: Ivanisevic (3) d. Rusedski (4) 3–6 6–7 7–6 6–2 6–3.
MEN'S DOUBLES – Final: E. Ferreira/Galbraith (1) d. Goellner/Prinosil 6-3 6-4.

HEINEKEN OPEN ($550,000)
SINGAPORE, 6–12 OCTOBER
MEN'S SINGLES – lst round: J. Stark d. M. Chang (1) 7–6 7–6; J. Novak d. N. Kulti (Q) 6–3 6–2; M. Sinner d. G. Pozzi 4–6 6–2 7–5; M. Gustafsson (7) d. P. Fredriksson 6–l 6–4; J. Courier (WC) (3) d. P. Srichaphan (WC) 2–6 6–4 6–3; M. Tebbutt (Q) d. P. McEnroe 6–3 6–2; M. Ondruska (Q) d. R. Furlan 6–3 7–6; T. Johansson (5) d. A. O'Brien 6–2 1–6 7–5; M. Damm (6) d. J. Kroslak 6–7 7–6 6–1; V. Spadea d. A. Radulescu 6–4 6–4; G. Stafford d. R. Reneberg 6–2 2–6 7–6; M. Tillstrom d. M. Woodforde (4) 6–4 6–4; N. Kiefer (8) d. S. Draper 6–4 6–2; C. Wilkinson (Q) d. K. Carlsen 3–6 6–3 6–2; B. Black d. D. Wheaton (WC) 6–2 6–4; M. Rios (2) d. J. Gimelstob 6–2 6–4.
2nd round: Stark d. Novak 6–3 2–6 6–3; Gustafsson (7) d. Sinner 7–6 4–6 6–3; Courier (WC) (3) d. Tebbutt (Q) 6–4 7–6; Johansson (5) d. Ondruska (Q) 6–4 6–4; Damm (6) d. Spadea 7–6 7–5; Tillstrom d. Stafford 7–6 6–4; Kiefer (8) d. Wilkinson (Q) 6–4 6–3; Rios (2) d. Black 6–2 6–7 7–6.
Quarter-finals: Gustafsson (7) d. Stark 6–7 6–2 6–2; Johansson (5) d. Courier (WC) (3) 3–6 6–3 6–2; Tillstrom d. Damm (6) 7–6 6–l; Kiefer (8) d. Rios (2) 6–1 7–5.
Semi-finals: Gustafsson (7) d. Johansson (5) 7–6 4–6 7–6; Kiefer (8) d. Tillstrom 6–7 6-3 6–3.
Final: Gustafsson (7) d. Kiefer (8) 4–6 6–3 6–3.
MEN'S DOUBLES – Final: Bhupathi/Paes (1) d. Leach/Stark (2) 6-4 6-4.

World Series

QATAR MOBIL OPEN ($600,000)

DOHA, 30 DECEMBER–5 JANUARY

MEN'S SINGLES – Quarter-finals: J. Courier (8) d. T. Muster (1) 6–3 7–5; S. Bruguera d. P. Korda (6) 6–1 2–6 6–3; T. Henman d. M. Gustafsson (5) 6–3 7–6; H. Arazi d. M. Larsson 7–6 7–6. ***Semi-finals:*** Courier (8) d. Bruguera 6–4 6–2; Henman d. Arazi 6–3 2–6 6–2. ***Final:*** Courier (8) d. Henman 7–5 6–7 6–2.
MEN'S DOUBLES – Final: Eltingh/Haarhuis (1) d. Fredriksson/Norman (Q) 6–3 6–2.

AUSTRALIAN MEN'S HARDCOURT CHAMPIONSHIPS ($303,000)

ADELAIDE, 30 DECEMBER–5 JANUARY

MEN'S SINGLES – Quarter-finals: M. Tillstrom d. A. Cherkasov (WC) 6–2 6–4; T. Woodbridge (4) d. A. O'Brien (5) 6–4 6–4; J. Tarango (Q) d. J. Bjorkman 6–1 6–7 7–6; S. Draper (WC) d. K. Kucera 6–4 7–5. ***Semi-finals:*** Woodbridge (4) d. Tillstrom 6–7 7–6 6–3; Draper (WC) d. Tarango (Q) 6–1 3–6 6–2. ***Final:*** Woodbridge (4) d. Draper (WC) 6–2 6–1.
MEN'S DOUBLES – Final: Rafter/Shelton (WC) d. Woodbridge/Woodforde (1) 6–4 1–6 6–3.

BELL SOUTH OPEN ($303,000)

AUCKLAND, 6–13 JANUARY

MEN'S SINGLES – Quarter-finals: M. Ondruska (Q) d. M. Rios (1) 0–6 6–3 6–3; J. Bjorkman d. J. Gambill (Q) 6–4 6–0; K. Carlsen d. H. Gumy (5) 6–4 7–6; J. Novak d. A. Radulescu 6–1 6–4. ***Semi-finals:*** Bjorkman d. Ondruska (Q) 6–1 6–1; Carlsen d. Novak 7–6 6–4. ***Final:*** Bjorkman d. Carlsen 7–6 6–0.
MEN'S DOUBLES – Final: E. Ferreira/Galbraith (1) d. Leach/Stark (3) 6–4 4–6 7–6.

SYDNEY INTERNATIONAL ($303,000)

SYDNEY, 6–12 JANUARY

MEN'S SINGLES – Quarter-finals: G. Ivanisevic (1) d. S. Stolle (WC) 6–4 6–2; T. Henman d. A. O'Brien 1–6 7–6 6–4; A. Costa (3) d. B. Black 6–4 6–2; C. Moya d. P. Rafter (WC) 7–6 6–3. ***Semi-finals:*** Henman d. Ivanisevic (1) 4–6 7–6 6–1; Moya d. Costa (3) 3–6 6–3 7–6. ***Final:*** Henman d. Moya 6–3 6–1.
MEN'S DOUBLES – Final: Lobo/J. Sanchez d. Haarhuis/Siemerink (2) 6–4 6–7 6–3.

CROATIAN INDOORS ($375,000)

ZAGREB, 27 JANUARY–2 FEBRUARY

MEN'S SINGLES – Quarter-finals: G. Ivanisevic (1) d. A. Radulescu 6–0 1–1 ret; J. Sanchez (5) d. G. Etlis (Q) 6–0 7–6; G. Rusedski d. M. Damm 7–5 6–3; T. Enqvist (2) d. H. Arazi 6–2 6–3. ***Semi-finals:*** Ivanisevic (1) d. Sanchez (5) 6–2 6–4; Rusedski d. Enqvist (2) 6–4 6–4. ***Final:*** Ivanisevic (1) d. Rusedski 7–6 4–6 7–6.
MEN'S DOUBLES – Final: Hirszon/Ivanisevic d. Haygarth/Keil 6–4 6–3.

SHANGHAI OPEN ($303,000)

SHANGHAI, 27 JANUARY–2 FEBRUARY

MEN'S SINGLES – Quarter-finals: A. Volkov (8) d. D. Flach 6–4 4–6 6–2; B. Steven d. G. Solves 6–7 6–2 6–2; L. Paes (Q) d. J. Tarango (4) 6–3 2–6 6–3; J. Kroslak (7) d. J. Golmard 6–2 3–6 6–3. ***Semi-finals:*** Volkov (8) d. Steven 7–6 7–5; Kroslak (7) d. Paes (Q) 6–2 6–4. ***Final:*** Kroslak (7) d. Volkov (8) 6–2 7–6.
MEN'S DOUBLES – Final: Mirnyi/Ullyett d. Nydahl/Pescosolido 7–6 6–7 7–5.

DUBAI TENNIS OPEN ($1,014,250)

DUBAI, 10–16 FEBRUARY

MEN'S SINGLES – Quarter-finals: G. Ivanisevic (1) d. B. Becker (7) w/o; J. Novak d. R. Krajicek (3) 6–2 6–2; J. Courier d. W. Ferreira (4) 6–2 7–5; T. Muster (WC) (2) d. C. Ruud 6–4 6–7 7–5. ***Semi-finals:*** Ivanisevic (1) d. Novak 6–1 3–6 6–3; Muster (WC) (2) d. Courier 7–6 2–6 6–3. ***Final:*** Muster (WC) (2) d. Ivanisevic (1) 7–5 7–6.
MEN'S DOUBLES – Final: Groen/Ivanisevic d. Stolle/Suk (3) 7–6 6–3.

MARSEILLE OPEN ($514,250)

MARSEILLE, 11–16 FEBRUARY

MEN'S SINGLES – Quarter-finals: M. Rios (1) d. M. Larsson 3–6 7–5 6–4; S. Bruguera d. A. Chesnokov 6–3 6–2; F. Santoro (WC) d. M. Rosset (4) 3–6 6–3 7–5; T. Enqvist (2) d. H. Dreekmann (8) 6–4 3–6 6–1. ***Semi-finals:*** Rios (1) d. Bruguera 6–3 6–7 6–4; Enqvist (2) d. Santoro (WC) 6–4 6–3. ***Final:*** Enqvist (2) d. Rios (1) 6–4 1–0 ret.
MEN'S DOUBLES – Final: Enqvist/Larsson (WC) d. Delaitre/Santoro 6–3 6–4.

SYBASE OPEN ($303,000)
SAN JOSE, 10–16 FEBRUARY
MEN'S SINGLES – Quarter-finals: P. Sampras (1) d. C. Woodruff (8) 6–2 6–3; T. Martin (WC) (4) d. R. Reneberg (6) 6–1 6–4; A. Agassi (3) d. G. Doyle (Q) 6–2 6–1; G. Rusedski (7) d. M. Chang (2) 7–6 6–4. ***Semi-finals:*** Sampras (1) d. Martin (WC) (4) 6–2 6–3; Rusedski (7) d. Agassi (3) 6–3 6–4. ***Final:*** Sampras (1) d. Rusedski (7) 3–6 5–0 ret.
MEN'S DOUBLES – Final: MacPhie/Muller d. Knowles/Nestor (2) 4–6 7–6 7–5.

ABN/AMRO WORLD TENNIS TOURNAMENT ($725,000)
ROTTERDAM, 3–9 MARCH
MEN'S SINGLES – Quarter-finals: G. Ivanisevic (1) d. P. Korda (8) w/o; D. Vacek d. R. Furlan 6–4 1–6 6–3; T. Enqvist (WC) (3) d. A. Radulescu 7–6 6–3; R. Krajicek (2) d. M. Stich 7–6 7–6. ***Semi-finals:*** Vacek d. Ivanisevic (1) 6–4 1–6 7–6; Krajicek (2) d. Enqvist (WC) (3) 6–7 6–3 6–4. ***Final:*** Krajicek (2) d. Vacek 7–6 7–6.
MEN'S DOUBLES – Final: Eltingh/Haarhuis (1) d. Pimek/Talbot (3) 7–6 6–4.

FRANKLIN TEMPLETON TENNIS CLASSIC ($303,000)
SCOTTSDALE, 3–9 MARCH
MEN'S SINGLES – Quarter-finals: M. Philippoussis d. B. Black 7–5 6–3; C. Woodruff d. C. Moya (3) 7–6 5–7 6–3; J. Bjorkman d. A. Costa (4) 6–4 2–6 6–4; R. Reneberg (8) d. J. Golmard (Q) 6–4 6–2. ***Semi-finals:*** Philippoussis d. Woodruff 4–6 7–6 6–2; Reneberg (8) d. Bjorkman 6–3 6–3. ***Final:*** Philippoussis d. Reneberg (8) 6–4 7–6.
MEN'S DOUBLES – Final: Lobo/J. Sanchez (4) d. Bjorkman/Leach (3) 6–3 6–3.

COPENHAGEN OPEN ($203,000)
COPENHAGEN, 10–16 MARCH
MEN'S SINGLES – Quarter-finals: L. Burgsmuller (Q) d. T. Carbonell 6–4 6–4; T. Johansson (5) d. J. Kroslak 4–6 6–3 6–2; K. Kucera (6) d. G. Raoux 6–4 6–2; M. Damm (2) d. F. Fetterlein (WC) 6–4 6–3. ***Semi-finals:*** Johansson (5) d. Burgsmuller (Q) 6–2 6–4; Damm (2) d. Kucera (6) 6–4 3–6 6–3. ***Final:*** Johansson (5) d. Damm (2) 6–4 3–6 6–2.
MEN'S DOUBLES – Final: Olhovskiy/Steven d. Carlsen/Fetterlein (WC) 6–4 6–2.

ST PETERSBURG OPEN ($300,000)
ST PETERSBURG, 17–23 MARCH
MEN'S SINGLES – Quarter-finals: M. Stich (1) d. K. Carlsen (8) 6–2 6–4; T. Johansson (5) d. O. Delaitre (Q) 6–2 6–4; J. Kroslak d. M. Norman 6–3 2–6 7–5; R. Furlan (7) d. A. Clement (Q) 5–7 6–4 6–2. ***Semi-finals:*** Johansson (5) d. Stich (1) 6–3 6–1; Furlan (7) d. Kroslak 6–3 6–3. ***Final:*** Johansson (5) d. Furlan (7) 6–3 6–4.
MEN'S DOUBLES – Final: Olhovskiy/Steven d. Prinosil/Vacek (2) 6–4 6–3.

GRAND PRIX HASSAN II ($203,000)
CASABLANCA, 24–30 MARCH
MEN'S SINGLES – Quarter-finals: K. Alami (1) d. F. Vicente 6–7 6–1 7–5; F. Squillari d. Y. El Aynaoui 6–4 6–1; G. Schaller (4) d. T. Carbonell (6) 6–4 6–4; H. Arazi (2) d. E. Alvarez (8) 6–2 6–1. ***Semi-finals:*** Squillari d. Alami (1) 6–3 6–3; Arazi (2) d. Schaller (4) 6–2 7–6. ***Final:*** Arazi (2) d. Squillari 3–6 6–1 6–2.
MEN'S DOUBLES – Final: Cunha-Silva/Marques (4) d. Alami/Arazi (WC) 7–6 6–2.

ESTORIL OPEN ($600,000)
LISBON, 7–13 APRIL
MEN'S SINGLES – Quarter-finals: J. Sanchez (8) d. G. Schaller 6–0 4–1 ret; A. Corretja (6) d. F. Santoro 6–3 4–0 ret; F. Mantilla (4) d. A. Berasategui (5) 6–4 6–1; F. Clavet (7) d. C. Moya (2) 6–1 6–3. ***Semi-finals:*** Corretja (6) d. Sanchez (8) 6–3 6–1; Clavet (7) d. Mantilla (4) 3–6 7–5 6–0. ***Final:*** Corretja (6) d. Clavet (7) 6–3 7–5.
MEN'S DOUBLES – Final: Kuerten/Meligeni (WC) d. Gaudenzi/Messori 6–2 6–2.

MADRAS OPEN ($405,000)
MADRAS, 7–13 APRIL
MEN'S SINGLES – Quarter-finals: A. Pavel d. M. Norman (7) 6–0 6–2; M. Tillstrom (6) d. J. Stark (4) 7–5 6–3; A. Radulescu (5) d. M. Washington (3) 6–3 6–4; G. Solves d. R. Schuttler (Q) 6–4 1–6 6–2. ***Semi-finals:*** Tillstrom (6) d. Pavel 6–3 6–3; Radulescu (5) d. Solves 6–3 6–2. ***Final:*** Tillstrom (6) d. Radulescu (5) 6–4 4–6 7–5.
MEN'S DOUBLES – Final: Bhupathi/Paes (3) d. Ogorodov/Ran 7–6 7–5.

SALEM OPEN ($303,000)
HONG KONG, 7–13 APRIL
MEN'S SINGLES – Quarter-finals: M. Chang (1) d. D. Prinosil (7) 6–1 7–6; T. Johansson (4) d. J. Gimelstob 6–4 6–4; P. Rafter (5) d. T. Woodbridge (3) 6–3 6–1; B. MacPhie (Q) d. S. Lareau 6–3 6–3. ***Semi-finals:*** Chang (1) d. Johansson (4) 7–6 6–4; Rafter (5) d. MacPhie (Q) 3–6 6–1 3–0 ret. ***Final:*** Chang (1) d. Rafter (5) 6–3 6–3.
MEN'S DOUBLES – Final: Damm/Vacek (3) d. Braasch/Tarango 6–3 6–4.

US MEN'S CLAY COURT CHAMPIONSHIPS ($264,250)

ORLANDO, 21–27 APRIL

MEN'S SINGLES – Quarter-finals: M. Chang (1) d. B. Black (7) 7–5 6–3; J. Stoltenberg (5) d. M. Filippini 6–7 6–4 6–4; C. Woodruff (6) d. A. O'Brien (4) 6–4 6–7 6–4; G. Stafford d. F. Meligeni 6–3 6–4. ***Semi-finals:*** Chang (1) d. Stoltenberg (5) 4–6 6–3 6–3; Stafford d. Woodruff (6) 6–3 4–6 6–4. ***Final:*** Chang (1) d. Stafford 4–6 6–2 6–1.

MEN'S DOUBLES – Final: Merklein/Spadea (WC) d. O'Brien/Salzenstein (WC) 6–4 4–6 6–4.

BMW OPEN ($400,000)

MUNICH, 28 APRIL–4 MAY

MEN'S SINGLES – Quarter-finals: M. Philippoussis (8) d. A. Gaudenzi 7–5 4–6 6–4; C. Dosedel d. F. Fetterlein (Q) 7–6 6–4; A. Corretja (6) d. M. Sinner (Q) 5–7 6–2 6–1; M. Rosset (7) d. C. Moya (2) 7–5 7–6. ***Semi-finals:*** Philippoussis (8) d. Dosedel 7–5 7–5; Corretja (6) d. Rosset (7) 6–3 6–1. ***Final:*** Philippoussis (8) d. Corretja (6) 7–6 1–6 6–4.

MEN'S DOUBLES – Final: Albano/Corretja d. Braasch/Knippschild 3–6 7–5 6–2.

CZECH OPEN ($340,000)

PRAGUE, 28 APRIL–4 MAY

MEN'S SINGLES – Quarter-finals: E. Alvarez d. M. Craca (Q) 6–3 7–5; C. Pioline (4) d. R. Fromberg 6–4 4–6 6–2; B. Ulihrach (3) d. A. Portas (Q) 2–6 6–4 6–4; F. Santoro d. M. Rios (2) 4–6 6–3 6–0. ***Semi-finals:*** Pioline (4) d. Alvarez 6–3 6–7 6–1; Ulihrach (3) d. Santoro 6–4 6–2. ***Final:*** Pioline (4) d. Ulihrach (3) 6–2 5–7 7–6.

MEN'S DOUBLES – Final: Bhupathi/Paes d. Luxa/Skoch (WC) 6–1 6–1.

AT & T CHALLENGE ($303,000)

ATLANTA, 28 APRIL–4 MAY

MEN'S SINGLES – Quarter-finals: J. Stoltenberg (7) d. F. Meligeni 3–1 ret; M. Norman d. P. Korda (5) 6–4 6–4; M. Filippini d. G. Schaller 6–1 6–2; C. Woodruff (8) d. S. Stolle 6–1 4–6 6–3. ***Semi-finals:*** Stoltenberg (7) d. Norman 6–4 5–7 6–3; Filippini d. Woodruff (8) 7–5 3–6 6–4. ***Final:*** Filippini d. Stoltenberg (7) 7–6 6–4.

MEN'S DOUBLES – Final: Bjorkman/Kulti (2) d. Davis/Jones 6–2 7–6.

AMERICA'S RED CLAY CHAMPIONSHIPS ($245,000)

CORAL SPRINGS, 5–11 MAY

MEN'S SINGLES – Quarter-finals: J. Bjorkman (1) d. J. Viloca 6–4 7–6; S. Campbell (Q) d. S. Sargsian 6–1 6–3; J. Stoltenberg (4) d. D. Witt (Q) 6–1 7–5; J. van Herck d. M. Woodforde 3–6 6–2 6–3. ***Semi-finals:*** Bjorkman (1) d. Campbell (Q) 6–4 4–6 6–4; Stoltenberg (4) d. van Herck 6–3 6–3. ***Final:*** Stoltenberg (4) d. Bjorkman (1) 6–0 2–6 7–5.

MEN'S DOUBLES – Final: Randall/van Emburgh d. L. Jensen/M. Jensen (3) 6–7 6–2 7–6.

INTERNATIONALER RAIFFEISEN GRAND PRIX ($400,000)

ST. POLTEN, 19–24 MAY

MEN'S SINGLES – Quarter-finals: P. Rafter (7) d. T. Muster (1) 6–3 7–6; M. Norman d. S. Schalken 1–6 6–1 6–3; M. Filippini d. T. Nydahl (Q) 7–5 6–1; D. Hrbaty d. K. Alami 6–1 6–2. ***Semi-finals:*** Rafter (7) d. Norman 6–1 4–6 6–3; Filippini d. Hrbaty 7–6 6–1. ***Final:*** Filippini d. Rafter (7) 7–6 6–2.

MEN'S DOUBLES – Final: Jones/Melville d. L. Jensen/M. Jensen 6–2 7–6.

GERRY WEBER OPEN ($875,000)

HALLE, 9–15 JUNE

MEN'S SINGLES – Quarter-finals: Y. Kafelnikov (1) d. M. Stich (7) 7–6 6–7 6–3; B. Becker (4) d. J. Tarango 6–4 6–2; P. Haarhuis d. R. Reneberg 6–2 6–1; P. Korda (8) d. T. Muster (2) 6–3 6–4. ***Semi-finals:*** Kafelnikov (1) d. Becker (4) 6–3 6–4; Korda (8) d. Haarhuis 7–6 6–4. ***Final:*** Kafelnikov (1) d. Korda (8) 7–6 6–7 7–6.

MEN'S DOUBLES – Final: Braasch/Stich (WC) d. Adams/Barnard 7–6 6–2.

THE STELLA ARTOIS GRASS COURT CHAMPIONSHIPS ($675,000)

LONDON, 9–15 JUNE

MEN'S SINGLES – Quarter-finals: J. Bjorkman (8) d. P. Sampras (WC) (1) 3–6 6–3 6–4; M. Philippoussis (6) d. J. Knippschild 6–2 6–7 6–4; G. Ivanisevic (3) d. J. Golmard 6–3 7–6; G. Rusedski (16) d. P. Rafter (9) 4–6 7–5 6–3. ***Semi-finals:*** Philippoussis (6) d. Bjorkman (8) 2–6 7–6 6–2; Ivanisevic (3) d. Rusedski (16) 4–6 6–4 7–6. ***Final:*** Philippoussis (6) d. Ivanisevic (3) 7–5 6–3.

MEN'S DOUBLES – Final: Philippoussis/Rafter (6) d. Stolle/Suk (7) 6–2 4–6 7–5.

INTERNAZIONALI DE TENNIS CARISBO ($303,000)

BOLOGNA, 9–15 JUNE

MEN'S SINGLES – Quarter-finals: G. Kuerten (8) d. A. Berasategui (1) 6–3 6–7 7–5; M. Martelli d. H. Arazi (5) 2–6 6–3 6–4; K. Alami (6) d. A. Gaudenzi 3–6 6–3 6–3; F. Mantilla (WC) (2) d. N. Lapentti 4–6 6–4 6–3. ***Semi-finals***: Kuerten (8) d. Martelli 6–1 6–2; Mantilla (WC) (2) d. Alami (6) 6–3 6–2. ***Final:*** Mantilla (WC) (2) d. Kuerten (8) 4–6 6–2 6–1.

MEN'S DOUBLES – Final: Kuerten/Meligeni (4) d. Randall/Waite (3) 6–2 7–5.

HEINEKEN TROPHY ($475,000)

ROSMALEN, 16–22 JUNE

MEN'S SINGLES – Quarter-finals: M. Chang (1) d. F. Clavet (8) 6–7 7–6 6–1; R. Krajicek (3) d. M. Damm 7–6 7–6; J. Bjorkman (4) d. F. Wibier (Q) 6–2 6–4; G. Raoux (Q) d. S. Schalken 7–6 6–4. ***Semi-finals:*** Krajicek (3) d. Chang (1) 6–7 6–3 6–4; Raoux (Q) d. Bjorkman (4) 6–0 6–1. ***Final:*** Krajicek (3) d. Raoux (Q) 6–4 7–6.
MEN'S DOUBLES – Final: Eltingh/Haarhuis (1) d. Kronemann/MacPherson 6–4 7–5.

THE NOTTINGHAM OPEN ($303,000)

NOTTINGHAM, 16–21 JUNE

MEN'S SINGLES – Quarter-finals: K. Kucera d. S. Draper 4–6 6–2 7–5; T. Henman (WC) (4) d. G. Stafford 3–6 6–3 7–6; G. Rusedski d. J. Stoltenberg 6–3 7–6; S. Stolle d. A. O'Brien (8) 7–6 4–6 7–6. ***Semi-finals:*** Kucera d. Henman (WC) (4) 6–4 2–6 6–4; Rusedski d. Stolle 6–3 6–4. ***Final:*** Rusedski d. Kucera 6–4 7–5.
MEN'S DOUBLES – Final: E. Ferreira/Galbraith (1) d. Sapsford/Wilkinson (WC) 4–6 7–6 7–6.

RADO SWISS OPEN ($525,000)

GSTAAD, 7–13 JULY

MEN'S SINGLES – Quarter-finals: W. Ferreira (8) d. M. Rosset 7–5 7–6; F. Mantilla (6) d. J. Sanchez 6–4 6–3; J. Viloca d. N. Kiefer (WC) 6–4 6–3; A. Corretja (2) d. A. Berasategui (7) 6–4 6–0. ***Semi-finals:*** Mantilla (6) d. Ferreira (8) 6–3 6–4; Viloca d. Corretja (2) 3–6 7–6 6–4. ***Final:*** Mantilla (6) d. Viloca 6–1 6–4 6–4.
MEN'S DOUBLES – Final: Kafelnikov/Vacek (1) d. Kronemann/MacPherson 4–6 7–6 6–3.

SWEDISH OPEN ($303,000)

BASTAD, 7–13 JULY

MEN'S SINGLES – Quarter-finals: C. Costa d. P. Fredriksson 6–2 6–3; M. Norman (4) d. J. Tarango 6–2 6–3; K. Kucera (5) d. M. Larsson (3) 6–4 ret; J. Marin d. T. Nydahl (WC) 6–2 6–1. ***Semi-finals:*** Norman (4) d. Costa 7–5 6–3; Marin d. Kucera (5) 7–6 6–3. ***Final:*** Norman (4) d. Marin 7–5 6–2.
MEN'S DOUBLES – Final: Kulti/Tillstrom (WC) d. Gustafsson/Larsson (WC) 6–0 6–3.

MILLER LITE HALL OF FAME CHAMPIONSHIPS ($255,000)

NEWPORT, 7–13 JULY

MEN'S SINGLES – Quarter-finals: L. Paes (7) d. A. Radulescu (1) 6–3 7–6; S. Sargsian (5) d. S. Stolle (4) 6–3 7–5; G. Stafford (3) d. D. Wheaton 4–6 6–3 6–2; B. Steven (8) d. M. Woodforde (2) 6–0 6–0. ***Semi-finals:*** Sargsian (5) d. Paes (7) 7–6 2–6 6–3; Steven (8) d. Stafford (3) 6–3 5–7 6–4. ***Final:*** Sargsian (5) d. Steven (8) 7–6 4–6 7–5.
MEN'S DOUBLES – Final: Gimelstob/Steven (4) d. Kinnear/Kitinov 6–3 6–4.

GENERALI OPEN ($500,000)

KITZBUHEL, 21–27 JULY

MEN'S SINGLES – Quarter-finals: C. Dosedel (15) d. M. Filippini (9) 7–5 6–4; J. Alonso-Pintor d. H. Gumy 4–6 6–3 7–6; G. Blanco (14) d. S. Koubek (WC) 6–7 6–2 6–4; F. Dewulf (10) d. Y. Kafelnikov (2) 7–5 7–5. ***Semi-finals:*** Alonso-Pintor d. Dosedel (15) 6–3 6–4; Dewulf (10) d. Blanco (14) 6–3 6–2. ***Final:*** Dewulf (10) d. Alonso-Pintor 7–6 6–4 6–1.
MEN'S DOUBLES – Final: Arthurs/Fromberg (Q) d. Buchmayer/Strengberger (WC) 6–4 6–3.

INTERNATIONAL CHAMPIONSHIP OF CROATIA-UMAG ($375,000)

UMAG, 21–27 JULY

MEN'S SINGLES – Quarter-finals: S. Bruguera (1) d. P. Haarhuis (8) 6–3 6–4; A. Martin d. J. Sanchez (4) 4–6 6–4 6–1; F. Mantilla (3) d. D. Hrbaty (5) 3–6 6–3 6–4; C. Moya (2) d. A. Portas (7) 1–6 6–3 7–5. ***Semi-finals:*** Bruguera (1) d. Martin 6–3 6–1; Mantilla (3) d. Moya (2) 7–6 5–7 6–3. ***Final:*** Mantilla (3) d. Bruguera (1) 6–3 7–5.
MEN'S DOUBLES – Final: Pescariu/Sanguinetti d. Hrbaty/Kucera 7–6 6–4.

INFINITI OPEN ($303,000)

LOS ANGELES, 21–27 JULY

MEN'S SINGLES – Quarter-finals: G. Ivanisevic (WC) (1) d. B. Black 7–6 6–2; J. Courier (6) d. R. Krajicek (4) 7–6 7–5; G. Raoux d. M. Philippoussis (3) 7–6 6–4; T. Enqvist (2) d. K. Carlsen 6–3 7–5. ***Semi-finals:*** Courier (6) d. Ivanisevic (WC) (1) 6–3 6–4; Enqvist (2) d. Raoux 6–4 6–1. ***Final:*** Courier (6) d. Enqvist (2) 6–4 6–4.
MEN'S DOUBLES – Final: Lareau/O'Brien (1) d. Bhupathi/Leach (4) 7–6 6–4.

GRÖLSCH OPEN ($475,000)

AMSTERDAM, 28 JULY–3 AUGUST

MEN'S SINGLES – Quarter-finals: C. Moya (1) d. F. Clavet (8) 6–3 6–4; M. Norman (4) d. C. Ruud 6–3 7–6; M. Filippini d. J. Sanchez (6) 7–6 6–1; C. Dosedel d. J. van Lottum (WC) 6–4 4–6 6–2. ***Semi-finals:*** Moya (1) d. Norman (4) 6–4 6–3; Dosedel d. Filippini 7–6 6–2. ***Final:*** Dosedel d. Moya (1) 7–6 7–6 6–7 6–2.
MEN'S DOUBLES – Final: Kilderry/Lapentti d. Kratzmann/Pimek (3) 3–6 7–5 7–6.

INTERNAZIONALI DI TENNIS DI SAN MARINO ($275,000)
SAN MARINO, 4–10 AUGUST
MEN'S SINGLES – Quarter-finals: F. Mantilla (1) d. C. Ruud (8) 6–3 6–1; D. Hrbaty (6) d. A. Voinea 7–6 4–6 7–5; C. Costa d. J. Sanchez (4) 6–3 6–3; M. Gustafsson d. A. Pavel 6–4 4–6 6–1. ***Semi-finals:*** Mantilla (1) d. Hrbaty (6) 6–4 6–4; Gustafsson d. Costa 1–6 6–1 6–3. ***Final:*** Mantilla (1) d. Gustafsson 6–4 6–1.
MEN'S DOUBLES – Final: Brandi/Messori (3) d. Coupe/Roditi 7–5 6–4.

US PRO TENNIS CHAMPIONSHIPS ($303,000)
BOSTON, 18–24 AUGUST
MEN'S SINGLES – Quarter-finals: S. Schalken d. A. Corretja (1) 6–3 3–6 6–3; A. Costa (5) d. J. van Herck 6–7 6–2 6–1; J. Tarango d. G. Rusedski (6) 7–6 7–6; M. Rios (2) d. H. Gumy 6–4 6–3. ***Semi-finals:*** Schalken d. Costa (5) 6–4 5–7 6–3; Rios (2) d. Tarango 6–4 6–3. ***Final:*** Schalken d. Rios (2) 7–5 6–3.
MEN'S DOUBLES – Final: Eltingh/Haarhuis (1) d. Randall/Waite (4) 6–4 6–2.

WALDBAUM'S HAMLET CUP ($303,000)
LONG ISLAND, 18–24 AUGUST
MEN'S SINGLES – Quarter-finals: P. Rafter (WC) (8) d. M. Chang (1) 6–4 3–6 6–1; T. Enqvist (WC) (6) d. R. Reneberg 5–7 6–4 6–2; C. Moya (5) d. M-K. Goellner 6–4 6–4; J. Alonso-Pintor (Q) d. G. Ivanisevic (WC) (2) 7–6 3–6 6–3. ***Semi-finals:*** Rafter (WC) (8) d. Enqvist (WC) (6) 6–4 6–4; Moya (5) d. Alonso-Pintor (Q) 6–2 6–3. ***Final:*** Moya (5) d. Rafter (WC) (8) 6–4 7–6.
MEN'S DOUBLES – Final: Ondruska/Prinosil d. Keil/Middleton 6–4 6–4.

THE PRESIDENT'S CUP ($380,000)
TASHKENT, 8–14 SEPTEMBER
MEN'S SINGLES – Quarter-finals: Y. Kafelnikov (1) d. A. Stoliarov (Q) 6–4 6–4; M. Rosset (3) d. H. Arazi (5) 6–2 6–4; F. Clavet (6) d. J. Sanchez (4) 6–1 6–2; T. Henman (WC) (2) d. V. Spadea (8) 6–3 6–4. ***Semi-finals:*** Rosset (3) d. Kafelnikov (1) 3–6 7–6 6–2; Henman (WC) (2) d. Clavet (6) 6–3 7–5. ***Final:*** Henman (WC) (2) d. Rosset (3) 7–6 6–4.
MEN'S DOUBLES – Final: Santopadre/Spadea (4) d. Arazi/Ran 6–4 6–7 6–0.

BOURNEMOUTH INTERNATIONAL OPEN ($375,000)
BOURNEMOUTH, 8–14 SEPTEMBER
MEN'S SINGLES – Quarter-finals: C. Moya (1) d. D. Scala (Q) 6–3 6–4; G. Rusedski (3) d. L. Arnold 7–6 6–3; M. Ondruska d. J. Diaz 7–5 6–3; F. Mantilla (2) d. C. van Garsse 6–3 7–6. ***Semi-finals:*** Moya (1) d. Rusedski (3) 6–2 6–2; Mantilla (2) d. Ondruska 6–7 6–1 6–1. ***Final:*** Mantilla (2) d. Moya (1) 6–2 6–2.
MEN'S DOUBLES – Final: Kinnear/Kitinov (4) d. Martin/Wilkinson 7–6 6–2.

MARBELLA OPEN ($303,000)
MARBELLA, 8–14 SEPTEMBER
MEN'S SINGLES – Quarter-finals: A. Costa (1) d. A. Gaudenzi 6–3 7–6; G. Blanco (6) d. F. Roig 7–6 6–3; D. Hrbaty (4) d. K. Alami (5) 6–3 7–5; A. Berasategui (2) d. J. Alonso-Pintor (7) 6–1 6–4. ***Semi-finals:*** Costa (1) d. Blanco (6) 7–5 6–2; Berasategui (2) d. Hrbaty (4) 6–4 6–4. ***Final:*** Costa (1) d. Berasategui (2) 6–3 6–2.
MEN'S DOUBLES – Final: Alami/Alonso-Pintor d. Berasategui/Burillo (3) 4–6 6–3 6–0.

OPEN ROMANIA ($475,000)
BUCHAREST, 22–28 SEPTEMBER
MEN'S SINGLES – Quarter-finals: M-K. Goellner (7) d. C. Costa 6–2 7–6; A. Gaudenzi d. N. Lapentti 6–2 6–4; R. Fromberg d. A. Portas (4) 6–4 6–3; F. Clavet d. J. Sanchez 4–6 6–2 6–3. ***Semi-finals:*** Gaudenzi d. Goellner (7) 6–2 7–6; Fromberg d. Clavet 4–6 6–3 6–4. ***Final:*** Fromberg d. Gaudenzi 6–1 7–6.
MEN'S DOUBLES – Final: Lobo/J. Sanchez (1) d. Davids/Orsanic 7–5 7–5.

GRAND PRIX DE TENNIS DE TOULOUSE ($375,000)
TOULOUSE, 22–28 SEPTEMBER
MEN'S SINGLES – Quarter-finals: V. Spadea d. J. Gimelstob 6–3 7–6; M. Philippoussis (WC) (3) d. A. Clement (LL) 7–5 3–6 7–6; A. Radulescu d. T. Haas 6–1 6–4; N. Kiefer d. G. Raoux (8) 6–2 6–7 7–5. ***Semi-finals:*** Philippoussis (WC) (3) d. Spadea 7–5 6–4; Kiefer d. Radulescu 6–3 2–6 7–6. ***Final:*** Kiefer d. Philippoussis (WC) (3) 7–5 5–7 6–4.
MEN'S DOUBLES – Final: Eltingh/Haarhuis (1) d. Fleurian/Mirnyi 6–3 7–6.

DAVIDOFF SWISS INDOORS ($975,000)
BASEL, 29 SEPTEMBER–5 OCTOBER
MEN'S SINGLES – Quarter-finals: M. Philippoussis d. Y. Kafelnikov (1) 6–3 6–7 6–2; T. Henman d. M. Norman 6–3 6–2; G. Rusedski (4) d. T. Enqvist (6) 7–6 4–6 6–3; P. Korda (7) d. L. Roux (LL) 6–3 6–4. ***Semi-finals:*** Philippoussis d. Henman 7–6 6–4; Rusedski (4) d. Korda (7) 6–7 6–3 7–5. ***Final:*** Rusedski (4) d. Philippoussis 6–3 7–6 7–6.
MEN'S DOUBLES – Final: Henman/Rosset (WC) d. Braasch/Grabb 7–6 6–7 7–6.

BEIJING OPEN ($303,000)

BEIJING, 29 SEPTEMBER–5 OCTOBER

MEN'S SINGLES – Quarter-finals: J. Courier (WC) (1) d. J. Kroslak 6–4 6–3; T. Johansson (3) d. G. Pozzi 6–2 6–4; M. Gustafsson (5) d. B. Black 6–4 6–3; K. Carlsen d. A. O'Brien 7–5 5–7 7–6. ***Semi-finals:*** Courier (WC) (1) d. Johansson (3) 6–3 6–4; Gustafsson (5) d. Carlsen 6–2 6–4. ***Final:*** Courier (WC) (1) d. Gustafsson (5) 7–6 3–6 6–3.

MEN'S DOUBLES – Final: Bhupathi/Paes (1) d. Courier/O'Brien (WC) 7–5 7–6.

CAMPIONATI INTERNAZIONALI DE SICILIA ($303,000)

PALERMO, 29 SEPTEMBER–5 OCTOBER

MEN'S SINGLES – Quarter-finals: A. Corretja (WC) (1) d. F. Clavet (8) 7–6 6–2; D. Hrbaty (6) d. A. Portas (3) 7–5 6–4; J. Sanchez d. M. Filippini (5) 6–3 1–6 6–4; A. Berasategui (2) d. K. Alami (7) 7–6 6–2. ***Semi-finals:*** Hrbaty (6) d. Corretja (WC) (1) 6–4 6–4; Berasategui (2) d. Sanchez 6–2 6–3. ***Final:*** Berasategui (2) d. Hrbaty (6) 6–4 6–2.

MEN'S DOUBLES – Final: Kratzmann/Pimek (3) d. Davids/Orsanic (4) 3–6 6–3 7–6.

GRAND PRIX DE TENNIS DE LYON ($725,000)

LYON, 13–19 OCTOBER

MEN'S SINGLES – Quarter-finals: M. Philippoussis (7) d. C. Pioline 6–3 3–6 7–6; F. Santoro d. F. Mantilla (WC) (4) 6–1 6–1; T. Haas d. T. Enqvist (5) 6–3 6–3; Y. Kafelnikov (2) d. M-K. Goellner 6–4 7–5. ***Semi-finals:*** Santoro d. Philippoussis (7) 6–4 6–2; Haas d. Kafelnikov (2) 4–6 6–4 6–3. ***Final:*** Santoro d. Haas 6–4 6–4.

MEN'S DOUBLES – Final: E. Ferreira/Galbraith (1) d. Delaitre/Santoro 3–6 6–2 6–4.

IPB CZECH INDOOR ($975,000)

OSTRAVA, 13–19 OCTOBER

MEN'S SINGLES – Quarter-finals: K. Kucera (8) d. J. Novak 6–4 6–2; G. Ivanisevic (3) d. B. Ulihrach 7–6 6–2; T. Muster (4) d. D. Nargiso (Q) 7–6 6–1; M. Norman (7) d. S. Bruguera (2) 6–4 6–7 7–5. ***Semi-finals:*** Kucera (8) d. Ivanisevic (3) 6–3 0–0 ret; Norman (7) d. Muster (4) 6–7 6–2 7–5. ***Final:*** Kucera (8) d. Norman (7) 6–2 ret.

MEN'S DOUBLES – Final: Novak/Rikl d. Johnson/Montana (3) 6–2 6–4.

ABIERTO MEXICANO DE TENIS ($305,000)

MEXICO CITY, 20–26 OCTOBER

MEN'S SINGLES – Quarter-finals: F. Clavet (1) d. A. Sa (Q) 6–3 7–6; N. Lapentti d. E. Alvarez 6–2 4–6 7–5; F. Meligeni d. L. Arnold (Q) 2–6 7–6 6–0; J. Viloca d. J. Marin 6–4 6–2. ***Semi-finals:*** Clavet (1) d. Lapentti 7–5 7–6; Viloca d. Meligeni 6–3 6–1. ***Final:*** Clavet (1) d. Viloca 6–4 7–6.

MEN'S DOUBLES – Final: Lapentti/Orsanic (3) d. Herrera/M. Sanchez (WC) 4–6 6–3 7–6.

CERVEZA CLUB COLOMBIA OPEN ($303,000)

BOGOTA, 27 OCTOBER–2 NOVEMBER

MEN'S SINGLES – Quarter-finals: F. Clavet (1) d. E. Alvarez 7–6 2–3 ret; D. Sanguinetti d. J. Burillo 6–4 6–3; N. Lapentti d. C. Costa (6) 7–5 4–6 6–3; V. Spadea d. F. Meligeni (8) 7–5 7–6. ***Semi-finals:*** Clavet (1) d. Sanguinetti 6–3 6–7 7–6; Lapentti d. Spadea 6–2 7–5. ***Final:*** Clavet (1) d. Lapentti 6–3 6–3.

MEN'S DOUBLES – Final: Lobo/Meligeni (1) d. Alami/Ruah (Q) 6–1 6–3.

KREMLIN CUP ($1,125,000)

MOSCOW, 3–9 NOVEMBER

MEN'S SINGLES – Quarter-finals: Y. Kafelnikov (1) d. S. Sargsian 6–1 6–2; D. Nestor (Q) d. M. Damm 6–3 6–4; W. Black (Q) d. D. Vacek 6–1 6–2; P. Korda (2) d. A. O'Brien 7–5 6–3. ***Semi-finals:*** Kafelnikov (1) d. Nestor (Q) 6–4 6–3; Korda (2) d. Black (Q) 6–7 6–3 7–5. ***Final:*** Kafelnikov (1) d. Korda (2) 7–6 6–4.

MEN'S DOUBLES – Final: Damm/Suk d. Adams/Santoro 6–4 6–3.

STOCKHOLM OPEN ($800,000)

STOCKHOLM, 3–9 NOVEMBER

MEN'S SINGLES – Quarter-finals: P. Rafter (1) d. T. Henman (8) 6–3 6–3; J. Bjorkman (4) d. K. Kucera 6–3 6–2; J. Siemerink d. C. Pioline 6–4 6–2; G. Rusedski (2) d. M. Larsson w/o. ***Semi-finals:*** Bjorkman (4) d. Rafter (1) 7–6 7–6; Siemerink d. Rusedski (2) 4–6 7–6 6–4. ***Final:*** Bjorkman (4) d. Siemerink 3–6 7–6 6–2 6–4.

MEN'S DOUBLES – Final: Goellner/Reneberg (Q) d. E. Ferreira/Galbraith (1) 6–3 3–6 7–6.

HELLMANN'S CUP ($303,000)

SANTIAGO, 3–9 NOVEMBER

MEN'S SINGLES – Quarter-finals: M. Rios (1) d. F. Meligeni 1–6 7–6 6–1; M. Filippini (5) d. R. Vasek 6–1 7–5; J. Alonso-Pintor (4) d. M. Puerta (Q) 6–4 6–2; J. Burillo d. O. Gross 6–4 6–4. ***Semi-finals:*** Rios (1) d. Filippini (5) 6–1 6–4; Alonso-Pintor (4) d. Burillo 6–1 4–6 6–3. ***Final:*** Alonso-Pintor (4) d. Rios (1) 6–2 6–1.

MEN'S DOUBLES – Final: Davids/Kratzmann (4) d. Alonso-Pintor/Lapentti 7–6 5–7 6–4

ATP Tour World Championship

Barry Flatman

Pete Sampras is a man of several habits. A propensity for stating the obvious has never been one of them; not, that is, until the time had come to celebrate victory in the ATP Tour World Championship for a fourth time.

The man now universally accepted not just as the greatest player of the nineties but quite possibly of all time has always been suitably modest at post-match press conferences. But after emphatically dismissing the challenge of Yevgeny Kafelnikov in the same fashion he had dealt with Carlos Moya to win a second Australian Open, Cedric Pioline to take a fourth Wimbledon title and Patrick Rafter, just a few weeks earlier, to reclaim the Grand Slam Cup in Munich, Sampras felt the time was right to announce what those four opponents already knew to their cost. 'When everything clicks in my game, I am unbeatable,' he said.

The 26-year-old had arrived in Hanover already assured that he would finish 1997 as the world number one for the fifth year running. He left, seven days later, with everyone aware that the gap that exists between him and the rest is still growing.

Sampras's week in Bavaria was not, however, without its problems. His game grated rather than clicked in his opening match against Spain's Moya. In any tournament not employing the charitable round-robin format, that defeat would have resulted in the eventual champion looking for a seat on the first available return flight across the Atlantic. But the American is a long-time campaigner in the ATP Tour's end-of-year climax and knows that a temporary setback can be a blessing in disguise.

Indeed, each time he had lifted the trophy previously he had reached the final after losing one of his group matches. It had happened three times in the event's former home of Frankfurt and again the previous year in Hanover after a memorable five-set battle royal with Boris Becker.

To expect such a magnificent finish two years running would have been greedy. Yet, in its way, the 1997 final was equally impressive. Whereas those fortunate spectators of 1996 had watched a contest of the very highest calibre, those who sat through the 88 minutes of Sampras's 6–3 6–2 6–2 victory over Kafelnikov witnessed an exhibition, albeit one-sided, of complete tennis mastery.

The statistically minded can point to figures as a demonstration of Sampras' superiority. His victory earned him $1,134,000 and took his career prize fortune through the $30 million mark. Try as he might, an increasingly disspirited Kafelnikov could win only three service games without having to battle break points. Furthermore, as Sampras zeroed in on victory, he allowed the Russian only eight points in his last ten service games.

Those who prefer to savour the overall splendor of a performance without needing numbers to reinforce their impression will certainly recall the potency of Sampras's serve and the devastating power of his groundshots. But most of all they will think back to his superhuman reflexes at the net which caused a particularly over-excited master of ceremonies to summarise the display as 'tennis from outer space'.

Apart from an inexplicably slack opening game, when he somehow misdirected the easiest of forehand volleys into the net and then despatched two double-faults in succession, Sampras's show was certainly alien to Kafelnikov who was almost apologetic at the end. 'I felt so embarrassed,' said the 23-year-old from Sochi.

Kafelnikov had been the last of the eight original contestants to qualify for the right to play in Hall 13 of the giant Messe that will house Expo 2000. In fact he had left it until the previous Sunday to book his ticket by winning Moscow's Kremlin Cup. But the confidence of that win soon evaporated under a deluge of Sampras winners. 'Pete had an answer for everything. Everyone knows my groundstrokes are good but his are five times better. He was totally devastating and I had no chance'.

Ominously, that appeared to be the case throughout 1997 whenever anyone walked out for a final against Sampras. Adding eight more titles to his collection throughout the course of the year, he mantained a 100 per cent record in finals. According to the man himself, he had kept the best for last.

Despite a loss to Moya in the round-robin section, Pete Sampras retained his ATP Tour World Championship title with considerable style in Hanover. (Stephen Wake)

'That was right up there with my best matches of the year,' thought Sampras, fittingly voted the best player of the Open era in a poll of all the former world no.1's plus the ATP Tour's tournament directors and members of the international press corps. 'It's an unbelievable feeling when I play the way I did against Yevgeny. All the shots came together and I seemed to get the feeling that everything I tried would work.'

Things had been very different for Sampras just five days earlier against Moya. Despite being widely accepted as the Spaniard most likely to succeed away from clay, the Australian finalist was still regarded as one of the tournament's two rank outsiders, along wih compatriot Sergi Bruguera. The draw had placed Moya in the same group as a trio of attacking players – Patrick Rafter and Greg Rusedski, both first-timers like himself, plus defending champion Sampras. But the 21-year-old's indoor form in the later part of the year had been unspectacular to say the least.

However, Moya had rapidly become aware that he had caught Sampras off form and he did not waste the opportunity. Nothing seemed to please the world No.1 that day. His movement, his motivation, the speed of the court and even the tension of his rackets – all seemed to be a problem. Meanwhile Moya immediately appeared to feel at home and delivered a stream of the most precise lobs that would have been out of the range of the feared Sampras Slam Dunk, even if the shot's inventor had been having a good day.

Moya won 6–3 6–7 6–2 to become the only member of the top ten to beat Sampras in 1997. Meanwhile Rafter triumphed 4–6 6–3 6–4 against Greg Rusedski in a re-run of the US Open final. The British No.1 could count himself unlucky over some debatable service calls at crucial stages of the match.

It was ironic that the draw had bunched all the players with big serves in one group and all the top returners in the other. Kafelnikov found himself doing battle with Michael Chang, newcomer Jonas Bjorkman and Sergi Bruguera. The man in form was Bjorkman who had arrived fresh from winning the Stockholm Open after an impressive autumnal run which had seen him move up to fourth place in the rankings.

All that counted for nothing against Kafelnikov, although he did manage to break the Russian as he served for the match. It was, however, no more than a stay of execution. Nevertheless Bjorkman was still in line for a place in the semi-finals after ably coping with Bruguera who also lost in straight sets to Chang before deciding that a rib injury was too painful for him to complete his group matches.

Rusedski also had to bow out without a win to his name. The morning after his defeat by Rafter he awoke to find the thigh muscle of his right leg knotted with pain. Facing any opponent that day would have been arduous enough. Against Sampras on an occasion when it was a case of victory or likely elimination, it becomes an almost impossible task.

So it turned out. Although Britain's big server fought gamely he decided, after consulting two local doctors, that completing his schedule against Moya would lay him open to the risk of serious injury. Therefore discretion became the better part of valour and heralded the entrance of on-site replacement Thomas Muster.

Finding a substitute for Bruguera proved an altogether more complicated affair for the ATP Tour heirachy who worked the telephone lines out of Germany long into the night before coming up with the name of seventh alternative Tim Henman. Those giving their apologies numbered Marcelo Rios and Gustavo Kuerten who would have been unable to get to Hanover in time from their homes in South America, and the trio of Richard Krajicek, Goran Ivanisevic and Petr Korda who were all convalescing after surgery.

Felix Mantilla's name was next on the list. According to the organisers he did not answer their message. According to the Spaniard himself he was never contacted in the first place. With a new day fast approaching and no opponent for Kafelnikov, a decision had to be made. Accordingly the SOS went out to Henman who was playing the British National Championships 500 miles away in Telford near Birmingham.

The problem was not as unsettling as it might have been for Kafelnikov. He was already assured of a place in the semi-finals after a masterful 6–3 6–0 destruction of Chang who, a day later, found himself unable to take even a set off the determined Bjorkman.

Kafelnikov's hopes of entering the weekend with a 100 per cent record were dashed by the English jet-setter. For Henman it was a most unusual day. After winning a match in England he flew to Hanover on a chartered jet, thrashed Kafelnikov 6–4 6–4, then flew back to Birmingham airport. There a car was waiting to whisk him back to Telford for a short night's sleep before his semi-final.

If Henman, unexpectedly $100,000 richer, was the fortunate man of the tournament, Rafter could consider himself one of the most hard done by. After excellent displays to beat both Rusedski and Moya, he walked on court with Sampras in the knowledge the world no.1 still had to win to survive. Furthermore, Rafter knew he would make it to the weekend if he could win just one more set. But stopping such a talented individual as Sampras in such a mood proved too much for the Australian. He was despatched 6–4 6–1.

The semi-finals paired Kafelnikov with Moya and Sampras with Bjorkman – a repeat of the Mercedes Super 9 final in Paris less than a fortnight previously. Moya, perhaps as surprised as anyone by his unexpected success at getting through the group matches, squandered a gilt edged opportunity to reach the final. He squandered four set points in the first set and then had the upper hand in the second tie-break but let it slip to give his opponent a 7–6 7–6 win.

Bjorkman, on the other hand, could only concur with Sampras's assessment. After winning comfortably 6–3 6–4 the eventual champion claimed he was getting better and better with every match.

Before the final the ATP Tour's President, Mark Miles, took time out to explain the revolutionary thinking which could come into affect in the year 2000. There would be a restructured ranking system, a trimmed Mercedes Super 7, closer links with the women's tour and a different home for these Championships each year.

As for Sampras, he now stands just one win short of Ivan Lendl's haul of five ATP titles. By the Millennium he could well have claimed that record. If the awe in which his opponents hold him continues for the next few years, Sampras should have no problems. Rafter, who finished the year as the American's nearest challenger in second place on the ranking list, summed it all up. 'Do we give Pete too much respect?' he wondered. 'When somebody plays like that, it's difficult to do anything to the man except respect him.'

ATP TOUR CHAMPIONSHIP 1997

HANOVER, 11–16 NOVEMBER

ROUND ROBIN SECTION – Red Group: 1st P. Sampras (1) d. G. Rusedski (5) 6–4 7–5; d. P. Rafter (3) 6–4 6–1; 2nd C. Moya (7) d. P. Sampras (1) 6–3 6–7(4) 6–2; d. T. Muster (Alt) 6–2 6–3; 3rd P. Rafter (3) d. G. Rusedski (5) 4–6 6–3 6–4; d. C. Moya (7) 6–4 6–2; 4th G. Rusedski (5); T. Muster (Alt). ***White Group:*** 1st Y. Kafelnikov (6) d. J. Bjorkman (4) 6–3 7–6(6); d. M. Chang (2) 6–3 6–0; 2nd J. Bjorkman (4) d. S. Bruguera (8) 6–3 6–1; d. M. Chang (2) 6–4 7–5; 3rd M. Chang (2) d. S. Bruguera (8) 7–6(8) 6–2; 4th S. Bruguera (8); T. Henman (Alt) d. Y. Kafelnikov (6) 6–4 6–4.

PLAY-OFFS – Semi-finals: Sampras (1) d. Bjorkman (4) 6–3 6–4; Kafelnikov (2) d. Moya (7) 7–6(2) 7–6(3). ***Final:*** Sampras (1) d. Kafelnikov (6) 6–3 6–2 6–2.

PRIZE MONEY AND POINTS: Sampras $1,340,000 (630); Kafelnikov $640,000 (350); Bjorkman $280,000 (160); Moya $280,000 (160); Rafter $280,000 (160); Chang $180,000 (80); Henman* $100,000 (80); Rusedski $80,000 (–); Bruguera $80,000 (–); Muster * $40,000 (–).

* = Alternate

ATP TOUR DOUBLES CHAMPIONSHIP 1997

HARTFORD CT, 19–23 NOVEMBER

ROUND ROBIN SECTION – Green Group: 1st S. Lareau/A. O'Brien (6) d. D. Johnson/F. Montana (8) 6–3 3–6 6–3, d. T. Woodbridge/M. Woodforde (1) 7–6(4) 7–5; 2nd R. Leach/J. Stark (4) d. S. Lareau/A. O'Brien (6) 6–4 3–6 6–3, d. D. Johnson/F. Montana (8) 6–3 6–4; 3rd T. Woodbridge/M. Woodforde (1) d. D. Johnson/F. Montana (8) 6–4 6–1, d. R. Leach/J. Stark (4) 6–3 6–7(4) 7–6(5); 4th D. Johnson/F. Montana (8). ***Yellow Group:*** 1st J. Eltingh/P. Haarhuis (1) d. M. Knowles/D. Nestor (7) 6–4 7–6(4), d. M. Bhupathi/L. Paes (5) 6–3 6–2, d. E. Ferreira/P. Galbraith (3) 7–6(1) 6–7(5) 6–2; 2nd M. Bhupathi/L. Paes (5) d. E. Ferreira/P. Galbraith (3) 7–5 6–4, d. T. Kronemann/D. MacPherson (Alt) 6–4 7–6(5); 3rd E. Ferreira/P. Galbraith (3) d. M. Knowles/D. Nestor (7) 6–2 6–7(6) 7–5; 4th M. Knowles/D. Nestor (7).

PLAY-OFFS – Semi-finals: Bhupathi/Paes (5) d. Lareau/O'Brien (6) 6–4 6–4; Leach/Stark (4) d. Eltingh/Haarhuis (2) 6–3 6–4. ***Final:*** Leach/Stark (4) d. Bhupathi/Paes (5) 6–3 6–4 7–6(3).

PRIZE MONEY AND POINTS: Leach/Stark $145,000 (630); Bhupathi/Paes $80,000 (350); Eltingh/Haarhuis $80,000 (240); Lareau/O'Brien $50,000 (160); Woodbridge/Woodforde $80,000 (160); Ferreira/Galbraith $35,000 (80); Knowles/Nestor $10,000 (–); Johnson/Montana $10,000 (–); Kronemann/MacPherson * $10,000 (–).

* = Alternate

Corel WTA Tour

Corel WTA Tour Year • Points Explanation and Allocation • Corel WTA Tour Tournaments – Tiers I, II, III and IV • Corel WTA Chase Championships

With relatively little tournament experience it was astonishing that the 17-year-old unseeded American, Venus Williams, should have been able to reach the final of the US Open at the first attempt. (Michael Cole)

With incredible poise for a 16-year-old, Russia's Anna Kournikova swept to the semi-finals of Wimbledon to emphasise the challenge being made by a fine group of new teenage stars. (Michael Cole)

Corel WTA Tour Year

Barry Wood

The Corel WTA Tour could have chosen a song by '60's group The Association as their theme for 1997. 'Enter the Young' would have been entirely appropriate, as many of the headlines throughout the year were generated by an exciting collection of teenagers. The impact they made also led to an adjustment of the age eligibility rules.

The tennis group was, of course, dominated by Martina Hingis. Her rise in 1996 had been impressive to say the least, and she consolidated her advance in equally remarkable fashion during 1997. She won all but five of her matches, with her first defeat not coming until the final of the French Open. Her preparation had been reduced to just one clay court event in the United States, after which she suffered a knee injury when she fell from a horse. Surgery was required, cancelling her entire European clay court season before she arrived in Paris. Despite the dangers of horse-riding, a passion that matches her love of tennis, and the fact that it ultimately cost her the Grand Slam, Hingis vowed to continue riding.

By the time Hingis suffered her injury she had already set several new records. She became the first woman to win consecutive tournaments on four continents – Sydney and the Australian Open (Australia), Tokyo (Asia), Paris Indoors (Europe) and the Lipton and Hilton Head events (North America). By winning the Lipton in March, she passed the $1 million mark in prize money for the year, reaching that milestone faster than any other woman. Later, by winning the US Open, she became the first woman player to win over $3 million in a season. By winning the Lipton, Hingis also replaced the injured Steffi Graf as the world number one, at 16 years and six months the youngest ever to top the rankings. Monica Seles had previously held the record, at 17 years, three months when she passed Graf in March 1991.

When the year drew to a close, Hingis had won 12 titles and was able to count her defeats on one hand – to Iva Majoli at the French Open, Lindsay Davenport in Los Angeles, Amanda Coetzer in Leipzig, Lisa Raymond in Zurich and Mary Pierce at the Chase Championships.

The door for Hingis was opened by the absence of Graf, who missed almost the entire season, first with illness and then injury, but knee surgery indicated her determination to continue her career rather than settle for an early retirement. She competed though in just four events, defaulting the final in Tokyo in February, suffering the heaviest defeat of her career in Berlin when she earned just one game against Amanda Coetzer, winning Strasbourg but then losing to Coetzer again at the French Open.

Graf's victory in Strasbourg came against 15-year-old Mirjana Lucic of Croatia, who had earlier become the first player ever to win a Tour event on her debut, on home ground in Bol. It was there that she defeated Coetzer in the semi-finals, and she won her first 15 matches on the Corel WTA Tour. Lucic entered the rankings at 69, second only to Capriati's 25 in 1990.

It was Anna Kournikova, though, who attracted more attention – often as much for her model-girl looks and controversial lifestyle as for her tennis. There was a great deal of substance behind the hyping of the young Russian, however, as she demonstrated in no uncertain fashion by reaching the semi-finals of Wimbledon upon her senior debut, emulating Chris Evert's 1972 feat. In one of her Wimbledon matches, against Barbara Rittner, she showed remarkable composure in recovering from a set and 1–5 down, saving two match points on her way to victory.

Both Lucic and Kournikova complained repeatedly about the age restriction rules, introduced a couple of years earlier to protect young players from physical and emotional burnout. Their argument revolved around a new ranking system that rewarded players who played more tournaments, and they considered they were now at an unfair disadvantage.

The WTA responded to their concerns by adjusting the rules, prompted by the US Open who ignored them in allowing Lucic, who was ranked highly enough for direct entry, to play. Previously, 15-year-olds were restricted to eight tournaments a year, none with more than $164,250 in total prize money, and one exhibition or non-tour event. They were not allowed to play in Grand Slam tournaments.

Under the new rules, 15-year-old players who have completed a player development course can play eight regular tournaments regardless of the size of the event, plus Grand Slams and the season-ending Chase Championships if their ranking qualifies them to do so. Kournikova, who turned 16 during the year and had been limited to 14 tournaments, including the Grand Slams and the Chase Championships, will be able to play in three more events. No changes were made in the rules for 14-year-olds, who are permitted to play only in small ITF events.

A lack of playing opportunities has never been an issue with Venus Williams, who has often been criticised for playing so few events. However, she expanded her schedule during 1997 to include overseas tournaments and Grand Slams. Her results though were patchy, and her father/coach, Richard, controversially declined to travel to Europe with her for the French Open and Wimbledon. After a win over Iva Majoli at Indian Wells, Venus failed to make a major impact again until the US Open where, with Richard again strangely absent, she reached the final, the first unseeded woman to do so. That, surely, endorsed Richard's coaching ability.

His positive influence was further emphasised when younger sister Serena, often rumoured to be a better prospect than Venus, defeated both Mary Pierce and Monica Seles in Chicago in November. Ranked 304th, Serena became the lowest ranked player to defeat a player in the top five since Stephanie Rehe defeated Gabriela Sabatini in 1990. She also became the lowest ranked player in Tour history to defeat two top 10 players in the same tournament.

Lindsay Davenport found the consistency that had so long been missing from her game. She claimed six titles, second only to Hingis, winning in Oklahoma, Indian Wells, Amelia Island, Atlanta (where she had won Olympic gold a year before), Zurich and Chicago. In addition, she reached the semi-finals of the US Open and headed the doubles rankings in October.

Jana Novotna and Amanda Coetzer also achieved career-high rankings. Novotna climbed to two in July and finished the year there, after reaching her second Wimbledon final and winning the Chase Championships. She also won titles, in Madrid, Leipzig and Moscow, and shared the Eastbourne title with Arantxa Sanchez Vicario after the final was uncompleted due to rain. Coetzer achieved a ranking of three in November, after winning in Budapest and Luxembourg, and reaching the semi-finals of both the Australian and French Opens.

Impressive strides were made by Iva Majoli, Irina Spirlea, Sandrine Testud and Mary Pierce. Majoli surprised everyone by winning the French Open. She had though already triumphed in Hanover and Hamburg, and she went on to win her first ever match on grass on the way to reaching the Wimbledon quarter-finals. Spirlea held match points to reach her first Grand Slam final at the US Open before losing to Venus Williams, reached the final of Indian Wells, and the semi-finals of Birmingham, Filderstadt and Philadelphia.

Testud won Palermo and reached the final in Atlanta, and excelled with victories over Monica Seles, Arantxa Sanchez Vicario, Lindsay Davenport and Iva Majoli to end the year knocking on the door of the top 10. Mary Pierce was named as the comeback player of the year, winning the Italian Open, and reaching the final at four other venues.

Monica Seles had a solid year, despite missing the first three months with a broken finger. Upon her comeback, she reached the final of both Lipton and Hilton Head, losing twice to Hingis, and later the final of Madrid, losing to Novotna. Hingis also beat her in the semi-finals of the French Open and the final of San Diego. However, the latter part of the year saw her collect titles in Los Angeles, Toronto and Tokyo. At one stage she played seven consecutive events, more than at any other stage of her career. All in all, an impressive achievement against the emotionally anguished background of her father's struggle against cancer.

Seven players won their first career titles – Marion Maruska in Auckland, Ai Sugiyama at the Japan Open, Chanda Rubin in Linz, Mirjana Lucic in Bol, Virginia Ruano-Pascual in Cardiff, Sandrine Testud in Palermo and Henrietta Nagyova in Pattaya.

The escape of the year belonged to Arantxa Sanchez Vicario, who in September saved seven match points against Yayuk Basuki in the semi-finals of the Toyota Princess Cup in Tokyo.

For the first time in the history of the Corel WTA Tour, stretching back to 1971, a top 10 player was unseeded at a regular Tour event. It occurred in Filderstadt, where nine of the top 10 were entered. World number 10, Conchita Martinez, went unseeded. The tournament set another record when, for the first time, three top five players were eliminated in the opening round.

In doubles, 1997 saw the retirement of Gigi Fernandez. In her 15-year career she won 68 titles, including 17 Grand Slams and two Olympic gold medals. She won 36 of her titles, including 14 Grand slams, with Natasha Zvereva, making them one of the most successful teams of all time. She also won two singles titles, and was a Wimbledon semi-finalist.

A highly successful year for the WTA, then, with several young players emerging to offer the promise of an exciting future. It is little wonder that, by the end of October, the Corel WTA Tour had already broken their annual attendance record.

POINTS EXPLANATION

The new Corel WTA Tour ranking system, which came into effect on 26 December 1996, is based on the accumulation of points over a moving 52-week period. A player's points are no longer averaged according to the number of events played as they were in the system that had been in use since 1983.

A player's ranking in singles and doubles depends upon the points won at each tournament, according to the round reached. To these are added 'quality points' which are awarded for beating players ranked in the top 500 (different for singles and doubles).

POINTS ALLOCATION

Equal points are awarded for singles and doubles. The figures beneath each Tier heading indicate minimum prize money.

Category	*W*	*F*	*S/F*	*Q/F*	*R16*	*R32*	*R64*	*R128*	*QFR*	*Q3*	*Q2*	*Q1*
Grand Slams	520	364	234	130	72	44	26	2	16.5	12	6	2
Chase Chps	390	273	175	97	54	—	—	—	—	—	—	—
Tier I (16) $926,250	260	182	117	65	36	—	—	—	—	—	—	—
Tier I (32) $926,250	260	182	117	65	36	1	—	—	11	6	3	1
Tier I (64) $926,250	260	182	117	65	36	22	1	—	6	—	3	1
Tier I (128) $926,250	260	182	117	65	36	22	13	1	11	6	3	1
Tier II (16) $450,000	200	140	90	50	1	—	—	—	—	—	—	—
Tier II (32) $450,000	200	140	90	50	26	1	—	—	9	5	3	1
Tier II (64) $450,000	200	140	90	50	26	14	1	—	5	—	3	1
Tier III (16) $164,250	140	98	63	35	1	—	—	—	—	—	—	—
Tier III (32) $164,250	140	98	63	35	18	1	—	—	7	3	2	1
Tier III (64) $164,250	140	98	63	35	18	10	1	—	4	—	2	1
Tier IV (16) $107,500	80	56	36	20	1	—	—	—	—	—	—	—
Tier IV (32) $107,500	80	56	36	20	10	1	—	—	4.5	3	2	1
Tier IV (64) $107,500	80	56	36	20	10	6	1	—	2.5	—	1.5	1
Other Tournaments												
$75,000 (16)	54	38	24	14	1	—	—	—	—	—	—	—
$75,000	54	38	24	14	7	1	—	—	2.5	2	1.5	1
$50,000 (16)	36	25	16	9	1	—	—	—	—	—	—	—
$50,000	36	25	16	9	5	1	—	—	2.5	2	1.5	1
$25,000 (16)	22	15	10	6	1	—	—	—	—	—	—	—
$25,000	22	15	10	6	3	1	—	—	1.5	1	5	0.25
$10,000 (8)	10	7	5	1	—	—	—	—	—	—	—	—
$10,000 (M)	10	7	5	3	1	—	—	—	—	—	—	—
$10,000 (16)	5	4	2	1.5	1	—	—	—	—	—	—	—
$ 5,000 (8)	5	4	2	1	—	—	—	—	—	—	—	—
$ 5,000 (M)	5	4	2	1.5	1	—	—	—	—	—	—	—

POINTS ALLOCATION *(continued)*

Notes for Qualifiers
1) No points are awarded for doubles qualifying.
2) Players who qualify and then lose in the first round of the main draw receive points indicated in the QFR column on the previous page.
3) Players who qualify and lose after the first round of the main draw will receive QFR points, plus round and quality points.
4) Lucky Losers who lose in the first round of the main draw will receive round points plus any quality points earned in the qualifying.

QUALITY POINTS – SINGLES

Loser's Rank	Points	Grand Slam Points
1	100	150
2	75	113
3	66	99
4	55	83
5	50	75
6–10	43	65
11–16	35	53
17–25	23	35
26–35	15	23
36–50	10	15
51–75	8	12
76–150	4	6
151–250	2	3
251–500	1	1.5

QUALITY POINTS – DOUBLES

Loser's Rank	Points	Grand Slam Points
3–5	100	150
6–10	90	135
11–20	65	97.5
21–30	45	67.5
31–50	30	45
51–80	20	30
81–130	14	21
131–200	9	13.5
201–300	6	9
301–500	4	6
Both Ranked	2	3

GRAND SLAM CHAMPIONSHIPS AND WTA TOUR 1997

DATE	VENUE	SURFACE	SINGLES FINAL	DOUBLES WINNERS
30 Dec–5 Jan	Queensland	Hard	E. Likhovtseva d. A. Sugiyama 3–6 7–6 6–3	Kijimuta/Miyagi
30 Dec–4 Jan	Auckland	Hard	M. Maruska d. J. Wiesner 6–3 6–1	Husarova/van Roost
6–11 Jan	Sydney	Hard	M. Hingis d. J. Capriati 6–1 5–7 6–1	G. Fernandez/Sanchez Vicario
6–12 Jan	Hobart	Hard	D. van Roost d. M. Werdel-Witmeyer 6–3 6–3	Kijimuta/Miyagi
13–26 Jan	**Ford Australian Open**	**Hard**	**M. Hingis d. M. Pierce 6–2 6–2**	**Hingis/Zvereva**
27 Jan–2 Feb	Tokyo, Pan Pacific	Carpet	M. Hingis d. S. Graf w/o	Davenport/Zvereva
3–9 Feb	Linz	Carpet	C. Rubin d. K. Habsudova 6–4 6–2	Fusai/Tauziat
10–16 Feb	Paris	Carpet	M. Hingis d. A. Huber 6–3 3–6 6–3	Hingis/Novotna
17–23 Feb	Hanover	Carpet	I. Majoli d. J. Novotna 4–6 7-6 6–4	Arendt/Bollegraf
17–23 Feb	Oklahoma City, OK	Hard	L. Davenport d. L. Raymond 6–4 6–2	Hiraki/Miyagi
3–16 Mar	Indian Wells, CA	Hard	L. Davenport d. I. Spirlea 6–2 6–1	Davenport/Zvereva
20–30 Mar	Key Biscayne, FL	Hard	M. Hingis d. M. Seles 6–2 6–1	Sanchez Vicario/Zvereva
31 Mar–6 Apr	Hilton Head, SC	Clay	M. Hingis d. M. Seles 3–6 6–3 7-6	M. J. Fernandez/Hingis
7–13 Apr	Amelia Island, FL	Clay	L. Davenport d. M. Pierce 6–2 6–3	Davenport/Novotna
14–20 Apr	Tokyo, Japan Open	Hard	A. Sugiyama d. A. Frazier 4–6 6–4 6–4	Dechaume-Balleret/Hiraki
21–27 Apr	Jakarta	Hard	N. Sawamatsu d. Y. Yoshida 6–3 6–2	Guse/Radford
21–27 Apr	Budapest	Clay	A. Coetzer d. S. Appelmans 6–1 6–3	Coetzer/Fusai
28 Apr–4 May	Hamburg	Clay	I. Majoli d. R. Dragomir 6–3 6–2	Huber/Pierce
28 Apr–4 May	Bol	Clay	M. Lucic d. C. Morariu 7-5 6–7 7-6	Montalvo/Nagyova
5–11 May	Rome	Clay	M. Pierce d. C. Martinez 6–4 6–0	Arendt/Bollegraf
12–18 May	Berlin	Clay	M. J. Fernandez d. M. Pierce 6–4 6–2	Davenport/Novotna
13–18 May	Cardiff	Clay	V. Ruano-Pascual d. A. Dechaume-Balleret 6–1 3–6 6–2	Graham/Guse
19–24 May	Madrid	Clay	J. Novotna d. M. Seles 7–5 6–1	M. J. Fernandez/ Sanchez Vicario
19–24 May	Strasbourg	Clay	S. Graf d. M. Lucic 6–2 7–5	Sukova/Zvereva
19–24 May	Edinburgh, World Doubles Cup	Clay	—	Arendt/Bollegraf
26 May–8 Jun	**French Open**	**Clay**	**I. Majoli d. M. Hingis 6–4 6–2**	**G. Fernandez/Zvereva**
9–16 Jun	Birmingham	Grass	N. Tauziat d. N. Basuki 2–6 6–2 6–2	Adams/Neiland
17–22 Jun	Eastbourne	Grass	J. Novotna & A. Sanchez Vicario (Joint Winners)	McNeil/ Sukova & Arendt/ Bollegraf (Joint Winners)
16–22 Jun	Rosmalen	Grass	R. Dragomir d. M. Oremans 5–7 6–2 6–4	Melicharova/Vildova
23 June–6 Jul	**Wimbledon**	**Grass**	**M. Hingis d. J. Novotna 2–6 6–3 6–3**	**G. Fernandez/Zvereva**
14–20 Jul	Prague	Clay	J. Kruger d. M. Maruska 6–1 6–1	Dragomir/Habsudova
14–20 Jul	Palermo	Clay	S. Testud d. E. Makarova 7–5 6–3	Farina/Schett
21–27 Jul	Stanford, CA	Hard	M. Hingis d. C. Martinez 6–0 6–2	Davenport/Hingis
21–27 Jul	Warsaw	Clay	B. Paulus d. H. Nagyova 6–4 6–4	Dragomir/Gorrochategui
28 Jul–3 Aug	San Diego, CA	Hard	M. Hingis d. M. Seles 7–6 6–4	Hingis/Sanchez Vicario
28 Jul–3 Aug	Maria Lankowitz	Clay	B. Schett d. H. Nagyova 3–6 6–2 6–3	Melicharova/Vildova
4–10 Aug	Manhattan Beach	Hard	M. Seles d. L. Davenport 5–7 7–5 6–4	Basuki/Vis
11–17 Aug	Toronto	Hard	M. Seles d. A. Huber 6–2 6–4	Basuki/Vis
18–24 Aug	Atlanta, GA	Hard	L. Davenport d. S. Testud 6–4 6–1	Arendt/Bollegraf
25 Aug–7 Sep	**US Open**	**Hard**	**M. Hingis d. V. Williams 6–0 6–4**	**Davenport/Novotna**
15–21 Sep	Tokyo, Nichirei	Hard	M. Seles d. A. Sanchez Vicario 6–1 3–6 7–6	Seles/Sugiyama
22–28 Sep	Surabaya	Hard	D. van Roost d. L. Nemeckova 6–1 6–3	Guse/Hiraki
22–28 Sep	Leipzig	Carpet	J. Novotna d. A. Coetzer 6–2 4–6 6–3	Hingis/Novotna
4–5 Oct	**KB Fed Cup Final, Netherlands**	**Carpet**	**France d. Netherlands 4–1**	
6–12 Oct	Filderstadt	Hard	M. Hingis d. L. Raymond 6–4 6–2	Hingis/Sanchez Vicario
13–19 Oct	Zurich	Carpet	L. Davenport d. N. Tauziat 7–6 7–5	Hingis/Sanchez Vicario
20–26 Oct	Quebec City	Hard	B. Schultz-McCarthy d. D. van Roost 6–4 6–7 7–5	Raymond/Stubbs
20–26 Oct	Luxembourg	Carpet	A. Coetzer d. B. Paulus 6–4 3–6 7–5	Neiland/Sukova
27 Oct–2 Nov	Moscow	Carpet	J. Novotna d. A. Sugiyama 6–3 6–4	Sanchez Vicario/Zvereva
3–9 Nov	Chicago, IL	Carpet	L. Davenport d. N. Tauziat 6–0 7–5	Fusai/Tauziat
10–16 Nov	Philadelphia, PA	Carpet	M. Hingis d. L. Davenport 7–5 6–7 7–6	Raymond/Stubbs
17–23 Nov	**Corel WTA Chase Championship**	**Carpet**	**J. Novotna d. M. Pierce 7–6 6–2 6–3**	**Davenport/Novotna**
17–23 Nov	Pattaya	Hard	H. Nagyova d. D. van Roost 7–5 6–7 7–5	Kunce/Morariu

PLAYER NATIONALITIES AND BIRTHDAYS (WOMEN)

The following players have competed in the 1997 Grand Slam Championships, the WTA Tour and Fed Cup ties. (Birthdays dd-mm-yy).

Surname / Forename	*Nation*	*DOB*
ADAMS, Katrina	(USA)	05-08-68
AHL, Lucie	(GBR)	23-07-74
ALAIN, Catherine	(CAN)	13-12-80
ALCAZAR, Ana	(ESP)	08-06-79
ALLEY, Keirsten	(USA)	17-09-73
ANDRETTO, Laurence	(FRA)	12-02-79
ANDRIYANI, Liza	(INA)	02-12-79
ANUCHAN, Montika	(THA)	16-01-80
APPELMANS, Sabine	(BEL)	22-04-72
ARENDT, Nicole	(USA)	26-08-69
ARYANI, Tina	(INA)	
ASAGOE, Shinobu	(JPN)	28-06-76
ATAKA, Miyako	(JPN)	05-04-69
BABEL, Meike	(GER)	22-11-74
BAJIN, Sanja	(CAN)	22-02-80
BARABANSCHIKOVA, Olga	(BLR)	02-11-79
BARCLAY, Catherine	(AUS)	12-06-73
BARNA, Adriana	(GER)	21-05-78
BARNA, Anca	(GER)	14-05-77
BASUKI, Nany 'Yayuk'	(INA)	30-11-70
BEGEROW, Petra	(GER)	14-04-75
BERGER, Segolene	(FRA)	25-03-78
BERNARD, Melanie	(CAN)	14-09-74
BIGGS, Gail	(AUS)	25-08-70
BLESZYNSKI, Anna	(USA)	21-10-76
BOBKOVA, Radka	(CZE)	12-02-73
BOLLEGRAF, Manon	(NED)	10-04-64
BOOGERT, Kristie	(NED)	16-12-73
BRADTKE, Nicole	(AUS)	22-09-69
BRANDI, Kristina	(USA)	29-03-77
BRAVERMAN, Brandis	(USA)	13-02-80
BRIOUKHOVETS, Elena	(UKR)	08-06-71
BUTH, Dawn	(USA)	29-05-76
CACIC, Sandra	(USA)	10-09-74
CALLENS, Els	(BEL)	20-08-70
CANEPA, Alice	(ITA)	30-04-78
CANO, Marta	(ESP)	27-09-75
CAPRIATI, Jennifer	(USA)	29-03-76
CARLSSON, Asa	(SWE)	16-06-75
CASONI, Giulia	(ITA)	19-04-78
CAVANAUGH, Leslie	(USA)	09-02-72
CECCHINI, Anna-Maria 'Sandra'	(ITA)	27-02-65
CENKOVA, Lenka	(CZE)	24-01-77
CHEN, Li Ling	(CHN)	13-03-71
CHERNOVA, Daria	(UKR)	01-01-75
CHERNOVITA, Mimma	(INA)	11-11-74
CHI, Jane	(USA)	21-06-74
CHLADKOVA, Denisa	(CZE)	08-02-79
CHO, Yoon-Jeong	(KOR)	02-04-79
CHOUDHURY, Jasmine	(GBR)	05-04-78
CIANFAGNA, Maria Florencia	(ARG)	30-01-74
COCHETEUX, Amelie	(FRA)	27-03-78
COETZER, Amanda	(RSA)	22-10-71
COURTOIS, Laurence	(BEL)	18-01-76
CRISTEA, Catalina	(ROM)	02-06-75
CROSS, Karen	(GBR)	19-02-74
CSURGO, Virag	(HUN)	10-11-72
CURUTCHET, Emmanuelle	(FRA)	19-12-78
DAVENPORT, Lindsay	(USA)	08-06-76
DE LONE, Erika	(USA)	14-10-72
DE SWARDT, Mariaan	(RSA)	18-03-71
DE VILLE, Stephanie	(BEL)	24-07-76
DE WEILLE, Kim	(NED)	12-04-76
DECHAUME-BALLERET, Alexia	(FRA)	03-05-70
DECHY, Nathalie	(FRA)	21-02-79
DELISLE, Caroline	(CAN)	05-10-69
DELL'ANGELO, Laura	(ITA)	17-05-81
DEMENTIEVA, Elena	(RUS)	15-10-81
DEWI, Cynthia	(INA)	09-01-81
DHENIN, Caroline	(FRA)	13-06-73
DIAZ-OLIVA, Mariana	(ARG)	11-03-76
DOMINIKOVICH, Evie	(AUS)	29-05-80
DOPFER, Sandra	(AUT)	25-05-70
DRAGOMIR, Ruxandra	(ROM)	24-10-72
DRAKE, Maureen	(CAN)	21-03-71
DRAKE-BROCKMAN, Siobhan	(AUS)	07-04-78
DUANGCHAN, Suvimol	(THA)	10-04-74
ELLWOOD, Annabel	(AUS)	02-02-78
ENDO, Mana	(JPN)	06-02-71
ESCOBAR, Marina	(ESP)	02-02-77
FARINA, Silvia	(ITA)	27-04-72
FAUTH, Evelyn	(AUT)	27-11-76
FEBER, Nancy	(BEL)	05-02-76
FEISTEL, Magdalena	(POL)	22-08-70
FERNANDEZ, Gigi	(USA)	22-02-64
FERNANDEZ, Mary Joe	(USA)	19-08-71
FRAZIER, Amy	(USA)	19-09-72
FREYE, Kirstin	(GER)	29-05-75
FRITZ, Lisa	(GER)	28-04-80
FULCO-VILLELLA, Bettina	(ARG)	23-10-68
FUSAI, Alexandra	(FRA)	22-11-73
GAGLIARDI, Emmanuelle	(SUI)	09-07-76
GAIDANO, Maria Jose	(ARG)	25-05-73
GARRISON, Zina	(USA)	16-11-63
GARRONE, Laura	(ITA)	15-11-67
GAVALDON, Angelica	(MEX)	03-10-73
GEORGES, Sophie	(FRA)	08-02-77
GERSI, Adriana	(CZE)	26-06-76
GHIRARDI-RUBBI, Lea	(FRA)	10-02-74
GLASS, Andrea	(GER)	17-07-76
GOLARSA, Laura	(ITA)	27-11-67
GOLOVIZNINA, Maria	(RUS)	05-06-79
GORROCHATEGUI, Ines	(ARG)	13-06-73
GRAF, Stefanie	(GER)	14-06-69
GRAHAM, Deborah 'Debbie'	(USA)	25-08-70
GRANDE, Rita	(ITA)	23-03-75
GROSSMAN, Ann	(USA)	13-10-70
GRZYBOWSKA, Magdalena	(POL)	22-11-78
GUBACSI, Zsofia	(HUN)	06-04-81
GUNAWAN, Marieke	(INA)	14-10-78
GUSE, Kerry-Anne	(AUS)	04-12-72
HAAS, Sabine	(GER)	24-04-75
HABELER, Elisabeth	(AUT)	18-11-74
HABSUDOVA, Karina	(SVK)	02-08-73
HACK, Sabine	(GER)	12-07-69
HAKAMI, Elly	(USA)	25-08-69
HALARD-DECUGIS, Julie	(FRA)	10-09-70
HEISE, Ines	(GER)	09-11-75

Surname / Forename	*Nation*	*DOB*
HELGESON-NIELSEN, Ginger	(USA)	14-09-68
HETHERINGTON, Jill	(CAN)	27-10-64
HIETE, Tracey	(USA)	29-01-71
HINGIS, Martina	(SUI)	30-09-80
HIRAKI, Rika	(JPN)	06-12-71
HOPMANS, Amanda	(NED)	11-02-76
HORN, Liezel	(RSA)	21-08-76
HOSOKI, Yuko	(JPN)	12-11-68
HOTTA, Tomoe	(JPN)	16-04-75
HOULE, Genevieve	(CAN)	08-11-80
HUBER, Anke	(GER)	04-12-74
HUDSON, Rewa	(NZL)	15-09-80
HUSAROVA, Janette	(SVK)	04-06-74
HY-BOULAIS, Patricia	(CAN)	22-08-65
INOUE, Haruka	(JPN)	07-06-77
INOUE, Maiko	(JPN)	05-02-79
IRVIN, Marissa	(USA)	23-06-80
ISKANDAR, Irawati	(INA)	31-10-69
JAGIENIAK, Karolina	(FRA)	04-06-79
JECMENICA, Tatjana	(YUG)	04-07-78
JENSEN, Amy	(AUS)	31-07-78
JENSEN, Rebecca	(USA)	19-11-72
JEON, Mi-Ra	(KOR)	06-02-78
JEYASEELAN, Sonya	(CAN)	24-04-76
JONES, Danielle	(AUS)	04-03-69
JOOSTEN, Franke	(NED)	05-08-74
JOSEPH, Christine	(CAN)	06-05-75
KANDARR, Jana	(GER)	21-09-76
KHELEFI, Ines	(CAN)	15-08-81
KHOO, Chin-Bee	(MAS)	04-05-77
KIJIMUTA, Naoko	(JPN)	26-03-72
KIM, Eun-Ha	(KOR)	08-03-75
KLEINOVA, Sandra	(CZE)	08-05-78
KLOESEL, Sandra	(GER)	22-06-79
KOCHTA, Marketa	(GER)	14-07-75
KOLBOVIC, Renata	(CAN)	30-07-76
KORNIENKO, Irina	(RUS)	16-01-78
KOULIKOVSKAYA, Eugenia	(RUS)	21-12-78
KOURNIKOVA, Anna	(RUS)	07-06-81
KOVES, Nora	(HUN)	13-06-71
KRAJCOVICOVA, Denisa	(SVK)	18-10-68
KREMER, Anne	(LUX)	17-10-75
KRIVENCHEVA, Svetlana	(BUL)	30-12-73
KRIZAN, Tina	(SLO)	18-03-74
KROUPOVA, Katerina	(CZE)	20-02-74
KRUGER, Joannette	(RSA)	03-09-73
KSCHWENDT, Karin	(AUT)	14-09-68
KUKI, Madoka	(JPN)	19-06-76
KUNCE, Kristine	(AUS)	03-03-70
KUTI-KIS, Rita	(HUN)	13-02-78
LABAT, Florencia	(ARG)	12-06-71
LAKE, Valda	(GBR)	11-10-68
LAMARRE, Magali	(FRA)	24-02-78
LANGROVA, Petra	(CZE)	27-06-70
LEE, Janet	(USA)	22-10-76
LEE, Lindsay	(USA)	28-06-77
LEON-GARCIA, Gala	(ESP)	23-12-73
LETTIERE, Angela	(USA)	04-04-72
LI, Fang	(CHN)	01-01-73
LIKHOVTSEVA, Elena	(KAZ)	08-09-75
LIMANTO, Augustine	(INA)	04-08-78
LIMMER, Joanne	(AUS)	29-03-74
LINDSTEDT, Annica	(SWE)	13-04-78
LOIT, Emilie	(FRA)	09-06-79
LOUARSABISHVILI, Nino	(GEO)	03-02-77

Surname / Forename	*Nation*	*DOB*
LUBIANI, Francesca	(ITA)	12-07-77
LUCIC, Mirjana	(CRO)	09-03-82
LUGINA, Olga	(UKR)	08-01-74
LUTROVA, Julia	(RUS)	09-01-75
MAJOLI, Iva	(CRO)	12-08-77
MAKAROVA, Elena	(RUS)	01-02-73
MALEEVA, Magdalena	(BUL)	01-04-75
MANDULA, Petra	(HUN)	17-01-78
MAROSI, Katalin	(HUN)	12-11-79
MARTINCOVA, Eva	(CZE)	04-03-75
MARTINEK, Veronika	(GER)	03-04-72
MARTINEZ, Conchita	(ESP)	16-04-72
MARTINEZ-GRANADOS, Conchita	(ESP)	20-01-76
MARUSKA, Marion	(AUT)	15-12-72
MASANTE, Luciana	(ARG)	04-12-78
MAURESMO, Amelie	(FRA)	05-07-79
MAZZOTTA, Melissa	(VEN)	21-06-72
McGRATH, Meredith	(USA)	28-04-71
McNEIL, Lori	(USA)	18-12-63
McQUILLAN, Rachel	(AUS)	02-12-71
McSHEA, Lisa	(AUS)	29-10-74
MEDVEDEVA, Natalia	(UKR)	15-11-71
MEIER, Silke	(GER)	13-07-68
MEISS, Katrin	(GER)	21-05-77
MELICHAROVA, Eva	(CZE)	20-02-70
MIKKERS, Anne-Marie	(NED)	13-05-73
MILLER, Anne	(USA)	19-01-77
MIYAGI, Nana	(JPN)	10-04-71
MIYAUCHI, Misumi	(JPN)	06-09-71
MOCHIZUKI, Hiroko	(JPN)	23-07-75
MONTALVO, Laura	(ARG)	29-03-76
MONTERO, Araceli	(ESP)	23-03-67
MONTOLIO, Maria-Angeles	(ESP)	06-08-75
MORARIU, Corina	(USA)	26-01-78
MOROS, Cristina	(USA)	10-02-77
MULEJ, Barbara	(SLO)	29-05-74
MURIC, Maja	(CRO)	27-02-74
MUSGRAVE, Trudi	(AUS)	10-09-77
NAGATOMI, Keiko	(JPN)	22-11-74
NAGATSUKA, Kyoko	(JPN)	22-02-74
NAGYOVA, Henrieta	(SVK)	15-12-78
NAREE, Sawitre	(THA)	24-01-81
NEILAND, Larisa	(LAT)	21-07-66
NEJEDLY, Jana	(CAN)	09-06-74
NEJEDLY, Martina	(CAN)	26-05-75
NEKVAPILOVA, Milena	(CZE)	09-05-77
NEMECKOVA, Lenka	(CZE)	20-04-76
NICKITAS, Stephanie	(USA)	08-04-77
NIDEFFER, Rosalyn	(RSA)	02-11-60
NIROJ, Marissa	(THA)	26-04-79
NITTINGER, Nina	(GER)	16-06-76
NOORLANDER, Seda	(NED)	22-05-75
NOVOTNA, Jana	(CZE)	02-10-68
OBATA, Saori	(JPN)	23-04-78
OLSZA, Aleksandra	(POL)	08-12-77
OREMANS, Maria 'Miriam'	(NED)	09-09-72
ORTUNO, Alicia	(ESP)	02-05-76
OSTERLOH, Lilia	(USA)	07-04-78
PALAVERSIC, Maja	(CRO)	24-03-73
PANOVA, Tatiana	(RUS)	13-08-76
PAPADAKI, Christina	(GRE)	24-02-73
PARK, Sung-Hee	(KOR)	17-02-75
PAULUS, Barbara	(AUT)	01-09-70
PAZ, Mercedes	(ARG)	27-06-66

Surname / Forename	*Nation*	*DOB*
PELIKANOVA, Radka	(CZE)	03-04-77
PENA, Laura	(ESP)	01-11-79
PERFETTI, Flora	(ITA)	29-01-69
PIERCE, Mary	(FRA)	15-01-75
PISNIK, Tina	(SLO)	19-02-81
PITKOWSKI, Sarah	(FRA)	13-11-75
PIZZICHINI, Gloria	(ITA)	24-07-75
PLEMING, Louise	(AUS)	22-06-67
PLESU, Ioana	(CAN)	17-12-80
PLISCHKE, Sylvia	(AUT)	20-07-77
PO, Kimberly	(USA)	20-10-71
PORURI, Laxmi	(USA)	09-11-72
PORWIK, Claudia	(GER)	14-11-68
POSPISILOVA, Jana	(CZE)	23-03-70
PRAKUSYA, Wynne	(INA)	26-04-81
PRATT, Nicole	(AUS)	05-03-73
PRAZERES, Sofia	(POR)	19-06-74
PROBST, Wiltrud	(GER)	29-05-69
PULLIN, Julie	(GBR)	05-11-75
QUAST, Isabell	(GER)	17-12-75
RADFORD, Kristine	(AUS)	03-03-70
RANDRIANTEFY, Dally	(MAD)	23-02-77
RAYMOND, Lisa	(USA)	10-08-73
RICHTEROVA, Ludmila	(CZE)	07-03-77
RINALDI-STUNKEL, Kathy	(USA)	24-03-67
RIPPNER, Aubrie 'Brie'	(USA)	21-01-80
RITTNER, Barbara	(GER)	25-04-73
ROESCH, Angelika	(GER)	08-06-77
ROSEN, Hila	(ISR)	05-09-77
RUANO-PASCUAL, Virginia	(ESP)	21-09-73
RUBIN, Chanda	(USA)	18-02-76
SAEKI, Miho	(JPN)	18-03-76
SALVADOR, Elena	(ESP)	15-05-79
SANCHEZ LORENZO, Maria Antonia	(ESP)	07-11-77
SANCHEZ VICARIO, Arantxa	(ESP)	18-12-71
SANDU, Raluca	(ROM)	03-02-80
SANGARAM, Benjamas	(THA)	11-01-75
SAWAMATSU, Naoko	(JPN)	23-03-73
SAWONDARI, Wurtraish	(INA)	20-11-80
SCHETT, Barbara	(AUT)	10-03-76
SCHLUKEBIR, Katrina 'Katie'	(USA)	29-04-75
SCHMIDLE, Syna	(GER)	20-11-78
SCHNEIDER, Caroline	(GER)	01-06-73
SCHNELL, Melanie	(AUT)	22-01-77
SCHNITZER, Miriam	(GER)	14-01-77
SCHNYDER, Patty	(SUI)	14-12-78
SCHULTZ-McCARTHY, Brenda	(NED)	28-12-70
SCHWARTZ, Barbara	(AUT)	27-01-79
SCHWARZ, Petra	(AUT)	24-05-72
SCOTT, Julie	(USA)	16-10-75
SELES, Monica	(USA)	02-12-73
SERNA, Maria-Luisa	(ESP)	01-09-79
SERRA-ZANETTI, Adriana	(ITA)	05-03-76
SERRA-ZANETTI, Antonella	(ITA)	25-07-80
SHAUGHNESSY, Meghann	(USA)	13-04-79
SHRIVER, Pamela 'Pam'	(USA)	04-07-62
SIDDALL, Shirli-Ann	(GBR)	20-06-74
SIDOT, Anne-Gaelle	(FRA)	24-07-79
SIMPSON, Rene	(CAN)	14-01-66
SINGER, Christina	(GER)	27-07-68
SMITH, Samantha 'Sam'	(GBR)	27-11-71
SMYLIE, Elizabeth 'Liz'	(AUS)	11-04-63
SNYDER, Tara	(USA)	26-05-77
SPIRLEA, Irina	(ROM)	26-03-74

Surname / Forename	*Nation*	*DOB*
SRIHADI, Ninisita	(INA)	25-09-80
SROMOVA, Hana	(CZE)	10-04-78
STECK, Jessica	(RSA)	06-08-78
STEINBACH, Lydia	(GER)	30-07-80
STEVEN, Julie	(USA)	24-04-76
STEVENSON, Alexandra	(USA)	15-12-80
STEWART, Bryanne	(AUS)	09-12-79
STOJANOVA, Pavlina	(BUL)	14-07-74
STRANDLUND, Maria	(SWE)	17-08-69
STUBBS, Rennae	(AUS)	26-03-71
STUDENIKOVA, Katerina	(SVK)	02-09-72
SUAREZ, Paola	(ARG)	23-06-76
SUGIYAMA, Ai	(JPN)	05-07-75
SUKOVA, Helena	(CZE)	23-02-65
SULISTYOWATI, Eny	(INA)	14-01-80
TAKUMA, Kazue	(JPN)	04-08-74
TALAJA, Silvija	(CRO)	14-01-78
TAMEISHI, Keiko	(JPN)	22-04-77
TANASUGARN, Tamarine	(THA)	24-05-77
TARABINI, Patricia	(ARG)	06-08-68
TATARKOVA, Elena	(UKR)	22-08-76
TAUZIAT, Nathalie	(FRA)	17-10-67
TAYLOR, Claire	(GBR)	17-02-75
TAYLOR, Jane	(AUS)	07-11-72
TAYLOR, Sarah	(USA)	06-11-81
TEMESVARI, Andrea	(HUN)	26-04-66
TEODOROWICZ, Katarzyna	(POL)	28-11-72
TESTUD, Sandrine	(FRA)	03-04-72
THIMJAPO, Chattida	(THA)	05-10-82
THOMS, Heike	(GER)	01-11-68
TOLU, Suzanne	(FRA)	20-05-79
TORDOFF, Abigail	(GBR)	18-07-79
TORRENS-VALERO, Cristina	(ESP)	12-09-74
TRAIL, Jacqueline 'Jackie'	(USA)	26-11-80
TRISKA, Kristina	(SWE)	06-03-80
TU, Meilen	(USA)	17-01-78
URABE, Nami	(JPN)	29-08-78
URBIN, Karin	(CAN)	19-07-81
VAIDYANATHAN, Nirupama	(IND)	08-12-76
VAN DE ZANDE, Daphne	(BEL)	21-07-74
VAN LOTTUM, Noelle	(FRA)	12-07-72
VAN ROOST, Dominique	(BEL)	31-05-73
VARMUZA, Ludmila	(SMR)	25-02-79
VASKOVA, Alena	(CZE)	08-11-75
VAVRINEC, Miroslava	(SUI)	01-04-78
VENTO, Maria Alejandra	(VEN)	24-05-74
VENTURA, Sara	(ITA)	30-04-76
VILDOVA, Helena	(CZE)	19-03-72
VIS, Caroline	(NED)	04-03-70
WAGNER, Elena	(GER)	17-05-72
WAINWRIGHT, Amanda 'Mandy'	(GBR)	24-03-76
WANG, Shi-Ting	(TPE)	19-10-73
WARD, Jo	(GBR)	22-06-75
WARTUSCH, Patricia	(AUT)	05-08-78
WASHINGTON, Mashona	(USA)	31-05-76
WATANABE, Jolene	(USA)	31-08-68
WEINGARTNER, Marlene	(GER)	30-01-80
WERDEL-WITMEYER, Marianne	(USA)	17-10-67
WHITLINGER-JONES, Tami	(USA)	13-11-68
WIESNER, Judith	(AUT)	02-03-66
WILD, Linda	(USA)	11-02-71
WILLIAMS, Serena	(USA)	26-09-81
WILLIAMS, Venus	(USA)	18-03-77
WITOONPANICH, Pirada	(THA)	21-07-81

Despite injury problems, Brenda Schultz-McCarthy had a good year which included a first win over Monica Seles and a run to the final of the Fed Cup with the Dutch team that was beaten by the French on home soil. (Michael Cole)

Surname / Forename	*Nation*	*DOB*
WOHR, Jasmin	(GER)	21-08-80
WONGKAMALASAI, Orawan	(THA)	25-08-81
WOOD, Clare	(GBR)	08-03-68
WOOD, Jane	(GBR)	20-03-68
WOODROFFE, Lorna	(GBR)	18-08-76
YAMAGISHI, Yoriko	(JPN)	11-03-72
YAZAWA, Kiyoko	(JPN)	08-08-72
YI, Jing-Qian	(CHN)	28-02-74
YOSHIDA, Yuka	(JPN)	01-04-76
ZDENOVCOVA, Magdalena	(CZE)	17-05-78
ZIVEC-SKULJ, Maja	(GER)	25-09-73
ZRUBAKOVA, Radomira 'Radka'	(SVK)	26-12-70
ZULUAGA, Fabiola	(COL)	07-01-79
ZVEREVA, Natalia 'Natasha'	(BLR)	16-04-71

With six tournament wins and a semi-final finish at the US Open, America's Lindsay Davenport rose to No.3 in the year-end rankings, a career high. (Michael Cole)

Corel WTA Tour

Tier I and II Tournaments

SYDNEY INTERNATIONAL ($342,500)
SYDNEY, 6–12 JANUARY
WOMEN'S SINGLES – 1st round: A. Sanchez Vicario (1) bye; A. Frazier d. S. Dopfer (LL) 6–2 6–3; J. Capriati d. C. Rubin 6–3 4–6 6–3; R. Simpson (Q) d. K. Habsudova (6) 6–4 7–5; L. Davenport (4) bye; L. Raymond d. A. Sugiyama 6–1 6–0; N. Sawamatsu d. M. Tu (Q) 7–5 6–3; R. McQuillan (WC) d. B. Schultz-McCarthy (7) 6–4 6–7 6–4; M. J. Fernandez d. A. Coetzer (9) 6–1 3–6 6–2; K. Po d. J. Wiesner 6–2 3–6 6–4; S. Pitkowski (Q) d. N. Zvereva 6–0 6–0; I. Majoli (3) bye; M. Pierce d. I. Spirlea (5) 6–3 4–6 6–4; N. Basuki d. N. Bradtke (WC) 6–3 3–6 6–0; S. Appelmans d. J. Kandarr (Q) 6–0 6–1; M. Hingis (2) bye.
2nd round: Frazier d. Sanchez-Vicario (1) 6–3 6–3; Capriati d. Simpson (Q) 6–3 6–2; Davenport (4) d. Raymond 6–3 6–4; Sawamatsu d. McQuillan (WC) 7–5 6–3; Fernandez d. Po 6–2 6–4; Majoli (3) d. Pitkowski (Q) 6–2 6–1; Basuki d. Pierce 6–4 6–4; Hingis (2) d. Appelmans 6–3 3–6 6–1.
Quarter-finals: Capriati d. Frazier 6–4 6–1; Davenport (4) d. Sawamatsu 6–3 6–7 6–1; Fernandez d. Majoli (3) 7–5 6–4; Hingis (2) d. Basuki 7–6 6–1.
Semi-finals: Capriati d. Davenport (4) 2–6 6–4 6–2; Hingis (2) d. Fernandez 6–3 6–2.
Final: Hingis (2) d. Capriati 6–1 5–7 6–1.
WOMEN'S DOUBLES – Final: G. Fernandez/Sanchez Vicario (1) d. Davenport/Zvereva (2) 6–3 6–1.

TORAY PAN PACIFIC OPEN ($926,250)
TOKYO, 27 JANUARY–2 FEBRUARY
WOMEN'S SINGLES – 1st round: S. Graf (1) bye; L. Raymond d. S. Noorlander (Q) 7–5 6–7 7–5; A. Sugiyama d. A. Dechaume-Balleret (Q) 7–6 6–7 6–4; I. Majoli (5) d. L. Varmuzova (Q) 6–4 7–5; C. Martinez (3) bye; K. Boogert (Q) d. N. Kijimuta 6–2 4–6 6–4; N. Sawamatsu d. H. Nagyova 4–6 6–3 6–3; B. Schultz-McCarthy (8) d. R. Dragomir 5–7 6–4 6–2; L. Davenport (6) d. S-T. Wang 6–1 6–2; T. Tanasugarn (WC) d. N. Zvereva 6–2 6–1; K. Studenikova d. K. Po 6–4 6–1; A. Huber (4) bye; I. Spirlea (7) d. E. Likhovtseva 6–3 6–4; A. Coetzer d. N. Basuki 6–4 6–1; G. Pizzichini d. R. Hiraki (WC) 7–6 4–6 7–6; M. Hingis (2) bye.
2nd round: Graf (1) d. Raymond 6–3 6–2; Majoli (5) d. Sugiyama 7–5 7–5; Martinez (3) d. Boogert (Q) 7–6 1–6 6–3; Schultz-McCarthy (8) d. Sawamatsu 7–6 7–5; Davenport (6) d. Tanasugarn (WC) 6–3 6–1; Huber (4) d. Po 6–4 6–3; Coetzer d. Spirlea (7) 6–4 2–6 6–4; Hingis (2) d. Pizzichini 6–1 6–0.
Quarter-finals: Graf (1) d. Majoli (5) 6–2 6–3; Schultz-McCarthy (8) d. Martinez (3) 6–1 6–0; Huber (4) d. Davenport (6) 6–3 4–6 6–2; Hingis (2) d. Coetzer 6–0 6–1.
Semi-finals: Graf (1) d. Schultz-McCarthy (8) 6–1 7–5; Hingis (2) d. Huber (4) 6–1 5–7 6–2.
Final: Hingis (2) d. Graf (1) w/o.
WOMEN'S DOUBLES – Final: Davenport/Zvereva (2) d. G. Fernandez/Hingis (1) 6–4 6–3.

OPEN GAZ DE FRANCE ($450,000)
PARIS, 10–16 FEBRUARY
WOMEN'S SINGLES – 1st round: M. Hingis (1) bye; S. Farina d. K. Studenikova 3–6 6–1 6–3; N. Tauziat d. F. Labat 6–1 6–2; K. Habsudova (6) d. N. Dechy (WC) 2–6 6–4 6–3; I. Majoli (4) bye; A. Sidot (WC) d. M. Strandlund (Q) 6–2 6–7 6–1; N. Basuki d. B. Schett 6–4 7–5; B. Schultz-McCarthy (7) d. H. Nagyova 4–6 6–1 6–2; I. Spirlea (5) d. E. Likhovtseva 6–4 7–5; C. Rubin d. N. Arendt (Q) 6–1 6–1; S. Appelmans d. M. Maleeva 7–5 6–2; A. Huber (3) bye; M. Pierce (8) d. A. Carlsson 6–2 6–3; A. Gersi (Q) d. A. Glass (Q) 7–5 6–0; K. Boogert (LL) d. S. Testud 0–6 6–1 7–6; J. Novotna (2) bye.
2nd round: Hingis (1) d. Farina 6–3 6–4; Tauziat d. Habsudova (6) 6–4 7–6; Majoli (4) d. Sidot (WC) 6–4 6–3; Basuki d. Schultz-McCarthy (7) 6–4 3–6 6–2; Spirlea (5) d. Rubin 6–3 6–4; Huber (3) d. Appelmans 6–3 6–2; Pierce (8) d. Gersi (Q) w/o; Novotna (2) d. Boogert (LL) 6–2 6–4.
Quarter-finals: Hingis (1) d. Tauziat 6–3 6–2; Majoli (4) d. Basuki 7–6 3–6 6–3; Huber (3) d. Spirlea (5) 6–4 6–2; Novotna (2) d. Pierce (8) 6–1 6–2.
Semi-finals: Hingis (1) d. Majoli (4) 6–1 6–3; Huber (3) d. Novotna (2) 6–3 6–4.
Final: Hingis (1) d. Huber (3) 6–3 3–6 6–3.
WOMEN'S DOUBLES – Final: Hingis/Novotna (1) d. Fusai/Grande 6–3 6–0.

FABER GRAND PRIX ($450,000)
HANOVER, 17–23 FEBRUARY
WOMEN'S SINGLES – 1st round: J. Novotna (1) bye; R. Dragomir (WC) d. B. Rittner 4–6 6–3 7–5; D. van Roost d. D. Chladkova (Q) 7–6 4–6 6–3; E. Likhovtseva (8) d. N. Tauziat 4–6 7–6 6–2; K. Habsudova (4) bye; M. Maleeva d. S. Farina 6–2 6–1; S. Testud (Q) d. S. Kleinova (Q) 4–6 6–4 6–2; B. Schultz-McCarthy (5) d. F. Labat 6–4 7–6; S. Appelmans (7) d. K. Studenikova 6–2 6–3; A. Sidot d. C. Singer (WC) 7–6 6–2; N. Basuki

d. E. Callens 3–6 6–1 6–4; I. Majoli (3) bye; B. Paulus (6) d. A. Miller 6–0 6–0; A. Carlsson d. F. Perfetti (Q) 3–6 6–3 6–4; M. Oremans d. B. Schett 4–6 6–3 7–5; A. Huber (2) bye.
2nd round: Novotna (1) d. Dragomir (WC) 6–2 6–3; Likhovtseva (8) d. van Roost 6–1 6–2; Maleeva d. Habsudova (4) 0–6 6–3 6–2; Testud (Q) d. Schultz-McCarthy (5) 6–4 6–3; Sidot d. Appelmans (7) 6–3 4–6 7–5; Majoli (3) d. Basuki 7–5 6–1; Paulus (6) d. Carlsson 6–3 7–5; Oremans d. Huber (2) 6–0 5–7 6–4.
Quarter-finals: Novotna (1) d. Likhovtseva (8) 6–4 6–2; Maleeva d. Testud (Q) 6–1 6–4; Majoli (3) d. Sidot 4–6 7–6 6–4; Paulus (6) d. Oremans 7–6 6–4.
Semi-finals: Novotna (1) d. Maleeva 6–0 7–5; Majoli (3) d. Paulus (6) 7–6 6–4.
Final: Majoli (3) d. Novotna (1) 4–6 7–6 6–4.
WOMEN'S DOUBLES – Final: Arendt/Bollegraf (2) d. Neiland/Schultz-McCarthy (1) 4–6 6–3 7–6.

STATE FARM EVERT CUP ($1,250,000)

INDIAN WELLS, 7–15 MARCH
WOMEN'S SINGLES – 1st round: A. Sanchez Vicario (1) bye; S. Farina d. N. Miyagi (Q) 6–3 6–4; A. Carlsson d. B. Schett 6–7 6–2 6–2; B. Paulus (10) d. F. Lubiani (LL) 6–7 6–1 6–4; L. Raymond (16) d. J. Kandarr (Q) 7–6 6–2; S. Testud d. A. Sidot 6–7 7–5 6–2; F. Labat d. K. Triska (WC) 6–2 6–1; A. Coetzer (8) bye; A. Huber (3) bye; A. Kournikova d. P. Hy-Boulais 1–6 6–1 6–4; H. Sukova d. G. Pizzichini 6–1 5–7 6–2; N. Tauziat (13) d. S. de Ville 6–1 6–0; E. Likhovtseva (12) d. K. Studenikova 7–6 4–6 7–5; O. Barabanschikova (WC) d. A. Stevenson (WC) 6–4 7–5; A. Dechaume-Balleret (Q) d. K. Kschwendt 6–2 6–2; I. Spirlea (6) bye; I. Majoli (5) bye; N. Zvereva d. M. Endo 6–4 6–1; V. Williams (Q) d. A. Miller 6–2 6–4; A. Sugiyama d. N. Kijmuta 6–4 6–7 7–6; R. Dragomir (14) d. K. Brandi (Q) 6–4 7–5; E. Makarova d. P. Suarez 6–4 7–6; T. Whitlinger-Jones (Q) d. K. Boogert 5–7 6–4 6–3; L. Davenport (4) bye; M. J. Fernandez (9) bye; L. Neiland d. M. Grzybowska (Q) 6–7 6–3 6–2; B. Rittner d. T. Tanasugarn 5–7 6–0 6–2; K. Po (11) d. A. Grossman 5–7 6–0 6–0; C. Rubin (15) d. A. Frazier 6–3 4–6 7–6; N. Sawamatsu d. M. Weingartner (Q) 5–7 6–2 6–2; P. Begerow d. C. Cristea (LL) 6–7 6–1 6–1; C. Martinez (2) bye.
2nd round: Sanchez Vicario (1) d. Farina 6–4 6–2; Carlsson d. Paulus (10) 6–4 6–4; Testud d. Raymond (16) 5–7 6–3 6–4; Labat d. Coetzer (8) 1–6 7–5 7–5; Huber (3) d. Kournikova 3–6 6–2 6–2; Tauziat (13) d. Sukova 6–2 6–2; Likhovtseva (12) d. Barabanschikova (WC) 6–2 6–2; Spirlea (6) d. Dechaume-Balleret (Q) 6–7 7–6 6–2; Majoli (5) d. Zvereva 6–4 6–4; Williams (Q) d. Sugiyama 3–6 6–3 6–2; Dragomir (14) d. Makarova 6–2 3–6 6–2; Davenport (4) d. Whitlinger-Jones (Q) 6–4 6–0; Fernandez (9) d. Neiland 6–3 6–3; Po (11) d. Rittner 7–5 6–2; Rubin (15) d. Sawamatsu 7–5 2–6 7–5: Martinez (2) d. Begerow 6–4 6–2.
3rd round: Sanchez Vicario (1) d. Carlsson 6–1 6–3; Testud d. Labat 6–2 6–2; Tauziat (13) d. Huber (3) 6–4 6–3; Spirlea (6) d. Likhovtseva (12) 6–3 6–4; Williams (Q) d. Majoli (5) 7–5 3–6 7–5; Davenport (4) d. Dragomir (14) 6–2 6–1; Fernandez (9) d. Po (11) 6–2 6–3; Martinez (2) d. Rubin (15) 6–1 1–6 7–5.
Quarter-finals: Sanchez Vicario (1) d. Testud 3–6 6–2 6–2: Spirlea (6) d. Tauziat (13) 6–4 6–2; Davenport (4) d. Williams (Q) 6–4 5–7 7–6; Fernandez (9) d. Martinez (2) 6–4 6–4.
Semi-finals: Spirlea (6) d. Sanchez Vicario (1) 4–6 6–3 6–3; Davenport (4) d. Fernandez (9) 6–1 6–1.
Final: Davenport (4) d. Spirlea (6) 6–2 6–1.
WOMEN'S DOUBLES – Final: Davenport/Zvereva (3) d. Raymond/Tauziat (4) 6–3 6–2.

LIPTON CHAMPIONSHIPS ($1,750,000)

KEY BISCAYNE, 20–30 MARCH
WOMEN'S SINGLES – 1st round: M. Hingis (1) bye; P. Hy-Boulais d. N. Dechy 6–2 6–4; V. Williams (WC) d. G. Helgeson-Nielsen 6–1 4–6 6–3; J. Capriati (23) bye; R. Dragomir (20) bye; I. Gorrochategui d. A. Rippner (WC) 6–4 7–6; J. Watanabe (WC) d. M. Montolio (Q) 2–6 6–3 6–2; E. Likhovtseva (16) bye; M. J. Fernandez (10) bye; A. Ellwood d. D. Chladkova 6–2 6–1; L. Lee (WC) d. C. Cristea 6–3 6–4; M. Maleeva (18) bye; L. Wild (28) bye; M. Grzybowska (Q) d. C. Morariu (WC) 6–1 7–6; A. Sidot d. P. Suarez 6–1 6–4; L. Davenport (5) bye; J. Novotna (3) bye; M. Saeki (Q) d. R. Grande 0–6 6–1 6–3; R. Hiraki d. M. Endo 4–6 6–4 6–3; L. Raymond (22) bye; K. Studenikova (29) bye; T. Tanasugarn d. G. Pizzichini 6–4 6–4; A. Kournikova d. N. Miyagi 6–2 6–0; A. Coetzer (12) bye; K. Po (14) bye; F. Labat d. M. de Swardt 6–2 6–3; M. Serna (Q) d. K. Brandi (WC) 6–3 6–3; B. Schett (32) bye; A. Sugiyama (25) bye; A. Dechaume-Balleret d. H. Sukova 6–3 6–4; S-T. Wang d. R. Zrubakova 6–3 6–4; I. Majoli (8) bye; I. Spirlea (7) bye; F. Perfetti d. M. Shaughnessy (WC) 6–0 4–6 6–3; P. Begerow d. S. Kleinova 7–6 7–6; S. Appelmans (19) bye; C. Rubin (21) bye; A. Grossman d. K. Kschwendt 6–3 6–1; E. Callens d. M. Sanchez Lorenzo (Q) 6–1 6–3; J. Wiesner (13) bye; K. Habsudova (9) bye; N. Zvereva d. P. Langrova 6–4 6–0; M. Tu (WC) d. A. Miller 7–6 6–1; A. Carlsson (30) bye; A. Frazier (27) bye; B. Rittner d. S. de Ville 6–3 6–1; N. Sawamatsu d. S. Farina 4–6 6–1 6–2; M. Seles (4) bye; A. Huber (6) bye; L. McNeil (WC) d. M. Oremans 6–4 6–4; A. Fusai d. M. Maruska 6–4 5–7 6–3; D. van Roost (26) bye; N. Tauziat (17) bye; L. Neiland d. L. Richterova 6–3 7–5; E. Wagner d. T. Whitlinger-Jones 2–6 6–4 6–3; B. Paulus (11) bye; B. Schultz-McCarthy (15) bye; T. Panova (Q) d. D. Randriantefy (Q) 7–6 6–3; P. Schnyder d. A. Gersi 6–1 6–3; S. Testud (24) bye; H. Nagyova (31) bye; J. Kandarr d. S. Smith (Q) 6–7 6–1 7–5; N. Kijimuta d. E. Makarova 7–5 6–1; A. Sanchez Vicario (2) bye.
2nd round: Hingis (1) d. Hy-Boulais 3–6 6–3 6–2; Williams (WC) d. Capriati (23) 7–6 3–6 6–2; Dragomir (20) d. Gorrochategui 2–6 6–3 7–6; Likhovtseva (16) d. Watanabe (WC) 6–2 6–0; Fernandez (10) d. Ellwood 6–4 6–4; Maleeva (18) d. Lee (WC) 6–3 6–3; Grzybowska (Q) d. Wild (28) 6–3 6–3; Davenport (5) d. Sidot 6–4 6–2; Novotna (3) d. Saeki (Q) 4–6 6–3 6–3; Raymond (22) d. Hiraki 6–3 4–6 6–2; Studenikova (29) d. Tanasugarn 6–0 6–2; Kournikova d. Coetzer (12) 6–1 3–6 6–3; Po (14) d. Labat 6–4 6–0; Schett (32) d. Serna

(Q) 6–3 6–3; Sugiyama (25) d. Dechaume-Balleret 6–0 6–1; Majoli (8) d. Wang 6–4 1–6 7–6; Spirlea (7) d. Perfetti 6–2 6–0; Appelmans (19) d. Begerow 6–2 7–5; Rubin (21) d. Grossman 6–2 6–0; Wiesner (13) d. Callens 6–2 6–3; Zvereva d. Habsudova (9) 6–4 6–3; Carlsson (30) d. Tu (WC) 5–7 6–1 6–4; Frazier (27) d. Rittner 6–4 6–3; Seles (4) d. Sawamatsu 6–3 2–6 6–2; Huber (6) d. McNeil (WC) 6–3 6–3; Fusai d. van Roost (26) 6–4 7–6; Tauziat (17) d. Neiland 4–6 7–6 6–4; Paulus (11) d. Wagner 6–1 6–3; Panova (Q) d. Schultz-McCarthy (15) 1–6 7–6 6–4; Testud (24) d. Schnyder 6–4 6–4; Nagyova (31) d. Kandarr 7–6 6–0; Sanchez Vicario (2) d. Kijimuta 4–6 6–3 6–2.
3rd round: Hingis (1) d. Williams (Q) 6–4 6–2; Likhovtseva (16) d. Dragomir (20) 6–7 6–4 7–5; Fernandez (10) d. Maleeva (18) 3–6 6–2 6–4; Davenport (5) d. Grzybowska (Q) 6–2 6–0; Novotna (3) d. Raymond (22) 6–2 6–1; Kournikova d. Studenikova (29) 1–6 6–4 6–0; Schett (32) d. Po (14) 6–3 7–5; Majoli (8) d. Sugiyama (25) 6–3 3–6 6–3; Spirlea (7) d. Appelmans (19) 2–6 6–2 6–3; Rubin (21) d. Wiesner (13) 3–6 6–3 7–5; Carlsson (30) d. Zvereva 6–4 1–6 6–1; Seles (4) d. Frazier (27) 6–3 6–3; Fusai d. Huber (6) 7–6 6–3; Paulus (11) d. Tauziat (17) 6–1 6–7 6–1; Testud (24) d. Panova (Q) 7–6 6–1; Sanchez Vicario (2) d. Nagyova (31) 7–5 4–6 6–4.
4th round: Hingis (1) d. Likhovtseva (16) 6–3 2–6 6–3; Fernandez (10) d. Davenport (5) 6–2 6–4; Novotna (3) d. Kournikova 6–3 6–4; Majoli (8) d. Schett (32) 6–2 4–6 6–2; Spirlea (7) d. Rubin (21) 1–6 7–6 7–6; Seles (4) d. Carlsson (30) 6–2 6–1; Paulus (11) d. Fusai 6–1 2–6 6–1; Testud (24) d. Sanchez Vicario (2) 6–0 7–5.
Quarter-finals: Hingis (1) d. Fernandez (10) 6–4 6–1; Novotna (3) d. Majoli (8) 6–2 3–6 7–6; Seles (4) d. Spirlea (7) 3–6 6–2 6–3; Paulus (11) d. Testud (24) 6–3 6–3.
Semi-finals: Hingis (1) d. Novotna (3) 6–3 2–6 6–4; Seles (4) d. Paulus (11) 6–1 6–0.
Final: Hingis (1) d. Seles (4) 6–2 6–1.
WOMEN'S DOUBLES – Final: Sanchez Vicario/Zvereva (1) d. Appelmans/Oremans (11) 6–2 6–3.

FAMILY CIRCLE MAGAZINE CUP ($926,250)
HILTON HEAD ISLAND, 31 MARCH–6 APRIL
WOMEN'S SINGLES – 1st round: M. Hingis (1) bye; B. Rittner d. G. Pizzichini 6–1 4–6 7–5; B. Schett d. J. Kruger 4–6 6–0 6–0; A. Fusai d. K. Habsudova (10) 7–6 6–3; M. Maleeva (16) d. P. Langrova 7–5 6–4; W. Probst (Q) d. A. Glass (Q) 6–3 3–6 6–4; C. Torrens-Valero (Q) d. F. Perfetti 3–6 7–5 6–1; I. Spirlea (8) bye; J. Novotna (3) bye; P. Schnyder d. T. Whitlinger-Jones (WC) 6–2 7–5; G. Leon-Garcia (Q) d. T. Tanasugarn 6–1 6–4; B. Schultz-McCarthy (14) d. E. Makarova 3–6 7–6 6–4; B. Paulus (12) d. S. Dopfer (Q) 6–0 6–2; V. Ruano-Pascual (Q) d. P. Hy-Boulais 6–2 6–3; M. de Swardt d. N. Zvereva 6–4 2–1 ret; L. Davenport (6) bye; A. Huber (7) bye; L. Raymond d. L. Wild 6–0 6–1; R. Dragomir d. K. Studenikova 5–7 7–6 6–4; I. Majoli (9) d. R. Simpson (Q) 4–6 6–4 6–4; S. Farina d. E. Likhovtseva (15) 1–6 6–3 6–4; A. Gersi d. C. Cristea 6–4 6–0; S-T. Wang d. M. Weingartner (WC) 6–4 7–6; M. Seles (4) bye; C. Martinez (5) bye O. Barabanschikova (Q) d. L. Neiland 7–5 6–0; A. Sugiyama d. A. Grossman 1–6 6–2 6–3; J. Capriati d. M. J. Fernandez (11) 6–3 4–6 7–6; A. Coetzer (13) d. H. Nagyova 6–2 6–3; P. Suarez d. I. Gorrochategui (WC) 7–6 6–2; S. Pitkowski d. F. Labat 0–6 6–4 7–5; A. Sanchez Vicario (2) bye.
2nd round: Hingis (1) d. Rittner 6–0 6–4; Schett d. Fusai 6–1 6–0; Probst (Q) d. Maleeva (16) w/o; Spirlea (8) d. Torrens-Valero (Q) 7–6 6–4; Novotna (3) d. Schnyder 3–6 7–5 6–1; Schultz-McCarthy (14) d. Leon-Garcia (Q) 6–4 6–4; Paulus (12) d. Ruano-Pascual (Q) 6–4 6–1; Davenport (6) d. de Swardt 6–2 6–0; Huber (7) d. Raymond 6–0 6–2; Majoli (9) d. Dragomir 3–6 6–4 6–1; Gersi d. Farina 6–4 6–3; Seles (4) d. Wang 6–3 6–3; Martinez (5) d. Barabanschikova 6–7 6–4 6–3; Capriati d. Sugiyama 6–1 6–0; Coetzer (13) d. Suarez 4–6 6–2 4–0 ret; Sanchez Vicario(2) d. Pitkowski 6–2 6–2.
3rd round: Hingis (1) d. Schett 6–3 6–3; Probst (Q) d. Spirlea (8) 4–1 ret; Schultz-McCarthy (14) d. Novotna (3) 6–3 6–3; Davenport (6) d. Paulus (12) 6–2 6–4; Huber (7) d. Majoli (9) 3–6 7–6 6–3; Seles (4) d. Gersi 6–2 7–6; Martinez (5) d. Capriati 6–0 5–7 6–4; Coetzer (13) d. Sanchez Vicario (2) 6–2 5–7 6–0.
Quarter-finals: Hingis (1) d. Probst (Q) 6–2 6–0; Schultz-McCarthy (14) d. Davenport (6) 4–6 6–4 6–2; Seles (4) d. Huber (7) 6–3 6–0; Martinez (5) d. Coetzer (13) 6–1 6–3.
Semi-finals: Hingis (1) d. Schultz-McCarthy (14) 5–7 6–3 6–2; Seles (4) d. Martinez (5) 6–3 6–4.
Final: Hingis (1) d. Seles (4) 3–6 6–3 7–6.
WOMEN'S DOUBLES – Final: M. J. Fernandez/Hingis (2) d. Davenport/Novotna (1) 7–5 4–6 6–1.

BAUSCH & LOMB CHAMPIONSHIPS ($450,000)
AMELIA ISLAND, 7–13 APRIL
WOMEN'S SINGLES – 1st round: J. Novotna (1) bye; B. Schett d. C. Morariu (Q) 6–4 6–1; A. Mauresmo (WC) d. G. Leon-Garcia (Q) 4–6 7–6 6–2; A. Coetzer (12) d. E. Martincova (Q) 7–5 6–1; M. J. Fernandez (9) d. S. Pitkowski 6–3 6–0; P. Hy-Boulais d. R. McQuillan (Q) 4–6 6–2 6–1; M. Weingartner (WC) d. J. Steck (WC) 7–5 6–3; T. Jecmenica (LL) bye; M. Diaz-Oliva (LL) bye; J. Capriati d. C. Cristea 7–6 6–2; S. Farina d. M. Maruska 7–5 7–5; J. Kandarr (LL) d. C. Torrens-Valero (Q) 6–3 6–2; B. Schultz-McCarthy (13) d. A. Gersi 6–1 6–1; S. Kleinova d. B. Fulco-Villella (Q) 5–7 6–4 6–0; S-T. Wang d. M. Serna 4–6 6–2 6–1; L. Davenport (6) bye; I. Majoli (8) bye; M. Montolio (Q) d. P. Suarez 2–6 6–4 7–6; A. Fusai d. L. Neiland 6–2 7–6; E. Likhovtseva (14) d. T. Whitlinger-Jones 2–6 6–4 6–1; C. Rubin d. B. Paulus (10) 6–4 7–6; V. Williams (Q) d. J. Watanabe 1–6 6–4 6–1; J. Kruger d. P. Schnyder 7–6 5–7 6–4; C. Martinez (4) bye; A. Huber (5) bye; R. Zrubakova d. I. Gorrochategui 6–4 6–3; H. Nagyova d. E. Makarova 6–1 6–4; M. Pierce (11) d. E. Wagner 6–0 6–1; R. Dragomir (16) d. D. Chladkova 6–4 6–2; A. Grossman d. P. Langrova 6–2 6–4; F. Labat d. K. Kschwendt 6–3 6–1; A. Sanchez Vicario (2) bye.
2nd round: Novotna (1) d. Schett 4–6 6–4 6–0; Coetzer (12) d. Mauresmo (WC) 6–4 1–6 6–1; Fernandez (9) d. Hy-Boulais 6–3 6–0; Weingartner (WC) d. Jecmenica (LL) 2–6 7–6 7–5; Diaz-Oliva (LL) d. Capriati w/o;

Kandarr (LL) d. Farina 6–4 7–6; Schultz-McCarthy (13) d. Kleinova 7–5 6–3; Davenport (6) d. Wang 6–2 6–0; Majoli (8) d. Montolio (Q) 6–3 6–2; Fusai d. Likhovtseva (14) 1–6 7–6 6–4; Rubin d. Williams (Q) 6–4 6–0; Martinez (14) d. Kruger 6–3 6–1; Huber (5) d. Zrubakova 6–2 6–2; Pierce (11) d. Nagyova 7–5 6–0; Dragomir (16) d. Grossman 6–2 6–3; Sanchez Vicario (2) d. Labat 3–6 6–2 6–3.
3rd round: Coetzer (12) d. Novotna (1) 6–2 1–6 6–1; Fernandez (9) d. Weingartner (WC) 6–1 6–2; Kandarr (LL) d. Diaz-Oliva (LL) 6–3 6–1; Davenport (6) d. Schultz-McCarthy (13) 6–2 6–1; Majoli (8) d. Fusai 6–0 6–2; Martinez (4) d. Rubin 6–3 6–3; Pierce (11) d. Huber (5) 7–6 6–2; Sanchez Vicario (2) d. Dragomir (16) 6–3 1–6 6–4.
Quarter-finals: Coetzer (12) d. Fernandez (9) 6–2 6–4; Davenport (6) d. Kandarr (LL) 6–2 6–2; Majoli (8) d. Martinez (4) 1–6 6–3 6–3; Pierce (11) d. Sanchez Vicario (2) 6–2 6–1.
Semi-finals: Davenport (6) d. Coetzer (12) 7–5 6–2; Pierce (11) d. Majoli (8) 2–6 7–5 7–6.
Final: Davenport (6) d. Pierce (11) 6–2 6–3.
WOMEN'S DOUBLES – Final: Davenport/Novotna (3) d. Arendt/Bollegraf (4) 6–3 6–0.

REXONA CUP ($450,000)
HAMBURG, 28 APRIL – 4 MAY
WOMEN'S SINGLES – 1st round: A. Sanchez Vicario (1) bye; P. Langrova d. F. Lubiani 6–3 6–3; O. Lugina (Q) d. F. Perfetti 6–4 6–1; A. Sidot d. B. Schultz-McCarthy (5) 6–2 6–1; A. Huber (3) bye; B. Schett d. A. Olsza (Q) 6–2 6–0; F. Labat d. A. Carlsson 6–3 6–2; R. Dragomir (7) d. A. Gersi 6–4 6–3; M. Pierce (6) d. P. Schnyder 6–1 6–1; P. Suarez d. A. Grossman 6–4 6–3; M. Serna d. C. Cristea 4–6 6–3 7–5; I. Majoli (4) bye; M. Sanchez Lorenzo (Q) d. S. Testud (8) 6–3 6–1; J. Kandarr (WC) d. S. Krivencheva (Q) 6–1 7–6; B. Rittner d. S. Kloesel (WC) 6–1 5–7 6–3; C. Martinez (2) bye.
2nd round: Langrova d. Sanchez Vicario (1) 7–5 6–3; Sidot d. Lugina (Q) 6–3 6–3; Schett d. Huber (3) 6–4 7–6; Dragomir (7) d. Labat 7–5 6–3; Pierce (6) d. Suarez 3–6 7–6 6–3; Majoli (4) d. Serna 6–4 7–5; Sanchez Lorenzo (Q) d. Kandarr (WC) 6–2 6–1; Martinez (2) d. Rittner 7–5 6–0.
Quarter-finals: Sidot d. Langrova 6–1 4–6 6–1; Dragomir (7) d. Schett 6–1 7–5; Majoli (4) d. Pierce (6) 2–6 6–4 6–4; Sanchez Lorenzo (Q) d. Martinez (2) 7–5 5–7 6–2.
Semi-finals: Dragomir (7) d. Sidot 6–4 6–0; Majoli (4) d. Sanchez Lorenzo (Q) 6–2 6–3.
Final: Majoli (4) d. Dragomir (7) 6–3 6–2.
WOMEN'S DOUBLES – Final: Huber/Pierce d. Dragomir/Majoli 2–6 7–6 6–2.

ITALIAN OPEN ($926,250)
ROME, 5–11 MAY
WOMEN'S SINGLES – 1st Round: M. Seles (1) bye; B. Schett d. S. Kleinova (Q) 4–6 6–2 7–5; A. Grossman (Q) d. T. Tanasugarn 6–4 6–3; M. Pierce (10) d. A. Cecchini (WC) 6–1 6–1; R. Dragomir (14) d. A. Canepa (Q) 6–3 6–0; E. Callens d. A. Ellwood 6–4 3–6 6–4; N. Arendt (Q) d. L. Golarsa (WC) 6–3 6–2; I. Majoli (5) bye; A. Huber (4) bye; F. Lubiani (WC) d. D. Chladkova 6–2 6–4; A. Gersi d. M. Diaz-Oliva (Q) 7–5 6–3; B. Paulus (11) d. K. Brandi (Q) 3–6 6–3 7–5; N. Tauziat (15) d. H. Sukova 6–4 6–2; D. van Roost d. P. Begerow 6–3 6–0; C. Torrens-Valero (Q) d. S. Pitkowski 2–6 6–3 6–3; I. Spirlea (7) bye; K. Habsudova (8) bye; F. Labat d. O. Barabanschikova (Q) 6–1 7–6; J. Kruger d. A. Sugiyama 6–3 6–2; B. Schultz-McCarthy (9) d. H. Nagyova 6–3 6–4; E. Likhovtseva (12) d. A. Sidot 6–4 6–3; L. Neiland d. F. Perfetti 6–2 3–6 6–2; C. Rubin d. J. Capriati 7–6 6–2; C. Martinez (3) bye; A. Coetzer (6) bye; A. Kournikova d. S-T. Wang 6–4 6–3; P. Schnyder d. N. Basuki 6–0 6–1; S. Testud (16) d. M. Oremans 6–3 3–6 7–6; S. Appelmans (13) d. N. Sawamatsu 6–3 6–1; G. Pizzichini d. A. Fusai 3–6 6–2 7–5; P. Suarez d. K. Studenikova 7–5 7–6; A. Sanchez Vicario (2) bye.
2nd round: Seles (1) d. Schett 7–5 6–0; Pierce (10) d. Grossman (Q) 6–2 6–2; Dragomir (14) d. Callens 3–6 6–2 6–0; Majoli (5) d. Arendt (Q) 7–6 4–6 6–3; Lubiani (WC) d. Huber (4) 6–2 6–2; Paulus (11) d. Gersi 6–1 6–3; van Roost d. Tauziat (15) 6–7 6–1 6–2; Spirlea (7) d. Torrens-Valero (Q) 7–5 7–6; Habsudova (8) d. Labat 6–4 6–3; Kruger d. Schultz-McCarthy (9) 6–2 7–5; Likhovtseva (12) d. Neiland 6–3 6–3; Martinez (3) d. Rubin 6–2 6–3; Coetzer (6) d. Kournikova 6–2 4–6 6–1; Schnyder d. Testud (16) 7–6 6–0; Appelmans (13) d. Pizzichini 6–4 6–3; Sanchez Vicario (2) d. Suarez 6–2 6–2.
3rd round: Pierce (10) d. Seles (1) 7–6 7–6; Dragomir (14) d. Majoli (5) 4–6 6–4 6–3; Paulus (11) d. Lubiani (WC) 6–2 6–1; Spirlea (7) d. van Roost 6–1 6–3; Kruger d. Habsudova (8) 6–2 6–4; Martinez (3) d. Likhovtseva (12) 6–2 6–1; Schnyder d. Coetzer (6) 7–6 7–5; Sanchez Vicario (2) d. Appelmans (13) 6–3 6–4.
Quarter-finals: Pierce (10) d. Dragomir (14) 6–3 6–4; Paulus (11) d. Spirlea (7) 6–4 6–2; Martinez (3) d. Kruger 6–0 6–4; Schnyder d. Sanchez Vicario (2) 6–1 6–1.
Semi-finals: Pierce (10) d. Paulus (11) 4–6 6–3 6–1; Martinez (3) d. Schnyder 6–2 6–2.
Final: Pierce (10) d. Martinez (3) 6–4 6–0.
WOMEN'S DOUBLES – Final: Arendt/Bollegraf (2) d. Martinez/Tarabini (6) 6–2 6–4.

GERMAN OPEN ($926,250)
BERLIN, 12–18 May
WOMEN'S SINGLES – 1st round: S. Graf (1) bye; C. Rubin d. P. Hy-Boulais 7–5 6–2; A. Fusai d. T. Tanasugarn 7–5 6–3; R. Dragomir (15) d. N. Zvereva 7–6 6–2; J. Wiesner (14) d. L. Courtois 6–0 6–2; L. Neiland d. A. Sidot 6–3 6–4; K. Studenikova d. J. Kruger (Q) 6–1 6–4; A. Coetzer (7) bye; C. Martinez (4) bye; N. Basuki d. S-T. Wang 6–4 6–3; S. Kleinova d. J. Kandarr 6–4 6–2; M. Pierce (12) d. E. Wagner (WC) 6–2 6–3; K. Habsudova (9) d. S. Kloesel (WC) 7–5 6–3; G. Pizzichini d. P. Suarez 7–6 4–6 6–1; I. Gorrochategui (Q)

d. W. Probst (Q) 6–4 6–3; I. Majoli (6) bye; A. Sanchez Vicario (5) bye; B. Schett d. F. Labat 6–1 6–0; A. Kournikova d. S. Plischke (Q) 6–2 6–2; A. Gersi d. B. Paulus (13) 7–5 6–7 6–4; M. J. Fernandez (10) d. F. Perfetti 6–4 3–6 6–1; M. Sanchez Lorenzo (Q) d. H. Nagyova 6–2 4–6 6–3; S. Testud d. A. Sugiyama 6–2 6–1; L. Davenport (3) bye; I. Spirlea (8) bye; T. Panova (Q) d. M. Serna (LL) 6–2 7–6; S. Appelmans d. E. Makarova (Q) 6–2 7–6; B. Schultz-McCarthy (11) d. P. Schnyder 6–1 6–4; E. Martincova (Q) d. E. Likhovtseva (16) 6–1 6–4; N. Tauziat d. A. Glass (WC) 6–7 6–1 6–1; B. Rittner d. E. Callens 6–1 6–0; J. Novotna (2) bye.
2nd round: Graf (1) d. Rubin 6–3 3–6 6–1; Dragomir (15) d. Fusai 6–2 6–2; Wiesner (14) d. Neiland 7–6 6–1; Coetzer (7) d. Studenikova 6–0 6–0; Martinez (4) d. Basuki 6–3 5–7 6–3; Pierce (12) d. Kleinova 6–3 2–6 6–2; Pizzichini d. Habsudova (9) 6–4 4–2 ret; Majoli (6) d. Gorrochategui (Q) 6–3 7–5; Sanchez Vicario (5) d. Schett 6–2 4–6 7–5; Kournikova d. Gersi 6–0 6–3; Fernandez (10) d. Sanchez Lorenzo (Q) 6–4 1–6 6–3; Testud d. Davenport (3) 7–6 7–6; Spirlea (8) d. Panova (Q) 7–6 6–1; Appelmans d. Schultz-McCarthy (11) 1–0 ret; Tauziat d. Martincova (Q) 6–2 6–4; Novotna (2) d. Rittner 6–4 2–6 7–5.
3rd round: Graf (1) d. Dragomir (15) 6–3 6–2; Coetzer (7) d. Wiesner (14) 6–1 6–1; Pierce (12) d. Martinez (4) 6–2 6–0; Majoli (6) d. Pizzichini 6–4 6–2; Kournikova d. Sanchez Vicario (5) 3–6 6–0 6–3; Fernandez (10) d. Testud 6–2 6–2; S. Appelmans d. Spirlea (8) 7–6 2–6 6–3; Novotna (2) d. Tauziat 6–0 6–2.
Quarter-finals: Coetzer (7) d. Graf (1) 6–0 6–1; Pierce (12) d. Majoli (6) 6–1 6–4; Fernandez (10) d. Kournikova 6–1 6–4; Novotna (2) d. Appelmans 1–6 6–2 6–0.
Semi-finals: Pierce (12) d. Coetzer (7) 6–4 6–4; Fernandez (10) d. Novotna (2) 6–3 6–1.
Final: Fernandez (10) d. Pierce (12) 6–4 6–2.
WOMEN'S DOUBLES – Final: Davenport/Novotna (2) d. G. Fernandez/Zvereva (1) 6–2 3–6 6–2.

OPEN PAGINAS AMARILLAS VILLE DE MADRID ($175,000)
MADRID, 19–24 MAY
WOMEN'S SINGLES – 1st round: M. Seles (1) bye; M. Sanchez Lorenzo d. V. Martinek 6–1 6–0; V. Ruano-Pascual d. L. Wild 4–6 7–6 6–1; A. Frazier (8) d. L. Pena (WC) 6–4 6–3; I. Spirlea (4) d. A. Ellwood 6–3 6–4; A. Cecchini d. R. Grande 7–5 6–3; F. Labat d. L. Nemeckova 6–2 6–1; M. Maruska d. K. Po (6) 3–6 6–2 6–4; P. Schnyder d. L. Raymond (7) 6–1 6–2; A. Grossman d. F. Lubiani 7–5 7–5; C. Cristea d. T. Whitlinger-Jones 7–6 6–4; A. Sanchez Vicario (3) d. M. Serna 6–2 6–1; I. Gorrochategui d. M. J. Fernandez (5) 6–2 6–3; G. Leon-Garcia d. R. Hiraki 6–2 6–4; A. Carlsson d. E. Salvador (WC) 6–0 6–0; J. Novotna (2) bye.
2nd round: Seles (1) d. Sanchez Lorenzo 6–0 6–1; Ruano-Pascual d. Frazier (8) 6–0 6–0; Spirlea (4) d. Cecchini 6–1 6–2; Labat d. Maruska 6–2 6–2; Grossman d. Schnyder 7–6 4–6 7–5; Sanchez Vicario (3) d. Cristea 4–6 6–0 6–0; Leon-Garcia d. Gorrochategui 6–3 3–6 6–2; Novotna (2) d. Carlsson 6–2 6–2.
Quarter-finals: Seles (1) d. Ruano-Pascual 6–2 6–1; Labat d. Spirlea (4) 6–2 7–5; Sanchez Vicario (3) d. Grossman 6–1 6–1; Novotna (2) d. Leon-Garcia 6–3 6–4.
Semi-finals: Seles (1) d. Labat 6–7 6–1 6–2; Novotna (2) d. Sanchez Vicario (3) 6–4 6–4.
Final: Novotna (2) d. Seles (1) 7–5 6–1.
WOMEN'S DOUBLES – Final: M. J. Fernandez/Sanchez Vicario (1) d. Gorrochategui/ Spirlea 6–3 6–2.

DIRECT LINE INSURANCE CHAMPIONSHIPS ($450,000)
EASTBOURNE, 17–22 JUNE
WOMEN'S SINGLES – 1st round: M. Seles (1) bye; N. Sawamatsu d. J. Ward (Q) 6–2 7–5; S. Farina d. L. Raymond 7–5 6–4; B. Schultz-McCarthy (8) d. H. Sukova 6–3 7–6; A. Sanchez Vicario (4) bye; K. Guse (Q) d. S-T. Wang 6–3 5–7 6–4; A. Sidot d. L. Ahl (WC) 6–3 6–4; I. Spirlea (6) d. I. Gorrochategui (Q) 6–0 3–6 6–4; N. Tauziat d. M. J. Fernandez (5) 7–6 7–5; V. Williams (Q) d. C. Rubin 6–4 6–4; N. Zvereva d. A. Frazier 7–6 6–0; I. Majoli (3) bye; K. Po (7) d. K. Studenikova 0–6 7–6 6–2; A. Sugiyama d. S. Siddall (WC) 6–2 5–7 8–6; N. Basuki d. E. Likhovtseva 6–3 6–0; J. Novotna (2) bye.
2nd round: Seles (1) d. Sawamatsu 6–2 7–5; Schultz-McCarthy (8) d. Farina 4–6 6–1 6–2; Sanchez Vicario (4) d. Guse (Q) 7–5 6–0; Spirlea (6) d. Sidot 6–4 6–3; Tauziat d. Williams (Q) 6–3 5–7 6–4; Zvereva d. Majoli (3) 6–2 7–5; Sugiyama d. Po (7) 6–3 6–1; Novotna (2) d. Basuki 7–5 6–4.
Quarter-finals: Schultz-McCarthy (8) d. Seles (1) 7–5 7–5; Sanchez Vicario (4) d, Spirlea (6) 6–4 6–4; Zvereva d. Tauziat 6–4 5–7 6–4; Novotna (2) d. Sugiyama 6–2 6–7 6–4.
Semi-finals: Sanchez Vicario (4) d. Schultz-McCarthy (8) 7–5 6–1; Novotna (2) d. Zvereva 6–7 6–0 7–5.
Final: Abandoned due to rain. Novotna and Sanchez Vicario shared the title.
WOMEN'S DOUBLES – Final: Abandoned due to rain.

BANK OF THE WEST CLASSIC ($450,000)
STANFORD, 21–27 JULY
WOMEN'S SINGLES – 1st round: M. Hingis (1) bye; M. Maleeva d. J. Nejedly (Q) 6–0 6–3; L. Wild d. L. McNeil (WC) 6–4 7–5; A. Kremer (WC) d. M. Pierce (5) 3–6 6–1 6–4; L. Davenport (4) bye; S. Cacic (LL) d. A. Grossman 6–2 6–2; E. Likhovtseva d. P. Hy-Boulais 6–3 6–2; L. Raymond (8) d. F. Lubiani 6–4 6–3; K. Po (7) d. M. Schnitzer (Q) 6–2 6–4; A. Sugiyama d. A. Miller 6–2 2–6 6–3; M. Tu d. E. de Lone (Q) 7–5 5–7 6–0; A. Coetzer (3) bye; C. Martinez (6) d. S. Drake-Brockman (Q) 6–3 6–2; A. Frazier d. N. Kijimuta 4–6 6–0 6–0; R. Grande d. O. Barabanschikova 6–4 7–6; M. Seles (2) bye.
2nd round: Hingis (1) d. Maleeva 6–1 6–2; Wild d. Kremer (WC) 6–3 6–4; Davenport (4) d. Cacic (LL) 6–2 6–2; Likhovtseva d. Raymond (8) 6–4 6–3; Po (7) d. Sugiyama 6–3 6–1; Coetzer (3) d. Tu 6–2 6–0; Martinez (6) d. Frazier 6–1 6–1; Seles (2) d. Grande 6–2 6–1.

Quarter-finals: Hingis (1) d. Wild 6–1 6–7 6–3; Davenport (4) d. Likhovtseva 7–6 6–3; Coetzer (3) d. Po (7) 7–5 6–4; Martinez (6) d. Seles (2) 7–6 6–4.
Semi-finals: Hingis (1) d. Davenport (4) 6–3 1–6 6–2; Martinez (6) d. Coetzer (3) 6–4 6–0.
Final: Hingis (1) d. Martinez (6) 6–0 6–2.
WOMEN'S DOUBLES – Final: Davenport/Hingis (1) d. Martinez/Tarabini (3) 6–1 6–3.

TOSHIBA TENNIS CLASSIC ($450,000)

SAN DIEGO, 28 JULY–3 AUGUST
WOMEN'S SINGLES – 1st round:
M. Hingis (1) bye; V. Williams (Q) d. F. Labat 6–3 6–2; H. Sukova d. C. Rubin 7–5 3–0 ret; C. Martinez (7) d. L. Raymond 6–3 3–6 6–1; A. Sanchez Vicario (WC) (4) bye; S. Testud d. A. Carlsson 6–1 6–2; N. Tauziat d. R. Grande (Q) 7–5 6–1; M. Pierce (6) d. A. Frazier 6–3 6–7 6–3; A. Huber (5) d. M. Maleeva 7–5 1–6 6–3; N. Basuki d. A. Miller (Q) 6–1 6–3; A. Sidot d. S. Drake-Brockman (Q) 7–5 6–3; A. Coetzer (3) bye; I. Spirlea (8) d. E. Likhovtseva 6–3 6–3; N. Zvereva d. K. Po 7–6 2–6 6–1; A. Sugiyama d. A. Stevenson (WC) 6–3 6–1; M. Seles (2) bye.
2nd round: Hingis (1) d. Williams (Q) 6–2 6–1; Martinez (7) d. Sukova 6–1 6–0; Testud d. Sanchez Vicario (WC) (4) 6–1 6–2; Pierce (6) d. Tauziat 6–2 6–1; Basuki d. Huber (5) 6–2 2–6 6–2; Coetzer (3) d. Sidot 6–2 6–1; Zvereva d. Spirlea (8) 6–2 6–0; Seles (2) d. Sugiyama 6–4 6–4.
Quarter-finals:. Hingis (1) d. Martinez (7) 6–4 6–4; Pierce (6) d. Testud 6–3 6–2; Coetzer (3) d. Basuki 6–3 6–4; Seles (2) d. Zvereva 6–1 6–3.
Semi-finals: Hingis (1) d. Pierce (6) 6–0 6–2; Seles (2) d. Coetzer (3) 6–3 6–4.
Final: Hingis (1) d. Seles (2) 7–6 6–4.
WOMEN'S DOUBLES – Final: Hingis/Sanchez Vicario (2) d. Frazier/Po (1) 6–3 7–5.

ACURA CLASSIC ($450,000)

MANHATTAN BEACH, 4–10 AUGUST
WOMEN'S SINGLES – 1st round: M. Hingis (1) bye; A. Sidot d. E. Likhovtseva 6–3 6–2; V. Williams (WC) d. A. Grossman (Q) 6–0 6–3; A. Huber (6) d. A. Kournikova (WC) 6–0 6–1; L. Davenport (4) bye; N. Basuki d. S. Appelmans 3–6 7–6 6–1; N. Tauziat d. M. Maleeva 6–4 7–6; K. Po (8) d. M. Serna (Q) 7–5 6–1; A. Sanchez Vicario (5) d. N. Sawamatsu 6–2 7–6; A. Sugiyama d. H. Sukova 3–6 6–2 6–3; A. Frazier d. T. Panova (Q) 6–1 6–0; A. Coetzer (3) bye; N. Zvereva d. I. Spirlea (7) 6–4 6–3; R. Dragomir d. N. Kijimuta (Q) 7–6 7–5; S. Testud d. C. Rubin 6–4 6–2; M. Seles (2) bye.
2nd round: Hingis (1) d. Sidot 6–2 6–2; Huber (6) d. Williams (WC) 7–6 6–4; Davenport (4) d. Basuki 6–1 6–1; Tauziat d. Po (8) 7–6 4–6 6–4; Sanchez Vicario (5) d. Sugiyama 6–3 7–5; Frazier d. Coetzer (3) 6–1 6–3; Zvereva d. Dragomir 6–2 4–6 7–6; Seles (2) d. Testud 6–7 7–6 6–3.
Quarter-finals: Hingis (1) d. Huber (6) 6–3 6–0; Davenport (4) d. Tauziat 6–1 3–6 6–3; Frazier d. Sanchez Vicario (5) 3–6 6–1 6–3; Seles (2) d. Zvereva 6–1 6–1.
Semi-finals: Davenport (4) d. Hingis (1) 6–2 4–6 6–4; Seles (2) d. Frazier 6–0 6–2.
Final: Seles (2) d. Davenport (4) 5–7 7–5 6–4.
WOMEN'S DOUBLES – Final: Basuki/Vis d. Neiland/Sukova (4) 7–6 6–3.

DU MAURIER OPEN ($926,250)

TORONTO, 11–17 AUGUST
WOMEN'S SINGLES – 1st round: M. Seles (1) bye; A. Carlsson d. A. Grossman (Q) 6–4 6–3; A. Fusai d. S. Pitkowski 6–1 6–0; S. Appelmans (16) d. P. Hy-Boulais (WC) 6–3 6–3; T. Tanasugarn d. R. Dragomir (13) 6–0 6–1; R. Grande (Q) d. B. Rittner 6–2 3–6 6–3; S. Jeyaseelan (Q) d. M. Babel 6–4 7–6; M. Pierce (6) bye; L. Davenport (WC) (4) bye; A. Sugiyama d. E. Callens 6–4 6–3; M. Serna d. R. Kolbovic (Q) 6–2 6–2; M. Saeki (Q) d. I. Spirlea (9) 4–6 6–3 6–2; N. Kijimuta d. B. Schultz-McCarthy (12) 6–4 2–6 6–3; N. Basuki d. S. Kleinova 6–3 6–0; Y. Yoshida d. A. Ellwood 5–7 6–3 6–1; C. Martinez (7) bye; A. Huber (8) bye; F. Labat d. L. Wild 6–2 6–0; L. Raymond d. A. Glass (Q) 6–2 6–1; S. Testud (15) d. M. Sanchez Lorenzo 7–5 6–2; K. Po (11) d. N. Tauziat 6–1 7–6; J. Capriati d. S. Farina 6–4 6–3; N. Dechy (Q) d. V. Williams 6–1 1–6 6–1; A. Coetzer (3) bye; A. Sanchez Vicario (5) bye; A. Miller d. E. Likhovtseva 7–6 2–6 6–3; N. Arendt d. H. Sukova 6–2 6–4; M. J. Fernandez (10) d. J. Kruger 6–4 7–5; M. Maleeva d. K. Habsudova (14) 6–3 6–3; F. Lubiani (LL) d. T. Panova (Q) 6–2 7–6; N. Sawamatsu d. C. Rubin 6–1 6–4; I. Majoli (2) bye.
2nd round: Seles (1) d. Carlsson 6–2 6–4; Appelmans (16) d. Fusai 6–3 6–3; Grande (Q) d. Tanasugarn 6–4 2–6 6–2; Pierce (6) d. Jeyaseelan (Q) 6–1 6–1; Davenport (WC) (4) d. Sugiyama 6–2 7–6; Serna d. Saeki (Q) 7–6 4–6 6–3; Basuki d. Kijimuta 6–4 6–2; Martinez (7) d. Yoshida 6–3 3–6 6–1; Huber (8) d. Labat 6–2 6–1; Testud (15) d. Raymond 6–3 6–3; Po (11) d. Capriati 6–3 6–2; A. Coetzer (3) d. N. Dechy (Q) 4–6 6–4 6–2; Sanchez Vicario (5) d. Miller 6–2 6–1; Fernandez (10) d. Arendt 6–4 6–2; Maleeva d. Lubiani (LL) 6–7 6–4 6–4; Sawamatsu d. Majoli (2) 7–5 6–7 6–1.
3rd round: Seles (1) d. Appelmans (16) 6–3 7–5; Grande (Q) d. Pierce (6) 6–2 6–2; Davenport (WC) (4) d. Serna 7–5 6–4; Martinez (7) d. Basuki 6–1 6–4; Huber (8) d. Testud (15) 6–3 6–4; Coetzer (3) d. Po (11) 6–3 6–3; Fernandez (10) d. Sanchez Vicario (5) 6–4 6–3; Maleeva d. Sawamatsu 7–5 6–4.
Quarter-finals: Seles (1) d. Grande (Q) 6–0 6–0; Martinez (7) d. Davenport (WC) (4) 6–4 4–6 6–2; Huber (8) d. Coetzer (3) 2–6 6–1 6–4; Fernandez (10) d. Maleeva 6–2 6–7 6–4.
Semi-finals: Seles (1) d. Martinez (7) 6–2 7–6; Huber (8) d. Fernandez (10) 3–6 6–2 ret.

Final: Seles (1) d. Huber (8) 6–2 6–4.
WOMEN'S DOUBLES – Final: Basuki/Vis (6) d. Arendt/Bollegraf (2) 3–6 7–5 6–4.

US HARDCOURT CHAMPIONSHIPS ($450,000)

ATLANTA, 18–24 AUGUST

WOMEN'S SINGLES – 1st round: J. Novotna (1) bye; N. Basuki d. M. Babel 6–4 7–6; N. Tauziat (Q) d. A. Carlsson 6–4 6–3; A. Coetzer (5) d. L. Wild (WC) 6–1 6–2; L. Davenport (4) bye; P. Schnyder d. F. Labat (Q) 6–3 6–2; D. van Roost d. A. Miller (Q) 6–1 6–3; R. Dragomir (7) d. A. Sidot 6–3 6–3; B. Schultz-McCarthy (6) d. P. Hy-Boulais (Q) 7–6 7–6; S. Farina (LL) d. M. Maleeva 6–3 7–6; E. Likhovtseva d. S. Appelmans 4–6 7–6 4–2 ret; I. Majoli (3) bye; S. Testud d. K. Habsudova (8) 6–3 6–1; C. Rubin d. H. Sukova 6–1 6–2; N. Sawamatsu d. A. Sugiyama 7–6 6–4; M. Seles (2) bye.
2nd round: Novotna (1) d. Basuki 4–6 6–2 6–2; Coetzer (5) d. Tauziat (Q) 6–2 5–7 6–2; Davenport (4) d. Schnyder 6–3 6–2; van Roost d. Dragomir (7) 6–0 6–2; Schultz-McCarthy (6) d. Farina (LL) 1–1 ret; Majoli (3) d. Likhovtseva 6–2 3–6 6–4; Testud d. Rubin 6–4 6–1; Seles (2) d. Sawamatsu 6–4 6–3.
Quarter-finals: Coetzer (5) d. Novotna (1) 1–6 6–3 6–1; Davenport (4) d. van Roost 6–1 7–5; Majoli (3) d. Schultz-McCarthy (6) 6–2 7–5; Testud d. M. Seles (2) w/o .
Semi-finals: Davenport (4) d. Coetzer (5) 6–2 6–4; Testud d. Majoli (3) 7–5 6–3.
Final: Davenport (4) d. Testud 6–4 6–1.
WOMEN'S DOUBLES – Final: Arendt/Bollegraf (1) d. Fusai/Tauziat (3) 6–7 6–3 6–2.

NICHIREI INTERNATIONAL LADIES CHAMPIONSHIPS ($450,000)

TOKYO, 15–21 SEPTEMBER

WOMEN'S SINGLES – 1st round: M. Seles (1) bye; T. Tanasugarn d. M. Maleeva 0–6 6–4 6–2; A. Sugiyama d. A. Ellwood 6–3 6–2; N. Zvereva (8) d. J. Halard-Decugis 4–6 6–3 6–2; C. Martinez (3) bye; S-T. Wang d. N. Kijimuta 4–6 6–3 6–1; M. Endo (Q) d. C. Torrens-Valero 6–4 7–5; N. Sawamatsu d. H. Nagyova (9) 2–6 6–4 6–1; N. Basuki (5) d. S. Pitkowski 7–5 7–6; M. Saeki (WC) d. H. Inoue (LL) 6–4 6–4; R. Hiraki (WC) d. Y. Yoshida 6–4 6–1; K. Po (4) bye; M. Vento (Q) d. P. Schnyder (7) 6–4 6–0; F. Li (Q) d. M. Serna 7–5 7–5; S. Asagoe (Q) d. C. Rubin 6–4 6–3; A. Sanchez Vicario (2) bye.
2nd round: Seles (1) d. Tanasugarn 6–1 6–4; Zvereva (8) d. Sugiyama 6–2 6–3; Martinez (3) d. Wang 6–1 6–3; Sawamatsu d. Endo (Q) 3–6 6–4 6–2; Basuki (5) d. Saeki (WC) 6–7 6–4 6–2; Po (4) d. Hiraki (WC) 3–6 7–6 6–3; Li (Q) d. Vento (Q) 7–5 6–2; Sanchez Vicario (2) d. Asagoe (Q) 6–0 6–0.
Quarter-finals: Seles (1) d. Zvereva (8) 6–1 6–0; Sawamatsu d. Martinez (3) 7–6 6–4; Basuki (5) d. Po (4) 7–5 6–3; Sanchez Vicario (2) d. Li (Q) 6–3 7–5.
Semi-finals: Seles (1) d. Sawamatsu 6–3 6–1; Sanchez Vicario (2) d. Basuki (5) 1–6 7–6 6–4.
Final: Seles (1) d. Sanchez Vicario (2) 6–1 3–6 7–6.
WOMEN'S DOUBLES – Final: Seles/Sugiyama d. Halard-Decugis/Rubin 6–1 6–0.

PORSCHE TENNIS GRAND PRIX ($450,000)

FILDERSTADT, 6–12 OCTOBER

WOMEN'S SINGLES – 1st round: M. Hingis (1) bye; N. Zvereva d. C. Martinez (WC) 6–1 6–0; R. Grande (Q) d. S. Testud 7–6 6–3; M. Maleeva d. A. Sidot (LL) 6–7 6–4 6–3; I. Majoli (3) bye; P. Schnyder (Q) d. H. Sukova 7–6 6–2; A. Kournikova (WC) d. B. Schett (Q) 6–3 7–6; A. Coetzer (5) d. B. Schultz-McCarthy 7–6 6–3; I. Spirlea (8) d. R. Dragomir 6–2 6–0; K. Habsudova d. J. Capriati 6–2 6–1; A. Sanchez Vicario d. J. Wiesner 6–2 7–5; L. Davenport (4) bye; M. J. Fernandez d. A. Huber (6) 6–4 6–4; N. Sawamatsu d. S. Appelmans 6–3 6–2; L. Raymond d. S. Farina (Q) 6–3 6–2; J. Novotna (2) bye.
2nd round: Hingis (1) d. Zvereva 4–6 6–1 6–4; Maleeva d. Grande (Q) 6–2 6–3; Schnyder (Q) d. Majoli (3) 6–2 6–2; Coetzer (5) d. Kournikova (WC) 3–6 6–3 6–4; Spirlea (8) d. Habsudova 6–2 6–0; Sanchez Vicario d. Davenport (4) 6–4 7–6; Sawamatsu d. Fernandez 6–2 0–6 6–3; Raymond d. Novotna (2) 3–6 6–4 6–4.
Quarter-finals: Hingis (1) d. Maleeva 6–2 6–3; Coetzer (5) d. Schnyder (Q) 6–2 7–5; Spirlea (8) d. Sanchez Vicario 7–5 6–4; Raymond d. Sawamatsu 6–2 6–3.
Semi-finals: Hingis (1) d. Coetzer (5) 6–2 6–1; Raymond d. Spirlea (8) 6–3 6–1.
Final: Hingis (1) d. Raymond 6–4 6–2.
WOMEN'S DOUBLES – Final: Hingis/Sanchez Vicario (3) d. Davenport/Novotna (1) 7–6 3–6 7–6.

EUROPEAN INDOORS ($926,250)

ZURICH, 12–19 OCTOBER

WOMEN'S SINGLES – 1st round: M. Hingis (1) bye; A. Sidot (LL) d. K. Habsudova 6–2 7–6; L. Raymond d. H. Sukova 7–5 6–3; A. Coetzer (5) d. P. Schnyder (WC) 7–6 6–3; I. Majoli (3) bye; S. Appelmans d. B. Schultz-McCarthy 6–3 6–7 7–5; N. Tauziat d. K. Po 6–3 5–7 7–5; D. van Roost (Q) d. A. Sanchez Vicario (8) 7–5 5–7 6–4; A. Huber (6) d. M. J. Fernandez 7–5 6–0; V. Williams (Q) d. R. Dragomir 6–0 6–3; N. Zvereva d. M. Oremans (Q) 6–2 2–6 6–3; L. Davenport (4) bye; I. Spirlea (7) d. N. Sawamatsu 6–4 3–6 6–2; S. Kleinova (Q) d. M. Maleeva 6–3 6–3; A. Sugiyama d. B. Schett (WC) 6–2 1–0 ret; J. Novotna (2) bye.
2nd round: Hingis (1) d. Sidot (LL) 6–3 6–2; Raymond d. Coetzer (5) 7–5 6–3; Appelmans d. Majoli (3) 7–6 6–2; Tauziat d. van Roost (Q) 6–3 6–7 7–6; Williams (Q) d. Huber (6) w/o; Davenport (4) d. Zvereva 6–4 2–2 ret; Kleinova (Q) d. Spirlea (7) 3–6 5–1 ret; Novotna (2) d. Sugiyama 6–0 6–7 6–2.
Quarter-finals: Raymond d. Hingis (1) 4–6 6–2 7–5; Tauziat d. Appelmans 4–6 6–1 7–5; Davenport (4) d.

Williams (Q) 6–0 6–4; Novotna (2) d. Kleinova (Q) 6–2 7–6.
Semi-finals: Tauziat d. Raymond 6–3 7–5; Davenport (4) d. Novotna (2) 6–4 6–1.
Final: Davenport (4) d. Tauziat 7–6 7–5.
WOMEN'S DOUBLES – Final: Hingis/Sanchez Vicario (2) d. Neiland/Sukova 4–6 6–4 6–1.

LADIES KREMLIN CUP ($926,250)

MOSCOW, 27 OCTOBER–2 NOVEMBER
WOMEN'S SINGLES – 1st round: J. Novotna (1) bye; K. Po d. S. Williams (Q) 6–3 7–6; V. Williams d. E. Likhovtseva 7–6 6–3; S. Farina (Q) d. S. Appelmans (8) 3–6 7–6 6–1; C. Martinez (4) bye; P. Schnyder d. E. Dementieva (Q) 6–2 6–1; K. Habsudova d. M. Maleeva 6–1 6–3; S. Testud (6) d. J. Kruger 6–3 7–6; B. Schultz-McCarthy (7) d. B. Paulus 7–5 6–3; A. Sugiyama d. N. Zvereva 6–4 7–6; E. Makarova (WC) d. N. Basuki 5–4 ret; A. Sanchez Vicario (3) bye; D. van Roost d. A. Huber (5) 5–7 6–4 6–3; H. Sukova d. M. Lucic (Q) 6–2 6–4; L. Neiland (WC) d. F. Labat 3–6 6–3 6–1; I. Spirlea (2) bye.
2nd round: Novotna (1) d. Po 6–0 6–2; Williams d. Farina (Q) 6–4 6–0; Martinez (4) d. Schnyder 7–5 2–6 6–1; Testud (6) d. Habsudova 6–2 3–6 7–6; Sugiyama d. Schultz-McCarthy (7) 6–4 7–5; Sanchez Vicario (3) d. Makarova (WC) 6–3 6–0; van Roost d. Sukova 6–2 7–6; Spirlea (2) d. Neiland (WC) 6–4 7–6.
Quarter-finals: Novotna (1) d. Williams 7–5 6–4; Martinez (4) d. Testud (6) 6–1 6–4; Sugiyama d. Sanchez Vicario (3) 6–1 7–6; van Roost d. Spirlea (2) 6–2 6–4.
Semi-finals: Novotna (1) d. Martinez (4) 6–4 6–1; Sugiyama d. van Roost 6–2 4–6 6–3.
Final: Novotna (1) d. Sugiyama 6–3 6–4.
WOMEN'S DOUBLES – Final: Sanchez Vicario/Zvereva (1) d. Basuki/Vis (2) 5–3 def.

AMERITECH CUP ($450,000)

CHICAGO, 3–9 NOVEMBER
WOMEN'S SINGLES – 1st round: J. Novotna (1) bye; A. Frazier d. J. Nejedly (Q) 6–3 6–3; N. Tauziat d. R. Dragomir 6–3 5–7 6–2; S. Appelmans d. M. J. Fernandez (6) 6–2 6–1; I. Majoli (4) bye; L. Courtois d. A. Mauresmo (Q) 5–7 7–6 6–4; N. Basuki d. L. Osterloh (WC) 6–0 6–3; B. Schultz-McCarthy (7) d. C. Rubin 6–4 7–5; L. Raymond (8) d. H. Sukova 6–2 6–2; A. Sugiyama d. T. Snyder (Q) 6–4 6–3; J. Kruger d. A. Carlsson 5–7 6–3 6–3; L. Davenport (3) bye; M. Pierce (5) d. C. Cristea (Q) 6–3 6–3; S. Williams (WC) d. E. Likhovtseva 6–3 7–5; M. Grzybowska d. J. Capriati 6–3 7–5; M. Seles (2) bye.
2nd round: Novotna (1) d. Frazier 5–7 6–2 6–3; Tauziat d. Appelmans 6–1 6–2; Majoli (4) d. Courtois 7–5 6–1; Basuki d. Schultz-McCarthy (7) 6–2 4–6 6–4; Raymond (8) d. Sugiyama 6–4 6–2; Davenport (3) d. Kruger 6–2 6–4; Williams (WC) d. Pierce (5) 6–3 7–6; Seles (2) d. Grzybowska 3–6 6–3 6–2.
Quarter-finals: Tauziat d. Novotna (1) 7–5 6–3; Majoli (4) d. Basuki 4–6 7–5 6–4; Davenport (3) d. Raymond (8) 6–4 6–4; Williams (WC) d. Seles (2) 4–6 6–1 6–1.
Semi-finals: Tauziat d. Majoli (4) 6–2 6–3; Davenport (3) d. Williams (WC) 6–4 6–4.
Final: Davenport (3) d. Tauziat 6–0 7–5.
WOMEN'S DOUBLES – Final: Fusai/Tauziat (4) d. Davenport/Seles 6–3 6–2.

ADVANTA CHAMPIONSHIPS ($450,000)

PHILADELPHIA, 10–16 NOVEMBER
WOMEN'S SINGLES – 1st round: M. Hingis (1) bye; S. Appelmans d. R. Dragomir 6–4 6–1; L. Raymond d. H. Sukova 6–3 6–4; A. Huber d. I. Majoli (6) 6–3 1–6 6–3; A. Coetzer (3) bye; C. Rubin d. F. Li (Q) 7–6 7–6; A. Sugiyama d. J. Capriati 6–1 6–2; A. Sanchez Vicario (8) d. N. Basuki 6–2 6–0; I. Spirlea (7) d. V. Williams (WC) 6–3 6–2; M. Vento (Q) d. M. Weingartner (Q) 6–2 6–3; B. Schultz-McCarthy d. S. Taylor (WC) 6–2 6–2; M. Seles (4) bye; L. Davenport (5) d. N. Tauziat 6–3 6–3; C. Martinez d. S. Cacic (Q) 6–3 6–1; A. Frazier d. J. Kruger (LL) 7–5 6–1; J. Novotna (2) bye.
2nd round: Hingis (1) d. Appelmans 6–2 4–6 6–2; Huber d. Raymond 2–6 6–2 7–5; Coetzer (3) d. Rubin 6–4 7–6; Sanchez Vicario (8) d. Sugiyama 6–1 7–6; Spirlea (7) d. Vento (Q) 6–2 6–1; Seles (4) d. Schultz-McCarthy 4–3 ret; Davenport (5) d. Martinez 6–3 6–0; Novotna (2) d. Frazier 6–2 6–1.
Quarter-finals: Hingis (1) d. Huber 7–6 5–7 6–4; Sanchez Vicario (8) d. Coetzer (3) 6–2 6–2; Spirlea (7) d. Seles (4) 6–4 7–6; Davenport (5) d. Novotna (2) 6–3 6–2.
Semi-finals: Hingis (1) d. Sanchez Vicario (8) 1–6 7–6 6–3; Davenport (5) d. Spirlea (7) 6–2 6–4.
Final: Hingis (1) d. Davenport (5) 7–5 6–7 7–6.
WOMEN'S DOUBLES – Final: Raymond/Stubbs d. Davenport/Novotna (2) 6–3 7–5.

Corel WTA Tour

Tier III and IV Tournaments

AUSTRALIAN WOMEN'S HARDCOURT ($164,250)
HOPE ISLAND, 30 DECEMBER–5 JANUARY
WOMEN'S SINGLES – Quarter-finals: B. Schultz-McCarthy (1) d. M. Serna (Q) 6–1 6–4; E. Likhovtseva (3) d. R. McQuillan (WC) 3–6 6–3 7–6; A. Sugiyama (6) d. S. Appelmans (4) 6–2 3–6 7–6; A. Sidot d. A. Carlsson 6–2 6–2.
Semi-finals: Likhovtseva (3) d. Schultz-McCarthy (1) 6–4 6–3; Sugiyama (6) d. Sidot 6–2 6–4.
Final: Likhovtseva (3) d. Sugiyama (6) 3–6 7–6 6–3.
WOMEN'S DOUBLES – Final: Kijimuta/Miyagi (3) d. Dragomir/Farina 7–6 6–1.

AMWAY CLASSIC ($107,500)
AUCKLAND, 30 DECEMBER–5 JANUARY
WOMEN'S SINGLES – Quarter-finals: M. Maruska (Q) d. A. Huber (1) 6–4 2–6 6–2; T. Tanasugarn d. S. Cacic 3–6 6–4 6–4; E. Wagner d. R. Hiraki (Q) 6–3 0–6 6–4; J. Wiesner (2) d. A. Dechaume-Balleret 6–4 7–6.
Semi-finals: Maruska (Q) d. Tanasugarn 3–6 6–3 6–3; Weisner (2) d. Wagner 6–2 6–1.
Final: Maruska (Q) d. Weisner (2) 6–3 6–1.
WOMEN'S DOUBLES – Final: Husarova/van Roost d. Olsza/Wagner 6–2 6–7 6–3.

TASMANIAN INTERNATIONAL ($107,500)
HOBART, 6–12 JANUARY
WOMEN'S SINGLES – Quarter-finals: E. Callens d. A. Sidot 6–3 3–6 6–0; M. Werdel-Witmeyer d. S-T. Wang (6) 6–4 6–2; D. van Roost d. L. Cenkova (Q) 6–0 1–0 ret; M. Endo d. A. Ellwood (WC) 3–6 6–4 6–2.
Semi-finals: Werdel-Witmeyer d. Callens 6–3 6–0; van Roost d. Endo 6–3 6–4.
Final: van Roost d. Werdel-Witmeyer 6–3 6–3.
WOMEN'S DOUBLES – Final: Kijimuta/Miyagi (2) d. Rittner/van Roost 6–3 6–1.

EA-GENERALI LADIES AUSTRIAN OPEN ($164,250)
LINZ, 3–9 FEBRUARY
WOMEN'S SINGLES – Quarter-finals: J. Novotna (1) d. M. Maleeva (5) 6–0 6–3; C. Rubin (7) d. B. Rittner 4–6 7–6 6–4; J. Wiesner (3) d. N. Tauziat (6) 7–5 6–2; K. Habsudova (2) d. A. Carlsson (8) 6–2 6–2.
Semi-finals: Rubin (7) d. Novotna (1) 7–5 5–7 6–3; Habsudova (2) d. Wiesner (3) 6–3 4–6 6–3.
Final: Rubin (7) d. Habsudova (2) 6–4 6–2.
WOMEN'S DOUBLES – Final: Fusai/Tauziat (1) d. Melicharova/Vildova 4–6 6–3 6–1.

IGA TENNIS CLASSIC ($164,250)
OKLAHOMA, 17–23 FEBRUARY
WOMEN'S SINGLES – Quarter-finals: L. Davenport (1) d. J. Capriati (5) 6–3 6–4; K. Po (3) d. S. Cacic 6–3 6–3; L. Raymond (4) d. P. Shriver (WC) 7–5 7–6; F. Lubiani d. A. Coetzer (2) 6–0 6–4.
Semi-finals: Davenport (1) d. Po (3) 1–6 6–2 6–3; Raymond (4) d. Lubiani 6–1 6–0.
Final: Davenport (1) d. Raymond (4) 6–4 6–2.
WOMEN'S DOUBLES – Final: Hiraki/Miyagi (4) d. Werdel-Witmeyer/Whitlinger-Jones 6–4 6–1.

JAPAN OPEN ($164,250)
TOKYO, 14–20 APRIL
WOMEN'S SINGLES – Quarter-finals: A. Ellwood (9) d. J. Lee (Q) 6–1 6–4; A. Frazier (3) d. N. Sawamatsu (6) 7–6 7–6; A. Sugiyama (4) d. C. Morariu 7–6 6–2; K. Po (2) d. S-T. Wang (5) 4–6 6–3 6–3.
Semi-finals: Frazier (3) d. Ellwood (9) 6–2 6–3; Sugiyama (4) d. Po (2) 5–7 6–4 6–1.
Final: Sugiyama (4) d. Frazier (3) 4–6 6–4 6–4.
WOMEN'S DOUBLES – Final: Dechaume-Balleret/Hiraki (3) d. Guse/Morariu 6–4 6–2.

DANAMON OPEN ($107,500)
JAKARTA, 21–27 APRIL
WOMEN'S SINGLES – Quarter-finals: Y. Yoshida (7) d. S-T. Wang (1) 6–4 3–2 ret; A. Dechaume-Balleret d. E. Kim (Q) 6–4 6–2; R. Grande (6) d. N. Feber w/o; N. Sawamatsu (2) d. N. Miyagi 7–5 6–1.
Semi-finals: Yoshida (7) d. Dechaume-Balleret 3–6 7–6 6–1; Sawamatsu (2) d. Grande (6) 7–6 3–6 6–1.
Final: Sawamatsu (2) d. Yoshida (7) 6–3 6–2.
WOMEN'S DOUBLES – Final: Guse/Radford (4) d. Nemeckova/Yoshida 6–4 5–7 7–5.

BUDAPEST LOTTO LADIES OPEN ($107,500)
BUDAPEST, 21–27 APRIL
WOMEN'S SINGLES – Quarter-finals: K. Habsudova (1) d. A. Fusai (8) 6–4 6–3; S. Appelmans (4) d. C. Torrens-Valero 6–4 6–4; H. Nagyova (7) d. J. Kruger (Q) 4–6 6–4 6–3; A. Coetzer (2) d. E. Wagner 6–1 6–7 6–2.
Semi-finals: Appelmans (4) d. Habsudova (1) 6–2 6–4; Coetzer (2) d. Nagyova (7) 6–7 6–1 6–0.
Final: Coetzer (2) d. Appelmans (4) 6–1 6–3.
WOMEN'S DOUBLES – Final: Coetzer/Fusai (1) d. Martincova/Wagner (3) 6–3 6–1.

CROATIAN BOL LADIES OPEN ($107,500)
BOL, 28 APRIL–4 MAY
WOMEN'S SINGLES – Quarter-finals: A. Coetzer (1) d. S. Pitkowski 6–4 7–6; M. Lucic (Q) d. K. Studenikova (4) 7–5 6–4; C. Morariu d. J. Kruger 6–1 2–6 6–4; E. Gagliardi d. M. Maruska 6–4 6–1.
Semi-finals: Lucic (Q) d. Coetzer (1) 6–4 6–3; Morariu d. Gagliardi 6–1 1–6 6–3.
Final: Lucic (Q) d. Morariu 7–5 6–7 7–6.
WOMEN'S DOUBLES – Final: Montalvo/Nagyova d. Gaidano/Maruska (Q) 6–3 6–1.

THE ROVER CHAMPIONSHIPS ($107,500)
CARDIFF, 13–18 MAY
WOMEN'S SINGLES – Quarter-finals: R. Grande d. D. van Roost (1) 1–6 6–2 7–5; V. Ruano-Pascual d. P. Langrova (4) 6–4 6–2; A. Dechaume-Balleret d. F. Lubiani 2–6 6–4 6–2; S. Pitkowski (5) d. A. Carlsson (2) 7–5 6–4.
Semi-finals: Ruano-Pascual d. Grande 6–3 3–6 6–4; Dechaume-Balleret d. Pitkowski (5) 6–3 6–4.
Final: Ruano-Pascual d. Dechaume-Balleret 6–1 3–6 6–2.
WOMEN'S DOUBLES – Final: Graham/Guse (1) d. Pullin/Woodroffe 6–3 6–4.

INTERNATIONAUX DE STRASBOURG ($250,000)
STRASBOURG, 19–24 MAY
WOMEN'S SINGLES – Quarter-finals: S. Graf (WC) (1) d. S. Testud 3–6 6–2 6–1; A. Coetzer (3) d. N. Kijimuta 6–2 6–3; J. Wiesner (4) d. S. Appelmans (6) 6–3 6–4; M. Lucic (Q) d. N. Zvereva 7–5 6–3.
Semi-finals: Graf (WC) (1) d. Coetzer (3) 4–6 7–5 7–6; Lucic (Q) d. Wiesner (4) 7–5 6–7 7–6.
Final: S. Graf (WC) (1) d. M. Lucic (Q) 6–2 7–5.
WOMEN'S DOUBLES – Final: Sukova/Zvereva (1) d. Likhovtseva/Sugiyama 6–1 6–1.

WORLD DOUBLES CUP ($188,125)
EDINBURGH, 21–24 MAY
WOMEN'S DOUBLES – Final: N. Arendt/M. Bollegraf (1) d. R. McQuillan/N. Miyagi 6–1 3–6 7–5.

DFS CLASSIC ($164,250)
BIRMINGHAM, 9–16 JUNE
WOMEN'S SINGLES – Quarter-finals: I. Spirlea (1) d. D. van Roost (6) 6–4 6–4; N. Basuki (4) d. M. Maleeva (7) 7–6 6–2; K. Kunce (Q) d. L. Raymond (3) 6–4 6–7 6–3; N. Tauziat (2) d. N. Zvereva (8) 6–1 2–6 6–2.
Semi-finals: Basuki (4) d. Spirlea (1) 7–6 6–1; Tauziat (2) d. Kunce (Q) 6–4 6–4.
Final: Tauziat (2) d. Basuki (4) 2–6 6–2 6–2.
WOMEN'S DOUBLES – Final: Adams/Neiland (1) d. Tauziat/Wild (2) 6–2 6–3.

WILKINSON LADY CHAMPIONSHIPS ($164,250)
ROSMALEN, 16–22 JUNE
WOMEN'S SINGLES – Quarter-finals: A. Huber (1) d. S. Appelmans (5) 6–2 4–6 7–6; M. Oremans d. K. Habsudova (4) 6–2 7–5; R. Dragomir (3) d. D. van Roost (6) 6–1 2–6 6–4; A. Carlsson (8) M. Pierce (2) w/o .
Semi-finals: Oremans d. Huber (1) 4–6 6–4 ret; Dragomir (3) d. Carlsson (8) 6–4 6–2.
Final: Dragomir (3) d. Oremans 5–7 6–2 6–4.
WOMEN'S DOUBLES – Final: Melicharova/Vildova d. Habsudova/Labat 6–3 7–6.

PUPP CZECH OPEN ($160,000)
PRAGUE, 14–20 JULY
WOMEN'S SINGLES – Quarter-finals: J. Kruger d. A. Dechaume-Balleret 4–6 7–6 6–1; V. Martinek (Q) d. D. Chladkova (5) 6–4 6–0; M. Maruska d. K. Habsudova (3) 7–5 1–6 6–4; C. Cristea d. L. Richterova (WC) 6–2 2–6 7–5.
Semi-finals: Kruger d. Martinek (Q) 7–5 6–1; Maruska d. Cristea 6–2 6–1.
Final: Kruger d. Maruska 6–1 6–1.
WOMEN'S DOUBLES – Final: Dragomir/Habsudova (1) d. Martincova/Vildova (3) 6–1 5–7 6–2.

TORNEO INTERNAZIONALE ($163,000)
PALERMO, 14–20 JULY
WOMEN'S SINGLES – Quarter-finals: B. Paulus (1) d. I. Gorrochategui 2–6 6–3 6–2; E. Makarova d. S. Farina (5) 7–5 7–6; B. Schett (3) d. V. Ruano-Pascual (6) 6–3 5–7 7–6; S. Testud (2) d. E. Gagliardi 6–7 6–2 6–3.

Semi-finals: Makarova d. Paulus (1) 6–4 7–5; Testud (2) d. Schett (3) 0–6 6–3 7–6.
Final: Testud (2) d. Makarova 7–5 6–3.
WOMEN'S DOUBLES – Final: Farina/Schett (1) d. Labat/Paz (2) 2–6 6–1 6–4.

WARSAW CUP BY HEROS ($164,250)

WARSAW, 21–27 JULY
WOMEN'S SINGLES – Quarter-finals: B. Paulus (1) d. G. Leon-Garcia (Q) 6–2 6–0; V. Ruano-Pascual d. J. Kruger 7–5 7–5; H. Nagyova (6) d. C. Torrens-Valero 6–3 6–1; R. Dragomir (2) d. K. Studenikova (8) 6–2 6–3.
Semi-finals: Paulus (1) d. Ruano-Pascual 6–2 6–1; Nagyova (6) d. Dragomir (2) 6–4 7–5.
Final: Paulus (1) d. Nagyova (6) 6–4 6–4.
WOMEN'S DOUBLES – Final: Dragomir/Gorrochategui (2) d. Babel/Barclay 6–4 6–0.

STYRIA OPEN MARIA LANKOWITZ ($107,500)

MARIA LANKOWITZ, 28 JULY–3 AUGUST
WOMEN'S SINGLES – Quarter-finals: M. Sanchez Lorenzo d. B. Paulus (Q) w/o ; B. Schett (5) d. J. Wiesner (3) 3–6 7–5 6–0; H. Nagyova (6) d. P. Schnyder (4) 0–6 6–4 6–2; M. Babel d. G. Leon-Garcia (Q) 6–3 6–1.
Semi-finals: Schett (5) d. Sanchez Lorenzo 6–4 6–1; Nagyova (6) d. Babel 6–1 7–6.
Final: Schett (5) d. Nagyova (6) 3–6 6–2 6–3.
WOMEN'S DOUBLES – Final: Melicharova/Vildova (2) d. Bobkova/Probst 6–2 6–2.

WISMILAK INTERNATIONAL ($107,500)

SURABAYA, 22–28 SEPTEMBER
WOMEN'S SINGLES – Quarter-finals: D. van Roost (1) d. D. Randriantefy (WC) 6–0 6–2; R. McQuillan (7) d. N. Pratt 3–6 6–2 6–2; M. Vento d. S. Pitkowski (6) 6–3 6–2; L. Nemeckova d. H. Inoue 6–2 6–3.
Semi-finals: van Roost (1) d. McQuillan (7) 6–2 7–5; Nemeckova d. Vento 6–4 6–3.
Final: van Roost (1) d. Nemeckova 6–1 6–3.
WOMEN'S DOUBLES – Final: Guse/Hiraki (2) d. Drake/Kolbovic 6–1 7–6.

SPARKASSEN CUP INTERNATIONAL GRAND PRIX ($450,000)

LEIPZIG, 22–28 SEPTEMBER
WOMEN'S SINGLES – Quarter-finals: M. Hingis (1) d. S. Appelmans (7) 6–3 6–2; A. Coetzer (4) d. M. Grzybowska (Q) 6–1 7–6; A. Huber (5) d. I. Majoli (3) 4–6 7–6 6–4; J. Novotna (2) d. S. Kleinova (Q) 6–4 6–2.
Semi-finals: Coetzer (4) d. Hingis (1) 6–4 4–6 7–6; Novotna (2) d. Huber (5) 6–7 7–5 6–4.
Final: Novotna (2) d. Coetzer (4) 6–2 4–6 6–3.
WOMEN'S DOUBLES – Final: Hingis/Novotna (1) d. Basuki/Sukova (2) 6–2 6–2.

BELL CHALLENGE ($164,250)

QUEBEC CITY, 20–26 OCTOBER
WOMEN'S SINGLES – Quarter-finals: B. Schultz-McCarthy (1) d. C. Morariu 1–6 6–2 6–1; C. Rubin (5) d. M. Vento 6–4 6–1; D. van Roost (4) d. J. Watanabe (Q) 6–1 6–2; L. Raymond (2) d. M. Grzybowska (7) 6–2 7–6.
Semi-finals: B. Schultz-McCarthy (1) d. C. Rubin (5) 6–2 6–4; D. van Roost (4) d. L. Raymond (2) 6–2 3–6 6–1.
Final: B. Schultz-McCarthy (1) d. D. van Roost (4) 6–4 6–7 7–5.
WOMEN'S DOUBLES – Final: Raymond/Stubbs (1) d. Fusai/Tauziat (2) 6–4 5–7 7–5.

SEAT OPEN LUXEMBOURG ($164,250)

LUXEMBOURG, 20–26 OCTOBER
WOMEN'S SINGLES – Quarter-finals: A. Coetzer (1) d. M. Oremans (WC) 7–5 6–7 6–4; K. Studenikova (Q) d. J. Kruger 6–3 6–4; B. Paulus (5) d. S. Appelmans (4) 3–6 6–3 6–2; A. Sidot d. H. Nagyova 6–4 7–6.
Semi-finals: Coetzer (1) d. Studenikova (Q) 6–1 3–6 6–0; Paulus (5) d. Sidot 6–3 6–4.
Final: Coetzer (1) d. Paulus (5) 6–4 3–6 7–5.
WOMEN'S DOUBLES – Final: Neiland/Sukova (1) d. Babel/Courtois 6–2 6–4.

VOLVO WOMEN'S OPEN ($107,500)

PATTAYA, 17–23 NOVEMBER
WOMEN'S SINGLES – Quarter-finals: R. Dragomir (1) d. C. Morariu 4–6 6–3 6–0; H. Nagyova (4) d. S. Kleinova (7) 6–3 6–4; O. Barabanschikova d. N. Pratt 6–0 6–3; D. van Roost (2) d. L. Courtois 6–2 6–1.
Semi-finals: Nagyova (4) d. Dragomir (1) 4–6 7–5 6–2; Van Roost (2) d. Barabanschikova 6–3 6–2.
Final: Nagyova (4) d. van Roost (2) 7–5 6–7 7–5.
WOMEN'S DOUBLES – Final: Kunce/Morariu d. Labat/van Roost (4) 6–3 6–4

Jana Novotna won her first major title at the Chase Championships, some compensation for her loss to Hingis in the Wimbledon final. (Stephen Wake)

Corel WTA Chase Championships

John Parsons

At a time when all the talk about the future of women's tennis was concentrated on youth, especially on Martina Hingis, Anna Kournikova, Mirjana Lucic and the Williams sisters – Venus and Serena – one member of the old guard demonstrated in the showpiece end-of-year Chase Championships that she was not yet ready to leave the stage entirely to them.

Few have ever doubted the ability of Jana Novotna to produce the most skilful, stylish and indeed some of most thoughtful tennis, even if at times the latter quality has seemed in doubt as emotions have overwhelmed her. Yet the style and steadfastness with which the 29-year-old not just played but competed throughout the week in New York on the way to winning both the singles and the doubles titles indicated that it still may not be too late for her to win the biggest prize of all, and the one for which her game is best suited – Wimbledon.

Novotna, who described her 7–6 6–2 6–3 defeat of Mary Pierce in a Madison Square Garden final watching by nearly 14,000 spectators as 'the greatest moment of my tennis career', has twice been runner up at The Championships and might have won on both occasions. In 1993, she led Steffi Graf 4–1, with a point for 5–1 in the final set before crumbling in a manner which meant that not only the Duchess of Kent, but millions more watching on television, felt like offering her a shoulder to cry on. Last year, when it looked as if her time had come at last, a pulled stomach muscle ended her chances of building on the first set lead she had won so impressively against Hingis.

After winning the 21st title of her career, Novotna, who has always been best remembered for the finals she has lost rather than those she has won, said 'I've now proved to myself that I am a great champion. Even if I don't win another match, no-one can take that away from me. I never doubted that I could do it.' She was equally insistent that it could be the springboard for even more noteworthy successes in the year ahead.

Far from bemoaning the teenage invasion, Novotna, who ended the year with a career best second place in the world rankings, welcomed it. 'It makes it really interesting to have the contrast between the youngsters and the older players,' she said. 'Women's tennis needed a boost and the young players are providing that but I think I'm now playing the best tennis of my life.'

Pierce, without a set from their four previous meetings, went storming to the net at every opportunity in the early stages of the final. She certainly had nothing to lose but it only briefly deflected Novotna in a performance which was well planned and impressively executed.

'I knew for her to beat me she had to come up with something new but I wasn't surprised. I was ready for it,' said Novotna, who won £350,000 for her effort. The match began to turn her way in the closing stages of the first set. Pierce, who had missed a break point in the second game, had two set points as Novotna wavered from 40–15 in the 12th, missing a backhand when there was a real chance on the first of them.

Although Pierce tried to compensate with a well played rally to force the second break point, Novotna this time did not need gratuitous help. She aced her opponent in a way which lifted her whole approach, for she went on to win the tie-break on another ace to 7–4, from 2–4, as the Pierce forehand, which had been her great strength throughout the week, began going to pieces. Once Novotna had saved two more break points on Pierce errors at the start of the second set and then broken for 2–0 with even more of the same kind of help, the psychological battle was effectively over.

The way Novotna broke in the third set typified the difference between the two players. Whereas Pierce was desperate for added power and frequently overhit, Novotna preferred precision and the net-skimming backhand with which she broke for 5–3 and then served out to love to round off the triumph in style, underlined her confidence.

On her way to the final Novotna overcame a poor start to produce exquisite tennis as she beat Conchita Martinez 6–4 6–4 in the first round and then defeated Arantxa Sanchez Vicario, 6–4 3–6 6–1 after the Spaniard had achieved the first of many upsets in the week by dismissing fifth seeded Monica Seles 3–6 6–4 6–4. The former world champion was not even remotely close to the form which had made her such an illustrious champion before the stabbing incident in Hamburg in 1993. Lacking both concentration and consistency, two of the qualities which used to be among her greatest strengths, she lost eight consecutive games, many of them on errors, from leading 4–2 in the second set.

In the semi-finals Novotna steadily wore down Irina Spirlea, 7–5 6–2. It was hardly surprising. The Romanian had already won two tough three setters, the first against Sandrine Testud, the other, in which she saved two match points, against Mary Joe Fernandez, whose big moment had come in the first round when she beat fellow American, Lindsay Davenport – or rather Davenport essentially beat herself.

Davenport, who had briefly assumed second place in the rankings, resorted to all her old wasteful ways. Despite leading by a set and 4–1, then 4–2 in the third (in which she also had three match points), she went down 2–6 6–4 7–6. It was one of those frustrating matches which provided gripping excitement for an appreciative crowd but which only became seriously competitive for all the wrong reasons. Davenport, never the fastest on court, lost four consecutive games to concede the second set and then, after breaking to lead 5–4 in the third, lost two match points with timid backhands, one of which barely reached the net. By the time the third match point came along, lost by an overhit backhand, Fernandez had also lost four match points of her own and only won her fifth on another missed backhand by her opponent. It was that kind of match.

For many the biggest upset of the week was the 6–3 2–6 7–5 victory for Pierce over top seeded Hingis. Pierce, who had rarely played with such consistent aggression, won the first five games in 14 minutes. She richly deserved her success but anyone who had seen the way Hingis had struggled against Brenda Schultz-McCarthy in the first round, knew it was an upset waiting to happen. Hingis, less than two months past her 17th birthday, was already playing more on instinct than inspiration in her 7–6 5–2 win against the Dutch player, who largely beat herself with extravagant, all too familiar knockabout overhitting in the first set before having to retire because of a torn off toe-nail in the second.

Having been taken to three sets in her five previous matches, it was clear that Hingis was mentally and physically exhausted. Hard though she tried to sustain her second set recovery against Pierce, she could no longer patch up the wear and tear of 82 earlier matches during the year. She admitted that she had committed to too many end of the year tournaments to compensate for time lost by her horse riding accident before Paris but added 'I won't make the same mistake again.'

The match lasted 2 hours 6 minutes and ended with two extraordinary games. With Hingis serving at 5–5, 15–30, Pierce missed a simple backhand but then reached break point with a mishit forehand. Hingis escaped but still lost the game and then slung her racket along the ground from the baseline to beyond the net and was warned.

At 15–15 in the next game, Pierce won a fabulous rally of 28 shots but was so exhausted that she then double faulted. Over the next eight minutes, Pierce missed two match points, saved three break points and received a time warning as she waited to serve on her third and last match point. The Hingis backhand return went wide. By then everyone, including the 13,000 spectators, felt exhausted and hardly any stayed to watch Nathalie Tauziat punish Iva Majoli for errors in a 7–6 7–6 victory which took her through to an all-French semi-final which Pierce won 6–2 5–7 6–4.

Yet the week belonged, rightly, to Novotna and this time the tears were of joy, especially when she gave the credit to her coach, Hana Mandlikova. 'She was a great champion herself and she's simply taught me how to be one,' said Novotna, who one day earlier, had teamed with Davenport to take the doubles title as they beat the French pair, Alexandra Fusai and Tauziat, 6–7 6–3 6–2. It made her the first to win both events since Martina Navratilova in 1983.

COREL WTA CHASE CHAMPIONSHIPS 1997 ($2,000,000)
MADISON SQUARE GARDENS, 17–23 NOVEMBER
WOMEN'S SINGLES – 1st round: M. Hingis (1) d. B. Schultz-McCarthy 7–6 5–2 ret; M. Pierce (7) d. S. Appelmans 6–3 6–4; N. Tauziat d. A. Coetzer (4) 6–3 6–3; I. Majoli (6) d. A. Huber 7–6 7–6; I. Spirlea (8) d. S. Testud 6–3 5–7 6–4; M. J. Fernandez d. L. Davenport (3) 2–6 6–4 7–6; A. Sanchez Vicario d. M. Seles (5) 3–6 6–4 6–4; J. Novotna (2) d. C. Martinez 6–4 6–4.
Quarter-finals: Pierce (7) d. Hingis (1) 6–3 2–6 7–5; Tauziat d. Majoli (6) 7–6 7–6; Spirlea (8) d. Fernandez 5–7 6–2 7–5; Novotna (2) d. Sanchez Vicario 6–4 3–6 6–1.
Semi-finals: Pierce (7) d. Tauziat 6–2 5–7 6–4; Novotna (2) d. Spirlea (8) 7–6 6–2.
Final: Novotna (2) d. Pierce (7) 7–6 6–2 6–3.
WOMEN'S DOUBLES – Final: Davenport/Novotna (3) d. Fusai/Tauziat 6–7 6–3 6–2.

Other Official Pro Tournaments

Men's Challenger Tournaments
Men's Satellite Series
ITF Women's Circuits

Magnus Larsson's defeat of the injured Pete Sampras on the opening day of the Davis Cup final opened the door for a Swedish victory. (Michael Cole)

Men's Challenger Tournaments 1997

In 1997 there were 107 Challenger tournaments for men in 42 countries with the introduction of a sixth prize money level at $37,500 + Hospitality. Where a tournament provides hospitality for its players the event is credited another $25,000 in terms of its ranking points level. The prize money and points levels were:

$125,000H	100 points to the champion
$125,000 (or $100,000H)	90 points to the champion
$100,000 (or $75,000H)	80 points to the champion
$75,000 (or $50,000H)	70 points to the champion
$37,500H	65 points to the champion
$50,000 (or $25,000H)	60 points to the champion

SINGAPORE (SIN) (50H) 6–12 JANUARY – ***Singles:*** A. Chesnokov (3) d. J. van Herck (6) 3–6 7–6 6–2. ***Doubles:*** M. Bhupathi/L. Paes (1) d. M. Joyce/S. Melville (2) 6–4 4–6 7–6.

HEILBRONN (GER) (100H) 20–26 JANUARY – ***Singles:*** H. Holm d. H. Dreekmann (WC) (1) 6–3 2–6 6–0. ***Doubles:*** O. Delaitre/S. Simian d. P. Baur/C. Ferreira 6–7 6–3 7–6.

LIPPSTADT (GER) (25H) 27 JANUARY–2 FEBRUARY – ***Singles:*** A. Thoms d. D. Dier 7–6 6–3. ***Doubles:*** H. Holm/N. Holm (WC) d. F. Bergh/R. Bergh 7–6 7–6.

WOLFSBURG (GER) (25H) 3–9 FEBRUARY – ***Singles:*** J. Knippschild (3) d. A. Thoms 6–4 6–3. ***Doubles:*** N. Bruno/L. Tieleman d. H. Holm/N. Holm (WC) 7–6 6–4.

LUBECK (GER) (25H) 10–16 FEBRUARY – ***Singles:*** G. Grant d. R. Schuttler 6–3 6–3. ***Doubles:*** M. Huning/J. Winnink (3) d. T. Phillips/C. Wilkinson 7–6 7–6.

CHERBOURG (FRA) (37.5H) 17–23 FEBRUARY – ***Singles:*** F. Fetterlein d. L. Roux (5) 6–3 6–4. ***Doubles:*** M. Mirnyi/K. Ullyett (1) d. S. Pescosolido/V. Santopadre 6–3 6–7 6–4.

KYOTO (JPN) (25H) 17–23 FEBRUARY – ***Singles:*** C. Arriens (Q) d. M. Bhupathi 3–6 6–2 7–6. ***Doubles:*** M. Bhupathi/W. Black (1) d. S. Iwabuchi/T. Suzuki (2) 6–4 6–7 6–1.

PUNTA DEL ESTE (URU) (25H) 17–23 FEBRUARY – ***Singles:*** M. Meneschincheri d. J. Marin 6–7 6–1 6–4. ***Doubles:*** D. Orsanic/M. Rodriguez (4) d. N. Aerts/F. Meligeni 6–2 6–4.

SALINAS (ECU) (50H) 24 FEBRUARY – 2 MARCH – ***Singles:*** O. Gross d. G. Schaller (1) 6–1 3–6 6–2. ***Doubles:*** F. Meligeni/A. Sa (WC) d. D. Johnson/F. Montana (1) 6–3 3–6 6–3.

MAGDEBURG (GER) (25H) 24 FEBRUARY – 2 MARCH – ***Singles:*** P. Luxa d. K. Ullyett (8) 6–3 2–6 7–5. ***Doubles:*** T. Phillips/C. Wilkinson d. P. Luxa/T. Zdrazila 6–3 6–4.

INDIAN WELLS (USA) (50H) 3–9 MARCH – ***Singles:*** J. Novak (1) d. C. Dosedel (4) 7–6 6–4. ***Doubles:*** N. Kulti/M. Tebbutt (1) d. S. Davis/K. Jones 6–2 4–6 6–3.

BARLETTA (ITA) (25H) 31 MARCH – 6 APRIL – ***Singles:*** C. Costa (3) d. D. Sanguinetti 6–3 6–2. ***Doubles:*** N. Marques/T. van Houdt (2) d. A. Martin/A. Portas (3) 6–3 6–4.

PUERTA VALLARTA (MEX) (25H) 31 MARCH – 6 APRIL – ***Singles:*** A. Merinov d. M. Knowles 6–3 7–6. ***Doubles:*** A. Hernandez/O. Ortiz d. F. Montana/J. Waite (1) 4–6 6–2 6–1.

NAPOLI (ITA) (75H) 7–13 APRIL – ***Singles:*** D. Pescariu d. O. Gross (6) 6–4 6–2. ***Doubles:*** A. Kitinov/T. van Houdt (4) d. T. Carbonell/F. Roig (1) 7–6 6–4.

BERMUDA (BER) (125H) 7–13 APRIL – ***Singles:*** J. van Herck d. S. Sargsian (7) 6–1 4–6 6–0. ***Doubles:*** J. Frana/M. Knowles (3) d. L. Arnold/D. Orsanic 6–3 6–7 6–3.

BIRMINGHAM (USA) (50H) 14–20 APRIL – ***Singles:*** J. van Herck (5) d. T. Haas 7–6 6–7 6–4. ***Doubles:*** L. Jensen/M. Jensen (4) d. F. Bergh/R. Bergh 6–2 7–6.

SPLIT (CRO) (50H) 14–20 APRIL – ***Singles:*** D. Pescariu (8) d. J. Marin (7) 3–6 6–2 6–1. ***Doubles:*** D. Bowen/D. Pescariu (3) d. T. Phillips/D. Roditi (4) 7–6 6–3.

PRAGUE (CZE) (25H) 21–27 APRIL – ***Singles:*** A. Portas d. F. Vicente 6–1 6–4.
Doubles: M. Bhupathi/L. Paes (1) d. D. Bowen/T. Ketola (Q) 6–4 6–0.

LJUBLJANA (SLO) (125H) 5–11 MAY – ***Singles:*** B. Steven (6) d. A. Pavel (7) 7–6 6–2.
Doubles: L. Arnold/D. Orsanic (2) d. D. Skoch/F. Wibier 6–0 6–4.

JERUSALEM (ISR) (50) 5–10 MAY – ***Singles:*** W. Black d. M. Ruah 6–2 6–1.
Doubles: M. Bhupathi/L. Paes (1) d. W. Black/K. Ullyett (2) 6–7 6–2 7–6.

BRATISLAVA (SVK) (50) 5–11 MAY – ***Singles:*** S. Grosjean (Q) d. R. Vasek 6–4 6–1.
Doubles: J. Palmer/C. van Rensburg (1) d. J. Balcells/D. Bowen (4) 4–6 6–3 7–5.

KOSICE (SVK) (125H) 12–18 MAY – ***Singles:*** D. Hrbaty (WC) (1) d. N. Lapentti 6–4 6–4.
Doubles: P. Cash/A. Kratzmann (2) d. B. Haygarth/M. Mirnyi (3) 4–6 6–2 6–4.

CURITIBA (BRA) (50H) 12–18 MAY – ***Singles:*** G. Kuerten (2) d. R. Sabau (4) 3–6 6–4 6–3.
Doubles: G. Weiner/H. Wiltschnig d. E. Medica/M. Puerta 6–3 6–4.

DRESDEN (GER) (50H) 12–18 MAY – ***Singles:*** D. Norman d. J. Alonso-Pintor 6–4 6–4.
Doubles: M. Merklein/J. Salzenstein (3) d. C. Mamiit/J. Szymanski (Q) 7–6 6–1.

BUDAPEST I (HUN) (50H) 19–25 MAY – ***Singles:*** S. Randjelovic (Q) d. J. Munoz-Hernandez (Q) 4–6 6–3 6–0.
Doubles: N. Marques/T. van Houdt (3) d. A. Kitinov/G. van Emburgh (4) 2–6 6–4 6–3.

PROSTEJOV (CZE) (125H) 3–8 JUNE – ***Singles:*** B. Ulihrach (WC) (1) d. F. Meligeni 6–2 4–6 6–1.
Doubles: J. Novak/D. Rikl (1) d. S. Melville/D. Nargiso (WC) 6–4 6–2.

FURTH (GER) (50) 3–8 JUNE – ***Singles:*** D. Sanguinetti d. T. Nydahl (3) 6–4 6–2.
Doubles: B. Coupe/P. Rosner d. M. Sinner/J. Winnink (WC) 7–5 6–3.

WEIDEN (GER) (25H) 9–15 JUNE – ***Singles:*** D. Dier d. T. El Sawy (6) 7–6 6–3.
Doubles: G. Grant/M. Merklein (1) d. G. Doyle/M. Wakefield 6–4 7–6.

ZAGREB (CRO) (75H) 16–22 JUNE – ***Singles:*** A. Berasategui (WC) (1) d. I. Ljubicic (WC) 6–1 6–2.
Doubles: D. Roditi/T. Zdrazila d. B. Coupe/P. Rosner 3–6 7–6 7–6.

EISENACH (GER) (25H) 16–22 JUNE – ***Singles:*** T. Nydahl (2) d. D. Sanguinetti (3) 6–3 6–1.
Doubles: G. Grant/M. Merklein (1) d. E. Couto/A. Savolt (4) 6–2 6–2.

BRAUNSCHWEIG (GER) (125H) 23–29 JUNE – ***Singles:*** F. Roig (Q) d. F. Mantilla (WC) (2) 6–2 2–6 6–2.
Doubles: B. Coupe/P. Rosner d. N. Djordjevic/O. Ortiz (4) 6–4 6–3.

VENICE (ITA) (100H) 1–6 JULY – ***Singles:*** J. Alonso-Pintor d. M. Craca 6–3 6–7 6–0.
Doubles: G. Galimberti/M. Valeri (Q) d. D. Roditi/M. Rodriguez (4) 6–4 0–6 7–6.

FLUSHING MEADOW (USA) (50H) 1–6 JULY – ***Singles:*** G. Pozzi d. T. Ho (Q) 6–1 6–4.
Doubles: G. Grant/M. Merklein (1) d. M. Joyce/D. Witt 6–1 6–4.

ULM (GER) (50H) 1–6 JULY – ***Singles:*** D. Pescariu (3) d. S. Koubek 7–5 6–1.
Doubles: K. Goossens/T. van Houdt d. P. Luxa/P. Pala (1) 6–3 6–0.

MONTAUBAN (FRA) (25H) 1–6 JULY – ***Singles:*** O. Mutis (WC) d. H. Skoff 6–3 7–6.
Doubles: G. Castrichella/D. Musa d. L. Rehmann/A. Savolt 7–6 2–6 7–6.

BRASOV (ROM) (50H) 7–13 JULY – ***Singles:*** I. Moldovan (3) d. D. Pescariu (1) 6–2 6–4.
Doubles: G. Cosac/M. MacLagan d. I. Moldovan/D. Pescariu 6–4 7–6.

GRANBY (CAN) (50H) 7–13 JULY – ***Singles:*** W. Black d. C. Caratti (6) 6–1 6–2.
Doubles: G. Doyle/M. Merklein (2) d. E. Erlich/L. Manta (4) 7–5 6–3.

BRISTOL (GBR) (50) 7–13 JULY – ***Singles:*** S. Pescosolido d. M. Petchey (1) 7–6 7–6.
Doubles: Not played due to rain.

CALI (COL) (25H) 7–13 JULY – ***Singles:*** R. Delgado (4) d. S. Prieto 6–3 1–6 7–6.
Doubles: E. Medica/M. Puerta d. B. Martinez/M. Osorio 7–6 7–5.

OBERSTAUFEN (GER) (25H) 7–13 JULY – ***Singles:*** D. Sanguinetti (2) d. A. Gaudenzi (4) 4–6 7–6 6–3.
Doubles: J. Carrasco/J. Mas d. G. Blumauer/A. Gaudenzi (2) 6–2 7–6.

CONTREXEVILLE (FRA) (75H) 14–20 JULY – ***Singles:*** J. Alonso-Pintor (1) d. A. Gaudenzi (3) 6–4 6–3.
Doubles: P. Luxa/D. Skoch (2) d. B. Haygarth/G. van Emburgh (1) 6–4 6–2.

QUITO (ECU) (50H) 14–20 JULY – ***Singles:*** M. Puerta d. R. Delgado (3) 6–1 7–5.
Doubles: B. Martinez/M. Osorio d. R. Delgado/M. Garcia 6–4 6–4.

SCHEVENINGEN (NED) (50H) 14–20 JULY – ***Singles:*** I. Moldovan (4) d. S. Navarro 3–6 7–5 6–2.
Doubles: A. Calatrava/T. van Houdt d. R. Sluiter/P. Wessels (WC) 6–7 6–2 7–6.

APTOS (USA) (50) 14–20 JULY – ***Singles:*** J. Gambill d. W. McGuire 6–0 4–6 6–3.
Doubles: S. le Blanc/J. Robichaud (4) d. D. Caldwell/A. Peterson 7–6 6–4.

MANCHESTER (GBR) (50) 14–20 JULY – ***Singles:*** O. Burrieza (8) d. S. Pescosolido 7–6 2–6 6–1.
Doubles: M. Petchey/D. Sapsford (4) d. N. Behr/F. Veglio 6–3 6–7 7–6.

PORTSCHACH (AUT) (25H) 14–20 JULY – ***Singles:*** C. van Garsse (2) d. J. Perlant (4) 7–5 6–1.
Doubles: J. Crabb/M. Stadling d. D. Petrovic/G. Silcock (4) 7–5 6–3.

OSTEND (BEL) (75H) 21–27 JULY – ***Singles:*** J. Burillo (5) d. A. Calatrava 7–6 3–6 7–5.
Doubles: K. Goossens/T. van Houdt (3) d. T. Benhabiles/J. Boutter (Q) 3–6 6–4 6–0.

NEWCASTLE (GBR) (50H) 21–27 JULY – ***Singles:*** F. Santoro (WC) (2) d. S. Grosjean (4) 2–6 6–3 6–3.
Doubles: O. Burrieza/F. Veglio d. A. Clement/R. Gilbert 7–5 4–0 ret.

TAMPERE (FIN) (50H) 21–27 JULY – ***Singles:*** A. Savolt (4) d. T. Larkham 7–5 6–0.
Doubles: C. Buscaglione/R. Lavergne d. T. Ketola/B. Urh (2) 6–4 6–3.

WINNETKA (USA) (50) 21–27 JULY – ***Singles:*** G. Pozzi (5) d. W. Black 6–4 6–2.
Doubles: M. Sell/M. Wakefield (1) d. C. Clark/B. Ellwood (3) 6–3 7–6.

POZNAN (POL) (125H) 28 JULY–3 AUGUST – ***Singles:*** J. Tarango (1) d. D. Rikl 7–5 6–3.
Doubles: D. Rikl/T. Zdrazila (2) d. J. Burillo/L. Markovits (4) 6–3 6–2.

MERANO (ITA) (100H) 28 JULY–3 AUGUST – ***Singles:*** L. Arnold d. V. Santopadre 6–1 6–4.
Doubles: M. Hood/S. Prieto (3) d. C. Brandi/F. Messori (1) 6–1 4–6 7–6.

ISTANBUL (TUR) (50) 28 JULY–3 AUGUST – ***Singles:*** J. Fleurian (6) d. M. Petchey (3) 6–3 6–1.
Doubles: J. Cunha-Silva/J. Fleurian (1) d. C. Haggard/M. Petchey (2) w/o.

LEXINGTON (USA) (50H) 28 JULY–3 AUGUST – ***Singles:*** W. Black (8) d. G. Pozzi (6) 6–4 6–1.
Doubles: W. Black/B. MacPhie (1) d. D. di Lucia/B. Shelton (2) 6–4 7–5.

SEGOVIA (ESP) (100H) 4–10 AUGUST – *Singles:* J. Burillo (5) d. N. Escude (8) 6–3 2–1 ret.
Doubles: J. Cunha-Silva/N. Marques (2) d. J. Carrasco/B. Eagle 6–7 6–2 6–4.

BINGHAMTON (USA) (37.5H) 4–10 AUGUST – ***Singles:*** D. Witt (WC) d. B. MacPhie 6–2 6–4.
Doubles: B. MacPhie/J. Salzenstein (2) d. E. Couto/T. El Sawy 7–5 6–7 6–3.

BELO HORIZONTE (BRA) (25H) 4–10 AUGUST – ***Singles:*** R. Jabali d. A. Sa (6) 2–6 7–5 6–3.
Doubles: G. Trifu/G. Weiner (3) d. N. Aerts/A. Sa (2) 1–6 6–3 6–4.

PILZEN (CZE) (25H) 4–10 AUGUST – ***Singles:*** V. Santopadre (2) d. M. Tabara 6–3 5–7 6–3.
Doubles: P. Pala/B. Urh d. R. Stepanek/R. Vasek 2–4 ret.

GRAZ (AUT) (125H) 11–17 AUGUST – ***Singles:*** R. Vasek d. A. Portas (1) 6–1 6–3.
Doubles: L. Arnold/T. van Houdt (1) d. A. Martin/A. Portas (3) 6–1 6–2.

OLBIA (ITA) (50H) 11–17 AUGUST – ***Singles:*** D. Nargiso (WC) d. D. Musa 5–7 6–2 6–3.
Doubles: G. Grant/M. Ruah (1) d. M. Navarra/S. Pescosolido 3–6 6–2 7–5.

BRONX (USA) (50) 11–17 AUGUST – ***Singles:*** M. Sell d. G. Pozzi (2) 3–6 6–4 6–3.
Doubles: N. Aerts/A. Sa d. M. Sell/M. Wakefield (4) 4–6 7–5 6–1.

GENEVA (SUI) (50H) 18–24 AUGUST – ***Singles:*** A. Gaudenzi (1) d. A. Martin (4) 6–2 6–1.
Doubles: D. del Rio/M. Puerta (4) d. G. Marx/O. Morel 6–3 6–4.

NETTINGSDORF (AUT) (25H) 18–24 AUGUST – ***Singles:*** R. Vasek (3) d. C. Vinck 6–3 6–3.
Doubles: B. Jacob/M. Kohlmann d. T. Buchmayer/T. Strengberger 6–2 3–6 6–3.

ALPIRSBACH (GER) (37.5H) 25–31 AUGUST – ***Singles:*** F. Maggi d. S. Koubek (8) 6–4 5–7 6–4.
Doubles: M. Huning/G. Silcock (1) d. A. Lopez-Moron/F. Maggi 5–7 6–4 7–5.

SANTA CRUZ (BOL) (25H) 25–31 AUGUST – ***Singles:*** G. Canas (1) d. M. Carlsson (2) 6–2 4–6 6–2.
Doubles: M. Hood/S. Prieto (1) d. E. Caldas/A. Ferreira 7–6 4–6 6–3.

EDINBURGH (GBR) (50H) 1–7 SEPTEMBER – ***Singles:*** D. Pescariu (1) d. A. Gaudenzi (2) 4–6 7–5 6–1.
Doubles: W. Arthurs/G. Doyle (4) d. C. Haggard/J. Holmes (2) 4–6 6–2 6–2.

GUADALAJARA (MEX) (25H) 1–7 SEPTEMBER – ***Singles:*** A. Hernandez (2) d. R. Kokavec 6–4 5–7 6–2.
Doubles: N. Aerts/A. Sa (1) d. A. Hernandez/O. Ortiz (2) 3–6 6–2 6–4.

AZORES (POR) (75H) 2–7 SEPTEMBER – ***Singles:*** C. Caratti d. O. Burrieza 3–6 6–3 6–4.
Doubles: A. Cherkasov/G. Etlis d. N. Holm/L-A. Wahlgren 6–7 7–5 6–3.

BUDAPEST II (HUN) (50H) 8–14 SEPTEMBER – ***Singles:*** J-F. Andersen d. F. Costa (2) 7–6 2–6 6–2.
Doubles: N. Djordjevic/D. Vemic (2) d. K. Bardoczky/M. Jancso 6–1 3–6 6–4.

ESPINHO (POR) (100H) 8–14 SEPTEMBER – ***Singles:*** M. Safin d. S. Huet 7–5 6–0. ***Doubles:*** J-I. Carrasco/A. Lopez-Moron (3) d. A. Calatrava/B. Moto (2) 4–6 6–2 7–5.

SZCZECIN (POL) (125H) 15–21 SEPTEMBER – ***Singles:*** R. Fromberg (6) d. N. Lapentti (4) 6–7 6–4 6–1. ***Doubles:*** T. Kempers/D. Orsanic (1) d. C. Brandi/F. Messori (2) 6–3 7–5.

URBANA (USA) (25H) 15–21 SEPTEMBER – ***Singles:*** A. Richardson (7) d. C. Mamiit (5) 6–7 7–6 6–3. ***Doubles:*** M. Sell/K. Ullyett (2) d. G. Motomura/T. Suzuki 3–6 7–6 6–2.

DELRAY BEACH (USA) (50) 22–28 SEPTEMBER – ***Singles:*** T. Martin (1) d. E. Ran 6–2 6–0. ***Doubles:*** M. Sell/K. Ullyett (2) d. O. Motevassel/D. Musa 6–3 6–3.

SAO PAULO (BRA) (100) 22–28 SEPTEMBER – ***Singles:*** L. Arnold (6) d. F. Meligeni (1) 6–4 1–0 ret. ***Doubles:*** N. Aerts/B. Martinez (3) d. M. Carlsson/F. Costa 6–0 6–0.

SEVILLE (ESP) (25H) 22–27 SEPTEMBER – ***Singles:*** A. Calatrava (1) d. A. Lopez-Moron (5) 6–2 6–4. ***Doubles:*** T. Ketola/M. Kohlmann (3) d. A. Calatrava/J. Imaz-Ruiz 4–6 6–1 6–3.

SKOPJE (MKD) (25H) 22–28 SEPTEMBER – ***Singles:*** D. Vemic d. C. Trimmel 6–3 6–7 6–3. ***Doubles:*** T. Buchmayer/T. Strengberger (2) d. N. Djordjevic/D. Vemic (1) 6–4 7–6.

MALLORCA (ESP) (50) 29 SEPTEMBER–5 OCTOBER – ***Singles:*** A. Lopez-Moron d. O. Stanoytchev 6–4 6–4. ***Doubles:*** M. Ardinghi/G. Marx d. D. Bowen/T. El Sawy (2) 6–3 6–2.

SAN ANTONIO (USA) (50) 29 SEPTEMBER–5 OCTOBER – ***Singles:*** D. Nestor d. G. Grant (7) 6–4 6–2. ***Doubles:*** D. Flach/J. Salzenstein (4) d. C. Clark/B. Hawk 4–6 6–2 6–1.

SANTIAGO (CHI) (100) 30 SEPTEMBER–5 OCTOBER – ***Singles:*** G. Canas (5) d. D. van Scheppingen (6) 4–6 7–5 6–3. ***Doubles:*** L. Arnold/J. Oncins d. D. del Rio/M. Puerta (4) 6–2 6–2.

BARCELONA (ESP) (100) 6–12 OCTOBER – ***Singles:*** C. Costa (7) d. J-A. Marin 6–1 6–4. ***Doubles:*** T. El Sawy/N. Marques d. D. Pescariu/D. Sanguinetti 6–1 6–2.

LIMA (PER) (100) 6–12 OCTOBER – ***Singles:*** T. Nydahl (2) d. O. Gross (3) 4–6 6–0 6–4. ***Doubles:*** M. Hood/S. Prieto (4) d. K. Goossens/J. Szymanski 6–2 6–1.

SEDONA (USA) (50) 6–12 OCTOBER – ***Singles:*** M. Sell d. G. Weiner 6–4 6–4. ***Doubles:*** J-L. de Jager/R. Koenig (4) d. A. Peterson/E. Taino 6–2 6–2.

GUAYAQUIL (ECU) (100) 13–19 OCTOBER – ***Singles:*** T. Nydahl (2) d. M. Zabaleta (WC) 6–0 6–3. ***Doubles:*** G. Koves/T. Nydahl d. D. del Rio/M. Puerta 2–6 6–3 7–6.

CAIRO (EGY) (100H) 13–19 OCTOBER – ***Singles:*** A. Berasategui (WC) (1) d. K. Alami (3) 7–5 6–3. ***Doubles:*** T. Carbonell/F. Roig (1) d. W. Arthurs/E. Ran 6–3 6–3.

BREST (FRA) (100H) 20–26 OCTOBER – ***Singles:*** J. van Herck (5) d. S. Grosjean 4–6 6–2 6–4. ***Doubles:*** D. Randall/J. Waite (1) d. J-L. de Jager/R. Koenig 3–6 7–6 6–4.

ECKENTAL (GER) (25H) 20–26 OCTOBER – ***Singles:*** R. Schuttler (5) d. P. Luxa 6–4 6–1. ***Doubles:*** L. Rehmann/R. Schuttler d. G. Blumauer/M. Mirnyi (3) 6–4 1–6 6–3.

SEOUL (KOR) (50H) 20–26 OCTOBER – ***Singles:*** P. Tramacchi d. R. Lavergne 6–3 6–3. ***Doubles:*** E. Kempes/G. Motomura (1) d. J. Golmard/R. Lavergne 7–5 7–5.

AACHEN (GER) (50H) 27 OCTOBER–2 NOVEMBER – ***Singles:*** H. Dreekmann (4) d. J. Novak (1) 5–7 7–6 6–3. ***Doubles:*** J-L. de Jager/C. Haggard d. D. Randall/J. Waite (1) 3–6 6–1 7–6.

NEUMUNSTER (GER) (25H) 3–9 NOVEMBER – ***Singles:*** D. Norman (4) d. J. van Lottum 6–7 7–6 7–6. ***Doubles:*** J-L. de Jager/C. Haggard (2) d. L. Burgsmuller/M. Hantschk 6–3 6–1.

PUEBLA (MEX) (25H) 3–9 NOVEMBER – ***Singles:*** L-E. Herrera d. W. McGuire 7–6 4–6 6–4. ***Doubles:*** T. El Sawy/M. Ruah (2) d. M. Ardinghi/V. Santopadre (3) 7–6 7–5.

ANDORRA (AND) (100H) 10–16 NOVEMBER – ***Singles:*** G. Pozzi d. N. Escude 7–6 4–6 6–3. ***Doubles:*** N. Escude/J. Golmard d. T. Kempers/M. Oosting (3) 6–4 6–4.

LAS VEGAS (USA) (50H) 10–16 NOVEMBER – ***Singles:*** C. Vinck d. A. Agassi (5) 6–2 7–5. ***Doubles:*** D. di Lucia/M. Sell d. P. Goldstein/J. Thomas 6–4 6–4.

PUERTO RICO (PUR) (100H) 10–16 NOVEMBER – ***Singles:*** F. Squillari d. M. Carca 6–3 6–4. ***Doubles:*** L. Arnold/D. Orsanic (1) d. M. Hood/S. Prieto 7–5 3–6 6–3.

AMARILLO (USA) (50) 17–23 NOVEMBER – ***Singles:*** P. Tramacchi d. T. Ketola 6–4 5–7 6–3. ***Doubles:*** G. Grant/M. Merklein (2) d. M. Petchey/A. Rueb 6–2 6–2.

GUADALAJARA II (MEX) (100) 17–23 NOVEMBER – ***Singles:*** Y. El Aynaoui d. R. Wassen 6–4 6–7 6–4. ***Doubles:*** N. Aerts/A. Sa (3) d. R. Kokavec/M-A. Osorio 7–6 6–3.

PORTOROZ (SLO) (25H) 17–23 NOVEMBER – ***Singles:*** O. Stanoytchev d. L. Burgsmuller 1–6 7–6 6–0.
Doubles: D. Sapsford/C. Wilkinson (1) d. S. Hirszon/U. Plamberger (3) 6–0 3–6 6–3.

BOMBAY (IND) (25H) 24–29 NOVEMBER – ***Singles:*** T. Suzuki d. B. Cowan 6–1 6–0.
Doubles: E. Couto/J. Cunha-Silva (1) d. M. Hilpert/D. Nainkin 1–6 6–6 def.

BUENOS AIRES (ARG) (100) 24–30 NOVEMBER – ***Singles:*** F. Squillari (3) d. D. Moyano 6–1 6–4.
Doubles: D. del Rio/D. Orsanic (2) d. P. Albano/L. Lobo (1) 6–4 4–6 6–1.

BURBANK (USA) (50) 24 NOVEMBER–1 DECEMBER – ***Singles:*** A. Agassi (3) d. S. Sargsian (1) 6–2 6–1.
Doubles: D. Flach/B. MacPhie (2) d. G. Bastl/P. Gottesleben 7–6 6–4.

IXTAPA (MEX) (25H) 24–30 NOVEMBER – ***Singles:*** S. Campbell (3) d. T. Ketola 7–6 6–1.
Doubles: C. Haggard/M. Ruah (1) d. B. Martinez/R. Wassen (3) 6–4 7–6.

REUNION ISLAND (REU) (50H) 24–30 NOVEMBER – ***Singles:*** J. Apell d. A. Clement (3) 6–4 7–6.
Doubles: C. Ferreira/J. Siemerink (2) d. A. Calatrava/J. Golmard (3) 6–2 6–3.

AHMEDABAD (IND) (25H) 1–6 DECEMBER – ***Singles:*** V. Kutsenko d. H. Wiltschnig 6–1 6–4.
Doubles: E. Couto/J. Cunha-Silva (1) d. G. Motomura/O. Ogorodov (2) 6–4 3–6 6–3.

BAD LIPPSPRINGE (GER) (50) 1–7 DECEMBER – ***Singles:*** M. Kohlmann d. R. Schuttler (4) 4–6 7–6 6–5.
Doubles: T. Ketola/M. Kohlmann d. D. Dier/L. Koslowski 4–6 6–3 7–5.

WISMAR (GER) (25H) 8–13 DECEMBER – ***Singles:*** C. Vinck (6) d. I. Heuberger 6–3 7–6.
Doubles: L. Burgsmuller/M. Kohlmann d. B. Martinez/O. Ortiz (2) 6–4 7–6.

SANTIAGO II (CHI) (25H) 8–13 DECEMBER – ***Singles:*** O. Gross (2) d. F. Cabello (4) 6–2 6–2.
Doubles: M. Hood/S. Prieto (1) d. D. del Rio/M. Puerta (2) 7–5 6–3.

EILAT (ISR) (50H) 8–13 DECEMBER – ***Singles:*** T. Ketola d. N. Godwin 6–3 6–4.
Doubles: P. Baur/A. Cherkasov d. S. Groen/R. Wassen (3) 6–3 7–6.

PERTH (AUS) (25H) 8–13 DECEMBER – ***Singles:*** W. Arthurs (Q) d. T. Larkham (5) 7–5 7–6.
Doubles: J. Holmes/P. Kilderry (3) d. L. Hewitt/L. Smith 6–1 3–6 7–6.

Men's Satellite Circuits 1997

In 1997 there were 111 Satellite Circuits for men in 53 countries, each comprising three tournaments plus a Masters play-off at which prize money and ranking points were awarded. Each circuit was organised and run by the National Association of the country in which the circuit took place. Below are listed the winners of each circuit, with the ATP Tour ranking points won in brackets (based on the total number of circuit points plus bonuses during the four weeks).

VALUE *CIRCUIT + US$'000*	*START*	*SINGLES WINNERS (+PTS)*	*DOUBLES WINNERS (+PTS)*
India (25H)	28–12	A. Merinov (LAT) (58)	J. Winnink (NED)/T. Zdrazila (CZE) (57)
Spain I (25)	03–01	S. Koubek (AUT) (55)	A. Portas (ESP)/J-L. Rascon (ESP) (50)
Portugal I (25)	03–01	M. Craca (GER) (56)	J. Cunha-Silva (POR)/N. Marques (POR) (54)
Central America (25)	04–01	L. Gloria (USA) (37)	S. Ladipo (NGR)/G. Trifu (ROM) (48)
France I (25)	04–01	C. van Garsse (BEL) (40)	G. Marx (FRA)/O. Morel (FRA) (40)
Italy I (25)	04–01	N. Timfjord (SWE) (50)	M. Bertolini (ITA)/I. Gaudi (ITA) (52)
Spain II (50)	31–01	A. Calatrava (ESP) (63)	A. Martin (ESP)/S. Navarro (ESP) (62)
France II (25)	01–02	F. Vitoux (FRA) (46)	G. Marx (FRA)/O. Morel (FRA) (49)
Portugal II (25)	01–02	E. Couto (POR) (48)	E. Couto (POR)/B. Mota (POR) (45)
Great Britain I (50)	03–02	A. Richardson (GBR) (59)	M. Bertolini (ITA)/I. Gaudi (ITA) (60)
Austria I (25)	08–02	G. Mandl (AUT) (48)	B. Galik (SVK)/B. Urh (SLO) (49)
Israel I (25)	08–02	A. Ilie (AUS) (53)	D. Poliakov (UKR)/D. Tomashevich (UZB) (40)
Philippines (25)	17–02	Y-I. Yoon (KOR) (55)	H-T. Lee (KOR)/Y-I. Yoon (KOR) (49)
Spain III (25)	28–02	M. Rodriguez (ARG) (51)	J. Balcells (ESP)/A. Lopez-Moron (ESP) (50)
Australia I (25H)	02–03	A. Belobrajdic (AUS) (60)	A. Foster (GBR)/D. Sapsford (GBR) (46)
France III (50H)	08–03	R. Gilbert (FRA) (60)	L. Barthez (FRA)/G. Carraz (FRA) (64)
Greece I (25)	08–03	N. Escude (FRA) (48)	W. Neefs (BEL) (37)/C. Singer (USA) (35)
Mexico I (25)	08–03	G. Weiner (USA) (46)	C. Clark (USA)/A. Peterson (USA) (45)
Egypt I (25)	22–03	Z. Nagy (HUN) (48)	R. Hanak (CZE)/T. Krupa (CZE) (48)
USA I (50)	04–04	E. Erlich (ISR) (46)	C. Haggard (RSA)/M. Hilpert (GER) (60)
Argentina I (25)	05–04	F. Dondo (URU) (50)	J-I. Garat (ARG)/L. Olguin (ARG) (42)
Brazil I (25)	05–04	M. Carlsson (BRA) (50)	N. Aerts (BRA)/A. Sa (BRA) (53)
Croatia I (25)	05–04	M. Belgraver (NED) (46)	I. Ljubicic (CRO)/G. Oresic (CRO) (44)
Italy II (25)	05–04	M. Hipfl (AUT) (48)	F. Beraldo (ITA)/M. Bertolini (ITA) (48)
Mexico II (25)	05–04	M. Sanchez (MEX) (46)	J. Knowle (AUT)/T. Strengberger (AUT) (48)
Malaysia I (25)	07–04	N. Thomann (FRA) (49)	J. Coetzee (RSA)/D. Roberts (RSA) (46)
New Zealand (25H)	07–04	P. Tramacchi (AUS) (52)	M. Tebbutt (AUS)/P. Tramacchi (AUS) (61)
Bulgaria (25)	12–04	N. Escude (FRA) (49)	M. Schmidtmann (GER)/D. Sistermans (NED) (42)
Germany I (50)	13–04	J-B. Perlant (FRA) (46)	H. Capell (GER)/M. Kohlmann (GER) (50)
Great Britain II (50)	21–04	A. Belobrajdic (AUS) (61)	B. Cowan (GBR)/N. Weal (GBR) (52)
Brazil II (25)	03–05	A. Sa (BRA) (50)	A. Ferreira (BRA)/J. Zwetsch (BRA) (49)
Chile I (25)	03–05	S. Prieto (ARG) (49)	H. Gamonal (CHI)/R. Gamonal (CHI) (39)
Croatia II (25)	03–05	Z. Krajan (CRO) (46)	I. Ljubicic (CRO)/G. Oresic (CRO) (41)
Portugal III (25)	03–05	J. Cunha-Silva (POR) (46)	J. Cunha-Silva (POR)/B. Fragoso (POR) (47)
Yugoslavia I (25)	03–05	D. Vemic (YUG) (52)	D. Petrovic (AUS)/G. Silcock (AUS) (49)
Spain IV (25)	09–05	A. Calatrava (ESP) (52)	C. Martinez (ESP)/E. Nicolas (ESP) (43)
Greece II (25)	10–05	L. Tieleman (ITA) (51)	T. Ketola (FIN)/L. Tieleman (ITA) (45)
Australia II (25)	10-05	A. Hunt (NZL) 48	B. Ellwood (AUS)/P. Tramacchi (AUS) (53)
USA II (50)	16-05	R. Mena (PAR) (53)	C. Groer (USA)/A. Hamadeh (LIB) (54)
Germany II (50)	19-05	A. Garizzio (ARG) (53)	O. Fukarek (CZE)/R. Stephanek (CZE) (59)
Korea (25)	24-05	H-T. Lee (KOR) (50)	D-H. Kim (KOR)/H-T. Lee (KOR) (50)
Mexico III (24)	24-05	G. Motomura (JPN) (50)	M. Puerta (ARG)/K. Orellana (VEN) (44)
Brazil III (25)	31-05	A. Sa (BRA) (48)	N. Aerts (BRA)/A. Sa (BRA) (51)
Finland (25)	31-05	J-B. Perlant (FRA) (48)	C. Rochus (BEL)/R. Willems (BEL) (49)
Italy III (25)	31-05	E. Grossi (ITA) (42)	S. Iwabuchi (JPN)/T. Suzuki (JPN) (38)
Yugoslavia/ Macedonia (25)	31-05	A. Schneiter (ARG) (47)	D. Petrovic (AUS)/G. Silcock (AUS) (52)
Spain V (25)	06-06	J. Imaz-Ruiz (ESP) (49)	M. Roy (ESP) (40)/A. Gonzalez (ESP) (35)

VALUE *CIRCUIT + US$'000*	*START*	*SINGLES WINNERS (+PTS)*	*DOUBLES WINNERS (+PTS)*
Canada (25)	08-06	G. Bastl (SUI) (50)	B. Eagle (USA)/A. Peterson (USA) (42)
Croatia III (25)	16-06	M. Nielsen (NZL) (42)	J. Dumanic (CRO)/V. Sever (CRO) (44)
Netherlands (25H)	16-06	E. Kempes (NED) (56)	E. Kempes (NED)/P. Wessels (NED) (59)
USA III (50)	16-06	R. Bryan (USA) (45)	L. Smith (AUS)/E. Taino (USA) (59)
Venezuela (25)	16-06	A. Aramburu (PER) (46)	F. Ruiz (CHI)/A. Venero (PER) (44)
Austria II (25)	23-06	M. Hipfl (AUT) (50)	O. Fukarek (CZE)/T. Strengberger (AUT) (49)
China PR (25)	23-06	D-H. Kim (KOR) (46)	D-H. Kim (KOR)/H-T. Lee (KOR) (47)
Denmark (25)	30-06	T. Larsen (DEN) (50)	P. Sommer (GER)/M. Wislsperger (GER) (48)
Italy IV (25H)	30-06	E. Grossi (ITA) (57)	G. Gatto (ITA)/G. Montenet (ITA) (59)
Japan I (25)	07-07	J-F. Bachelot (FRA) (50)	T. Shimada (JPN)/M. Takada (JPN) (40)
Spain VI (50)	07-07	J-M. Vicente (ESP) (56)	D. Hipperdinger (ARG)/M. Roy (ESP) (50)
Colombia (25)	14-07	M. Rincon (COL) (46)	F. Ruiz (CHI)/A. Venero (PER) (45)
Hungary (25)	14-07	M. Delfino (ARG) (43)	R. Hanak (CZE)/T. Krupa (CZE) (50)
Slovenia (25)	14-07	J. Vacek (CZE) (46)	L. Friedl (CZE)/P. Kovacka (CZE) (50)
France IV (25)	21-07	S. de Chaunac (FRA) (46)	R. du Pre (FRA)/A. la Porte (FRA) (42)
Belarus/Russia (25)	21-07	A. Stoliarov (RUS) (52)	M. Boye (FRA)/V. Voltchkov (BLR) (47)
USA VI (50)	21-07	J. Szymanski (VEN) (58)	J. Weir-Smith (RSA)/T. Budgen (AUS) (54)
Egypt II (25)	28-07	L. Milligan (GBR) (47)	J. Gould (AUS)/J. Kerr (AUS) (50)
Great Britain III (25)	28-07	C. Wilkinson (GBR) (49)	J. Fox (GBR)/N. Gould (GBR) (41)
Baltic (25)	28-07	J-F. Andersen (NOR) (46)	H. Andersson (SWE)/M. Hellstrom (SWE) (47)
Belgium/ Luxembourg (25H)	04-08	J. Boutter (FRA) (49)	X. Malisse (BEL)/W. Neefs (BEL) (48)
Italy V (25H)	04-08	O. Fukarek (CZE) (55)	M. Bertolini (ITA)/J. Margotto (ITA) (59)
Croatia IV (25)	11-08	R. Hanak (CZE) (50)	R. Hanak (CZE)/T. Krupa (CZE) (51)
Ecuador/Peru (25)	11-08	A. Calleri (ARG) (51)	S. Barron (IRL)/J. Coetzee (RSA) (49)
Spain VII (50)	11-08	D. Sanchez (ESP) (55)	C. Martinez (ESP)/E. Nicolas (ESP) (55)
Yugoslavia II (25)	11-08	J. Vanek (CZE) (46)	M. Pampoulov (AUT)/M. Velev (BUL) (47)
Cuba/Mexico (25)	18-08	M. Sanchez (MEX) (46)	R. Omana (VEN)/J. Romero (VEN) (44)
Iran, Republic (25H)	18-08	Y. Doumbia (SEN) (60)	Y. Doumbia (SEN)/I. Gaudi (ITA) (59)
Slovak Republic (25)	18-08	T. Zib (CZE) (50)	D. Fiala (CZE)/L. Friedl (CZE) (49)
Turkey II (25)	18-08	A. Hadad (ISR) (47)	R. Chess (USA)/T. Shimada (JPN) (41)
Indonesia (25)	25-08	J. Stasiak (AUS) (49)	S. Wibowo (INA)/B. Wiryawan (INA) (43)
Switzerland I (25)	25-08	A. Garizzio (ARG) (49)	M. Hantschk (GER)/M. Menzler (GER) (42)
France V (50H)	08-09	J-F. Bachelot (FRA) (69)	R. Sluiter (NED)/N. Zimonjic (YUG) (70)
Bolivia/Paraguay (25)	08-09	F. Browne (ARG) (48)	D. Furmanski (ARG)/M. Garcia (ARG) (43)
Sweden/Norway (25)	08-09	F. Jonsson (SWE) (47)	M. Boye (FRA)/P. Pala (CZE) (48)
USA V (50)	08-09	G. Bastl (SUI) (43)	M. Sprengelmeyer (USA)/C. Groer (USA) (56)
Great Britain IV (25)	16-09	D. Sapsford (GBR) (49)	B. Cowan (GBR)/T. Spinks (GBR) (48)
Uzbekistan (25)	22-09	T. Catar (SVK) (40)	D. Fitzgerald (SUI)/M. Jorquera (ARG) (38)
Greece III (25)	22-09	K. Flygt (SWE) (49)	N. Behr (ISR)/J. Knowle (AUT) (47)
Australia III (25H)	29-09	J. Stasiak (AUS) (55)	J. Crabb (AUS)/P. Kilderry (AUS) (50)
Portugal IV (25)	29-09	T. Ketola (FIN) (49)	T. Ketola (FIN) (48)/V. Pest (GER) (42)
Argentina II (25)	06-10	D. Moyano (ARG) (49)	E. Artoni (ARG)/M. Pastura (ARG) (49)
France VI (25)	06-10	S. de Chaunac (FRA) (46)	G. Carraz (FRA)/J. Hanquez (FRA) (44)
Italy VI (25)	06-10	N. Kischkewitz (FRA) (41)	G. Oresic (CRO) (41)/I. Ljubicic (CRO) (35)
Tunisia (25)	13-10	Y. Doumbia (SEN) (51)	Y. Doumbia (SEN)/Z. Nagy (HUN) (50)
USA VI (50)	13-10	P. Goldstein (USA) (45)	R. Sluiter (NED)/N. Zimonjic (YUG) (56)
Czech Moravian (25)	20-10	L. Friedl (CZE) (49)	L. Friedl (CZE) (38)/T. Krupa (CZE) (30)
Spain IX (25)	20-10	D. Sanchez (ESP) (50)	C. Martinez (ESP)/D. Sanchez (ESP) (45)
Switzerland II (50)	20-10	F. Veglio (SUI) (58)	M. Bertolini (ITA)/F. Veglio (SUI) (59)
Brazil IV (25)	27-10	A. Ferreira (BRA) (51)	B. Borgula (SVK)/F. Costa (BRA) (47)
Central Africa (25)	27-10	O. Motevassel (USA) (43)	J. Coetzee (RSA)/D. Roberts (RSA) (48)
Greece IV (25)	27-10	G. Gatto (ITA) (50)	W. Neefs (BEL)/D. Sistermans (NED) (44)
Australia IV (25H)	02-11	A. Belobrajdic (AUS) (62)	J. Holmes (AUS)/A. Painter (AUS) (60)
Israel II (25)	03-11	N. Behr (ISR) (48)	J. Erlich (ISR)/A. Hadad (ISR) (44)
Thailand (25)	03-11	P. Srichaphan (THA) (49)	W. Arthurs (AUS)/B. Larkham (AUS) (48)
Uruguay (25)	03-11	D. Furmanski (ARG) (38)	D. Furmanski (ARG)/M. Wowk (ARG) (42)
Chile II (25)	10-11	F. Browne (ARG) (48)	F. Ruiz (CHI)/T. Venero (PER) (42)
Egypt III (25)	17-11	M. Velev (BUL) (50)	T. Lenho (FIN)/T. Nurminen (FIN) (46)
Japan II (25)	17-11	Y. Yamamoto (JPN) (47)	A. Matsushita (JPN)/M. Takada (JPN) (50)
USA VII (50)	17-11	T. Zib (USA) (57)	S. Aspelin (USA)(59)/C. Groer (USA) (58)
Brazil V (25)	24-11	M. Carlsson (BRA) (48)	J. Zwetsch (BRA)(51)/ A. Ferreira (BRA) (37)
Portugal V (25)	24-11	N. Marques (POR) (49)	M. Merry (NED)/R. Sluiter (NED) (41)
South Africa (25)	24-11	J. Bower (RSA) (49)	R. Koenig (RSA)/W. Whitehouse (RSA) (47)

ITF Women's Circuit

Ingrid Lofdahl-Bentzer

The ITF Women's Circuit, previously known as the Futures Circuit, continues to grow both in the number of events and the amount of prize money on offer. In 1997, the Circuit consisted of some 280 tournaments, with the total prize money available being close to $5 million.

The country by country breakdown of events for 1997 shows good global representation, with Europe hosting the most tournaments. There has been a very positive increase in the number of events and prize money in general, and in particular in the USA.

In an effort to create a more structured circuit, the ITF has encouraged the tournaments in the lower prize money categories to up-grade to the $50,000 and $75,000 level, with the possibility of help from the Grand Slam Development Fund. With twenty nine events in the higher level prize money category, the Women's Circuit is therefore in a position to service the middle-ranked players, as well as providing an important spring board before they make a full commitment to the COREL WTA TOUR. The ITF Women's Circuit has concentrated its efforts on increasing the number of $25,000 events to keep a balanced structure, facilitating the route for players to reach the highest level of tournaments possible according to their individual ability.

The ITF Women's Circuit and the ITF Junior Department work very closely together. The Junior Exempt Project, which was instigated in 1996, came into full effect in April 1997. This programme has helped the top juniors counter the possible ramifications of the 1997's 'Rolling Race Ranking System' as well as further improve, develop and integrate the Junior players into the Women's Circuit. The top ten junior girls on the ITF Junior World Ranking at the end of 1996 were given the opportunity to select two events on the 1997 ITF Women's Circuit, where they were given a place in the Main Draw. This creates an important bridge between the junior and senior circuits and also offers tournaments the chance to have one of the world's top juniors competing at their event.

The system operates as follows, in accordance with the Age Eligibility Rule:

- Number 1 and 2 ranked players may choose an ITF event with prize money up to and including $75,000 prize money level events
- Number 3 to 6 ranked players may choose an ITF event with prize money up to and including $50,000 prize money level events
- Number 7 to 10 ranked players may choose an ITF event with prize money up to and including $25,000 prize money level events

The Women's Department has also worked closely with the Age Eligibility Commission in their effort to up-date and modify the Age Eligibility Rule.

The minor changes in officiating implemented from 1 January, have helped to ensure that the events are run to the high standards which the players are now coming to expect.

In an effort to consolidate the partnership between the ITF Women's Circuit and the COREL WTA TOUR, a feed-up system has been in effect for the last few years. During 1997, the winner or finalist in most of the $75,000 and $50,000 events were offered a place in the Main Draw of a COREL WTA TOUR Tier III or IV event and the winner or finalist in selected $25,000 events were offered a place in the Qualifying Draw of a COREL WTA TOUR Tier III or IV event.

With the above mentioned projects, as well as the continued co-operation and positive interaction with our national associations, we are confident that the future of the ITF Women's Circuit will be exciting and progressive.

ITF WOMEN'S CIRCUIT RESULTS 1997

ITF WOMEN'S $20,000 CIRCUITS

Mexico, Reynosa (Circuit I) – February 24–March 2 – ***Singles:*** S. Chi (TPE) d. M. d'Agostini (BRA) 6–2 7–6. ***Doubles:*** S. Chi (TPE)/S. Huang (CAN) d. K. Palme (MEX)/G. Velez (MEX) 6–1 6–3.

Mexico, Matamoros (Circuit II) – March 3–9 – ***Singles:*** A. Zhidkova (RUS) d. K. Palme (MEX) 6–4 6–0. ***Doubles:*** S. Chi (TPE)/S. Huang (CAN) d. K. Palme (MEX)/G. Velez (MEX) 6–0 6–1.

Mexico, Victoria (Circuit III) – March 10–16 – ***Singles:*** S. Chi (TPE) d. A. Zhidkova (MEX) 6–1 6–1. ***Doubles:*** L. Becarra (MEX)/M. d'Agostini (BRA) d. K. Palme (MEX)/G. Velez (MEX) 6–1 6–4.

Mexico, Mante (Masters) – March 17–23 – ***Singles:*** S. Chi (TPE) d. M. d'Agostini (BRA) 6–2 6–3. ***Doubles:*** P. Arrangoiz (MEX)/A. Zhidkova (RUS) d. K. Palme (MEX)/G. Velez (MEX) 5–7 6–0 6–3.

México, Circuit I – May 26–June 1 – ***Singles:*** A. P. Gonzalez (MEX) d. A. Garcia (MEX) w/o. ***Doubles:*** L. Becerra (MEX)/A. P. Gonzalez (MEX) d. A. Hernandez (MEX)/R. Raiss (USA) 6–2 7–5.

México, Circuit II – June 2–8 – ***Singles:*** L. Becerra (MEX) d. A. Hernandez (MEX) 6–4 6–1. ***Doubles:*** L. Becerra (MEX)/A. P. Gonzalez (MEX) d. Y. Cordoval (CUB)/Y. Montesino (CUB) 6–3 6–1.

México, Circuit III – June 9–15 – ***Singles:*** H. Hernandez (MEX) d. L. Becerra (MEX) 7–6 (4) 4–6 6–2. ***Doubles:*** L. Becerra (MEX)/A. P. Gonzalez (MEX) d. A. Hernandez (MEX)/ R. Raiss (USA) 6–2 6–2.

México Masters – June 16–22 – ***Singles:*** A. P. Gonzalez (MEX) d. A. Hernandez (MEX) 6–4 7–5. ***Doubles:*** A. P. Gonzalez (MEX)/L. Becerra (MEX) d. A. Hernandez (MEX)/R. Rochelle (USA) 6–4 6–3.

ITF WOMEN'S $40,000 CIRCUITS

Australia, Warrnambool (Circuit I) – March 3–9 – ***Singles:*** S-A. Siddall (GBR) d. L. Ahl (GBR) 6–3 6–3. ***Doubles:*** N. de Villiers (RSA)/S-A. Siddal (GBR) d. J. Limmer (AUS)/L. McShea (AUS) 6–4 4–6 7–6.

Australia, Canberra (Circuit II) – March 10–16 – ***Singles:*** J. Taylor (AUS) d. E. Dominikovic (AUS) 7–5 4–6 6–4. ***Doubles:*** J. Ward (GBR)/L. Woodroffe (GBR) d. E. Dominikovic (AUS)/A. Grahame (AUS) 4–6 6–4 6–2.

Australia, Wodonga (Circuit III) – March 17–23 – ***Singles:*** M. Dittmann (AUS) d. L. Woodroffe (GBR) 3–6 7–6 6–4. ***Doubles:*** N. de Villiers (RSA)/S-A. Siddall (GBR) d. J. Ward (GBR)/L. Woodroffe (GBR) 3–6 6–2 6–3.

Australia, Corowa (Masters) – March 24–30 – ***Singles:*** E. Dominikovic (AUS) d. J. Taylor (AUS) 6–4 6–2. ***Doubles:*** T. Musgrave (AUS)/J. Taylor (AUS) d. N. de Villiers (RSA)/S. A. Siddall (GBR) 6–4 4–6 6–2.

Australia, Warwick (Circuit I) – April 14–20 – ***Singles:*** J. A. Fetch (AUS) d. N. de Villiers (RSA) 6–2 4–6 7–6(2). ***Doubles:*** T. Musgrave (AUS)/B. Stewart (AUS) d. K. Moulds (AUS)/S. Stanley (AUS) 6–4 6–0.

Australia, Dalby (Circuit II) –April 21–27– ***Singles:*** N. de Villers (RSA) d. E. Dominikovic (AUS) 7–5 7–6(5). ***Doubles:*** N. de Villers (RSA)/L. McShea (AUS) d. J. A. Fetch (AUS)/R. Reid (AUS) 6–0 6–3.

Australia, Circuit III – April 28–May 4 – ***Singles:*** E. Dominikovic (AUS) d. N. de Villers (RSA) 6–2 6–4. ***Doubles:*** N. de Villers (RSA)/L. McShea (AUS) d. J. A. Fetch (AUS)/R. Reid (AUS) 6–7(4) 6–1 6–3.

Australia, Circuit I – May 12–18 – ***Singles:*** C. Watson (AUS) d. R. Reid (AUS) 6–4 6–2. ***Doubles:*** N. de Villers (RSA)/L. Mc Shea (AUS) d. J. A. Fetch (AUS)/R. Reid (AUS) 6–4 6–4.

Australia, Circuit II – May 19–25 – ***Singles:*** R. Reid (AUS) d. S. Asogoe (JPN) 3–6 6–3 6–4. ***Doubles:*** S. Asogoe (JPN)/B. Sangaram (THA) d. N. de Villiers (RSA)/L. McShea (AUS) 5–7 6–3 6–3.

Australia, Circuit III – May 26 – June 1 – ***Singles:*** L. McShea (AUS) d. N. de Villers (RSA) 6–4 6–2. ***Doubles:*** N. de Villers (RSA)/L. McShea (AUS) d S. Asogoe (JPN)/B. Sangaram (THA) 4–6 6–1 6–1.

Australia Masters – June 2–8 – ***Singles:*** C. Watson (AUS) d. R. Reid (AUS) 6–4 6–2. ***Doubles:*** N. de Villiers (RSA)/L. McShea (AUS) d. R. Reid (AUS)/J. A. Fetch (AUS) 6–4 6–4.

Japan Circuit I – September 8–14 – ***Singles:*** S. Umehara (JPN) d. C. Grunes (GER) 6–2 2–6 7–6 (6). ***Doubles:*** A. Matsuda (JPN)/S. Honda (JPN) d. S. Hisamatsu (JPN)/A. Grahame (AUS) 2–6 6–1 6–3.

Japan Circuit II – September 15–21 – ***Singles:*** K. Moulds (AUS) d. S. de Beer (RSA) 2–6 7–5 6–3. ***Doubles:*** S. de Beer (RSA)/N. Urabe (JPN) d. Y. Sasano (JPN)/R. Otakeyama (JPN) 6–2 6–3.

Japan Circuit III – September 22–28 – ***Singles:*** R. Takemura (JPN) d. A. Grahame (AUS) 6–3 5–7 6–4. ***Doubles:*** S. de Beer (RSA)/N. Urabe (JPN) d. S. Katsumi (JPN)/K. Kojima (JPN) 6–3 6–3.

Japan Masters – 29 September–5 October – ***Singles:*** S. de Beer (RSA) d. A. Narvaez (USA) 6–2 7–6(4). ***Doubles:*** S. de Beer (RSA)/N. Urabe (JPN) d. Y. Kitamur (JPN)/N. Yuki (JPN) 6–2 6–3.

ITF WOMEN'S $10,000 TOURNAMENTS

USA, Delray, Beach, FL. – January 6–12 – ***Singles:*** S. Mabry (USA) d. K. Triska (USA) 6–3 6–1.
Doubles: C. Black (ZIM)/I. Seljutina (KAZ) d. B. Rippner (USA)/P. Yaroshuk (USA) 6–3 6–3.

Spain, Pontevedra, – January 13–19 – ***Singles:*** H. van Aalderen (NED) d. L. Dominguez (ESP) 6--4 6–2.
Doubles: A. Ortuno (ESP)/S. Prazeres (POR) d. T. Garbin (ITA)/S. Ventura (ITA) 4–6 6–1 6–4.

Finland, Helsinki – January 13–19 – ***Singles:*** G. Navratilova (CZE) d. S. Rottier (NED) 3–6 6–4 2–2 ret.
Doubles: O. Blahotova (CZE)/G. Navratilova (CZE) d. M. Koutstaal (NED)/A. Linkova (RUS) 6–2 6–1.

USA, Delray Beach, FL – January 13–19 – ***Singles:*** T. Snyder (USA) d. B. Rippner (USA) 6–2 6–4.
Doubles: Re. Jensen (USA)/K. Phebus (USA) d. P. Nelson (USA)/V. Webb (CAN) 6–7 6–2 6–2.

Sweden, Bastad – January 20–26 – ***Singles:*** P. van Acker (BEL) d. A-K. Svensson (SWE) 4–6 7–5 6–1.
Doubles: A. Lindstedt (SWE)/Z. Dragana (YUG) d. A-K. Svensson (SWE)/P. van Acker (BEL) 6–7 7–6 6–3.

Turkey, Istanbul – January 20–26 – ***Singles:*** M. Froelich (GER) d. E. Fauth (AUT) 6–2 6–2.
Doubles: J. Ondrouchova (CZE)/H. Sromova (CZE) d. M. Mastalirova (CZE)/M. Nekvapilova (CZE) 6–2 6–1.

Spain, Orense – January 20–26 – ***Singles:*** A. Ortuño (ESP) d. L. Sentis (NED) 6–3 6–2.
Doubles: A. Ortuño (ESP)/S. Prazares (POR) d. L. Sentis (NED)/S. Trik (NED) 6–2 6–3.

USA, San Antonio, TX – January 20–26 – ***Singles:*** B. Rippner (USA) d. M. Muric (CRO) 6–2 6–4.
Doubles: J. Chi (USA)/K. Pace (USA) d. K. Alley (USA)/P. Nelson (USA) 6–4 4–6 6–4.

France, Dinan – January 27–February 2 – ***Singles:*** E. Loit (FRA) d. E. Curutchet (FRA) 6–1 7–6.
Doubles: C. Dewinne (FRA)/S. Georges (FRA) d. E. Loit (FRA)/L. Sanchez (FRA) 7–5 6–2.

Denmark, Rungsted – January 27–February 2 – ***Singles:*** M. Zdenovcova (CZE) d. K. Freye (GER) 7–6 7–6.
Doubles: L. Jasson (FIN)/A. Lindstedt (SWE) d. D. Zaric (YUG)/K. Pojatina (CRO) 4–6 7–5 6–4.

Spain, Mallorca I – February 3–9 – ***Singles:*** M-P. Zavagli (ITA) d. P. Garcia (ESP) 6–2 6–2.
Doubles: C. Salvi (ITA)/A. Vanc (ROM) d. A. Capena (ITA)/S. Ventura (ITA) 6–3 3–6 6–2.

Iceland, Reykjavik – February 3–9 – ***Singles:*** A. Hegedus (HUN) d. M. Losey (SUI) 6–2 6–4.
Doubles: A. Lindsted (SWE)/L. Jansson (FIN) d. N. Koves (HUN)/A. Hegedus (HUN) 4–6 6--1 6–2.

Great Britain, Sunderland – February 3–9 – ***Singles:*** L. Woodroffe (GBR) d. A. Lombardi (ITA) 6–4 2–6 6–4.
Doubles: S-A. Siddall (GBR)/A. Wainwright (GBR) d. M. Miller (GBR)/R. Viollet (GBR) 7–6 6–4.

Spain, Mallorca II – February 10–16 – ***Singles:*** A. Canepa (ITA) d. K. Kilsch (GER) 6–2 7–5.
Doubles: C. Salvi (ITA)/A. Vanc (ROM) d. V. Mracnova (SVK)/M. Ondrejkova (SVK) 6–2 6–1.

Great Britain, Birmingham – February 10–16 – ***Singles:*** S-A. Siddall (GBR) d. C. Taylor (GBR) 6–4 6–4.
Doubles: J. Pullin (GBR)/L. Woodroffe (GBR) d. S-A. Siddall (GBR)/A. Wainwright (GBR) 6–2 6–4.

Portugal, Faro – February 17–26 – ***Singles:*** P. Stojanova (BLR) d. A. Briegel (GER) 6–4 6–1.
Doubles: M. Inoue (JPN)/R. Otakeyama (JPN) d. S. Sallaberry (FRA)/A. Tricerri (SUI) 6–3 6–2.

Israel, Jaffa – February 24–March 2 – ***Singles:*** T. Oblziler (ISR) d. N. Koves (HUN) 7–5 6–4.
Doubles: H. Sromova (CZE)/M. Nekvapilova (CZE) d. N. Koves (HUN)/P. Markova (SVK) 6–4 6–2.

Germany, Buchen – March 3–9 – ***Singles:*** M. Schnitzer (GER) d. M. Zdenovcova (CZE) 6–2 4–6 7–5.
Doubles: N. Dubbers (GER)/L. Fritz (GER) d. O. Blahotova (CZE)/J. Macurova (CZE) 5–7 6–3 6–4.

New Zealand, Blenheim – March 3–9 – ***Singles:*** L. Chen (CHN) d. B. Sangaram (THA) 6–2 6–2.
Doubles: Abandoned due to rain.

Israel, Tel Aviv – March 3–9 – ***Singles:*** M. Vavrinec (SUI) d. N. Cahana (ISR) 6–3 7–6.
Doubles: H. van Aalderen (NED)/A. van der Hurk (NED) d. M. Nekvapilova (CZE)/H. Sromova (CZE) 0–6 6–3 6–4.

France, Dinard – March 24–30 – ***Singles:*** C. Black (ZIM) d. M. Lamarre (FRA) 4–6 6–4 6–2.
Doubles: G. di Natalie (ITA)/ F. Fortuni (ITA) d. M. Lamarre (FRA)/A. Svensson (SWE) 6–4 7–5.

Croatia, Makarska – March 31–6 April – ***Singles:*** G. Casoni (ITA) d. A. Foldenyi (HUN) 2–6 6–6 6–4.
Doubles: E. Koulikovskaya (RUS)/C. Schneider (GER) d. N. Koves (HUN)/H. Vildova (CZE) 6–1 4–6 6–4.

Indonesia, Bandung – March 31–6 April – ***Singles:*** Y. J. Cho (KOR) d. Y. J. Choi (KOR) 6–4 6–1.
Doubles: T. Hotta (JPN)/Y. Yamagishi (JPN) d. W. Prakusya (INA)/E. Sulistyowati (INA) 2–6 7–6(5) 7–5.

Indonesia, Jakarta – April 7–13 – ***Singles:*** Y. J. Cho (KOR) d. Y. J Choi (KOR) 6–1 7–5.
Doubles: E. Jelfs (GBR)/J. Choudhury (GBR) d. K. J. Won (KOR)/Y. J. Cho (KOR) 6–4 7–6(6).

Calvi, France – April 7–13 – ***Singles:*** S. Georges (FRA) d. S. Berger (FRA) 7–5 6–4.
Doubles: E. Curutchet (FRA)/S. Georges (FRA) d. S. Rizzi (FRA)/L. Sanchez (FRA) 6–1 6–1.

Hvar, Croatia – April 7–13 – ***Singles:*** M. Nekvapilova (CZE) d. H. Vildova (CZE) 7–6(2) 6–4.
Doubles: P. Markova (SVK)/Z. Valekova (SVK) d. J. Pullin (GBR)/A. Wainwright (GBR) 7–6 (3) 6–4.

Angillua, Italy – April 7–13 – ***Singles:*** Z. Malkova (CZE) d. L. Fodorean (ROM) 5–7 6–4.
Doubles: O. Hostakova (CZE)/Z. Malkova (CZE) d. L. Fodorean (ROM)/O. Golimbioschi (ROM) 3–6 6–2.

Viña del Mar, Chile– April 7–13 – ***Singles:*** K. Marosi (HUN) d. M. C. Contin (ARG) 6–1 6–4.
Doubles: K. Marosi (HUN)/V. Stelle (ARG) d. M. C. Contin (ARG)/L. Masante (ARG) 6–1 5–7 6–2.

Dubrovnik, Croatia – April 14–20 – ***Singles:*** M. Nekvapilova (CZE) d P. Stoyanova (BUL) 6–2 0–6 6–2.
Doubles: : P. Markova (SVK)/Z. Valekova (SVK) d. M. Nekvapilova (CZE)/H. Sromova (CZE) 2–6 7–5 6–4.

Anguilli, Italy – April 14–20 – ***Singles:*** O. Golimbioschi (ROM) d. G. di Natalie (ITA) 7–5 6–2.
Doubles: S. Nacuk (YUG)/D. Zaric (YUG) d. T. Obziler (ISR)/A. Smashnova (ISR) 6–2 6–4.

Elvas, Portugal – April14–20 – ***Singles:*** A. Ortuno (ESP) d. P. Hermida (ESP) 6–4 6–3.
Doubles: T. Samara (USA)/A. Soukup (CAN) d. M. d'Agostini (BRA)/A. Ortuño (ESP) 6–4 7–5

Bournemouth, Great Britain – April 21–27 – ***Singles:*** J. Pullin (GBR) d. J. Ward (GBR) 6–0 6–3.
Doubles: S. Siddall (GBR)/A Wainwright (GBR) d. L. Woodroffe (GBR)/J. Pullin (GBR) 6–3 7–5.

Prostejov, Czech Republic – April 21–27 – ***Singles:*** K. Kroupova (CZE) d. L. Prusova (CZE) 0–6 6–2 6–3.
Doubles: M. Nekvapilova (CZE)/S. Nesvadbova (CZE) d. O. Blahotova (CZE)/H. Sromova (CZE) 6–2 7–6(6).

San Severo, Italy – April 21–27 – ***Singles:*** O. Golimbioschi (ROM) d. O. Ivanova (RUS) 6–3 6–2.
Doubles: S. da Ponte (ITA)/L. Dell Angelo (ITA) d. A. Vanc (ROM)/M. P. Zavagli (ITA) 6–4 4–6 6–4.

Guimaraes, Portugal – April 21–27 – ***Singles:*** S. Prazares (POR) d. K. Alley (USA) 6–3 6–1.
Doubles: E. Lebescond (FRA)/S. Sfar (TUN) d. K. Chevalier (FRA)/J. Gabrisova (CZE) 6–4 6–2.

Spain, Balaguer– April 28–May 4 – ***Singles:*** N. Serra (ESP) d. C. Barclay (AUS) 3–6 6–3 6–3.
Doubles: Z. L. Dominguez (ESP)/N. Montero (ESP) d. C. Contin (ARG)/C. Martinez (ESP) 0–6 6–2 6–4.

Bulgaria, Sophia – April 28–May 4 –***Singles:*** M Lazarovska (FYR) d. S. Gallovits (SVK) 3–6 7–6(5) 7–6(4).
Doubles: M. Lazarovska (FYR)/T. Nedeva (BUL) d. M. Caiazzo (FRA)/K. Misic (YUG) 6–4 6–2.

Great Britain, Hatfield – April 28–May 4 – ***Singles:*** S. Siddall (GBR) d. L. Ahl (GBR) 6–2 6–0.
Doubles: S. Siddall (GBR)/J Ward (GBR) d. L. Ahl (GBR)/J. Steck (RSA) 3–6 6–4 7–5.

Portugal, Azemeis – April 28–May 4 – ***Singles:*** Final abandoned due to rain.
Doubles: P. Hermida (ESP)/A. Soukup (CAN) d. S. Burnstein(ISR)/L. Gabai (ISR) 6–0 6–4.

Spain, Tortosa – May 5–11 – ***Singles:*** N. Montero (ESP) d. V. Stele (ARG) 6–4 6–1.
Doubles: M. Cano (ESP)/N Montero (ESP) d. V. Stele (ARG)/ M d'Agostini (BRA) 6–3 1–6 6–4.

Slovak Republic, Nitra – May 5–11 – ***Singles:*** J. Macurova (CZE) d. A. Zarska (POL) 6–4 4–6 6–3.
Doubles: J. Blahotova (CZE)/J. Macurova (CZE) d. E. Sebova (SVK)/G. Volekova (SVK) 6–0 0–6 7–6(4).

France, Gelos –May 5–11 – ***Singles:*** E. Loit (FRA) d. K. Jagienak (FRA) 6–4 6–2.
Doubles: K. Jagienak (FRA)/L. Ghirardi-Rubbi (FRA) d. S. Berger (FRA)/L. Sanchez (FRA) 7–5 6–1.

Great Britain, Lee-on-Solent – May 5–11 – ***Singles:*** J. Steck (RSA) d. M. Lamarre (FRA) 6–3 6–2.
Doubles: S. Siddall (GBR)/J. Ward (GBR) d. R. Jensen (USA)/N. Egorova (RUS) 6–2 7–5.

Slovak Republic, Presov – May 12–18 – ***Singles:*** J. Macurova (CZE) d. J. Ondrouchova (CZE) 2–6 6–2 6–3.
Doubles: J. Sromova (CZE)/M. Nekvapilova (CZE) d. O. Blahotova (CZE)/T. Macurova (CZE) 2–6 6–4 6–2.

France, Le Touquet – May 12–18 – ***Singles:*** J. Henin (BEL) d. C. Kremer (GBR) 6–2 6–3.
Doubles: N. Arendt (FRA)/M. Lamarre (FRA) d. L. Masante (ARG)/V. Stele (ARG) 6–2 6–3.

Yugoslavia, Novi Sad – May 12–18 – ***Singles:*** T. Garbin (ITA) d. D. Zaric (YUG) 6–4 6–1.
Doubles: T. Garbin (ITA)/F. Guardigli (ITA) d. D. Zaric (YUG)/N. Teodora (BUL) 6–4 6–4.

Austria, Brixen – May 19–25 – ***Singles:*** A. Hegedus (HUN) d. A. Barna (GER) 6–3 6–3.
Doubles: P. Wartusch (AUT)/C. Schneider (GER) d. M. Vavrinec (SUI)/L. Masante (ARG) 6–3 6–0.

Spain, Zaragoza – May 19–25 – ***Singles:*** K. de Weille (NED) d. L. Dominguez (ESP) 6–4 6–3.
Doubles: K. de Weille (NED)/N. Koves (HUN) d. E. Bes (ESP)/L. Dominguez (ESP) 7–6 (4) 6–4.

FYROM, Skopje – May 19–25 – ***Singles:*** A. Gallovits (ROM) d. L. Fodorean (ROM) 6–2 6–1.
Doubles: D. Zaric (YUG)/T. Nedeva (BUL) d. L. Fodorean (ROM)/K. Altilla (ITA) 6–3 6–2.

Austria, Salzburg – May 26–June 1 – ***Singles:*** S. Lutter (AUT) d. Y. Hosoki (JPN) 3–6 6–1 6–1.
Doubles: C. Schneider (GER)/P. Wartusch (AUT) d. L. dell'Angelo (ITA)/T. Garbin (ITA) 1–6 6–3 6–2.

Spain, Barcelona – May 26–June 1 – ***Singles:*** K. Marosi (HUN) d. M. Cano (ESP) 6–2 6–3.
Doubles: K. de Weille (NED)/A. Hopmans (NED) d. K. Marosi (HUN)/V. Stele (ARG) 6–4 5–7 6–4.

Bulgaria, Bourgas – May 26–June 1 – ***Singles:*** A. Lombardi (ITA) d. M. Froehlich (GER) 4–6 6–4 6–2.
Doubles: T. Nedeva (BUL)/P. Stoyanova (BUL) d. M. Froehlich (GER)/K. Pojatina (CRO) 6–1 6–2.

Poland, Warsaw – May 26–June 1 – ***Singles:*** L. Prusova (CZE) d. H. Sromova (CZE) 6–2 6–7 6–4.
Doubles: H. Sromova (CZE)/M. Nekvapilova (CZE) d. O. Blahotova (CZE)/J. Ondrouchova (CZE) w/o.

USA, El Paso, TX – May 26–June 1 – ***Singles:*** H. Parkinson (USA) d. S. Reeves (USA) 3–6 6–4 6–2. ***Doubles:*** K. Smashey (USA)/S. Walker (USA) d. R. Kolbovic (CAN)/A. Mall (USA) 6–7 (4) 6–4 6–0.

El Salvador, San Salvador – May 26–June 1 – ***Singles:*** C. Tortorella (ARG) d. M. d'Agostini (BRA) 6–7 (1) 6–4 6–1. ***Doubles:*** M. d'Agostini (BRA)/C. Tortorella (ARG) d. J. Rosen (USA)/M. E. Rojas (PER) 6–4 6–0.

USA, El Paso, TX – May 26–June 1 – ***Singles:*** H. Parkinson (USA) d. S. Reeves (USA) 3–6 6–4 6–2. ***Doubles:*** K. Smashey (USA)/S. Walker (USA) d. A. Mall d (USA)/R. Kolbovic (CAN) 6–7 (4) 6–4 6–0.

Turkey, Antalya – June 2–8 – ***Singles:*** T. Obziler (ISR) d. G. Gultekin (TUR) 6–0 6–4. ***Doubles:*** G. Gultekin (TUR)/D. Aksit (TUR) d. M. Bobedova (RUS)/A. Soukup (CAN) w/o.

Poland, Bytom – June 2–8 – ***Singles:*** J. Pospisilova (CZE) d. M. Vavrinec (SUI) 7–6 (4) 6–7 (0) 6–1. ***Doubles:*** K. Kroupova (CZE)/J. Ondrouchova (CZE) d. K. Teodorowicz (POL)/A. Zarska (POL) 2–6 6–2 6–3 .

Slovenia, Velenje – June 9–15 – ***Singles:*** A. M. Foldenyi (HUN) d. M. Froehlich (GER) 6–1 6–1. ***Doubles:*** T. Hergolt (SLO)/T. Pisnik (SLO) d. H. Fremuthova (CZE)/A. Soukup (CAN) w/o.

Italy, Camucia – June 9–15 – ***Singles:*** S. Finer (SWE) d. F. Fortuni (ITA) 6–3 6–1. ***Doubles:*** C. Salvi (ITA)/A. Vanc (ROM) d. A. Serra-Zanetti (ITA)/M. P. Zavagli (ITA) 6–4 6–1.

Poland, Kedzierzyn-Kozle – June 9–15 – ***Singles:*** M. Nekvapilova (CZE) d. Z. Hejdova (CZE) 6–3 2–6 6–3. ***Doubles:*** M. Nekvapilova (CZE)/J. Macurova (CZE) d. L. Prusova (CZE)/Z. Prusova (CZE) 6–4 6–2 .

Switzerland, Bossonens – June 9–15 – ***Singles:*** T. Singian (USA) d. C. Charbonnier (SUI) 6–4 6–4. ***Doubles:*** J. Mens (NED)/K. Kilsdonk (NED) d. C. Charbonnier (SUI)/L. Bao (SUI) 6–4 6–2.

USA, Hilton Head, SC – June 9–15 – ***Singles:*** S. Mabry (USA) d. S. Reeves (USA) 0–6 6–4 7–6 (6). ***Doubles:*** V. Webb (CAN)/V. Sureephong (USA) d. N. Kaiwai (NZL)/G. McManus (NZL) 6–1 6–3.

Italy, Nino Palumbo – June 16–22 – ***Singles:*** T. Hotta (JPN) d. M. Goloviznina (RUS) 6–4 6–4. ***Doubles:*** L. Gabai (ISR)/L. Skavronskaia (RUS) d. C. Giraldo (COL)/P. Racedo (ARG) 6–3 6–3.

Switzerland, Klosters – June 16–22 – ***Singles:*** M. Vavrinec (SUI) d. E. Fauth (AUT) 4–6 7–5 6–2. ***Doubles:*** K. Kilsdonk (NED)/J. Mens (NED) d. E. Juricich (URU)/M. Sequera (VEN) 6–7 (8) 6–4 6–2.

Estonia, Kukulinn – June 16–22 – ***Singles:*** N. Koves (HUN) d. E. Voropaeva (RUS) 6–1 6–2. ***Doubles:*** G. Kucerova (GER)/M. Kucerova (GER) d. N. Koves (HUN)/K. Lampinen (FIN) 6–4 6–1.

Czech Republic, Stare Splavy – June 16–22 – ***Singles:*** K. Kroupova (CZE) d. M. Nekvapilova (CZE) 6–3 3–6 7–6 (6). ***Doubles:*** J. Macurova (CZE)/G. Navratilova (CZE) d. K. Kroupova (CZE)/J. Ondrouchova (CZE) 6–2 6–2.

Brazil, Manaus – June 23–29 – ***Singles:*** M. Nejedly (CAN) d. C.Tortorela (ARG) 6–4 6–1. ***Doubles:*** J. Moore (GBR)/X. Rodriguex (COL) d. C. Germar (GBR)/K. Liggan (IRL) 6–0 6–2.

Czech Republic, Plzen – June 23–29 – ***Singles:*** M. Pastikova (CZE) d. K. Kroupova (CZE) 6–2 6–7 (8) 6–4. ***Doubles:*** L. Cervanova (SVK)/Z. Valekova (SVK) d. P. Kucova (CZE)/E. Krejcova (CZE) 5–7 6–1 6–2.

Sweden, Bastad – June 23–29 – ***Singles:*** N. Koves (HUN) d. A. Lindstedt (SWE) 4–6 7–6 (4) 6–2. ***Doubles:*** A. Lindstedt (SWE)/A. K. Svensson (SWE) d. S. Finer (SWE)/L. Jansson (FIN) w/o.

Italy, Milan – June 23–29 – ***Singles:*** A. Vanc (ROM) d. M. Kovacavic (CRO) 6–2 6–3. ***Doubles:*** Y. Yamagishi (JPN)/T. Hotta (JPN) d. A. Linkova (RUS)/M. Goloviznina (RUS) 6–3 5–7 6–4.

Netherlands, Velp – June 23–29 – ***Singles:*** E. Bes (ESP) d. J. Mens (NED) 6–4 6–7 (2) 7–5. ***Doubles:*** G. Dimitrova (BUL)/D. Topalova (BUL) d. J. Mens (NED)/K. Kilsdonk (NED) 5–7 7–5 6–4.

USA, Greenwood, SC – June 23–29 – ***Singles:*** J. Nejedly (CAN) d. H. Parkinson (USA) 7–5 6–3. ***Doubles:*** M. Beadman (AUS)/A. Jensen (AUS) d. K. Alley (USA)/T. Samara (USA) 4–6 6–2 6–4.

France, Mont-de-Marsan – June 30–July 6 – ***Singles:*** E. Nunes (FRA) d. S. Obata (JPN) 6–2 6–4. ***Doubles:*** K. Marosi (HUN)/V. Stele (ARG) d. S. Obata (JPN)/N. Urabe (JPN) 6–4 6–1.

USA, Oklahoma City, OK – June 30–July 6 – ***Singles:*** J. Scott (USA) d. K. Schlukeblr (USA) 6–2 6–4. ***Doubles:*** J. Scott (USA)/K. Schlukeblr (USA) d. J. Embry (USA)/C. Sessions-Bailey (USA) 6–2 6–2.

Finland, Lohja – June 30–July 6 – ***Singles:*** M. Persson (SWE) d. M. Vavrinec (SUI) 3–6 6–4 6–3. ***Doubles:*** A. Lindstedt (SWE)/A. Mikkers (NED) d. H. K. Aalto (FIN)/K. Lampinen (FIN) 6–1 6–1.

Italy, Sezze – June 30–July 6 – ***Singles:*** A. Vanc (ROM) d. M. P Zavaglil (ITA) 6–4 0–6 6–2. ***Doubles:*** L Garrone (ITA)/E. Savoldi (ITA) d. A. Vanc (ROM)/A. Linkova (RUS) 6–3 6–0.

Spain, Vigo – July 7–13 – ***Singles:*** C. Martinez-Granados (ESP) d. N. Montero (ESP) 6–2 6–4 ***Doubles:*** N. Montero (ESP)/L. Dominguez (ESP) d. G Riera (ESP)/C. Martinez-Granados (ESP) 6–3 6–0.

USA, Easton, MD – July 7–13 – ***Singles:*** N. de Villiers (RSA) d. K. Miller (USA) 6–3 6–3. ***Doubles:*** N. de Villiers (RSA)/L. McShea (AUS) d. K. Miller (USA)/M. Catlin (USA) 6–0 3–6 6–2.

Great Britain, Felixstowe – July 7–13 – ***Singles:*** K. Cross (GBR) d. S. de Beer (RSA) 6–1 7–5. ***Doubles:*** S. de Beer (RSA)/E. Jelfs (GBR) d. H. Crook (GBR)/V. Davies (GBR) 7–5 7–5.

Italy, Fiumicno – July 7–13 – ***Singles:*** E. Fauth (AUT) d. A. Lombardi (ITA) 6–3 6–4. ***Doubles:*** Z. Hejdova (CZE)/J. Macurova (CZE) d. S. Finer (SWE)/A. Linkova (RUS) 6–1 6–1.

Netherlands, Amersfoort – July 7–13 – ***Singles:*** N. Tijssen (NED) d. Y. Basting (NED) 6–1 6–3. ***Doubles:*** D. Haak (NED)/E. Bes (ESP) d. A. Klim (AUS)/Z. Lesenarova (CZE) 4–3 ret.

Great Britain, Frinton – July 13–20 – ***Singles:*** S. de Beer (RSA) d. M. Joubert (RSA) 6–4 6–4. ***Doubles:*** J. Ward (GBR)/L. Woodroffe (GBR) d. K. Cross (GBR)/N. Egorova (RUS) 6–2 6–4.

Italy, Civitanova – July 13–20 – ***Singles:*** K. Kovacevic (CRO) d. K. Piccolini (ITA) 6–0 6–0. ***Doubles:*** K. Kovacevic (CRO)/K. Pojatina (CRO) d. R. Lamagni (ITA)/F. Pennetta (ITA) 6–4 6–1.

Poland, Torun – July 13–20 – ***Singles:*** A. Lindstedt (SWE) d. S. Rynarzewska (POL) 6–1 6–0. ***Doubles:*** R. Kucerova (CZE)/M. Sucha (SVK) d. P. Kucova (CZE)/L. Zacharova (SVK) 6–3 6–3.

Italy, Lido di Camaiore – July 21–27 – ***Singles:*** F. Fortuni (ITA) d. J. Lubasova (CZE) 6–3 4–6 6–3. ***Doubles:*** F. Fortuni (ITA)/G. Casoni (ITA) d. J. A. Fetch (AUS)/C. Dock (AUS) 6–4 6–1.

Indonesia, Jakarta – July 21–27 – ***Singles:*** W. Sawondari (INA) d. I. Iskandar (INA) 6–0 6–3. ***Doubles:*** S-T. Wang (TPE)/H. L. Hsu (TPE) d. T. Hotta (JPN)/Y. Yamagishi (JPN) 6–4 6–4.

Great Britain, Ilkley – July 28–August 3 – ***Singles:*** S. de Beer (RSA)d. J. Lutrova (RUS) 7–5 6–1. ***Doubles:*** C. Watson (AUS)/T. Musgrave (AUS) d. G. Biggs (AUS)/J. Lutrova (RUS) 6–1 6–1.

Italy, Muri Antichi – July 28–August 3 – ***Singles:*** A. Serra-Zanetti (ITA) d. G. Casoni (ITA) 6–7 (3) 6–3 6–3. ***Doubles:*** G. Casoni (ITA)/F. Fortuni (ITA) d. N. Gondarenko (UKR)/B. Pablova (BUL) 7–6(7) 6–2.

Germany, Horb – July 28–August 3 – ***Singles:*** A. Foldenyi (HUN) d. J. Abe (GER) 6–4 6–1. ***Doubles:*** J. Abe (GER)/R. Reid (AUS) d. A. Pirsu (ROM)/M. Mihalache (ROM) 6–3 6–3.

France, Les Contamines – July 28–August 3 – ***Singles:*** E. Curutchet (FRA) d. S. Berger (FRA) 5–7 7–6 (4) 6–4. ***Doubles:*** E. Curutchet (FRA)/S. Georges (FRA) d. E. Belbl (GER)/A. Roesch (GER) 6–2 6–1.

Morocco, Rabat – July 28–August 3 – ***Singles:*** B. Mouthassine (MAR) d. J. Carballal (ESP) 6–2 6–0. ***Doubles:*** B. Mouthassine (MAR)/N. van de Walle (NED) d. B. Loogen (GER)/L. McDonald (GBR) 6–3 6–3.

Indonesia, Bandung – July 2–August 3 – ***Singles:*** W. Prakusya (INA) d. K. J. Won (KOR) 6–4 7–6 (8). ***Doubles:*** B. Sangaram (THA)/K. Ishida (JPN) d. T. Hotta (JPN)/Y. Yamagishi (JPN) 6–2 3–6 6–4.

Great Britain, Southsea – August 4–10 – ***Singles:*** N Egorova (RUS) d. L. Gabai (ISR) 6–3 6–3. ***Doubles:*** N/A.

Germany, Paderborn – August 4–10 – ***Singles:*** J. Schofeldova (CZE) d. J. Macurova (CZE) 6–1 7–6 (3). ***Doubles:*** G. Kucerova (GER)/M. Kucerova (GER) d. K. Pohlman (GER)/S. Lutter (AUT) 6–4 6–2.

Belgium, Rebecq – August 4–10 – ***Singles:*** L. Bacheva (BUL) d. K. Chevalier (FRA) 6–3 4–6 6–3. ***Doubles:*** K. Kilsdonk (NED)/J. Mens (NED) d. A. Lindstedt (SWE)/M. Mikkers (NED) 6–3 6–4.

Italy, Catania – August 4–10 – ***Singles:*** A. Serra-Zanetti (ITA) d. M. Dittman (AUS) 2–6 6–4 6–4. ***Doubles:*** G. Casoni (ITA)/S. da Ponte (ITA) d. D. Ding (CHN)/W. Ni (CHN) 6–4 6–2.

France, Perigueux – August 4–10 – ***Singles:*** R. M. Andres (ESP) d. N. Callen (FRA) 3–6 6–2 7–5. ***Doubles:*** M. Andres (ESP)/S. Martinovic (BOS) d. G. Bimes (FRA)/V. Courmes (FRA) 6–4 6–3.

Turkey, Istanbul – August 11–17 – ***Singles:*** E. Dementieva (RUS) d. D. Topalova (BUL) 7–5 6–4. ***Doubles:*** E. Dementieva (RUS)/A. Myskina (RUS) d. S. Ozlu (TUR)/S. Penciu (TUR) 6–0 6–2.

Belgium, Koksijde – August 11–17 – ***Singles***: J. Henin (BEL) d. N. Serra (ESP) 6–3 7–6 (4). ***Doubles:*** A. Lindstedt (SWE)/A. Mikkers (NED) d. K. Chevalier (FRA)/L. Sanchez (FRA) 6–1 7–5.

Italy, Nicolosi – August 11–17 – ***Singles:*** M. P. Zavagli (ITA) d. L. dell'Angelo (ITA) 5–7 7–6(1) 6–3. ***Doubles:*** N. Cahana (ISR)/M. Vosseberg (NED) d. M. Brusati (ITA)/S. Ventura (ITA) 7–5 4–6 6–4.

France, Saint Gaudens – August 11–17 – ***Singles***: P. Garcia (ESP) d. R. M Andres (ESP)2–6 6–4 7–5. ***Doubles:*** I. Kakoulia (GEO)/M. Rautajoki (FRA) d. S. Bouilleau (FRA)/V. Courmes (FRA) 6–2 6–2.

Venezuela, Isla de Margarita – August 11–17 – ***Singles:*** A. Engel (USA) d. M. d'Agostini (BRA) 7–6 (4) 6–4. ***Doubles:*** E. Jurichich (URU)/M. Sequera (VEN) d. M. Lopez (ARG)/J. Torti (ARG) 7–6 (4) 7–5.

Czech Republic, Valasske – August 18–24 – ***Singles*** : K. Kroupova (CZE) d. L. Prusova (CZE) 6–2 6–1. ***Doubles:*** K. Kroupova (CZE) /J. Ondrouchova (CZE) d. B. Kumbarova (CZE)/P. Plackova (CZE) 5–7 7–6 (6) 7–6 (2).

Italy, Carraba – August 18–24 – ***Singles:*** E. Brusati (ITA) d. A. Risuleo (ITA) 6–3 6–2. ***Doubles:*** N/A.

Slovenia, Mribor – August 18–24 – ***Singles:*** T. Pisnik (SLO) d. N. Schwartz (AU) 6–0 6–2. ***Doubles:*** Pisnik (SLO)/T. Hergold (SLO) d. N. Culum (SLO)/T. Hojnik (SLO) 6–3 6–2.

Thailand, Samutpakaran – August 18–24 – ***Singles*** : A. Hegedus (HUN) d. G. Duangchan (THA) 6–4 6–4. ***Doubles:*** W. Sawondari (INA)/W. Prakusya (INA) d. S. Y. Park (KOR)/E. J. Lee (KOR) 6–4 7–5.

Ukraine, Kiev – August 25–31 – ***Singles***: O. Ivanova (RUS) d. L. Masante (ARG) 6–0 6–2. ***Doubles:*** N. Ostrovska (BLR)/V. Zhukovets (BLR) d. I. Kornienko (RUS)/E. Krutko (LAT) 6–3 1–6 7–5.

Thailand, Bankok – August 25–31 – ***Singles*** : A. Hegedus (HUN) d. E. K Kim (KOR) 6–0 6–3. ***Doubles:*** E.K Kim (KOR)/Y.J. Chung (KOR) d. S. Naee (THA)/O. Wongkamalasai (THA) 6–2 6–2.

Ecuador, Guayaquil – August 25–31 – ***Singles***: M. d'Agostini (BRA) d. P. Cabezas (CHI) 6–7 (0) 7–5 7–6 (4). ***Doubles:*** M. d'Agostini (BRA)/P. Cabezas (CHI) d. M. Lopez (ARG)/R. Ottoboni (ARG) 6–1 6–4.

Romania, Cluj – September 1–7 – ***Singles***: B. Topalova (BUL) d. A. Pirsu (ROM) 6–3 5–7 6–3. ***Doubles:*** O. Blahotova (CZE)/B. Kumbarova (CZE) d M. Mihalache (ROM)/A. Pirsu (ROM) 7–6 (3) 6–4.

Poland, Olsztyn – September 1–7 – ***Singles***: K. Teodorowicz (POL) d. P. Plackova (CZE) 6–4 6–1. ***Doubles:*** J. Ondrouchova (CZE)/A. Vaskova (CZE) d. R. Kucerova (CZE)/D. Olszewska (POL) 6–2 6–3.

Croatia, Supetar – September 1–7 – ***Singles***: M. Kovacevic (CRO) d. D. Mecova (CZE) 2–6 6–3 6–3. ***Doubles:*** D. Mecova (CZE)/S. Sosnarova (CZE) d. L. Seelen (NED)/Y. Basting (NED) 6–3 4–6 6–2.

Germany, Bad Nauheim – September 1–7 – ***Singles***: L. Masante (ARG) d. I. Quast (GER) 6–4 6–3. ***Doubles:*** A. Lindstedt (SWE)/L. Masante (ARG) d. M. Koutstaal (NED)/D. Haak (NED) 6–2 6–2.

Perú, Lima – September 1–7 September – ***Singles:*** M. d'Agostini (BRA) d. R. Ottoboni (ARG) 6–3 6–0. ***Doubles:*** R. Ottoboni (ARG)/P. Racedo (ARG) d. M. Rojas (PER)/J. Rosen (USA) 6–0 6–4.

Romania, Cluj — September 8–14 – ***Singles***: M. Sucha (SVK) d. M. Mihalache (ROM) 7–5 3–6 6–4. ***Doubles:*** H. Fremuthova (CZE)/P. Bartunkova (CZE) d. O. Blahtova (CZE)/M. Mihalache (ROM) 6–4 6–4.

Bolivia, La Paz – September 8–14 – ***Singles***: V. Menga (BRA) d. L. Montalvo (ARG) 6–3 7–5. ***Doubles:*** K. Palme (MEX)/M. Mastarilova (CZE) d. M. Lopez (ARG)/L. Montalvo (ARG) 4–6 6–3 6–2.

Italy, Fano – September 8–14 – ***Singles:*** A. Vanc (ROM) d. E. Zardo (SUI) 6–3 7–5. ***Doubles:*** A. Vanc (ROM)/F. Fortuni (ITA) d. T. Musgrave (AUS)/J. A. Fetch (AUS) 6–1 6–4.

Spain, Madrid – September 8–14 – ***Singles:*** K. Nagy (HUN) d. N. Montero (ESP) 6–1 6–0. ***Doubles:*** P. Aznar (ESP)/P. Hermida (ESP) d. M. Cano (ESP)/G. Leon (ESP) 5–7 6–3 6–3.

Croatia, Sibenik – September 8–14 September – ***Singles:*** M. Palaversic (CRO) d. M. Kovacevic (CRO) 6–2 4–6 6–2. ***Doubles:*** M. Kovacevic (CRO)/K. Pojatina (CRO) d. A. Radeljevic (CRO)/K. Valkyova (SVK) 6–3 6–2.

Chile, Santiago – September 15–21 – ***Singles:*** M. d'Agostini (ARG) d. L. Montalvo (ARG) 4–6 6–2 6–1. ***Doubles:*** M. Mastalirova (CZE)/A. Tricerri (SLO) d. L. Montalvo (ARG)/M. Lopez (ARG) 6–4 6–3.

Romania, Cluj 3 – September 15–21 – ***Singles:*** M. Radu (ROM) d. T. Kovalchuk (UKR) 6–7(3) 6–0 6–1. ***Doubles:*** T. Kovalchuk (UKR)/A. Zaporozhanova (UKR) d. A. Barna (GER)/M. Mihalache (ROM) 6–4 5–7 6–3.

Croatia, Biograd – September 15–21 – ***Singles:*** L. Cervanova (SVK) d. K. Srebotnik (SLO) 6–4 6–2. ***Doubles:*** K. Srebotnik (SLO)/J. Kostanic (CRO) d. C. Aagaard (DEN)/K. Altlia (ITA) 6–4 6–2.

Great Britain, Sunderland – September 22–28 – ***Singles:*** M. Joubert (RSA) d. N. Egorova (RUS) 6–3 1–6 7–5. ***Doubles:*** M. Joubert (RSA)/H. Crook (GBR) d. V. Davie (GBR)/L. Gabai (ISR) 6–2 6–4.

Croatia, Zadar – September 22–28 – ***Singles:*** K. Srebotnik (SLO) d. J. Kostanic (CRO) 4–6 6–4 6–4. ***Doubles:*** K. Srebotnik (SLO)/J. Kostanic (CRO) d. Y. Basting (NED)/S. Trik (NED) 7–5 7–5.

Bulgaria, Albena – September 22–28 – ***Singles:*** D. Topalova (BUL) d. L. Bacheva (BUL) 2–6 6–4 6–0. ***Doubles:*** D. Topalova (BUL)/G. Dimitrova (BUL) d. A. Pandjerova (BUL)/L. Bacheva (BUL) 7–5 6–1.

Argentina, Buenos Aires – September 29–October 5 – ***Singles:*** M. A. Landa (ARG) d. B. Fulco-Villella (ARG) 6–4 6–1. ***Doubles:*** L. Montalvo (ARG)/P. Mercedes (ARG) d. C. Contin (ARG)/R. Ottoboni (ARG) 4–6 6–2 6–4.

Spain, Lerida – September 29–October 5 – ***Singles:*** K. de Weille (NED) d. G. C. Martinez (ESP) 7–6 6–2. ***Doubles:*** N. Montero (ESP)/L. Dominguez (ESP) d. C. Buis (NED)/N. Serra (ESP) 6–7(1) 6–2 6–1.

Great Britain, Nottingham – September 29–October 5 – ***Singles:*** N. Egorova (RUS) d. A. Wainwright (GBR) 6–2 6–7(3) 6–1. ***Doubles:*** L. Ahl (GBR)/J. Ward (GBR) d. K. Cross (GBR)/E. Jelfs (GBR) 7–6(6) 6–2.

Switzerland, Langenthal – September 29–October 5 – ***Singles:*** H. Vildova (CZE) d. G. Kucerova (GER) 6–3 6–2. ***Doubles:*** G. Kucerova (GER)/H. Vildova (CZE) d. D. Asensio (SUI)/A. Buergis (SUI) 7–5 6–4.

Italy, Lecce – September 29–October 5 – ***Singles:*** N. Remis (AUT) d. B. Auer (AUT) 6–2 6–3 ret. ***Doubles:*** K. Altilia (ITA)/O. Golimbioschi (ITA) d. S. Sallaberry (FRA)/A. Wilmart (BEL) 6–0 6–2.

Georgia, Tiblisi – September 29–October 5 – ***Singles:*** N. Petrova (RUS) d. A. Zaporozhnova (UKR) 6–1 6–4. ***Doubles:*** E. Dementieva (RUS)/A. Myskina (RUS) d. A. Zaporozhnova (UKR)/V. Zhukomets (BLR) 3–6 6–0 6–4.

México, México DF – September 29–October 5 – ***Singles:*** D. Ospina (USA) d. J. Rosen (USA) 6–2 7–6(5). ***Doubles:*** K. Schlukebir (USA)/M. Zimpfer (USA) d. M. Vossberg (NED)/N. Cahana (ISR) 6–4 6–2.

Japan, Saga – October 6–12 – ***Singles:*** S. de Beer (RSA) d. S. A. Sagoe (JPN) 6–1 5–7 6–3. ***Doubles:*** D. Jones (AUS)/S. Obata (JPN) d. S. de Beer (RSA)/N. Urabe (JPN) 6–3 6–4.

Uruguay, Montevideo – October 6–12 – ***Singles:*** C. Fernandez (ARG) d. C. Contin (ARG) 7–6(4) 6–4. ***Doubles:*** M. Mastalirova (CZE)/P. Racedo (ARG) d. V. Menga (BRA)/L. Bernal (PAR) 6–1 4–6 6–4.

Georgia, Batumi – October 6–12 – ***Singles:*** A. Myskina (RUS) d. E. Dementieva (RUS) 6–7(1) 6–4 7–5. ***Doubles:*** A. Myskina (RUS)/E. Dementieva (RUS) d. D. Kovacova (SVK)/I. Nossenko (UKR) 6–1 1–0 ret.

Spain, Gerona – October 6–12 –***Singles:*** E. Salvador (ESP) d. N. Sierra (ESP) 6–3 6–2. ***Doubles:*** G. Riera (ESP)/C. Martinez (ESP) d. L. Dominguez (ESP)/N. Montero (ESP) 2–6 6–3 6–4.

Greece, Thessaloniki – October 6–12 – ***Singles:*** A. Panderova (BUL) d. A. Pirsu (ROM) 6–2 6–2. ***Doubles:*** K. Altilia (ITA)/C. A. Aagaard (DEN) d. A. Hegedus (HUN)/N. Koves (HUN) 7–6(5) 6–7(3).

Switzerland, Biel – October 6–12 – ***Singles:*** E. Zardo (SUI) d. C. Charbonnier (SUI) 3–6 6–1 7–5 ***Doubles:*** S. Lohrmann (GER)/K. Marent (AUS) d. D. Asensco (SUI)/A. Buergis (SUI) 2–6 6–0 6–4

Japan, Haibara – October 13–19 – ***Singles:*** R. Takemura (JPN) d. K. Ishida (JPN) 3–6 6–4 6–4. ***Doubles:*** R. Takemura (JPN)/N. Akahori (JPN) d. K. Ishida (JPN)/K. J. Won (KOR) 6–2 6–1.

Cyprus, Nicosia – October 13 –19 – ***Singles:*** E. Krejcova (CZE) d. K. Nagy (HUN) 6–3 2–6 6–4. ***Doubles:*** K. Altilia (ITA)/C. A. Aagaard (DEN) d. E. Krejcova (CZE)/L. Cervanova (SVK) 6–4 7–5.

France, St Rapahel – October 13–19 – ***Singles:*** S. Erre (FRA) d. Y. Basting (NED) 6–4 6–1. ***Doubles:*** H. Sromova (CZE)/A. Vaskova (CZE) d. S. Lohrmann (GER) /K. Marent (AUT) 6–3 6–3.

Lithuania, Siauliai – October 13–19 – ***Singles:*** M. Stets (BLR) d. N. Ostrovskaya (BLR) 6–3 4–6 6–1. ***Doubles:*** T. Poutchek (BLR)/O. Glouschenko (BLR) d. N. Ostrovskaya (BLR)/V. Zhukovets (BLR) 7–5 6–3.

Paraguay, Asuncion – October 13–19 – ***Singles:*** L. Schaerer (PAR) d. M. V. Beortegui (ARG) 6–1 6–2. ***Doubles:*** L. Schaerer (PAR)/V. Menga (BRA) d. P. Raccedo (ARG)/M. Mastalirova (CZE) w/o.

México, Coatzacoalcos – October 13–19 – ***Singles:*** A. Paulenkova (CZE) d. I. Petrov (MEX) 7–6(6) 7–6(3). ***Doubles:*** Cancelled.

France, Joue-les-Tours – October 20–26 – ***Singles:*** K. Nowak (POL) d. K. Miskolczy (HUN) 6–1 6–2. ***Doubles:*** H. Sromova (CZE)/M. Nekvapilova (CZE) d. P. Dyberg (DEN)/M. Pape (DEN) 5–7 6–3 6–4.

Spain, Ceuta – October 20–26 – ***Singles:*** B. Mouthassine (MAR) d. A. Salas (ESP) 6–2 2–6 7–5. **Doubles*:*** A. Ortuño (ESP)/P. Aznar (ESP) d. A. Goni (ESP)/Y. Goni (ESP) ret.

Brazil, Rio Grade do Sul – October 20–26 – ***Singles:*** L. Montalvo (ARG) d. V. Menga (BRA) 6–3 6–0. ***Doubles:*** J. Cortez (BRA)/A. P. Zannoni (BRA) d. M. d'Agostini (BRA)/V. Menga (BRA) 6–3 6–7(4) 6–1.

México, Puerto Vallarta – October 20–26 – ***Singles:*** K. Schlukebir (USA) d. J. Ondrouchova (CZE) 6–1 7–6 (7). ***Doubles:*** K. Schlukebir (USA)/E. Adams (USA) d. G. Gultekin (TUR)/C. Udofa (NIG) 6–3 6–4.

Latvia, Jurmala – October 20–26 – ***Singles:*** M. Wagner (GER) d. A. Zarska (POL) 6–4 3–6 6–1. ***Doubles:*** N. Ostroyvskaya (BLR)/V. Zhukvets (BLR) d. N. Bondarenko (UKR)/M. Stets (BLR) 3–6 6–3 6–4.

México, Culiacan – October 27–November 2 – ***Singles:*** A. Zhidkova (RUS) d. P. Marinova (CAN) 6–3 6–0. ***Doubles:*** I. Petrov (MEX)/L. Becerra (MEX) d. P. Arrangoiz (MEX)/A. Zhidkova (RUS) 7–5 6–0.

Sweden, Stockholm – October 27–November 2 – ***Singles:*** G. Arn (GER) d. A. Briegel (GER) 6–2 6–3. ***Doubles:*** A. Lindstedt (SWE)/A. K. Svensson (SWE) d. O. Blahtova (CZE)/J. Macurova (CZE) 3–6 7–5 6–3.

Belarus, Minsk – October 27–November 2 ***Singles:*** N. Ostrovskaya (BEL) d. O. Glouschenko (BEL) 4–6 6–4 6–2. ***Doubles:*** A. Crib (BLR)/M. Stets (BLR) d. H. Laupa (EST)/E. Krutko (LAT) 6–2 6–1.

Brazil, Suzano, SP – November 3–9 – ***Singles:*** M. d'Agostini (BRA) d. A. Narvaez (USA) 4–6 6–3 6–3. ***Doubles:*** L. Bernal (PAR)/L. Schaerer (PAR) d. C. Martinez-Granado (ESP)/G. Riera (ESP) 3–6 6–3 7–6(4).

France, Moulins – November 3–9 – ***Singles:*** E. Nunes (FRA) d. L. Bacheva (BUL) 6–2 6–1. ***Doubles:*** M. Schnell (AUT)/J. Steven (USA) d. K. Freye (GER)/K. Pace (USA) 6–1 4–2 ret.

Dominican Republic, Santo Domingo – November 3–9 – ***Singles:*** M. Sequera (VEN) d. A. Trcierri (SUI) 6–2 4–6 6–0. ***Doubles:*** E. Adams (USA)/R. Jensen (USA) d. J. Rosen (USA)/M. Sequera (VEN) 6–3 6–3.

Philippines, Manila – November 10–16 – ***Singles:*** J. Y. Choi (KOR) d. W. Prakusya (INA) 0–6 6–1 6–4. ***Doubles:*** D. Ding (CHN)/L. Ting (CHN) d. C. B. Khoo (MAS)/T. T. Weng (TPE) 7–5 6–3.

Brazil, Rio de Janeiro – November 10–16 – ***Singles:*** Z. Valekova (SVK) d. L. Cervanova (SVK) 6–3 4–6 6–1. ***Doubles:*** P. Markova (SVK)/Z. Valekova (SVK) d. M. Mastalirova (CZE)/P. Racedo (ARG) 6–0 6–7(4) 6–2.

France, Le Havre – November 10–16 – ***Singles:*** M. Schnell (AUT) d. K. Nowak (POL) 6–2 7–5. ***Doubles:*** M Schnell (AUT)/J. Steven (USA) d. K. Marosi (HUN)/C. Schneider (GER) 6–2 3–6 7–6(3).

France, Deauville – 17–23 November – ***Singles:*** G. Kucerova (GER) d. L. Bacheva (BUL) 6–3 7–6(5). ***Doubles:*** L. Bacheva (BUL)/J. Abe (GER) d. K. Marosi (HUN)/C. Schneider (GER) 6–2 6–4.

Brazil, Sao Paulo – 17–23 November – ***Singles:*** A. Narvaez (USA) d. L. Cervanova (SVK) 6–4 5–7 6–3. ***Doubles:*** M. d'Agostini (BRA)/V. Menga (BRA) d. M. A. Contin (ARG)/C. Torterella (ARG) 6–1 6–3.

Israel, Jaffa – 17–23 November – ***Singles:*** A. Smashnova (ISR) d. T. Obziler (ISR) 6–3 6–2. ***Doubles:*** N. Cahana (ISR)/M. Koutstaal (NED) d. A. Smashnova (ISR)/T. Obziler (ISR) 6–2 6–1.

Philippines, Manila – 17–23 November – ***Singles:*** J. J. Chen (CHN) d. C. B. Khoo (MAS) 6–1 7–6(2). ***Doubles:*** J. J. Chen (CHN)/Q. Yang (CHN) d. J. Y. Choi (KOR)/E.Y. Ha (KOR) 6–7 (6) 6–3 6–1.

Venezuela, Caracas – 17–23 November – ***Singles:*** K. Schlukebir (USA) d. M. Mazzota (VEN) 7–5 7–5. ***Doubles:*** W. Fix (USA)/K. Schlukebir (USA) d. R. Jensen (USA)/J. Moore (GBR) 7–6 (8) 4–6 7–5.

Spain, Mallorca – 24–30 November – ***Singles:*** N. Serra (ESP) d. M. Schnell (AUT) 6–4 6–1. ***Doubles:*** R. M. Andres (ESP)/M. Escobar (ESP) d. K. Marosi (HUN)/M. Schnell (AUT) 6–4 6–2.

Brazil, Campiñas – 24–30 November – ***Singles:*** L. Cervanova (SVK) d. I. Kurta (USA) 6–0 6–0. ***Doubles:*** Cancelled due to rain.

South Africa, Pretoria – 1–7 December – ***Singles:*** G. Swart (RSA) d. P. Murren (USA) 6–3 4–6 7–5. ***Doubles:*** H. Crook (GBR)/M. Joubert (RSA) d. G. Swart (RSA)/L. Gibbs (RSA) 6–2 7–5.

Spain, Mallorca – 1–7 December – ***Singles:*** C. Martinez (ESP) d. E. Bes (ESP) 6–3 5–7 6–3. ***Doubles:*** K. Marosi (HUN)/M. Schnell (AUT) d. M. Cano (ESP)/C. Martinez (ESP) 6–4 4–6 7–5.

Egypt, Cairo – 1–7 December – ***Singles:*** A. Paulenkova (SVK) d. N. Remis (AUT) 6–3 6–2. ***Doubles:*** N. Remis (AUT)/B. Kamper (AUT) d. J. Adlbrecht (AUT)/B. Auer (AUT) 6–1 7–5.

Portugal, Espinho – 8–14 December – ***Singles:*** M. P. Zavagli (ITA) d. G. Casoni (ITA) 7–5 7–6(8). ***Doubles:*** P. Zavagli (ITA)/G. Casoni (ITA) d. T. Aranda (ESP) /J. Carballal (ESP) 6–2 6–4.

Czech Republic, Victovice – 8–14 December – ***Singles:*** K. Studenikova (SVK) d. M. Pastikova (CZE) 6–3 6–3. ***Doubles:*** G. Kucerova (GER)/M. Kucerova (GER) d. M. Pastikova (CZE)/L. Prusova (CZE) 6–3 6–4.

Egypt, Ismalia – 8–14 December – ***Singles:*** S. Sfar (TUN) d. T. Obziler (ISR) 5–7 7–5 6–4. ***Doubles:*** S. Sfar (TUN)/B. Karpenschef (FRA) d. B. Kamper (AUT)/N. Remis (AUT) 6–3 7–6(5).

Portugal, Estoril – 15–21 December – ***Singles:*** L. Latimer (GBR) d. A. Brigel (GER) 6–3 3–6 7–5. ***Doubles:*** K. Freye (GER)/A. Zarska (POL) d. A. Bachmann (GER)/M. Mihalache (ROM) 6–7 (4) 6–0 6–4.

ITF WOMEN'S $25,000 TOURNAMENTS

USA, Mission, TX. – January 27–February 2 – ***Singles:*** C. Black (ZIM) d. K. Phebus (USA) 6–3 6–3. ***Doubles:*** A. Mall (USA)/K. Phebus (USA) d. K. Alley (USA)/P. Nelson (USA) 1–6 6–1 6–1.

Slovenia, Rogaska Slatina – February 10–16 – ***Singles:*** M. Schnitzer (GER) d. E. Syssoeva (RUS) 7–6 6–4. ***Doubles:*** B. Schwartz (AUT)/P. Wartusch (AUT) d. H. Rosen (ISR)/D. Zaric (YUG) 6–1 6–4.

Colombia, Cali – February 10–16 – ***Singles:*** L. Pena (ESP) d. S. Plischke (AUT) 7–6 6–3. ***Doubles:*** R. McQuillan (AUS)/S. Schmidle (GER) d. S. Prazeres (POR)/L. Schaerer (PAR) 6–2 6–3.

Great Britain, Redbridge – February 17–23 – ***Singles:*** M. A. Sanchez Lorenzo (ESP) d. E. Tatarkova (UKR) 6–1 6–1. ***Doubles:*** J. Pullin (GBR)/L. Woodroffe (GBR) d. K-A. Guse (UAS)/C. Wood (GBR) 2–6 6–4 6–4.

Great Britain, Bushey – February 24–March 2 – ***Singles:*** O. Barabanschikova (BLR) d. R. Sandu (ROM) 6–1 7–6. ***Doubles:*** O. Lugina (UKR)/C. Wood (GBR) d. K. Freye (GER)/E. Tatarkova (UKR) 7–6 6–7 6–1.

USA, Rockford, IL – March 3–9 – ***Singles:*** S. Jeyaseelan (CAN) d. S. Drake-Brockman (AUS) 7–6 6–3. ***Doubles:*** J. Lee (USA)/M. Strandlund (SWE) d. E. Brioukhovets (UKR)/N. van Lottum (FRA) 7–6 6–3.

Japan, Noda – March 17–23 – ***Singles:*** K-A. Guse (AUS) d. Y-J. Choi (KOR) 0–6 6–4 6–2. ***Doubles:*** Y. Hosoki (JPN)/K. Nagatomi (JPN) d. Y-J. Choi (KOR)/M-R. Jeon (KOR) 6–2 6–2.

USA, Woodlands, TX – March 17–23 – ***Singles:*** K. Phebus (USA) d. K. Triska (SWE) 6–1 7–5. ***Doubles:*** N. Feber (BEL)/L. Horn (RSA) d. S. Haas (GER)/K. Triska (SWE) 6–1 6–2.

France, Reims – March 17–23 – ***Singles:*** S. Pitkowski (FRA) d. S. Krivencheva (BUL) 7–5 6–1. ***Doubles:*** S. Krivencheva (BUL)/E. Tatarkova (UKR) d. S. Meier (GER)/P. Schwarz (AUT) 6–2 6–2.

Athens, Greece – April 7–13 – ***Singles:*** M. A. Sanchez Lorenzo (ESP) d. S. Prazeres (POR) 6–7 (3) 6–1 7–6 (4). ***Doubles: :*** C. Black (ZIM)/I. Seljutina (KAZ) d. V. Csurgo (HUN)/S. Krivencheva (BUL) 6–3 6–4.

Monterrey, Mexico – April 21–27 – ***Singles:*** S. Cacic (FRA) d. A. Gavaldon (MEX) 6–3 6–2. ***Doubles:*** E. de Lone (USA)/L. Plemming (USA) d. S. Mabry (USA)/B. Rippner (USA) 7–6 3–6 7–6 (3).

Korea, Seoul – May 5 – 11 ***Singles:*** M. Miyauchi (JPN) d. K.A Guse (AUS)1– 6 6–3 6–1. ***Doubles:*** S. H. Kim (KOR)/Y. J. Cho (KOR) d. J. Y. Choi (KOR)/ S. H. Park (KOR) 6–3 7–6(6).

Russia, Sochi – May 19–25 – ***Singles:*** N. Louarsabishvili (GEO) d. J. Steck (RSA) 7–5 6–1. ***Doubles:*** E. Syssoeva (RUS)/E. Koulikovskaya (RUS) d. N. Louarsabishvili (GEO)/K. Shibata (JPN) 3–6 6–3 6–0.

Great Britain, Surbiton – June 2–8 – ***Singles:*** T. Tanasugarn (THA) d. A. Olsza (POL) 5–7 7–6 (5) 5–0 ret. ***Doubles:*** C. Barclay (AUS)/K. A. Guse (AUS) d. D. Graham (USA)/K. Kunck (AUS) 3–6 6–4 7–6 (5).

USA, Mount Pleasant, SC – June 16–22 – ***Singles:*** G. Biggs (AUS) d. J. Fernandez (MEX) 6–3 4–6 7–5. ***Doubles:*** K. Alley (USA)/L. Andriyani (INA) d. A. Augustustus (UAS)/T. Samara (USA) 2–6 6–3 6–4.

France, Bordeaux – June 23–29 – ***Singles:*** E. Curutchet (FRA) d. J. Abe (GER) 7–6 6–3. ***Doubles:*** C. Dhenin (FRA)/N. Louarsabishivili (GEO) d. M. F. Landa (ARG)/M. Weingartner (GER) 6–7 (6) 6–4 7–5.

Brazil, Campinas – June 30–July 6 – ***Singles:*** S. Schaerer (PAR) d. L. Varmuza (SMR) 6–4 6–1. ***Doubles:*** S. Schaerer (PAR)/C. Tortorela (ARG) d. R. Burzagli (BRA)/J. Cortez (BRA) 5–7 6–3 6–3.

Germany, Vaihingen – June 30–July 6 – ***Singles:*** A. Alcazar (ESP) d. S. Kloesel (GER) 6–3 6–4. ***Doubles:*** S. Noorlander (NED)/N. Vaidyanathan (IND) d. M. F. Landa (ARG)/M. Weingartner (GER) 6–3 6–1.

Germany, Pucheim – July 7–13 – ***Singles:*** N. van Lottum (FRA) d. V. Csurgo (HUN) 6–0 6–2. ***Doubles:*** N. van Lottum (FRA)/K. Freye (GER) d. M. F. Landa (ARG)/S. Noorlander (NED) 6–1 6–2.

USA, Clearwater, FL – July 13–20 – ***Singles:*** K. Miller (USA) d. M. Drake (CAN) 6–3 7–6 (6). ***Doubles:*** A. Wainwright (GBR)/J. Pullin (GBR) d. M. Drake (CAN)/L. Lee (USA) 6–4 6–4.

Germany, Darmstadt – July 13–20 – ***Singles:*** P. Stoyanova (BUL) d. R. Sandu (ROM) 6–4 6–1. ***Doubles:*** P. Stoyanova (BUL)/S. Krivencheva (BUL) d. M. Feistel (POL)/O. Ivanova (RUS) 6–0 2–6 6–3.

Spain, Gexto – July 13–20 – ***Singles:*** S. Berger (FRA) d. A. Smashnova (ISR)3–6 6–3 6–1. ***Double:*** A. Hopmans (NED)/P. van Acker (BEL) d. A. Ortuno (ESP)/H. Rosen (ISR) 7–5 4–6 7–5.

Ireland, Dublin – July 21–August 3 – ***Singles:*** S. de Beer (RSA) d. P. Wartusch (AUT) 6–4 3–6 7–6(2). ***Doubles:*** S. de Beer (RSA)/E. Jelfs (GBR) d. A. August (USA)/A. Jensen (AUS) 6–3 4–6 6–4.

Germany, Rostock – July 21–August 3 – ***Singles:*** S. Meier (GER) d. S. Schmilde (GER) 6–3 7–5. ***Doubles:*** S. Krivencheva (BUL)/P. Stoyanova (BUL) d. R. Reid (AUS)/R. Vidats (HUN) w/o.

Spain, Valladolid – July 21–August 3 – ***Singles:*** M. Froehlich (GER) d. D. van de Zande (BEL) 6–3 4–6 6–2. ***Doubles:*** S. Finer (SWE)/A. K. Svensson (SWE) d. P. Rampre (SWE)/D. van de Zande (BEL) 6–4 6–3.

USA, Lexington, KY – July 28–August 3 – ***Singles:*** K. Miller (USA) d. L. Horn (RSA) 6–7(2) 6–1 6–2. ***Doubles:*** E. Hakami(USA)/D. Jones (AUS) d. K. Shibata (JPN)/K. Srebotnik (SLO) 6–2 7–5.

Tunisia, Carthage – August 4–10 – ***Singles:*** S. Kloesel (GER) d. M. Zivec-Skulj (GER) 3–6 7–5 6–0. ***Doubles:*** A. Ortuno (ESP)/Z. Valekova (SVK) d. E. Bes (ESP)/E. Salvador (ESP) 4–6 6–4 6–4.

USA, Bronx, NY – August 11–17 – ***Singles*:** R. McQuillan (AUS) d. E. de Lone (USA) 6–1 6–4. ***Doubles:*** R. McQuillan (AUS)/L. McShea (AUS) d. S. Siddall (GBR)/L. Woodroffe (GBR) 6–2 6–1.

Ukraine, Kiev – August 18–24 – ***Singles*:** B. Schwartz (AUT) d. M. F Landa (ARG) 6–3 6–2. ***Doubles:*** C. Black (ZIM)/I. Seljutina (KAZ) d. N. Egorova (RUS)/O. Ivanova (RUS) 6–2 6–4.

Greece, Athens – August 25–31 – ***Singles* :** A. Pirsu (ROM) d. E. Koulikovskaya (RUS) 4–6 7–5 6–3. ***Doubles:*** E. Koulikovskaya (RUS)/S. Nacuk (YUG) d. R. Andres (ESP)/M. Escobar (ESP) 6–4 6–3.

Italy, Ortobello – August 25–31 – ***Singles* :** R. Bobkova (UKR) d. A. Ortuno (ESP) 6–2 6–4. ***Doubles:*** K. Kroupova (CZE)/S. Meier (GER) d. K. de Weille (RSA)/H. van Aalderen (RSA) 6–3 2–6 6–2.

Italy, Spoleto – September 1–7 – ***Singles:*** L. Garrone (ITA) d. A. Ortuno (ESP) w/o. ***Doubles:*** K. Kroupova (CZE)/J. Pospisilova (CZE) d. A. Alkazar (ESP)/E. Bes (ESP) 6–1 6–0.

Ukraine, Kiev – September 8–14 – ***Singles*:** A. Foldenyi (HUN) d. K. Nowak (POL) 6–2 6–3 ret. ***Doubles:*** A. Lindestedt (SWE)/C. Schneider (GER) d. N. Medvedeva (UKR)/A. Zdorovitsk (UKR) 6–1 6–2.

Bulgaria, Sophia – September 15–21 – ***Singles:*** A. Alcazar (ESP) d. P. Stoyanova (BUL) 2–6 6–3 6–1. ***Doubles:*** S. Kloesel (GER)/K. Kschwendt (AUT) d. S. Nacuk (YUG)/D. Zaric (YUG) 6–4 6–4.

USA, Newport Beach, CA – September 22–28 – ***Singles:*** S. Cacic (USA) d. S. Reeves (USA) 6–4 4–6 6–4. ***Doubles:*** J. Lee (USA)/G. Helgeson-Nielson (USA) d. A. Jensen (USA/A. Agustus (USA) 6–3 6–3.

Romaina, Bucharest – September 22–28 – ***Singles:*** A. Hopmans (NED) d. S. Kloesel (GER) 4–6 6–2 7–5. ***Doubles:*** V. Csurgo (HUN)/I. Husarova (SVK) d. O. Glouschenko (BLR)/T. Poutcheck (BLR) 6–0 6–0.

Argentina, Tucuman – September 22–28 – ***Singles:*** M. Diaz-Oliva (ARG) d. L. Montalvo (ARG) 6–2 6–7(3) 7–6(0). ***Doubles:*** C. Black (ZIM)/I. Selyutina (KAZ) d. M. d'Agostini (BRA)/V. Menga (BRA) 6–3 6–1.

Slovenia, Otocec – September 29–October 5 – ***Singles:*** A. Alcazar (ESP) d. B. Schwartz (AUT) 6–3 6–2. ***Doubles:*** L. Cenkova CZE)/K. Kroupova (CZE) d. P. Mandula (HUN)/K. Marosi (HUN) 7–5 7–6(3).

Japan, Saga – October 6–12 – ***Singles:*** S. de Beer (RSA) d. S. Asagoe (JPN) 6–1 5–7 6–3. ***Doubles:*** D. Jones (AUS)/S. Obata (JPN) d. N. Urabe (JPN)/S. de Beer (RSA) 6–3 6–4.

México, Tampico – October 6–12 – ***Singles:*** C. Papadaki (GRE) d. S. Noorlander (NED) 6–3 6–4. ***Doubles:*** Cancelled due to rain.

Germany, Flensberg – October 13–19 – ***Singles:*** S. Schmidle (GER) d. K. Hrdlickova (CZE) 6–4 6–4. ***Doubles:*** P. Wartusch (AUT)/J. Woehr (GER) d. V. Csurgo (HUN)/K. Freye (GER) 6–3 3–6 6–3.

Great Britain, Edinburgh – October 27–November 2 – ***Singles:*** B. Schwartz (AUT) d. S. Nacuk (YUG) 3–6 6–3 6–4. ***Doubles:*** J. Pullin (GBR)/L. Woodroffe (GBR) d. A. Hopmans(NED)/S. Noorlander (NED) 6–3 6–1.

Brazil, Mogi Das Cruzes – October 27–November 2 – ***Singles:*** M. Diaz-Oliva (ARG) d. C. Martinez-Granados (ESP) 6–0 6–0.
Doubles: L. Montalvo (ARG)/M. Paz (ARG) d. V. Menga (BRA)/M. d'Agostini (BRA) 6–2 6–0.

Israel, Ramat Hasharon – October 27–November 2 – ***Singles:*** A. Serra-Zanetti (ITA) d. K. Srebotnik (SLO) 6–4 6–2. ***Doubles:*** K. Freye (GER)/H. Rosen (ISR) d. K. Srebotnik (SLO)/P. Rampre (SLO) 6–1 6–1.

Australia, Mt Gambier – November 10–16 – ***Singles:*** H. Rosen (ISR) d. A. Olsza (POL) 6–1 6–3. ***Doubles:*** C. Barclay (AUS)/E. H. Kim (KOR) d. R. Reid (AUS)/R. Vidats (HUN) 6–3 6–2.

Australia, Port Pirie – 17–23 November – ***Singles:*** K. Miller (USA) d. J. Okada (USA) 4–6 6–1 7–6 (5). ***Doubles:*** N. de Villers (RSA)/L. McShea (AUS) d. A Olsza (POL)/J. Steck (RSA) 6–4 6–3.

Australia, Nuriootpa – 24–30 November – ***Singles:*** A. Olzsa (POL) d. A. Serra-Zanetti (ITA) 6–1 6–1. ***Doubles:*** C. Barclay (AUS)/K. A. Guse (AUS) d. N. de Villiers (RSA)/L. McShea (AUS) 6–3 7–5.

Colombia, Bogota – 8–14 December – ***Singles:*** F. Zuluaga (COL) d. M. Nejedly (CAN) 6–2 6–1. ***Doubles:*** M. d'Agostini (BRA)/V. Menga (BRA) d. E. Maia (BRA)/L. Schaerer (PAR) 6–2 6–2.

ITF WOMEN'S $50,000 TOURNAMENTS

Czech Republic, Prostejov – 27 January–2 February – ***Singles:*** K. Habsudova (SVK) d. B. Paulus (AUT) 6–7 6–1 6–3. ***Doubles:*** D. Krajcovicova (SVK)/A. Temesvari (HUN) d. A. Olfza (POL)/E. Tatarkova (UKR) 6–2 6–3.

USA, Midland, MI – 10–16 February – ***Singles:*** K. Po (USA) d. M. Tu (USA) 6–2 6–3. ***Doubles:*** A. Lettiere (USA)/N. Miyagi (JPN) d. J. Lee (USA)/L. Lee (USA) 6–3 6–2.

USA, Phoenix, AZ – March 31–April 6 – ***Singles:*** F. Li (CHN) d. K. Brandi (USA) 6–1 6–2. ***Doubles:*** L. Ghirardi-Rubbi (FRA)/ N. Louarsabishvili (GEO) d. M. J. Gaido (ARG)/ M. A. Vento (VEN) 6–0 6–2.

Japan, Gifu – April 28–May 4 ***Singles:*** K. A. Guse (AUS) d. M. R. Jeon (KOR) 7–5 7–5. ***Doubles:*** S. Obata (JPN)/K. Shibata (JPN) d. S. Asagoe (JPN)/Y. Nishimata (JPN) 6–3 7–5.

Uzbekistan, Tashkent – 2–8 June– ***Singles:*** A. Gavaldon (MEX) d. A. Smashnova (ISR) 6–3 6–2. ***Doubles:*** E. de Lone (USA)/N. Pratt (AUS) d. A. Ortuño (ESP)/H. Rosen (ISR) 6–3 6–1.

Hungary, Budapest – 9–15 June– ***Singles:*** G. Leon-Garcia (ESP) d. M. Diaz-Oliva (ARG) 7–5 6–2. ***Doubles:*** K. Marosi (HUN)/V. Stele (ARG) d. E. Tatarkova (UKR)/F. Zuluaga (COL) 6–3 6–3.

France, Marseille – 9–15 June – ***Singles:*** A. Cocheteux (FRA) d. M. Lucic (CRO) 4–6 7–5 6–4. ***Doubles:*** K. Marosi (HUN)/V. Stele (ARG) d. C. Dhenin (FRA)/N. Louarsabishvili (GEO) 6–2 4–6 6–1.

USA, Queens, NY – June 30–July 6 –***Singles:*** F. Li (CHN) d. L. Lee (USA) 7–5 7–5. ***Doubes:*** J. Lee (USA)/L. Lee (USA) d. F. Li (CHN)/K. Phebus (USA) 6–2 2–6 6–3.

USA, Peachtree, GA – 21–27 July– ***Singles:*** M. A. Vento (VEN) d. S. Jeyaseelan (CAN) 6–4 6–0. ***Doubles:*** S. Jeyaseelan (CAN)/K. Shibata (JPN) d. J. Pullin (GBR)/A. Wainwright (GBR) 6–4 6–1.

Indonesia, Jakarta – 4–10 August – ***Singles:*** S-T. Wang (TPE) d. G. Aizenberg (ARG) 6–1 6–4. ***Doubles:*** Y. J. Choi (KOR)/E. H. Kim (KOR) d. K. A. Guse (AUS)/K. Kunce (AUS) 6–3 6–4.

Korea, Seoul – 8–14 September – ***Singles*** : S. H. Park (KOR) d. K. A. Guse (AUS) 6–3 6–4. ***Doubles:*** K. A. Guse (AUS)/C. Barclay (AUS) d. S. H. Park (KOR)/S-T. Wang (TPE) 4–6 6–4 6–1.

Russia, Samara – 8–14 September – ***Singles***: T. Panova (RUS) d. L. Cenkova (CZE) 6–0 6–2. ***Doubles:*** Cancelled.

Chinese Taipei, Taipei – 15–21 September – ***Singles:*** K. A. Guse (AUS) d. C. Barclay (AUS) 6–4 7–6(2). ***Doubles:*** Y. J. Choi (KOR)/E. H. Kim (KOR) d. K. A. Guse (AUS)/C. Barclay (AUS) 1–6 6–4 6–3.

Greece, Thessaloniki – 22–28 September – ***Singles:*** A. Mauresmo (FRA) d. E. Bes (ESP) 6–0 6–0. ***Doubles:*** J. Pospisilova (CZE)/R. Bobkova (CZE) d. M. Goloviznina (RUS)/E. Koulikovskaya (RUS) 6–2 6–3.

USA, Santa Clara – 29 September–5 October – ***Singles:*** M. Grzybowska (POL) d. K. Nagatsuka (JPN) 6–1 7–5. ***Doubles:*** E. de Villers (RSA)/L. McShea (AUS) d. R. McQuillan (AUS)/N. Miyagi (JPN) 7–6 7–6.

USA, Sedona – 6–12 October – ***Singles:*** R. McQuillan (AUS) d. S. Dopfer (AUT) 6–3 7–6 (5). ***Doubles:*** C. Cristea (ROM)/C. Morariu (USA) d. L. Horn (RSA)/P. Suarez (ARG) 7–5 6–2.

Great Britain, Southampton – 13–19 October – ***Singles:*** E. Koulikovskaya (RUS) d. E. Tatarkova (UKR) 6–0 4–6 7–6(5). ***Doubles:*** J. Pulin (GBR)/L. Woodroffe (GBR) d. L. Cenkova (CZE)/S. Nacuk (YUG) 6–2 6–1.

France, Poitiers – 27 October–2 November– ***Singles***: K. Boogert (NED) d. A. Cocheteux (FRA) 6–4 7–5. ***Doubles:*** N. Feber (BEL)/P. Langrova (CZE) d. L. Ghirardi-Rubbi (FRA)/S. Krivencheva (BUL) 3–6 6–3 6–1.

France, Cergy Pontoise – 1–7 December – ***Singles:*** L. Golarsa (ITA) d. A. Sidot (FRA) 4–6 7–5 7-6(4). ***Doubles:*** K. Boogert (NED)/M. Oremans (NED) d. J. Hallard-Decugis (FRA)/A. Sidot (FRA) 7–5 6–4.

Germany, Bad Gogging – 8–14 December – ***Singles***: N. Dechy (FRA) d. E. Callens (BEL) 6–4 6–1. ***Doubles:*** T. Krizan (SLO)/S. Plischke (AUT) d. S. Georges (FRA)/E. Curutchet (FRA) 6–3 6–3.

ITF WOMEN'S $75,000 TOURNAMENTS

Colombia, Bogota – 17–23 February – ***Singles:*** C. Morariu (USA) d. L. Nemeckova (CZE) 6–2 6–3. ***Doubles:*** S. Noorlander (NED)/C. Papadaki (GRE) d. L. Montalvo (AGR)/M. Paz (ARG) 7–6 4–6 7–5.

Wichita, USA – 14–20 April – ***Singles:*** F. Li (CHN) d. S. Cacic (USA) 6–2 6–2. ***Doubles:*** K. McCarthy (USA)/K. Pace (USA) d. L. Plemming (AUS)/N. Pratt (AUS) 4–6 7–5 6–2.

Turkey, Istanbul – 21–27 July – ***Singles:*** G. Pizzichini (ITA) d. S. Noorlander (NED) 0–6 6–4 7–6(4). ***Doubles:*** L. Golarsa (ITA)/M. Paz (ARG) d. S. Plischke (AUT)/M. Weingartner (GER) 3–6 6–3 6–3.

Croatia, Makarska – 28 July–3 August – ***Singles:*** M. Lucic (CRO) d. S. Dopfer (AUT) 6–1 6–4. ***Doubles:*** O. Lugina (UKR)/E. Wagner (GER) d. M. Goloviznina (RUS)/E. Koulikovskaya (RUS) 5–7 7–5 7–5.

Poland, Sopot – 4–10 August – ***Singles:*** M. Grzybowska (POL) d. D. Chladkova (CZE) 6–3 6–2. ***Doubles:*** E. Tatarkova (UKR)/S. Kriovencheva (BUL) d. R. Bobkova (CZE)/L. Nemeckova (CZE) 7–6 (7) 6–3.

USA, Salt Lake City, UT – 4–10 August – ***Singles:*** F. Li (CHN) d. L. Golarsa (ITA) 6–3 6–2. ***Doubles:*** M. de Swardt (RSA)/D. Graham (USA) d. R. McQuillan (USA)/N. Miyagi (JPN) 7–6 (1) 7–5.

Slovak Republic, Bratislava – 11–17 August – ***Singles***: H. Nagyova (SVK) d. G. Leon-Garcia (ESP) 6–4 6–0. ***Doubles:*** H. Nagyova (SVK)/L. Courtois (BEL) d. S. Krivencheva (BUL)/P. Stojanova (BUL) 6–1 6–0.

USA, Austin TX – 27 October–2 November – ***Singles:*** E. Gagliardi (ITA) d. N. Miyagi (JPN) 6–3 3–6 6–4. ***Doubles:*** S-H. Park (KOR)/S. Miho (JPN) d. D. Graham (USA)/M. McGrath (USA) 6–4 5–7 6–2.

Colombia, Bogota – 17–23 February – ***Singles:*** C. Morariu (USA) d. L. Nemeckova (CZE) 6–2 6–3. ***Doubles:*** S. Noorlander (NED)/C. Papadaki (GRE) d. L. Montalvo (AGR)/M. Paz (ARG) 7–6 4–6 7–5.

USA, Wichita, KS – 14–20 April – ***Singles:*** F. Li (CHN) d. S. Cacic (USA) 6–2 6–2. ***Doubles:*** K. McCarthy (USA)/K. Pace (USA) d. L. Plemming (AUS)/N. Pratt (AUS) 4–6 7–5 6–2.

Turkey, Istanbul – 21–27 Jul – ***Singles:*** G. Pizzichini (ITA) d. S. Noorlander (NED) 0–6 6–4 7–6(4). ***Doubles:*** L. Golarsa (ITA)/M. Paz (ARG) d. S. Plischke (AUT) /M. weingartner (GER) 3–6 6–3 6–3.

Croatia, Makarska – 28 July–3 Aug – ***Singles:*** M. Lucic (CRO) d. S. Dopfer (AUT) 6–1 6–4. ***Doubles:*** O.Lugina (UKR)/E. Wagner (GER) d. M. Goloviznina (RUS) /E. Koulikovskaya (RUS) 5–7 7–5 7–5.

Poland, Sopot – 4–10 Aug – ***Singles:*** M. Grzybowska (POL) d. D. Chladkova (CZE) 6–3 6–2. ***Doubles:*** E. Tatarkova (UKR)/S. Kriovencheva (BUL) d. R. Bobkova (CZE) /L. Nemeckova (CZE) 7–6 (7) 6–3.

USA, Salt Lake City, UT – 4–10 Aug – ***Singles:*** Fang Li (CHN) d. L. Golarsa (ITA) 6–3 6–2. ***Doubles:*** M. De Swardt (RSA)/D. Graham (USA) d. R. McQuillan (UAS) /N. Miyagi (JPN) 7–6 (1) 7–5.

Slovak Republic, Bratislava – 11–17 August – ***Singles***: H. Nagyova (SVK) d. G. Leon-Garcia (ESP) 6–4 6–0. ***Doubles:*** H. Nagyova (SVK)/L. Courtois (BEL) d. S. Krivencheva (BUL) /P. Stojanova (BUL) 6–1 6–0.

USA, Austin, TX – 27 October–2 November – ***Singles***: E. Gagliardi (ITA) d. N. Miyagi (JPN) 6–3 3–6 6–4. ***Doubles:*** S. H. Park (KOR)/S. Miho (JPN) d. D. Graham (USA) /M. mcGrath (USA) 6–4 5–7 6–2.

International Team Competitions

European Cups – Men and Women
Peugeot ATP Tour World Team Championship

As well as winning five tounaments in 1997, Felix Mantilla remained unbeaten in leading Spain to victory in the Peugeot World Team Championship. (Stephen Wake)

European Cups

Henry Wancke

MEN

Not since they won the old King's Cup between 1964 and 1967 have British teams experienced that level of success in European Cup competition. Although the 1997 victory was important psychologically, it must be remembered that Britain, like every other team, chose to go into battle without their strongest players.

For team captain David Lloyd, himself a former strong King's Cup campaigner, it was the first experience of leading a team to overall victory. Since his ultimate goal is to carry off the Davis Cup, he sensibly used the European Men's Team Championship to blood two inexperienced 19-year-olds, Arvind Parmar and Martin Lee.

Alongside them Lloyd included 28-year-old Danny Sapsford, now a veteran of such campaigns. While both youngsters benefitted from the experience, it was Sapsford who kept the team on track by remaining unbeaten in all three ties.

In the opening round Italy beat Portugal easily while the Netherlands had an excellent 2–1 win against Sweden after losing the opening rubber. In the other half Britain, seeded 3, made light work of Germany with a decisive 3–0 win. Progress became more treacherous in the semi-finals when they faced the No.2 seeds, the Czech Republic, who had beaten Israel 2–0.

Here Sapsford had the responsibility of levelling the tie following Parmar's earlier 6–7 6–4 6–2 defeat by Radek Stepanek. This he achieved with an excellent 6–2 6–1 win over the 1992 Wimbledon junior champion, David Skoch. Later Sapsford returned with Lee to secure a place in the final with an emphatic 6–3,6–1 victory over Skoch and Stepanek.

In the other semi-finals the Netherlands had surprised and delighted the home crowds by ousting the top seeds, Italy, 2–0.

In the Championship tie Lloyd preferred Lee for the opening singles against the Netherlands. Despite a strong performance, the former junior world No.1 had to give best to Martin Verkerk, 4–6 7–6 6–2. Again it fell to Sapsford to save the day and his 7–6 6–4 defeat of Peter Wessels forced the tie into a deciding doubles. Once again Lee and Sapsford came through safely, beating Wessels and Kempes 6–3 7–5.

With the previous week's announcement involving the expansion of the top Divisions for 1998, no nation was relegated from the Champions Division. Next year will see the addition of Spain and Bulgaria who gained promotion from Division One. By the same token, no team dropped out of Division One, though four nations gained promotion from Division Two. They were Malta, Poland, Croatia and Romania.

First Round: Italy d. Portugal 2–0. Netherlands d. Sweden 2–1; Great Britain d. Germany 3–0; Czech Republic d. Israel 2–0.
Semi-finals: Netherlands d. Italy 2–0. Martin Verkerk (NED) d. Vincenzo Santopadre (ITA) 4–6 7–6(1) 7–6(3); Peter Wessels (NED) d. Davide Sanguinetti (ITA) 6–4 6–2. ***Great Britain d. Czech Republic 2–1.*** Radek Stepanek (CZE) d. Arvind Parmar (GBR) 6–7(5) 6–4 6–2; Danny Sapsford (GBR) d. David Skoch (CZE) 6–2 6–1; Martin Lee/Sapsford (GBR) d. Stepanek/Skoch 6–3 6–1.
Final: Great Britain d. Netherlands 2–1. Martin Verekerk (NED) d. Martin Lere (GBR) 4–6 7–6(5) 6–2; Danny Sapsford (GBR) d. Peter Wessels (NED) 7–6(4) 6–4; Lee/Sapsford (GBR) d. Kempes /Wessels 6–3 7–5.

WOMEN

Having gained promotion to the Champion's Division twelve months earlier, Spain's second string of players went on to add the European Women's Team Championship in 1997. They exploited their choice of ground advantage by staging the event in Barcelona, on outdoor clay, early in December.

That decision did not suit the defending champions, Germany, or the team they had beaten for the 1996 title, the Netherlands. Both nations had players committed to an indoor tournament the following week. All were reluctant to play outdoors. Accordingly Germany and Sweden withdrew.

With the Championship wide open Spain and Italy, the new top seeds, gained first round byes. Belgium disposed of Finland 2–1, to provide the hosts with their first opponents, while Hungary took out Greece, also 2–1, to earn a tie against Italy.

In the semi-finals Spain looked confident in beating Belgium 3–0 while Italy were forced into a deciding doubles rubber before coming through to beat Hungary 2–1.

Although, Spain got off to a good start in the final when Gala Leon beat Flora Perfetti 6–4 7–6, they did not have matters all their own way. Again Italy forced the issue into a deciding rubber when Francesca Lubiani claimed the third set tie-break 8–6 to level the contest with her 4–6 6–4 7–6 defeat of Virginia Ruano.

Confident from her singles success, Leon was able to lift her team-mate Ruano in the doubles to claim the final rubber 6–2 6–2 against Perfetti and Giulia Casoni.

Meanwhile in Division One, all four teams in both round-robin groups were in contention for promotion on the final day with similar win–loss results. For the record, Austria and the Czech Republic gained promotion to the Champions Division, while Croatia, Denmark, Israel and Switzerland elevated themselves from Division Two.

First Round: Belgium d. Finland 2–1; Hungary d. Greece 2–1.
Semi-finals: Spain d. Belgium 3–0. Gala Leon (ESP) d. Kim Clysters (BEL) 6–1 6–3; Virginia Ruano (ESP) d. Daphne Van de Zande (BEL) 6–4 6–3; Ana Alcazar/Leon d. Clysters/E Last 6–0 6–3; ***Italy d. Hungary 2–1.*** Annamaria Foldenyi (HUN) d. Gloria Pizzichini (ITA) 6–0 6–4; Francesca Lubiana (ITA) d. Petra Mandula (HUN) 6–1 2–6 6–4; Giulia Casoni/Flora Perfetti (ITA) d. Foldenyi/Mandula 6–0 6–3.
Final: Spain d. Italy 2–1. Gala Leon (ESP) d. Flora Perfetti (ITA) 6–4 7–6(3); Francesca Lubiani (ITA) d. Virginia Ruano (ESP) 4–6 6–4 7–6(6); Leon/Ruano (ESP) d. Giulia Casoni/ Perfetti (ITA) 6–2 6–2.

(Above) *Danny Sapsford, ably supported by Martin Lee (right), led Britain to their first European Cup success with a 2–1 win over the Netherlands.* (Michael Cole)

PEUGEOT ATP TOUR WORLD TEAM CHAMPIONSHIP

DUSSELDORF, GERMANY, 19–25 MAY 1997
Eight-team draw: $1,650,000. Surface: Clay.

RED GROUP
USA: Pete Sampras, Michael Chang, Alex O'Brien, Jonathan Stark.
Australia: Mark Woodforde, Mark Philippoussis, Todd Woodbridge.
Czech Republic: Petr Korda, Bohdan Ulihrach, Jiri Novak, Daniel Vacek.
Croatia: Goran Ivanisevic, Sasa Hirszon, Josip Dumanic.

BLUE GROUP
Spain: Albert Costa, Felix Mantilla, Javier Sanchez, Francisco Roig.
Sweden: Thomas Enqvist, Magnus Gustafsson, Magnus Larsson, Nicklas Kulti.
Netherlands: Richard Krajicek, Paul Haarhuis, Jacco Eltingh.
Germany: Mchael Stich, David Prinosil, Martin Sinner.

TEAM STANDINGS
RED GROUP W–L: Australia 3–1*; Croatia 1–2; USA 1–2; Czech Republic 1–2.
BLUE GROUP W–L: Spain 4–0*; Netherlands 2–1; Germany 1–2; Sweden 0–3.
**Includes final.*

RED GROUP RESULTS: ***Australia d. USA 2–1:*** Michael Chang (USA) d. Woodforde (AUS) 6–3 4–6 7–5; Philippoussis (AUS) d. Pete Sampras (USA) 4–6 6–4 0–1 Ret.; Woodbridge/Woodforde (AUS) d. O'Brien/Stark (USA) 6–4 4–6 6–2. ***Croatia d. Czech Republic 2–1:*** Goran Ivanisevic (CRO) d. Bohdan Ulihrach (CZE) 6–4 3–6 6–4; Petr Korda (CZE) d. Sasa Hirszon (CRO) 7–5 6–4; Hirszon/Ivanisevic (CRO) d. Novak/Vacek (CZE) 5–7 6–4 6–3. ***Australia d. Czech Republic 3–0:*** Philippoussis (AUS) d. Ulihrach (CZE) 6–4 4–6 6–3; Woodforde (AUS) d. Korda (CZE) 3–6 7–5 6–1; Woodbridge/Woodforde (AUS) d. Vacek/Damm (CZE) 6–4 6–3. ***USA d. Croatia 2–1:*** Ivanisevic (CRO) d. Chang (USA) 6–2 2–6 6–3; O'Brien (USA) d. Hirszon (CRO) 6–1 6–2; O'Brien/Stark (USA) d. Hirszon/Ivanisevic (CRO) 6–3 7–6(6). ***Australia d. Croatia 3–0:*** Philippoussis (AUS) d. Ivanisevic (CRO) 6–1 6–2; Woodbridge (AUS) d. Hirszon (CRO) 6–4 6–1; Woodbridge/Woodforde (AUS) d. Hirszon/Ivanisevic (CRO) 6–2 7–5. ***Czech Republic d. USA 2–1:*** Korda (CZE) d. O'Brien (USA) 3–6 7–6(5) 6–3; Chang (USA) d. Ulihrach (CZE) 6–3 7–6(3); Korda/Vacek (CZE) d. O'Brien/Stark (USA) 6–2 6–2.

BLUE GROUP RESULTS: ***Netherlands d. Germany 2–1:*** Michael Stich (GER) d. Jan Siemerink (NED) 6–3 6–2; Paul Haarhuis (NED) d. David Prinosil (GER) 7–5 6–4; Eltingh/Haarhuis (NED) d. Stich/Sinner (GER) 6–2 6–3. ***Spain d. Sweden 2–1:*** Mantilla (ESP) d. Magnus Larsson (SWE) 1–6 7–6(5) 6–4; Costa (ESP) d. Magnus Gustafsson (SWE) 6–4 6–1; Enqvist/Kulti (SWE) d. Roig/Sanchez (ESP) 1–6 6–1 6–4. ***Spain d. Germany 3–0:*** Costa (ESP) d. Stich (GER) 6–1 6–3; Mantilla (ESP) d. Prinosil (GER) 6–2 6–1; Carbonell/Roig (ESP) d. Prinosil/Sinner (GER) 5–7 7–5 6–3 ***Netherlands d. Sweden 2–1:*** Larsson (SWE) d. Haarhuis (NED) 2–6 6–3 6–2; Siemerink (NED) d. Enqvist (SWE) 6–2 7–6(11); Eltingh/Haarhuis (NED) d. Enqvist/Kulti (SWE) 6–2 6–3. ***Germany d. Sweden 2–1:*** Stich (GER) d. Gustafsson (SWE) 2–6 7–6(4) 6–4; Sinner (GER) d. Larsson (SWE) 7–6(4) 7–6(6); Larsson/Kulti (SWE) d. Stich/Sinner (GER) 6–2 6–4. ***Spain d. Netherlands 2–1:*** Costa (ESP) d. Siemerink (NED) 6–1 7–6; Mantilla (ESP) d. Haarhuis (NED) 6–1 6–1; Eltingh/Haarhuis (NED) d. Carbonell/Roig (ESP) 7–6(5) 7–6(4).

FINAL: ***Spain d. Australia 3–0:*** Felix Mantilla (ESP) d. Mark Woodforde (AUS) 7–5 6–2; Albert Costa (ESP) d. Mark Philippoussis (AUS) 3–6 7–6(3) 7–6(7); Tomas Carbonell/Francisco Roig (ESP) d. Todd Woodbridge/Mark Woodforde (AUS) 6–3 7–5.

Rankings

World Rankings
ATP Tour Rankings and Prize Money
History of the ATP Tour No.1 Men's Ranking
Corel WTA Tour Rankings and Prize Money
History of the WTA Tour No.1 Women's Ranking

With a consistently high percentage of winning serves, plus improved all-round play, Greg Rusedski reached a career-high ranking of four and finished the year at No.6, the first Briton ever to appear in the top ten. (Michael Cole)

1997 World Rankings

John Barrett

1997 WORLD RANKINGS (last year's ranking in brackets)

	Men		Women
1	Pete Sampras (1)	1	Martina Hingis (8)
2	Patrick Rafter (–)	2	Jana Novotna (5)
3	Michael Chang (4)	3	Lindsay Davenport (7)
4	Jonas Bjorkman (–)	4	Monica Seles (2)
5	Greg Rusedski (–)	5	Iva Majoli (–)
6	Yevgeny Kafelnikov (3)	6	Mary Pierce (–)
7	Carlos Moya (–)	7	Amanda Coetzer (10)
8	Marcelo Rios (–)	8	Arantxa Sanchez Vicario (3)
9	Gustavo Kuerten (–)	9	Irina Spirlea (–)
=10	Sergi Bruguera (–)	10	Mary Joe Fernandez (–)
=10	Thomas Muster (7)		

It wasn't a race; more of a procession really. So completely did Pete Sampras and Martina Hingis dominate the scene in 1997 that when they reached the finishing post in November and looked back, their nearest challengers appeared as small dots on the horizon.

Sampras started and finished the year strongly. With a second Australian and a fourth Wimbledon title among his eight tournament successes, the 26-year-old American brought his tally of Grand Slam titles to 10, just two short of Roy Emerson's all-time record. In between he had lost early at the French Open – no real surprise, that. But he did falter at the US Open in the fourth round. Like an actor who had forgotten his lines he allowed the brilliant but erratic Czech, Peter Korda, to steal the scene in a dramatic tie-break that brought down the curtain. The loss of his title served only to sharpen Sampras's resolve for the remainder of the season. At the Grand Slam Cup and the ATP Tour Championship, the world champion was word perfect.

Hingis also kept to the script until fatigue caught up with her at the end of a tiring but spectacular year. The remarkable Swiss Miss was just 16 years 4 months old when she scored the first of her three 1997 Grand Slam success in Melbourne on 26 January. She thus became the youngest woman this century to win one of the four major Championships. Exactly nine weeks later, in the middle of a winning streak of six tournaments and 37 matches that would end in the French Open final, she thrashed Monica Seles in Key Biscayne to earn the world No.1 ranking, the youngest player ever to achieve that pinnacle. Had she not arrived in Paris without any match play for five weeks following a riding accident that led to arthroscopic surgery on a damaged knee, she would probably have become the fourth woman to achieve a Grand Slam. On last year's evidence it will only be a matter of time before that honour falls to her.

The men's season was remarkable for the number of different players who reached the quarter-finals of the Grand Slams, 27 in all. At the end of Wimbledon Pete Sampras was the only player to have reached the last eight twice. I cannot remember that ever happening before.

The best of the rest were Patrick Rafter, Michael Chang and Jonas Bjorkman. Besides winning his first major crown at the US Open, Rafter was a semi-finalist in Paris and led Australia to the last but one round of the Davis Cup. With his athletic good looks and ready smile he led the field in female admirers, too.

Chang won five tournament and banked more than $2.5 million in prize money to bring his career earnings to $26.25 million, but once again had no major titles to show for his efforts.

Bjorkman was a revelation. His consistency, especially on return of serve, was remarkable in the latter half of the year. He was always there or thereabouts. A semi-finalist at the US Open and the ATP Championship he also anchored the Swedes in their successful Davis Cup run.

The British No.1 Greg Rusedski had a fabulous year that might have been even more spectacular if he had not suffered an injury to his left wrist in the Spring. After reaching his first quarter-final at Wimbledon he served his way to the final of the US Open, the first Briton to reach that stage in America since Fred Perry in 1934. He also won twice on the ATP Tour.

Yevgeny Kafelnikov won three tournaments and reached the final in Hanover but only once reached the last eight at a Grand Slam. Surprisingly for a man bred on clay courts, that had happened at Wimbledon.

Like Rusedski, Carlos Moya reached a Grand Slam final for the first time (in Melbourne) while the Chilean left-hander Marcelo Rios was the only man apart from Sampras to win two Super Nine tournaments.

In many ways the success of Gustavo Kuerten at the French Open was the story of the year. This was a romantic rags-to-riches tale whose plot would have been rejected by any respectable publisher.

When the colourful Brazilian made himself the champion by beating three former winners – Muster, Kafelnikov and Bruguera – he was scoring his first success on the main tour. A telephone call from Sports Minister Pele on the eve of the final was one of the things that inspired him, he said.

It was difficult to adjudge the last place. Richard Krajicek kept looking as if he would catch fire. Despite three tournament wins, he never did and had to be rejected. The most successful tournament winner, apart from Sampras and Chang, was Felix Mantilla, a quarter-finalist in Melbourne. However, the Spaniard's five titles were all minor affairs.

Sergi Bruguera's performance in reaching another French Open final, plus three other final round appearances was just enough to earn him the last place. But he must share it with Thomas Muster who started well with a run to the semi-finals in Australia and then won in Dubai and Key Biscayne. What a pity the Austrian left-hander faded on clay, the surface on which he has had so much success.

At a time of change, the women were only slightly less volatile than the men with 21 players distributed among Grand Slam quarter-finals. Jana Novotna's strong finish at the season-ending Chase Championships made up for the disappointment of losing to Hingis in the Wimbledon final. The popular Czech won on four other occasions to claim second place in this year's list, an improvement of three places over 1996.

Next is Lindsay Davenport whose greater consistency earned her six tournament wins and a semi-final finish at Flushing Meadows.

Monica Seles, whose year was clouded by her father's illness, had one of those frustrating seasons when the promise of success was constantly dashed by young players reaching new heights. Unable to play in Australia she lost narrowly to Hingis in a Paris semi-final, failed to convert a match-point against Sandrine Testud in Wimbledon's third round and did the same thing against Irina Spirlea in the quarter-finals at the US Open.

Majoli's spectacular win over Hingis in the French Open final plus two other tournament wins earns her fifth place, one ahead of Australian Open finalist Mary Pierce who ended the season as she had begun it by reaching a final at the Chase Championships.

The indefatigable Amanda Coetzer worked harder than anyone but revealed the flaw in the WTA ranking system which rewards quantity over quality. Her 27 tournaments brought her two minor titles and semi-final finishes in Melbourne and Paris but gave her 4th place in the WTA year-end rankings. I can place her no higher than seventh.

Arantxa Sanchez Vicario slips from No.3 to No.8 after a season she will want to forget. The former world No.1 won no titles but at least she was a semi-finalist at Wimbledon and reached the quarter-finals at the French and US Opens plus the Chase Championships.

Irina Spirlea made great strides. By reaching the semi-finals at the US Open and the Chase, the quarters in Melbourne and one other final she pips Mary Joe Fernandez for 9th place. The American, though, will be delighted that she is fit again and playing more like her old self.

JOHN BARRETT'S WORLD RANKINGS 1982–96

MEN

	1982		1983		1984		1985		1986
1	Connors	1	McEnroe	1	McEnroe	1	Lendl	1	Lendl
2	Lendl	2	Connors	2	Lendl	2	Wilander	2	Becker
3	McEnroe	3	Wilander	3	Connors	3	Edberg	3	Edberg
4	Vilas	4	Lendl	4	Wilander	4	Becker	4	Leconte
5	Wilander	5	Noah	5	Gomez	5	McEnroe	5	Nystrom
6	Gerulaitis	=6	Arias	6	Cash	6	Connors	6	Mecir
7	Mayer G.	=6	Higueras	7	Sundstrom	7	Jarryd	7	Wilander
8	Noah	8	Solomon	8	Jarryd	8	Leconte	8	Noah
9	Clerc	9	Clerc	9	Nystrom	9	Nystrom	9	McEnroe
10	Higueras	10	Teltscher	10	Arias	=10	Gunthardt	10	Gomez
						=10	Noah		

	1987		1988		1989		1990		1991
1	Lendl	1	Wilander	1	Becker	1	Edberg	1	Edberg
2	Edberg	2	Edberg	2	Lendl	2	Lendl	2	Courier
3	Wilander	3	Lendl	3	Edberg	3	Agassi	3	Becker
4	Cash	4	Becker	4	McEnroe J.	4	Sampras	4	Stich
5	Mecir	5	Agassi	5	Chang	5	Becker	5	Lendl
6	Connors	6	Mayotte	6	Gilbert	6	Gomez	6	Forget
7	Becker	7	Mecir	7	Krickstein	7	Muster	7	Agassi
8	Noah	8	Carlsson K.	8	Mecir	8	Ivanisovic	8	Sampras
9	Mayotte	9	Cash	9	Mayotte	9	Sanchez	9	Novacek
10	Gomez	=10	Leconte	10	Agassi	10	McEnroe J.	10	Korda
		=10	Svensson						

	1992		1993		1994		1995		1996
1	Courier	1	Sampras	1	Sampras	1	Sampras	1	Sampras
2	Edberg	2	Courier	2	Agassi	2	Agassi	2	Becker
3	Agassi	3	Stich	3	Bruguera	3	Muster	3	Kafelnikov
4	Ivanisevic	4	Bruguera	4	Becker	4	Becker	4	Chang
5	Sampras	5	Edberg	5	Martin	5	Chang	5	Krajicek
6	Becker	6	Medvedev	6	Ivanisevic	6	Kafelnikov	6	Agassi
7	Rossetl	7	Chang	7	Chang	7	Enqvist	7	Muster
8	Chang	8	Ivanisevic	8	Stich	8	Courier	8	Ivanisevic
9	Korda	9	Pioline	9	Edberg	9	Ferreira	=9	Washington
=10	Lendl	10	Muster	10	Berasategui	10	Ivanisevic	=9	Stich
=10	Ferreira								

WOMEN

	1982		1983		1984		1985		1986
1	Navratilova	1	Navratilova	1	Navratilova	1	Navratilova	1	Navratilova
2	Evert Lloyd	2	Evert Lloyd	2	Evert Lloyd	2	Evert Lloyd	2	Evert
3	Jaeger	3	Jaeger	3	Mandlikova	3	Mandlikova	3	Graf
4	Mandlikova	4	Durie	4	Shriver	4	Garrison	4	Sukova
5	Austin	5	Shriver	5	Bassett	5	Kohde-Kilsch	5	Mandlikova
6	Ruzici	6	Mandlikova	6	Maleeva Man	6	Sukova	6	Sabatini
7	Bunge	7	Turnbull	7	Garrison	7	Shriver	7	Shriver
8	Shriver	8	Hanika	8	Jordan K.	8	Graf	8	Garrison
9	Potter	9	Temesvari	9	Turnbull	9	Maleeva Man	9	Maleeva
=10	Garrison	10	Potter	10	Kohde-Kilsch	=10	Rinaldi	10	Rinaldi
=10	Turnbull					=10	Sabatini		

	1987		1988		1989		1990		1991
1	Graf	1	Graf	1	Graf	1	Graf	1	Seles
2	Navratilova	2	Sabatini	2	Navratilova	2	Seles	2	Graf
3	Evert	3	Navratilova	3	Sanchez-Vicario	3	Sabatini	3	Sabatini
4	Mandlikova	4	Evert	4	Sabatini	4	Navratilova	4	Navratilova
5	Sabatini	5	Shriver	5	Seles	5	Fernandez	5	Sanchez-Vic.
6	Shriver	6	Sukova	6	Evert	6	Maleeva, K.	6	Fernandez
7	Sukova	7	Zvereva	7	Garrison	7	Garrison	7	Capriati
8	Kohde-Kilsch	8	Garrison	8	Sukova	8	Sanchez-Vicario	8	Novotna
9	Maleeva Frag.	9	Maleeva Frag.	9	Maleeva Frag.	9	Maleeva Frag.	9	Martinez
10	McNeil	10	Kohde-Kilsch	10	Lindqvist	10	Capriati	10	Maleeva Fra.

	1992		1993		1994		1995		1996
1	Seles	1	Graf	1	Sanchez Vicario	1	Graf	1	Graf
2	Graf	2	Seles	2	Graf	2	Seles	2	Seles
3	Sanchez-Vicario	3	Sanchez-Vicario	3	Martinez	3	Sanchez-Vicario	3	Sanchez-Vicario
4	Capriati	4	Martinez	4	Pierce	4	Martinez	4	Martinez
5	Sabatini	5	Navratilova	5	Novotna	5	Pierce	5	Novotna
6	Fernandez	6	Novotna	6	Sabatini	6	Sabatini	6	Huber
7	Maleeva Fragniere	7	Sabatini	7	Davenport	7	Date	7	Davenport
8	Navratilova	8	Huber	8	Navratilova	8	Fernandez	8	Hingis
9	Martinez	9	Fernandez	9	Date	9	Novotna	9	Date
10	Zvereva	10	Maleeva Fragniere	10	Zvereva	10	Huber	10	Coetzer

The retirement of Michael Stich (left) *and the partial retirement from competition of Boris Becker (below) marked the end of Germany's greatest era in men's tennis. Their future lies with young men like Nicolas Kiefer* (middle left) *Daniel Elsner* (bottom left) *and Tommy Haas* (bottom right).
(Tommy Hindley, Stephen Wake, Michael Cole)

VAN DER MEER
TENNISUNIVERSITY

These manufacturers & groups are members of the ITF Foundation

Any commercial tennis organisation is welcome to apply for membership to:

The International Tennis Federation
Palliser Road Barons Court London W14 9EN
Telephone 44 171 381 8060 Fax 44 171 381 3898
Website http://www.itftennis.com

Open Tennis – The First Thirty Years

Ronald Atkin

It all began on a raw Monday in April 1968 at the English seaside resort of Bournemouth. Here, at the British Hard Court Championships, a little-known Briton, John Clifton, won the first point but lost the match to Australia's Owen Davidson. The first open tournament in the history of tennis was under way, at the unlikely setting of the West Hants LTC. From this modest beginning has mushroomed in 30 years one of the richest and most popular of professional sports.

In August 1967, with the backing of Britain's Lawn Tennis Association, an eight-man professional tournament, won by Rod Laver, had been staged on the hallowed lawns of the All England Club, one month after the traditional Championships. At the end of that year the LTA had taken the historic decision to remove in future all distinction between amateur and professional players at all their tournaments, including Wimbledon. Thus the hand of the International Lawn Tennis Federation was forced, after years of opposition to the move, and approval was given to stage twelve open tournaments in 1968.

Official misgivings that the professionals would swamp the amateurs were confounded in Bournemouth's second round when Mark Cox, ranked only third in Britain, overcame the mighty Pancho Gonzales in five sets to become the first amateur to defeat a professional. The pros had their way in the end, however, with Ken Rosewall beating Laver to take the winner's money in a total prize fund of just £5,490.

Then, a month later, came the first of the open Grand Slams at Roland Garros, and to underline the fact that tennis was experiencing a time of revolution the French Open was staged amid a general strike and student riots. With public transport non-existent, spectators walked or hitch-hiked out to Auteuil in the city's suburbs to see that persistent little fellow Rosewall win again, 15 years after capturing his first French title. The women's crown went to the American, Nancy Richey, and, with prize money officially on offer for the first time, Rosewall walked away with 15,000 francs while Richey collected one-third of that amount.

At Wimbledon, what then seemed the mouth-watering prize money of £26,150 was on offer. Rod Laver, picking up as the Centre Court's champion where he had left off in 1961 and 1962, was the recipient of men's top money of £2,000, while Billie Jean King, winning her third straight Wimbledon, collected £750.

No starker example of the astonishing growth of tennis in three decades can be offered than to detail the 1997 Wimbledon champions' earnings: Pete Sampras £415,000 and Martina Hingis £373,500. And all of it set in motion by what the late General Secretary of the ITF, David Gray, called, 'the most astonishing year in the history of lawn tennis.'

At first, the prize money of the open era merely accelerated. Then, as sponsors moved in, the cash on offer soared virtually out of sight. Whenever a sponsoring company opted out, another one was eagerly jostling for somewhere to put its money. Though that eagerness has abated somewhat, particularly in the women's game, the rewards have outstripped most other sports quite comfortably, thanks largely to the formation of two players' bodies – the Association of Tennis Professionals (1972) and the Women's Tennis Association (1973).

In fact, everything has gone through the roof – attendances, TV and media coverage, the number of tournaments, the power of rackets, the percentage of injuries and burn-outs, fitness requirements, arguments and lawsuits and – not least – the quality of the biggest theatres where the players perform.

To deal with the last first: it was the Americans who stirred the Grand Slam pot, taking their championships away from a private club, Forest Hills, and building in an astonishing 12 months a completely new facility on the site of a former World Fair at Flushing Meadows in New York. The place was stark and unattractively functional and it generated problems galore. But it was home, a new home which the US Tennis Association could call its own.

Then, under the wise guidance of Philippe Chatrier, the French Federation president who had worn more hats than most during the open era, Roland Garros was dusted down, smartened up and sold to the Paris public as the place to be seen in late May and early June.

Next came the Australian Open, turning its back on the grass of Kooyong and building a stunning new facility at Flinders Park which had its baptismal year in 1988.

Two new stadiums at Roland Garros expanded the French Open even further before Wimbledon announced its long-term plans to take the world's premier tournament into the new millenium. The first tangible result of these plans was unveiled for the public last summer, a sumptuous new No. 1 Court. The US Open facilities had been dismissed as not worthy of a Grand Slam, with the result that a massive new arena, a stadium named in memory of Arthur Ashe, was opened for the first time last September.

Whether the players are better than in the past is a matter for earnest debate. They are certainly fitter and faster and required to run further in pursuit of all that money. When he won Wimbledon for a fourth time in 1969 and then captured the US Open for a second time Rod Laver was hailed as the greatest-ever; twenty-eight years later the same phrase was applied to Pete Sampras when he won a second Compaq Grand Slam Cup. So the standard has not deteriorated, though there have been peaks and valleys in both men's and women's tennis.

After the Australians, Laver, Newcombe et al, came an American pair whose ability was matched only by their ability to earn headlines, good and bad: Jimmy Connors and John McEnroe. But European men's tennis, quiescent since the days of Fred Perry and the Musketeers of France, took its place in the forefront again with the emergence of the Swedes Bjorn Borg, Mats Wilander and Stefan Edberg, the Czech-born but eventually American-based Ivan Lendl and Germany's very own 'boom boom', Boris Becker. In the Nineties it has been Sampras all the way.

The best of the women at the start of open tennis were Billie Jean King and the Australian pair, Margaret Court and Evonne Goolagong. They were supplanted by Chris Evert and, after her defection from Czechoslovakia in 1975, Martina Navratilova. These two then proceeded to stage the greatest-ever women's rivalry until a young German called Steffi Graf broke the mould by beating them both in the same Florida tournament and proceeded to take over. Graf's career struck a glorious peak in 1988 when she won all four Grand Slams and Olympic gold at the first Games to which tennis was fully readmitted.

Though more prone to injury than most, Graf comfortably extended her domination into the Nineties and was not usurped until Monica Seles started to win all her titles. Then Martina Hingis came along to shatter most of the 'youngest-ever' records in the Grand Slams.

The Davis Cup, too, went 'open' in 1972 with the overdue abolition of the Challenge Round. With that abolition disappeared the hegemony of Australia and the United States, who between them had won the trophy every year since 1937. They won the next two as well, but then Europe got it on the act, first Italy, then the Czechs and, as the pace of European tennis gathered, Sweden, Germany and France. The interest in the Davis Cup kept pace on the graph of popularity with the rest of professional tennis. In 1997 the number of competing nations had shot up to 127, and sponsorship for this (and the women's team event, the Fed Cup) was strong.

The open era has delivered just about everything: the bizarre contest between Billie Jean King and Bobby Riggs, labelled 'Battle of the Sexes' in 1973; the emergence, and virtual disappearance, of the game's vaudeville branch, known as World Team Tennis; the spaghetti racket – outlawed in less than 12 months; the appearance of a transsexual, Renee Richards, formerly Dr Richard Raskind, in the US Open women's draw in 1976; the introduction of a Code of Conduct and then drug testing; and the tragedies of burn-out among the girls who had played too much too soon – Tracy Austin, Andrea Jaeger and then Jennifer Capriati. And the normal on-court dramas of tennis spun wickedly out of control at Hamburg in April 1993 when a crazedly devoted follower of Steffi Graf stabbed her greatest rival, Monica Seles.

Since the open era came out of its starting blocks the din of argument has been loud as various factions whose multiplicity of initials merely served to bewilder the public, struggled for control of the professional game, abetted by that booming fraternity, agents. The ATP took its tour away from the Grand Slam segment of the year and expanded vigorously to 77 tournaments in 34 countries; the women's tour had 54 in 23 countries last year.

Now, in the shadow of the millennium, those who went their own way are seeking to get together again, to streamline the circuit, simplify the rankings system and the playing calendar and to put right the wrongs which have crept in over 30 years of the professional game.

I wonder if Messrs Clifton and Davidson had realised just what they were starting on that April morning at Bournemouth in 1968.

30 Years of Open Tennis

1968–1998

Above: Australia's Ken Rosewall, having won the world's first open tournament, the 1968 British Hard Court Championships at Bournemouth, also claims the first open Grand Slam title in Paris, where the women's singles is won by the US No.1, Nancy Richey *(Right)*. *(Michael Cole)*

SETS GAMES POINTS
W.KING
2 40
JONES
3 30

Above: Rod Laver at Forest Hills in 1972, where, three years earlier, he had won the second of his two Grand Slams. *(Michael Cole)*

Left: At the age of 30, Ann Jones, having surprised top seeded Margaret Court in the semi-finals, beats three-time defending champion and No. 2 seed, Billie Jean King, to win Wimbledon in 1969, the first left-hander to hold the title. *(Michael Cole)*

Facing page:

Billie Jean King, beats Ann Jones in the semi-finals of the first open Wimbledon in 1968 en route to the third of her six singles titles which earned her £750. *(Michael Cole)*

Inset: With Martina Navratilova after the Czech-born left-hander has won her record 20th Wimbledon title in 1979. *(Michael Cole)*

Right: Czechoslovakia's Jan Kodes winning the first of his two consecutive French Open titles in 1970. *(Michael Cole)*

Below: At Forest Hills in 1970 Margaret Court completes her Grand Slam to equal the 1953 record of Maureen Connolly. *(Michael Cole)*

Inset: The same year at Wimbledon she had beaten Billie Jean King 14–12 11–9 in Wimbledon's longest final and receives her trophy from Princess Margaret. *(Michael Cole)*

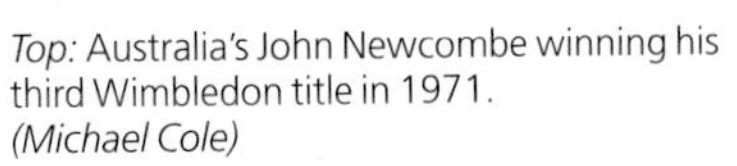

Top: Australia's John Newcombe winning his third Wimbledon title in 1971. *(Michael Cole)*

Above: Among the 57 career titles of the gifted Romanian, Ilie Nastase, was the 1972 US Open, one of his two Grand Slam successes (the other was the 1973 French Open). *(Michael Cole)*

Right: Stan Smith winning the 1971 US Open, the year before he won Wimbledon and led the United States to victory in the first-ever Davis Cup final in Bucharest. *(Michael Cole)*

Left: The 1975 Wimbledon victory of Arthur Ashe over fellow American and defending champion Jimmy Connors was a tactical triumph. *(Michael Cole)*

Below: Already twice the winner in France, Bjorn Borg, aged 20, wins the 1976 Wimbledon title against Romania's Ilie Nastase. *(Michael Cole)*

Inset: Five years in a row (1976–80) the ice-cool Swede would hold the men's singles trophy, a modern record. *(Michael Cole)*

Left: Guillermo Vilas, four times a finalist in Paris, wins the title in 1977, losing only three games to the American, Brian Gottfried. Three months later he claimed the last of the three US Opens played on clay during a spell of dominance which brought the Argentine left-hander 46 consecutive winning matches, an open era record. *(Michael Cole)*

Above: An ecstatic Virginia Wade wins Wimbledon's centennial championships in 1977 in front of the Queen who is celebrating her jubilee year. *(Michael Cole)*

Left: Vitas Gerulaitis lost a magnificent Wimbledon semi-final to his great friend and rival Bjorn Borg in 1977 but finished the year as the Australian Open champion. *(Michael Cole)*

DOUBLES PARTNERSHIPS

Clockwise from the right: Six of the greatest doubles pairs of the open era: John Newcombe and Tony Roche (AUS) *(Michael Cole)*; Todd Woodbridge and Mark Woodforde (AUS) *(Tommy Hindley)*; Rosie Casals and Billie Jean King (USA) *(Michael Cole)*; Natasha Zvereva (BEL) and Gigi Fernandez (USA) *(Michael Cole)*; Pam Shriver and Martina Navratilova (USA) *(Michael Cole)*; Peter Fleming and John McEnroe (USA) *(Michael Cole)*

Right: The graceful Australian Evonne Goolagong Cawley won two Wimbledon titles – the first in 1971 as a 19-year-old, the second in 1980 after the birth of her daughter Kelly. Not since the 1914 success of Dorothea Lambert Chambers had a mother won the title. *(Michael Cole)*

Below: Tracy Austin, aged 16 years 9 months, became the youngest winner of the US Open in 1979, a title the American would win again in 1981 after achieving a No. 1 world ranking the previous year. *(Michael Cole)*

Above: Martina Navratilova, aged 21, wins Wimbledon for the first time in 1978 and *(Right)* claims a record ninth title in 1990. *(Michael Cole)*

Above: Czech-born Hana Mandlikova winning the French Open in 1981, one year after her first Grand Slam success in Australia as an 18-year-old. She would also claim the 1985 US and the 1987 Australian titles before becoming an Australian citizen in 1988. *(Michael Cole)*

Right and Below: John McEnroe's raging genius wins him the 1981 Wimbledon title which he would win twice more (1983, 1984). His turbulent career included four US Opens, three Masters and five WCT crowns among his 77 singles titles, plus 77 doubles wins and a 59-10 Davis Cup record. *(Michael Cole)*

Below: In 1982 Mats Wilander of Sweden, aged 17 years 9 months, becomes the youngest French Open champion, a title he would win again in 1985 and 1988. He also won twice in Australia on grass (1983, 1984) and once on hard courts (1988). *(Michael Cole)*

Above: Jimmy Connors, aged 29, winning the 1982 Wimbledon title which he had also won in 1974, the year he also captured the first of his five US Opens. During this period the American left-hander was ranked No. 1 for a record 160 consecutive weeks. *(Michael Cole)*

Below: Aged 17 years 7 months, Boris Becker became Wimbledon's youngest men's champion at the start of a career which brought him six Grand Slam titles, two Davis Cup successes and a world No.1 ranking. *(Michael Cole)*

Top: The 1984 French Open was the first of Ivan Lendl's eight Grand Slam titles during a brilliant career in which he was ranked No.1 for a record 270 weeks. *(Michael Cole)*

Above: The first of Stefan Edberg's two consecutive US Open wins comes in 1991 after the Swede had already won two Australian and two Wimbledon titles. *(Michael Cole)*

Right: America's Chris Evert winning the 1986 French Open, the first of a record seven Paris titles in a long and brilliant career that saw her amass 18 Grand Slam titles and a massive $8.89 million in prize money. *(Michael Cole)*

Left: Argentina's Gabriela Sabatini whose only Grand Slam success was a stunning defeat of defending champion Steffi Graf at the 1990 US Open. *(Michael Cole)*

Below: At the 1988 US Open Germany's new Olympic champion Steffi Graf completes a unique Golden Grand Slam. *(Tommy Hindley)*

Above: Aged 19, Californian
Pete Sampras is the youngest man to hold the US Open trophy after beating Andre Agassi in the 1990 final. *(Michael Cole)*

Left: One year earlier, fellow American Michael Chang, 17, had become the youngest-ever winner of the French Open when he shocked Stefan Edberg in the 1989 final. *(Michael Cole)*

Left: Monica Seles of Croatia winning the first of her nine Grand Slam titles at the 1990 French Open when, aged 16 years 6 months, she was the youngest Grand Slam winner since 15-year-old Lottie Dod won Wimbledon in 1887. *(Michael Cole)*

Below: The relentless American Jim Courier winning the first of his two French Open titles in 1991. *(Michael Cole)*

Above: After failing in two French Open finals on friendly clay Andre Agassi confounds his critics when he wins the first of his three Grand Slam titles on Wimbledon's grass in 1992. *(Michael Cole)*

Right: The feisty Spaniard, Arantxa Sanchez Vicario, winning the 1994 US Open from defending champion Steffi Graf. *(Tommy Hindley)*

Below: Sergi Bruguera in Paris, 1993, winning the first of his two consecutive French opens. *(Michael Cole)*

Right: Gustavo Kuerten's spectacular victory at the 1997 French Open was the first ever by a Brazilian man. *(Tommy Hindley)*

Pat Rafter on his way to the 1997 US Open, the first Grand Slam success by an Australian since Pat Cash won Wimbledon in 1987. *(Michael Cole)*

Aged just 16 years 3 months, Martina Hingis wins the 1997 Australian Open, to become the youngest Grand Slam winner this century. *(Stephen Wake)*

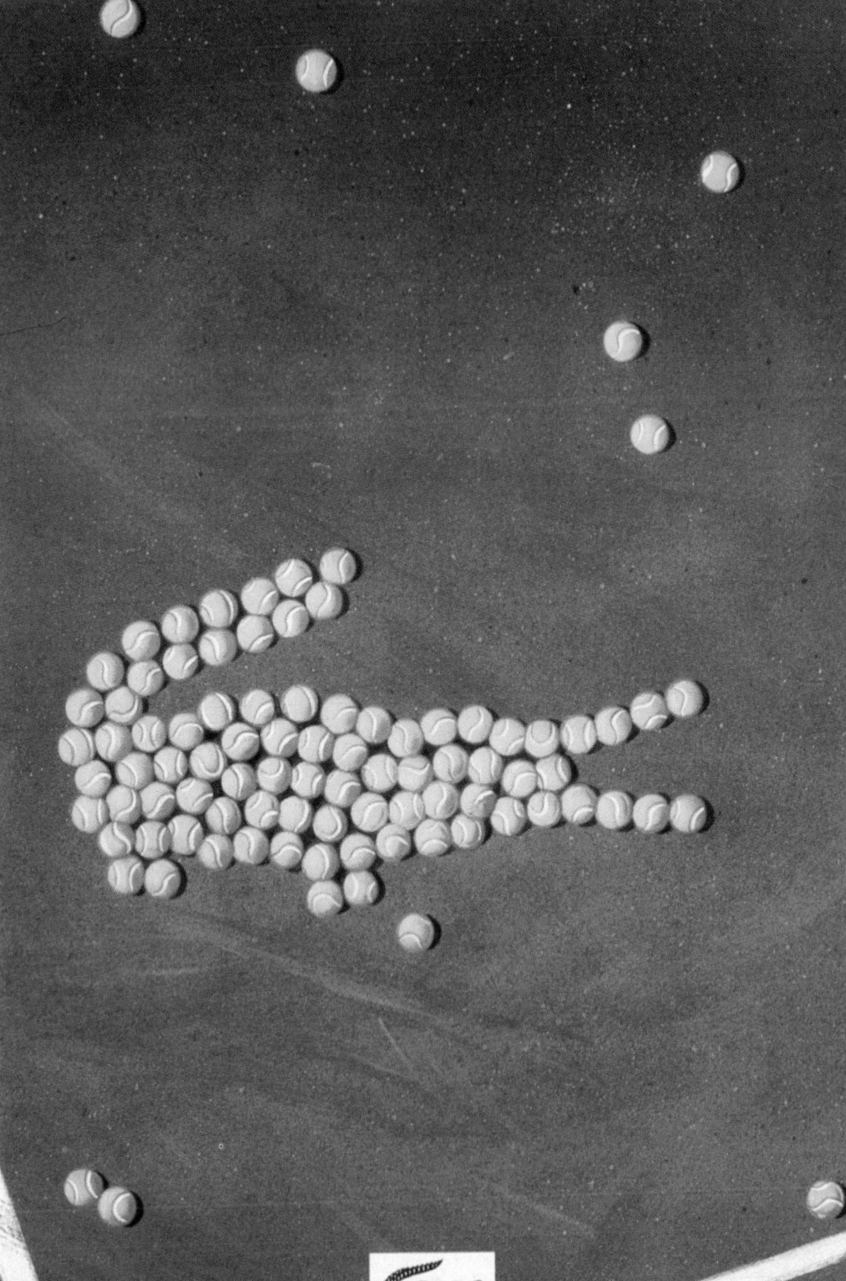

LACOSTE

ATP Tour Rankings and Prize Money 1997

The following tables show the rankings of the top 300 men in singles, the top 180 in doubles and the top 300 on the prize money list, plus those players whose career earnings exceed $1 million. For the purposes of rankings and prize money, the season is deemed to have ended on 16 November rather than 31 December. Nevertheless, points earned by players who took part in Challenger and Satellite events taking place between the November date and the end of the year still had them added to subsequent lists. Besides the four Grand Slam Championships, all official ATP Tour tournaments, including Championship Series, World Series and Challenger Series events, as well as the Satellite Circuits administered by member nations of the ITF, were eligible for ranking purposes. Rankings for 1997, adjusted every week, were based on a player's best 14 results (including bonus points) during a moving twelve-month period. All players had to commit to at least 11 tournaments during the year. Somewhat controversially, in 1997, as in every year since 1991, points were also given for the season-ending IBM/ATP Tour World Championship. (Statistics supplied by ATP Tour.)

The nationalities and birthdays of players can be found on pp 142–146.

SINGLES

		Tmts	*Points*
1	Pete Sampras	16	4547
2	Patrick Rafter	26	3210
3	Michael Chang	22	3189
4	Jonas Bjorkman	26	2949
5	Yevgeny Kafelnikov	27	2690
6	Greg Rusedski	22	2617
7	Carlos Moya	29	2508
8	Sergi Bruguera	25	2367
9	Thomas Muster	23	2353
10	Marcelo Rios	26	2317
11	Richard Krajicek	22	2299
12	Alex Corretja	26	2275
13	Petr Korda	24	2261
14	Gustavo Kuerten	15	2215
15	Goran Ivanisevic	23	2176
16	Felix Mantilla	27	2110
17	Tim Henman	26	1929
18	Mark Philippoussis	21	1809
19	Albert Costa	22	1778
20	Cedric Pioline	25	1534
21	Jim Courier	22	1528
22	Magnus Norman	27	1450
23	Alberto Berasategui	31	1425
24	Karol Kucera	30	1423
25	Magnus Larsson	21	1376
26	Todd Woodbridge	20	1319
27	Andrei Medvedev	24	1314
28	Thomas Enqvist	22	1312
29	Fabrice Santoro	29	1294
30	Chris Woodruff	22	1234
31	Marc Rosset	32	1222
32	Nicolas Kiefer	20	1209
33	Francisco Clavet	28	1198
34	Bohdan Ulihrach	29	1143
35	Albert Portas	26	1082
36	Julian Alonso	24	1035
37	Magnus Gustafsson	19	990
38	Hicham Arazi	32	960
39	Thomas Johansson	29	959
40	Filip Dewulf	26	942
41	Tommy Haas	21	933
42	Dominik Hrbaty	30	928
43	Wayne Ferreira	22	910
44	Slava Dosedel	20	899
45	Marcelo Filippini	28	886
46	Mark Woodforde	25	866
47	Guillaume Raoux	27	861
48	Jiri Novak	23	848
49	Jeff Tarango	31	843
50	Brett Steven	20	817
51	Marc-Kevin Goellner	34	812
52	Galo Blanco	31	790
53	Daniel Vacek	30	782
54	Javier Sanchez	36	776
55	Karim Alami	33	748
56	Carlos Costa	31	739
57	Andrea Gaudenzi	34	739
58	Sargis Sargsian	32	736
59	Scott Draper	25	735
60	Sjeng Schalken	29	725
61	Lionel Roux	29	721
62	Martin Damm	26	718
63	Boris Becker	12	715
64	Nicolas Lapentti	30	715
65	Michael Stich	13	711
66	Christian Ruud	26	708
67	Johan van Herck	25	694
68	Fernando Meligeni	27	691
69	Mikael Tillstrom	24	677
70	Richard Fromberg	33	675
71	Paul Haarhuis	25	666
72	Alex Radulescu	29	665

		Tmts	*Points*
73	Juan Albert Viloca	34	655
74	Richey Reneberg	20	654
75	Grant Stafford	24	649
76	Kenneth Carlsen	29	640
77	Byron Black	26	633
78	Jan Siemerink	27	622
79	Jason Stoltenberg	17	617
80	Jan Kroslak	23	586
81	Todd Martin	8	579
82	Dinu Pescariu	29	577
83	Tomas Nydahl	25	570
84	Sandon Stolle	20	555
85	Hernan Gumy	28	545
86	Juan Atonio Marin	29	537
87	Vincent Spadea	31	536
88	David Prinosil	26	533
89	Jordi Burillo	27	532
90	Hendrik Dreekmann	24	525
91	Marcello Craca	24	522
92	Davide Sanguinetti	27	519
93	Nicolas Escude	15	514
94	Gilbert Schaller	29	510
95	Jonathan Stark	23	507
96	Gianluca Pozzi	22	503
97	Wayne Black	19	499
98	Alex O'Brien	29	489
99	Renzo Furlan	28	486
100	Emilio Alvarez	32	481
101	Arnaud Clement	23	479
102	Justin Gimelstob	29	479
103	Jens Knippschild	19	475
104	Arnaud Boetsch	23	459
105	Oliver Gross	23	453
106	Franco Squillari	25	444
107	Radomir Vasek	20	443
108	Alex Calatrava	21	443
109	Andrei Pavel	26	443
110	Alberto Martin	25	441
111	Marcos Ondruska	24	437
112	Daniel Nestor	25	426
113	Guillermo Canas	24	422
114	Leander Paes	25	420
115	Lucas Arnold	26	420
116	Dick Norman	21	416
117	Jerome Golmard	27	412
118	Ramon Delgado	21	405
119	Jacobo Diaz	24	400
120	Dennis van Scheppingen	23	399
121	Fernando Vicente	29	393
122	Andre Agassi	14	375
123	Rainer Schuttler	25	366
124	Stefan Koubek	22	365
125	Alex Lopez-Moron	24	363
126	Oscar Burrieza	18	352
127	Geoff Grant	22	350
128	Vincenzo Santopadre	25	349
129	Marzio Martelli	27	348
130	Gaston Etlis	27	347
131	Martin Sinner	24	345
132	Francisco Cabello	20	339
133	Andrei Cherkasov	35	334
134	Frederik Fetterlein	20	333
135	John van Lottum	18	330
136	Cristiano Caratti	25	328
137	Oleg Ogorodov	28	327
138	Christophe van Garsse	12	326
139	Olivier Delaitre	21	321
140	Adrian Voinea	25	319
141	Sebastien Grosjean	20	313
142	Michael Tebbutt	22	313
143	Andrew Richardson	21	312
144	Alejandro Hernandez	28	312
145	Steve Campbell	24	311
146	David Wheaton	11	306
147	Mariano Puerta	16	304
148	Davide Scala	23	304
149	Francisco Roig	18	299
150	Marco Meneschincheri	29	299
151	Chris Wilkinson	18	295
152	Gabriel Silberstein	21	294
153	Nicklas Kulti	23	294
154	Mark Petchey	20	292
155	Sebastien Lareau	22	292
156	Andrei Merinov	24	292
157	Michael Sell	14	287
158	Diego Nargiso	15	287
159	Allen Belobrajdic	18	284
160	Ion Moldovan	27	282
161	Christian Vinck	20	281
162	Dirk Dier	22	275
163	Doug Flach	25	273
164	Sebastian Prieto	17	271
165	Andre Sa	14	269
166	Eyal Erlich	17	269
167	Gerard Solves	26	268
168	Tomas Carbonell	22	264
169	Jeff Salzenstein	24	262
170	Javier Frana	14	260
171	David Rikl	16	260
172	Martin Rodriguez	19	253
173	Henrik Holm	15	251
174	Luis Herrera	22	251
175	Jaime Oncins	22	247
176	Jan-Michael Gambill	18	246
177	Petr Luxa	24	245
178	Jose 'Pepe' Imaz	14	244
179	Stephane Simian	26	241
180	Jean-Baptiste Perlant	11	240
181	Kevin Ullyett	22	238
182	Todd Larkham	19	235
183	Glenn Weiner	16	227
184	Raviv Weidenfeld	19	227
185	Francisco Costa	18	226
186	Attila Savolt	22	225
187	Brian Macphie	12	224
188	Orlin Stanoytchev	34	223
189	Alexander Volkov	17	220
190	Wade McGuire	17	219
191	Stephane Huet	25	219
192	Horst Skoff	12	215
193	Cecil Mamiit	29	213
194	Marat Safin	9	211
195	Agustin Garizzio	10	211
196	Lars Burgsmuller	18	209
197	Frederic Fontang	24	209
198	Rodolphe Gilbert	15	207
199	Oren Motevassel	23	207
200	Eyal Ran	29	207
201	Salvador Navarro	19	206
202	Grant Doyle	25	206

		Tmts	Points
203	Yong-il Yoon	13	205
204	Marcio Carlsson	16	205
205	Fernon Wibier	21	204
206	Andrei Chesnokov	8	202
207	David Witt	9	201
208	Marcelo Charpentier	17	201
209	Daniele Musa	19	201
210	Danny Sapsford	14	200
211	Gerald Mandl	15	199
212	Roberto Jabali	24	199
213	Neville Godwin	17	198
214	Rainer Falenti	18	198
215	Nuno Marques	18	194
216	Bernardo Mota	16	192
217	Jean-Francois Bachelot	8	190
218	Dusan Vemic	8	190
219	Peter Tramacchi	9	189
220	Michael Joyce	20	188
221	Martijn Belgraver	14	187
222	Stefano Pescosolido	18	186
223	Quino Munoz	13	185
224	Tamer el Sawy	21	180
225	Ivo Heuberger	22	179
226	Gabriel Trifu	16	178
227	Regis Lavergne	15	177
228	Mahesh Bhupathi	14	176
229	Alistair Hunt	17	175
230	Karsten Braasch	10	174
231	Alex Reichel	16	174
232	Bobby Kokavec	15	172
233	Jurek Stasiak	8	171
234	Julien Chauvin	19	170
235	Ben Ellwood	19	170
236	Edwin Kempes	9	168
237	Andrei Stoliarov	10	168
238	Markus Hipfl	11	168
239	Fabio Maggi	12	168
240	Wolfgang Schranz	11	165
241	Tuomas Ketola	14	165
242	Jean-Philippe Fleurian	11	164
243	James Sekulov	17	164
244	Bernd Karbacher	18	164
245	Tommy Ho	7	163
246	Peter Wessels	10	162
247	Charles Auffray	15	159
248	Goichi Motomura	20	159
249	Razvan Sabau	22	158
250	Nicolas Thomann	12	157
251	Agustin Calleri	4	156

		Tmts	Points
252	Mariano Zabaleta	20	156
253	Mark Merklein	23	156
254	David Sanchez	9	155
255	Michael Kohlmann	17	155
256	Malivai Washington	5	154
257	Thomas Larsen	8	154
258	Jaymon Crabb	12	154
259	Mark Knowles	13	154
260	David Skoch	20	154
261	Olivier Mutis	12	153
262	Michal Tabara	12	152
263	Patrik Fredriksson	26	152
264	Carsten Arriens	10	151
265	Emanuel Couto	18	146
266	Gabrio Castrichella	18	143
267	Jan Frode Andersen	4	139
268	Lorenzo Manta	11	138
269	Lars Jonsson	23	138
270	Maurice Ruah	16	137
271	Thierry Champion	24	137
272	Markus Zillner	9	136
273	Joao Cunha-Silva	11	136
274	Federico Browne	6	135
275	German Puentes	15	135
276	Tomas Behrend	8	134
277	David Nainkin	20	134
278	Elia Grossi	7	133
279	Martin Stringari	18	133
280	Luis Adrian Morejon	16	132
281	Bryan Shelton	17	131
282	Steven Randjelovic	14	130
283	Alexandre Strambini	17	130
284	Arne Thoms	6	129
285	Martin Lee	10	129
286	Alejandro Aramburu	14	129
287	Ivan Ljubicic	11	128
288	Ota Fukarek	7	126
289	Stefano Cobolli	7	125
290	Mariano Sanchez	7	124
291	Laurence Tieleman	11	123
292	Paul Goldstein	8	122
293	Pier Gauthier	9	122
294	Luke Milligan	11	121
295	Markus Hantschk	13	121
296	Steve Bryan	20	121
297	Jan Weinzierl	7	120
298	Roberto Carretero	17	120
299	Yahiya Doumbia	5	118
300	Clemens Trimmel	7	118

DOUBLES

		Tnts	Points
1	Todd Woodbridge	16	4624
2	Mark Woodforde	17	4624
3	Paul Haarhuis	23	3180
4	Jacco Eltingh	24	3635
5	Daniel Vacek	23	3314
6	Yevgeny Kafelnikov	27	2690
7	Alex O'Brien	26	2909
8	Rick Leach	24	2658
9	Patrick Galbraith	27	2573
10	Ellis Ferreira	25	2527
11	Mahesh Bhupathi	25	2519
12	Patrick Rafter	21	2498
13	Jonathan Stark	22	2481
14	Leander Paes	26	2412
15	Sebastien Lareau	19	2395
16	Nicklas Kulti	19	2300
17	Jonas Bjorkman	22	2240
18	Daniel Nestor	19	2221
19	Mark Knowles	16	2166
20	Martin Damm	19	2145
21	Luis Lobo	25	2058
22	Javier Sanchez	26	1982
23	Cyril Suk	29	1931
24	Neil Broad	26	1886
25	David Adams	36	1827
26	Donald Johnson	31	1826
27	Francisco Montana	29	1791
28	Piet Norval	29	1776
29	Andrei Olhovskiy	26	1766
30	Mark Philippoussis	12	1682
31	Daniel Orsanic	23	1635
32	Jim Grabb	20	1568
33	Marc-Kevin Goellner	20	1500
34	Fabrice Santoro	26	1479
35	Pablo Albano	31	1478
36	Karsten Braasch	21	1407
37	Olivier Delaitre	21	1382
38	Wayne Black	21	1358
39	Sandon Stolle	18	1323
40	Libor Pimek	33	1317
41	David Macpherson	25	1287
42	Lucas Arnold	20	1269
43	Trevor Kronemann	22	1267
44	Fernando Meligeni	22	1262
45	Luke Jensen	29	1259
45	Murphy Jensen	29	1259
47	Aleksandar Kitinov	33	1240
48	Joshua Eagle	27	1219
49	Fernon Wibier	33	1172
50	Pavel Vizner	31	1151
51	Francisco Roig	23	1146
52	Brett Steven	18	1142
53	Tomas Carbonell	25	1128
54	David Rikl	19	1119
55	Byron Talbot	32	1119
56	Jack Waite	33	1112
57	Menno Oosting	33	1100
58	Gustavo Kuerten	19	1090
59	Dave Randall	23	1084
60	Justin Gimelstob	23	1084
61	Hendrik Jan Davids	27	1083
62	Jiri Novak	18	1074
63	Andrew Kratzmann	28	1057
64	Peter Nyborg	31	1053
65	Alberto Berasategui	14	1051
66	Sander Groen	25	1044
67	David Prinosil	19	1012
68	Andrew Florent	25	997
69	Goran Ivanisevic	17	976
70	Byron Black	22	968
71	Jeff Salzenstein	24	960
72	Nicolas Lapentti	27	932
73	Kelly Jones	21	929
74	Tom Kempers	30	927
75	Jeff Tarango	26	887
76	Alex Corretja	17	886
77	Alberto Martin	21	854
78	Tom Vanhoudt	20	823
79	Filippo Messori	23	821
80	Kevin Ullyett	25	817
81	Brandon Coupe	37	815
82	Grant Stafford	20	803
83	Nuno Marques	21	803
84	Kent Kinnear	34	802
85	Max Mirnyi	26	795
86	Mark Merklein	23	794
87	T.J. Middleton	31	783
88	Gary Muller	20	779
89	Paul Rosner	27	760
90	Cristian Brandi	28	757
91	Stephen Noteboom	34	748
92	Mikael Tillstrom	7	745
93	David Roditi	25	743
94	Tom Nijssen	29	741
95	Marcos Ondruska	26	733
96	Chris Wilkinson	17	729
97	Brian Macphie	23	727
98	Grant Connell	19	708
99	Brent Haygarth	32	708
100	Michael Tebbutt	20	705
101	Jordi Burillo	20	704
102	Jens Knippschild	15	691
103	Julian Alonso	22	691
104	Scott Davis	17	688
105	Wayne Arthurs	17	677
106	Richey Reneberg	17	674
107	Greg Van Emburgh	31	673
108	Tomas Zdrazila	26	668
109	Maurice Ruah	20	660
110	Nebojsa Djordjevic	28	648
111	Wayne Ferreira	13	642
112	Gabor Koves	30	641
113	John-Laffnie de Jager	21	633
114	Neville Godwin	14	621
115	Geoff Grant	21	614
116	Paul Kilderry	22	609
117	Jan Siemerink	20	606
118	Marius Barnard	31	603
119	Joao Cunha-Silva	15	587
120	Chris Haggard	22	583
121	Robbie Koenig	14	576
122	Sargis Sargsian	15	569
123	Mark Keil	27	562
124	Danny Sapsford	15	543
125	Nelson Aerts	18	542
126	Bernardo Mota	19	534
127	Petr Luxa	20	532
128	Devin Bowen	31	532
129	Tamer el Sawy	19	529
130	Michael Sell	18	524
131	Bryan Shelton	16	519
132	Tim Henman	10	512
133	Sebastian Prieto	21	512
134	Vincenzo Santopadre	22	508
135	Jean-Philippe Fleurian	19	505
136	Emanuel Couto	19	499

		Tnts	Points
137	Karim Alami	9	498
138	Tomas Nydahl	19	490
139	Patrik Fredriksson	20	489
140	Guillaume Raoux	20	488
141	Sasa Hirszon	17	484
142	Mariano Puerta	15	481
143	Dinu Pescariu	21	477
144	Bill Behrens	21	473
145	Andre Sa	18	471
146	Oscar Ortiz	27	470
147	Mariano Hood	18	458
148	Scott Melville	17	452
149	Vincent Spadea	13	445
150	Bernardo Martinez	21	438
151	David Dilucia	28	438
152	Thomas Strengberger	16	428
153	Juan Ignacio Carrasco	15	425
154	Pat Cash	17	421
155	Oleg Ogorodov	20	417
156	Davide Sanguinetti	17	402
157	David Skoch	15	401
158	Mathias Huning	22	397
159	Albert Portas	14	391
160	Magnus Larsson	5	389
161	Myles Wakefield	19	389
162	Richard Fromberg	6	386
163	Eyal Ran	20	386
164	Patrick Baur	16	383
165	Thomas Buchmayer	12	382
166	Tuomas Ketola	17	382
167	Magnus Norman	10	378
168	Grant Silcock	15	372
169	Rikard Bergh	18	372
170	Doug Flach	19	372
171	Georg Blumauer	21	371
172	Alex Lopez-Moron	14	368
173	Martin Rodriguez	17	363
174	Jamie Holmes	14	361
175	Borut Urh	10	360
176	Michael Kohlmann	17	360
177	Henrik Holm	13	358
178	Edwin Kempes	13	357
179	Massimo Ardinghi	15	357
180	Grant Doyle	16	354

ATP TOUR BOARD OF DIRECTORS 1998 (Chief Executive Officer: Mark Miles)

Tournament Representatives
Franco Bartoni (Europe)
Sanji Arisawa (International Group)
Charlie Pasarell (North America)

Player Representatives
Paul Annacone
Brad Drewett
David Felgate

ATP TOUR PLAYER COUNCIL

President: Alex Corretja. **Vice President:** Jim Grabb
Members: Josh Eagle, David Ekerot, Hernan Gumy, Tim Henman, Magnus Larsson, Thomas Muster, Javier Sanchez. **Alumni:** Harold Solomon

ATP TOUR TOURNAMENT COUNCIL

EUROPE: Franco Bartoni, Jacques Hermenjat, Leo Huemer, Wim Buitendijk, Gunter Sanders
INTERNATIONAL: Sanji Arisawa (Chairman), Ayman Azmy, Graham Pearce, Marcus Stapleton
AMERICAS: Butch Buchholz, Tom Buford, Bob Kramer, Charlie Pasarell

ADDRESSES OF ATP TOUR OFFICES

United States
200 ATP Tour Boulevard
Ponte Vedra Beach
Florida
32082, USA
Tel:1-904-285 8000
Fax:1-904-285 5966

Europe
Monte Carlo Sun
74 Boulevard D'Italie
98000, Monaco
Tel: 377-93-159 565
Fax: 377-93-159 794

International Group
Level 6
20 Alfred Street
Milsoms Point
2061, NSW, Australia
Tel: 612 9964 9900
Fax: 612 9964 9977

ANNUAL ATP TOUR AWARDS FOR 1996

For the first time, the ATP TOUR and the COREL WTA TOUR staged a combined Awards Gala at the Jackie Gleason Theater, Miami on 19 March 1997. The following awards were made to recognise performances in 1996.

Player of the Year:	Pete Sampras
Doubles Team of the Year:	Todd Woodbridge/Mark Woodforde
Most Improved Player:	Tim Henman
Rado Player to Watch:	Dominik Hrbaty
Comeback Player of the Year:	Stephane Simian
Stefan Edberg Sportsmanship Award:	Alex Corretja
Senior Tour Player of the Year:	Jimmy Connors
Ron Bookman Media Excellence Award:	Brett Haber
Arthur Ashe Humanitarian Award:	Paul Flory
Championship Series Tournament of the Year:	Indianapolis
World Series Tournament of the Year:	Gstaad

PRIZE MONEY 1997

Total prize money on the men's tour exceeded $75 million in 1997. Pete Sampras's $6,498,311 breaks all men's and women's records for prize money won in a single year. Five men exceeded $2 million last year, one fewer than in 1996. There were 18 men who earned more than $1 million during the year, four more than in 1996. As last year, 39 took home more than $500,000. Further down the list, 165 men earned more than $100,000, seven more than in 1996.

Note: Prize money figures issued by the ATP Tour represent earnings from all official tournaments, including the Compaq Grand Slam Cup. They also include circuit bonuses, play-offs, and team events where entry is based purely on merit. They do not include earnings from Davis Cup ties, invitation tournaments, exhibitions or special events, nor do they include income from commercial contracts or endorsements. (Figures are supplied by the ATP Tour.)

(The nationalities and birthdays of players can be found on pp 142–146)

1	Pete Sampras	$6,498,311
2	Yevgeny Kafelnikov	3,207,757
3	Patrick Rafter	2,923,519
4	Michael Chang	2,541,830
5	Thomas Muster	2,166,590
6	Jonas Bjorkman	1,950,375
7	Gustavo Kuerten	1,586,753
8	Petr Korda	1,515,483
9	Greg Rusedski	1,515,473
10	Goran Ivanisevic	1,458,257
11	Richard Krajicek	1,434,564
12	Marcelo Rios	1,397,445
13	Todd Woodbridge	1,295,918
14	Sergi Bruguera	1,227,428
15	Alex Corretja	1,182,807
16	Carlos Moya	1,137,400
17	Mark Woodforde	1,126,627
18	Felix Mantilla	1,105,593
19	Cedric Pioline	999,701
20	Mark Philippoussis	904,211
21	Albert Costa	864,684
22	Tim Henman	802,746
23	Paul Haarhuis	794,450
24	Daniel Vacek	786,605
26	Boris Becker	674,245
27	Chris Woodruff	631,646
28	Fabrice Santoro	626,434
29	Alberto Berasategui	597,985
30	Alex O'Brien	591,828
31	Jim Courier	588,084
32	Marc Rosset	584,879
33	Thomas Enqvist	566,615
34	Javier Sanchez	562,048
35	Magnus Norman	541,933
36	Jacco Eltingh	532,266
37	Martin Damm	526,568
38	Bohdan Ulihrach	526,454
39	Magnus Larsson	515,772
40	Karol Kucera	492,333
41	Filip Dewulf	492,104
42	Jonathan Stark	477,798
43	Marc-Kevin Goellner	474,502
44	Daniel Nestor	465,190
45	Jan Siemerink	462,832
46	Wayne Ferreira	456,171
47	Francisco Clavet	422,936
48	Leander Paes	422,383
49	Nicolas Kiefer	417,269
50	Jeff Tarango	411,650
51	Hicham Arazi	397,741
52	Nicklas Kulti	395,400
53	David Prinosil	378,727
54	Byron Black	372,633
55	Michael Stich	370,474
56	Jiri Novak	369,784
57	Thomas Johansson	363,967
58	Magnus Gustafsson	360,912
59	Guillaume Raoux	359,522
60	Tommy Haas	350,926
61	Sebastien Lareau	330,980
62	Brett Steven	324,379
63	Mikael Tillstrom	314,551
64	Sjeng Schalken	312,824
65	Sandon Stolle	311,287
66	Fernando Meligeni	306,665
67	Richey Reneberg	305,643
68	Lionel Roux	305,459
69	Andre Agassi	305,132
70	Slava Dosedel	301,843
71	Mark Knowles	300,511
72	Mahesh Bhupathi	296,522
73	Albert Portas	293,996
74	Alex Radulescu	292,898
75	Dominik Hrbaty	292,807
76	Karim Alami	290,249
77	Christian Ruud	288,557
78	Patrick Galbraith	281,624
79	Sargis Sargsian	278,427
80	Richard Fromberg	276,008
81	Grant Stafford	275,775
82	Scott Draper	274,925
83	Marcelo Filippini	273,482
84	Tomas Carbonell	272,356
85	Ellis Ferreira	270,969
86	Nicolas Lapentti	266,758
87	Justin Gimelstob	261,285
88	Vincent Spadea	259,172
89	Rick Leach	247,353
90	Carlos Costa	247,024
91	Olivier Delaitre	246,025
92	Julian Alonso	245,982
93	Hendrik Dreekmann	244,535
94	Arnaud Boetsch	240,654
95	Wayne Black	240,623
96	Juan Viloca	237,375
97	Andrea Gaudenzi	233,766
98	Galo Blanco	232,314
99	Kenneth Carlsen	231,236

100	Hernan Gumy	224,016
101	Renzo Furlan	222,946
102	Andrei Olhovskiy	221,141
103	Donald Johnson	220,102
104	Luis Lobo	219,328
105	Francisco Montana	214,016
106	Cyril Suk	211,069
107	Marcos Ondruska	209,387
108	David Adams	209,079
110	Jim Grabb	198,083
111	Jan Kroslak	193,718
112	Norval Piet	193,554
113	Johan van Herck	190,821
114	Neil Broad	188,629
115	Karsten Braasch	183,893
116	Fernon Wibier	182,810
117	Jens Knippschild	177,916
118	Emilio Alvarez	175,501
119	David Rikl	174,609
120	Jordi Burillo	170,989
121	Lucas Arnold	170,882
122	Francisco Roig	166,283
123	Michael Tebbutt	161,072
124	Todd Martin	161,050
125	Adrian Voinea	154,033
126	Jerome Golmard	153,562
127	Dennis van Scheppingen	150,751
128	Alberto Martin	150,095
129	Dinu Pescariu	149,807
130	Andrei Pavel	147,935
131	Arnaud Clement	146,105
132	Pablo Albano	145,457
133	Patrik Fredriksson	144,916
134	Martin Sinner	144,360
135	Tomas Nydahl	144,305
136	Nicolas Escude	143,462
137	Gilbert Schaller	140,245
138	Jeff Salzenstein	139,954
139	Libor Pimek	136,329
140	Doug Flach	135,031
141	Stephane Simian	134,585
142	Neville Godwin	133,316
143	Davide Sanguinetti	131,326
144	Juan Marin	130,479
145	Joshua Eagle	129,521
146	Hendrik Davids	127,329
147	Luke Jensen	126,658
148	Byron Talbot	122,664
149	David Macpherson	121,098
150	Marzio Martelli	121,006
151	Pavel Vizner	115,161
152	Oliver Gross	114,894
153	Peter Nyborg	113,700
154	Trevor Kronemann	112,330
155	Gaston Etlis	112,055
156	Daniel Orsanic	111,017
157	Murphy Jensen	110,767
158	Sander Groen	107,614
159	Eyal Ran	106,797
160	David Wheaton	106,605
161	Alexander Volkov	106,357
162	Jack Waite	106,261
163	Kevin Ullyett	105,820
164	Aleksandar Kitinov	105,238
165	Oleg Ogorodov	101,990
166	Andrei Cherkasov	99,256
167	Pat Cash	98,937
168	Javier Frana	98,760
169	Nuno Marques	98,714
170	Fernando Vicente	97,027
171	Thierry Champion	96,440
172	Bernd Karbacher	95,517
173	Filippo Messori	94,004
174	Jean-Philippe Fleurian	93,580
175	Menno Oosting	93,342
176	Marcello Craca	93,088
177	Jacobo Diaz	92,136
178	Brian Macphie	91,916
179	Gianluca Pozzi	91,526
180	Roberto Carretero	91,409
181	Dick Norman	90,861
182	Franco Squillari	89,905
183	Frederik Fetterlein	88,696
184	Chris Wilkinson	88,393
185	John van Lottum	87,444
186	Andrew Florent	87,251
187	Kelly Jones	83,215
188	Patrick McEnroe	82,619
189	Orlin Stanoytchev	82,066
190	Andrew Kratzmann	81,250
191	Steve Campbell	80,891
192	Cristiano Caratti	80,034
194	Andrew Richardson	79,652
195	Diego Nargiso	79,405
196	Geoff Grant	79,177
197	Gerard Solves	78,308
198	Max Mirnyi	77,853
199	Marius Barnard	77,329
200	Dave Randall	76,806
201	Sebastien Grosjean	76,736
202	Petr Luxa	75,316
203	Tom Kempers	75,152
204	Christophe van Garsse	75,039
205	Omar Camporese	74,308
206	Mark Petchey	74,118
207	Radomir Vasek	72,850
208	Ramon Delgado	72,815
209	Henrik Holm	71,475
210	Kent Kinnear	71,376
211	Danny Sapsford	71,208
212	Michael Joyce	71,176
213	Davide Scala	71,035
214	Stephen Noteboom	70,778
215	Bryan Shelton	70,316
216	Marcos Gorriz	69,286
217	Vincenzo Santopadre	68,287
218	Nicolas Pereira	68,072
219	Grant Connell	66,809
220	Tom Nijssen	66,491
221	Marcelo Charpentier	64,897
222	Cristian Brandi	63,619
223	T.J. Middleton	63,330
224	Gary Muller	63,147
225	Cecil Mamiit	61,618
226	Mark Merklein	61,115
227	Jaime Oncins	60,991
228	Tamer el Sawy	60,416
229	Brent Haygarth	59,786
230	Guillermo Canas	59,216
231	Frederic Fontang	59,005
232	Oscar Burrieza	58,753
233	Rainer Schuttler	58,384
234	Andrei Merinov	58,315
235	Alex Lopez-Moron	58,176
236	Grant Doyle	58,032
237	Alejandro Hernandez	56,684
238	Paul Kilderry	56,072
239	Ion Moldovan	55,870
240	Michael Sell	55,487
241	Tommy Ho	55,035

242	Scott Davis	54,833	272	Peter Tramacchi	42,359
243	Stephane Huet	54,262	273	Tom Vanhoudt	41,736
244	Todd Larkham	54,217	274	Gabor Koves	41,632
245	Lars Jonsson	53,395	275	Salvador Navarro	41,435
246	Malivai Washington	53,210	276	Scott Melville	41,315
247	Mark Keil	52,774	277	Dirk Dier	40,134
248	Luis Herrera	52,717	278	Sebastian Prieto	39,985
249	Razvan Sabau	52,475	279	Wade McGuire	39,910
250	Patrick Baur	52,287	280	Mariano Puerta	39,890
251	Steve Bryan	50,140	281	Guy Forget	39,450
252	Wayne Arthurs	49,956	282	Maurice Ruah	39,076
253	Jan-Michael Gambill	49,542	283	Martin Rodriguez	37,873
254	Greg van Emburgh	48,666	284	Chris Haggard	37,497
255	David Nainkin	48,574	285	David Roditi	37,310
256	Stefano Pescosolido	48,353	286	Martin Lee	36,292
257	Stefan Koubek	48,302	287	Lars Burgsmuller	35,605
258	Marco Meneschincheri	47,866	288	Robbie Koenig	35,567
259	Rodolphe Gilbert	47,582	289	Emanuel Couto	34,785
260	Francisco Cabello	47,433	290	Marat Safin	34,775
261	Mariano Zabaleta	47,430	291	Jozsef Krocsko	34,615
262	Gabriel Silberstein	46,666	292	Emilio Sanchez	34,514
263	John-Laffnie de Jager	45,806	293	Regis Lavergne	34,510
264	Brandon Coupe	45,735	294	Paul Rosner	34,435
266	Eyal Erlich	44,553	295	Roberto Jabali	34,426
267	Alex Calatrava	44,287	296	Andre Sa	33,930
268	Andrei Chesnokov	44,229	297	Nebojsa Djordjevic	33,584
269	Bernardo Mota	44,180	298	Bill Behrens	32,933
270	David Skoch	42,982	299	Attila Savolt	32,831
271	Ben Ellwood	42,774	300	Roger Smith	32,750

THE MILLIONAIRES

Below is a list of players who, by the end of November 1997, had won at least US$1 million in prize money during the course of their careers. The list, which contains 19 new millionaires, includes earnings at all official tournaments, including the ATP Tour Championship and the Compaq Grand Slam Cup. It does not include income from Davis Cup ties, special events, exhibitions or commercial endorsements.
Note: *Indicates players who appear in the list for the first time.

1	Pete Sampras	$32,060,658	27	David Wheaton	5,155,434
2	Boris Becker	24,515,647	28	Andrei Medvedev	5,042,085
3	Ivan Lendl	21,262,417	29	Guillermo Vilas	4,923,882
4	Stefan Edberg	20,630,941	30	Todd Martin	4,824,749
5	Michael Chang	16,286,739	31	Magnus Larsson	4,766,883
6	Goran Ivanisevic	16,206,537	32	Marc Rosset	4,681,550
7	Jim Courier	13,322,569	33	Patrick Rafter	4,515,712
8	Andre Agassi	13,206,463	34	Andres Gomez	4,385,040
9	Michael Stich	12,628,890	35	Jonas Bjorkman	4,218,490
10	John McEnroe	12,539,622	36	Jacco Eltingh	4,170,253
11	Thomas Muster	11,640,654	37	Thomas Enqvist	4,054,560
12	Sergi Bruguera	10,748,329	38	Javier Sanchez	4,017,055
13	Yevgeny Kafelnikov	9,604,741	39	Cedric Pioline	3,974,668
14	Petr Korda	9,039,709	40	Henri Leconte	3,918,146
15	Jimmy Connors	8,641,040	41	Richey Reneberg	3,816,568
16	Mats Wilander	7,976,256	42	Karel Novacek	3,739,175
17	Richard Krajicek	6,835,339	43	Aaron Krickstein	3,710,447
18	Mark Woodforde	6,727,181	44	Tomas Smid	3,699,738
19	Todd Woodbridge	6,169,747	45	Bjorn Borg	3,655,751
20	Wayne Ferreira	5,928,744	46	Alberto Berasategui	3,584,117
21	Jakob Hlasek	5,784,225	47	Yannick Noah	3,440,390
22	Guy Forget	5,657,293	48	Magnus Gustafsson	3,433,494
23	Paul Haarhuis	5,518,152	49	Alexander Volkov	3,362,786
24	Brad Gilbert	5,508,745	50	John Fitzgerald	3,204,572
25	Anders Jarryd	5,377,067	51	Byron Black	3,160,041
26	Emilio Sanchez	5,337,724	52	Daniel Vacek	3,146,367

Sweden's Stefan Edberg, who retired at the end of 1996, was given a special award at Wimbledon by the Club's President, the Duke of Kent to recognise his services to The Championships which he won twice, successes which contributed to his career prize-money total of more than $20.6 million. (Tommy Hindley)

53	Wally Masur	3,134,447
54	Malivai Washington	3,124,982
55	Patrick McEnroe	3,093,541
56	Kevin Curren	3,055,060
57	Andrei Chesnokov	3,049,903
58	Arnaud Boetsch	3,005,156
59	Jan Siemerink	2,966,903
60	Jim Grabb	2,915,928
61	Grant Connell	2,911,095
62	Carlos Costa	2,872,962
63	Alex Corretja	2,845,215
64	Brian Gottfried	2,782,514
65	Vitas Gerulaitis	2,778,748
66	Wojtek Fibak	2,725,133
67	Marcelo Rios	2,715,549
68	Jonathan Stark	2,670,735
69	Tim Mayotte	2,663,672
70	Greg Rusedski	2,637,814
71	Andrei Olhovskiy	2,635,584
72	Miloslav Mecir	2,632,538
73	Rick Leach	2,612,056
74	Tomas Carbonell	2,574,403
75	Jason Stoltenberg	2,497,788
76	Jonas Svensson	2,439,702
77	Amos Mansdorf	2,427,691
78	Johan Kriek	2,381,844
79	Patrick Galbraith	2,373,164
80	Francisco Clavet	2,373,025
81	Carl-Uwe Steeb	2,320,082
82	Nicklas Kulti	2,283,304
83	Scott Davis	2,277,873
84	Jaime Yzaga	2,235,560
85	Albert Costa	2,222,342
86	Raul Ramirez	2,217,971
87	Martin Damm	2,164,765
88	Renzo Furlan	2,154,915

89	Sergio Casal	2,107,745
90	Ilie Nastase	2,076,761
91	Joakim Nystrom	2,074,947
92	Olivier Delaitre	2,068,298
93	Fabrice Santoro	2,066,906
94	Ken Flach	2,061,390
95	Alex O'Brien	2,060,749
96	Marc-Kevin Goellner	2,057,329
97	David Pate	2,028,197
98	Eddie Dibbs	2,016,426
99	Andrei Cherkasov	2,015,421
100	Jeff Tarango	1,993,058
101	Brett Steven	1,991,859
102	Jose-Luis Clerc	1,987,036
103	Peter Fleming	1,986,529
104	Pat Cash	1,946,669
105	Christo van Rensburg	1,925,392
106	Robert Seguso	1,881,888
107	Guillaume Raoux	1,874,102
108	Martin Jaite	1,873,881
109	Jordi Arrese	1,846,849
110	Mark Philippoussis*	1,844,837
111	Jimmy Arias	1,830,340
112	Tim Henman	1,828,358
113	Cyril Suk	1,803,499
114	Harold Solomon	1,802,769
115	Jim Pugh	1,780,455
116	Stan Smith	1,774,811
117	Bernd Karbacher	1,768,335
118	Richard Fromberg	1,762,899
119	Andrea Gaudenzi	1,760,344
120	Carlos Moya*	1,729,980
121	Gustavo Kuerten*	1,726,638
122	David Prinosil	1,713,315
123	Marcelo Filippini	1,712,346
124	Ronald Agenor	1,712,305
125	Roscoe Tanner	1,696,108
126	Javier Frana	1,691,847
127	Henrik Holm	1,689,080
128	Felix Mantilla*	1,686,314
129	Guillermo Perez-Roldan	1,685,721
130	Eliot Teltscher	1,653,997
131	Paul Annacone	1,646,806
132	Patrik Kuhnen	1,646,328
133	Horst Skoff	1,642,168
134	Derrick Rostagno	1,621,535
135	Sherwood Stewart	1,602,565
136	Ken Rosewall	1,600,300
137	Arthur Ashe	1,584,909
138	Omar Camporese	1,582,561
139	Rod Laver	1,564,213
140	Heinz Gunthardt	1,550,007
14A	Alberto Mancini	1,543,120
142	Sandon Stolle	1,539,326
143	Mark Knowles	1,528,018
144	Danie Visser	1,527,930
145	Luiz Mattar	1,493,136
146	Diego Nargiso	1,476,808
147	Marcos Ondruska	1,456,923
148	Tom Nijssen	1,452,330
149	Slava Dosedel	1,452,168
150	Daniel Nestor*	1,450,942
151	Mark Edmondson	1,450,890
152	Slobodan Zivojinovic	1,450,384
153	Gary Muller	1,447,444
154	Libor Pimek	1,445,908
155	Balazs Taroczy	1,437,443
156	Bill Scanlon	1,427,007
157	Brian Teacher	1,426,244
158	Todd Witsken	1,420,910
159	Jared Palmer	1,413,373
160	Jose Higueras	1,406,355
161	Manuel Orantes	1,398,303
162	Gene Mayer	1,381,562
163	Mark Kratzmann	1,378,936
164	Mikael Pernfors	1,361,603
165	David Adams	1,351,762
166	Darren Cahill	1,349,247
167	Jan Apell	1,349,240
168	David Rikl	1,346,840
169	Jeremy Bates	1,339,964
170	Vijay Amritraj	1,330,503
171	Jean-Philippe Fleurian	1,321,616
172	Bohdan Ulihrach*	1,320,209
173	Sebastien Lareau*	1,312,729
174	Goran Prpic	1,303,207
175	Tim Wilkison	1,287,675
176	Jan Gunnarsson	1,285,040
177	Stefano Pescosolido	1,285,033
178	Gilbert Schaller	1,281,043
179	Ramesh Krishnan	1,263,130
180	Christian Bergstrom	1,261,262
181	Tom Okker	1,257,200
182	Thierry Champion	1,249,659
183	Bryan Shelton	1,236,508
184	Karol Kucera*	1,235,208
185	Horacio de la Pena	1,234,768
186	Paul McNamee	1,232,825
187	Luke Jensen	1,231,836
188	Gianluca Pozzi	1,220,419
189	John Alexander	1,214,079
190	Francisco Roig	1,185,442
191	Robert Lutz	1,165,276
192	Kelly Jones	1,163,123
193	Kenneth Carlsen*	1,140,671
194	Peter Lundgren	1,130,516
195	Michiel Schapers	1,124,730
196	Tim Gullikson	1,121,430
197	Filip Dewulf*	1,116,084
198	Shuzo Matsuoka	1,114,362
199	Franco Davin	1,108,860
200	Eric Jelen	1,100,059
201	David Macpherson*	1,091,767
202	Jiri Novak*	1,090,053
203	Piet Norval*	1,088,737
204	Steve Denton	1,084,214
205	Nicolas Pereira	1,083,441
206	Glenn Michibata	1,081,397
207	Dick Stockton	1,063,385
208	John Newcombe	1,062,408
209	Thierry Tulasne	1,058,412
210	Sandy Mayer	1,057,783
211	Cristiano Caratti*	1,053,588
212	Peter McNamara	1,046,145
213	Diego Perez	1,042,224
214	Karsten Braasch*	1,040,124
215	Chris Woodruff*	1,038,384
216	Jordi Burillo*	1,026,073
217	Alex Antonitsch	1,024,171
218	Hendrik Dreekmann*	1,021,226
219	Rodolphe Gilbert*	1,003,051

History of the ATP Tour No.1 World Ranking

August 1973 – end of 1997

(Figures supplied by ATP Tour)

	Player	*Age*	*First date No.1*		*Total weeks*
1	Ivan Lendl	22.11	28 Feb	1983	270
2	Jimmy Connors	21.11	29 Jul	1974	268
3	Pete Sampras	21.8	12 Apr	1993 (current)	206
4	John McEnroe	21 (& 15 days)	2 Mar	1980	170
5	Bjorn Borg	21.2	23 Aug	1977	109
6	Stefan Edberg	24.9	13 Aug	1990	66
7	Jim Courier	21.5	10 Feb	1992	55
8	Ilie Nastase	27.1	23 Aug	1973	40
9	Andre Agassi	24.11	10 Apr	1995	30
10	Mats Wilander	24.1	12 Sep	1988	20
11	Boris Becker	23.2	28 Jan	1991	12
12	John Newcombe	30 (& 11 days)	3 Jun	1974	8
13	Thomas Muster	28.4	12 Feb	1996	5

HISTORY OF THE NO.1 RANKING

Ranking date		*Player*	*Weeks at No. 1*
1973	**23 August**	**Ilie Nastase (1)**	**40**
1974	**3 June**	**John Newcombe (2)**	**8**
1974	**29 July**	**Jimmy Connors (3)**	**160**
1975			
1976			
1977	**23 August**	**Bjorn Borg (4)**	**1**
1977	30 August	Connors	84
1978			
1979	9 April	Borg	6
1979	21 May	Connors	7
1979	9 July	Borg	34
1980	**3 March**	**John McEnroe (5)**	**3**
1980	24 March	Borg	20
1980	11 August	McEnroe	1
1980	18 August	Borg	46
1981	6 July	McEnroe	2
1981	20 July	Borg	2
1981	3 August	McEnroe	58
1982	13 September	Connors	7
1982	1 November	McEnroe	1
1982	8 November	Connors	1
1982	15 November	McEnroe	11
1983	31 January	Connors	1
1983	7 February	McEnroe	1
1983	14 February	Connors	2
1983	**28 February**	**Ivan Lendl (6)**	**11**
1983	16 May	Connors	3
1983	6 June	McEnroe	1
1983	13 June	Connors	3
1983	4 July	McEnroe	17
1983	31 October	Lendl	6
1983	12 December	McEnroe	4

Ranking date		*Player*	*Weeks at No. 1*
1984	9 January	Lendl	9
1984	12 March	McEnroe	13
1984	11 June	Lendl	1
1984	18 June	McEnroe	3
1984	9 July	Lendl	5
1984	13 August	McEnroe	53
1985	19 August	Lendl	1
1985	26 August	McEnroe	2
1985	9 September	Lendl	157
1986			
1987			
1988	**12 September**	**Mats Wilander (7)**	**20**
1989	30 January	Lendl	80
1990	**13 August**	**Stefan Edberg (8)**	**24**
1991	**28 January**	**Boris Becker (9)**	**3**
1991	18 February	Edberg	20
1991	8 July	Becker	9
1991	9 September	Edberg	22
1992	**10 February**	**Jim Courier (10)**	**6**
1992	23 March	Edberg	3
1992	13 April	Courier	22
1992	14 September	Edberg	3
1992	5 October	Courier	27
1993	**12 April**	**Pete Sampras (11)**	**19**
1993	23 August	Courier	3
1993	13 September	Sampras	82
1994			
1995	**10 April**	**Andre Agassi (12)**	**30**
1995	6 November	Sampras	14
1996	29 January	Agassi	2
1996	**12 February**	**Thomas Muster (13)**	**1**
1996	19 February	Sampras	3
1996	11 March	Muster	4
1996	15 April	Sampras	88

Corel WTA Tour Rankings and Prize Money 1997

RANKINGS

The following tables show the season-ending rankings in singles and doubles. The rankings, updated weekly, are based on points won on the Corel WTA Tour, including the four Grand Slam Championships. (Statistics supplied by Corel WTA Tour)

Note: Players' nationalities and birthdays can be found on pp 174–177.

SINGLES

		Tnts	Points
1	Martina Hingis	17	6264
2	Jana Novotna	20	3753
3	Lindsay Davenport	22	3696
4	Amanda Coetzer	27	3360
5	Monica Seles	17	2988
6	Iva Majoli	24	2874
7	Mary Pierce	16	2861
8	Irina Spirlea	23	2577
9	Arantxa Sanchez Vicario	23	2361
10	Mary Joe Fernandez	17	2114
11	Nathalie Tauziat	22	2003
12	Conchita Martinez	19	1988
13	Sandrine Testud	23	1841
14	Anke Huber	24	1829
15	Brenda Schultz-McCarthy	26	1543
16	Sabine Appelmans	26	1502
17	Lisa Raymond	21	1437
18	Dominique van Roost	19	1394
19	Ruxandra Dragomir	27	1333
20	Ai Sugiyama	26	1252
21	Yayuk Basuki	22	1230
22	Venus Williams	14	1173
23	Kimberly Po	21	1147
24	Barbara Paulus	18	1133
25	Natasha Zvereva	20	1066
26	Patty Schnyder	24	928
27	Joannette Kruger	23	926
28	Steffi Graf	5	888
29	Karina Habsudova	24	880
30	Chanda Rubin	22	876
31	Elena Likhovtseva	26	853
32	Anna Kournikova	10	852
33	Anne-Gaelle Sidot	25	842
34	Naoko Sawamatsu	20	810
35	Henrieta Nagyova	22	757
36	Magdalena Maleeva	23	710
37	Amy Frazier	17	685
38	Barbara Schett	22	684
39	Florencia Labat	28	657
40	Magdalena Grzybowska	23	637
41	Magui Serna	21	620
42	Sandra Kleinova	28	606
43	Silvia Farina	23	597
44	Rita Grande	26	571
45	Asa Carlsson	27	564
46	Tamarine Tanasugarn	24	560
47	Miriam Oremans	18	554
48	Maria Alejandra Vento	20	537
49	Rachel McQuillan	25	532
50	Denisa Chladkova	27	526
51	Alexandra Fusai	23	513
52	Mirjana Lucic	6	511
53	Maria Sanchez Lorenzo	25	495
54	Virginia Ruano-Pascual	17	488
55	Marion Maruska	26	479
56	Sarah Pitkowski	25	463
57	Sandra Cacic	26	459
58	Garcia Leon Gala	20	458
59	Olga Barabanschikova	28	455
60	Corina Morariu	22	446
61	Francesca Lubiani	27	435
62	Kerry-Anne Guse	25	423
63	Nicole Arendt	14	421
64	Patricia Hy-Boulais	19	417
65	Alex Dechaume-Balleret	21	413
66	Jennifer Capriati	13	412
67	Shi-Ting Wang	20	407
68	Fang Li	12	399
69	Yuka Yoshida	22	374
70	Laura Golarsa	24	373
71	Barbara Rittner	20	368
72	Katarina Studenikova	24	363
73	Catalina Cristea	30	353
74	Naoko Kijimuta	20	352
75	Miho Saeki	24	347
76	Ann Grossman	20	343
77	Emmanuelle Gagliardi	24	342
78	Kristina Brandi	33	339
79	Meilen Tu	25	338
80	Helena Sukova	21	335
81	Lenka Nemeckova	24	328
82	Jana Kandarr	27	324
83	Cristin Torrens-Valero	25	320
84	Kristie Boogert	17	317
85	Larisa Neiland	19	312
86	Gloria Pizzichini	19	312
87	Elena Makarova	15	310
88	Wiltrud Probst	19	308
89	Ines Gorrochategui	19	304
90	Nathalie Dechy	25	303
91	Rika Hiraki	24	301
92	Andrea Glass	24	300
93	Annabel Ellwood	27	297
94	Adriana Gersi	18	296
95	Flora Perfetti	19	289
96	Sonya Jeyaseelan	22	284
97	Tatiana Panova	25	283
98	Jolene Watanabe	29	259
99	Serena Williams	5	257
100	Elena Wagner	14	253
101	Nana Miyagi	24	248
102	Nicole Pratt	30	247
103	Olga Lugina	17	246
104	Els Callens	19	243
105	Mariana Diaz-Oliva	28	242
106	Amelie Cocheteux	23	238
107	Angelica Gavaldon	24	237
108	Rene Simpson	18	231

		Tnts	Points
109	Amelie Mauresmo	20	231
110	Sung-Hee Park	22	226
111	Sandra Dopfer	26	222
112	Janet Lee	25	220
113	Tara Snyder	27	219
114	Sylvia Plischke	23	218
115	Paola Suarez	24	216
116	Mana Endo	21	215
117	Meike Babel	15	211
118	Anne Miller	20	210
119	Pavlina Stoyanova	28	209
120	Sandra Kloesel	27	209
121	Siobhan Drake-Brockman	29	207
122	Haruka Inoue	19	207
123	Seda Noorlander	24	205
124	Kristine Kunce	16	204
125	Marketa Kochta	25	198
126	Samantha Smith	27	193
127	Radka Zrubakova	18	193
128	Lea Ghirardi-Rubbi	17	190
129	Anne Kremer	14	186
130	Lenka Cenkova	18	186
131	Marlene Weingartner	23	186
132	Noelle van Lottum	22	185
133	Eva Martincova	19	177
134	Lindsay Lee	27	176
135	Petra Langrova	22	173
136	Elena Tatarkova	19	170
137	Jana Nejedly	21	168
138	Veronika Martinek	23	166
139	Eugenia Koulikovskaya	16	158
140	Anna Smashnova	18	153
141	Petra Begerow	16	148
142	Ana Alcazar	15	146
143	Kyoko Nagatsuka	16	143
144	Mi-Ra Jeon	22	141
145	Caroline Dhenin	19	140
146	Karen Cross	23	140
147	Lorna Woodroffe	24	139
148	Erika de Lone	19	138
149	Liezel Horn	25	135
150	Miriam Schnitzer	19	135
151	Raluca Sandu	20	133
152	Aleksandra Olsza	24	132
153	Maureen Drake	22	130
154	Brie Rippner	18	129
155	Marian Werdel-Witmeyer	5	129
156	Syna Schmidle	23	128
157	Shinobu Asagoe	16	127
158	Ludmila Richterova	19	126
159	Nancy Feber	15	125
160	Karin Miller	17	122
161	Mariaan de Swardt	11	120
162	Ginger Helgeson Nielsen	18	120
163	Larissa Schaerer	16	120
164	Meghann Shaughnessy	38	120
165	Svetlana Krivencheva	18	119
166	Emmanuelle Curutchet	18	118
167	Kristina Triska	28	117
168	Conchita Martinez-Granados	23	115
169	Karin Kschwendt	25	115
170	Eun-Ha Kim	18	114
171	Samantha Reeves	22	114
172	Radka Bobkova	13	114
173	Eva Bes	18	114
174	Nino Louarsabishvili	20	114
175	Nannie de Villiers	26	113
176	Jane Taylor	25	112
177	Tina Krizan	21	111
178	Renee Reid	28	110
179	Lucie Ahl	26	110
180	Sofia Prazeres	19	110
181	Laura Pena	17	109
182	Alicia Ortuno	24	108
183	Shirli-Ann Siddall	26	108
184	Gigi Fernandez	3	108
185	Magalie Lamarre	19	107
186	Evie Dominikovic	17	107
187	Jessica Steck	20	105
188	Laurence Courtois	12	105
189	Cara Black	14	104
190	Nirupama Vaidyanathan	24	103
191	Stephanie de Ville	16	103
192	Virag Csurgo	20	101
193	Geraldine Aizenberg	20	101
194	Lilia Osterloh	13	100
195	Silvija Talaja	15	100
196	Julie Pullin	25	99
197	Patricia Wartusch	17	99
198	Laurence Andretto	19	99
199	Martina Nejedly	27	99
200	Surina de Beer	10	97
201	Barbara Schwartz	13	96
202	Dally Randriantefy	11	96
203	Keri Phebus	20	95
204	Sandra Cecchini	7	95
205	Gail Biggs	24	94
206	Tathiana Garbin	19	93
207	Maria Fernanda Landa	18	93
208	Fabiola Zuluaga	17	93
209	Maria Jose Gaidano	18	93
210	Sandra Nacuk	11	92
211	Daphne van de Zande	18	92
212	Katalin Marosi	22	90
213	Tami Jones	14	89
214	Melissa Mazzotta	26	88
215	Ludmilla Varmuza	20	88
216	Hila Rosen	17	88
217	Yuko Hosoki	14	86
218	Amanda Hopmans	14	86
219	Milena Nekvapilova	26	85
220	Young-Ja Choi	11	85
221	Saori Obata	22	85
222	Linda Wild	15	85
223	Misumi Miyauchi	13	84
224	Laura Garrone	5	84
225	Petra Gaspar	19	84
226	Adriana Serra-Zanetti	19	83
227	Renata Kolbovic	21	82
228	Pam Nelson	25	81
229	Katerina Kroupova	15	81
230	Dragana Zaric	16	79
231	Tatiana Poutchek	18	78
232	Silke Meier	16	78
233	Bettina Fulco-Villella	23	78
234	Alice Pirsu	20	77
235	Meike Froehlich	15	77
236	Julia Abe	14	77
237	Mashona Washington	15	76
238	Jane Chi	21	76
239	Kvetoslava Hrdlickova	10	74
240	Segolene Berger	18	74
241	Christina Papadaki	12	74
242	Melissa Beadman	25	73
243	Alice Canepa	12	73
244	Miriam D'Agostini	21	73
245	Laura Montalvo	12	72
246	Maja Zivec-Skulj	22	72
247	Elena Salvador	21	71
248	Katarzyna Nowak	26	71
249	Sophie Georges	17	71
250	Petra Rampre	13	71

DOUBLES

		Tnts	Points
1	Natasha Zvereva	18	5435
2	Lindsay Davenport	19	5377
3	Martina Hingis	16	4409
4	Gigi Fernandez	18	4175
5	Arantxa Sanchez Vicario	21	4129
6	Jana Novotna	15	3997
7	Manon Bollegraf	23	3982
8	Nicole Arendt	19	3720
9	Larisa Neiland	26	3327
10	Helena Sukova	22	3046
11	Caroline Vis	29	2963
12	Lisa Raymond,	17	2853
13	Nathalie Tauziat	21	2842
14	Alexandra Fusai	25	2820
15	Yayuk Basuki	24	2721
16	Mary Joe Fernandez	16	2463
17	Patricia Tarabini	27	2322
18	Nana Miyagi	29	2102
19	Conchita Martinez	19	1928
20	Naoko Kijimuta	22	1787
21	Ruxandra Dragomir	26	1577
22	Katrina Adams	19	1540
23	Kimberly Po	20	1438
24	Elena Likhovtseva	26	1432
25	Ai Sugiyama	23	1391
26	Anke Huber	16	1321
27	Chanda Rubin	21	1310
28	Sabine Appelmans	19	1280
29	Miriam Oremans	16	1231
30	Rika Hiraki	24	1170
31	Amanda Coetzer	18	1142
32	Debbie Graham	19	1103
33	Iva Majoli	21	1064
34	Rennae Stubbs	9	1055
35	Amy Frazier	15	1036
36	Ines Gorrochategui	17	946
37	Lori McNeil	16	943
38	Irina Spirlea	21	931
39	Kristine Kunce	19	914
40	Anna Kournikova	10	897
41	Linda Wild	15	895
42	Helena Vildova	25	888
43	Kerry-Anne Guse	23	887
44	Rachel McQuillan	27	881
45	Brenda Schultz-McCarthy	20	868
46	Mercedes Paz	20	846
47	Kristie Boogert	16	845
48	Rita Grande	20	844
49	Florencia Labat	24	841
50	Silvia Farina	18	835

COREL WTA TOUR AWARDS WINNERS

ANNUAL AWARDS GALA

For the first time, the COREL WTA TOUR and the ATP TOUR staged a combined Awards Gala at the Jackie Gleason Theater, Miami on 19 March 1997. The following awards were made to recognise performances in 1996.

Player of the Year: Steffi Graf
Doubles Team of the Year: Jana Novotna/Arantxa Sanchez Vicario
Most Improved Player: Martina Hingis
Most Impressive Newcomer: Anna Kournikova
Comeback Player of the Year: Jennifer Capriati
Ted Tinling Media Award: Mary Carillo
Karen Krantzcke Sportsmanship: Yayuk Basuki
Player Service Award: Katrina Adams
David Gray Special Service: Martina Navratilova
Diamond Aces Award: Gabriela Sabatini
Most Exciting Player Award: Steffi Graf
Tier I and II Tournament of the Year: Toshiba Classic, San Diego
Tier III and IV Tournament of the Year: Bell Challenge, Quebec City
Tournament Achievement Award: The Lipton Championships, Key Biscayne

WTA ANNUAL AWARDS FOR 1997

Presented during the week of 17 November 1997 at Madison Square Garden, NY during the Chase Championships to recognise performances in 1997.

Player of the Year: Martina Hingis
Doubles Team of the Year: Gigi Fernandez/Natasha Zvereva
Most Improved Player: Amanda Coetzer
Most Impressive Newcomer: Venus Williams
Comeback Player of the Year: Mary Pierce
Ted Tinling Media Award: L'Equipe
Karen Krantzcke Sportsmanship Award: Amanda Coetzer
Player Service Award: Katrina Adams
Diamond Aces Award: Amanda Coetzer
Most Exciting Player Award: Monica Seles
David Gray Special Service Award: Pam Shriver
Tournament of the Year (Tier I-II): State Farm Evert Cup, Indian Wells
Tournament of the Year (Tier III-IV): Bell Challenge, Quebec City

PRIZE MONEY (As at 24 November 1997)

The following table shows the prize money (including bonuses) won at all recognized tournaments which adopted the WTA guidelines, where direct entry was based solely upon merit. It does not include income from the Fed Cup, other team events, exhibitions, special events or commercial contracts. (Figures supplied by Corel WTA Tour.)

Note: Players' nationalities and birthdays can be found on pp 174–177.

1	Martina Hingis	$3,400,196
2	Jana Novotna	1,685,115
3	Lindsay Davenport	1,533,101
4	Iva Majoli	1,227,332
5	Monica Seles	914,020
6	Arantxa Sanchez Vicario	890,512
7	Mary Pierce	881,639
8	Mary Joe Fernandez	769,132
9	Natasha Zvereva	746,643
10	Irina Spirlea	720,758
11	Amanda Coetzer	701,994
12	Nathalie Tauziat	600,642
13	Conchita Martinez	528,544
14	Venus Williams	466,863
15	Gigi Fernandez	454,432
16	Lisa Raymond	450,070
17	Sandrine Testud	417,753
18	Anke Huber	411,315
19	Yayuk Basuki	385,824
20	Ruxandra Dragomir	381,500
21	Manon Bollegraf	374,574
22	Helena Sukova	362,457
23	Nicole Arendt	357,052
24	Brenda Schultz-McCarthy	348,247
25	Sabine Appelmans	339,845
26	Ai Sugiyama	307,837
27	Larisa Neiland	306,340
28	Anna Kournikova	292,362
29	Kimberly Po	286,866
30	Dominique van Roost	274,010
31	Alexandra Fusai	265,781
32	Elena Likhovtseva	260,662
33	Barbara Paulus	252,231
34	Steffi Graf	230,249
35	Chanda Rubin	226,106
36	Karina Habsudova	225,396
37	Patty Schnyder	210,374
38	Florencia Labat	207,224
39	Miriam Oremans	180,804
40	Henrieta Nagyova	175,589
41	Barbara Schett	175,052
42	Rika Hiraki	168,806
43	Nana Miyagi	168,222
44	Joannette Kruger	167,307
45	Naoko Kijimuta	166,242
46	Rachel McQuillan	163,310
47	Amy Frazier	161,989
48	Magdalena Maleeva	161,647
49	Silvia Farina	160,439
50	Anne-Gaelle Sidot	159,026
51	Magui Serna	155,386
52	Caroline Vis	153,819
53	Asa Carlsson	151,989
54	Tamarine Tanasugarn	151,238
55	Naoko Sawamatsu	150,262
56	Rita Grande	141,892
57	Denisa Chladkova	139,896
58	Patricia Hy-Boulais	137,894
59	Magdalena Grzybowska	137,433
60	Patricia Tarabini	131,630
61	Kristie Boogert	126,879
62	Virginia Ruano-Pascual	125,986
63	Shi-Ting Wang	124,080
64	Paola Suarez	122,968
65	Alexi Dechaume-Balleret	120,848
66	Ines Gorrochategui	120,290
67	Barbara Rittner	119,548
68	Flora Perfetti	117,671
69	Els Callens	116,269
70	Ann Grossman	115,848
71	Corina Morariu	115,512
72	Kerry-Anne Guse	112,983
73	Lori McNeil	108,356
74	Gloria Pizzichini	108,083
75	Yuka Yoshida	107,720
76	Sandra Kleinova	106,000
77	Katarina Studenikova	105,484
78	Linda Wild	105,276
79	Annabel Ellwood	103,580
80	Catalina Cristea	103,070
81	Olga Barabanschikova	98,215
82	Sarah Pitkowski	97,676
83	Elena Makarova	96,624
84	Laura Golarsa	96,208
85	Ma. Alejandra Vento	94,209
86	Miho Saeki	92,864
87	Gala Leon Garcia	92,350
88	Mercedes Paz	91,476
89	Marion Maruska	91,411
90	Mirjana Lucic	91,285
91	Elena Wagner	90,077
92	Francesca Lubiani	90,012
93	Wiltrud Probst	89,534
94	Katrina Adams	89,037
95	Jana Kandarr	86,635
96	Radka Zrubakova	84,574
97	Ma. Ant Sanchez Lorenzo	83,625
98	Judith Wiesner	83,489
99	Petra Langrova	82,547
100	Meilen Tu	82,465
101	Ginger Helgeson-Nielsen	81,560
102	Sung-Hee Park	81,275
103	Lenka Nemeckova	80,980
104	Kristina Brandi	80,904
105	Emmanuelle Gagliardi	80,422
106	Rene Simpson	80,353
107	Jennifer Capriati	79,852
108	Aleksandra Olsza	78,562
109	Sandra Cacic	78,191
110	Fang Li	75,317
111	Meike Babel	74,682
112	Tami Jones	74,585
113	Kristine Kunce	73,295
114	Noelle van Lottum	72,797
115	Nathalie Dechy	71,682
116	Adriana Gersi	71,619
117	Janet Lee	69,048
118	Cristina Torrens-Valero	68,018

119	Andrea Glass	67,891
120	Mariana Diaz-Oliva	67,622
121	Tatiana Panova	66,155
122	Sonya Jeyaseelan	65,677
123	Jolene Watanabe	65,464
124	Sandra Dopfer	63,254
125	Nicole Pratt	62,951
126	Debbie Graham	62,465
127	Olga Lugina	61,443
128	Petra Begerow	59,728
129	Eva Martincova	59,232
130	Mana Endo	58,337
131	Lindsay Lee	57,893
132	Mariaan de Swardt	57,007
133	Ludmila Richterova	56,797
134	Anne Miller	56,372
135	Seda Noorlander	55,779
136	Erika de Lone	51,628
137	Marketa Kochta	51,330
138	Laurence Courtois	47,644
139	Samantha Smith	47,469
140	Amelie Mauresmo	47,371
141	Rennae Stubbs	46,745
142	Elena Tatarkova	46,008
143	Lorna Woodroffe	44,486
144	Stephanie de Ville	42,802
145	Amelie Cocheteux	41,462
146	Nancy Feber	40,786
147	Tina Krizan	40,702
148	Karin Kschwendt	40,300
149	Angelica Gavaldon	40,061
150	Helena Vildova	38,894
151	Marlene Weingartner	38,664
152	Siobhan Drake Brockman	38,549
153	Lenka Cenkova	38,507
154	Shirli-Ann Siddall	38,300
155	Clare Wood	38,056
156	Sylvia Plischke	38,022
157	Serena Williams	37,927
158	Tara Snyder	37,862
159	Caroline Dhenin	37,446
160	Lilia Osterloh	36,674
161	Haruka Inoue	36,522
162	Catherine Barclay	36,399
163	Pavlina Stoyanova	36,247
164	Lea Ghirardi-Rubbi	35,511
165	Eva Melicharova	34,781
166	Virag Csurgo	34,132
167	Svetlana Krivencheva	33,829
168	Silvija Talaja	33,755
169	Julie Pullin	33,484
170	Sandra Kloesel	33,314
171	Natalia Medvedeva	33,008
172	Laura Montalvo	32,996
173	Anne Kremer	32,872
174	Brie Rippner	32,355
175	Karen Cross	30,469
176	Maureen Drake	29,746
177	Evgenia Koulikovskaya	29,509
178	Angeles Montolio	29,057
179	Liezel Horn	28,629
180	Radka Bobkova	28,541
181	Magalie Lamarre	27,830
182	Maja Muric	27,321
183	Sandra Cecchini	27,196
184	Mariann Werdel-Witmeyer	26,868
185	Bettina Fulco-Villella	26,715
186	Jana Nejedly	26,016
187	Emmanuelle Curutchet	25,914
188	Meghann Shaughnessy	25,611
189	Lucie Ahl	25,567
190	Kyoko Nagatsuka	25,215
191	Miriam Schnitzer	25,066
192	Maria Jose Gaidano	24,943
193	Kristina Triska	24,598
194	Silke Meier	24,515
195	Nirupama Vaidyanathan	24,476
196	Louise Pleming	24,377
197	Nino Louarsabishvili	24,204
198	Jane Taylor	24,090
199	Larissa Schaerer	23,314
200	Kirstin Freye	23,177
201	Veronika Martinek	23,142
202	Danielle Jones	23,050
203	Ludmilla Varmuza	22,807
204	Mi-Ra Jeon	21,950
205	Sofia Prazeres	21,725
206	Lisa Mcshea	21,658
207	Nannie de Villiers	21,439
208	Shinobu Asagoe	21,106
209	Tatjana Jecmenica	20,561
210	Anna Smashnova	20,547
211	Nicole Bradtke	20,452
212	Christina Papadaki	20,423
213	Dally Randriantefy	20,362
214	Emilie Loit	20,340
215	Raluca Sandu	20,255
216	Alicia Ortuno	19,702
217	Laura Garrone	19,168
218	Ana Alcazar	18,883
219	Syna Schmidle	18,656
220	Amanda Wainwright	18,334
221	Fabiola Zuluaga	18,330
222	Karin Miller	18,312
223	Surina de Beer	18,233
224	Eun-Ha Kim	17,863
225	Laurence Andretto	17,731
226	Milena Nekvapilova	17,695
227	Katerina Kroupova	17,684
228	Samantha Reeves	17,632
229	Renata Kolbovic	16,802
230	Jane Chi	16,790
231	Carolina Jagienak	16,732
232	Renee Reid	16,606
233	Saori Obata	16,584
234	Claire Taylor	16,548
235	Elena Brioukhovets	16,467
236	Evie Dominikovic	16,002
237	Katalin Marosi	16,001
238	Melissa Mazzotta	15,955
239	Young-Ja Choi	15,953
240	Katarzyna Nowak	15,699
241	Jacqueline Trail	15,650
242	Laura Pena	15,602
243	Kathy Rinaldi-Stunkel	15,486
244	Yuko Hosoki	15,454
245	Caroline Schneider	15,412
246	Martina Nejedly	15,396
247	Trudi Musgrave	15,117
248	Miriam D'Agostini	14,894
249	Conchita Martinez-Granados	14,773
250	Keri Phebus	14,696

THE MILLIONAIRESSES

The players listed below have won at least US$1 million in prize money during the course of their careers. The totals include earnings at all official tournaments recognized by the WTA Tour, as well as official bonuses. They do not include income from special events, exhibitions or commercial endorsements.

NOTE: *Indicates players who appear in the list for the first time.

1	Martina Navratilova	$20,344,061
2	Steffi Graf	20,076,565
3	Arantxa Sanchez Vicario	12,523,488
4	Monica Seles	9,874,510
5	Chris Evert	8,896,195
6	Gabriela Sabatini	8,785,850
7	Jana Novotna	8,257,780
8	Conchita Martinez	6,877,810
9	Helena Sukova	6,308,521
10	Natasha Zvereva	6,082,686
11	Pam Shriver	5,460,566
12	Martina Hingis	4,948,617
13	Mary Joe Fernandez	4,903,886
14	Gigi Fernandez	4,680,456
15	Zina Garrison-Jackson	4,590,816
16	Lindsay Davenport	3,692,454
17	Larisa Neiland	3,533,154
18	Hana Mandlikova	3,340,959
19	Lori McNeil	3,284,785
20	Manuela Maleeva-Fragniere	3,244,811
21	Mary Pierce	3,219,509
22	Iva Majoli	3,173,232
23	Anke Huber	3,119,900
24	Nathalie Tauziat	3,014,864
25	Wendy Turnbull	2,769,024
26	Amanda Coetzer	2,613,328
27	Brenda Schultz-McCarthy	2,501,489
28	Claudia Kohde-Kilsch	2,227,116
29	Katerina Maleeva	2,220,371
30	Tracy Austin	1,992,380
31	Kimiko Date	1,974,253
32	Billie Jean King	1,966,487
33	Manon Bollegraf	1,795,930
34	Magdalena Maleeva	1,792,768
35	Judith Wiesner	1,738,253
36	Rosalyn Nideffer	1,701,944
37	Elizabeth Smylie	1,701,837
38	Jennifer Capriati	1,688,628
39	Irina Spirlea*	1,687,268
40	Amy Frazier	1,592,516
41	Kathy Jordan	1,592,111
42	Patty Fendick	1,574,956
43	Virginia Wade	1,542,278
44	Sabine Appelmans	1,448,330
45	Julie Halard-Decugis	1,439,961
46	Meredith McGrath	1,429,330
47	Kathy Rinaldi-Stunkel	1,416,878
48	Evonne Goolagong	1,399,431
49	Chanda Rubin	1,391,349
50	Andrea Jaeger	1,379,066
51	Barbara Potter	1,376,580
52	Lisa Raymond*	1,372,170
53	Rosie Casals	1,364,955
54	Yayuk Basuki*	1,328,765
55	Nicole Bradtke	1,298,972
56	Sylvia Hanika	1,296,560
57	Sandra Cecchini	1,292,608
58	Jo Durie	1,224,016
59	Katrina Adams	1,200,066
60	Barbara Paulus*	1,184,119
61	Virginia Ruzici	1,183,728
62	Leila Meskhi	1,179,720
63	Karina Habsudova*	1,176,653
64	Robin White	1,174,349
65	Andrea Temesvari	1,162,635
66	Anne Smith	1,159,717
67	Dianne Balestrat	1,145,377
68	Mercedes Paz	1,129,260
69	Catarina Lindqvist	1,126,665
70	Bettina Bunge	1,126,424
71	Linda Wild	1,124,733
72	Elna Reinach	1,114,668
73	Ann Grossman*	1,100,821
74	Nicole Arendt*	1,094,802
75	Rachel McQuillan*	1,070,571
76	Radka Zrubakova*	1,052,517
77	Betty Stove	1,047,356
78	Marianne Werdel-Witmeyer	1,045,983
79	Sandrine Testud*	1,019,870
80	Betsy Nagelsen	1,016,519
81	Laura Arraya	1,005,589
82	Kimberly Po*	1,005,359

COREL WTA TOUR

CORPORATE HEADQUARTERS: 1266 East Main Street, 4th Floor, Stamford, CT 06902-3546, USA
Tel: 1-203-978 1740; Fax: 1-203-978 1702

TOUR HEADQUARTERS USA: 133 First Street, St.Petersburg, FL 33701, USA
Tel: 1-813 895 5000; Fax: 1-813 894 1982; Telex: 441761
TOUR HEADQUARTERS EUROPE: P.O.Box 1227, London, SW18 5ZQ, England
Tel: 44-181-877 9250; Fax: 44-181-877 9238
INTERNET ADDRESS: http://www.corelwtatour.com
FAXBACK NUMBER: 1-813 822 8868

On 1 January 1995, the Women's Tennis Association and the Women's Tennis Council merged to form the WTA TOUR with Ann Person Worcester, the former Managing Director of the Council, becoming the first Chief Executive Officer of the new body, a post she filled until her retirement at the end of 1997.

COREL WTA TOUR BOARD OF DIRECTORS
Katrina Adams (Active Player)
Robert Arrix (Bausch & Lomb Championships)
Ingrid Bentzer (ITF Women's Circuit Manager)
Franco Bartoni (Tournament Director, Italian Open)
Ray Benton (RHB Ventures)
Sara Fornaciari (Executive Director WTA TOUR Players' Association)
Geoff Pollard (President, Tennis Australia)
Gunter Sanders (General Secretary, German Tennis Federation)
Brian Tobin (President, ITF)
Gunter Sanders (General Secretary, German Tennis Federation)
Brian Tobin (President, ITF)
Marianne Werdel Witmeyer (Former President, WTA TOUR Players' Association)

ALTERNATE DIRECTORS
John Beddington (Masters International)
John Feaver (Events and Tournaments Director, LTA)
Raquel Giscafre (Tournament Director, Toshiba Tennis Classic)
Heinz Grimm (Vice President, ITF)
Kathleen Horvath (Former player, WTA TOUR Players' Association)
Mercedes Paz (Active Player)

OBSERVERS
Bill Babcock (Administrator, International Tennis Federation)
Julia (Judy) Levering (First Vice-President, USTA)
Paul Munick (Vice-President, Madison Square Gerden)

WTA TOUR PLAYERS' ASSOCIATION – BOARD OF DIRECTORS (As of 8 December 1997)

President:	Patricia Hy-Boulais		
Vice-Presidents:	Karin Kschwendt	Kimberley Po	
Officers:	Brenda Schultz-McCarthy	Linda Wild	
Executive Director:	Sara Fornaciari		
Members:	Mary Joe Fernandez	Joanette Kruger	Irina Spirlea
	Rika Hiraki	Florencia Labat	Nathalie Tauziat
	Anke Huber	Mercedes Paz	Dominique van Roost
Former Top Player:	Kathleen Horvath		
Business Advisors:	Jane Brown	John Korff	Loretta McCarthy

COREL WTA TOUR EXECUTIVE STAFF

Chief Executive Officer:	Ric Clarson
VP of Tour Operations and Player Relations:	Peachy Kellmeyer
Director of Communications:	Joe Favorito
Director of Public Relations:	Jim Fuhse
Director of Management Information Systems:	Jim Hill
Director of Marketing:	Marc Lowitz
Director of Tour Operations:	Joan Mattraw
Director of Player Relations:	Jean Nachand
Director of Sports Sciences and Medicine:	Kathleen Stroia

History of the WTA Tour No.1 World Ranking

November 1975 – end of 1997

(Figures supplied by WTA Tour)

	Player	Age	First date No.1		Total weeks
1	Steffi Graf (+)	18.2	17 Aug	1987	374
2	Martina Navratilova	21.9	10 Jul	1978	331
3	Chris Evert	20.11	1 Nov	1975	262
4	Monica Seles (+)	17.3	11 Mar	1991	178
5	Martina Hingis	16.6	31 Mar	1997 (current)	40
6	Tracy Austin	17.3	7 Apr	1980	22
7	Arantxa Sanchez Vicario	23.2	6 Feb	1995	12

(+) including 65 weeks as joint No.1

HISTORY OF THE NO.1 RANKING

Ranking date		Player	Weeks at No. 1
1975	**1 Nov**	**Chris Evert (1)**	**140**
1978	**10 July**	**Martina Navratilova (2)**	**27**
1979	14 January	Chris Evert	2
1979	28 January	Martina Navratilova	4
1979	25 February	Chris Evert	7
1979	16 April	Martina Navratilova	10
1979	25 June	Chris Evert	11
1979	10 September	Martina Navratilova	30
1980	**7 April**	**Tracy Austin (3)***	**2**
1980	21 April	Martina Navratilova	10
1980	1 July	Tracy Austin	20
1980	18 November	Chris Evert	76
1981			
1982	3 May	Martina Navratilova	2
1982	17 May	Chris Evert	4
1982	14 June	Martina Navratilova **+**	156
1983			
1984			
1985	10 June	Chris Evert	18
1985	14 October	Martina Navratilova	2
1985	28 October	Chris Evert	4
1985	25 November	Martina Navratilova	90
1986			
1987	**17 August**	**Steffi Graf (4) ++**	**186**
1988			
1989			
1990			
1991	**11 March**	**Monica Seles (5)****	**21**
1991	5 August	Steffi Graf	1
1991	12 August	Monica Seles	1
1991	19 August	Steffi Graf	3
1991	9 September	Monica Seles	91
1992			
1993	7 June	Steffi Graf	87
1994			
1995	**6 Feb**	**Arantxa Sanchez Vicario (6)**	**2**
1995	20 February	Steffi Graf	1

It was a year of disappointment for Steffi Graf, for so long the world's No. 1 player. An injured knee required an operation after the French Open so that she missed the rest of the season and was unsure if, and when, she would return to action. (Tommy Hindley)

Ranking date		***Player***	***Weeks at No. 1***
1995	27 February	Arantxa Sanchez Vicario	6
1995	10 April	Steffi Graf	5
1995	15 May	Arantxa Sanchez Vicario	4
1995	12 June	Steffi Graf	9
1995	14 August	Steffi Graf	64
		and Monica Seles +++	64
1996	4 November	Steffi Graf	2
1996	18 November	Steffi Graf	1
		and Monica Seles +++	1
1996	25 November	Steffi Graf	18
1997	**31 March**	**Martina Hingis (7) *** **	**40**

* Tracy Austin is the youngest player to reach No. 1 at 17 years, 3 months, 26 days.
** Monica Seles becomes No.1 aged 17 years, 3 months, 19 days, 7 days younger than Austin.
*** Martina Hingis becomes the youngest woman ever to be ranked No.1, aged 16 years, 6 months and 1 day.
+ Martina Navratilova held the No.1 position for 156 weeks consecutively.
++ Steffi Graf held the No.1 position for a record 186 weeks consecutively, more than any man or woman.
+++ Steffi Graf and Monica Seles co-ranked No. 1.

A joyous moment for Martina Hingis, her first Wimbledon singles title at the age of 16. The only player to have won the title at a younger age is Lottie Dod, who was 15 at the time of her first win in 1887 – but that year there were only five players in the draw. (Tommy Hindley)

Hingis – The Prodigious Achiever

Peter Bodo

If one of the most reliable distinguishing characteristics of a 'genius' is that he or she shatters conventional wisdom and forces us to re-think attitudes that have become articles of faith or cozy truisms, then Martina Hingis qualifies for the accolade in more ways than her brilliant, historically important results suggest.

But ponder the glory and implications of that record for a moment. A Czech native whisked off to Switzerland at an early age by her coach and mother, Melanie Molitor, Hingis turned professional the instant she turned 14 years of age. At 15, she began to win with regularity on the pro tour. At 16, Hingis became the youngest-ever singles winner at a Grand Slam event this century (she achieved that distinction in January 1997, when she captured the Australian Open). Hingis went on to amass a 37-match winning streak before she fell from a horse and injured a knee later in the spring, scaring the wits out of the entire tennis establishment. The injury was serious enough to require surgery, but in her very first event after that trauma, Hingis reached the final of the French Open (losing to Iva Majoli).

Undeterred, Hingis went on another tear, winning Wimbledon and crafting another 17-match winning streak before she was beaten by Lindsay Davenport at a US Open tune-up tournament in California. She retaliated for that by carving up the entire field at Flushing Meadow en route to her third Grand Slam title of the year. So, in a year in which Hingis had endured surgery, she fell one match short of becoming only the fourth woman in history (after Maureen Connolly, Margaret Court and Steffi Graf) to capture a calendar-year Grand Slam. And all of that transpired before her 17th birthday on 30 September.

Clearly, Hingis is a prodigy. Her forebears in the game are women like 'Little Mo' Connolly, Evonne Goolagong Cawley, Chris Evert, Andrea Jaeger, Tracy Austin, Jennifer Capriati, Steffi Graf and Monica Seles. But one of the more interesting aspects of Hingis's personality is that she is unlike those other precocious champions in as many ways as she resembles them. And one of her first unconscious statements as a champion was an implicit denunciation of our contemporary stereotype of prodigy.

That stereotype was implanted by Evert, and then perpetuated with slight variations by her Open-era descendants – all of whom preferred to play from the baseline, and shared a precocious, steely will and deep concentration. As the years rolled on, each new prodigy seemed to play with greater and more comprehensive power in addition to improved consistency and precision – an evolution greatly accelerated by developments in racquet technology. In some ways, each successive model was an improved version of the last.

Who would have thought, as little as two years ago, that the most precocious of all the Open era prodigies would be a relatively short (five-foot-six), plump, confident but not entirely focused young lady who was named after Martina Navratilova, but who almost never strikes a blistering groundstroke, nor a second serve that qualifies as anything but a puffball?

Hingis's emergence was particularly unlikely, considering the messages sent by the two prodigies who preceded her. The success of Graf, whose game often looked as if it was cobbled together by a basement hobbyist, suggested that tennis was becoming the domain of a new breed – the world class athlete. Then came Seles, whose success implied that there was no strategic answer to the baseline game played with minimalist fury. If you just hit hard enough and sufficiently close to the lines most of the time, you won – no matter what tools or athletic gifts the player opposite possessed.

Graf subsequently earned her place in the tennis pantheon, proving the value of superior athletic assets and skills. Seles did not fare quite as well, partly for reasons over which she had no control. Although she was unstoppable until she was stabbed by a deranged fan, it seems impossible that anyone could play as fiercely and fearlessly as young Seles did throughout an entire career. The bottom line is that without the confidence and focus of her most youthful, halcyon days, Seles has proved to be a player of a different, slightly lower class.

Then along came Hingis, to show us that even in this *fin de siecle* era there is still such a thing as a TENNIS PLAYER, and that this creature occupies a unique niche in the sporting stable. Hingis'

Martina's mother, Melanie Molitor, named her daughter after the great Navratilova and has been her only coach. As the young Martina claims, they are a great team, with three Grand Slams already in the trophy bag. The third of those was the US Open (opposite), where Martina parried a strong challenge from the unexpected finalist Venus Williams. (Michael Cole & Stephen Wake)

demonstrates that the great tennis player doesn't have to be an extraordinary athlete like Graf, nor a remarkable competitor able to employ a pre-emptive strategy in the manner of Seles.

Hingis shows that some of the most critical assets a tennis player can have, including a sense of anticipation, and an innate understanding of the court's dimensions and how best to use them, are not typical, generic athletic endowments. Nor are they talents or skills that can be learned, although like anything else they can be marginally improved through practice. By and large, some of the things that help make a great tennis players are sport-specific gifts. One of the reasons that so many young players, including some prodigies, develop power games is because they lack what Hingis innately has – that special 'feel' for the game and how it is played. If the others had it, or if they could learn it, they wouldn't have to hit the ball as hard.

In this regard, Hingis has a lot in common with Evert. If you knew nothing about tennis and watched some old video footage of practice sessions featuring Evert and her great rival, Martina Navratilova, you would be hard pressed to believe that the American girl could hold her own. But there always was a kind of clairvoyance about Evert's game, an alertness and anticipation that were neurological rather than muscular skills. She had a great instinct of where to be on the court, of where to put the ball, and of where her opponent was going to put the ball. Evert was one of the greatest tennis players who ever lived. But I shudder at the image of her as, say, a high jumper.

'Martina (Hingis) reminds me of myself,' Evert told the *New York Times* last September. 'I can finally say there's one player who does. Like her, I wasn't lightning fast, but I was there; and then there's the fact that even though she doesn't have one big weapon and she's not going to blow you off the court, she doesn't fear anyone.'

But the comparison with Evert only goes so far, on a number of counts. For one thing, Evert concedes that Hingis already has a great deal more variety in her game. Hingis also is much more comfortable approaching the net and hitting the volley. And she already varies the pace and spin of the ball more comprehensively than did Evert, who makes the astute observation that 'In all round terms, I was more mechanical than Martina is. She is one of the most fluid players I've ever seen.'

But the signature difference between Hingis and every other prodigy but one is mental. Prodigies typically compete with an abundance of concentration. The quality called 'intensity' gradually became the trademark of the Open-era prodigy. Who can forget the screwed-up, ferret face of Austin in her heyday, or the orgasmic shriek with which Seles punctuated each of her groundstrokes? Hingis is a different breed of cat. She loses concentration, she pouts, she engages spectators and freely allows her unpredictable emotions to influence the way in which she plays. Ironically, this makes her precociously mature. She is anything but a one-dimensional doomsday stroking machine, living in the oxygen tent of her own youthful talent, determination and energy.

In that respect, Hingis resembles that great Australian prodigy and player, Evonne Goolagong. She also lacked the prodigy's trademark intensity. Known for her blithe spirit, her jazzy and inventive style, and the lapses of concentration that were dubbed 'walkabouts' in deference to her aboriginal roots, Goolagong won seven Grand Slam titles and reached four consecutive US Open finals (losing each time). She was wildly popular and beloved for her personality, sportsmanship, and overall demeanor.

But unlike the young Goolagong, Hingis has a bit of an edge – a self-assuredness that strikes some people as pure conceit, and others as insouciance. She can be saucy, impertinent, and playful, in a way that is reminiscent of the young Tracy Austin. Over the years, Hingis' self-assurance may mature into quiet confidence, but for now she obviously enjoys being young, gifted, and successful beyond her wildest dreams.

Hingis sometimes appears to be made up of bits and pieces of former prodigies, but ultimately the whole seems greater than the sum of her parts. This is no less true of her personality than her tennis game. She has never been called a 'clone' of anyone, as have so many other erstwhile prodigies. This is why there is an aura of genius about her.

With seven doubles wins as her only successes in 1997, Arantxa Sanchez Vicario slipped to No.9 in the year-end singles rankings, her lowest finish since 1988. (Michael Cole)

Reference Section

Biographies • All-Time Greats
Obituaries • Championship Rolls

INDEX TO BIOGRAPHIES

The top 75 singles and top 25 doubles players on both the ATP and WTA tours are shown, together with senior and junior Grand Slam winners and all those who competed in the season-ending championships. Players ranked in the top 10 in singles are shown in bold. Figures following players' names indicate their singles ranking, junior ranking where applicable, and those in brackets show the doubles ranking where appropriate.

MEN

WOMEN

Biographies

Christine Forrest

Abbreviations used in this section:

f	final	RH	right-handed	Inv	Invitation
sf	semi-final	LH	left-handed	Jun	Junior
qf	quarter-final	2HB	2-handed backhand	Nat	National
r/u	runner-up	2HF	2-handed forehand	Pro	Professional
def.	defaulted	US CC	US Clay Court Championships	Tourn	Tournament
ret'd	retired			CS	Colgate Series
fs	final set	LIPC	Lipton International Players Championships	TS	Toyota Series
rr	round-robin			HC	Hard Court
bp	break-point	W Cup	Wightman Cup	VS	Virginia Slims
sp	set-point	FC Cup	Family Circle Cup	WT Cup	World Team Cup
mp	match-point	GS Cup	Grand Slam Cup	D Cup	Davis Cup
tb	tie-break	Champ	Champion/ Championship		
1r	first round				
2s	second set	GP	Grand Prix		

TOP TEN

Full biographical and statistical details of the top ten men and top ten women head separate men's and women's sections. Each individual's record contains personal details, followed by his or her 1997 prize money, career prize money, the number of career titles won and year-end rankings. A paragraph on style is followed by annual notes of career highlights, beginning with the tournaments won each year. A section giving principal singles results in full for 1997 includes all matches where a player has reached at least the semi-final. There follows a complete career record of every singles match played at each of the four Grand Slam Championships, at the Olympic Games and in Davis Cup or Fed Cup ties, in the Grand Slam Cup and in the season ending Tour Championships.

REMAINING BIOGRAPHIES

Within the two sections are the principal 1997 results, the annual notes and the career highlights of the next 65 ranked singles players of each sex, the top 25 doubles players, all Grand Slam winners and the juniors who have won Grand Slam titles. The final ranking for each year is shown in brackets following the year.

John Barrett's annual world rankings, as well as the year-end rankings published by the ATP Tour and the Corel WTA Tour, and total prize money together with lists of the men and women whose career earnings exceed $1 million, can be found in the Rankings Section (pp 217–245).

We gratefully acknowledge the assistance of the ATP Tour, the Corel WTA Tour, and Nola Hendon of the WTA European office in supplying statistical information.

1 PETE SAMPRAS (USA)

Born: Washington, DC, 12 August 1971. **Lives:** Tampa, Fla, son of Greek immigrants. **Father:** Sam. **Mother:** Georgia. **Sisters:** Stella and Marion. **Brother:** Gus (older) who sometimes travels with him.
Agent: IMG. **Coaches:** Paul Annacone; formerly the late Tim Gullikson. Coached first by Dr Pete Fischer and after they split in 1989 Robert Lansdorp coached him on forehand, Larry Easley on volley and Del Little on footwork. Went to Bollettieri Academy and worked with Joe Brandi. They parted in Dec. 1990, to be reunited briefly during 1991, and Sampras started working with Pat Etcheberry for strength.
Personal trainer: Todd Snyder. **Turned pro:** 1988.
Height: 6ft 1in (1.83m). **Weight:** 170lb (77kg).

Rankings: 1988: 97; **1989:** 81; **1990:** 5; **1991:** 6; **1992:** 3; **1993:** 1; **1994:** 1; **1995:** 1; **1996:** 1; **1997:** 1. **Highest:** 1 (12 April 1993).

1997 Prize Money: $6,498,311. **Career Earnings:** $32,060,658. **Career Titles:** 52.

Style: Right-handed, ever since changing from 2HB to 1HB in 1987 on advice of his then coach, Dr Pete Fischer. Sampras is one of the finest servers and volleyers on the tour and has flat, orthodox groundstrokes, hit on the rise with awesome power. He is vulnerable to shin splints that have affected his career at important moments, and his stamina is questionable.

CAREER HIGHLIGHTS (year: (titles))
1988: Reached sf Schenectady and qf Detroit (d. Mayotte). **1989:** Upset Wilander *en route* to last 16 US Open and reached qf Adelaide. In doubles with Courier won Italian Open, and took 7th place at Masters. **1990: (4)** *US OPEN, Philadelphia, Manchester, GS Cup*. Upset Mayotte in 70-game struggle 1r Australian Open on his way to last 16, unseeded, and in Feb. won his 1st tour title at Philadelphia. In Sept. he won his 1st GS title at US Open and moved into the top 10. At 19 yrs 28 days he was the youngest champion there (the previous youngest was Oliver Campbell, who won in 1890 aged 19 yrs 6 mths). Shin splints had been troubling him since US Open, and although he was able to play ATP World Champ, he did not progress beyond rr. Won inaugural GS Cup and 1st prize $2m. Voted Most Improved Player of The Year. **1991: (4)** *Los Angeles, Indianapolis, Lyon, IBM/ATP World Champ*. Suffered a string of injuries to shin, foot and ham-string, returning to action in Feb. He finished the year in tremendous style by winning ATP World Champ in Frankfurt, the youngest since J. McEnroe in 1979. After Frankfurt sacked Brandi again and sought new coach on eve of D Cup f v France in Lyon where, in his 1st ever tie, he was humiliated by an inspired Leconte on opening day and lost decisive 3rd rubber to Forget. **1992: (5)** *Philadelphia, Kitzbuhel, Cincinnati, Indianapolis, Lyon*. Broke into top 3 after winning Philadelphia and on 5 Oct. took 2nd place ahead of Edberg. In US Open he upset Courier but lost f to Edberg in 4s. In July he won his 1st title on clay at Kitzbuhel. **1993: (8)** *WIMBLEDON, US OPEN, Sydney Outdoor, LIPC, Tokyo Japan Open, Hong Kong, Lyon, Antwerp*. Ousted Edberg from the No. 2 position after Australian Open, closed the gap behind Courier after winning LIPC and finally took over the top spot on 12 April, the 11th man to reach the top since rankings began in 1973. He lost the No. 1 position to Courier again on 22 Aug. after 19 weeks, but regained it 13 Sept. He won his 1st Wimbledon and 2nd US Open to take 8 titles across the year, including 3 in succession with LIPC, Tokyo Japan Open and Hong Kong. His 83 matches won in the year were the most since Lendl's 84 in 1985 and his 8 titles the most since Lendl's 10 in 1989. He was also r/u in IBM/ATP World Champ, where he lost to an inspired Stich, and reached sf GS Cup where Korda beat him in an exhausting 4½ hour match. He appeared in 5 other sf and was in winning US WT Cup squad. **1994: (10)** *AUSTRALIAN OPEN, WIMBLEDON, Sydney NSW Open, Indian Wells, LIPC, Osaka, Tokyo Japan Open, Italian Open, Antwerp, IBM/ATP Champ*. It was another extraordinary year in which he won 10 tourns – 3 more than anyone else and the most since Lendl's 10 in 1989 – including a 1st Australian Open, 2nd Wimbledon and 2nd IBM/ATP Champ. After Wimbledon he looked unassailable at the top of the rankings by the biggest margin ever and was the 1st man since Lendl in 1987 to remain unmoved at No. 1 all year. He was also the only

player in 1994 to win titles on all 4 surfaces. Yet he began surprisingly by losing to qualifier Alami in 1r Qatar, his 1st tourn of the year, but then overcame a stomach upset to retain his LIPC title over Agassi, who agreed to delay their f for 50 mins to allow Sampras to recover. He took a 4-week break from the tour in spring, returning to win Italian Open in May, his 5th consec. tourn success, and extended to 29 matches his winning streak (the longest since Lendl's 31 in 1985), which was ended by Stich at WT Cup after Sampras had held 2 mps. He then lost to Courier in qf French Open, 3 matches short of becoming the 1st man to win a GS on 4 different surfaces. Martin beat him in f Queen's, but at Wimbledon he was superb, sweeping to f, where he demolished Ivanisevic in ss to retain the title. In addition to the quality of his tennis, for which he was voted Player of the Year, his outfits attracted attention, for he wore baggy, knee-length shorts specially designed for him by Nike. By the end of Wimbledon, he had already qualified for the year-end IBM/ATP World Champ – the earliest ever. However, thereafter he was plagued by injury. He withdrew from Washington suffering from tendinitis in left ankle, was out for 6 weeks before US Open and was not fully fit there, suffering from exhaustion, dehydration and blisters as he lost to Yzaga in 5s in last 16. There was further disappointment when US lost D Cup sf to SWE after he was forced to retire v Edberg with hamstring injury, after having hurt his knee beating Larsson on the 1st day. He suffered a rare defeat at the hands of an inspired Becker in sf Stockholm in Oct. and his victory at Antwerp was his 1st since Wimbledon. He was still not invincible at IBM/ATP Champ, where Becker beat him in rr, although the tables were turned in their f. After beating Ivanisevic in magnificent 5s sf in GS Cup, he lost f to Larsson, again affected by fatigue. **1995: (5)** *WIMBLEDON, US OPEN, Indian Wells, Queen's, Paris Open*. His year was overshadowed by the illness of his coach, Tim Gullikson, who was receiving treatment throughout for 4 brain tumours. When the diagnosis was first made and Gullikson was flown back to US during the Australian Open, Sampras broke down during an emotional qf v Courier, recovering from 2 sets down to win the match, although he eventually lost the f to Agassi. It was an unsettled year for him as he flew back and forth over the Atlantic to visit Gullikson between tourns and he was coached on the spot at Wimbledon by Paul Annacone. Won his 1st title of the year at Indian Wells in March, but lost the No.1 ranking to Agassi 10 April after 82 consec. weeks. He regained the top spot on 6 Nov. after winning Paris Open, from which Agassi had withdrawn injured, and with Agassi sidelined for the rest of the year with a chest muscle injury, he finished the year at the top – the 1st since Lendl in 1987 to hold that position for 3 years in succession. Withdrew 2r Monte Carlo v Haarhuis with right ankle injury, returning at Hamburg in May. In an attempt to become only the 5th man to win all 4 GS titles, he changed his schedule to allow himself 2 months on European clay in preparation for French Open, but fell there 1r to Schaller. However, he retained his Wimbledon crown and won a 3rd US Open, taking 5 titles in all from 9 f and was named ATP Player of the Year. He was disappointing at IBM/ATP Champ, where it seemed that, once he had secured his year-end position at the top of the rankings, he lost interest, losing his 3rd rr match to W. Ferreira and capitulating tamely to Chang in ss in sf. In D Cup f, however, he played a heroic part, winning both his singles and then doubles (with Martin) as USA d. RUS 3–2 in Moscow. **1996: (8)** *US OPEN, San Jose, Memphis, Hong Kong, Tokyo Japan Open, Indianapolis, Basel, ATP Champs*. It was a year in which he was challenged for the top ranking at different times by Agassi, Muster, M. Chang and Kafelnikov, although he finished as No. 1 for the 4th time in succession and was again voted Player of the Year. On 29 Jan., after losing 3r Australian Open to Philippoussis, he dropped behind Agassi and Muster to be ranked as low as No. 3 for 1st time since Jan. 1993. He was back at No. 2 on 12 Feb. and returned to the top a week later after winning San Jose. The title at Memphis the following week consolidated his position, but he slipped again after withdrawing qf Rotterdam with a metatarsal sprain of his right ankle. Back-to-back titles at Hong Kong and Tokyo Japan Open saw him return to the top on 14 April and become the 10th man to reach win 40 titles. Withdrew from Italian Open after the death of his former coach, Tim Gullikson, and missed some of WT Cup with back spasms, although he was back later in the tourn, losing to Kafelnikov. He had played only 2 CC matches before French Open, where he recovered from 2 sets to 0 down v Courier, but was exhausted when losing sf to Kafelnikov again and withdrew from Queen's to recover. He was still below his best at Wimbledon, where Krajicek beat him in qf, and although he claimed to be feeling better at Indianapolis in August, where he won his 1st title since April, he was struggling again at US Open. In 5s of his 3 hr 52 min qf v Corretja, he was ill from severe dehydration, vomiting on court and leaning on his racket between points. However, he saved mp at 7–6 in 5s tb and then, hardly able to stand with stomach pains, produced an ace to take an 8–7 lead, whereupon Corretja served a double-fault. He was almost certainly saved by the US Open rule of playing 5s tb. Amazingly, he went on to beat

Ivanisevic in 4s sf 2 days later and take the title over M. Chang 2 days after that. His final victory was particularly poignant, coming as it did on what would have been Tim Gullikson's 45th birthday, and he paid tribute to his former coach. He added the title at Basel, r/u Stuttgart Eurocard and sf LIPC, plus 3 qf, and was already confirmed as World Champion before ATP Champs. There his year finished in triumph as he and Becker played a magnificent f, which Sampras eventually took in 5s, in front of Becker's home crowd. Withdrew from GS Cup with bilateral peroneal tendinitis and ankle pain. **1997: (8)** *AUSTRALIAN OPEN, WIMBLEDON, San Jose, Philadelphia, Cincinnati, GS Cup, Paris Open, ATP Champs.* On 28 April he had been at No. 1 for 171 weeks, overtaking J. McEnroe to become 3rd on the all-time list (after Lendl, 270, and Connors, 268), and was still at the top at end of year – only 2nd after Connors to finish No. 1 for 5th consec. year. He won his 1st 17 matches of the year, including a 2nd Australian Open, before a 2r defeat by Ulihrach at Indian Wells heralded a relatively lean patch. He was hampered at LIPC by a wrist injury, although he refused to blame that for his sf defeat by Bruguera, and missed 2 tourns with the injury thereafter. After being beaten qf Queen's by Bjorkman, he went into Wimbledon having failed to reach f in previous 7 tourns. However, he was back on top there, winning the Championships for a 4th time. When he won his next tourn at Cincinnati, his 49th career title, he drew level with Becker at the top amongst active players, moving ahead on his own after taking a 50th at GS Cup. He finished the season with 52 titles, having won all 8 f he played. In French Open, however, he lost to M. Norman 3r while suffering from stomach upset (although, in his usual style, he refused to make that an excuse for his defeat) and at US Open he fell in 5s tb in last 16 to Korda, who had also stretched him to 5s at Wimbledon. In his 8th consec. ATP Champs, he lost 1st match to Moya, but was magnificent thereafter as he swept to his 4th title there, finishing the year head and shoulders above the rest of the pack. After leading US to f of D Cup, he was forced to retire injured v Larsson in 2nd rubber when trailing 6–3 6–7 1–2 as USA went down 5–0 to SWE.

PRINCIPAL 1997 RESULTS – won 8, sf 1 (detailed Grand Slam results follow)
won Australian Open, **won** Wimbledon, **won** San Jose (d. Radulescu 7–6 6–3, Gimelstob 6–2 6–3, Woodruff 6–2 6–3, Martin 6–2 6–3, Rusedski 3–6 5–0 ret'd), **won** Philadelphia (d. Filippini 6–4 6–1, Bjorkman 7–5 7–6, D. Flach 6–4 6–2, Schalken 3–6 7–5 6–3, Rafter 5–7 7–6 6–3), **won** Cincinnati (d. Gimelstob 6–2 6–4, Rafter 7–6 6–4, Kafelnikov 6–2 6–2, A. Costa 6–3 6–4, Muster 6–3 6–4), **won** GS Cup, **won** Paris Open (d. Becker 7–6 3–6 6–3, Korda 4–6 7–6 6–4, Muster 6–1 4–6 6–2, Kafelnikov 7–6 6–3, Bjorkman 6–3 4–6 6–3 6–1), **won** ATP Champs; **sf** LIPC (d. Voinea 6–2 6–0, Clavet 6–3 7–6, Larsson 6–2 6–0, Dreekmann w.o., lost Bruguera 5–7 7–6 6–4).

CAREER GRAND SLAM RECORD
AUSTRALIAN OPEN – Played 7, won 2, r/u 1, sf 1
1989: 1r lost Saceanu 6–4 6–4 7–6. **1990: last 16** d. Mayotte [6] 7–6 6–7 4–6 7–5 12–10, Arrese 0–6 6–2 3–6 6–1 6–3, Woodbridge 7–5 6–4 6–2, lost Noah 6–3 6–4 3–6 6–2. **1991–92:** Did not play. **1993: sf** [seed 3] d. Steeb 6–1 6–2 6–1, Larsson 6–3 3–6 6–3 6–4, Antonitsch 7–6 6–4 6–2, Washington [13] 6–3 6–4 6–4, Steven 6–3 6–2 6–3, lost Edberg [2] 7–6 6–3 7–6. **1994: won** [seed 1] d. Eagle 6–4 6–0 7–6, Kafelnikov 6–3 2–6 6–3 1–6 9–7, Simian 7–5 6–1 1–6 6–4, Lendl [15] 7–6 6–2 7–5, Gustafsson [10] 7–6 2–6 6–3 7–6, Courier 6–3 6–4 6–4, Martin 7–6 6–4 6–4). **1995: r/u** [seed 1] d. Pozzi 6–3 6–2 6–0, Kroslak 6–2 6–0 6–1, Jonsson 6–1 6–2 6–4, Larsson [15] 4–6 6–7 7–5 6–4 6–4, Courier [9] 6–7 6–7 6–3 6–4 6–3, Chang [5] 6–7 6–3 6–4 6–4, lost Agassi [2] 4–6 6–1 7–6 7–4. **1996: 3r** seed 1, lost Philippoussis 6–4 7–6 7–6. **1997: won** [seed 1] d. Pescariu 6–2 6–4 6–2, Voinea 3–6 6–2 6–3 6–2, Woodforde 6–1 6–0 6–1, Hrbaty 6–7 6–3 6–4 3–6 6–4, A. Costa [10] 6–3 6–7 6–1 3–6 6–2, Muster [5] 6–1 7–6 6–3, Moya 6–2 6–3 6–3.
FRENCH OPEN – Played 8, sf 1, qf 3
1989: 2r d. Lozano 6–3 6–2 6–4, lost Chang [15] 6–1 6–1 6–1. **1991: 2r** [seed 6] d. Muster 4–6 4–6 6–4 6–1 6–4, lost Champion 6–3 6–1 6–1. **1992: qf** [seed 3] d. Rosset 7–6 4–6 6–4 3–6 6–3, Prades 7–6 6–4 7–6, R. Gilbert 6–3 6–2 6–3, Steeb 6–4 6–3 6–2, lost Agassi [11] 7–6 6–2 6–1. **1993: qf** [seed 1] d. Cherkasov 6–1 6–2 3–6 6–1, Ondruska 7–5 6–0 6–3, Svensson 6–4 6–4 6–2, Washington 6–3 7–6 6–1, lost Bruguera [10] 6–3 4–6 6–1 6–4. **1994: qf** [seed 1] d. A. Costa 6–3 6–4 6–4, Rios 7–6 7–6 6–4, Haarhuis 6–1 6–4 6–1, Tillstroem 6–4 6–4 1–6 6–4, lost Courier [7] 6–4 5–7 6–4 6–4. **1995: 1r** [seed 2] lost Schaller 7–6 4–6 6–7 6–2 6–4. **1996: sf** [seed 1] d. Gustafsson 6–1 7–5 7–6, Bruguera 6–3 6–4 6–7 2–6 6–3, Martin 3–6 6–4 7–5 4–6 6–2, Draper 6–4 7–5 6–2, Courier [7] 6–7 4–6 6–4 6–4 6–4, lost Kafelnikov [6] 7–6 6–0 6–2. **1997: 3r** [seed 1] d. Santoro 6–3 7–5 6–1, Clavet 6–1 6–2 6–2, lost M. Norman 6–2 6–4 2–6 6–4.
WIMBLEDON – Played 9, won 4, sf 1, qf 1
1989: 1r lost Woodbridge 7–5 7–6 5–7 6–3. **1990: 1r** lost van Rensburg 7–6 7–5 7–6. **1991: 2r** [seed 8] d. Marcellino 6–1 6–2 6–2, lost Rostagno 6–4 3–6 7–6 6–4. **1992: sf** [seed 5] d. Cherkasov 6–1 6–3 6–3, Woodbridge 7–6 7–6 6–7 6–4, S. Davis 6–1 6–0 6–2, Boetsch 6–3 7–5 7–6, Stich [3] 6–3 6–2 6–4, lost Ivanisevic [8] 6–7 7–6 6–4 6–2. **1993: won** [seed 1] d. Borwick 6–7 6–3 7–6 6–3, Morgan 6–4 7–6 6–4, Black 6–4 6–1 6–1, Foster 6–1 6–2 7–6, Agassi [8] 6–2 6–2 3–6 3–6 6–4, Becker [4] 7–6 6–4 6–4, Courier [3] 7–6

7–6 3–6 6–3. **1994: won** [seed 1] d. Palmer 7–6 7–5 6–3, Reneberg 6–3 6–4 6–2, C. Adams 6–1 6–2 6–4, Vacek 6–4 6–1 7–6, Chang [10] 6–4 6–1 6–3, Martin [6] 6–4 6–4 3–6 6–3, Ivanisevic 7–6 7–6 6–0. **1995: won** [seed 2] d. Braasch 7–6 6–7 6–4 6–1, Henman 6–2 6–3 7–6, Palmer 4–6 6–4 6–1 6–2, Rusedski 6–4 6–2 7–5, Matsuoka 6–7 6–3 6–4 6–2, Ivanisevic [4] 7–6 4–6 6–3 4–6 6–3, Becker [3] 6–7 6–2 6–4 6–2. **1996: qf** [seed 1] d. Reneberg 4–6 6–4 6–3 6–3, Philippoussis 7–6 6–4 6–4, Kucera 6–4 6–3 6–7 7–6, Pioline [16] 6–4 6–4 6–2, lost Krajicek 7–5 7–6 6–4. **1997: won** [seed 1] d. Tillstrom 6–4 6–4 6–2, Dreekmann 7–6 7–5 7–5, B. Black 6–1 6–2 6–2, Korda [16] 6–4 6–3 6–7 6–7 6–4, Becker [8] 6–1 6–7 6–1 6–4, Woodbridge 6–2 6–1 7–6, Pioline 6–4 6–2 6–4.

US OPEN – Played 10, won 4, r/u 1, qf 1

1988: 1r lost Yzaga 6–7 6–7 6–4 7–5 6–2. **1989:** last 16 d. Moreno 6–3 5–7 6–4 6–1, Wilander [5] 5–7 6–3 1–6 6–4, Yzaga 4–6 6–4 6–3 6–2, lost Berger [11] 7–5 6–2 6–1. **1990: won** [seed 12] d. Goldie 6–1 7–5 6–1, Lundgren 6–4 6–3 6–3, Hlasek 6–3 6–4 6–1, Muster [6] 6–7 7–6 6–4 6–3, Lendl [3] 6–4 7–6 3–6 4–6 6–2, J. McEnroe 6–2 6–4 3–6 6–3, Agassi 6–4 6–3 6–2. **1991: qf** [seed 6] d. van Rensburg 6–0 6–3 6–2, Ferreira 6–1 6–2 2–2 ret'd, Simian 7–6 6–4 6–3, Wheaton [11] 3–6 6–2 6–2 6–4, lost Courier [4] 6–2 7–6 7–6. **1992: r/u** [seed 3] d. di Lucia 6–3 7–5 6–2, Damm 7–5 6–1 6–2, Martin 7–6 2–6 4–6 7–5 6–4, Forget [13] 6–3 1–6 1–6 6–4 6–3, Volkov 6–4 6–1 6–0, Courier [1] 6–1 3–6 6–2 6–2, lost Edberg [2] 3–6 6–4 7–6 6–2. **1993: won** [seed 2] d. Santoro 6–3 6–1 6–2, Vacek 6–4 5–7 6–2 7–6, Boetsch 6–4 6–4 7–6, Enqvist 6–4 6–4 7–6, M. Chang [7] 6–7 7–6 6–1 6–1, Volkov [14] 6–4 6–3 6–2, Pioline 6–4 6–4 6–3. **1994: last 16** [seed 1] d. Ullyett 6–2 6–2 6–2, Vacek 6–3 6–4 6–4, Smith 4–6 6–2 6–4 6–3, lost Yzaga 3–6 6–3 4–6 7–6 7–5. **1995: won** [seed 2] d. Meligeni 6–0 6–3 6–4, Yzaga 6–1 6–4 6–3, Philippoussis 6–7 7–5 7–5 6–3, Martin [15] 7–6 6–3 6–4, B. Black 7–6 6–4 6–0, Courier [14] 7–5 4–6 6–4 7–5, Agassi [2] 6–4 6–3 4–6 7–5. **1996: won** [seed 1] d. Szymanski 6–2 6–2 6–1, Novak 6–3 1–6 6–3 4–6 6–4, Volkov 6–3 6–4 6–2, Philippoussis 6–3 6–3 6–4, Corretja 7–6 5–7 5–7 6–4 7–6, Ivanisevic [4] 6–3 6–4 6–7 6–3, M. Chang [2] 6–3 6–2 6–2. **1997: last 16** [seed 1] d. Larkham 6–3 6–1 6–3, Baur 7–5 6–4 6–3, Radulescu 6–3 6–4 6–4, lost Korda [15] 6–7 7–5 7–6 3–6 7–6.

OLYMPIC RECORD

1992: (Barcelona) last 16 [seed 3] d. Masur 6–1 7–6 6–4, Yzaga 6–3 6–0 3–6 6–1, lost Cherkasov [13] 6–7 1–6 7–5 6–0 6–3.

CAREER DAVIS CUP RECORD

1991: November – *World Group Final FRA d. USA 3–1 in FRA (Carpet).* R2 lost H. Leconte 6–4 7–5 6–4; R4 lost G. Forget 7–6 3–6 6–3 6–4. **1992: January** – *World Group 1R USA d. ARG 5–0 in USA (Hard).* R1 d. M. Jaite 3–6 6–4 6–2 6–4; R4 d. A. Mancini 6–4 6–1. **March** – *World Group qf USA d. TCH 3–2 in USA (Hard).* R1 d. K. Novacek 6–3 6–4 6–2; R4 lost P. Korda 6–4 6–3 2–6 6–3. **September** – *World Group sf USA d. SWE 4–1 in USA (Clay).* R3 (with J. McEnroe) d. S. Edberg/A. Jarryd 6–1 6–7 4–6 6–3 6–3. **December** – *World Group Final USA d. SWZ 3–1 in USA (Hard).* R3 (with J. McEnroe) d. J. Hlasek/M. Rosset 6–7 6–7 7–5 6–1 6–2. **1994: July** – *World Group 2r USA d. NED 3–2 in NED (Hard).* R2 d. J. Eltingh 6–2 6–2 6–0; R4 lost R. Krajicek 2–6 7–5 7–6 7–5. **September** – *World Group sf SWE d. USA 3–2 in SWE (Carpet).* R2 d. M. Larsson 6–7 6–4 6–2 7–6; R4 lost S. Edberg 6–3 ret'd. **1995: March** – *World Group qf USA d. ITA 5–0 in ITA (Clay).* R2 d. R. furlan 7–6 6–3 6–0; R 4 d. A. Gaudenzi 6–3 1–6 6–3. **September** – *World Group sf USA d. SWE 4–1 in USA (Hard).* R1 d. T. Enqvist 6–3 6–4 3–6 6–3; R5 d. M. Wilander 2–6 7–6 6–3. **December** – *World Group Final USA d. RUS 3–2 in Moscow (Clay).* R1 d. A. Chesnokov 3–6 6–4 6–3 6–7 6–4. R3 (+ T. Martin) d. Y. Kafelnikov/A. Olhovskiy) 7–5 6–4 6–3; R4 d. Kafelnikov 6–2 6–4 7–6. **1997: September** – *World Group sf USA d. AUS 4–1 in USA (Hard).* R2 d. M. Philippoussis 6–1 6–2 7–6; R3 (with T. Martin) lost T. Woodbridge/M. Woodforde 3–6 7–6 6–2 6–4; R4 d. P. Rafter 6–7 6–1 6–1 6–4. **November** – *World Group Final SWE d. USA 5–0 in SWE (Hard).* R2 lost M. Larsson 3–6 7–6 2–1 ret'd.

GRAND SLAM CUP RECORD – Played 6, won 2, r/u 2, sf 1

1990: won [seed 4] d. Cherkasov 5–7 6–2 7–5, Ivanisevic [5] 7–6 6–7 8–6, Chang 6–3 6–4 6–4, Gilbert 6–3 3–6 7–6 2–6 6–4. **1992: sf** [seed 3] d. Volkov 6–3 6–4, Leconte 7–6 6–4, lost Stich 7–6 7–6 3–6 7–6. **1993: r/u** [seed 1] d. Muster 6–3 6–1, Chang 7–6 6–3, lost Korda 3–6 7–6 3–6 7–6 13–11. **1994: r/u** [seed 1] d. Yzaga 6–2 6–4, Chang 6–4 6–3, Ivanisevic 5–7 6–3 6–4 6–7 10–8, lost Larsson 7–6 4–6 7–6 6–4. **1995: qf** [seed 1] d. P. McEnroe 6–1 7–6, lost Ivanisevic [8] def. **1996:** Did not play. **1997: won** [seed 1] d. Mantilla 6–4 3–6 6–2, Bjorkman [8] 7–6 6–4, Rusedski [4] 3–6 7–6 7–6 6–2, Rafter [2] 6–2 6–4 7–5.

GRAND PRIX MASTERS/ATP TOUR CHAMPIONSHIP – Played 8, won 4, r/u 1, sf 2

1990: Equal 3rd in rr lost Edberg 7–5 6–4, lost Agassi 6–4 6–2, d. E. Sanchez 6–2 6–4. **1991: won** in rr d. Stich 6–2 7–6, d. Agassi 6–3 1–6 6–3, lost Becker 6–4 6–7 6–1; sf d. Lendl 6–2 6–3; f d. Courier 3–6 7–6 6–3 6–4. **1992: sf** in rr d. Becker 7–6 7–6, d. Edberg 6–3 3–6 7–5, d. Korda 3–6 6–3 6–3; sf lost Courier 7–6 7–6. **1993: r/u** in rr d. Ivanisevic 6–3 4–6 6–2, d. Edberg 6–3 7–6, d. Bruguera 6–3 1–6 6–3; sf d. Medvedev 6–3 6–0; f lost Stich 7–6 2–6 7–6 6–2. **1994: won** in rr lost Becker 7–5 7–5, d. Edberg 4–6 6–3 7–6, d. Ivanisevic 6–3 6–4; sf d. Agassi 4–6 7–6 6–3; f d. Becker 4–6 6–3 7–5 6–4. **1995: sf** in rr d. Kafelnikov 6–3 6–3, d. Becker 6–2 7–6, lost W. Ferreira 7–6 4–6 6–3; sf lost M. Chang 6–4 6–4. **1996: won** in rr d. Agassi 6–2 6–1, lost Becker 7–6 7–6, d. Kafelnikov 6–4 6–4; sf d. Ivanisevic 6–7 7–6 7–5; f d. Becker 3–6 7–6 7–6 6–7 6–4. **1997: won** in rr lost Moya 6–3 6–7 6–2, d. Rusedski 6–4 7–5, d. Rafter 6–4 6–1; sf d. Bjorkman 6–3 6–4; f d. Kafelnikov 6–3 6–2 6–2.

2 PATRICK RAFTER (AUS)

Born: Mount Isa, Queensland, 28 December 1972.
Lives: Pembroke, Bermuda.
Father: Jim. **Mother:** Jocelyn. **Siblings:** Third youngest of nine children (Stephen, Teresa, Geoff, Marie, Peter, Louise, Patrick, Michael and David).
Agent: His brother, Stephen; ProServ for marketing opportunities. **Coaches:** His brother, Geoff, and Tony Roche.
Turned pro: 1991.
Height: 6ft 1in (1.85m). **Weight:** 175lb (79kg).

Rankings: 1990: 751; **1991:** 294; **1992:** 301; **1993:** 57; **1994:** 21; **1995:** 68; **1996:** 62; **1997:** 2 singles, 12 doubles.
Highest: 2 (17 November 1997).

1997 Prize Money: $2,923,519. **Career Earnings:** $4,515,712. **Career titles:** 2.

Style: A forthright, attacking serve-and-volley right-hander, he uses his natural athletic ability to move quickly about the court, taking the ball early and moving constantly forward. Fast reflexes enable him to blanket the net, and his excellent overhead makes him a difficult man to lob. Improving groundstrokes and return of serve have lifted him into the top ten where he belongs.

CAREER HIGHLIGHTS (year: (titles))
1991: Began to make his mark on the Satellite circuits. **1993:** Emerging from the Challenger circuit, where he won Aptos, he broke into top 100 after reaching sf Indianapolis upset Chesnokov, Ferreira and Sampras. Voted ATP Newcomer of the Year. **1994: (1)** *Manchester.* In a remarkable 18-month period he moved from 301 to 21 in the rankings. He upset Courier 1r Indian Wells, surprised Rosset and M. Chang on his way to sf LIPC, and broke into top 25 after reaching his 1st tour f at Hong Kong in April, where the match was delayed 1 hour to allow him to recover from food poisoning. He upset Muster at French Open, where he was unseeded, and after he had won his 1st title at Manchester, he played a 5-set marathon v Bruguera in 2r Wimbledon, succumbing only 13–11 after being overtaken by cramp. He also reached sf Adelaide and Sydney Indoor, 4 more qf and last 16 French Open, unseeded. Played 3 doubles f, winning Bologna with Fitzgerald. **1995:** A 4, F 1, W 1, US 2. Having achieved so much so fast, he felt somewhat drained and disillusioned, as well as being hampered during the year by a torn cartilage in his racket wrist, for which he underwent surgery on 30 Oct., missing the rest of the season. His best performances were sf Washington, qf Adelaide, Los Angeles, Ostrava and Lyon and an upset of Medvedev at Cincinnati. Played 2 doubles f, winning Adelaide with Courier. **1996:** Returning at Australian Open, he was forced to retire 2r with a recurrence of the wrist injury, and was out with that and an ankle injury until April. However, he felt more optimistic and under less pressure once Philippoussis had replaced him at the top of the Australian rankings. He did not progress beyond qf, but reached that stage at US CC (where he won the doubles with Cash), Queen's, Washington (d. Agassi) and Toronto (d. MaliVai Washington) and upset Rosset at Wimbledon, where he was unseeded. **1997: (1)** *US OPEN.* The climax of an superb season came at US Open, where, playing his 3rd f in consec. tourns and his 6th of the year, he won his 1st title of the year in tremendous style. He was the 1st Australian since Cash at Wimbledon in 1987 to win a GS title and the 1st to win US Open since Newcombe in 1973. It was his 1st title for 3 years. Hampered by a sore shoulder, he had not even been sure of competing and was grateful for his Wednesday start. His success swept him through the rankings to No. 3, the highest by an Australian since Laver was No. 2 in 1975, and at end of season he ousted M. Chang to take the No. 2 slot himself. He also performed well on clay in spring: unseeded at French Open, he upset Krajicek on his way to becoming the 1st Australian man to reach qf there since Phil Dent in 1977 and progressing to sf, unseeded. In other tourns, he was r/u Philadelphia, Hong Kong, St Polten (d. Muster on clay), New Haven, Long Island (d. M. Chang and Enqvist) and GS Cup, adding sf Tokyo Japan Open, Stuttgart Eurocard and Stockholm and qf Sydney (d. Haarhuis) and Queen's (d. Courier). Qualified for his 1st ATP Champs, where he was just beaten to sf by Moya, whom he had beaten in rr. In doubles he

played 5 f with 3 different partners, winning Adelaide with Shelton and Queen's with Philippoussis. When he was playing Pioline at Paris Open, a laser beam was shone in his eyes from the crowd, but he went on to save 3 mps and win the match.

PRINCIPAL 1997 RESULTS – w 1, r/u 6, sf 4 (detailed Grand Slam results follow)
won US Open; **r/u** Philadelphia (d. Woodforde 6–2 6–2, Gimelstob 6–3 5–7 7–5, B. Black 6–3 1–6 6–1, Stafford 6–3 6–4, lost Sampras 5–7 7–6 6–3), **r/u** Hong Kong (d. Woodforde 2–6 7–6 6–4, Arriens 4–6 7–6 6–3, Woodbridge 6–3 6–1, MacPhie 3–6 6–1 3–0 ret'd, lost M. Chang 6–3 6–3), **r/u** St Polten (d. Fromberg 7–6 7–6, Tarango 6–7 6–2 6–1, Muster 6–3 7–6, M. Norman 6–1 4–6 6–3, lost Filippini 7–6 6–2), **r/u** New Haven (d. Martelli 6–3 6–4, Medvedev 6–3 2–6 6–4, Bruguera 7–5 2–6 6–2, Rusedski 7–5 4–6 6–3, lost Kafelnikov 7–6 6–4), **r/u** Long Island (d. Kucera 6–3 3–6 6–3, Ulihrach 7–5 7–5, M. Chang 6–4 3–6 6–1, Enqvist 6–4 6–4, lost Moya 6–4 7–6), **r/u** GS Cup; **sf** French Open, **sf** Tokyo Japan Open (d. Ran 6–0 6–4, Holm 6–1 6–2, Woodbridge 6–4 7–6, lost Krajicek 7–6 6–3), **sf** Stuttgart Eurocard (d. Enqvist w.o., Prinosil 3–6 6–2 6–1, R. Martin 4–6 7–6 6–4, lost Korda 6–4 7–6), **sf** Stockholm (d. Tillstrom 6–3 6–0, Van Herck 6–3 6–4, Henman 6–3 6–3, lost Bjorkman 7–6 7–6). **1997 HIGHLIGHTS – DOUBLES:** (with Philippoussis unless stated) (with Shelton) **won** Adelaide (d. Woodbridge/Woodforde 6–4 1–6 6–3), **won** Queen's (d. Stolle/Suk 6–2 4–6 7–5); **r/u** Indian Wells (lost Knowles/Nestor 7–6 4–6 7–5), (with Gimelstob) **r/u** Tokyo Japan Open (lost Damm/Vacek 2–6 6–2 7–6), **r/u** Cincinnati (lost Woodbridge/Woodforde 7–6 4–6 6–4).

CAREER GRAND SLAM RECORD

AUSTRALIAN OPEN – Played 6

1992: 1r lost Grabb 3-6 6-0 7-6 6-2. **1993: 1r** lost Siemerink 4–6 2–6 6–3 6–4 6–2. **1994: 3r** d. Wekesa 6–1 3–6 6–1 6–2, Eltingh 6–4 6–4 6–4, lost Daufresne 5–7 6–2 6–1 6–4. **1995: last 16** [unseeded] d. Hlasek 6–3 1–6 5–7 7–6 6–3, Campbell 6–4 7–6 6–2, Ondruska 6–3 1–6 3–6 6–2 6–2, lost Agassi [2] 6–3 6–4 6–0. **1996: 2r** d. Rios 6–3 6–4 6–3, lost Hadad 7–6 6–4 2–2 ret'd. **1997: 1r** lost A. Costa [10] 7–5 6–2 7–5.

FRENCH OPEN – Played 4, sf 1

1994: last 16 [unseeded] d. Davin 6–7 6–4 2–6 6–4 7–5, Roux 6–2 6–4 6–4, Muster [11] 6–4 5–7 6–3 6–3, lost Bruguera [6] 6–4 6–3 6–1. **1995: 1r** lost Bruguera [7] 6–3 6–1 7–6. **1996: 1r** lost Moya 6–4 7–6 6–2. **1997: sf** [unseeded] d. Gaudenzi 3–6 7–6 6–3 6–4, Fontang 6–3 6–4 6–3, Krajicek [6] 6–3 4–6 6–4 6–2, Woodforde 6–2 5–7 6–1 6–2, Blanco 6–3 7–6 6–3, lost Bruguera [16] 6–7 6–1 7–5 7–6.

WIMBLEDON – Played 5

1993: 3r d. Youl 6–3 6–3 6–4, Nelson 7–6 6–4 6–2, lost Agassi [d 8] 6–1 6–7 6–0 6–3. **1994 2r** d. Morgan 6–4 5–7 6–4 7–6, lost Bruguera [8] 7–6 3–6 4–6 7–5 13-11. **1995: 1r** lost Woodforde 3–6 6–1 7–6 6–4. **1996: last 16** d. Vacek 6–2 6–4 7–6, Pozzi 6–1 7–5 6–4, Rosset [14] 4–6 6–3 4–6 6–1 6–3, lost Ivanisevic [4] 7–6 4–6 7–6 6–3. **1997: last 16** [12] d. Stafford 2–6 4–6 6–3 6–2 6–2, Knippschild 6–3 4–6 6–3 6–0, Van Garsse 7–5 6–4 4–6 6–3, lost Woodbridge 6–7 6–4 7–6 6–3.

US OPEN – Played 5, won 1

1993: 1r lost D. Flach 3–6 6–3 6–2 6–1. **1994: 3r** d. Rikl 6–4 6–1 6–4, Apell 7–5 4–6 7–6 6–3, lost Martin [9] 7–5 6–3 6–7 6–2. **1995: 2r** d. Reneberg 7–6 6–3 6–4, lost Rosset 6–4 6–4 3–6 6–3. **1996: 1r** lost Carlsen 7–6 6–3 7–6. **1997: won** [seed 13] d. Medvedev 6–3 6–4 7–5, M. Norman 6–2 6–1 6–2, Roux 6–1 6–1 6–2, Agassi 6–3 7–6 4–6 6–3, Larsson 7–6 6–4 6–2, M. Chang [2] 6–3 6–3 6–4, Rusedski 6–3 6–2 4–6 7–5.

OLYMPIC RECORD

Has never competed.

CAREER DAVIS CUP RECORD

1994: March – *World Group 1r RUS d. AUS 4–1 in RUS (Carpet).* R1 lost Y. Kafelnikov 6–3 6–0 6–4; R4 lost A. volkov 6–4 7–6 6–3. **September** – *World Group Qualifying AUS d. NZL 4–1 in NZL (Carpet).* R2 d. J. Greenhalgh 7–5 6–2 6–3; R4 d. B. Steven 7–5 6–4 6–1. **1995: February** – *World Group 1r RSA d. AUS 3–2 in RSA (Hard).* R1 d. M. Ondruska 6–3 6–4 2–6 6–4; R4 lost W. Ferreira 6–2 3–6 6–4 6–2. **1996: September** – *World Group Qualifying AUS d. CRO 4–1 in CRO (Clay).* R3 (with M. Woodforde) d. S. Hirszon/G. Ivanisevic 6–3 6–2 6–4. **1997: February** – *World Group 1r AUS d. FRA 4–1 in AUS (Grass).* R1 d. C. Pioline 3–6 6–7 6–4 7–5 6–4; R5 lost A. Boetsch 4–6 4–6 6–7. **April** – *World Group qf AUS d. CZE 5–0 in AUS (Grass)* R1 d. M. Damm 6–1 7–6 4–6 6–4; R5 d. D. Rikl 7–6 0–6 6–2. **September** – *World Group sf USA d. AUS 4–1 in USA (Hard).* R1 lost M. Chang 6–4 1–6 6–3 6–4; R4 lost P. Sampras 6–7 6–1 6–1 6–4.

GRAND SLAM CUP RECORD – Played 1, r/u 1

1997: r/u [seed 2] d. Muster 6–2 6–3, Rios 6–1 7–6, Korda 7–5 3–6 6–7 7–6 9–7, lost Sampras [seed 1] 6–2 6–4 7–5.

GRAND PRIX MASTERS/ATP TOUR CHAMPIONSHIP – Played 1

1997: 3rd in rr d. Rusedski 4–6 6–3 6–2, d. Moya 6–4 6–2, lost Sampras 6–4 6–1.

3 MICHAEL CHANG (USA)

Born: Hoboken, NJ, 22 February 1972. **Lives:** Henderson, Nev. **Father:** Joe. **Mother:** Betty. Parents are research chemists from Taipei. **Brother:** Carl (older).
Agent: Advantage International. **Coaches:** His brother, Carl, since July 1991. First introduced to the game by his father who still guides him, and has been coached by Brian Gottfried, Jose Higueras and Phil Dent. **Turned pro:** 1988.
Height: 5ft 8in (1.73m). **Weight:** 145lb (65kg).

Rankings: 1987: 63; **1988:** 30; **1989:** 5; **1990:** 15; **1991:** 15; **1992:** 6; **1993:** 8; **1994:** 6; **1995:** 5; **1996:** 2. **1997:** 3.
Highest: 2 (9 September 1996).

1997 Prize Money: $2,541,830. **Career Earnings:** $16,286,739. **Career Titles:** 31.

Style: A small but athletic right-hander with a two-handed backhand whose astonishing speed about the court and indomitable will-to-win enable him to beat larger and stronger men. His return of serve and passing shots make him the bane of every serve-and-volley player. A much improved serve and a greater willingness to volley make him an even more formidable opponent.

CAREER HIGHLIGHTS (year: (titles))
1987: At 15 yrs 6 mths he was the youngest player to compete in men's singles at US Open since 1918, and was the youngest ever to win a match in GS tourn, having been granted a wild card after winning US 18s at Kalamazoo. At 15 yrs 7 mths was youngest to win a pro tourn at Las Vegas Challenger and was the youngest ever GP semi-finalist at Scottsdale. **1988: (1)** *San Francisco*. At 16 yrs 4 mths was the youngest for 60 years to win a match in Wimbledon main draw, and when he won his 1st title at San Francisco at 16 yrs 7 mths, he was youngest to win a SS event and second-youngest after Krickstein to win a GP title. **1989: (2)** *FRENCH OPEN, Wembley*. At the French Open aged 17 yrs 3 mths, he became the youngest male winner of a GS tourn and the 1st American since Trabert in 1955 to win that title. In 5s of his 4r match v Lendl, he was so badly affected with cramp that he had to serve underarm. Was the youngest to play D Cup for USA, making his debut v PAR, and the youngest to break into top 5. **1990: (1)** *Canadian Open*. Out until March with stress fracture of cup of left hip suffered Dec. 1989. Won 1st HC title at Canadian Open. In winning US D Cup team, in sf coming back from 2 sets to 1 down v Skoff to take US into f, where USA d. AUS 3–2. **1991: (1)** *Birmingham*. He had to wait until Nov. before winning his 1st title of the year at Birmingham. R/u to Wheaton in GS Cup, winning $1 million. **1992: (3)** *Indian Wells, LIPC, San Francisco*. Returned to top 10 1st time since July 1991 after winning Indian Wells, following with LIPC (d. Sampras and Courier) and San Francisco (d. Courier again). Was also r/u Hong Kong and appeared in sf Tokyo Suntory (losing both times to Courier) and reached same stage Cincinnati, Long Island and Tokyo Seiko (losing all 3 to Lendl). His best showing in GS was sf US Open, where he survived 5s matches v Washington and W. Ferreira, but lost a 3rd over the same length v Edberg. Qualified for ATP World Champ, but won no match there. Wore spectacles on court 1st time at Gstaad in July, switching from contact lenses after suffering build-up problems. **1993: (5)** *Jakarta, Osaka, Cincinnati, Kuala Lumpur Salem Open, Beijing*. He beat Agassi and Edberg back-to-back to win Cincinnati in Aug., but enjoyed his greatest success in Asia, where he won 4 of his 5 titles across the year. His GS record was more disappointing, though, with his best showing qf US Open. At Wimbledon he played 3 5s matches before falling 3r to Wheaton, who also beat him 2r Australian Open, and Karbacher beat him same stage French Open. A member of the winning US World Team Cup squad, he was r/u Los Angeles and Long Island (d. Edberg) and reached 4 more sf to qualify for IBM/ATP World Champ where he won only match 1 (v Courier) in rr. **1994: (6)** *Jakarta, Philadelphia, Hong Kong, Atlanta, Cincinnati, Beijing*. After winning Jakarta in Jan., he took a 3-month break, missing Australian Open, to work on fitness and strength. He returned to take 5 more titles, including Beijing in Oct. – his 7th title in Asia. Atlanta was his 1st title on clay since 1989 and his 3rd on a different surface in 1994. He was r/u both Tokyo tourns and San Jose, and at Antwerp beat Ivanisevic for the 1st time. However,

he disappointed again at IBM/ATP World Champ, where he beat only Berasategui. Playing GS Cup for fifth time (the only man to do so), lost qf to Sampras. **1995: (4)** *Hong Kong, Atlanta, Tokyo Seiko, Beijing*. He played during the year with a slightly longer-handled racket. Continued his success in Asia, taking 3 of his 4 titles of the year there to complete 10 out of 23 in his career. Working on his serve to make it more of a weapon, he rediscovered his CC form in reaching f French Open – his best performance since he won in 1989. He also reached f San Jose, Philadelphia and Cincinnati, sf Australian Open and Tokyo Japan Open and 4 more qf. His year finished on a high note when he upset Sampras in sf IBM/ATP Champ and finished r/u to Becker, never before having progressed beyond rr. **1996: (3)** *Indian Wells, Washington, Los Angeles*. At Australian Open he defied a stomach injury to beat Agassi in ss and extend Becker to 4s in f, then upset Agassi again on his way to the title at Indian Wells. However, at French Open he could not overcome a pulled abdominal muscle as he lost to an inspired Edberg in 3r, and at Wimbledon A. Costa beat him 1r. Things looked up again after that as he reached the top 3 1st time after winning Washington. He then won his next tourn at Los Angeles and reached f the following week at Cincinnati. At US Open, where he was controversially seeded 2 ahead of Muster, who was ranked above him, he upset Agassi again and was r/u to Sampras. This result took him to the No. 2 slot, and had he beaten Sampras, he would have passed him at the top of the rankings. Although his results in Asia were less impressive than before, he was r/u Hong Kong and Singapore, and also reached sf San Jose, Memphis, Atlanta and Stuttgart Eurocard, plus 3 more qf. His season tailed off in disappointment at ATP Champs, where he won only 1 rr match, and he missed GS Cup 1st time after withdrawing with tendinitis in ankle. **1997: (5)** *Memphis, Indian Wells, Hong Kong, Orlando, Washington*. Although he never looked likely to displace Sampras at the top of the rankings, he held on to his 2nd position until Rafter overtook him at the end of the year. He won all 5 f he played, winning Memphis, Indian Wells, Hong Kong (his 11th title in Asia), Orlando and Washington. He did not find his best form in GS, and although he reached sf Australian Open and US Open, he fell to Bruguera last 16 French Open and at Wimbledon Woodbridge eventually ousted him 8–6 fs 1r. He also appeared in sf Rosmalen, Montreal and Cincinnati, plus qf San Jose and Long Island. Yet again he was disappointing at ATP Champs, winning only 1 match, and lost his No. 2 ranking to Rafter. In D Cup f lost vital opening rubber to Bjorkman and final dead rubber to Larsson as USA went down 5–0 to SWE.

PRINCIPAL 1997 RESULTS – won 5, sf 5 (detailed Grand Slam results follow)
won Memphis (d. Rafter 6–2 6–4, Carlsen 6–7 6–2 6–0, Reneberg 7–6 6–4, Martin 3–6 6–4 6–4, Woodbridge 6–3 6–4), **won** Indian Wells (d. Schalken 6–4 6–3, Rosset 6–2 7–5, Pioline 6–3 6–2, Muster 6–1 7–6, Ulihrach 4–6 6–3 6–4 6–3), **won** Hong Kong (d. Tong 6–0 6–1, Tarango 6–4 4–6 6–1, Prinosil 6–1 7–6, Johansson 7–6 6–4, Rafter 6–3 6–3), **won** Orlando (d. Gambill 6–3 6–3, Viloca 6–2 6–7 7–5, B. Black 7–5 6–3, Stoltenberg 4–6 6–3 6–3, Stafford 4–6 6–2 6–1), **won** Washington (d. Herrera 6–3 6–7 7–6, Joyce 4–6 6–1 6–2, Draper 6–2 6–3, Steven 6–2 7–6, Korda 5–7 6–2 6–1); **sf** Australian Open, **sf** US Open, **sf** Rosmalen (d. Santoro 4–6 6–4 6–3, Radulescu 7–6 6–1, Clavet 6–7 7–6 6–1, lost Krajicek 6–7 6–3 6–4), **sf** Montreal (d. Stolle 6–1 1–0 ret'd, O'Brien 4–6 6–2 6–3, Krajicek 7–6 6–4, lost Kuerten 6–3 6–1), **sf** Cincinnati (d. W. Ferreira 6–7 6–1 6–2, Medvedev 3–6 6–1 6–4, Kuerten 6–1 6–2, lost Muster 6–3 4–6 7–6)

CAREER GRAND SLAM RECORD
AUSTRALIAN OPEN – Played 5, r/u 1, sf 2
1992: 3r [seed 14] d. Roese 6–2 6–3 6–0, Caratti 6–3 3–6 6–4 6–4, lost Krajicek 6–4 6–1 5–7 1–6 6–3. **1993: 2r** [seed 6] d. Bailey 6–3 6–1 6–1, lost Wheaton 6–4 6–3 1–6 6–3. **1994:** Did not play. **1995: sf** [seed 5] d. Kilderry 6–2 6–4 5–7 6–2, Alami 6–3 6–4 6–1, Damm 6–3 7–5 6–3, Delaitre 6–3 6–2 6–4, Medvedev [seed 13] 7–6 7–5 6–3, lost Sampras [seed 1] 6–7 6–3 6–4 6–4. **1996: r/u** [seed 5] d. Rikl 6–2 6–1 6–2, Hlasek 6–1 6–3 6–3, Raoux 6–2 6–2 7–6, Fleurian 6–3 6–3 6–4, Tillstrom 6–0 6–2 6–4, Agassi [2] 6–1 6–4 7–6, lost Becker [4] 6–2 6–4 2–6 6–2. **1997: sf** [seed 2] d. Goossens 6–0 6–3 6–1, Reneberg 6–3 7–5 6–1, Henman 6–1 7–6 6–3, Medvedev 4–6 6–2 6–2 6–1, Rios [9] 7–5 6–1 6–4, lost Moya 7–5 6–2 6–4.
FRENCH OPEN – Played 10, won 1, r/u 1, qf 2
1988: 3r d. Seguso 7–5 6–2 6–3, Svantesson 6–4 6–1 6–3, lost McEnroe [16] 6–0 6–3 6–1. **1989: won** [seed 15] d. Masso 6–7 6–3 6–0 6–3, Sampras 6–1 6–1 6–1, Roig 6–0 7–5 6–3, Lendl [1] 4–6 4–6 6–3 6–3 6–3, Agenor 6–4 2–6 6–4 7–6, Chesnokov 6–1 5–7 7–6 7–5, Edberg [3] 6–1 2–6 4–6 6–4 6–2. **1990 qf** [seed 11] d. Motta 6–2 7–6 6–1, Rosset 7–5 4–6 6–4 6–3, Bergstrom 2–6 5–7 6–0 6–2 6–4, E. Sanchez [6] 6–4 6–4 6–2, lost Agassi [3] 6–1 6–2 4–6 6–2. **1991: qf** [seed 10] d. Siemerink 6–2 6–0 6–3, Jonsson, 7–6 4–6 6–4 3–6 6–3, Connors 4–6 7–5 6–2 4–6 0–15 ret'd, Forget [7] 6–1 6–1 4–6 6–3, lost Becker [2] 6–4 6–4 6–2. **1992: 3r** [seed 5] d. Haarhuis 6–4 6–3 6–3, Gorriz 6–3 2–6 6–3 6–0, lost Kulti 7–5 2–6 6–3 3–6 8–6. **1993: 2r** [seed 8] d. Vitoux 6–4 6–2 6–3, lost Karbacher 1–6 6–3 6–4 6–2. **1994: 3r** [seed 8] d. Grabb 6–3 7–6 6–1,

Arrese 4–6 6–0 6–4 6–2, lost Yzaga 6–2 6–3 5–7 1–6 7–6. **1995: r/u** [seed 6] d. Nargiso 6–3 6–4 6–1, Vacek 6–3 5–7 6–4 6–4, Carbonell 6–1 6–2 7–6, Stich [12] 1–6 6–0 6–2 6–3, Voinea 7–5 6–0 6–1, Bruguera [7] 6–4 7–6 7–6, lost Muster [5] 7–5 6–2 6–4. **1996: 3r** [seed 4] d. Prinosil 6–1 6–1 6–2, Fromberg 6–4 3–6 7–6 6–4, lost Edberg 4–6 7–5 6–0 7–6. **1997: last 16** [seed 2] d. R. Gilbert 6–2 6–3 6–2, Golmard 6–2 6–3 3–6 6–2, Simian 6–1 5–2 ret'd, lost Bruguera [16] 3–6 6–4 6–3 6–4.

WIMBLEDON – Played 10, qf 1

1988: 2r d. Layendecker 7–5 1–6 6–4 6–2, lost Leconte [7] 2–6 7–6 6–2 6–3. **1989: last 16** [seed 9] d. Scanlon 6–4 6–3 2–6 6–3, Agenor 4–6 6–2 6–1 7–5, Schapers 4–6 6–3 7–5 7–5, lost Mayotte [8] 6–3 6–1 6–3. **1990: last 16** [seed 13] d. Altur 5–7 6–4 6–3 7–5, Pugh 6–3 6–2 6–2, Kratzmann 3–6 4–6 6–4 6–2 6–2, lost Edberg [3] 6–3 6–2 6–1. **1991: 1r** [seed 9] lost Mayotte 6–7 4–6 6–1 7–6 6–2. **1992: 1r** [seed 7] lost Bates 6–4 6–3 6–3. **1993: 3r** [seed 12] d. Haarhuis 6–2 6–2 4–6 6–7 6–4, Woodbridge 6–7 6–3 6–4 3–6 6–4, lost Wheaton 6–4 6–4 5–7 4–6 6–4. **1994: qf** [seed 10] d. A. Costa 7–6 6–4 6–2, Tebbutt 3–6 6–3 7–6 6–7 6–4, Connell 7–6 6–4 6–2, Bruguera [8] 6–4 7–6 6–0, lost Sampras [seed 1] 6–4 6–1 6–3. **1995: 2r** [seed 5] d. Roux 6–3 6–4 4–6 6–2, lost Korda 6–4 6–4 6–4. **1996: 1r** [seed 6] lost A. Costa 3–6 7–6 7–6 6–4. **1997: 1r** [seed 5] lost Woodbridge 7–6 3–6 6–2 3–6 8–6.

US OPEN – Played 11, r/u 1, sf 2, qf 1

1987: 2r d. McNamara 6–3 6–7 6–4 6–4, lost Odizor 6–1 6–2 6–7 3–6 6–4. **1988: last 16** d. Mattar 6–4 6–3 7–5, Svensson [13] 5–7 6–4 2–6 6–1 6–4, Wilkison 4–6 3–6 6–3 6–4 7–5, lost Agassi [4] 7–5 6–3 6–2. **1989: last 16** [seed 7] d. Wilkison 7–5 6–3 6–2, Hogstedt 6–1 6–3 6–3, Aldrich 6–0 7–6 6–4, lost Mayotte [9] 7–5 6–1 1–6 6–3. **1990: 3r** [seed 11] d. Pernfors 6–0 6–2 6–3, Arias 7–6 6–3 6–2, lost Cherkasov 6–4 6–4 6–3. **1991: last 16** d. Woodforde 6–3 6–0 6–2, Witsken 6–3 6–0 6–2, J. McEnroe [16] 6–4 4–6 7–6 2–6 6–3, lost Edberg [2] 7–6 7–5 6–3. **1992: sf** [seed 4] d. E. Ferreira 6–3 6–4 7–6, P. McEnroe 6–3 6–3 6–4, Boetsch 6–3 6–3 6–1, Washington [14] 6–2 2–6 3–6 6–3 6–1, W. Ferreira [12] 7–5 2–6 6–3 6–7 6–1, lost Edberg [2] 6–7 7–5 7–6 5–7 6–4. **1993: qf** [seed 7] d. Cannon 6–1 7–5 6–2, Pereira 6–1 6–2 4–6 6–3, Karbacher 4–6 6–4 6–3 6–4, Ferreira 6–4 6–3 6–4, lost Sampras [2] 6–7 7–6 6–1 6–1. **1994: last 16** [seed 6] d. Cherkasov 6–4 6–2 6–2, MaliVai Washington 4–6 6–2 6–3 7–6, Grabb 6–1 4–1 ret'd, lost Agassi 6–1 6–7 6–3 3–6 6–1. **1995: qf** [seed 5] d. Pozzi 6–0 6–1 6–0, Pescosolido 4–6 6–3 6–4 6–4, Woodbridge 6–3 6–2 6–0, Tebbutt 6–2 6–2 4–6 6–3, lost Courier [seed 14] 7–6 7–6 7–5. **1996: r/u** [seed 2] d. Oncins 3–6 6–1 6–0 7–6, Godwin 6–1 6–3 6–1, Spadea 6–4 5–7 2–6 7–5 6–3, Hlasek 6–3 6–4 6–2, J. Sanchez 7–5 6–3 6–7 6–3, Agassi [6] 6–3 6–2 6–2, lost Sampras [1] 6–1 6–4 7–6. **1997: sf** [seed 2] d. Fredriksson 6–3 6–4 6–2, Salzenstein 4–6 6–2 6–3 6–4, Pioline 6–3 0–6 5–7 7–5 6–1, Rios [10] 7–5 6–2 4–6 4–6 6–3, lost Rafter 6–3 6–3 6–4.

OLYMPIC RECORD

1992: (Barcelona) 2r [seed 6] d. Mancini 6–1 6–4 3–6 6–0, lost Oncins 6–2 3–6 6–3 6–3.

CAREER DAVIS CUP RECORD

1989: February – *World Group 1r USA d. PAR 5–0 in USA (Hard).* R1 d. V. Pecci 6–7 6–3 6–4 6–2; R4 d. H. Chapacu 5–7 6–0 6–1. **1990: September** – *World Group sf USA d. AUT 3–2 in AUT (Clay).* R1 lost T. Muster 4–6 6–2 6–2 6–4; R5 d. H. Skoff 3–6 6–7 6–4 6–4 6–3. **1990: December** – *World Group Final USA d. AUS 3–2 in USA (Clay).* R2 d. D. Cahill 6–2 7–6 6–0; R5 lost R. Fromberg 7–5 2–6 6–3. **1996: February** – *World Group 1r USA d. MEX 5–0 in USA (Hard).* R1 d. L. Lavalle 6–1 6–2 6–4; R4 d. A. Hernandez 6–0 6–2. **1997: September** – *World Group sf USA d. AUS 4–1 in USA (Hard).* R1 d. P. Rafter 6–4 1–6 6–3 6–4; R5 d. M. Philippoussis 7–6 7–6). **November** – *World Group Final SWE d. USA 5–0 in SWE (Hard)* R1 lost Bjorkman 7–5 1–6 6–3 6–3; R5 lost Larsson 7–6 6–7 6–4.

GRAND SLAM CUP RECORD – Played 6, r/u 2, sf 1, qf 2

1990: sf [unseeded] d. Edberg [1] 6–4 4–6 7–5, Leconte 7–6 6–3, lost Sampras [4] 6–3 6–4 6–4. **1991: r/u** [unseeded] d. Courier [2] 6–4 6–2, P. McEnroe [8] 6–2 6–4, Lendl [4] 2–6 4–6 6–4 7–6 9–7, lost Wheaton 7–5 6–2 6–4. **1992: r/u** [unseeded] d. Agassi [2] 6–4 6–2, Korda [7] 6–3 6–4, Ivanisevic [4] 6–7 6–2 6–4 3–6 6–3, lost Stich 6–2 6–3 6–2. **1993: qf** [unseeded] d. Masur [8] 6–2 4–6 7–5, lost Sampras [1] 7–6 6–3. **1994: qf** [seed 8] d. Berasategui 6–1 7–5, lost Sampras 6–4 6–3. **1995: 1r** [seed 4] lost Eltingh 7–6 6–3. **1996–97:** Did not play.

GRAND PRIX MASTERS/ATP TOUR CHAMPIONSHIP (from 1990) – Played 7, r/u 1

1989: Equal 4th in rr lost Lendl 6–1 6–3, lost McEnroe 6–2 5–7 6–4, lost Krickstein 6–3 7–6. **1992: Equal 4th in rr** lost Ivanisevic 7–6 6–2, lost Krajicek 2–6 6–3 7–6, lost Courier 7–5 6–2. **1993: 3rd in rr** d. Courier 6–4 6–0, lost Stich 4–6 7–6 6–2, lost Medvedev 2–6 6–4 6–2. **1994: 3rd in rr** lost Bruguera 7–6 7–5, d. Berasategui 6–1 6–0, lost Agassi 6–4 6–4. **1995: r/u** in rr d. Muster 4–6 6–2 6–3, lost Enqvist 6–1 6–4, d. Courier 6–2 7–5; sf d. Sampras 6–4 6–4; f lost Becker 7–6 6–0 7–6. **1996: Equal 3rd in rr** lost Krajicek 6–4 6–4, d. Ivanisevic 6–7 7–6 6–1, lost Muster 6–4 6–3. **1997: 4th in rr** d. Bruguera 7–6 6–2, lost Kafelnikov 6–3 6–0, lost Bjorkman 6–4 7–5.

4 JONAS BJORKMAN (SWE)

Born: Vaxjo, 23 March 1972. **Lives:** Monte Carlo, Monaco.
Father: Lars. **Mother:** Margareta. **Siblings:** One sister.
Agent: Advantage International. **Coach:** Fredrik Rosengren.
Turned pro: 1991.
Height: 6ft (1.84m). **Weight:** 166lb (76kg).

Rankings: 1991: 691; **1992:** 331; **1993:** 95; **1994:** 50; **1995:** 30; **1996:** 69; **1997:** 4 singles, 17 doubles.
Highest: 4 (10 November 1997).

1997 Prize Money: $1,950,375.
Career Earnings: $4,218,490. **Career titles:** 3.

Style: A right-hander with one of the finest service returns in the modern game, he creates early openings which are despatched from mid-court with fierce forehands and flat double-handed backhands of great power and penetration. Fitter and faster than he used to be, he is now happy to mount attacks at the net, where his volleys are sound. A much improved serve makes him a well-rounded performer capable of beating anyone.

CAREER HIGHLIGHTS (year: (titles))
Former Nat Jun champ. **1992:** Began to make his mark on the satellite circuit. **1993:** Reached qf Kuala Lumpur Salem Open and won 3 Challenger titles, which took him into the top 100. **1994:** Unseeded at Wimbledon, he took advantage of the removal of Edberg by Carlsen and the Dane's retirement during their encounter next day to reach last 16, and at US Open he upset Edberg himself on his way to qf, again unseeded. Reached sf Schenectady (d. Bruguera) plus qf Marseille, Tel Aviv and Antwerp. In doubles he appeared in his 1st GS f at French Open with Apell, and with various partners he won 8 titles from 11 other f. He and Apell won 6 titles on 4 different surfaces during the year, including their 1st World Doubles Champ. Member of victorious SWE D Cup team, winning doubles with Apell. **1995:** In singles he broke into top 25 after reaching his 1st f at Hong Kong. He also reached sf LIPC and Vienna, plus 4 more qf, and played on winning SWE WT Cup team. He played 5 doubles f, winning 1 with regular partner Apell and 1 each with de Jager and Frana after Apell underwent shoulder surgery in Sept. **1996:** Although it was a less impressive year in singles, he reached sf Rosmalen (d. Siemerink) and qf US CC and Los Angeles. At Australian Open, where he was unseeded, he upset Martin and extended Agassi to 5s. Played 7 doubles f with 3 different partners, winning Antwerp and New Delhi with Kulti, with whom he qualified for World Doubles Champ, although they did not pass rr. Lost vital doubles with Kulti as SWE lost 3–2 to FRA in D Cup f. **1997: (3)** *Auckland, Indianapolis, Stockholm.* In by far his his best year to date, he won his 1st career singles title at Auckland and broke into the top 20 after taking his 2nd at Indianapolis. He moved on into the top 5 in Oct., moving to a career-high No. 4 after winning Stockholm. He was consistent through the year with r/u Coral Springs and Paris Open, sf Memphis (d. Haarhuis), Scottsdale (d. Rafter and A. Costa), Indian Wells, Queen's (d. Sampras), Rosmalen, Stuttgart Eurocard, US Open (unseeded, extended Rusedski to 7–5 fs), plus qf Adelaide (losing 15–17 on tb v Tarango), LIPC (d. Rios) and GS Cup (d. Becker). Qualifying for his 1st ATP Champs, he reached sf before losing in ss to Sampras. From 4 doubles f won Atlanta and was r/u US Open, both with Kulti. Played No.1 in winning SWE D Cup team against the Americans in Gothenburg, contributing two singles wins.

PRINCIPAL 1997 RESULTS – won 3, r/u 2, sf 6 (detailed Grand Slam results follow)
SINGLES: won Auckland (d. C. Costa 6–4 6–2, Ruud 6–0 7–5, Gambill 6–4 6–0, Ondruska 6–1 6–1, Carlsen 7–5 6–0), **won** Indianapolis (d. Smith 6–2 7–6, Roux 6–3 6–3, Woodbridge 6–2 7–5, Ho 5–7 6–4 7–5, Woodforde 6–0 6–2, Moya 6–4 6–2), **won** Stockholm (d. Goellner 6–4 5–2 ret'd, Johansson 6–4 7–5, Kucera 6–3 6–2, Rafter 7–6 7–6, Siemerink 3–6 7–6 6–2 6–4); **r/u** Coral Springs (d. Zabaleta 6–3 6–2, L. Jensen 6–1 6–2, Viloca 6–4 7–6, Campbell 6–4 4–6 6–4, lost Stoltenberg 6–0 2–6 7–5), **r/u** Paris Open (d. Johansson 6–3 6–7 7–6, Woodbridge 7–6 7–5, Krajicek 6–4 0–1 ret'd, Enqvist 7–6 7–5, lost Sampras 6–3 4–6 6–3 6–1); **sf** Memphis (d. Fromberg 6–4 6–3, Frana 6–0 6–4, Haarhuis 6–3 6–4, lost Woodbridge 6–1 7–5), **sf** Scottsdale (d. O'Brien 6–4 1–6 7–5, Rafter 3–6 6–1 7–6, A. Costa 6–4 2–6 6–4, lost Reneberg 6–3 6–3), **sf** Indian Wells (d. Gaudenzi 6–1 6–3, Tarango 6–4 6–2, Woodruff 2–6 7–5 6–1, Berasategui 6–2 6–3,

lost Ulihrach 6–3 6–2), **sf** Queen's (d. Herrera 7–5 7–5, Simian 6–4 7–5, Sampras 3–6 6–3 6–4, lost Philippoussis 2–6 7–6 6–2), **sf** Rosmalen (d. Kroslak 5–7 7–5 6–1, Vacek 6–1 6–2, Wibier 6–2 6–4, lost Raoux 6–0 6–1), **sf** Stuttgart Eurocard (d. Siemerink 6–3 6–4, Henman 6–2 3–6 6–3, Kiefer 6–4 6–2, lost Krajicek 6–4 3–6 6–3). **DOUBLES:** (with Kulti unless stated) **r/u US Open** (lost Kafelnikov/Vacek 7–6 6–3); **won** Atlanta (d. Davis/Jones 6–2 7–6); (with Leach) **r/u** Scottsdale (lost Lobo/J. Sanchez 6–3 6–3), **r/u** Indianapolis (lost Tebbutt/Tillstrom)

CAREER GRAND SLAM RECORD

AUSTRALIAN OPEN – Played 4

1994: 2r d. Thorne 3–6 6–4 6–7 7–5 6–2, lost Martin [9] 6–1 5–7 6–2 6–2. **1995: 3r** d. Ruud 6–3 6–3 6–2, Forget 6–4 1–6 2–6 6–4 6–3, lost Kafelnikov [10] 4–6 6–1 6–2 7–6. **1996: last 16** [unseeded] d. Ilie 7–5 6–3 6–7 6–7 6–4, Henman 6–1 6–3 6–2, Martin [15] 6–3 3–6 6–3 2–6 6–4, lost Agassi [2] 4–6 6–2 4–6 6–1 6–2. **1997: last 16** [unseeded] d. Ulihrach 1–6 6–1 6–4 6–2, Goellner 6–4 3–6 6–4 6–1, Braasch 6–4 7–6 6–3, lost Moya 6–3 1–6 3–6 6–2 6–4.

FRENCH OPEN – Played 4

1994: 3r d. Arnold 6–7 7–6 6–1 3–6 9–7, Dosedel 6–0 7–5 6–3, lost Courier [7] 6–3 6–1 6–1. **1995: 1r** lost Draper 6–7 6–3 6–3 3–6 6–2. **1996: last 16** [unseeded] d. Dewulf 6–4 6–4 6–3, Champion 6–7 6–1 6–4 6–0, Woodruff 7–6 2–4 4–6 7–5 6–4, lost Krajicek [13] 6–3 6–2 6–4. **1997: 2r** d. Reneberg 6–2 6–1 1–6 6–2, lost Kuerten 6–4 6–2 4–6 7–5.

WIMBLEDON – Played 4

1994: last 16 [unseeded] d. Petchey 6–2 6–1 2–6 2–6 6–1, Ondruska 6–3 4–6 6–3 3–6 6–3, Carlsen 6–4 6–4 1–0 ret'd, lost W. Ferreira 6–3 6–7 6–4 6–3. **1995: 2r** d. Burgsmuller 6–1 6–1 6–1, lost W. Ferreira [7] 6–2 6–4 6–3. **1996: 1r** lost Milligan 4–6 6–1 2–6 7–5 6–4. **1997: 1r** [seed 17] lost Wilkinson 7–6 0–6 5–7 6–3 6–4.

US OPEN – Played 5, sf 1, qf 1

1993: 2r d. Simian 6–4 6–3 6–3, lost Mansdorf 6–3 6–3 7–5. **1994: qf** [unseeded] d. Stark 6–2 6–2 7–5, O'Brien 6–2 6–3 6–4, Edberg [5] 6–4 6–4 6–3, Renzenbrink 3–6 6–3 6–2 6–7 6–3, lost Stich [4] 6–4 6–4 6–7 6–3. **1995: 3r** d. Knowles 6–1 7–5 6–1, Haarhuis 6–4 6–4 6–3, lost B. Black 6–3 7–6 6–1. **1996: 3r** d. Kucera 6–2 5–7 7–6 7–5, Nainkin 6–4 6–1 6–1, lost Corretja 6–2 4–6 6–4 6–4 6–3. **1997: sf** [unseeded] d. Clavet 6–2 6–4 6–4, T. Martin 7–5 6–4 6–0, Kuerten 6–3 6–1 7–5, Draper 6–3 6–3 1–6 7–6, Korda [15] 7–6 6–2 1–0 ret'd, lost Rusedski 6–1 3–6 3–6 6–3 7–5.

OLYMPIC RECORD

1996: (Atlanta) 1r lost Agassi [1] 7–6 7–6.

CAREER DAVIS CUP RECORD

1994: March – *World Group 1r SWE d. DEN 5–0 in SWE (Carpet).* R3 (+ J. Apell) d. K. Carlsen/M. Christensen 6–7 7–6 7–6 2–6 6–2. **July** – *World Group qf SWE d. FRA 3–2 in FRA (Hard).* R3 (+ Apell) d. O. Delaitre/J. P. Fleurian 6–1 6–4 6–4. **September** – *World Group sf SWE d. USA 3–2 in SWE (Carpet).* R3 (+ Apell) d. J. Palmer/J. Stark 6–4 6–4 3–6 6–2. **December** – *World Group final SWE d. RUS 4–1 in RUA (Carpet).* R3 (+ Apell) d. Y. Kafelnikov/A. Olhovskiy 6–7 6–2 6–3 1–6 8–6. **1995: February** – *World Group 1r SWE d. DEN 3–2 in DEN (Carpet).* R1 lost K. Carlsen 4–6 6–3 6–4 6–4; R3 (+ J. Apell) d. Carlsen/M. Christensen 6–7 6–3 6–4 6–2. R5 d. F. Fetterlein 6–7 6–4 6–7 6–3 6–4. **April** – *World Group qf SWE d. AUT 5–0 in SWE (Carpet).* R3 (+ Apell) d. A. Antonitsch/T. Muster 7–5 6–3 6–3. **September** – *World Group sf USA d. SWE 4–1 (Hard).* R3 (+ S. Edberg) d. T. Martin/J. Stark 6–3 6–4 6–4. **1996: February** – *World Group 1r SWE d. BEL 4–1 in SWE (Carpet).* R3 (+ N. Kulti) d. F. Dewulf/D. Norman 6–3 6–1 6–4. **April** – *World Group qf SWE d. IND 5–0 in IND (Grass).* R1 d. L. Paes 1–6 6–4 5–7 6–3 7–5; R3 (+ Kulti) d. M. Bhupathi/Paes 6–7 6–3 6–4 6–1. R5 d. Bhupathi 6–2 6–4. **September** – *World Group sf SWE d. CZE 4–1 in CZE (Carpet).* R3 (+ Kulti) lost P. Korda/D. Vacek 4–6 6–3 6–4 6–4. **November** – *World Group final FRA d. SWE 3–2 in SWE (Hard).* R3 (+ Kulti) lost G. Forget/G. Raoux 6–3 1–6 6–3 6–3. **1997: April** – *World Group qf SWE d. RSA 3–2 in SWE (Carpet).* R2 lost W. Ferreira 6–3 6–4 2–6 7–6; R3 (+ N. Kulti) d. D. Adams/E. Ferreira 7–5 2–6 6–4 6–7 6–2. R5 d. G. Stafford 3–6 6–0 3–6 6–2 6–2. **September** – *World Group sf SWE d. ITA 4–1 in SWE (Carpet).* R1 d. O. Camporese 6–7 6–3 6–2 3–6 6–3; R3 (+ Kulti) d. Camporese/D. Nargiso 6–1 6–1 6–2. R4 d. R. Furlan 4–6 6–4 6–0 6–4. **November** – *World Group Final SWE d. USA 5–0 in SWE (Hard).* R1 d. M. Chang 7–5 1–6 6–3 6–3; R4 d. J. Stark 6–1 6–1.

GRAND SLAM CUP RECORD – Played 1, qf 1

1997: qf d. Becker 6–3 6–2, lost Sampras [1] 7–6 6–4.

GRAND PRIX MASTERS/ATP TOUR CHAMPIONSHIP – Played 1, sf 1

1997: sf in rr lost Kafelnikov 6–3 7–6, d. Bruguera 6–3 6–1, d. M. Chang 6–4 7–5; sf lost Sampras 6–3 6–4.

5 YEVGENY KAFELNIKOV (RUS)

Born: Sochi, 18 February 1974. **Lives:** Sochi.
Father: Aleksandre. **Mother:** Valentina.
Agent: IMG. **Coach:** Anatoli Lepeshin. **Turned pro:** 1992.
Height: 6ft 3in (1.90m). **Weight:** 173lb (78kg).

Rankings: 1992: 314; **1993:** 104; **1994:** 11; **1995:** 6; **1996:** 3; **1997:** 5 singles, 6 doubles. **Highest:** 3 (4 November 1996).

1997 Prize Money: $3,207,757.
Career Earnings: $9,604,741. **Career Titles:** 14.

Style: An elegant groundstroke artist whose returns of serve on both wings, single-handed on forehand, double on backhand, are the foundation of his powerful game. A sound serve-and-volley technique makes him a threat on any surface.

CAREER HIGHLIGHTS (year: (titles))
1990: In winning USSR World Youth Cup team. **1992:** Began to make his mark on the Eastern European satellite circuits. **1993:** Upset Stich on his way to qf Barcelona in spring and again at Lyon in autumn. **1994: (3)** *Adelaide, Copenhagen, Long Island*. He sprang to prominence and the top 100 by winning his 1st tour title in his 1st f at Adelaide on HC. In 2r Australian Open he took Sampras to 9–7 5s, followed with the title at Copenhagen on carpet in Feb. and was ranked as high as 36 by March. In April he upset Agassi and Stich to reach sf Monte Carlo; in May he upset Ivanisevic and Stich on his way to f Hamburg, moving into the top 20, and in June he surprised Courier to reach sf Halle. He continued his winning ways by upsetting M. Chang on his way to the title at Long Island in Aug., upset Muster *en route* to sf Gstaad, Edberg and Bruguera to reach sf Stockholm and appeared in the same stage New Haven, plus 5 more qf across the year, to finish the year poised just outside the top 10. He was also a successful doubles player, winning 4 titles from 6 f with various partners. Led RUS to their first ever D Cup f and was voted Most Improved Player of the Year. **1995: (4)** *Milan, St Petersburg, Gstaad, Long Island*. Broke into the top 10 after his qf appearance at Australian Open. Upset Agassi, who was injured, at French Open and removed both Ivanisevic and Becker on his way to the title at Milan, going on to win St Petersburg, Gstaad and Long Island. He was r/u Nice, and reached sf Rotterdam, Barcelona, Gstaad, New Haven and Lyon, plus 6 more qf. In doubles played 6 f with various partners, winning 3, and was the 1st player since E. Sanchez in 1990 to end the year in top 10 both singles and doubles. In D Cup with Olhovskiy saved 5 mps to upset Becker and Stich, although he won only 1 of his 3 matches in f as RUS lost 3–2 to USA. **1996: (4)** *FRENCH OPEN, Adelaide, Prague, Lyon*. The high point of his career came with a magnificent performance at French Open, where he won both singles and doubles (with Vacek, in only their 3rd tourn together). He became 1st Russian since Metreveli in 1973 to reach GS f and 1st player since Rosewall in 1968 to win both singles and doubles there. He played a heavy schedule, winning Adelaide, Prague and Lyon, as well as r/u Rotterdam, St Petersburg, Halle, Stuttgart, Paris Open and Moscow, plus sf Milan, Hamburg, Gstaad, Basel and GS Cup (lost in 5s to Ivanisevic), and 4 qf, including Australian Open. Upset Sampras at both WT Cup and French Open (although the No. 1 was below his best on both occasions) and had hoped to overtake him at the top of the rankings by the end of HC season. However, he threw away an outside chance of achieving that when he withdrew from US Open, offended at being seeded lower than his ranking and using a slight injury as a legitimate excuse. He might still have been in with a chance had he not lost f Paris Open to Enqvist, although he reached career-high No. 3 on 4 Nov. The only man to qualify for end-of-season champs in both singles and doubles (with Vacek), he decided not to compete in the doubles, which were played in US the week before the singles in Hannover. There, in a tough group, he won only 1 match in rr. He and Vacek played 7 f together, winning 4, and he also took a 5th with Olhovskiy. **1997: (3)** *Halle, New Haven, Moscow.* Broke a finger on right hand in gym the week before Australian Open and was out 3 months, returning at end April – still not fully fit but missing the game and keen to play again. He was back to form by June, when he won his 1st GC title at Halle, following with New Haven and Moscow to qualify for ATP Champs, where he was r/u to Sampras. Across

The only man to figure in the top ten in singles and doubles, Russia's Yevgeny Kafelnikov won a second French Open doubles title with Daniel Vacek and together they won the US Open for the first time. (Michael Cole)

the year he also reached sf Hamburg, Montreal, Tashkent, Lyon and Paris Open, plus qf French Open, Stuttgart Mercedes, Kitzbuhel, Cincinnati, Basel and GS Cup, although he was generally disappointing in GS singles. In doubles with Vacek, he won all 3 f he played – at French Open, US Open and Gstaad – and was again the only man to qualify for the season-ending champs in both singles and doubles, although injury prevented him from taking up his doubles place.

PRINCIPAL 1997 RESULTS – won 3, r/u 1, sf 5 (detailed Grand Slam results follow)
won Halle (d. Schalken 6–0 6–2, Kiefer 7–6 7–6, Stich 7–6 6–7 6–3, Becker 6–3 6–4, Korda 7–6 6–7 7–6), **won** New Haven (d. Mamiit 5–7 6–1 6–3, Dosedel 6–2 6–3, Henman 5–7 6–3 6–4, Korda 6–4 7–6, Rafter 7–6 6–4), **won** Moscow (d. Stark 6–7 6–1 6–3, B. Black 6–4 6–3, Sargsian 6–1 6–2, Nestor 6–4 6–3, Korda 7–6 6–4); **r/u** ATP Champs, **sf** Hamburg (d. Fromberg 7–6 7–6, Dosedel 6–2 6–1, A. Costa 6–3 6–0, lost Medvedev 6–3 6–1), **sf** Montreal (d. Spadea 4–6 6–3 7–6, W. Ferreira 7–5 6–3, Enqvist 7–5 6–7 6–1, lost Woodruff 5–7 7–5 6–3), **sf** Tashkent (d. Tomashevich 6–4 6–2, Welgreen 6–1 6–4, Stoliarov 6–4 6–4, lost Rosset 3–6 7–6 6–2), **sf** Lyon (d. Steven 6–1 6–2, Wibier 6–3 6–4, Goellner 6–4 7–5, lost Haas 4–6 6–4 6–3), **sf** Paris Open (d. Vacek 6–1 6–2, Escude 6–3 6–4, Rusedski 6–4 3–6 6–3, lost Sampras 7–6 6–3). **DOUBLES:** (with Vacek) **won French Open** (d. Woodbridge/Woodforde 7–6 4–6 6–3), **won US Open** (d. Bjorkman/Kulti 7–6 6–3); **won** Gstaad (d. Kronemann/Macpherson 4–6 7–6 6–3).

CAREER GRAND SLAM RECORD
AUSTRALIAN OPEN – Played 3, qf 2

1994: 2r d. Bryan 4–6 ret'd, lost Sampras [1] 6–3 2–6 6–3 1–6 9–7. **1995: qf** [seed 10] d. Larkham 6–3 6–0 6–1, Carlsen 4–6 6–3 6–1 6–3, Bjorkman 4–6 6–1 6–2 7–6, Martin 6–1 6–4 6–2, lost Agassi [2] 6–2 7–5 6–0. **1996: qf** [seed 6] d. Santoro 6–1 6–1 7–5, Corretja 6–1 6–2 6–3, Tebbutt 7–5 5–7 6–4 6–2, MaliVai Washington 6–3 6–2 6–4, lost Becker [4] 6–4 7–6 6–1. **1997:** Did not play.

FRENCH OPEN – Played 5, won 1, sf 1, qf 1

1993: 2r d. Kucera 6–3 6–4 6–4, lost Dosedel 6–3 6–1 6–0). **1994: 3r** d. Guardiola 4–6 7–5 6–4 4–6 6–4, Karbacher 6–2 1–6 6–2 6–2, lost Berasategui 6–3 6–2 6–2. **1995: sf** [seed 9] d. Siemerink 6–1 6–2 6–7 6–3, Gustafsson 6–3 6–7 6–1 7–5, Wheaton 6–2 6–1 4–6 6–3, Corretja 6–3 6–2 6–2, Agassi [1] 6–4 6–3 7–5, lost Muster [5] 6–4 6–0 6–4. **1996: won** [seed 6] d. Blanco 6–1 6–3 6–3, Johansson 6–2 7–5 6–3, Mantilla 6–4 6–2 6–2, Clavet 6–4 6–3 6–3, Krajicek [13] 6–3 6–4 6–7 6–2, Sampras [1] 7–6 6–0 6–2, Stich [15] 7–6 7–5 7–6. **1997: qf** [seed 3] d. Damm 6–2 6–4 6–4, Raoux 7–5 6–3 6–4, Pioline 7–5 6–4 6–7 1–6 6–4, Philippoussis 6–2 6–3 7–5, lost Kuerten 6–2 5–7 2–6 6–0 6–4.

WIMBLEDON – Played 4, qf 1

1994 3r [seed 16] d. Tieleman 7–5 6–7 7–5 6–7 11–9, Braasch 6–1 6–1 6–3, lost Vacek 4–6 7–5 6–4 3–6 6–4. **1995: qf** d. Dewulf 6–3 7–5 6–3, Karbacher 6–4 6–4 7–5, Volkov 7–6 6–2 6–4, Krickstein 6–3 6–3 6–2, lost Ivanisevic [4] 7–5 7–6 6–3. **1996: 1r** [seed 5] lost Henman 7–6 6–3 6–7 4–6 7–5. **1997: last 16** [seed 3] d. Marin 6–4 6–2 6–0, J. Sanchez 6–2 4–6 6–3 6–4, Stoltenberg 6–3 7–6 4–6 6–3, lost Kiefer 6–2 7–5 2–6 6–1.

US OPEN – Played 3

1994: last 16 [seed 14] d. Eltingh 7–6 7–5 6–3, Damm 6–3 7–6 7–6, C. Costa 6–3 6–4 6–2, lost Stich [4] 7–6 6–3 6–2. **1995: 3r** [seed 7] d. Tarango 6–0 6–4 7–5, Marques 6–3 6–4 6–4, lost Spadea 6–2 6–4 6–4. **1996:** Did not play. **1997: 2r** [seed 3] d. Caratti 6–2 6–4 7–6, lost Woodforde 6–3 6–4 7–6.

OLYMPIC RECORD

Has never competed.

CAREER DAVIS CUP RECORD

1993: March – *World Group 1r GER d. RUS 4–1 in RUS (Carpet).* R5 lost M. Stich 6–3 6–4. **September** – *World Group qualifying RUS d. CUB 5–0 in RUS (Carpet).* R1 d. M. Tabares 6–2 6–3 6–2; R5 d. J. Pino 7–6 6–7 6–2. **1994: March** – *World Group 1r RUS d. AUS 4–1 in RUS (Carpet).* R1 P. Rafter 6–3 6–0 6–4; R3 (+ A. Olhovskiy) d. T. Woodbridge/M. Woodforde 6–4 6–0 3–6 4–6 6–3; R5 d. J. Morgan 6–3 6–7 7–5. **July** – *World Group qf RUS d. CZE 3–2 in RUS (Carpet).* R1 d. C. Dosedel 6–2 6–3 6–4; R3 (+ Olhovskiy) lost P. Korda/C. Suk 3–6 6–4 4–6 6–3 7–5; R4 d. Korda 6–4 6–1 2–6 6–4. **September** – *World Group sf RUS d. GER 4–1 in GER (Hard).* R1 d. B. Karbacher 7–6 6–1 2–6 6–4; R3 (+ Olhovskiy) d. K. Braasch/M. Stich 6–4 7–6 3–6 6–7 10–8; R4 d. Stich 7–5 6–3. **December** – *World Group Final SWE d. RUS 4–1 in RUS (Carpet).* R2 lost M. Larsson 6–0 6–2 3–6 2–6 6–3; R3 (+ Olhovskiy) lost J. Apell/J. Bjorkman 6–7 6–2 3–6 1–6 8–6; R4 d. S. Edberg 4–6 6–4 6–0. **1995: February** – *World Group 1r RUS d. BEL 4–1 in BEL (Clay).* R2 d. K. Goossens 4–6 6–4 6–3 6–4; R3 (+ A. Olhovskiy) d. F. Dewulf/L. Pimek 2–6 7–5 7–5 6–3; R4 lost J. van Herck 7–6 6–3 6–1. **March** – *World Group qf RUS d. RSA 4–1 in RUS (Carpet).* R1 d. M. Ondruska 6–1 6–4 6–4; R3 (+ Olhovskiy) d. W. Ferreira/G. Muller 4–6 4–6 7–6 7–6 6–3; R4 d. Ferreira 6–4 7–5 6–1. **September** – *World Group sf RUS d. GER 3–2 in RUS (Clay).* R2 lost M. Stich 6–1 4–6 6–3 6–4; R3 (+ Olhovskiy) d. B. Becker/Stich 7–6 6–4 2–6 6–7 7–5; R4 d. B. Karbacher 6–1 7–6 6–2. **December** – *World Group Final USA d. RUS 3–2 in RUS (Clay).* R2 d. J. Courier 7–6 7–5 6–3; R3 (+ Olhovskiy) lost T. Martin/P. Sampras 7–5 6–4 6–3; R4 lost Sampras 6–2 6–4 7–6. **1996: February** – *World Group 1r ITA d. RUS 3–2 in ITA (Clay).* R2 d. R. Furlan 6–3 5–7 6–4 6–3; R3 (+ A. Olhovskiy) lost A. Gaudenzi/R. Furlan 6–4 2–6 5–7 7–6 6–4; R4 d. Gaudenzi 6–3 3–6 7–6 7–5. **September** – *World Group Qualifying RUS d. HUN 4–1 in RUS (Carpet).* R1 d. A. Savolt 7–5 3–6 6–3 6–4; R3 (+ A. Olhovskiy) d. G. Koves/S. Noszaly 7–6 6–3 6–1; R4 d. J. Krocsko 6–0 6–3). **1997: September** – *World Group Qualifying RUS d. ROM 3–2 in ROM (Carpet).* R2 d. I. Moldovan 6–4 7–6 6–4; R3 (with A. Olhovskiy) lost A. Pavel/G. Trifu 6–4 6–4 6–4. R4 lost Pavel 6–4 3–6 6–4 6–1.

GRAND SLAM CUP RECORD – Played 3, sf 2, qf 1

1995: sf [seed 6] d. Furlan 6–4 6–1, Eltingh 3–6 6–3 6–2, lost Ivanisevic [8] 7–6 4–6 6–3 6–4. **1996: sf** [seed 3] d. Corretja 6–4 7–6, d. Courier 2–6 6–4 8–6, last Ivanisevic 6–7 2–6 6–3 6–2 6–4. **1997: qf** d. Bruguera [5] 6–4 6–3, lost Rusedski [4] 6–7 6–3 6–1.

GRAND PRIX MASTERS/ATP TOUR CHAMPIONSHIP – Played 3, r/u 1

1995: 4th in rr lost Sampras 6–3 6–3, lost W. Ferreira 3–6 7–6 6–1, lost Becker 6–4 7–5. **1996: Equal 3rd in rr** lost Becker 6–4 7–5, d. Enqvist 6–3 7–6, lost Sampras 6–4 6–4. **1997: r/u** in rr d. Bjorkman 6–3 7–6, d. M. Chang 6–3 6–0, lost Henman 6–4 6–4; sf d. Moya 7–6 7–6; f lost Sampras 6–3 6–2 6–2.

6 GREG RUSEDSKI (GBR)

Born: Montreal, Canada, 6 September 1973. **Lives:** London.
Father: Tom. **Mother:** Helen.
Agent: ProServ. **Coaches:** Tony Pickard. Formerly coached by Brad Schultz, Keith Diepraam, Louis Cayer, Scott Brooke, and Brian Teacher from May 1996 to Sept. 1997; also works with sports psychologist Wayne Halliwell.
Fitness trainer: Pat Etcheberry. **Turned pro:** 1991.
Height: 6ft 3in (1.90m). **Weight:** 190lb (86kg).

Rankings: 1989: 1103; **1990:** 679; **1991:** 603; **1992:** 158; **1993:** 48; **1994:** 117; **1995:** 38; **1996:** 48; **1997:** 6.
Highest: 4 (6 October 1997).

1997 Prize Money: $1,515,473. **Career Earnings:** $2,637,814. **Career titles:** 5.

Style: With the fastest timed serve in the world (143 mph at the 1997 US Open), his game is built around this fierce left-handed delivery in which he has tremendous confidence. Confidence is also growing in his improving groundstrokes. The forehand is his main attacking weapon while topspin backhand drives and returns of serve have been added to his natural slice on that wing. For a tall man he moves well and is refining his net game, which now combines subtlety with power.

CAREER HIGHLIGHTS (year: (titles))
A British passport-holder, he switched to play for Great Britain in May 1995, qualifying through his English mother and having satisfied residency qualifications. He had not played D Cup for Canada: although he was named in the squad in 1992, he was injured, and by 1993 had decided he wanted to qualify to play for GBR. Girlfriend Lucy Connor. Canadian Under-14 and Under-18 Champ and won 6 Nat Jun titles. **1991:** Won Wimbledon Jun doubles with Alami and began to make his mark on the Challenger circuit. **1992:** Won Newcastle Challenger. **1993: (1)** *Newport.* Burst into prominence on the main tour when he reached qf Osaka after qualifying, then won his 1st tour title at Newport, unseeded. He was also r/u Beijing and appeared in sf Tokyo Seiko (d. Ferreira, Krajicek and M. Chang back-to-back) and shot up the rankings from 130 to 55 in 2 weeks in Oct. **1994:** Although he could not maintain the standards of the previous year, he reached qf Hong Kong and Manchester and upset Muster at Indianapolis. **1995: (1)** *Seoul.* A month after being accepted to play for Great Britain, he upset Forget at Wimbledon, where he was unseeded. Won Seoul (d. Volkov), r/u Coral Springs and reached sf Basel, qf Jakarta, San Jose and Memphis (d. Krickstein) and upset Krajicek at Cincinnati. **1996: (1)** *Beijing.* At Beijing in Oct. he won his 1st singles title since switching his allegiance to GB. He extended Becker to 5s 1r Australian Open, upset Gustafsson at Olympics, and on his way to sf Sydney upset Krajicek 1r and beat Arriens 6–0 6–0 in 29 mins 2r. He reached the same stage Nottingham (d. A. Costa) and Singapore, as well as qf Adelaide, San Jose, Seoul, Stockholm (d. W. Ferreira) and Bournemouth, where he won the doubles with Goellner. At Wimbledon, however, he was restricted by a hip injury, which caused him to withdraw from D Cup tie v NIG. **1997: (2)** *Nottingham, Basel.* The highlight of an extraordinary year came at US Open, where he had never before won a match, but now became the 1st British player since Fred Perry in 1936 to reach f there. A throat infection had prevented him from practising the day before his sf v Bjorkman, in which he recovered from 2–1 sets down to win on his 24th birthday. On 15 Sept. he became the 1st ever British player to break into the top 10 since rankings began, and on 6 Oct., after winning Basel, he rose to No. 4. On 27 Jan. he had fallen as low as 56, but immediately upset Siemerink and Enqvist *en route* to f Zagreb, where he extended Ivanisevic to fs tb. At San Jose a week later, he upset M. Chang and Agassi and took a set off Sampras in f, before retiring 0–5 down in 2s with a wrist injury, which kept him out of LIPC. Played a 20-minute tb against Ivanisevic sf Queen's, eventually losing 18–16. At Wimbledon he upset Philippoussis before winning a 5s encounter v Stark 11–9, going on to reach qf, unseeded. These results, plus the title at Nottingham, a 6th f at Vienna (where the loss of 3s tb saw him squander a 2-sets-to-0 lead v Ivanisevic), sf GS Cup, Queen's, New Haven (d. A. Costa and Krajicek), Bournemouth and Stockholm and qf Boston and Paris Open, saw

him overtake Henman as No. 1 GBR. Despite crediting his then coach Brian Teacher for much of his success – especially improved return of serve and more relaxed attitude on court – he split with him end Sept. and began working with Tony Pickard, Edberg's former coach. He became the 1st GBR player to qualify for the season-ending champs, but his heavy schedule took its toll and, after losing his 1st 2 rr matches, he was forced to withdraw with a hamstring injury.

PRINCIPAL 1997 RESULTS – won 2, r/u 4, sf 5 (detailed Grand Slam results follow)
won Nottingham (d. Kuerten 6–1 7–5, Woodforde 6–4 7–6, Stoltenberg 6–3 7–6, Stolle 6–3 6–4, Kucera 6–4 7–5), **won** Basel (d. Prinosil 4–6 6–4 7–5, W. Ferreira 6–3 7–6, Enqvist 7–6 4–6 6–3, Korda 6–7 6–3 7–5, Philippoussis 6–3 7–6 7–6); **r/u** US Open; **r/u** Zagreb (d. Montana 6–3 6–4, Siemerink 4–6 6–3 6–2, Damm 7–5 6–3, Enqvist 6–4 6–4, lost Ivanisevic 7–6 4–6 7–6), **r/u** San Jose (d. Hernandez 6–3 6–4, Nestor 6–3 6–3, M. Chang 7–6 6–4, Agassi 6–3 6–4, lost Sampras 3–6 5–0 ret'd), **r/u** Vienna (d. Medvedev 7–6 6–4, M. Norman 6–4 6–2, T. Martin 6–1 6–7 6–3, Henman 6–4 6–4, lost Ivanisevic 3–6 6–7 7–6 6–2 6–3); **sf** GS Cup, **sf** Queen's (d. Woodforde 4–6 6–4 6–3, Ulyett 7–5 4–6 7–6, Draper 6–3 6–2, Rafter 4–6 7–5 6–3, lost Ivanisevic 4–6 6–4 7–6), **sf** New Haven (d. Wessels 6–3 6–2, Salzenstein 6–4 6–0, A. Costa 6–3 7–6, Krajicek 7–6 3–6 6–3, lost Rafter 7–5 4–6 6–3), **sf** Bournemouth (d. A. Martin 6–3 4–6 6–2, Fromberg 7–6 7–6, Arnold 7–6 6–3, lost Moya 6–2 6–2), **sf** Stockholm (d. Kulti 7–6 6–4, Roux 6–4 7–6, Larsson w.o., lost Siemerink 4–6 7–6 6–4).

CAREER GRAND SLAM RECORD
AUSTRALIAN OPEN – Played 4
1994: 1r lost Lendl [15] 6–4 7–6 7–5. **1995: 3r** d. Volkov 6–4 6–2 6–3, Kulti 7–6 4–6 2–6 6–2 6–3, lost Agassi [2] 6–2 6–4 6–2. **1996: 1r** lost Becker [4] 6–4 3–6 4–6 6–3 6–3. **1997: 1r** lost Mantilla [14] 6–4 5–7 7–5 6–2.
FRENCH OPEN – Played 3
1994: 3r d. Goellner 7–6 6–3 7–6, Volkov 7–5 6–3 2–6 6–3, lost Medvedev [4] 2–6 6–3 6–4 3–6 6–2. **1995:** Did not play. **1996: 2r** d. Doyle 6–2 1–6 7–5 2–6 7–5, lost Stich [15] 6–3 7–5 6–3. **1997: 1r** lost M. Norman 6–3 6–2 3–6 4–6 9–7.
WIMBLEDON – Played 5, qf 1
1993: 1r lost Edberg [2] 7–6 6–4 6–7 7–6. **1994: 2r** d. Kulti 6–3 6–4 6–2, lost Bergstrom 6–4 6–4 5–7 7–6. **1995: last 16** [unseeded] d. Simian 6–3 6–3 6–3, Forget [16] 1–6 7–6 7–6 7–5, Delaitre 6–7 6–4 6–4 7–6, lost Sampras [2] 6–4 6–2 7–5. **1996: 2r** d. Nestor 7–6 7–6 6–2, lost Steven 7–6 4–6 7–6 6–2. **1997: qf** [unseeded] d. Philippoussis [7] 7–6 7–6 6–3, Stark 4–6 6–7 6–4 6–3 11–9, Richardson 6–3 6–4 6–4, Reneberg 7–6 6–4 7–6, lost Pioline 6–4 4–6 6–4 6–3.
US OPEN – Played 4, r/u 1
1994: 1r lost Holm 6–3 6–2 3–6 7–5. **1995: 1r** lost Winnink 7–6 6–4 6–7 6–1. **1996: 1r** lost Dreekmann 6–2 6–4 6–2. **1997: r/u** [unseeded] d. Wheaton 6–2 6–3 6–3, Ondruska 7–6 6–4 6–1, Knippschild 7–6 6–3 6–1, Vacek 7–6 6–2 6–2, Krajicek 7–5 7–6 7–6, Bjorkman 6–1 3–6 3–6 6–3 7–5, lost Rafter [13] 6–3 6–2 4–6 7–5.

OLYMPIC RECORD
1996: (Atlanta) 3r d. Frana 4–6 7–5 6–3, Gustafsson [13] 6–7 7–6 6–3, lost Bruguera 7–6 6–3.

CAREER DAVIS CUP RECORD
1995: July – *Zone 2 Relegation GBR d. MON 5–0 in GBR (Grass).* R1 d. Ch. Boggetti 6–2 6–2 7–6; R4 d. S. Graeff 6–0 6–1. **1996: May** – *Zone 2 1r GBR d. SLO 4–1 in GBR (Carpet).* R1 d. Borut Urh 6–1 6–4 6–7 6–3; R3 (with N. Broad) d. G. Krusic/Urh 7–6 6–2 6–3. R4 d. I. Bozic 6–1 6–2 6–2. **September** – *Zone 2 sf GBR d. EGY 5–0 in GBR (Grass).* R1 d. T. El Sawy 6–2 6–4 7–5; R5 d. A. E. S. Ghoneim 6–4 6–2. **1997: July** – *Zone 1 Relegation GBR d. UKR 3–2 in UKR (Clay).* R2 lost A. Medvedev 6–1 6–1 2–6 6–2; R3 (with T. Henman) d. Medvedev/D. Poliakov 6–1 6–4 7–6; R5 d. A. Rybalko 7–5 6–3 6–3.

GRAND SLAM CUP RECORD – Played 1, sf 1
1997: sf [seed 4] d. Woodbridge 4–6 6–1 7–5, Kafelnikov 6–7 6–3 6–1, lost Sampras [1] 3–6 7–6 7–6 6–2.

ATP TOUR CHAMPIONSHIP – Played 1
1997: 4th in rr lost Rusedski 4–6 6–3 6–4, lost Sampras 6–4 7–5, withdrew.

7 CARLOS MOYA (ESP)

Born: Palma da Mallorca, 27 August 1976. **Lives:** Barcelona.
Father: Andres. **Mother:** Pilar. **Sister:** Caroline (29).
Brother: Andres (27).
Agent: IMG. **Coach:** Jose Perlas. **Turned pro:** 1995.
Height: 6ft 3in (1.90m). **Weight:** 177lb (80kg).

Rankings: 1994: 346; **1995:** 63; **1996:** 28; **1997:** 7.
Highest: 5 (8 September 1997).

1997 Prize Money: $1,137,400.
Career Earnings: $1,729,980. **Career Titles:** 3.

Style: His heavy semi-Western forehand is a match-winning shot and his double-handed topspin backhand is also a fearsome stroke. From the back of the court he likes to control the rallies until a short ball allows him the chance to run to the net, where he volleys with increasing skill. He has a powerful but erratic serve, covers the court well and is tactically intelligent.

CAREER HIGHLIGHTS (year: (titles))
1994: European Jun champ in singles and doubles and played on winning Galea Cup team. A qualifier at St Polten, he upset Clavet on the way to his 1st main tour qf. **1995: (1)** *Buenos Aires.* After taking 2 Challenger titles, he finished the year in style with his 1st success on the senior tour at Buenos Aires, unseeded and without dropping a set. **1996: (1)** *Umag.* He recorded some significant upsets on his way to the title at Umag, r/u Munich (d. MaliVai Washington, Ivanisevic and Muster) and Bucharest, sf Barcelona (d. Rosset and Berasategui and took a set off Muster) and Oporto, and qf Casablanca and Amsterdam. He also surprised MaliVai Washington again at Italian Open, breaking into the top 20 in May, and removed Becker at Paris Open. **1997: (1)** *Long Island.* He began the year in style by upsetting W. Ferreira and A. Costa on the way to f Sydney, and followed with the high point of his career to date at Australian Open where, unseeded, he was r/u, upsetting Becker and M. Chang on the way. This performance took him into top 10, and he moved on up to top 5 in autumn. He became 1st Spaniard since Higueras in 1983 to win a title in US when he took Long Island in Aug., and also reached f Amsterdam, Indianapolis and Bournemouth, sf Barcelona, Monte Carlo and Umag, plus qf Scottsdale, Estoril and Munich. These results took him to his 1st ATP Champs, where he upset Sampras in rr and qualified for sf, where he lost to Kafelnikov.

PRINCIPAL 1997 RESULTS – won 1, r/u 4, sf 3 (detailed Grand Slam results follow)
won Long Island (d. J. Sanchez 0–6 7–5 6–2, Rosset 6–2 3–1 ret'd, Goellner 6–4 6–4, Alonso 6–2 6–3, Rafter 6–4 7–6); **r/u** Sydney (d. W. Ferreira 2–6 6–0 6–3, Stafford 6–2 6–3, Rafter 7–6 6–3, A. Costa 3–6 6–3 7–6, lost Henman 6–3 6–1), **r/u** Amsterdam (d. Carraz 6–4 6–4, Vicente 6–4 6–3, Clavet 6–3 6–4, M. Norman 6–4 6–3, lost Dosedel 7–6 6–7 7–6), **r/u** Indianapolis (d. Campbell 7–6 5–7 7–6, Fromberg 6–2 6–4, Novak 6–3 7–5, W. Ferreira 6–4 6–2, lost Bjorkman 6–3 7–6), **r/u** Bournemouth (d. Motevassel 6–4 6–0, Van Scheppingen 6–1 6–3, Scala 6–3 6–4, Rusedski 6–2 6–2, lost Mantilla 6–2 6–2); **sf** Barcelona (d. Clavet 6–4 6–4, Arazi 7–5 4–6 6–1, Medvedev 6–4 6–2, lost A. Costa 7–6 7–5), **sf** Monte Carlo (d. Clavet 6–1 4–6 6–1, Medvedev 6–4 7–6, Krajicek 1–6 6–2 6–4, lost Rios 6–4 7–6), **sf** Umag (d. Sanguinetti 5–7 4–2 ret'd, Vicente 2–6 6–1 7–5, Portas 1–6 6–3 7–5, lost Mantilla 7–5 5–7 6–3)

CAREER GRAND SLAM RECORD
AUSTRALIAN OPEN – Played 2, r/u 1
1996: 1r lost Medvedev 6–4 7–5 2–6 7–6. **1997: r/u** [unseeded] d. Becker [6] 5–7 7–6 3–6 6–1 6–4, McEnroe 3–6 6–0 6–3 6–1, Karbacher 6–2 6–2 6–2, Bjorkman 6–3 1–6 3–6 6–2 6–4, Mantilla 7–5 6–2 6–7 6–2, M. Chang [2] 7–5 6–2 6–4, lost Sampras [1] 6–2 6–3 6–3.
FRENCH OPEN – Played 2
1996 2r d. Rafter 6–4 7–6 6–2, lost Edberg 6–2 6–2 6–1. **1997: 2r** [seed 9] d. A. Martin 6–3 6–7 5–7 6–3 6–3, lost Portas 6–4 4–6 7–5 6–3.
WIMBLEDON – Played 2
1996 1r lost Bouteyre 6–7 7–6 2–6 6–4 10–8. **1997: 2r** [seed 10] d. Bryan 7–6 6–3 4–6 6–2, lost Reneberg 6–4 6–3 6–3.

Carlos Moya, the highest ranking Spaniard, had lost to Pete Sampras in the Australian Open final but was the only man to beat the world No.1 at the ATP Tour Championship where his challenge ended in the semi-finals at the hands of Yevgeny Kafelnikov. (Michael Cole)

US OPEN – Played 2

1996: 2r d. Humphries 6–1 6–7 6–7 6–4 6–4, lost Siemerink 7–6 6–4 6–4. **1997: 1r** [seed 8] lost Raoux 6–4 7–6 6–2.

OLYMPIC RECORD

Has never competed.

CAREER DAVIS CUP RECORD

1996: September – *World Group Qualifying ESP d. DEN 4–1 in ESP (Clay).* R2 d. K. Carlsen 6–1 6–2 6–1; R5 d. T. Larsen 6–3 6–4. **1997: February** – *World Group 1r ESP d. GER 4–1 in ESP (Clay).* R1 d. M. Goellner 6–4 6–3 6–3. R4 d. H. Dreekmann 6–4 6–4 7–5. **April** – *World Group qf ITA d. ESP 4–1 in ITA (Carpet).* R1 lost O. Camporese 6–7 6–7 6–1 6–3 6–3. R4 d. M. Martelli 7–6 4–6 6–3.

GRAND SLAM CUP RECORD

Has never played.

GRAND PRIX MASTERS/ATP TOUR CHAMPIONSHIP – Played 1, sf 1

1997: sf in rr d. Sampras 6–3 6–7 6–2, lost Rafter 6–4 6–2, d. Muster 6–2 6–3; sf lost Kafelnikov 7–6 7–6.

8 SERGI BRUGUERA (ESP)

Born: Barcelona, 16 January 1971, and lives there.
Father: Luis.
Agent: IMG. **Coach:** His father, Luis.
Turned pro: 1988 (aged 17).
Height: 6ft 2in (1.88m). **Weight:** 167lb (76kg).

Rankings: 1988: 333; **1989:** 26; **1990:** 28; **1991:** 11; **1992:** 16; **1993:** 4; **1994:** 4; **1995:** 13; **1996:** 81; **1997:** 8.
Highest: 4 (13 September 1993).

1997 Prize Money: $1,227,428.
Career Earnings: $10,748,329. **Career Titles:** 14.

Style: A fluent, forceful baseliner with semi-Western forehand and two-handed backhand who thrives on clay where he has the power to hit early winners. His consistency, fine return of serve and speed about the court, plus an uncanny ability to pick the right shot on his passes and lobs, make him a formidable adversary. His natural flair and touch on the volley also make him a fine all-court player. With a powerful serve he is capable of playing well on all surfaces.

CAREER HIGHLIGHTS (year: (titles))
1987: Nat Jun Champ. **1989:** Upset Gomez and Connors *en route* to 1st GP sf at Italian Open, following with his 2nd and 3rd at Gstaad and Stuttgart, as well as reaching last 16 French Open. Voted ATP Newcomer of the Year. **1990:** Recorded some big upsets during the year. Removed top seed Edberg in ss 1r French Open; r/u Gstaad (d. Chesnokov) and Geneva; sf Adelaide (took Muster to 3s) and Paris Open (d. Gomez). Won 2 doubles titles. **1991: (1)** *Estoril.* Enjoyed an extraordinary month in April, when he upset Chesnokov at Estoril *en route* to his 1st career title, upset the same player and Becker back-to-back in reaching f Barcelona and beat Becker again in f Monte Carlo, these triumphs taking him into top 10 1st time. He also won Athens (d. Muster); r/u Gstaad (d. Gomez and Ivanisevic); sf Italian Open and Lyon. **1992: (3)** *Madrid, Gstaad, Palermo.* Continued his winning ways in taking Madrid, Gstaad (d. Ivanisevic) and Palermo, was r/u Lisbon, Bordeaux and Athens (where he retired v Arrese with a hand injury) and reached sf Barcelona. Won all his matches as ESP won World Team Cup. **1993: (5)** *FRENCH OPEN, Monte Carlo, Gstaad, Prague, Bordeaux.* The highlight of his year came with victory over Courier in f French Open, when he became the 1st Spaniard since Orantes in 1975 to win a major title. Followed by winning Gstaad in his next tourn and at Bordeaux took his 1st title on a surface other than clay. Earlier he upset Krajicek and Korda on his way to f Milan, surprised Agassi in reaching same stage Barcelona and was also a finalist at Palermo and Madrid. He appeared in qf Marseille, Estoril, Italian Open and Long Island and qualified for IBM/ATP Champ 1st time, but won no match there. **1994: (3)** *FRENCH OPEN, Gstaad, Prague.* Having missed Hamburg and Rome with shoulder problems in spring and won no title since Sept. 1993, he returned to play WT Cup, going on to retain his French Open crown in a great year for Spanish tennis. He followed with Gstaad and Prague and also appeared in f Dubai, Monte Carlo (d. Ivanisevic and Edberg) and Madrid, plus sf Milan, Stuttgart Eurocard and Paris Open. He qualified again for IBM/ATP Champ, where he reached sf, losing to Becker. **1995:** After injuring his knee at Stuttgart Eurocard Eurocard in Feb., he underwent surgery in March and was out of action until April. After his return, he upset Agassi on his way to sf Hamburg, was r/u Italian Open, made his mark again at French Open and reached sf Gstaad and Stuttgart Mercedes, plus 4 qf. However, he finished the year without a title and dropped out of the top 10. Needing help to adapt to HC for US Open and concerned at his discomfort on any surface other than clay, he turned to J. McEnroe for advice and as a practice partner – but still lost 2r. **1996:** Missed the start of the season, having torn ligaments in right ankle in Dec. Returned in Feb. to reach qf Marseille, following with the same stage Hamburg and Bastad. His best performance, though, came at Olympics where, unseeded, he upset Boetsch and MaliVai Washington to take a silver medal. He surprised Pioline at New Haven and Enqvist in WT Cup, but was still troubled by his ankle through the year and plummeted in the rankings. **1997:** He was back to his old form, returning to top 20 in April and top 10 after French Open. Although he won no title, he played 4 f and scored some significant upsets on the way to f French Open (d. M. Chang), Milan (d. Krajicek in marathon fs tb 1r), LIPC (unseeded, d. M.

Chang and Sampras) and Umag. He also appeared in sf Qatar and Marseille, plus qf Hamburg (d. W. Ferreira), Stuttgart Mercedes, Cincinnati, New Haven and Ostrava to qualify for ATP Champs, where he lost 2 rr matches before withdrawing with a rib injury.

PRINCIPAL 1997 RESULTS – r/u 4, sf 2 (detailed Grand Slam results follow)
r/u French Open; **r/u** Milan (d. Krajicek 4–6 7–6 7–6, J. Sanchez 6–4 6–0, Boetsch 6–3 5–7 7–6, Kiefer 6–3 6–4, lost Ivanisevic 6–2 6–2), **r/u** LIPC (d. Stoltenberg 6–3 3–6 7–5, M. Chang 6–4 6–3, Etlis 7–6 6–4, Medvedev 6–-0 6–3, Sampras 6–7 7–6 6–4, lost Muster 7–6 6–3 6–1), **r/u** Umag (d. Silberstein 6–0 6–4, Merinov 6–0 6–1, Haarhuis 6–3 6–4, A. Martin 6–3 6–1, lost Mantilla 6–3 7–5); **sf** Qatar (d. Stich 6–3 6–1, J. Sanchez 6–0 6–1, Korda 6–1 2–6 6–3, lost Courier 6–4 6–2), **sf** Marseille (d. Pioline 6–1 6–7 6–1, Roux 4–6 6–3 6–2, Chesnokov 6–3 6–2, lost Rios 6–3 6–7 6–4).

CAREER GRAND SLAM RECORD

AUSTRALIAN OPEN – Played 4

1990: 2r [seed 13] d. Shiras 6–1 6–4 6–3, lost Pernfors 6–4 6–3 1–6 6–4. **1991: 1r** lost Ivanisevic [5] 6–4 0–6 6–1 6–4. **1992:** Did not play. **1993: last 16** [seed 15] d. Enqvist 6–3 6–7 4–6 6–1 6–2, Grabb 6–1 6–7 7–5 6–0, Siemerink 7–6 4–6 6–3 3–6 9–7, lost Courier [1] 6–1 6–3 7–6. **1994-96:** Did not play. **1997: 3r** d. Hewitt 6–3 6–4 6–3, Larsson 4–6 6–3 6–4 7–6, lost Enqvist [7] 7–6 7–5 6–2.

FRENCH OPEN – Played 8, won 2, r/u 1, sf 1

1989: last 16 d. Marques 6–4 4–6 4–6 6–4 6–3, Jelen 5–7 7–6 7–6 7–6, Novacek 6–4 6–1 1–6 6–3, lost Agenor 2–6 3–6 6–3 6–1 6–2. **1990: 2r** d. Edberg [1] 6–4 6–2 6–1, lost Svensson 2–6 2–6 6–4 6–4 6–0. **1991: 2r** [5] d. S. Davis 6–2 6–2 6–1, lost Camporese 1–6 2–6 6–4 1–0 ret_d. **1992: 1r** lost Lendl [10] 6–4 6–2 6–1. **1993: won** [seed 10] d. Leconte 7–6 6–1 6–0, Champion 6–0 6–0 6–0, M. Larsson 6–1 6–3 6–1, Meligeni 6–3 6–1 7–5, Sampras 6–3 4–6 6–1 6–4 [1], Medvedev 6–0 6–4 6–2 [11], Courier [2] 6–4 2–6 6–2 3–6 6–3. **1994: won** [seed 6] d. Damm 6–1 6–1 7–6, Ruud 6–2 6–2 7–6, Agenor 6–3 6–3 6–3, Rafter 6–4 6–3 6–1, Medvedev [4] 6–3 6–2 7–5, Courier [7] 6–3 5–7 6–3 6–3, Berasategui 6–3 7–5 2–6 6–1. **1995: sf** [seed 7] d. Rafter 6–3 6–1 7–6, Alvarez 6–4 6–4 6–2, Steven 6–3 6–2 6–4, Larsson [10] 6–1 2–6 7–6 7–6, Furlan 6–2 7–5 6–2, lost M. Chang [6] 6–4 7–6 7–6. **1996:** Did not play. **1997: r/u** [seed 16] d. Van Herck 6–3 0–6 6–2 6–0, Van Scheppingen 6–2 6–3 6–3, D. Norman 6–3 6–1 6–3, M. Chang [2] 3–6 6–4 6–3 6–4, Arazi 4–6 6–3 6–2 6–2, Rafter 6–7 6–1 7–5 7–6, lost Kuerten 6–3 6–4 6–2.

WIMBLEDON – Played 3

1989: 1r lost Mansdorf [16] 6–2 6–1 6–4. **1990: 2r** d. Castle 6–7 6–4 6–3 6–1, lost Shelton 5–7 2–6 6–4 6–4 6–4. **1991–93:** Did not play. **1994: last 16** [seed 8] d. Cowan 6–2 4–6 6–4 6–3, Rafter 7–6 3–6 4–6 7–5 13-11, Fleurian 7–6 6–4 2–6 7–5, lost Chang [10] 6–4 7–6 6–0. **1995-97:** Did not play.

US OPEN – Played 8

1989: 1r lost Shiras 6–1 2–6 6–3 4–6 6–4. **1990: 2r** d. Hogstedt 6–3 6–2 6–2, lost Mansdorf 7–6 6–2 2–6 6–3. **1992: 2r** d. R. Gilbert 4–6 6–3 6–4 6–3, lost W. Ferreira [12] 6–7 6–2 3–6 6–1 6–2. **1993: 1r** [seed 5] lost J. Sanchez 7–6 6–3 6–4. **1994: last 16** [seed 3] d. Shelton 6–0 6–2 7–5, Olhovskiy 7–5 6–2 7–6, Goellner 1–6 6–4 6–2 6–7 6–1, lost Muster [13] 6–4 7–6 6–4. **1995: 2r** [seed 11] d. Van Herck 6–3 6–4 6–4, lost Vacek 6–2 6–3 6–4. **1996: 3r** d. Goossens 6–2 6–0 7–6, Stich 6–3 6–2 6–4, lost Muster [3] 6–2 6–4 6–3. **1997: last 16** [seed 7] d. Tebbutt 3–6 4–6 6–3 6–2 6–2, Stafford 6–4 6–2 7–5, Gumy 6–1 6–4 5–7 3–6 6–4, lost Rios [10] 7–5 6–2 6–4.

OLYMPIC RECORD

1992: (Barcelona) 2r [seed 11] d. Castle 6–1 6–2 6–3, lost Koevermans 1–6 6–3 6–3 6–2. **1996: (Atlanta) silver medal** [unseeded] d. Pavel 2–6 6–1 6–0, Boetsch [7] 7–6 4–6 6–2, Rusedski 7–6 6–3, MaliVai Washington [4] 7–6 4–6 7–5, Meligeni 7–6 6–2, lost Agassi [1] 6–2 6–3 6–1.

CAREER DAVIS CUP RECORD

1990: February – *World Group 1r AUT d. ESP 3–2 in ESP (Clay).* R2 lost H. Skoff 4–6 5–7 0–6; R4 lost T. Muster 5–7 1–6 6–7. **September** – *World Group qualifying ESP d. RUS 4–1 in RUS (Carpet).* R1 d. A. Chesnokov 6–2 6–7 6–2 6–3; R4 lost A. Cherkasov 4–6 6–7. **1991: February** – *World Group 1r ESP d. CAN in ESP (Clay) 4–1.* R1 d. A. Sznajder 6–4 6–2 1–6 6–1; R5 d. M. Wostenholme 6–1 7–6. **1992: January** – *World Group 1r ITA d. ESP 4–1 in ITA (Carpet).* R1 lost O. Camporese 4–6 1–6 6–4 1–6; R5 lost C. Caratti 4–6 7–6 1–6. **1993: March** – *World Group 1r NED d. ESP in ESP (Clay).* R1 lost P. Haarhuis 3–6 6–4 6–4 3–6 2–6; R5 lost M. Koevermans 6–3 7–6 4–6 4–6 4–6. **September** – *World Group qualifying – ESP d. KOR 5–0 In KOR (Hard).* R1 d. E. Chang 6–4 6–4 6–2; R4 d. H. C. Shin 6–3 6–1. **1994: March** – *World Group 1r ESP d. ITA in ESP (Clay).* R1 d. A. Gaudenzi 6–3 7–5 6–1; R3 (with T. Carbonell) d. P. Cane/D. Nargiso 6–3 3–6 6–1 6–1; R4 d. S. Pescosolido 6–4 1–6 0–6 6–2 6–3. **July** – *World Group 2r GER d. ESP in GER (Grass).* R1 d. M. Goellner 7–6 6–3 6–2; R3 (with T. Carbonell) lost K. Braasch/M. Stich 6–3 7–6 6–2; R4 lost M. Stich 7–6 5–7 7–5 6–2. **1995: February** – *World Group 1r AUT d. ESP 4–1 in AUT (Hard).* R1 d. G. Schaller 6–1 6–2 6–2; R3 (with E. Sanchez) lost A. Antonitsch/T. Muster 6–2 3–6 6–3 6–3); R4 lost Muster 6–4 7–5 6–3). **September** – *World Group Qualifying MEX d. ESP 3–2 in MEX (Hard).* R 1 d. L. Herrera 6–4 4–6 3–6 6–1 6–2; R3 d. L. Lavalle 6–3 6–7 1–6 6–2 6–4.

Back in the top ten after two years of frustrating injuries, Sergi Bruguera of Spain reached four finals in 1997 but failed to add to his 14 career titles. (Michael Cole)

GRAND SLAM CUP RECORD – Played 4, qf 2

1993: qf [seed 3] d. Larsson 6–3 6–4, lost Korda 4–6 6–0 6–4. **1994: qf** [seed 4] d. Medvedev 5–7 6–4 6–0, lost Martin [5] 7–6 6–4. **1995: 1r** lost Martin 7–6 6–4. **1996:** Did not play. **1997: 1r** [seed 5] lost Kafelnikov 6–4 6–3.

GRAND PRIX MASTERS/ATP TOUR CHAMPIONSHIP – Played 3, sf 1.

1993: 4th in rr lost Edberg 6–2 6–4, lost Ivanisevic 6–4 7–6, lost Sampras 6–3 1–6 6–3. **1994: sf** in rr d. Chang 7–6 7–5, d. Berasategui 6–3 6–2, lost Agassi 6–4 1–6 6–3; sf lost Becker 6–7 6–4 6–1. **1997: 4th in rr** lost M. Chang 7–6 6–2, lost Bjorkman 6–3 6–1, withdrew.

9 THOMAS MUSTER (AUT)

Born: Leibnitz, 2 October 1967. **Lives:** Monte Carlo, Monaco.
Father: Heinz. **Mother:** Inge. **Fiancee:** Mariella Theiner.
Agent: AMI Pro Management. **Coach:** Ronald Leitgeb until end 1990 when he became business manager only.
Turned pro: 1985.
Height: 5ft 11in (1.80m). **Weight:** 165lb (75kg).

Rankings: 1984: 309; **1985:** 98; **1986:** 47; **1987:** 56; **1988:** 16; **1989:** 21; **1990:** 7; **1991:** 35; **1992:** 18; **1993:** 9; **1994:** 16; **1995:** 3; **1996:** 5. **1997:** 9.
Highest: 1 (12 February 1996)

1997 Prize Money: $2,166,590.
Career Earnings: $11,640,654. **Career Titles:** 42.

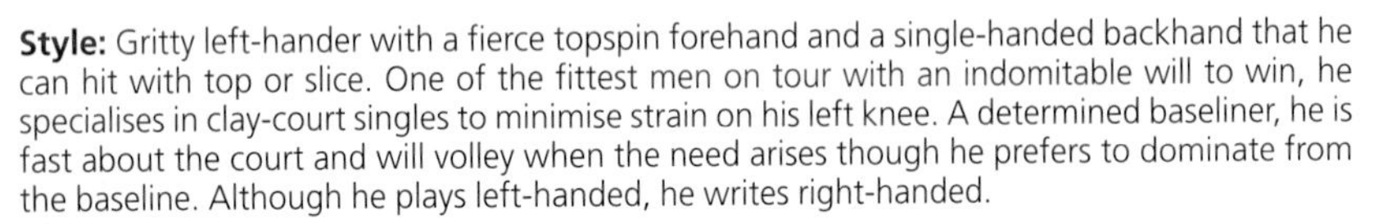

Style: Gritty left-hander with a fierce topspin forehand and a single-handed backhand that he can hit with top or slice. One of the fittest men on tour with an indomitable will to win, he specialises in clay-court singles to minimise strain on his left knee. A determined baseliner, he is fast about the court and will volley when the need arises though he prefers to dominate from the baseline. Although he plays left-handed, he writes right-handed.

CAREER HIGHLIGHTS (year: (titles))
1986: (1) *Hilversum*. Won his first GP title in Hilversum. **1987:** Won Young Masters. **1988: (4)** *Boston, Bordeaux, Prague, Bari*. In the space of 5 weeks he won Boston, Bordeaux and Prague, following with Bari later in year. **1989:** Reached 1st GS sf at Australian Open. On 1 April, 2 hours after beating Noah to reach f LIPC, which took him into top 10 for 1st time, he was knocked down by a drunken driver in Miami and suffered 2 torn ligaments and torn cartilage in his left knee, requiring reconstructive surgery. In plaster 6 weeks and was expected to be out of action for about 10 months, but in May he was already practising in a specially designed wheelchair. In Sept., after only 4 months' rehabilitation, he played doubles at Geneva then reached qf Barcelona in singles, following with sf Vienna. **1990: (3)** *Adelaide, Casablanca, Rome*. At Adelaide in Jan. won 1st tour title since injury 10 months earlier, following with Casablanca in March, Italian Open in May and reaching sf French Open to regain his place in the top 10. R/u Monte Carlo and Munich; sf Vienna; qualified for ATP World Champ but failed to reach sf and fell 1r GS Cup to Leconte. Still in pain and advised by doctors to concentrate on CC tourns in 1990. Suspended 5 weeks from 22 Oct. and fined $15,000 (reduced on appeal from a ten-week suspension from US Open plus $25,000 fine) by ATP for 'violation of best efforts' and 'unsportsmanlike conduct' – after accepting guarantee to play at Prague he pulled out after just 1 game, having previously expressed his intention to do so. Voted Comeback Player of the Year. **1991: (2)** *Florence, Geneva*. Underwent arthroscopic surgery on his left knee in March and won no match in his 1st 6 tourns until Italian Open, where he reached 3r, following with qf Bologna. Having dropped out of top 100 for the 1st time since April 1986, he returned after taking the title at Florence, following with Geneva and beating Skoff in f both times. He also reached sf Genova, Prague and Athens. **1992: (3)** *Monte Carlo, Florence, Umag*. He returned to the top 20 with the titles in Monte Carlo, Florence and Umag, plus sf showings at Stuttgart, Kitzbuhel and Tel Aviv. **1993: (7)** *Mexico City, Florence, Genova, Kitzbuhel, San Marino, Umag, Palermo*. In a particularly productive year he won 7 titles; only Sampras with 8 won more in 1993. Florence and Genova came in successive weeks in spring and he repeated the double in summer with his 1st title in Austria at Kitzbuhel, followed the next week with San Marino – and then Umag 2 weeks after that. These performances made him the 1st since Wilander in 1983 to win 6 titles on clay in one year, although he was disappointed on carpet in Vienna in Oct., when he lost f in 4s tb to Ivanisevic. He was also r/u Sydney Outdoor and reached 5 more sf, but his GS record was disappointing, with qf US Open his best showing. In Oct. he returned to top 10 for 1st time since March 1991, but just failed to qualify for IBM/ATP Champs. **1994: (3)** *Mexico City, Madrid, St Polten*. He won 3 titles and reached sf Kitzbuhel, Tel Aviv and Vienna, plus 8 more qf – including Australian Open and US Open (d. Bruguera) – but this was not enough to keep his place in the top 10. **1995: (12)** *FRENCH OPEN, Mexico City, Estoril, Barcelona, Monte Carlo, Italian Open, St*

Polten, San Marino, Stuttgart Mercedes, Umag, Bucharest, Essen. He returned to the top in style with 12 titles – the most since McEnroe's 13 in 1984. His 86 victories across the year were the most since Lendl's 106 in 1982. The climax came when he won his 1st GS title at French Open, becoming the 1st Austrian ever to win a GS. He put together a winning streak of 40 CC matches from Oct. 1994 until Corretja beat him 1r Gstaad in July; it was the 3rd-best run in the Open era, behind Vilas (53) and Borg (44). He declined to compete at Wimbledon and withdrew after 1r Amsterdam with a cyst on his right big toe, connected with a fracture he had not been aware of. At Kitzbuhel after that he lost his 1st CC f since Munich 1990, but at Umag he returned to his winning ways after saving 3 mps in f v C. Costa. Earlier in the year he had recovered from 2 sets down v Becker to win Monte Carlo. By Nov., after he'd won the 1st indoor title of his career at Essen over Sampras and with Agassi injured, he was beginning to look a contender for the No. 1 spot. Going into IBM/ATP Champ, he had an outside chance of overtaking Sampras at the top, but lost all his rr matches and finished the year behind both Sampras and Agassi. **1996: (7)** *Mexico City, Estoril, Barcelona, Monte Carlo, Italian Open, Stuttgart, Bogota*. Moved to No. 2 behind Agassi after Australian Open and to No. 1 for 1st time on 12 Feb., becoming the 13th man to top the rankings. However, Sampras overtook him a week later and it became a see-saw event as Muster regained the top spot on 11 March, Sampras took it back on 21 April, M. Chang overtook him as No. 2 after US Open, and he slipped further down to No. 5. To complete his record and aiming to remove any doubts as to the justification of his top ranking, he aimed to play well on surfaces other than clay – especially grass, on which he won his 1st senior match in D Cup v Ondruska in Johannesburg in Jan. and reached sf Queen's in June. Playing a heavy schedule to maintain his ranking in the top 10, he won seven titles – surpassed only by Sampras – at Mexico City, followed by Estoril, Barcelona and Monte Carlo back-to-back, Italian Open, Stuttgart and Bogota. Having taken his 7th successive CC title at Monte Carlo, he suffered a surprise defeat at Munich at the hands of Moya, and Alvarez beat him qf Kitzbuhel. He also reached sf Qatar, Munich and Cincinnati, but was again disappointing at ATP Champs, where the fast court did not suit his game and he beat only M. Chang. He withdrew qf St Polten with a minor injury, and injured a thigh at Queen's, aggravating the injury at Halle and withdrawing from Wimbledon. He was irritated at being seeded only 7 there, despite his No. 2 ranking, and that at US Open he was seeded behind M. Chang, contrary to the rankings. Declined to play Olympics and in D Cup tie v BRA in Sept., he walked off court, complaining of behaviour of Brazilian spectators and forfeiting the match. AUT forfeited the rest of the tie and were fined $58,760, while Muster was fined $2,000 for a visible obscenity and $6,000 for leaving the court and refusing to play. He suffered a recurrence of an old injury to his left hip, which forced him to retire 2r Stuttgart Eurocard, and he was conscious that most of his injuries resulted from playing on hard surfaces. Did not take up his place in GS Cup. **1997: (2)** *Dubai, LIPC.* He returned to No. 2 in Feb., after sf finish at Australian Open (d. Ivanisevic), but it was not to be one of his better years and he dropped out of the top 10 for a while in autumn. Developing his game on surfaces other than clay, on which he struggled (by his standards), he won HC titles at Dubai and then LIPC (d. Courier 1st time since 1990). This title was particularly poignant, coming as it did 8 years almost to the day after he last reached f there, only to suffer the accident that almost ended his career. His only other f of year was also HC at Cincinnati (d. M. Chang), although he added sf Indian Wells and Ostrava, plus qf Qatar, St Polten, Halle and Paris Open. He withdrew from Wimbledon with a hip injury and lost to Henman 1r US Open, where he could have been distracted by unsubstantiated reports of his having tested positive for drugs – a rumour condemned by ATP. Played 1 match at ATP Champs (lost Moya) as alternate when Rusedski withdrew after 2 matches.

PRINCIPAL 1997 RESULTS – won 2, r/u 1, sf 3

won Dubai (d. Nydahl 6–4 6–3, Sinner 6–4 6–4, Ruud 6–4 6–7 7–5, Courier 7–6 2–6 6–3, Ivanisevic 7–5 7–6), **won** LIPC (d. Stafford 6–4 2–6 6–1, Corretja 6–4 6–4, Bjorkman 7–5 6–2, Courier 6–3 6–4, Brugera 7–6 6–3 6–1); **r/u** Cincinnati (d. Santoro 6–3 5–7 6–4, Damm 6–3 3–6 7–5, Siemerink 6–7 7–6 7–6, M. Chang 6–3 4–6 7–6, lost Sampras 6–3 6–4); **sf** Australian Open, **sf** Indian Wells (d. Voinea 6–2 6–4, Dosedel 6–4 6–4, Philippoussis 6–3 7–6, lost M. Chang 6–1 7–6), **sf** Ostrava (d. Kralert 6–1 6–3, Haarhuis 6–3 7–6, Nargiso 7–6 6–1, lost M. Norman 6–7 6–2 7–5).

CAREER GRAND SLAM RECORD
AUSTRALIAN OPEN – Played 9, sf 2, qf 1

1988: 1r lost Cash [4] 7–5 6–1 6–4. **1989: sf** [seed 11] d. Rive 6–4 6–2 6–4, Wekesa 4–6 7–6 6–2 6–3, Visser 6–7 6–3 3–6 6–3 1–9, Gustafsson 6–3 6–2 7–5, Edberg [4] w.o., lost Lendl [2] 6–2 6–4 5–7 7–5. **1990: 3r** [seed 15] d. Vojtisek 6–3 6–2 6–4, Van Rensburg 1–6 7–5 7–5 2–6 8–6, lost Youl 3–6 6–4 6–3 6–2. **1991:** Did not play. **1992: 3r** d. Fleurian 7–6 6–1 7–5, Haarhuis 6–4 6–4 7–6, lost Courier [2] 6–1 6–4 6–2. **1993: 2r** d. Haarhuis 4–6 6–3 7–6 6–1, lost Steven 6–2 7–6 6–4. **1994: qf** [seed 8] d. Weiss 6–3 6–3, Carlsen 6–4 6–4 6–2, Raoux 6–3 6–3 6–2, Volkov [12] 6–3 6–3 6–2, lost Edberg [4] 6–2 6–3 6–4. **1995: 3r** [seed 14] d. Reneberg 2–6 6–2 7–6 4–6 6–3, Guardiola 6–3 7–6 6–2, lost Eltingh 6–3 6–2 2–6 7–5. **1996: last 16** [seed 3] d. Guardiola 6–3 6–3 6–2, Frana 6–4 6–4 1–6 7–6, Kulti 6–4 7–6 6–4, lost Tillstrom 6–5 4–6 6–3 6–2. **1997: sf** [seed 5] d. Grant 6–3 6–4 6–2, Stafford 6–3 6–2 6–2, Knippschild 6–4 7–6 6–3, Courier [11] 6–2 3–6 7–6 6–3, Ivanisevic [3] 6–4 6–2 6–3, lost Sampras [1] 6–1 7–6 6–3.

FRENCH OPEN – Played 12, won 1, sf 1

1985: 1r lost Taroczy 7–5 6–3 7–5. **1986: 2r** d. Wilkison 6–3 6–4 6–3, lost Forget 6–2 6–3 4–6 7–6. **1987: 3r** d. Perez Roldan 6–1 6–3 6–2, Stenlund 6–2 6–2 6–2, lost Jaite [14] 6–2 3–6 7–6 6–0. **1988: 3r** d. Flach 6–0 6–1 6–2, Hennemann 6–1 6–0 6–2, lost Becker [5] 6–1 4–6 7–5 6–3. **1989:** Did not play. **1990: sf** [seed 7] d. Jonsson 7–5 6–3 6–2, Winogradsky 6–2 6–3 6–1, Haarhuis 3–6 7–5 6–2 7–6, Jaite [10] 7–6 6–3 6–2, Ivanisevic 6–2 4–6 6–4 6–3, lost Gomez [4] 7–6 6–1 7–5. **1991: 1r** lost Sampras [6] 4–6 4–6 6–4 6–1 6–4. **1992: 2r** d. Motta 6–4 6–4 5–7 6–2, lost Courier [1] 6–1 6–4 6–4. **1993: last 16** [seed 15] d. Skoff 0–6 6–3 6–4 6–2, Pioline 7–5 2–6 6–4 6–2, B. Gilbert 7–5 6–2 6–4, lost Courier [2] 6–3 2–6 6–4 6–2. **1994: 3r** [seed 11] d. Cherkasov 6–0 7–5 6–1, Agassi 6–3 6–7 7–5 2–6 7–5, lost Rafter 6–4 5–7 6–3 6–3. **1995: won** [seed 5] d. Solves 3–6 6–4 6–2 6–1, Pioline 6–1 6–3 6–3, C. Costa 6–3 7–5 6–2, Medvedev 6–3 6–3 6–0, A. Costa 6–2 3–6 6–7 7–5 6–2, Kafelnikov [9] 6–4 6–0 6–4, Chang [seed 6] 7–5 6–2 6–4. **1996: last 16** [seed 2] d. Fetterlein 6–4 6–2 6–1, Solves 6–1 6–3 6–0, Voinea 6–2 6–2 ret'd, lost Stich [15] 4–6 6–4 6–1 7–6. **1997: 3r** [seed 5] d. Goellner 4–6 7–6 6–2 6–7 6–4, Tarango 7–5 1–6 6–2 6–1, lost Kuerten 6–7 6–1 6–3 3–6 6–4.

WIMBLEDON – Played 4

1987: 1r lost Forget 6–4 6–4 6–4. **1988–91:** Did not play. **1992: 1r** lost Stafford 6–3 6–3 7–6. **1993: 1r** [seed 16] lost Delaitre 7–5 6–4 6–2. **1994: 1r** lost Mronz 5–7 7–6 6–7 6–4 8–6). **1995–97:** Did not play.

US OPEN – Played 9, qf 3

1986: 1r lost Curren 6–0 5–7 6–3 7–5. **1987: 3r** d. Lozano 7–6 6–2 6–4, Bergstrom 6–7 6–2 6–7 6–3 6–4, lost Gomez [9] 1–6 6–7 6–3 6–3 6–3. **1988: 1r** lost Pernfors 7–6 6–2 3–6 6–1. **1989:** Did not play. **1990: last 16** [seed 6] d. Rahunen 5–7 6–4 6–0 3–0 ret'd, Jarryd 6–4 6–3 4–6 6–1, Yzaga 6–2 6–2 4–6 5–7 7–6, lost Sampras [12] 6–7 7–6 6–4 6–3. **1993: qf** [seed 12] d. Corretja 6–4 6–4 6–3, Krickstein 6–4 6–0 6–3, McEnroe 6–2 7–5 6–7 6–2, B. Gilbert 6–2 7–5 6–7 6–2, lost Volkov [14] 7–6 6–3 3–6 2–6 7–5. **1994: qf** [seed 13] d. Musa 6–3 6–2 6–0, Ruah 6–4 4–6 6–4 6–2, Enqvist 6–0 6–4 6–2, Bruguera 6–4 7–6 6–4 [3], lost Agassi 7–6 6–3 6–0. **1995: last 16** [seed 3] d. L. Jensen 7–6 6–3 6–0, Woodforde 4–6 6–2 6–2 6–4, Clavet 0–6 6–4 6–3 7–5, lost Courier 6–3 6–0 7–6. **1996: qf** [seed 3] d. Frana 6–1 7–6 6–2, Dier 6–3 6–2 6–4, Bruguera 6–2 6–4 6–3, Enqvist [13] 7–6 6–2 4–6 6–1, lost Agassi [6] 6–2 7–5 4–6 6–2. **1997: 1r** [seed 5] lost Henman 6–3 7–6 4–6 6–4.

OLYMPIC RECORD

1992: (Barcelona) 1r [seed 10] lost Leconte 7–6 7–6 6–4.

CAREER DAVIS CUP RECORD

1984: June – *European Zone A qf AUT d. NOR 5–0 in AUT (Clay).* R5 d. T. Jonsson 6–0 6–3. **1985: June** – *European Zone A qf AUT d. GRE 3–2 in GRE (Clay).* R1 d. G. Kavelonis 6–4 6–1 6–1. **August** – *European Zone A sf ISR d. AUT 3–2 in AUT (Clay).* R1 d. A. Mansdorf 7–5 1–6 6–3 6–0; R5 d. S. Glickstein 3–6 10–8 6–2. **1986: June** – *European Zone A qf AUT d. POR 5–0 in AUT (Clay).* R2 d. N. Marques 6–0 6–1 6–2; R3 (+A. Antonitsch) d. J. Cunha-Silva/Marques 6–3 3–6 6–3 6–4; R5 d. Cunha–Silva 6–2 6–1. **July** – *European Zone A sf AUT d. ROM 3–2 in AUT (Clay).* R1 d. F. Segarceanu 6–4 6–4 5–7 6–4; R3 (+ Antonitsch) lost A. Dirzu/Segarceanu 4–6 7–9 3–6; R5 d. Dirzu 6–2 6–3 6–2. **October** – *European Zone A final FRA d. AUT 4–1 in FRA (Carpet).* R2 lost T. Tulasne 6–4 3–6 6–3 5–7 2–6; R3 (+ Antonitsch) lost G. Forget/H. Leconte 4–6 2–6 2–6; R4 lost Leconte 3–6 2–6. **1987: June** – *European Zone A qf AUT d. GRE 4–1 in AUT (Clay).* R2 d. T. Bavelas 7–5 6–0 6–1; R3 (+ A. Antonitsch) d. G. Kalovelonis/J. Rigas 6–2 6–2 6–2; R4 d. Kalovelonis 6–1 7–5. **July** – *European Zone A sf AUT d. POR 4–1 in POR (Clay).* R2 d. J. Cunha-Silva 6–1 9–7 6–3; R3 (+ Antonitsch) d. P. Cordeiro/Cunha-Silva 6–3 4–6 6–4 6–3; R4 d. N. Marques 6–3 5–7 7–5. **October** – *European Zone A final DEN d. AUT 3–2 in DEN (Carpet).* R1 lost M. Christensen 4–6 2–6 2–6; R3 (+ Antonitsch) d. Christensen/M. Mortensen 7–5 3–6 12–10 6–3; R5 lost M. Tauson 8–6 10–12 6–2 3–6 4–6. **1988: June** – *European Zone 1 AUT d. NGR 5–0 in AUT (Clay).* R2 d. Mmoh 6–2 6–4 6–3; R3 (+ A. Antonitsch) d. Mmoh/N. Odizor 12–10 6–3 6–3; R5 d. Odizor 6–4 10–8. **July** – *European Zone A final AUT d. GBR 5–0 in AUT (Clay).* R1 d. S. Shaw 6–4 6–2 6–2. R3 (+ Antonitsch) d. J. Bates/A. Castle 6–3 6–4 3–6 6–3; R2 d. R. Whichello 6–1 6–3. **1989: February** – *World Group 1r AUT d. AUS 5–0 in AUT (Clay).* R2 d. M. Woodforde 6–4 6–7 6–2 6–3; R3 (+ A. Antonitsch) d. P. Cash/J. Fitzgerald 6–3 7–6 3–6 3–6 6–2; R5 d. Cash 6–2 6–0. **1990: February** – *World Group 1r AUT d. ESP 3–2 in ESP (Clay).* R1 d. E. Sanchez 1–6 6–2 4–6 6–3 6–4; R3 (+ A. Antonitsch) lost S. Casal/Sanchez 6–1 3–6 6–7 4–6; R4 d. S. Bruguera 7–5 6–1 7–6. **March** – *World Group qf AUT d. ITA 5–0 in AUT (Clay).* R2 d. P. Cane 7–5 7–5 1–6 4–6 6–3; R3 (+ Antonitsch) d. Cane/D. Nargiso 7–6 1–6 6–2 6–2; R5 d. Nargiso 6–3 6–2. **September** – *World Group sf USA d. AUT 3–2 in AUT (Clay).* R1 d. M. Chang 4–6 6–2 6–2 6–4; R3 (+ Antonitsch) lost R. Leach/J. Pugh 6–7 6–3 0–6 5–7; R4 d. A. Agassi 6–2 6–2 7–6. **1991: September** – *World Group qualifying GBR d. AUT 3–1 in GBR (Grass).* R2 lost M. Petchey 6–2 3–6 7–6 6–2; R3 (+ A. Antonitsch) lost J. Bates/N. Brown 6–7 6–3 6–0 7–5. **1994: March** – *World Group 1r GER d. AUT 3–2 in AUT (Clay).* R2 d. M. Goellner 6–3 6–3 6–3; R3 (+ A. Antonitsch) lost P. Kuhnen/M. Stich 6–4 3–6

Curiously for a clay-court expert, the Austrian left-hander Thomas Muster failed to win a clay court title in 1997 but did well on hard courts, reaching the Australian Open semi-finals and winning titles in Dubai and Key Biscayne. (Tommy Hindley)

6–2 2–6 6–1; R4 d. M. Stich 6–4 6–7 4–6 6–3 12–10. **September** – *World Group qualifying AUT d. URU 3–2 in URU (Clay).* R1 d. M. Perez 6–3 6–2 6–3; R4 d. M. Filippini 7–5 6–1 6–1). **1995: February** – *World Group 1r AUT d. ESP 4–1 in AUT (Hard).* R2 d. C. Costa 6–4 6–4 6–4; R 3 (+ A. Antonitsch) d. S. Bruguera/E. Sanchez 6–2 3–6 6–3 6–3; R4 d. S. Bruguera 6–4 7–5 6–3. **March** – *World Group qf SWE d. AUT 5–0 in SWE (Carpet).* R 1 lost M. Larsson 6–1 7–6 7–5; R3 (+ Antonitsch) lost J. Appell/J. Bjorkman 7–5 6–3 6–3; R4 lost S. Edberg 6–4 6–2. **1996: February** – *World Group 1r RSA d. AUT 3–2 in RSA (Grass/Hard).* R1 d. M. Ondruska 6–2 7–5 6–2; R3 (+ A. Antonitsch) lost W. Ferreira/G. Muller 6–3 7–6 6–7 3–6 6–3; R4 d. Ferreira 7–5 6–7 6–4 7–6. **September** – *World Group Qualifying BRA d. AUT 4–1 in BRA (Carpet).* R1 d. F. Meligeni 6–3 6–3 6–3; R3 (+ U. Plamberger) lost G. Kuerten/J. Oncins 7–6 4–6 6–3 3–6 2–0 def. **1997: April** – *Zone 1 2r AUT d. CRO 3–2 in AUT (Clay).* R2 d. S. Hirszon 6–0 6–4 3–6 6–1; R3 (+ U. Plamberger) lost Hirszon/G. Ivanisevic 7–5 6–2 6–2; R4 lost Ivanisevic 6–7 7–5 6–7 6–2 7–5. **September** – *World Group Qualifying ZIM d. AUT 3–2 in ZIM (Hard).* R2 d. W. Black 6–3 6–0 6–4; R4 d. B. Black 3–6 6–3 2–6 6–3 6–1.

GRAND SLAM CUP RECORD – Played 5

1990: 1r [seed 7] lost Leconte 6–3 6–4. **1993: 1r** lost Sampras [1] 6–3 6–1. **1994: 1r** lost Agassi [2] 6–3 7–5). **1995: 1r** [seed 5] lost B. Black 7–6 2–6 6–1. **1996** Did not play. **1997: 1r** lost Rafter [2] 6–2 6–3.

GRAND PRIX MASTERS/ATP TOUR CHAMPIONSHIP – Played 3

1990: 3rd in rr d. Gomez 7–5 5–7 6–4, lost Becker 7–5 6–4, lost Lendl 6–3 6–3. **1991–94:** Did not play. **1995: 4th in rr** lost M. Chang 4–6 6–2 6–3, lost Courier 6–4 4–6 6–4, lost Enqvist 6–4 6–7 6–4. **1996: Equal 3rd in rr** lost Ivanisevic 6–4 6–4, lost Krajicek 7–6 6–7 6–3, d. M. Chang 6–4 6–3.

10 MARCELO RIOS (CHI)

Born: Santiago, 26 December 1975. **Lives:** Santiago.
Father: Jorge, an engineer. **Mother:** Alicia, a teacher.
Sister: Paula.
Agent: IMG. **Coach:** Larry Stefanki, formerly Nick Bollettieri.
Turned pro: 1994.
Height: 5ft 9in (1.75m). **Weight:** 140lb (63kg).

Rankings: 1992: 487; **1993:** 549; **1994:** 107; **1995:** 25; **1996:** 11. **1997:** 10. **Highest:** 7 (15 September 1997).

1997 Prize Money: $1,397,445.
Career Earnings: $2,715,549. **Career Titles:** 5.

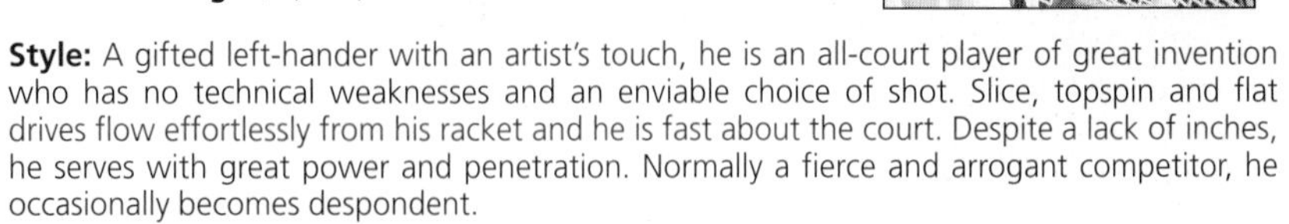

Style: A gifted left-hander with an artist's touch, he is an all-court player of great invention who has no technical weaknesses and an enviable choice of shot. Slice, topspin and flat drives flow effortlessly from his racket and he is fast about the court. Despite a lack of inches, he serves with great power and penetration. Normally a fierce and arrogant competitor, he occasionally becomes despondent.

CAREER HIGHLIGHTS (year: (titles))
1992: Won Chilean satellite aged 16. **1993:** No. 1 in ITF Jun rankings after winning US Open Jun over Downs. Joined the Chilean D Cup squad and was named his country's Athlete of the Year. **1994:** He reached sf Hilversum and qf Gstaad and at French Open, after qualifying, he kept Sampras on court more than 2½ hours in 2r. Took over the No. 1 ranking in Chile from Sergio Cortes in summer. **1995: (3)** *Bologna, Amsterdam, Kuala Lumpur.* Won his 1st tour title at Bologna and broke into the top 50, becoming the 1st Chilean to reach that level since Acuna in 1986. In July he won both singles and doubles titles at Amsterdam, having played through the qualifying after applying too late for a regular place in the draw, and in Oct. reached top 25 after winning a 3rd title in Kuala Lumpur and r/u Santiago. **1996: (1)** *St Polten.* In an impressive year he continued to shoot up the rankings, becoming in May the 1st Chilean to appear in the top 10. He won St Polten, was r/u Scottsdale, Barcelona (d. Courier and took a set off Muster) and Santiago and reached sf Indian Wells (d. W. Ferreira), Monte Carlo (d. Becker), Hamburg (d. W. Ferreira again), Toronto and Toulouse, plus 4 more qf. **1997: (1)** *Monte Carlo.* In a consistent, if not spectacular, year, he maintained his ranking, finishing just inside the top 10, and narrowly missed a berth at the season-ending champs. He won Monte Carlo, was r/u Marseille (ret'd with leg injury), Rome, Boston and Santiago, and reached qf Australian Open (d. Enqvist), US Open (d. Bruguera and extended M. Chang to 5s), GS Cup, Auckland, Prague, Singapore and Stuttgart Eurocard (d. Kafelnikov).

PRINCIPAL 1997 RESULTS – won 1, r/u 4 (detailed Grand Slam results follow)
won Monte Carlo (d. Gaudenzi 6–2 6–2, A. Costa 7–6 6–4, Larsson 6–2 6–1, Moya 6–4 7–6, Corretja 6–4 6–3 6–3); **r/u** Marseille (d. Viloca 7–6 6–4, Van Herck 6–2 6–4, Larsson 3–6 7–5 6–4, Bruguera 6–3 6–7 6–4, lost Enqvist 6–4 1–0 ret'd), **r/u** Rome (d. Camporese 6–3 7–5, Santoro 6–2 6–2, Larsson 4–6 7–5 6–4, Courier 6–3 3–6 7–6, Berasategui 6–3 3–6 6–1, lost Corretja 7–5 7–5 6–3), **r/u** Boston (d. Stark 6–7 6–2 7–6, Furlan 6–4 6–4, Gumy 6–4 6–3, Tarango 6–4 6–3, lost Schalken 7–5 6–3), **r/u** Santiago (d. Sanguinetti 6–2 7–5, Prieto 5–7 6–1 6–4, Meligeni 1–6 7–6 6–1, Filippini 6–1 6–4, lost Alonso 6–2 6–1)

CAREER GRAND SLAM RECORD
AUSTRALIAN OPEN – Played 2, qf 1
1996: 1r lost Rafter 6–3 6–4 6–3. **1997: qf** [seed 9] d. Korda 7–6 6–3 6–3, Joyce 6–0 6–4 6–2, Schaller 4–6 7–6 6–1 6–1, Enqvist [7] 4–6 6–4 7–6 6–7 6–3, lost M. Chang [2] 7–5 6–1 6–4.
FRENCH OPEN – Played 4
1994: 2r d. Eagle 6–2 6–3 6–2, lost Sampras [1] 7–6 7–6 6–4. **1995: 2r** d. Spadea 6–4 6–4 6–7 6–3, lost Berasategui [11] 6–4 7–5 6–7 3–6 6–1. **1996: last 16** [seed 9] d. Joyce 7–6 6–1 6–4, Stoltenberg 6–4 6–3 6–3, Korda 6–3 6–3 6–2, lost Pioline 6–4 6–1 6–2. **1997: last 16** [seed 7] d. W. Black 6–4 5–7 4–6 6–2 6–1, B. Black 6–7 6–7 6–4 7–6 6–0, Boetsch 7–6 6–3 6–4, lost Arazi 6–2 6–1 5–7 7–6.
WIMBLEDON – Played 2
1995: 1r lost Knowles 4–6 6–3 6–4 7–6. **1997: last 16** [seed 9] d. Bhapathi 6–4 6–4 6–4 6–3, Van Scheppingen 6–2 6–3 6–7 7–6, Van Lottum 7–6 6–3 6–7 6–4, lost Becker [seed 8] 6–2 6–2 7–6.

It was a breakthrough year for the gifted Chilean, Marcelo Rios, who entered the top ten for the first time after winning his fifth career title in Monte Carlo. (Stephen Wake)

US OPEN – Played 4, qf 1

1994: 2r d. Palmer 6–2 7–6 6–2, lost W. Ferreira [12] 6–2 6–2 6–4. **1995: 1r** lost Enqvist [9] 2–6 6–2 4–6 6–3 7–6. **1996: 2r** [seed 10] d. Pavel 4–6 6–1 6–4 6–2, lost Tarango 6–4 4–6 7–6 6–2. **1997: qf** [seed 10] d. Smith 6–1 6–1 6–4, Carlsen 6–4 5–7 3–6 6–1 7–6, Haas 6–4 3–6 6–3 1–6 6–1, Bruguera [7] 7–5 6–2 6–4, lost M. Chang [2] 7–5 6–2 4–6 4–6 6–3.

OLYMPIC RECORD

Has never competed.

CAREER DAVIS CUP RECORD

1993: February – *Zone 1 1r BAH d. CHI 3–2 in CHI (Clay).* R3 (+ G. Silberstein) lost M. Knowles/R. Smith 6–2 6–1 6–3. **1996: February** – *Zone 1 1r BRA d. CHI 3–2 in CHI (Clay).* R2 d. J. Oncins 6–3 6–2 7–5; R3 (+ M. Rebolledo) lost G. Kuerten/Oncins 7–5 6–3 4–6 6–2. R4 d. F. Meligeni 6–2 7–6 6–3. **April** – *Zone 1 Relegation CAN d. CHI 3–2 in CAN (Carpet).* R1 d. D. Nestor 6–4 7–6 6–7 3–6 14–12. R3 (+ O. Bustos) lost G. Connell/S. Lareau 6–3 6–4 7–5. **September** – *American Zone 1 Play-off CHI d. PER 5–0 in CHI (Clay).* R1 d. A. Venero 7–5 6–2 6–4; R3 (+ O. Bustos) d. L. Horna/Venero 6–4 6–3 6–7 3–6 8–6; R4 d. A. Aramburu 6–2 6–3. **1997: February** – *Zone 1 1r CHI d. ECU 4–1 in CHI (Clay).* R2 d. L. Morejon 6–1 6–3 3–6 6–2; R3 (with O. Bustos) lost P. Campana/N. Lapentti 4–6 6–4 6–0 6–3. R4 d. Lapentti 7–5 6–7 6–3 6–7 8–6. **April** – *Zone 1 2r CHI d. ARG 3–2 in CHI (Clay).* R1 d. J. Frana 6–1 6–4 7–6; R3 (with G. Silberstein) d. J. Frana/L. Lobo 3–6 7–6 4–6 6–4 6–2. R4 d. H. Gumy 6–4 7–5 6–4. **September** – *World Group Qualifying IND d. CHI 3–2 in IND (Grass).* R2 d. M. Bhupathi 6–2 3–6 6–3 6–4; R3 lost Bhupathi/L. Paes 3–6 6–3 6–4 6–7 6–3. R4 d. Paes 6–7 6–4 6–0 7–6.

GRAND SLAM CUP RECORD – Played 1, qf 1

1997: qf [seed 7] d. Woodforde 6–7 6–3 6–1, lost Rafter [2] 6–1 7–6.

GRAND PRIX MASTERS/ATP TOUR CHAMPIONSHIP

Has never played.

REMAINING MEN'S BIOGRAPHIES

The following biographies show the players' progress each year in the four Grand Slam Championships. It is shown thus: A (Australian Open), F (French Open), W (Wimbledon), US (US Open), followed by the round reached or '–' if a player did not compete. Where a player's career prize money exceeds $1 million, it is shown in brackets after his 1997 prize money.

KARIM ALAMI (MAR)

Born Casablanca, 24 May 1973, and lives there; RH; 6ft 1in; 187lb; turned pro 1990; career singles titles 2; final 1997 ATP ranking 55; 1997 prize money $290,249.

Coached by Carlos Gattiker. Fluent in six languages. **1990:** (340). **1991:** (405) Ranked No. 2 in ITF Jun Singles after being r/u US Open to Paes and Orange Bowl to Charpentier; No. 1 in ITF Jun Doubles after winning Wimbledon with Rusedski and US Open with de Jager. **1992:** (402). **1993:** (212). **1994:** (100) A –, F –, W 2, US 2. Upset Sampras 1r Qatar after qualifying and became the lowest-ranked player to beat the current No. 1. Then in March at Casablanca he appeared in his 1st f, unseeded; upset Volkov at Italian Open and reached qf Jakarta. **1995:** (70) A 2, F –, W –, US –. Reached qf Qatar, Bologna, Prague, Bogota and Montevideo, but could progress no further. **1996:** (56) A 1, F 1, W 1, US 1. Having won only 1 match in 10 tourns all year, he came into his own at Atlanta, where he upset Frana and M. Chang on the way to his 1st tour title and the 1st ever by a Moroccan. He followed in Sept. with Palermo (unseeded) when Voinea retired in f, and also appeared in qf Bologna, where he was r/u doubles with Koves. **1997:** A 1, F 1, W –, US 1. He reached sf Casablanca and Bologna, qf Barcelona (d. Ivanisevic), Rome (d. Bruguera), St Polten, Marbella and Palermo, and upset Muster 1r Rosmalen. Played 3 doubles f with different partners, winning Marbella with Alonso. **1997 HIGHLIGHTS – SINGLES: Australian Open 1r** (lost Kulti 6–4 6–2 6–4), **French Open 1r** (lost Corretja [seed 8] 6–3 6–4 6–1), **US Open 1r** (lost Philippoussis 6–3 6–4 3–6 6–4); **sf** Casablanca (d. Solves 6–4 6–3, Craca 7–5 7–6, Vicente 6–7 6–1 7–5, lost Squillari 6–3 6–3), **sf** Bologna (d. Pescariu 6–3 6–1, Munoz 3–6 6–0 6–3, Gaudenzi 3–6 6–3 6–3, lost Mantilla 6–3 6–2). **1997 HIGHLIGHTS – DOUBLES:** (with Alonso) **won** Marbella (d. Berasategui/Burillo 4–6 6–3 6–0); (with Arazi) **r/u** Casablanca (lost Cunha-Silva/Marques 7–6 6–2), (with Ruah) **r/u** Bogota (lost Lobo/Meligeni 6–1 6–3).

JULIAN ALONSO (ESP)

Born Mataro, 2 August 1977; lives Barcelona; RH; 6ft 1in; 180lb; turned pro 1996; career singles titles 1; final 1997 ATP ranking 36; 1997 prize money $245,982.

Coached by Pato Alvarez. **1994:** Won nat 18s. **1996:** (289) Began to make his mark on the satellite circuits in both singles and doubles. **1997:** A –, F –, W –, US 1. Broke into top 100 in July after winning Venice and Contrexville Challengers in consecutive weeks, then followed the next week with his 1st f on the main tour at Kitzbuhel (unseeded). His year finished on a high note as he upset Rios for his 1st title at Santiago, where he was r/u doubles with Lapentti. Earlier he had upset Bjorkman and Ivanisevic *en route* to sf Long Island, reached qf Marbella, where he won the doubles with Alami, and upset Corretja at Lyon. **1997 HIGHLIGHTS – SINGLES: US Open 1r** (lost Sargsian 2–6 0–6 6–0 6–4 6–4); **won** Santiago (d. Pescariu 6–4 6–7 6–1, Craca 6–4 1–6 7–5, Puerta 6–4 6–2, Burillo 6–1 4–6 6–3, Rios 6–2 6–1), **won** Venice Challenger (d. Craca 6–3 6–7 6–4), **won** Contrexville Challenger (d. Gaudenzi 6–4 6–3); **r/u** Kitzbuhel (d. Hipfl 7–5 4–6 6–1, Ulihrach 6–2 6–3, Karbacher 6–3 6–2, Gumy 4–6 6–3 7–6, Dosedel 6–3 6–4, lost Dewulf 7–6 6–4 6–1); **sf** Long Island (d. Ruud 3–6 6–4 6–0, Bjorkman 6–3 6–4, Ivanisevic 7–6 3–6 6–3, lost Moya 6–2 6–3). **1997 HIGHLIGHTS – DOUBLES:** (with Alami) **won** Marbella (d. Berasategui/Burillo 4–6 6–3 6–0); (with Lapentti) **r/u** Santiago (lost Davids/Kratzmann 7–6 5–7 6–4).

HICHAM ARAZI (MAR)

Born Casablanca, 19 October 1973; lives Magny, France; LH; 5ft 9in; 143lb; turned pro 1993; career singles titles 1; final 1997 ATP ranking 38; 1997 prize money $397,741.

Coached by Alberto Castellani. Moved to France at age 2. **1991:** (1093). **1992:** (533). **1993:** (340) Began to make his mark on the satellite circuits. **1994:** (185). **1995:** (148) A –, F –, W –, US 1. Reached 3 f on the Challenger circuit. **1996:** (78) A –, F –, W 2, US 1. Won 2 Challenger titles and on the main tour reached qf Palermo and Toulouse, breaking into the top 100. **1997:** A 1, F qf, W 1, US 1. He began the year with his 1st sf on the at Qatar, the delighted the home crowds at Casablanca by winning his 1st career singles title there. He made his mark at French Open, upsetting Rios to reach qf, unseeded, and reached the same stage Zagreb, Hamburg (d. Muster), Bologna and Tashkent. Played 2 doubles f, but won no title. **1997 HIGHLIGHTS – SINGLES: Australian Open 1r** (lost Fleurian 7–5 6–0 6–3), **French Open qf** [unseeded] (d. Dreekmann 6–3 6–4 6–2, Woodbridge 6–4 7–5 6–2, Larsson 6–2 6–3 7–5, Rios [seed 7] 6–2 6–1 5–7 7–6, lost Bruguera [seed 16] 4–6 6–3 6–2 6–2), **Wimbledon 1r** (lost Reneberg 7–6 6–4 7–6), **US Open 1r** (lost Golmard 6–4 1–6 7–6 4–6 7–5); **won** Casablanca (d. Krocsko 6–3 6–1, Skoch 6–3 6–3, Alvarez 6–2 6–1, Schaller 6–2 7–6, Squillari 3–6 6–1 6–2); **sf** Qatar (d. Paes 6–2 6–3, McEnroe 2–6 7–5 7–5, Larsson 7–6 7–6, lost Henman 6–3 2–6 6–2). **1997 HIGHLIGHTS – DOUBLES:** (with Alami) **r/u** Casablanca (lost Cunha-Silva/Marques 7–6 6–2), (with Ran) **r/u** Tashkent (lost Santopadre/Spadea 6–4 6–7 6–0).

BORIS BECKER (GER)

Born Leimen, 22 November 1967; lives Munich; RH; 6ft 3in; 187lb; turned pro 1984; career singles titles 49; 1997 ATP ranking 63; 1997 prize money $674,245 ($24,515,647).

Wife Barbara Feltus (married 17 December 1993); son Noah Gabriel (born 18 January 1994). Played both tennis and soccer as a boy, giving up soccer for tennis at the age of 12. **1982:** Won first of three consecutive German Nat Jun Champs. **1983:** (563) R/u Orange Bowl 16s. **1984:** (65) A qf, F –, W 3, US –. R/u US Open Jun and in the men's game made a surprise appearance in qf Australian Open. **1985:** (6) A 2, F 2, W won, US 4. Won Queen's and then Wimbledon, at 17 yrs 7 mths becoming youngest men's titlist, the first German, and the first unseeded player to capture the world's most prestigious event. He also won Cincinnati and closed the year with D Cup wins over Edberg and Wilander in f as FRG lost 3–2 to SWE. Won inaugural Young Masters, was r/u to Lendl in ATP Masters and was voted ATP Most Improved Player. **1986:** (2) A –, F qf, W won, US sf. Won Wimbledon again in even more convincing fashion, dismissing Lendl in f without loss of a set and still younger than any other champ. Through the year he also won Chicago, Toronto, Sydney Indoor, Tokyo Indoor and Paris Open, closing the year with streak of 3 straight tourns and 21 matches in a row before losing Masters f to Lendl. Won Young Masters in Jan. and Dec. **1987:** (4) A 4, F sf, W 2, US 4. Split with coach Gunther Bosch Jan. At end of year Bob Brett became coach and Frank Dick his trainer. Missed LIPC suffering from a form of typhus which seemed to weaken him and restrict his performance for several weeks, and he was further restricted by tendinitis of left knee for last 5 months of year. Won only 3 titles all year and, going for his 3rd consec. Wimbledon singles title, fell 2r to Doohan. After US Open took time off in Germany with his family, returning refreshed in Oct. and qualified for Masters, where he extended Lendl to 3s, but lost his Young Masters title. **1988:** (4) A –, F 4, W r/u, US 2. He was again plagued by injury problems, withdrawing from Toronto and the Olympics and playing Masters only 10 days after his foot had been removed from plaster following injury in Stockholm sf. However, he still won titles at Indian Wells, WCT Dallas, Queen's, Indianapolis, Tokyo Indoor, Stockholm and finished the year by taking his 1st Masters title in a thrilling f v Lendl, as well as leading FRG to victory over SWE in D Cup f. **1989:** (2) A 4, F sf, W won, US won. The high spot of his year was a convincing third title at Wimbledon where he beat Lendl in a stirring sf and Edberg in f. This was followed by his first triumph at US Open, where he d. Lendl in f, and r/u spot at Masters to Edberg. He won in Milan and on clay reached f Monte Carlo and sf French Open. He also won Philadelphia and Paris Open, as well as leading FRG to victory in WT Cup and D Cup. Voted ATP Player of the Year. **1990:** (2) A qf, F 1, W r/u, US sf. His 1r loss to Ivanisevic at French Open was his 1st at that stage in GS. From 9 f he won Brussels, Stuttgart Indoor, Indianapolis, Sydney Indoor and Stockholm, strongly challenging Edberg for the No. 1 spot at end of year. He gave a stunning performance at Stockholm, beating the Swede in f and taking his indoor match record since 1988 to 77–5. However, in f Paris Open he had to withdraw v the same player with a pulled left thigh, which was still undergoing treatment when he began play on 2nd day of ATP World Champ, where he fell to Agassi in sf. **1991:** (3) A won, F sf, W r/u, US 3. Reached No. 1 for the 1st time on 28 Jan. after winning his 1st Australian Open; his 5 hr 22 min match in 3r with Camporese was the longest ever played there and lasted only 1 min less than the marathon at Wimbledon in 1969 between Gonzales and Pasarell. He was overtaken again by Edberg on 18 Feb., after retiring v Cherkasov at Brussels with a right thigh strain, but returned to the top after his appearance in f Wimbledon, where he lost in ss to countryman Stich. His disappointing 3r loss to Haarhuis at US Open saw him slip again to No. 2, and by year's end he had fallen to 3 behind Courier, having narrowly failed to qualify for sf ATP World Champ in Frankfurt. However, he played his best ever CC season, although he again failed to win his 1st title on that surface, losing f Monte Carlo to Bruguera, who had also beaten him at Barcelona. Withdrew from Italian Open with back trouble, but played French Open, where he reached sf for 3rd time. He outlasted Edberg in 5s f Stockholm in Oct. for only his 2nd title of the year; also reached f Indianapolis and sf Brussels and Cincinnati. **1992:** (5) A 3, F –, W qf, US 4. In Jan. he dropped out of top 3 1st time since April 1989, and in losing 3r Australian Open to J. McEnroe, he fell from top 5 for 1st time since 1988, eventually slipping as low as 9 in Nov. However, working since Sept. with Gunther Bresnik, he found his best form again and finished the year in tremendous style by taking ATP World Champ, surviving a close sf v Ivanisevic and sweeping Courier aside in f. Missed French Open to avoid aggravating a thigh strain and lost qf Wimbledon to Agassi. His titles at Brussels, Rotterdam, Basel, Paris Open and ATP Champ were all indoors and he also reached sf Hamburg and Indianapolis. In doubles he won an Olympic gold medal and Monte Carlo with Stich, plus Brussels with J. McEnroe. **1993:** (11) A 1, F 2, W sf, US 4. After winning singles and doubles at Qatar (d. Edberg and Ivanisevic), he put behind him 1r loss at Australian Open to Jarryd and took Milan, but was then forced to withdraw from sf Stuttgart Eurocard with a viral infection which kept him out 2 months. He suffered a disastrous CC season and split with Bresnik a week before French Open. He took the title at Indianapolis and also reached sf Antwerp, but failed to qualify for IBM/ATP World Champ for 1st time since 1985 and dropped out of the top 10 for the 1st time in 8 years. By then his mind was on the expected birth of his child in Jan. Playing the GS Cup 1st time he lost 1r to W. Ferreira and then announced that, having split from his boyhood friend and practice partner, Eric Jelen, he had appointed Nick Bollettieri as his coach. **1994:** (3) A –, F –, W sf, US 1. Inspired by the birth of his son in Jan. and giving Bollettieri much of the credit for putting the enjoyment back in his game, he moved up the rankings again. When he successfully defended his title at Milan in Feb., he ended his longest spell without a title (21 tourns), then upset Stich at Stuttgart Eurocard. He returned to the top 10 after enjoying unusual success on clay at Italian Open, where he beat Ivanisevic before falling tamely in f to Sampras. He was surrounded by controversy at Wimbledon, where he illegally received physiotherapy during a toilet break and was frequently accused of unacceptable gamesmanship on his way to sf, where he fell to Ivanisevic. At Los Angeles he won his 1st title in US for four years, and at Stockholm he was superb, becoming the only player all year to beat the current top 3 in 1 tourn (Stich, Sampras and Ivanisevic), to qualify for IBM/ATP World Champ. He seemed in peak form there, unbeaten in rr and beating Sampras in ss for 2nd time in a fortnight, but when they met in f, Sampras had the better of him in 4s. However, Becker's performance that week took him past Ivanisevic and Bruguera to the No. 3 spot. Refused to play D Cup sf v RUS, in which GER were defeated, but had stated his willingness to play in f. In GS Cup he beat W. Ferreira, his conqueror of 1993, but was thrashed by Ivanisevic. **1995:** (4) A 1, F 3, W r/u, US –. In summer he split with Bollettieri, who left to concentrate on his tennis academy. Until he finished the year on a high note by winning IBM/ATP Champ, his only title had been Marseille, although he was r/u 3 times. He reached that stage at Milan, then, still looking for a 1st CC title, he failed to capitalise on a 2-set lead over Muster at Monte Carlo. He continued to excite at Wimbledon, where he beat Pioline only 9–7 5s in qf, recovered from a set down v Agassi to upset the top seed, and took 1s in f v Sampras before letting the match slip away. Suffered back problems at Essen, but recovered in time to progress to f Paris Open the following week and also appeared in sf US Open, Stuttgart Eurocard, Indian Wells, Queen's and Basel, reaching qf or better in 11 of 16 tourns across the year. Thrilled the German crowds on his way to victory at IBM/ATP Champ, with a few scares along the way: having lost to Sampras in rr, he needed to beat Kafelnikov in ss to go through to the knockout rounds, and several times looked to have failed. **1996:** (6) A won, F –, W 3, US –. At Australian Open, where he took his 1st GS title since 1991, he was stretched to 5s in 1r by Rusedski and in 2r by Johansson, against whom he recovered from 2 sets down. He missed French Open after suffering a torn thigh muscle in WT Cup rr v Rosset, but was back in action at Queen's, where he lost no set and won his 100th GC match on the way to his 7th GC title. However, disaster struck again at Wimbledon, where, executing a late and awkward return of serve v Godwin, he suffered a badly sprained tendon in his right wrist and was forced to withdraw, also missing US Open and having already declined to play Olympics. Returning in Sept., he withdrew 1r Bucharest with a recurrence of the injury, but later in the month at Basel was encouraged to survive uninjured through a 3s match v Ulihrach, although he lost 2r to Novak. Then in Oct. he won his 2nd title of the year at Vienna, surviving 4s in f against Siemerink, and at the end of the month he beat Sampras in 5s to take the title at Stuttgart Eurocard – surprised and delighted to have made such a rapid recovery. Sampras was again his opponent in a truly memorable match in f ATP Champs, when both men were at their glorious best and Becker was eventually beaten 6–4 5s after a match of 3 tbs. Earlier he had beaten Sampras in another close encounter in their rr match. He also reached sf Antwerp and Munich and moved back into the top 3 after Stuttgart. The year ended on a high note when he beat the holder Ivanisevic in f GS Cup on home soil in Munich – his first success there. **1997:** A 1, F –, W qf, US –. He was restricted all year by injury, withdrawing from Qatar with an ankle injury and being plagued throughout by recurring wrist problems. After losing qf Wimbledon to Sampras, he announced that that would be his last Wimbledon, although he would continue to play ATP tour. He withdrew US Open following the death of his manager, Axel Meyer-Wolden, so Wimbledon turned out to be his last GS tourn of all. Sf Halle marked his best performance and he dropped out of the top 10 for 1st time since 1994. By end of year, he had dropped out of top 50 for 1st time since 1984 and was intending to play only very occasionally on ATP tour. He was appointed GER D Cup manager for 1998, and became actively involved in development of younger German players, including Kiefer, who had replaced him in Oct. as No. 1 in GER. **1997 HIGHLIGHTS – SINGLES: Australian Open 1r** [seed 6] (lost Moya 6–7 7–6 3–6 6–1 6–4), **Wimbledon qf** [seed 8] (d. Aurelio Gorriz 6–3 6–2 6–3, Johansson 6–1 6–4 6–4, Petchey 6–3 6–3 6–2, Rios [seed 9] 6–2 6–2 7–6, lost Sampras [seed 1] 6–1 6–7 6–1 6–4); **sf** Halle (d. Radulescu 6–3 7–6, Dreekmann 6–3 6–4, Tarango 6–4 6–2, lost Kafelnikov 6–3 6–4). **CAREER HIGHLIGHTS – SINGLES: Australian Open – won 1991** (Bates 6–4 6–2 6–3, Vajda 6–4 6–1 6–3, Camporese 7–6 7–6 0–6 4–6 14–12, Ferreira 6–4 7–6 6–4, Forget 6–2 7–6 6–3, P. McEnroe 7–6 6–3 4–6 4–6 6–2, Lendl 1–6 6–4 6–4 6–4), **won 1996** (d. Rusedski 6–4 3–6 4–6 6–3 6–3, Johansson 4–6 3–6 6–2 6–1 6–4, Larsson 7–6 6–3 6–3, Steven 1–6 6–4 6–3 6–2, Kafelnikov 6–4 7–6 6–1, Woodforde 6–4 6–2 6–0, M. Chang 6–2 6–4 2–6 6–2); **Wimbledon – won 1985** [unseeded] (d. Pfister 4–6 6–3 6–2 6–4, Anger 6–0 6–1 6–3, Nystrom 3–6 7–6 6–1 4–6 9–7, Mayotte 6–3 4–6 6–7 7–6 6–2, Leconte 7–6 3–6 6–3 6–4, Jarryd 2–6 7–6 6–3 6–3, Curren 6–3 6–7 7–6 6–4), **won 1986** (d. Bengoechea 6–4 6–2 6–1, Tom Gullikson 6–4 6–3 6–2, McNamee 6–4 6–4 4–6 6–4, Pernfors 6–3 7–6 6–2, Mecir 6–4 6–2 7–6, Leconte 6–2 6–4 6–7 6–3, Lendl 6–4 6–3 7–5), **won 1989** (d. Shelton 6–1 6–4 7–6, Matuszewski 6–3 7–5 6–4, Gunnarsson 7–5 7–6 6–3, Krickstein 6–4 6–4 7–5, Chamberlin 6–1 6–2 6–0, Lendl 7–6 6–7 2–6 6–4 6–3, Edberg 6–0 7–6 6–4), **r/u 1988** (d. Frawley 6–3 6–1 6–2, Novacek 6–3 6–4 6–4, Giammalva 7–6 6–4 6–4, Annacone 6–3 6–4 6–4, Cash 6–4 6–3 6–4, Lendl 6–4 6–3 6–7 6–4, lost Edberg 4–6 7–6 6–4 6–2), **r/u 1990** (d. Herrera 7–6 7–6 7–5, Masur 6–7 6–2 6–3 6–2, Goldie 6–3 6–4 4–6 7–5, Cash 7–6 6–1 6–4, Gilbert 6–4 6–4 6–1, Ivanisevic 4–6 7–6 6–0 7–6, lost Edberg 6–2 6–2 3–6 3–6 6–4), **r/u 1991** (d. Steeb 6–4 6–2 6–4, Lundgren 7–6 7–5 7–5, Olhovskiy 6–1 6–4 3–6 6–3, Bergstrom 6–4 6–7 6–1 7–6, Forget 6–7 7–6 6–2 7–6, Wheaton 6–4 7–6 6–5, lost Stich 6–4 7–6 6–4), **r/u 1995** (d. Alvarez 6–3 6–3 6–4, Apell 6–3 3–6 6–1 6–2, Siemerink 2–6 6–2 6–2 6–4, D. Norman 7–6 6–3 6–4, Pioline 6–3 6–1 6–7 6–7 9–7, Agassi 2–6 7–6 6–4 7–6, lost Sampras 6–7 6–2 6–4 6–2), **sf 1993** (d. Goellner 4–6 6–3 6–2 6–4, Volkov 7–6 6–1 6–3, Hlasek 6–3 3–6 6–2 6–3, Leconte 6–4 6–4 3–6 6–3, Stich 7–5 6–7 6–7 6–2 6–4, lost Sampras 7–6 6–4 6–4), **sf 1994** (d. Wheaton 6–2 6–4 6–3, Thoms 7–6 6–2 6–4, Frana 7–6 6–4 1–6 6–3, Medvedev 6–7 7–5 7–6 6–7 7–5, Bergstrom 7–6 6–4 6–3, lost Ivanisevic 6–2 7–6 6–4); **US Open – won 1989** (d. Pate 6–1 6–3 6–1, Rostagno 1–6 6–7 6–3 7–6 6–3, Mecir 6–4 3–6 6–4 6–3, Pernfors 5–7 6–3 6–2 6–1, Noah 6–3 6–3 6–2, Krickstein 6–4 6–3 6–4, Lendl 7–6 1–6 6–3 7–6), **sf 1986** (d. Michibata 6–2 5–7 6–4 6–2, Motta 6–3 6–0 6–2, Casal 7–5 6–4 6–2, Donnelly 6–4 6–3 6–7 6–4, Srejber 6–3 6–2 6–1, lost Mecir 4–6 6–3 6–4 3–6 6–3), **sf 1990** (d. Aguilera 7–5 6–3 6–2, Noah 6–4 6–2 7–6, Carbonell 6–4 6–2

6–2, Cahill 2–6 6–2 6–3 3–6 6–4, Krickstein 3–6 6–3 6–3 6–3, lost Agassi 6–7 6–3 6–2 6–3), **sf 1995** (d. Lopez-Moron 6–1 6–0 6–3, Arriens 6–1 6–3 7–5, Stoltenberg 6–2 4–6 6–0 6–4, Rosset 7–6 6–3 6–3, P. McEnroe 6–4 7–6 6–7 7–6, lost Agassi 7–6 7–6 4–6 6–4); **ATP Champs – won 1988** (d. Wilander 7–6 6–7 6–1, Leconte 6–0 1–0 ret'd, lost Edberg 7–6 3–6 6–4 in rr, d. Hlasek 7–6 7–6, Lendl 5–7 7–6 3–6 6–2 7–6), **won 1992** (d. Korda 6–4 6–2, Edberg 6–4 6–0, lost Sampras 7–6 7–6 in rr, d. Ivanisevic 4–6 6–4 7–6, Courier 6–4 6–3 7–5), **won 1995** (d. W. Ferreira 4–6 6–2 7–6, lost Sampras 6–2 7–6, d. Kafelnikov 6–4 7–5 in rr, d. Enqvist 6–4 6–7 7–5, d. M. Chang 7–6 6–0 7–6), **r/u 1985** (d. Annacone 3–6 6–3 6–2, Wilander 6–4 4–6 6–3, Jarryd 6–3 6–4, lost Lendl 6–2 7–6 6–3), **r/u 1986** (d. Nystrom 6–1 6–3, Leconte 0–6 6–1 6–1, Wilander 6–3 3–6 6–3 in rr, d. Edberg 6–4 6–4, lost Lendl 6–4 6–4 6–4), **r/u 1989** (d. Gilbert 2–6 6–3 6–4, Agassi 6–1 6–3, Edberg 6–1 6–4 in rr, d. J. McEnroe 6–4 6–4, lost Edberg 2–6 7–6 6–3 6–1), **r/u 1994** (d. Ivanisevic 6–3 3–6 7–6, Sampras 7–5 7–5, Edberg 6–7 6–4 7–5 in rr, d. Bruguera 6–7 6–4 6–1, lost Sampras 4–6 6–3 7–5 6–4), **r/u 1996** (d. Kafelnikov 6–4 7–5, Sampras 7–6 7–6, lost Enqvist 6–3 7–6 in rr, d. Krajicek 6–7 7–6 6–3, lost Sampras 3–6 7–6 7–6 6–7 6–4), **sf 1990** (d. Gomez 4–6 6–3 6–3, Muster 7–5 6–4, Lendl 1–6 7–6 6–4 in rr, lost Agassi 6–2 6–4); **French Open – sf 1987** (d. Perez 6–0 6–1 7–5, Buckley 6–1 4–6 6–3 6–2, Sundstrom 6–1 3–6 6–3 6–1, Arias 5–7 6–3 6–2 6–0, Connors 6–3 6–3 7–5, lost Wilander 6–4 6–1 6–2), **sf 1989** (d. Pugh 6–4 6–2 6–3, Winogradsky 7–6 7–5 6–3, Bates 7–5 6–1 6–2, Perez Roldan 3–6 6–4 6–2 4–6 7–5, Berger 6–3 6–4 6–1, lost Edberg 6–3 6–4 5–7 3–6 6–2), **sf 1991** (d. Arrese 6–2 7–5 6–2, Woodbridge 5–7 1–6 6–4 6–4 6–4, Masur 6–3 6–3 6–2, Clavet 7–6 6–4 6–3, Chang 6–4 6–4 6–2, lost Agassi 7–5 6–3 3–6 6–1). **CAREER HIGHLIGHTS – DOUBLES:** (with Stich) **Olympics – won gold medal** (d. Ferreira/Norval 7–6 4–6 7–6 6–3).

ALBERTO BERASATEGUI (ESP)

Born Bilbao, 28 June 1973; lives Andorra; RH; 5ft 8in; 145lb; turned pro 1991; career singles titles 13; final 1997 ATP ranking 23; 1997 prize money $597,985 ($3,584,117).

Coached by Javier Duarte. Attended school in US and trained at the Harry Hopman Academy in Saddlebrook, Fla., from age 13 to 16. **1990:** (495) Began playing the Spanish satellite circuit. **1991:** (301) European Jun champ and a member of winning Sunshine Cup and Galea Cup teams, he enjoyed some success on the Spanish satellite circuit and tested the waters on the Challenger circuit. **1992:** (115) A –, F 1, W –, US –. Reached sf Casablanca after qualifying. **1993:** (36) A –, F 2, W –, US 2. Broke into top 50 after r/u appearance at Umag (d. Gustafsson), followed with same stage Athens and then in Nov. took his 1st tour title at Sao Paulo and appeared in f Buenos Aires the next week. He reached 3 more qf and upset Bruguera at Stuttgart Mercedes. **1994:** (8) A –, F r/u, W –, US 1. Upset Edberg and Courier on his way to the title at Nice and moved into the top 20 in May. The climax of his year came when, unseeded, he swept to f French Open without dropping a set, although Bruguera was too much for him at that stage. He broke into the top 10 in Aug. after winning Stuttgart Mercedes, and then in autumn, concentrating on CC tourns to give himself the best chance of earning a berth in his 1st IBM/ATP Champs, he won 4 more consec. titles. That took his tally of titles in the year to 7, second only to the 10 won by Sampras. However, they all came on clay – he won only 2 matches all year on surfaces other than clay – and his dismal showing at IBM/ATP Champs, where he won only 8 games in 3 matches in the weakest group, called into question the true ability of a player who can play effectively on only one surface. **1995:** (33) A –, F 3, W –, US –. He could not maintain his standards on his favourite surface in the European CC season, failing to pass 2r in 9 tourns, and had dropped out of the top 10 in May before another disappointing performance at French Open. At Oporto in June he won his 1st title since Oct. 1994, and reached f Montevideo at end of year, but otherwise his best showings were 7 qf. **1996:** (19) A –, F 3, W –, US 2. He returned to top 20 with the titles at Bologna, Kitzbuhel and Bucharest, as well as sf finishes at Scottsdale, Casablanca, Stuttgart and Santiago, qf Barcelona and Gstaad and an upset of Krajicek at Paris Open. At Casablanca v Filippini, he played and won the longest known singles game in ATP history – it lasted 20 minutes and included 28 deuces. **1997:** A 3, F 1, W –, US 1. Palermo was his only title on the main tour, with Zagreb and Cairo on the Challenger circuit. At Marbella he was r/u both singles and doubles, and he also reached sf Barcelona (where he won the doubles with Burillo) and Rome (d. Rafter and Kafelnikov), plus qf Indian Wells, Estoril, Hamburg (d. Rios), Bologna, Gstaad and Stuttgart Mercedes. **1997 HIGHLIGHTS – SINGLES: Australian Open 3r** [seed 16] (d. Larkham 6–1 6–2 6–4, Carbonell 6–3 7–5 6–4, lost Hrbaty 6–3 7–6 6–7 2–0 ret'd), **French Open 1r** [seed 12] (lost Medvedev 6–4 4–6 2–6 6–2 6–1), **US Open 1r** (lost W. Ferreira 6–7 2–6 6–3 6–1 6–3); **won** Palermo (d. Vicente 6–4 5–7 6–4, C. Costa 6–4 4–6 6–3, Alami 7–6 6–2, J. Sanchez 6–2 6–3, Hrbaty 6–4 6–2), **won** Zagreb Challenger (d. Ljubicic 6–1 6–2), **won** Cairo Challenger (d. Alami 7–5 6–3); **r/u** Marbella (d. C. Costa 6–0 6–3, Nydahl 4–6 7–5 6–1, Alonso 6–1 6–4, Hrbaty 6–4 6–4, lost A. Costa 6–3 6–2); **sf** Barcelona (d. J. Sanchez 6–1 6–2, Fromberg 6–4 6–3, Mantilla 7–6 6–1, Meligeni 6–2 7–5, lost Portas 6–3 7–5), **sf** Rome (d. Vacek 6–3 6–4, Rafter 3–6 6–4 7–5, Kafelnikov 6–3 6–2, Goellner 7–5 7–5, lost Rios 6–3 3–6 6–1). **1997 HIGHLIGHTS – DOUBLES:** (with Burillo) **won** Barcelona (d. Albano/Corretja 6–3 7–5); **r/u** Marbella (lost Alami/Alonso 4–6 6–3 6–0). **CAREER HIGHLIGHTS – SINGLES: French Open – r/u 1994** [unseeded] (d. W. Ferreira 6–3 ret'd, Pioline 6–4 7–5 6–3, Kafelnikov 6–3 6–2 6–2, Frana 6–2 6–0 ret'd, Ivanisevic 6–4 6–3 6–3, Larsson 6–3 6–4 6–1, lost Bruguera 6–3 7–5 2–6 6–1).

MAHESH BHUPATHI (IND)

Born Madras, 7 June 1974; lives Bangalore; RH; 6ft 1in; 183lb; turned pro 1995; career singles titles 0; final 1997 ATP ranking 228 singles, 11 doubles; 1997 prize money $336,522.

1992: (944). **1993:** (532). **1994:** (284). **1995:** (350) A –, F –, W –, US 1. **1996:** (418). **1997:** A –, F –, W 1, US –. Formed a successful doubles partnership with Paes, winning the 6 f they played together and qualifying for a first World Doubles Champ. There they squeaked past Lareau/O'Brien in sf before denting their record of f won by losing to Leach/Stark. In mixed, he won French Open with Hiraki. **1997 HIGHLIGHTS – SINGLES: Wimbledon 1r** (lost Rios [seed 9] 6–4 6–4 6–3). **1997 HIGHLIGHTS – DOUBLES:** (with Paes unless stated) **won** Chennai (d. Ogorodov/Ran 7–6 7–5), **won** Prague (d. Luxa/Skoch 6–1 6–1), **won** Montreal (d. Lareau/O'Brien 7–6 6–3), **won** New Haven (d. Goellner/Olhovskiy 4–6 6–7 6–2), **won** Beijing (d. Courier/O'Brien 7–5 7–6), **won** Singapore (d. Leach/Stark 6–4 6–4); (with Leach) **r/u** Los Angeles (lost Lareau/O'Brien 7–6 6–4), **r/u** World Doubles (lost Leach/Stark 6–3 6–4 7–6). **MIXED DOUBLES:** (with Hiraki) **won French Open** (d. Galbraith/Raymond 6–4 6–1).

GALO BLANCO (ESP)

Born Oviedo, 8 October 1976; lives Barcelona; RH; 5ft 8in; 145lb; turned pro 1995; career singles titles 0; final 1997 ATP ranking 52; 1997 prize money $232,314.

Coached by Enrique Perez. **1993:** (1130). **1994:** (469) Won Nat Jun Champ over Moya. **1995:** (171) Won Tampere Challenger and on the main tour reached qf Buenos Aires. **1996:** (97) A –, F 1, W –, US 1. Qf Bastad and won Prague Challenger, breaking into top 100 in July. **1997:** A 1, F qf, W –, US 1. Until French Open, where he was unseeded, he had won only 1 of 7 matches in 1997. However, there he made his mark by removing Gustafsson and Korda on the way to qf, and followed with sf Kitzbuhel (d. Corretja) and Marbella. **1997 HIGHLIGHTS – SINGLES: Australian Open 1r** (lost Simian 6–4 6–2 6–4), **French Open qf** [unseeded] (d. Godwin 6–3 6–2 1–6 7–5, Gustafsson 6–4 4–6 6–4 7–6, Woodruff 7–6 6–3 7–6, Korda 1–6 6–1 7–5 6–4, lost Rafter 6–3 7–6 6–3), **US Open 1r** (lost Haarhuis 7–6 6–0 6–7 6–7 6–3); **sf** Kitzbuhel (d. Squillari 6–3 6–2, Corretja 7–6 7–5, Koubek 6–7 6–2 6–4, lost Dewulf 6–3 6–2), **sf** Marbella (d. Lozano 6–2 4–6 7–6, Alvarez 6–4 6–4, Roig 7–6 6–3, lost A. Costa 7–5 6–2).

FRANCISCO CLAVET (ESP)

Born Aranjuez, 24 October 1968; lives Madrid; LH; 6ft; 156lb; turned pro 1988; career singles titles 6; final 1997 ATP ranking 33; 1997 prize money $422,936 ($2,373,025).

Coached by his older brother Pepo (Jose), who used to play the circuit. **1986:** (870). **1987:** (638). **1988:** (290). **1989:** (188) Qf Kitzbuhel. **1990:** (90) A –, F 1, W –, US –. Won his 1st tour title at Hilversum as a lucky loser, upsetting Jaite on the way. **1991:** (30) A 2, F 4, W 1, US 3. Reached sf Stuttgart Mercedes (d. Muster and Gomez), Kitzbuhel, Schenectady, Athens and Sao Paulo, plus 3 more qf and last 16 French Open, unseeded. **1992:** (22) A 2, F 1, W 1, US 1. Enjoying another consistent year, he was r/u Gstaad and San Marino and reached sf Philadelphia, Indian Wells, Madrid, Athens and Palermo. **1993:** (99) A –, F 2, W –, US 1. In a less successful year, his best showing was sf Genova, plus qf Hilversum, Bucharest and Sao Paulo (d. Yzaga) and an upset of Novacek at Buenos Aires. **1994:** (38) A –, F 2, W –, US 2. On the main tour he was r/u Santiago and Montevideo (losing both to Berasategui) and reached sf Athens and Buenos Aires (d. Berasategui on clay), plus qf Pinehurst, Florence, St Polten and Palermo. He also won 2 titles on the Challenger circuit. **1995:** (49) A –, F 3, W –, US 3. At Palermo he won his 1st title since 1990, as well as reaching sf Mexico City, Oporto, Umag and Montevideo. **1996:** (34) A 3, F 4, W 1, US 1. In another productive year, he won Amsterdam and appeared in sf Mexico City and Bologna, plus qf Antwerp, Estoril, St Polten, Gstaad (d. MaliVai Washington), Stuttgart Eurocard, Bucharest and Palermo. Upset A. Costa at French Open, where he was unseeded. **1997:** A –, F 2, W 2, US 1. His best performances came in Oct., when he won Mexico City and Bogota back-to-back, having earlier reached f Estoril (d. Kuerten, Moya and Mantilla), sf Tashkent and Bucharest, and qf Antwerp (d. Enqvist), Rosmalen, Amsterdam and Palermo. **1997 HIGHLIGHTS – SINGLES: French Open 2r** (d. Charpentier 3–6 6–4 6–7 6–1 6–3, lost Sampras [seed 1] 6–1 6–2 6–2), **Wimbledon 2r** (d. Lapentti 7–5 6–1 6–3, lost Rikl 6–4 7–6 6–4), **US Open 1r** (lost Bjorkman 6–2 6–4 6–4); **won** Mexico City (d. Gaudenzi 4–6 6–2 6–0, Burillo 3–6 6–4 7–5, Sa 6–3 7–6, Lapentti 7–5 7–6, Viloca 6–4 7–6), **won** Bogota (d. Pescariu 6–7 6–0 6–1, Vicente 6–1 6–4, Alvarez 7–6 2–3 ret'd, Sanguinetti 6–3 6–7 7–6, Lapentti 6–3 6–3); **r/u** Estoril (d. Gaudenzi 3–6 6–3 6–2, Kuerten 1–6 6–1 7–6, Moya 6–1 6–3, Mantilla 3–6 7–5 6–0, lost Corretja 6–3 7–5); **sf** Tashkent (d. Canas 6–3 6–3, Erlich 3–6 6–4 6–3, J. Sanchez 6–1 6–2, lost Henman 6–3 7–5), **sf** Bucharest (d. Alami 6–3 6–3, Behrend 7–6 6–4, J. Sanchez 4–6 6–2 6–3, lost Fromberg 4–6 6–3 6–4).

ALEX CORRETJA (ESP)

Born Barcelona, 11 April 1974, and lives there; RH; 5ft 11in; 155lb; turned pro 1991; career singles titles 4; final 1997 ATP ranking 12; 1997 prize money $1,182,807 ($2,845,215).

Coached by Javier Duarte. **1990:** Won Orange Bowl 16s. **1991:** (232) Began to make his mark on the satellite circuits. **1992:** (86) A –, F 1, W –, US 1. Reached his 1st tour f at Guaruja in Nov. and moved into top 100. Upset E. Sanchez 1r Hamburg. **1993:** (76) A –, F 1, W –, US 1. Reached sf Florence and Sao Paulo, plus qf Monte Carlo. **1994:** (22) A –, F 3, W 2, US 1. His 1st tour title came at the very end of the season at Buenos Aires in his 3rd career f. He had scored some big upsets during the year on his way to f Palermo (where he held 2 mps v Berasategui), sf Mexico City (d. Berasategui), Barcelona (d. Courier), Madrid (d. Berasategui again), Indianapolis (d. Courier and Edberg), Athens and Santiago, as well as beating Becker at Hamburg. At French Open, he was 2-sets-to-love up v Ivanisevic 3r before letting the match slip away. **1995:** (48) A –, F 4, W –, US 2. Upset W. Ferreira at French Open and at Gstaad he ended Muster's 40-match CC winning streak. He also reached sf Mexico City, Munich and Buenos Aires and in doubles won Palermo with Santoro. **1996:** (23) A 2, F 2, W 2, US qf. He was again a dangerous opponent, as he confirmed on his way to r/u Hamburg

(d. A. Costa, Rosset and Rios), Kitzbuhel and Marbella, sf Estoril (d. A. Costa and took a set off Muster) and Stuttgart Eurocard (d. Moya), plus qf Indianapolis (d. Reneberg) and Palermo. He was on the verge of causing the upset of the year in qf US Open (unseeded) v Sampras, when he held mp at 7–6 in fs tb, with Sampras suffering so severely from dehydration that he was hardly able to stand. However, the No. 1 drew level, served an ace for 8–7 and Corretja let the match go with a double-fault after 3 hr 52 min. Won Stefan Edberg Sportsmanship award. **1997:** A 2, F 4, W –, US 3. In his best year to date, he broke into top 10 with titles at Estoril, Rome (d. Ivanisevic and Rios) and Stuttgart Mercedes. He also reached f Monte Carlo and Munich (where he won the doubles with Albano), sf Gstaad and Palermo and qf Boston. In GS he overruled an 'out' call on a crucial bp when losing to Dewulf at French Open, and was forced to withdraw from 3r US Open after injuring his left thigh while warming up. **1997 HIGHLIGHTS – SINGLES: Australian Open 2r** (d. Mitchell 7–6 6–0 6–2, lost Schaller 4–6 6–3 6–3 4–6 6–3), **French Open last 16** [seed 8] (d. Alami 6–3 6–4 6–1, Knippschild 4–6 6–1 6–1 7–6, Champion 6–1 3–0 ret'd, lost Dewulf 5–7 6–1 6–4 7–5), **US Open 3r** [seed 8] (d. Rosset 4–6 6–3 6–2 6–2, Ulihrach 7–5 6–4 3–6 6–4, lost Krajicek w.o.); **won** Estoril (d. Gumy 6–2 6–3, Filippini 6–4 4–6 6–1, Santoro 6–3 4–0 ret'd, J. Sanchez 6–3 6–1, Clavet 6–3 7–5), **won** Rome (d. Arazi 6–0 6–3, Boetsch 6–2 6–3, Moya 6–4 6–4, Alami 4–6 7–5 6–3, Ivanisevic 7–6 7–6, Rios 7–5 7–5 6–3), **won** Stuttgart Mercedes (d. Goellner 7–5 6–1, Larsson 7–6 6–4, Berasategui 6–4 6–4, A. Costa 6–4 6–4, Kucera 6–2 7–6); **r/u** Monte Carlo (d. Marques 6–0 6–0, Pioline 6–4 6–3, Ulihrach 4–6 7–6 6–0, Ruud 6–2 6–0, Santoro 6–4 6–4, lost Rios 6–4 6–3 6–3), **r/u** Munich (d. Camporese 6–1 6–3, Medvedev 7–5 2–6 6–1, Sinner 5–7 6–2 6–1, Rosset 6–3 6–1, lost Philippoussis 7–6 1–6 6–4); **sf** Gstaad (d. Novak 6–3 7–5, Pioline 6–3 3–2 ret'd, Berasategui 6–4 6–0, lost Viloca 3–6 7–6 6–4), **sf** Palermo (d. Martelli 5–7 6–3 6–2, Fromberg 6–1 6–4, Clavet 7–6 6–2, lost Hrbaty 6–4 6–4). **1997 HIGHLIGHTS – DOUBLES:** (with Albano) **won** Munich (d. Braasch/Knippschild 3–6 7–5 6–2); **r/u** Barcelona (lost Berasategui/Burillo 6–3 7–5). **CAREER HIGHLIGHTS – SINGLES: US Open – qf 1996** [unseeded] (d. B. Black 7–6 3–6 6–2 6–2, Veglio 6–7 6–4 6–4 6–0, Bjorkman 6–2 4–6 4–6 6–4 6–3, Forget 6–4 6–3 7–6, lost Sampras 7–6 5–7 5–7 6–4 7–6).

ALBERT COSTA (ESP)

Born Lerida, 25 June 1975; lives Barcelona; RH; 5ft 11in; 163lb; turned pro 1993; career singles titles 6; final 1997 ATP ranking 19; 1997 prize money $864,684 ($2,222,342).

Coached by Lorenzo Fargas. A Catalan, he prefers to be known as Albert, rather than Alberto. No relation to Carlos Costa. **1991:** On winning ESP World Youth Cup team. **1993:** Ranked No. 4 in ITF Jun rankings, he won Orange Bowl and was r/u French Open Jun to Carretero. In the senior game he reached qf Santiago (d. Berasategui) after qualifying. **1994:** (52) A –, F 1, W 1, US 1. He was voted Newcomer of the Year, in which he reached sf Estoril, Prague (d. Chesnokov) and Bucharest (d. Gaudenzi), and won 2 Challenger titles. **1995:** (24) A –, F qf, W –, US –. Unseeded at French Open, he upset Courier and was the only player to take a set off Muster, whom he extended to 5s. At Casablanca he reached his 1st f on the main tour, following with the same stage Estoril (d. Medvedev) and in Aug. won his 1st title at Kitzbuhel, upsetting Muster on clay. He also reached sf Nice and Santiago, plus 2 qf, to break into top 25. **1996:** (13) A 2, F 2, W 2, US 1. He continued his march through the rankings with the titles at Gstaad (d. Kafelnikov), San Marino and Bournemouth. He removed Agassi on the way to f Monte Carlo, where he extended Muster to 5s, reached his 1st HC f at Dubai and upset M. Chang at Wimbledon in only his 4th tourn on grass as he developed his skills on surfaces other than clay. He also appeared in sf Italian Open and Tel Aviv, plus qf Scottsdale and Umag. **1997:** A qf, F 3, W –, US 1. Broke into top 10 after winning Barcelona and consolidated with the title at Marbella, although he was unable to maintain that position, despite reaching sf Sydney, Stuttgart Mercedes (d. Kafelnikov), Cincinnati (d. Corretja) and Boston, and qf Australian Open (extended Sampras to 5s), Scottsdale and Hamburg. Played in winning ESP WT Cup team. **1997 HIGHLIGHTS – SINGLES: Australian Open qf** [seed 10] (d. Rafter 7–5 6–2 7–5, Kroslak 6–1 7–6 7–6, Draper 6–4 6–2 7–5, W. Ferreira [seed 8] 6–3 6–2 3–2 ret'd, lost Sampras [seed 1] 6–3 6–7 6–1 3–6 6–2), **French Open 3r** [seed 11] (d. Voinea 6–4 7–5 6–4, Pavel 6–1 4–6 0–6 6–3 6–4, lost Woodforde 6–4 7–6 6–3), **US Open 1r** [seed 16] (lost Boetsch 6–2 6–4 6–4); **won** Barcelona (d. Viloca 6–4 6–3, Goellner w.o., Pioline 6–4 6–2, Moya 7–6 7–5, Portas 7–5 6–4 6–4), **won** Marbella (d. Vicente 6–1 6–2, Burillo 7–6 6–3, Gaudenzi 6–3 7–6, Blanco 7–5 6–2, Berasategui 6–3 6–2); **sf** Sydney (d. Roux 6–4 6–2, Ulihrach 6–2 6–2, B. Black 6–4 6–2, lost Moya 3–6 6–3 7–6), **sf** Stuttgart Mercedes (d. Dosedel 6–3 7–5, Becker w.o., Kafelnikov 6–4 6–4, lost Corretja 6–4 6–4), **sf** Cincinnati (d. Courier 4–6 7–6 6–3, Haas 6–3 6–4, Corretja 6–1 7–6, Bruguera 4–6 6–3 5–2 ret'd, lost Sampras 6–3 6–4), **sf** Boston (d. Hrbaty 6–2 6–2, Carlsen 6–3 6–4, Van Herck 6–7 6–2 6–1, lost Schalken 6–4 5–7 6–3). **CAREER HIGHLIGHTS – SINGLES: Australian Open – qf 1997; French Open – qf 1995** unseeded (d. Renzenbrink 6–3 6–4 6–0, Raoux 6–4 6–4 6–4, Karbacher 7–5 6–2 6–2, Courier 6–4 1–6 7–6 6–4, lost Muster 6–2 3–6 6–7 7–5 6–2).

CARLOS COSTA (ESP)

Born Barcelona, 22 April 1968, and lives there; RH; 6ft; 175lb; turned pro 1988; career singles titles 6; final 1997 ATP ranking 56; 1997 prize money $247,024 ($2,872,962).

Coached by Jose Perlas. No relation to Albert. Wife Itziar (married 2 December 1994). **1986:** (870) Nat Jun champ. **1988:** (243). **1989:** (201) Won Madrid doubles with Carbonell. **1990:** (151) A –, F –, W 1, US –. Won Zaragoza Challenger; upset Korda and Cherkasov at Barcelona. **1991:** (55) A –, F 3, W –, US –. Reached sf Florence and sf Guaruja Bliss; won Venice and Siracusa Challengers. Played 2 doubles f, winning San Marino with Arrese. **1992:** (14) A –, F 4, W 2, US 4. Really came into his own during the year and broke into top 20 after upsetting E. Sanchez and Bruguera *en route* to his first tour title at Lisbon and following with Barcelona in April. R/u Madrid and Italian Open; sf Hamburg (d. Agassi). **1993:** (26) A 3, F 4, W 2, US 3. He made his mark in GS: unseeded at French Open, he upset Ivanisevic and extended Krajicek to 10–8 5s in last 16; at Wimbledon he extended W. Ferreira to 8–6 5s 2r and at US Open he upset Ivanisevic again. Won Hilversum and Buenos Aires (where he also took the doubles with Carbonell), r/u Mexico City and reached sf Schenectady, as well as upsetting Sampras 2r Stockholm. **1994:** (27) A –, F 2, W 2, US 3. Won Estoril and San Marino, r/u Barcelona and reached 4 more qf. **1995:** (31) A –, F 3, W –, US –. R/u Oporto and Umag (d. Berasategui and held 3 mps v Muster before letting the title slip away), reached sf Bastad and Amsterdam and won Graz Challenger. Upset Eltingh at Stuttgart Mercedes. **1996:** (61) A 2, F 1, W 1, US 1. It was a less productive year in which he slipped out of the top 50, despite appearances in f Bologna, sf Bastad and qf Indian Wells (d. Becker), Estoril and Monte Carlo (d. M. Chang). **1997:** A –, F 2, W –, US 1. His best performances were sf Bastad and San Marino, plus qf Monte Carlo (d. W. Ferreira), Bucharest (d. Moya) and Bogota. On the Challenger circuit he won Barletta and Barcelona. **1997 HIGHLIGHTS – SINGLES: French Open 2r** (d. D. Flach 6–4 6–0 6–1, lost Korda 6–3 7–5 6–4), **US Open 1r** (lost Paes 6–1 7–5 6–4); **won** Barletta Challenger (d. Sanguinetti 6–3 6–2), **won** Barcelona Challenger (d. Marin 6–1 6–4); **sf** Bastad (d. Pavel 3–6 6–3 6–1, Craca 6–3 6–4, Fredriksson 6–2 6–3, lost M. Norman 7–5 6–3), **sf** San Marino (d. Arazi 6–4 6–3, Furlan 5–7 6–3 6–3, J. Sanchez 6–3 6–3, lost Gustafsson 1–6 6–1 6–3).

JIM COURIER (USA)

Born Sanford, Fla., 17 August 1970; lives Miami, Fla.; RH; 2HB; 6ft 1in; 175lb; turned pro 1988; career singles titles 22; final 1997 ATP ranking 21; 1997 prize money $588,084 ($13,322,569).
Coached by Harold Solomon; trained by Pat Etcheberry. **1986:** A prominent junior who was a product of the Nick Bollettieri Tennis Academy. Played on US Jun World Cup team r/u to AUS; won Orange Bowl. **1987:** (346) Won French Open Jun doubles with Stark and won Orange Bowl again. **1988:** (43) A –, F –, W –, US 2. Sf US CC and Stockholm (d. Jarryd and Pernfors back-to-back); qf Stratton Mountain and Detroit. R/u US Nat 18s to Chang. **1989:** (24) A –, F 4, W 1, US 3. Upset Agassi *en route* to last 16 French Open and beat Edberg to win his 1st GP title at Basel in autumn. In doubles won Italian Open and qualified for Masters with Sampras. **1990:** (25) A 2, F 4, W 3, US 2. Although he won no title, he reached sf Indian Wells, plus qf Milan, Philadelphia, LIPC, Munich, Gstaad and Cincinnati. **1991:** (2) A 4, F won, W qf, US r/u. He began an extraordinary year by extending Edberg to 5s in last 16 Australian Open, then in March won both singles and doubles (with J. Sanchez) at Indian Wells, following immediately with the title at LIPC over Wheaton, which took him into top 10 for 1st time. Then followed the high spot of his career to date, when he won the French Open. Swept to f US Open, ending Connors' romantic run in sf, but was completely outplayed by Edberg at the last hurdle. **1992:** (1) A won, F won, W 3, US sf. He won his 2nd and 3rd GS titles at Australian and French Opens, but lost the chance of a GS when he was beaten by Olhovskiy at Wimbledon and at US Open fell in sf to Sampras. After reaching f San Francisco in Feb., he displaced Edberg from the top of the rankings, becoming the 10th man to hold that position since rankings began, but lost his place 6 weeks later (23 March) when he fell to Chang sf LIPC. Throughout the year the top ranking shifted between the two, Courier regaining it in April after winning Tokyo Suntory, where Edberg fell sf. The titles at Hong Kong and Italian Open kept him in the lead until after US Open. However, he returned to No. 1 again on 5 Oct., with Edberg dropping to 3 behind Sampras, and after taking r/u spot at ATP World Champ to an inspired Becker, he finished the year at the top. **1993:** (3) A won, F r/u, W r/u, US 4. His year began well when he retained his Australian Open title, but he was overtaken at the top of the rankings by Sampras 12 April after losing to Mansdorf in sf Osaka and then lost to Stark 3r Tokyo Japan Open. He regained the top spot briefly 19 weeks later after winning Indianapolis and beating Becker 1st time in 7 meetings, but gave it up again to Sampras after US Open. He also won Memphis, Indian Wells and Italian Open, was r/u French Open to Bruguera and played his 1st Wimbledon f, losing to Sampras, but at US Open fell in last 16 to Pioline. As usual he was less impressive after end Aug. and at IBM/ATP Champ, where he won no match, he behaved very strangely in his rr match v Medvedev. In contrast to his usual professionalism and dedication, he read a book between points, abandoned his baseball cap, without which he never played, and gave extraordinarily facile and vague answers at the press conference afterwards. He finished the year ranked 3 behind Stich, with Sampras firmly at the top. **1994:** (13) A sf, F sf, W 2, US 2. Again he began the year well, apparently back to normal after his strange performance v Medvedev at end of 1993, and feeling generally optimistic, although he was still struggling for motivation. In spring he decided to ease off his single-minded approach to the game and smell the roses more, playing for fun and taking breaks when he wanted to. At French Open, seeded as low as 7, he looked a likely winner when beating Sampras, before falling to Bruguera. Then at Wimbledon he lost to Forget 2r, a result which saw him slip out of the top 10. After 1r loss to Corretja at Indianapolis, feeling the lack of mental application and commitment, he decided to take an indefinite break from the game, although he did play US Open, where Gaudenzi beat him. He was then out of action until Lyon in Oct. R/u finishes at Nice and Lyon and sf showings at Philadelphia, LIPC and Toronto plus 5 more qf were not enough to prevent him finishing the year still outside the top 10 and with a question mark over his future. **1995:** (8) A qf, F 4, W 2, US sf. Having won no title for 16 months, he returned to form at the start of the year by winning both singles and doubles at Adelaide, following with the singles at Scottsdale (d. Edberg), Tokyo Japan Open (d. M. Chang and Agassi). He upset Muster and M. Chang on his way to sf US Open and celebrated his return to the top 10 on Sept. 18 by winning Basel the next week. He was also r/u Toulouse and reached sf San Jose, Hong Kong and Paris Open to qualify for IBM/ATP Champ, but did not progress beyond rr. **1996:** (26) A qf, F qf, W 1, US –. Although it was not one of his best years, he was enjoying his tennis more

and took the title at Philadelphia, as well as reaching sf Barcelona and qf LIPC and Halle. At Australian Open he was 2s and a break up v Agassi in qf before letting the match slip away, and at French Open was similarly 2s up against Sampras before losing the next 3. He injured his knee at New Haven and was out 2 months, missing US Open. **1997:** A 4, F 1, W 1, US 1. Despite being hampered in early season by a hamstring strain, he succeeded in his aim of regaining his place in top 25, having dropped out for 1st time in 8 years. He scored some major upsets on his way to the title at Qatar (d. Muster), Los Angeles (d. Krajicek, Ivanisevic and Enqvist back-to-back) and Beijing, sf Dubai and LIPC (d. Krajicek and Ivanisevic), and qf Rome (d. Sampras) and Singapore. **1997 HIGHLIGHTS – SINGLES: Australian Open last 16** [seed 11] (d. Schalken 6–7 6–3 4–6 6–1 8–6, Dosedel 4–6 6–2 3–6 6–4 6–4, Tarango 6–1 7–6 6–3, lost Muster [seed 5] 6–2 3–6 7–6 6–3), **French Open 1r** (lost Larsson 6–1 6–2 4–6 1–6 6–4), **Wimbledon 1r** (lost Stich 7–6 7–5 7–6), **US Open 1r** (lost T. Martin 3–6 6–3 6–4 6–2); **won** Qatar (d. Schalken 7–6 7–5, Sabau 6–3 6–4, Muster 6–3 7–5, Bruguera 6–4 6–2, Henman 7–5 6–7 6–2), **won** Los Angeles (d. Stafford 7–5 7–5, Bhupathi 7–6 6–3, Krajicek 7–6 7–5, Ivanisevic 6–3 6–4, Enqvist 6–4 6–4), **won** Beijing (d. Radulescu 6–3 6–4, Ondruska 6–4 6–3, Kroslak 6–4 6–3, Johansson 6–3 6–4, Gustafsson 7–6 3–6 6–3); **sf** Dubai (d. Medvedev 6–3 6–3, A. Costa 6–2 6–3, W. Ferreira 6–2 7–5, lost Muster 7–6 2–6 6–3), **sf** LIPC (d. Stolle 6–2 6–2, Draper 4–6 6–1 6–4, Krajicek 7–6 6–4, Ivanisevic 6–2 7–6, lost Muster 6–3 6–4). **1997 HIGHLIGHTS – DOUBLES:** (with O'Brien) **r/u** Beijing (lost Bhupathi/Paes 7–5 7–6). **CAREER HIGHLIGHTS – SINGLES: Australian Open – won 1992** (d. Gilbert 6–4 7–6 6–3, Enqvist 2–6 6–3 6–1 6–4, Muster 6–1 6–4 6–2, Rosset 6–3 6–1 6–3, Mansdorf 6–3 6–2 6–2, Krajicek w.o., Edberg 6–3 3–6 6–4 6–2), **won 1993** (d. Jonsson 7–5 6–0 6–3, Weiss 6–2 7–5 6–4, Raoux 6–4 6–3 6–4, Bruguera 6–1 6–3 7–6, Korda 6–1 6–0 6–4, Stich 7–6 6–4 6–2, Edberg 6–2 6–1 2–6 7–5), **sf 1994** (d. Shelton 4–6 6–1 6–7 6–2 6–4, Ondruska 6–1 6–4 6–4, Kulti 6–3 6–3 7–6, W. Ferreira 6–3 6–4 6–2, Ivanisevic 7–6 6–4 6–2, lost Sampras 6–3 6–4 6–4), **qf 1995** (d. Rikl 6–4 6–0 7–6, Caratti 6–2 6–2 6–1, Woodforde 6–3 6–3 6–3, Novacek 6–2 6–3 6–2, lost Sampras 6–7 6–7 6–3 6–4 6–3), **qf 1996** (d. van Herck 7–5 7–6 6–4, Tarango 7–5 6–7 6–4 6–3, Woodbridge 6–3 6–7 7–6 3–6 6–4, Ondruska 7–5 2–6 4–6 6–4 6–2, lost Agassi 6–7 2–6 6–3 6–4 6–2); **French Open – won 1991** (d. Rostagno 6–3 6–3 6–0, Ferreira 6–2 6–3 6–4, Larsson 6–3 4–6 4–6 7–5 6–2, Martin 6–2 6–3 6–3, Edberg 6–4 2–6 6–3 6–4, Stich 6–2 6–7 6–2 6–4, Agassi 3–6 6–4 2–6 6–1 6–4), **won 1992** (d. Kroon 7–6 6–4 6–2, Muster 6–1 6–4 6–4, Mancini 6–4 6–2 6–0, Medvedev 6–1 6–4 6–2, Ivanisevic 6–2 6–1 2–6 7–5, Agassi 6–3 6–2 6–2), **r/u 1993** (d. Azar 6–3 6–3 6–3, Carbonell 6–4 6–1 6–0, Tarango 6–1 6–7 6–3 7–5, Muster 6–3 2–6 6–4 6–2, Prpic 6–1 4–6 6–0 7–5, Krajicek 6–1 6–7 7–5 6–2, lost Bruguera 6–4 2–6 6–2 3–6 6–3), **sf 1994** (d. Fleurian 6–1 6–4 6–4, Pescosolido 7–5 6–0 6–7 6–4, Bjorkman 6–3 6–1 6–1, Delaitre 6–1 6–7 6–1 7–6, Sampras 6–4 5–7 6–4 6–4, lost Bruguera 6–3 5–7 6–3 6–3), **qf 1996** (d. Olhovskiy 6–1 3–6 7–6 6–4, Rikl 6–3 6–2 6–3, Kucera 6–7 7–5 6–4 6–4 ret'd, W. Ferreira 4–6 6–1 6–3 6–3, lost Sampras 6–7 4–6 6–4 6–4 6–4); **Wimbledon – r/u 1993** (d. Pozzi 6–0 7–5 6–4, Agenor 7–5 6–1 7–6, Stoltenberg 6–4 7–6 3–6 6–4, W. Ferreira 4–6 7–6 7–5 6–4, Martin 6–2 7–6 6–3, Edberg 4–6 6–4 6–2 6–4, lost Sampras 7–6 7–6 3–6 6–3), **qf 1991** (d.Gilbert 6–4 6–2 7–6, Grabb 6–4 7–6 2–6 4–6 6–4, Boetsch 6–2 6–2 6–0, Novacek 6–3 6–4 6–2, lost Stich 6–3 7–6 6–2); **US Open – r/u 1991** (d. Kulti 6–3 6–4 6–4, Arias 6–3 6–2 6–0, Jarryd 6–3 6–2 6–2, E. Sanchez 6–4 6–4 6–3, Sampras 6–2 7–6 7–6, Connors 6–3 6–3 6–2, lost Edberg 6–2 6–4 6–0), **sf 1992** (d. O'Brien 4–6 6–1 6–4 7–6, Chesnokov 4–6 6–3 6–3 6–1, Pioline 7–6 6–4 3–6 6–3, J. McEnroe 6–2 6–2 7–6, Agassi 6–3 6–7 6–1 6–4, lost Sampras 6–1 3–6 6–2 6–2), **sf 1995** (d. Karbacher 6–3 6–4 3–6 6–3, Lareau 6–3 6–4 6–4, Carlsen 6–3 6–4 6–2, Muster 6–3 6–0 7–6, M. Chang 7–6 7–6 7–5, lost Sampras 7–5 4–6 6–4 7–5); **ATP Champs – r/u 1991** (lost Lendl 6–2 6–3, d. Novacek 6–7 7–5 6–2, d. Forget 7–6 6–4 in rr; d. Agassi 6–3 7–5, lost Sampras 3–6 7–6 6–3 6–4), **r/u 1992** (d. Krajicek 6–7 7–6 7–5, lost Ivanisevic 6–3 6–3, d. M. Chang 7–5 6–2 in rr, d. Sampras 7–6 7–6, lost Becker 6–4 6–3 7–5).

MARTIN DAMM (CZE)

Born Liberec, 1 August 1972; lives Monte Carlo, Monaco; RH; 6ft 2in; 177lb; turned pro 1990; career singles titles 0; final 1997 ATP ranking 61 singles, 20 doubles; 1997 prize money $526,568 ($2,164,765).

Coached by Tomas Petera. Wife Vlasta (married 11 September 1993). **1988:** In winning Czech World Youth Cup team. **1989:** (722) Ranked 4 in singles and 2 in doubles in ITF Jun Rankings and was r/u US Open Jun doubles with Kodes. **1990:** (317). **1991:** (144) Won Warsaw Challenger. **1992:** (90) A –, F –, W 2, US 2. Won Dublin and Aachen Challengers and at Wimbledon extended a lacklustre Becker to 5s. **1993:** (77) A 2, F 1, W 1, US 2. A qualifier at Basel, he reached his 1st tour sf, saving mps in both 2r and qf. Upset Haarhuis 1r Copenhagen and Stich at Bolzano and on the Challenger circuit he won Munich. In doubles he played 4 f, winning Munich with Holm and Zaragoza with Novacek, with whom he reached his 1st GS f at US Open. **1994:** (99) A 4, F 1, W 3, US 2. Upset Pioline on his way to last 16 Australian Open, unseeded, and in 3r Wimbledon extended Martin to 11–9 5s. Reached sf Ostrava and qf Hong Kong (d. Krickstein). In doubles with various partners won 3 titles from 6 f. **1995:** (61) A 3, F 1, W –, US 1. Upset Berasategui and Siemerink back-to-back to reach sf Stuttgart Eurocard and also appeared in qf Rotterdam and Basel. In doubles won 2 titles with Jarryd. **1996:** (50) A 1, F 1, W 2, US 1. He appeared with his 1st f on the main tour at Seoul, following with the same stage Long Island and Beijing (d. M. Chang), and reached sf Adelaide and Ostrava (d. Stich), plus qf Rotterdam and Hong Kong. From 3 doubles f, he won Beijing with Olhovskiy. **1997:** A 1, F 1, W 1, US 3. In singles he was r/u Copenhagen and reached qf Zagreb, Antwerp (d. Rios), Tokyo Japan Open, Rosmalen, Singapore and Moscow, as well as upsetting Krajicek at Cincinnati. In doubles he won Hong Kong and Tokyo Japan Open with Vacek and Moscow with Suk. **1997 HIGHLIGHTS – SINGLES: Australian Open**

1r (lost Johansson 6–4 6–2 3–6 6–7 6–2), **French Open 1r** (lost Kafelnikov [seed 3] 6–2 6–4 6–4), **Wimbledon 1r** (lost Frana 6–7 6–4 6–3 6–2), **US Open 3r** (d. Ho 6–3 6–4 6–7 6–4, Steven 6–4 6–4 3–6 7–6, lost Korda [seed 15] 4–6 6–3 6–4 7–5); **r/u** Copenhagen (d. Langvardt 6–2 6–3, Marques 6–3 3–6 6–3, Fetterlein 6–4 6–3, Kucera 6–4 3–6 6–3, lost Johansson 6–4 3–6 6–2). **1997 HIGHLIGHTS – DOUBLES:** (with Vacek unless stated) **won** Hong Kong (d. Braasch/Tarango 6–3 6–4), **won** Tokyo Japan Open (d. Gimelstob/Rafter 2–6 6–2 7–6), (with Suk) **won** Moscow (d. D. Adams/Santoro 6–4 6–3). **CAREER HIGHLIGHTS – DOUBLES:** (with Novacek) **US Open – r/u 1993** (lost K. Flach/Leach 6–7 6–4 6–2).

JOSE DE ARMAS (VEN)

Born Florida, USA, 25 March 1981; lives Caracas; RH; 6ft; 105lb; career singles titles 0; final 1997 ATP ranking 1122.

Coached by Victor Perez. **1997:** Won French Open Jun doubles with Horna.

FILIP DEWULF (BEL)

Born Mol, 15 March 1972; lives Leopoldsburg; RH; 6ft 3in; 176lb; turned pro 1990; career singles titles 2; final 1997 ATP ranking 40; 1997 prize money $492,104 ($1,116,084).

Coached by Gabriel Gonzales. **1990:** (517). **1991:** (277) Won Nat Champ and joined Belgian D Cup squad. **1992:** (164) Enjoyed some success on the Challenger circuit. **1993:** (164) Reached his 1st qf on main tour at Florence. **1994:** (134) Took over his country's top ranking. **1995:** (67) A , F –, W 1, US –. The highlight of his year came at Vienna in Oct. when, after qualifying, he went on to win the title, upsetting Muster in f and breaking into the top 100. He was only the 2nd Belgian to win a title on the main tour and the 1st since Bernard Mignot at Dusseldorf in 1975. Earlier he had reached his 1st sf at San Marino and qf Oporto and Toulouse. **1996:** (96) A 2, F 1, W 2, US 1. Although it was a less spectacular year, he performed steadily, reaching sf St Petersburg and qf Zagreb (d. Gaudenzi), Marseille, Copenhagen and Kitzbuhel, as well as upsetting Haarhuis 1r Australian Open. **1997:** A 2, F sf, W 1, US 1. At French Open he became the 1st Belgian man in the open era to reach GS sf and was the 1st qualifier for 20 years to reach sf at any GS. This result, which included an upset of Corretja, shot him through the rankings from 122 to 58. He continued his progress with the title at Kitzbuhel (d. Kafelnikov), without dropping a set, but his only other qf was at Antwerp (as LL), and although he qualified for GS Cup, he ret'd 1r v Korda with left ankle sprain. **1997 HIGHLIGHTS – SINGLES: Australian Open 2r** (d. Wibier 6–4 6–2 7–5, lost Draper 7–6 7–5 6–0); **French Open sf** [unseeded] (d. Caratti 6–3 6–3 6–1, Meligeni 6–4 6–2 3–6 1–6 6–3, Portas 6–3 7–6 4–6 6–7 8–6, Corretja [seed 8] 5–7 6–1 6–4 7–5, M. Norman 6–2 6–7 6–4 6–3, lost Kuerten 6–1 3–6 6–1 7–6), **Wimbledon 1r** (lost Pavel 6–1 4–6 2–6 6–2 6–3), **US Open 1r** (lost Van Herck 6–4 4–6 7–6 7–6); **won** Kitzbuhel (d. Sinner 6–1 6–0, Viloca 6–4 6–2, Kafelnikov 7–5 7–5, Blanco 6–3 6–2, Alonso 7–6 6–4 6–1). **CAREER HIGHLIGHTS – SINGLES: French Open – sf 1997.**

ARNAUD DI PASQUALE (FRA)

Born Casablanca, 11 February 1979; lives Paris; RH; 6ft 1in; 172lb; career singles titles 0; final 1997 ATP ranking 572; Junior ranking 1.

Coached by Georges Goven and Alain Solves. **1996:** R/u Orange Bowl. **1997:** Won US Open Jun over Whitehouse and took European Jun Champs.

SLAVA DOSEDEL (CZE)

Born Prerov, 14 August 1970; lives Monte Carlo, Monaco; RH; 6ft; 168lb; turned pro 1989; career singles titles 3; final 1997 ATP ranking 44; 1997 prize money $301,843 ($1,452,168).

Formerly named Ctislav, but is now known as Slava, which is a more easily pronounced version of the same name. Coached by Petr Hutka. Former Nat 18s champ. **1988:** (561). **1989:** (265) Won Yugoslav satellite. **1990:** (146) Won Bangkok Challenger. **1991:** (202) A 2, F 2, W –, US –. **1992:** (170) A –, F –, W – , US 1. Qf Bologna and won Poznan Challenger. **1993:** (75) A –, F 4, W 1, US 1. Finished the year in style with his 1st main tour f at Sao Paulo, having never before passed qf. He reached that stage at Dubai, Bologna and San Marino and made an unexpected appearance in last 16 French Open. **1994:** (29) A –, F 2, W 2, US –. Broke into the top 50 with sf showings at Nice, Italian Open (d. Medvedev and Courier), Bologna, St Polten, Prague, Palermo and Santiago, plus 3 qf. **1995:** (62) A –, F 2, W 2, US –. Returning in Oct. after a 6-week absence with a shoulder injury, he ended the year on a high note with his 1st title at Santiago. Earlier he had reached sf St Polten, plus qf Milan (d. Berasategui), Bologna and San Marino. **1996:** (66) A –, F 2, W –, US –. He proved to be a dangerous opponent, recording some useful upsets on his way to f Munich (unseeded, d. Becker), sf St Polten (d. Edberg) and Umag (d. A. Costa), qf Amsterdam (d. C. Costa) and San Marino, as well as surprising Kafelnikov at Marseille and Pioline at Hamburg. In doubles he won St Polten with Vizner. **1997:** A 2, F 1, W 1, US 1. Won Amsterdam, upset Berasategui on his way to sf Munich and removed Muster and Filippini *en route* to the same stage Kitzbuhel. **1997 HIGHLIGHTS – SINGLES: Australian Open 2r** (d. Forget 6–2 3–6 6–3 6–4, lost Courier [seed 11] 4–6 6–2 3–6 6–4 6–4), **French Open 1r** (lost Kuerten 6–0 7–5 6–1), **Wimbledon 1r** (lost Larkham 6–7 6–3 6–4 7–5), **US Open 1r** (lost Knippschild 7–5 5–7 6–4 6–7 6–4); **won** Amsterdam (d. Wibier 6–3 6–1, Arazi 7–5 7–6, Van Lottum 6–4 4–6 6–2, Filippini 7–6 6–2, Moya 7–6 6–7 7–6); **sf** Munich (d. Knippschild 6–4 6–1, Berasategui 4–6 6–1 6–4, Fetterlein 7–6 6–4, lost Philippoussis 7–5 7–5), **sf** Kitzbuhel (d. Champion 6–3 6–2, Muster 2–6 6–3 6–4, Filippini 7–5 6–4, lost Alonso 6–3 6–4).

SCOTT DRAPER (AUS)

Born Brisbane, 5 June 1974, and lives there; LH; 5ft 10in; 170lb; turned pro 1994; career singles titles 0; final 1997 ATP ranking 59; 1997 prize money $274,925.

Trained by Mark Waters. **1992:** (1098) Won Wimbledon Jun doubles with Baldas. **1993:** (882). **1994:** (420) Made his mark on the satellite circuits in both singles and doubles. **1995:** (81) A 1, F 4, W 1, US 3. He sprang to prominence at French Open, where he was a qualifier; he was a wild card at Australian Open, lucky loser at Wimbledon and gained direct acceptance at US Open. Reached his 1st qf on the main tour at Tokyo Japan Open, following with the same stage at Beijing and Moscow, and won Nagoya Challenger. **1996:** (94) A 1, F 4, W 1, US 2. Reached qf Sydney, Los Angeles (d. Stich), Beijing and Tel Aviv. He was again prominent at French Open, where he was unseeded. **1997:** A 3, F 1, W 1, US 4. Reached his 1st career f at Adelaide, having almost withdrawn before the tourn with wrist problems. He also appeared in qf Rome (d. Muster), Nottingham and Washington, upset Agassi at LIPC and M. Chang at Queen's, and extended W. Ferreira to 7–5 5s at Wimbledon. **1997 HIGHLIGHTS – SINGLES: Australian Open 3r** (d. Radulescu 6–2 6–4 6–7 6–3, Dewulf 7–6 7–5 6–0, lost A. Costa [seed 10] 6–4 6–2 7–5), **French Open 1r** (lost Krajicek [seed 6] 7–6 6–2 6–1), **Wimbledon 1r** (lost W. Ferreira [seed 15] 6–7 3–6 6–4 6–0 7–5), **US Open last 16** [unseeded] (d. Gambill 6–4 6–3 7–6, Novak 7–5 7–6 3–6 6–3, Tarango 7–6 3–6 2–6 6–4 6–4, lost Bjorkman 6–3 6–3 1–6 7–6); **r/u** Adelaide (d. Radulescu 6–3 3–6 6–3, Ulihrach 7–6 1–6 6–3, Kucera 6–4 7–5, Tarango 6–1 3–6 6–2, lost Woodbridge 6–2 6–1).

DANIEL ELSNER (GER)

Born Memmingen, 4 January 1979; lives Kirchberg, Austria; RH; 6ft 1in; 177lb; career singles titles 0; final 1997 ATP ranking 608; Junior ranking 2; 1997 prize money $22,350.

Coached by Peter Pfannkoch. **1995:** In winning GER World Youth Cup team. **1996:** Won US Open Jun over Hipfl. **1997:** Won Aus Jun over Whitehouse, French Jun over Horna, and was r/u Wimbledon to Whitehouse (thus missing out on holding all 4 GS at once).

JACCO ELTINGH (NED)

Born Heerde, 29 August 1970; lives Monte Carlo, Monaco; RH; 6ft 2in; 180lb; turned pro 1989; career singles titles 4; final 1997 ATP ranking 604 singles, 4 doubles; 1997 prize money $572,266 ($4,170,253).

Coached by Alex Reynders. Wife Hellas Ter Riet, who used to play on the women's tour (married 11 July 1997). **1988:** (439) European 18s Champ and won Orange Bowl doubles with Siemerink. **1989:** (286). **1990:** (128) Reached first ATP tour sf at Sao Paulo. **1991:** (110) A 3, F 1, W 4, US 1. In singles he reached qf Madrid and Newport and made an unexpected appearance in last 16 Wimbledon, where he took a set off Agassi. In doubles won 4 titles with 4 different partners. **1992:** (78) A 2, F 1, W 1, US 1. Scored some big upsets during the year, surprising Wheaton and Washington *en route* to his 1st tour title at Manchester, Svensson in reaching qf Copenhagen, Novacek 1r Auckland and Agassi at Barcelona. In doubles he won Schenectady with Haarhuis and was r/u Wimbledon mixed with Oremans. **1993:** (62) A 2, F 1, W 2, US 2. Continued his record of big upsets, surprising Sampras on the way to his 1st title on clay at Atlanta and removing Courier on the way to qf Kuala Lumpur Salem Open. He reached the same stage at US CC and Manchester. Played 10 doubles f, winning 1 with Davis and 6 with Haarhuis, including ATP World Doubles when they beat Woodbridge/Woodforde. **1994:** (23) A 2, F 4, W 2, US 1. In singles he won his 1st HC title at Schenectady, unseeded, and at Kuala Lumpur won both singles and doubles. He also appeared in sf Tokyo Seiko and Moscow (d. Korda), 6 more qf, upsetting Sampras at Philadelphia and Chang at Italian Open, and last 16 French Open, unseeded. Played 12 doubles f with Haarhuis, being voted Doubles Team of the Year. They won Australian Open, US Open and 6 others to qualify for World Doubles Champ as top pairing, although they lost sf to Woodbridge/Woodforde. **1995:** (43) A qf, F 3, W qf, US 2. Unseeded at all GS, he upset Muster at Australian Open and Stich and W. Ferreira at Wimbledon. He reached sf Halle and qf Kuala Lumpur in singles and in doubles with Haarhuis won French Open and 6 more titles to qualify for World Doubles Champ. There they advanced to f without dropping a set, but were then surprisingly beaten by Connell/Galbraith. **1996:** (305) A 1, F –, W 1, US –. In D Cup v IND, he injured his knee v Bhupathi in the last match and was forced to retire in 4s, giving the tie to IND. He was out for much of the year with recurring tendinitis in both knees and played only a restricted schedule. However, he and Haarhuis made the most of their appearances together, winning 2 of 5 doubles f, r/u US Open, and qualifying for World Doubles Champ. **1997:** A 1, F –, W –, US –. Announced in June that he would play doubles only, owing to recurring knee problems, and won 6 titles from 8 f with Haarhuis, with whom he qualified for World Doubles Champ again. There they were the only partnership to win all their rr matches, but lost sf to Leach/Stark. However, they still finished the year as the season's 2nd pairing. Aiming to become the 1st duo in the open era to win all GS titles, they just failed to win the missing title when they lost Wimbledon f in 4s to Woodbridge/Woodforde. **1997 HIGHLIGHTS – SINGLES: Australian Open 1r** (lost MaliVai Washington 6–3 6–7 6–3 6–2). **1997 HIGHLIGHTS – DOUBLES:** (with Haarhuis) **r/u Wimbledon** (lost Woodbridge/Woodforde 7–6 7–6 5–7 6–3); **won** Qatar (d. Fredriksson/M. Norman 6–3 6–2), **won** Rotterdam (d. Pimek/Talbot 7–6 6–4), **won** Rosmalen (d. Kronemann/Macpherson 6–4 7–5), **won** Boston (d. Randall/Waite 6–4 6–2), **won** Toulouse (d. Fleurian/Mirny 6–3 7–6), **won** Paris Open (d. Leach/Stark 6–2 7–6); **r/u** Monte Carlo (lost Johnson/Montana 7–6 2–6 7–6). **CAREER HIGHLIGHTS – SINGLES: Australian Open – qf 1995** [unseeded] (d. Wilander 6–3 7–6 6–4, Lareau 7–6 5–7 7–6 7–5, Muster 6–3 6–2 2–6 7–5, P. McEnroe 6–4 6–4 6–7 5–7 6–4, lost Krickstein 7–6 6–4 5–7 6–4); **Wimbledon – qf 1995** [unseeded] (d. Stich 6–4 7–6 6–1, Olhovskiy 5–7 6–3 6–4 7–6, Wilander 7–5 6–3 7–6, W. Ferreira 6–4 4–6 7–6 6–3, lost Agassi 6–2 6–3 6–4). **CAREER HIGHLIGHTS – DOUBLES:** (with Haarhuis) **Australian Open – won 1994** (d. B. Black/Stark 6–7 6–3 6–4 6–3); **French Open – won 1995** (d. Kulti/Larsson 6–7 6–4 6–1); **US Open – won 1994** (d. Woodbridge/Woodforde 6–3 7–6), **r/u 1996** (lost Woodbridge/Woodforde 4–6 7–6 7–6); **ATP World Doubles Champ** – **won 1993** (d. Woodbridge/Woodforde 7–6 7–6 6–4), **r/u 1995** (lost Connell/Galbraith 7–6 7–6 3–6 7–6); **Wimbledon – r/u 1997.**

THOMAS ENQVIST (SWE)

Born Stockholm, 13 March 1974; lives Monte Carlo, Monaco; RH; 6ft 3in; 187lb; turned pro 1991; career singles titles 11; final 1997 ATP ranking 28; 1997 prize money $566,615 ($4,054,560).

Coached by Joachim Nystrom. Won Donald Duck Cup in 1985, 1987 and 1988. **1988:** Won European 14s. **1989:** (1103). **1990:** (472) R/u French Open Jun to Gaudenzi. **1991:** (229) In Jun singles won Australian Open over Gleeson, Wimbledon over Joyce and was r/u French Open to Medvedev to finish the year at No. 1 in the ITF Jun singles rankings. In Jun doubles won French Open with Martinelle. **1992:** (63) A 2, F –, W –, US –. Made his mark in the senior game right from the start of the year at Australian Open, where he was the only player apart from Edberg to take a set off Courier. Reached qf Adelaide, Bastad and Indianapolis and in autumn won his 1st tour title at Bolzano. **1993:** (87) A 1, F 1, W 1, US 4. Having failed to pass 2r all year to date, he won Schenectady in Aug., upsetting Lendl on the way, and followed with sf Vienna (d. Volkov) and qf Bordeaux. At US Open he upset Agassi 1r *en route* to last 16, unseeded. **1994:** (60) A 2, F 1, W –, US 3. Reached sf Auckland, qf Memphis (d. MaliVai Washington), Toronto (d. Korda and Yzaga), Washington (d. Yzaga again), Indianapolis and Schenectady; upset Korda 1r Australian Open and Kafelnikov at Cincinnati. **1995:** (7) A 3, F 1, W 1, US 2. Continuing to cause some big upsets, he beat Volkov on his way to the title at Auckland, Agassi and M. Chang to take Philadelphia, Ivanisevic and M. Chang at Montreal (where he lost sf to Sampras only 7–6 fs), and surprised Ivanisevic three times more on his way to f Los Angeles, sf Cincinnati and then the title at Indianapolis. That last result took him into the top 10 and ahead of Larsson to the No. 1 slot in Sweden. He also won US CC and reached 6 more qf, being voted ATP Most Improved Player of the Year. **1996:** (9) A qf, F 1, W 2, US 4. After taking the title at New Delhi in April, without losing a set, he was less consistent and dropped out of the top 10 in July. However, he found form again later in the year, upsetting Sampras on his way to sf Cincinnati and removing Kafelnikov on the way to his 1st Mercedes Super 9 title at Paris Open in Nov., which saw him back in the top 10. He also appeared in sf Lyon and qf Australian Open, Dubai, Memphis, Tokyo Japan Open, Indianapolis and Toronto. **1997:** A 4, F –, W –, US –. Hampered during the year by infected blisters, an arm injury and flu, he played only Australian Open of GS and slipped out of the top 25. However, he won both singles and doubles at Marseille (with Larsson), reached f Los Angeles and sf Zagreb, Rotterdam and Paris Open, plus qf Montreal, Basel and Lyon. **1997 HIGHLIGHTS – SINGLES: Australian Open last 16** [seed 7] (d. Pereira 6–1 6–2 6–4, Fromberg 6–4 6–4 7–5, Bruguera 7–6 7–5 6–2, lost Rios [seed 9] 4–6 7–6 6–7 6–3); **won** Marseille (d. Fredriksson 6–1 6–2, Hrbaty 6–3 6–2, Dreekmann 6–4 3–6 6–1, Santoro 6–4 6–3, Rios 6–4 1–0 ret'd); **r/u** Los Angeles (d. Bryan 6–3 6–2, Spadea 7–6 6–1, Carlsen 6–3 7–5, Raoux 6–4 6–1, lost Courier 6–4 6–4); **sf** Zagreb (d. Fredriksson 6–7 6–3 6–3, Alami 6–3 6–0, Arazi 6–2 6–3, lost Rusedski 6–4 6–4), **sf** Rotterdam (d. Ulihrach 7–5 6–7 6–3, Kiefer 6–2 6–2, Radulescu 7–6 6–3, lost Krajicek 6–7 6–3 6–4), **sf** Paris Open (d. Prinosil 7–5 6–1, Gustafsson 6–1 6–4, Raoux 7–5 6–2, lost Bjorkman 7–6 7–5). **1997 HIGHLIGHTS – DOUBLES:** (with Larsson) **won** Marseille (d. Delaitre/Santoro 6–3 6–4). **CAREER HIGHLIGHTS – SINGLES: Australian Open – qf 1996** (d. Goellner 6–3 6–2 6–4, Voinea 6–4 6–4 6–1, Gumy 6–2 7–6 3–6 6–1, Furlan 7–5 6–0 6–3, lost Woodforde 6–4 6–4 6–4).

ELLIS FERREIRA (RSA)

Born Pretoria 19 February 1970; lives Atlanta, Ga.; LH; 6ft 2in; 185lb; turned pro 1991; career singles titles 0; final 1997 ATP ranking 10 doubles; 1997 prize money $288,469.

Wife Ashley (married 19 September 1992); daughter Camden Lanier born 24 July 1997. No relation to Wayne Ferreira. **1991:** (503) All-American in doubles for 3rd year at Univ. of Alabama. **1992:** (387) A –, F –, W –, US 1 . **1993:** (362) A –, F –, W –, US –. **1994:** (240) A –, F –, W 1, US 2. R/u Sun City doubles with Stafford. **1995:** (519) A –, F –, W –, US –. In doubles with Siemerink won Vienna and r/u Stuttgart Mercedes. **1996:** (–) A –, F –, W –, US –. Played 3 doubles f, winning Sydney and Monte Carlo with Siemerink. **1997:** Won 5 doubles titles from 7 f with Galbraith, with whom he qualified for his 1st World Doubles Champ, where they won only 1 match. **1997 HIGHLIGHTS – DOUBLES:** (with Galbraith) **won** Auckland (d. Leach/Stark 6–4 4–6 7–6), **won** Memphis (d. Leach/Stark 6–3 3–6 6–1), **won** Nottingham (d. Sapsford/Wilkinson 4–6 7–6 7–6), **won** Vienna (d. Goellner/Prinosil 6–3 6–4), **won** Lyon (d. Delaitre/Santoro 3–6 6–2 6–4); **r/u** Philadelphia (lost Lareau/O'Brien 6–3 6–3), **r/u** Stockholm (lost Goellner/Reneberg 6–3 3–6 7–6).

WAYNE FERREIRA (RSA)

Born Johannesburg, 15 September 1971, and lives there; RH; 2HB: 6ft; 168lb; turned pro 1989; career singles titles 7; final 1997 ATP ranking 43; 1997 prize money $456,171 ($5,928,744).

Coached by Danie Visser; physical trainer Walt Landers. Wife Liesl (married 16 Dec. 1994). No relation to Ellis Ferreira. Has represented Transvaal at cricket, football and badminton. **1989:** (229) Finished the year No. 1 doubles player in ITF Jun Rankings, having won US Open Jun with Stafford and r/u Wimbledon Jun with de Jager. **1990:** (173) A –, F –, W 2, US –. Upset Noah 1r Wimbledon. **1991:** (50) A 4, F 2, W 2, US 2. In singles reached last 16 Australian Open after qualifying and qf Sydney Indoor (d. Lendl), Brisbane and Birmingham. In doubles won LIPC with Norval and Adelaide with Kruger. **1992:** (12) A sf, F 3, W 4, US qf. Having never before progressed beyond qf on the main tour, he put in a tremendous performance at Australian Open, where he upset Wheaton and Novacek *en route* to sf, unseeded. Took his 1st tour title at Queen's in June and broke into top 20, progressing to top 10 in Sept. after reaching qf US Open. Won a second title at Schenectady, r/u Memphis and Stuttgart and sf Johannesburg. Played 4 doubles f, winning Olympic silver medal with Norval and taking Auckland with Grabb. **1993:** (22) A 4, F 2, W 4, US 4. It was a less spectacular year in which he slipped out of the top 20 and was unseeded at US Open, where he survived 3 5s matches. He won no title but was r/u Indian Wells and Queen's and reached sf Durban and Sydney Indoor. **1994:** (12) A 4, F 1, W qf, US 3. Won Hawaii, Indianapolis, Bordeaux, Basel, Tel Aviv; r/u Rotterdam (d. Ivanisevic), Manchester; sf Dubai and Toronto. Unseeded at Wimbledon, he upset Rosset on his way to qf, where he took Martin to 7-5 5s. **1995:** (9) A 2, F 3, W 4, US 1. Returned to top 10 after winning his 1st CC title at Munich in May, although he slipped out again later in year. Was asked to try a different racket, but did not get on with it and lost 1r or 2r of 5 tourns before returning to his old type, whereupon he won Ostrava 2 weeks later, following the next week with Lyon, where he beat Sampras in f. He also won Dubai and reached sf Tokyo Japan Open, Italian Open and Paris Open, plus 4 qf. **1996:** (10) A 2, F 4, W 3, US 1. He edged up the rankings in what was a solid, if not spectacular, year. Although his GS performances were disappointing, he won the titles at Scottsdale and Toronto, was r/u Washington and reached sf Italian Open, Queen's and New Haven, as well as qf Dubai, Indian Wells, Hamburg, Cincinnati, Ostrava and Olympics. **1997:** A –, F 3, W 3, US 4. He began the year by winning Hopman Cup singles and followed with sf Gstaad and Indianapolis and qf Dubai. However, restricted by a thigh strain, he missed Australian Open, withdrew during French Open and struggled for much of the year. **1997 HIGHLIGHTS – SINGLES: French Open 3r** [seed 13] (d. Tillstrom 6–7 7–6 6–7 6–3 6–1, Carretero 7–6 4–6 6–1 2–6 6–4, lost Korda w.o.), **Wimbledon 3r** [seed 15] (d. Draper 6–7 3–6 7–6 6–4, R. Gilbert 7–6 4–6 6–3 3–6 9–7, lost Pioline 6–4 6–3 6–3), **US Open last 16** [unseeded] (d. Berasategui 6–7 2–6 6–3 6–1 6–3, Henman 6–3 6–2 6–4, Gimelstob 5–7 7–6 6–3 6–0, lost Larsson 6–3 7–6 6–3); **sf** Gstaad (d. Clavet 3–6 6–4 6–4, Vicente 2–6 6–3 6–4, Rosset 7–6 6–3, lost Mantilla 6–3 6–4), **sf** Indianapolis (d. Tebbutt 6–4 6–3, Ran 6–2 6–3, Stafford 6–4 7–6, Larsson 3–6 6–3 7–6, lost Moya 6–4 6–2). **CAREER HIGHLIGHTS – SINGLES: Australian Open – sf 1992** (d. Lavalle 6–2 6–4 1–6 6–3, Novacek 3–6 6–3 7–6 7–6, Woodforde 4–6 6–3 6–2 6–2, Wheaton 6–7 6–4 6–2 6–2, J. McEnroe 6–4 6–4 6–4, lost Edberg 7–6 6–1 6–2), **Wimbledon – qf 1994** (d. Hadad 6–4 3–6 7–5 6–3, Rosset [14] 6–7 6–3 6–4 6–4, Wilkinson 6–2 6–2 6–3, Bjorkman 6–3 6–7 6–4 6–3, lost Martin 6–3 6–2 3–6 5–7 7–5), **US Open – qf 1992** (d. Arrese 3–6 7–5 6–3 6–3, Bruguera 6–7 6–2 3–6 6–1 6–2, Masur 6–4 6–4 6–2, E. Sanchez 6–2 6–4 2–6 6–4, lost Chang 7–5 2–6 6–3 6–7 6–1).

MARCELO FILIPPINI (URU)

Born Montevideo, 4 August 1967, and lives there; RH; 5ft 10in; 145lb; turned pro 1987; career singles titles 5; final 1997 ATP ranking 45; 1995 prize money $273,482 ($1,712,346).

Coached by Jose-Luis Damiani. **1986:** (415). **1987:** (118) Played his best tennis at Sao Paulo, where he won the Challenger title and reached qf of GP event. **1988:** (53) A –, F 2, W –, US –. Won his 1st GP singles title at Bastad in July – the 1st time he had passed qf in a GP tourn – r/u Bari, sf St Vincent and Barcelona. **1989:** (43) A –, F 1, W –, US –. Won Prague and reached 5 more qf, finishing the year with an upset of Hlasek at Itaparica. **1990:** (49) A –, F 2, W –, US 1. R/u Itaparica; sf Bastad (d. Wilander), San Remo and San Marino. **1991:** (107) A –, F 2, W –, US –. R/u Madrid. **1992:** (60) A –, F 4, W –, US –. Reached last 16 French Open, unseeded; sf Florence, Genova and Kitzbuhel; qf Casablanca, Tampa, Cologne and Buzios. **1993:** (84) A 3, F 1, W –, US –. Reached sf Santiago and upset Lendl on his way to qf Italian Open. **1994:** (61) A –, F –, W –, US –. At Florence he won his 1st title for 5 years, and also reached sf Birmingham, San Marino (d. Berasategui) and Montevideo, where he won the doubles with Mattar. **1995:** (103) A –, F 1, W –, US –. He reached sf Bologna, sf Munich and qf Amsterdam and Montevideo, but slipped out of the top 100. **1996:** (80) A –, F –, W –, US 1. Serving for the title at Bermuda v MaliVai Washington at 5–3 40–30 3s, he lost the point and let the match slip away. In other tourns he reached qf Marbella and Santiago and won Barcelona Challenger. At Casablanca v Berasategui, he played and lost the longest known singles game in ATP history, lasting 20 mins and featuring 28 deuces. **1997:** A –, F 1, W 1, US 2. Unseeded at Atlanta in May, he took his 1st title since 1994, following 3 weeks later by winning his next tourn at St Polten, unseeded again. He also reached sf Amsterdam and Santiago and qf Orlando, Kitzbuhel and Palermo. **1997 HIGHLIGHTS – SINGLES: French Open 1r** (lost Tarango 4–6 6–2 5–7 7–6 6–4), **Wimbledon 1r** (lost Korda [seed 16] 4–6 7–6 6–1 6–4), **US Open 2r** (d. O'Brien 6–2 6–4 6–4, lost Krajicek 7–6 6–2 7–5); **won** Atlanta (d. Spadea 6–4 7–6, O'Brien 7–6 6–4, Schaller 6–1 6–2, Woodruff 7–5 3–6 6–4, Stoltenberg 7–6 6–4), **won** St Polten (d. Viloca 7–6 7–5, Rosset 4–0 ret'd, Nydahl 7–5 6–1, Hrbaty 7–6 6–1, Rafter 7–6 6–2); **sf** Amsterdam (d. Goellner 7–5 1–6 6–4, Alami 6–3 3–6 6–0, J. Sanchez 7–6 6–1, lost Dosedel 7–6 6–2), **sf** Santiago (d. Alvarez 6–2 7–6, A. Martin 7–5 6–3, Vasek 6–1 7–5, lost Rios 6–1 6–4).

RICHARD FROMBERG (AUS)

Born Ulvestone, Tas., 28 April 1970; lives Newtown, Tas.; RH; 6ft 5in; 195lb; turned pro 1988; career singles titles 4; final 1997 ATP ranking 70; 1997 prize money $276,008 ($1,762,899).

Played in winning World Youth Cup team in 1985 and 1986. Coached by Ray Ruffels and working with David Tunbridge. **1988:** (103) A 2, F –, W –, US –. Qf Brisbane and r/u Australian Open Jun doubles with J. Anderson. **1989:** (126) A 1, F 1, W –, US –. Won Bahia Challenger. **1990:** (32) A 1, F 1, W 2, US 1. Reached f Singapore then won 1st tour title at Bologna, following with Bastad. Joined AUS D Cup squad for f v USA, where he took Agassi to 5s in 1st rubber and beat Chang in dead 5th rubber. **1991:** (93) A 2, F 1, W 1, US 1. Began the year in style by winning Wellington, followed by qf showing at Italian Open. Sidelined for 5 weeks in July/August with rotator cuff tendinitis, he returned to reach qf Indianapolis and Brisbane. **1992:** (83) A 1, F 2, W 1, US 3. Won 2 Challenger titles and appeared in qf US CC (d. Rostagno), Prague and Schenectady. **1993:** (40) A 4, F 3, W 1, US 3. Was r/u Tampa and reached sf Adelaide, Hilversum (d. Haarhuis) and Lyon. In GS he upset C. Costa to reach last 16 Australian Open, unseeded, and on the Challenger circuit he won Turin. Won Australia's only rubber (v Goellner) in D Cup final as AUS lost 4–1 to GER. **1994:** (59) A 2, F 2, W 3, US 3. After suffering problems with rotator cuff muscle in right shoulder during 1st 3 months of year, he reached f Florence and Hilversum (d. Berasategui) plus sf Bastad. **1995:** (93) A 2, F 1, W –, US –. Upset Rosset on his way to f Sydney and reached qf Nice, Oporto and Valencia. Out of action June to Sept. after breaking his left wrist. **1996:** (82) A 1, F 2, W 1, US –. He could not advance beyond qf, although he reached that stage at Sydney, Casablanca, Estoril, Coral Springs (d. Woodforde) and Oporto, where he also won the Challenger title. **1997:** A 2, F 1, W 1, US 2. Having reached only one qf all year – at Prague – he came good in autumn, winning Bucharest for his 1st title since 1991, and also took Szczecin Challenger. **1997 HIGHLIGHTS – SINGLES: Australian Open 2r** (d. Steven 4–6 2–6 7–5 6–3 6–1, lost Enqvist [seed 7] 6–4 6–4 7–5), **French Open 1r** (lost Mantilla [seed 10] 6–3 6–2 6–2), **Wimbledon 1r** (lost Van Scheppingen 5–7 6–4 3–6 6–1 6–4), **US Open 2r** (d. McEnroe 6–2 6–2 6–7 6–3, lost Radulescu 3–6 6–4 6–3 3–6 6–4); **won** Bucharest (d. Arazi 6–4 6–0, Voinea 7–5 6–3, Portas 6–4 6–3, Clavet 4–6 6–3 6–4, Gaudenzi 6–1 7–6), **won** Szczecin Challenger (d. Lapentti 6–7 6–4 6–1). **1997 HIGHLIGHTS – DOUBLES:** (with Arthurs) **won** Kitzbuhel (d. Buchmayer/Strengberger 6–4 6–3).

PATRICK GALBRAITH (USA)

Born Tacoma, Wash., 16 April 1967; lives Seattle, Wash.; LH; 6ft; 160lb; turned pro 1989; career singles titles 0; final 1997 ATP ranking 9 doubles; 1997 prize money $299,124 ($2,373,164).

Coached by Dean Goldfine. A 3-times All-American at UCLA in doubles with Garrow, with whom he won NCAA doubles in 1988. **1989:** (438) Won Newport doubles with Garrow. **1990:** (581) Playing with various partners, he reached 3 doubles f, winning 2. **1991:** (670) Continuing to make his mark in doubles, he won 3 titles with Witsken and a 4th with Jarryd. Qualified with Witsken for ATP Doubles Champ, but they were eliminated after rr. **1992:** (–) Again made his mark in doubles, winning 5 titles with different partners. **1993:** (–) In doubles with Connell reached 7 f, including his 1st GS f at Wimbledon, and won titles at Auckland, Tokyo Seiko and Antwerp. They were voted ATP Doubles Team of the year and qualified for IBM/ATP Finals as 1st pairing but fell sf to Eltingh/Haarhuis. **1994:** (–) Continued his successful partnership with Connell, reaching f Wimbledon and winning 4 titles from 6 more f to qualify for World Doubles Champ. In mixed doubles with Reinach won US Open. **1995:** (–) Played 9 doubles f, winning 6 with Connell, including World Doubles Champ. There they qualified for the knockout stages only by virtue of their won-lost sets percentage in rr, where they lost 2 of their 3 matches. Having found the fun missing from their partnership since April, they decided in Aug. to split at end of year. **1996:** (–) Appeared in 5 doubles f with different partners, winning Scottsdale with Leach, Hong Kong with Olhovskiy, Toronto with Haarhuis and Stockholm with Stark. In mixed he won US Open with Raymond. **1997:** Teaming with E. Ferreira, he won 5 doubles titles from 7 f to qualify for World Doubles Champ, where they won only 1 match. **1997 HIGHLIGHTS – DOUBLES:** (with E. Ferreira) **won** Auckland (d. Leach/Stark 6–4 4–6 7–6), **won** Memphis (d. Leach/Stark 6–3 3–6 6–1), **won** Nottingham (d. Sapsford/Wilkinson 4–6 7–6 7–6), **won** Vienna (d. Goellner/Prinosil 6–3 6–4), **won** Lyon (d. Delaitre/Santoro 3–6 6–2 6–4); **r/u** Philadelphia (lost Lareau/O'Brien 6–3 6–3), **r/u** Stockholm (lost Goellner/Reneberg 6–3 3–6 7–6). **MIXED DOUBLES:** (with Raymond) **r/u French Open** (lost Bhupathi/Hiraki 6–4 6–1). **CAREER HIGHLIGHTS – DOUBLES:** (with Connell) **World Doubles Champ – won 1995** (d. Eltingh/Haarhuis 7–6 7–6 3–6 7–6); **Wimbledon – r/u 1993** (lost Woodbridge/Woodforde 7–5 6–3 7–6), **r/u 1994** (lost Woodbridge/Woodforde 7–6 6–3 6–1). **MIXED DOUBLES:** (with Reinach) **US Open – won 1994** (d. Woodbridge/Novotna 6–2 6–4), (with Raymond) **won 1996** (d. Leach/Bollegraf 7–6 7–6).

ANDREA GAUDENZI (ITA)

Born Faenza, 30 July 1973; lives Monte Carlo, Monaco; RH; 2HB; 6ft; 183lb; turned pro 1990; career singles titles 0; final 1997 ATP ranking 57; 1997 prize money $233,766 ($1,760,344).

Coached by Ronnie Leitgeb. **1990:** (861) No. 1 in ITF Jun rankings after winning French Open Jun over Enqvist and US Open Jun over Tillstrom. **1991:** (620) Restricted by torn ligaments in left ankle. **1992:** (258) Was again hampered by a string of injuries, but enjoyed some success on the satellite circuits. **1993:** (60) Having won 2 Challenger titles, he reached his 1st main tour sf at San Marino, following with the same stage at Bucharest and Palermo and upset B. Gilbert at Athens. **1994:** (24) A 2, F 4, W 1, US 3. He scored some big upsets during the year in reaching his 1st tour f at Stuttgart Mercedes (d. Stich and Chesnokov), plus sf Gstaad (d. Pioline), qf Estoril (d. Kafelnikov), Barcelona (d. Muster), Bologna, Italian Open (d. Muster again) and Vienna. Unseeded in GS, he upset Korda 1r French Open and Courier 2r US Open. **1995:** (22) A 2, F 1, W 1, US 1. Upset Rosset 1r Australian Open and Ivanisevic on his way to f Dubai, a result which took him into the top 20. He was also r/u San Marino as well as reaching sf Sydney, Monte Carlo (d. Kafelnikov and Bruguera), Umag, plus 4 qf. **1996:** (55) A 1, F 2, W –, US 2. A finalist at Estoril, he also reached sf St Polten and qf Mexico City and Italian Open (d. Enqvist). He upset Muster 1r Milan, where he won the doubles with Ivanisevic, and at Olympics upset C. Costa and took a set off Agassi. Underwent arthroscopic surgery on his shoulder on 17 Oct., expecting to be out 3 months. **1997:** A 1, F 1, W –, US –. Still looking for his 1st title on the main tour, he played his 5th f at Bucharest, as well as reaching qf Munich (d. Enqvist), Bologna and Marbella and winning Geneva Challenger. **1997 HIGHLIGHTS – SINGLES: Australian Open 1r** (lost Kroslak 4–6 6–4 6–2 6–2), **French Open 1r** (lost Rafter 3–6 7–6 6–3 6–4); **won** Geneva Challenger (d. A. Martin 6–2 6–1); **r/u** Bucharest (d. Alonso 6–1 6–4, Marin 6–4 7–5, Lapentti 6–2 6–4, Goellner 6–2 7–6, lost Fromberg 6–1 7–6). **1997 HIGHLIGHTS – DOUBLES:** (with Messori) **r/u** Estoril (lost Kuerten/Meligeni 6–2 6–2).

MARC-KEVIN GOELLNER (GER)

Born Rio de Janeiro, Brazil, 22 September 1970; lives Bonn; RH; 6ft 5in; 178lb; turned pro 1991; career singles titles 2; final 1997 ATP ranking 51; 1997 prize money $474,502.

Coached by Andreas Maurer. Brought up in Australia, he later lived in Bonn, before moving to England in 1996. Wife Ira Patricia (married 18 February 1994); daughter Nina Jacqueline (born 28 September 1995); son Yannick-Keanu (born 4 June 1997). His trademark is playing in odd shoes. **1991:** (223) Restricted himself to the Satellite and Challenger circuits. **1992:** (107) A –, F –, W –, US 2. Won 2 Challenger titles and reached qf Athens on the main tour. In doubles won Rotterdam with Prinosil as lucky loser. **1993:** (31) A 2, F 4, W 1, US 3. He scored some notable upsets in a year that saw him move up the rankings into the top 50 and beyond. After qualifying at Nice, he beat Edberg and Lendl back-to-back as he swept to his 1st tour title. He followed with an upset of Korda on his way to an unscheduled appearance in last 16 French Open, and also reached the doubles f there with Prinosil, upsetting Woodbridge/Woodforde in sf. He surprised M. Chang at Hamburg and Arrese at Casablanca and reached sf Gstaad and Stuttgart Mercedes. **1994:** (81) A –, F 1, W 1, US 3. He was unable to pass qf in any tourn on the main tour, but reached that stage on 3 different surfaces at Dubai (d. Novacek), Florence, Halle (d. Medvedev), New Haven and Schenectady and upset Medvedev again at Stuttgart. **1995:** (78) A 1, F 2, W 2, US 2. Upset Rosset on his way to sf Queen's, where he extended Sampras to 13–11 fs after holding 3 mps, reached qf Casablanca, Bastad and Palermo, and surprised Gaudenzi at Stuttgart Mercedes. Played 2 doubles f with Nargiso, but won no title. **1996:** (53) A 1, F 1, W 1, US –. Although he often struggled to pass 1r of tourns, he won Marbella (d. Mantilla and Corretja), r/u Bournemouth, reached sf Zagreb, qf Stuttgart (d. Rios) and Basel and upset W. Ferreira at Munich. In doubles he won an Olympic bronze medal with Prinosil and took Bournemouth with Rusedski. **1997:** A 2, F 1, W 1, US 1. Reached sf Antwerp and Bucharest, plus qf Rome (d. Krajicek and A. Costa), Long Island (d. Kuerten) and Lyon. Played 3 doubles f with different partners, winning Stockholm with Reneberg. **1997 HIGHLIGHTS – SINGLES: Australian Open 2r** (d. Carlsen 6–4 6–1 6–7 6–4, lost Bjorkman 6–4 3–6 6–4 6–1), **French Open 1r** (lost Muster [seed 5] 4–6 7–6 6–2 6–7 6–1), **Wimbledon 1r** (lost Viloca 7–5 4–6 7–6 7–6), **US Open 1r** (lost Ruud 6–4 4–6 1–6 6–4 6–3); **sf** Antwerp (d. Stich 7–6 6–4, Van Garsse 6–3 6–4, Damm 3–1 ret'd, lost Henman 6–4 6–4), **sf** Bucharest (d. Viloca 6–3 6–3, Ruud 6–2 5–7 6–2, C. Costa 6–2 7–6, lost Gaudenzi 6–2 7–6). **1997 HIGHLIGHTS – DOUBLES:** (with Reneberg) **won** Stockholm (d. E. Ferreira/Galbraith 6–3 3–6 7–6); (with Olhovskiy) **r/u** New Haven (lost Bhupathi/Paes 4–6 6–7 6–2), (with Prinosil) **r/u** Vienna (lost E. Ferreira/Galbraith 6–3 6–4). **CAREER HIGHLIGHTS – DOUBLES:** (with Prinosil) **French Open – r/u 1993** (lost L./M. Jensen 6–4 6–7 6–4).

FERNANDO GONZALEZ (CHI)

Born Santiago, 29 July 1980, and lives there; RH; 6ft; 160lb; career singles titles 0.

Coached by Marco Colignon. **1997:** Won US Open Jun doubles with Massu and took S. American Jun singles.

MAGNUS GUSTAFSSON (SWE)

Born Lund, 3 January 1967; lives Monte Carlo, Monaco; RH; 6ft 1in; 172lb; turned pro 1986; career singles titles 10; final 1997 ATP ranking 37; 1997 prize money $360,912 ($3,433,494).

Coached by Stefan Simonsson from 1996. **1986:** (273) Nat 18 Champ. **1987:** (53) Reached 1st GP sf at Stockholm, won Tampere Challenger and broke into top 50. **1988:** (51) A 3, F 4, W 2, US –. Upset Mayotte to reach last 16 French Open; sf Hilversum and Barcelona (d. Jaite and Leconte). **1989:** (34) A 4, F 1, W 1, US 1. Played his 1st GP f at Gstaad, then in autumn upset Wilander and Agassi *en route* to 1st SS f at Stockholm. **1990:** (31) A 2, F 4, W –, US –. Took a break in March, suffering from shin splints. Reached sf Brussels, Stuttgart (d. E. Sanchez and took Lendl to 3s) and upset Agassi at Hamburg. Forced to default last 16 French Open to Gomez owing to a knee injury. **1991:** (12) A 3, F 3, W 2, US –. Won 1st GP title at Munich, upsetting Lendl on the way, and followed with Bastad and Hilversum to break into the top 10 in July. R/u Hamburg, Kitzbuhel and Prague; sf Sydney NSW and reached 2 doubles f. Withdrew from US Open with chronic inflammation of the right elbow. **1992:** (47) A 2, F 2, W –, US 1. Won Bastad and was r/u Barcelona as well as reaching sf Florence and 2 more qf, but was plagued by injuries and slipped down the rankings.

1993: (14) A 1, F 1, W 1, US 1. In a more successful year on the circuit, he returned to the top 20, winning Stuttgart Mercedes and reaching f Antwerp (d. Stich and Becker back-to-back), f Genova and Hilversum, plus sf Estoril, Barcelona, Prague and Umag. Upset Courier at Paris Open. **1994:** (33) A qf, F 2, W –, US –. After taking up transcendental meditation at the start of the year, he won his 1st career HC title at Auckland in Jan., following 3 weeks later with Dubai (d. Bruguera in f), which took him back to the top 10 for the 1st time since Aug. 1991. He also reached qf Stuttgart Eurocard, Copenhagen, Munich, Hamburg, but in Oct. he underwent surgery to his right shoulder to remove bone aggravating the tendon and was expected to be out for 8 months. **1995:** (88) A –, F 2, W –, US –. Back in action slightly ahead of schedule in May, he reached qf Stuttgart Mercedes, Umag and Valencia, and won Braunschweig Challenger. Threatened with foot surgery in Sept., he avoided it after trying a new sole on his shoe. **1996:** (17) A –, F 1, W 4, US 2. Returning to form, he won St Petersburg (d. Kafelnikov) and Bastad (d. Edberg) on the main tour and took Hamburg on the Challenger circuit. He also reached sf Coral Springs and Paris Open (d. Agassi, W. Ferreira and Rosset), qf Copenhagen, Monte Carlo (d. Ivanisevic), Halle, Lyon and Stuttgart Eurocard, and upset W. Ferreira at Wimbledon, where he was unseeded. These performances took him back to the top 20 in Nov. **1997:** A 2, F 2, W 2, US 2. It was a quieter year in which he won Singapore and was r/u San Marino and Beijing, but the only other qf he played was at Qatar. His 2 biggest upsets were Ivanisevic 1r French Open and M. Chang at Paris Open. **1997 HIGHLIGHTS – SINGLES: Australian Open 2r** [seed 12] (d. Doyle 6–7 6–3 7–5 6–1, lost Braasch 3–6 7–6 6–4 6–4), **French Open 2r** (d. Ivanisevic [seed 4] 4–6 6–3 7–6 6–3, lost Blanco 6–4 4–6 6–4 7–6), **Wimbledon 2r** (d. Spadea 6–2 6–1 6–3, lost Van Garsse 6–4 6–4 6–1), **US Open 2r** (d. Stark 6–3 6–2 7–5, lost Gimelstob 6–3 3–6 7–6 4–6 6–1); **won** Singapore (d. Fredriksson 6–1 6–4, Sinner 7–6 4–6 6–3, Stark 6–7 6–2 6–2, Johansson 7–6 4–6 7–6, Kiefer 4–6 6–3 6–3); **r/u** San Marino (d. Filippini 6–2 6–4, A. Martin 7–6 6–2, Pavel 6–4 4–6 6–1, C. Costa 1–6 6–1 6–3, lost Mantilla 6–4 6–1), **r/u** Beijing (d. Sinner 7–6 1–6 7–6, Rikl 6–2 6–4, B. Black 6–4 6–3, Carlsen 6–2 6–4, lost Courier 7–6 3–6 6–3). **1997 HIGHLIGHTS – DOUBLES:** (with Larsson) **r/u** Bastad (lost Kulti/Tillstrom 6–0 6–3). **CAREER HIGHLIGHTS – SINGLES: Australian Open – qf 1994** (d. Smith 3–6 7–5 6–2 2–6 6–2, Steven 7–6 6–2 4–6 6–2, Renzenbrink 6–2 6–2 6–2, Damm 2–6 6–3 6–1 6–1, lost Sampras 7–6 2–6 6–3 7–6).

PAUL HAARHUIS (NED)

Born Eindhoven, 19 February 1966; lives Monte Carlo, Monaco; RH; 2HB; 6ft 2in; 177lb; turned pro 1989; career singles titles 1; final 1997 ATP ranking 71 singles, 3 doubles; 1997 prize money $834,450 ($5,518,152).

Coached by Alex Reynders. Wife Anja (married 12 September 1996). **1987:** (397) Finished 2nd on Dutch satellite circuit. **1988:** (462) Graduated from Florida State Univ. **1989:** (57) A –, F 3, W –, US 4. After winning Lagos Challenger, he qualified for French Open, where he upset Zivojinovic 1r, and again as a qualifier upset J. McEnroe at US Open. Qf Hilversum (d. K. Carlsson) and Itaparica. **1990:** (54) A 1, F 3, W 3, US 1. Qf Philadelphia (d. Gilbert and took Gomez to 3s) and Estoril. Reached 4 f in doubles with various partners, winning Moscow. **1991:** (37) A 2, F 3, W 1, US qf. He again excelled at US Open, upsetting top seed Becker *en route* to qf, unseeded. Reached sf Rotterdam, won Lagos Challenger and scored some other big upsets – E. Sanchez at Estoril and Ivanisevic at Italian Open and French Open. In doubles reached 5 f, winning 3 with different partners, and was r/u French Open mixed with Vis. **1992:** (39) A 2, F 1, W 2, US 2. Scored some useful upsets during the year on his way to f Singapore, sf Rotterdam (d. Lendl) and qf Wellington, Memphis (d. Wheaton), Philadelphia (d. Wheaton again), Hamburg (d. Muster and Chang), Schenectady and Sydney Indoor. Reached 4 doubles f, winning Hilversum with Koevermans and Schenectady with Eltingh. **1993:** (42) A 1, F 4, W 1, US 2. He was still a dangerous opponent, surprising W. Ferreira at French Open, where he was unseeded, and removing Ivanisevic and Medvedev on his way to sf Tokyo Seiko. He reached the same stage at Kuala Lumpur Malaysian Open and Jakarta, plus qf at Prague, Hilversum (d. Bruguera) and Moscow and upset Volkov at LIPC. In doubles he reached 11 f, winning 1 with Koevermans and 6 with Eltingh, including IBM/ATP World Doubles where they beat Woodbridge/Woodforde in ss. **1994:** (37) A 3, F 3, W 1, US 1. In singles r/u Qatar (d. Ivanisevic) and Philadelphia and reached sf Rotterdam (d. Becker and Volkov). Voted Doubles Team of the Year with Eltingh: their partnership flourished as they won their 1st GS title at Australian Open, following with US Open, and won a total of 8 titles from 12 f to qualify for World Doubles Champ as top pairing, but lost to Woodbridge/Woodforde. **1995:** (19) A 1, F 1, W 2, US 2. Won his 1st career singles title at Jakarta, r/u Memphis and Rotterdam (d. Kafelnikov) and reached sf Philadelphia (d. Sampras) and Halle (d. Kafelnikov again), plus 2 qf. Then after upsetting Ivanisevic at Paris Open in Nov., he broke into the top 20. In doubles with Eltingh, he won French Open and all 6 other f they played to qualify for World Doubles Champ. There they advanced to f without dropping a set before being surprisingly beaten by Connell/Galbraith. **1996:** (26) A 1, F 3, W 4, US 3. R/u Indian Wells (d. Enqvist, Sampras and Ivanisevic), sf Jakarta, Estoril and Rosmalen (d. Krajicek) and qf Washington and Paris Open (d. Ivanisevic and Martin). Other upsets across the year included Boetsch at French Open and Enqvist again at Halle. His regular doubles partner, Eltingh, was restricted for much of the year by tendinitis in both knees, but they still won 2 of 5 doubles f, were r/u US Open and qualified for World Doubles Champ. He took a 3rd title with Galbraith. **1997:** A 1, F 1, W 3, US 2. Reached sf Halle and qf Memphis and Umag, as well as upsetting Medvedev at Halle, A. Costa at Toulouse and Muster at Stuttgart Eurocard. In 3r Wimbledon he served for the match v Henman at 5–4 40–30 5s, but double-faulted, going on to lose 12–14. He played 9 doubles f in all, including 8 with Eltingh, with whom he aimed to become 1st pair in open era to win all GS titles. However, although they won 5 titles, they failed to take the missing GS when they lost Wimbledon f in 4s to Woodbridge/Woodforde. Qualified for World Doubles Champ again, and were the only duo to win all their rr matches. However, they lost sf to Leach/Stark, but still finished the year as the season's 2nd paring. **1997 HIGHLIGHTS – SINGLES: Australian Open 1r** (lost Kucera 6–1 3–6 6–3 4–6 6–4), **French Open 1r** (lost Van Scheppingen 6–2 6–4 5–7 6–4, lost Bruguera [seed 16] 6–2 6–3 6–3), **Wimbledon 3r** (d. Lareau 6–1 6–2 7–6, Larkham 3–6 6–3 6–1 6–2, lost Henman [seed 14] 6–7 6–3 6–2 4–6 14–12), **US Open 2r** (d. Blanco 7–6 6–0 6–7 6–7 6–3, lost Roux 7–6 6–3 6–7 6–7 6–4); **sf** Halle (d. Medvedev 7–6 6–3, Damm 6–7 6–3 7–6, Reneberg 6–2 6–1, lost Korda 7–6 6–4). **1997 HIGHLIGHTS – DOUBLES:** (with Eltingh unless stated) **r/u Wimbledon** (lost Woodbridge/Woodforde 7–6 7–6 5–7 6–3); **won** Qatar (d. Fredriksson/M. Norman 6–3 6–2), **won** Rotterdam (d. Pimek/Talbot 7–6 6–4), **won** Rosmalen (d. Kronemann/Macpherson 6–4 7–5), **won** Boston (d. Randall/Waite 6–4 6–2), **won** Toulouse (d. Fleurian/Mirny 6–3 7–6), **won** Paris Open (d. Leach/Stark 6–2 7–6); (with Siemerink) **r/u** Sydney (lost Lobo/J. Sanchez 6–4 6–7 6–3), **r/u** Monte Carlo (lost Johnson/Montana 7–6 2–6 7–6). **CAREER HIGHLIGHTS – SINGLES: US Open – qf 1991** [unseeded] (d. Jelen 2–6 6–2 6–1 3–6 6–2, Chesnokov 6–1 4–6 6–2 7–6, Becker 6–3 6–4 6–2, Steeb 6–2 6–3 6–4, lost Connors 4–6 7–6 6–4 6–2). **CAREER HIGHLIGHTS – DOUBLES:** (with Eltingh) **Australian Open – won 1994** (d. B. Black/ Stark 6–7 6–3 6–4 6–3); **French Open – won 1995** (d. Kulti/Larsson 6–7 6–4 6–1); **US Open – won 1994** (d. Woodbridge/Woodforde 6–3 7–6), **r/u 1996** (lost Woodbridge/ Woodforde 4–6 7–6 7–6); **IBM/ATP World Doubles Champ – won 1993** (d. Woodbridge/Woodforde 7–6 7–6 6–4), **r/u 1995** (lost Connell/Galbraith 7–6 7–6 3–6 7–6); **Wimbledon – r/u 1997**.

TOMMY HAAS (GER)

Born Hamburg, 3 April 1978; lives Bradenton, Fla.; RH; 6ft 2in; 175lb; turned pro 1996; career singles titles 0; final 1997 ATP ranking 41; 1997 prize money $350,926.

Coached by Nick Bollettieri. **1993:** (1072). **1994:** (1192). **1995:** (–). **1996:** (196) A –, F –, W –, US 1. Upset Furlan and Woodforde *en route* to qf Indianapolis and extended Stich to 4s at US Open. **1997:** A –, F –, W 2, US 3. Reached his 1st career sf at Hamburg (d. Moya and Berasategui) and followed in Oct. at Lyon with his 1st f (unseeded, d. Enqvist and Kafelnikov), breaking into top 50. His other qf appearances came at Washington and Toulouse. **1997 HIGHLIGHTS – SINGLES: Wimbledon 2r** (d. Ruud 6–2 6–1 6–2, lost Petchey 7–6 6–4 6–2), **US Open 3r** (d. Gross 6–3 6–4 2–6 6–4, Kroslak 6–4 6–1 6–2, lost Rios [seed 10] 6–4 3–6 6–3 1–6 6–1); **r/u** Lyon (d. Portas 6–1 6–3, Alonso 6–2 6–3, Enqvist 6–3 6–3, Kafelnikov 4–6 6–4 6–3, lost Santoro 6–4 6–4); **sf** Hamburg (d. Hrbaty 7–6 6–3, Moya 6–4 6–1, Gross 5–7 7–5 6–3, Berasategui 2–6 6–2 6–3, lost Mantilla 4–6 6–3 6–4).

TIM HENMAN (GBR)

Born Oxford, 6 September 1974, and lives there; RH; 6ft 1in; 155lb; turned pro 1993; career singles titles 2; final 1997 ATP ranking 17; 1997 prize money $802,746 ($1,828,358).

Coached by David Felgate; trained by Tim Newenham, who travels with him. Great-grandson of Ellen Stawell-Brown, the 1st woman to serve overarm in the ladies' singles at Wimbledon, and grandson of Henry Billington, who played at Wimbledon in 1940s and 1950s. **1992:** (771) Nat Jun champ in singles and doubles. **1993:** (434). **1994:** (161) A –, F –, W 1, US –. Began to make an impact on the satellite circuits and made his D Cup debut, but in September he broke his leg in 3 places and was out 5 months. **1995:** (99) A –, F –, W 2, US 2. A mixed year finished on a high note when he broke into the top 100 after winning both singles and doubles at Seoul Challenger in Oct., following with Nat Champs and singles title at Reunion Challenger. On the main tour he reached his 1st qf at Nottingham, but hit a low point at Wimbledon, where he was disqualified and fined $3,000 after a ball he hit in frustration during a doubles match accidentally hit a ball-girl on the head. **1996:** (29) A 2, F 1, W qf, US 4. In contrast to the previous year, Wimbledon provided the highlight of his career to date. Against Kafelnikov in 1r, he squandered a 2-set lead and stood 2 mps down at 3–5 fs, but served 2 aces before going on to win 7–5. He further thrilled his home crowds by progressing to qf, unseeded, a performance which took him into top 50 1st time. He went on to take an Olympic silver medal in doubles with Broad – Britain's 1st in tennis since 1924 – and at US Open, again unseeded, he avenged his Wimbledon defeat by Martin. After reaching sf Shanghai, Rotterdam (d. Siemerink and Moya), Copenhagen, Seoul, Lyon (d. Siemerink again) and Ostrava (d. W. Ferreira) and qf Nottingham (d. MaliVai Washington), he moved into top 25 in Oct., but slipped down again as he struggled at end of year. He took over No. 1 British ranking from Rusedski on 29 April and confirmed his position by winning Nat Champ in Nov. By reaching sf GS Cup he became the 200th man to exceed prize money of $1m. Won Most Improved Player award. **1997:** A 3, F 1, W qf, US 2. He began the year in style with his 1st f on the main tour at Qatar, following the next week with his 1st title at Sydney (d. Ivanisevic) and then a 3rd consec f at Antwerp. After Qatar he became 1st GBR player since Mottram in 1983 to reach the top 20, progressing to No. 14 after Antwerp. However, he was restricted at LIPC by an elbow injury, which required arthroscopic surgery on 26 March to remove pieces of bone from the elbow joint, causing him to miss D Cup tie v Zimbabwe. At Wimbledon he reached qf again, inspired by the middle-Sunday home crowd as he d. Haarhuis 14–12 5s before upsetting Krajicek. After that, he hit a low point in losing 1r Montreal to LeBlanc, ranked more than 800 places below him, was brilliant in beating Muster 1r US Open, but dreadful in losing to W. Ferreira 2r. Avoiding clay at home at Bournemouth, he then opted instead to play in Tashkent, where he won his 2nd title of the year. By then, though, Rusedski had overtaken him as No. 1 in GBR and confirmed his dominance by winning their sf at Vienna. He reached the same

World No. 17, Tim Henman, whose rivalry with Greg Rusedski for leadership of the British game helped both men to achieve career-best rankings in 1997. (Tommy Hindley)

stage at Nottingham and Basel (where he won the doubles with Rosset) and qf New Haven and Stockholm. Played 1 match at ATP Champs (d. Kafelnikov, who had already qualified for sf) as alternate when Bruguera withdrew after playing 2. **1997 HIGHLIGHTS – SINGLES: Australian Open 3r** (d. Pavel 7–5 6–4 6–2, Raoux 6–3 6–3 6–4, lost M. Chang 6–1 7–6 6–3), **French Open 1r** [seed 14] (lost Delaitre 6–2 2–6 1–6 6–2 6–4), **Wimbledon qf** [seed 14] (d. Nestor 7–6 6–1 6–4, Golmard 7–6 6–3 6–3, Haarhuis 6–7 6–3 6–2 4–6 14–12, Krajicek [seed 4] 7–6 6–7 7–6 6–4, lost Stich 6–3 6–2 6–4), **US Open 2r** (d. Muster [seed 5] 6–3 7–6 4–6 6–4, lost W. Ferreira 6–3 6–2 6–4); **won** Sydney (d. Furlan 6–4 6–4, Bruguera 3–6 6–3 6–3, O'Brien 1–6 7–6 6–4, Ivanisevic 4–6 7–6 6–1, Moya 6–3 6–1), **won** Tashkent (d. Champion 6–4 6–7 7–6, Volkov 6–3 6–3, Spadea 6–3 6–4, Clavet 6–3 7–5, Rosset 7–6 6–4); **r/u** Qatar (d. Wiltschnig 6–3 6–2, El Sawy 6–3 6–2, Gustafsson 6–3 7–6, Arazi 6–3 2–6 6–2, lost Courier 7–5 6–7 6–2), **r/u** Antwerp (d. Bruguera 6–3 4–6 6–4, Tillstrom 6–2 6–3, Clavet 7–6 6–4, Goellner 6–4 6–4, lost Rosset 6–2 7–5 6–4); **sf** Nottingham (d. Richardson 6–3 6–7 6–4, Fromberg 6–4 6–7 7–6, Stafford 3–6 6–3 7–6, lost Kucera 6–4 2–6 6–4), **sf** Basel (d. Goellner 7–6 6–3, Kucera 6–4 6–1, M. Norman 6–3 6–2, lost Philippoussis 7–6 6–4), **sf** Vienna (d. Mantilla 6–4 4–6 6–4, Apell 6–3 6–3, Kucera 6–4 6–1, lost Rusedski 6–4 6–4). **1997 HIGHLIGHTS – DOUBLES:** (with Rosset) **won** Basel (d. Braasch/Grabb 7–6 6–7 7–6). **CAREER HIGHLIGHTS – SINGLES: Wimbledon – qf 1996** [unseeded] (d. Kafelnikov 7–6 6–3 6–7 4–6 7–5, Sapsford 6–1 6–7 6–0 6–1, Milligan 6–1 6–3 6–4, Gustafsson 7–6 6–4 7–6, lost Martin 7–6 7–6 6–4), **qf 1997. CAREER HIGHLIGHTS – DOUBLES:** (with Broad) **Olympics – silver medal 1996** (lost Woodbridge/Woodforde 6–4 6–4 6–2).

LUIS HORNA (PER)

Born Lima, 14 September 1980, and lives there; RH; 5ft 11in; 155lb; career singles titles 0; final 1997 ATP ranking 903; Junior ranking 4; 1997 prize money $2,425.

Coached by Julio Victorero and Carlos Alvarado. **1996:** Won S. American Jun Champs. **1997:** R/u French Open Jun to Elsner; won doubles there with De Armas and Wimbledon Jun doubles with Massu. Won S. American Jun Champs.

DOMINIK HRBATY (SVK)

Born Bratislava, 4 January 1978, and lives there; RH; 6ft; 165lb; turned pro 1996; career singles titles 0; final 1997 ATP ranking 42; 1997 prize money $292,807.

Coached by Marian Vajda. **1994:** (1024). **1995:** (364) Enjoyed some success on the satellite circuits. **1996:** (77) Joined his country's D Cup squad and was voted Player to Watch after winning 2 Challenger titles from 6 f. **1997:** A 4, F 1, W 1, US 1. In May, he upset Kafelnikov as he swept to his 1st sf on the main tour, following in Oct. with an upset of Corretja to reach his 1st f. He also reached sf San Marino and Marbella, and qf Umag, as well as taking Kosice Challenger. At Australian Open, unseeded in his 1st GS, he led 4–2 and 15–40 on Sampras's serve in 5s last 16. **1997 HIGHLIGHTS – SINGLES: Australian Open last 16** [unseeded] (d. Stolle 1–6 7–5 7–5 6–7 6–1, Kulti 6–2 6–1 6–2, Berasategui [seed 16] 6–3 7–6 6–7 2–0 ret'd, lost Sampras [seed 1] 6–7 6–3 6–4 3–6 6–4), **French Open 1r** (lost Rosset [seed 15] 7–5 3–6 7–6 6–4), **Wimbledon 1r** (lost Johansson 7–5 6–3 6–1), **US Open 1r** (lost Gumy 6–7 6–3 6–7 6–3 6–2); **won** Kosice Challenger (d. Lapentti 6–4 6–4); **r/u** Palermo (d. Marin 6–4 6–3, Gumy 6–3 3–2 ret'd, Portas 7–5 6–4, Corretja 6–4 6–4, lost Berasategui 6–4 6–2); **sf** St Polten (d. Kafelnikov 6–3 6–3, Silberstein 6–2 7–6, Alami 6–1 6–2, lost Filippini 7–6 6–1), **sf** San Marino (d. Charpentier 7–6 6–2, Dreekmann 5–7 7–5 ret'd, Voinea 7–6 4–6 7–5, lost

Mantilla 6–4 6–4), **sf** Marbella (d. Lapentti 6–3 6–2, Clement 6–4 6–4, Alami 6–3 7–5, lost Berasategui 6–4 6–4). **1997 HIGHLIGHTS – DOUBLES:** (with Kucera) **r/u** Umag (lost Pescariu/Sanguinetti 7–6 6–4).

GORAN IVANISEVIC (CRO)

Born Split, 13 September 1971; lives there and Monte Carlo, Monaco; LH; 6ft 4in; 180lb; turned pro 1988; career singles titles 17; final 1997 ATP ranking 15; 1997 prize money $1,458,257 ($16,206,537).

Coached by Vedran Martic. **1987:** (954) Won US Open Jun doubles with Nargiso. **1988:** (371) A –, F –, W 1, US –. Joined Yugoslav D Cup squad. R/u French Open Jun doubles with Caratti and was No. 3 in ITF Jun singles rankings. **1989:** (40) A qf, F 4, W 2, US 2. Qf Australian Open after qualifying and last 16 French Open, unseeded. Upset Leconte *en route* to 1st GP sf at Nice, following with 2nd at Palermo and then 1st f at Florence. **1990:** (9) A 1, F qf W sf, US 3. Helped his country to win WT Cup in May, then upset Becker 1r French Open *en route* to qf, following with sf appearance at Wimbledon, both unseeded. Won his 1st career title at Stuttgart, reached 2r GS Cup and broke into the top 10. R/u French Open doubles with Korda. **1991:** (16) A 3, F 2, W 2, US 4. After a good year in 1990, his game fell apart at the beginning of 1991, and he withdrew from LIPC with compact fracture of left index finger. But then he played through the qualifying to gain a place at Manchester, where he won both singles and doubles. Did not play for YUG in D Cup and, with Prpic, announced in Tokyo in October that henceforth he wanted to be known as a Croatian. **1992:** (4) A 2, F qf, W r/u US 3. At Wimbledon he upset Edberg on his way to a thrilling f v Agassi, which he lost in 5s. At Olympics, where he won 4 consec. 5s matches, he won a bronze medal in both singles and doubles (with Prpic). Finished the year by qualifying 1st time for ATP World Champ, losing a close sf to Becker. Withdrew from Monte Carlo with arrythmia heartbeat and also missed Munich. **1993:** (7) A –, F 3, W 3, US 2. Missed Australian Open with a stress fracture of the foot which kept him out 7 weeks early in year and had to wait until Sept. before winning his 1st title of the year at Bucharest. He followed with Vienna and Paris Open, where he upset Edberg and Sampras, and also upset Sampras at Italian Open. He was r/u Qatar, Italian Open and Stockholm and reached 3 more sf, including IBM/ATP World Champ. He squeezed in there, taking the last place after Sampras d. Pioline at Antwerp, but this time the No. 1 turned the tables, inflicting his only defeat in rr before the Croat was removed in sf by Stich. His GS record was disappointing; he lost 3r French Open and 2r US Open – to C. Costa both times – and bowed out in 3r Wimbledon, after all three of his encounters had gone to 5s. **1994:** (5) A qf, F qf, W r/u, US 1. He reached his 2nd Wimbledon f for the loss of only 1 set (to Volkov), but was then overpowered by Sampras. His performance and Stich's 1r defeat saw the Croat overtake the German for the 2nd slot in the rankings, behind Sampras, although he slipped back to 5th behind Agassi, Bruguera and Becker by the end of the season. During his qf v Forget, he delivered a serve at 136 mph, the fastest ever recorded, and during the year he served a record 1,241 aces, a new record which easily beat his own 1992 record of 1,066. He was r/u Stuttgart Eurocard, Bucharest and Stockholm, reached sf Qatar, Rotterdam, Italian Open and Vienna, and played 4 more qf, including Australian Open. In French Open, where he was fined (£333) for racket abuse, he lost in last 16 to Berasategui, and at US Open Zoecke removed him 1r. He qualified for IBM/ATP World Champ, but failed to win a match. Another fine there for his outbursts earned him an 8-week suspension for accumulating fines of more than $10,000 (for the 2nd year). However, as GS Cup and Australian Open were not included in the ban, he was inconvenienced only in missing Sydney in Jan. Lost thrilling 5s sf to Sampras at GS Cup. **1995:** (10) A 1, F 1, W sf, US 1. In a difficult year he won no title and reached only one f – at Hamburg – although he appeared in sf Wimbledon, Milan, Barcelona, Monte Carlo, Italian Open, Los Angeles and Indianapolis and 4 more qf. He was plagued by injury during the year, undergoing surgery on 23 Feb. after aggravating a knee injury at Stuttgart Eurocard and returning to action at Barcelona in April. Was forced to retire 1r US Open after badly spraining his ankle and did not qualify for IBM/ATP Champ. After Bob Brett left him end Oct., unable to cope with the Croatian's wild ways, he hired Vedran Martic, a fellow-Croatian whom he'd known since he was 9. Took a complete break for a week before GS Cup, returning refreshed and in better control of his head. **1996:** (4) A 3, F 4, W qf, US sf. Under the calming influence of Martic, and travelling with Father Joe, his personal priest, masseur and trainer, he felt more relaxed, working harder off court and trying to stay cooler on it. He began the year in tremendous style, with 4 wins from 5 f in consec tourns from 29 Jan. to 10 March, taking the inaugural Croatian Indoors at Zagreb and Dubai in consec weeks and then winning Milan and Rotterdam back-to-back to add to Hopman Cup – which he won with Majoli – and r/u finishes at Sydney and Antwerp. At LIPC, where he played his 7th f in 9 tourns, he was saved by rain from 2–6 0–1 down in sf v Sampras, but a stiff neck forced him to retire in f v Agassi. Thereafter he was less impressive, his only other f being at Indianapolis, until winning Moscow over Kafelnikov in Nov. At ATP Champs, he took advantage of the fast surface to reach sf, where he lost to Sampras only 7–5 fs. He also reached sf US Open and Indian Wells and qf Wimbledon, Munich, Cincinnati, Vienna and Stuttgart Eurocard, and broke his world record for aces. **1997:** A qf, F 1, W 2, US 1. Again his best results came in early season, when he delighted home crowds by winning both singles and doubles (with Hirszon) at Zagreb in Feb., following next week with r/u Dubai, where he won the doubles with Groen. He took Milan 3 weeks later, but his only other title came in Oct. at Vienna, where he recovered from 2-sets-to-0 down in f v Rusedski, taking 3s tb and finally the match. He withdrew Antwerp in April after breaking the middle finger on his right hand, returning 3 weeks later to reach sf Rome. He was r/u Queen's and appeared in sf Sydney, Rotterdam, Los Angeles and Ostrava, where he retired with an arm injury, plus qf Australian Open, LIPC and Long Island. His GS performances were disappointing, with qf Australian Open his best showing. In 2r Wimbledon he served a record 46 aces v M.

Norman but lost 14–12 fs and stalked out, being fined for missing the press conference. **1997 HIGHLIGHTS – SINGLES: Australian Open qf** [seed 3] (d. Ellwood 6–2 7–5 6–3, Kucera 6–4 6–2 6–2, Woodruff 6–3 6–7 6–3 6–1, Ruud 4–6 6–2 6–7 6–3 6–3, lost Muster [seed 5] 6–4 6–2 6–3), **French Open 1r** [seed 4] (lost Gustafsson 4–6 6–3 7–6 6–3), **Wimbledon 2r** [seed 2] (d. Pescariu 6–1 6–3 6–3, lost M. Norman 6–3 2–6 7–6 4–6 14–12), **US Open 1r** [seed 4] (lost Pescariu 4–6 7–5 6–1 7–6); **won** Zagreb (d. M. Norman 7–6 6–7 7–5, Johansson 7–6 6–4, Radulescu 6–0 1–1 ret'd, J. Sanchez 6–2 6–4, Rusedski 7–6 4–6 7–6), **won** Milan (d. Olhovskiy 7–6 6–7 6–2, Pioline 7–6 7–6, Vacek 6–3 6–7 6–4, Prinosil 6–0 7–6); **r/u** Dubai (d. El Aynaoui 6–3 6–4, Ulihrach 7–6 6–4, Becker w.o., Novak 6–1 3–6 6–3, lost Muster 7–5 7–6), **r/u** Queen's (d. Paes 7–6 6–3, M. Lee 6–1 7–5, Golmard 6–3 7–6, Rusedski 4–6 6–4 7–6, lost Philippoussis7–5 6–3); **sf** Sydney (d. Goellner 6–3 6–4, J. Sanchez 6–4 0–6 6–4, Stolle 6–4 6–2, lost Henman 4–6 7–6 6–1), **sf** Rotterdam (d. Santoro 6–3 6–4, Raoux 7–5 6–7 6–3, Korda w.o., lost Vacek 6–4 1–6 7–6), **sf** Rome (d. Woodforde 6–2 6–7 6–4, Ruud 6–2 6–2, Becker 7–6 6–3, Draper 6–4 6–4, lost Corretja 7–6 7–6), **sf** Los Angeles (d. Godwin 7–6 6–3, Delaitre 7–5 7–6, B. Black 7–6 6–2, lost Courier 6–3 6–4). **1997 HIGHLIGHTS – DOUBLES:** (with Hirszon) **won** Zagreb (d. Haygarth/Keil 6–4 6–3), (with Groen) **won** Dubai (d. Stolle/Suk 7–5 6–3). **CAREER HIGHLIGHTS – SINGLES: GS Cup – won 1995** (d. Korda 7–6 6–3, Sampras w.o., Kafelnikov 7–6 4–6 6–3 6–4, Martin 7–6 6–3 6–4), **r/u 1996** (d. Tillstrom 6–4 6–2, Woodforde 6–4 6–4, Kafelnikov 6–7 2–6 6–3 6–2 6–4, lost Becker 6–3 6–4 6–4), **sf 1992** (d. Forget 7–5 6–4, J. McEnroe 3–6 6–4 6–2, lost Chang 6–7 6–2 6–4 3–6 6–3), **sf 1994** (d. Bjorkman 6–4 6–2, Becker 6–4 6–1, lost Sampras 5–7 6–3 6–4 6–7 10–8), **Wimbledon – r/u 1992** (d. Koslowski 6–2 6–2 6–3, Woodforde 6–4 6–4 6–7 6–3, Rosset 7–6 6–4 6–4, Lendl 6–7 6–1 6–4 1–0 ret'd, Edberg 6–7 7–5 6–1 3–6 6–3, Sampras 6–7 7–6 6–4 6–2, lost Agassi 6–7 6–4 6–4 1–6 6–4), **r/u 1994** (d. Meligeni 6–1 6–3 6–4, Mronz 6–2 7–6 6–1, Mansdorf 6–3 7–5 6–4, Volkov 7–6 7–6 4–6 6–2, Forget 7–6 7–6 6–4, Becker 6–2 7–6 6–4, lost Sampras 7–6 7–6 6–0), **sf 1990** (d. Leach 6–4 6–0 6–4, Delaitre 6–2 6–0 4–6 6–7 6–3, Rostagno 6–2 6–2, 6–4, Koevermans 4–6 6–3 6–4 7–6, Curren 4–6 6–4 6–4 6–7 6–3, lost Becker 4–6 7–6 6–0 7–6), **sf 1995** (d. Lareau 6–2 6–4 6–4, Stark 6–4 6–2 7–5, Boetsch 6–4 6–4 6–4, Martin 6–4 7–6 6–7 7–6, Kafelnikov 7–5 7–6 6–3, lost Sampras 7–6 4–6 6–3 4–6 6–3); **US Open – sf 1996** (d. Chesnokov 1–6 6–2 6–4 6–4, Draper 6–7 6–3 6–4 6–4, Dreekmann 6–3 6–2 7–6, Medvedev 6–4 3–6 6–3 7–6, Edberg 6–3 6–4 7–6, lost Sampras 6–3 6–4 6–7 6–3); **Olympics – sf bronze medal 1992** (d. Mota 6–2 6–2 6–7 4–6 6–3, Haarhuis 6–7 6–2 1–6 6–3 6–2, Hlasek 3–6 6–0 4–6 7–6 6–7, Santoro 6–7 6–7 6–4 6–4 8–6, lost Rosset 6–3 7–5 6–2); **ATP Champs – sf 1992** (d. M. Chang 7–6 6–2, Courier 6–3 6–3, Krajicek 6–4 6–3 in rr, lost Becker 6–4 6–4 7–6), **sf 1993** (d. Bruguera 6–4 7–6, Edberg 7–6 6–7 6–3, lost Sampras 6–3 4–6 6–2 in rr, lost Stich 7–6 7–6), **sf 1996** (d. Muster 6–4 6–4, Krajicek 7–6 6–7 6–3, lost M. Chang 6–4 6–3in rr, lost Sampras 6–7 7–6 7–5).

THOMAS JOHANSSON (SWE)

Born Linkoping, 24 March 1975, and lives there; RH; 5ft 11in; 165lb; turned pro 1994; career singles titles 0; final 1997 ATP ranking 39; 1997 prize money $363,967.

Coached by Magnus Tideman. **1989:** European 14s champ in singles and doubles (with M. Norman). **1991:** R/u Orange Bowl 16s to Corrales. **1992:** Underwent surgery in Oct. and did not play for rest of year. **1993:** (418) Unranked at the time, he upset Novacek *en route* to qf Bolzano in his 1st ATP tourn. **1994:** (485) A 1, F –, W –, US –. **1995:** (126) A –, F 1, W –, US –. Won Jerusalem and Napoli on the Challenger circuit. **1996:** (60) A 2, F 2, W 4, US 2. He attracted attention at Australian Open, where he led Becker 2-sets-to-love 2r, before letting the match slip from his grasp, and at Wimbledon, where he was unseeded, he removed Eltingh in 5s before taking a set off Martin. Moved into top 100 with sf finishes at Singapore, Beijing and Moscow (d. Haarhuis), and qf Gstaad and Long Island, looking ready to crack the top 50 in 1997. **1997:** A 2, F 1, W 2, US 1. His best performances came in spring, beginning with his 1st singles title at Copenhagen, in his 1st f. He followed the next week with St Petersburg, upsetting Stich on the way, and reached sf of his next 2 tourns at Hong Kong and Tokyo Japan Open. After a quieter summer, he appeared in 2 more Asian sf at Beijing and Singapore. **1997 HIGHLIGHTS – SINGLES: Australian Open 2r** (d. Damm 6–4 6–2 3–6 6–7 6–2, lost Karbacher 6–3 6–2 7–6), **French Open 1r** (lost Escude 6–3 2–6 7–5 7–6), **Wimbledon 2r** (d. Hrbaty 7–5 6–3 6–1, lost Becker [seed 8] 6–1 6–4 6–4), **US Open 1r** (lost Woodruff 6–3 6–0 3–6 6–0); **won** Copenhagen (d. Van Herck 6–4 7–5, Volkov 4–6 6–3 6–2, Kroslak 4–6 6–3 6–2, Burgsmuller 6–2 6–4, Damm 6–4 3–6 6–3), **won** St Petersburg (d. Volkov 6–4 6–1, Simian 3–6 6–3 6–2, Delaitre 6–2 6–4, Stich 6–3 6–1, Furlan 6–3 6–4); **sf** Hong Kong (d. Simian 4–6 6–2 6–4, Grabb 6–1 6–2, Gimelstob 6–4 6–4, lost M. Chang 7–6 6–4), **sf** Tokyo Japan Open (d. Nestor 6–4 6–4, Matsuoka 6–2 6–2, Woodforde 6–3 6–4, lost Roux 4–6 7–5 6–3), **sf** Beijing (d. Kulti 7–5 6–3, Paes 7–5 6–1, Pozzi 6–2 6–4, lost Courier 6–3 6–4), **sf** Singapore (d. O'Brien 6–1 1–6 7–5, Ondruska 6–4 6–4, Courier 3–6 6–3 6–2, lost Gustafsson 7–6 4–6 7–6).

DONALD JOHNSON (USA)

Born Allentown, Pa, 9 September 1968; lives Chapel Hill, NC; LH; 6ft 3in; 185lb; turned pro 1992; career singles titles 0; final 1997 ATP ranking 26 doubles; 1997 prize money $225,102.

Coached by Sam Paul. Wife Krista (married 21 May 1995). **1989:** (943). **1990:** (–). **1991:** (518). **1992:** (295) Won his 1st doubles titles on the Challenger circuit. **1993:** (415) Won 3 more Challenger doubles titles. **1994:** (320). **1995:** (199) A –, F 2, W –, US –. Spent his honeymoon playing through qualifying at French Open. **1996:** (460) A –, F –, W –, US –. Emerging from the satellite circuits, he extended Sampras to 3s 1r Indianapolis. Won his 1st doubles title on the main tour when he took Mexico City with Montana, following with Amsterdam – and 5 more on the Challenger circuit. **1997:** A –, F –, W –, US –. Appeared in 3 doubles f with Montana, winning Monte Carlo. They played as alternates at World Doubles Champ when Kafelnikov/Vacek withdrew, but lost all 3 rr matches. **1997 HIGHLIGHTS – DOUBLES:** (with Montana) **won** Monte Carlo (d. Eltingh/Haarhuis 7–6 2–6 7–6); **r/u** Stuttgart Mercedes (lost Kuerten/Meligeni 6–4 6–4), **r/u** Ostrava (lost Novak/Rikl 6–2 6–4).

NICOLAS KIEFER (GER)

Born Holzminden, 5 July 1977; lives Sievershansen; RH; 5ft 11in; 160lb; turned pro 1995; career singles titles 1; final 1997 ATP ranking 32; 1997 prize money $417,269.

Coached by Karl Meiler with German Tennis Federation. **1993:** Won Nat Jun. **1994:** (1212). **1995:** (202) No. 2 in ITF Jun rankings after winning Australian Open over J. Lee and US Open over Seetzen, and r/u Wimbledon to Mutis. In the senior game he followed the title at Garmisch Challenger with qf St Petersburg on the main tour. **1996:** (127) A 1, F –, W –, US –. Qf Kitzbuhel. **1997:** A –, F 1, W qf, US –. Reached his 1st sf at Milan, then upset Medvedev and Kafelnikov back-to-back on his way to qf Wimbledon, unseeded. A severe ankle injury suffered at Stuttgart Mercedes in July kept him out until Sept., but 2 weeks after his return he upset Henman and Philippoussis to take his 1st tour title in his 1st f at Toulouse, following with f Singapore (d. Rios). He also played qf Gstaad and Stuttgart Eurocard (d. Rusedski) and overtook Becker as No. 1 in GER. **1997 HIGHLIGHTS – SINGLES: French Open 1r** (lost Ulihrach 6–3 6–3 6–3), **Wimbledon qf** [unseeded] (d. Volkov 6–4 6–4 6–2, Baur 7–5 7–6 6–1, Medvedev [seed 13] 6–4 6–2 6–7 6–4, Kafelnikov [seed 3] 6–2 7–5 2–6 6–1, lost Woodbridge 7–6 2–6 6–0 6–4); **won** Toulouse (d. Fredriksson 4–6 6–3 6–1, Henman 4–6 7–6 6–2, Raoux 6–2 6–7 7–5, Radulescu 6–3 2–6 7–6, Philippoussis 7–5 5–7 6–4); **r/u** Singapore (d. Draper 6–4 6–2, Wilkinson 6–4 6–3, Rios 6–1 7–5, Tillstrom 6–7 6–3 6–3, lost Gustafsson 4–6 6–3 6–3); **sf** Milan (d. Forget 6–1 6–4, Martelli 6–3 6–4, Kucera 2–6 6–3 6–4, lost Bruguera 6–3 6–4). **CAREER HIGHLIGHTS – SINGLES: Wimbledon – qf 1997.**

MARK KNOWLES (BAH)

Born Nassau, 4 September 1971, and lives there; RH; 6ft 3in; 185lb; turned pro 1992; career singles titles 0; final 1997 ATP ranking 259 singles, 19 doubles; 1997 prize money $305,511 ($1,528,018).

Coached by Glenn Michibata. **1986:** Nat 16s champ. **1987:** (918). **1988:** (728). **1989:** (430) Joined his country's D Cup squad. **1990:** (–). **1991:** (293) Won All-American honours in singles and doubles at UCLA. **1992:** (255) A –, F –, W 2, US –. **1993:** (175) A –, F –, W –, US –. Upset Volkov at Washington and won Montreal doubles with Courier. **1994:** (255) A 1, F –, W 2, US –. In doubles he won Bogota with Nestor and r/u LIPC with Palmer. **1995:** (147) A –, F –, W 2, US 1. In singles he won 2 Challenger titles but reached no qf on the main tour. Continued to make his mark in doubles, joining with Nestor to upset Woodbridge/Woodforde on their way to a 1st GS f at Australian Open. They played 2 more f together, winning Indianapolis and qualifying for World Doubles Champ – although they won no match there – and he also won Japan Open with Stark. **1996:** (126) A –, F 2, W 2, US 2. The highlight of his year came at Shanghai, where he became the 1st Bahamian to reach a singles f and won the doubles with Smith. He played 6 other doubles f, winning Qatar, Memphis, Hamburg and Cincinnati with Nestor, with whom he qualified for World Doubles Champ. However, they were forced to withdraw after 2 rr matches when Nestor suffered a rib injury. **1997:** A 1, F –, W –, US –. He was out of action for 3 months, suffering from a stress fracture of the 7th rib, which continued to plague him. Played 4 f with Nestor, winning Indian Wells and Rome and taking the last berth at World Doubles Champ, where they lost 2 matches before an aggravation of the rib injury forced them to withdraw. **1997 HIGHLIGHTS – SINGLES: Australian Open 1r** (lost Woodbridge 6–4 6–2 6–1). **1997 HIGHLIGHTS – DOUBLES:** (with Nestor) **won** Indian Wells (d. Philippoussis/Rafter 7–6 4–6 7–5), **won** Rome (d. B. Black/O'Brien 6–3 4–6 7–5); **r/u** San Jose (lost MacPhie/ Muller 4–6 7–6 7–5), **r/u** LIPC (lost Woodbridge/ Woodforde 7–6 7–6). **CAREER HIGHLIGHTS – DOUBLES:** (with Nestor) **Australian Open – r/u 1995** (lost Palmer/ Reneberg 6–3 3–6 6–3 6–2).

PETR KORDA (CZE)

Born Prague, 23 January 1968; lives Monte Carlo, Monaco; LH; 6ft 3in; 160lb; turned pro 1987; career singles titles 8; final 1997 ATP ranking 13; 1997 prize money $1,515,483 ($9,039,709).

Trained by Ivan Machytka. Wife former circuit player, Regina Rajchrtova (married 19 September 1992); daughter Jessica Regina (born 27 February 1993). **1984:** Won Nat 18s at age 16. **1985:** In Jun doubles with Suk won French Open, r/u Australian Open and Wimbledon and was joint No. 1 in ITF rankings. **1986:** (511) Won Wimbledon Jun doubles with Carbonell. **1987:** (87) Won Budapest Challenger and on the senior tour upset Srejber on his way to his 1st qf showing at Prague. **1988:** (188) A –, F 2, W 3, US 1. Broke into top 100 in May and upset E. Sanchez in his 1st tourn on grass at Wimbledon. In doubles won Gstaad and Prague. Out of action with shoulder and ankle injuries following a car accident. **1989:** (59) A –, F –, W –, US –. Reached his 1st GP f at Frankfurt in autumn after sf showing at Vienna. In doubles won Stuttgart and reached 3 other f. **1990:** (38) A 2, F 2, W 1, US 2. Reached sf Philadelphia, Munich (d. Chang) and Moscow, and upset Gomez at Toronto World Tennis. In doubles r/u French Open with Ivanisevic and reached 3 more f, winning Monte Carlo with Smid. **1991:** (9) A 2, F 2, W 1, US 1. Made tremendous strides as he moved into the top 10 in autumn. Won his 1st tour singles title at New Haven, following with Berlin and also winning the doubles at both tourns. R/u Tampa, Washington (d. B. Gilbert), Montreal (d. Agassi and Courier); sf Umag and Vienna, and upset Lendl *en route* to qf Stockholm. **1992:** (7) A 1, F r/u, W 2, US 1. Having never before passed 3r GS singles, he was r/u French Open to Courier, who was the 1st seeded player he encountered in the tourn. Won Washington, Long Island (d. Edberg and Lendl) and Vienna, moving into top 5 in Oct. He was also r/u Munich, Toulouse and Basel, reached sf Italian Open and Stuttgart and qualified for ATP World Champ but won no match there. **1993:** (12) A qf, F 2, W 4, US 1. In the spring he suffered from a viral infection, which caused inflammation of the heart and build-up of fluids. Although he dropped out of the top 10, he finished the year spectacularly by winning GS Cup, beating Bruguera, Sampras and Stich back-to-back. He was also r/u Sydney Indoor and New Haven and reached sf Milan, LIPC (upset Edberg), Halle, Montreal and Vienna, plus 5 more qf. In doubles he won 3 titles with 3 different partners. **1994:** (18) A 1, F 1, W 2, US –. R/u Milan (d. Ivanisevic and Bruguera), Indian Wells (where he extended Sampras to 5s) and Munich (where he won doubles with Becker) and reached sf Sydney NSW Open. Upset Edberg on his way to qf Paris Open at end of season. He was out of action 2 months to Oct. with groin and hip problems which had hampered him since French Open. **1995:** (41) A 3, F 1, W 4, US qf. In singles he reached sf Dubai and Milan, plus qf Basel and US Open, being unseeded both there and at Wimbledon, where he upset M. Chang. Reached 2 doubles f but won no title. Underwent a hernia operation on 13 Oct., having suffered groin problems (amongst other ailments) since May 1994 and considered retiring. **1996:** (24) A 1, F 3, W –, US 3. Having been talked out of retirement by his wife and friends, he was back in style at Qatar, where, unseeded and feeling better than for a long time, he won his 1st singles title since GS Cup in December 1993. He upset Ivanisevic at Ostrava, where he was r/u, played through the qualifying to reach sf Paris Open (d. Rios), and appeared in qf Basel and Moscow. He won all his matches at WT Cup, although CZE lost f to SUI, and in doubles with Edberg he won a 1st GS title at Australian Open. **1997:** A 1, F 4, W 4, US qf. Free from pain and enjoying the game more than ever, he aimed to return to top 20 for 1st time since Feb. 1995. He achieved that goal after reaching f Halle (d. Muster) and Washington, and progressed to top 10 again after winning Stuttgart Eurocard in Oct., consolidating his position with r/u Moscow. The only player to take a set off Sampras at Wimbledon, he extended the eventual champion to 5s in last 16. At US Open, he went one better, removing the top seed in 5s tb, but was forced to retire in qf against Bjorkman, suffering from a cold and breathing difficulties. In another thrilling 5s match, he lost sf GS Cup to Rafter 9–7 fs. He also reached sf Antwerp, New Haven and Basel, plus qf Qatar, Milan, Rotterdam, Prague and Atlanta. **1997 HIGHLIGHTS – SINGLES: Australian Open 1r** (lost Rios [seed 9] 7–6 6–3 6–3), **French Open last 16** [unseeded] Burillo 6–4 6–0 7–6, C. Costa 6–3 7–5 6–4, W. Ferreira [seed 13] w.o., lost Blanco 1–6 6–1 7–5 6–4), **Wimbledon last 16** [seed 16] (d. Filippini 4–6 7–6 6–1 6–4, Rosset 6–3 6–0 7–6, O'Brien 6–3 4–6 6–3 6–7 6–4, lost Sampras [seed 1] 6–4 6–3 6–7 6–7 6–4), **US Open qf** [seed 15] (d. Spadea 2–6 7–5 7–6 6–4, Martelli 6–3 7–6 7–6, Damm 4–6 6–3 6–4 7–5, Sampras [seed 1] 6–7 7–5 7–6 3–6 7–6, lost Bjorkman 7–6 6–2 1–0 ret'd); **won** Stuttgart Eurocard (d. Woodruff 6–3 6–3, Pioline 6–3 ret'd, Rios 6–3 6–4, Rafter 6–4 7–6, Krajicek 7–6 6–2 6–4); **r/u** Halle (d. Carbonell 7–5 2–6 6–2, Escude 6–3 6–3, Muster 6–3 6–4, Haarhuis 7–6 6–4, lost Kafelnikov 7–6 6–7 7–6), **r/u** Washington (d. Nainkin 6–4 6–2, Wibier 6–4 6–4, Haas 6–7 6–4 6–4, Wheaton 6–2 6–3, lost M. Chang 5–7 6–2 6–1), **r/u** Moscow (d. Tarango 4–6 7–5 6–3, Carlsen 7–6 5–7 6–1, O'Brien 7–5 6–3, W. Black 6–7 6–3 7–5, lost Kafelnikov 7–6 6–4); **sf** Antwerp (d. Van Scheppingen 6–3 6–2, J. Sanchez 6–3 6–3, D. Norman 6–3 6–4, lost Rosset 7–6 6–3), **sf** New Haven (d. Gambill 6–3 6–3, J. Sanchez 6–2 6–4, Wheaton 4–6 7–6 6–4, lost Kafelnikov 6–4 7–6), **sf** Basel (d. Escude 6–1 6–4, Woodruff 7–5 6–4, Roux 6–3 6–4, lost Rusedski 6–7 6–3 7–5), **sf** GS Cup (d. Kuerten 6–3 5–3 ret'd, Pioline 7–5 6–3, lost Rafter 7–5 3–6 6–7 7–6 9–7). **CAREER HIGHLIGHTS – SINGLES: French Open – r/u 1992** (d. Bergstrom 6–4 6–2 6–2, Matsuoka 1–6 4–6 6–4 6–4 6–4, Schapers 6–4 6–2 3–6 6–1, Oncins 6–4 6–3 6–3, Cherkasov 6–4 6–7 6–2 6–4, Leconte 6–2 7–5 6–3, lost Courier 7–5 6–2 6–1); **Australian Open – qf 1993** (d. C. Adams 6–3 3–6 6–3 6–3, Eltingh 7–6 6–2 6–3, Medvedev 6–4 4–6 6–3 7–6, Garner 7–5 6–3 6–1, lost Courier 6–1 6–0 6–4), **US Open – qf 1995** [unseeded] (d. Matsuoka 7–6 6–7 6–7 6–5 ret'd, Eltingh 6–2 6–4 3–6 6–1, Ondruska 6–3 6–2 7–5, Spadea 6–2 7–5 6–4, lost Agassi 6–4 6–2 1–6 7–5), **qf 1997**; **GS Cup – won 1993** (d. Volkov 6–2 6–3, Bruguera 4–6 6–0 6–4, Sampras 3–6 7–6 3–6 7–6 13–11, Stich 2–6 6–4 7–6 2–6 11–9). **CAREER HIGHLIGHTS – DOUBLES:** (with Edberg) **Australian Open – won 1996** (d. Lareau/O'Brien 7–5 7–5 4–6 6–1); (with Ivanisevic) **French Open – r/u 1990** (lost Casal/E. Sanchez 7–5 6–3).

RICHARD KRAJICEK (NED)

Born Rotterdam, 6 December 1971; lives The Hague; RH; 6ft 5in; 190lb; turned pro 1989; career singles titles 13; final 1997 ATP ranking 11; 1997 prize money $1,434,564 ($6,835,339).
Coached by Rohan Goetzke. Son of Czech immigrants. Switched from 2HB to 1HB at age 12. Won Nat 12s and 14s. **1990:** (129) Won Verona and Casablanca Challengers. **1991:** (40) A 4, F 2, W 3, US 1. Reached last 16 Australian Open, unseeded, then at Hong Kong in April he won his 1st tour title in his 1st f. At New Haven he upset Edberg *en route* to qf (where he retired) and Hlasek and J. McEnroe in reaching sf Toulouse. At US Open held 2 mps v Lendl 1r before losing in 5s, and in doubles reached 2 f with Siemerink, winning Hilversum. **1992:** (10) A sf, F 3, W 3, US 4. Upset Lendl 1r Sydney NSW Open, then made a tremendous impact at Australian Open where, unseeded, he surprised Chang and Stich before being forced to def. sf v Courier with tendinitis of right shoulder. He followed by winning Los Angeles and Antwerp (d. Courier), r/u

Tokyo Suntory (d. Stich and Edberg) and sf Sydney Indoor (d. Lendl again). These performances saw him become the 1st Dutchman in the top 20 since Tom Okker in 1976 and at end of year he broke into the top 10. His late surge at Antwerp gained him the last place at his 1st ATP Champs when Agassi and Lendl were forced to withdraw, but he won only 1 match there (v Chang). **1993:** (15) A 2, F sf, W 4, US 4. At French Open he outlasted 3 opponents in consec. 5s encounters before falling to Courier in 4s and at US Open he saved 2 mps in 3s v Martin in a match lasting 5 hr 10 min. Won Los Angeles, r/u Stuttgart Eurocard (d. Becker) and upset Agassi *en route* to qf LIPC, where he won the doubles with Siemerink. Out of action from Nov. with tendinitis in both knees. **1994:** (17) A –, F 3, W 1, US 2. He returned from injury to play doubles only at Estoril in March; then in his 1st singles tourn at Barcelona in April, he won his 1st ever CC title, upsetting Bruguera on the way. Won 1st GC title at Rosmalen in June and in Sept. won Sydney Indoor, for his 3rd title on a different surface during the year. This last success and sf finish at Los Angeles took him back to the top 20. **1995:** (11) A 2, F 2, W 1, US 3. Upset W. Ferreira and Stich on his way on his way to the title at Stuttgart Eurocard, took Rotterdam the following week, and upset Kafelnikov and Becker to reach f New Haven. He also reached sf Adelaide and 7 more qf, including Essen, where he upset Becker again. Won Rosmalen doubles with Siemerink. **1996:** (7) A 3, F qf, W won, US 1. The climax of his career came at Wimbledon, where, unseeded owing to his previous disappointing performances there and record of injury, he became the 1st Dutchman to win a GS title. He upset Stich and Sampras and lost only one set along the way, returning to top 10. The rest of the year was less spectacular, with no other title, but r/u showings at Italian Open (unseeded, d. W. Ferreira) and Los Angeles, sf ATP Champs and qf appearances at French Open, Antwerp, Hong Kong, Tokyo Japan Open, Rosmalen, New Haven and Singapore. He also upset Bruguera at LIPC and was the only player to take a set off Kafelnikov at French Open. After he withdrew 3r Australian Open with a back injury, Agassi had remarked that every time Krajicek thought about tennis, he was mysteriously injured; thereafter he changed his attitude, became less worried about getting injured and thus relieved the pressure on himself. However, it was not all plain sailing and he retired from qf Singapore in Oct. with a right knee injury and pulled out of Stockholm with recurring knee problems. At GS Cup he lost tamely 1r to MaliVai Washington, his victim in Wimbledon f, and immediately sought a solution to his knee problem, undergoing surgery to repair torn meniscus on 9 Dec. **1997:** A –, F 3, W 4, US qf. After returning in Feb., he won Rotterdam (d. Enqvist), Tokyo Japan Open and Rosmalen (d. Chang), but by US Open (d. Mantilla) had slipped far enough down the rankings to be unseeded. However, he picked up again, upsetting Sampras in ss *en route* to f Stuttgart Eurocard and returning to top 10. He also reached sf Vienna and qf Dubai, Monte Carlo, Los Angeles, Montreal, New Haven and Paris Open, where he withdrew with a knee injury – the 10th time in his career he'd pulled out mid-tourn. **1997 HIGHLIGHTS – SINGLES: French Open 3r** [seed 6] (d. Draper 7–6 6–2 6–1, Ulihrach 6–2 3–6 6–2 6–3, lost Rafter 6–3 4–6 6–4 6–2), **Wimbledon last 16** [seed 4] (d. Craca 7–5 6–2 6–4, Pavel 3–6 6–4 6–7 6–3 6–3, Rikl 6–4 6–3 7–5, lost Henman [seed 14] 7–6 6–7 7–5 6–4), **US Open qf** [unseeded] (d. W. Black 6–4 6–2 6–2, Filippini 7–6 6–2 7–5, Corretja [seed 6] w.o., Mantilla [seed 12] 7–5 6–3 6–4, lost Rusedski 7–5 7–6 7–6); **won** Rotterdam (d. Damm 6–4 6–2, Prinosil 7–6 7–6, Stich 7–6 7–6, Enqvist 6–7 6–3 6–4, Vacek 7–6 7–6), **won** Tokyo Japan Open (d. Godwin 6–3 6–4, M. Norman 7–5 6–0, Prinosil 6–4 6–3, Rafter 7–6 6–3, Roux 6–2 3–6 6–1), **won** Rosmalen (d. Haarhuis 7–5 7–6, Dreekmann 6–0 6–3, Damm 7–6 7–6, M. Chang 6–7 6–3 6–4, Raoux 6–4 7–6); **r/u** Stuttgart Eurocard (d. Becker 7–6 6–4, Sampras 6–4 6–4, Larsson 6–2 7–5, Bjorkman 6–4 3–6 6–3, lost Korda 7–6 6–2 6–4); **sf** Vienna (d. Dewulf 6–2 6–4, Clement 3–6 6–4 6–2, Larsson 6–4 6–4, lost Ivanisevic 5–7 6–4 7–6). **CAREER HIGHLIGHTS – SINGLES: Wimbledon – won 1996** [unseeded] (d. J. Sanchez 6–4 6–3 6–4, Rostagno 6–4 6–3 6–3, Steven 7–6 6–7 6–4 6–2, Stich 6–4 7–6 6–4, Sampras 7–5 7–6 6–4, Stoltenberg 7–5 6–2 6–1, MaliVai Washington 6–3 6–4 6–3); **Australian Open – sf 1992** [unseeded] (d. Saceanu 6–3 6–3 6–3, Grabb 6–2 7–6 6–1, Chang 6–4 6–1 5–7 1–6 6–3, Bergstrom 7–5 7–6 6–3, Stich 5–7 7–6 6–7 6–4 6–4, lost Courier w.o.); **French Open – sf 1993** (d. Bergstrom 7–5 6–3 7–5, Rosset 6–2 6–3 6–1, Arrese 2–6 6–2 6–2 6–7 6–2, C. Costa 7–5 3–6 6–3 5–7 10–8, Novacek 3–6 6–3 3–6 6–3 6–4, lost Courier 6–1 6–7 7–5 6–2), **qf 1996** (d. Noszaly 4–6 6–4 6–4 7–6, Carbonell 6–2 4–6 7–6 6–2, Woodbridge 7–5 6–2 6–2, Bjorkman 6–3 6–2 6–4, lost Kafelnikov 6–3 6–4 6–7 6–2).

TREVOR KRONEMANN (USA)

Born Edina, Minn. 3 September 1968; lives Bradenton, Fla.; RH; 6ft 4in; 225lb; turned pro 1991; career singles titles 0; final 1997 ATP ranking 43 doubles; 1997 prize money $117,330.

Wife Melanie (married 26 March 1994). **1989:** (–) R/u NCAA doubles with Briggs, with whom he was an All-American 2 years. **1990:** (727) All-American in singles at Univ. Cal-Irvine for 4th straight year. **1991:** (589) Moved on to the Challenger circuit, where he won 2 doubles titles with Briggs. **1992:** (–) Won Tampa doubles with Briggs after qualifying. **1993:** (662) Won US CC doubles with Bergh. **1994:** (790) Won 4 doubles titles on the Challenger circuit with 3 different partners. **1995:** (–) Developing his doubles partnership with Macpherson, won Barcelona, Munich and Scottsdale. **1996:** (–) Despite winning only San Jose from 2 f, he and Macpherson played World Doubles Champ as alternates after Forget/Hlasek and Kafelnikov/Vacek withdrew, and progressed to sf before losing to Lareau/O'Brien. **1997:** He and Macpherson played 2 doubles f, winning no title, but played (and lost) 1 match at World Doubles Champ as alternates again after Knowles and Nestor withdrew after 2 matches. **1997 HIGHLIGHTS – DOUBLES:** (with Macpherson) **r/u** Rosmalen (lost Eltingh/Haarhuis 6–4 7–5), **r/u** Gstaad (lost Kafelnikov/Vacek 4–6 7–6 6–3).

KAROL KUCERA (SVK)

Born Bratislava, 4 March 1974, and lives there; RH; 6ft 2in; 165lb; turned pro 1992; career singles titles 2; final 1997 ATP ranking 24; 1997 prize money $492,333 ($1,235,208).

Coached by Miloslav Mecir. **1990:** (862). **1991:** (351) Member of Czech Galea Cup team for 1st of 2 years. **1992:** (214) Won Prague Challenger. **1993:** (181) Enjoyed some success on the Challenger circuit, although he won no title. **1994:** (57) After winning 2 Challenger titles, he reached his 1st main tour qf at St Polten, following with his 1st f at Umag, unseeded. Upset Dosedel *en route* to qf Bucharest and surprised Bruguera at Moscow. **1995:** (74) A 1, F 1, W 1, US 1. Never before having won a match on grass, he won his 1st title on the main tour at Rosmalen, as well as reaching sf Copenhagen, qf Marseille and Toulouse and upsetting Siemerink at Moscow. **1996:** (63) A 3, F 3, W 3, US 1. He upset W. Ferreira at Australian Open, surprised M. Chang on the way to sf Long Island, took a set off Sampras at Wimbledon and reached qf Lyon. **1997:** A 2, F 1, W 1, US 1. Won Ostrava, where his opponents in both sf and f ret'd after 1s, and r/u Nottingham (d. Henman) and Stuttgart Mercedes (d. Medvedev, Rios and Bruguera). He also reached sf Copenhagen and Bastad, qf Adelaide (d. Woodforde), Milan, Vienna (d. Kafelnikov) and Stockholm (d. Muster) and upset Ivanisevic at Basel. **1997 HIGHLIGHTS – SINGLES: Australian Open 2r** (d. Haarhuis 6–1 3–6 6–3 4–6 6–4, lost Ivanisevic 6–4 6–2 6–2), **French Open 1r** (lost Boetsch 6–1 6–1 6–4), **Wimbledon 1r** (lost Rosset 7–5 6–3 6–2), **US Open 1r** (lost M. Norman 6–7 6–4 6–2 6–3); **won** Ostrava (d. Braasch 7–5 6–4, Carlsen 6–3 6–7 7–6, Novak 6–4 6–2, Ivanisevic 6–3 ret'd, M. Norman 6–2 ret'd); **r/u** Nottingham (d. M. Lee 6–1 6–1, B. Black 7–5 6–3, Draper 4–6 6–2 7–5, Henman 6–4 2–6 6–4, lost Rusedski 6–4 7–5), **r/u** Stuttgart Mercedes (d. Kiefer 1–2 ret'd, Medvedev 6–2 6–4, Rios 6–4 6–4, Bruguera 6–3 2–6 7–5, Portas 6–4 6–3, lost Corretja 6–2 7–6); **sf** Copenhagen (d. Stanoytchev 6–3 6–0, Santoro 6–1 4–6 6–1, Raoux 6–4 6–2, lost Damm 6–4 3–6 6–3), **sf** Bastad (d. Apell 6–3 3–6 6–2, Dosedel 7–6 6–3, Larsson 6–4 ret'd, lost Marin 7–6 6–3). **1997 HIGHLIGHTS – DOUBLES:** (with Hrbaty) **r/u** Umag (lost Pescariu/Sanguinetti 7–6 6–4).

GUSTAVO KUERTEN (BRA)

Born Florianapolis, 10 September 1976, and lives there; RH; 6ft 3in; 180lb; turned pro 1995; career singles titles 1; final 1997 ATP ranking 14; 1997 prize money $1,586,753 ($1,726,638).

Coached by Larri Passos. **1993:** (665). **1994:** (421) Won French Open Jun doubles with Lapentti, to whom he was r/u Orange Bowl 18s. **1995:** (197) Made an impact on the satellite circuits. **1996:** (88) A –, F 1, W –, US –. Reached qf Umag (d. Berasategui) and Beijing and finished the season by winning Campinas Challenger. In doubles he won Santiago with Meligeni. **1997:** A 2, F won, W 1, US 3. The title at Curitiba Challenger restored his confidence after a poor start to the year, which gave no hint of what was to come at French Open. There he upset CC specialists Muster, Medvedev, Kafelnikov and Bruguera to win his 1st title, having never before passed qf. He was the 1st Brazilian to win a GS title (or even to pass qf in GS), 3rd unseeded player to win French Open, and 1st since Wilander in 1982 to win his 1st career title in GS. Only Mark Edmondson, winning Australian Open in 1976 from a ranking of 212, had won a GS ranked lower than his 66. However, that triumph saw him become the 1st Brazilian to break into top 20 at No. 15, and after r/u showing at Montreal (d. M. Chang), he moved into top 10. He also reached f Bologna (d. Berasategui) and qf Cincinnati, as well as recording other useful upsets during the year, including Agassi at Memphis and W. Ferreira at Indian Wells. In doubles with Meligeni, he played and won 3 f. **1997 HIGHLIGHTS – SINGLES: Australian Open 2r** (d. Tillstrom 7–5 7–6 3–6 6–4, lost Godwin 6–7 6–0 6–1 6–0), **won French Open** [unseeded] (d. Dosedel 6–0 7–5 6–1, Bjorkman 6–4 6–2 4–6 7–5, Muster [seed 5] 6–7 6–1 6–3 3–6 6–4, Medvedev 5–7 6–1 6–2 1–6 7–5, Kafelnikov [seed 3] 6–2 5–7 2–6 6–0 6–4, Dewulf 6–1 3–6 6–1 7–6, Bruguera 6–3 6–4 6–2), **Wimbledon 1r** [seed 11] (lost Gimelstob 6–3 6–4 4–6 1–6 6–4), **US Open 3r** [seed 9] (d. Grant 6–4 3–6 6–7 6–2 6–2, Schalken 6–4 6–4 6–2, lost Bjorkman 6–3 6–1 7–5); **won** Curitiba Challenger (d. Sabau 3–6 6–4 6–3); **r/u** Bologna (d. Charpentier 6–1 6–3, Diaz 6–4 6–2, Berasategui 6–3 6–7 7–5, Martelli 6–1 6–2, lost Mantilla 4–6 6–2 6–1), **r/u** Montreal (d. Stark 6–2 6–4, Tebbutt 5–7 6–4 6–4, Santoro 6–3 7–6, M. Chang 6–3 6–1, lost Woodruff 7–5 4–6 6–3). **1997 HIGHLIGHTS – DOUBLES:** (with Meligeni) **won** Estoril (d. Gaudenzi/Messori 6–2 6–2), **won** Bologna (d. Randall/Waite 6–2 7–5), **won** Stuttgart Mercedes (d. Johnson/Montana 6–4 6–4). **CAREER HIGHLIGHTS – SINGLES: French Open – won 1997.**

NICKLAS KULTI (SWE)

Born Stockholm, 22 April 1971; lives Monte Carlo, Monaco; RH; 6ft 3in; 172lb; turned pro 1989; career singles titles 3; final 1997 ATP ranking 153 singles, 16 doubles; 1997 prize money $395,400 ($2,283,304).

Coached by Martin Bohm. Won 11 Nat Jun titles. **1985:** Won Orange Bowl 14s. **1986:** Won European Jun doubles with Larsson. **1988:** (176) R/u US Open Jun to Pereira. **1989:** (110) A 3, F 1, W –, US –. In Jun tennis won Australian Open and Wimbledon, r/u US Open to Stark and finished the year ranked No. 1 in ITF Jun rankings. On the senior tour reached sf Bastad. **1990:** (57) A 1, F 3, W –, US –. Reached 1st tour f at Prague and sf San Marino. **1991:** (79) A 1, F 2, W 1, US 1. Won his 1st tour title at Adelaide. **1992:** (79) A 2, F qf, W 2, US 1. Upset Chang in reaching his 1st GS qf at French Open, where he took Leconte to 5s. He appeared at the same stage in Copenhagen and Munich and won 2 doubles titles. **1993:** (46) A 2, F 1, W 1, US 2. Won Adelaide again (d. Volkov), r/u Copenhagen and reached qf Sydney Indoor, Munich, Bastad, Prague and Antwerp. **1994:** (98) A 3, F 2, W 1, US 2. In singles he reached sf Adelaide (d. Rosset) and qf

Sydney NSW Open (d. MaliVai Washington and Chesnokov). In doubles he played 3 f with different partners, winning Monte Carlo with Larsson. **1995:** (173) A 2, F –, W –, US 1. Reached his 1st GS f at French Open doubles with Larsson and in singles appeared in sf Prague. However, in Sept. he underwent surgery to repair inflamed tendon on left foot and was out for rest of year. **1996:** (64) A 3, F 1, W 1 US 1. Returning in Jan., he was back in the top 100 after r/u showing at Atlanta in May (d. Reneberg), then at Halle he upset Kafelnikov *en route* to his 1st GC title after qualifying. At Stockholm, Edberg's last tourn, he beat the former No. 1 in 1r. From 6 doubles f he won Antwerp and New Delhi with Bjorkman, with whom he qualified for his 1st World Doubles Champ. After losing doubles with Bjorkman in D Cup f v FRA, he played as substitute for Edberg in decisive 5th rubber, held 3 Cup points as Boetsch served at 6–7 0–40 in 5s, but lost 10–8 after 4 hrs 48 min of drama. **1997:** A 2, F 1, W 2, US –. Reached no qf in singles, but in doubles played 4 f, winning Bastad with Tillstrom and Atlanta with Bjorkman, with whom he was r/u US Open. **1997 HIGHLIGHTS – SINGLES: Australian Open 2r** (d. Alami 6–4 6–2 6–4, lost Hrbaty 6–2 6–1 6–2), **French Open 1r** (lost Philippoussis 6–2 4–6 3–6 6–4 6–4), **Wimbledon 2r** (d. Sinner 7–6 6–2 6–3, lost Stoltenberg 6–2 3–6 6–2 6–3). **1997 HIGHLIGHTS – DOUBLES:** (with Bjorkman unless stated) **r/u US Open** (lost Kafelnikov/Vacek 7–6 6–3); **won** Atlanta (d. Davis/Jones 6–2 7–6), (with Tillstrom) **won** Bastad (d. Gustafsson/Larsson 6–0 6–3); **r/u** Indianapolis (lost Tebbutt/Tillstrom). **CAREER HIGHLIGHTS – SINGLES: French Open – qf 1992** (d. J. McEnroe 6–2 7–5 6–7 7–5, Zillner 4–6 6–1 2–6 7–6 6–2, Chang 7–6 2–6 6–3 8–6, Perez 6–0 3–6 7–5 6–4, lost Leconte 6–7 3–6 6–3 6–3 6–3). **CAREER HIGHLIGHTS – DOUBLES: French Open –** (with Larsson) **r/u 1955** (lost Eltingh/ Haarhuis 6–7 6–4 6–1), **US Open –** (with Bjorkman) **r/u 1997**.

NICOLAS LAPENTTI (ECU)

Born Guyaquil, 13 August 1976, and lives there; RH; 6ft 2in; 180lb; turned pro 1995; career singles titles 1; final 1997 ATP ranking 64; 1997 prize money $266,758.

Coached by Raul Viver. **1991:** (922). **1992:** (–) Joined his country's D Cup squad. **1993:** (323). **1994:** (632) Won Orange Bowl 18s over Kuerten; in Jun doubles won French Open with him and US Open with Ellwood, finishing No. 2 in ITF Jun rankings in both singles and doubles. **1995:** (125) On the satellite circuits he won all his singles matches in 4 weeks on the Colombia satellite, following with the 1st 2 on the Ecuador circuit. Five days later he qualified for his 1st main tour event at Bogota and won the title. He then rounded off his season by winning Santiago Challenger. **1996:** (121) A 1, F 1, W 2, US 1. R/u Bogota in both singles and doubles (with Campana). **1997:** A –, F 2, W 1, US 2. Bogota was again the venue for his best performance: he was r/u there, having reached sf Mexico City the week before and qf Bologna and Bucharest (d. Berasategui) earlier in year. Played 3 doubles f with different partners, winning Amsterdam with Kilderry and Mexico City with Orsanic. **1997 HIGHLIGHTS – SINGLES: French Open 2r** (d. Fetterlein 6–4 6–1 6–2, lost Woodruff 6–4 5–7 3–6 6–4 6–1), **Wimbledon 1r** (lost Clavet 7–5 6–1 6–3), **US Open 2r** (d. Pavel 6–4 5–0 ret'd, lost Pioline 6–0 6–4 6–2); **r/u** Bogota (d. Pavel 6–2 6–2, Rincon 6–3 6–3, C. Costa 7–5 4–6 6–3, Spadea 6–2 7–5, lost Clavet 6–3 6–3); **sf** Mexico City (d. Ogorodov 6–2 6–2, Blanco 6–3 6–0, Alvarez 6–2 4–6 7–5, lost Clavet 7–5 7–6). **1997 HIGHLIGHTS – DOUBLES:** (with Kilderry) **won** Amsterdam (d. A. Kratzmann/Pimek 3–6 7–5 7–6), (with Orsanic) **won** Mexico City (d. Herrera/M. Sanchez 4–6 6–3 7–6); (with Alonso) **r/u** Santiago (lost Davids/Kratzmann 7–6 5–7 6–4).

SEBASTIEN LAREAU (CAN)

Born Montreal, 27 April 1973; lives Boucherville, Quebec; RH; 6ft; 175lb; turned pro 1991; career singles titles 0; final 1997 ATP ranking 155 singles, 15 doubles; 1997 prize money $355,980 ($1,312,729).

Coached by Martin Laurendeau. Won Nat 12s, 16s and 18s in singles and doubles. **1989:** (1015). **1990:** (633) Won French Open and Wimbledon Jun doubles with LeBlanc. **1991:** (348) Began to make his mark on the satellite circuits and joined his country's D Cup squad. **1992:** (193) Won Nova Scotia Challenger. **1993:** (167) Won Calgary Challenger in singles and doubles. **1994:** (102) He reached his 1st qf on the main tour at Antwerp (d. Stich) and won 2 Challenger titles. R/u 3 times in doubles with different partners. Won Nat singles and doubles and took over the No. 1 ranking in Canada. **1995:** (138) A 2, F 1, W 1, US 2. In singles he moved into top 100 1st time with qf showings at Philadelphia and St Petersburg, and in doubles he won Seoul with Tarango and Beijing with Ho. **1996:** (104) A 2, F –, W –, US –. In doubles with O'Brien he reached his 1st GS f at Australian Open and from 3 more f won Stuttgart Eurocard. Qualifying as 8th pairing for World Doubles Champ, they d. Woodbridge/Woodforde in rr but lost f to them 7–6 4s. **1997:** A 1, F 2, W 1, US –. Qf Hong Kong was his best singles performance. Played 4 doubles f with O'Brien, winning Philadelphia and Los Angeles and r/u Australian Open, to qualify for World Doubles Champ. In their last rr match there, needing to d. Woodbridge/Woodforde in ss to qualify for sf on game percentage, they did so, but then lost in 3s to Bhupathi/Paes. **1997 HIGHLIGHTS – SINGLES: Australian Open 1r** (lost Knippschild 6–2 6–7 7–6 6–3), **French Open 2r** (d. Gumy 2–6 6–4 6–4 4–6 8–6, lost Roux 7–5 6–2 6–4), **Wimbledon 1r** (lost Haarhuis 6–1 6–2 7–6). **1997 HIGHLIGHTS – DOUBLES:** (with O'Brien) **r/u Australian Open** (lost Woodbridge/Woodforde 4–6 7–5 7–5 6–3); **won** Philadelphia (d. E. Ferreira/Galbraith 6–3 6–3), **won** Los Angeles (d. Bhupathi/Leach 7–6 6–4); **r/u** Montreal (lost Bhupathi/Paes 7–6 6–3). **CAREER HIGHLIGHTS – DOUBLES:** (with O'Brien) **Australian Open – r/u 1996** (lost Edberg/Korda 7–5 7–5 4–6 6–1), **r/u 1997**, **World Doubles Champ – r/u 1996** (lost Woodbridge/Woodforde 6–4 5–7 6–2 7–6).

MAGNUS LARSSON (SWE)

Born Olofstrom, 25 March 1970; lives Vaxjo; RH; 6ft 4in; 194lb; turned pro 1989; career singles titles 5; final 1997 ATP ranking 25; 1997 prize money $515,772 ($4,766,883).

Coached by Carl Axel Hageskog and Stefan Simonsson. **1986:** Won European Jun doubles with Kulti. **1988:** (381) R/u French Open Jun to Pereira. **1989:** (145) A 1, F –, W –, US –. Won Geneva Challenger. **1990:** (56) A 2, F –, W 1, US –. Won Florence after qualifying, r/u Bastad and won Ljubliana Challenger. **1991:** (61) A 1, F 3, W 2, US 3. He sprung some big upsets during the year, surprising Becker *en route* to sf Adelaide, Edberg at Monte Carlo, Gomez at US Open and Cherkasov on his way to qf Bastad. He reached the same stage at Prague and Florence and extended Courier to 5s French Open, at one stage being 2 sets to 1 ahead. **1992:** (34) A 1, F 3, W 3, US 2. Won both singles and doubles at Copenhagen, following with the singles title at Munich (d. Stich and Korda). He also made an unexpected appearance in last 16 Olympics (d. Forget) and reached 3 qf. **1993:** (39) A 2, F 3, W 2, US qf. Usually a CC specialist, he was playing only his 6th HC tourn at US Open, where he upset Becker to reach qf, unseeded. He also appeared in sf Copenhagen and Bastad plus 4 more qf. Qualified for GS Cup but lost 1r Bruguera. **1994:** (19) A 1, F sf, W 1, US 1. At French Open he continued his unexpected success in GS when, unseeded, he upset Martin and saved 6 mps v Dreekmann to reach sf. Again rising to the big occasion, he won the dramatic final rubber in D Cup sf v US, beating Martin to take SWE to f. He finished the year in triumph, winning both his matches as SWE won D Cup over RUS in Moscow, and took his first GS Cup by beating Sampras in f. He also won Zaragoza and Toulouse, was r/u Halle and Antwerp and upset Chang at Stockholm, breaking into top 20 1st time after Antwerp. **1995:** (17) A 4, F 4, W –, US –. Upset Stich on the way to f Qatar, where he won the doubles, and removed Ivanisevic to reach f Barcelona. Extended Sampras to 5s Australian Open and Agassi to fs tb in sf LIPC, reaching the same stage at Atlanta and US CC, plus 3 more qf, and broke into top 10 in April. However, he broke a bone in 2 places in his right foot playing an exhibition match in June and was out 5 months, missing Wimbledon and US Open. Played on winning SWE team in WT Cup and reached his 1st GS f in doubles with Kulti at French Open. **1996:** (46) A 3, F 1, W 2, US 1. He struggled to regain his form, with his best performances being r/u Toulouse (d. Rios) and qf Qatar, Barcelona (d. Bruguera), Hamburg, Halle and Bastad. **1997:** A 2, F 3, W –, US qf. He was always a dangerous opponent and the only player to upset Sampras twice in 1997. Although he did not progress beyond qf, he was consistent in reaching that stage at US Open, Qatar (d. Enqvist), Marseille (d. Clavet), Monte Carlo (d. Sampras), Bastad, Indianapolis (d. Sampras), Vienna (d. Enqvist), Stuttgart Eurocard (d. Corretja) and Stockholm (d. Enqvist), adding upsets of Kafelnikov at Barcelona, Rios at Indian Wells and Mantilla at French Open. Played 2 doubles f, winning Marseille with Enqvist. **1997 HIGHLIGHTS – SINGLES: Australian Open 2r** (d. Viloca 6–3 6–3 7–6, lost Bruguera 4–6 6–3 6–4 7–6), **French Open 3r** (d. Courier 6–1 6–2 4–6 1–6 6–4, Mantilla 6–2 6–4 3–6 6–3 [seed 10], lost Arazi 6–2 6–3 7–5), **US Open qf** [unseeded] (d. Siemerink 6–4 6–2 6–3, Escude 6–4 6–2 7–6, Meligeni 6–2 6–4 6–3, W. Ferreira 6–3 7–6 6–3, lost Rafter [seed 13] 7–6 6–4 6–2). **1997 HIGHLIGHTS – DOUBLES:** (with Enqvist) **won** Marseille (d. Delaitre/Santoro 6–3 6–4); (with Gustafsson) **r/u** Bastad (lost Kulti/Tillstrom 6–0 6–3). **CAREER HIGHLIGHTS – SINGLES: GS Cup – won 1994** [unseeded] (d. Edberg 6–4 6–7 8–6, Agassi 6–3 1–6 6–0, Martin 6–4 6–1 6–1, Sampras 7–6 4–6 7–6 6–4); **French Open – sf 1994** [unseeded] (d. Steven 6–2 6–2 6–2, Tarango 6–2 6–4 6–3, Martin 6–7 6–3 6–0 1–6 6–3, Yzaga 6–3 6–2 6–2, Dreekmann 3–6 6–7 7–6 6–0 6–1, lost Berasategui 6–3 6–4 6–1); **US Open – qf 1993** (d. Raoux 6–2 6–4 7–6, Borwick 6–4 6–4 6–4, Fromberg 6–2 7–5 7–6, Becker 6–2 6–3 3–6 7–5, lost Masur 6–2 7–5 7–5), **qf 1997**. **CAREER HIGHLIGHTS – DOUBLES:** (with Kulti) **French Open – r/u 1995 Open** (lost Eltingh/ Haarhuis 6–7 6–4 6–1).

RICK LEACH (USA)

Born Arcadia, Cal., 28 December 1964; lives Laguna Beach, Cal.; LH; 6ft 2in; 175lb; turned pro 1987; career singles titles 0; final 1997 ATP ranking 8 doubles; 1997 prize money $319,853 ($2,612,056).

Wife Christi Bondra (married 26 December 1992); daughter Paulina Christine (born 23 February 1994). Won 19 nat jun titles. **1986:** (201) Coached by his father, Dick, at USC, where he was an All-American. Won NCAA doubles with Pawsat and took 3 singles titles on USTA circuit. **1987:** (148) A –, F –, W –, US 2. Won NCAA doubles again (with Melville) and won 2 GP doubles titles. **1988:** (258) A 2, F –, W –, US 2. In doubles with Pugh won Australian Open and Masters doubles on 1st appearance there but, suffering from flu and food poisoning, was forced to default US Open doubles f. Won 6 other titles (1 with Goldie). **1989:** (195) A 1, F –, W –, US 2. In doubles with Pugh won Australian Open, r/u Wimbledon and took 4 other titles to qualify for Masters, where they surprisingly took only 6th place. **1990:** (279) A –, F –, W 1, US 2. In doubles with Pugh won a 1st Wimbledon title, plus LIPC and Philadelphia, to qualify for IBM/ATP World Doubles Final, where they failed to reach sf, and played together in winning US D Cup team. In mixed doubles with Garrison won Wimbledon and r/u US Open. **1991:** (402) A –, F –, W –, US 1. Won 2 doubles titles with Pugh and r/u French Open. **1992:** (429) A –, F –, W 1, US –. In doubles with Jones was r/u Australian Open and US Open, won Tokyo Suntory and New Haven and qualified for World Doubles final. **1993:** (632) A –, F –, W –, US –. Teamed with K. Flach to win his 1st US Open doubles. They won another 2 titles together, just missing IBM/ATP World Doubles, and he had a 4th win with Black. **1994:** (536) A –, F –, W –, US –. Won 2 doubles titles with different partners. **1995:** (–) A –, F –, W –, US –. Won New Haven doubles with Melville, with whom he qualified for World Doubles Champ, although they did not progress beyond rr. In mixed he took Australian Open with Zvereva. **1996:** (–) A –, F –, W –, US –. In men's doubles he won 4 of 5 f, each with a different partner, and in mixed he was r/u US Open with

Bollegraf. **1997:** A –, F –, W –, US –. Until the World Doubles f, it was the 1st time in 11 years that he had won no doubles title, although he had played 7 f – 5 with Stark and 1 each with Bjorkman and Bhupathi. However, playing his 7th season-ending champs in 10 years and with his 5th different partner (Stark), he won the title for the 2nd time. It was a triumphant end for the partnership, for he and Stark had decided in Aug. to part company at end of year. He also collected 2 mixed doubles titles, taking Australian Open and US Open with Bollegraf. **1997 HIGHLIGHTS – DOUBLES:** (with Stark unless stated) **won** World Doubles Champ (d. Bhupathi/Paes 6–3 6–4 7–6); **r/u** Auckland (lost E. Ferreira/Galbraith 6–4 4–6 7–6), **r/u** Memphis (lost E. Ferreira/Galbraith 6–3 3–6 6–1), (with Bjorkman) **r/u** Scottsdale (lost Lobo/J. Sanchez 6–3 6–3), (with Bhupathi) **r/u** Los Angeles (lost Lareau/O'Brien 7–6 6–4), **r/u** Singapore (lost Bhupathi/Paes 6–4 6–4), **r/u** Stuttgart Eurocard (lost Woodbridge/Woodforde 6–4 6–4), **r/u** Paris Open (lost Eltingh/Haarhuis 6–2 7–6). **MIXED DOUBLES:** (with Bollegraf) **won Australian Open** (d. de Jager/Neiland 6–3 6–7 7–5), **won US Open** (d. Albano/Paz 3–6 7–5 7–6). **CAREER HIGHLIGHTS - DOUBLES:** (with Pugh unless stated) **Australian Open - won 1988** (d. Bates/Lundgren 6–3 6–2 6–3), **won 1989** (d. Cahill/Kratzmann 6–4 6–4 6–4), [Jones] **r/u 1992** (lost Woodbridge/Woodforde 6–4 6–3 6–4); **Wimbledon - won 1990** (d. Aldrich/Visser 7–6 7–6 7–6), **r/u 1989** (lost Fitzgerald/Jarryd 3–6 7–6 6–4 7–6); **US Open** – (with Flach) **won 1993** (d. Damm/Novacek 6–7 6–4 6–2), **r/u 1988** (lost Casal/E. Sanchez def.), (with Jones) **r/u 1992** (lost Grabb/Reneberg 3–6 7–6 6–3 6–3); **Masters/World Doubles Champ - won 1988** (d. Casal/E. Sanchez 6-4 6-3 2-6 6-0), (with Stark) **won 1997**; **French Open - r/u 1991** (lost Fitzgerald/Jarryd 6–0 7–6). **MIXED DOUBLES:** (with Bollegraf unless stated) **Australian Open –** (with Zvereva) **won 1995** (d. Suk/G. Fernandez 7–6 6–7 6–4), **won 1997; Wimbledon –** (with Garrison) **won 1990** (d. Smylie/Fitzgerald 7–5 6–2), **US Open – won 1997**.

LUIS LOBO (ARG)

Born Buenos Aires, 9 November 1970, and lives there; RH; 5ft 11in; 168lb; turned pro 1990; career singles titles 0; final 1997 ATP ranking 21 doubles; 1997 prize money $219,328.

1989: (1103). **1990:** (785) Began to play the satellite circuit. **1991:** (431). **1992:** (275) Continued to make his mark on the Challenger circuit. **1993:** (427). **1994:** (411) Moving on to the main tour, he won Athens doubles with J. Sanchez. **1995:** (775) Won 2 doubles titles from 6 f with J. Sanchez to qualify for World Doubles Champ. **1996:** (591) Appeared in 3 doubles f, winning Barcelona with J. Sanchez and Umag with Albano. **1997:** From 5 doubles f, he won 4 with J. Sanchez and 1 with Meligeni. **1997 HIGHLIGHTS – DOUBLES:** (with J. Sanchez unless stated) **won** Sydney (d. Haarhuis/Siemerink 6–4 6–7 6–3), **won** Scottsdale (d. Bjorkman/Leach 6–3 6–3), **won** Hamburg (d. Broad/Norval 6–3 7–6), **won** Bucharest (d. Davids/Orsanic 7–5 7–5), (with Meligeni) **won** Bogota (d. Alami/Ruah 6–1 6–3)

DAVID MACPHERSON (AUS)

Born Launceston, Tas., 3 July 1967; lives Sarasota, Fla.; LH; 5ft 9in; 140lb; turned pro 1985; career singles titles 0; final 1997 ATP ranking, 41 doubles; 1997 prize money $126,098 ($1,091,767).

Wife Charlene (married 24 March 1990); daughter Alexandra Grace (born 20 November 1993). Won Nat Jun doubles with Custer in 14s, 16s and 18s (3 times). **1983:** (480) A 1, F –, W –, US –. **1984:** (552) A –, F –, W –, US –. **1985:** (389) A 1, F –, W –, US –. R/u US Open Jun doubles with Flynn. **1986:** (505) A –, F –, W –, US –. **1987:** (436) A 2, F –, W –, US –. **1988:** (509) A –, F –, W –, US –. Won Raleigh Challenger doubles with Youl. **1989:** (352) A –, F –, W –, US –. Won 3 doubles titles on the Challenger circuit and took both singles and doubles on Australian satellite circuit. **1990:** (521) A 1, F –, W –, US –. Won Toronto doubles with Galbraith. **1991:** (811) A –, F –, W –, US –. Won Rotterdam and Lyon doubles with DeVries. **1992:** (–) A –, F –, W –, US –. Won doubles titles in Milan, Indian Wells, Atlanta, US CC, Manchester and Brisbane with 3 different partners, qualifying for World Doubles Final with DeVries. **1993:** (1186) A –, F –, W –, US –. In doubles won Nice with Warder and reached 2 more f with DeVries. **1994:** (–) Won 2 Challenger doubles titles with Kronemann. **1995:** (–) Developing his doubles partnership with Kronemann, he won Scottsdale, Barcelona, Munich and r/u Sydney. **1996:** (–) It had been a less successful year, in which he and Kronemann won San Jose from only 2 f. However, they played World Doubles Champ as alternates after Forget/Hlasek and Kafelnikov/Vacek withdrew and reached sf before falling to Lareau/O'Brien. **1997:** In doubles with Kronemann he played 2 f, but won no title. However, they played as alternates again at World Doubles Champ, losing their only match after Knowles/Nestor withdrew after 2 matches. **1997 HIGHLIGHTS – DOUBLES:** (with Kronemann) **r/u** Rosmalen (lost Eltingh/Haarhuis 6–4 7–5), **r/u** Gstaad (lost Kafelnikov/Vacek 4–6 7–6 6–3).

FELIX MANTILLA (ESP)

Born Barcelona, 23 September 1974, and lives there; RH; 5ft 10in; 162lb; turned pro 1993; career singles titles 6; final 1997 ATP ranking 16; 1997 prize money $1,105,593 ($1,686,314).

Coached by Jordi Vilaro. **1992:** (680) Member of the winning Spanish Sunshine Cup team. **1993:** (432). **1994:** (301) Enjoyed some success on the satellite circuits. **1995:** (84) A –, F –, W –, US –. Broke into the top 100 at end of year, following his 1st r/u showing on the main tour at Buenos Aires. He had played through the qualifying there, as he had before reaching sf Valencia and qf Casablanca. **1996:** (18) A –, F 3, W 1, US –. He shot up into the top 20 with his 1st title on the main tour at Oporto (unseeded, d. Moya), r/u St Polten, Gstaad, San Marino and Umag, sf Marbella and Santiago, plus qf Monte Carlo (d. Bruguera), Stuttgart and Amsterdam. He also won 3 Challenger titles and upset Enqvist at Prague. **1997:** A qf, F 2, W –, US 4. In an 8-

week period in summer, he won Bologna, Gstaad, Umag and San Marino, reaching qf Stuttgart Mercedes in the middle of that sequence. He followed with a 5th title at Bournemouth a month later to add to f Hamburg (d. Becker), sf Estoril and qf Australian Open and Lyon. Won all his matches in winning ESP WT Cup team. Felt he should have been called ahead of Henman as alternate for last rr match ATP Champs when Bruguera withdrew, and did not accept claims by the organisers that they had been unable to contact him. **1997 HIGHLIGHTS – SINGLES: Australian Open qf** [seed 14] (d. Rusedski 6–4 5–7 7–5 6–2, Meligeni 6–2 6–4 6–1, Boetsch 6–3 1–6 7–6 6–4, MaliVai Washington 7–5 6–2 6–1, lost Moya 7–5 6–2 6–7 6–2), **French Open 2r** [seed 10] (d. Fromberg 6–3 6–2 6–2, lost Larsson 6–2 6–4 3–6 6–3), **US Open last 16** [seed 12] (d. Stoltenberg 7–6 6–3 6–2, J. Sanchez 7–5 6–4 6–2, Van Lottum 6–7 6–2 4–6 7–6 6–2, lost Krajicek 7–5 6–3 6–4); **won** Bologna (d. Gorriz 4–6 6–3 6–4, Meligeni 6–7 7–5 6–2, Lapentti 4–6 6–4 6–3, Alami 6–3 6–2, Kuerten 4–6 6–2 6–1), **won** Gstaad (d. Arnold 7–5 6–1, Blanco 7–6 6–2, J. Sanchez 6–4 6–3, W. Ferreira 6–3 6–4, Viloca 6–1 6–4 6–4), **won** Umag (d. Cherkasov 6–3 7–6, Caballero 6–3 6–3, Hrbaty 3–6 6–3 6–4, Moya 7–6 5–7 6–3, Bruguera 6–3 7–5), **won** San Marino (d. Fromberg 6–4 4–6 7–6, Sanguinetti 6–4 4–6 6–3, Ruud 6–3 6–1, Hrbaty 6–4 6–4, Gustafsson 6–4 6–1), **won** Bournemouth (d. Roux 6–3 6–3, Wilkinson 6–3 6–2, Van Garsse 6–3 7–6, Ondruska 6–7 6–1 6–1, Moya 6–2 6–2); **r/u** Hamburg (d. Larsson 6–7 6–4 6–3, Carretero 6–1 6–1, Becker 7–6 6–2, Arazi 4–6 7–6 6–4, Haas 4–6 6–3 6–4, lost Medvedev 6–0 6–4 6–2); **sf** Estoril (d. Carretero 6–3 6–1, Arazi 6–3 6–3, Berasategui 6–4 6–1, lost Clavet 3–6 7–5 6–0)

NICOLAS MASSU (CHI)

Born Vina Del Mar, 10 October 1979, and lives there; RH; 2HB; 5ft 11in; 156lb; career singles titles 0; final 1997 ATP ranking 583; Junior ranking 5; 1997 prize money $9,700.

Coached by Leonardo Zuleta. **1997:** Won Wimbledon Jun doubles with Horna and US Open Jun doubles with Gonzalez.

ANDREI MEDVEDEV (UKR)

Born Kiev, 31 August 1974, and lives there; RH; 6ft 4in; 192lb; turned pro 1991; career singles titles 11; final 1997 ATP ranking 27; 1997 prize money $731,068 ($5,042,085).

Coached by Bob Brett, formerly Boris Breskvar. Brother of Natalia Medvedeva, who plays on the women's tour. Soviet Union Jun champ in 14s, 16s and 18s. **1990:** (1007) Won Orange Bowl over Fernandez and won Sunshine Cup and World Youth Cup for USSR. **1991:** (226) Won French Open Jun over Enqvist. **1992:** (24) A –, F 4, W –, US –. His run of success began at French Open, where he played through the qualifying and on to the last 16, upsetting Hlasek on the way. Unable to obtain a visa to play the Wimbledon qualifying, he accepted a wild card for Genova and won his 1st tour title there, breaking into the top 100. He followed with the title in Stuttgart, after qualifying and upsetting 5 seeds (including Edberg), and continued to sweep up the rankings. His 3rd title, at Bordeaux, took him into the top 25, where he finished the year and was voted ATP Newcomer of the Year. **1993:** (6) A 3, F sf, W 2, US qf. The title at Estoril took him into the top 20 in April and, following that immediately with Barcelona (d. Lendl, Muster and Bruguera) and then sf appearance at French Open (d. Edberg), he moved on to the top 10. Working on developing an all-court game, he won his 1st HC title at New Haven (d. Agassi), was r/u Halle and Paris Open and appeared in sf Stuttgart and Kitzbuhel, as well as his 1st IBM/ATP World Champ. **1994:** (15) A –, F qf, W 4, US 2. In Jan. he underwent arthroscopic surgery for tendinitis and bone chips in his knee, returning in March to reach f Estoril, and then won Monte Carlo in his 3rd tourn of year, despite suffering from a fever. Won Hamburg, playing his 3rd f in 5 tourns to date, but at Italian Open he suffered pain again, having done too much too soon. In GS he reached qf French Open and extended Becker to 7–5 5s in last 16 Wimbledon, but at US Open he fell 2r to Novacek. He was also r/u Prague and reached sf Lyon. In May he parted company with his coach, Dolgopolov, who needed to spend more time with his increasing family, and started working with Brad Stine. **1995:** (16) A qf, F 4, W 2, US 2. Split with Stine early in the year, worked with Marco Dulis from end Feb. and in May began working with his friend Boris Breskvar. He lost confidence after a poor run following a broken wrist suffered at Australian Open, but returned to form in May with the title at Hamburg, where he beat Sampras and Ivanisevic back-to-back, and an upset of Berasategui at French Open. He also reached sf Nice, qf Rotterdam, LIPC, Estoril, Indianapolis and Ostrava. **1996:** (35) A 2, F 2, W 1, US 4. Although it was a less impressive year, he won Long Island, r/u Bastad, and reached sf Antwerp (d. Kafelnikov), plus qf Milan and Italian Open (d. Kafelnikov again). **1997:** A 4, F 4, W 3, US 1. His best performance came at Hamburg, where he upset Krajicek, Bruguera and Kafelnikov on his way to the title, unseeded, and returned for a while to the top 20. His only other qf showings were at LIPC and Barcelona, although he upset Stich at Australian Open and Berasategui at French Open, unseeded both times. **1997 HIGHLIGHTS – SINGLES: Australian Open last 16** [unseeded] (d. Champion 7–5 6–2 6–2, Stich [seed 15] 4–6 6–1 6–2 4–6 9–7, Van Scheppingen 6–1 6–1 6–1, lost M. Chang [seed 2] 4–6 6–2 6–2 6–1), **French Open last 16** [unseeded] (d. Berasategui 6–4 4–6 2–6 6–2 6–1, Viloca 6–4 6–3 6–4, Escude 7–6 6–4 6–3, lost Kuerten 5–7 6–1 6–2 1–6 7–5), **Wimbledon 3r** [seed 13] (d. Santoro 6–2 6–3 6–4, Sargsian 6–1 6–4 7–5, lost Kiefer 6–4 6–2 6–7 6–4), **US Open 1r** (lost Rafter [seed 13] 6–3 6–4 7–5); **won** Hamburg (d. Krajicek 6–1 6–1, Diaz 6–3 6–3, Bruguera 6–4 7–6, Kafelnikov 6–3 6–1, Mantilla 6–0 6–4 6–2). **CAREER HIGHLIGHTS – SINGLES: French Open – sf 1993** (d. Perez-Roldan 6–7 4–6 6–4 6–3 6–4, Furlan 6–3 6–3 6–4, Markus 7–6 3–6 7–5 6–4, Goellner 6–4 6–4 4–6 6–3, Edberg 6–0 6–7 7–5 6–4, lost Bruguera 6–0 6–4 6–2), **qf 1994** (d. Masur 6–2 6–4 6–2, Kulti 6–4 7–6 4–6 7–5, Rusedski 2–6 6–3 6–4 3–6 6–2, Eltingh 6–4 3–6 6–4 6–1, lost Bruguera 6–3 6–2 7–5);

Australian Open – qf 1995 (d. Paes 6–1 7–5 7–6, Rehmann 7–5 6–4 6–1, Pescosolido 6–4 6–3 6–3, Wheaton 3–6 6–3 6–4 6–7 10–8, lost M. Chang [seed 5] 7–6 7–5 6–3); **US Open – qf 1993** (d. Meligeni 6–2 6–2 4–6 6–1, Reneberg 4–6 7–6 6–4 6–3, Braasch 6–1 6–4 7–6, Krajicek 6–4 3–6 6–1 7–6, lost Pioline 6–3 6–1 3–6 6–2).

FRANCISCO MELIGENI (BRA)

Born Buenos Aires, Argentina, 12 April 1971; lives Sao Paulo; LH; 5ft 11in; 142lb; turned pro 1990; career singles titles 2; final 1997 ATP ranking 68; 1997 prize money $306,665.

Coached by Marcelo Mayer. **1989:** (615) Won Orange Bowl over Lopez and was No. 3 in ITF Jun rankings. **1990:** (391). **1991:** (203). **1992:** (167) A –, F –, W –, US 1. Reached his 1st tour qf at Maceio. **1993:** (98) A –, F 4, W –, US 1. Won 3 Challenger titles, reached qf Sao Paulo on the main tour and appeared in last 16 French Open after qualifying. **1994:** (92) A 1, F 1, W 1, US 1. He reached sf Coral Springs, qf Kitzbuhel, Bogota and Santiago (d. Novacek) and played 3 Challenger f, winning Ribeiro Preto. **1995:** (66) A –, F 3, W –, US 1. His 1st tour f at Mexico City in Feb., was followed 5 months later by his 1st title at Bastad. He also appeared in sf Bogota, qf US CC and Montevideo and upset Rosset at French Open. **1996:** (93) A 1, F 1, W –, US –. Came from behind in 3 matches on his way to the US CC title, unseeded. At Olympics, again unseeded, he upset A. Costa on the way to sf, losing the bronze medal contest to Paes. He reached the same stage Mexico City, plus qf Atlanta and Santiago, where he won the doubles with Kuerten, and on the Challenger circuit won Cairo. **1997:** A –, F 2, W –, US 3. In singles he reached sf Mexico City again and qf Barcelona, Orlando, Atlanta (d. M. Chang), Bogota and Santiago. Played 4 doubles f, winning 3 with Kuerten and 1 with Lobo. **1997 HIGHLIGHTS – SINGLES: French Open 2r** (d. Frana 6–4 6–7 6–4 7–5, lost Dewulf 6–4 6–2 3–6 1–6 6–3), **US Open 3r** (d. Szymanski 6–2 6–2 6–1, Ruud 6–3 6–4 6–3, lost Larsson 6–2 6–4 6–3); **sf** Mexico City (d. Filippini 4–6 7–6 6–1, Delgado 6–3 7–5, Arnold 2–6 7–6 6–0, lost Viloca 6–3 6–1). **1997 HIGHLIGHTS – DOUBLES:** (with Kuerten unless stated) **won** Estoril (d. Gaudenzi/Messori 6–2 6–2), **won** Bologna (d. Randall/Waite 6–2 7–5), **won** Stuttgart Mercedes (d. Johnson/Montana 6–4 6–4), (with Lobo) **won** Bogota (d. Alami/Ruah 6–1 6–3). **CAREER HIGHLIGHTS – SINGLES: Olympics – sf 1996** [unseeded] (d. Pescosolido 6–4 6–2, A. Costa 7–6 6–4, Philippoussis 7–6 4–6 8–6, Olhovskiy 6–7 7–5 6–3, lost Bruguera 7–6 6–2, lost Paes 3–6 6–2 6–4).

FRANCISCO MONTANA (USA)

Born Miami, Fla, 5 November 1969, and lives there; RH; 6ft; 163lb; turned pro 1990; career singles titles 0; final 1997 ATP ranking 739 singles, 27 doubles; 1997 prize money $219,016.

Coached by his father, Francisco. Won 10 nat jun champs. **1987:** (745). **1988:** (–). **1989:** (643) All-American at Univ. of Georgia. **1990:** (239). **1991:** (137) A –, F –, W –, US 1. **1992:** (117) A –, F –, W 1, US 1. Reached his 1st qf on the main tour at San Marino and broke into top 100 1st time in May. Played 2 doubles f, winning Long Island with Van Emburgh. **1993:** (179) A 1, F –, W –, US –. Reached sf Mexico City singles and r/u doubles there with Shelton. **1994:** (280) A –, F –, W –, US –. Won Mexico City with Shelton and r/u Atlanta with Pugh. **1995:** (326) A –, F –, W –, US –. In doubles he won Kitzbuhel with Van Emburgh and r/u Santiago with Cannon. **1996:** (296) A –, F 1, W –, US –. Won Mexico City and Amsterdam doubles with Johnson. **1997:** A –, F –, W –, US –. Appeared in 3 doubles f with Johnson, winning Monte Carlo. They played at World Doubles Champs as alternates when Kafelnikov and Vacek withdrew, but lost all 3 matches. **1997 HIGHLIGHTS – DOUBLES:** (with Johnson) **won** Monte Carlo (d. Eltingh/Haarhuis 7–6 2–6 7–6; **r/u** Stuttgart Mercedes (lost Kuerten/Meligeni 6–4 6–4), **r/u** Ostrava (lost Novak/Rikl 6–2 6–4).

DANIEL NESTOR (CAN)

Born Belgrade, Yugoslavia, 4 September 1972; lives Willowdale, Ontario; LH; 6ft 2in; 170lb; turned pro 1991; career singles titles 0; final 1997 ATP ranking 112 singles, 18 doubles; 1997 prize money $470,190 ($1,450,942).

Coached by Glenn Michibata. Moved to Canada in 1976. **1989:** (823). **1990:** (741). **1991:** (247) Won Nat doubles with Pridham. **1992:** (239) A 1, F –, W –, US –. Upset Edberg in D Cup and began to make his mark on the satellite circuit. **1993:** (186) A –, F –, W –, US 1. Out of action April to July with tendinitis of left wrist. R/u Nat singles and won doubles with Lareau. **1994:** (169) A –, F –, W –, US –. Upset Volkov at Toronto and reached qf Bogota, where he won the doubles with Knowles. **1995:** (180) A 2, F –, W 2, US 2. In singles he won Aptos Challenger but reached no qf on the main tour. In partnership with Knowles, upset Woodbridge/Woodforde on the way to a 1st GS f at Australian Open and won Indianapolis from 2 more f to qualify for World Doubles Champ, although they won no match there. **1996:** (114) A 1, F –, W 1, US –. Reached sf Newport and upset Muster at Toronto. In doubles he played 6 f, winning Qatar, Memphis, Hamburg and Cincinnati with Knowles. They qualified for World Doubles Champ, but were forced to withdraw after 2 rr matches when Nestor suffered a rib injury. **1997:** A 1, F 1, W 1, US 1. In singles he reached sf Moscow, upset Enqvist at LIPC, and won San Antonio Challenger. From 4 doubles f with Knowles, he won Indian Wells and Rome to take the last berth at World Doubles Champ. There they lost their 1st 2 matches and were forced to withdraw when Knowles aggravated a rib injury. **1997 HIGHLIGHTS – SINGLES: Australian Open 1r** (lost Raoux 7–6 6–2 6–2), **French Open 1r** (lost Volkov 6–1 6–1 3–6 6–2), **Wimbledon 1r** (lost Henman [seed 14] 7–6 6–1 6–4), **US Open 1r** (lost Gimelstob 7–6 6–7 6–3 6–2); **won** San Antonio Challenger (d. Grant 6–4 6–2); **sf** Moscow (d. Gimelstob 4–6 6–2 6–4, J. Sanchez 6–4 6–4, Damm 6–3 6–4, lost Kafelnikov 6–4 6–3). **1997 HIGHLIGHTS – DOUBLES:** (with Knowles) **won** Indian Wells (d.

Philippoussis/Rafter 7–6 4–6 7–5), **won** Rome (d. B. Black/O'Brien 6–3 4–6 7–5); **r/u** San Jose (lost MacPhie/Muller 4–6 7–6 7–5), **r/u** LIPC (lost Woodbridge/Woodforde 7–6 7–6). **CAREER HIGHLIGHTS – DOUBLES:** (with Knowles) **Australian Open – r/u 1995** (lost Palmer/ Reneberg 6–3 3–6 6–3 6–2).

MAGNUS NORMAN (SWE)

Born Filipstad, 30 May 1976, and lives there; RH; 6ft 2in; 167lb; turned pro 1995; career singles titles 1; final 1997 ATP ranking 22; 1997 prize money $541,933.

Coached by Thomas Hogstedt. **1992:** (679). **1993:** (733). **1994:** (686). **1995:** (174) Qf Bastad and upset Berasategui at Palermo, as well as making his mark on the satellite circuits. **1996:** (86) A 1, F 2, W –, US –. Reached sf Bournemouth and Stockholm, qf Casablanca and won 2 Challenger titles. **1997:** A 1, F qf, W 3, US 2. Caused one of the upsets of the year at French Open when he removed Sampras 3r, following with Rosset to reach qf, unseeded. He upset Agassi and Korda *en route* to sf Atlanta, then at Wimbledon surprised Ivanisevic in an epic 2r battle, prevailing 14–12 5s. He followed with his 1st tour title at Bastad, having saved mp when 1–5 down 3s 2r v Voinea. He continued to challenge top players by upsetting Bruguera and Muster on his way to f Ostrava, where he was forced to retire with a thigh injury that also kept him out of Stuttgart. He reached sf St Polten and Amsterdam, plus qf St Petersburg, Chennai and Basel (d. Bjorkman), finishing the year in top 25. During his long fs v Ivanisevic at Wimbledon, he suffered irregular heartbeat for 3rd time in his career, although this time it lasted only 30 sec. (as opposed to 40 min. before), and he was able to continue after receiving treatment on court. The condition is not believed to be dangerous. **1997 HIGHLIGHTS – SINGLES: Australian Open 1r** (lost Woodruff 6–4 6–1 6–1), **French Open qf** [unseeded] (d. Rusedski 6–3 6–2 3–6 4–6 9–7, Paes 6–3 6–2 3–6 6–3, Sampras [seed 1] 6–2 6–4 2–6 6–4, Rosset [seed 15] 4–6 6–3 7–6 6–3, lost Dewulf 6–2 6–7 6–4 6–3), **Wimbledon 3r** (d. Herrera 7–6 6–1 6–4, Ivanisevic [seed 2] 6–3 2–6 7–6 4–6 14–12, lost Steven 6–7 6–2 6–3 6–1), **US Open 2r** (d. Kucera 6–7 6–4 6–2 6–3, lost Rafter [seed 13] 6–2 6–1 6–2); **won** Bastad (d. Kulti 6–4 7–5, Voinea 6–3 3–6 7–6, Tarango 6–3 6–3, C. Costa 7–5 6–3, Marin 7–5 6–2); **r/u** Ostrava (d. Vasek 7–5 6–2, Prinosil 6–2 6–4, Bruguera 6–4 6–7 7–5, Muster 6–7 6–2 7–5, lost Kucera 6–2 ret'd); **sf** Atlanta (d. Fredriksson 6–3 6–0, Agassi 7–6 3–6 6–3, Korda 6–4 6–4, lost Stoltenberg 6–4 5–7 6–3), **sf** St Polten (d. Schranz 6–3 7–5, Trimmel 6–2 7–5 Schalken 1–6 6–1 6–3, lost Rafter 6–1 4–6 6–3), **sf** Amsterdam (d. Hrbaty 5–7 6–1 6–0, Gustafsson 6–4 6–4, Ruud 6–3 7–6, lost Moya 6–4 6–3). **1997 HIGHLIGHTS – DOUBLES:** (with Fredriksson) **r/u** Qatar (lost Eltingh/Haarhuis 6–3 6–2). **CAREER HIGHLIGHTS – SINGLES: French Open – qf 1997.**

JIRI NOVAK (CZE)

Born Zlin, 22 March 1975; lives Prostejov; RH; 6ft 3in; 176lb; turned pro 1993; career singles titles 1; final 1997 ATP ranking 48; 1997 prize money $369,784 ($1,090,053).

Coached by Daniel Traunicek. **1993:** (280) R/u in singles and won doubles in European Jun Champs. **1994:** (218) Won Prague Challenger. **1995:** (55) A –, F –, W –, US 1. He reached his 1st sf on the main tour at Buenos Aires, upset Korda at Ostrava and won 2 doubles titles from 4 f with Rikl. On the Challenger circuit he took 3 singles titles from 7 f. **1996:** (52) A 1, F 2, W 2, US 2. Playing his 1st career singles f on the main tour, he won the title at Auckland and broke into top 50. He followed with r/u Mexico City, sf Basel (d. Becker), qf Memphis, Casablanca, Bucharest and Ostrava, and upset Rios at Gstaad. From 4 doubles f with 3 different partners, he won Casablanca with Rikl and Gstaad with Vizner. **1997:** A 2, F –, W 1, US 2. At Dubai, he upset Moya and Krajicek before extending Ivanisevic to 3s in sf, having earlier reached same stage Auckland. He also appeared in qf Indianapolis (d. Enqvist) and Ostrava (d. Moya and won doubles with Rikl), and finished the year with an upset of Bruguera at Moscow. **1997 HIGHLIGHTS – SINGLES: Australian Open 2r** (d. Jonsson 6–3 6–3 6–2, lost Woodruff 6–2 7–6 6–2), **Wimbledon 1r** (lost Fetterlein 4–6 3–6 6–4 7–6 6–4), **US Open 2r** (d. Sanguinetti 5–7 6–2 7–6 6–2, lost Draper 7–5 7–6 3–6 6–3); **won** Indian Wells Challenger (d. Dosedel 7–6 6–4); **sf** Auckland (d. Draper 3–6 7–6 7–6, Mamiit 6–4 6–2, Radulescu 6–1 6–4, lost Carlsen 7–6 6–4), **sf** Dubai (d. Moya 2–6 6–0 7–5, Davids 6–3 6–3, Krajicek 6–2 6–2, lost Ivanisevic 6–1 3–6 6–3). **1997 HIGHLIGHTS – DOUBLES:** (with Rikl) **won** Ostrava (d. Johnson/Montana 6–2 6–4).

ALEX O'BRIEN (USA)

Born Amarillo, Texas, 7 March 1970, and lives there; RH; 6ft 1in; 185lb; turned pro 1992; career singles titles 1; final 1997 ATP ranking 98 singles, 7 doubles; 1997 prize money $616,828 ($2,060,749).

Coached by Keith Diepraam. **1989:** (666). **1990:** (689). **1991:** (256) Won New Haven Challenger. **1992:** (127) A –, F –, W –, US 1. All-American at Stanford for 3rd year in singles and 4th in doubles, he led them to NCAA team title and won NCAA individual singles and doubles titles – the 1st player to take all 3 in a season. On the Challenger circuit, he won Monterrey singles and both singles and doubles at Aptos. **1993:** (121) A 1, F 2, W 1, US 1. Won Fairfield Challenger and on the senior tour appeared in qf Adelaide (d. Krajicek) and Coral Springs. **1994:** (90) A 1, F 2, W 1, US 2. Reached his 1st sf on the main tour at Memphis, plus qf Manchester and Cincinnati (as LL), and upset Forget at New Haven. From 3 doubles f, he won Cincinnati with Stolle. **1995:** (210) A 2, F –, W 1, US 1. Appeared in 3 doubles f with Stolle, including a 1st in GS at US Open, but won no title. **1996:** (38) A –, F –, W –, US 3. Upset Kafelnikov, Boetsch and Siemerink on the way to his 1st singles title, unseeded, at New Haven, a result which enabled him to rise more than 200 places to 76 in 4 weeks. He also appeared in sf Moscow (d. Corretja), qf Los Angeles (d. Enqvist) and Toronto and upset MaliVai Washington at US Open. In doubles with Lareau he played 3 f, including Australian Open, and won Stuttgart Eurocard, qualifying for World Doubles Champ as 8th pairing. There they were surprise finalists, losing 7–6 4s to Woodbridge/ Woodforde, whom they had beaten in rr. **1997:** A 1, F –, W 3, US 1. Extended Korda to 5s at Wimbledon and reached qf Adelaide, Sydney, Orlando, Nottingham, Beijing and Moscow in singles. Played 7 doubles f with various partners, winning Philadelphia and Los Angeles and r/u Australian Open with Lareau, with whom he qualified for World Doubles Champ. In their last rr match there, needing to d. Woodbridge/Woodforde in ss to qualify for sf on game percentage, they did so, but then lost 7–6 fs to Bhupathi/Paes. Suffering from a stress fracture of the left foot, he was forced to withdraw from D Cup f the following week. **1997 HIGHLIGHTS – SINGLES: Australian Open 1r** (lost Braasch 3–6 6–3 6–4 7–5), **Wimbledon 3r** (d. Holm 7–6 6–4 7–6, Godwin 6–3 6–3 6–7 7–6, lost Korda [seed 16] 6–3 4–6 6–3 6–7 6–4), **US Open 1r** (lost Filippini 6–2 6–4 6–4). **1997 HIGHLIGHTS – DOUBLES:** (with Lareau unless stated) **r/u Australian Open** (lost Woodbridge/Woodforde 4–6 7–5 7–5 6–3); **won** Philadelphia (d. E. Ferreira/Galbraith 6–3 6–3), **won** Los Angeles (d. Bhupathi/Leach 7–6 6–4); (with Salzenstein) **r/u** Orlando (lost Merklein/Spadea 6–4 4–6 6–4), (with B. Black) **r/u** Rome (lost Knowles/Nestor 6–3 4–6 7–5), **r/u** Montreal (lost Bhupathi/Paes 7–6 6–3), (with Courier) **r/u** Beijing (lost Bhupathi/Paes 7–5 7–6). **CAREER HIGHLIGHTS – DOUBLES: Australian Open** – (with Lareau unless stated) **r/u 1996** (lost Edberg/Korda 7–5 7–5 4–6 6–1), **r/u 1997**; **US Open** – (with Stolle) **r/u 1995** (lost Woodbridge/Woodforde 6–3 6–3).

LEANDER PAES (IND)

Born Calcutta, 17 June 1973; lives there and Orlando, Fla.; RH; 5ft 10in; 171lb; turned pro 1991; career singles titles 0; final 1997 ATP ranking 114 singles, 14 doubles; 1997 prize money $462,383.

Trains at LGE Sports Science Center in Orlando. **1990:** Won Wimbledon Jun and finished the year at No. 2 in ITF Jun rankings, as well as making his D Cup debut. **1991:** (275). **1992:** (273) Won Guangzhoa Challenger. **1993:** (178). **1994:** (133) Won Challenger titles at Bombay and Binghampton and reached his 1st qf on the main tour at Kuala Lumpur. Upset W. Ferreira in D Cup tie. **1995:** (132) A 1, F –, W –, US –. Reached qf Beijing on the main tour, won Brasilia Challenger, and made his mark in D Cup again, upsetting Ivanisevic as IND d. CRO 3–2. **1996:** (128) A –, F –, W 1, US 2. The highlight of his year was winning a bronze medal at the Olympics – India's 1st for 16 years – upsetting Enqvist and Furlan on the way. It was particularly satisfying, as his father had been in that bronze-winning hockey team in 1972 and his mother had captained India's Olympic basketball team the same year. He also reached sf Newport (d. B. Black) and qf Rosmalen and won Mauritius Challenger. **1997:** A 2, F 2, W 1, US 3. In singles he reached sf Shanghai and Newport and in doubles he developed a formidable partnership with Bhupathi. They won all 6 f they played through the year to qualify for a 1st World Doubles Champ, where they were beaten in f by Leach/Stark. **1997 HIGHLIGHTS – SINGLES: Australian Open 2r** (d. Grabb 6–4 6–3 6–4, lost Ruud 6–2 6–2 6–2), **French Open 2r** (d. Stafford 6–4 3–6 6–3 6–2, lost M. Norman 6–3 6–2 3–6 6–3), **Wimbledon 1r** (lost Woodforde 6–3 7–5 6–4), **US Open 3r** (d. C. Costa 6–1 7–5 6–4, Boetsch 6–4 6–0 2–1 ret'd, lost Pioline 3–6 7–6 1–6 6–3 6–4); **sf** Shanghai (d. Sargsian 7–6 6–4, Nydahl 6–3 6–3, Tarango 6–3 2–6 6–3, lost Kroslak 6–2 6–4), **sf** Newport (d. Wibier 7–5 6–7 6–4, Simian 6–2 6–3, Radulescu 6–3 7–6, lost Sargsian 7–6 2–6 6–3). **1997 HIGHLIGHTS – DOUBLES:** (with Bhupathi) **won** Chennai (d. Ogorodov/Ran 7–6 7–5), **won** Prague (d. Luxa/Skoch 6–1 6–1), **won** Montreal (d. Lareau/O'Brien 7–6 6–3), **won** New Haven (d. Goellner/Olhovskiy 4–6 6–7 6–2), **won** Beijing (d. Courier/O'Brien 7–5 7–6), **won** Singapore (d. Leach/Stark 6–4 6–4); **r/u** World Doubles Champ (lost Leach/Stark 6–3 6–4 7–6). **CAREER HIGHLIGHTS – SINGLES: Olympics – bronze medal 1996** [unseeded] (d. Reneberg [seed 11] 6–7 7–6 1–0 ret'd, Pereira 6–2 6–3, Enqvist [seed 3] 7–5 7–6, Furlan [seed 14] 6–1 7–5, lost Agassi [seed 1] 7–6 6–3, d. Meligeni 3–6 6–2 6–4). **CAREER HIGHLIGHTS – DOUBLES:** (with Bhupathi) **World Doubles Champ – r/u 1997.**

MARK PHILIPPOUSSIS (AUS)

Born Melbourne, 7 November 1976; lives there and Monte Carlo, Monaco; RH; 6ft 4in; 202lb; turned pro 1994; career singles titles 4; final 1997 ATP ranking 18; 1997 prize money $904,211 ($1,844,837).

Coached by his father, Nick, and works for fitness with Todd Viney. Speaks fluent Greek but has been to Greece only once – as a baby. **1993:** (1072) Won Victorian satellite. **1994:** (304) A 1, F –, W –, US –. R/u Wimbledon Jun singles to Humphries and in Jun doubles won Australian Open and Wimbledon with Ellwood. **1995:** (32) A 1, F –, W –, US 3. After qualifying and having never before reached qf, he upset Martin on his way to f Scottsdale in only his 5th main tour event. Upset Haarhuis on his way to f Kuala Lumpur, following the next week with f Tokyo Seiko (d. Edberg), and also reached sf Bologna. Missed Wimbledon because he did not get the wild card he had requested and his father would not let him try to qualify. Won 2 doubles titles with different partners and was voted Player to Watch. **1996:** (30) A 4, F 2, W 2, US 4. Played near-perfect tennis to beat Sampras in ss at Australian Open and upset Pioline at US Open, unseeded both times. He won his 1st ATP tour title at Toulouse in the week his manager, Brad Robinson, died of lymphoma; reached sf Memphis (d. Haarhuis) and New Haven (d. Courier and Rosset); qf Olympics (d. Haarhuis again) Munich and Toronto (d. Rosset). **1997:** A –, F 4, W 1, US 3. Missed Australian Open with tendinitis in right arm, returning to win Scottsdale, unseeded. At Munich he played and won his 1st CC f, and followed with his 1st GC title at Queen's, where he also won the doubles with Rafter. It was an anticlimax when he drew, and lost to, Rusedski 1r Wimbledon. He reached f Toulouse and Basel (d. Kafelnikov), sf Lyon and qf Indian Wells (d. Agassi and Moya), Los Angeles and Montreal. **1997 HIGHLIGHTS – SINGLES: French Open last 16** [unseeded] (d. Kulti 6–2 4–6 3–6 6–4 6–4, Delaitre 6–4 3–6 6–1 6–4, Siemerink 6–4 6–4 6–2, lost Kafelnikov [seed 3] 6–2 6–3 7–5), **Wimbledon 1r** [seed 7] (lost Rusedski 7–6 7–6 6–3), **US Open 3r** [seed 14] (d. Alami 6–3 6–4 3–6 6–4, Golmard 7–6 6–2 1–0 ret'd, lost Vacek 7–6 7–5 6–2); **won** Scottsdale (d. Haas 2–6 6–3 6–4, Shelton 6–4 6–1, B. Black 7–6 6–3, Woodruff 4–6 7–6 6–2, Reneberg 6–4 7–6), **won** Munich (d. Radulescu 7–6 7–6, Gumy 6–7 6–4 6–4, Gaudenzi 7–5 4–6 6–4, Dosedel 7–5 7–5, Corretja 7–6 1–6 6–4), **won** Queen's (d. Stark 7–6 3–6 6–3, B. Black 6–3 6–3, Knippschild 6–2 6–7 6–4, Bjorkman 2–6 7–6 6–2, Ivanisevic 7–5 6–3); **r/u** Toulouse (d. Thomann 6–4 7–6, Roux 6–3 6–7 6–3, Clement 7–5 3–6 7–6, Spadea 7–5 6–4, lost Kiefer 7–5 5–7 6–4), **r/u** Basel (d. A. Costa 7–6 6–3, Santoro 6–3 6–3, Kafelnikov 6–3 6–7 6–2, Henman 7–6 6–4, lost Rusedski 6–3 7–6 7–6); **sf** Lyon (d. Thomann 7–6 4–6 6–3, Reneberg 4–6 7–6 6–4, Pioline 6–3 3–6 7–6, lost Santoro 6–4 6–2). **1997 HIGHLIGHTS – DOUBLES:** (with Rafter) **won** Queen's (d. Stolle/Suk 6–2 4–6 7–5); **r/u** Indian Wells (lost Knowles/Nestor 7–6 4–6 7–5), **r/u** Cincinnati (lost Woodbridge/Woodforde 7–6 4–6 6–4).

CEDRIC PIOLINE (FRA)

Born Neuilly-sur-Seine, 15 June 1969; lives Paris; RH; 6ft 2in; 175lb; turned pro 1989; career singles titles 2; final 1997 ATP ranking 20; 1997 prize money $999,701 ($3,974,668).

Coached by Pierre Cherret; physical trainer Luc Pausicles. Wife Mireille Bercot; son Andrea (born 14 March 1993). His mother was a member of Romania's World Championship volleyball squad, and he might have concentrated on that sport, but took up tennis instead after undergoing surgery to shorten one leg to match the other. **1987:** (954) R/u Nat Jun Champ. **1988:** (461). **1989:** (202) A –, F 1, W –, US –. Enjoyed some success on the Challenger circuit. **1990:** (118) A 1, F 1, W –, US –. Won his 1st pro title at Brest Challenger. **1991:** (51) A 1, F 2, W 2, US 1. Broke into top 100 after reaching sf Nice (d. Volkov and Leconte back-to-back). **1992:** (33) A 2, F 4, W 2, US 3. He reached his 1st tour f at Lyon (d. Forget) and upset B. Gilbert on his way to last 16 French Open, unseeded. **1993:** (10) A 2, F 2, W qf, US r/u. The highlight of his career came at US Open, where he swept aside Courier and Medvedev to become the 1st Frenchman since Cochet in 1932 to reach f there, eventually losing to Sampras. R/u Monte Carlo (d. Edberg), Toulouse, Bolzano and Lyon; sf Munich and Antwerp (d. Ivanisevic); upset Medvedev *en route* to qf Wimbledon, unseeded. He broke into top 10 in Oct., becoming only 2nd player after Pernfors to reach top 10 without a title. **1994:** (51) A 1, F 2, W 1, US 3. That 1st title still evaded him as he slipped out of the top 50. He was a finalist at Long Island, but otherwise reached qf only in Milan and Bordeaux. **1995:** (56) A 1, F 2, W qf, US 2. His best showing was sf Toulouse, plus qf Auckland, Nice, Long Island, Lyon and Wimbledon, where, unseeded, he upset Courier and recovered from 2s down to extend Becker to 9–7 5s. **1996:** (21) A –, F qf, W 4, US 3. After reaching f Zagreb and Marseille, he had played 9 f without winning that elusive 1st title: it came at last at Copenhagen in March, in his 10th f. He also appeared in sf Monte Carlo (d. Kafelnikov) and qf Rotterdam (d. Krajicek), Toulouse and French Open (d. Rios), where he was unseeded. Member of winning FRA D Cup team v SWE, he d. an injured Edberg in 1st rubber and served for the tie at 5–3 in 5s 4th, but lost to Enqvist 9–7. **1997:** A –, F 3, W r/u, US 4. The highlight of his year came at Wimbledon, where, ranked 44 and unseeded, he became the 1st French finalist there since Petra in 1946. He had missed Australian Open with a back injury and in other GS lost only in 5s to both Kafelnikov at French Open and M. Chang at US Open. He won his 2nd career title at Prague, but otherwise did not pass qf, although he reached that stage at Indian Wells, Barcelona (d. Muster), GS Cup, Ostrava and Stockholm, and upset M. Chang at Stuttgart Eurocard. **1997 HIGHLIGHTS – SINGLES: French Open 3r** (d. Gross 6–4 6–4 3–6 7–5, Etlis 2–6 6–3 6–3 7–6, lost Kafelnikov [seed 3] 7–5 6–4 6–7 1–6 6–4), **r/u Wimbledon** [unseeded] (d. Charpentier 5–7 6–3 7–5 6–2, Frana w.o., W. Ferreira [seed 15] 6–4 6–3 6–3, Steven 3–6 6–3 6–4 7–5, Rusedski 6–4 4–6 6–4 6–3, Stich 6–7 6–2 6–1 5–7 6–4, lost Sampras [seed 1] 6–4

A spectacular run to the Wimbledon final, unseeded, made Cedric Pioline the first Frenchman to reach that stage since the 1946 champion Yvon Petra. (Michael Cole)

6–2 6–4), **US Open last 16** [unseeded] (d. Wessels 6–4 6–2 6–2, Lapentti 6–0 6–4 6–2, Paes 3–6 7–6 1–6 6–3 6–4, lost M. Chang [seed 2] 6–3 0–6 5–7 7–5 6–1); **won** Prague (d. Kucera 7–5 4–6 6–4, Kroslak 6–3 6–1, Fromberg 6–4 4–6 6–2, Alvarez 6–3 6–7 6–1, Ulihrach 6–2 5–7 7–6). **CAREER HIGHLIGHTS – SINGLES: Wimbledon – r/u 1997, qf 1993** (d. Damm 6–4 7–5 3–6 7–5, Medvedev 6–7 7–6 6–3 6–4, Carlsen 6–4 6–4 6–3, Masur 6–3 6–2 3–6 6–7 8–6, lost Edberg 7–5 7–5 6–3), **qf 1995** (d. Lopez-Moron 6–1 6–2 6–4, Courier [seed 11] 6–4 6–4 6–4, Baur 6–4 6–4 6–3, Korda 7–6 6–3 6–2, lost Becker [seed 3] 6–3 6–1 6–7 6–7 9–7); **US Open – r/u 1993** (d. Prinosil 6–7 7–5 6–4 3–6 6–1, Palmer 6–4 3–6 5–7 7–5 6–1, Wilander 6–4 6–4 6–4, Courier 7–5 6–7 6–4 6–4, Medvedev 6–3 6–1 3–6 6–2, Masur 6–1 6–7 7–6 6–1, lost Sampras 6–4 6–4 6–3); **French Open – qf 1996** [unseeded] (d. Frana 6–1 6–3 6–2, Reneberg 7–5 6–2 6–3, Berasategui 4–6 6–1 6–4 6–0, Rios [seed 9] 6–4 6–1 6–2, lost Stich [seed 15] 6–4 4–6 6–3 6–2).

ALBERT PORTAS (ESP)

Born Barcelona, 15 November 1973, and lives there; RH; 6ft 2in; 172lb; turned pro 1993; career singles titles 0; final 1997 ATP ranking 35; 1997 prize money $293,996.

Coached by Jordi Plana. **1991:** (732). **1992:** (502). **1993:** (388). **1994:** (263) Began to make an impression on the satellite circuits. **1995:** (120) He enjoyed his greatest success in Prague, where he reached sf main tour event and won Challenger. **1996:** (180) R/u Santiago doubles with Pescariu. **1997:** A –, F 3, W –, US 1. He burst into prominence in the spring when he upset Rios and Berasategui on the way to his 1st career f at Barcelona, after qualifying, reached qf Prague (again as a qualifier), and (still a qualifier) upset Moya 2r French Open. He followed that with sf Stuttgart Mercedes (d. Muster and Mantilla) and also reached qf Umag, Bucharest and Palermo, as well as winning Prague Challenger again. **1997 HIGHLIGHTS – SINGLES: French Open 3r** (d. Solves 7–5 6–1 6–3, Moya [seed 9] 6–4 4–6 7–5 6–3, lost Dewulf 6–3 7–5 4–6 6–7 8–6), **US Open 1r** (lost J. Sanchez 7–5 6–2 7–5); **won** Prague Challenger (d. Vicente 6–1 6–4); **r/u** Barcelona (d. Kuerten 6–2 6–1, Rios 7–5 7–6, Vicente 7–5 3–6 6–1, Alami 6–2 7–5, Berasategui 6–3 7–5, lost A. Costa 7–5 6–4 6–4); **sf** Stuttgart Mercedes (d. Ruud 5–7 6–0 7–6, Muster 6–4 7–5, Gumy 3–6 6–2 7–6, Mantilla 6–2 6–4, lost Kucera 6–4 6–3).

ALEX RADULESCU (GER)

Born Bucharest, Romania, 7 December 1974; lives Bad Homburg; RH; 6ft 2in; 165lb; turned pro 1992; career singles titles 0; final 1997 ATP ranking 72; 1997 prize money $292,898.

Coached by Ulf Fischer. Moved to Germany from Romania in 1987 and has German nationality through his German grandmother. Took up the game because his father wanted a playing partner. Suffered a host of injuries as a junior – especially to his foot and left knee – but physiotherapy enabled him to play injury-free in 1996. **1991:** (863). **1992:** (468) Won Swiss satellite and r/u French Open Jun with Kafelnikov. **1993:** (202) Reached his 1st Challenger f at Gothenburg. **1994:** (249) Continued to play the satellite circuits, enjoying some success in doubles. **1995:** (249) Won Andorra and Velenje Challengers. **1996:** (71) A –, F –, W qf, US 1. Emerging from the satellite circuits, he sprang to prominence at Wimbledon, where, unseeded and playing in his 1st GS tourn, he upset Boetsch and proved his fitness by playing 4 5s matches. He also reached his 1st sf on the main tour at New Delhi (d. W. Ferreira), upset A. Costa at Stockholm and won Annenheim Challenger. **1997:** A 1, F 1, W 3, US 3. Progressed to his 1st f at Chennai, and reached sf Toulouse, plus qf Auckland, Zagreb, Memphis (d. Stoltenberg), Rotterdam and Newport. **1997 HIGHLIGHTS – SINGLES: Australian Open 1r** (lost Draper 6–2 6–4 6–7 6–3), **French Open 1r** (lost Stoltenberg 6–0 6–4 4–6 6–4), **Wimbledon 3r** (d. Voinea 7–6 3–6 6–1 3–6 6–4, Martelli 6–3 7–5 6–4, lost Woodbridge 6–4 6–4 6–4), **US Open 3r** (d. Ogorodov 3–6 6–4 7–6 6–1, Fromberg 3–6 6–4 6–3 3–6 6–4, lost Sampras [seed 1] 6–3 6–4 6–4); **r/u** Chennai (d. Motomura 5–7 6–4 6–4, Wibier 6–4 7–5, MaliVai Washington 6–3 6–4, Solves 6–3 6–2, lost Tillstrom 6–4 4–6 7–5); **sf** Toulouse (d. Escude 6–4 7–6, Santoro 6–2 6–3, Haas 6–1 6–4, lost Kiefer 6–3 2–6 7–6). **CAREER HIGHLIGHTS – SINGLES: Wimbledon – qf 1996** [unseeded] (d. Boetsch 6–3 6–4 6–7 5–7 9–7, Pescosolido 4–6 6–7 7–6 6–1 10–8, Wheaton 6–7 6–4 6–4 4–6 6–3, Godwin 6–3 6–0 6–4, lost MaliVai Washington 6–7 7–6 5–7 7–6 6–4).

GUILLAUME RAOUX (FRA)

Born Bagnol-sur-Cèze, 14 February 1970; lives Paris; RH; 5ft 11in; 170lb; turned pro 1989; career singles titles 1; final 1997 ATP ranking 47; 1997 prize money $359,522 ($1,874,102).

Coached by Thierry Tulasne. Wife Caroline (married 1 August 1992); son Romain (born 15 July 1993). **1986:** (870). **1987:** (938). **1988:** (448) A –, F 1, W –, US –. R/u Wimbledon Jun to Pereira and was ranked 2 on ITF Jun list. Won Nat 18s. **1989:** (220) A 1, F 1, W –, US –. Won Guadeloupe Challenger. **1990:** (84) A –, F 1, W 2, US –. Upset Sampras *en route* to qf Paris Open and won Martinique and Dijon Challengers. **1991:** (104) A 1, F 1, W 1, US 2. Reached his 1st f on the main tour at Birmingham. **1992:** (93) A 1, F 1, W 1, US 1. Won his 1st primary circuit title at Brisbane in autumn after winning Segovia Challenger earlier in year; qf Seoul, Queen's and Washington (d. Krickstein). **1993:** (82) A 3, F 1, W 1, US 1. He reached qf Copenhagen, Osaka and Manchester, upset Muster *en route* to last 16 LIPC, and won Jakarta doubles with Nargiso. **1994:** (118) A 3, F 1, W 1, US 1. His best performances were qf Adelaide, Osaka and Bordeaux. **1995:** (83) A 1, F 2, W 1, US 1. Reached f in 2 consec. tourns at St Petersburg and Johannesburg (here he d. Berasategui and won the doubles with R. Gilbert), appeared in qf Jakarta and Bordeaux and won Nantes Challenger. **1996:** (73) A 3, F 1, W 2, US 2. Upset Rosset on his way to sf Rotterdam, as well as reaching qf Qatar, Jakarta and Zagreb (d.

Boetsch). From 2 doubles f, he won Marseille with Fleurian. **1997:** A 2, F 2, W 3, US 2. He returned to the top 50 with r/u Rosmalen (d. Bjorkman), sf Los Angeles (d. Rafter and Philippoussis), qf Copenhagen, Toulouse and Paris Open (d. Bruguera) and an upset of Moya 1r US Open. **1997 HIGHLIGHTS – SINGLES: Australian Open 2r** (d. Nestor 7–6 6–2 6–2, lost Henman 6–3 6–3 6–4), **French Open 2r** (d. Spadea 6–2 6–0 6–1, lost Kafelnikov [seed 3] 7–5 6–3 6–4), **Wimbledon 3r** (d. Boetsch 6–3 6–4 6–1, D. Flach 6–3 6–7 6–3 6–1, lost Reneberg 7–5 6–7 7–6 6–3), **US Open 2r** (d. Moya [seed 8] 6–4 7–6 6–2, lost Tarango 6–4 6–7 6–7 6–2 6–4); **r/u** Rosmalen (d. Voltchkov 7–5 6–3, Alami 6–4 2–6 7–6, Schalken 7–6 6–4, Bjorkman 6–0 6–1, lost Krajicek 6–4 7–6); **sf** Los Angeles (d. Etlis 6–3 6–4, Rafter 6–4 7–6, Philippoussis 7–6 6–4, lost Enqvist 6–4 6–1).

RICHEY RENEBERG (USA)

Born Phoenix, Ariz., 5 October 1965; lives Minneapolis, Minn.; RH; 2HB; 5ft 11in; 170lb; turned pro 1987; career singles titles 3; final 1997 ATP ranking 74; 1997 prize money $305,643 ($3,816,568).

Coached by Keith Diepraam. Wife Marget Davis (married 16 November 1991); son Christopher Davis (born 31 December 1996). **1985:** (794) All-American at Southern Methodist Univ. for 1st of 3 straight years. **1986:** (337) R/u NCAA singles to Goldie. **1987:** (79) A –, F –, W 3, US 2. **1988:** (128) A 1, F 2, W 2, US 2. The No. 1 Collegiate player in US, he was voted ATP Newcomer of the Year after reaching his 1st GP qf at US CC and following with the same stage Vienna. **1989:** (80) A 2, F 1, W 2, US 2. Appeared in his 1st sf at Auckland and upset Noah *en route* to the same stage at Washington. **1990:** (23) A 1, F 1, W 1, US 1. Shot up the rankings into the top 25 with r/u showing at Wellington (d. Chesnokov), plus sf Rosmalen, Indianapolis (d. Sampras) and Tokyo Seiko, and an upset of J. McEnroe at Philadelphia. **1991:** (27) A –, F 1, W 2, US 1. Sidelined at start of year with rotator cuff tendinitis in his right shoulder, he missed the indoor season, but returned to make a surprise appearance in sf LIPC. He went on to win his 1st career singles title at Tampa, breaking into the top 20 in May, and following with sf Birmingham and a surprise defeat of Cherkasov 1r Wimbledon. In doubles won 2 titles with Grabb and reached 2 more f with different partners. **1992:** (95) A 3, W 1, F 1, US 1. In singles reached sf Lyon, qf Rosmalen and Los Angeles. Continued his successful doubles partnership with Grabb, winning US Open and r/u Wimbledon to J. McEnroe and Stich, playing a marathon 36-game 5s. They also won San Francisco, Rosmalen and Indianapolis, played 2 more f and qualified for World Doubles Champ. **1993:** (29) A 1, F 1, W 1, US 2. Won Kuala Lumpur Malaysian Open and reached sf Washington and Montreal, plus 6 more qf, and returned to the top 30. He won 3 doubles titles with 3 different partners and played in winning US WT Cup squad. **1994:** (34) A 2, F 3, W 2, US 4. R/u Hawaii and reached sf San Jose and Long Island, plus 3 more qf, including Indianapolis, where he upset Pioline. Unseeded at US Open, he surprised Becker 1r and held a one-set lead v Martin in last 16 before retiring with a groin injury. Won 2 doubles titles from 4 f with 3 partners. **1995:** (59) A 1, F 3, W 1, US 1. In singles he upset Martin and Larsson *en route* to sf Stockholm and reached qf Philadelphia (d. Eltingh), Rosmalen, Halle (d. Courier) and Indianapolis (d. W. Ferreira). Won his 1st Australian Open doubles with Palmer, with whom he also took Memphis. **1996:** (32) A 2, F 2, W 1, US 1. He won his 1st GC title at Rosmalen, r/u Tokyo Japan Open (d. M. Chang) and reached sf Atlanta and Halle (d. W. Ferreira and Courier), plus qf San Jose, Scottsdale, US CC, Washington and Moscow. Upset W. Ferreira again at Stuttgart Eurocard and surprised Enqvist 1r French Open. He played 4 doubles f with 3 different partners, winning Indianapolis and Lyon with Grabb. **1997:** A 2, F 1, W 4, US 1. R/u Scottsdale, but passed no other qf, although he reached that stage at San Jose, Memphis, Halle (d. Krajicek) and Long Island. In GS he upset Moya at Wimbledon, where he was unseeded, and in doubles won Stockholm with Goellner. **1997 HIGHLIGHTS – SINGLES: Australian Open 2r** (d. Burrieza 2–2 ret'd), **French Open 1r** (lost Bjorkman 6–2 6–1 1–6 6–2), **Wimbledon last 16** [unseeded] (d. Arazi 7–6 6–4 7–6, Moya [seed 10] 6–4 6–3 6–3, Raoux 7–5 6–7 7–6 6–3, lost Rusedski 7–6 6–4 7–6), **US Open 1r** (lost Van Lottum 6–1 6–4 2–6 6–4); **r/u** Scottsdale (d. Spadea 7–6 0–6 6–1, Gumy 2–6 6–1 6–2, Golmard 6–4 6–2, Bjorkman 6–3 6–3, lost Philippoussis 6–4 7–6). **1997 HIGHLIGHTS – DOUBLES:** (with Goellner) **won** Stockholm (d. E. Ferreira/Galbraith 6–3 3–6 7–6). **CAREER HIGHLIGHTS – DOUBLES:** (with Grabb unless stated) **Australian Open** – (with Palmer) **won 1995** (d. Knowles/Nestor 6–3 3–6 6–3 6–2); **US Open – won 1992** (d. Jones/Leach 3–6 7–6 6–3 6–3); **Wimbledon – r/u 1992** (lost J. McEnroe/Stich 5–7 7–6 3–6 7–6 19–17).

MARC ROSSET (SUI)

Born Geneva, 7 November 1970; lives Monte Carlo, Monaco; RH; 2HB; 6ft 7in; 194lb; turned pro 1988; career singles titles 11; final 1997 ATP ranking 31; 1997 prize money $584,879 ($4,681,550).

Coached by Stephane Oberer. **1988:** (474) Won Orange Bowl and was No. 4 on ITF Jun Rankings. **1989:** (45) On Challenger circuit he reached qf or better in 10 tourns, winning 2, and broke into the top 100 in Sept. after winning Geneva on the main tour. **1990:** (22) A 1, F 2, W 3, US 1. Broke into the top 25 in autumn, following some big upsets during the year. Won his 1st tour title at Lyon (d. Wilander); r/u Madrid (d. E. Sanchez) and Bologna; sf Nice (d. Noah), Gstaad (d. E. Sanchez) and Geneva. **1991:** (60) A 1, F 1, W 1, US 1. Sf New Haven (d. Lendl and Chang back-to-back); qf Brussels, LIPC and Hilversum. **1992:** (35) A 4, F 1, W 3, US 1. The highlight of his career came in August when he won an Olympic gold medal, unseeded, upsetting Courier (in ss), E. Sanchez and Ivanisevic. He also won Moscow in Nov., reached last 16 Australian Open, unseeded (d. Gustafsson), sf Basle and qf Adelaide, Scottsdale (d. Agassi) and Madrid (d. E. Sanchez). In partnership with

Hlasek won his 1st GS title at French Open, plus Italian Open and Lyon, and took Adelaide with Ivanisevic. Played in D Cup squad as SUI reached f, upsetting FRA in qf. **1993:** (16) A –, F 2, W 1, US 1. Began the year slowly, suffering from tonsillitis, and struggled to find his best form until Feb. when he won Marseille, following with Long Island (d. Ivanisevic and M. Chang) and then Moscow at end of year. He reached sf Bordeaux, Basle and Stockholm (d. Courier), and upset Agassi at Indian Wells, Becker at Monte Carlo and Muster at Italian Open. **1994:** (14) A 3, F 1, W 2, US 3. Still a dangerous opponent, he scored some big upsets during the year as he won Marseille (d. Stich) and Lyon (d. Courier), r/u New Haven (d. Lendl and Medvedev) and Paris Open (d. Becker and Chang) and reached sf Nice, Bordeaux and Moscow (d. Kafelnikov). **1995:** (15) A 1, F 2, W 1, US 4. Out 2 months early in year after fracturing a bone in his right foot in D Cup tie v NED in Feb. He returned to win Nice in his 1st tourn back, following with Halle (saving 7 mps v Stich), and sf Gstaad, Long Island, Toulouse and Moscow and 3 more qf. Broke into top 10 1st time in July but could not maintain his position. **1996:** (22) A –, F sf, W 3, US 1. At French Open, where he recovered from 2s down v Karbacher to win their qf, he became 1st Swiss to reach sf any GS. In WT Cup, he was undefeated in winning Swiss squad, having never before won any of his 9 matches in the competition. In other tourns he upset Kafelnikov *en route* to f Milan and reached qf Antwerp, Rotterdam, New Haven, Vienna (d. W. Ferreira) and Paris Open (d. Sampras in ss). At Hopman Cup in Jan. he injured his hand in a gesture of frustration after he and Hingis wasted 4 champ points in mixed doubles and was forced to def. after playing 2 more points. **1997:** A 2, F 4, W 2, US 1. He recorded some notable upsets on his way to winning Antwerp (d. Korda), r/u Tashkent (d. Kafelnikov), sf Munich (d. Moya) and qf Marseille and Gstaad (d. Kafelnikov). In doubles he won Basel with Henman. **1997 HIGHLIGHTS – SINGLES: Australian Open 2r** (d. J. Sanchez 6–4 7–6 6–1, lost Tarango 6–4 6–1 6–1), **French Open last 16** [seed 15] (d. Hrbaty 7–5 3–6 7–6 6–4, Stoltenberg 6–2 6–3 6–4, Roux 6–3 5–7 6–2 6–3, lost M. Norman 4–6 6–3 7–6 6–3), **Wimbledon 2r** (d. Kucera 7–5 6–2 6–3, lost Korda [seed 16] 6–3 6–0 7–6), **US Open 1r** (lost Corretja [seed 6] 4–6 6–3 6–2 6–2); **won** Antwerp (d. Medvedev 7–6 6–2, Kiefer 3–6 6–3 6–1, Dewulf 4–6 6–1 6–4, Korda 7–6 6–3, Henman 6–2 7–5 6–4); **r/u** Tashkent (d. Cherkasov 6–4 6–2, Santopadre 6–3 6–7 6–2, Arazi 6–2 6–4, Kafelnikov 3–6 7–6 6–2, lost Henman 7–6 6–4); **sf** Munich (d. Prinosil 2–6 6–3 6–2, Alami 6–4 2–6 6–4, Moya 7–5 7–6, lost Corretja 6–3 6–1). **1997 HIGHLIGHTS – DOUBLES:** (with Henman) **won** Basel (d. Braasch/Grabb 7–6 6–7 7–6). **CAREER HIGHLIGHTS – SINGLES: Olympics – gold medal 1992** [unseeded] (d. Alami 6–2 4–6 2–1 ret'd, W. Ferreira 6–4 6–0 6–2, Courier 6–4 6–2 6–1, E. Sanchez 6–4 7–6 3–6 7–6, Ivanisevic 6–3 7–5 6–2, Arrese 7–6 6–3 3–6 4–6 8–6); **French Open – sf 1996** (d. Steeb 6–4 6–4 6–0, Novak 6–2 6–4 6–3, Hlasek 6–4 6–4 6–1, Edberg 7–6 6–3 6–3, Karbacher 4–6 4–6 6–3 7–5 6–0, lost Stich 6–3 6–4 6–2). **CAREER HIGHLIGHTS – DOUBLES:** (with Hlasek) **French Open – won 1992** (d. D. Adams/ Olhovskiy 7–6 6–7 7–5).

LIONEL ROUX (FRA)

Born Lyon, 12 April 1973; lives Diemoz; RH; 6ft 1in; 175lb; turned pro 1991; career singles titles 0: final 1997 ATP ranking 61; 1997 prize money $305,459.

1991: (527) Nat Jun champ. **1992:** (190) A –, F 2, W –, US –. Won Singapore Challenger. **1993:** (212) A –, F 1, W –, US –. Continued to concentrate on the satellite circuits. **1994:** (64) A –, F 2, W –, US –. Never before having passed 2r on the main tour, he upset Lendl on the way to his 1st tour f at Osaka after qualifying. At Paris Open in Nov. he upset Stich, a setback that saw the German lose his last chance of a place at the Masters. He also reached qf Basel (d. Kafelnikov) and Lyon and upset Korda at Ostrava. **1995:** (96) A 1, F 1, W 1, US 1. His best results came in his own country, with sf showings at Marseille and Bordeaux, plus qf Johannesburg. **1996:** (101) A 1, F 2, W –, US –. He did not advance beyond qf, but reached that stage at Indianapolis (d. Stoltenberg and Edberg) and Lyon. **1997:** A 2, F 3, W 1, US 3. Against Stark 1r Australian Open, he recovered from 2s down by winning 3s tb and eventually taking 5s 13–11. Upset Becker and Johansson *en route* to f Tokyo Japan Open and appeared in qf Basel (d. Moya). **1997 HIGHLIGHTS – SINGLES: Australian Open 2r** (d. Stark 1–6 4–6 7–6 6–2 13–11, lost Boetsch 6–4 6–4 6–1), **French Open 3r** (d. Merinov 6–0 6–2 7–6, Lareau 7–5 6–2 6–4, lost Rosset [seed 15] 6–3 5–7 6–2 6–3), **Wimbledon 1r** (lost Steven 6–2 6–2 7–6), **US Open 3r** (d. Schaller 4–6 0–6 6–3 6–2 6–1, Haarhuis 7–6 6–3 6–7 6–7 6–4, lost Rafter [seed 13] 6–1 6–1 6–2); **r/u** Tokyo Japan Open (d. D. Adams 6–1 6–4, Fleurian 7–6 6–4, Becker 4–6 6–3 6–1, Damm 6–3 6–1, Johansson 4–6 7–6 6–3, lost Krajicek 6–2 3–6 6–1).

CHRISTIAN RUUD (NOR)

Born Oslo, 24 August 1972, and lives there; RH; 6ft 2in; 165lb; turned pro 1991; career singles titles 0; final 1997 ATP ranking 66; 1997 prize money $288,557.

Coached by Anders Haaseth and John-Erik Rustad. No. 1 Jun in Norway from age 15–18. His sister, Hedda, is a prominent Jun in Norway. **1988:** (1054) Joined his country's D Cup squad. **1989:** (1103) Won Nat Champ. **1990:** (1007). **1991:** (391) Began to make his mark on the satellite circuits. **1992:** (306) A –, F –, W –, US 1. Extended Becker to 5s in 4-hr battle 1r Olympics. **1993:** (143) A –, F –, W –, US –. Won 2 Challenger titles back-to-back. **1994:** (103) A –, F 2, W –, US –. Continued his success on the Challenger circuit with 4 titles. **1995:** (64) A 1, F 3, W 1, US 1. Moving on to the senior tour, he reached his 1st qf at Atlanta, following with sf Bucharest and then r/u Bastad, as well as winning Furth Challenger. **1996:** (59) A 2, F 1, W 1, US 1. In his best year to date, he reached sf Prague (where he took a set off Kafelnikov), Oporto (d. C. Costa), Umag and Bucharest, plus qf San Marino and Marbella and the title at Agadir Challenger. **1997:** A 4, F 1, W 1, US 2. Upset Corretja at Auckland, and, unseeded at Australian Open, he removed Siemerink 10–8 fs 1r before going on to extend Ivanisevic to 5s in last 16. He played qf Dubai, Monte Carlo (d. Kafelnikov),

Amsterdam and San Marino, but could not progress further. **1997 HIGHLIGHTS – SINGLES: Australian Open last 16** [unseeded] (d. Siemerink [seed 13] 3–6 4–6 7–5 6–2 10–8, Paes 6–2 6–2 6–2, Godwin 7–6 6–7 6–2 7–6, lost Ivanisevic [seed 3] 4–6 6–2 6–7 6–3 6–3), **French Open 1r** (lost Viloca 5–7 6–4 6–1 4–1 ret'd), **Wimbledon 1r** (lost Haas 6–2 6–1 6–2), **US Open 2r** (d. Goellner 6–4 4–6 1–6 6–4 6–3, lost Meligeni 6–3 6–4 6–3).

JAVIER SANCHEZ (ESP)

Born Pamplona, 1 February 1968; lives Andorra; RH; 5ft 10in; 155lb; turned pro 1986; career singles titles 4; final 1997 ATP ranking 54 singles, 22 doubles; 1997 prize money $562,048 ($4,017,055).

Has no coach, having split with Pato Alvarez after 10 years and feeling able to cope alone. Brother of Arantxa and Emilio, whom he overtook in the rankings 1st time on 30 Aug. 1993. Wife Isabel Ruiz (married 16 September 1994). **1986:** (225) No. 1 in ITF Jun rankings. Won Orange Bowl 18s, US Open Jun singles and doubles (with Carbonell), r/u Wimbledon Jun singles and French Open Jun doubles (with Carbonell). **1987:** (110) A –, F 2, W 1, US 1. R/u Madrid to his brother, Emilio. **1988:** (55) A –, F 2, W 1, US 1. Won 1st GP titles at Buenos Aires in both singles and doubles; sf Itaparica and qf Bologna. **1989:** (51) A –, F 1, W – US 2. Won both singles and doubles at Bologna, r/u Sao Paulo singles and took 3 more doubles titles with various partners. **1990:** (70) A 3, F 4, W –, US 1. Reached sf Madrid and last 16 French Open, unseeded. In doubles with various partners reached 6 f, winning 3. **1991:** (32) A 1, F 1, W 2, US qf. R/u Umag and Brasilia; sf Buzios and Madrid, upsetting Bruguera there and *en route* to qf US Open, unseeded. In doubles won 3 titles with different partners. **1992:** (41) A 1, F 1, W 2, US 2. Upset Forget *en route* to f Nice; sf Madrid, Cologne and Athens. Played 3 doubles f with different partners, winning Barcelona with Gomez. **1993:** (34) A 1, F 2, W 1, US 3. Enjoyed one of his best years and overtook his brother in the rankings for the 1st time on 30 Aug. On the main tour he was r/u Kitzbuhel and reached sf Genova, Hilversum (d. Muster) and Athens, plus 6 other qf. He upset Muster again *en route* to qf Stuttgart Mercedes and removed Bruguera 1r US Open. **1994:** (42) A 1, F 1, W –, US 1. At Bologna he took his 1st singles title since winning there in 1989 and broke into the top 25 1st time, although he could not maintain that ranking. He also reached sf Estoril and Hamburg (d. Korda). Won 2 doubles titles from 3 f with different partners. **1995:** (37) A 1, F 2, W –, US 1. It was another productive year in which he was r/u Prague (d. Rosset) and Tel Aviv; reached sf Dubai and Bologna, plus qf Qatar (d. Eltingh), Estoril, Gstaad and Umag; and upset Medvedev at Barcelona. Played 6 doubles f with Lobo, winning 2 and qualifying for World Doubles Champ. **1996:** (37) A 1, F 1, W 1, US qf. Upset MaliVai Washington on his way to the title at Tel Aviv, as well as reaching sf Dubai and San Marino (d. Gaudenzi) and qf Mexico City, Prague, Bologna and US Open, where (unseeded) he extended M. Chang to 4s. He was less prominent in doubles, in which he won Barcelona from 2 f with Lobo. **1997:** A 1, F 1, W 2, US 2. In singles, he reached sf Zagreb, Estoril and Palermo, plus qf Gstaad (d. Bruguera), Umag, Amsterdam, San Marino, Tashkent and Bucharest (d. Corretja). In doubles with Lobo, played and won 4 f. **1997 HIGHLIGHTS – SINGLES: Australian Open 1r** (lost Rosset 6–4 7–6 6–1), **French Open 1r** (lost Woodforde 5–7 7–6 6–7 6–4 8–6), **Wimbledon 2r** (d. Tebbutt 3–6 4–6 6–4 7–5 14–12), **US Open 2r** (d. Portas 7–5 6–2 7–5, lost Mantilla [seed 12] 7–5 6–4 6–2); **sf** Zagreb (d. Viloca 7–6 7–6, Schaller 6–3 7–5, Etlis 6–0 7–6, lost Ivanisevic 6–2 6–4), **sf** Estoril (d. Fragoso 6–2 6–2, Fontang 6–4 3–6 7–5, Schaller 6–0 4–1 ret'd, lost Corretja 6–3 6–1), **sf** Palermo (d. Arazi 7–5 6–3, Alonso 6–4 6–4, Filippini 6–3 1–6 6–4, lost Berasategui 6–2 6–3). **1997 HIGHLIGHTS – DOUBLES:** (with Lobo) **won** Sydney (d. Haarhuis/Siemerink 6–4 6–7 6–3), **won** Scottsdale (d. Bjorkman/Leach 6–3 6–3), **won** Hamburg (d. Broad/Norval 6–3 7–6), **won** Bucharest (d. Davids/Orsanic 7–5 7–5). **CAREER HIGHLIGHTS – SINGLES: US Open – qf 1996** [unseeded] (d. Skoch 6–2 7–6 6–3, Grabb 6–2 7–6 2–6 6–3, Stoltenberg 6–4 3–6 4–6 6–2 7–6, Boetsch 6–4 7–6 7–6, lost Chang 7–5 6–3 6–7 6–3).

FABRICE SANTORO (FRA)

Born Tahiti, 7 December 1972; lives Paris; RH; 5ft 10in; 160lb; turned pro 1989; career singles titles 1; final 1997 ATP ranking 29; 1997 prize money $626,434 ($2,066,906).

Coached by Henri Dumont. Nat champ in 12s, 14s and 16s. **1988:** (571) Won Orange Bowl 16s. **1989:** (235) A –, F 1, W –, US –. Won French Open Jun over Palmer and was No. 2 in ITF Jun rankings. Upset Gomez at Stuttgart. **1990:** (62) A –, F 2, W 1, US 3. After winning Telford Challenger, he upset Gomez again *en route* to his 1st tour f at Toulouse. Qf Nice (d. Chesnokov) and Bordeaux. Voted Newcomer of the Year. **1991:** (43) A 1, F 4, W –, US 1. Won Barcelona (d. Bruguera) and Brest Challenger; qf Adelaide, Sydney, Italian Open, Florence, Indianapolis and Bordeaux; last 16 French Open, unseeded. **1992:** (43) A –, F 1, W –, US 1. Made his mark at the Olympics, where he upset Becker and extended Ivanisevic to 8–6 fs in qf. Scored other big upsets during the year as he moved to sf Nice (d. Chesnokov), Gstaad (d. Novacek), Hilversum and New Haven (d. Korda). **1993:** (55) A 2, F 1, W –, US 1. Upset Volkov on his way to f Dubai and appeared in sf Nice (d. Krickstein) plus 3 more qf, including Indian Wells, where he upset Stich. Out 4 months from May to Aug. with a serious thumb injury. **1994:** (47) A 3, F 3, W –, US –. His best performance came at Kitzbuhel, where he upset Gaudenzi and Muster and extended Ivanisevic to 5s in f. He also won Venice Challenger and reached sf Tel Aviv, plus qf Pinehurst, Bordeaux and Montevideo. **1995:** (104) A 2, F 1, W 1, US 1. Reached sf Estoril and qf Palermo, where he won the doubles with Corretja, as well as upsetting Edberg 1r Monte Carlo and Sampras 1r Italian Open. Military service left him with limited opportunities for training and practice. **1996:** (118) A 1, F –, W –, US –. Military service again restricted his schedule. **1997:** A –, F 1, W 1, US 1. After winning Newcastle Challenger, he went on in Oct. to take his 1st title on the main tour at Lyon, unseeded (d. Krajicek, Mantilla and Philippoussis). He scored other big upsets on his way to sf Marseille (d. Korda), Monte Carlo (d. Muster and Bruguera), Prague (d. Kuerten and Rios), qf Estoril and Montreal (d. Muster) and removed Bruguera Stuttgart Eurocard. In doubles he played 2 f with Delaitre and 1 with D. Adams, but won no title. **1997 HIGHLIGHTS – SINGLES: French Open 1r** (lost Sampras [seed 1] 6–3 7–5 6–1), **Wimbledon 1r** (lost Medvedev [seed 13] 6–2 6–3 6–4), **US Open 1r** (lost Ondruska 5–7 6–4 4–6 6–2 6–3); **won** Lyon (d. Van Garsse 6–3 6–2, Krajicek 2–6 7–6 7–6, Mantilla 6–1 6–1, Philippoussis 6–4 6–2, Haas 6–4 6–4); **won** Newcastle Challenger (d. Grosjean 2–6 6–3 6–3); **sf** Marseille (d. Grosjean 6–4 5–7 6–1, Korda 6–4 6–4, Rosset 3–6 6–3 7–5, lost Enqvist 6–4 6–3), **sf** Monte Carlo (d. Roig 6–4 6–1, Muster 6–2 7–6, Bruguera 3–6 7–5 6–1, C. Costa 6–3 7–5, lost Corretja 6–4 6–4), **sf** Prague (d. Vacek 7–5 6–0, Kuerten 7–6 3–6 6–1, Rios 4–6 6–3 6–0, lost Ulihrach 6–4 6–2). **1997 HIGHLIGHTS – DOUBLES:** (with Delaitre unless stated) **r/u** Marseille (lost Enqvist/Larsson 6–3 6–4), **r/u** Lyon (lost E. Ferreira/Galbraith 2–6 6–2 6–4), (with D. Adams) **r/u** Moscow (lost Damm/Suk 6–4 6–3).

SARGIS SARGSIAN (ARM)

Born Yerevan, 3 June 1973; lives there and Orange, Conn.; RH; 5ft 11in; 165lb; turned pro 1995; career singles titles 1; final 1997 ATP ranking 58; 1997 prize money $278,427.

Won 2 nat jun titles. Ranked No. 1 in Armenia. **1992:** (626). **1993:** (594). **1994:** (–). **1995:** (253) A –, F –, W –, US 3. NCAA Champ and All-American for 2nd year in singles, 1st in doubles, at Arizona State Univ. Upset Medvedev at US Open. **1996:** (113) A –, F –, W –, US –. Upset Philippoussis at Stuttgart Mercedes and won Challenger titles at Zagreb and Austin. **1997:** A 2, F 1, W 2, US 3. At Newport he became the 1st Armenian to win a title on the main tour. He also reached qf Coral Springs and Moscow and upset Rosset at New Haven. **1997 HIGHLIGHTS – SINGLES: Australian Open 2r** (d. Ondruska 7–6 7–5 4–6 6–2, lost MaliVai Washington 6–1 6–0 6–2), **French Open 1r** (lost D. Norman 6–2 7–5 6–3), **Wimbledon 2r** (d. Van Herck 7–6 6–2 6–4, lost Medvedev [seed 13] 6–1 6–4 7–5), **US Open 3r** (d. Alonso 2–6 0–6 6–0 6–4 6–4, Woodruff w.o., lost M. Chang [seed 2] 6–1 6–3 7–5); **won** Newport (d. Nestor 7–6 7–5, Dilucia 7–5 6–2, Stolle 6–3 7–5, Paes 7–6 2–6 6–3, Steven 7–6 4–6 7–5).

SJENG SCHALKEN (NED)

Born Weert, 8 September 1976; lives Kessenich, Belgium; RH; 6ft 3in; 178lb; turned pro 1994; career singles titles 3; final 1997 ATP ranking 60; 1997 prize money $312,824.

Coached by Henk van Hulst and Alex Reynders. Won Nat 14s, 16s and 18s. **1994:** (187) Won US Open Jun over Tahiri. In the men's game he won Guayaquil Challenger and upset Vacek at Rosmalen. **1995:** (54) A –, F –, W 1, US 1. Upset Berasategui at Valencia on the way to his 1st title from his 1st f on the senior tour; reached sf Casablanca, qf Rotterdam (as LL), Munich (d. Korda), Palermo (d. Gaudenzi) and Santiago and won Monte Carlo Challenger. In doubles he won Amsterdam with Rios. **1996:** (65) A 1, F 2, W 1, US 3. Won Jakarta and reached qf Monte Carlo (d. Enqvist), Bogota, Beijing and Moscow (d. Courier). **1997:** A 1, F 1, W 1, US 2. A qualifier at Philadelphia, he upset Stoltenberg and took a set off Sampras in sf. Then at Boston in Aug., unseeded and defying a knee injury that had almost caused him to withdraw, he upset Corretja, A. Costa and Rios back-to-back to win the title. In other tourns he reached qf St Polten (d. Henman) and Rosmalen and extended Courier to 8–6 5s at Australian Open. **1997 HIGHLIGHTS – SINGLES: Australian Open 1r** (lost Courier [seed 11] 6–7 6–3 4–6 6–1 8–6), **French Open 1r** (lost Delgado 2–6 7–6 7–5 6–4), **Wimbledon 1r** (lost Ondruska 3–6 7–5 6–0 0–1 ret'd), **US Open 2r** (d. Van Scheppingen 6–4 6–3 6–4, lost Kuerten [seed 9] 6–4 6–4 6–2); **won** Boston (d. Roux 6–7 6–4 6–4, Dosedel 2–6 6–1 7–5, Corretja 3–6 6–3 6–3, A. Costa 6–4 5–7 6–3, Rios 7–5 6–3); **sf** Philadelphia (d. Stoltenberg 6–2 6–4, Carlsen 7–6 4–6 6–3, Stark 6–2 6–4, lost Sampras 3–6 7–5 6–3).

DAVID SHERWOOD (GBR)

Born Sheffield, 6 May 1980; lives Bisham Abbey; RH; 6ft 3in; 172lb; career singles titles 0.

Coached by Ian Barclay. **1997:** Won Australian Open Jun doubles with Trotman.

GRANT STAFFORD (RSA)

Born Johannesburg, 27 May 1971, and lives there; RH; 6ft 2in; 175lb; turned pro 1990; career singles titles 0; final 1997 ATP ranking 75; 1997 prize money $275,775.

Coached by Dennis Van Der Meer and works at Hilton Head Academy. Wife Wendy (Married 11 May 1997). **1988:** (564). **1989:** (712) Won US Open Jun doubles with W. Ferreira and finished No. 3 on ITF Jun doubles rankings. Nat champ in singles and doubles. **1990:** (264) Began to play the Challenger circuit. **1991:** (182) A –, F –, W –, US 1. **1992:** (188) A 1, F –, W 3, US –. Won 2 Challenger doubles titles with Ulyett. **1993:** (86) A 1, F –, W 1, US 1. Appeared in his 1st f on the main tour at Durban (d. W. Ferreira) and reached sf Kuala Lumpur Salem, plus qf Newport and Tel Aviv (d. E. Sanchez) and upset Sampras at Queen's. **1994:** (157) A 4, F 1, W 1, US 1. Qf Adelaide (d. Muster) and upset Rosset at Australian Open, where he was unseeded. **1995:** (282) A 1, F –, W –, US –. Won gold medals in singles and doubles (with De Jager) at African Games. **1996:** (84) A –, F –, W 2, US 1. Returned to the top 100 after reaching f Newport and qf Tel Aviv (won doubles with Ondruska), as well as taking 3 Challenger titles. **1997:** A 2, F 1, W 1, US 2. He reached his 1st CC f at Orlando, appeared in sf Philadelphia (d. Courier) and Newport, qf Nottingham (d. Siemerink) and upset Pioline at Indianapolis.

1997 HIGHLIGHTS – SINGLES: Australian Open 2r (d. Burillo 6–0 6–1 3–0 ret'd, lost Muster [seed 5] 6–3 6–2 6–2), **French Open 1r** (lost Paes 6–4 3–6 6–3 6–2), **Wimbledon 1r** (lost Rafter [seed 12] 2–6 4–6 6–3 6–2 6–2), **US Open 2r** (d. Alvarez 6–4 6–2 6–2, lost Bruguera [seed 7] 6–4 6–2 7–6); **r/u** Orlando (d. Champion 6–2 6–1, Stolle 6–2 6–3, Meligeni 6–3 6–4, Woodruff 6–3 4–6 6–4, lost M. Chang 4–6 6–2 6–1); **sf** Philadelphia (d. Radulescu 6–4 6–3, Courier 6–3 5–7 6–2, Stolle 6–4 6–2, lost Rafter 6–3 6–4), **sf** Newport (d. Salzenstein 7–5 6–3, L. Jensen 6–2 6–2, Wheaton 4–6 6–3 6–2, lost Steven 6–3 5–7 6–4).

JONATHAN STARK (USA)

Born Medford, Oregon, 3 April 1971; lives Seattle, Wash.; RH; 2HB; 6ft 2in; 185lb; turned pro 1991; career singles titles 2; final 1997 ATP ranking 95 singles, 13 doubles; 1997 prize money $550,298 ($2,670,735).

Coached by Brad Stine. Wife Dana Astle (married 19 July 1997). Won 4 Nat Jun titles. **1987:** Won French Open Jun doubles with Courier. **1988**: (403) Won US Open Jun doubles with Yoncey and in the senior game won Coquitlam Challenger. **1989:** (875) Won US Open Jun singles over Kulti and Wimbledon Jun doubles with Palmer. **1990:** (1001) All-American at Stanford, where he played No. 1 singles in his freshman year. **1991:** (243) All-American again and r/u NCAA doubles with Palmer. Outside collegiate tennis he won Ponte Vedra Challenger. **1992:** (85) A –, F –, W 1, US 2. Out in May with patellar tendinitis, he returned to reach his 1st GP f at Rosmalen, a performance which took him into the top 100. He also reached qf Newport and Brisbane and played 3 doubles f with P. McEnroe, winning Sydney Indoor. **1993:** (38) A 3, F 3, W 1, US 1. Won his 1st main tour singles title at Bolzano, upsetting Chesnokov and Pioline, and surprised Courier at Tokyo Japan Open. He moved into top 50, thanks to these results plus sf appearances at Adelaide and Halle. In doubles he played 8 f, winning 2 with McEnroe and 4 with Black. In an extraordinary 5-week spell in autumn he won 6 titles – 1 singles and 4 doubles with Black on main tour plus 1 Challenger singles. **1994:** (66) A 2, F 2, W 1, US 1. In singles he reached sf Hawaii, qf Philadelphia (d. Lendl), Indianapolis (d. Volkov) and Tokyo Seiko, and upset Becker 1r French Open. In doubles with Black he won French Open, r/u Australian Open, and took 2 more titles from a total of 9 f with him and 1 with O'Brien, qualifying with Black for their 1st World Doubles Champ. **1995:** (98) A 1, F 1, W 2, US 1. Upset MaliVai Washington and M. Chang on his way to sf Memphis and surprised Rafter in reaching qf Philadelphia. In doubles he won 2 titles from 3 f with different partners and took Wimbledon mixed with Navratilova. **1996:** (68) A 1, F –, W 1, US 1. A qualifier at Singapore, and ranked only 101, he upset M. Chang to take the title. He also reached sf New Delhi, qf Long Island (d. Siemerink) and upset Courier 1r Wimbledon. From 3 doubles f with different partners, he won Seoul with Leach and Stockholm with Galbraith. **1997:** A 1, F 2, W 2, US 1. He upset Ivanisevic at Indian Wells and reached qf Chennai, Philadelphia and Singapore (d. M. Chang), although he could progress no further. Played 5 doubles f with Leach, and although they won no title, their consistency earned them a place at World Doubles Champ. There they won that elusive title, beating Bhupathi/Paes in ss in f, to finish the 3rd-ranked doubles team. On the eve of that match, he was called up to the US squad for D Cup f in place of the injured O'Brien. **1997 HIGHLIGHTS – SINGLES: Australian Open 1r** (lost Roux 1–6 4–6 7–6 6–2 13–11), **French Open 2r** (d. Zabaleta 6–4 7–6 7–6, lost Escude 6–4 6–2 6–2), **Wimbledon 2r** (d. Huet 7–6 6–7 6–3 2–6 6–3, lost Rusedski 4–6 6–7 6–4 6–3 11-9), **US Open 1r** (lost Gustafsson 6–3 6–2 7–5). **1997 HIGHLIGHTS – DOUBLES:** (with Leach) **won** World Doubles Champ (d. Bhupathi/Paes 6–3 6–4 7–6); **r/u** Auckland (lost E. Ferreira/Galbraith 6–4 4–6 7–6), **r/u** Memphis (lost E. Ferreira/Galbraith 6–3 3–6 6–1), **r/u** Singapore (lost Bhupathi/Paes 6–4 6–4), **r/u** Stuttgart Eurocard (lost Woodbridge/Woodforde 6–4 6–4), **r/u** Paris Open (lost Eltingh/Haarhuis 6–2 7–6). **CAREER HIGHLIGHTS - DOUBLES:** (with Black) **Australian Open - r/u 1994** (lost Eltingh/Haarhuis 6-7 6-3 6-4 6-3)**; French Open - won 1994** (d. Apell/Bjorkman 6-4 7-6)**. MIXED DOUBLES:** (with Navratilova) **Wimbledon – won 1995** (d. Suk.G. Fernandez 6–4 6–4)**.**

BRETT STEVEN (NZL)

Born Auckland, 27 April 1969, and lives there; RH; 6ft 1in; 170lb; turned pro 1988; career singles titles 0; final 1997 ATP ranking 50; 1997 prize money $324,379 ($1,991,859).

Coached by Jeff Simpson. Wife Heather (married 11 December 1995); son Ryan James (born 28 July 1996). Won Nat Jun 12s, 14s, 16s and 18s. **1986:** (870) Won USTA GC 18s and took Nat doubles with Mustard. **1987:** (556). **1988:** (357). **1989:** (497). **1990:** (213) Won Canberra Challenger and joined his country's D Cup squad. **1991:** (225) Won Newport doubles with Pozzi. **1992:** (73) Reached his 1st qf on main tour at Indianapolis, following with Taipei, which took him into the top 100. **1993:** (43) A qf, F 2, W 2, US 1. Progressed into the top 50 in Feb. after upsetting Muster on his way to an unscheduled appearance in qf Australian Open. Reached his 1st senior f at Schenectady (d. Novacek) as well as sf Copenhagen, plus qf Auckland, Hong Kong and Montreal (d. Sampras). **1994:** (87) A 2, F 1, W 2, US 1. Appeared in sf Beijing (d. Olhovskiy), qf Auckland, Seoul, Washington (d. Mansdorf and Agassi) and Tokyo Seiko (d. Becker) and surprised Pioline 1r Wimbledon. In doubles he won 3 titles with different partners. **1995:** (42) A 2, F 3, W 3, US 2. In singles he reached sf Rosmalen, qf Auckland, Philadelphia, Scottsdale (d. Karbacher), Atlanta (d. Krickstein), Coral Springs and Halle (d. W. Ferreira), upset Enqvist at Vienna and won Wellington Challenger. Played 4 doubles f, winning Indian Wells with Ho, with whom he qualified for World Doubles Champ, where they could not progress beyond rr. **1996:** (100) A 4, F 2, W 3, US –. At Auckland, where he was r/u singles, he played 2 doubles matches on Saturday night, singles sf Sunday morning, finishing only 7.30pm after rain, and was back on court at 9.00 for the singles final. Not surprisingly he was in no state to play the doubles f and was forced to def. At Australian Open, where he was unseeded, he took a set off Becker. **1997:** A 1, F –, W 4, US 2. His best performance came at Newport, where he was r/u singles and won doubles with Gimelstob. He also reached sf Shanghai and Washington, qf Memphis, and won 2 more doubles titles with Olhovskiy. **1997 HIGHLIGHTS – SINGLES: Australian Open 1r** (lost Fromberg 4–6 2–6 7–5 6–3 6–1), **Wimbledon last 16** [unseeded] (d. Roux 6–2 6–2 7–6, Fetterlein 4–6 7–5 6–3 6–2, M. Norman 6–7 6–2 6–3 6–1, lost Pioline 3–6 6–3 6–4 7–5), **US Open 2r** (d. Viloca 4–6 6–2 6–1 6–2, lost Damm 6–4 6–4 3–6 7–6); **won** Ljubljana Challenger (d. Pavel 7–6 6–2); **r/u** Newport (d. Herrera 6–3 6–2, Shelton 4–6 6–3 6–4, Woodforde 6–0 6–0, Stafford 6–3 5–7 6–4, lost Sargsian 7–6 4–6 7–5); **sf** Shanghai (d. Knowles 7–6 7–6, Dewulf 6–3 4–6 7–5, Solves 6–7 6–2 6–2, lost Volkov 7–6 7–5), **sf** Washington (d. L. Jensen 7–6 6–3, Merinov 6–0 6–1, Smith 7–6 6–2, Schuttler 6–3 6–3, lost M. Chang 6–2 7–6). **1997 HIGHLIGHTS – DOUBLES:** (with Olhovskiy unless stated) **won** Copenhagen (d. Carlsen/Fetterlein 6–4 6–2), **won** St Petersburg (d. Prinosil/Vacek 6–4 6–3), (with Gimelstob) **won** Newport (d. Kinnear/Kitinov 6–3 6–4). **CAREER HIGHLIGHTS –SINGLES: Australian Open – qf 1993** [unseeded] (d. Randall 4–6 6–1 6–3 6–4, Muster 6–2 7–6 6–4, Olhovskiy 6–3 7–5 3–6 6–3, Fromberg 7–6 6–7 6–7 6–1 8–6, lost Sampras [seed 3] 6–3 6–2 6–3).

MICHAEL STICH (GER)

Born Pinneberg, 18 October 1968; lives Salzburg, Austria; RH; 6ft 4in; 175lb; turned pro 1988; career singles titles 18; final 1997 ATP ranking 67; 1997 prize money $370,474 ($12,628,890).
Coached by Sven Groeneveld; trained by Alex Stober. Wife actress Jessica Stockman (married 19 September 1992). Waited to turn pro until he had finished his exams and gained a place at university. Unlike Becker, he has completed his National Service. **1986:** Nat Jun Champ. **1987:** (564). **1988:** (269) Won Munster Challenger. **1989:** (100) A –, F 2, W 1, US 1. Played his 1st GP qf at Queen's, where he took Lendl to 3s. **1990:** (42) A 3, F 2, W 3, US 2. Won his 1st tour title at Memphis. In doubles reached 6 f, winning Munich and Vienna with Riglewski and Rosmalen with Hlasek. **1991:** (4) A 3, F sf, W won, US qf. Began a remarkable year by reaching f Adelaide and Sydney NSW and following with Memphis. He broke into the top 10 after French Open, but the triumph of his year was his straight-sets victory over Becker on grass to win Wimbledon – only the second title of his career – which took him to No. 4 ahead of Courier and Agassi. After winning Stuttgart Mercedes (on clay) he replaced Lendl at No. 3, but was overtaken again by Courier. With titles also at Schenectady (HC) and Vienna (Supreme), he became the 1st player since Mecir in 1987 to win titles on 4 different surfaces. Qualified for ATP World Champ in Frankfurt, but, shaken by the overwhelming support for his opponent when he played Becker, he won none of his rr matches. Ended year by reaching sf GS Cup where Wheaton beat him. **1992:** (15) A qf, F 3, W qf, US 2. Until he finished in triumph by winning GS Cup, it had been a less spectacular year in which he won only Rosmalen, r/u Hamburg and sf Indian Wells, plus 4 more qf. Although he lost his Wimbledon singles crown, he won the doubles there with J. McEnroe, unseeded, taking the title over Grabb/Reneberg in a f lasting 5 hrs 1 min. In partnership with Becker, he took an Olympic gold medal and won Monte Carlo. **1993:** (2) A sf, F 4, W qf, US 1. He confirmed his all-round ability by again taking titles on 4 different surfaces – Stuttgart Eurocard and Stockholm (d. Edberg) on carpet, Hamburg on clay, Queen's on grass and Basel (d. Edberg) on HC. He was also r/u Munich and Stuttgart Mercedes and reached 5 more qf, before crowning his year by winning ATP World Champ over Sampras and leading GER to victory in D Cup f v AUS. His golden run was ended by Korda in a spectacular f at GS Cup, but he had done enough already to overtake Courier for the No. 2 ranking. **1994:** (9) A 1, F 2, W 1, US r/u. It was a mixed year in which he won only Rotterdam, Munich and Halle and was disappointing in GS – particularly at Wimbledon, where he fell 1r to Shelton, a qualifier. This defeat cost him the No. 2 ranking as Ivanisevic overtook him. At end Oct. he slipped to 4 behind Becker, and by end of year, having failed to qualify for IBM/ATP World Champ, he had fallen as low as 9. In other tourns, he was r/u Vienna and reached sf Marseille, Hamburg, Cincinnati and New Haven, plus 5 more qf. He played in winning German WT Cup squad and at that tourn saved 2 mps to end Sampras' 29-match winning streak as the No. 1 was beginning to look unbeatable. **1995:** (12) A 3, F 4, W 1, US 4. Los Angeles was his only title, although he was r/u Stuttgart Eurocard (d. Becker), Munich and Halle (where he squandered 7 mps v Rosset), upset Sampras *en route* to sf Cincinnati and reached the same stage at Qatar. However, this was not enough to maintain his top 10 ranking, and he slipped out on 11 Sept. He suffered severe ligament injuries to his left ankle in a bad fall during qf Vienna and was out for rest of year, hoping to avoid surgery. **1996:** (16) A –, F r/u, W 4, US 2. The ankle injury kept him out until Feb., when he won his 2nd tourn back at Antwerp (d. Ivanisevic). However, he aggravated the injury again when dressing for his 2r match at Milan and was forced to withdraw, eventually undergoing surgery on 7 March. Returning refreshed but short of match practice, he made a big impact at French Open, where, benefiting from the unusually fast, dry surface, he upset Muster and Rosset on his way to f. Smiling more and reacting better with the crowds, he seemed set to return to the top 10, but that proved to be the high point of his year, for he passed no other qf, reaching that stage only at Queen's and Ostrava, and was restricted at US Open by a shoulder injury. **1997:** A 2, F –, W sf, US –. Having lost his fight to overcome a chronic shoulder injury, he announced his retirement on 2 May, but promised to honour his commitments, intending to finish his pro career at D Cup in Sept. In the event, he quit in July, deciding to go out on a high after losing a thrilling 5s sf to Pioline at Wimbledon, where he was unseeded. He reached the same stage St Petersburg, plus qf Rotterdam and Halle, where he won the doubles with Braasch. **1997 HIGHLIGHTS – SINGLES: Australian Open 2r** [seed 15] (d. Fredriksson 6–3 6–2 6–2, lost Medvedev 4–6 6–1 6–2 4–6 9–7), **Wimbledon sf** [unseeded] (d. Courier 7–6 7–5 7–6, Gimelstob 7–5 6–1 6–1, Stolle 6–3 6–7 6–2 7–6, Woodforde 6–4 6–7 6–3 7–5, Henman [seed 14] 6–3 6–2 6–4, lost Pioline 6–7 6–2 6–1 5–7 6–4); **sf** St Petersburg (d. Fromberg

4–6 7–5 7–6, Camporese 6–4 6–4, Carlsen 6–2 6–4, lost Johansson 6–3 6–1). **1997 HIGHLIGHTS – DOUBLES:** (with Braasch) **won** Halle (d. D. Adams/Barnard 7–6 6–3). **CAREER HIGHLIGHTS – SINGLES: Wimbledon – won 1991** (d. Goldie 6–4 6–1 6–2, Nargiso 6–3 6–4 6–7 6–2, Camporese 7–6 6–2 6–7 6–4, Volkov 4–6 6–3 7–6 1–6 7–5, Courier 6–3 7–6 6–2, Edberg 4–6 7–6 6–7 7–6, Becker 6–4 7–6 6–4), **sf 1997**, **qf 1992** (d. Pescosolido 6–3 6–3 6–2, Mansdorf 4–6 7–6 6–3 6–3, Larsson 6–4 6–1 6–3, Masur 3–6 6–1 6–4 6–4, lost Sampras 6–3 6–2 6–4); **qf 1993** (d. Siemerink 6–2 7–6 6–1, Stolle 4–6 6–1 7–5 6–4, van Rensburg 6–3 6–4 6–4, Korda 7–6 6–4 7–6, lost Becker 7–5 6–7 6–7 6–2 6–4); **ATP Champ – won 1993** (d. Medvedev 6–3 6–4, Chang 4–6 7–6 6–2, Courier 7–5 6–3 in rr, Ivanisevic 7–6 7–6, Sampras 7–6 2–6 7–6 6–2); **GS Cup – won 1993** (d. Edberg 7–6 6–7 7–6, Krajicek 7–6 7–5, Sampras 7–6 7–6 7–6, Chang 6–2 6–3 6–2), **r/u 1993** (d. Washington 6–3 6–1, Steven 5–7 6–4 6–4, Edberg 2–6 3–6 6–3 6–3 6–1, lost Korda 2–6 6–4 7–6 2–6 11–9); **French Open – r/u 1996** (d. Fredriksson 6–4 7–5 6–4, Rusedski 6–3 7–5 6–3, Tillstrom 4–6 6–0 6–4 7–6, Muster 4–6 6–4 6–1 7–6, Pioline 6–4 4–6 6–3 6–2, Rosset 6–3 6–4 6–2, lost Kafelnikov 7–6 7–5 7–6), **sf 1994** (d. Pearce 6–3 6–3 7–5, Krajicek 6–7 7–6 6–3 6–2, Costa 3–6 7–5 7–6 6–2, Santoro 6–3 6–1 6–2, Davin 6–4 6–4 6–4, lost Courier 6–2 6–7 6–2 6–4); **US Open – r/u 1994** (d. Delaitre 7–6 6–3 6–3, Bryan 6–1 6–4 6–2, B. Black 7–6 6–2 6–1, Kafelnikov 7–6 6–3 6–2, Bjorkman 6–4 6–4 5–7 6–3, Novacek 7–5 6–3 7–6, lost Agassi 6–1 7–6 7–5), **qf 1991** (d. Eltingh 7–6 6–1 6–0, J. Brown w.o., Washington 5–7 7–5 6–2 4–6 6–3, Rostagno 6–2 3–6 6–1 7–6, lost Lendl 6–3 3–6 4–6 7–6 6–1); **Australian Open – sf 1993** (d. O'Brien 6–4 7–5 6–2, Santoro 6–7 6–2 6–2 4–6 6–4, Stoltenberg 5–7 6–4 7–6 4–6 6–1, Carlsen 6–7 6–4 6–4 6–0, Forget 6–4 6–4 6–4, lost Courier 7–6 6–4 6–2), **qf 1992** (d. J. Sanchez 7–5 6–1 4–6 6–3, Svensson 6–4 6–1 1–6 6–4, Jaite 6–0 2–6 7–5 6–2, Masur 3–6 6–4 7–6 6–4, lost Krajicek 5–7 7–6 6–7 6–4 6–4). **CAREER HIGHLIGHTS – DOUBLES:** (with Becker) **Olympics – won gold medal 1992** (d. W. Ferreira/Norval 7–6 4–6 7–6 6–3).

CYRIL SUK (CZE)

Born Prague, 29 January 1967; lives Monte Carlo, Monaco; RH; 5ft 11in; 158lb; turned pro 1988; career singles titles 0; final 1997 ATP ranking – 23 doubles; 1997 prize money $211,069 ($1,803,499).

Coached by Zdenek Zofka; trained by Ivan Machytka. Brother of Helena Sukova; son of the 1962 Wimbledon finalist, the late Vera Sukova, and Cyril Suk, former President of Czech Tennis Federation. Wife Lenka (married 26 March 1991); son Cyril IV (born 21 October 1992); daughter Natalie Mia (born 8 May 1996). **1985:** No. 1 in Jun doubles rankings with Korda. **1988:** (184). **1989:** (231) A 1, F –, W –, US –. Won St Vincent doubles with Cihak. **1990:** (288) A 1, F –, W –, US –. **1991:** (532) A –, F –, W –, US –. Reached 6 doubles f, winning Prague with Flegl and Toulouse and Lyon with Nijssen, with whom he qualified for ATP Doubles Champ. In mixed doubles won French Open with his sister, Helena. **1992:** (723) A –, F –, W –, US –. Won Stuttgart and Basle doubles with Nijssen, qualifying for World Doubles Final, and in mixed won Wimbledon with Savchenko-Neiland. **1993:** (–) A –, F –, W –, US –. Appeared in 5 doubles f, winning Halle with Korda, New Haven with Vacek and Stuttgart Mercedes with Nijssen, with whom he qualified again for World Doubles Finals. **1994:** (653) A –, F –, W –, US –. Won 2 doubles titles with Nijssen, qualifying for World Doubles Champ for 4th straight year. **1995:** (–) A –, F –, W –, US –. Played 8 men's doubles f, winning 4 with Vacek, with whom he qualified for World Doubles Champ. He won a match there for the 1st time in 5 appearances, winning 2 in rr before losing sf to Eltingh/Haarhuis. In mixed with G. Fernandez was r/u Australian Open, Wimbledon and US Open. **1996:** (–) In men's doubles he appeared in 4 f with 3 different partners, winning Ostrava with Stolle, and in mixed he won Wimbledon with his sister, Helena. **1997:** A –, F –, W –, US –. Won Moscow doubles with Damm and was r/u 3 other tourns with Stolle, as well as retaining his Wimbledon mixed doubles title with his sister, Helena. **1997 HIGHLIGHTS – DOUBLES:** (with Stolle unless stated) (with Damm) **won** Moscow (d. D. Adams/Santoro 6–4 6–3); **r/u** Dubai (lost Groen/Ivanisevic 7–6 6–3), **r/u** Antwerp (lost D. Adams/Delaitre 3–6 6–2 6–1), **r/u** Queen's (lost Philippoussis/Rafter 6–2 4–6 7–5). **MIXED DOUBLES:** (with Sukova) **won Wimbledon** (d. Olhovskiy/Neiland 4–6 6–3 6–4). **CAREER HIGHLIGHTS – MIXED DOUBLES:** (with Sukova unless stated) **French Open – won 1991** (d. Haarhuis/Vis 3–6 6–4 6–1); **Wimbledon** – (with Savchenko-Neiland) **won 1992** (d. Eltingh/Oremans 7–6 6–2), **won 1996** (d. Woodforde/Neiland 1–6 6–3 6–2), **won 1997**.

JEFF TARANGO (USA)

Born Manhattan Beach, Cal., 20 November 1968, and lives there and Pezenas, France; LH; 5ft 11in; 160lb; turned pro 1989; career singles titles 2; final 1997 ATP ranking 49; 1997 prize money $411,650 ($1,993,058).

Coached by Joe Brandi. Wife Benedicte (married 4 July 1994); daughter Nina Rose (born 28 September 1997). **1986:** Won USTA Boys 18s. **1987:** (377) All-American at Stanford. **1988:** (96) A –, F –, W –, US 1. Upset Zivojinovic *en route* to 1st GP f at Livingston. **1989:** (137) A 2, F –, W 1, US 3. Qf Schenectady. All-American 3rd time singles, 2nd doubles, he led Stanford to 2nd consec. NCAA Team Champ. **1990:** (131) A –, F –, W 1, US 1. Qf Kiawah Island, d. Leconte and Bruguera at LIPC and won Furth Challenger. **1991:** (106) A 1, F 1, W 1, US 2. R/u Seoul, sf Bologna and qf Memphis. **1992:** (45) A 2, F 2, W 1, US 2. Won his 1st tour title at Wellington and followed with his second at Tel Aviv in autumn (d. Mansdorf and Muster), breaking into top 50. During the year he also upset Krickstein *en route* to sf US CC and surprised Korda 1r Australian Open. **1993:** (91) A 1, F 3, W 1, US 1. Reached sf San Francisco, plus qf Mexico City and Tampa. **1994:** (79) A 1, F 2, W 1, US 2. R/u Bordeaux (d. Kafelnikov and Rosset), sf Seoul, qf San Jose and Bologna (d. Rafter).

1995: (76) A 1, F 1, W 3, US 1. Upset Medvedev at Wimbledon, then in 3r v Mronz he stormed off the court after umpire Bruno Rebeuh (whom Tarango felt had been biased against him on previous occasions) declined to overrule what Tarango considered to be an ace, called out, and gave him a code of conduct warning for his response to the jeering and booing crowd. He became the 1st in history to be def. from singles at Wimbledon, was banned for 1996, and eventually fined $28,256 (reduced from $43,756). On the positive side, he reached qf Rotterdam (d. W. Ferreira), Italian Open (d. MaliVai Washington) and Vienna and upset Stich at Bucharest. In doubles he won 3 titles with different partners. **1996:** (105) A 2, F 3, W –, US 3. In singles he played qf Shanghai and St Petersburg and upset Rios at US Open. In doubles won Bastad and Bucharest with Ekerot. **1997:** A 3, F 2, W 1, US 3. Reached sf Adelaide (d. Bjorkman 17–15 in fs tb) and Boston, plus qf Shanghai, Memphis, Halle and Bastad, and won Poznan Challenger. **1997 HIGHLIGHTS – SINGLES: Australian Open 3r** (d. Shelton 2–6 7–6 7–6 6–2, Rosset 6–4 6–1 6–1, lost Courier [seed 11] 6–1 7–6 6–3), **French Open 2r** (d. Filippini 4–6 6–2 5–7 7–6 6–4, lost Muster [seed 5] 7–5 1–6 6–2 6–1), **Wimbledon 1r** (lost R. Gilbert 3–6 7–5 7–6 6–4), **US Open 3r** (d. Prinosil 6–4 6–2 7–5, Raoux 6–4 6–7 6–7 6–2 6–4, lost Draper 7–6 3–6 2–6 6–4 6–4); **won** Poznan Challenger (d. Rikl 7–5 6–3); **sf** Adelaide (d. Damm 6–3 6–3, Prinosil 6–2 6–4, Bjorkman 6–1 6–7 7–6, lost Draper 6–1 3–6 6–2), **sf** Boston (d. O'Brien 6–2 6–7 6–3, Mantilla 6–0 6–4, Rusedski 7–6 7–6, lost Rios 6–4 6–3). **1997 HIGHLIGHTS – DOUBLES:** (with Braasch) **r/u** Hong Kong (lost Damm/Vacek 6–3 6–4).

MIKAEL TILLSTROM (SWE)

Born Jonkoping, 5 March 1972; lives Gothenburg; RH; 6ft 1in; 155lb; turned pro 1991; career singles titles 1; final 1997 ATP ranking 69; 1997 prize money $314,551.

Coached by Martin Bohm. **1989:** (912). **1990:** (941) R/u US Open Jun to Gaudenzi and won Jun doubles there with Renstrom. **1991:** (329) Began to make his mark on the satellite circuits. **1992:** (141) Sf Hilversum after reaching qf Monte Carlo in his 1st ever primary circuit tourn (d. Rosset after qualifying), and following with the same stage San Marino, where he won the doubles with Kulti. **1993:** (428) Suffered an injury to his left foot in Jan. and was out until July, playing only 6 tourns all year. **1994:** (149) A –, F 4, W –, US –. He sprang to prominence at French Open where, unseeded, he upset Krajicek and gave Sampras a scare in last 16: after being 4–3 up in 4s and 3 points ahead for 5–3, he the match slip away. On the Challenger circuit, he won Weiden singles and 3 doubles titles. **1995:** (113) A –, F 2, W –, US –. Out of action until April with knee problems and played mostly on the satellite circuits. On the main tour, he upset Ivanisevic 1r French Open, after qualifying, and reached qf Stockholm (d. Krajicek) at end of year. **1996:** (47) A qf, F 3, W 3, US 2. Once again he made an impact in GS: at Australian Open, unseeded, he upset Muster to reach qf, and he ended Edberg's Wimbledon career 2r. In other tourns he reached qf Jakarta, Copenhagen, St Petersburg and Basel, surprised Berasategui at Oporto and Ivanisevic at Toronto. He moved swiftly up the rankings, cracking the top 100 in Jan. and top 50 in April. **1997:** A 1, F 1, W 1, US –. His 1st tour singles title came at Chennai, and he also reached sf Adelaide (d. Kafelnikov) and Singapore, as well as upsetting Siemerink at Sydney and Moya at LIPC. In doubles he won Bastad with Kulti and Indianapolis with Tebbutt. **1997 HIGHLIGHTS – SINGLES: Australian Open 1r** (lost Kuerten 7–5 7–6 3–6 6–4), **French Open 1r** (lost W. Ferreira [seed 13] 6–7 7–6 6–7 6–3 6–1), **Wimbledon 1r** (lost Sampras [seed 1] 6–4 6–4 6–2); **won** Chennai (d. El Sawy 5–7 7–5 6–4, Delaitre 6–1 3–6 6–0, Stark 7–5 6–3, Pavel 6–3 6–3, Radulescu 6–4 4–6 7–5); **sf** Adelaide (d. Kafelnikov 6–2 6–2, B. Black w.o., Cherkasov 6–2 6–4, lost Woodbridge 6–7 7–6 6–3), **sf** Singapore (d. Woodforde 6–4 6–4, Stafford 7–6 6–4, Damm 7–6 6–1, lost Kiefer 6–7 6–3 6–3). **1997 HIGHLIGHTS – DOUBLES:** (with Kulti) **won** Bastad (d. Gustafsson/Larsson 6–0 6–3), (with Tebbutt) **won** Indianapolis (d. Bjorkman/Kulti 6–3 6–2). **CAREER HIGHLIGHTS – SINGLES: Australian Open – qf 1996** [unseeded] (d. Krickstein 6–4 6–4 1–6 5–7 6–2, Ruud 6–3 3–6 6–4 4–6 6–4, McEnroe 1–6 6–4 7–6 6–3, Muster [seed 3] 7–5 4–6 6–3 6–2, lost M. Chang [seed 5] 6–0 6–2 6–4).

JAMES TROTMAN (GBR)

Born Ipswich, 16 February 1979; lives Bisham Abbey; RH; 2HB; 6ft; 154lb; career singles titles 0; final 1997 ATP ranking doubles 1313; 1997 prize money $3,241.

Coached by Ian Barclay. Restricted for 2 years with stress fractures of both feet and glandular fever from Jan. 1995. Ranked No. 1 in Nat 16s. **1995:** Delighted home crowds by winning Wimbledon Jun doubles with Lee. **1997:** Won Australian Open Jun doubles with Sherwood.

BOHDAN ULIHRACH (CZE)

Born Kolin, 23 February 1975; lives Prague and Monte Carlo, Monaco; RH; 6ft 2in; 170lb; turned pro 1993; career singles titles 2; final 1997 ATP ranking 34; 1997 prize money $526,454 ($1,320,209).

1992: 1098. **1993:** (462). **1994:** (150) Made his mark on the Challenger circuit, winning Oberstaufen. **1995:** (28) A –, F 2, W 1, US 2. Never before having reached qf on main tour, he was r/u St Polten, then in Aug. won his 1st title at Prague, breaking into top 50, and followed in Nov. with Montevideo, where he upset Berasategui in f. He also won Birmingham Challenger, reached qf Amsterdam and upset Kafelnikov at Ostrava. **1996:** (41) A 2, F 3, W 3, US 2. In another solid year he was r/u Prague and reached sf Bologna, Gstaad (d. Pioline) and Indianapolis, as well as upsetting Becker at Milan and A. Costa at US Open. **1997:** A 1, F 2, W –, US 2. At Indian Wells, unseeded, he upset Sampras in ss 2r and took a set off M. Chang in f. He reached the same stage Prague, plus qf Vienna (d. Kuerten) and Ostrava (d. Rosset), and upset Moya at Monte Carlo. **1997 HIGHLIGHTS – SINGLES: Australian Open 1r** (lost Bjorkman 1–6 6–1 6–4 6–2), **French Open 2r** (d. Kiefer 6–3 6–3 6–3, lost Krajicek [seed 6] 6–2 3–6 6–2 6–3), **US Open 2r** (d. Rake 6–2 6–3 6–2, lost Corretja 7–5 6–4 3–6 6–4); **won** Prostejov Challenger (d. Meligeni 6–2 4–6 6–1); **r/u** Indian Wells (d. Gumy 4–6 6–1 6–0, Sampras 7–6 7–5, Clavet 7–5 7–6, B. Black 6–4 6–2, Bjorkman 6–3 6–2, lost M. Chang 4–6 6–3 6–4 6–3), **r/u** Prague (d. Squillari 6–0 6–3, Blanco 6–4 6–0, Portas 2–6 6–4 6–4, Santoro 6–4 6–2, lost Pioline 6–2 5–7 7–6).

DANIEL VACEK (CZE)

Born Prague, 1 April 1971; lives Bradenton, Fla.; RH; 6ft 3in; 179lb; turned pro 1990; career singles titles 0; final 1997 ATP ranking 53 singles, 5 doubles; 1997 prize money $786,605 ($3,146,367).

Coached by Vojtech Flegl; trains at Nick Bollettieri's Academy. **1989:** (711). **1990:** (607) Won doubles titles at Umag, Prague and San Marino. **1991:** (464) A 1, F –, W –, US –. Reached 2 doubles f with different partners. **1992:** (113) A –, F –, W –, US –. Won Caracas and Munich Challengers. **1993:** (113) A 2, F 1, W 1, US 2. Upset Edberg in ss at New Haven and won the doubles there with Suk. **1994:** (46) A 3, F 3, W 4, US 2. In March he reached his 1st tour f at Copenhagen, then surprised Kafelnikov at Wimbledon, where he was unseeded. He also upset Muster twice in reaching qf Sydney NSW Open and Moscow and won Rennes Challenger. In doubles he played 4 f, winning Marseille with Siemerink and Toulouse with Oosting. **1995:** (27) A 1, F 2, W 1, US 4. Upset Kafelnikov on his way to f both Marseille and Moscow (where he also beat Volkov), removed Bruguera at US Open, where he was unseeded, and surprised M. Chang at Essen, as well as reaching qf Toulouse and Paris Open. In doubles he played 7 f with Suk, winning 4 and qualifying for World Doubles Champ, where they reached sf before losing to Eltingh/Haarhuis. **1996:** (72) A 1, F 1, W 1, US 1. In singles he reached sf Halle, plus qf Adelaide, Milan (d. Krajicek), St Petersburg, Prague and New Haven (d. Rios). Formed an effective doubles partnership with Kafelnikov, winning French Open and 3 other titles from 6 f to qualify for World Doubles Champ. However, with Kafelnikov qualifying also for ATP Champs in Hannover the following week, they did not take up their place. **1997:** A 1, F 1, W 1, US 4. Upset Siemerink and Ivanisevic *en route* to f Rotterdam, played qf Milan and Moscow, and removed Philippoussis at US Open, where he was unseeded. From 6 doubles f with 3 different partners, he won French Open, US Open and Gstaad with Kafelnikov, with whom he qualified for World Doubles Champ, plus Hong Kong and Tokyo Japan Open with Damm. With Kafelnikov injured after a gruelling week at ATP Champs, once again they did not take up their place at World Doubles Champ. **1997 HIGHLIGHTS – SINGLES: Australian Open 1r** (lost Carbonell 6–2 7–6 7–5), **French Open 1r** (lost Woodruff 6–4 6–2 6–3), **Wimbledon 1r** (lost Rikl 6–1 6–3 6–3), **US Open last 16** [unseeded] (d. Tieleman 4–6 6–4 1–6 6–3 6–2, Sell 4–6 7–6 6–1 6–2, Philippoussis [seed 14] 7–6 7–5 6–2, lost Rusedski 7–6 6–2 6–2); **r/u** Rotterdam (d. Siemerink 7–6 7–6, Van Scheppingen 7–6 4–6 6–1, Furlan 6–4 1–6 6–3, Ivanisevic 6–4 1–6 7–6, lost Krajicek 7–6 7–6). **1997 HIGHLIGHTS – DOUBLES:** (with Kafelnikov unless stated) **won French Open** (d. Woodbridge/Woodforde 7–6 4–6 6–3), **won US Open** (d. Bjorkman/Kulti 7–6 6–3); (with Damm) **won** Hong Kong (d. Braasch/Tarango 6–3 6–4), (with Damm) **won** Tokyo Japan Open (d. Gimelstob/Rafter 2–6 6–2 7–6), **won** Gstaad (d. Kronemann/Macpherson 4–6 7–6 6–3); (with Prinosil) **r/u** St Petersburg (lost Olhovskiy/Steven 6–4 6–3). **CAREER HIGHLIGHTS – DOUBLES:** (with Kafelnikov) **French Open – won 1996** (d. Forget/Hlasek 6–2 6–3), **won 1997; US Open – won 1997**.

JOHAN VAN HERCK (BEL)

Born Herentals, 24 May 1974; lives Herentmout; RH; 6ft 1in; 165lb; turned pro 1993; career singles titles 0; final 1997 ATP ranking 67; 1997 prize money $190,821.

Coached by Koen Gonnissen. **1991:** (1115). **1992:** (818). **1993:** (218) Won Spanish satellite event. **1994:** (167) Began to make his presence known on the Challenger circuit. **1995:** (107) A –, F 2, W –, US 1. Broke into top 100 1st time after winning 3 Challenger titles, 2 back-to-back in July. Made his D Cup debut, winning BEL's only point when he beat Kafelnikov in dead rubber. **1996:** (91) A 1, F 1, W 1, US –. A week after winning Stockholm Challenger, he reached his 1st sf on the main tour at Copenhagen, upset Mantilla to reach same stage Palermo, and played qf Oporto. **1997:** A 1, F 1, W 1, US 2. He reached sf Coral Springs and qf Boston on the main tour, and added 3 Challenger titles. **1997 HIGHLIGHTS – SINGLES: Australian Open 1r** (lost Tramacchi 6–7 6–3 6–4 3–2), **French Open 1r** (lost Bruguera [seed 16] 6–3 0–6 6–2 6–0), **Wimbledon 1r** (lost Sargsian 7–6 6–2 6–4), **US Open 2r** (d. Dewulf 6–4 4–6 7–6 7–6, lost Van Lottum 6–3 6–4 6–4); **won** Bermuda Challenger (d. Sargsian 6–1 4–6 6–0), **won** Birmingham Challenger (d. Haas 7–6 6–7 6–4), **won** Brest Challenger (d. Grosjean 4–6 6–2 6–4); **sf** Coral Springs (d. Delgado 7–6 6–3, Stolle 6–3 4–6 6–3, Woodforde 3–6 6–2 6–3, lost Stoltenberg 6–3 6–3).

JUAN ALBERT VILOCA (ESP)

Born Barcelona, 17 January 1973, and lives there; RH; 6ft 1in; 175lb; turned pro 1992; career singles titles 0; final 1997 ATP ranking 73; 1997 prize money $237,375.

Coached by Pato Alvarez. **1991:** (601). **1992:** (379). **1993:** (334) Began to make his mark on the Challenger circuit. **1994:** (168) Reached his 1st qf on the main tour at Buenos Aires. **1995:** (220) A –, F –, W –, US 1. **1996:** (83) A –, F –, W –, US –. A qualifier at Kitzbuhel, he upset Rios on the way to his 1st main tour sf, and on the Challenger circuit won 3 titles. **1997:** A 1, F 2, W 2, US 1. Broke into top 50 after reaching his 1st f at Gstaad, following with the same stage Mexico City, and also reached qf Coral Springs. **1997 HIGHLIGHTS – SINGLES: Australian Open 1r** (lost Larsson 6–3 6–3 7–6), **French Open 2r** (d. Ruud 5–7 6–4 6–1 4–1 ret'd, lost Medvedev 6–4 6–3 6–4), **Wimbledon 2r** (d. Goellner 7–5 4–6 7–6 7–6, lost Richardson 6–3 3–6 6–4 2–6 6–2), **US Open 1r** (lost Steven 4–6 6–2 6–1 6–2); **r/u** Gstaad (d. Heuberger 6–3 6–4, Rios 6–3 7–6, Kiefer 6–4 6–3, Corretja 3–6 7–6 6–4, lost Mantilla 6–1 6–4 6–4), **r/u** Mexico City (d. Vasek 1–6 6–1 6–4, C. Costa 6–4 6–3, Marin 6–4 6–2, Meligeni 6–3 6–1, lost Clavet 6–4 7–6).

WESTLEY WHITEHOUSE (RSA)

Born Empangeni, 13 March 1979; lives Pretoria; LH; 2HB; 6ft 5in; 172lb; career singles titles 0; final 1997 ATP ranking 650; Junior ranking 3.

Coached by Gerrie Dippenaar. **1996:** Won African Jun Champs. **1997:** Won Wimbledon Jun over Elsner (thus denying him all 4 Jun GS titles at once), was r/u to the same player at Australian Open and r/u US Open to Di Pasquale.

TODD WOODBRIDGE (AUS)

Born Sydney, 2 April 1971; lives there and Orlando, Fla; RH; 5ft 10in; 158lb; turned pro 1988; career singles titles 2; final 1997 ATP ranking 26 singles, 1 doubles; 1997 prize money $1,335,918 ($6,169,747).

Coached by Ray Ruffels. Wife Natasha Provis (sister of Nicole Bradtke who plays women's tour; married 8 April 1995). **1987:** (420) R/u Australian Open Jun to Stoltenberg, with whom he won the doubles there and at Wimbledon, and in winning AUS World Youth Cup team for 2nd straight year. **1988:** (213) A 2, F 1, W 1, US –. Won Tasmania and in Jun doubles with Stoltenberg won Australian Open, French Open and Wimbledon. **1989:** (131) A 2, F –, W 2, US –. Won Brisbane Challenger, upset Fitzgerald *en route* to sf GP event there and finished the year by winning Hobart Challenger. In Jun doubles won Australian and French Open with J. Anderson and in Jun singles was r/u Wimbledon to Kulti. **1990:** (50) A 2, F 2, W 1, US 1. Upset Chang on the way to his 1st tour f at New Haven and Gilbert *en route* to sf Sydney Indoor. In doubles with various partners he reached 4 f, winning 2, and took US Open mixed with Smylie. **1991:** (77) A 4, F 2, W 3, US 3. Upset Svensson at Australian Open, where he was unseeded, and at French Open extended Becker to 5s. In doubles won 6 titles, 4 with Woodforde, with whom he qualified for ATP Doubles Champ. **1992:** (54) A 1, F 3, W 2, US 2. R/u Seoul (d. Chang), sf Hong Kong, qf Tokyo Suntory and upset Stich at Sydney NSW Open. In doubles with Woodforde won a 1st men's GS title at Australian Open, World Doubles Final and 6 other titles, winning every f they played to finish the year as the top-ranked pairing and were voted ATP Doubles Team of year. In mixed doubles with Sanchez Vicario won French Open and r/u Australian Open. **1993:** (107) A 3, F 2, W 2, US 2. Was r/u Seoul and reached qf Tokyo Japan Open (d. M. Chang) in singles and continued to excel in doubles. Won his 1st Wimbledon and 4 other titles with Woodforde, took Hong Kong with Wheaton and qualified for ATP World Doubles with Woodforde. They were beaten there in f by Eltingh/Haarhuis, thus ending their record of having won all 17 finals they played since Feb. 1991, equalling McEnroe/Fleming's string in 1979–80. This defeat also ended Woodbridge's personal sequence of winning 21 consec. doubles f, which overtook J. McEnroe's record of 19. Their year ended on another disappointing note when they lost their match in 4–1 D Cup defeat by GER. In mixed doubles he won Australian Open with Sanchez Vicario and US Open with Sukova. **1994:** (91) A 2, F –, W –, US 3. In singles he was r/u Newport, reached sf Kuala Lumpur and won Wellington Challenger. His year began badly, with a slide down the singles rankings and a lacklustre performance in doubles with Woodforde, notably when they were defeated in D Cup 1r v RUS as AUS were eliminated. However, they regained form to win Wimbledon and finished the year with a total of 5 titles and r/u US Open to qualify for World Doubles Champ where they were r/u. In mixed doubles with Sukova he won Wimbledon and was r/u Australian Open. **1995:** (34) A 1, F 2, W 3, US 3. Won his 1st tour singles title at Coral Springs, where he also took the doubles; was r/u Nottingham and reached sf Vienna, plus 3 more qf. In doubles with Woodforde he won a 3rd Wimbledon, 1st US Open and 5 other titles to qualify for World Doubles Champ, where they lost sf to Connell/Galbraith, although they retained their position as top-ranked pairing and were named Doubles Team of the Year. **1996:** (36) A 3, F 3, W 2, US 1. In singles he was r/u Toronto (d. Rios), reached sf Sydney, Philadelphia, Hong Kong (d. Krajicek) and Nottingham, and upset Siemerink at Olympics, breaking into top 25 in March. He enjoyed another spectacular year in doubles with Woodforde, with whom he was named Doubles Team of the Year again. Despite missing that elusive 1st French Open, they won a 4th consec. Wimbledon, and after winning US Open, they tied with Newcombe/Roche and Fleming/J. McEnroe on a record 7 GS titles as a pairing. They crowned their year with Olympic gold, surviving some close matches along the way and playing an Olympic record 34-game 3rd set v Goellner/Prinosil. Their record of 12 titles from 13 f during the year was the most since Fleming/McEnroe's 15 in 1979 and included a 2nd World Doubles Champ. **1997:** A 3, F 2, W sf, US 2. A good year in singles brought him a 2nd career title at Adelaide, r/u Memphis, sf Wimbledon and qf Hong Kong and Tokyo Japan Open, with an upset of Moya at Paris Open. Wimbledon saw him in superb form as he upset M. Chang (8–6 fs) and Rafter in the singles, unseeded, and won the doubles with Woodforde. They were again the season's top doubles pairing, overtaking Fleming/McEnroe and Newcombe/Roche when they won their 8th GS title at Australian Open. A 1st French Open title still eluded them, despite their 1st f there, but their 5th consec. Wimbledon equalled the record of the Dohertys in 1987–1901 and their 9th GS title as a pairing was a record in the open era. With 5 titles across the year, they overtook Casal/E. Sanchez on the all-time list and finished the year with 50 titles, in 3rd place behind Fleming/McEnroe and Hewitt/McMillan on 57. At World Doubles Champ, they needed only to win 1s v Leach/Stark in their last rr match to qualify for sf, but lost in ss. However, they were still clearly the season's top doubles team. **1997 HIGHLIGHTS – SINGLES: Australian Open 3r** (d. Knowles 6–4 6–2 6–1, Simian 6–3 6–3 7–6, lost MaliVai Washington 4–6 6–2 6–3 6–1), **French Open 2r** (d. Carlsen 7–6 4–6 6–4 6–0, lost Arazi 6–4 7–5 6–2), **Wimbledon sf** [unseeded] (d. M. Chang [seed 5] 7–6 3–6 6–2 3–6 8–6, Ondruska 7–5 6–1 7–6, Radulescu 6–4 6–4 6–4, Rafter [seed 12] 6–7 6–4 7–6 6–3, Kiefer 7–6 2–6 6–0 6–4, lost Sampras [seed 1] 6–2 6–1 7–6), **US Open 2r** (d. Marin 7–6 6–3 4–6 6–1, lost Gumy 7–5 6–4 6–2); **won** Adelaide (d. Vacek 4–6 6–3 6–3, Novak 6–3 7–6, O'Brien 6–4 6–4, Tillstrom 6–7 7–6 6–3, Draper 6–2 6–1); **r/u** Memphis (d. Lareau 6–4 7–6, M. Norman 7–5 6–3, Taranto 6–3 6–1, Bjorkman 6–1 7–5, lost M. Chang 6–3 6–4). **1997 HIGHLIGHTS – DOUBLES:** (with Woodforde) **won Australian Open** (d. Lareau/O'Brien 4–6 7–5 7–5 6–3), **r/u French Open** (lost Kafelnikov/Vacek 7–6 4–6 6–3), **won Wimbledon** (d. Eltingh/Haarhuis 7–6 7–6 5–7 6–3); **won** LIPC (d. Knowles/Nestor 7–6 7–6), **won** Cincinnati (d. Philippoussis/Rafter 7–6 4–6 6–4), **won** Stuttgart Eurocard (d. Leach/Stark 6–3 6–3); **r/u** Adelaide (lost Rafter/Shelton 6–4 1–6 6–3). **CAREER HIGHLIGHTS – DOUBLES:** (with Woodforde) **Australian Open – won 1992** (d. Jones/Leach 6–4 6–3 6–4), **won 1997**; **Wimbledon – won 1993** (d. Connell/Galbraith 6–3 6–4 6–4), **won 1994** (d. Connell/Galbraith 7–6 6–3 6–1), **won 1995** (d. Leach/Melville 7–5 7–6 7–6), **won 1996** (d. B. Black/ Connell 4–6 6–4 6–3 6–2), **won 1997**; **US Open – won 1995** (d. O'Brien/Stolle 6–3 6–3), **won 1996** (d. Eltingh/Haarhuis 4–6 7–6 7–6), **r/u 1994** (lost Eltingh/Haarhuis 6–3 7–6); **Olympics – won 1996** (d. Broad/Henman 6–4 6–4 6–2); **World Doubles Final – won 1992** (d. Fitzgerald/Jarryd 6–2 7–6 5–7 3–6 6–3), **won 1996** (d. Lareau/O'Brien 6–4 5–7 6–2 7–6), **r/u 1993** (lost Eltingh/Haarhuis 7–6 7–6 6–4), **r/u 1994** (lost Apell/Bjorkman 6–4 4–6 4–6 7–6 7–6); **French Open – r/u 1997. CAREER HIGHLIGHTS – MIXED DOUBLES:** (with Sanchez Vicario unless stated) **Australian Open – won 1993** (d. Leach/Garrison-Jackson 7–5 6–4); **French Open – won 1992** (d. Shelton/McNeil 6–2 6–3); **Wimbledon** – (with Sukova) **won 1994** (d. Middleton/McNeil 3–6 7–5 6–3); **US Open** – (with Smylie) **won 1990** (d. Pugh/Zvereva 6–4 6–2), (with Sukova) **won 1993** (d. Woodforde/Navratilova 7–5 6–3).

MARK WOODFORDE (AUS)

Born Adelaide, 23 September 1965; lives there and Monte Carlo, Monaco; LH; 2HB; 6ft 1½in; 172lb; turned pro 1984; career singles titles 4; final 1997 ATP ranking 46 singles, 2 doubles; 1997 prize money $1,166,627 ($6,727,181).

Coached by Ray Ruffels; trained by Mark Waters. **1984:** (385). **1985:** (127) A 3, F –, W –, US –. **1986:** (181) A –, F 1, W 1, US 1. Won 1st pro title at Auckland and reached sf Bristol. **1987:** (67) A 2, F –, W 2, US 4. Upset Mayotte on his way to last 16 US Open after qualifying. **1988:** (42) A 2, F 2, W 4, US 4. Enjoyed a remarkable year, with success on all surfaces, in which he extended Lendl to 5 close sets in 4 hr 46 min match at Wimbledon, conceding only 10–8 in 5s, upset Edberg and J. McEnroe to reach sf Toronto and beat McEnroe again at US Open, where he was unseeded. Formed a useful doubles partnership with J. McEnroe in autumn. **1989:** (75) A 3, F 3, W 1, US 2. In singles won Adelaide and r/u Brisbane. In doubles won US Open with J. McEnroe and Monte Carlo with Smid. **1990:** (101) A 3, F –, W 4, US –. Upset Chesnokov 2r Australian Open, but was forced to retire in 3r v Wheaton when he tore 2 ligaments in his ankle, requiring surgery. Out of action until June, when he progressed to last 16 Wimbledon, unseeded and a wild card, and in Aug. reached sf New Haven. **1991:** (101) A 4, F 1, W 1, US 1. Upset E. Sanchez at Australian Open (unseeded), Chesnokov in reaching qf Copenhagen and Korda 1r Moscow. Won 4 doubles titles with Woodbridge to qualify for ATP Doubles Champ. **1992:** (40) A 3, F 1, W 2, US 3. In singles he was r/u Los Angeles and Antwerp (d. Lendl and Chang) and reached qf Singapore, Tampa and US CC. With Woodbridge took Australian Open doubles, World Doubles Final and 6 other titles, winning every f they played to finish the year as the top pairing and voted ATP Doubles Team of year. In mixed doubles with Provis, he won Australian Open and US Open. **1993:** (28) A 2, F 3, W 2, US 1. Won Philadelphia singles, beating Clavet and M. Chang on his way to f, where Lendl was forced to retire, and followed with an upset of Washington *en route* to sf Scottsdale. He also appeared in qf Sydney (d. Medvedev), LIPC (d. Courier), New Haven and Paris Open and broke into the top 25. At Wimbledon he won a 2nd men's doubles GS title with Woodbridge and took mixed with Navratilova. After Stockholm he and Woodbridge had won all 17 finals they played since Feb. 1991, equalling McEnroe/Fleming's string in 1979–80, but their run was ended by Eltingh/Haarhuis in f ATP World Doubles. Further disappointment followed when they lost in D Cup f as GER beat AUS 4–1. **1994:** (43) A 1, F 3, W 2, US 1. Upset Krajicek *en route* to f Los Angeles, Costa at LIPC, Lendl on his way to sf Coral Springs, Muster at Cincinnati, Ivanisevic at Indianapolis, and Courier at Paris Open, as well as reaching sf Pinehurst and Sydney Indoor. In doubles he and Woodbridge made a poor start to the year with failure again in D Cup as AUS lost to RUS, but they went on to win Wimbledon and r/u US Open. With various partners, he won 7 titles from 10 f, qualifying with Woodbridge for World Doubles Champ, where they were r/u. **1995:** (51) A 3, F 2, W 3, US 2. In singles he reached sf Adelaide (d. Kafelnikov), Coral Springs and Nottingham, played 3 more qf and upset Courier at LIPC. In doubles with Woodbridge he won Wimbledon, US Open and 5 other titles to qualify for World Doubles Champ, where they lost sf to Connell/Galbraith, although they still finished the year as top-ranked pairing and were named Doubles Team of the Year. When he won French Open mixed with Neiland, he had won a mixed title at all 4 GS tourns. **1996:** (27) A sf, F 1, W 1, US 1. The highlight of his singles year came at Australian Open where, unseeded, he took advantage of Sampras's removal from his half of the draw to sweep to sf, upsetting Enqvist on the way. He reached the same stage Philadelphia, Tokyo Japan Open (d. Enqvist again) and Toulouse, plus qf Sydney, Memphis and Queen's and made a 1st appearance in the top 20 on 22 April. In doubles with Woodbridge won a record 4th consec. Wimbledon and, after winning US Open, they tied with Newcombe/Roche and Fleming/J. McEnroe on a record 7 GS titles as a pairing. They also won Olympic gold, surviving some close matches along the way and playing an Olympic record 34-game 3rd set v Goellner/Prinosil. They finished a superb season with the World Doubles title, taking to 12 their titles from 13 f during the year – the most since Fleming/McEnroe's 15 in 1979 – and were voted Doubles Team of the Year again. In mixed doubles with Neiland he won Australian Open (where he and Woodbridge were surprisingly beaten 1r) and was r/u Wimbledon. **1997:** A 3, F 4, W 4, US 3. Although it was a quieter year in singles, he reached sf Indianapolis (d. Rios and Agassi), qf Tokyo Japan Open (d. Rosset), Coral Springs and Newport, as well as upsetting A. Costa at French Open and Kafelnikov at US Open. He and Woodbridge were again the season's top duo with 5 titles across the year, which took them to 50, ahead of Casal/E. Sanchez and into 3rd place on the all-time list behind Fleming/McEnroe and Hewitt/McMillan on 57. Their 8th GS title at Australian Open took them ahead of Fleming/McEnroe and Newcombe/Roche in GS titles, and their 5th consec. Wimbledon, equalled the record of the Dohertys in 1987–1901. This 9th GS title as a pairing was a record in the open era, but they were still unable to add an elusive 1st French Open title, despite reaching f there 1st time. At World Doubles Champ they needed only to take a set off Leach/Stark in their last rr match to qualify for sf, but they were beaten in ss. However, they still finished the season head and shoulders above any other pairing. **1997 HIGHLIGHTS – SINGLES: Australian Open 3r** (d. Tebbutt 6–4 6–4 7–5, Gumy 6–0 6–1 7–5, lost Sampras [seed 1] 6–1 6–0 6–1), **French Open last 16** [unseeded] (d. J. Sanchez 5–7 7–6 6–7 6–4 8–6, Volkov 7–6 6–3 7–5, A. Costa [seed 11] 6–4 7–6 6–3, lost Rafter 6–2 5–7 6–1 6–2), **Wimbledon last 16** [unseeded] (d. Paes 6–3 7–5 6–4, Wilkinson 5–7 5–7 6–2 6–4 6–1, Clement 6–2 6–3 6–3, lost Stich 6–4 6–7 6–3 7–5), **US Open 3r** (d. B. Black 7–6 6–3 6–2, Kafelnikov [seed 3] 6–3 6–4 7–6, lost Agassi 6–2 6–2 6–4); **sf** Indianapolis (d. Van Herck 6–1 6–2, Woodruff 6–3 6–3, Rios 7–6 6–4, Agassi 6–3 5–7 6–3, lost Bjorkman 6–0 6–2). **1997 HIGHLIGHTS – DOUBLES:** (with Woodbridge) **won Australian Open** (d. Lareau/O'Brien 4–6 7–5 7–5 6–3), **r/u French Open** (lost Kafelnikov/Vacek 7–6 4–6 6–3), **won Wimbledon** (d. Eltingh/Haarhuis 7–6 7–6 5–7 6–3); **won** LIPC (d. Knowles/Nestor 7–6 7–6), **won** Cincinnati (d. Philippoussis/Rafter 7–6 4–6 6–4), **won** Stuttgart Eurocard (d. Leach/Stark 6–3 6–3); **r/u** Adelaide (lost Rafter/Shelton 6–4 1–6 6–3). **CAREER HIGHLIGHTS – SINGLES: Australian Open – sf 1996** [unseeded] (d. Matsuoka 2–1 ret'd, Sinner 6–4 6–1 6–4, Clavet 4–6 7–6 6–2 6–4, Philippoussis 6–2 6–2 6–2, Enqvist 6–4 6–4 6–4, lost Becker 6–4 6–2 6–0), **CAREER HIGHLIGHTS – DOUBLES:** (with Woodbridge unless stated) **Australian Open – won 1992** (d. Jones/Leach 6–4 6–3 6–4), **won 1997**; **Wimbledon – won 1993** (d. Connell/Galbraith 6–3 6–4 6–4), **won 1994** (d. Connell/Galbraith 7–6 6–3 6–1), **won 1995** (d. Leach/Melville 7–5 7–6 7–6), **won 1996** (d. B. Black/Connell 4–6 6–4 6–3 6–2), **won 1997**; **US Open** – (with J. McEnroe) **won 1989** (d. Flach/Seguso 6–4 4–6 6–3 6–3), **won 1995** (d. O'Brien/Stolle 6–3 6–3), **won 1996** (d. Eltingh/Haarhuis 4–6 7–6 7–6), **r/u 1994** (lost Eltingh/Haarhuis 6–3 7–6); **Olympics – won 1996** (d. Broad/Henman 6–4 6–4 6–2); **World Doubles Final – won 1992** (d. Fitzgerald/Jarryd 6–2 7–6 5–7 3–6 6–3), **won 1996** , **r/u 1993** (lost Eltingh/Haarhuis 7–6 7–6 6–4), **r/u 1994** (lost Apell/Bjorkman 6–4 4–6 4–6 7–6 7–6); **French Open – r/u 1997**. **CAREER HIGHLIGHTS – MIXED DOUBLES:** (with Provis unless stated) **Australian Open – won 1992** (d. Woodbridge/Sanchez Vicario 6–3 4–6 11–9), (with Neiland) **won 1996** (d. L. Jensen/Arendt 4–6 7–5 6–0); **French Open** – (with Neiland) **won 1995** (d. de Jager/Hetherington 7–6 7–6); **Wimbledon** – (with Navratilova) **won 1993** (d. Nijssen/Bollegraf 6–3 6–4); **US Open – won 1992** (d. Nijssen/Sukova 4–6 6–3 6–3).

CHRIS WOODRUFF (USA)

Born Knoxville, Tenn., 2 January 1973, and lives there; RH; 6ft 2in; 170lb; turned pro 1993; career singles titles 1; final 1997 ATP ranking 30; 1997 prize money $631,646 ($1,038,384).
Coached by Scott Perelman. **1993:** (335) A –, F –, W –, US 1. An All-American in singles and doubles, he won NCAA Champ as a sophomore at Univ. of Tenn. **1994:** (310) A –, F –, W –, US –. Began to play the satellite circuits. **1995:** (135) A –, F –, W –, US 1. Won Aruba Challenger in singles and Lexington in doubles. However, depressed at his lack of progress, he nearly quit in summer, before his father, coach and sports psychologist persuaded him to continue. **1996:** (43) A –, F 3, W 1, US 1. His perseverance paid off as he broke into the top 100 in March and was in top 50 by autumn. After winning Heilbronn Challenger, he went on to reach f Philadelphia (d. Rios, after qualifying for his 1st senior tour event) and Coral Springs. Then at French Open, he recovered from 2 sets to 1 down to remove Agassi 2r French Open and upset Muster 1r Lyon. **1997:** A 3, F 3, W 1, US 2. His 1st title came in style at Montreal, with back-to-back upsets of Ivanisevic, Philippoussis, Kafelnikov and Kuerten. In other tourns he reached sf Scottsdale (d. Moya), Orlando, Atlanta, qf San Jose and upset Enqvist at Indian Wells. **1997 HIGHLIGHTS – SINGLES: Australian Open 3r** (d. M. Norman 6–4 6–1 6–1, Novak 6–2 7–6 6–2, lost Ivanisevic [seed 3] 6–3 6–7 6–3 6–1), **French Open 3r** (d. Vacek 6–4 6–2 6–3, Lapentti 6–4 5–7 3–6 6–4 6–1, lost Blanco 7–6 6–3 7–6), **Wimbledon 1r** (lost Stolle 6–2 6–2 6–4), **US Open 2r** (d. Johansson 6–3 6–0 3–6 6–0, lost Sargsian w.o.); **won** Montreal (d. Robichaud 7–6 6–3, Siemerink 6–7 7–5 7–6, Ivanisevic 7–6 6–2, Philippoussis 6–4 6–4, Kafelnikov 5–7 7–5 6–3, Kuerten 7–5 4–6 6–3); **sf** Scottsdale (d. Tarango 7–6 6–2, J. Sanchez 4–6 6–3 7–6, Moya 7–6 5–7 6–3, lost Philippoussis 4–6 7–6 6–2), **sf** Orlando (d. Frana 4–6 6–4 6–4, Gross 7–5 7–6, O'Brien 6–4 6–7 6–4, lost Stafford 6–3 4–6 6–4), **sf** Atlanta (d. Carlsen 6–2 6–2, Frana 7–6 6–2, Stolle 6–1 4–6 6–3, lost Filippini 7–5 3–6 6–4).

When she won the French Open junior title aged 12 and became the Wimbledon junior champion a year later, it was obvious that Martina Hingis had enormous potential. In 1997 the remarkable Swiss teenager fulfilled that potential by winning three Grand Slam titles and becoming the youngest world No. 1 since the rankings began. (Michael Cole)

1 MARTINA HINGIS (SUI)

Born: Kosice, Czechoslovakia, 30 September 1980.
Lives: Trubbach (moved to Switzerland at age 7).
Father: Karol. **Mother:** Melanie Molitor, a former Czech champion, who named her daughter after Martina Navratilova.
Agent: IMG. **Coach:** Her mother, Melanie Molitor.
Turned pro: 1994.
Height: 5ft 6in (1.67m). **Weight:** 115lb (52kg).

Rankings: 1994: 87; **1995:** 16; **1996:** 4. **1997:** 1.
Highest: 1 (31 March 1997).

1997 Prize Money: $3,400,196.
Career Earnings: $4,948,617. **Career Titles:** 14.

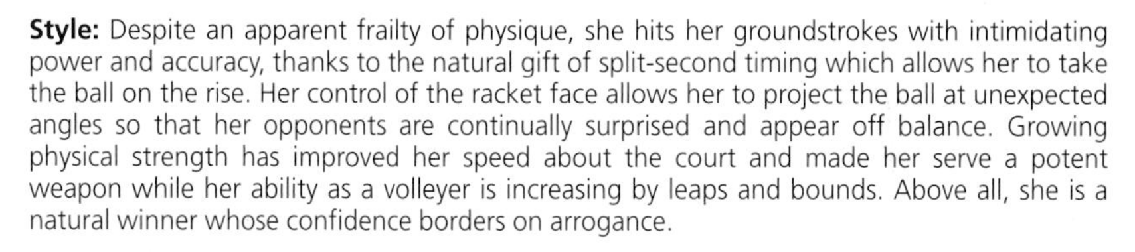

Style: Despite an apparent frailty of physique, she hits her groundstrokes with intimidating power and accuracy, thanks to the natural gift of split-second timing which allows her to take the ball on the rise. Her control of the racket face allows her to project the ball at unexpected angles so that her opponents are continually surprised and appear off balance. Growing physical strength has improved her speed about the court and made her serve a potent weapon while her ability as a volleyer is increasing by leaps and bounds. Above all, she is a natural winner whose confidence borders on arrogance.

CAREER HIGHLIGHTS (year: (titles))
1993: Won French Open Jun over Courtois, becoming, at age 12, the youngest to win a Jun GS title. Won the title at Langentha in her 1st Futures event. **1994:** Ranked No. 1 in ITF Jun singles after she won French Open over Jeyaseelan and Wimbledon over Jeon (becoming the youngest Jun champ there at 13 years 276 days), was r/u US Open to Tu and won European Champs; in Jun doubles, she won French Open with Nagyova. Having played 3 satellite events, she made her debut on the senior tour earlier than expected in Oct., in order to beat the new eligibility rules coming into effect in Jan. 1995. She was allowed to play only 3 tourns before returning to her private school. Her 1st appearance was at Zurich, where she beat Fendick (becoming, at 14 years 3 months 17 days, the youngest player to win a singles match in Open era) before losing to Pierce. She followed with qf at both Filderstadt and Essen where she beat Hack. **1995:** In a year in which she was voted Most Impressive Newcomer, she reached her 1st tour f at Hamburg, upsetting Novotna and Huber, surprised M. Maleeva at US Open and broke into top 20 in June, only 8 months after joining the tour. She also reached qf Paris Open (d. Halard) and played 2 doubles f, winning Hamburg with G. Fernandez. When she beat Watanabe at Australian Open, she became the youngest to win a singles match there in the Open era. **1996: (2)** *Filderstadt, Oakland.* At 15 years 3 months 22 days and unseeded, she became the youngest to reach qf Australian Open, upsetting Schultz-McCarthy on the way, and followed in May with one of the major upsets of the year when she removed Graf on her way to f Italian Open. At Wimbledon, aged 15 years 282 days, she became the youngest to win a title there when she and Sukova took the doubles – being 3 days younger than Lottie Dod when she won the singles in 1887 – and was the 1st Swiss woman to win a title at Wimbledon. She broke into the top 10 on 7 Oct., took her 1st title on the main tour at Filderstadt a week later (upsetting Sanchez Vicario, Davenport and Huber back-to-back), and played her next f the week after that, losing in Zurich to Novotna. Her 2nd title came in tremendous style at Oakland, where she upset Seles 6–2 6–0 in f, inflicting the most lop-sided defeat of the former No. 1's career. After qualifying for her 1st Chase Champs in both singles and doubles (with Sukova), she extended Graf to 5s in f, but was virtually immobilised towards the end by cramp and was unable to take advantage of Graf's back and knee injuries. She also reached sf Tokyo Toray (d. Sabatini), following with the same stage at US Open (d. Sanchez Vicario and Novotna) and Chicago (d. Davenport), plus qf Hamburg and the title at Prostejov Futures. At 16 years 1 month and 11 days, she became the youngest player, male or female, to pass $1m in earnings in a season. Voted Most Improved Player of the Year. **1997: (12)** *AUSTRALIAN OPEN, WIMBLEDON, US OPEN, Sydney, Tokyo Pan Pacific, Paris Open, LIPC, FC Cup, Stanford, San Diego, Filderstadt, Philadelphia.* She began a remarkable year in

tremendous style at Australian Open, where she became the youngest GS winner this century, losing no set on her way to the title, and was the 1st to win both singles and doubles there since Navratilova in 1985. On 31 March, she overtook the injured Graf at the top of the rankings, becoming the 7th woman to be ranked No. 1, and the youngest of all, aged 16 years 6 months and 1 day. At LIPC she d. Seles in f in 44 mins, becoming the 1st woman to have earned $1m by end March. She beat Seles again in f FC Cup, coming from 2–5 down in 3s tb having earlier led 5–2 fs. In April she fell from a horse and suffered a slight tear of the posterior cruciate ligament in her left knee, for which she underwent arthroscopic surgery on 21 April. She was back in action at French Open, where Majoli inflicted her 1st defeat of the year in f. She interrupted their match with a 5-minute bathroom break and later incurred a code violation for slamming down her racket. This ended her winning streak of 37 matches, but by end of French Open she had already qualified for Chase Champs. At Wimbledon she became the youngest singles champion there this century and youngest GS singles winner in the Open era. Until Chase Champs, she had failed to reach sf only at Zurich in Oct., when Raymond beat her in qf, and through the year she had been beaten only by Majoli, Davenport, Coetzer and Raymond. However, towards the end of the year, she was showing signs of tiring both physically and mentally, missing Chicago with an injury to her right heel and being extended to 3s in all 4 matches at Philadelphia. At Chase Champs, Schultz-McCarthy stretched her before retiring and Pierce was eventually too much for her, winning their qf 7–5 3s. So Hingis finished an extraordinary year firmly at the top of the rankings, but looking less invincible than she had in the summer. In addition to her singles triumphs, she was also a considerable force in doubles. She had been approached by Navratilova, who suggested that they might play GS doubles together, but she turned down the invitation from her former idol, wanting to pair with someone with whom she could play more often, although in fact she played with 6 different partners in reaching 9 doubles f. She won both singles and doubles at Australian Open (with Zvereva), Paris Open (Novotna), FC Cup (M. J. Fernandez), Stanford (Davenport), plus San Diego and Filderstadt (both with Sanchez Vicario), and also took doubles titles at Leipzig (with Novotna) and Zurich (with Sanchez Vicario). It was with Sanchez Vicario that she qualified for Chase Champs, but they fared little better than she had in the singles, losing 1r to finish the year on a surprisingly downbeat note.

Unquestionably the greatest-ever player for her age, Martina Hingis remains a refeshingly normal teenager who enjoys horse-riding, skateboarding and pop music. (Tommy Hindley)

PRINCIPAL 1997 RESULTS – won 12, r/u 1, sf 2 (detailed Grand Slam results follow)
won Australian Open, **won** Wimbledon, **won** US Open, **won** Sydney (d. Appelmans 6–3 3–6 6–1, Basuki 7–6 6–1, M. J. Fernandez 6–3 6–2, Capriati 6–1 5–7 6–1), **won** Tokyo Pan Pacific (d. Pizzichini 6–1 6–0, Coetzer 6–0 6–1, Huber 6–1 5–7 6–2, Graf def.), **won** Paris Open (d. Farina 6–3 6–4, Tauziat 6–3 6–2, Majoli 6–1 6–3, Huber 6–3 3–6 6–3), **won** LIPC (d. Hy-Boulais 3–6 6–3 6–2, V. Williams 6–4 6–2, Likhovtseva 6–3 2–6 6–3, M. J. Fernandez 6–4 6–1, Novotna 6–3 2–6 6–4, Seles 6–2 6–1), **won** FC Cup (d. Rittner 6–0 6–4, Schett 6–3 6–3, Probst 6–2 6–0, Schultz-McCarthy 5–7 6–3 6–2, Seles 3–6 6–3 7–6), **won** Stanford (d. Maleeva 6–1 6–2, Wild 6–1 6–7 6–3, Davenport 6–3 1–6 6–2, Martinez 6–0 6–2), **won** San Diego (d. V. Williams 6–2 6–1, Martinez 6–4 6–4, Pierce 6–0 6–2, Seles 7–6 6–4), **won** Filderstadt (d. Zvereva 4–6 6–1 6–4, Maleeva 6–2 6–3, Coetzer 6–2 6–1, Raymond 6–4 6–2), **won** Philadelphia (d. Appelmans 6–2 4–6 6–2, Huber 7–6 5–7 6–4, Sanchez Vicario 1–6 7–6 6–3, Davenport 7–5 6–7 7–6); **r/u** French Open; **sf** Los Angeles (d. Sidot 6–2 6–2, Huber 6–3 6–0, lost Davenport 6–2 4–6 6–4), **sf** Leipzig (d. Maruska 6–3 7–5, Appelmans 6–3 6–2, lost Coetzer 6–4 4–6 7–6). **DOUBLES:** (with Sanchez Vicario unless stated) (with Zvereva) **won Australian Open** (d. Davenport/Raymond 6–2 6–2); (with Novotna) **won** Paris Open (d. Fusai/Grande 6–3 6–0), (with M. J. Fernandez) **won** FC Cup (d. Davenport/Novotna 7–5 4–6 6–1), (with Davenport) **won** Stanford (d. Coetzer/Pierce 6–1 6–3), **won** San Diego (d. Frazier/Po 6–3 7–5), (with Novotna) **won** Leipzig (d. Basuki/Sukova 6–2 6–2), **won** Filderstadt (d. Davenport/Novotna 7–6 3–6 7–6), **won** Zurich (d. Neiland/Sukova 4–6 6–4 6–1); (with G. Fernandez) **r/u** Tokyo Pan Pacific (lost Davenport/Zvereva 6–4 6–3).

CAREER GRAND SLAM RECORD

AUSTRALIAN OPEN – Played 3, won 1, qf 1

1995: 2r d. Watanabe 6–0 7–6, lost Nagatsuka 6–3 6–4. **1996: qf** [unseeded] d. Nejedly 6–1 6–1, Paulus 6–1 6–4, Endo 6–1 6–4, Schultz-McCarthy [11] 6–1 6–4, lost Coetzer [16] 7–5 4–6 6–1. **1997: won** [seed 4] d. Rittner 6–1 7–5, Raymond 6–4 6–2, Schett 6–2 6–1, Dragomir 7–6 6–1, Spirlea [8] 7–5 6–2, M. J. Fernandez [14] 6–1 6–3, Pierce 6–2 6–2.

FRENCH OPEN – Played 3, r/u 1

1995: 3r d. Wiesner 2–6 6–3 7–5, de Swardt 6–1 6–7 6–2, lost Davenport [7] 4–6 6–2 6–2. **1996: 3r** [seed 15] d. Schett 6–3 6–0, Begerow 7–5 7–5, lost Habsudova 4–6 7–5 6–4. **1997: r/u** [seed 1] (d. Nagyova 6–0 6–2, Pizzichini 3–6 6–4 6–1, Kournikova 6–1 6–3, Paulus [16] 6–3 0–6 6–0, Sanchez Vicario [6] 6–2 6–2, Seles [3] 6–7 7–5 6–4, lost Majoli [6] 6–4 6–2.

WIMBLEDON – Played 3, won 1

1995: 1r lost Graf [1] 6–3 6–1. **1996: last 16** [seed 16] d. Nejedly 6–2 6–2, Viollet 6–1 6–1, Wild 6–3 2–6 6–1, lost Graf [1] 6–1 6–4. **1997: won** [seed 1] d. Kremer 6–4 6–4, Barabanschikova 6–2 6–2, Arendt 6–1 6–3, Appelmans 6–1 6–3, Chladkova 6–3 6–2, Kournikova 6–3 6–2, Novotna [3] 2–6 6–3 6–3.

US OPEN – Played 3, won 1, sf 1

1995: last 16 [unseeded] d. Feber 6–2 6–3, M. Maleeva [8] 4–6 6–4 6–2, Hy-Boulais 4–6 6–1 6–4, lost Sabatini [9] 6–2 6–4. **1996: sf** [seed 16] d. Montolio 6–1 6–0, Oremans 6–4 6–4, Kijimuta 6–2 6–2, Sanchez Vicario [3] 6–1 3–6 6–4, Novotna [7] 7–6 6–4, lost Graf [1] 7–5 6–3. **1997: won** [seed 1] d. Whitlinger-Jones 6–0 6–1, Chladkova 6–1 6–2, Likhovtseva 7–5 6–2, Labat 6–0 6–2, Sanchez Vicario [10] 6–3 6–2, Davenport [6] 6–2 6–4, V. Williams 6–0 6–4.

OLYMPIC RECORD

1996: (Atlanta) 2r [seed 15] d. Schad 6–0 6–1, lost Sugiyama 6–4 6–4.

CAREER FED CUP RECORD

1995: April *(Euro/Africa Group 1 in ESP, Clay): Round-robin LAT d. SUI 2–1.* R2 d. L. Neiland 6–1 6–2; R3 (with G. Dondit) lost A. Blumberga/Neiland 7–5 5–7 7–5. *Round-robin SUI d. FIN 3–0.* R2 d. N. Dahlman 6–1 7–6; R3 (with J. Manta) d. H. Aalto/Dahlman 6–1 6–1. *Round-robin BLR d. SUI 2–1.* R2 lost N. Zvereva 6–3 3–6 6–3; R3 (with Manta) d. M. Stets/V. Zhukovets 6–1 6–1. **1996: April** *(Euro/Africa Group 1 in ESP, Clay): Round-robin SUI d. YUG 3–0.* R2 d. B. Ivanovic 6–2 6–1; R3 (with A. Burgis) d. S. Nacuk/D. Zaric 6–1 6–3. *Round-robin SUI d. GEO 3–0.* R2 d. N. Louarsabishvili 6–1 6–1. *Round-robin SUI d. CRO 2–1.* R2 d. I. Majoli 5–7 6–1 6–1; R3 (with Burgis) d. M. Lucic/Majoli 6–1 7–5. *Qf SUI d. HUN 2–1.* R2 d. A. Temesvari 6–0 6–3. *Final SUI d. RUS 2–1.* R2 d. E. Likhovtseva 6–3 6–0. **July** – *Group 1 play-off SUI d. INA 3–2 in INA (Hard).* R2 d. L. Andriyani 6–0 6–0; R3 lost Y. Basuki 5–7 6–3 6–1; R5 (with P. Schnyder) d. Basuki/Tedjakusuma 6–3 6–2. **1997: March** – *Group I qf SUI d. SVK 3–2 in SVK (Carpet).* R1 d. K. Studenikova 6–1 6–3; R3 d. K. Habsudova 6–2 6–0. R5 (with P. Schnyder) d. Habsudova/R. Zrubakova 6–0 6–1. **July** – *World Group play-off SUI d. ARG 5–0 in SUI (Carpet).* R1 d. M. Gaidano 6–1 6–2; R3 d. F. Labat 6–2 6–1. R5 (with E. Gagliardi) d. L. Montalvo/M. Paz 6–3 6–4.

SEASON ENDING CHAMPIONSHIPS – Played 2, r/u 1, qf 1

(1996–97 Chase)
1996: r/u d. Spirlea 6–1 6–2, Date 6–1 6–2, Majoli 6–2 4–6 6–1, lost Graf 6–3 4–6 6–0 4–6 6–0. **1997: qf** d. Schultz-McCarthy 7–6 5–2 ret'd, lost Pierce 6–3 2–6 7–5.

2 JANA NOVOTNA (CZE)

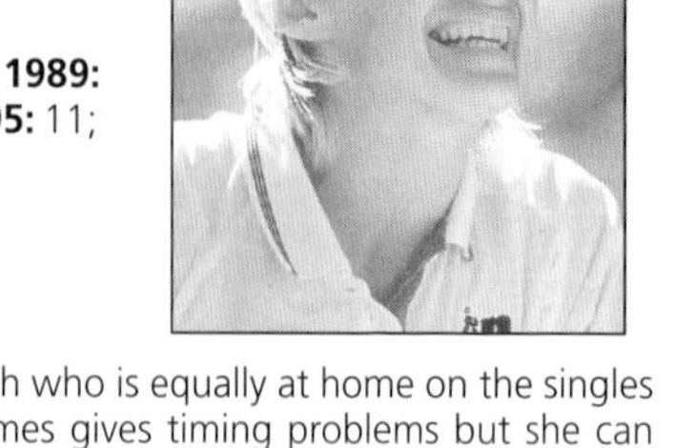

Born: Brno, 2 October 1968. **Lives:** Brno. **Father:** Frank. **Mother:** Libuse. **Brother:** Paul (older). **Agent:** Advantage International. **Coach:** Hana Mandlikova since 1990; formerly Mike Estep. **Turned pro:** 1987. **Height:** 5ft 9in (1.75m). **Weight:** 139lb (63kg).

Rankings: 1985: 305; **1986:** 172; **1987:** 49; **1988:** 45; **1989:** 11; **1990:** 13; **1991:** 7; **1992:** 10; **1993:** 6; **1994:** 4; **1995:** 11; **1996:** 3; **1997:** 2. **Highest:** 2 (July 1997).

1997 Prize Money: $1,685,115.
Career Earnings: $8,257,780. **Career Titles:** 19.

Style: A right-handed natural volleyer with good touch who is equally at home on the singles or doubles court. The high toss on her serve sometimes gives timing problems but she can serve-and-volley with the best. She has a large swing on the sometimes erratic forehand and can hit her backhand with slice or topspin.

CAREER HIGHLIGHTS (year: (titles))
1986: Won US Open Jun doubles with Zrubakova. **1987:** Reached last 16 Wimbledon and US Open, plus qf VS Kansas. In doubles she developed a formidable partnership with Suire, qualifying for VS Champs and taking a set off Navratilova/Shriver. **1988: (1)** *Adelaide*. Won her 1st title on the main tour at Adelaide, r/u Brisbane and upset Sabatini 1r Filderstadt. In doubles won Olympic silver medal with Sukova and took 5 doubles titles with 3 different partners. In mixed, with Pugh, won Australian and US Opens. **1989: (1)** *Strasbourg*. Was r/u Hamburg and Zurich and reached 4 more sf, as well as qf French Open, to qualify for VS Champs in both singles (lost Graf 1r) and doubles for 1st time. In doubles won 6 women's titles, including Wimbledon and LIPC with Sukova, plus Australian Open and Wimbledon mixed with Pugh. Won WTA Most Improved Player award. **1990: (1)** *Albuquerque*. She continued her successful doubles partnership with Sukova, with whom she won 8 of her 9 titles across the year. The duo were unbeaten until US Open, where, having won Australian Open, French Open and Wimbledon, they failed in their bid for a GS when they lost f to Navratilova/G. Fernandez. They were also disappointed at VS Champs, where they fell 1r to Medvedeva/Meskhi. In singles she upset Sabatini and K. Maleeva *en route* to her 1st GS sf at French Open and followed with qf Wimbledon and US Open. Extended Navratilova to 3s in sf Eastbourne. Qualified for VS Champs in both singles and doubles. **1991: (2)** *Sydney, Oklahoma*. Showing the benefits of her partnership with new coach, Mandlikova, she made a tremendous start to the year, upsetting Garrison, Graf and Sanchez Vicario back-to-back in ss to reach her 1st GS singles f at Australian Open, where she took the 1st set off Seles. R/u Leipzig, reached sf Berlin and VS Champs, upsetting Graf on the way, and appeared in qf French Open. Was voted WTA Doubles Team of the Year with G. Fernandez, with whom she won French Open and was r/u Australian Open, Wimbledon and VS Champs. She completed a full hand of GS doubles f, being r/u US Open with Savchenko, and appeared in 14 f altogether, winning 3 with Fernandez, 3 with Savchenko and 1 with Navratilova. **1992:** Upset Graf *en route* to f VS Chicago and extended her to 3s in f both Leipzig and Brighton and sf Zurich, losing twice only on tb. She reached 4 more qf and qualified again for VS Champs, where she took a set off Seles in qf singles and was r/u doubles with Savchenko-Neiland. This new pairing was as successful as her previous partnerships and brought 7 titles, plus r/u Wimbledon and US Open. **1993: (2)** *Osaka, Brighton*. The high point of her year came at Wimbledon, where she beat Navratilova for the first time and, playing an all-out aggressive game, was on the brink of upsetting Graf in f before losing faith in herself and letting the match slip away. At Osaka she won her 1st singles title for 2 years and followed in autumn with Brighton, as well as reaching f Leipzig and sf 5 other tourns. She reached last 16 US Open, but, hampered by an ankle injury, fell to Date. Qualified for VS Champs in both singles and doubles, reaching qf singles and r/u doubles with Neiland. It was the 6th time they'd lost to G. Fernandez/Zvereva during the year, including f French Open and Wimbledon. In all she reached 12 doubles f, winning 3 with Neiland and 1 each with Strnadova and Sanchez Vicario. **1994: (3)** *Leipzig, Brighton, Essen*. She played her best tennis in autumn, when she won 3 consec. tourns,

with Brighton the 1st time she had retained a title or won 2 in succession and her victory at Essen the following week extending the run to 3. In GS her best performance was sf US Open, for she fell qf Australian Open to Sabatini and lost 1r French Open to Smashnova, whereupon she withdrew from doubles with Sanchez Vicario, complaining of muscle strain in right shoulder. She also withdrew from Eastbourne, suffering with a painful bicep, but played Wimbledon, where she progressed to qf. There she again demonstrated her inability to cope with the big situation and tendency to 'choke' with a match apparently within her grasp when she won 1s v Navratilova, but then submitted tamely for the addition of only 1 more game. She also reached sf Hamburg and Berlin, plus 3 more qf, including VS Champs. In doubles with Sanchez Vicario she won US Open and was r/u Wimbledon and VS Champs; together they played 9 f, winning 5, and she also reached 2 more f with different partners. In mixed doubles, she was r/u US Open with Woodbridge. **1995: (1)** *Linz*. In 3r French Open v Rubin she choked again, letting a 5–0 40–0 fs lead slip away, although she claimed afterwards simply to have been upset by the rain and cramp in both legs, and at Wimbledon she allowed Graf to recover from a set down in sf. She won the only f she reached – at Linz – and also appeared in sf Paris Open, LIPC and Toronto, plus 2 qf. In doubles she won Australian Open and Wimbledon plus 2 other titles with Sanchez Vicario and took a 5th with M. J. Fernandez. Qualified for WTA Champs in both singles and doubles, falling 1r singles to Date but winning doubles with Sanchez Vicario. **1996: (4)** *Madrid, Zurich, Chicago, Philadelphia*. Victory in both singles and doubles (with Sanchez Vicario) at Madrid in May took her back into the top 10 and by end of year she had climbed to a career-high No. 3. She won 3 more singles titles in consec. tourns in autumn at Zurich, Chicago and Philadelphia (when Graf retired), was r/u Essen, and reached sf French Open, Olympics, FC Cup, Eastbourne and San Diego. In a major upset at French Open, she removed a below-par Seles in ss in qf: serving for the match at 5–3, she overcame her tendency to choke, although she slipped to 15–40 before taking the game and match. She repeated the feat on her way to a bronze medal at the Olympics, becoming the first player to beat Seles twice since her comeback the previous year. Coming into Chase Champs after her 3 consec. titles, she upset Sanchez Vicario 1st time in 5 years but lost sf to Graf, again failing to capitalise on a strong lead. In doubles, she played 9 f, winning 4 and being r/u US Open and Chase Champs with Sanchez Vicario, winning one each with Boogert and Arendt, and taking Olympic silver with Sukova. Voted Doubles Team of Year with Sanchez Vicario. **1997: (4)** *Madrid, Leipzig, Moscow, Chase Champs*. Beat Sanchez Vicario and Seles back-to-back to take the title at Madrid, winning 8 successive games in f to recover from 3–5 down v Seles. She also won Leipzig (both singles and doubles) and Moscow and shared Eastbourne with Sanchez Vicario after f was abandoned. She moved ahead of Graf to No. 2 in the rankings after Wimbledon, where she reached her 2nd f. She was superb there in 1s v Hingis before an abdominal muscle injury began to trouble her, although she refused to make that an excuse for her eventual defeat. She had already withdrawn from the doubles and pulled out of Prague afterwards. In singles she also reached sf Linz, Paris Open, LIPC, Berlin and Zurich, plus qf US Open, Atlanta, Chicago and Philadelphia. On 17 Nov. she was briefly overtaken in the rankings by Davenport, and slipped to No. 3. However, she was back at No. 2 the following week after a magnificent performance to win Chase Champs over Pierce, where she held her nerve to take her first major title. She completed her triumph by winning the doubles with Davenport. She played a total of 9 doubles f across the year, winning 4, including US Open, with Davenport, and 2 with Hingis.

PRINCIPAL 1997 RESULTS – won 4, shared 1, r/u 1, sf 5 (detailed Grand Slam results follow)
won Chase Champs, **won** Madrid (d. Carlsson 6–2 6–2, Leon-Garcia 6–3 6–4, Sanchez Vicario 6–4 6–4, Seles 7–5 6–1), **won** Leipzig (d. Kruger 6–0 6–4, Kleinova 6–4 6–2, Huber 6–7 7–5 6–4, Coetzer 6–2 4–6 6–3), **won** Moscow (d. Po 6–0 6–2, V. Williams 7–5 6–4, Martinez 6–4 6–1, Sugiyama 6–3 6–4); **shared** Eastbourne (with Sanchez Vicario) (d. Basuki 7–5 6–4, Sugiyama 6–2 6–7 6–4, Zvereva 6–7 6–0 7–5, final abandoned); **r/u** Hannover (d. Dragomir 6–2 6–3, Likhovtseva 6–4 6–2, M. Maleeva 6–0 7–5, lost Majoli 4–6 7–6 6–4); **sf** Linz (d. Farina 6–4 1–6 6–3, Maleeva 6–0 6–3, lost Rubin 7–5 5–7 6–3), **sf** Paris Open (d. Boogert 6–2 6–4, Pierce 6–1 6–2, lost Huber 6–3 6–4), **sf** LIPC (d. Saeki 4–6 6–3 6–3, Raymond 6–2 6–1, Kournikova 6–3 6–4, Majoli 6–2 3–6 7–6, lost Hingis 6–3 2–6 6–4), **sf** Berlin (d. Rittner 6–0 6–2, Tauziat 6–0 6–2, Appelmans 1–6 6–2 6–0, lost M. J. Fernandez 6–3 6–1), **sf** Zurich (d. Sugiyama 6–0 6–7 6–2, Kleinova 6–2 7–6, lost Davenport 6–4 6–1). **DOUBLES:** (with Davenport unless stated) **won US Open** (d. G. Fernandez/Zvereva 6–3 6–4); (with Hingis) **won** Paris Open (d. Fusai/Grande 6–3 6–0); **won** Amelia Island (d. Arendt/Bollegraf 6–3 6–0), **won** Berlin (d. G. Fernandez/Zvereva 6–2 3–6 6–2), (with Hingis) **won** Leipzig (d. Basuki/Sukova 6–2 6–2), **won** Chase Champs (d. Fusai/Tauziat 6–7 6–3 6–2); **r/u** FC Cup (lost M. J. Fernandez/Hingis 7–5 4–6 6–1), **r/u** Filderstadt (lost Hingis/Sanchez Vicario 7–6 3–6 7–6), **r/u** Philadelphia (lost Raymond/Stubbs 6–3 7–5).

Persistence was rewarded when 29-year-old Jana Novotna, having failed in three Grand Slam finals, at last won a major title – the season-ending Chase Championships. (Michael Cole)

CAREER GRAND SLAM RECORD

AUSTRALIAN OPEN – Played 8, r/u 1, qf 1

1988: 1r lost Inoue 7–6 6–4. **1989: 3r** d. Ingram 7–5 7–5, Cunningham 6–2 6–2, lost Navratilova [2] 6–2 6–2. **1990: 3r** [seed 5] d. Martin 6–7 6–0 6–0, Temesvari 6–1 6–1, lost Fendick 1–6 7–6 6–4. **1991: r/u** [10] d. A.Minter 7–6 6–2, Quentrec 6–2 6–2, Stafford 6–7 6–1 8–6, Garrison [7] 7–6 6–4, Graf [1] 5–7 6–4 8–6, Sanchez Vicario [6] 6–2 6–4, lost Seles [2] 5–7 6–3 6–1. **1992: last 16** [seed 6] d. Zrubakova 7–6 6–3, Alter 6–3 6–2, Li 6–3 6–1, lost Huber [12] 5–7 7–6 6–4. **1993: 2r** [seed 8] d. Testud 6–2 6–4, lost R. White 4–6 7–5 6–2. **1994: qf** [seed 5] d. Li 6–1 6–3, Kelesi 6–3 6–1, Taylor 6–4 6–2, Zardo 6–2 7–5, lost Sabatini [4] 6–3 6–4. **1995: last 16** [seed 3] d. Hy-Boulais 6–2 3–6 6–0, Sukova 3–6 6–3 6–2, Raymond 6–3 3–6 9–7, lost Gavaldon 7–5 6–0. **1996-97:** Did not play.

FRENCH OPEN – Played 12, sf 2, qf 3

1986: 1r lost Drescher 6–2 6–3. **1987: 3r** d. Durie 6–3 6–1, Zrubakova 6–3 4–6 6–4, lost Graf [2] 6–0 6–1. **1988: 1r** lost Tarabini 1–6 6–3 6–2. **1989: qf** [seed 11] d. Halard 6–3 6–2, Porwik 6–3 7–5, Simpson 6–1 6–0, Hanika 6–1 6–4, lost Sanchez Vicario [7] 6–2 6–2. **1990: sf** [seed 11] d. Demongeot 6–0 6–7 10–8, Schultz 6–3 6–1, Sviglerova 7–5 6–2, Sabatini [4] 6–4 7–5, K. Maleeva [8] 4–6 6–2 6–4, lost Graf [1] 6–1 6–2. **1991: qf** [seed 6] d. Farina 7–5 6–2, Hy 6–2 6–1, Brioukhovets 7–6 6–2, Meskhi [14] 6–0 7–6, lost Sabatini [3] 5–7 7–6 6–0. **1992: last 16** [seed 10] d. Graham 6–3 6–2, Medvedeva 6–4 6–1, Schultz 6–3 6–4, lost Graf [2] 6–1 6–4. **1993: qf** [seed 7] d. Porwik 6–3 6–3, Papadaki 3–6 6–2 6–2, Kroupova 2–6 6–2 6–3, Zvereva 6–3 6–3, lost Sanchez Vicario [2] 6–2 7–5. **1994: 1r** [seed 6] lost Smashnova 6–4 6–2. **1995: 3r** [seed 5] d. Dopfer 6–1 2–6 6–1, Schwarz-Ritter 6–4 6–3, lost Rubin 7–6 4–6 8–6. **1996: sf** [seed 10] d. Richterova 6–0 6–2, Wang 6–4 6–3, Makarova 6–1 7–5, Spirlea 6–1 7–5, Seles [1] 7–6 6–3, lost Sanchez Vicario 6–3 7–5. **1997: 3r** [seed 4] d. Torrens-Valero 6–3 6–2, Kandarr 6–4 6–0, lost Arendt 3–6 6–4 6–4.

WIMBLEDON – Played 12, r/u 2, sf 1, qf 3

1986: 1r lost Mascarin 3–6 7–6 7–2. **1987: last 16** d. Reis 6–3 3–6 8–6, Hu Na 6–2 6–3, Walsh-Pete 6–2 4–6 6–4, lost Graf [2] 6–4 6–3. **1988: 2r** d. Scheuer-Larsen 6–3 7–5, lost Sukova [6] 6–2 6–2. **1989: last 16** [seed 10] d. Simpson 6–2 6–1, Burgin 6–4 3–6 6–2, K. Adams 6–4 6–1, lost Golarsa 7–6 2–6 6–4. **1990: qf** [seed 13] d. Golarsa 3–6 7–6 6–2, Cunningham 6–2 6–1, Faull 6–2 6–1, Fendick 6–2 6–4, lost Graf [1] 7–5 6–2. **1991: 2r** [seed 6] d. Pratt 6–3 6–0, lost Schultz 4–6 7–6 6–4. **1992: 3r** [seed 11] d. Monami 6–1 6–2, Lindqvist 6–3 6–2, lost Fendick 6–3 6–3. **1993: r/u** [seed 8] d. Zardo 6–1 6–3, Gorrochategui 6–0 7–5, Werdel 6–3 6–1, Oremans 7–5 4–6 6–4, Sabatini [4] 6–4 6–3, Navratilova [2] 6–4 6–4, lost Graf [1] 7–6 1–6 6–4. **1994: qf** [seed 5] d. Oremans 6–4 4–6 6–4, Probst 6–2 6–1, Monami 6–0 4–6 6–0, Sawamatsu 6–3 6–3, lost Navratilova [4] 5–7 6–0 6–1. **1995: sf** [seed 4] d. Kschwendt 6–4 6–4, Durie 6–2 6–2, Wiesner 7–5 6–4, Bradtke 6–0 5–7 6–4, Date [6] 6–2 6–3, lost Graf [1] 5–7 6–4 6–2. **1996: qf** [seed 6] (d. Martinek 6–4 6–0, Courtois 7–6 6–3, Dragomir 6–3 6–1, Hy-Boulais 6–3 6–1, lost Graf [1] 6–3 6–2). **1997: r/u** [seed 3] d. Probst 6–4 4–6 6–0, Likhovtseva 6–1 4–6 6–4, Leon-Garcia 6–4 6–2, M. J. Fernandez [11] 5–7 6–4 7–5, Basuki 6–3 6–3, Sanchez Vicario [8] 6–4 6–2, lost Hingis 2–6 6–3 6–3.

US OPEN – Played 11, sf 1, qf 4

1987: last 16 d. Parkhomenko 6–1 7–6, Turnbull [16] 6–2 6–4, Halard 6–4 6–0, lost Shriver [5] 6–3 7–6. **1988: 1r** lost Wiesner 6–2 6–3. **1989: 2r** [seed 11] d. McGrath 7–5 6–2, lost Paulus 3–6 6–3 6–2. **1990: qf** [seed 12] d. Lapi 6–3 6–1, Rinaldi 6–4 6–3, Gildemeister 6–3 6–1, K. Maleeva [7] 6–4 6–2, lost Graf [1] 6–3 6–1. **1991: last 16** [seed 9] d. Grossman 6–3 4–6 6–1, Harper 6–2 6–3, Monami 6–1 6–2, lost Sabatini [3] 6–4 7–6. **1992: 1r** [seed 10] lost Fairbank-Nideffer 6–3 7–6. **1993: last 16** [seed 8] d. Gavaldon 6–2 6–4, Majoli 6–3 6–0, Golarsa 6–4 6–3, lost Date 6–4 6–4. **1994: sf** [seed 7] d. Makarova 7–5 7–5, Habsudova 6–2 6–3, Hy 6–1 6–2, Mag. Maleeva [15] 6–0 6–4, Pierce [4] 6–4 6–0, lost Graf [1] 6–3 7–5. **1995: qf** [seed 5] d. Cecchini 6–2. 6–0, Carlsson 6–1 6–2, Testud 6–4 7–5, Studenikova 6–4 6–3, lost Seles [2] 7–6 6–2. **1996: qf** [seed 7] d. Lubiani 6–1 7–5, Labat 6–2 4–6 6–2, Whitlinger-Jones 6–2 6–3, Habsudova 6–2 6–0, lost Hingis [16] 7–6 6–4. **1997: qf** [seed 3] d. Ruano-Pascual 6–0 6–4, Basuki 6–4 6–2, Lucic 6–2 6–7 6–3, M. J. Fernandez [12] 7–5 6–4, lost Davenport [6] 6–2 4–6 7–6.

OLYMPIC RECORD

1988: (Seoul) 2r d. Demongeot 6–4 6–3, lost Paulus 6–4 6–3. **1992: (Barcelona) 1r** [seed 9] lost Zvereva 6–1 6–0. **1996: (Atlanta) sf bronze medal** [seed 6] d. Dragomir 6–4 4–4 ret'd, Wiesner 6–4 3–6 6–3, Sugiyama 6–3 6–4, Seles [1] 7–5 3–6 8–6, lost Sanchez Vicario [3] 6–4 1–6 6–3; bronze medal play-off d. M. J. Fernandez [7] 7–5 6–4.

CAREER FED CUP RECORD

1987 (in CAN, Hard): *1r TCH d. SWE 3–0.* R3 (with H. Mandlikova) d. C. Lindqvist/M. Lindstrom 6–3 6–2. *2r TCH d. YUG 3–0.* R3 (with R. Rajchrtova) d. S. Goles/R. Sasak 6–4 5–7 6–4. **1988 (in AUS, Hard):** *1r TCH d. BRA 3–0.* R3 (with J. Pospisilova) d. N. Dias/L. Tella 6–3 6–2. *2r TCH d. NZL 3–0.* R3 (with Pospisilova) d. B. Cordwell/J. Richardson 7–6 7–6. *Qf TCH d. DEN 3–0.* R3 (with Pospisilova) d. H. Kjaer-Nielsen/T. Scheuer-Larsen 6–3 6–2. *Sf TCH d. CAN 3–0.* R3 (with Pospisilova) d. H. Kelesi/R. Simpson 7–6 6–2. *Final TCH d. URS 2–1.* R3 (with Pospisilova) lost L. Savchenko/N. Zvereva (URS) 7–6 7–5. **1989 (in JPN, Hard):** *1r TCH d. BEL 3–0.* R1 d. C. van Reneterghem 6–0 6–2. *2r TCH d. HUN 2–1.* R1 d. A. Noszaly 6–3 6–3. *Qf TCH d. FRG 2–1.* R1 d. C. Kohde-Kilsch 6–3 6–3; R3 (with H. Sukova) d. S. Graf/Kohde-Kilsch 6–2 6–2. *Final USA d. TCH 2–0.* R1 lost C. Evert 6–2 6–3. **1990 (in USA, Hard):** *1r TCH d. KOR 3–0.* R2 d. S. Im 6–0 6–1. *2r TCH d. AUS 2–1.* R2 d. R. McQuillan 6–4 6–4. *Qf USA d. TCH 2–1.* R2 d. Z. Garrison 6–3 6–3; R3 (with R. Rajchrtova) lost G. Fernandez/Garrison 7–6 6–4. **1991 (in GBR, Hard):** *1r TCH d. SWE 2–0.* R2 d. C. Dahlman 7–6 6–2. *2r TCH d. URS 2–1.* R2 d. N. Zvereva 6–4 6–1. *Qf TCH d. SUI 2–1.* R2 d. M. Maleeva-Fragniere 6–4 6–4. *Sf USA d. TCH 3–0.* R2 lost M. J. Fernandez 6–4 0–6 9–7. **1992 (in GER, Clay):** *1r TCH d. HUN 3–0.* R2 d. A. Temesvari-Trunkos 6–2 6–1; R2 (with A. Strnadova) d. V. Csurgo/Temesvari-Trunkos 1–6 7–5 7–5. *2r TCH d. KOR 3–0.* R2 d. S. Park 4–6 6–2 6–3; R3 (with Strnadova) d. I. Kim/J. Lee 6–3 6–3. *Qf AUS d. TCH 2–1.* R2 lost N. Provis 7–5 6–0; R3 (with Strnadova) lost Provis/R. Stubbs 6–3 6–3. **1993 (in GER, Clay):** *1r TCH d. RSA 2–1.* R2 d. A. Coetzer 6–1 6–4. *2r TCH d. ITA 2–1.* R2 lost S. Cecchini 0–6 6–2 6–3; R3 (with H. Sukova) d. Cecchini/ S. Farina 6–2 6–2. *Qf FRA d. TCH 3–0.* R2 lost Tauziat 6–1 0–6 6–3. **1995: April (in ESP, Clay)** *EA1 round-robin CZE d. POL 3–0.* R2 d. K. Nowak 6–4 6–3. Round-robin CZE d. GBR 3–0. R2 d. C. Wood 6–2 6–2; R3 (with H. Sukova) d. J. Durie/Wood 6–7 6–1 6–2. *Round-robin SLO d. CZE 2–1.* R2 lost T. Krizan 0–6 6–3 6–3. *EA1 qf CZE d. SLO 3–0.* R2 d. Krizan 6–0 7–5. *EA1 sf CZE d. BLR 3–0.* R2 d. N. Zvereva 0–6 7–6 6–3. **1996: April** – *Group 1 qf CZE d. CAN 3–0 in CAN (Hard).* R1 d. J. Nejedly 6–1 6–1; R3 d. P. Hy-Boulais 6–7 6–0 6–1. **July** – *World Group play-off CZE d. ARG 3–1 in CZE (Carpet).* R2 d. M. Paz 6–1 6–2. **1997: July** – *World Group sf NED d. CZE 3–2 in CZE (Clay).* R2 d. M. Oremans 6–3 6–0; R3 d. B. Schultz-McCarthy 7–6 6–3; R5 (with E. Martincova) lost M. Bollegraf/Oremans 6–4 7–6.

SEASON ENDING CHAMPIONSHIPS – Played 8, won 1, sf 2, qf 3

(1983–94 Virginia Slims, 1995 Corel, 1996–97 Chase)

1990: 1r lost Sabatini 6–1 5–7 7–6. **1991: sf** d. Maleeva-Fragniere 6–0 3–6 6–3, Graf 6–3 3–6 6–1, lost Navratilova 6–1 6–4. **1992: qf** d. Fernandez 7–6 6–2, lost Seles 3–6 6–4 6–1. **1993: qf** d. Garrison-Jackson 6–4 6–7 6–3, lost Sanchez Vicario 6–7 7–6 6–4. **1994: qf** d. Majoli 6–3 3–6 6–1, lost Davenport 6–2 6–2. **1995: 1r** lost Date 5–7 6–3 6–4. **1996: sf** d. Coetzer 6–4 6–1, Sanchez Vicario 6–0 6–3, lost Graf 4–6 6–4 6–3. **1997: won** d. Martinez 6–4 6–4, Sanchez Vicario 6–3 3–6 6–1, Spirlea 7–6 6–2, Pierce 7–6 6–2 6–3.

3 LINDSAY DAVENPORT (USA)

Born: Palos Verdes, Cal., 8 June 1976. **Lives:** Murrieta, Cal.
Father: Wink, a former Olympic volleyball player.
Mother: Ann. **Sisters:** Shannon and Leiann (both older).
Agent: ProServ. **Coaches:** Robert Van't Hof since Jan 1996. Formerly Lynn Rolley and Craig Kardon.
Turned pro: 22 February 1993.
Height: 6ft 2in (1.88m). **Weight:** 165lb (78kg).

Rankings: 1991: 339; **1992:** 159; **1993:** 20; **1994:** 6; **1995:** 12; **1996:** 9; **1997:** 3.
Highest: 2 (17 November 1997).

1997 Prize Money: $1,533,101.
Career Earnings: $3,692,454. **Career Titles:** 13.

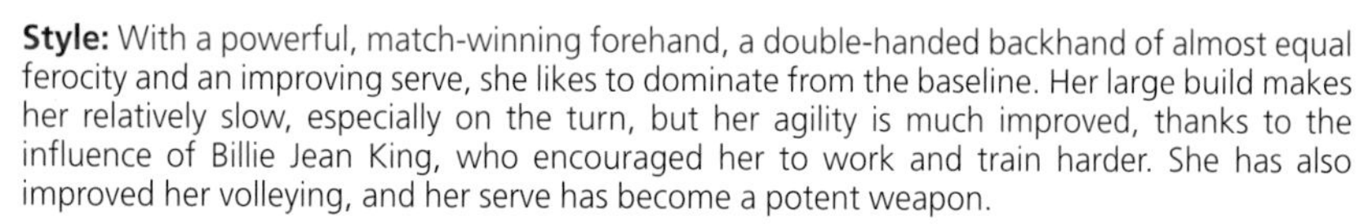

Style: With a powerful, match-winning forehand, a double-handed backhand of almost equal ferocity and an improving serve, she likes to dominate from the baseline. Her large build makes her relatively slow, especially on the turn, but her agility is much improved, thanks to the influence of Billie Jean King, who encouraged her to work and train harder. She has also improved her volleying, and her serve has become a potent weapon.

CAREER HIGHLIGHTS (year: (titles))
1991: Won USTA 18s singles and doubles. **1992:** Ranked No. 1 in Nat 18s, in Jun tennis she won US Open over Steven, was r/u Australian Open to Limmer and won Australian Open and US Open doubles with London. **1993: (1)** *Lucerne*. She burst into prominence on the senior tour and swept up the rankings, improving by more than 100 places to 25 in May when she won her 1st title at Lucerne, and breaking into top 20 by autumn. She reached sf Oakland, where she took a set off Navratilova, plus qf VS Florida (d. Sabatini), Indian Wells (d. Schultz) and Tokyo Nicherei. At US Open, unseeded, she upset Coetzer on her way to last 16, where she extended Sabatini to 3s. Made her Fed Cup debut. **1994: (2)** *Brisbane, Lucerne*. In the year in which she graduated from high school, she established herself as one of the top women players. She broke into the top 20 in Jan. after winning Brisbane and moved into top 10 in spring, winning Lucerne in May. At Australian Open she upset M. J. Fernandez to reach qf and reached the same stage Wimbledon, removing Sabatini and taking a set off eventual champ Martinez. She also appeared in sf Indian Wells, LIPC (d. Sabatini), Amelia Island (d. Martinez) and Oakland, plus 4 more qf. These results took her to her 1st VS Champs, where she removed Novotna and Pierce before Sabatini demolished her in f. In doubles she was r/u French Open and won Indian Wells with Raymond, with whom she qualified for VS Champs, and took Oakland with Sanchez Vicario. **1995: (1)** *Strasbourg*. She won both singles and doubles titles at Strasbourg, and achieved r/u finish at Sydney and Tokyo Pan Pacific, sf Oakland and qf Indian Wells, Manhattan Beach and Tokyo Nicherei. Qualified for VS Champs, but lost 1r to Sabatini. In doubles she played 5 f, winning 2 with M. J. Fernandez and 1 each with Novotna and Raymond. Injury restricted her towards the end of the year: she withdrew from San Diego with a tendon injury in her left leg and from Oakland with back problems, and dropped out of the top 10. **1996: (3)** *OLYMPICS, Strasbourg, Los Angeles*. She enjoyed the performance of her life at the Olympics, where she upset Huber, Majoli, M. J. Fernandez and Sanchez Vicario – for the 1st time in 6 meetings – to take the gold medal, never before having progressed beyond qf in GS. Yet, discouraged by injury, illness and lack of self-belief, she had come close to quitting towards the end of the previous year, before being talked out of it by M. J. Fernandez. Her rehabilitation and motivation were completed by Billie Jean King in her role as coach to the US Fed Cup and Olympic squads. Fitter and 20lb lighter, she learned how to use her size and strength to advantage, playing with renewed dedication after her split with Craig Kardon. She began the year on a high note at Sydney, where she upset Date and came near to doing the same to Seles in f (letting slip mp in 2s), as well as winning the doubles with M. J. Fernandez. At Indian Wells in March she extended Graf to 2 tb in sf before losing in 3s, following with the title at Strasbourg. Then at LA, where she won both singles and doubles (with Zvereva), she became the 1st player since 1994 to d. Graf in ss. She also reached sf LIPC and Filderstadt, plus qf French Open, Tokyo Toray,

Leipzig and Chicago. In other doubles tourns, she and M. J. Fernandez won French Open (upsetting Novotna/Sanchez Vicario and G. Fernandez/ Zvereva on the way), Sydney and Oakland and were r/u Australian Open. Her year ended less dramatically in singles, as she fell to Wild at US Open and Graf 2r Chase Champs, but she finished on a high note by taking the doubles there with M. J. Fernandez. **1997: (6)** *Oklahoma City, Indian Wells, Amelia Island, Atlanta, Zurich, Chicago.* After winning Oklahoma City in Feb., she followed the next week by taking both singles and doubles at Indian Wells, coming from 1–4 and 5–6 behind in 3s qf v V. Williams. A month later she won both singles and doubles at Amelia Island, adding singles titles at Atlanta, Zurich (d. Novotna) and Chicago. Only Hingis won more tournaments across the year. She was always a dangerous opponent: at Los Angeles she became the 2nd of only 5 players all year to beat Hingis, before extending Seles to 3s in f; at French Open she was 7–5 4–0 up v Majoli, before letting the match slip away; and at US Open she upset Novotna to reach sf. She seriously challenged Hingis again at Philadelphia, losing their f only 7–5 6–7 7–6. She had upset Novotna a 3rd time there and immediately replaced her as No. 2 in the rankings on 17 Nov. However, at Chase Champs the following week, Novotna's triumph and Davenport's 1r defeat by M. J. Fernandez reversed their positions again. She had also reached sf Sydney and Stanford (where she extended Hingis to 3s) and 3 more qf, as well as being a major force in doubles. When M. J. Fernandez talked of retiring at end 1996, Davenport established a new doubles partnership with Novotna, causing some bad feeling for a while between the former best friends. During the year she reached 12 f in all with 5 different partners, winning 3 with Novotna (including US Open), 2 with Zvereva and 1 with Hingis, as well as being r/u Australian Open with Raymond. She qualified for Chase Champs in both singles and doubles, falling 1r singles to M. J. Fernandez but winning the doubles with Novotna.

PRINCIPAL 1997 RESULTS – won 6, r/u 2, sf 3 (detailed Grand Slam results follow)
won Oklahoma City (d. Cristea 6–2 6–1, Capriati 6–3 6–4, Po 1–6 6–2 6–3, Raymond 6–1 6–0), **won** Indian Wells (d. Whitlinger-Jones 6–4 6–0, Dragomir 6–2 6–1, V. Williams 6–4 5–7 7–6, M. J. Fernandez 6–1 6–1, Spirlea 6–2 6–1), **won** Amelia Island (d. Wang 6–2 6–0, Schultz-McCarthy 6–2 6–1, Kandarr 6–2 6–2, Coetzer 7–5 6–2, Pierce 6–2 6–3), **won** Atlanta (d. Schnyder 6–3 6–2, Van Roost 6–1 7–5, Coetzer 6–2 6–4, Testud 6–4 6–1), **won** Zurich (d. Zvereva 6–4 2–2 ret'd, V. Williams 6–0 6–4, Novotna 6–4 6–1, Tauziat 7–6 7–5), **won** Chicago (d. Kruger 6–2 6–4, Raymond 6–4 6–4, S. Williams 6–4 6–4, Tauziat 6–0 7–5); **r/u** Los Angeles (d. Basuki 6–1 6–1, Tauziat 6–1 3–6 6–3, Hingis 6–2 4–6 6–4, lost Seles 5–7 7–5 6–4), **r/u** Philadelphia (d. Tauziat 6–3 6–3, Martinez 6–3 6–0, Novotna 6–3 6–2, Spirlea 6–2 6–4, lost Hingis 7–5 6–7 7–6); **sf** US Open; **sf** Sydney (d. Raymond 6–3 6–4, Sawamatsu 6–3 6–7 6–1, lost Capriati 2–6 6–4 6–2), **sf** Stanford (d. Cacic 6–2 6–2, Likhovtseva 7–6 6–3, lost Hingis 6–3 1–6 6–2). **DOUBLES:** (with Novotna unless stated) (with Raymond) **r/u Australian Open** (lost Hingis/Zvereva 6–2 6–2), **won US Open** (d. G. Fernandez/Zvereva 6–3 6–4); (with Zvereva) **won** Tokyo Pan Pacific (d. G. Fernandez/Hingis 6–4 6–3), (with Zvereva) **won** Indian Wells (d. Raymond/Tauziat 6–3 6–2), **won** Amelia Island (d. Arendt/Bollegraf 6–3 6–0), **won** Berlin (d. G. Fernandez/Zvereva 6–2 3–6 6–2), (with Hingis) **won** Stanford (d. Coetzer/Pierce 6–1 6–3), **won** Chase Champs (d. Fusai/Tauziat 6–7 6–3 6–2); (with Zvereva) **r/u** Sydney (lost G. Fernandez/Sanchez Vicario 6–3 6–1), **r/u** FC Cup (lost M. J. Fernandez/Hingis 7–5 4–6 6–1), **r/u** Filderstadt (lost Hingis/Sanchez Vicario 7–6 3–6 7–6), (with Seles) **r/u** Chicago (lost Fusai/Tauziat 6–3 6–2), **r/u** Philadelphia (lost Raymond/Stubbs 6–3 7–5).

CAREER GRAND SLAM RECORD

AUSTRALIAN OPEN – Played 5, qf 2

1993: 3r d. Fusai 7–5 6–1, Kiene 7–5 6–4, lost Pierce [10] 6–3 6–0. **1994: qf** [seed 16] d. Hy 3–6 6–2 7–5, Probst 6–1 7–5, Makarova 6–1 6–2, M. J. Fernandez [6] 6–2 6–7 6–2, lost Graf [1] 6–3 6–2. **1995: qf** [seed 6] d. Graham 4–6 6–3 6–2, Probst 6–2 6–2, Testud 6–3 6–4, Schultz 6–2 3–6 6–2, lost Martinez [2] 6–3 4–6 6–3. **1996: last 16** [seed 10] d. Singer 6–1 6–2, Stubbs 7–6 6–3, N. Dahlman 6–4 7–5, lost Martinez [2] 6–3 6–1. **1997: last 16** [seed 7] d. Dechy 4–6 6–1 6–1, Perfetti 6–2 7–5, Tanasugarn 6–1 6–0, lost Po 7–6 6–4.

FRENCH OPEN – Played 5, qf 1

1993: 1r lost Wiesner 6–3 6–1. **1994: 3r** [seed 9] d. Rubin 6–7 6–4 6–3, Nowak 6–4 6–2, lost Halard 6–4 6–2. **1995: last 16** [seed 7] d. Tang 7–6 6–0, Testud 6–3 7–5, Hingis 4–6 6–2 6–2, lost Date [9] 6–4 6–3. **1996: qf** [seed 10] d. Perfetti 6–4 6–1, Park 6–1 6–2, Basuki 6–3 6–2, Date [7] 3–6 6–4 8–6, lost Martinez [3] 6–1 6–3). **1997 last 16** [seed 5] d. Kruger 6–2 6–3, Makarova 6–1 6–1, Schnyder 4–6 6–3 9–7, lost Majoli [9] 5–7 6–4 6–2.

WIMBLEDON – Played 5, qf 1

1993: 3r d. Martinek 6–0 4–6 7–5, Rittner 6–0 7–6, lost Tauziat [16] 6–3 7–6. **1994: qf** [seed 9] d. Halard 6–1 6–4, Price 6–4 6–2, Rittner 6–4 3–6 6–1, Sabatini [10] 6–1 6–3, lost Martinez [3] 6–2 6–7 6–3. **1995: last 16** [seed 7] d. G. Fernandez 6–2 4–6 7–5, Labat 6–1 6–1, Singer 6–7 6–3 6–2, lost M. J. Fernandez [seed] 7–6 6–1. **1996: 2r** [seed 8] d. Schnell 6–4 6–1, lost Neiland 6–3 6–2. **1997: 2r** [seed 5] d. Whitlinger-Jones 5–7 6–2 6–2, lost Chladkova 7–5 6–2.

The popular American, Lindsay Davenport, enjoyed her best season to date, winning six titles and reaching a career-high No.2 before ending the year one place lower. (Michael Cole)

US OPEN – Played 7, sf 1

1991: 1r lost Graham 6–3 6–2. **1992: 2r** d. Basuki 6–4 6–4, lost Sanchez Vicario [5] 6–1 6–3). **1993: last 16** [unseeded] d. Probst 6–4 6–2, Hy 6–4 6–2, Coetzer [15] 6–1 6–2, lost Sabatini [5] 6–7 6–4 6–4. **1994: 3r** [seed 6] d. Grossi 6–1 6–1, Shriver 6–1 6–2, lost Endo 6–3 7–6. **1995: 2r** [seed 10] d. Kamstra 6–2 6–2, lost Garrison-Jackson 6–1 6–3. **1996: last 16** [seed 8] d. Serra-Zanetti 6–2 6–1, Nagyova 6–0 6–4, Sidot 6–0 6–3, lost Wild 6–2 3–6 6–0. **1997 sf** [seed 6] d. McNeil 6–2 7–6, Probst 6–2 6–3, Schnyder 1–6 6–1 6–4, Serna 6–0 6–3, Novotna [3] 6–2 4–6 7–6, lost Hingis [1] 6–2 6–4.

OLYMPIC RECORD

1996: (Atlanta) gold medal [seed 9] d. Kremer 6–2 6–1, Sawamatsu 6–2 6–2, Huber [5] 6–1 3–6 6–3, Majoli [4] 7–5 6–3, M. J. Fernandez [7] 6–2 7–6, Sanchez Vicario [2] 7–6 6–2.

CAREER FED CUP RECORD

1993 (in GER, Clay): *1r USA d. SUI 3–0.* R1 d. C. Fauche 6–4 6–3. *2r USA d. CHN 2–1.* R1 d. Y. Bi 6–1 6–3; R3 (+ L. McNeil) d. L. Chen/F. Li 6–3 6–0. *Qf ARG d. USA 2–1.* R1 lost I. Gorrochategui 7–6 5–7 5–7. **1994 (in GER, Clay):** *1r USA d. CZE 3–0.* R2 d. L. Richterova 4–6 6–1 6–4. *2r USA d. CAN 3–0.* R2 d. P. Hy 6–2 6–4. *Qf USA d. AUT 3–0.* R2 d. J. Wiesner 2–6 6–2 6–2. *Sf USA d. FRA 3–0.* R2 d. M. Pierce 5–7 6–2 6–2. *Final ESP d. USA 3–0.* R2 lost A. Sanchez Vicario 6–2 6–1. **1995: July** – *USA d. FRA 3–2 in USA (Carpet).* R2 d. J. Halard-Decugis 7–6 7–5; R3 d. M. Pierce 6–3 4–6 6–0; R5 (+ G. Fernandez) d. Halard-Decugis/N. Tauziat 6–1 7–6. **November** – *World Group Final ESP d. USA 3–2 in ESP (Clay).* (+ G. Fernandez) R5 D. Ruano-Pascual/ M. Sanchez Lorenzo 6–3 7–6. **1996: July** – *World Group I sf USA d. JPN 5–0 in JPN (Carpet).* R1 d. K. Date 6–2 6–1; R4 d. A. Sugiyama 7–6 7–5; R5 (+ L. Wild) d. K. Nagatsuka/A. Sugiyama 6–2 6–1. **September** – *World Group I final USA d. ESP 5–0 in USA (Carpet).* R2 d. A. Sanchez Vicario 7–5 6–1; R4 d. G. Leon-Garcia 7–5 6–2. **1997: July** – *World Group play-off USA d. JPN 5–0 in USA (Hard).* R2 d. N. Sawamatsu 6–1 6–3; R3 d. A. Sugiyama 6–4 7–6. R5 (with L. Raymond) d. N. Kijimuta/N. Miyagi 6–4 6–4.

SEASON ENDING CHAMPIONSHIPS – Played 4, r/u 1

(1983–94 Virginia Slims, 1995 Corel, 1996–97 Chase)

1994: r/u d. Huber 6–2 6–3, Novotna 6–2 6–2, Pierce 6–3 6–2, lost Sabatini 6–3 6–2 6–4. **1995: 1r** lost Sabatini 6–4 6–3. **1996: 2r** d. Paulus 6–3 6–2, lost Graf 6–4 7–6. **1997: 1r** lost M. J. Fernandez 2–6 6–4 7–6.

4 AMANDA COETZER (RSA)

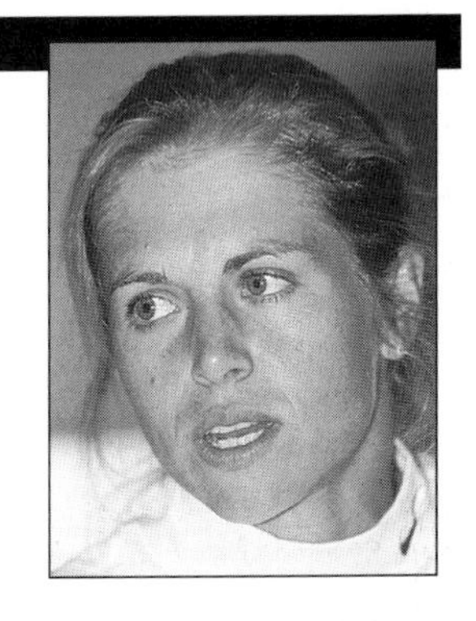

Born: Hoopstad, 22 October 1971. **Lives:** Hoopstad.
Father: Nico. **Mother:** Susta.
Sisters: Isabel, Martelle, Nicola.
Agent: Advantage International. **Coach:** Gavin Hopper since January 1995. **Turned pro:** 1988.
Height: 5ft 2in (1.57m). **Weight:** 122lb (55kg).

Rankings: 1987: 442; **1988:** 153; **1989:** 63; **1990:** 75; **1991:** 67; **1992:** 17; **1993:** 15; **1994:** 18; **1995:** 19; **1996:** 17; **1997:** 4. **Highest:** 4 (17 November 1997).

1997 Prize Money: $701,994.
Career Earnings: $2,613,328. **Career Titles:** 5.

Style: She compensates for lack of height with good anticipation and tremendous speed of foot, which allows her to reach shots that would have beaten most players. Her groundstrokes, single-handed on forehand, double-handed on backhand, are her great strength, both in attack and defence. One of the fittest players on the tour, she is feared by all opponents for her relentless determination.

CAREER HIGHLIGHTS (year: (titles))
1988: Won 4 titles on the satellite circuits. **1989:** Made an unexpected appearance in last 16 French Open and reached sf VS Arizona. **1990:** Reached qf VS Florida, Geneva and VS Albuquerque. **1991:** Upset K. Maleeva at Berlin and G. Fernandez on the way to her 1st primary circuit f at Puerto Rico. **1992:** Scored some big upsets during the year, surprising Garrison on her way to last 16 Olympics, unseeded, Wiesner and Sabatini *en route* to sf VS Florida, Capriati and Zvereva in reaching the same stage Italian Open and Tauziat at US Open. She also appeared in sf Kitzbuhel and Taipei, plus 5 more qf. In doubles she played 4 f with different partners, winning Taranto with Gorrochategui and Puerto Rico with Reinach. **1993: (2)** *Melbourne Open, Tokyo Nicherei.* Won her 1st Kraft tour title at Melbourne Open, following in autumn with Tokyo Nicherei (d. Sanchez Vicario). She was r/u Indian Wells, where she extended M. J. Fernandez to 3s tb and reached sf VS Florida, Amelia Island (d. Capriati) and Barcelona. In doubles she was r/u US Open with Gorrochategui and reached 3 other f. Qualified for VS Champs 1st time in both singles, where she upset M. J. Fernandez before falling qf to Graf, and doubles, in which she and Gorrochategui lost 1r. **1994: (1)** *Prague.* Won both singles and doubles (with Harvey-Wild) at Prague in May, was r/u Indian Wells (d. M. J. Fernandez and Davenport) and reached sf Stratton Mountain and Schenectady. Unseeded at French Open, she upset Date on her way to last 16, as she embarked on her best year yet in GS, reaching qf US Open. She qualified for VS Champs singles, but fell 1r to Pierce. **1995:** Her best moments came at Toronto, where she was unseeded: after becoming the 1st of only 2 players all year to beat Graf, ending her 32-match winning streak 1r, she went on to upset Pierce and Novotna before losing f to Seles, who was playing in her 1st tourn for 2½ years. She met Graf again 1r US Open, where she held 7 sps before taking 1s tb, but lost the next 2 sets. She was also r/u Brighton (d. M. Maleeva), reached sf Barcelona and Tokyo Nicherei plus 2 more qf, upset Pierce in Fed Cup and qualified for WTA Champs, where she lost 1r to Graf. In doubles she played 3 f, winning 2 with Gorrochategui. She won the Karen Krantzcke Sportsmanship Award. **1996:** She made her mark in GS, at Australian Open becoming the 1st South African in the open era to reach sf in any GS, and upsetting Huber at US Open, where she reached qf, unseeded. In other tourns she was r/u Oklahoma and appeared in qf Indian Wells, Madrid, Los Angeles and Tokyo Nicherei to qualify for Chase Champs, where Novotna removed her 1r. **1997: (2)** *Budapest, Luxembourg.* In her best year to date, she became only the 2nd South African woman to crack the top 10, after Greer Stevens in 1979, and in Nov. overtook Seles to reach a career-high No. 4. She continued to cause many significant upsets on her way to the titles at Budapest (singles and doubles, with Fusai) and Luxembourg, r/u Leipzig and sf Australian Open, French Open, Amelia Island, Bol, Berlin, Strasbourg, Stanford, San Diego, Atlanta and Filderstadt, plus qf Tokyo Pan Pacific, Oklahoma City, FC Cup (d. Sanchez Vicario), Toronto and Philadelphia. At Australian Open she ended Graf's run of 25 GS matches won, she beat her

again at Berlin 6–0 6–1 (inflicting the worst defeat of her career in 57 mins on the former No. 1, who was returning from injury), and upset her a third time at French Open, before extending Majoli to 7–5 3s in their sf. At Leipzig she became only the 3rd of 5 players all year to beat Hingis, and other upsets included Novotna at Amelia Island and Atlanta, M. J. Fernandez at Amelia Island, Martinez at French Open and Sanchez Vicario at FC Cup. At Chase Champs, however, she was unexpectedly beaten 1r by Tauziat.

PRINCIPAL 1997 RESULTS – won 2, r/u 1, sf 10 (detailed Grand Slam results follow)
won Budapest (d. Temesvari 7–6 6–2, Maruska 6–0 6–4, Wagner 6–1 6–7 6–2, Nagyova 6–7 6–1 6–0, Appelmans 6–2 6–4), **won** Luxembourg (d. Farina 6–2 3–6 6–2, Oremans 7–5 6–7 6–4, Studenikova 6–1 3–6 6–0, Paulus 6–4 3–6 7–5); **r/u** Leipzig (d. Maleeva 6–3 7–5, Grzybowska 6–1 7–6, Hingis 6–4 4–6 7–6, lost Novotna 6–2 4–6 6–3); **sf** Australian Open, **sf** French Open, **sf** Amelia Island (d. Martincova 7–5 6–1, Mauresmo 6–4 1–6 6–1, Novotna 6–2 1–6 6–1, M. J. Fernandez 6–2 6–4, lost Davenport 7–5 6–2), **sf** Bol (d.

Fast-improving Amanda Coetzer, one of only five players to beat Martina Hingis in 1997, ended her best year at No.4, the highest ranking ever by a South African woman. (Michael Cole)

Brandi 2–6 6–0 6–3, Pitkowski 6–4 7–6, lost Lucic 6–4 6–3), **sf** Berlin (d. Studenikova 6–0 6–0, Wiesner 6–1 6–1, Graf 6–0 6–1, lost Pierce 6–4 6–4), **sf** Strasbourg (d. Sawamatsu 6–1 6–2, Sidot 7–5 6–4, Kijimuta 6–2 6–3, lost Graf 4–6 7–5 7–6), **sf** Stanford (d. Tu 6–2 6–0, Po 7–5 6–4, lost Martinez 6–4 6–0), **sf** San Diego (d. Sidot 6–2 6–1, Basuki 6–3 6–4, lost Seles 6–3 6–4), **sf** Atlanta (d. Wild 6–1 6–2, Tauziat 6–2 5–7 6–2, Novotna 1–6 6–3 6–1, lost Davenport 6–2 6–4), **sf** Filderstadt (d.Schultz-McCarthy 7–6 6–3, Kournikova 3–6 6–3 6–4, Schnyder 6–2 7–5, lost Hingis 6–2 6–1). **DOUBLES:** (with Fusai) **won** Budapest (d. Martincova/Wagner 6–3 6–1); (with Pierce) **r/u** Stanford (lost Davenport/Hingis 6–1 6–3).

CAREER GRAND SLAM RECORD

AUSTRALIAN OPEN – Played 5, sf 2

1993: 1r lost Garrison-Jackson [16]. **1994: 2r** [seed 12] d. Begerow 6–1 6–3, lost Rubin 6–1 2–6 6–3. **1995: 3r** d. Montolio 6–2 6–2, Dragomir 6–4 4–6 6–4, lost M. J. Fernandez [13] 6–3 5–7 6–2. **1996: sf** [seed 16] d. Schnell 6–2 6–2, Hack 6–1 6–1, Hiraki 6–3 6–3, Likhovtseva 6–3 6–3, Hingis 7–5 4–6 6–1, lost Huber [8] 4–6 6–4 6–2. **1997: sf** [seed 12] d. Kournikova 6–2 6–2, Kandarr 6–2 7–6, Serna 6–3 6–2, Graf [1] 6–2 7–5, Po 6–4 6–1, lost Pierce 7–5 6–1.

FRENCH OPEN – Played 9, sf 1

1989: last 16 [unseeded] d. Martinek 6–4 6–1, Stafford 6–3 6–3, Gomer 7–6 6–1, lost Sanchez [7] 6–3 6–2. **1990: 1r** lost Sloane 6–4 6–3. **1991: 2r** d. A. Minter 5–7 7–5 6–3, lost Appelmans 6–3 5–7 6–1. **1992: 3r** d. Dechaume 6-4 3-6 6-3, Dopfer 7-6 4-6 6-3, lost Graf [2] 6-2 6-1. **1993: 2r** [seed 11] d. Neiland 6–0 6–4, lost Zvereva 6–2 7–6. **1994: last 16** [unseeded] d. Date [6] 6–2 6–1, Bobkova 6–4 6–4, Kochta 6–0 6–3, lost Pierce [12] 6–1 6–1. **1995: 2r** d. Frankl 6–0 6–4, lost Sabatini [8] 7–5 6–3. **1996: last 16** [seed 14] d. Sugiyama 6–1 7–5, Lubiani 6–4 6–1, Zvereva 6–3 3–6 6–2, lost Martinez [3] 6–2 6–3. **1997: sf** [seed 11] d. Grande 6–4 6–0, Frazier 7–6 6–4, Babel 6–4 6–2, Martinez [7] 6–7 6–4 6–3, Graf [2] 6–1 6–4, lost Majoli [9] 6–3 4–6 7–5.

WIMBLEDON – Played 8

1989: 1r lost K. Adams 7–5 6–3. **1990: 2r** d. Medvedeva 4–6 6–2 6–1, lost McNeil 6–3 6–2. **1991: 2r** d. F. Romano 7–6 6–2, lost Sanchez Vicario [4] 6–4 6–1. **1992:** Did not play. **1993: 2r** [seed 14] d. Testud 6–3 3–6 6–3, lost Stafford 6–3 6–2. **1994: last 16** [seed 14] d. Likhovtseva 6–4 6–0, Field 6–4 6–0, Helgeson 6–0 6–3, lost Neiland 1–6 6–3 6–4. **1995: 2r** d. Schwarz-Ritter 4–6 6–2 6–2, lost Graf [1] 6–3 7–5. **1996: 2r** [seed 14] d. Wagner 6–1 6–1, lost McGrath 7–6 2–6 6–3. **1997: 2r** [seed 6] d. Fusai 7–6 6–1, lost Hy-Boulais 6–2 6–1.

US OPEN – Played 9, qf 2

1989: 1r lost G. Fernandez 6–3 6–3. **1990: 1r** lost Kelesi 7–5 4–6 6–3. **1991: 1r** lost Halard 7–5 6–1. **1992: 3r** d. Paz 6-2 4-6 6-4, Tauziat [12] 6-0 6-0, lost Labat 6-3 4-6 6-4. **1993: 3r** [seed 15] d. Provis 6–3 6–2, Wang 6–1 6–3, lost Davenport 6–1 6–2. **1994: qf** [seed 11] d. Ritter 6–1 7–6, Maniokova 6–2 6–0, de Swardt 6–1 6–3, Endo 6–3 6–0, lost Graf [1] 6–0 6–2. **1995: 1r** lost Graf [seed 1] 6–7 6–1 6–4. **1996: qf** [unseeded] d. Huber [6] 6–1 2–6 6–2, De Swardt 6–2 7–5, Spirlea 7–6 7–5, Raymond 6–4 6–1, lost Seles [2] 6–0 6–3. **1997: last 16** [seed 5] d. Arendt 6–3 6–2, Dechaume-Balleret 6–1 6–1, Perfetti 6–2 7–5, lost Spirlea [11] 7–6 6–4.

OLYMPIC RECORD

1992: (Barcelona) last 16 [unseeded] d. Garrison [12] 7-5 6-1, Blumberga 6-2 6-4, lost Martinez [5] 6-4 6-3. **1996: (Atlanta) 2r** [seed 14] d. McQuillan 6–4 7–6, lost Zvereva 6–1 6–0 6–2.

CAREER FED CUP RECORD

1992 – April *(Qualifying in GRE Clay): Round-robin RSA d. EST 3–0.* R2 d. H. Holter 6–0 6–0. R3 (with E. Reinach) d. Holter/K. Bond 6–0 6–1. *Round-robin RSA d. IRL 3–0.* R2 d. G. Niland 6–1 6–1. *Round-robin RSA d. LUX 3–0.* R2 d. A. Kremer 6–0 6–0. *Qf RSA d. YUG 3–0.* R2 d. L. Pavlov 6–3 6–0. *Sf RSA d. SLO 3–0.* R2 d. B. Mulej 6–4 4–6 6–1. *Final RSA d. CRO 2–1.* R2 d. N. Ercegovic 7–5 4–6 6–2. **July** *(World Group in GER, Clay): 1r CAN d. RSA 2–1.* R2 lost P. Hy-Boulais 2–6 6–2 6–2. *Play-off 1r RSA d. BEL 2–1.* R2 lost S. Appelmans 6–3 6–3. *Play-off 2r RSA d. MEX 3–0.* R2 d. A. Gavaldon 6–2 6–1. **1993 (in GER, Clay):** *World Group 1r TCH d. RSA 2–1.* R2 lost J. Novotna 6–1 6–4. R3 (with E. Reinach) d. A. Strnadova/R. Zrubakova 7–5 6–4. *World Group play-off RSA d. ISR 2–1.* R2 d. Y. Segal 6–3 6–2. R3 (with Reinach) d. Segal/L. Zaltz 6–3 6–0. **1995: April** – *World Group qf FRA d. RSA 3–2 in FRA (Clay).* R1 d. J. Halard-Decugis 6–2 6–4; R3 d. M. Pierce 6–4 6–3. **July** – *World Group play-off RSA d. BUL 5–0 in RSA (Hard).* R2 d. P. Stojanova 6–0 6–1; R3 d. L. Bacheva 6–2 6–4. R5 (with E. Reinach) d. Bacheva/D. Djilianova 6–1 6–4. **1996: April** – *World Group qf ESP d. RSA 3–2 in ESP (Clay).* R2 lost C. Martinez 7–5 6–3; R3 d. A. Sanchez Vicario 6–4 6–1. R5 (with M. De Swardt) d. V. Ruano-Pascual/M. Sanchez Lorenzo 6–4 7–6. **July:** – *World Group play-off BEL d. RSA 4–1 in RSA (Hard).* R2 lost D. Van Roost 6–2 6–3; R3 lost S. Appelmans 6–3 3–6 6–0. R5 (with De Swardt) lost L. Courtois/N. Feber 6–2 3–6 6–0. **1997: March** – *Group 1 qf AUS d. RSA 3–2 in RSA (Hard).* R2 lost R. McQuillan 6–3 7–6; R3 d. A. Ellwood 1–6 6–1 6–0. **July** – *Group 1 play-off AUT d. RSA 3–2 in AUT (Clay).* R2 d. B. Schett 6–1 7–6; R3 d. B. Paulus 6–2 6–0. R5 (with J. Steck) lost Schett/J. Wiesner 6–1 6–4.

SEASON-ENDING CHAMPIONSHIPS – Played 5, qf 1

(1983-94 Virginia Slims, 1995 Corel, 1996–97 Chase)

1993: qf d. M. J. Fernandez 6–1 1–6 6–3, lost Graf 6–1 6–2. **1994: 1r** lost Pierce 5–7 6–3 6–3. **1995: 1r** lost Graf 6–2 6–2. **1996: 1r** lost Novotna 6–4 6–1. **1997: 1r** lost Tauziat 6–3 6–3.

5 MONICA SELES (USA)

Born: Novi Sad, 2 December 1973. **Lives:** Laurel Oak Estates and Country Club, Sarasota, Fla. **Father:** Karolj is cartoonist and TV director. **Mother:** Esther. **Brother:** Zoltan (older). Both parents travel with her, and her brother helps to train her. Discovered at 1985 Orange Bowl by Nick Bollettieri, who moved her family to USA from Yugoslavia in 1986.
Agent: IMG. **Coach:** Her father, Karolj. **Turned pro:** 1989.
Height: 5ft 10in (1.79m). **Weight:** 145lb (65kg).

Rankings: 1988: 86; **1989:** 6; **1990:** 2; **1991:** 1; **1992:** 1; **1993:** 8; **1994:** Not ranked; **1995:** 1 (jointly with Graf); **1996:** 2 (jointly with Sanchez Vicario); **1997:** 5.
Highest: 1 (March 1991).

1997 Prize Money: $914,020. **Career Earnings:** $9,874,510. **Career Titles:** 34.

Style: A naturally competitive left-hander who hits with two hands on both forehand and backhand. Her ability to hit a rising ball with perfect timing allows her to project thunderous drives on both wings that have destroyed all opposition. An improving serve that is now the equal of any of the women, plus a greater willingness to volley, allied to an acute tactical awareness, make her arguably among the finest match players of all time. Since her return in 1995, she has lost some of her speed of shot and of movement.

Ranking: Her ranking was protected when she returned in 1995, an arrangement set to last until she had played 14 tourns or after 18 months. During that time, she was co-ranked with the player whose average was immediately below hers (calculated by dividing points total by tourns played in past 52 weeks, but a minimum of 6).

CAREER HIGHLIGHTS (year: (titles))
Became a US citizen 16 March 1994. **1983:** At age 9, reached last 16 Sport Goofy singles. **1984:** Won Sport Goofy singles. **1985:** Won Sport Goofy singles and doubles. **1988:** Upset Kelesi at VS Florida in 1st pro match, took Sabatini to 1s tb 1r LIPC and upset Magers and McNeil to reach sf New Orleans. **1989: (1)** *Houston*. Won Houston over Evert and was r/u Dallas and Brighton. Unseeded at French Open, she upset Garrison and Manuela Maleeva before extending Graf to 3s sf. **1990: (9)** *FRENCH OPEN, Berlin, Los Angeles, Oakland, VS Champs, LIPC, San Antonio, Tampa, Italian Open*. Following her acrimonious split in March with Bollettieri, who she considered was spending too much time coaching Agassi, she was coached only by her father. At 16 years 6 months became the youngest French Open women's champion and second-youngest GS champion (after Lottie Dod, who was 15 years 10 months when she won Wimbledon in 1897). She went into the French Open having won 5 consec tourns without dropping a set, but her unbeaten run of 36 matches was ended by Garrison in qf Wimbledon. She in turn had ended Graf's 66-match unbeaten run at Berlin. Her season finished in triumph when she beat Sabatini in 5s in f VS Champs to finish with 9 titles. She beat Graf twice and Navratilova 3 times and by year's end had displaced Navratilova to finish ranked 2. Won WTA Most Improved Player award. **1991: (10)** *AUSTRALIAN OPEN, FRENCH OPEN, US OPEN, VS Champs, LIPC, Houston, Los Angeles, Tokyo Nicherei, Milan, Philadelphia*. Enjoyed a spectacular year in which she reached f in all 16 tourns she entered. At 17 years 2 months she became the youngest to take the Australian Open, being 4 months younger than Margaret Smith in 1960, and in March she ousted Graf from the top ranking to become the youngest (17 years 3 months) to reach that spot (Tracy Austin had been 1 month older). Although Graf overtook her again briefly on and off during the summer, Seles finished the year firmly fixed at the top, was voted WTA Singles Player of the Year and was the youngest to be named Official World Champion. She pulled out of Wimbledon 72 hours before the start, losing her chance of completing a GS. She first said she had suffered 'a minor accident' but eventually she claimed she had panicked after being given conflicting advice that the shin splints from which she was suffering might keep her out of the game for 6 months or a year. She was fined $6,000 for withdrawing and $20,000 for subsequently appearing in an exhibition tournament. She also missed Fed Cup, claiming injury,

although she played an exhibition tournament at the same time. **1992: (10)** *AUSTRALIAN OPEN, FRENCH OPEN, US OPEN, VS Champs, Essen, Indian Wells, Houston, Barcelona, Tokyo Nicherei, Oakland*. After she had won Australian Open and become the 1st woman since Hilde Sperling in 1937 to win 3 consec French Opens, she seemed on course for a GS. But Graf, who had stretched her to 10–8 fs in Paris, demolished her in Wimbledon f and thereafter she seemed less invincible, although she won her 3rd GS title of the year at US Open and finished the season with ss win over Navratilova in f of VS Champs. She was beaten all year only 5 times – by Capriati at LIPC (the only tourn she entered in which she failed to reach the f), by Sabatini at Italian Open, Graf at Wimbledon, Navratilova at Los Angeles and by Sanchez Vicario at Montreal. She took a total of 10 titles, including Houston for the loss of only 8 games, and when she won Barcelona at 18 years 4 months, she beat Tracy Austin's record of 18 years 8 months as youngest to achieve 25 singles titles. Controversy was never far away, and in 1992 it was her grunting which was the main subject. She played the Wimbledon final almost silently (refusing to make that an excuse for her defeat) and for the rest of the year made an attempt to control the noise, which players and spectators alike found distasteful and disturbing. She was voted Player of Year for the second straight year and set a new record for prize money won in one season, beating Edberg's record $2,363,575 in 1991. **1993: (2)** *AUSTRALIAN OPEN, VS Chicago*. She suffered a nightmare year, at the end of which there was still some question whether she would return to competitive play. Having taken a 2-month break, she returned to win Australian Open but was then sidelined for 2 months with a viral infection, missing LIPC. She returned to action at Hamburg where, on 30 April, during a changeover after she had recovered from 0–3 down to 4–3 v Magdalena Maleeva, she was stabbed in the back by Gunther Parche, a German who wanted to put her out of action to enable Steffi Graf to return to the No. 1 position. She and the rest of the world were horrified when Parche was given only a two-year suspended sentence in autumn, while Seles was sidelined for more than 2 years as the injury, which required only 2 stitches, was worse than first thought – and the psychological damage was considerable, requiring more than 100 hours of therapy. In the other 2 tourns she played, she won VS Chicago and was r/u Paris Open to Navratilova. **1994:** She did not play at all and dropped off the rankings on 14 Feb., a month before becoming US citizen. **1995: (1)** *Toronto*. She returned to the public arena in a much-publicised exhibition match v Navratilova at Atlantic City on 29 July, which she won 6–3 6–2. Two inches taller, 10lb heavier and with some new one-handed strokes in her repertoire, she was co-ranked No. 1 with Graf when she returned to the tour, a position it was agreed she should hold for her 1st 6 matches. Despite her extra weight and suffering from tendinitis in her left knee, she was still head and shoulders above anyone else apart from Graf, sweeping to the title at her 1st tourn back at Toronto, where she dropped only 14 games in 5 matches. She then moved as convincingly to f US Open, losing no set until Graf beat her there, and was given a special invitation to play in WTA Champs. However, when her knee and ankle problems flared up again, despite a rest until end Oct., she was forced to withdraw first from Oakland and then from WTA Champs. Voted Comeback Player of the Year and Most Exciting Player. **1996: (5)** *AUSTRALIAN OPEN, Sydney, Eastbourne, Montreal, Tokyo Nicherei*. Having won her 1st 2 tourns of year at Sydney and Australian Open, she suffered only the 2nd defeat since her return when Majoli upset her in qf Tokyo Toray. At Australian Open she had recovered from 2–5 down in 3s sf v Rubin and maintained her record of never having lost a match at the event. However, she suffered tendinitis and a small tear to the lining of the shoulder socket, which may in the long term require surgery and in the short term caused her to withdraw from Indian Wells, LIPC, FC Cup and before sf Madrid. That was her 1st tourn on European red clay since her stabbing on that surface in Hamburg, and although not fully fit, she had wanted to overcome the mental barrier of returning to Europe before French Open. She was determined to play in Paris, regardless of her injury, and was magnificent in beating M. Maleeva, whom she had been playing when stabbed, but was below par (particularly her serve) when losing to Novotna. It ended her run of 25 consec. match wins there since 1989, and was only her 5th defeat on clay. Still receiving 2 hours' treatment a day on her shoulder, she won her 1st title on grass at Eastbourne, but her timing deserted her at Wimbledon and she fell 2r to Studenikova. Novotna inflicted a second defeat in qf Olympics and Graf beat her again in f US Open, but she won Montreal and Tokyo Nicherei and was in the winning USA Fed Cup team that d. ESP 5–0 in f, after making her debut in Japan in July. In Oct. she began a rehabilitation programme for her shoulder in the hope of avoiding surgery, returning at the end of the month at Chicago, where she lost sf to Capriati. On 4 Nov. she slipped from the top to No. 2, co-ranked with Sanchez Vicario, and at Oakland suffered the most one-sided defeat of her career at the hands of Hingis. Losing 6–2 6–0, she recorded her 1st set lost to love since Nov. 1990 and only the 4th of her pro career. The year ended in further disappointment when her shoulder injury forced her to retire v Date 1r Chase Champs, and she was left seriously considering surgery. That, however, would necessitate an absence of several months from the tour and another setback in her psychological rehabilitation. Then in Dec., warming up for an exhibition match, she broke a finger on her right hand. **1997: (3)** *Los Angeles, Toronto, Tokyo Nicherei.* Having missed 4 tourns, including Australian Open, she returned in March at LIPC, where she appeared overwhelmed both physically and mentally by Hingis in f, losing in 44 mins. She lost to the same player in 3s tb in f FC Cup, having recovered from 2–5 down in 3s, and withdrew from Amelia Island with bronchitis. She was further distracted by the absence of her father, fighting in US against stomach cancer and unable to be with her for French Open, where she lost sf in 3s to Hingis, and Wimbledon, where she was beaten 3r by Testud. From 21 July, however, she played 7 tourns in 9 weeks, winning her 1st title of the year at Los Angeles in Aug. She followed with Toronto the next week and then Tokyo Nicherei, where she also took the doubles with Sugiyama (the 5th doubles title of her career – each won with a different partner). She was also r/u Madrid and San Diego, and played qf Eastbourne, Stanford, Atlanta, Chicago and Philadelphia, qualifying for Chase Champs by end Sept. At US Open, she held mp in 2s tb v Spirlea, but went on to lose the match. She was encouraged to have played through 4 months without injury, and although she withdrew Moscow in Oct. with a shoulder injury, she was back in action the following week at Chicago, where she was r/u doubles with Davenport. At the start of Chase Champs, where she fell 1r to Sanchez Vicario, she had slipped to No. 5 in the rankings.

A year of mixed emotions for Monica Seles, who was supplanted by Martina Hingis as the youngest player ever to be ranked No. 1, yet retained her top ten place despite injuries and the worry of her father's serious illness. (Tommy Hindley)

PRINCIPAL 1997 RESULTS – won 3, r/u 4, sf 1 (detailed Grand Slam results follow)
won Los Angeles (d. Testud 6–7 7–6 6–3, Zvereva 6–1 6–1, Frazier 6–0 6–2, Davenport 5–7 7–5 6–4), **won** Toronto (d. Carlsson 6–2 6–4, Appelmans 6–3 7–5, Grande 6–2 7–6, Martinez 6–2 7–6, Huber 6–2 6–4), **won** Tokyo Nicherei (d. Tanasugarn 6–1 6–4, Zvereva 6–1 6–0, Sawamatsu 6–3 6–1, Sanchez Vicario 6–1 3–6 7–6); **r/u** LIPC (d. Sawamatsu 6–3 2–6 6–2, Frazier 6–3 6–3, Carlsson 6–2 6–1, Spirlea 3–6 6–2 6–3, Paulus 6–3 6–3, lost Hingis 6–2 6–1), **r/u** FC Cup (d. Wang 6–3 6–3, Gersi 6–2 7–6, Huber 6–3 6–0, Martinez 6–3 6–4, lost Hingis 3–6 6–3 7–6), **r/u** Madrid (d. Sanchez-Lorenzo 6–0 6–1, Ruano-Pascual 6–2 6–1, Labat 6–7 6–1 6–2, lost Novotna 7–5 6–1), **r/u** San Diego (d. Sugiyama 6–4 6–4, Zvereva 6–1 6–3, Coetzer 6–3 6–4, lost Hingis 7–6 6–4); **sf** French Open. **DOUBLES:** (with Sugiyama) **won** Tokyo Nicherei (d. Halard-Decugis/Rubin 6–1 6–0); (with Davenport) **r/u** Chicago (lost Fusai/Tauziat 6–3 6–2).

CAREER GRAND SLAM RECORD

AUSTRALIAN OPEN – Played 4, won 4

1991: won [seed 2] d. Hack 6–0 6–0, Caverzasio 6–1 6–0, Kschwendt 6–3 6–1, Tanvier 6–2 6–1, Huber 6–3 6–1, Fernandez [3] 6–3 0–6 9–7, Novotna [10] 5–7 6–3 6–1. **1992: won** [seed 1] d. Kijimuta 6–2 6–0, Date 6–2 7–5, Basuki 6–1 6–1, Meskhi [13] 6–4 4–6 6–2, Huber [12] 7–5 6–3, Sanchez Vicario [4] 6–2 6–2, M. J. Fernandez [7] 6–2 6–3. **1993: won** [seed 1] d. Pizzichini 6–1 6–2, Strandlund 6–2 6–0, Fendick 6–1 6–0, Tauziat [13] 6–2 6–0, Halard 6–2 6–7 6–0, Sabatini [3] 6–1 6–2, Graf [2] 4–6 6–3 6–2. **1994–95:** Did not play. **1996: won** [seed 1] d. J. Lee 6–3 6–0, Studenikova 6–1 6–1, Halard-Decugis 7–5 6–0, Sawamatsu 6–1 6–3, Majoli [7] 6–1 6–2, Rubin [13] 6–7 6–1 7–5, Huber [8] 6–4 6–1. **1997:** Did not play.

FRENCH OPEN – Played 6, won 3, sf 2, qf 1

1989: sf d. Reis 6–4 6–1, Martin 6–0 6–2, Garrison [4] 6–3 6–2, Faull 6–3 6–2, M. Maleeva [6] 6–3 7–5, lost Graf [1] 6–3 3–6 6–3. **1990: won** [seed 2] d. Piccolini 6–0 6–0, Kelesi 4–6 6–4 6–4, Meskhi 7–6 7–6, Gildemeister [16] 6–4 6–0, Maleeva-Fragniere [6] 3–6 6–1 7–5, Capriati 6–2 6–2, Graf [1] 7–6 6–4. **1991: won** [seed 1] d. Zrubakova 6–3 6–0, de Swardt 6–0 6–2, Quentrec 6–1 6–2, Cecchini 3–6 6–3 6–0, Martinez [7] 6–0 7–5, Sabatini [3] 6–4 6–1, Sanchez Vicario [5] 6–3 6–4. **1992: won** [seed 1] d. Mothes 6–1 6–0, Kschwendt 6–2 6–2, McNeil 6–0 6–1, Kijimuta 6–1 3–6 6–4, Capriati [5] 6–2 6–2, Sabatini [3] 6–3 4–6 6–4, Graf [2] 6–2 3–6 10–8. **1993–95:** Did not play. **1996: qf** [seed 1] d. Chenin 6–1 6–1, Sawamatsu 7–6 6–2, Appelmans 6–2 7–5, M. Maleeva [13] 6–1 6–1, lost Novotna [10] 7–6 6–3. **1997: sf** [seed 3] d. Saeki 6–0 6–3, Pitkowski 6–3 7–5, Tauziat 6–0 6–1, Pierce [10] 6–4 7–5, M. J. Fernandez [12] 3–6 6–2 7–5, lost Hingis [1] 6–7 7–5 6–4.

WIMBLEDON – Played 5, r/u 1, qf 1

1989: last 16 [seed 11] d. Schultz 7–6 1–6 6–4, Porwik 6–2 6–4, Sviglerova 6–4 6–3, lost Graf [1] 6–0 6–1. **1990: qf** [seed 3] d. Strandlund 6–2 6–0, Benjamin 6–3 7–5, A. Minter 6–3 6–3, Henricksson 6–1 6–0, lost Garrison [5] 6–3 3–6 6–4. **1991:** Did not play. **1992: r/u** [seed 1] d. Byrne 6–2 6–2, Appelmans 6–3 6–2, Gildemeister 6–4 6–1, G. Fernandez 6–4 6–2, Tauziat [14] 6–1 6–3, Navratilova [4] 6–2 6–7 6–4, lost Graf 6–2 6–1. **1993–95:** Did not play. **1996: 2r** [seed 2] d. Grossman 6–1 6–2, lost Studenikova 7–5 6–7 6–4. **1997: 3r** [seed 2] d. McQuillan 6–0 6–2, Brandi 5–7 6–3 6–3, lost Testud 0–6 6–4 8–6.

US OPEN – Played 7, won 2, r/u 2, qf 1

1989: last 16 [seed 12] d. Henricksson 4–6 6–2 6–2, A. Smith 7–5 6–2, Stafford 7–6 6–2, lost Evert [4] 6–0 6–2. **1990: 3r** [seed 3] d. Pampoulova 6–0 6–0, Fairbank-Nideffer 6–2 6–2, lost Ferrando 1–6 6–1 7–6. **1991: won** [seed 2] d. Arendt 6–2 6–0, Zardo 7–5 6–1, Gomer 6–1 6–4, Rajchrtova 6–1 6–1, G. Fernandez 6–2 6–2, Capriati [7] 6–3 3–6–7–6, Navratilova [6] 7–6 6–1. **1992: won** [seed 1] d. Keller 6–1 6–0, Raymond 7–5 6–0, Porwik 6–4 6–0, G. Fernandez 6–1 6–2, Hy 6–1 6–2, M. J. Fernandez [7], Sanchez Vicario [5] 6–3 6–3. **1993–94:** Did not play. **1995: r/u** [seed 2] d. Dragomir 6–3 6–1, de Lone 6–2 6–1, Kamio 6–1 6–1, Huber [11] 6–1 6–4, Novotna [seed 5] 7–6 6–2, Martinez [4] 6–2 6–2, lost Graf [1] 7–6 0–6 6–3. **1996: r/u** [seed 2] d. Miller 6–0 6–1, Courtois w.o., Randriantefy 6–0 6–2, Testud 7–5 6–0, Coetzer 6–0 6–3, Martinez [4] 6–4 6–3, lost Graf [1] 7–5 6–4. **1997: qf** [seed 2] d. Boogert 6–1 6–2, Snyder 6–2 6–3, Oremans 6–1 6–1, Pierce [9] 1–6 6–2 6–2, lost Spirlea [seed 11] 6–7 7–6 6–3.

OLYMPIC RECORD

1996: (Atlanta) qf [seed 1] d. Chen 6–0 6–4, Hy-Boulais 6–3 6–2, Sabatini 6–3 6–3, lost Novotna [6] 7–5 3–6 8–6).

CAREER FED CUP RECORD

1996: July – *World Group sf USA d. JPN 5–0 in JPN (Carpet).* R2 d. A. Sugiyama 6–2 6–2; R3 d. K. Date 6–0 6–2. **September** – *World Group Final USA d. ESP 5–0 in USA (Carpet).* R1 d. C. Martinez 6–2 6–4; R3 d. A. Sanchez Vicario 3–6 6–3 6–1.

SEASON ENDING CHAMPIONSHIPS – Played 6, won 3, qf 1

(1983–94 Virginia Slims, 1995 Corel, 1996–97 Chase)

1989: qf lost Navratilova 6–3 5–7 7–5. **1990: won** d. Paulus 6–2 6–2, Sanchez Vicario 5–7 7–6 6–4, M. J. Fernandez 6–3 6–4, Sabatini 6–4 5–7 3–6 6–4 6–2. **1991: won** d. Halard 6–1 6–0, M. J. Fernandez 6–3 6–2, Sabatini 6–1 6–1, Navratilova 6–4 3–6 7–5 6–0. **1992: won** d. Tauziat 6–1 6–2, Novotna 3–6 6–4 6–1, Sabatini 7–6 6–1, Navratilova 7–5 6–3 6–1. **1993–95:** Did not play. **1996: 1r** lost Date 5–4 ret'd. **1997: 1r** lost Sanchez Vicario 3–6 6–4 6–4.

6 IVA MAJOLI (CRO)

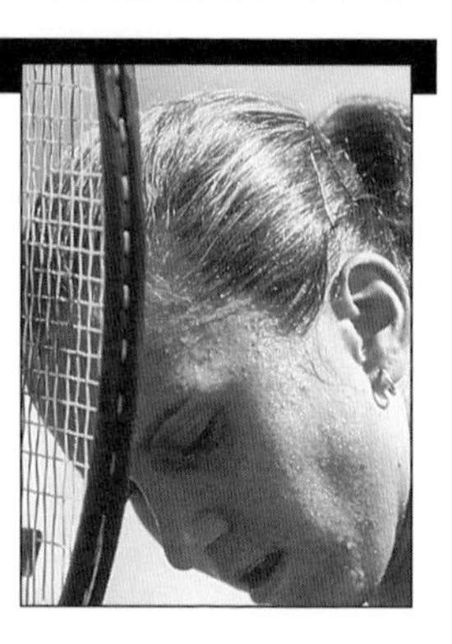

Born: Zagreb, 12 August 1977. **Lives:** Zagreb.
Father: Stanko. **Mother:** Dradica. **Brother.** Drago, older.
Sister: Nina, older.
Agent: IMG. **Coaches:** Her father and brother Drago. Worked with Nikki Pilic at start of 1995 and with Goran Prpic in 1996.
Turned pro: 1991.
Height: 5ft 8in (1.73m). **Weight:** 136lb (61kg).

Rankings: 1991: 798; **1992:** 50; **1993:** 46; **1994:** 13; **1995:** 9; **1996:** 7; **1997:** 6. **Highest:** 4 (February 1996).

1997 Prize Money: $1,227,332.
Career Earnings: $3,173,232. **Career Titles:** 7.

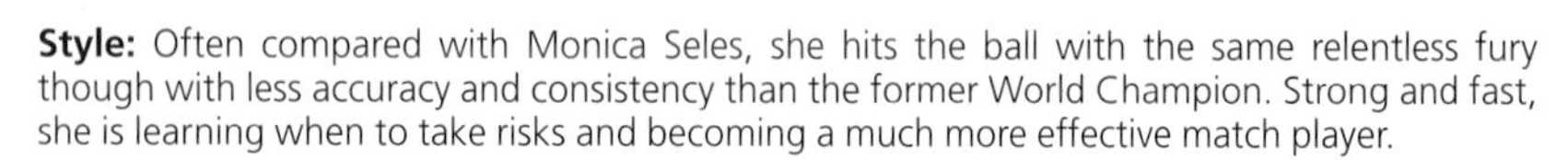

Style: Often compared with Monica Seles, she hits the ball with the same relentless fury though with less accuracy and consistency than the former World Champion. Strong and fast, she is learning when to take risks and becoming a much more effective match player.

CAREER HIGHLIGHTS (year: (titles))
At 12, she moved with her father and brother to USA to attend Bollettieri Tennis Academy, where they were joined later by her sister and mother. However, missing the rest of her family and friends, she returned home. **1992:** Reached qf VS Houston (d. McNeil), Oakland (d. McNeil again) and Indianapolis (d. Tauziat) to break into top 50. Won St Simons and Evansville Challengers back-to-back. **1993:** Reached qf VS Chicago and Oakland. Unseeded at French Open, she upset Hack on her way to last 16, where she extended Graf to 2s tb. Voted WTA Most Impressive Newcomer. **1994:** She proved to be a dangerous opponent and recorded some big upsets during the year as she moved into the top 20. Reached her 1st tour f at Osaka, following with the same stage Barcelona (d. Martinez and Mag. Maleeva) and Essen (d. Huber), sf Indian Wells (d. Zvereva), FC Cup (d. Sabatini and Davenport) and Stratton Mountain (d. M. J. Fernandez) and 3 more qf. In GS she made an unexpected appearance in last 16 French and US Opens and qualified for VS Champs 1st time, losing 1r to Novotna. **1995: (2)** *Zurich, Filderstadt.* She continued her upsetting ways in spring when she surprised Pierce at French Open and took a set off Sanchez Vicario in f Barcelona. She went on to win her 1st title at Zurich in Oct. (d. Pierce again and Novotna) and broke into the top 10 after following with Filderstadt next week (d. Pierce a 3rd time and Sabatini). She also appeared in sf Tokyo Pan Pacific and Paris Open, plus qf FC Cup, Italian Open and Toronto to qualify for VS Champs, where she lost 1r to Martinez. **1996: (2)** *Tokyo Toray, Essen.* At Tokyo Toray in Jan. she became only the 2nd player (after Graf) to beat Seles since her comeback, going on to upset Sanchez Vicario for the title and following in Feb. with Essen over Novotna. She was playing her 3rd consec. singles f, having appeared at that stage at Paris Open in between. She was also r/u Leipzig and reached sf Italian Open, Berlin and Zurich, plus qf Australian Open, French Open, Olympics, FC Cup, Rosmalen and Filderstadt, as well as winning the Hopman Cup with Ivanisevic. At Chase Champs she upset Huber and Martinez (overcoming a displaced rib during that match) before extending Hingis to 3s sf. **1997: (3)** *FRENCH OPEN, Hannover, Hamburg.* The high point of her career came at French Open, where she won her 1st GS title and ended Hingis's unbeaten run in 1997 of 37 matches. In 4r she recovered from 5–7 0–4 down v Davenport, and in sf had to overcome the debilitating effect of a virus. Earlier, she had won Hannover over Novotna and retained her record in Germany with the title at Hamburg, where she was r/u doubles with Dragomir. She also reached sf Paris Open, Amelia Island, Atlanta and Chicago, plus qf Sydney, Tokyo Pan Pacific, LIPC, Leipzig and Chase Champs.

PRINCIPAL 1997 RESULTS – won 3, sf 4 (detailed Grand Slam results follow)
won French Open, **won** Hannover (d. Basuki 7–5 6–1, Sidot 4–6 7–6 6–4, Paulus 7–6 6–4, Novotna 4–6 7–6 6–4), **won** Hamburg (d. Serna 6–4 7–5, Pierce 2–6 6–4 6–4, Sanchez-Lorenzo 6–2 6–3, Dragomir 6–4 6–0); **sf** Paris Open (d. Sidot 6–4 6–3, Basuki 7–6 3–6 6–3, lost Hingis 6–1 6–3), **sf** Amelia Island (d. Montolio 6–3 6–2, Fusai 6–0 6–2, Martinez 1–6 6–3 6–3, lost Pierce 2–6 7–5 7–6), **sf** Atlanta (d. Likhovtseva 6–2 3–6 6–4, Schultz-McCarthy 6–2 7–5, lost Testud 7–5 6–3), **sf** Chicago (d. Courtois 7–5 6–1, Basuki 4–6 7–5 6–4, lost Tauziat 6–2 6–3). **DOUBLES:** (with Dragomir) **r/u** Hamburg (lost Huber/Pierce 2–6 7–6 6–2).

CAREER GRAND SLAM RECORD

AUSTRALIAN OPEN – Played 2, qf 1.

1996: qf [seed 7] d. Makarova 6–4 6–2, McNeil 6–3 6–2, Fusai 6–2 6–1, Appelmans 6–2 6–2, lost Seles [1] 6–1 6–2. **1997: 1r** [seed 5] lost Schnyder 7–5 6–1.

FRENCH OPEN – Played 5, won 1, qf 2

1993: last 16 [unseeded] d. Dopfer 6–2 6–4, Louise Allen 6–0 6–1, Hack [15] 6–0 7–6, lost Graf [1] 6–4 7–6. **1994: last 16** [unseeded] (d. Monami 6–1 7–5, Farina 6–4 6–1, Kschwendt 3–6 6–3 6–1, lost Gorrochategui 7–5 6–4. **1995: qf** [seed 12] d. Endo 6–3 6–3, Gaidano 6–1 6–0, Wang 7–5 6–2, Pierce [3] 6–2 6–3, lost Date [9] 7–5 6–1. **1996: qf** [seed 5] d. Meier 6–3 6–4, Grande 6–3 7–6, Testud 4–6 7–5 6–4, Leon Garcia 6–3 6–1, lost Graf [1] 6–3 6–1. **1997: won** [seed 9] d. Kleinova 7–5 6–4, Fusai 6–2 6–3, Grossman 6–1 4–6 6–1, Davenport [5] 5–7 6–4 6–2, Dragomir 6–3 5–7 6–2, Coetzer [11] 6–3 4–6 7–5, Hingis [1] 6–4 6–2.

WIMBLEDON – Played 3, qf 1

1994: 1r lost Cacic 4–6 6–3 6–4. **1995: 1r** [seed 11] lost Gavaldon 1–6 6–3 6–1. **1996:** Did not play. **1997: qf** [seed 4] d. Diaz-Oliva 2–6 6–0 6–3, Maruska 6–3 6–3, Cross 4–6 7–6 6–4, Spirlea [12] 6–7 6–1 9–7, lost Kournikova 7–6 6–4.

US OPEN – Played 6

1992: 2r d. de Swardt 6–4 6–4, lost Labat 6–3 6–3. **1993: 2r** d. McQuillan 6–3 6–3, lost Novotna [8] 6–3 6–0. **1994: last 16** [unseeded] d. Van Lottum 6–1 2–0 ret'd, Reinach 6–2 6–2, Smashnova 6–2 6–3, lost Pierce [12] 6–1 6–2. **1995: 1r** [seed 13] lost Paulus 6–4 6–4. **1996: 1r** [seed 5] lost Wiesner 2–6 6–3 6–1. **1997: 2r** [seed 4] d. Cristea 6–3 6–2, lost Testud 6–4 2–6 6–1.

OLYMPIC RECORD

1996: (Atlanta) qf [seed 4] d. Bradtke 3–6 6–3 6–4, Ruano-Pascual 7–5 6–3, Habsudova 6–4 3–6 6–4, lost Davenport [9] 7–5 6–3.

CAREER FED CUP RECORD

1993 (in GBR, Hard): *Qualifying round-robin CRO d. EST 3–0.* R2 d. H. Holter 6–3 6–2; R3 (with M. Muric) d. Holter/A. Tulp 6–2 7–5. *Qualifying round-robin CRO d. TUR 3–0.* R1 d. I. Aksit 6–2 6–1; R3 (with Muric) d. E. Bayburt/G. Giltekin 6–1 6–0. *Qualifying knock-out CRO d. RUS 2–1.* R2 lost E. Makarova 7–5 6–4; R3 (with Muric) d. Makarova/E. Maniokova 6–3 7–5. **1994 (in GER, Clay):** *World Group 1r BUL d. CRO 2–1.* R2 d. M. Maleeva 3–6 6–4 6–4; R3 (with M. Muric) lost K./M. Maleeva 6–2 6–3. **1995** *(Euro/Africa Regional Qualifying 1 in ESP, Clay): Round-robin BEL d. CRO 2–1.* R2 lost S. Appelmans 6–2 6–2. *Round-robin CRO d. ISR 3–0.* R2 d. A. Smashnova 6–1 4–6 6–3. *Round-robin ROM d. CRO 2–1.* R2 d. R. Dragomir 6–4 6–2; R3 (with N. Ercegovic) lost C. Cristea/Dragomir 4–6 6–3 6–1. **1996:** *(Euro/Africa Group 1 in ESP, Clay): Round-robin CRO d. GEO 3–0.* R2 d. N. Louarsabishvili 7–5 0–6 6–4. *Round-robin CRO d. YUG 3–0.* R2 d. D. Zaric 6–2 6–2. *Round-robin SUI d. CRO 2–1.* R2 lost M. Hingis 5–7 6–1 6–1; R3 (with M. Lucic) lost A. Burgis/Hingis 6–1 7–5. *Qf CRO d. ROM 3–0.* R2 d. R. Dragomir 6–2 6–3. *Final CRO d. BUL 2–1.* R1 d. N. Zvereva 6–1 6–2. **1997: March** – *Group I qf CRO d. AUT 4–1 in CRO (Hard).* R1 d. B. Schett 7–5 4–6 6–2; R3 lost J. Wiesner 6–4 6–4. **July** – *World Group play-off GER d. CRO 3–2 in GER (Carpet).* R1 d. M. Babel 6–2 6–3; R3 lost A. Huber 6–7 6–2 6–0; R5 (with M. Lucic) lost Babel/Huber 7–6 6–7 6–1.

SEASON ENDING CHAMPIONSHIPS – Played 4, sf 1, qf 1

(1983–94 Virginia Slims, 1995 Corel, 1996–97 Chase)

1994: 1r lost Novotna 6–3 3–6 6–1. **1995: 1r** lost Martinez 1–6 7–5 6–0. **1996: sf** d. Huber 7–5 6–3, Martinez 7–6 7–6, lost Hingis 6–2 4–6 6–1. **1997: qf** d. Huber 7–6 7–6, lost Tauziat 7–6 7–6.

7 MARY PIERCE (FRA)

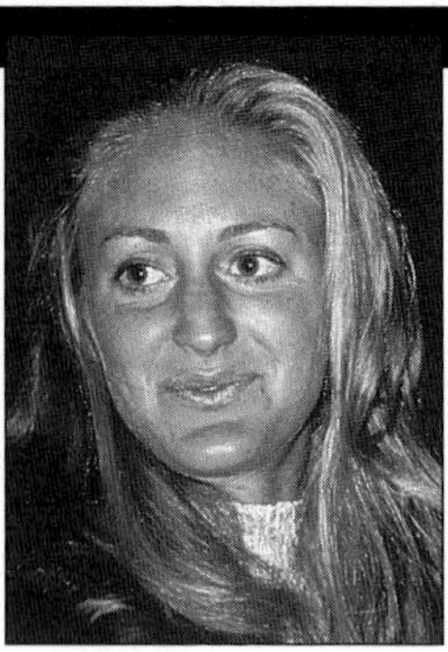

Born: Montreal, Canada, 15 January 1975. **Lives:** Paris and Bradenton, Fla., USA. **Father:** Jim. **Mother:** Yannick, who is French. **Brother:** David (younger).
Agent: IMG. **Coach:** Craig Kardon from February 1997; formerly her father, then Nick Bollettieri, Sven Groeneveld, Joe Giuliano and Brad Gilbert. **Trainer:** Jose Rincon.
Turned pro: March 1989.
Height: 5ft 10in (1.80m). **Weight:** 143lb (65kg).

Rankings: 1989: 236; **1990:** 106; **1991:** 26; **1992:** 13; **1993:** 12; **1994:** 5; **1995:** 5. **1996:** 20. **1997:** 7.
Highest: 3 (February 1995).

1997 Prize Money: $881,639. **Career Earnings:** $3,219,509. **Career Titles:** 7.

Style: An exciting, forceful baseliner with uncompromising attitude whose forehand rivals Graf's for pace. Her two-handed backhand is also powerful, though somewhat erratic. Not a natural volleyer. Has improved her movement and also her awareness of when to take risks.

CAREER HIGHLIGHTS (year: (titles))
Decided to play for France, her mother's country, when the USTA, put off by her father's aggressive manner, were not interested in supporting her. He was banned indefinitely from all her tournaments from French Open 1993 – mainly as a consequence of his disruptive behaviour, but also after bruises on her arms and shoulders, which he had inflicted, were noticed. Free from his dominance, she gained in confidence and was advised until Feb. 1996 by Nick Bollettieri. **1989:** At 14 yrs 2 mths at Hilton Head, she was the youngest to make her pro debut – a record broken the following year by Capriati. Won York on the USTA satellite circuit. **1990:** Reached sf Athens and moved to France, representing that country in Fed Cup. **1991: (1)** *Palermo.* At Palermo she won both singles and doubles for her 1st career title, which took her into the top 50. Upset Fairbank-Nideffer *en route* to last 16 LIPC and appeared in sf Puerto Rico. **1992: (3)** *Cesena, Palermo, Puerto Rico.* Broke into the top 20 after winning Cesena and followed with Palermo and Puerto Rico, plus sf Essen. Reached last 16 French Open and US Open, but was forced to withdraw from LIPC with leg and back strains. **1993: (1)** *Filderstadt.* She won Filderstadt, was r/u Palermo and reached sf Brighton plus 6 more qf, including Australian Open, where she extended Sabatini to 3s. From May onwards, once her aggressive father was excluded from her affairs, she was noticeably more relaxed in her game. She confirmed this improvement and crowned her year by upsetting Sabatini and Navratilova (her 1st victories over top 10 players) on her way to sf VS Champs, for which she qualified 1st time. **1994:** The highlight of her career came at French Open, where she swept to f with the loss of only 10 games – 4 in her sf v Graf, whom she demolished, having managed to win only one game against the same opponent in 1993 US Open. Her loss of only 6 games to qf was a modern-day record. Playing Under-21 at Eastbourne to get used to grass (which she finds difficult to play on), she lost 1r and then announced her withdrawal from Wimbledon 'for reasons beyond my control', later claiming that she could not face the threat that her father might appear there, brought over by a British tabloid newspaper. Although she won no title, she was r/u Houston, Leipzig, Filderstadt, Philadelphia and reached sf FC Cup (upsetting Sanchez Vicario) and Montreal. At VS Champs she again made her mark, upsetting Graf before falling to Davenport in sf. **1995: (2)** *AUSTRALIAN OPEN, Tokyo Nicherei.* She began the year in tremendous style at Australian Open when she took her 1st GS title without losing a set. However, things went downhill thereafter as she was restricted by a series of illness and injury problems. She suffered a groin pull in Feb., then a bad reaction to antibiotics for a kidney infection caused her to withdraw 2r Hamburg, so that the French Open was only her 7th tourn of the year. Despite complaining of shoulder and groin injuries after her defeat in last 16 there, she did appear at Wimbledon for 1st time, although Tauziat beat her 2r. She upset Sanchez Vicario to win Tokyo Nicherei and appeared in f Paris Open and Zurich, as well as sf Italian Open and San Diego, plus 4 more qf. She moved as high as No. 3 behind Sanchez Vicario in Feb., although she had slipped back to No. 6 by Nov. Qualified for WTA Champs but lost 1r to

The glamorous French No. 1, Mary Pierce, battling against injuries, played her full part in helping her country to win the Fed Cup for the first time. (Tommy Hindley)

Huber. **1996:** She seemed to have lost her way in what turned out to be a disappointing year in which she was affected by injuries. She began the year badly when she became the 1st defending Australian Open champ in the Open era to lose before qf. Her 2r loss saw her fall from the top 10 for 1st time since June 1994, and Nick Bollettieri resigned as her coach in an acrimonious split. She was booed off the court after her defeat at the hands of Rittner 3r French Open and departed without waiting for her opponent after a display of stalling and gamesmanship. Her best performances were at Amelia Island, where she upset Martinez *en route* f, and Hamburg, where she upset Hingis to reach sf. Otherwise her only qf appearances were at Tokyo Nicherei and at Wimbledon, where, on her least favourite surface, she performed better than expected. On that occasion, she wore a demure white outfit, in contrast to the low-cut black number that aroused such interest at the French Open. She withdrew from Filderstadt, Zurich and Oakland to rest her right shoulder, which had been troubling her for much of the year. **1997:** Returning after 3 months' absence, she had slipped so far down the rankings that she was unseeded at Australian Open, where she upset Huber and Coetzer on her way to f. Then she withdrew Indian Wells with a right calf strain suffered at Fed Cup and was out for another 5 weeks. On her return, she upset Sanchez Vicario and Majoli on her way to f Amelia Island and surprised Majoli again to reach the same stage Berlin. She also reached sf San Diego and qf Paris Open, Hamburg and Rosmalen, and played in winning FRA Fed Cup team in Oct., although an elbow injury had kept her out of sf in July. After missing another 3 tourns in autumn with a kidney infection, she was beaten by S. Williams at Chicago on her return and withdrew from Philadelphia to recover and prepare for Chase Champs. She obviously did that to good effect, for in qf she became only the 5th player all year to beat Hingis. In her 1st f there, she seriously challenged Novotna for 1s, but went on to lose in ss. Played 2 doubles f, winning Hamburg with Huber.

PRINCIPAL 1997 RESULTS – r/u 4, sf 1 (detailed Grand Slam results follow)
r/u Australian Open, **r/u** Amelia Island (d. Wagner 6–0 6–1, Nagyova 7–5 6–0, Huber 7–6 6–2, Sanchez Vicario 6–2 6–1, Majoli 2–6 7–5 7–6, lost Davenport 6–2 6–3), **r/u** Berlin (d. Wagner 6–2 6–3, Kleinova 6–3 2–6 6–2, Martinez 6–2 6–0, Majoli 6–1 6–4, lost M. J. Fernandez 6–4 6–2), **r/u** Chase Champs; **sf** San Diego (d. Frazier 6–3 6–7 6–3, Tauziat 6–2 6–1, Testud 6–3 6–2, lost Hingis 6–0 6–2). **DOUBLES:** (with Huber) **won** Hamburg (d. Dragomir/Majoli 2–6 7–6 6–2); (with Coetzer) **r/u** Stanford (lost Davenport/Hingis 6–1 6–3).

CAREER GRAND SLAM RECORD

AUSTRALIAN OPEN – Played 5, won 1, r/u 1, qf 1

1993: qf [seed 10] d. Byrne 6–2 6–2, Date 6–1 6–1, Davenport 6–3 6–0, G. Fernandez 6–0 6–0, lost Sabatini [3] 4–6 7–6 6–0). **1994: last 16** [seed 9] d. Baudone 6–2 6–1, Harvey-Wild 6–7 7–5 6–3, Appelmans 6–3 6–2, lost Sabatini [4] 6–3 6–3. **1995: won** [seed 4] d. Krizan 6–1 6–0, Reinach 6–1 6–2, Randriantefy 6–3 6–3, Huber [10] 6–2 6–4, Zvereva [8] 6–1 6–4, Martinez [2] 6–3 6–1, Sanchez Vicario 6–3 6–2. **1996: 2r** [seed 4] d. Schwarz 6–3 6–1, lost Likhovtseva 7–6 4–6 7–5. **1997: r/u** [unseeded] d. Likhovtseva 3–6 6–2 6–4, Medvedeva 6–2 6–2, Kochta 6–0 6–2, Huber [5] 6–2 6–3, Appelmans 1–6 6–4 6–4, Coetzer [12] 7–5 6–1, lost Hingis [4] 6–2 6–2.

FRENCH OPEN – Played 8, r/u 1

1990: 2r d. Fulco 6–0 6–1, lost M. J. Fernandez [7] 6–4 6–4. **1991: 3r** d. Dahlman 7–6 6–0, Martinek 6–3 6–0, lost Sabatini [3] 6–2 6–1. **1992: last 16** [seed 13] d. Rajchrtova 6–1 6–1, Savchenko Neiland 6–2 6–3, Strnadova 7–6 6–4, lost Capriati [5] 6–4 6–3. **1993: last 16** [seed 12] d. Mothes 6–0 6–0, McQuillan 6–4 6–0, Po 6–7 6–3 6–3, lost Capriati [6] 6–4 7–6. **1994: r/u** [seed 12] d. Provis 6–1 6–0, Bentivoglio 6–0 6–1, McNeil 6–0 6–0, Coetzer 6–1 6–1, Ritter 6–0 6–2, Graf [1] 6–2 6–2, lost Sanchez Vicario [2] 6–4 6–4). **1995: last 16** [seed 3] d. Bradtke 6–1 6–3, Singer 7–5 6–0, Labat 6–2 6–2, lost Majoli [12] 6–2 6–3. **1996: 3r** [seed 12] d. Schnell 7–5 6–2, Randriantefy 6–3 2–6 6–2, lost Rittner 6–4 6–2. **1997: last 16** [seed 10] d. Panova 6–2 4–6 6–4, Hy-Boulais 6–1 6–3, Testud 6–1 6–3, lost Seles [3] 6–4 7–5.

WIMBLEDON – Played 3, qf 1

1995: 2r [seed 5] d. Dopfer 6–1 6–2, lost Tauziat 6–4 3–6 6–1. **1996: qf** [seed 13] d. Schnyder 6–3 6–2, Taylor 6–4 6–2, Medvedeva 6–4 6–1, Likhovtseva 6–2 6–3, lost Date [12] 3–6 6–3 6–1. **1997: last 16** [seed 9] d. Van Roost 6–3 6–4, Ruano-Pascual 6–0 2–6 6–3, Serna 6–4 6–3, lost Sanchez Vicario [8] 6–1 6–3.

US OPEN – Played 6, qf 1

1991: 3r d. Garrone 4–6 6–0 7–6, McNeil 6–3 3–6 7–6, lost Maleeva-Fragniere [10] 4–6 5–1 ret'd. **1992: last 16** [seed 16] d. Vento 6–2 6–2, L. Ferrando 7–5 6–4, R. White 6–2 6–1, lost M. J. Fernandez [7] 6–0 6–4. **1993: last 16** [seed 13] d. Baudone 6–0 6–7 7–6, Arendt 6–2 6–4, Schultz 7–5 7–6, lost Graf [1] 6–1 6–0. **1994: qf** [seed 4] d. Temesvari 6–3 6–2, Studenikova 6–3 2–6 6–4, Wiesner 6–2 6–4, Majoli 6–1 6–2, lost Novotna [7] 6–4 6–0. **1995: 3r** [seed 6] d. de Swardt 6–4 6–1, Jecmenica 6–3 6–0, lost Frazier 6–3 7–6. **1996:** Did not play. **1997: last 16** [seed 9] d. G. Fernandez 6–1 6–2, Farina 6–2 3–0 ret'd, Zvereva 7–6 6–1, lost Seles [2] 1–6 6–2 6–2.

OLYMPIC RECORD

1996: (Atlanta) 2r [seed 12] d. Barabanschikova 6–3 7–6, lost Gorrochategui 6–4 1–6 7–5.

CAREER FED CUP RECORD

1990 (in USA, Hard): *1r FRA d. TPE 3–0.* R3 (with I. Demongeot) d. S. Lai/Y. Lin 6–2 6–2. *2r FRA d. NZL 3–0.* R3 (with Demongeot) d. B. Cordwell/J. Richardson 6–3 6–4. *Qf ESP d. FRA 3–0.* R3 (with Demongeot) lost C. Martinez/A. Sanchez Vicario 6–4 6–4. **1991 (in GBR, Hard):** *1r POL d. FRA 2–1.* R1 d. M. Mroz 6–4 6–2; R3 (with N. Tauziat) lost Mroz/K. Teodorowicz 6–4 6–4. *Play-off FRA d. YUG 2–0.* R1 d. L. Pavlov 6–0 6–1. **1992 (in GER, Clay):** *1r FRA d. CHN 2–1.* R1 d. L. Chen 6–2 6–2. *2r FRA d. RUS 3–0.* R1 d. E. Makarova 6–1 6–2. *Qf USA d. FRA 2–1.* R1 lost G. Fernandez 6–1 6–4. **1994 (in GER, Clay):** *1r FRA d. KOR 3–0.* R2 d. S. Park 6–3 6–1. *2r FRA d. ITA 3–0.* R2 d. S. Cecchini 6–0 6–3. *Qf FRA d. BUL 2–1.* R2 lost Mag. Maleeva 6–7 6–4 6–4. *Sf USA d. FRA 3–0.* R2 lost Davenport 5–7 6–2 6–2. **1995: April** – *World Group qf FRA d. RSA 3–2 in FRA (Clay).* R2 d. J. Kruger 6–4 6–3; R3 lost A. Coetzer 6–4 6–3. **July** – *World Group sf USA d. FRA 3–2 in USA (Carpet).* R1 d. M. J. Fernandez 7–6 6–3; R3 lost L. Davenport 6–3 4–6 6–0. **1996: July** – *World Group sf ESP d. FRA 3–2 in FRA (Carpet).* R2 d. A. Sanchez Vicario 6–3 6–4; R3 lost C. Martinez 7–5 2–1. **1997: March** – *World Group qf FRA d. JPN 4–1 in JPN (Hard).* R1 d. N. Sawamatsu 6–0 7–6; R3 lost A. Sugiyama 7–5 6–7 6–4. **October** – *World Group Final FRA d. NED 4–1 in NED (Carpet).* R2 d. M. Oremans 6–4 6–1; R3 lost B. Schultz-McCarthy 4–6 6–3 6–4.

SEASON ENDING CHAMPIONSHIPS – Played 4, r/u 1, sf 2

(1983–94 Virginia Slims, 1995 Corel, 1996–97 Chase)

1993: sf d. Sabatini 7–6 6–3, Navratilova 6–1 3–6 6–4, lost Sanchez Vicario 6–2 5–7 6–3. **1994: sf** d. Coetzer 5–7 6–3 6–3, Graf 6–4 6–4, lost Davenport 6–3 6–2. **1995: 1r** lost Huber 6–2 6–3. **1996:** Did not play. **1997: r/u** d. Appelmans 6–3 6–4, Hingis 6–3 2–6 7–5, Tauziat 6–2 5–7 6–4, lost Novotna 7–6 6–2 6–3.

8 IRINA SPIRLEA (ROM)

Born: Bucharest, 26 March 1974. **Lives:** Bucharest.
Father: Dumitru. **Mother:** Georgeta.
Brother: Daniel (younger).
Agent: Stefano Lopez. **Coaches:** Chris Garner and Francesco Elia; formerly Florenta Mihai. **Turned pro:** 1990.
Height: 5ft 9in (1.75m). **Weight:** 150lb (68kg).

Rankings: 1990: 310; **1991:** 208; **1992:** 165; **1993:** 63; **1994:** 43; **1995:** 21; **1996:** 11; **1997:** 8.
Highest: 7 (October 1997).

1997 Prize Money: $720,758.
Career Earnings: $1,687,268. **Career Titles:** 3.

Style: Her fierce forehand is her chief weapon and she uses her cleverly varied backhand to create openings. At her best on clay where she outmanoeuvres opponents from the back of the court. She is improving fast on other surfaces because she is an instinctively good match player.

CAREER HIGHLIGHTS (year: (titles))
1990: Won French Open Jun doubles with Dragomir. **1991:** Won her 1st title on the satellite circuit at Milan. **1992:** Won Jakarta on the Futures circuit. **1993:** Qf Palermo on the main tour and the Challenger title at Brindisi were her best showings until Oct., when she upset Coetzer and Endo to reach her 1st main tour f at Sapporo and followed with sf Curitiba. **1994: (1)** *Palermo.* She enjoyed her greatest success in Italy. In April she appeared in both singles and doubles f at Taranto, winning the doubles with Van Lottum but losing the singles to Halard, and the following week she upset Sabatini on her way to sf Italian Open. Then in July she won her 1st main tour title at Palermo, upsetting Schultz. She also surprised M. J. Fernandez to reach last 16 French Open, unseeded, and broke into the top 50. Voted WTA Most Impressive Newcomer. **1995: (1)** *Palermo.* She began the year in style with r/u showing at Jakarta, where she won the doubles with Porwik, and then, unseeded at Australian Open, she upset Halard and took a set off Martinez in last 16. Continuing her progress, she won Palermo again, upset Coetzer and M. J. Fernandez before taking a set off Sanchez Vicario in sf Berlin and reached the same stage at Zagreb, as well as upsetting Frazier at Wimbledon and Zvereva at Philadelphia. **1996: (1)** *Amelia Island.* The year began badly as she failed to pass 2r in her 1st 4 tourns. In her next 3, though, she reached qf LIPC and FC Cup (d. Sabatini), then upset Sanchez Vicario and Pierce at Amelia Island to take her 1st title in America and move into the top 20. She followed with another upset of Sanchez Vicario to reach sf Italian Open, appeared in same stage Oakland, surprised Schultz-McCarthy at French Open, where she was unseeded, and upset Pierce again at Eastbourne, as well as reaching qf Madrid, Los Angeles and Chicago (d. M. J. Fernandez). These results took her to her 1st Chase Champs, where she lost 1r to Hingis. In doubles, she played 3 f, winning Italian Open with Sanchez Vicario. She was fined $10,000 and defaulted for abusive language v de Ville in 2r Palermo when the score stood at 15–15 3s. **1997:** She broke into the top 10 in March after reaching f Indian Wells (d. Sanchez Vicario). She was always a tough opponent in GS, extending Graf to 3s at French Open, losing to Majoli at Wimbledon only 9–7 fs and at US Open she upset Coetzer and then saved mp in 2s tb v Seles, going on to win the match, before losing sf in 3s tb to V. Williams. She also reached sf Birmingham, Philadelphia (d. Seles) and Chase Champs, plus qf Australian Open, Paris Open, LIPC, Madrid, Eastbourne and Moscow.

PRINCIPAL 19970 RESULTS – r/u 1, sf 5 (detailed Grand Slam results follow)
r/u Indian Wells (d. Dechaume-Balleret 6–7 7–6 6–2, Likhovtseva 6–3 6–4, Tauziat 6–4 6–2, Sanchez Vicario 4–6 6–3 6–3, lost Davenport 6–2 6–1); **sf** US Open; **sf** Birmingham (d. McQuillan 7–5 7–6, Arendt 6–3 6–4, Van Roost 6–4 6–4, lost Basuki 7–6 6–1), **sf** Filderstadt (d. Dragomir 6–2 6–0, Habsudova 6–2 6–0, Sanchez Vicario 7–5 6–4, lost Raymond 6–3 6–1), **sf** Philadelphia ld. V. Williams 6–3 6–2, Vento 6–2 6–1, Seles 6–4 7–6, lost Davenport 6–2 6–4), **sf** Chase Champs. **DOUBLES:** (with Gorrochategui) **r/u** Madrid (lost M. J. Fernandez/Sanchez Vicario 6–3 6–2).

CAREER GRAND SLAM RECORD

AUSTRALIAN OPEN – Played 4, qf 1

1994: 1r lost Singer 6–2 6–4. **1995: last 16** [unseeded] d. Halard [16] 6–0 7–5, Maniokova 6–0 6–2, Kamio 2–6 6–3 6–3, lost Martinez [2] 6–2 6–7 6–2. **1996: 2r** d. Testud 6–4 6–7 8–6, lost Appelmans 6–3 6–3. **1997 qf** [seed 8] d. Kijimuta 6–2 6–4, Kruger 6–1 6–1, Farina 6–4 6–3, Habsudova 6–4 6–4, lost Hingis [4] 7–5 6–2.

FRENCH OPEN – Played 5

1992: 1r lost Hy 6-2 4-6 2-1 ret'd. **1994: last 16** [unseeded] d. Kroupova 6–3 6–1, Quentrec 7–5 6–0, M. J. Fernandez [10] 6–4 6–1, lost Graf [1] 6–0 6–1. **1995: 3r** d. Keller 6–0 6–1, Mothes 6–0 6–1, lost Sabatini 6–3 6–4. **1996: last 16** [unseeded] d. Mothes 6–0 6–1, Farina 4–0 ret'd, Schultz-McCarthy [8] 6–3 3–6 6–2, lost Novotna [10] 6–1 7–5. **1997: last 16** [seed 13] d. J. Lee 6–1 6–0, Gorrochategui 6–4 4–6 6–2, Ruano-Pascual 6–1 6–1, lost Graf [2] 6–7 6–2 6–2.

WIMBLEDON – Played 4

1994: 2r d. Javer 6–1 6–2, lost Radford 7–5 3–6 6–4. **1995: 3r** d. Kruger 6–2 3–6 6–4, Frazier [12] 6–1 6–3, lost Raymond 6–4 2–6 6–4. **1996: 2r** [seed 15] d. S. Smith 3–6 6–1 6–2. **1997: last 16** [seed 12] d. Nagyova 6–1 6–0, Makarova 4–6 6–1 10–8, G. Fernandez 6–3 6–1, lost Majoli [4] 6–7 6–1 9–7.

US OPEN – Played 4, sf 1

1994: 1r lost Huber [14] 6–4 6–2. **1995: 1r** lost G. Fernandez 4–6 6–1 7–5. **1996: 3r** d. Begerow 6–3 6–2, Gaidano 6–1 6–2, lost Coetzer 7–6 7–5. **1997: sf** [seed 11] d. Frazier 6–1 6–1, Kournikova 6–1 3–6 6–3, Osterloh 6–2 7–5, Coetzer [5] 7–6 6–4, Seles [2] 6–7 7–6 6–3, lost V. Williams 7–6 4–6 7–6.

OLYMPIC RECORD

1992: (Barcelona) 1r lost Sanchez Vicario [seed 2] 6-1 6-3.

CAREER FED CUP RECORD

1991 (in GBR, Hard): *Prelim 1r ROM d. THA 2–1.* R2 lost S. Duangchan 6–2 6–4. R3 (with R. Dragomir) d. K./T. Summa 6–2 4–6 6–0. *Prelim 2r ROM d. CUB 3–0.* R2 d. R. Pichardo 6–3 4–6 6–3. R3 (with L. Bujor) d. I. Concepcion/B. Rodriguez 6–2 6–4. *World Group 1r FIN d. ROM 3–0.* R2 lost P. Thoren 6–2 6–2. R3 (with Dragomir) lost A. Aallonen/N. Dahlman 6–4 2–6 6–2. *World Group play-off ROM d. POR 2–0.* R2 d. S. Prazeres 2–6 6–1 6–2. **1992 (in GER, Clay):** *1r AUT d. ROM 2–1.* R2 lost J. Wiesner 6–0 6–3. R3 (with R. Dragomir) lost P. Ritter/Wiesner 7–5 6–3. *Play-off BUL d. ROM 2–1.* R2 lost K. Maleeva 6–1 6–0. R3 (with Dragomir) d. M. Maleeva/E. Pampoulova-Wagner 7–6 6–2. **1994 (in AUT, Clay):** *Qualifying round-robin ROM d. HUN 3–0.* R2 d. P. Gaspar 6–1 7–6. R3 (with C. Cristea) d. R. Kuti-Kis/P. Mandula 6–3 6–3. *Round-robin ROM d. NOR 3–0.* R2 d. L. Andersen 6–1 6–4. R3 (with Cristea) d. Andersen/K. Brekke-Borgerson 6–2 6–0. *Knock-out ROM d. HUN 2–1.* R2 d. P. Gaspar 6–3 6–0. R3 (with Cristea) lost Kuti-Kis/Mandula 6–1 2–1 ret'd. *Knock-out final BLR d. ROM 2–1.* R2 lost N. Zvereva 6–3 3–6 6–1.

SEASON ENDING CHAMPIONSHIPS – Played 2, sf 1

(1996–97 Chase)

1996: 1r lost Hingis 6–1 6–2. **1997: sf** d. Testud 6–3 5–7 6–4, M. J. Fernandez 5–7 6–2 7–5, lost Novotna 7–6 6–2.

9 ARANTXA SANCHEZ VICARIO (ESP)

Born: Barcelona, 18 December 1971. **Lives:** Andorra.
Father: Emilio. **Mother:** Marisa, whose maiden name, Vicario, she added to her own, travels with her. **Sister:** Marisa (older).
Brothers: Emilio and Javier (both older) who compete on the men's tour.
Agent: IMG. **Coach:** Her brother, Emilio; formerly Gabriel Urpi, Mervyn Rose, Carlos Kirmayr, Juan Nunez, Mike Estep, Eduardo Osta, Sven Groeneveld and David de Migues.
Turned pro: 1986.
Height: 5ft 6½in (1.69m). **Weight:** 124lb (56kg).

Rankings: 1986: 124; **1987:** 47; **1988:** 18; **1989:** 5; **1990:** 7; **1991:** 5; **1992:** 4; **1993:** 2;. **1994:** 2; **1995:** 3; **1996:** 2 (jointly with Seles); **1997:** 9.
Highest: 1 (February 1995).

1997 Prize Money: $890,512. **Career Earnings:** $12,523,488. **Career Titles:** 24.

Style: One of the fastest movers on a tennis court whose attacking, all-round game and cheerful demeanour has created an enormous following round the world. A right-hander with a good forehand, accurate double-handed backhand and excellent touch on the volley, Arantxa has enjoyed outstanding success both in singles and doubles.

CAREER HIGHLIGHTS (year: (titles))
1986: Emerging from the satellite circuits, she reached sf Spanish Open and played Fed Cup. **1987:** Qf French Open in 1st GS appearance. **1988: (1)** *Brussels*. Upset Evert (suffering from a foot injury) at French Open *en route* to qf again and reached last 16 US Open. Won her 1st pro singles title at Brussels and was r/u Tampa. **1989: (2)** *FRENCH OPEN, Barcelona*. At 17 yrs 6 mths became the youngest woman and the 1st Spaniard to win French Open women's title. Qf Wimbledon and US Open, won Barcelona and was r/u Italian Open and Canadian Open, qualifying for 1st VS Champs, where she reached sf. Voted WTA Most Improved Player for 2nd year running. **1990: (2)** *Barcelona, Newport*. In some disappointing performances she fell to Harvey-Wild 1r VS Chicago, to Paz 2r French Open and to Nagelsen 1r Wimbledon. Won 2 titles, r/u Tokyo Toray, VS Houston, Amelia Island, Leipzig and Hamburg, where she d. Navratilova and took Graf to 3s. She lost 1r VS Champs to K. Maleeva and in GS her best showing was sf US Open, but she won French Open mixed doubles with Lozano. In women's doubles won 1 title with Navratilova and 3 with Paz, with whom she was r/u VS Champs. **1991: (1)** *Washington*. Upset Sabatini *en route* to sf Australian Open and Graf on her way to f French Open, inflicting on the former No. 1 her worst defeat and 1st love set since 1984. In other GS lost qf Wimbledon to M. J. Fernandez and same round US Open to Navratilova, who also stopped her at that stage VS Champs. Had to wait until late Aug. to win her 1st title of the year at VS Washington, although she had reached qf or better in all 13 tourns until then. R/u Sydney, Berlin, Eastbourne, VS Philadelphia and appeared in 6 more sf. Played in the victorious Spanish Fed Cup team, winning all her matches. In doubles won Barcelona with Navratilova and took Sydney and Amelia Island with Sukova, with whom she qualified for VS Champs. In mixed doubles r/u US Open with her brother, Emilio. **1992: (2)** *LIPC, Montreal*. Again she was remarkably consistent if not spectacular. She upset Graf qf US Open on her way to f, where she lost to Seles, whom she had beaten 3 weeks earlier at Montreal – one of only 5 defeats the No. 1 suffered all year. Reached sf Australian Open and French Open and won an Olympic bronze medal; took 2 titles and was r/u Sydney, Barcelona, Hamburg, Berlin and Philadelphia, reaching 4 more sf and losing qf VS Champs to Navratilova. She enjoyed a terrific year in doubles, winning Australian Open, VS Champs and 4 more titles with Sukova; r/u French Open, Olympic silver medal and 1 title with Martinez; plus 3 more titles with other partners. In mixed with Woodbridge won French Open and r/u Australian Open. **1993: (4)** *LIPC, Amelia Island, Barcelona, Hamburg*. Following a heavy schedule which left her exhausted and struggling to finish her f v Graf at VS Champs, she moved up to No. 2 in the rankings. She beat Graf twice during the year in winning LIPC and Hamburg (ending the German's unbeaten record there), and also won Amelia Island and

Barcelona. She was r/u VS Florida, FC Cup, San Diego, VS Los Angeles and VS Champs and appeared in 4 more sf. In GS she reached sf Australian Open, French Open and US Open and played in winning Spanish Fed Cup team, unbeaten in all her matches. She also played 7 women's doubles f, winning US Open and two others with Sukova, with whom she reached sf VS Champs, and one each with Martinez and Novotna. In mixed, she took Australian Open with Woodbridge. **1994: (8)** *FRENCH OPEN, US OPEN, Amelia Island, Barcelona, Hamburg, Montreal, Tokyo Nicherei, Oakland*. In a great year for her and for Spanish tennis, she won French Open and a 1st US Open and, with new Wimbledon champion Martinez, took ESP to victory in Fed Cup. Graf was the only player to beat her 3 times, including f Australian Open, although she beat the German in Hamburg and Montreal, both matches being decided in 3s tb, and in 3s at US Open. She was r/u VS Florida, Stratton Mountain and San Diego, but her Wimbledon singles bid ended at last 16 stage, when she lost to Garrison-Jackson, and at VS Champs she surprisingly fell 1r to Halard. She played 16 doubles f with various partners, winning 11 – including US Open with Novotna, with whom she was also r/u Wimbledon and VS Champs – and 7 times she won both singles and doubles titles at same tourn, most notably at US Open. The only woman to earn more than $2m prize money in 1994, she won almost $3m. **1995: (2)** *Barcelona, Berlin*. Took over the No. 1 ranking for the 1st time on 6 Feb., becoming the 1st Spanish player and only the 6th woman to hold that position since rankings began, and on 13 Feb. she became the 1st since Navratilova in August 1987 to top both singles and doubles rankings. However, Graf deposed her again a week later, and when she regained the top singles spot on 27 Feb., Zvereva had replaced her at the top of the doubles. She topped both rankings again twice more, on 27 March and 1 May, but Graf took over the top singles spot after French Open and by Oct. she had slipped to No. 3 behind Martinez, although she finished the year No. 1 in doubles. She had to wait until 30 April before winning her 1st title of year at Barcelona, where she also won the doubles, and Berlin was her only other singles title, although she was r/u Australian Open, French Open, Wimbledon, Italian Open and Tokyo Nicherei and reached 2 more sf. The outcome of her memorable f v Graf at Wimbledon hung on the result of a remarkable game on her serve at 5–5 fs, which covered 32 points and 20 min. For the 1st time in her 10-year career she was restricted by illness and injury, suffering a stomach virus at French Open, withdrawing qf FC Cup with a badly sprained right ankle and tenderness to the fibula and taking a break in autumn, suffering from fatigue. She still seemed below her best at WTA Champs, where she lost 1r singles to Zvereva, although she and Novotna won the doubles. Also with Novotna she won Australian Open and Wimbledon, was r/u French Open and took 2 more titles, plus a 5th with Neiland. Contributed 1 singles win as ESP d. USA 3–2 in f Fed Cup. **1996: (2)** *FC Cup, Hamburg*. Between April and August, her ranking fluctuated with that of Martinez between No. 2 and No. 3, before she settled at No. 2 on 5 Aug. after taking a silver medal at the Olympics, and was co-ranked in that spot with Seles from 4 Nov. She won both singles and doubles in 2 tourns – at FC Cup (with Novotna) and Hamburg (with Schultz-McCarthy). At French Open, she lost f to Graf only 10–8 fs in what was probably the match of the year. Earlier, though, she had been booed off the court after a disappointing display of gamesmanship in qf v Habsudova; after missing 2 mps at 5–4 in 2s, she lost tb and played dolly-shots in 3s, which she eventually won 10–8. Apparently forgetting the need to entertain, she claimed she was simply doing her job by winning. In contrast to their French Open f, her Wimbledon f defeat by Graf was disappointingly one-sided. She was also r/u Tokyo Toray, Montreal, San Diego and Tokyo Nicherei, reaching 2 more sf and 5 more qf, including Chase Champs, where she lost in ss to Novotna. In qf Australian Open v Rubin, she played (and lost) the longest women's match in the history of the tourn; it lasted 3 hours 33 min, comprising the most games in a set (30) and most in a woman's match (48) and being the 6th-longest on the WTA tour. The pair then joined together to win the doubles. Retaining her top doubles ranking, she took 9 titles from 12 f, winning a total of 4 with Novotna – with whom she was also r/u US Open and Chase Champs – 2 with Rubin and 1 each with Schultz-McCarthy, Spirlea and Neiland, as well as an Olympic bronze medal with Martinez. Her Fed Cup record suffered a setback as she won only one singles and one doubles match, losing to players she would normally expect to beat. She was restricted in the spring by a shoulder injury, caused by playing too much tennis, and in autumn took a 3-week break, feeling physically and mentally exhausted by the game. **1997:** It was another generally disappointing year in which she dropped out of the top 10 for a while and was seeded as low as 10 at US Open. She won no title, although she shared Eastbourne (where f was rained off) with Novotna and in f Tokyo Nicherei was 3–1 up in 3s v Seles before letting the match slip away. In November, she showed her old form again at Philadelphia, where she upset Coetzer in ss and was on the point of doing the same to Hingis in sf before losing 2s tb and eventually the match. Then at Chase Champs, where she qualified in both singles and doubles, she upset Seles before losing qf in 3s to her former doubles partner Novotna, and, in partnership with Hingis, fell 1r doubles to Fusai/Tauziat. Her best GS performance was sf Wimbledon, and she reached the same stage Indian Wells, Madrid and Philadelphia, as well as qf French Open, US Open, Amelia Island, Los Angeles, Filderstadt and Moscow. In doubles she played and won 7 f, taking 3 titles with Hingis, 2 with Zvereva and 1 each with G. Fernandez and M. J. Fernandez.

PRINCIPAL 1997 RESULTS – shared 1, r/u 1, sf 4 (detailed Grand Slam results follow)
shared Eastbourne (with Novotna) (d. Guse 7–5 6–0, Spirlea 6–4 6–4, Schultz-McCarthy 7–5 6–1, final abandoned); **r/u** Tokyo Nicherei (d. Asagoe 6–0 6–0 Li 6–3 7–5, Basuki 1–6 7–6 6–4, lost Seles 6–1 3–6 7–6); **sf** Wimbledon, **sf** Indian Wells (d. Farina 6–4 6–2, Carlsson 6–1 6–3, Testud 3–6 6–2 6–2, lost Spirlea 4–6 6–3 6–3), **sf** Madrid (d. Serna 6–2 6–1, Cristea 4–6 6–0 6–0, Grossman 6–1 6–1, lost Novotna 6–4 6–4), **sf** Philadelphia (d. Basuki 6–2 6–0, Sugiyama 6–1 7–6, Coetzer 6–2 6–2, lost Hingis 1–6 7–6 6–3). **DOUBLES:** (with Hingis unless stated) (with G. Fernandez) **won** Sydney (d. Davenport/Zvereva 6–3 6–1), (with Zvereva) **won** LIPC (d. Appelmans/Oremans 6–2 6–3), (with M. J. Fernandez) **won** Madrid (d. Gorrochategui/Spirlea 6–3 6–2), **won** San Diego (d. Frazier/Po 6–3 7–5), **won** Filderstadt (d. Davenport/Novotna 7–6 3–6 7–6), **won** Zurich (d. Neiland/Sukova 4–6 6–4 6–1), (with Zvereva) **won** Moscow (d. Basuki/Vis 5–3 ret'd).

CAREER GRAND SLAM RECORD

AUSTRALIAN OPEN – Played 7, r/u 2, sf 3, qf 1

1991: sf [seed 6] d. Medvedeva 6–0 6–2, Javer 4–6 6–4 6–2, McNeil 6–4 3–6 6–0, Frazier [13] 6–3 6–2, Sabatini [4] 6–1 6–3, lost Novotna 6–2 6–4. **1992: sf** [seed 4] d. Provis 6–2 6–1, Testud 6–1 6–1, Strnadova 1–6 6–0 6–3, Savchenko-Neiland 6–1 7–6, Maleeva-Fragniere def., lost Seles [1] 6–2 6–2. **1993: sf** [seed 4] d. van Lottum 6–2 6–3, Arraya 6–0 6–1, Zrubakova 6–1 6–3, Huber [11] 7–5 6–2, M. J. Fernandez [5] 7–5 6–4, lost Graf [2] 7–5 6–4. **1994: r/u** [seed 2] d. Habsudova 6–1 6–3, Wang 6–2 6–4, Grossman 6–2 6–3, Mag. Maleeva [14] 4–6 6–1 6–3, Maleeva-Fragniere [8] 7–6 6–4, Sabatini [4] 6–1 6–2, lost Graf [1] 6–0 6–2. **1995: r/u** [seed 1] d. Li 6–2 6–0, Whitlinger-Jones 6–2 6–1, Garrison-Jackson 6–1 6–3, Habsudova 7–5 6–0, Sawamatsu 6–4 7–6, Werdel-Witmeyer 6–4 6–1, lost Pierce [4] 6–3 6–2. **1996: qf** [seed 3] d. Reinstadler 6–2 6–2, Rittner 6–3 6–2, Cacic 6–3 6–3, M. J. Fernandez [9] 6–3 6–3, lost Rubin [13] 6–4 2–6 16–14. **1997: 3r** [seed 2] d. Pizzichini 6–4 6–4, De Ville 1–0 ret'd, lost Van Roost 1–6 6–4 8–6.

FRENCH OPEN – Played 11, won 2, r/u 3, sf 2, qf 3

1987: qf d. Burgin 7–5 6–3, Dinu 6–0 6–2, Paulus 6–4 6–2, Karlsson 6–1 6–4, lost Sabatini [7] 6–4 6–0. **1988: qf** d. Kuczynska 6–2 6–0, Meier 7–5 6–0, Evert [3] 6–1 7–6, Tanvier 6–2 6–0, lost Provis 7–5 3–6 6–4. **1989: won** [seed 7] d. Rajchrtova 6–2 6–1, Demongeot 6–4 6–4, Medvedeva 6–0 3–6 6–2, Coetzer 6–3 6–2, Novotna [11] 6–2 6–2, M. J. Fernandez [15] 6–2 6–2, Graf [1] 7–6 3–6 7–5. **1990: 2r** [seed 3] d. van Lottum 6–1 6–3, lost Paz 7–5 3–6 6–1, **1991: r/u** [seed 5] d. McNeil 6–2 6–2, Godridge 6–1 6–2, Fulco 6–1 6–1, Tami Whitlinger 6–2 6–1, M. J. Fernandez [4] 6–3 6–2, Graf [2] 6–0 6–2, lost Seles [1] 6–3 6–4. **1992: sf** [seed 4] d. Oeljeklaus 6–0 6–2, Zardo 6–3 6–2, Wiesner 6–3 6–1, Date [14] 6–1 6–2, Bollegraf 6–2 6–3, lost Graf [2] 0–6 6–2 6–2. **1993: sf** [seed 2] d. Kiene 6–3 7–6, Sawamatsu 6–0 6–0, Meskhi 6–3 6–0, Dragomir 6–0 6–1, Novotna [7] 6–2 7–5, lost M. J. Fernandez [5] 6–2 6–2. **1994: won** [seed 2] d. Labat 6–4 6–1, van Lottum 6–1 6–0, Rittner 6–4 6–2, Huber [11] 6–3 6–2, Halard 6–1 7–6, Martinez [3] 6–3 6–1, Pierce [12] 6–4 6–4. **1995: r/u** [seed 1] d. Park 6–1 6–0, Pitkowski 6–3 6–0, Reinstadler 6–3 6–1, Smashnova 6–4 6–0, Rubin 6–3 6–1, Date [9] 7–5 6–2, lost Graf [2] 7–5 4–6 6–0. **1996: r/u** [seed 4] d. Glass 6–2 6–3, Martinek 6–0 6–1, Likhovtseva 6–0 6–0, Rittner 6–3 6–4, Habsudova 6–2 6–7 10–8, Novotna [10] 6–3 7–5, lost Graf [1] 6–3 6–7 10–8. **1997: qf** [seed 6] d. Jagieniak 6–0 6–2, Sugiyama 6–3 6–1, Van Roost 6–0 6–3, Zvereva 6–4 6–2, lost Hingis [1] 6–2 6–2.

WIMBLEDON – Played 11, r/u 2, sf 1, qf 2

1987: 1r lost Cordwell 6–1 2–6 6–4. **1988: 1r** lost Okamoto 6–3 6–4. **1989: qf** [seed 7] d. Pospisilova 6–2 7–5, Halard 6–4 6–3, Reggi 4–6 6–3 7–5, McNeil [15] 6–3 2–6 6–1, lost Graf [1] 7–5 6–1. **1990: 1r** [seed 6] lost Nagelsen 1–6 7–6 9–7. **1991: qf** [seed 3] d. Rittner 6–1 6–2, Coetzer 6–4 6–1, McNeil 6–2 6–4, A. Minter 7–5 3–6 6–1, lost M. J. Fernandez [6] 6–2 7–5. **1992: 2r** [seed 5] d. Meskhi 6–3 7–6, lost Halard 6–3 2–6 6–3). **1993: last 16** [seed 3] d. Zrubakova 6–1 6–1, Neiland 7–6 6–0, Fendick 6–3 6–2, lost Sukova [15] 6–3 6–4. **1994: last 16** [seed 2] d. K. Maleeva 6–1 6–2, Gaidano 6–2 6–1, Feber 6–2 6–1, lost Garrison-Jackson [13] 7–5 4–6 6–3. **1995: r/u** [seed 2] d. Studenikova 6–2 6–1, Endo 7–5 6–2, Garrison-Jackson 6–1 6–2, Huber [9] 7–5 6–4, Schultz-McCarthy [15] 6–4 7–6, Martinez [4] 6–3 6–7 6–1, lost Graf [1] 4–6 6–1 7–5. **1996: r/u** [seed 4] d. Serra-Zanetti 6–3 6–4, Oremans 7–6 6–3, Sawamatsu 6–4 6–1, Appelmans 3–6 6–2 6–1, Wiesner 6–4 6–0, McGrath 6–2 6–1, lost Graf [1] 6–3 7–5. **1997: sf** [seed 8] d. Wood 6–0 6–0 Gagliardi 6–4 6–2, Labat 6–1 6–2, Pierce [9] 6–1 6–3, Tauziat 6–2 7–5, lost Novotna [3] 6–4 6–2.

US OPEN – Played 11, won 1, r/u 1, sf 2, qf 1

1987: 1r lost Dias 6–4 6–2. **1988: last 16** d. Keil 6–3 6–0, Steinmetz 6–2 6–2, Sloane 6–3 6–3, lost Garrison [11] 4–6 7–5 6–2. **1989: qf** [seed 6] d. Faull 6–3 6–1, Cammy Macgregor 6–1 6–3, Wasserman 6–1 2–6 6–4, Paulus 6–2 6–2, lost Sabatini [3] 3–6 6–4 6–1. **1990: sf** [seed 6] d. Provis 6–0 6–3, Kuhlman 6–1 6–2, Fendick 6–2 6–1, Paulus [16] 6–4 6–3, Garrison [4] 6–2 6–2, lost Graf [1] 6–1 6–2. **1991: qf** [seed 4] d. Piccolini 6–0 6–1, Godridge 6–1 6–1, Herreman 6–2 6–2, Zvereva 6–3 7–6, lost Navratilova [6] 7–6 6–7 6–4. **1992: r/u** [seed 5] d. Savchenko-Neiland 5–7 6–2 6–2, Davenport 6–2 6–1, Sawamatsu 6–1 6–3, Garrison [14] 6–0

6–1, Graf [2] 7–6 6–3, Maleeva-Fragniere [9] 6–2 6–1, lost Seles 6–3 6–3. **1993: sf** [seed 2] d. Labat 6–4 6–3, Harvey-Wild 6–2 6–2, Rubin 6–0 6–0–1, Tauziat 6–4 6–3, Zvereva 3–0 ret'd, lost Sukova [12] 6–7 7–5 6–2. **1994: won** [seed 2] d. Ferrando 7–5 6–1, Tauziat 6–2 7–6, Cecchini 6–2 6–1, Grossman 6–2 6–0, Date [5] 6–3 6–0, Sabatini [8] 6–1 7–6, Graf [1] 1–6 7–6 6–4. **1995: last 16** [seed 3] d. Cristea 6–1 6–1, Kruger 6–4 6–3, Gaidano 6–3 6–0, lost M. J. Fernandez [14] 1–6 6–4 6–4. **1996: last 16** [seed 3] d. Poruri 6–2 6–1, Arendt 6–2 6–2, Likhovtseva 6–1 6–0, lost Hingis 6–1 3–6 6–4. **1997: qf** [seed 10] d. Guse 6–2 6–4, Tu 6–2 5–7 6–2, Fusai 6–2 6–1, McQuillan 6–1 6–2, lost Hingis [seed 1] 6–3 6–2.

OLYMPIC RECORD

SINGLES: 1988: (Seoul) 1r lost Goles 6–4 6–2. **1992: (Barcelona) sf bronze medal** [seed 2] d. Spirlea 6–1 6–3, Endo 6–0 6–1, Rittner 4–6 6–3 6–1, Martinez [5] 6–4 6–4, lost Capriati [3] 6–3 3–6 6–1. **1996: (Atlanta) r/u silver medal** [seed 3] d. van Roost 6–1 7–5, Farina 6–1 6–3, Schultz-McCarthy [11] 6–4 7–6, Date [8] 4–6 6–3 10–8, Novotna [6] 6–4 1–6 6–3, lost Davenport [9] 7–6 6–2). **DOUBLES:** (with Martinez): **1992: (Barcelona) r/u silver medal** d. McQuillan/Provis 6–3 6–3, lost G. Fernandez/M. J. Fernandez 7–5 2–6 6–2. **1996: (Atlanta) sf bronze medal** lost Novotna/Sukova; bronze medal play-off d. Bollegraf/ Schultz-McCarthy 6–1 6–3.

CAREER FED CUP RECORD

1986 (in TCH, Clay): *1r ESP d. INA 2–1.* R2 d. S. Anggarkusuma 7–6 6–3. R3 (with A. Almansa) d. Anggarkusuma/Y. Basuki 7–5 6–4. *2r USA d. ESP 3–0.* R2 lost M. Navratilova 6–3 6–0. **1987 (in CAN, Hard):** *1r ESP d. JAM 3–0.* R2 d. J. van Ryck de Groot 6–3 6–1; R3 (with M. J. Llorca) d. H. Harris/van Ryck de Groot 7–6 6–2. *2r AUS d. ESP 2–1.* R2 lost E. Smylie 6–1 4–6 6–1; R3 (with Llorca) lost Smylie/W. Turnbull 6–1 6–2. **1988 (in AUS, Hard):** *1r ESP d. NED 3–0.* R2 d. B. Schultz 6–2 7–6; R3 (with C. Martinez) d. M. Bollegraf/C. Vis 5–7 6–4 6–4. *2r ESP d. INA 3–0.* R2 d. Y. Basuki 6–1 6–1; R3 (with Martinez) d. S. Anggarkusuma/Basuki 6–0 5–7 6–2. *Qf URS d. ESP 2–1.* R2 d. N. Zvereva 7–6 6–1; R3 (with Martinez) lost L. Savchenko/Zvereva 4–6 6–4 6–4. **1989 (in JPN, Hard):** *1r ESP d. FRA 2–0.* R2 d. N. Tauziat 6–4 6–2. *2r ESP d. NED 2–0.* R2 d. B. Schultz 2–6 6–4 10–8. *Qf ESP d. URS 2–1.* R2 d. N. Zvereva 7–5 6–3; R3 (with C. Martinez) lost L. Savchenko/Zvereva 6–4 2–6 6–1. *Sf ESP d. AUS 2–0.* R2 d. A. Minter 6–1 4–6 6–2. *Final USA d. ESP 3–0.* R2 lost M. Navratilova (USA) 0–6 6–3 6–4; R3 (with Martinez) lost Z. Garrison/P. Shriver 7–5 6–1. **1990 (in USA, Hard):** *1r ESP d. CAN 2–1.* R2 d. H. Kelesi 6–3 6–2. *2r ESP d. ISR 3–0.* R2 d. Y. Segal 6–0 6–0; R3 (with C. Martinez) d. I. Berger/L. Zaltz 6–3 6–4. *Qf ESP d. FRA 3–0.* R2 d. N. Tauziat 7–6 6–1; R3 (with Martinez) d. I. Demongeot/M. Pierce 6–4 6–4. *Sf URS d. ESP 2–1.* R2 lost N. Zvereva 6–4 2–0 ret'd. **1991 (in GBR, Hard):** *1r ESP d. BEL 2–0.* R2 d. S. Appelmans 7–6 6–3. *2r ESP d. AUS 3–0.* R2 d. R. McQuillan 6–1 3–6 6–2; R3 (with C. Martinez) d. K. Godridge/E. Smylie 6–3 6–4. *Qf ESP d. INA 2–0.* R2 d. Y. Basuki 4–6 7–5 6–4. *Sf ESP d. GER 3–0.* R2 d. A. Huber 6–1 2–6 6–2; R3 (with Martinez) d. B. Rittner/Huber 6–1 6–1. *Final ESP d. USA 2–1.* R2 d. M. J. Fernandez 6–3 6–4; R3 (with Martinez) d. Z. Garrison/G. Fernandez 3–6 6–1 6–1. **1992 (in GER, Clay):** *1r ESP d. BEL 2–1.* R2 d. S. Appelmans 6–1 6–2; R3 (with N. Perez) lost D. Monami/S. Wasserman 7–5 6–4. *2r ESP d. CAN 2–1.* R2 d. P. Hy 6–4 6–2; R3 (with C. Martinez) d. J. Hetherington/Hy 6–4 6–0. *Qf ESP d. ARG 2–1.* R2 d. M. Paz 6–2 6–1. *Sf ESP d. AUS 3–0.* R2 d. N. Provis 6–2 6–0; R3 (with V. Ruano-Pascual) d. J. Byrne/R. Stubbs 6–3 6–3. *Final GER d. ESP 2–1.* R2 lost S. Graf 6–4 6–2; R3 (with Martinez) d. A. Huber/B. Rittner 6–1 6–2. **1993 (in GER, Clay):** *1r ESP d. GBR 3–0.* R2 d. C. Wood 6–3 6–0; R3 (with C. Martinez) d. J. Durie/Wood 6–1 4–6 6–1. *2r ESP d. INA 3–0.* R2 d. N. Basuki 6–1 6–2. *Qf ESP d. NED 3–0.* R2 d. M. Oremans 7–6 6–0. *Sf ESP d. FRA 2–1.* R2 d. N. Tauziat 6–1 6–4. *Final ESP d. AUS 3–0.* R2 d. N. Provis 6–2 6–3; R3 (with Martinez) d. E. Smylie/R. Stubbs 3–6 6–1 6–3. **1994 (in GER, Clay):** *1r ESP d. CHI 3–0.* R2 d. P. Cabezas 6–1 6–0; R3 (with C. Martinez) d. Cabezas/Castro 6–0 6–1. *2r ESP d. ARG 3–0.* R2 d. F. Labat 6–1 6–4. *Qf ESP d. JPN 3–0.* R2 d. K. Date 6–3 2–6 8–6. *Sf ESP d. GER 2–1.* R2 d. A. Huber 4–6 6–0 7–5; R3 (with Martinez) d. B. Rittner/C. Singer 7–5 6–1. *Final ESP d. USA 3–0.* R2 d. L. Davenport 6–2 6–1; R3 (with Martinez) d. G./ M. J. Fernandez 6–3 6–4. **1995: April** – *World Group qf ESP d. BUL 3–2 in BUL (Carpet).* R1 d. K. Maleeva 6–3 6–3; R2 lost M. Maleeva 6–3 6–3). **July** – *World Group sf ESP d. GER 3–2 in ESP (Clay).* R2 lost S. Hack 6–4 6–2; R3 d. A. Huber 6–3 1–6 6–2. **November** – *World Group Final ESP d. USA 3–2 in ESP (Clay).* R2 d. M. J. Fernandez 6–3 6–2; R4 lost C. Rubin 1–6 6–4 6–4. **1996: April** – *World Group sf ESP d. RSA 3–2 in ESP (Clay).* R1 d. J. Kruger 6–3 6–1; R3 lost A. Coetzer 6–4 6–1. **July** – *World Group sf ESP d. FRA 3–2 in FRA (Carpet).* R2 lost M. Pierce 6–3 6–4; R4 lost J. Halard-Decugis 2–6 6–4 7–5; R5 (with C. Martinez) d. Halard-Decugis/N. Tauziat 6–4 2–1. **September** – *World Group Final USA d. ESP 5–0 in USA (Carpet).* R2 lost L. Davenport 7–5 6–1; R3 lost M. Seles 3–6 6–3 6–1. **1997: March** – *World Group qf BEL d. ESP 5–0 in BEL (Hard).* R1 lost E. Callens 6–3 7–6; R3 lost S. Appelmans 6–3 2–6 8–6. **July** – *World Group play-off ESP d. AUS 3–2 in AUS (Hard).* R1 d. R. McQuillan 6–2 6–1; R3 d. A. Ellwood 6–2 6–0.

SEASON ENDING CHAMPIONSHIPS – Played 9, r/u 1, sf 1, qf 5

(1983–94 Virginia Slims, 1995 Corel, 1996–97 Chase)

1989: sf d. Man. Maleeva 7–5 7–6, lost Navratilova 6–2 6–2. **1990: qf** d. Zvereva 6–2 7–5, lost Seles 5–7 7–6 6–4. **1991: qf** d. Garrison 4–6 6–1 6–0, lost Navratilova 1–6 6–4 6–2. **1992: qf** d. Garrison-Jackson 7–6 6–1, lost Navratilova 6–1 2–6 6–2. **1993: r/u** d. Sukova 7–5 6–2, Novotna 6–7 7–6 6–4, Pierce 6–2 5–7 6–2, lost Graf 6–1 6–4 3–6 6–1. **1994: 1r** lost Halard 6–2 1–6 7–6. **1995: 1r** lost Zvereva 4–6 6–4 6–4. **1996: qf** d. Schultz-McCarthy 6–4 7–6, lost Novotna 6–0 6–3. **1997: qf** d. Seles 3–6 6–4 6–4, lost Novotna 6–3 3–6 6–1.

10 MARY JOE FERNANDEZ (USA)

Born: Dominican Republic, 19 August 1971. **Lives:** Miami, Fla.
Father: Jose, born in Spain. **Mother:** Sylvia comes from Cuba.
Sister: Sylvia (older).
Agent: IMG. **Manager:** Ion Tiriac. **Coach:** Harold Solomon since Dec. 1991; formerly Dean Goldfein, Juan Avendano and Tim Gullikson; trainer Ron Zelhov.
Fitness trainer: Pat Etcheberry. **Turned pro:** 1986.
Height: 5ft 10in (1.78m). **Weight:** 140lb (63kg).

Rankings: 1985: 99; **1986:** 27; **1987:** 20; **1988:** 15; **1989:** 12; **1990:** 4; **1991:** 8; **1992:** 7; **1993:** 7; **1994:** 14; **1995:** 8; **1996:** 14; **1997:** 10. **Highest:** 4 (October 1990).

1997 Prize Money: $769,132. **Career Earnings:** $4,903,886. **Career Titles:** 7.

Style: With Chris Evert as her model, she is a right-hander with a 2-handed backhand whose fierce, flat drives on both wings make her a fearsome opponent. Happiest at the back of the court swapping deep drives, she can volley and does so more frequently now in an attempt to broaden her game.

CAREER HIGHLIGHTS (year: (titles))
Junior record – 1982: Won Orange Bowl 12s, beating Sabatini in f. **1983:** Won Orange Bowl 14s, beating Sabatini in sf. **1984:** In 16s age group won Orange Bowl 16s, US Nat, US CC and was ranked No. 1 in US. **1985:** Won Orange Bowl 18s, ranked 2 behind Rehe in US 18s. **Prof. record – 1986:** Demonstrating her uncanny court sense, excellent anticipation, extraordinary determination and formidable flat forehand and 2HB, she stopped Kohde-Kilsch to reach qf French Open; had other good CC wins over Rehe and Sabatini during the year. **1987:** Reached last 16 Wimbledon, qf Geneva and Filderstadt. **1988:** Last 16 Wimbledon and upset Sabatini on her way to sf both LIPC and Eastbourne. **1989:** Upset Sabatini again *en route* to sf French Open; r/u Filderstadt and sf Pan Pacific Open. In doubles r/u US Open with Shriver, and with various partners reached 4 other f, winning VS Dallas. Qualified for VS Champs for 1st time, but lost 1r to Navratilova. **1990: (2)** *Tokyo Indoor, Filderstadt.* Her year began on a high note at Australian Open, where she was r/u to Graf in singles and r/u with Fendick in doubles. She continued to do well in GS, reaching qf French Open and sf US Open, having missed Wimbledon. In Sept. won her 1st career title at Tokyo Nicherei (indoors), following with Filderstadt in Oct. In other tourns she reached sf VS Florida, Barcelona, VS Los Angeles, VS New England and VS Champs to finish the year in the top 5, ahead of Sabatini. **1991:** Reached sf Wimbledon and Australian Open, where she extended Seles to 9–7 fs as she suffered the 1st of 6 defeats during the year at the hands of the new No. 1. R/u VS Houston, Tokyo Ariake; sf Tokyo Pan Pacific, LIPC, Italian Open, Eastbourne, VS Washington and Milan; and qualified for VS Champs, where she lost qf to Seles. Won her 1st GS title when she took Australian Open doubles with Fendick and from 5 more f with various partners she won LIPC with Garrison, with whom she qualified for VS Champs. Recruited Ion Tiriac to improve her game and image, feeling that although she was ranked in the top 5 she was relatively little known. **1992:** Working with Harold Solomon, with whom she developed a serve-and-volley attack, she began the year with a flourish at Australian Open, upsetting Sabatini to reach her 2nd f there and also r/u doubles with Garrison. At the Olympics she won a bronze medal in singles and gold in doubles with G. Fernandez and then upset Sabatini again to reached sf US Open. She was r/u Essen and appeared in 8 more singles sf – at Sydney, VS Florida, Italian Open, Berlin, Eastbourne, Tokyo Nicherei, Filderstadt and Brighton. As well as her major triumphs in doubles, she won Tokyo with R. White and reached 3 more f. So it was rather an anticlimax when, having qualified for VS Champs in singles and doubles (with Garrison), she lost 1r in both. **1993: (1)** *Indian Wells.* Her best performance of the year came at the French Open, where she was r/u to Graf, having taken the 1st set in their f. In qf at 1–6 1–5 and mp down v Sabatini, she realised the match had lasted only 54 minutes; determined to make the hour at least, she won that point and went on to win the match 1–6 7–6 10–8 in 3 hrs 35 mins (3rd-longest recorded women's singles match). She won her 1st title for 3 years at Indian Wells, reached sf VS Chicago, Italian Open and Berlin

plus 5 more qf, including Australian Open. Withdrew before her 1st match at US Open with abdominal pains and later underwent abdominal surgery. Returned at VS Champs, where she lost 1r to Garrison-Jackson and qualified for VS Champs but, still feeling below her best form, she fell 1r to Coetzer. **1994: (1)** *Strasbourg.* She was out of action for 6 weeks in spring with stomach problems, returning to win Strasbourg over Sabatini, and she beat the same player again on her way to f Sydney. However, she was plagued by a string of aliments all year and could never regain her best form. She reached no other sf and her only other qf appearances came at Indian Wells and Stratton Mountain as she slipped out of the top 10. **1995: (2)** *Indian Wells, Brighton.* She upset Martinez on the way to the title at Indian Wells in March and followed in autumn with Brighton. She also appeared in sf Sydney and Oakland, plus 3 more qf, upsetting Davenport at Wimbledon and Sanchez Vicario at US Open. She qualified for WTA Champs, where Graf beat her in qf, and her excellent autumn results took her back to the top 10. Played 4 doubles f, winning 2 with Davenport and 1 with Novotna. Lost both singles as USA went down to ESP 3–2 in f Fed Cup. **1996:** Although she gained no singles title, she won Olympic gold in doubles with G. Fernandez to become the most decorated American woman tennis player ever. A late addition to the US squad after Rubin withdrew injured, she upset Martinez qf singles, but lost the bronze medal play-off to Novotna. Earlier she had upset both players to reach f Eastbourne and also appeared in sf Amelia Island and qf Sydney and Montreal. In doubles with Davenport, upset Novotna/Sanchez Vicario and G. Fernandez/Zvereva to take both French Open and Chase Champs, r/u Australian Open and won Sydney and Oakland. Withdrew from US Open with tendinitis of right wrist. In Fed Cup won all her matches as USA d. AUT in qf and ESP in f. **1997: (1)** *Berlin.* At Berlin she upset Novotna and Pierce for her 1st title since October 1995. She was always a threat to the top players on her way to sf Sydney (d. Coetzer and Majoli), Indian Wells (d. Martinez), Toronto (d. Sanchez Vicario) and Australian Open, as well as qf LIPC, Amelia Island, Chase Champs and French Open. There she extended Seles to 7–5 3s, handed Novotna a similar challenge at Wimbledon, and at Chase Champs she upset Davenport and before losing to Spirlea only 7–5 fs in qf. Her doubles partnership with Davenport had ended acrimoniously when Davenport, believing her to be retiring, arranged to play in 1997 with Novotna. As they went their separate ways, Fernandez played 3 doubles f, winning FC Cup with Hingis, Madrid with Sanchez Vicario and r/u French Open with Raymond. However, she was again plagued by injury and illness, suffering during the year from lower back strain, a sprained wrist, tendinitis in her right wrist, and a stomach injury, which hampered her at US Open.

PRINCIPAL 1997 RESULTS – won 1, sf 4 (detailed Grand Slam results follow)
won Berlin (d. Perfetti 6–4 3–6 6–1, Sanchez-Lorenzo 6–4 1–6 6–3, Testud 6–2 6–2, Kournikova 6–1 6–4, Novotna 6–3 6–1, Pierce 6–4 6–2); **sf** Australian Open, **sf** Sydney (d. Coetzer 6–1 3–6 6–2, Po 6–2 6–4, Majoli 7–5 6–4, lost Hingis 6–3 6–2), **sf** Indian Wells (d. Neiland 6–3 6–3, Po 6–2 6–3, Martinez 6–4 6–4, lost Davenport 6–1 6–1), **sf** Toronto (d. Kruger 6–4 7–5, Arendt 6–4 6–2, Sanchez Vicario 6–4 6–3, Maleeva 6–2 6–7 6–4, lost Huber 3–6 6–2 ret'd). **DOUBLES:** (with Raymond) **r/u French Open** (lost G. Fernandez/Zvereva 6–2 6–3); (with Hingis) **won** FC Cup (d. Davenport/Novotna 7–5 4–6 6–1), (with Sanchez Vicario) **won** Madrid (d. Gorrochategui/Spirlea 6–3 6–2).

CAREER GRAND SLAM RECORD
AUSTRALIAN OPEN – Played 9, r/u 2, sf 2, qf 1
1989: 3r [seed 10] d. Phelps 6–1 4–6 6–1, Grossman 6–4 7–6, lost Tanvier 6–2 6–3. **1990: r/u** [seed 6] d. Jaggard 6–1 6–3, Rinaldi 6–4 6–4, Halard 6–0 3–6 6–3, Faber 6–4 6–2, Garrison [3] 1–6 6–2 8–6, Porwik 6–2 6–1, lost Graf [1] 6–3 6–4. **1991: sf** [seed 3] d. Gomer 6–1 6–0, Romano 6–1 6–2, Sawamatsu 6–3 6–3, Appelmans [16] 6–3 6–3, K. Maleeva [5] 6–3 6–2, lost Seles [2] 6–3 0–6 9–7. **1992: r/u** [seed 7] d. Javer 6–1 6–0, Rittner 6–4 6–4, McQuillan 6–1 2–6 6–1, Fendick 6–4 6–1, Frazier 6–4 7–6, Sabatini 6–1 6–4, lost Seles 6–2 6–3. **1993: qf** [seed 5] d. Bowes 6–3 6–1, Wang 7–6 6–4, Sawamatsu 2–6 6–3 6–1, Maleeva-Fragniere [9] 7–5 2–6 6–2, lost Sanchez Vicario [4] 7–5 6–4. **1994: last 16** [seed 6] d. Hakami 6–4 6–3, Gorrochategui 6–3 2–6 9–7, Kuhlman 6–4 6–1, lost Davenport [16] 6–2 6–7 6–2. **1995: last 16** [seed 11] d. Callens 7–5 6–4, Harvey-Wild 7–6 7–5, Coetzer 6–3 5–7 6–2, lost Sawamatsu 6–4 7–6. **1996: last 16** [seed 9] d. Ruano-Pascual 6–4 6–3, Sanchez Lorenzo 6–2 6–0, Arendt 6–1 6–1, lost Sanchez Vicario [3] 6–3 6–3. **1997: sf** [seed 14] d. Golarsa 6–2 4–6 6–2, Basuki 7–5 6–4, Nagyova 6–2 6–1, Schnyder 4–6 6–4 6–1, Van Roost 7–5 4–0 ret'd, lost Hingis [4] 6–1 6–3.
FRENCH OPEN – Played 12, r/u 1, sf 1, qf 4
1985: 1r lost Mandlikova [3] 6–1 7–5. **1986: qf** d. Kelesi 7–6 6–3, Temesvari 5–7 6–2 6–3, Hobbs 6–2 6–0, Kohde-Kilsch [4] 7–6 7–5, lost Sukova [6] 6–2 7–4. **1987: 2r** [seed 13] d. Horvath 4–6 6–0 6–2, lost Rehe 7–6 1–6 6–4. **1989: sf** [seed 15] d. Herreman 6–2 6–3, Farley 6–7 6–3 6–1, Dias 6–7 6–1 6–1, Sabatini [2] 6–4 6–4, Kelesi [10] 6–2 7–5, lost Sanchez Vicario [7] 6–2 6–2. **1990: qf** [seed 7] d. McDonald 6–4 6–2, Pierce

6–4 6–4, Cueto 7–6 6–2, Grossman 6–3 6–2, lost Capriati 6–2 6–4. **1991: qf** [seed 4] d. Romano 6–3 6–0, Hack 6–4 6–0, Thoren 6–4 6–3, Reinach 6–4 7–6, lost Sanchez Vicario [5] 6–3 6–2. **1992: 3r** [seed 6] d. Langrova 6–3 6–1, Stafford 6–1 6–4, lost Hack 7–6 6–2. **1993: r/u** [seed 5] d. Feber 6–2 6–3, Grossman 6–3 3–6 6–1, Rinaldi 6–2 6–2, Schultz 2–6 7–5 6–3, Sabatini [3] 1–6 7–6 10–8, Sanchez Vicario [2] 6–2 6–2, lost Graf [1] 4–6 6–2 6–4. **1994: 3r** [seed 10] d. Habsudova 6–4 3–6 6–1, Gavaldon 6–0 6–1, lost Spirlea 6–4 6–1. **1995: 1r** [seed 13] lost Suarez 6–4 6–3. **1996: last 16** [seed 11] d. Grzybowska 6–0 6–1, Nagyova 6–2 6–4, Pizzichini 6–2 6–3, lost Graf [1] 6–1 7–6. **1997: qf** [seed 12] (d. McNeil 6–2 6–3, Glass 6–1 6–0, Perfetti 6–3 7–6, Raymond 6–7 6–2 6–2, lost Seles [seed 3] 3–6 6–2 7–5.

WIMBLEDON – Played 11, sf 1, qf 2

1986: 1r lost Evert-Lloyd [2] 6–4 6–1. **1987: last 16** d. Bonder 6–0 6–2, Potter 6–0 6–1, Moulton 7–6 6–2, lost Balestrat 7–5 6–2. **1988: last 16** [seed 16] d. Jagerman 6–3 6–2, Meskhi 6–1 7–5, Kuczynska 6–4 6–1, lost Graf [1] 6–2 6–2. **1989: last 16** [seed 12] d. Daniels 6–4 7–5, Louise Allen 6–4 6–1, Tanvier 4–6 6–2 6–4, lost Fairbank 6–4 2–6 6–0. **1991: sf** [seed 6] d. Kamstra 6–2 6–4, Keller 7–6 6–1, Shriver 6–3 7–5, Wiesner [9] 6–0 7–5, Sanchez Vicario [3] 6–2 7–5, lost Graf [1] 6–2 6–4. **1992: 3r** [seed 7] d. Bentley 6–1 6–0, N. Dahlman 7–5 6–2, lost Frazier 6–3 6–3. **1993: 3r** [seed 5] d. Nagatsuka 6–3 6–0, Dragomir 6–3 6–2, lost Garrison-Jackson 6–0 6–1. **1994: 3r** [seed 11] d. Habsudova 6–4 6–2, Schultz 6–4 6–4, lost Sawamatsu 6–0 7–5. **1995: qf** [seed 13] d. Habsudova 5–7 6–3 6–3, Park 6–4 6–0, Oremans 6–1 6–2, Davenport [7] 7–6 6–1, lost Graf [1] 6–3 6–0. **1996 qf** [seed 9] d. Kandarr 6–0 6–0, Testud 6–4 6–4, Labat 6–2 6–0, Sugiyama 6–4 1–6 6–3, lost McGrath 6–3 6–1. **1997: last 16** [seed 11] (d. Van Lottum 6–2 6–2, Olsza 6–4 6–0, Tanasugarn 6–2 6–4, lost Novotna [seed 3] 5–7 6–4 7–5.

US OPEN – Played 11, sf 2, qf 1

1985: 2r d. Gomer 6–1 6–4, lost Henricksson 6–1 6–4. **1986: 3r** d. Garrone 3–6 6–1 6–3, Hanika 6–2 6–2, lost Evert-Lloyd [2] 6–4 6–2. **1987: 3r** d. Marsikova 6–3 6–0, Savchenko 6–1 6–4, lost M. Maleeva [10] 6–0 0–6 6–3. **1988: 3r** [seed 13] d. Byrne 6–1 6–2, Tauziat 6–4 6–4, lost Reinach 7–5 6–3. **1989: 1r** [seed 10] lost W. White 6–4 6–3. **1990: sf** [seed 8] d. Henricksson 6–1 6–1, Oremans 6–4 6–1, R. White 6–1 6–2, Wiesner [15] 6–3 6–2, Maleeva-Fragniere [9] 7–5 3–6 6–3, lost Sabatini [5] 7–5 5 7–6–3. **1991: 3r** [seed 5] d. Savchenko 6–3 6–3, Schultz 7–6 6–3, lost Zrubakova 6–1 6–2. **1992: sf** [seed 7] d. Faber 3–6 6–0 6–4, Medvedeva 3–6 6–3 6–1, Schultz 6–4 6–2, Pierce [16] 6–0 6–4, Sabatini [4] 6–2 1–6 6–4, lost Seles 6–3 6–2). **1993:** Did not play. **1994: 3r** [seed 9] d. Appelmans 6–4 6–3, Fendick 6–2 2–6 7–6, lost Grossman 6–4 6–4. **1995: qf** [seed 14] d. Wiesner 4–6 6–4 6–3, Hack 7–6 6–3, Adams 6–3 6–1, Sanchez Vicario [seed 3] 1–6 6–4 6–4, lost Sabatini [9] 6–1 6–3. **1996:** Did not play. **1997: last 16** [seed 12] d. Kijimuta 6–2 6–3, Grande 4–6 6–2 6–2, Suarez 6–1 6–2, lost Novotna [3] 7–5 6–4.

OLYMPIC RECORD

SINGLES – 1992: (Barcelona) sf bronze medal [seed 4] d. Chen 6–2 6–3, Hy 6–2 1–6 12–10, Zvereva 7–6 6–1, Maleeva-Fragniere [6] 5–7 6–1 6–0, lost Graf [1] 6–4 6–2. **1996 (Atlanta) Olympics sf** [seed 7] d. Likhovtseva 6–2 6–4, Wang 7–6 2–6 6–1, Gorrochategui 6–0 6–3, Martinez [2] 3–6 6–2 6–3, lost Davenport [9] 6–2 7–6; bronze medal play-off lost Novotna 7–5 6–4. **DOUBLES – 1992 (Barcelona)** (with G. Fernandez) **won gold medal** d. Muns/Schultz 6–0 6–0, Graf/Huber 7–6 6–4, de Swardt/Reinach 6–2 6–4, Meskhi/Zvereva 6–4 7–5, Martinez/Sanchez Vicario 7–5 2–6 6–2. **1996 (Atlanta)** (with G. Fernandez) **won gold medal** d. Novotna/Sukova 7–6 6–4.

CAREER FED CUP RECORD

1991 (in GBR, Hard): *2r USA d. BUL 3–0.* R2 d. K. Maleeva 6–2 6–1. *Qf USA d. AUT 2–1.* R2 d. B. Paulus 6–1 6–1. *Sf USA d. TCH 3–0.* R2 d. J. Novotna 6–4 0–6 9–7. *Final ESP d. USA 2–1.* R2 lost A. Sanchez Vicario 6–3 6–4. **1994 (in GER, Clay):** *1r USA d. CZE 3–0.* R1 d. P. Langrova 6–2 6–4. *2r USA d. CAN 3–0.* R1 d. H. Kelesi 6–1 4–1 ret'd. *Qf USA d. AUT 3–0.* R1 d. P. Ritter 6–2 6–4; R3 (with G. Fernandez) d. S. Plischke/P. Ritter 6–4 6–1. *Sf USA d. FRA 3–0.* R1 d. J. Halard 6–1 6–3. *Final ESP d. USA 3–0.* R1 lost C. Martinez 6–2 6–3; R3 (with G. Fernandez) lost Martinez/A. Sanchez Vicario 6–3 6–4. **1995: April** – *World Group qf USA d. AUT 5–0 in USA (Hard).* R2 d. B. Schett 6–2 6–4; R3 d. J. Wiesner 6–3 2–6 6–3. *World Group sf USA d. FRA 3–2 in USA (Carpet).* R1 lost M. Pierce 7–6 6–3; R4 lost J. Halard 1–6 7–5 6–1; R5 (with L. Davenport) d. Halard/Tauziat 6–1 7–6. **November** – *World Group Final ESP d. USA 3–2 in ESP (Clay).* R2 lost A. Sanchez Vicario 6–3 6–2; R3 lost C. Martinez 6–3 6–4. **1996: April** – *World Group qf USA d. AUT 3–2 in AUT (Clay).* R1 d. J. Wiesner 6–3 7–6; R3 d. B. Paulus 6–3 7–6; R5 (with G. Fernandez) d. P. Schwarz-Ritter/Wiesner 6–0 6–4. **September** – *World Group Final USA d. ESP 5–0 in USA (Carpet).* R5 (with L. Wild) d. G. Leon-Garcia/V. Ruano-Pascual 6–1 6–4. **1997: March** – *World Group qf NED d. USA 3–2 in NED (Carpet).* R1 lost M. Oremans 6–1 6–4; R3 lost B. Schultz-McCarthy 1–6 6–4 9–7. **July** – *World Group play-off USA d. JPN 5–0 in USA (Hard).* R1 d. A. Sugiyama 4–6 6–2 6–2.

SEASON ENDING CHAMPIONSHIPS – Played 5, sf 1, qf 3

(1983–93 Virginia Slims, 1995 Corel, 1996–97 Chase)

1990: sf d. Tauziat 6–1 7–6, Maleeva-Fragniere 6–1 7–6, lost Seles 6–3 6–4. **1991: qf** d. Sukova 2–6 7–6 2–2 ret'd, lost Seles 6–3 6–2. **1992: 1r** lost Novotna 7–6 6–2. **1993: 1r** lost Coetzer 6–1 1–6 6–3. **1994:** Did not play. **1995: qf** d. Rubin 3–6 6–2 6–3, lost Graf 6–3 6–4. **1996:** Did not play. **1997: qf** d. Davenport 2–6 6–4 7–6, lost Spirlea 5–7 6–2 7–5.

REMAINING WOMEN'S BIOGRAPHIES

The following biographies show the players' progress each year in the four Grand Slam Championships. It is shown thus: A (Australian Open), F (French Open), W (Wimbledon), US (US Open), followed by the round reached or '–' if a player did not compete. Where a player's career prize money exceeds $1 million, it is shown in brackets after her 1997 prize money.

KATRINA ADAMS (USA)

Born Chicago, Ill., 5 August 1968; lives Missouri City, Tex.; RH; 2HB; 5ft 5in; 145lb; turned pro 1988; career singles titles 0; final 1997 WTA ranking 312 singles, 22 doubles; 1997 prize money $89,037 ($1,200,066).

Coached by Charlton Eagle. **1986:** (393) Won NCAA doubles with Donnelly. **1987:** (158). **1988:** A 1, F 1, W 4, US 1. Upset Fendick *en route* to 1st VS f in Wellington and removed Hanika at Wimbledon. **1989:** (86) A 2, F 1, W 3, US 1. Upset Man. Maleeva and Fendick on her way to sf US HC. In doubles won 8 titles with different partners. **1990:** (254) A 1, F –, W 1, US 1. Reached 1 f and 10 sf in doubles but won no title on the main tour. **1991:** (93) A –, F –, W –, US –. In singles r/u VS Nashville and qf VS Albuquerque (d. Fendick). She won the doubles there with Demongeot and reached 3 more f with various partners. **1992:** (143) A 3, F 1, W 2, US –. Played 3 doubles f with different partners and won Indianapolis with Reinach. **1993:** (179) A –, F –, W –, US 1. From 6 doubles f won VS Houston, Quebec City and VS Philadelphia with Bollegraf and VS Chicago with Garrison-Jackson. Qualified for VS Champs with Bollegraf, but did not progress beyond 1r. **1994:** (143) A –, F –, W 1, US 1. Qf Oklahoma (d. Harvey-Wild) was her best performance in singles, and in doubles she played 2 f, but won no title. **1995:** (113) A –, F –, W 1, US 3. Upset Coetzer at Oklahoma but reached no qf in singles. She finished without a doubles title, but reached 2 f with different partners and qualified for VS Champs with Garrison-Jackson. **1996:** (120) A –, F 1, W 2, US 1. While qf Oklahoma was her best showing in singles, she played 3 doubles f, winning Budapest with Graham and Cardiff with de Swardt. Won Player Service Award. **1997:** A 1, F –, W –, US –. Won Birmingham doubles with Neiland. **1997 HIGHLIGHTS – SINGLES: Australian Open 1r** (lost Yoshida 7–5 6–3). **1997 HIGHLIGHTS – DOUBLES:** (with Neiland) **won** Birmingham (d. Tauziat/Wild 6–2 6–3).

SABINE APPELMANS (BEL)

Born Aalst, 22 April 1972; lives Asse; LH; 2HB; 5ft 6in; 127lb; turned pro 1989; career singles titles 7; final 1997 WTA ranking 16; 1997 prize money $339,845 ($1,448,330).

Coached by Steve Martens. Husband Serge Habourdin (married September 1996). She is naturally right-handed, but chose to join a left-handed group when learning to play tennis in order to be with a friend. **1987:** (283). **1988:** (215) A –, F 2, W –, US –. Enjoyed some success on the European satellite circuits and upset Burgin 1r French Open. **1989:** (149) A –, F –, W –, US –. Reached her 1st primary circuit qf at Taipei. **1990:** (22) A 3, F 1, W –, US 3. R/u Auckland (d. Cordwell) and reached sf Wellington and Singapore, breaking into top 100 and finishing the year in the top 25. **1991:** (18) A 4, F 4, W 1, US 1. Won her 1st singles title at Phoenix, following with VS Nashville; was r/u Tokyo Suntory, reached sf Oslo and Puerto Rico and appeared in 3 doubles f. Voted Belgian Sports Celebrity of the Year. **1992:** (26) A 1, F 2, W 2, US 4. Won Pattaya City and r/u Tokyo Suntory, as well as reaching qf Olympics, Essen, Berlin and Leipzig. In GS upset Huber *en route* to last 16 US Open, unseeded. **1993:** (36) A 1, F 2, W 3, US 2. Having won Porto Challenger but reached no qf on the main tour, she was r/u Budapest (d. Wiesner) in Oct. and followed the next week with sf Essen (d. Maleeva-Fragniere). **1994:** (27) A 3, F 2, W 1, US 1. Won Linz (d. Huber) and Pattaya City and reached sf Tokyo Japan Open, Los Angeles (d. Novotna) and Moscow. Ranked No. 1 in Belgium, she reached her highest world ranking of 17 in May, before slipping back out of the top 20. **1995:** (31) A 3, F 3, W 1, US 3. Won Zagreb and reached qf Paris Open, Linz, Strasbourg (d. Frazier) and Tokyo Nicherei. **1996:** (21) A 4, F 3, W 4, US 1. Upset Novotna, Sukova and Halard-Decugis on her way to the title at Linz and reached sf Moscow, plus qf Jakarta, Zurich (d. Martinez) and Luxembourg. She made her mark in GS: at French Open she was 5–2 up in 2s v Seles, but won no more games, and at Wimbledon, where she was unseeded, she scraped past Schultz-McCarthy 12–10 fs before extending Sanchez Vicario to 3s. In doubles she reached 2 f with Oremans, but won no title. **1997:** A qf, F 1, W 4, US 1. She was r/u Budapest, and although she reached no other f, she appeared in qf Australian Open, Gold Coast, Berlin, Strasbourg, Rosmalen, Leipzig, Zurich (d. Schultz-McCarthy and Majoli) and Luxembourg. Once again she impressed in GS, removing Martinez at Australian Open and Schultz-McCarthy at Wimbledon, where she was unseeded. Upset M. J. Fernandez at Chicago and surprised Sanchez Vicario in Fed Cup as BEL d. ESP. Qualified for Chase Champs 1st time, but fell 1r to Pierce at her best. **1997 HIGHLIGHTS – SINGLES: Australian Open qf** [seed 16] (d. Sukova 6–2 6–2, Grossman 6–4 6–1, Boogert 6–1 3–0 ret'd, Martinez [seed 3] 2–6 7–5 6–1, lost Pierce 1–6 6–4 6–4), **French Open 1r** (lost Dhenin 6–7 6–2 6–1), **Wimbledon last 16** [unseeded] (d. Simpson 6–2 3–6 6–0, Golarsa 6–2 6–0, Schultz-McCarthy [seed 14] 6–2 6–3, lost Hingis [seed 1] 6–1 6–3), **US Open 1r** (lost Kournikova 6–2 6–0); **r/u** Budapest (d. Langrova 6–1 4–6 6–4, Dechy 6–1 6–2, Torrens-Valero 6–4 6–4, Habsudova 6–2 6–4, lost Coetzer 6–1 6–3). **1997 HIGHLIGHTS – DOUBLES:** (with Oremans) **r/u** LIPC (lost Sanchez Vicario/Zvereva 6–2 6–3). **CAREER HIGHLIGHTS – Australian Open – qf 1997.**

NICOLE ARENDT (USA)

Born Somerville, NJ, 26 August 1969; lives Princeton, NJ; LH; 5ft 9½in; 150lb; turned pro 1991; career singles titles 0; final 1997 WTA ranking 63 singles, 8 doubles; 1997 prize money $357,052 ($1,094,802).

Coached by Charlton Eagle. **1986:** (–) A –, F –, W –, US 2. Won San Antonio Futures. **1987:** (366) A –, F –, W –, US 1. **1988:** (451) A –, F –, W –, US –. Began 3-year career at Univ. of Florida-Gainesville, where she was an All-American 8 times. **1989:** (–) A –, F –, W –, US –. **1990:** (388) A –, F –, W –, US –. R/u NCAA Champs and won Lady Lake Futures. **1991:** (211) A –, F –, W –, US 1. On the Futures circuit she took Sanibel and Greensboro, and won NCAA Champs doubles with Jillian Alexander. **1992:** (126) A 2, F –, W –, US 2. At Puerto Rico she reached her 1st qf on the senior tour. **1993:** (88) A 2, F –, W 2, US 2. Reached sf Jakarta, where she won the doubles with Radford and upset Paradis-Mangon on her way to qf Pattaya City. Won Karen Krantzcke Sportsmanship Award. **1994:** (73) A 1, F –, W 2, US 2. Upset Appelmans at Eastbourne, and appeared in sf Singapore and qf Pattaya City (d. Basuki) and Jakarta, where she won the doubles again with Radford. Sidelined for 2 months with pulled stomach muscle, suffered at Filderstadt. **1995:** A 1, F 1, W 1, US 3. In singles qf Birmingham was her best showing, but she made her mark in doubles, winning 3 titles with Bollegraf, with whom she qualified for WTA Champs, and 1 with Golarsa. **1996:** (70) A 3, F 1, W 3, US 2. From 4 women's doubles f with different partners, she won Edinburgh with Bollegraf and Filderstadt with Novotna. In mixed she was r/u Australian Open and French Open with L. Jensen. **1997:** A 1, F 4, W 3, US 1. Upset Novotna at French Open, where she was unseeded. In doubles with Bollegraf, she was r/u Wimbledon and reached 6 other f, winning Hannover, Edinburgh and Atlanta and sharing Eastbourne. They qualified together for Chase Champs but were forced to retire in sf v Fusai/Tauziat. **1997 HIGHLIGHTS – SINGLES: Australian Open 1r** (lost Boogert 3–6 6–3 6–4), **French Open last 16** [unseeded] (d.Hiraki 6–2 6–1, Golarsa 6–2 6–2, Novotna [seed 4] 3–6 6–4 6–4, lost Dragomir 6–1 6–1), **Wimbledon 3r** (d. Langrova 6–2 6–0, Raymond 1–6 6–4 6–3, lost Hingis [seed 1] 6–1 6–3), **US Open 1r** (lost Coetzer [seed 5] 6–3 6–2). **1997 HIGHLIGHTS – DOUBLES:** (with Bollegraf) **r/u Wimbledon** (lost G. Fernandez/Zvereva 7–6 6–4); **won** Hannover (d. Neiland/Schultz-McCarthy 4–6 6–3 7–6), **won** Edinburgh (d. McQuillan/Miyagi 6–1 3–6 7–5), **won** Atlanta (d. Fusai/Tauziat 6–7 6–3 6–2); **shared** Eastbourne (with McNeil/Sukova; final cancelled); **r/u** Amelia Island (lost Davenport/Novotna 6–3 6–0), **r/u** Toronto (lost Basuki/Vis 3–6 7–5 6–4). **CAREER HIGHLIGHTS – DOUBLES:** (with Bollegraf) **Wimbledon – r/u 1997**.

OLGA BARABANSCHIKOVA (BRS)

Born Minsk, 2 November 1979; lives London, England; RH; 5ft 7½in; 124lb; career singles titles 0; final 1997 WTA ranking 59; 1997 prize money $98,215.

Coached by Victor Archutowski. Has lived in Ealing since age 12. **1994:** Won Nat Jun Champs. **1995:** Won Astrid Bowl and took her 1st pro title on the French satellite circuit. **1996:** (152) Won Wimbledon Jun doubles with Mauresmo and was a member of the Belarus Olympic Team. **1997:** A –, F 1, W 2, US 3. Moving on to the women's tour, she upset Schultz-McCarthy at US Open and won Bushey Futures, before finishing the year on a high note with sf Pattaya. **1997 HIGHLIGHTS – SINGLES: French Open 1r** (lost Habsudova [seed 15] 6–3 6–3), **Wimbledon 2r** (d. Begerow 6–3 6–3, lost Hingis [seed 1] 6–2 6–2), **US Open 3r** (d. Golarsa 6–3 6–3, Schultz-McCarthy [seed 13] 6–3 6–3, lost Labat 4–6 7–6 6–1); **won** Bushey Futures (d. Sandu 6–1 7–6); **sf** Pattaya (d. Chladkova 3–6 7–6 6–2, Park 7–6 2–2 ret'd, Pratt 6–0 6–3, lost Van Roost 6–3 6–2).

YAYUK BASUKI (INA)

Born Yogyakarta, 30 November 1970; lives Jakarta; RH; 5ft 4½in; 125lb; turned pro 1990; career singles titles 6; final 1997 WTA ranking 21 singles, 15 doubles; 1997 prize money $385,824 ($1,328,765).

Coached by her husband, Hary Suharyadi (married 31 January 1994). Ranked No. 1 in Indonesia. **1986:** Joined her country's Fed Cup team. **1988:** (284). **1989:** (377) Made her mark on the satellite circuits, winning Jakarta. **1990:** (266) Continued to enjoy success on the satellite circuits. **1991:** (35) A –, F 1, W 3, US 2. At Pattaya City, she became 1st native Indonesian to win a primary circuit title and was voted Indonesian Athlete of the Year. Upset Kohde-Kilsch *en route* to qf Eastbourne and reached the same stage at VS Nashville. **1992:** (48) A 3, F –, W 4, US 1. Upset Huber at Wimbledon and Pierce at Olympics, making an unexpected appearance in last 16 both times. Won Kuala Lumpur and reached sf Pattaya City. **1993:** (43) A 1, F 2, W 4, US 1. Won Pattaya City (d. Probst and Fendick) and Jakarta and reached qf Kuala Lumpur. Unseeded at Wimbledon, she upset Mag. Maleeva and extended Martinez to 3s. In doubles with Basuki won Sapporo and Taipei back-to-back in autumn. **1994:** (29) A 2, F –, W 4, US 1. Won Beijing and Jakarta and reached sf Eastbourne (d. Sukova). She also upset Tauziat 1r Australian Open and surprised Mag. Maleeva at Wimbledon. In doubles she reached 3 f, winning Hong Kong with Tedjakusuma. **1995:** (24) A 3, F 1, W 4, US 1. Sf Jakarta and Manhattan Beach (d. M. J. Fernandez, Tauziat and Davenport); reached qf Eastbourne; and upset Sabatini in Fed Cup. **1996:** (26) A 1, F 3, W 1, US 1. Reached f Jakarta, but withdrew with a cold. Upset Majoli and Frazier on her way to sf Montreal before reaching same stage Philadelphia, and appeared in qf Eastbourne (d. Davenport) and Beijing. In doubles she won Hobart with Nagatsuka and Strasbourg with Bradtke, although it was with Vis that she played Chase Champs. Won Karen Krantzcke Sportsmanship Award. **1997:** A 2, F 2, W qf, US 2. She proved to be a dangerous opponent on her way to f Birmingham (d. Spirlea), sf Tokyo Nicherei, and qf Wimbledon (unseeded), Sydney (d. Pierce), Paris Open (d. Schultz-

McCarthy), San Diego (d. Huber) and Chicago (d. Schultz-McCarthy). In doubles she played 4 f and won Los Angeles and Toronto back-to-back with Vis, with whom she qualified for Chase Champs again. Was hampered in the spring by injury – tendinitis in right foot, ankle and calf. **1997 HIGHLIGHTS – SINGLES: Australian Open 2r** (d. Sawamatsu 6–3 4–1 ret'd, lost M. J. Fernandez [seed 14] 7–5 6–4), **French Open 2r** (d. Carlsson 6–4 4–6 6–1, lost Dragomir 7–5 4–6 8–6), **Wimbledon qf** [unseeded] (d. Sugiyama 6–3 6–0, Gorrochategui 6–2 6–0, Kijimuta 6–3 6–2, Hy-Boulais 6–0 7–6, lost Novotna [seed 3] 6–3 6–3), **US Open 2r** (d. Van Lottum 6–3 6–4, lost Novotna [seed 3] 6–4 6–2); **r/u** Birmingham (d. Kijimuta 6–1 4–6 6–1, Cacic 6–1 4–6 6–1, Maleeva 7–6 6–2, Spirlea 7–6 6–1, lost Tauziat 2–6 6–2 6–2); **sf** Tokyo Nicherei (d. Pitkowski 7–5 7–6, Saeki 6–7 6–4 6–2, Po 7–6 6–3, lost Sanchez Vicario 1–6 7–6 6–4). **1997 HIGHLIGHTS – DOUBLES:** (with Vis unless stated) **won** Los Angeles (d. Neiland/Sukova 7–6 6–3), **won** Toronto (d. Arendt/Bollegraf 3–6 7–5 6–4); (with Sukova) **r/u** Leipzig (lost Hingis/Novotna 6–2 6–2), **r/u** Moscow (lost Sanchez Vicario/Zvereva 5–3 ret'd).

CARA BLACK (ZIM)

Born Harare, 17 February 1979, and lives there; RH; 2HB; 5ft 4in; 120lb; career singles titles 0; final 1997 WTA ranking 189; Junior ranking 1; 1997 prize money $14,287.

Coached by her father, Don Black, and Daria Kopsic. Her brothers, Byron and Wayne, play the men's circuit. **1992:** All-Africa champ. **1994:** Won Nat Jun Champ in singles and doubles. **1995:** (489) Won Wimbledon Jun doubles with Olsza and Nat Jun Champ in singles and doubles again. In the women's game won 2 Futures singles titles, being r/u in both doubles. **1996:** Played Fed Cup and won Nitra Futures. **1997:** Missed Australian Open Jun, but in other Jun GS was r/u French Open to Henin, won Wimbledon over Rippner and US Open over Chevalier, as well as taking French Open and Wimbledon doubles with Selyutina. In the women's game, she won Futures titles at Dinard and Mission. **1997 HIGHLIGHTS – SINGLES: won** Dinard Futures (d. Lamarre 4–6 6–4 6–2), **won** Mission Futures (d. Phebus 6–3 6–3).

MANON BOLLEGRAF (NED)

Born Den Bosch, 10 April 1964; lives Ermelo; RH; 2HB; 5ft 8in; 150lb; turned pro 1985; career singles titles 1; final 1997 WTA ranking – 7 doubles; 1997 prize money $374,574 ($1,795,930).

Coached by Ron Timmermans and at tournaments by Charlton Eagle. **1986:** (148) Qf Singapore. **1987:** (120) A 2, F 2, W –, US –. Qf Little Rock and took over the No. 1 ranking in her country. **1988:** (117) A 2, F 1, W 2, US 2. Qf Brisbane. **1989:** (38) A 3, F 3, W 1, US 2. In singles won 1st primary circuit title at Oklahoma (unseeded), reached sf Brussels and Nashville and upset McNeil 2r French Open. In doubles won 4 women's titles plus French Open mixed with Nijssen. **1990:** (32) A 2, F 1, W 1, US 2. In singles r/u VS Oklahoma and reached sf Strasbourg. Appeared in 5 doubles f with various partners, winning Wichita with McGrath and Zurich with Pfaff. **1991:** (49) A 1, F 1, W 3, US 1. R/u Colorado and sf Oklahoma in singles, won Leipzig with Demongeot in doubles and took US Open mixed with Nijssen. **1992:** (44) A 1, F qf, W 2, US –. In singles she upset Maleeva-Fragniere and Tauziat in reaching qf French Open, unseeded, and reached sf VS Oklahoma and qf Chicago. In doubles she reached 4 f with different partners, winning Waregem with Vis. Missed Olympics and US Open after tearing several ligaments at Frankfurt, for which she underwent surgery, and was out for rest of year. **1993:** (161) A 1, F 1, W 1, US 1. At US Open she extended eventual finalist Sukova to 3s tb 1r, but it was in doubles that she excelled. In mixed she was r/u French Open with Nijssen and in partnership with Adams she played 5 women's f, winning 3 and qualifying for VS Champs, where they failed to pass 1r. **1994:** (109) A 1, F 1, W 1, US 1. She upset Garrison-Jackson at FC Cup, but reached no qf in singles. Again her strength lay in doubles, in which she appeared in 10 f with various partners, winning 1 with Neiland and 2 with Navratilova, with whom she qualified for VS Champs, where they reached sf. **1995:** (158) A 2, F –, W –, US 2. Played 9 doubles f with various partners, winning 4 with Arendt, with whom she qualified for WTA Champs, and 1 with Stubbs. **1996:** (–) A –, F –, W –, US –. In doubles she won Linz with McGrath and Edinburgh with Arendt; in mixed was r/u US Open with Leach. Underwent arthroscopic surgery on her left knee at end Sept., which prevented her playing at Chase Champs, for which she qualified in doubles. **1997:** A –, F –, W –, US –. Returning in time for Australian Open, she won the mixed doubles there with Leach, adding US Open later in year. In women's doubles with Arendt, she was r/u Wimbledon and from 6 other f won 3 titles and shared another, qualifying for Chase Champs. There, however, they were forced to retire sf v Fusai/Tauziat. **1997 HIGHLIGHTS – DOUBLES:** (with Arendt) **r/u Wimbledon** (lost G. Fernandez/Zvereva 7–6 6–4); **won** Hannover (d. Neiland/Schultz-McCarthy 4–6 6–3 7–6), **won** Edinburgh (d. McQuillan/Miyagi 6–1 3–6 7–5), **won** Atlanta (d. Fusai/Tauziat 6–7 6–3 6–2); **shared** Eastbourne (with McNeil/Sukova; final cancelled); **r/u** Amelia Island (lost Davenport/Novotna 6–3 6–0), **r/u** Toronto (lost Basuki/Vis 3–6 7–5 6–4). **MIXED DOUBLES:** (with Leach) **won Australian Open** (d. De Jager/Neiland 6–3 6–7 7–5), **won US Open** (d. Albano/Paz 3–6 7–5 7–6). **CAREER HIGHLIGHTS – SINGLES: French Open – qf 1992** [unseeded] (d. Maniokova 6–2 6–3, Thoren 6–2 4–6 7–5, Maleeva-Fragniere 7–5 6–2, Tauziat 6–4 1–6 6–2, lost Sanchez Vicario 6–2 6–3). **CAREER HIGHLIGHTS – DOUBLES:** (with Arendt) **Wimbledon – r/u 1997**. **CAREER HIGHLIGHTS – MIXED DOUBLES:** (with Nijssen unless stated) **Australian Open –** (with Leach) **won 1997; French Open – won 1989** (d. de la Pena/Sanchez Vicario 3–6 6–7 6–2); **US Open – won 1991** (d. E. Sanchez/Sanchez Vicario 6–2 7–6), (with Leach) **won 1997**.

SANDRA CACIC (USA)

Born Joliet, Ill., 10 September 1974; lives Bradenton, Fla.; RH; 2HB; 5ft 6½in; 140lb; turned pro 1990; career singles titles 1; final 1997 WTA ranking 57; 1997 prize money $78,191.

Coached by her father, Tony, who played soccer for Croatia. **1989:** (450). **1990:** (570). **1991:** (376) Out for 18 months with tendinitis of the wrist. **1992:** (249) Returned to action on the satellite circuits towards the end of the year. **1993:** (81) A –, F –, W –, US 2. Won Leon Futures and on the main tour upset Novotna and Neiland on the way to her 1st qf at Zurich. **1994:** (54) A 1, F 2, W 2, US 2. Reached qf Chicago (d. Sukova), Oklahoma (d. McNeil) and Houston, but could progress no further. **1995:** (112) A 2, F 1, W 2, US 1. Won Lakeland Futures. **1996:** (82) A 3, F 1, W 1, US 1. She began the year in style by taking her 1st senior tour title at Auckland, after qualifying, but struggled thereafter. **1997:** A 1, F 1, W 1, US 1. On the main tour she reached qf Auckland and Oklahoma City, and on the Futures circuit won Monterrey and Newport. **1997 HIGHLIGHTS – SINGLES: Australian Open 1r** (lost Probst 6–4 2–6 7–5), **French Open 1r** (lost Pizzichini 7–6 7–5), **Wimbledon 1r** (lost Frazier 7–5 6–4), **US Open 1r** (lost Grande 6–2 6–1); **won** Monterrey Futures (d. Gavaldon 6–3 6–2, **won** Newport Futures (d. Reeves 6–4 4–6 6–4).

JENNIFER CAPRIATI (USA)

Born New York, 29 March 1996; lives Wesley Chapel, Fla.; RH; 2HB; 5ft 8½in; 135lb; turned pro 1990; career singles titles 6; final 1997 WTA ranking 66; 1997 prize money $79,852 ($1,688,628).

1988: Won Nat 18s at age 12. **1989:** Won French Open Jun (losing no set, and being the youngest to win that title), US Open Jun, plus Wimbledon and US Open Jun doubles with McGrath, as well as US 18s HC and CC. At 13 years 6 months was youngest to play W Cup, making a sparkling debut with a 6–0 6–0 drubbing of Wood, but was still too young to compete on the pro tour until March. **1990:** (8) A –, F sf, W 4, US 4. At age 13 she became the 1st female to reach f of her 1st pro tourn at VS Florida, Boca Raton. She upset Sukova there and at LIPC, where she reached last 16, stunned Sanchez Vicario and Zvereva *en route* to 2nd tour f at FC Cup, and in Oct. beat Garrison at Puerto Rico to win her 1st tour title. Reached sf in 1st GS tourn at French Open, becoming youngest (at 14 years 66 days) to reach that stage; youngest seed at Wimbledon, youngest to win singles match at US Open, and youngest to qualify for VS Champs, where she lost 1r to Graf. Also youngest to reach top 10 at 14 years 235 days. She was a member of the winning US Fed Cup team and won WTA Most Impressive Newcomer award. **1991:** (6) A –, F 4, W sf, US sf. Caused the upset of the Championships when she stunned Navratilova in ss to become youngest semi-finalist at Wimbledon, and at US Open d. Sabatini to reach the same stage and took Seles to 3s tb. She had earlier upset the No. 1 as she won San Diego, following with Toronto and r/u VS Philadelphia. Also reached sf VS Florida and Berlin and qualified for VS Champs, where she lost qf to Sabatini. In doubles won Italian Open with Seles. **1992:** (7) A qf, F qf, W qf, US 3. Found it a hard year on the tour, despite winning the Olympic Gold medal. She struggled to recapture her enjoyment of the game and early in the year was rumoured to be contemplating retirement. By year's end she was beginning to feel more positive again and reached sf VS Champs, where she lost to Sabatini. Won San Diego and reached sf Berlin, Philadelphia and LIPC where, in qf, she became one of a handful of players to beat Seles during the year. **1993:** (9) A qf, F qf, W qf, US 1. She struggled again and, feeling more and more jaded and less interested in the game, she withdrew from VS Champs, lacking motivation. Her only title came at Sydney, with r/u Toronto and sf FC Cup, plus 5 more qf, including Australian Open, French Open and Wimbledon, but at US Open fell 1r to Meskhi. **1994:** (–) A –, F –, W –, US –. In Jan. she dropped out of the top 10 for 1st time since July 1991. Disillusioned with life on the circuit and showing behavioural problems, she was arrested on drug charges in mid-May and voluntarily entered a Miami drug abuse rehabilitation centre, uncertain whether she would ever return to the tennis circuit. However, she was back in action for her only tourn of the year at Philadelphia in Nov., where she lost 1r to Huber, but was still vague about her future plans. **1995:** (–) A –, F –, W –, US –. Still struggling with behavioural problems and motivation, she was out of action all year. **1996:** (24) A –, F 1, W –, US 1. At Paris Open in Feb. she was expected back for her 1st event since Nov. 1994, but withdrew citing a strained gluteal muscle sustained during practice. She eventually ended her absence of 1 year 9 months and 4 weeks on 19 Feb. at Essen, where she won 2 matches and extended Novotna to 3s in qf. Upset Coetzer at LIPC, after losing 2nd set to love, in her 3rd tourn back and still unranked, and played Fed Cup in April. Returned to the rankings at 103 on 1 April – for the first time since she fell off on 26 June 1994 – was back in the top 50 in Oct., and top 25 in Nov. Withdrew from Wimbledon, not feeling ready to compete at that level, and at Montreal retired 3r with a gluteal strain on her left side, after upsetting Spirlea 1r. She followed qf appearance at Zurich (d. M. Maleeva) with the high point of her year at sf Chicago, where she upset Seles in ss, before losing to Novotna in her 1st f since Toronto 1993. She was voted Comeback Player of the Year. Low points were her disappointing performance at Fed Cup qf, losing both her singles in ss v AUT, and occasional behavioural problems. **1997:** A 1, F –, W –, US 1. She began the year well by upsetting Davenport *en route* to f Sydney, where she extended Hingis to 3s. Thereafter, though, her best showing was qf Oklahoma City, as she withdrew from Amelia Island with a left hip adductor strain, sprained her right ankle during practice in Rome and withdrew from French Open and Wimbledon. **1997 HIGHLIGHTS – SINGLES: Australian Open 1r** (lost Watanabe 6–2 3–6 6–4), **US Open 1r** (lost Martinez [seed 7] 6–1 6–2); **r/u** Sydney (d. Rubin 6–3 4–6 6–3, Simpson 6–3 6–2, Frazier 6–4 6–1, Davenport 2–6 6–4 6–2, lost Hingis 6–1 5–7 6–1). **CAREER HIGHLIGHTS – SINGLES: Olympics – won gold medal 1992** (d. Reinach 6–1 6–0, Tarabini 6–4 6–1, Basuki 6–3 6–4,

Huber 6–3 7–6, Sanchez Vicario 6–3 3–6 6–1, Graf 3–6 6–3 6–4); **French Open – sf 1990** (d. Testud 6–1 6–1, Cammy Macgregor 6–1 6–0, Wiesner 6–4 6–4, Paz 6–0 6–3, M. J. Fernandez 6–2 6–4, lost Seles 6–2 6–2), **qf** 1992 (d. Reinstadler 6–1 6–7 6–3, Testud 6–4 6–4, Habsudova 4–6 6–4 6–3, Pierce 6–4 6–3, lost Seles 6–2 6–2), **qf** 1993 (d. Herreman 6–0 6–1, Fusai 6–1 7–5, Labat 6–0 3–6 6–4, Pierce 6–4 7–6, lost Graf 6–3 7–5); **Wimbledon – sf 1991** (d. Stafford 6–0 7–5, Zrubakova 6–2 6–3, Probst 6–3 1–6 6–3, Schultz 3–6 6–1 6–1, Navratilova 6–4 7–5, lost Sabatini 6–4 6–4), **qf** 1992 (d. Rubin 6–0 7–5, Shriver 6–2 6–4, Hy 6–3 6–1, Sawamatsu 6–3 4–6 6–4, lost Sabatini 6–1 3–6 6–3), **qf** 1993 (d. Siddall 6–7 6–2 6–1, Smylie 4–6 6–3 6–2, Schultz 7–5 4–6 6–2, Raymond 4–6 6–3 8–6, lost Graf 7–6 6–1); **US Open – sf 1991** (d. Pfaff 6–1 6–0, Ritter 6–3 6–0, Hy 6–1 6–4, Durie 6–1 6–2, Sabatini 6–3 7–6, lost Seles 3–6 6–3 7–6); **Australian Open – qf 1992** (d. Medvedeva 6–2 6–0, van Lottum 6–3 6–4, Adams 6–0 6–0, Garrison Jackson 6–4 6–4, lost Sabatini 6–4 7–6), **qf** 1993 (d. Harvey-Wild 6–0 6–1, Labat 6–7 7–5 6–2, Zvereva 7–5 7–5, K. Maleeva 6–7 6–3 6–1, lost Graf 7–5 6–2).

ASA CARLSSON (SWE)

Born Vasteras, 16 June 1975; lives Surahammar; RH; 2HB; 5ft 9½in; 138lb; turned pro 1992; career singles titles 0; final 1997 WTA ranking 45; 1997 prize money $151,989.

Coached by Roger Lofqvist. **1991:** (330) Won Ljusdals Futures and in jun tennis was r/u Australian Open doubles with Cristea. **1992:** (199) Won both singles and doubles at Helsinki Futures. **1993:** (167) She continued to enjoy some success on the satellite circuits and reached qf Schenectady on the main tour. **1994:** (69) A –, F 1, W 1, US 2. Reached 1st tour singles sf at Houston, following in May with her 1st f at Prague, having upset Harvey-Wild on the way. **1995:** (49) A 1, F 1, W 1, US 2. R/u Houston and appeared in sf Bournemouth plus qf Prague, San Diego and Moscow. **1996:** (44) A 2, F 1, W 1, US 4. Upset Sukova *en route* to sf Essen, surprised Sabatini at US Open, where she was unseeded, and reached qf Linz. **1997:** A 3, F –, W 1, US 1. Reached sf Rosmalen, plus qf Gold Coast, Linz and Cardiff, and upset Paulus at Indian Wells. **1997 HIGHLIGHTS – SINGLES: Australian Open 3r** (d. Langrova 6–3 6–2, Hy-Boulais 2–6 6–3 6–0, lost Martinez [seed 3] 6–0 6–1), **Wimbledon 1r** (lost Schett 2–6 6–3 6–0), **US Open 1r** (lost Schultz-McCarthy [seed 13] 6–3 6–3); **sf** Rosmalen (d. Torrens-Valero 6–3 3–6 7–5, Lubiani 6–7 6–2 7–5, Pierce w.o., lost Dragomir 6–4 6–2).

KILDINE CHEVALIER (FRA)

Born Lyon, 30 June 1980; lives Francheville; RH; 2HB; 5ft 8½in; 120lb; career singles titles 0; final 1997 WTA ranking 385; Junior ranking 12.

Coached by Gerbrand Appelboom. **1995:** In winning FRA World Youth Cup team. **1997:** R/u US Open Jun to Black.

DENISA CHLADKOVA (CZE)

Born Prague, 8 February 1979, and lives there; RH; 5ft 8in; 122lb; turned pro 1994; career singles titles 0; final 1997 WTA ranking 50; 1997 prize money $139,896.

Coached by Josef Cihak. **1995:** (276) A member of winning World Youth Cup team, she began to make an impact on the satellite circuits. **1996:** (99) Reached her 1st tour sf at Pattaya at end of year (d. Park and Labat) and broke into top 100. **1997:** A 1, F 1, W qf, US 2. Upset Davenport on her way to qf Wimbledon, where she was unseeded, and reached the same stage at Prague.**1997 HIGHLIGHTS – SINGLES: Australian Open 1r** (lost De Ville 6–3 6–7 8–6), **French Open 1r** (lost Frazier 6–4 6–0), **Wimbledon qf** [unseeded] (d. Kleinova 7–6 6–4, Davenport [seed 5] 7–5 6–2, Zrubakova 6–7 6–3 8–6, Vento 6–1 6–3, lost Hingis [seed 1] 6–3 6–2), **US Open 2r** (d. Sukova 6–1 1–6 6–1, lost Hingis [seed 1] 6–1 6–2).

CATALINA CRISTEA (ROM)

Born Bucharest, 2 July 1975, and lives there; RH; 2HB; 5ft 8in; 125lb; turned pro 1992; career singles titles 0; final 1997 WTA ranking 73; 1997 prize money $103,070.

1990: (806). **1991:** (504) R/u US Open Jun doubles with Carlsson. **1992:** (429). **1993:** (127) R/u Australian Open Jun doubles with Carlsson. On the senior tour she reached her 1st qf at Puerto Rico (d. Quentrec), following in Oct. with her 1st sf at Taipei. **1994:** (191) A 2, F 1, W –, US –. **1995:** (103) A –, F 3, W –, US 1. Upset Zvereva 1r French Open. **1996:** (125) A 1, F 1, W 1, US –. Reached qf Warsaw and on the ITF circuit won Bucharest. **1997:** A 1, F 2, W 1, US 1. Appeared in sf Prague, but reached no other qf on the main tour. **1997 HIGHLIGHTS – SINGLES: Australian Open 1r** (lost Sugiyama 7–6 6–4), **French Open 2r** (d. Probst 6–3 6–4, lost Testud 6–0 6–4), **Wimbledon 1r** (lost Gagliardi 3–6 7–6 6–1), **US Open 1r** (lost Majoli [seed 4] 6–3 6–2); **sf** Prague (d. Gersi 6–2 1–0 ret'd, Simpson 6–3 6–3, Richterova 6–2 2–6 7–5, lost Maruska 6–2 6–1).

ALEXIA DECHAUME-BALLERET (FRA)

Born La Rochelle, 3 May 1970; lives St Laurent; RH; 2HB; 5ft 5in; 132lb; turned pro 1985; career singles titles 0; final 1997 WTA ranking 65; 1997 prize money $120,848.

Coached by her husband Bernard Balleret (married 13 Nov. 1993). **1986:** (225) A –, F 2, W –, US –. **1987:** (127) A –, F 1, W –, US –. Appeared in her 1st VS qf at Athens. **1988:** (127) A –, F 1, W 1, US 1. Reached qf Taranto on the main tour and won Bayonne on the French satellite circuit, breaking into top 100 in June. **1989:** (173) A 2, F 2, W –, US –. **1990:** (84) Reached her 1st primary circuit f at Taranto and returned to the top 100 in Sept.

1991: (72) A 3, F 1, W 1, US 1. In singles her best showing was qf Barcelona; in doubles she reached 2 f, winning Taranto with Labat. **1992:** (54) A 3, F 1, W 2, US 1. In singles she reached sf San Marino, plus 3 more qf, and upset Wiesner at Australian Open. In partnership with Labat she won Kitzbuhel and San Marino back-to-back in July, followed by Schenectady in Aug. **1993:** (–) A –, F –, W –, US –. Withdrew Sydney with a wrist injury that kept her out all year. Married her coach, Bernard Balleret, at end of year. **1994:** (65) A –, F 4, W 2, US 3. Returned to action at Auckland in Feb. and received a wild-card at French Open, where she reached last 16. Otherwise her best showing was qf Beijing. **1995:** (132) A 1, F 1, W 1, US 1. Qf Puerto Rico and played 1 doubles f with Testud. **1996:** (95) A 2, F 1, W 1, US 1. Qf Strasbourg and reached Bol doubles with Fusai. **1997:** A 1, F 1, W 1, US 2. She reached her 1st career f at Cardiff and sf Jakarta, as well as qf Auckland and Prague (d. Schultz-McCarthy). In doubles she won Tokyo Japan Open with Hiraki. **1997 HIGHLIGHTS – SINGLES: Australian Open 1r** (lost Hy-Boulais 6–0 2–6 6–4), **French Open 1r** (lost Makarova 6–4 6–2), **Wimbledon 1r** (lost Golarsa 6–1 4–6 6–3), **US Open 2r** (d. Sidot 6–3 3–6 6–3, lost Coetzer [seed 5] 6–1 6–1); **r/u** Cardiff (d. Richterova 7–5 6–0, Cristea 6–4 6–4, Lubiani 2–6 6–4 6–2, Pitkowski 6–3 6–4, lost Ruano-Pascual 6–1 3–6 6–2); **sf** Jakarta (d. Jeon 6–4 6–1, Kijimuta 6–0 6–4, Kim 6–4 6–2, lost Yoshida 3–6 7–6 6–1). **1997 HIGHLIGHTS – DOUBLES:** (with Hiraki) **won** Tokyo Japan Open (d. Guse/Morariu 6–4 6–2).

RUXANDRA DRAGOMIR (ROM)

Born Pitesti, 24 October 1972; lives Bucharest; RH; 2HB; 5ft 6in; 127lb; career singles titles 4; final 1997 WTA ranking 19 singles, 21 doubles; 1997 prize money $381,500.

Coached by Emilian Negoita. **1990:** (294) Won 3 titles on the Futures circuits and took French Open Jun doubles with Spirlea. **1991:** (322) Won Supetar Challenger and joined her country's Fed Cup squad. **1992:** (175) Won Klagenfurt and Le Havre Challengers. **1993:** (74) A –, F 4, W 2, US 1. Upset Date on her way to an unexpected appearance in last 16 French Open and reached sf Curitiba. **1994:** (82) A 1, F 4, W 2, US 2. Upset Mag. Maleeva at French Open, where she was unseeded, and reached qf Prague. **1995:** (54) A 2, F 4, W 1, US 1. Still unseeded at French Open, she again made her mark and upset Sawamatsu. Reached her 1st f on the main tour at Styrian Open, appeared in qf Barcelona and won Bournemouth doubles with de Swardt. **1996:** (25) A 2, F 2, W 3, US 1. Won her 1st title on the main tour at Budapest (d. Halard-Decugis), followed in Sept. with Karlovy Vary at her 2nd tourn back after a hamstring injury suffered 1r Olympics, and finished the year on a high note with the title at Pattaya. She also reached sf Rosmalen and qf Hamburg and Moscow, breaking into top 25 1st time by end of year. **1997:** A 4, F qf, W 1, US 1. She moved into the top 20 with the title at Rosmalen, r/u Hamburg, sf Warsaw and Pattaya, as well as upsets of Wiesner at Australian Open and Habsudova at French Open, unseeded both times. In doubles she reached 4 f with different partners, winning Prague with Habsudova and Warsaw with Gorrochategui. **1997 HIGHLIGHTS – SINGLES: Australian Open last 16** [unseeded] (d. Wiesner 4–6 6–3 10–8, Ruano-Pascual 7–6 6–1, Brandi 6–1 6–1, lost Hingis [seed 4] 7–6 6–1), **French Open qf** [unseeded] (d. Jeyaseelan 6–3 6–2, Basuki 7–5 4–6 8–6, Habsudova [seed 15] 6–3 6–2, Arendt 6–1 6–1, lost Majoli [seed 9] 6–3 5–7 6–2), **Wimbledon 1r** [seed 15] (lost Glass 5–7 6–2 10–8), **US Open 1r** [seed 15] (lost Raymond 6–2 3–6 6–3); **won** Rosmalen (d. Tanasugarn 6–3 6–1, Rittner 6–1 2–0 ret'd, Van Roost 6–1 2–6 6–4, Carlsson 6–4 6–2, Oremans 5–7 6–2 6–4); **r/u** Hamburg (d. Gersi 6–4 6–3, Labat 7–5 6–3, Schett 6–1 7–5, Sidot 6–4 6–0, lost Majoli 6–3 6–2); **sf** Warsaw (d. Sanchez-Lorenzo 6–3 2–6 6–1, Studenikova 6–2 6–3, lost Nagyova 6–4 7–5), **sf** Pattaya (d. Horn 6–2 5–7 6–4, Golarsa 6–3 2–6 7–5, Morariu 4–6 6–3 6–0, lost Nagyova 4–6 7–5 6–2). **1997 HIGHLIGHTS – DOUBLES:** (with Habsudova) **won** Prague (d. Martincova/Vildova 6–1 5–7 6–2), (with Gorrochategui) **won** Warsaw (d. Babel/Barclay 6–4 6–0); (with Farina) **r/u** Gold Coast (lost Kijimuta/Miyagi 7–6 6–1), (with Majoli) **r/u** Hamburg (lost Huber/Pierce 2–6 7–6 6–2). **CAREER HIGHLIGHTS – French Open – qf 1997.**

SILVIA FARINA (ITA)

Born Milan, 27 April 1972, and lives there; RH; 5ft 7½in; 138lb; career singles titles 0; final 1997 WTA ranking 43; 1997 prize money $160,439.

Coached by Leonardo Lerda. **1989:** (165) Qf Taranto. **1990:** (192). **1991:** (68) A –, F 1, W –, US –. Upset Reggi *en route* to her 1st primary circuit f at San Marino and reached sf Taranto. **1992:** (167) A –, F 1, W 1, US –. Upset Gildemeister at LIPC and Paz on her way to sf Palermo. **1993:** (85) A –, F –, W 2, US 1. Reached qf Taranto (d. Zrubakova) and won Limoges Challenger. **1994:** (52) A 1, F 2, W 1, US 2. Reached sf Styria and qf Hobart (d. Wang), Eastbourne (d. Date and Fendick) and Moscow. Upset Sabatini at French Open, having failed to take a single game from her in their two previous meetings. **1995:** (53) A 2, F 1, W 2, US 1. Upset McNeil *en route* to sf FC Cup, reaching same stage Auckland, as well as qf Puerto Rico, Palermo and Styrian Open, where she won the doubles with Temesvari. **1996:** (40) A 2, F 2, W 1, US 1. She reached sf Paris Open (d. Hingis) and Palermo, plus qf Hobart (d. Basuki), Warsaw and Zurich (after qualifying). During the year she also upset Sukova at LIPC and Tauziat at Los Angeles. Withdrew 2r French Open with recurrence of a right ankle ligament sprain suffered at FC Cup. **1997:** A 3, F 3, W 1, US 2. Once again Palermo saw her at her best, reaching qf singles and winning the doubles with Schett. Other highlights were upsets of Likhovtseva at FC Cup and Appelmans at Moscow. **1997 HIGHLIGHTS – SINGLES: Australian Open 3r** (d. Olsza 6–3 6–2, Suarez 6–4 6–1, lost Spirlea 6–4 6–3), **French Open 3r** (d. Wiesner 6–2 1–6 6–0, Begerow 6–4 6–2, lost Paulus [seed 16] 6–4 6–1), **Wimbledon 1r** (lost Schultz-McCarthy [seed 14] 4–6 6–3 6–2), **US Open 2r** (d. Wild 6–4 6–7 6–4, lost Pierce [seed 9] 6–2 3–0 ret'd). **1997 HIGHLIGHTS – DOUBLES:** (with Schett) **won** Palermo (d. Labat/Paz 2–6 6–1 6–4); (with Dragomir) **r/u** Gold Coast (lost Kijimuta/Miyagi 7–6 6–1).

GIGI FERNANDEZ (USA)

Born San Juan, Puerto Rico, 22 February 1964; lives Aspen, Col.; RH; 5ft 7in; 145lb; turned pro 1983; career singles titles 2; final 1997 WTA ranking 184 singles, 4 doubles; 1997 prize money $454,432 ($4,680,456).

Coached by Julie Anthony. Name is Beatriz but she is always known as Gigi. **1983:** (84) A 2, F –, W –, US 1. Narrowly beaten 7–6 fs by Herr in f AIAW. **1984:** (27) A 2, F –, W 2, US 2. Buoyed by praise she received from Navratilova after coming within two points of upsetting Shriver at Wimbledon, she reached f Newport as Lucky Loser and pushed Navratilova to 2s tb. **1985:** (64) A 2, F –, W –, US 1. Won LIPC doubles with Navratilova. **1986:** (62) F 2, W 1, US 1. Qualified with R. White for VS Champ doubles in Nov. and in singles won her 1st primary circuit title at Singapore. **1987:** (39) A 2, F 2, W 4, US 1. Reached last 16 Wimbledon unseeded, qf VS Florida and San Diego and won 3 doubles titles with McNeil. **1988:** (52) A –, F –, W 2, US 1. In doubles won US Open and Japan Open with R. White, reaching 7 other f with various partners and qualifying for VS Champs. **1989:** (23) A –, F 1, W 1, US 2. R/u Puerto Rico, sf Eastbourne and Newport in singles; in doubles with various partners reached 8 f, winning 4. **1990:** (36) A 4, F –, W 2, US 1. In singles reached sf Puerto Rico and qf Tokyo, San Antonio and Birmingham. In doubles won US Open with Navratilova and with various partners took 4 other titles, reaching 3 more f. Played in winning US Fed Cup team. **1991:** (22) A 1, F 2, W 3, US qf. At VS Albuquerque she won her 1st singles title since 1986 and reached sf Eastbourne (d. Novotna). Upset Garrison at VS Houston and in GS she removed Sukova 1r Wimbledon and surprised Meskhi at US Open, where she was unseeded. Voted WTA Doubles Team of the Year with Novotna: together they won French Open, r/u Australian Open, Wimbledon and VS Champs and reached 5 other f, winning 2. In addition she reached 5 more f with 4 different partners, winning a further 3 to bring a total of 6 titles from 14 f. **1992:** (33) A 1, F –, W 4, US 4. In singles was r/u Puerto Rico, played 4 qf and reached last 16 Wimbledon and US Open, unseeded both times. In Oct. began a 5-month rest period, from which she emerged to play VS Champs doubles with Zvereva, progressing to sf. They enjoyed a successful partnership across the year, winning French Open, Wimbledon and US Open plus 2 other titles. She also took an Olympic gold medal with M. J. Fernandez and won a 7th doubles title with Fendick. Won the Eagle Award for Excellence in Sports. **1993:** (50) A 4, F 1, W 2, US 3. In singles she reached qf Eastbourne and upset Sukova at Tokyo Pan Pacific. She won the doubles there with Zvereva and the pair went on to win French Open and Wimbledon for 6 straight GS titles, second in the Open era only to the 8 in succession taken by Navratilova/Shriver. The string was broken and they were denied a traditional GS at US Open when, with Zvereva suffering from flu, they lost sf to Sanchez Vicario/Sukova. However, they maintained their record of never having lost a GS f together and were voted WTA Doubles Team of Year, confirming that assessment by winning VS Champs. In all Fernandez played a total of 15 doubles f, winning 11 with Zvereva and 1 with Sukova. **1994:** (32) A 3, F 1, W sf, US qf. By the time Wimbledon began, she had won no singles match between Feb. and Eastbourne in June, losing 1r last 7 tourns, and had dropped in the rankings to 99. At the Championships, however, she played the tennis of her life to reach sf singles, unseeded (becoming the lowest-ranked semi-finalist in GS in the Open era), and won the doubles with Zvereva. This despite being troubled by hamstring injuries to both legs, which caused her to def. from mixed doubles with Suk. She credited this success to determination and playing for each point. At US Open she reached qf, again unseeded, and appeared at the same stage Filderstadt (d. Coetzer). Her doubles partnership with Zvereva prospered as they won Australian Open, French Open and Wimbledon, taking their record to 9 titles from 10 consec. GS tourns. However, the GS eluded them again, when they unexpectedly fell to K. Maleeva/White in sf US Open, but they won another 8 titles together, including VS Champs. **1995:** (65) A 1, F –, W 1, US 3. She could not maintain the same standards in singles, although she did reach sf Puerto Rico and qf San Diego. However, her doubles partnership with Zvereva continued to thrive: they won French Open and US Open, but lost f Australian Open, Wimbledon and WTA Champs to Novotna/Sanchez Vicario, and won 5 more titles from another 8 f to be voted Doubles Team of the Year. She also won an 8th title with Hingis and in mixed with Suk she was r/u Australian Open, Wimbledon and US Open. **1996:** (101) A 1, F 1, W 3, US 1. With Zvereva often injured, she played doubles with 4 different partners, although it was with her regular partner that she qualified for VS Champs, losing sf to Davenport/M. J. Fernandez. In GS she won US Open and was r/u French Open with Zvereva, and at Olympics won a 2nd gold medal with M. J. Fernandez. From 6 other f, she won San Diego with Martinez and Tokyo Toray with Zvereva. **1997:** A 2, F –, W 3, US 1. Playing 6 doubles f with 3 different partners, she won French Open and Wimbledon and r/u US Open with Zvereva and took Sydney with Sanchez Vicario. She retired at the end of the season, but hopes of a stunning finale were ended when she and Zvereva were beaten 1r Chase Champs by Neiland/Sukova. **1997 HIGHLIGHTS – SINGLES: Australian Open 2r** (d. Callens 6–4 6–3, lost Gorrochategui 7–5 7–6), **Wimbledon 3r** (d. Oremans 7–6 6–3, Dechy 6–3 4–6 6–3, lost Spirlea [seed 12] 6–3 6–1), **US Open 1r** (lost Pierce [seed 9] 6–1 6–2). **1997 HIGHLIGHTS – DOUBLES:** (with Zvereva unless stated) **won French Open** (d. M. J. Fernandez/Raymond 6–2 6–3), **won Wimbledon** (d. Arendt/Bollegraf 7–6 6–4), **r/u US Open** (lost Davenport/Novotna 6–3 6–4); (with Sanchez Vicario) **won** Sydney (d. Davenport/Zvereva 6–3 6–1); (with Hingis) **r/u** Tokyo Pan Pacific (lost Davenport/Zvereva 6–4 6–3), (with Zvereva) **r/u** Berlin (lost Davenport/Novotna 6–2 3–6 6–2). **CAREER HIGHLIGHTS – SINGLES: Wimbledon – sf 1994** [unseeded] (d. Grossi 6–2 6–1, Po 6–2 1–6 9–7, Endo 4–6 6–3 6–3, Basuki 6–4 6–1, Garrison-Jackson 6–4 6–4, lost Navratilova 6–4 7–6); **US Open – qf 1991** [unseeded] (d. Frankl 6–0 6–4, Rinaldi 6–4 6–1, Meskhi 7–6 6–7 7–6, Zrubakova 6–2 6–2, lost Seles 6–1 6–2), **qf** 1994 [unseeded] (d. Hack 6–2 2–6 7–6, Testud 7–5 6–3, Wang 6–3 6–2, Helgeson 6–3 6–4, lost Sabatini 6–2 7–5). **CAREER HIGHLIGHTS – DOUBLES:** (with Zvereva unless stated) **Australian Open – won 1993** (d. Shriver/Smylie 6–4 6–3), **won 1994** (d. Fendick/McGrath

6–3 4–6 6–4), (with Novotna) **r/u 1991** (lost Fendick/M. J. Fernandez 7–6 6–1), **r/u 1995** (lost Novotna/Sanchez Vicario 6–3 6–7 6–4); **French Open** – (with Novotna) **won 1991** (d. Savchenko/Zvereva 6–4 6–0), **won 1992** (d. Martinez/Sanchez Vicario 6–3 6–2), **won 1993** (d. Neiland/Novotna 6–3 7–5), **won 1994** (d. Davenport/Raymond 6–2 6–2), **won 1995** (d. Novotna/Sanchez Vicario 6–7 6–4 7–5), **won 1997**, **r/u 1996** (lost Davenport/M. J. Fernandez 6–2 6–1); **Wimbledon – won 1992** (d. Novotna/Savchenko-Neiland 6–4 6–1), **won 1993** (d. Neiland/Novotna 6–4 6–7 6–4), **won 1994** (d. Novotna/Sanchez Vicario 6–4 6–1), **won 1997**, (with Novotna) **r/u 1991** (lost Savchenko/Zvereva 6–4 3–6 6–4), **r/u 1995** (lost Novotna/Sanchez Vicario 5–7 7–5 6–4); **US Open** – (with R. White) **won 1988** (d. Fendick/Hetherington 6–4 6–1), (with Navratilova) **won 1990** (d. Novotna/Sukova 6–2 6–4), **won 1992** (d. Novotna/Savchenko-Neiland 7–6 6–1), **won 1995** (d. Schultz/McCarthy 7–5 6–3), **won 1996** (d. Novotna/Sanchez Vicario 1–6 6–1 6–4), **r/u 1997**; **VS Champs – won 1993** (d. Neiland/Novotna 6–3 7–5), **won 1994** (d. Novotna/Sanchez Vicario 6–3 6–7 6–3), **won 1995** (lost Novotna/Sanchez Vicario 6–2 6–1), (with Novotna) **r/u 1991** (lost Navratilova/Shriver 4–6 7–5 6–4); **Olympics** – (with M. J. Fernandez) **gold medal 1992** (d. Martinez/Sanchez Vicario 7–5 2–6 6–2), (with M. J. Fernandez) **gold medal 1996** (d. Novotna/Sukova 7–6 6–4).

AMY FRAZIER (USA)

Born St Louis, Mo., 19 September 1972; lives Rochester Hills, Mich.; RH; 2HB; 5ft 8in; 140lb; turned pro 1990; career singles titles 5; final 1997 WTA ranking 37; 1997 prize money $161,989 ($1,592,516).

Coached by John Cook and John Austin. Won 7 Nat Jun titles. **1986:** (331). **1987:** (202) A –, F –, W –, US 1. Won Kona on USTA circuit. **1988:** (55) A 1, F 1, W 1, US 3. Appeared in sf Guaruja, plus qf LA (d. Shriver and Magers), Kansas and Indianapolis (d. Kelesi). **1989:** (33) A 3, F 1, W 2, US 1. Won 1st primary circuit singles title at VS Kansas as well as reaching sf Albuquerque (d. Maleeva-Fragniere) and VS Indianapolis. **1990:** (16) A 1, F –, W 3, US 1. Won VS Oklahoma and was r/u Tokyo Nicherei, where she beat Seles and K. Maleeva back-to-back and extended M. J. Fernandez to 3s. In other tourns reached sf Indian Wells and Sydney, where she upset Novotna and took Zvereva to 3s, and upset Fairbank-Nideffer at Wimbledon. **1991:** (28) A 4, F –, W 4, US 2. Although she won no title, she reached sf Tokyo Nicherei and qf VS Chicago, Tokyo Suntory, Toronto and VS California. **1992:** (19) A qf, F 2, W 4, US 1. Taking advantage of Graf's withdrawal from her part of the draw, she made an unexpected appearance in qf Australian Open, and, again unseeded, upset M. J. Fernandez at Wimbledon. Won both singles and doubles titles at Lucerne and also took the doubles at Tokyo Suntory. She reached sf singles there, as well as at VS Oklahoma and San Antonio, and qualified for VS Champs 1st time, losing 1r to Sabatini. **1993:** (39) A 1, F –, W –, US 2. Out of action for 6 months from Feb. with a chronic form of flu, she had a quieter year, in which her best showings were sf Sydney and VS Philadelphia (d. Pierce and Sabatini) and qf Tokyo Nicherei (d. K. Maleeva). **1994:** (16) A 3, F 1, W 1, US 2. At Tokyo Japan Open she reached her 1st f for 2 years, a result which took her back to the top 20. She upset Huber and Martinez on her way to the title at Los Angeles, surprised Sabatini again *en route* to f Tokyo Nicherei and reached sf Oklahoma and Lucerne. **1995:** (18) A 3, F 3, W 2, US qf. She was still a dangerous opponent, upsetting Pierce and Zvereva back-to-back at US Open, where she was unseeded, and removing Date to take the title at Tokyo Japan Open. She also reached sf Oklahoma, qf Chicago and Tokyo Nicherei. **1996:** (29) A 1, F 1, W 4, US 2. R/u Tokyo Japan Open and reached qf Oklahoma, Montreal (d. Pierce) and Los Angeles. Played 3 doubles f with Po, but won no title. **1997:** A 1, F 2, W 2, US 1. She began the year with an upset of Sanchez Vicario to reach qf Sydney, following with r/u Tokyo Japan Open and sf Los Angeles (d. Coetzer and Sanchez Vicario again). **1997 HIGHLIGHTS – SINGLES: Australian Open 1r** (lost Huber [seed 5] 0–6 6–2 7–5), **French Open 2r** (d. Chladkova 6–4 6–0, lost Coetzer [seed 11] 7–6 6–4), **Wimbledon 2r** (d. Cacic 7–6 6–4, lost Schultz-McCarthy [seed 14] 7–6 6–3), **US Open 1r** (lost Spirlea [seed 11] 6–1 6–1); **r/u** Tokyo Japan Open (d. Hosoki 6–1 6–2, Yoshida 6–4 6–3, Sawamatsu 7–6 7–6, Ellwood 6–2 6–3, lost Sugiyama 4–6 6–4 6–4); **sf** Los Angeles (d. Coetzer 6–1 6–3, Sanchez Vicario 3–6 6–1 6–3, lost Seles 6–0 6–2). **1997 HIGHLIGHTS – DOUBLES:** (with Po) **r/u** San Diego (lost Hingis/Sanchez Vicario 6–3 7–5). **CAREER HIGHLIGHTS – SINGLES: Australian Open – qf 1992** [unseeded] (d. Cunningham 6–3 7–5, de Vries 6–1 7–6, Hack 6–1 3–6 6–2, Monami 6–3 6–4, lost M. J. Fernandez 6–4 7–6); **US Open – qf 1995** [unseeded] (d. Rottier 6–0 6–0, Phebus 6–2 6–1, Pierce 6–3 7–6, Zvereva 6–4 4–6 6–3, lost Graf 6–2 6–3).

ALEXANDRA FUSAI (FRA)

Born St Cloud, 22 November 1973; lives Nantes; RH; 2HB; 5ft 9in; 132lb; turned pro 1991; career singles titles 0; final 1997 WTA ranking 51 singles, 14 doubles; 1997 prize money $265,781.

1990: (297) Won Sezze and Cherbourg Futures. **1991:** (184) A –, F 1, W –, US –. Won European Jun Champs and in the senior game won Limoges Futures. **1992:** (141) A –, F 1, W –, US 1. Won 2 Futures titles in Australia. **1993:** (77) A 1, F 2, W 1, US 2. In her best year to date, she reached sf Taranto and upset Probst on her way to the same stage Liege, as well as reaching qf Melbourne Open and Taipei. **1994:** (92) A –, F 3, W 1, US 2. She could advance no further than qf Taranto (d. Wiesner) and Prague. **1995:** (104) A 1, F 1, W 1, US –. She reached sf Warsaw on the main tour and won Szczeciu Futures. **1996:** (72) A 3, A 2, W 2, US 2. In singles qf Cardiff was her best showing, while in doubles she played 4 f with different partners, winning Surabaya with Guse. **1997:** A 2, F 2, W 1, US 3. Reached qf Budapest, upset Habsudova at FC Cup and played in winning FRA Fed Cup team. In doubles, she played 6 f with 3 different partners, winning Budapest with Coetzer and Linz and Chicago with Tauziat. At their 1st Chase champs, she and Tauziat upset Hingis/Sanchez Vicario *en route* to f, where they extended Davenport/Novotna to 3s. **1997 HIGHLIGHTS – SINGLES: Australian Open 2r** (d. Helgeson-Nielsen 6–2 6–2, lost Schett 2–6 7–5 7–5), **French Open 2r** (d. Richterova 7–5 3–0 ret'd, lost Majoli [seed 9] 6–2 6–3), **Wimbledon 1r** (lost Coetzer [seed 6] 6–2 1–6 6–2), **US Open 3r** (d. Gagliardi 6–1 6–1, Miyagi 6–3 3–6 6–4, lost Sanchez Vicario [seed 10] 6–2 6–1). **1997 HIGHLIGHTS – DOUBLES:** (with Tauziat unless stated) **won** Linz (d. Milicharova/Vildova 4–6 6–3 6–1), (with Coetzer) **won** Budapest (d. Martincova/Wagner 6–3 6–1), **won** Chicago (d. Davenport/Seles 6–3 6–2); (with Grande) **r/u** Paris Open (lost Hingis/Novotna 6–3 6–0), **r/u** Atlanta (lost Arendt/Bollegraf 6–7 6–3 6–2), **r/u** Quebec City (lost Raymond/Stubbs 6–4 5–7 7–5), **r/u** Chase Champs (lost Davenport/Novotna 6–7 6–3 6–2).

LAURA GOLARSA (ITA)

Born Milan, 27 November 1967, and lives there; RH; 5ft 5in; 125lb; turned pro 1986; career singles titles 0; final 1997 WTA ranking 70; 1997 prize money $96,208.

Coached by Walter Bertini. **1985:** (162). **1986:** (208) Qf Argentine Open. **1987:** (106) A –, F –, W 2, US 3. Qf Taipei. **1988:** (79) A –, F 1, W 2, US 1. R/u Athens. **1989:** (59) A 1, F 3, W qf, US 2. Unseeded, she reached qf Wimbledon, where she took Evert to 7–5 fs. She reached the same stage at Taranto and Moscow, and in doubles won Sofia with Garrone. **1990:** (61) A 1, F –, W 1, US 1. Reached qf Barcelona and Taranto and broke into top 50. **1991:** (221) A – F 1 W 1, US –. Won doubles at Bol with Magdalena Maleeva. **1992:** (120) A – F –, W 1, US 1. Reached sf Cesena, but no other qf. **1993:** (71) A 1, F –, W 2, US 3. In singles she reached qf Barcelona (d. Wiesner), Birmingham (d. Fendick) and Puerto Rico and in doubles won Brighton with Medvedeva. **1994:** (113) A 1, F 1, W 3, US 1. In singles she reached qf Hobart (d. Neiland) and Birmingham, and from 3 doubles f with different partners won Brisbane with Medvedeva. **1995:** (156) A 1, F –, W 1, US –. Again she achieved her best results in doubles, playing 4 f with different partners, of which she won Oklahoma with Arendt. In singles qf Zagreb was her best showing. **1996:** (185) A –, F 1, W 1, US –. **1997:** A 1, A 2, W 2, US 1. She extended M. J. Fernandez to 3s 1r Australian Open but reached no qf. **1997 HIGHLIGHTS – SINGLES: Australian Open 1r** (lost M. J. Fernandez [seed 14] 6–2 4–6 6–2), **French Open 2r** (d. Van Lottum 4–6 7–5 12–10, lost Arendt 6–2 6–2), **Wimbledon 2r** (d. Dechaume-Balleret 6–1 4–6 6–3, lost Appelmans 6–2 6–0), **US Open 1r** (lost Barabanschikova 6–3 6–3).

STEFFI GRAF (GER)

Born Neckerau, 14 June 1969; lives Bruhl and New York, USA; RH; 5ft 9in; 132lb; turned pro 1982; career singles titles 103; final 1997 WTA ranking 28; 1997 prize money $230,249 ($20,076,565).

Coached by Heinz Gunthardt. **1982:** (214) The youngest at the time to receive a WTA ranking at 13 years 4 months; won European 14s and European circuit Masters. **1983:** (98) A – 1, F 2, W –, US –. Reached her 1st tour sf at Freiburg. **1984:** (22) A 3, F 3, W 4, US 1. Won Olympic demonstration event in Los Angeles and reached last 16 Wimbledon. **1985:** (6) A –, F 4, W 4, US sf. Reached sf US Open and LIPC, plus last 16 French Open and Wimbledon. **1986:** (3) A –, F qf, W –, US sf. Won 8 of her last 11 tourns and 52 of her last 55 matches. Won her 1st pro tourn by beating Evert-Lloyd in Hilton Head f, then beat Navratilova in German Open f and had 3 mps in memorable US Open sf loss to Navratilova. Won 4 straight tourns and 23 consec matches in spring. A virus infection affected her performance in Paris and kept her out of Wimbledon, and a freak accident in Prague (a heavy umbrella stand blew over and broke a toe) prevented her from playing in Fed Cup. **1987:** (1) A –, F won, W r/u, US r/u. After a 2-month break Dec–Jan., missing Australian Open, she took over No. 2 ranking from Evert-Lloyd end Feb. and No. 1 from Navratilova 16 Aug. Won her 1st GS title at French Open, becoming, at 17 years 11 months and 23 days, the youngest-ever winner of the women's singles there. Unbeaten from 23 Nov. 1986 (VS Champs) until Wimbledon f, where she fell to Navratilova, losing to her again in f US Open when suffering from flu. She won 75 of 77 matches to take 11 titles, confirming her No. 1 ranking by taking VS Champs and being named Official World Champion by virtue of her position at head of VS points table. She became only the 2nd player after Navratilova to earn more than $1 million in prize money in a year. **1988:** (1) A won, F won, W won, US won. At the age of 19 she achieved a unique 'Golden Slam', becoming only the 3rd woman, after Connolly and Court, to achieve the traditional GS and topping her exceptional year with a gold medal at the Olympics in Seoul. She won 8 other titles and 71 of 74 matches, losing only to Sabatini – at VS Florida (following a 6–week break) and at Amelia Island – and to Shriver (when suffering from flu) at VS Champs, ending run of 46 winning results. Became the 2nd German woman to win Wimbledon after Cilly Aussem in 1931. In doubles won Wimbledon and LIPC with Sabatini, but was forced to default qf VS Champs. **1989:** (1) A won, F r/u, W won, US won. A second consec. GS slipped from her grasp when, feeling unwell after suffering from food poisoning, she lost f French Open to Sanchez Vicario. However, she retained her titles at Australian Open, Wimbledon and US Open, won VS Champs and took 10 other singles titles. With a record of 82 wins and 2 defeats, losing just 12 sets all year, she was beaten only by Sanchez Vicario at French Open and Sabatini at Amelia Island in spring. In doubles was r/u French Open with Sabatini. **1990:** (2) A won, F r/u, W sf, US r/u. Began the year in her usual style by winning Australian Open and recorded a 66-match winning streak (the 2nd-highest in women's tennis), which was broken when she lost to Seles in f Berlin. She lost f French Open (her 13th consec. GS f) to the same player, Garrison upset her in sf Wimbledon and Sabatini beat her in f US Open and sf VS Champs. These were the only players to beat her in a year in which she won 10 titles. She was out of action from Feb.

to April after breaking her thumb ski-ing, and was hampered through the year by allegations concerning her father and by sinus problems, which caused her to withdraw from the Fed Cup team and required an operation after Wimbledon. On 13 Aug. went into her 157th consec. week at No. 1 (starting 17 Aug. 1987), overtaking Navratilova's women's record of 156 (14 June 1982–9 June 1985); 3 weeks later she passed Jimmy Connors's all-time record of 159 weeks. **1991:** (1) A qf, F sf, W r/u, US sf. Her loss to Novotna in qf Australian Open was her 1st so early in GS since French Open 1986, and until she beat Seles to take San Antonio in April, she had gone 5 tourns since Nov. 1990 without winning a title. She went on to take Hamburg, Berlin, Leipzig, Zurich and Brighton and was r/u VS Florida and Amelia Island. However, she lost her No. 1 ranking to Seles in March, having held that position for a record 186 consec. weeks, regained it briefly after winning her 3rd Wimbledon in a thrilling f over Sabatini, but lost it again in Aug. In sf French Open Sanchez Vicario inflicted her worst defeat (6–0 6–2) and 1st love set since 1984, Navratilova beat her in sf US Open and Novotna removed her in qf VS Champs. When she d. Wiesner 2r Leipzig, she notched up her 500th career win, the youngest to reach that landmark, being 6 months younger than Evert, although Evert needed only 545 matches to Graf's 568. Split with Slozil in Nov., preferring to work on her own. **1992:** (2) A –, F r/u, W won, US qf. Misfortune continued to dog her as she was forced to withdraw at the last minute from Australian Open with German measles. When she returned, at VS Chicago in Feb., she fell sf to Novotna after winning the 1st set to love, but returned to the winner's circle in March when she won VS Florida. She followed with Hamburg, which took her past Evert's $8,827,034 career prize money to $8,907,534 in second place behind Navratilova. At French Open, with the crowd behind her, she saved 5 mps v Seles in f before losing 8–10 fs and at Wimbledon she ended the No. 1's chance of a GS by allowing her only 3 games in the final, for her 4th title there. She won an Olympic silver medal, losing to Capriati, and finished the year with 8 titles, but ended on a disappointing note when she fell 1r VS Champs to McNeil. Led GER to Fed Cup victory over ESP in f. **1993:** A r/u, F won, W won, US won. Her 10 titles across the year took her career total to 80, 4th in the Open era behind Navratilova, Evert and Goolagong Cawley. Was considerably upset when a fanatical supporter stabbed Seles, aiming to sideline her so that Graf could regain the No. 1 ranking. She did so on 7 June after winning French Open, delighting in her victory there but admitting that it was something of a hollow achievement without Seles on the scene. Played and won Wimbledon carrying a foot injury, which would have kept her out of any other tourn, and by end of US Open had reached qf or better in 29 GS from 1985, 2nd to Evert's Open era record 34 from 1971–1983. Underwent surgery 4 Oct. to remove bone splinters from her right foot, returning 8 Nov. at VS Philadelphia, where her winning sequence of 6 straight tourns ended when she lost f to Martinez. She won 10 titles across the year and reached 4 more f, including Australian Open, where she lost in 3s to Seles. She also lost once to Navratilova and twice to Sanchez Vicario, who inflicted her 1st-ever defeat at Hamburg, where she'd won 32 matches. She was voted WTA Player of the Year and won VS Champs, despite needing painkillers for a back injury, finishing the year well and truly at the top of the rankings, although in the continued absence of Seles there was something of a question mark over the achievement. **1994:** (1) A won, F sf, W 1, US r/u. She completed another non-calender GS at Australian Open, having won all 4 GS tourns during Seles's absence, and was still the only player, male or female, to win all 4 titles in the 1990s. When she won Berlin in May, she had reached 20 consec. f and until losing f Hamburg to Sanchez Vicario, she had won 36 consec. matches since Philadelphia in Nov. However, although she finished the year with another 7 titles, she was unable to maintain the impetus. At French Open she was swept away in sf by Pierce and later announced that she was pulling out of Fed Cup, saying she was too tired and needed 'a long period of rest'. Then at Wimbledon, having played no match since French Open, she suffered a shock defeat in 1r at the hands of McNeil – the player who had inflicted her only previous 1r defeat in her adult life at VS Champs in 1992. It was the 1st time for 9 years that she'd lost successive matches on tour, the 1st time for 32 years that the reigning champion at Wimbledon had been beaten in her 1st match and the 1st time ever that the reigning champion had lost 1r (Margaret Smith having received a bye before her 2r defeat). She played US Open, despite suffering stress fracture of back, and in f v Sanchez Vicario, a set up and 3–2 in 2s tb, she looked a likely winner, but by then her back was seriously bothering her and the match slipped from her grasp. At VS Champs she lost qf to Pierce, and although she refused to blame her back problems, it looked increasingly likely that she would require surgery, with the possibility that she might miss 1995 Australian Open. **1995:** (1) A –, F won, W won, US won. She refused to undergo back surgery yet, and it was a strain to her right calf muscle that caused her to withdraw from Australian Open. For the 1st time since 1987 she held none of the 4 GS titles, although that soon changed when she went on to win French Open, Wimbledon and US Open, becoming the 1st woman to win all 4 GS titles at least 4 times each. When she won LIPC, her 89th title, she passed Cawley to take 3rd place in the list of title-winners after Navratilova (167) and Evert (157), and took a total of 9 across the year. Her US Open title was her 18th GS in singles, equalling the record shared by Navratilova and Evert. However, she ended her 9-year record of having won at least 50 matches per year with 47 won and 2 lost across the year. She lost the No. 1 ranking to Sanchez Vicario 6 Feb., regained it 20 Feb., and the top position passed between them until her triumph at French Open. Her victory there was remarkable, for she had been out of action 6 weeks beforehand with flu and a recurrence of her back problems and was unable to practise until 8 days before the tourn started. She caught a virus in the 2nd week there and required drops in her eyes twice during the final – yet still she won. In her Wimbledon f v Sanchez Vicario, which will be remembered as one of the great matches, she played a game at 5–5 fs which involved 32 points and 20 mins. Graf rated it the greatest game she had ever played. Then came the 1st of only 2 defeats all year – at the hands of Coetzer 1r Toronto – ending a 32-match winning streak, and only her 3rd at that stage since 1985. Although she would make no excuses, she was hampered by her back injury and concern over her father (who had claimed to have suffered a heart attack while being held in prison over tax evasion charges) and struggled to beat the same player in her next match – 1r US Open. Further injury plagued her there and, suffering problems with her left foot, she had to go to hospital on the eve of the f to check that it was not a stress fracture. Her opponent there was Seles, ranked equal No. 1 with Graf for her 1st 6 tourns, who was beaten in the long-awaited 1st encounter between the two since the 1993 Australian Open f. She then lost 1r Brighton to de Swardt – at 54 the lowest-ranked player to have beaten her for 10 years – and although she generously gave credit to de Swardt, she played badly and was obviously seriously distracted by her father's situation, legal investigations into her finances and her back injury. She regained her winning habit at Philadelphia, although not without dropping a set each to Frazier and McNeil, and finished the year in triumph at WTA Champs, where Huber extended her to 5s f. On 15 Dec. she underwent surgery to remove bone splinters from her left foot. **1996:** (1) A –, F won, W won, US won. After missing Australian Open, she returned to action in March to win Indian Wells. When, in her next tourn, she took LIPC for a record 5th time, she became the 1st player, male or female, to win it 3 times in a row. In Fed Cup qf v Date, played on HC, she looked weary and lost 12–10 fs, also losing the doubles with Huber. Then, short of practice on clay, she was surprisingly beaten by Hingis in qf Italian Open – she claimed that her foot and back were as good as they ever are, but that she couldn't get her brain round it, undoubtedly distracted by her father having been charged on 17 April with evading $13 million taxes by failing to report $28m of Graf's earnings between 1989 and 1993. She was back in the winner's circle the following week in Berlin and was in fine form at French Open, losing no set on her way to f, where she played the longest ever f there, taking 3 hr 3 min to defeat Sanchez Vicario. Withdrew from Eastbourne with a minor inflammation of the patella tendon of her left knee, wanting to rest it before Wimbledon. Her 7th Wimbledon title took her past Wills-Moody with 20 GS titles, 2nd behind Court's 24 – and it was also her 100th career title (30 on clay, 7 on grass, 28 indoors and 35 on HC), achieved despite the handicap of a heavy cold and continuing knee problems. She looked in danger only in sf v Date, when she surrendered 6 consec. games to lose 2nd set before play was halted for the night. However, she took fs next morning and was not troubled by Sanchez Vicario in a disappointing f. In sf Los Angeles in Aug., Davenport inflicted her 1st ss defeat since 1994, but at US Open she managed to overcome the distraction of her father's trial in Germany for tax evasion (as well as calf and knee problems), moving smoothly to f, where she again d. Seles. On 13 May, she had passed Navratilova's record of 331 weeks in total at No. 1 and on 4 Nov., after Seles dropped to co-ranked No. 2, she regained the solo spot at the top of the rankings for the 8th time in all and 1st time since Aug. 1995, when Seles returned to the tour. Injuries plagued her throughout the year, for although her back problems were eased by her no longer having to compensate for her injured foot, her sacroiliac joint moves out of place and she still has to restrict her schedule, travelling with her personal masseur and chiropractor. A recurrence of the patella tendon injury in her left knee forced her to withdraw from sf Leipzig – the 1st time in her career that she'd withdrawn mid-tourn. She was a doubtful starter at Philadelphia in Nov. after the injury flared up yet again, but in the event it was a recurrence of her back injury that forced her to retire during her f v Novotna, soon after her father was released on bail. However, in typical fashion she lifted herself above the pain of both back and knee injuries for the big occasion at VS Champs, which she won for a 5th time after 5s f v Hingis. Voted Player of Year for record 8th time. **1997:** A 4, F qf, W –, US –. At Australian Open, suffering from an infected toe and the heat, and distracted again by an imminent court verdict concerning her father, she ended her run of 45 consec. GS matches. Her defeat there by Coetzer was only the 2nd time in 12 years that she'd lost before qf in GS. When Hingis overtook her at the top of the rankings on 31 March, she had been No. 1 for a total of 364 weeks – an all-time record. She withdrew f Tokyo Pan Pacific with a severely aggravated infection of the tip of the patella tendon of left knee, suffered in sf, and was out for 3½ months, the longest break of her career to date. Returning to action at Berlin, below her best and lacking in confidence, she managed to win only one game in 57-min qf v Coetzer, suffering the worst defeat of her career. The same player extended her to fs tb in sf Strasbourg, but this time she made it back to the winner's circle for the 1st time in 1997, despite still being below her best. It was Coetzer yet again who ended her challenge at French Open, where she fell in ss qf and slipped to No. 3 in the rankings behind Seles. On 10 June she underwent surgery to repair a fracture of cartilage and shortening and partial rupture of the patellar tendon of her left knee, an injury first suffered at Wimbledon a year earlier. She was out for the rest of the year. **1997 HIGHLIGHTS – SINGLES: Australian Open last 16** [seed 1] (d. Husarova 5–1 ret'd, Neiland 7–5 6–2, Gorrochategui 7–5 6–3, lost Coetzer [seed 12] 6–2 7–5); **French Open qf** [seed 2] (d. Suarez 6–1 6–4, Mauresmo 6–3 6–3, Serna 7–6 6–1, Spirlea [seed 13] 6–7 6–2 6–2, lost Coetzer [seed 11] 6–1 6–4); **won** Strasbourg (d. Hy-Boulais 6–3 6–2, Testud 3–6 6–2 6–1, Coetzer 4–6 7–5 7–6, Lucic 6–2 7–5); **r/u** Tokyo Pan Pacific (d. Raymond 6–3 6–2, Majoli 6–2 6–3, Schultz-McCarthy 6–1 7–5, lost Hingis def.). **CAREER HIGHLIGHTS – SINGLES: Australian Open – won 1988** (d. Jonsson 6–3 6–1, Thompson 6–0 6–1, Cammy MacGregor 6–1 6–2, Lindqvist 6–0 7–5, Mandlikova 6–2 6–2, Kohde-Kilsch 6–2 6–3, Evert 6–1 7–6), **won 1989** (d. Guse 6–2 6–1, Simpson 6–0 6–0, Werdel 6–0 6–1, Provis 6–4 6–0, Kohde-Kilsch 6–2 6–3, Sabatini 6–3 6–0, Sukova 6–4 6–4), **won 1990** (d. Cunningham 6–2 7–5, De Lone 6–1 6–2, Meskhi 6–4 6–1, Reggi 6–2 6–3, Fendick 6–3 7–5, Sukova 6–3 3–6 6–4, M. J. Fernandez 6–4 6–4), **won 1994** (d. Po 6–1 2–0 ret'd, Provis 6–1 6–4, Rittner 6–2 6–4, Testud 6–1 6–2, Davenport 6–3 6–2, Date 6–3 6–3, Sanchez Vicario 6–0 6–2), **r/u 1993** (d. Herreman 6–2 6–1, Santrock 6–1 6–1, Porwik 6–1 ret'd, Mag. Maleeva 6–3 6–3, Capriati 7–5 6–2, Sanchez Vicario 7–5 6–4, lost Seles 4–6 6–3 6–2); **French Open – won 1987** (d. Bartos-Cserepy 6–1 6–1, Budarova 6–1 6–1, Novotna 6–0 6–1, Kelesi 7–6 6–2, M. Maleeva 6–4 6–1, Sabatini 6–4 4–6 7–5, Navratilova 6–4 4–6

8–6), **won 1988** (d. Guerree 6–0 6–4, Reis 6–1 6–0, Sloane 6–0 6–1, Tauziat 6–1 6–3, Fulco 6–0 6–1, Sabatini 6–3 7–6, Zvereva 6–0 6–0), **won 1993** (d. C. Dahlman 7–6 6–1, Strnadova 6–1 6–1, Arraya 6–2 6–2, Majoli 6–4 7–6, Capriati 6–3 7–5, Huber 6–1 6–1, M. J. Fernandez 4–6 6–2 6–4), **won 1995** (d. Gorrochategui 6–1 7–5, Begerow 6–4 6–3, Baudone 6–2 6–1, Huber 6–0 6–3, Sabatini 6–1 6–0, Martinez 6–3 6–7 6–3, Sanchez Vicario 7–5 4–6 6–0), **won 1996** (d. Neiland 6–3 6–2, Bradtke 6–2 6–2, Langrova 6–0 1–0 ret'd, M. J. Fernandez 6–1 7–6, Majoli 6–3 6–1, Martinez 6–3 6–1, Sanchez Vicario 6–3 6–7 10–8), **r/u 1989** (d. Benjamin 6–1 6–1, Fulco 6–0 6–1, Jagerman 6–1 6–2, La Fratta 6–2 6–1, Martinez 6–0 6–4, Seles 6–3 3–6 6–3, lost Sanchez 7–6 3–6 7–5), **r/u 1990** (d. Paradis 6–0 6–2, Santrock 6–1 6–2, Cecchini 6–2 6–3, Tauziat 6–1 6–4, Martinez 6–1 6–3, Novotna 6–1 6–2, lost Seles 7–6 6–4), **r/u 1992** (d. Simpson-Alter 6–3 6–1, Housset 6–2 6–1, Coetzer 6–2 6–1, Novotna 6–1 6–4, Zvereva 6–3 6–7 6–3, Sanchez Vicario 0–6 6–2 6–2, lost Seles 6–2 3–6 10–8), **sf 1991** (d. Mag. Maleeva 6–3 7–6, Langrova 6–0 6–1, Stafford 6–0 6–1, Appelmans 6–2 6–2, Tauziat 6–3 6–2, lost Sanchez Vicario 6–0 6–2), **sf 1994** (d. Studenikova 6–2 6–2, Rottier 7–5 6–3, Kruger 6–0 4–6 6–2, Spirlea 6–0 6–1, Gorrochategui 6–4 6–1, lost Pierce 6–2 6–2); **Wimbledon – won 1988** (d. Na 6–0 6–0, Quentrec 6–2 6–0, Phelps 6–3 6–1, M. J. Fernandez 6–2 6–2, Paradis 6–3 6–1, Shriver 6–1 6–2, Navratilova 5–7 6–2 6–1), **won 1989** (d. Salmon 6–1 6–2, Kessaris 6–2 6–1, A. Minter 6–1 6–3, Seles 6–4 6–3, Sanchez 7–5 6–1, Evert 6–2 6–1, Navratilova 6–2 6–7 6–1), **won 1991** (d. Appelmans 6–2 6–2, Louie-Harper 6–0 6–1, Basuki 6–2 6–3, Frazier 6–2 6–1, Garrison 6–1 6–3, M. J. Fernandez 6–2 7–5, Sabatini 6–4 3–6 8–6), **won 1992** (d. Van Lottum 6–1 6–0, Werdel 6–1 6–1, De Swardt 5–7 6–0 7–5, Fendick 4–6 6–3 6–2, Zvereva 6–3 6–1, Sabatini 6–3 6–3, Seles 6–2 6–1), **won 1993** (d. Sharpe 6–0 6–0, Wood 6–2 6–1, Kelesi 6–0 6–0, McGrath 6–1 6–4, Capriati 7–6 6–1, Martinez 7–6 6–3, Novotna 7–6 1–6 6–4), **won 1995** (d. Hingis 6–3 6–1, Coetzer 6–3 7–5, Boogert 6–1 6–0, Gorrochategui 6–0 6–1, M. J. Fernandez 6–3 6–0, Novotna 5–7 6–4 6–2, Sanchez Vicario 4–6 6–1 7–5), **won 1996** (d. Richterova 6–4 6–1, Baudone 7–5 6–3, Arendt 6–2 6–1, Hingis 6–1 6–4, Novotna 6–3 6–2, Date 6–2 2–6 6–3, Sanchez Vicario 6–3 7–5), **r/u 1987** (d. Villagran 6–09 6–2, Scheuer-Larsen 6–0 6–0, Gildemeister 6–2 6–1, Novotna 6–4 6–3, Sabatini 4–6 6–1 6–1, Shriver 6–0 6–2, lost Navratilova 7–5 6–3), **sf 1990** (d. Porwik 6–1 6–2, McGrath 6–3 6–0, Kohde-Kilsch 6–0 6–4, Capriati 6–2 6–4, Novotna 7–5 6–2, lost Garrison 6–3 3–6 6–4); **US Open – won 1988** (d. E. Minter 6–1 6–1, Bollegraf 6–1 6–0, Herreman 6–0 6–1, Fendick 6–4 6–2, K. Maleeva 6–3 6–0, Evert w.o., Sabatini 6–3 3 6–6–1), **won 1989** (d. Inoue 6–3 6–2, Herreman 6–2 6–1, Phelps 6–1 6–1, Fairbank 6–4 6–0, Sukova 6–1 6–1, Sabatini 3–6 6–4 6–2, Navratilova 3–6 7–5 6–1), **won 1993** (d. White 6–3 6–0, McGrath 6–3 6–1, Wiesner def., Pierce 6–1 6–0, Sabatini 6–2 5–7 6–1, Maleeva-Fragniere 4–6 6–1 6–0, Sukova 6–3 6–3), **won 1995** (d. Coetzer 6–7 6–1 6–4, Grande 6–1 6–3, Tauziat 6–3 6–3, Rubin 6–2 6–2, Frazier 6–2 6–3, Sabatini 6–4 7–6, Seles 7–6 0–6 6–3), **won 1996** (d. Basuki 6–3 7–6, Kschwendt 6–2 6–1, Zvereva 6–4 6–2, Kournikova 6–2 6–1, Wiesner 7–5 6–3, Hingis 7–5 6–3, Seles 7–5 6–3), **r/u 1987** (d. Fulco 6–0 6–3, Huber 6–2 6–3, Tarabini 6–2 6–0, Hanika 7–5 6–2, Shriver 6–4 6–3, McNeil 4–6 6–2 6–4, lost Navratilova 7–6 6–1), **r/u 1990** (d. Drake 6–1 6–1, McQuillan 6–1 6–3, Reinach 6–4 3–6 6–1, Capriati 6–1 6–2, Novotna 6–3 6–1, Sanchez Vicario 6–1 6–2, lost Sabatini 6–2 7–6), **r/u 1994** (d. Mall 6–2 6–1, Cacic 6–0 6–2, Bobkova 6–2 6–3, Garrison-Jackson 6–1 6–2, Coetzer 6–0 6–2, Novotna 6–3 7–5, lost Sanchez Vicario 1–6 7–6 6–4), **sf 1985** (d. Fendick 4–6 6–1 7–5, A. Minter 6–3 7–6, A. White 6–4 6–2, M. Maleeva 6–4 6–2, Shriver 7–6 6–7 7–6, lost Navratilova 6–2 6–3), **sf 1986** (d. Mascarin 6–0 6–1, Temesvari 6–1 6–0, Bowes 6–1 1–0 ret'd, Reggi 6–1 3–6 6–0, Gadusek 6–3 6–1, lost Navratilova 6–1 6–7 7–6), **sf 1991** (d. Temesvari 6–1 6–2, Mothes 6–0 6–0, Sviglerova 6–4 7–5, Wiesner 7–5 6–4, Martinez 6–1 6–3, lost Navratilova 7–6 6–7 6–4); **Olympics – won 1984** [demonstration event, under 21] (d. Goles 1–6 6–3 6–4 in f), **won gold medal 1988** (d. Meskhi 7–5 6–1, Suire 6–3 6–0, Savchenko 6–2 4–6 6–3, Garrison-Jackson 6–2 6–0, Sabatini 6–3 6–3), **r/u silver medal 1992** (d. Novelo 6–1 6–1, Schultz 6–1 6–0, Mag. Maleeva 6–3 6–4, Appelmans [16] 6–1 6–0, M. J. Fernandez [4] 6–4 6–2, lost Capriati [3] 3–6 6–3 6–4); **VS/WTA Champs – won 1987** (d. Sukova 6–2 2–0 ret'd, Hanika 6–1 6–4, Sabatini 4–6 6–4 6–0 6–4), **won 1989** (d. Sukova 6–2 6–1, Sabatini 6–3 5–7 6–1, Navratilova 6–4 7–5 2–6 6–2), **won 1993** (d. Zvereva 6–2 6–4, Coetzer, 6–1 6–2, Huber 6–2 3–6 6–3, Sanchez Vicario 6–1 6–4 3–6 6–1), **won 1995** (d. Coetzer 6–2 6–2, M. J. Fernandez 6–3 6–4, Zvereva 6–4 6–3, Huber 6–1 2–6 6–1 4–6 6–3), **won 1996** (d. Habsudova 6–1 6–4, Davenport 6–4 7–6, Novotna 4–6 6–4 6–3, Hingis 6–3 4–6 6–0 4–6 6–0), **r/u 1986 (November)** (d. McNeil 7–5 4–6 6–2, Man. Maleeva 6–3 3–6 7–5, Sukova 7–6 3–6 6–1, lost Navratilova 7–6–6–3 6–2), **sf 1986 (March)** (d. Sabatini 1–6 6–4 6–3, Shriver 4–6 7–6 6–3, lost Navratilova 6–3 6–2), **sf 1988** (d. Man. Maleeva 6–1 6–2, lost Shriver 6–3 7–6), **sf 1990** (d. Capriati 6–3 5–7 6–3, K. Maleeva 6–3 6–0, lost Sabatini 6–4 6–4). **CAREER HIGHLIGHTS – DOUBLES:** (with Sabatini) **Wimbledon – won 1988** (d. Savchenko/Zvereva 6–3 1–6 12-10); **French Open – r/u 1986** (lost Navratilova/Temesvari 6–1 6–2), **r/u 1987** (lost Navratilova/Shriver 6–2 6–1), **r/u 1989** (lost Savchenko/Zvereva 6–4 6–4).

RITA GRANDE (ITA)

Born Napoli, 23 March 1975; lives Torino; RH; 5ft 9½in; 146lb; career singles titles 0; final 1997 WTA ranking 44; 1997 prize money $141,892.

Coached by Antonella Canapi and Pino Carnovale. **1990** (406). **1991:** (364). **1992:** (443). **1993:** (183) R/u Wimbledon Jun to Feber and in the women's game won Vilamoura Futures. **1994:** (140) She finished the year on a high note by reaching her 1st sf on the senior tour at Taipei. **1995:** (74) A –, F –, W–, US 2. Reached sf Pattaya City and qf Tokyo Japan Open (d. Werdel-Witmeyer). **1996:** (65) A 3, F 2, W 1, US 4. Qf Auckland was her best showing. **1997:** A 2, F 1, W 1, US 2. Reached sf Jakarta and Cardiff, plus qf Toronto (d. Pierce). **1997 HIGHLIGHTS – SINGLES: Australian Open 2r** (d. Montolio 6–2 6–4, lost Boogert 6–3 7–5), **French**

Open 1r (lost Coetzer [seed 11] 6–4 6–0), **Wimbledon 1r** (lost Labat 6–4 6–4), **US Open 2r** (d. Cacic 6–2 6–1, lost M. J. Fernandez 4–6 6–2 6–2); **sf** Jakarta (d. Radford 6–3 4–6 6–2, Nemeckova 6–4 6–0, Feber w.o., lost Sawamatsu 7–6 3–6 6–1), **sf** Cardiff (d. Guse 7–5 6–2, Torrens-Valero 6–3 6–2, Van Roost 1–6 6–2 7–5, lost Ruano-Pascual 6–3 3–6 6–4). **1997 HIGHLIGHTS – DOUBLES:** (with Fusai) **r/u** Paris Open (lost Hingis/Novotna 6–3 6–0).

MAGDALENA GRZYBOWSKA (POL)

Born Poznan, 22 November 1978; lives Krakow; RH; 2HB; 6ft ½in; 147lb; turned pro 1995; career singles titles 0; final 1997 WTA ranking 40; 1997 prize money $137,433.

Coached by her father, Marek, and Zbigniew Gorszczak. **1994:** (441) Won Szezecin Futures in only her 3rd pro event, having been r/u in her 1st at Olsztyn Futures. **1995:** (73) Upset Hack on her way to sf Warsaw after qualifying, won Bratislava Futures and joined her country's Fed Cup squad. **1996:** (130) A 2, F 1, W 1, US 1. Won Australian Open Jun over Dechy. **1997:** A 3, F 1, W 3, US 1. Won 2 titles on the Futures circuit and on the main tour upset Paulus *en route* to qf Leipzig, reaching the same stage Quebec City. **1997 HIGHLIGHTS – SINGLES: Australian Open 3r** (d. Pitkowski 4–6 6–3 6–1, Tu 6–4 6–7 6–1, lost Schnyder 7–6 6–1), **French Open 1r** (lost Begerow 3–6 6–3 6–4), **Wimbledon 3r** (d. V. Williams 4–6 6–2 6–4, Schett 4–6 6–3 6–2, lost Hy-Boulais 6–4 6–1), **US Open 1r** (lost Serna 6–4 1–6 6–3); **won** Santa Clara Futures (d. Nagatsuka 6–1 7–5), **won** Sopot Futures (d. Chladkova 6–3 6–2).

KERRY-ANN GUSE (AUS)

Born Brisbane, 4 December 1972, and lives there; RH; 5ft 3in; 154lb; turned pro 1987; career singles titles 0; final 1997 WTA ranking 62; 1997 prize money $112,983.

Coached by her father, Mauri Guse. **1988:** In winning AUS World Youth Cup team. **1989:** (598) A 1, F –, W –, US –. **1990:** (349) A –, F –, W –, US –. **1991:** (315) A –, F –, W –, US –. **1992:** (220) A –, F –, W –, US –. **1993:** (234) A 1, F –, W –, US –. **1994:** (207) A 1, F –, W –, US –. Played 2 doubles f with different partners. **1995:** (182) A 1, F –, W –, US –. Reached qf Nagoya, where she won the doubles with Radford. **1996:** (142) A 1, F 1, W 2, US –. Appeared in 2 doubles f, winning Surabaya with Fusai. **1997:** A –, F –, W 2, US 1. In singles she won 3 Futures titles, and in doubles played 4 f with different partners, winning Jakarta with Radford, Cardiff with Graham and Surabaya with Hiraki. **1997 HIGHLIGHTS – SINGLES: Wimbledon 2r** (d. Po 3–6 7–5 6–2, lost Tauziat 6–0 6–3), **US Open 1r** (lost Sanchez Vicario [seed 10] 6–2 6–4); **won** Noda Futures (d. Choi 0–6 6–4 6–2), **won** Gifu Futures (d. Jeon 7–5 7–5), **won** Taipei Futures (d. Barclay 6–4 7–6. **1997 HIGHLIGHTS – DOUBLES:** (with Radford) **won** Jakarta (d. Nemeckova/Yoshida 6–4 5–7 7–5), (with Graham) **won** Cardiff (d. Pullin/Woodroffe 6–3 6–4), (with Hiraki) **won** Surabaya (d. Drake/Kolbovic 6–1 7–6); (with Morariu) **r/u** Tokyo Japan Open (lost Dechaume-Balleret/Hiraki 6–4 6–2).

KARINA HABSUDOVA (SVK)

Born Bojnice, 2 August 1973; lives Bratislava; RH; 2HB; 5ft 7in; 132lb; career singles titles 0; final 1997 WTA ranking 29; 1997 prize money $225,396 ($1,176,653).

Coached by Branislav Stankovic. **1990:** (122) Won Wimbledon Jun doubles with Strnadova and finished the year ranked No. 1 in ITF Jun singles and doubles. In the senior game she won Katowice Challenger and reached qf Moscow on the main tour. **1991:** (54) A 4, F 1, W 2, US 2. Won US Open Jun over Mall and took Australian Open Jun doubles with Rittner. On the women's tour she made an unexpected appearance in last 16 Australian Open and reached sf Phoenix and VS Nashville. **1992:** (67) A 2, F 3, W 1, US 1. Upset Mag. Maleeva *en route* to her 1st Kraft tour sf at Osaka and reached qf San Antonio. **1993:** (111) A 2, F –, W –, US 3. She enjoyed some success in doubles on the satellite circuits, but missed 3 months with pneumonia. **1994:** (31) A 1, F 1, W 1, US 2. Despite being hampered by injuries to her left ankle and Achilles tendon, she moved into the top 50 with appearances in sf Italian Open (d. Pierce) and Filderstadt (d. Martinez) – as a qualifier both times – plus same stage Essen and qf Taranto and Styria. **1995:** (57) A 4, F 2, W 1, US 1. Won Prostejov Challenger and on the main tour reached qf Paris Open and Palermo. **1996:** (16) A 2, F qf, W 1, US 4. Returned to the top 50 after LIPC, where she removed Sanchez Vicario, Halard-Decugis and Spirlea before taking a set off Rubin in sf. Then at Berlin in May, she gave a sign of things to come by upsetting Hingis, Pierce and Huber to reach her 1st tour f, where she took a set off Graf. At French Open, unseeded, she again upset Hingis and Huber back-to-back, before extending Sanchez Vicario to 10–8 fs in qf, a result that took her into the top 20. She was the 1st Slovakian to rank so high and the 1st in the Open era to reach qf GS, other Czechs to do either having come from other parts of the country. She also reached a 2nd f at Luxembourg, upset Date on the way to sf Los Angeles, reached the same stage at Warsaw and surprised M. J. Fernandez at Filderstadt. These results enabled to her qualify 1st time for Chase Champs, although she lost 1r to Graf. In doubles she won Karlovy Vary with Sukova. **1997:** A 4, F 3, W 1, US 4. Although it was a less spectacular year, she was r/u Linz, reached sf Budapest, plus qf Rosmalen and Prague, and won Prostejov Futures over Paulus. From 2 doubles f, she won Prague with Dragomir. **1997 HIGHLIGHTS – SINGLES: Australian Open last 16** [seed 9] (d. Talaja 6–1 6–2, Bradtke 6–3 6–3, Wang 6–3 7–6, lost Spirlea [seed 8] 6–4 6–4), **French Open 3r** [seed 15] (d. Barabanschikova 6–3 6–3, Likhovtseva 6–2 6–2, lost Dragomir 6–3 6–2), **Wimbledon 1r** (lost Martinez [seed 10] 6–1 6–2), **US Open last 16** [unseeded] (d. Tauziat 7–5 7–6, Sugiyama 5–7 6–3 7–5, Maleeva 0–6 7–5 6–1, lost Testud 6–3 4–6 7–6); **won** Prostejov Futures (d. Paulus 6–7 6–1 6–3); **r/u** Linz (d. Glass 6–7 6–4 6–3, Carlsson 6–2 6–2, Wiesner 6–3 4–6 6–3, lost Rubin 6–4 6–2);

sf Budapest (d. Kleinova 6–2 6–4, Begerow 6–2 6–4, Fusai 6–4 6–3, lost Appelmans 6–2 6–4). **1997 HIGHLIGHTS – DOUBLES:** (with Dragomir) **won** Prague (d. Martincova/Vildova 6–1 5–7 6–2); (with Labat) **r/u** Rosmalen (lost Melicharova/Vildova 6–3 7–6).

JUSTINE HENIN (BEL)

Born Liege, 1 June 1982; lives Rochefort; RH; 5ft 4in; 118lb; career singles titles 0; Junior ranking 6.

Coached by Carlos Rodriguez. **1996:** Nat Jun champ. **1997:** Won French Open Jun over Black.

RIKA HIRAKI (JPN)

Born Beirut, Lebanon, 6 December 1971; lives Matsudo; RH; 2HF; 2HB; 5ft 2in; 99lb; turned pro 1991; career singles titles 0; final 1997 WTA ranking 91 singles, 30 doubles; 1997 prize money $168,806.

1987: (282). **1988:** (295). **1989:** (–). **1990:** (226) Won her 1st pro title at Matsuyama Futures. **1991:** (104) A –, F 1, W 1, US 1. Reached her 1st sf on the main tour at Tokyo Japan Open and followed with Pattaya City. From 2 doubles f won Puerto Rico with Labat. **1992:** (125) A 1, F 1, W 3, US –. Played 2 doubles f, winning Tokyo Suntory with Frazier. **1993:** (134) A 1, F 1, W 1, US –. She reached qf Tokyo Pan Pacific and joined the Japanese Fed Cup squad. **1994:** (184) A –, F –, W –, US 1. R/u Tokyo Nicherei doubles with Frazier. **1995:** (150) A 1, F –, W –, US –. Her best performance came at Nagoya, where she reached qf singles and was r/u doubles with Park. **1996:** (105) A 3, F 1, W 2, US 1. Qf Jakarta, where she won the doubles with Kijimuta. **1997:** A 3, F 1, W 1, US 2. In singles she reached qf Auckland and upset Schultz-McCarthy (affected with a back injury) at Australian Open. In mixed doubles she won a 1st GS title at French Open with Bhupathi, and in the women's game she won Oklahoma City with Miyagi, Tokyo Japan Open with Dechaume-Balleret and Surabaya with Guse. **1997 HIGHLIGHTS – SINGLES: Australian Open 3r** (d. Richterova 6–4 2–6 6–4, Schultz-McCarthy 0–6 6–1 6–4, lost Po 6–2 6–2), **French Open 1r** (lost Arendt 6–2 6–1), **Wimbledon 1r** (lost Yoshida 6–2 6–3), **US Open 2r** (d. Diaz/Oliva 6–4 4–6 6–2, lost McQuillan 6–0 6–2). **1997 HIGHLIGHTS – DOUBLES:** (with Miyagi) **won** Oklahoma City (d. Werdel-Witmeyer/Whitlinger-Jones 6–4 6–1), (with Dechaume-Balleret) **won** Tokyo Japan Open (d. Guse/Morariu 6–4 6–2), (with Guse) **won** Surabaya (d. Drake/Kolbovic 6–1 7–6). **MIXED DOUBLES:** (with Bhupathi) **won French Open** (d. Galbraith/Raymond 6–4 6–1).

ANKE HUBER (GER)

Born Bruchsal, 4 December 1974; lives Going, Austria; RH; 2HB; 5ft 8in; 128lb; turned pro 1989; career singles titles 10; final 1997 WTA ranking 14; 1997 prize money $411,315 ($3,119,900).

1986: Won Nat 12s. **1987:** Won Nat 14s. **1988:** Won Nat 16s. **1989:** (203) Won European Jun Champs and played in winning FRG World Youth Cup team. **1990:** (34) A 3, F –, W 2, US 1. She showed great fighting spirit in extending Sabatini to 2s tb in their 2r encounter at Wimbledon. At end Aug. won her 1st tour title at Schenectady after qualifying and followed with r/u Bayonne, upsetting Garrison and breaking into top 100, then shooting up to top 50 by Oct. Voted WTA Most Impressive Newcomer. **1991:** (14) A qf, F 3, W 4, US 2. Upset Maleeva-Fragniere and Zvereva *en route* to qf Australian Open, unseeded, reached last 16 Wimbledon and ended Sabatini's winning run as she reached qf Berlin. The high spot of her year, though, came at Filderstadt in autumn, where she upset Garrison, Sukova and Navratilova in fs tb to take the title. It was the 1st time for 8 years that Navratilova had been beaten by an unseeded player. **1992:** (11) A qf, F2, W 3, US 1. Upset Novotna *en route* to qf Australian Open and appeared at same stage Olympics; reached sf Sydney, Hamburg, San Diego, Brighton and Oakland and was a member of winning German Fed Cup team. **1993:** (10) A 4, F sf, W 4, US 3. Won a 3rd career title at Kitzbuhel, was r/u Sydney (d. Sanchez Vicario) and Brighton and reached sf VS Florida and VS Champs plus 4 more qf. **1994:** (12) A 3, F 4, W 2, US 2. Restricted early in year by injury, she did not pass qf until reaching sf Berlin in May. However, having split with coach Boris Breskvar after Wimbledon, she won Styria and Filderstadt (d. Navratilova and Pierce) before finishing the season with a flourish at Philadelphia, where she upset Sabatini and Pierce again to take the title. She also appeared in sf Leipzig and 4 more qf, but at VS Champs fell 1r to Davenport. **1995:** (10) A 4, F 4, W 4, US 4. Won Leipzig and reached sf Delray Beach, Hamburg, Filderstadt and Philadelphia (d. Sabatini), as well as qf Tokyo Pan Pacific, LIPC, Manhattan Beach and Toronto. However, she saved her best for the end, upsetting Pierce and Date on her way to f WTA Champs, where she extended Graf to 5s. **1996:** (6) A r/u, F 4, W 3, US 1. Her fine form continued into the new season, which she began on a high note by upsetting Martinez on the way to her 1st GS f at Australian Open, a performance that took her into top 5 1st time. Her 1st title on grass came at Rosmalen, followed by two indoors at Leipzig and Luxembourg. She also appeared in f Los Angeles and Filderstadt (d. Martinez again), sf Essen and Zurich, and qf Paris Open, LIPC, Berlin and Strasbourg. Her performance at Chase Champs was an anticlimax, though, as she lost 1r to Majoli. **1997:** A 4, F 1, W 3, US 3. Although she won no title and was disappointing in the major tourns, she was r/u Paris Open (d. Novotna) and Toronto, reached sf Tokyo Pan Pacific, Rosmalen and Leipzig (d. Majoli), plus qf Auckland, FC Cup, Los Angeles and Philadelphia (d. Majoli). She twice extended Hingis to 3s during her unbeaten run at start of year, and qualified for Chase Champs, although she lost there 1r to Majoli and finished the year outside the top 10. In doubles she won Hamburg with Pierce. **1997 HIGHLIGHTS – SINGLES: Australian Open last 16** [seed 5] (d. Frazier 0–6 6–2 7–5, Lubiani 4–6 6–2 6–0, Zvereva 7–5 6–0, lost Pierce 6–2 6–3), **French Open 1r** [seed 8] (lost Po 6–3 4–6 6–3), **Wimbledon 3r** [seed 7] (d. Inoue 6–3 6–3, Kruger 6–2 6–0, lost Kournikova 3–6 6–4 6–4), **US Open 3r** [seed 8] (d. Pizzichini 6–2 6–2, J. Lee 6–2 6–1, lost V. Williams 6–3 6–4); **r/u** Paris Open (d. Appelmans 6–3 6–2, Spirlea 6–4 6–2, Novotna 6–3 6–4, lost Hingis 6–3 3–6 6–3), **r/u** Toronto (d. Labat 6–2 6–1, Testud 6–3 6–4, Coetzer 2–6 6–1 6–1, M. J. Fernandez 3–6 6–2 ret'd, lost Seles 6–2 6–4); **sf** Tokyo Pan Pacific (d. Po 6–4 6–3, Davenport 6–3 4–6 6–2, lost Hingis 6–1 5–7 6–2), **sf** Rosmalen (d. Kleinova 6–4 2–6 6–4, Appelmans 6–2 4–6 7–6, lost Oremans 4–6 6–4 ret'd), **sf** Leipzig (d. Farina 6–4 6–2, Serna 6–2 6–3, Majoli 4–6 7–6 6–4, lost Novotna 6–7 7–5 6–4). **1997 HIGHLIGHTS – DOUBLES:** (with Pierce) **won** Hamburg (d. Dragomir/Majoli 2–6 7–6 6–2). **CAREER HIGHLIGHTS – SINGLES: Australian Open – r/u 1996** (d. Kleinova 6–1 6–4, Carlsson 6–1 6–2, Richterova 6–2 6–1, Schett 6–3 6–2, Martinez 4–6 6–2 6–1, Coetzer 4–6 6–4 6–2, lost Seles 6–4 6–1), **qf 1991** (d. Richardson 6–4 6–1, Maleeva-Fragniere 6–4 6–4, Shriver 6–3 7–5, Zvereva 6–3 6–4, lost Seles 6–3 6–1), **qf 1992** (d. Zivec-Skulj 2–6 6–3 6–1, Jaggard-Lai 6–0 6–1, Fairbank-Nideffer 6–0 7–5, Novotna 5–7 7–6 6–4, lost Seles 7–5 6–3); **WTA Champs – r/u 1995** (d. Pierce 6–2 6–3, Date 3–6 6–2 6–1, Schultz-McCarthy 6–3 6–3, lost Graf 6–1 2–6 6–1 4–6 6–3), **sf 1993** (d. Mag. Maleeva 6–4 1–6 7–6, Martinez 6–3 6–3, lost Graf 6–2 3–6 6–3); **Olympics – qf 1992** (d. Sawamatsu 6–0 4–6 6–2, Paulus 6–4 6–1, Muns-Jagerman 7–5 7–6, lost Capriati 6–3 7–6).

PATRICIA HY-BOULAIS (CAN)

Born Cambodia, 22 August 1965; lives Toronto; RH; 5ft 4in; 123lb; turned pro 1986; career singles titles 1; final 1997 WTA ranking 64; 1997 prize money $137,894.

Married her coach, Yves Boulais, 19 November 1994. At age 6 she moved from Cambodia to Hong Kong, where she was ranked No. 1 country at age 16. **1983:** (65) A –, F –, W 2, US 3. R/u Wimbledon Jun singles and won doubles there with Fendick. On the senior tour she reached sf Nashville. **1984:** (214) A –, F 1, W –, US –. An All-American at UCLA, she won Fort Lauderdale on USTA circuit. **1985:** (308) A –, F –, W –, US –. **1986:** (101) F –, W –, US –. Won Taipei and reached sf Singapore. **1987:** (101) A 2, F 1, W 1, US 2. Extended Graf to 3s in Fed Cup. **1988:** (205) A 1, F –, W –, US –. Won USTA Detroit. **1989:** (222) A –, F –, W –, US –. Won USTA Chicago. **1990:** (103) A –, F 1, W –, US 2. Qf Singapore was her best showing. **1991:** (57) A 2, F 2, W 3, US 3. Qf VS Indian Wells and upset Fairbank-Nideffer at Wimbledon. **1992:** (32) A 2, F 4, W 3, US qf. Unseeded both times, she reached last 16 French Open and at US Open upset Capriati and Sukova back-to-back to reach qf. She reached the same stage FC Cup (d. Mag. Maleeva and Novotna), Montreal (d. Maleeva-Fragniere) and extended M. J. Fernandez to 12–10 fs at Olympics. **1993:** (41) A 2, F 3, W 3, US 2. She reached sf Hong Kong, upset Sukova *en route* to same stage Quebec City and surprised Provis at Eastbourne. **1994:** (64) A 1, F 1, W 1, US 3. In a quieter year she reached sf Auckland, where she won the doubles with Paz, and appeared in qf Los Angeles and Quebec City. **1995:** (75) A 1, F 2, W 2, US 3. Having gone 6 tourns without passing 1r, she was r/u both singles and doubles at Bournemouth. Her 2r match v Rubin at Wimbledon, which she lost 7–6 6–7 17–15, set records for the longest women's match there: the 58 games exceeded by 4 the previous record set by A. Weiwers and O. Anderson in 1948, and the 32 games in the final set were 6 more than the previous longest, achieved 6 times since 1919. **1996:** (67) A 1, F 1, W 4, US 1. Beat De Swardt, Zvereva and Tauziat at Wimbledon, where she was unseeded, and reached sf Cardiff. **1997:** A 2, F 2, W 4, US 2. Upset Coetzer at Wimbledon, where she was unseeded, but was out of action at end of season with right knee problems. **1997 HIGHLIGHTS – SINGLES: Australian Open 2r** (d. Dechaume-Balleret 6–0 2–6 6–4, lost Carlsson 2–6 6–3 6–0), **French Open 2r** (d. Dechy 6–7 6–4 11–9, lost Pierce [seed 10] 6–1 6–3), **Wimbledon last 16** [unseeded] (d. Saeki 6–2 1–6 6–2, Coetzer [seed 6] 6–2 6–1, Grzybowska 6–4 6–1, lost Basuki 6–0 7–6), **US Open 2r** (d. Kochta 6–2 6–1, lost Wagner 6–3 0–6 7–6). **CAREER HIGHLIGHTS – SINGLES: US Open – qf 1992** [unseeded] (d. Sviglerova 6–1 6–1, Wiesner 6–2 6–2, Capriati 7–5 6–4, Sukova 6–1 7–6, lost Seles 6–1 6–2).

MARISSA IRVIN (USA)

Born Santa Monica, Cal., 23 June 1980, and lives there; RH; 2HB; 5ft 7in; 130lb; career singles titles 0.

1997: Won US Open Jun doubles with Stevenson.

NAOKO KIJIMUTA (JPN)

Born Yokohama, 26 March 1972, and lives there; RH; 2HB; 5ft 4½in; 120lb; turned pro 1992; career singles titles 0; final 1997 WTA ranking 74 singles, 20 doubles; 1997 prize money $166,242.

Coached by her older sister, Akiko, who used to play on the women's tour. **1991:** (432). **1992:** (316). **1993:** (222). **1994:** (154) A 1, F –, W –, US –. **1995:** (87) (A 1, F –, W –, US 2). Upset Wang on the way to her 1st sf on the main tour at Pattaya City and broke into the top 100. **1996:** (50) A 1, F 1, W 1, US 3. Reached sf Jakarta and Tokyo Japan Open in consec. tourns, appeared in qf Cardiff and Beijing and upset Schultz-McCarthy at Montreal. In doubles she won Jakarta with Hiraki and Beijing with Saeki. **1997:** A 1, A 2, W 3, US 1. Although her only qf was at Strasbourg (d. Maleeva), she upset Paulus at Wimbledon and Schultz-McCarthy at Toronto. In doubles with Miyagi, she won Gold Coast and Hobart. **1997 HIGHLIGHTS – SINGLES: Australian Open 1r** (lost Spirlea [seed 8] 6–2 6–4), **French Open 2r** (d. Andretto 6–3 6–3, lost Serna 3–6 6–4 6–2), **Wimbledon 3r** (d. Neiland 7–6 6–2, Paulus [seed 16] 5–7 6–3 6–3, lost Basuki 6–3 6–2), **US Open 1r** (lost M. J. Fernandez [seed 12] 6–2 6–3). **1997 HIGHLIGHTS – DOUBLES:** (with Miyagi) **won** Gold Coast (d. Dragomir/Farina 7–6 6–1), **won** Hobart (d. Rittner/Van Roost 6–3 6–1).

SANDRA KLEINOVA (CZE)

Born Prague, 8 May 1978, and lives there; RH; 2HB; 5ft 9½in; 136lb; turned pro 1993; career singles titles 0; final 1997 WTA ranking 42; 1997 prize money $106,000.

Coached by Martin Fasati; trained by Stefan Mester. Niece of former D Cup player Hiri Hrebec. Won Nat 12s, 16s, 18s. **1993:** (552). **1994:** (578). **1995:** (121) R/u Nagoya, in only her 2nd main tour event, having reached qf in her 1st at Prague. On the Futures circuit she won Turku and Rungsted. **1996:** (150) A 1, F –, W –, US 1. Qf Bol was her best performance. **1997:** A 3, F 1, W 1, US 1. She reached qf Leipzig (d. Basuki), Zurich (d. Maleeva) and Pattaya, and upset Van Roost at Bol. **1997 HIGHLIGHTS – SINGLES: Australian Open 3r** (d. Whitlinger-Jones 7–6 6–1, Sidot 6–4 4–6 8–6, lost Rubin [seed 15] 6–1 6–3), **French Open 1r** (lost Majoli [seed 9] 7–5 6–4), **Wimbledon 1r** (lost Chladkova 7–6 6–4), **US Open 1r** (lost Lucic 6–0 6–3).

ANNA KOURNIKOVA (RUS)

Born Moscow, 7 June 1981, and lives there; RH; 2HB; 5ft 6in; 112lb; turned pro 1995; career singles titles 0; final 1997 WTA ranking 32; 1997 prize money $292,362.

Coached by Nick Bollettieri, working at his academy since 1992. **1995:** (281) No. 1 in ITF Jun rankings after winning Orange Bowl and European Champs. **1996:** (57) A –, F –, W –, US 4. At US Open, having played through the qualifying in only her 2nd main draw event, she upset Paulus to reach last 16. She surprised Coetzer at Zurich and won 2 titles on the Futures circuit. Aged 14, she became the youngest to win a Fed Cup match when she helped RUS d. SWE 3–0. Voted Most Impressive Newcomer. **1997:** A 1, F 3, W sf, US 2. She upset Coetzer at LIPC and Sanchez Vicario on her way to qf Berlin, before impressing at Wimbledon, where, unseeded, she upset Huber and Majoli on her way to sf. **1997 HIGHLIGHTS – SINGLES: Australian Open 1r** (lost Coetzer [seed 12] 6–2 6–2), **French Open 3r** (d. Zrubakova 6–3 6–2, Cecchini 6–2 6–2, lost Hingis [seed 1] 6–1 6–3), **Wimbledon sf** [unseeded] (d. Rubin 6–1 6–1, Rittner 4–6 7–6 6–3, Huber [seed 7] 3–6 6–4 6–4, Sukova 2–6 6–2 6–3, Majoli [seed 4] 7–6 6–4, lost Hingis 6–3 6–2), **US Open 2r** (d. Appelmans 6–2 6–0, lost Spirlea [seed 11] 6–1 3–6 6–3). **CAREER HIGHLIGHTS – SINGLES: Wimbledon – sf 1997.**

JOANNETTE KRUGER (RSA)

Born Johannesburg, 3 September 1973; lives Benoni; RH; 2HB; 5ft 10½in; 130lb; career singles titles 2; final 1997 WTA ranking 27; 1997 prize money $167,307.

Coached by her mother, Petro Kruger. **1989:** (519). **1990:** (357) Won Bournemouth Futures. **1991:** (274). **1992:** (105) Won 3 titles on the Futures circuit and played Fed Cup. **1993:** (128) A 1, F 1, W 1, US –. Appeared in her 1st sf on the senior tour at San Marino. **1994:** (79) A 1, F 3, W 1, US 1. Reached qf Birmingham and took a set off Novotna at Brighton. **1995:** (30) A 2, F 2, W 1, US 2. Won her 1st main tour title in her 1st f at Puerto Rico, unseeded, and broke into the top 50 in April. She recorded some useful upsets on her way to qf Houston (d. Garrison-Jackson), Italian Open (d. Huber), Leipzig (d. Davenport) and Zurich (d. Sukova). **1996:** (112) A 2, F –, W 1, US 1. She reached qf Oklahoma and Bol. After passing out with heat stroke at Indian Wells, she underwent neurological tests both in US and at home, required anti-seizure medication, and missed French Open. **1997:** A 2, F 1, W 2, US 4. She won Prague and reached qf Budapest (d. Davenport), Warsaw (d. Habsudova) and Luxembourg, as well as upsetting Habsudova at Maria Lankowitz and Paulus at US Open, where she was unseeded. **1997 HIGHLIGHTS – SINGLES: Australian Open 2r** (d. Randriantefy 6–3 2–6 6–2, lost Spirlea 6–1 6–1), **French Open 1r** (lost Davenport [seed 5] 6–2 6–3), **Wimbledon 2r** (d. De ville 7–6 6–3, lost Huber [seed 7] 6–2 6–0), **US Open last 16** [unseeded] (d. Paulus [seed 14] 6–1 6–7 6–1, Nagyova 6–4 7–6, Tanasugarn 6–7 7–5 6–4, lost V. Williams 6–2 6–3); **won** Prague (d. Barabanschikova 6–3 6–2, Louarabishvili 6–2 5–7 6–4, Dechaume-Balleret 4–6 7–6 6–1, Martinek 7–5 6–1, Maruska 6–1 6–1).

FLORENCIA LABAT (ARG)

Born Buenos Aires, 12 June 1971, and lives there; LH; 5ft 7in; 135lb; turned pro 1989; career singles titles 0; final 1997 WTA ranking 39; 1997 prize money $207,224.

Coached by Jorge Gerosi. **1987:** Won S American Jun Champs and Orange Bowl 16s singles and doubles. **1988:** (389) No. 3 in ITF Jun rankings. **1989:** (70) A –, F –, W –, US 2. No. 1 in ITF Jun rankings. Won S American Jun Champs again. On the pro tour she reached qf Arcachon and VS Arizona as well as upsetting Lindqvist 1r US Open and winning 2 titles on the Futures circuit. **1990:** (118) A –, F 1, W 1, US 1. Qf Strasbourg and Puerto Rico and joined her country's Fed Cup team. **1991:** (56) A –, F 2, W –, US 3. Reached her 1st sf on the main tour at Sao Paulo, appeared in qf Taranto, Kitzbuhel (d. Kelesi) and Schenectady and upset Tauziat at US Open. In doubles won Taranto with Dechaume and Puerto Rico with Hiraki. **1992:** (51) A 1, F 1, W 1, US 4. Upset Wiesner *en route* to sf Kitzbuhel and Medvedeva and Zrubakova on her way to same stage Schenectady. In doubles with Dechaume she won both those tourns plus San Marino. Made an unexpected appearance in last 16 US Open. **1993:** (51) A 2, F 3, W 3, US 1. At end of year she played her 1st Kraft tour f at Curitiba, having earlier reached qf Brisbane (d. Zrubakova), Strasbourg, Kitzbuhel and San Marino. In GS she extended Capriati to 3s at Australian Open and again at French Open. Played 2 doubles f with Rittner but won no title. **1994:** (38) A 2, F 1, W 4, US 1. It was a good year for her, in which she reached f Brisbane (d. Mag. Maleeva), Singapore and Jakarta as well as sf Pattaya City and qf Tokyo Japan Open. In GS she upset Hack 1r Wimbledon, where she was unseeded. **1995:** (56) A 1, F 3, W 2, US 3. Reached sf Puerto Rico, qf Delray Beach and upset Sawamatsu at Berlin. **1996:** (43) A 2, F 1, W 3, US 2. Upset Kruger and Hack on her way to sf Auckland, followed with the same stage at Hobart the next week and played qf Montreal, Quebec City and Pattaya. **1997:** A 2, F 2, W 3, US 4. Her best performance came at Madrid, where she upset Spirlea and extended Seles to 3s in sf. She reached no other qf in singles, but played – and lost – 3 doubles f with different partners. **1997 HIGHLIGHTS – SINGLES: Australian Open 2r** (d. Kremer 7–5 4–6 6–2, lost Nagyova 6–3 6–2), **French Open 2r** (d. Boogert 7–5 6–0, lost Schultz-McCarthy [seed 14] 4–6 7–6 6–4), **Wimbledon 3r** (d. Grande 6–4 6–4, Callens 6–2 6–3, lost Sanchez Vicario [seed 8] 6–1 6–2), **US Open last 16** [unseeded] (d. Gavaldon 6–2 6–1, Lubiani 6–1 6–1, Barabanschikova 4–6 7–6 6–1, lost Hingis 6–0 6–2); **sf** Madrid (d. Nemeckova 6–2 6–1, Maruska 6–2 6–2, Spirlea 6–2 7–5, lost Seles 6–7 6–1 6–2). **1997 HIGHLIGHTS – DOUBLES:** (with Habsudova) **r/u** Rosmalen (lost Melicharova/Vildova 6–3 7–6), (with Paz) **r/u** Palermo (lost Farina/Schett 2–6 6–1 6–4), (with Van Roost) **r/u** Pattaya (lost Kunce/Morariu 6–3 6–4).

GALA LEON-GARCIA (ESP)

Born Madrid, 23 December 1973; lives Barcelona; LH; 5ft 4in; 124lb; career singles titles 0; final 1997 WTA ranking 58; 1997 prize money $92,350.

Coached by Gabriel Urpi; trained by Jordi Llacer. **1991:** (694). **1992:** (481). **1993:** (289). **1994:** (329). **1995:** (134) On the Futures circuit she won 3 singles and 2 doubles titles. **1996:** (85) A –, F 4, W 1, US 1. Broke into top 100 after reaching last 16 French Open as a qualifier (d. Paulus). Played in ESP Fed Cup team r/u to USA. **1997:** A 1, F 1, W 3, US 2. Reached her 1st qf on the main tour at Madrid, following with same stage Warsaw and Maria Lankowitz, and won Budapest Futures. **1997 HIGHLIGHTS – SINGLES: Australian Open 1r** (lost Po 4–6 7–6 6–2), **French Open 1r** (lost Kandarr 7–6 6–3), **Wimbledon 3r** (d. Endo 6–3 6–3, Torrens-Valero 3–6 6–2 6–3, lost Novotna [seed 3] 6–4 6–2), **US Open 2r** (d. A. Miller 4–6 6–2 6–3, lost V. Williams 6–0 6–1); **won** Budapest Futures (d. Diaz-Oliva 7–5 6–2).

FANG LI (CHN)

Born Hunan, 1 January 1973, and lives there; RH; 2HB; 5ft 5½in; 138lb, turned pro 1990; career singles titles 0; final 1997 WTA ranking 68; 1997 prize money $75,317.

Coached by Jiang Hongwei and Xie Fengsen. Ranked No. 1 in China. **1990:** (350) Won Murcia and Fayetteville Futures. **1991:** (153) A 3, F –, W –, US –. Won 9 Futures events. **1992:** (119) A 1, F 1, W 1, US 2. Emerging from the satellite circuits, she reached her 1st qf on main tour at Kuala Lumpur. **1993:** (132) A 1, F –, W 1, US 1. Upset Probst at Melbourne and played 2 doubles f, winning Kitzbuhel with Monami. **1994:** (66) A 1, F 2, W 2, US 1. Reached her 1st main tour sf at Singapore and appeared in qf Palermo and Beijing, where she won the doubles with Chen. **1995:** (95) A 1, F –, W –, US 1. At Hobart she upset Wiesner to reach her 1st f on the main tour and played qf Auckland and Surabaya. **1996:** (194) A –, F –, W –, US –. Reached sf Auckland after qualifying. **1997:** Although qf Tokyo Nicherei was her best showing on the senior tour, she won Phoenix, Queens, Wichita and Salt Lake City on the Futures circuit. **1997 HIGHLIGHTS – SINGLES: US Open 1r** (lost Lubiani 6–4 3–6 6–2); **won** Phoenix Futures (d. Brandi 6–1 6–2), **won** Queens Futures (d. J. Lee 7–5 7–5), **won** Wichita Futures (d. Cacic 6–2 6–2), **won** Salt Lake City Futures (d. Golarsa 6–3 6–2).

ELENA LIKHOVTSEVA (KAZ)

Born Alma-Ata, 8 September 1975; lives Moscow, Russia; RH; 2HB; 5ft 8½in; 142lb; turned pro 1992; career singles titles 2; final 1997 WTA ranking 31 singles, 25 doubles; 1997 prize money $260,662.

Coached by Dmitriy Degtiatev. **1991:** Won Orange Bowl 18s. **1992:** (353) Won Vilamoura Futures. **1993:** A –, F –, W –, US 1. Won her 1st tour title at Montpellier and reached qf San Diego (d. Medvedeva). **1994:** A 3, F –, W 1, US 4. After upsetting Sukova at Indian Wells and reaching qf Moscow, she reached last 16 US Open, unseeded. **1995:** (45) A 1, F 2, W 1, US 1. Upset Raymond and Frazier on her way to f Oklahoma and reached qf Hobart, Indian Wells (d. Frazier), Delray Beach, Moscow and Leipzig (d. Sukova). **1996:** (23) A 4, F 3, W 4, US 3. After removing defending champion Pierce at Australian Open, where she was unseeded, she went on to reach sf Oklahoma (d. Frazier), Berlin (d. Sanchez Vicario) and Quebec City, plus qf Oakland (d. M. J. Fernandez). **1997:** A 1, F 2, W 2, US 3. Her year began on a high note with the title at Gold Coast (d. Schultz-McCarthy). Although she did not maintain that level, she reached qf Hannover and Stanford (d. Raymond), upset Basuki at Luxembourg and extended Novotna to 3s at Wimbledon. **1997 HIGHLIGHTS – SINGLES: Australian Open 1r** (lost Pierce 3–6 6–2 6–4), **French Open 2r** (d. Nemeckova 6–4 6–3, lost Habsudova [seed 15] 6–2 6–2), **Wimbledon 1r** (lost Zvereva 6–2 6–2, lost Novotna [seed 3] 6–1 4–6 6–4), **US Open 3r** (d. Langrova 7–5 6–4, Richterova 7–5 6–1, lost Hingis [seed 1] 7–5 6–2); **won** Gold Coast (d. Suarez 6–3 6–4, McQuillan 3–6 6–3 7–6, Schultz-McCarthy 6–4 6–3, Sugiyama 3–6 7–6 6–3). **1997 HIGHLIGHTS – DOUBLES:** (with Sugiyama) **r/u** Strasbourg (lost Sukova/Zvereva 6–1 6–1).

FRANCESCA LUBIANI (ITA)

Born Bologna, 12 July 1977, and lives there; LH; 2HF; 2HB; turned pro 1992; career singles titles 0; final 1997 WTA ranking 61; 1997 prize money $90,012.

Coached by her father, Paolo Lubiani. R/u Orange Bowl 14s. **1992:** (541). **1993:** (439). **1994:** (316) Won Amadora Futures. **1995:** (173). **1996:** (92) A 2, F 2, W 1, US 1. **1997:** A 2, F 1, W 1, US 2. Burst on to the scene on the main tour when she upset Frazier and Coetzer to reach her 1st sf at Oklahoma City, and also appeared in qf Cardiff. **1997 HIGHLIGHTS – SINGLES: Australian Open 2r** (d. McQuillan 6–2 7–6, lost

Huber [seed 5] 4–6 6–2 6–0), **French Open 1r** (lost Pitkowski 7–6 6–2, lost Seles [seed 3] 6–3 7–5), **Wimbledon 1r** (lost Pitkowski 6–3 4–6 6–1), **US Open 2r** (d. Li 6–4 3–6 6–2, lost Labat 6–1 6–1); **sf** Oklahoma City (d. Frazier 7–6 7–5, Grzybowska 6–1 7–5, Coetzer 6–0 6–4, lost Raymond 6–1 6–0).

MIRJANA LUCIC (CRO)

Born Dortmund, Germany, 9 March 1982; lives Makarska; RH; 2HB; 5ft 11in; 145lb; career singles titles 1; 1997 WTA ranking 52; 1997 prize money $91,285.

Coached by Goran Prpic. **1996:** Won US Open Jun over Weingartner. **1997:** A –, F –, W –, US 3. Played Fed Cup for CRO at age 14 as CRO d. AUS 4–1. Then at 15 years 1 month 25 days, she became the youngest since Capriati in 1990 to take a title when she delighted home crowds by winning Bol in her 1st ever tourn on the main tour. She followed by reaching f of her second after qualifying at Strasbourg (d. Tauziat), took the title at ITF Makarska and came into the rankings at No. 69. A hard-hitter who plays with a maturity beyond her years, she extended Novotna to 3s at US Open, having been permitted by the tourn organisers to play there, although French Open and Wimbledon had excluded her from the women's tourn as being too young, and she was restricted in the number of tourns she could play during the year. In the Jun game, she won Australian Open over Weingartner and took the doubles there with Wohr. **1997 HIGHLIGHTS – SINGLES: US Open 3r** (d. Kleinova 6–0 6–3, Rippner 6–0 6–1, lost Novotna [seed 3] 6–2 6–7 6–3); **won** Bol (d. McQuillan 6–2 6–2, Fusai w.o., Studenikova 7–5 6–4, Coetzer 6–4 6–3, Morariu 7–5 6–7 7–6), **won** Makarska Futures (d. Dopfer 6–1 6–4); **r/u** Strasbourg (d. Begerow 6–2 4–6 6–2, Tauziat 6–1 3–6 7–5, Zvereva 7–5 6–3, Wiesner 7–5 6–7 7–6, lost Graf 6–2 7–5).

RACHEL McQUILLAN (AUS)

Born Merewether, NSW, 2 December 1971; lives Newcastle, NSW; RH; 2HB; 5ft 7in; 132lb; career singles titles 0; final 1997 WTA ranking 49; 1997 prize money $163,310 ($1,070,571).

Her father, Ted, travels with her. **1987:** (448) In winning World Youth Cup team. **1988:** (202) A 1, F –, W –, US –. Won Australian Open and Wimbledon Jun doubles with Faull; r/u US Open Jun to Cunningham. Ranked No. 2 in ITF Jun doubles and No. 5 in singles. **1989:** (79) A 1, F 1, W –, US 1. Reached qf Adelaide and Hamburg, then upset Cecchini *en route* to f Athens. R/u US Open Jun to Capriati. **1990:** (39) A 4, F 1, W 2, US 2. Upset Wiesner twice to make surprise appearances in f Brisbane and Kitzbuhel and overturned Kelesi at Australian Open, where she was unseeded. In doubles reached 2 f with Faull. **1991:** (36) A 4, F 4, W 1, US 2. Unseeded both times, she upset Paulus at Australian Open and Kelesi at French Open. R/u Strasbourg (d. Wiesner), sf Bayonne and won Schenectady doubles with Porwik. **1992:** (38) A 3, F –, W 1, US 3. R/u Brisbane, sf Bayonne and qf Osaka were her best performances in singles. In doubles she reached 4 f with different partners, winning an Olympic bronze medal with Provis. **1993:** (112) A 1, F 2, W 2, US 1. In a quieter year, her only qf showing in singles was at Brisbane, and she won 2 doubles titles with Porwik and Kschwendt. **1994:** (61) A 3, F 1, W 2, US 1. At Hobart she reached her 1st f for 2 years (d. Helgeson) and also appeared in qf Brisbane (d. Halard) and Jakarta. Played 3 doubles f but won no title. **1995:** (69) A 1, F 1, W 2, US 1. Did not progress beyond qf, but reached that stage at Auckland, LIPC (d. Frazier and Davenport) and San Diego (d. Tauziat). **1996:** (183) A 1, F 1, W –, US –. **1997:** A 1, F 1, W 1, US 4. On the main tour she reached sf Surabaya and qf Gold Coast, as well as upsetting Martinez at US Open (where she was unseeded), Schultz-McCarthy at Sydney and Coetzer in Fed Cup. On the Futures circuit she won both singles and doubles at Bronx Futures and singles at Sedona. **1997 HIGHLIGHTS – SINGLES: Australian Open 1r** (lost Lubiani 6–2 7–6), **French Open 1r** (lost Yoshida 6–3 4–6 6–3), **Wimbledon 1r** (lost Seles [seed 2] 6–0 6–2), **US Open last 16** [unseeded] (d. Torrens-Valero 4–6 7–5 6–4, Hiraki 6–0 6–2, Martinez [seed 7] 6–2 7–5, lost Sanchez Vicario [seed 10] 6–1 6–2); **won** Bronx Futures (d. De Lone 6–1 6–4), **won** Sedona Futures (d. Dopfer 6–3 7–6); **sf** Surabaya (d. Drake-Brockman 6–2 6–3, Miyagi 6–4 6–7 6–1, Pratt 3–6 6–2 6–2, lost Van Roost 6–2 7–5). **1997 HIGHLIGHTS – DOUBLES:** (with Miyagi) **r/u** Edinburgh (lost Arendt/Bollegraf 6–1 3–6 7–5).

MAGDALENA MALEEVA (BUL)

Born Sofia, 1 April 1975, and lives there; RH; 2HB; 5ft 6in; 127lb; turned pro 1989; career singles titles 6; final 1997 WTA ranking 36; 1997 prize money $161,647 ($1,792,768).

Coached by her brother-in-law François Fragniere, formerly by her mother, Yulia Berberian. Younger sister of Manuela and Katerina. **1988:** Won Orange Bowl 12s and became youngest Bulgarian nat champ at 13 yrs 4 mths. **1989:** (211) R/u Bari on Italian satellite circuit in first pro tourn. **1990:** (72) A –, F 3, W 2, US 1. In Jun singles won Australian Open (over Stacey), French Open (over Ignatieva) and US Open (over van Lottum). On the senior tour reached qf Wellington and after upsetting Lindqvist at Wimbledon moved into the top 100. **1991:** (38) A 4, F 1, W 1, US 2. Upset Fairbank-Nideffer on her way to an unexpected appearance in last 16 Australian Open and in April upset Kelesi *en route* to her 1st tour f at Bol, where she also teamed with Golarsa to win the doubles. **1992:** (20) A 1, F 3, W 1, US qf. Won her 1st tour title at San Marino and, unseeded, upset Navratilova 2r US Open on her way to qf, where she retired against her sister, Manuela, with a thigh injury. Upset Capriati and Sukova back-to-back at Tokyo Pan Pacific, where she reached sf, as she did at Brisbane, and surprised Date *en route* to last 16 Olympics, unseeded. **1993:** (16) A 4, F 4, W 3, US 4. Voted WTA Most Improved Player of the Year, she continued to progress with r/u showing at Brisbane, sf Zurich and Hamburg, plus qf Osaka, Indian Wells, Barcelona, Berlin, San Diego, VS Los Angeles and Leipzig. Qualified for VS Champs but was eliminated 1r by Huber. She was playing Seles in qf Hamburg when the No. 1 was stabbed in the back at the changeover. **1994:** (11) A 4, F 1, W 2, US 4. Won Zurich (d. Sukova) and Moscow and upset Navratilova on her way to sf Chicago, reaching the same stage Brisbane and Barcelona. Although she was disappointing in GS, she appeared in 2 more qf and finished the year poised outside the top 10. Stress fracture of the ribs prevented her taking her place at VS Champs. **1995:** (6) A 1, F 2, W –, US 2. Upset Sabatini on her way to the title at Chicago, following with Moscow and Oakland. She surprised Pierce twice – on her way to f Berlin and sf Tokyo Pan Pacific – and was also r/u FC Cup and Leipzig and reached sf Amelia Island, Hamburg and Brighton. Although she took her place in the top 10, her year was not all plain sailing, for a back injury forced her to withdraw from Wimbledon and from San Diego in Aug. and in autumn flu caused her to withdraw from f Leipzig and to miss Zurich. She qualified for her 1st VS Champs, but that, too, ended in disappointment as she was beaten 1r by Schultz-McCarthy. **1996:** (18) A –, F 4, W 2, US 1. She was still affected by injury, being forced to withdraw from Linz with lower back strain. Although she won no title and slipped from the top 10, she was r/u Madrid (d. Sanchez Vicario) and reached sf Paris Open, plus qf Tokyo Toray, Italian Open, Montreal and Leipzig. **1997:** A –, F 1, W 3, US 3. She tended to struggle again, with her best performance sf Hannover, and qf showings at Linz, Birmingham, Toronto and Filderstadt. **1997 HIGHLIGHTS – SINGLES: French Open 1r** (lost Raymond 4–6 7–5 6–3), **Wimbledon 3r** (d. Pullin 6–1 6–3, Helgeson-Nielsen 7–5 7–5, lost Vento 6–2 7–6), **US Open 3r** (d. Stojanova 6–2 6–3, Raymond 3–6 6–2 6–4, lost Habsudova 0–6 7–5 6–1); **sf** Hannover (d. Farina 6–2 6–1, Habsudova 0–6 6–3 6–2, Testud 6–1 6–4, lost Novotna 6–0 7–5). **CAREER HIGHLIGHTS – SINGLES: US Open – qf 1992** [unseeded] (d. Kroupova 6–2 6–1, Navratilova 6–4 0–6 6–3, Po 6–2 6–3, Rubin 7–5 5–7 6–1, lost Maleeva-Fragniere 6–2 5–3 ret'd).

CONCHITA MARTINEZ (ESP)

Born Monzon, 16 April 1972; lives Barcelona; RH; 2HB; 5ft 7in; 132lb; turned pro 1988; career singles titles 28; final 1997 WTA ranking 12 singles, 19 doubles; 1997 prize money $528,544 ($6,877,810).

Coached by Carlos Kirmayr; trained by Miguel Mir. **1988:** (40) A –, F 4, W –, US 1. Upset McNeil *en route* to last 16 French Open after qualifying and won her 1st pro titles in both singles and doubles (with Paulus) at Sofia. Won Nat Champs over Sanchez and played Fed Cup. **1989:** (7) A 2, F qf, W –, US 4. Won Wellington, Tampa (d. Sabatini) and VS Arizona, was r/u Geneva and Bayonne and reached qf French Open. She into the top 10 1st time, was voted WTA Most Impressive Newcomer. **1990:** (11) A –, F qf, W –, US 3. She won Clarins, Scottsdale and Indianapolis, reached sf LIPC (d. Sabatini), Tampa and Leipzig and appeared in qf French Open again. she appeared in her 1st VS Champs, but lost 1r to Garrison. **1991:** (9) A –, F qf, W –, US qf. She took 3 titles again – at Barcelona, Kitzbuhel and Clarins – upset Navratilova on her way to sf Italian Open, and reached the same stage at Geneva, San Diego and Milan, plus 4 more qf. She played in the successful Spanish Fed Cup team and qualified for VS Champs again, where she fell 1r to Graf. **1992:** (8) A 4, F qf, W 2, US 1. Although Kitzbuhel was her only title, she was r/u Indian Wells, VS Florida, FC Cup and San Diego and appeared in sf Amelia Island and Barcelona. She extended Sabatini to 3s in her 4th French Open qf and reached the same stage at Olympics. Qualified for VS Champs, where she beat K. Maleeva but lost qf to McNeil. In doubles with Sanchez Vicario she was r/u French Open and Olympic Games (silver medal) and won Barcelona, reaching 4 more f with various partners. **1993:** (4) A 4, F qf, W sf, US 4. When she won Italian Open, with defeats of Navratilova and Sabatini, she became the 1st Spanish woman to win the title since 1930. She also won Brisbane, VS Houston (d. Sabatini), Stratton Mountain and VS Philadelphia (ending Graf's 9–match winning streak against her), was r/u Linz, Barcelona and Essen and reached 4 more sf, including Wimbledon. Qualified for VS Champs, where she fell qf to Huber, and played in winning Spanish Fed Cup team. In doubles she played 4 f with 3 different partners, winning Brisbane with Neiland and Barcelona with Sanchez Vicario. **1994:** (3) A qf, F sf, W won, US 3. The highlight of an excellent year came when she won her first GS title at Wimbledon, ending Navratilova's dream of a 10th title in a thrilling f, where the Spaniard overcame a leg injury to play superb tennis. She was the 1st Spaniard to reach Wimbledon f since De Alvarez lost to Wills-Moody in 1928. She also won FC Cup, Italian Open and Stratton Mountain, and reached sf French Open, VS Houston and San Diego, plus qf Australian Open and same stage at 6 other tourns. One of these was Brighton, where she was accused of throwing the match v Neiland, the day before she was due to attend her coach's wedding in Switzerland. Played on the victorious Spanish Fed Cup team for the third time, and qualified for VS Champs, where she lost qf to Date. **1995:** (2) A sf, F sf, W sf, US sf. After splitting with Van Harpen, who left 'for family reasons', she was coached by Carlos Kirmayr from March 1995, whereupon her fortunes changed again and she won back-to-back titles at FC Cup, Amelia Island, Hamburg and Italian Open (d. Pierce and Sanchez Vicario), following with San Diego and Manhattan Beach. She was also r/u Delray Beach and reached sf of all 4 GS tourns. She had slipped down the rankings behind Pierce, but after beating her again at San Diego, she regained the No. 3 position and at end Oct. overtook Sanchez Vicario to take 2nd place (behind Graf and Seles jointly). Qualified for WTA Champs in both singles and doubles (with Tarabini), but was restricted by a neck injury, losing qf singles to Schultz-McCarthy and 1r doubles to Novotna/Sanchez Vicario. Contributed two singles wins as Spain d. USA 3–2 in f Fed Cup. **1996:** (5) A qf, F sf, W 4, US sf. She became the 1st to win 4 consec. Italian Open titles, following in autumn with Moscow, and was r/u Indian Wells and Hamburg, as well as reaching sf French Open, US Open, Tokyo Toray, FC Cup and San Diego. Her ranking fluctuated for much of the year between 2nd and 3rd spot: on 15 April she slipped to No. 3 behind Sanchez Vicario again, returned to No. 2 for 1 week on 29 April, but dropped back again after letting slip a 4–1 lead in 2s to lose f Hamburg to her countrywoman. She returned briefly to 2nd spot in Aug., before settling back at No. 3 and then dropping to No. 5 in Nov. She finished the year on a sour note at Chase Champs, losing to Majoli in a 2r encounter in which she received a warning for racket abuse and a point penalty for a visible obscenity. In doubles, she took an Olympic bronze medal with Sanchez Vicario and won San Diego with G. Fernandez. **1997:** A 4, F 4, W 3, US 3. She struggled to hold on to her top 10 ranking, slipping in and out of the elite before finishing the season just outside after another disappointing performance at Chase Champs, where Novotna beat her 1r. A highlight was at Stanford, where she was r/u, upsetting Seles (1st time in 12 meetings) and Coetzer. She reached no other f, but appeared in sf FC Cup, Toronto and Moscow, as well as qf Tokyo Pan Pacific, Oklahoma City, Amelia Island, Hamburg, San Diego and Tokyo Nicherei. She also qualified for Chase Champs in doubles with Tarabini, despite having reached no f all year. **1997 HIGHLIGHTS – SINGLES: Australian Open last 16** [seed 3] (d. Oremans 6–0 6–2, Gersi 6–2 7–6, Carlsson 6–0 6–1, lost Appelmans [seed 16] 2–6 7–5 6–1), **French Open last 16** [seed 7] (d. Loic 4–6 6–2 6–3, Rubin 6–3 6–0, Dhenin 6–2 6–1, lost Coetzer [seed 11] 6–7 6–4 6–3), **Wimbledon 3r** [seed 10] (d. Habsudova 6–1 6–2, Yoshida 6–0 6–0, lost Sukova 6–4 6–2), **US Open 3r** [seed 7] (d. Capriati 6–1 6–2, Smith 6–1 6–0, lost McQuillan 6–2 7–5); **r/u** Stanford (d. Drake-Brockman 6–3 6–2, Frazier 6–1 6–1, Seles 7–6 6–4, Coetzer 6–4 6–0, lost Hingis 6–0 6–2); **sf** FC Cup (d. Barabanschikova 6–7 6–4 6–3, Capriati 6–0 5–7 6–4, Coetzer 6–1 6–3, lost Seles 6–3 6–4), **sf** Toronto (d. Yoshida 6–3 3–6 6–1, Basuki 6–1 6–4, Davenport 6–4 4–6 6–2, lost Seles 6–2 7–5), **sf** Moscow (d. Schnyder 7–5 2–6 6–1, Testud 6–1 6–4, lost Novotna 6–4 6–1). **CAREER HIGHLIGHTS – SINGLES: Wimbledon – won 1994** (d. Simpson-Alter 6–1 6–3, Miyagi 6–1 7–6, Tauziat 6–1 6–3, Radford 3–6 6–3 6–4, Davenport 6–2 6–7 6–3, McNeil 3–6 6–2 10–8, Navratilova 6–4 3–6 6–3), **sf 1993** (d. Helgeson 7–5 6–3, Wiesner 6–1 4–6 6–1, Paradis-Mangon 7–5 6–0, Basuki 3–6 6–2 6–2, Sukova 6–1 6–4, lost Graf [1] 7–6 6–3), **sf 1995** (d. Carlsson 6–1 6–1, Kandarr 6–4 6–3, Stafford 6–1 6–1, Kamstra 6–2 6–3, Sabatini 7–5 7–6, lost Sanchez Vicario 6–3 6–7 6–1); **Australian Open – sf 1995** (d. Rittner 6–3 6–2, Martinek 6–1 6–3, Boogert 6–3 2–6 6–3, Spirlea 6–2 6–7 6–2, Davenport 6–3 4–6 6–3, lost Pierce 6–3 6–1), **qf 1994** (d. Zvereva 5–7 6–4 6–3, Fendick 6–7 6–1 6–4, Frazier 6–3 6–0, Rubin 7–6 6–3, lost Date 6–2 4–6 6–3), **qf 1996** (d. Wood 6–4 6–1, Labat 6–2 6–4, Kandarr 6–3 6–0, Davenport lost Huber 4–6 6–2 6–1); **French Open – sf 1994** (d. Neiland 6–2 6–3, Helgeson 6–2 6–3, Schultz 7–5 6–3, Dechaume-Balleret 6–1 6–2, Hack 2–6 6–0 6–2, lost Sanchez Vicario 6–3 6–1), **sf 1995** (d. Hack 6–0 6–0, Oremans 6–2 6–3, Halard 6–1 6–2, Serra-Zanetti 6–0 6–1, Ruano-Pascual 2–6 6–0 6–3, lost Graf 7–5 6–3), **sf 1996** (d. Callens 6–1 6–1, Zrubakova 6–3 7–5, Grossman 6–2 6–1, Coetzer 6–2 6–3, Davenport 6–1 6–3, lost Graf 6–3 6–1); **qf 1989** (d. Herr 6–3 6–2, Pospisilova 6–0 6–4, Amiach 6–3 6–3, K. Maleeva 6–0 6–1, lost Graf 6–0 6–4), **qf 1990** (d. Thompson 7–5 6–1, Etchemendy 7–6 6–3, Zrubakova 6–1 6–3, Probst 6–3 6–3, lost Graf 6–1 6–3), **qf 1991** (d. Wiesner 6–4 6–3, Rehe 6–1 7–6, Cunningham, 6–1 6–4, Capriati 6–3 6–3, lost Seles 6–0 7–5), **qf 1992** (d. Gildemeister 6–2 7–6, Martinek 6–2 6–0, Grossman 6–2 6–2, Meskhi 6–4 7–5, lost Sabatini 3–6 6–3 6–2), **qf 1993** (d. Ghirardi 7–5 3–6 6–4, Helgeson 7–5 6–2, Baudone 6–0 7–5, Wiesner 6–3 6–3, lost Huber 6–7 6–4 6–4); **US Open – sf 1995** (d. Rinaldi-Stunkel 6–2 6–2, Po 6–1 6–4, Sawamatsu 6–1 6–2, Garrison-Jackson 7–6 7–5, Schultz-McCarthy 3–6 7–6 6–2, lost Seles 6–2 6–2), **sf 1996** (d. Dragomir 6–2 6–0, Tauziat 6–1 6–3, Sukova 6–4 6–3, Carlsson 6–2 6–1, Wild 7–6 6–0, lost Seles 6–4 6–3), **qf 1991** (d. Dahlman 6–1 6–1, Basuki 6–3 6–4, Fendick 7–5 6–3, Garrison 6–4 6–4, lost Graf 6–1 6–3); **Olympics – qf 1992** (d. Wiesner 4–6 6–1 6–2, Cecchini 6–4 6–3, Coetzer 6–4 6–3, lost Sanchez Vicario 6–4 6–4), **qf 1996** (d. Schnyder 6–1 6–2, Zrubakova 6–1 6–4, Zvereva 6–2 7–5, lost M. J. Fernandez 3–6 6–2 6–3). **CAREER HIGHLIGHTS – DOUBLES:** (with Sanchez Vicario) **French Open – r/u 1992** (lost G. Fernandez/Zvereva 6–3 6–2); **Olympics – r/u silver medal 1992** (lost G./M. J. Fernandez 7–5 2–6 6–2).

MARION MARUSKA (AUT)

Born Modling, 15 December 1972; lives Hinterbruhl; RH; 2HB; 5ft 8in; 134lb; turned pro 1992; career singles titles 1: final 1997 WTA ranking 55; 1997 prize money $91,411.

1988: (594). **1989:** (341). **1990:** (179) Won European Jun 18s and Wels Futures. **1991:** (109) A –, F –, W –, US 1. **1992:** (234) A 1, F –, W –, US –. Won Ronneby Futures. **1993:** (351) A –, F –, W –, US –. **1994:** (206) A –, F –, W –, US –. R/u in 2 satellite events. **1995:** (179) Won Plovdiv Futures. **1996:** (145) A –, F –, W –, US –. **1997:** A –, F –, W 2, US 1. Upset Huber and Wiesner to take her 1st tour title at Auckland in Jan., surprised Habsudova on her way to f Prague and reached qf Bol, where she was r/u doubles with Gaidano. **1997 HIGHLIGHTS – SINGLES: Wimbledon 2r** (d. Gersi 7–6 6–2, lost Majoli [seed 4] 6–3 6–3), **US Open 1r** (lost Schett 6–1 6–0); **won** Auckland (d. Hudson 6–0 6–2, Labat 6–7 6–0 6–3, Huber 6–4 2–6 6–2, Tanasugarn 3–6 6–3 6–3, Wiesner 6–3 6–1); **r/u** Prague (d. Studenikova 6–0 6–2, Courtois w.o., Habsudova 7–5 1–6 6–4, Cristea 6–2 6–1, lost Kruger 6–1 6–1). **1997 HIGHLIGHTS – DOUBLES:** (with Gaidano) **r/u** Bol (lost Montalvo/Nagyova 6–3 6–1).

NANA MIYAGI (JPN)

Born Seattle, Wash., USA, 10 April 1971; lives Okinawa; RH; 2HF; 2HB; 5ft 4in; 118lb; turned pro 1988; career singles titles 0; final 1997 WTA ranking 101 singles, 18 doubles; 1997 prize money $168,222.

Coached by her father, Murray, a Canadian/American. Moved to Japan at age 13. **1988:** (198). **1989:** (102) Qf Canadian Open (d. Zvereva) and joined Japan's Fed Cup squad. **1990:** (110) A 2, F 2, W 1, US 1. In singles reached qf Tokyo Pan Pacific and in doubles won Schenectady with May. **1991:** (144) A 2, F 1, W 1, US –. Upset Date on her way to qf Tokyo Pan Pacific in singles and won Pattaya City doubles with Wibowo. **1992:** (116) A 1, F –, W –, US –. Reached sf Taipei on the main tour and won York Futures. Out of action for 5 months with right knee and shoulder injuries. **1993:** (308) A 1, F –, W –, US –. Although she was still restricted by her injuries, she won Sapporo and Taipei doubles with Basuki. **1994:** (58) A –, F –, W 2, US –. Appeared in sf Tokyo Nicherei (d. Davenport and Hack and took a set off Sanchez Vicario), reached qf Jakarta and Taipei and played 2 doubles f with Basuki. **1995:** (126) A 1, F –, W 1, US 1. Reached sf Tokyo Japan Open and qf Jakarta. **1996:** (60) A 2, F 1, W 1, US 1. Reached her 1st f on the main tour at Surabaya and during the year upset Kamio at Hobart, Hingis at LIPC and Appelmans at Tokyo Japan Open. Played 2 doubles f with different partners, but won no title. **1997:** A 1, F 1, W 1, US 2. In singles her best showing was qf Jakarta, but in doubles she reached 4 f with 3 different partners, joining with Kijimuta to win Gold Coast and Hobart, and taking Oklahoma with Hiraki. **1997 HIGHLIGHTS – SINGLES: Australian Open 1r** (lost Schett 7–6 7–6), **French Open 1r** (lost Perfetti 7–6 2–6 6–0), **Wimbledon 1r** (lost Tauziat 6–3 6–4), **US Open 2r** (d. Gorrochategui 6–2 7–5, lost Fusai 6–3 3–6 6–4). **1997 HIGHLIGHTS – DOUBLES:** (with Kijimuta unless stated) **won** Gold Coast (d. Dragomir/Farina 7–6 6–1), **won** Hobart (d. Rittner/Van Roost 6–3 6–1), (with Hiraki) **won** Oklahoma City (d. Werdel-Witmeyer/Whitlinger-Jones 6–4 6–1); (with McQuillan) **r/u** Edinburgh (lost Arendt/Bollegraf 6–1 3–6 7–5).

CORINA MORARIU (USA)

Born Detroit, Mich., 26 January 1978; lives Boca Raton, Fla.; RH; 5ft 8in; 130lb; career singles titles 0; final 1997 WTA ranking 60; 1997 prize money $115,512.

Coached by Andrew Turcinovich. **1994:** (622) Won Australian Open Jun doubles with Varmuzova. **1995:** (246) In Jun doubles with Varmuzova she won Australian Open, French Open and US Open, finishing No. 2 on the ITF Jun doubles rankings. In the senior game, she won 3 singles and 4 doubles titles on the Futures circuit. **1996:** (122) A –, F –, W 1, US 1. Reached qf Tokyo Japan Open after qualifying. **1997:** A 1, F –, W 2, US 2. Broke into top 100 at beginning of May after playing her 1st f on the main tour at Bol, having gained direct entry via the feed-up system. She also reached qf Luxembourg, Tokyo Japan Open (r/u doubles with Guse) and Pattaya (won doubles with Kunce) and took Bogota Futures. **1997 HIGHLIGHTS – SINGLES: Australian Open 1r** (lost Bradtke 6–3 6–2), **Wimbledon 2r** (d. Taylor 6–2 6–1, lost Testud 6–7 6–3 6–1), **US Open 2r** (d. Ellwood 7–6 7–6, lost Osterloh 6–7 6–1 3–0 ret'd); **r/u** Bol (d. Palaversic 6–4 6–4, Chladkova 6–3 7–6, Kruger 6–1 2–6 6–4, Gagliardi 6–1 1–6 6–3, lost Lucic 7–5 6–7 7–6). **1997 HIGHLIGHTS – DOUBLES:** (with Kunce) **won** Pattaya (d. Labat/Van Roost 6–4 7–6); (with Guse) **r/u** Tokyo Japan Open (lost Dechaume-Balleret/Hiraki 6–4 6–2).

HENRIETA NAGYOVA (SVK)

Born Nove Zamky, 15 December 1978, and lives there; RH; 2HB; 5ft 10in; 134lb; turned pro 1994; career singles titles 2; final 1997 WTA ranking 35; 1997 prize money $175,589.

Coached by Lubomir Kurhajec. **1994:** (379) Won French Open Jun doubles with Hingis and on the women's satellite circuit won Olsztyn and Porec back-to-back. **1995:** (137) Continuing to make her mark on the satellite circuit, she won Bordeaux and Athens, where she also took the doubles. **1996:** (42) A –, F 2, W 1, US 2. She broke into the top 100 in Feb., after winning Cali and later Bratislava on the Futures circuit. On the main tour, unseeded at Warsaw, she upset Paulus to take her 1st title in her 1st f at that level, upset Appelmans on her way to sf Cardiff, and reached same stage Pattaya, as well as qf Palermo, Karlovy Vary and Luxembourg (d. Coetzer). **1997:** A 3, F 1, W 1, US 2. The highlight of her year came at Pattaya, in the last tourn, when she upset Dragomir and Van Roost to take the title. She had earlier upset Dragomir on her way to f Warsaw, and reached the same stage Maria Lankowitz, plus sf Budapest and qf Luxembourg. She won Bol doubles with Montalvo and took both singles and doubles at Bratislava Futures. **1997 HIGHLIGHTS – SINGLES: Australian Open 3r** (d. Gagliardi 6–3 7–6, Labat 6–3 6–2, lost M. J. Fernandez [seed 14] 6–2 6–1), **French Open 1r** (lost Hingis [seed 1] 6–0 6–2), **Wimbledon 1r** (lost Spirlea [seed 12] 6–1 6–0), **US Open 2r** (d. Olsza 6–3 6–0, lost Kruger 6–4 7–6); **won** Pattaya (d. Endo 1–6 6–4 6–2, Wang 7–5 6–3, Kleinova 6–3 6–4, Dragomir 4–6 7–5 6–2, Van Roost 7–5 6–7 7–5), **won** Bratislava Futures (d. Leon-Garcia 6–4 6–0); **r/u** Warsaw (d. Kleinova 6–4 6–4, Lugina 6–2 6–1, Torrens-Valero 6–3 6–1, Dragomir 6–4 7–5, lost Paulus 6–4 6–4), **r/u** Maria Lankowitz (d. Begerow 3–6 6–4 3–2 ret'd, Gorrochategui 7–5 6–4, Schnyder 0–6 6–4 6–2, Babel 6–1 7–6, lost Schett 3–6 6–2 6–3); **sf** Budapest (d. Serna 6–0 7–5, Leon-Garcia 6–2 1–6 6–4, Kruger 4–6 6–4 6–3, lost Coetzer 6–7 6–1 6–0). **1997 HIGHLIGHTS – DOUBLES:** (with Montalvo) **won** Bol (d. Gaidano/Maruska 6–3 6–1).

LARISA NEILAND (LAT)

Born Lvov, Ukraine, 21 July 1966; lives Yurmala; RH; 5ft 6in; 134lb; turned pro 1988; career singles titles 2; final 1997 WTA ranking 85 singles, 9 doubles; 1997 prize money $306,340 ($3,533,154).

Husband Alex Neiland (married 21 December 1989). Maiden name Savchenko. 1983: A –, F –, W –, US 1. Ranked 10 on ITF Jun list. **1984:** (138) A 1, F 3, W 1, US –. Won 2 titles on satellite circuit. **1985:** (55) A –, F 1, W 3, US –. Reached sf VS Denver and joined Fed Cup team. **1986:** (35) F 2, W 2, US –. Showed affinity for grass courts, reaching sf Birmingham, qf Eastbourne, and upsetting Rehe at Wimbledon. Qualified with Parkhomenko for VS Champ doubles March and Nov. **1987:** (24) A –, F –, W 2, US 2. Won 4 doubles titles with Parkhomenko and ousted Navratilova/Shriver *en route* to sf Wimbledon. **1988:** (16) A –, F –, W 4, US qf. R/u VS California (d. Mandlikova and Sabatini), sf Pan Pacific Open (d. Zvereva) and qf Eastbourne (d. Kohde-Kilsch), US Open and Olympics. In doubles with Zvereva r/u Wimbledon and VS Champs, for which she qualified in both singles and doubles. **1989:** (20) A –, F 3, W 1, US 4. Upset Navratilova *en route* to f VS California but then, frustrated by her poor form in singles, she talked of retiring after US Open. However, there she reached last 16, upsetting Shriver, and followed up with sf Moscow and r/u VS Chicago. In doubles won French Open and r/u

Wimbledon and VS Champs with Zvereva, reaching 9 more f and winning 4. **1990:** (87) A 1, F 2, W 2, US 3. In singles qf Tokyo Toray and Birmingham. In doubles r/u French Open and won 3 titles with Zvereva, taking another with K. Jordan. Qualified for VS Champs with Zvereva but lost 1r to Adams/McNeil. **1991:** (48) A 2, F 2, W 2, US 1. Won her 1st singles title at St Petersburg and reached sf Brisbane, upsetting Novotna. In doubles played 8 f with Zvereva, winning Wimbledon plus 5 others and r/u French Open to qualify for VS Champs; reached another 4 f with Novotna, winning 3 and r/u US Open; and won Auckland with Fendick. **1992:** (59) A 4, F 2, W 1, US 1. In singles reached sf Auckland and last 16 Australian Open, unseeded. In doubles with Novotna won 7 titles and was r/u Wimbledon and US Open to qualify for VS Champs, where they were r/u to Sanchez Vicario/Sukova. She won 1 more title each with Zvereva and Sanchez Vicario and in mixed won Wimbledon with Suk. **1993:** (32) A 1, F 1, W 2, US 1. Won her 2nd career singles title at Schenectady, was r/u Tokyo Pan Pacific (upset McNeil and Novotna) and reached sf Birmingham. She continued to excel in doubles, playing 13 f, of which she won 1 with Martinez and 3 with regular partner Novotna, with whom she was r/u French Open and Wimbledon. They qualified together for VS Champs, where they were runners-up to G. Fernandez/Zvereva – as they were on 5 other occasions. **1994:** (41) A 1, F 1, W qf, US 1. It was a less spectacular year in singles, although she was r/u Schenectady and upset Martinez *en route* to sf Brighton. The highlight, however, came at Wimbledon, where, unseeded, she upset Date and Coetzer on her way to qf. In doubles she played 8 f, winning 6 titles with 5 different partners and in mixed with Olhovskiy won Australian and r/u French Open. **1995:** (97) A 1, F 1, W 2, US 2. Qf FC Cup was her best performance in singles. In doubles she played 13 f with various partners – winning 5 with McGrath, with whom she qualified for VS Champs, and 1 with Sanchez Vicario – and took French Open mixed with Woodforde. **1996:** (62) A 1, F 1, W 3, US 1. She reached qf Birmingham and Rosmalen (d. Schultz-McCarthy), and upset Sawamatsu at Indian Wells and Davenport at Wimbledon. In women's doubles she played 9 f, winning Essen and Berlin with McGrath, with whom she was r/u Wimbledon and qualified for Chase Champs, as well as taking Rosmalen with Schultz-McCarthy, Montreal with Sanchez Vicario and Moscow with Medvedeva. In mixed, with Woodforde, she won Australian Open and was r/u Wimbledon. **1997:** A 2, F 2, W 1, US 1. From 5 women's doubles f with 3 different partners, she won Birmingham with Adams and Luxembourg with Sukova, with whom she qualified for Chase Champs. There they upset G. Fernandez/Zvereva in Fernandez's farewell tourn, but lost sf to Davenport/Novotna. In mixed she was r/u Australian Open with De Jager and Wimbledon with Olhovskiy. **1997 HIGHLIGHTS – SINGLES: Australian Open 2r** (d. Dominikovic 6–2 5–7 6–0, lost Graf 7–5 6–2), **French Open 2r** (d. Sidot 6–2 7–5, lost Grossman 6–4 6–4), **Wimbledon 1r** (lost Kijimuta 7–6 6–2), **US Open 1r** (lost V. Williams 5–7 6–0 6–1). **1997 HIGHLIGHTS – DOUBLES:** (with Sukova unless stated) (with Adams) **won** Birmingham (d. Tauziat/Wild 6–2 6–3), **won** Luxembourg (d. Babel/Courtois 6–2 6–4); (with Schultz-McCarthy) **r/u** Hannover (lost Arendt/Bollegraf 4–6 6–3 7–6), **r/u** Los Angeles (lost Basuki/Vis 7–6 6–3), **r/u** Zurich (lost Hingis/Sanchez Vicario 4–6 6–4 6–1). **MIXED DOUBLES:** (with De Jager) **r/u Australian Open** (lost Leach/Bollegraf 6–3 6–7 7–5), (with Olhovskiy) **r/u** Wimbledon (lost Suk/Sukova 4–6 6–3 6–4). **CAREER HIGHLIGHTS – SINGLES: Wimbledon – qf 1994** [unseeded] (d. Adams 6–4 6–3, Smashnova 6–3 6–4, Date 6–3 6–2, Coetzer 1–6 6–3 6–4, lost McNeil 6–3 6–4); **US Open – qf 1988** (d. Golarsa 7–6 6–2, Burgin 5–7 7–5 6–4, Bassett-Seguso 6–4 6–3, Phelps 6–3 6–1, lost Sabatini 4–6 6–4 6–2). **CAREER HIGHLIGHTS – DOUBLES:** (with Zvereva unless stated) **French Open – won 1989** (d. Graf/Sabatini 6–4 6–4), **r/u 1990** (lost Novotna/Sukova 6–4 7–5), **r/u 1991** (lost G. Fernandez/Novotna 6–4 6–0), (with Novotna) **r/u 1993** (lost G. Fernandez/Zvereva 6–3 7–5); **Wimbledon – won 1991** (d. G. Fernandez/Novotna 6–4 3–6 6–4), **r/u 1988** (lost Graf/Sabatini 6–3 1–6 12–10), **r/u 1989** (lost Novotna/Sukova 6–1 6–2), (with Novotna) **r/u 1993** (lost G. Fernandez/Zvereva 6–4 6–7 6–4), (with McGrath) **r/u 1996** (lost Hingis/Sukova 5–7 7–5 6–1); **US Open** – (with Novotna) **r/u 1991** (lost Shriver/Zvereva 6–4 4–6 7–6); VS Champs – **r/u 1988** (lost Navratilova/Shriver 6–3 6–4), **r/u 1989** (lost Navratilova/ Shriver 6–3 6–2), (with Novotna) **r/u 1993** (lost G. Fernandez/Zvereva 6–3 7–5). **MIXED DOUBLES: Australian Open** – (with Woodforde unless stated) (with Olhovskiy) **won 1994** (d. Woodbridge/Sukova 7–5 6–7 6–2), **won 1996** (d. L. Jensen/Arendt 6–2 6–4), **French Open – won 1995** (d. de Jager/Hetherington 7–6 7–6).

MIRIAM OREMANS (NED)

Born Berlicum, 9 September 1972, and lives there; RH; 5ft 6½in; 143lb; turned pro 1989; career singles titles 0; final 1997 WTA ranking 47; 1997 prize money $180,804.

Coached by Hugo Ekker. At age 12 chose a career in tennis rather than competitive horse-riding, at which she also excelled. **1989:** (–) Won Nat 18s singles and European Jun doubles. In the women's game won 2 titles on the Israeli satellite circuit. **1990:** (191) A –, F –, W –, US 2. **1991:** (148) A 1, F –, W 1, US –. Upset Sawamatsu 1r Tokyo Suntory. **1992:** (132) A –, F –, W 1, US –. Upset Zardo 2r Brisbane, won Linz doubles with Kiene and r/u Wimbledon mixed with Eltingh. **1993:** (31) A 3, F 2, W 4, US 1. She showed she could be a dangerous opponent and swept into the top 50 with some useful upsets across the year. At Eastbourne she surprised Sukova and McNeil *en route* to f, where she took a set off Navratilova on grass; then, unseeded at Wimbledon, she extended Novotna to 3s in last 16. She also appeared in qf Indian Wells (d. Hy), Tokyo Japan Open and Zurich (d. Wiesner), as well as upsetting Huber at LIPC and Halard at Berlin. **1994:** (47) A 1, F 3, W 1, US 1. Restricted by a thigh strain in 1st part of year, she came into her own at French Open, where she upset Navratilova 1r, inflicting her 1st loss at that stage in GS since 1976. Reached sf Zurich (d. Pierce) and took a set off Novotna 1r Wimbledon. **1995:** (42) A 2, F 2, W 3, US 1. Although she reached qf Sydney (d. Frazier), Strasbourg (where she was r/u doubles with Appelmans) and Brighton (d. Novotna), she could progress no further. **1996:** (51) A 1, F 3, W 2, US 2. She reached sf Birmingham, plus qf Cardiff and Paris

Open, where she upset Wiesner in a match that lasted more than 3 hours and ran to 3 tbs. Played 2 doubles f with Appelmans, but won no title. **1997:** A 1, F 1, W 1, US 3. She was r/u Rosmalen (d. Habsudova), reached qf Hannover (d. Huber) and Luxembourg, and upset M. J. Fernandez in Fed Cup as NED d. USA. **1997 HIGHLIGHTS – SINGLES: Australian Open 1r** (lost Martinez [seed 3] 6–0 6–2), **French Open 1r** (lost Ghirardi-Rubbi 2–6 6–2 6–3), **Wimbledon 1r** (lost G. Fernandez 7–6 6–3), **US Open 3r** (d. Makarova 3–6 6–4 6–4, Babel 7–5 6–1, lost Seles [seed 2] 6–1 6–1); **r/u** Rosmalen (d. Schnyder 7–5 6–2, Maleeva 6–4 7–5, Habsudova 6–2 7–5, Huber 4–6 6–4 ret'd, lost Dragomir 5–7 6–2 6–4). **1997 HIGHLIGHTS – DOUBLES:** (with Appelmans) **r/u** LIPC (lost Sanchez Vicario/Zvereva 6–2 6–3).

BARBARA PAULUS (AUT)

Born Vienna, 1 September 1970; lives Hinterbruehl; RH; 5ft 9½in; 138lb; turned pro 1986; career singles titles 6; final 1997 WTA ranking 24; 1997 prize money $252,231 ($1,184,119).

Coached by Peter Eipeldauer. **1982:** Won Nat 12 for 2nd year. **1985:** Won Nat 18s. **1986:** (187) Won Nat Indoor and Outdoor, reached qf Bregenz and played Fed Cup. **1987:** (96) A –, F 3, W 1, US –. Appeared in qf Guaruja and won Wels on the Futures circuit. **1988:** (25) A –, F 3, W –, US –. Won her 1st primary circuit title at Geneva over McNeil, r/u Sofia and upset Kohde-Kilsch 1r Filderstadt. **1989:** (24) A –, F 2, W –, US 4. R/u Arcachon, sf Geneva (d. Evert) and surprised Novotna at US Open, where she was unseeded. **1990:** (15) A 4, F –, W 1, US 4. In her best year she won Geneva, was r/u Sydney, Palermo and Filderstadt (d. Garrison and Sabatini) and reached sf San Diego and Leipzig. **1991:** (25) A 2, F –, W –, US 2. Reached sf Sydney (d. Maleeva-Fragniere), Leipzig (d. K. Maleeva) and Brighton, where she was forced to def. ill. **1992:** (205) A 1, F –, W –, US 1. Out of action March to May following knee surgery and suffering from a wrist injury and out again from Oct. with recurring wrist problems. **1993:** (259) A –, F –, W –, US –. **1994:** (108) A –, F –, W –, US –. Reached qf Pattaya City (d. Harvey-Wild) and won Maribor Futures. **1995:** (23) A 4, F 1, W 2, US 2. Having won no title on the main tour for 5 years, she returned to her old place in the rankings with the titles at Warsaw and Pattaya City, r/u finish at Brighton, sf showing at Styrian Open and an upset of Majoli at US Open. **1996:** (10) A 2, F 3, W –, US 3. She returned to the top 20 and moved on into top 10 1st time in Nov. after winning Styria, r/u Auckland, FC Cup (unseeded, upsetting M. Maleeva and Martinez), Strasbourg, Warsaw and Moscow, as well as sf Luxembourg and qf Berlin and Philadelphia. She qualified for her 1st Chase Champs, but fell 1r to Davenport. **1997:** A –, F 4, W 2, US –. An injured thumb kept her out at the beginning of the year, but she returned to reach sf Hannover, following with the same stage LIPC and Palermo, then progressing to the title at Warsaw the following week. She reached a 2nd f at Luxembourg, where she extended Coetzer to 7–5 3s, reached qf Maria Lankowitz (but withdrew with tendinitis of right elbow), and took a set off Hingis at French Open. **1997 HIGHLIGHTS – SINGLES: French Open last 16** [seed 16] (d. Whitlinger-Jones 6–0 6–1, Wang 6–2 6–2, Farina 6–4 6–1, lost Hingis [seed 1] 6–3 0–6 6–0), **Wimbledon 2r** [seed 16] (d. Boogert 6–3 1–6 6–3, lost Kijimuta 5–7 6–3 6–3); **won** Warsaw (d. Babel 6–0 6–0, Leon-Garcia 6–2 6–0, Ruano-Pascual 6–2 6–1, Nagyova 6–4 6–4); **r/u** (d. Dechy 6–4 6–4, Mauresmo 7–6 6–3, Appelmans 3–6 6–3 6–2, Sidot 6–3 6–4, lost Coetzer 6–4 3–6 7–5); **sf** Hannover (d. A. Miller 6–0 6–0, Carlsson 6–3 7–5, Oremans 7–6 6–4, lost Majoli 7–6 6–4), **sf** LIPC (d. Wagner 6–1 6–3, Tauziat 6–1 6–7 6–1, Fusai 6–1 2–6 6–1, Testud 6–3 6–3, lost Seles 6–1 6–0), **sf** Palermo (d. Dopfer 7–5 2–1 ret'd, Cecchini 6–1 6–4, Gorrochategui 2–6 6–3 6–2, lost Makarova 6–4 7–5).

SARAH PITKOWSKI (FRA)

Born Seclin, 13 November 1975; lives Vallee d'Ascq; RH; 5ft 2½in; 103lb; turned pro 1993; career singles titles 0; final 1997 WTA ranking 56; 1997 prize money $97,676.

Coached by Niki Kelaidis. **1991:** (885). **1992:** (215) Won Nat 18s and took Futures titles in Swindon and Madeira. **1993:** (151) A –, F 1, W –, US –. In Jun tennis won European 18s and was a member of French team that won Annie Soisbault Cup. On the women's tour she took Caserta Futures. **1994:** (111) A –, F –, W –, US –. Won 2 Futures titles. **1995:** (107) A 2, F 2, W 1, US 1. Appeared in her 1st qf on the main tour at Surabaya and won 2 Futures titles again. **1996:** (87) A 1, F 3, W –, US 2. Reached qf Palermo and Surabaya. **1997:** A 1, F 2, W 2, US 2. Progressed to her 1st sf on the main tour at Cardiff, as well as qf Bol and Surabaya, and won Reims Futures. **1997 HIGHLIGHTS – SINGLES: Australian Open 1r** (lost Grzybowska 4–6 6–3 6–1), **French Open 2r** (d. Lubiani 7–6 6–2, lost Seles [seed 3] 6–3 7–5), **Wimbledon 2r** (d. Lubiani 6–3 4–6 6–1, lost Serna 6–2 6–0), **US Open 2r** (d. Simpson 6–1 4–6 7–6, lost Perfetti 6–4 6–3); **won** Reims Futures (d. Krivencheva 7–5 6–1); **sf** Cardiff (d. Leon-Garcia 6–3 6–2, Whitlinger-Jones 3–6 6–0 7–5, Carlsson 7–5 6–4, lost Dechaume-Balleret 6–3 6–4).

KIMBERLY PO (USA)

Born Los Angeles, Cal., 20 October 1971; lives Rolling Hills, Cal.; RH; 2HB; 5ft 3in; 120lb; turned pro 1991; career singles titles 0; final 1997 WTA ranking 23 singles, 23 doubles; 1997 prize money $286,866 ($1,005,359).

Coached by Donnie Young. **1988:** (541) Member of US National team. **1989:** (241) Won Fayetteville on the USTA circuit. **1990:** (459). **1991:** (103) A –, F –. W –, US 3. Reached qf Phoenix on the main tour and won Evansville Challenger. **1992:** (70) A 3, F 1, W 2, US 3. Extended Navratilova to 3s 2r Wimbledon and reached qf VS Los Angeles. **1993:** (42) A 3, F 3, W 1, US 3. She finished the year on a high note, upsetting Sukova on her way to sf VS Philadelphia. Reached qf Los Angeles again and upset Fendick at Oakland, as well as taking sets off Pierce at French Open and Magdalena Maleeva at US Open. **1994:** (71) A 1, F 2, W 2, US 1. She salvaged her season again at Philadelphia, where she reached her only qf on the main tour. Won the Karen Krantzcke Sportsmanship Award. **1995:** (164) A –, F 1, W 1, US 2. She reached no qf all year, and slipped down the rankings. **1996:** (28) A –, F –, W 2, US 3. Working more on strategies with her new coach, Donnie Young, she moved back into the top 50. Upset Huber and M. J. Fernandez on her way to sf Montreal, removed Pierce to reach same stage Tokyo Nicherei and surprised Date 1r US Open. She also reached qf Tokyo Japan Open (after qualifying), Quebec City and Oakland (d. M. Maleeva). In doubles with Frazier played 3 f but won no title. **1997:** A qf, F 3, W 1, US 3. She broke into the top 20 1st time with sf Oklahoma City and Tokyo Japan Open, qf Australian Open (unseeded), Stanford and Tokyo Nicherei, and the Midland Futures title. Her biggest upsets during the year were Davenport at Australian Open and Huber at French Open. **1997 HIGHLIGHTS – SINGLES: Australian Open qf** [unseeded] (d. Leon Garcia 4–6 7–6 6–2, Sugiyama 6–0 4–6 6–3, Hiraki 6–2 6–2, Davenport [seed 7] 7–6 6–4, lost Coetzer [seed 12] 6–4 6–1), **French Open 3r** (d. Huber [seed 8] 6–3 4–6 6–3, Yoshida 6–3 6–0, lost Raymond 6–4 2–6 6–1), **Wimbledon 1r** (lost Guse 3–6 7–5 6–2), **US Open 3r** [seed 16] (d. Martincova 6–4 6–1, Schett 6–3 4–6 7–5, lost Serna 6–4 6–3); **won** Midland Futures (d. Tu 6–2 6–3); **sf** Oklahoma City (d. Whitlinger Jones 7–6 6–4, Lee 6–1 6–4, Cacic 6–3 6–3, lost Davenport 1–6 6–2 6–3), **sf** Tokyo Japan Open (d. Watanabe 6–2 6–2, Wang 4–6 6–3 6–3, lost Sugiyama 5–7 6–4 6–1). **1997 HIGHLIGHTS – DOUBLES:** (with Frazier) **r/u** San Diego (lost Hingis/Sanchez Vicario 6–3 7–5). **CAREER HIGHLIGHTS – SINGLES: Australian Open – qf 1997.**

LISA RAYMOND (USA)

Born Norristown, Pa, 10 Aug 1973; lives Wayne, Pa; RH; 5ft 5in; 122lb; turned pro 1993; career singles titles 1; final 1997 WTA ranking 17 singles, 12 doubles; 1997 prize money $450,070 ($1,372,170).

Coached by Eric Riley. Won 5 Nat Jun Champs. **1988:** R/u USTA 18s GC. **1989:** (438) A –, F –, W –, US 1. No. 2 in USTA 18s. **1990:** (327) A –, F –, W –, US 1. R/u US Open Jun doubles with de Lone and was ranked No. 1 in USTA 18s. **1991:** (251) A –, F –, W –, US –. Qf Westchester. **1992:** (76) A –, F –, W –, US 2. A freshman at Univ. of Florida, she won NCAA Champs over McCarthy. In the women's game she reached qf Puerto Rico and Philadelphia. **1993:** (54) A –, F –, W 4, US 2. Took Nat Collegiate title 2nd straight year, winning all 34 of her matches. Turned pro at end of college year and at Wimbledon, unseeded and in only her 2nd tourn as pro, she took Capriati to 8–6 3s in last 16, breaking into top 50. At end of year she reached sf Sapporo and won Tokyo Nicherei doubles with Rubin. **1994:** (44) A 2, F 1, W 1, US 3. In singles she reached f Lucerne, unseeded (d. Mag. Maleeva and Frazier), and appeared in qf Eastbourne. In doubles with Davenport was r/u French Open, won Indian Wells and qualified for VS Champs. **1995:** (20) A 3, F –, W 4, US 2. Upset Zvereva, Frazier and Garrison-Jackson on her way to f Chicago (unseeded) and reached same stage San Diego, plus qf Oklahoma. Played 2 doubles f, winning Indian Wells with Davenport. **1996:** (33) A 1, F 1, W 2, US 4. Having failed to pass qf in singles all year, she upset Schultz-McCarthy on the way to her 1st main tour title at Quebec City in Oct. She also reached qf Oklahoma, Eastbourne and Philadelphia (d. Martinez) and extended M. Maleeva to 12–10 fs 1r French Open. In doubles she won Chicago and Philadelphia with Stubbs, with whom she qualified for Chase Champs, and took a 1st GS title at US Open mixed with Galbraith. **1997:** A 2, F 4, W 2, US 2. An impressive 10-day period in Oct., with 4 major upsets, saw her move into the top 15 1st time. She upset Novotna and Spirlea on her way to f Filderstadt, where she lost to Hingis, then at Zurich the following week, she removed Coetzer before becoming one of just 5 players all year to beat Hingis – only to lose sf to Tauziat. She was also r/u Oklahoma City, reached sf Quebec City and qf Chicago, and upset Dragomir at US Open. She played 5 women's doubles f, winning Luxembourg and Philadelphia with Stubbs, r/u Australian Open with Davenport and r/u French Open with G. Fernandez. In mixed she was r/u Australian Open with Galbraith. **1997 HIGHLIGHTS – SINGLES: Australian Open 2r** (d. Drake-Brockman 6–2 6–2, lost Hingis [seed 4] 6–4 6–2), **French Open last 16** [unseeded] (d. Maleeva 4–6 7–5 6–3, Tanasugarn 6–1 6–1, Po 6–4 2–6 6–1, lost M. J. Fernandez [seed 12] 6–7 6–2 6–2), **Wimbledon 2r** (d. Martincova 6–4 6–2, lost Arendt 1–6 6–4 6–3), **US Open 2r** (d. Dragomir [seed 15] 6–2 3–6 6–3, lost Maleeva 3–6 6–2 6–4); **r/u** Oklahoma City (d. Kschwendt 5–7 6–2 7–5, Dechaume-Balleret 7–5 7–6, Lubiani 6–1 6–0, lost Davenport 6–4 6–2), **r/u** Filderstadt (d. Farina 6–3 6–2, Novotna 3–6 6–4 6–4, Sawamatsu 6–2 6–3, Spirlea 6–3 6–1, lost Hingis 6–4 6–2); **sf** Zurich (d. Sukova 7–5 6–3, Coetzer 7–5 6–3, Hingis 4–6 6–2 7–5, lost Tauziat 6–3 7–5), **sf** Quebec City (d. Lubiani 6–3 6–7 6–4, Grzybowska 6–2 7–5, lost Van Roost 6–2 3–6 6–1). **1997 HIGHLIGHTS – DOUBLES:** (with Stubbs unless stated) (with Davenport) **r/u Australian Open** (lost Hingis/Zvereva 6–2 6–2), (with G. Fernandez) **r/u French Open** (lost G. Fernandez/Zvereva 6–2 6–3); **won** Luxembourg (d. Fusai/Tauziat 6–4 5–7 7–5), **won** Philadelphia (d. Davenport/Novotna 6–3 7–5); (with Tauziat) **r/u** Indian Wells (lost Davenport/Zvereva 6–3 6–2). **MIXED DOUBLES:** (with Galbraith) **r/u French Open** (lost Bhupathi/Hiraki 6–4 6–1). **CAREER HIGHLIGHTS – DOUBLES:** (with Davenport unless stated) **Australian Open – r/u 1997; French Open – r/u 1994** (lost G. Fernandez/Zvereva 6–2 6–2), (with G. Fernandez) **r/u 1997**. **MIXED DOUBLES:** (with Galbraith) **US Open – won 1996** (d. Leach/Bollegraf 7–6 7–6).

AUBRIE RIPPNER (USA)

Born Cal., 21 January 1980, and lives there; RH; 2HB; 5ft 8in; 118lb; career singles titles 0; final 1997 WTA ranking 154; 1997 prize money $32,355.

Known as Brie Rippner. Coached by her father, Rob Rippner. **1995:** Won USTA Nat Jun Champs. **1997:** R/u Wimbledon Jun to Black and won San Antonio on the ITF circuit. **1997 HIGHLIGHTS – SINGLES: US Open 2r** (d. Medvedeva 6–2 6–2, lost Lucic 6–0 6–1); **won** San Antonio ITF (d. Muric 6–2 6–4)

BARBARA RITTNER (GER)

Born Krefeld, 25 April 1973; lives Cologne; RH; 2HB; 5ft 8in; 145lb; turned pro 1989; career singles titles 1; final 1997 WTA ranking 76; 1997 prize money $119,548.

Coached by Karsten Saniter. **1989:** (349) Won Nat Jun Champs **1990:** (107) Enjoyed some success on the satellite circuits. **1991:** (43) A 2, F 1, W 1, US 3. Won Wimbledon Jun over Makarova and Australian Open Jun doubles with Habsudova. In the senior game she reached her 1st tour f at St Petersburg and appeared in qf Wellington, Puerto Rico and Leipzig. **1992:** (32) A 2, F 2, W 3, US 1. A member of the winning German Fed Cup team, she won her 1st primary circuit title at Schenectady and upset Tauziat on her way to last 16 Olympics, unseeded. She also surprised Zrubakova at Sydney and Cecchini *en route* to sf Essen. **1993:** (34) A 3, F 3, W 2, US 2. R/u San Marino and reached qf Sydney (d. Sukova), VS Florida (d. Zvereva), Leipzig and Filderstadt as well as appearing in 2 doubles f with Labat. **1994:** (40) A 3, F 3, W 3, US 3. Out for a month following an appendectomy in Feb. She did not advance beyond qf all year, but reached that stage at Brisbane, Sydney (d. Wiesner), Hamburg, Styria, Schenectady (d. Hack) and Zurich (d. Appelmans). **1995:** (52) A 1, F 1, W –, US 1. Upset Majoli on her way to f Linz, where she took a set off Novotna, and reached qf Delray Beach, Zagreb and Hamburg. **1996:** (52) A 2, F 4, W 1, US 3. Removed Pierce at French Open, where she was unseeded; incensed by Pierce's gamesmanship, she began to retaliate in an ill-humoured match, after which Pierce was booed off the court. Upset Schultz-McCarthy at US Open and Appelmans on her way to qf Essen. From 2 doubles f, she won Luxembourg with Van Roost. **1997:** A 1, F 1, W 2, US 1. Upset Appelmans *en route* to qf Linz. **1997 HIGHLIGHTS – SINGLES: Australian Open 1r** (lost Hingis [seed 4] 6–1 7–5), **French Open 1r** (lost Van Roost 3–0 ret'd), **Wimbledon 2r** (d. Sidot 7–6 6–4, lost Kournikova 4–6 7–6 6–3), **US Open 1r** (lost Osterloh 6–3 1–6 6–3). **1997 HIGHLIGHTS – DOUBLES:** (with Van Roost) **r/u** Hobart (lost Kijimuta/Miyagi 6–3 6–1).

VIRGINIA RUANO-PASCUAL (ESP)

Born Madrid, 21 September 1973; lives Valencia; RH; 5ft 6½in; 134lb; turned pro 1992; career singles titles 1; final 1997 WTA ranking 54; 1997 prize money $125,986.

1989: (496). **1990:** (309). **1991:** (261). **1992:** (123) A –, F –, W –, US 1. Qf Sao Paulo (d. F. Bonsignori) and won Bilbao Futures. **1993:** (125) A –, F –, W –, US 1. Reached qf Liege (d. Zardo) and Kitzbuhel (d. Rittner) and played on winning Spanish Fed Cup team. **1994:** (161) A 1, F –, W –, US –. **1995:** (64) A –, F qf, W 1, US 1. Having stretched Sanchez Vicario to 3s in Rome, she made an impact at French Open, where she was unseeded. On the Futures circuit she won Zaragoza. **1996:** (98) A 1, F 1, W 1, US 1. Reached qf Hobart (d. Hack) and won Bronx Futures. Played in ESP Fed Cup team r/u to USA. **1997:** A 2, F 3, W 2, US 1. Won her 1st title on the main tour at Cardiff, unseeded, and reached sf Warsaw, plus qf Madrid (d. Frazier) and Palermo. **1997 HIGHLIGHTS – SINGLES: Australian Open 2r** (d. Torrens-Valero 6–0 3–6 6–3, lost Dragomir 7–6 6–1), **French Open 3r** (d. Montolio 6–0 6–0, Cocheteux 6–4 6–2, lost Spirlea [seed 13] 6–1 6–1), **Wimbledon 2r** (d. Dopfer 6–2 6–2, lost Pierce [seed 9] 6–0 2–6 6–3), **US Open 1r** (lost Novotna [seed 3] 6–0 6–4); **won** Cardiff (d. Ellwood 3–6 7–6 7–6, Grossman 6–0 6–0, Langrova 6–4 6–2, Grande 6–3 3–6 6–4, Dechaume-Balleret 6–1 3–6 6–2); **sf** Warsaw (d. Schett 6–1 5–7 7–5, Nemeckova 6–4 4–6 6–1, Kruger 7–5 7–5, lost Paulus 6–2 6–1). **CAREER HIGHLIGHTS – SINGLES: French Open – qf 1995** [unseeded] (d. Demongeot 7–6 6–2, Fendick 7–5 6–1, Tauziat 6–2 7–6, Dragomir 2–6 6–0 6–3, lost Martinez 6–0 6–4).

CHANDA RUBIN (USA)

Born Lafayette, La, 18 February 1976, and lives there; RH; 2HB; 5ft 6in; 128lb; turned pro 1991; career singles titles 1; final 1997 WTA ranking 30; 1997 prize money $226,106 ($1,391,349).

Coached by Marcel Freeman. Did not attend a tennis academy, as her parents put an academic background before tennis. **1988:** Won Nat 12s and Orange Bowl in same age group. **1989:** Won Nat 14s. **1990:** (522) A –, F –, W –, US 1. **1991:** (83) A –, F –, W –, US 2. She announced her presence on the senior tour by upsetting Bollegraf at LIPC in spring, and at end of year broke into the top 100 after reaching her 1st tour f at Phoenix. **1992:** (68) A 1, F 1, W 1, US 4. Surprised K. Maleeva at US Open, where she was unseeded, and upset Zvereva VS Florida. In the Jun game won Wimbledon over Courtois. **1993:** (69) A 1, F –, W 2, US 3. Reached her 1st main tour sf at Birmingham (d. Coetzer) and appeared in qf FC Cup. In doubles won Tokyo Nicherei with Raymond. **1994:** (25) A 4, F 1, W 1, US 1. Broke into top 50, after a fine start to the year in which she followed sf appearance at Hobart with upsets of K. Maleeva and Coetzer at Australian Open. She went on to reach f Chicago (d. Mag. Maleeva) and sf VS Florida (d. Coetzer), Lucerne (d. Sukova) and Quebec City. Played 2 doubles f with Harvey-Wild, winning Hobart. **1995:** (15) A 2, F qf, W 3, US 4. She broke into the top 20 after reaching f Eastbourne (d. Date), and surprised Sabatini and Sanchez Vicario on her way to the same stage Manhattan Beach, where she took a set off Martinez. She also reached sf Zurich and Filderstadt (d. Davenport and Zvereva and extended Majoli to fs tb), plus 3 more qf, being voted WTA Most Improved Player. She made her mark in GS: unseeded at French Open, she upset Novotna – 0–5 0–40 down in fs, she was aiming simply to win just 1 game in the set, but Novotna let the game slip away as Rubin saved 9 mps. In 2r Wimbledon she beat Hy-Boulais 7–6 6–7 17–15, breaking the Championship records for the longest women's singles match (beating by 4 games the previous record of 54 by A. Weiwers and O. Anderson in 1948) and the longest set (their 32 games being 6 more than the previous record of 26, achieved 6 times since 1919). Then she upset Sukova at US Open, where she was unseeded, and beat Sanchez Vicario in Fed Cup f. She also won Midland Futures in both singles and doubles and from 2 doubles f on the main tour won Prague with Harvey-Wild. Qualified for her 1st WTA Champs, but lost 1r to M. J. Fernandez. **1996:** (12) A sf, F –, W –, US –. It was a frustrating year for her. She broke into top 10 1st time after reaching her 1st GS sf at Australian Open, with upsets of Sabatini and then Sanchez Vicario 6–4 2–6 16–14 in qf. Continuing her record of lengthy matches, it was the longest women's match in the history of the tourn – lasting 3 hours 33 min, comprising the most games in a set (30) and most in a woman's match (48) – and being the 6th-longest on the WTA tour. In sf against Seles, she let slip a lead of 5–2 in 3s and at 5–3 30–15 served a double fault to let Seles back into the match, but was the only player to take a set off the eventual winner. She and Sanchez Vicario were on court together again, upsetting G. Fernandez and Zvereva on their way to the doubles title. LIPC was her 1st major singles f, but it was at that tourn that she suffered a fracture of the hook of the hamate bone of her right hand. She missed Fed Cup and French Open with recurring tendinitis of the wrist, which caused her to retire during her 1st match at Eastbourne and withdraw from Wimbledon and then the Olympics and US Open. Underwent surgery in Sept. to remove hook of hamate bone in right wrist and was out until Nov., when she lost 1r Oakland to Wild, before upsetting Majoli on her way to qf Philadelphia. During the year she also reached sf Oklahoma, plus qf Sydney and Indian Wells. In doubles she teamed with Schultz-McCarthy to win Oklahoma and Indian Wells and with Sanchez Vicario to add Amelia Island to their Australian title. **1997:** A 4, F 2, W 1, US 1. She began the year by winning Hopman Cup with Gimelstob and made a stunning come-back at Linz, upsetting Novotna and Habsudova on the way to her 1st career title. Thereafter, though, she struggled to recapture her best form and reached no other qf until Quebec City, where she advanced to sf. **1997 HIGHLIGHTS – SINGLES: Australian Open last 16** [seed 15] (d. Zrubakova 7–6 6–3, Testud 6–2 6–1, Kleinova 6–1 6–3, lost Van Roost 7–5 6–4), **French Open 2r** (d. Diaz-Oliva 7–6 7–5, lost Martinez [seed 7] 6–3 6–0), **Wimbledon 1r** (lost Kournikova 6–1 6–1), **US Open 1r** (lost Tanasugarn 6–4 6–0); **won** Linz (d. Schnyder 7–5 6–0, Testud 6–4 6–3, Rittner 4–6 7–5 6–4, Novotna 7–5 5–7 6–3, Habsudova 6–4 6–2); **sf** Quebec City (d. Pitkowski 7–5 6–7 7–5, Hy-Boulais 6–3 6–4, Vento 6–4 6–1, lost Schultz-McCarthy 6–2 6–4). **1997 HIGHLIGHTS – DOUBLES:** (with Halard-Decugis) **r/u** Tokyo Nicherei (lost Seles/Sugiyama 6–1 6–0). **CAREER HIGHLIGHTS – SINGLES: Australian Open** – **sf 1996** (d. McQuillan 4–6 6–3 6–2, Krizan 6–7 6–2 6–3, Courtois 6–0 6–2, Sabatini 6–2 6–4, Sanchez Vicario [seed 3] 6–4 2–6 16–14, lost Seles 6–7 6–1 7–5); **French Open** – **qf 1995** [unseeded] (d. Makarova 7–6 6–3, Babel 6–3 6–2, Novotna 7–6 4–6 8–6, Sugiyama 6–2 1–6 6–2, lost Sanchez Vicario 6–3 6–1). **CAREER HIGHLIGHTS – DOUBLES:** (with Sanchez Vicario) **Australian Open** – **won 1996** (d. Davenport/ M. J. Fernandez 6–4 2–6 6–2).

MIHO SAEKI (JPN)

Born New York, USA, 18 March 1976; lives Tokyo; RH; 2HB; 5ft 6in; 125lb; turned pro 1994; career singles titles 0; final 1997 WTA ranking 75; 1997 prize money $92,868.

Coached by Ms Iida. **1993:** (697). **1994:** (454). **1995:** (234) Won Tokyo Japan Open doubles with Yoshida and took 2 singles titles on the Futures circuit. **1996:** (128) In singles reached qf Pattaya and won Wilmington Futures. In doubles won Beijing with Kijimuta and Pattaya with Yoshida. **1997:** A 1, F 1, W 1, US 1. Upset Spirlea at Toronto. **1997 HIGHLIGHTS – SINGLES: Australian Open 1r** (lost Serna 6–3 7–6 7–5), **French Open 1r** (lost Seles [seed 3] 6–0 6–3), **Wimbledon 1r** (lost Hy-Boulais 6–2 1–6 6–2), **US Open 1r** (lost J. Lee 6–3 6–7 6–3).

MARIA ANTONIA SANCHEZ LORENZO (ESP)

Born Salamanca, 7 November 1977; lives Barcelona; LH; 2HF; 2HB; 5ft 7in; 131lb; career singles titles 0; final 1997 WTA ranking 53; 1997 prize money $83,628.

Coached by Xavier Torner; trained by Salvador Sosa. **1992:** (912). **1993:** (440) Won Tortosa Futures. **1994:** (131) Won Caceres Futures. **1995:** (125) Reached her 1st qf on the main tour at Styria. **1996:** (117) A 2, F 2, W 1, US 1. Upset Sugiyama at Madrid. **1997:** A 1, F –, W 2, US 1. Upset Martinez on her way to sf Hamburg after qualifying, reached the same stage San Diego, and won 2 Futures titles. **1997 HIGHLIGHTS – SINGLES: Australian Open 1r** (lost Taylor 7–5 4–6 7–5), **Wimbledon 2r** (d. Perfetti 6–4 6–4, lost Cross 6–4 6–0), **US Open 1r** (lost Testud 6–3 6–3); **won** Redbridge Futures (d. Tatarkova 6–1 6–1), **won** Athens Futures (d. Prazares 6–7 6–1 7–6); **sf** Hamburg (d. Testud 6–3 6–1, Kandarr 6–2 6–1, Martinez 7–5 6–0, lost Majoli 6–2 6–3), **sf** San Diego (d. Kandarr 7–5 6–0, Ruano-Pascual 7–6 3–6 6–2, Paulus w.o., lost Schett 6–4 6–1).

NAOKO SAWAMATSU (JPN)

Born Nishinomiya, 23 March 1973; lives Tokyo; RH; 2HB; 5ft 6in; 127lb; turned pro 1991; career singles titles 4; final 1997 WTA ranking 34; 1997 prize money $150,262.

Coached by Ricky Brown. Her mother, Junko, played pro tennis, appearing at Wimbledon in 1970 with her sister, Kazuko Sawamatsu, who went on to win the title there in 1975 with Kiyomura. **1988:** Won nat champ. **1989:** (256) Won Nagasaki on satellite circuit. **1990:** (31) A –, F 2, W 1, US 2. Won Moulins Challenger, then, a wild-card entry, she beat 3 seeded players to win Singapore, having reached sf Tokyo Suntory 2 weeks earlier. These results saw her break into the top 100 and then top 50 in April. **1991:** (33) A 3, F 4, W 2, US 2. Unseeded at French Open, she upset Garrison 1r and took Tauziat to 12–10 fs in last 16; r/u Pattaya City and reached sf Strasbourg. **1992:** (24) A –, F 1, W 4, US 3. At Wimbledon, where she was unseeded, she upset Wiesner and took a set off Capriati. She was also r/u Strasbourg and reached sf Tokyo Suntory. **1993:** (28) A 3, F 2, W 3, US 1. Won Strasbourg, r/u Melbourne Open and upset Maleeva-Fragniere

2r Wimbledon. **1994:** (26) A 2, F 2, W 4, US 1. Won Singapore and reached sf Tokyo Japan Open, plus qf Italian Open and Strasbourg. She upset M. J. Fernandez at Wimbledon, where she was unseeded, and surprised Coetzer at Sydney. **1995:** (17) A qf, F 3, W 3, US 3. When news of the Japanese earthquake came through before her 1st match at Australian Open, she learned that her home had been destroyed. Determined to give people from her region some good news, she played the tennis of her life, reaching her 1st GS qf, unseeded, and upsetting Date. Fired with the same determination, she moved on to a career high of 14, upsetting Davenport to reach sf Indian Wells and appearing in qf Tokyo Pan Pacific (d. Zvereva) and Tokyo Nicherei. **1996:** (34) A 4, F 2, W 3, US 2. In a less impressive year, her best performances came in Tokyo, where she reached qf both tourns, upsetting Date at Tokyo Toray. **1997:** A 1, F 1, W 2, US 2. Her 1st title since 1994 came at Jakarta in April. She also reached sf Tokyo Nicherei (d. Martinez), qf Sydney, Tokyo Japan Open and Filderstadt, and upset Majoli at Toronto. In losing to Tauziat 7–5 4–6 17–15 in Fed Cup, she played the longest singles set and equalled the longest rubber (Baldovonis d. Connor 6–4 11-13 11-9 in 1974). **1997 HIGHLIGHTS – SINGLES: Australian Open 1r** (lost Basuki 6–3 6–1 ret'd), **French Open 1r** (lost V. Williams 6–2 6–7 7–5), **Wimbledon 2r** (d. Smith 6–1 6–3, lost Tanasugarn 6–2 6–2), **US Open 2r** (d. De Lone 6–4 6–3, lost Zvereva 6–4 3–6 6–3); **won** Jakarta (d. Morariu 6–0 3–6 6–4, Guse 6–3 6–0, Miyagi 7–5 6–1, Grande 7–6 3–6 6–1, Yoshida 6–3 6–2); **sf** Tokyo Nicherei (d. Likhovtseva 2–6 6–4 6–1, Endo 3–6 6–4 6–2, Martinez 7–6 6–4, lost Seles 6–3 6–1). **CAREER HIGHLIGHTS – SINGLES: Australian Open – qf 1995** [unseeded] (d. Sugiyama 6–3 6–3, Courtois 6–0 6–4, Date 3–6 6–3 6–3, M. J. Fernandez 6–4 7–6, lost Sanchez Vicario 6–1 6–3).

BARBARA SCHETT (AUT)

Born Innsbruck, 10 March 1976, and lives there; RH; 2HB; 5ft 9½in; 149lb; turned pro 1992; career singles titles 2; final 1997 WTA ranking 38; 1997 prize money $175,052.

Coached by Thomas Prerovsky. **1991:** (753). **1992:** (299) Won Zaragoza Futures. **1993:** (136) Upset K. Maleeva after qualifying for her 1st event on the main tour at Kitzbuhel and reached same stage Montpellier. **1994:** (100) A –, F 1, W 1, US 1. In jun tennis she was r/u Australian Open Jun to Musgrave. She made her mark in the senior game with another upset of K. Maleeva on her way to sf Linz, as well as reaching qf Tokyo Japan Open and Prague to move into the top 100. **1995:** (83) A 1, F 1, W –, US 1. Upset McNeil LIPC and Cecchini on her way to sf Palermo and appeared in qf Prague. **1996:** (38) A 4, F 1, W 2, US 2. The high point of her year came at Palermo, where she won her 1st main tour singles and doubles titles (with Husarova). She reached sf Moscow, upset Frazier at Australian Open, where she was unseeded, surprised M. Maleeva on her way to qf Amelia Island and held 5 mps v Seles at Madrid, before letting the match slip away. **1997:** A 3, F 1, W 2, US 2. At Maria Lankowitz she upset Wiesner on the way to her 2nd career title and 1st in her own country. She also reached sf Palermo, where she took the doubles with Farina, and upset Huber *en route* to qf Hamburg. **1997 HIGHLIGHTS – SINGLES: Australian Open 3r** (d. Miyagi 7–6 7–6, Fusai 2–6 7–5 7–5, lost Hingis [seed 4] 6–2 6–1), **French Open 1r** (lost Lamarre 6–1 ret'd), **Wimbledon 2r** (d. Carlsson 2–6 6–3 6–0, lost Grzybowska 4–6 6–3 6–2), **US Open 2r** (d. Maruska 6–1 6–0, lost Po 6–3 4–6 7–5); **won** Maria Lankowitz (d. Fauth 6–3 6–2, Torrens-Valero w.o., Wiesner 3–6 7–5 6–0, Sanchez-Lorenzo 6–4 6–1, Nagyova 6–1 7–6); **sf** Palermo (d. Meier 6–1 1–0 ret'd, Van Lottum 6–1 6–3, Ruano-Pascual 6–3 5–7 7–6, lost Testud 0–6 6–3 7–6). **1997 HIGHLIGHTS – DOUBLES:** (with Farina) **won** Palermo (d. Labat/Paz 2–6 6–1 6–4).

PATTY SCHNYDER (SUI)

Born Basel, 14 December 1978; lives Bottmingen; LH; 2HB; 5ft 6½in; 125lb; turned pro 1994; career singles titles 0; final 1997 WTA ranking 26; 1997 prize money $210,374.

1994: (786) Nat Jun champ for 2nd year. **1995:** (152) On the Futures circuit she won Nitra and Presov back-to-back, following with Cureglia, and on the main tour upset Spirlea 1r Zurich. **1996:** (58) A –, F 1, W 1, US –. She reached her 1st f on the main tour at Karlovy Vary, removing Paulus on the way, and joined the Swiss Fed Cup squad. **1997:** A 4, F 3, W 1, US 3. She upset Majoli at Australian Open, where she was unseeded, surprised Raymond at Madrid, and extended Davenport to 9–7 fs at French Open, taking her to 3s again at US Open. Although she did not progress beyond qf all year, she reached that stage at Maria Lankowitz and Filderstadt (d. Sukova and Majoli after qualifying). **1997 HIGHLIGHTS – SINGLES: Australian Open last 16** [unseeded] (d. Majoli 7–5 6–1, Endo 6–0 6–4, Grzybowska 7–6 6–1, lost M. J. Fernandez [seed 14] 4–6 6–4 6–1), **French Open 3r** (d. Maruska 6–3 6–3, Studenikova 6–0 2–0 ret'd, lost Davenport [seed 5] 4–6 6–3 9–7), **Wimbledon 1r** (lost Woodroffe 6–4 6–4), **US Open 3r** (d. Van Roost 6–2 6–2, Yoshida 4–6 6–2 6–4, lost Davenport [seed 6] 1–6 6–1 6–4).

BRENDA SCHULTZ-McCARTHY (NED)

Born Haarlem, 28 December 1970; lives Heemstede and Delray Beach, Fla.; RH; 6ft 2in; 170lb; turned pro 1986; career singles titles 7; final 1997 WTA ranking 15 singles; 1997 prize money $348,247 ($2,501,489).

Has no regular coach, but works with Stan Franker and practises regularly with Paul Dogger. Husband Sean McCarthy (married 8 April 1995). **1987:** (150) A –, F –, W –, US 1. Won Chicago on USTA circuit and reached qf Paris Open. **1988:** (39) A 1, F 4, W 1, US 1. Won Wimbledon Jun over Derly and on the senior tour was a finalist at Oklahoma and Taipei. Upset Cecchini at French Open and also scored upsets during the year over Lindqvist, Hanika, Reggi and Fendick. **1989:** (85) A 4, F 1, W 1, US 1. R/u Brisbane was her best performance.

1990: (43) A 2, F 2, W 4, US 1. Reached sf Brisbane (d. Rinaldi) and qf Tokyo Toray and Oklahoma (d. Reggi). **1991:** (30) A 1, F 1, W 4, US 1. Produced some excellent results on grass: after upsetting Kohde-Kilsch and Tauziat on her way to sf Birmingham, she surprised Novotna and extended Capriati to 3s at Wimbledon, where she was unseeded. In Aug. she went on to win her 1st main tour title at Schenectady. In partnership with Schapers, she won longest set (56 games) and longest match in games (77) ever recorded in Wimbledon mixed doubles when they beat Temesvari/Nijssen 6–3 5–7 29–27). **1992:** (34) A 1, F 3, W 1, US 3. Won Birmingham, r/u Palermo and Schenectady and reached sf FC Cup. **1993:** (40) A –, F 4, W 3, US 3. The highlight of her year came at Taranto, where she won both singles and doubles (with Graham). She upset Maleeva-Fragniere at French Open and reached qf VS Chicago (where she extended Seles to 3s for 3rd time in 3 meetings) and Berlin (d. Capriati). **1994:** (15) A –, F 3, W 3, US 1. It was another year of improvement as she broke into the top 20. Although she took no title on the main tour (Midland Challenger was her only success), she was r/u Oklahoma, Berlin (d. Huber), Palermo and Quebec City and reached sf LIPC (d. Sanchez Vicario), Taranto and Birmingham, plus qf Leipzig, Essen and Philadelphia (d. Davenport). In beating Majoli at Birmingham, she served 22 aces, comfortably beating the previous women's record of 16. Qualified for VS Champs 1st time, but fell 1r to Graf. **1995:** (13) A 4, F 2, W qf, US qf. In another excellent year she won Oklahoma and Quebec, and appeared in sf Delray Beach and qf Wimbledon, US Open (d. Date), Chicago, Zurich and Filderstadt to qualify for VS Champs, where she upset M. Maleeva and Martinez to reach sf. In doubles she was r/u US Open with Stubbs and played 4 more f with various partners, winning 2 with Sabatini, with whom she qualified for WTA Champs. **1996:** (13) A 4, F 3, W 3, US 2. Broke into top 10 1st time in March, after winning both singles and doubles at Oklahoma, although she could not maintain that ranking. In singles she also reached sf Sydney (d. M. J. Fernandez), Birmingham and Oakland (d. Davenport), as well as qf Hamburg, Madrid, Zurich, Quebec City and Chicago, to qualify for Chase Champs, where she lost 1r to Sanchez Vicario. In doubles she won a total of 5 titles with 4 different partners. She broke her own 5-year-old record for the fastest serve by a woman when she achieved 121.8 mph against Hingis at Australian Open. **1997:** A 2, F 3, W 3, US 2. It was Oct. before she played her 1st f of year, winning Quebec City, although she made her presence felt all year – notably at FC Cup as she upset Novotna and Davenport *en route* to sf, where she took a set off Hingis. She reached the same stage at Gold Coast, Tokyo/Japan Open and Eastbourne, where she beat Seles 1st time, coming back from 2–5 down 1s to win in ss and finishing with an ace in a match that was spread over 3 days. She also appeared in qf Atlanta and played in NED Fed Cup team that d. USA, but was restricted during the year by a lower back strain, Achilles and ankle problems and a recurring thigh muscle strain. She qualified for Chase Champs, where she was offering a serious challenge to Hingis before tripping and tearing a toenail, which forced her retirement a few games later. **1997 HIGHLIGHTS – SINGLES: Australian Open 2r** [seed 10] (d. Park 6–2 2–6 6–2, lost Hiraki 0–6 6–1 6–4), **French Open 3r** [seed 14] (d. Cenkova 6–3 7–5, Labat 4–6 7–6 6–4, lost Zvereva 7–6 6–4), **Wimbledon 3r** [seed 14] (d. Farina 4–6 6–3 6–2, Frazier 7–6 6–3, lost Appelmans 6–2 6–3), **US Open 2r** [seed 13] (d. Carlsson 6–7 6–3 6–4, lost Barabanschikova 6–3 6–3); **won** Quebec City (d. Jeyaseelan 6–4 6–1, Morariu 1–6 6–2 6–1, Rubin 6–2 6–4, Van Roost 6–4 6–7 7–5); **sf** Gold Coast (d. Oremans 7–6 6–0, Serna 6–1 6–4, lost Likhovtseva 6–4 6–3), **sf** Tokyo Pan Pacific (d. Dragomir 5–7 6–4 6–2, Sawamatsu 7–6 7–5, Martinez 6–1 6–0, lost Graf 6–1 7–5), **sf** FC Cup (d. Makarova 3–6 7–6 6–4, Leon-Garcia 6–4 6–4, Novotna 6–3 6–3, Davenport 4–6 6–4 6–2, lost Hingis 5–7 6–3 6–2), **sf** Eastbourne (d. Sukova 6–3 7–6, Farina 4–6 6–1 6–2, Seles 7–5 7–5, lost Sanchez Vicario 7–5 6–1). **1997 HIGHLIGHTS – DOUBLES:** (with Neiland) **r/u** Hannover (lost Arendt/Bollegraf 4–6 6–3 7–6). **CAREER HIGHLIGHTS – SINGLES: Wimbledon – qf 1995** (d. Bobkova 6–7 7–6 6–1, Neiland 6–2 6–4, Zrubakova 6–4 7–5, Basuki 6–3 6–1, lost Sanchez Vicario 6–4 7–6); **US Open – qf 1995** (d. Keller 7–6 2–6 7–6, L. Lee 4–6 6–3 6–4, Gavaldon 6–2 7–5, Date 7–5 3–6 6–2, lost Martinez 3–6 7–6 6–2). **CAREER HIGHLIGHTS – DOUBLES:** (with Stubbs) **US Open – r/u 1995** (lost G. Fernandez/Zvereva 7–5 6–3).

IRINA SELYUTINA (KAZ)

Born Almaty, 1 November 1979, and lives there; RH; 5ft 10in; 146lb; career singles titles 0; Junior ranking 7; 1997 prize money $6,720.

Coached by Valery Kovalev and Daria Kopsic. **1996:** Won both singles and doubles at Sao Paulo ITF. **1997:** In Jun doubles won French Open and Wimbledon with Black.

MAGUI SERNA (ESP)

Born Las Palmas, 1 March 1979; lives Barcelona; LH; 5ft 6in; 143lb; turned pro 1993; career singles titles 0; final WTA ranking 41; 1997 prize money $155,386.

Coached by Eric Van Harpen. Formerly nat champ in 12s and 14s. **1994:** (342) Won 2 Futures tourns back-to-back. **1995:** (357) Continued to make her mark on the satellite circuit with the title at Mallorca. **1996:** (138) R/u Wimbledon Jun to Mauresmo and in the senior game she won 3 Futures titles in the space of four weeks. **1997:** A 3, F 3, W 3, US 4. Reached qf Gold Coast after qualifying (d. Dragomir) and upset Po at US Open, where she was unseeded. **1997 HIGHLIGHTS – SINGLES: Australian Open 3r** (d. Saeki 6–3 7–6 7–5, L. Lee 7–5 7–6, lost Coetzer [seed 12] 6–3 6–2), **French Open 3r** (d. Wild 7–6 6–0, Kijimuta 3–6 6–4 6–2, lost Graf [seed 2] 7–6 6–1), **Wimbledon 3r** (d. Watanabe 6–3 6–1, Ruano-Pascual 6–2 6–0, lost Pierce [seed 9] 6–4 6–3), **US Open last 16** [unseeded] (d. Grzybowska 6–4 1–6 6–3, Dechy 6–4 6–4, Po [seed 16] 6–4 6–3, lost Davenport [seed 6] 6–0 6–3).

ANNE-GAELLE SIDOT (FRA)

Born Enghien-les-Bains, 24 July 1979; lives Montlignon; LH; 5ft 7½in; 124lb; turned pro 1994; career singles titles 0; final 1997 WTA ranking 33; 1997 prize money $159,026.

Coached by Bruno Dadillon. **1995:** (163) A –, F 1, W –, US –. Won Flensburg Futures. **1996:** (55) A –, F 1, W 2, US 3. After winning Wurzburg Futures, she extended Date to 3s 2r Wimbledon and upset Halard-Decugis *en route* to her 1st sf on the main tour at Luxembourg, before closing her season with the title at Cardiff Futures. **1997:** A 2, F 1, W 1, US 1. She recorded some useful upsets on her way to sf Gold Coast, Hamburg (d. Schultz-McCarthy) and Luxembourg (d. Habsudova, whom she had earlier beaten at Zurich), qf Hobart (d. Hack) and Hannover (d. Appelmans). **1997 HIGHLIGHTS – SINGLES: Australian Open 2r** (d. Jecmenica 5–7 7–5 6–4, lost Kleinova 6–4 4–6 8–6), **French Open 1r** (lost Neiland 6–2 7–5), **Wimbledon 1r** (lost Rittner 7–6 6–4), **US Open 1r** (lost Dechaume-Balleret 6–3 3–6 6–3); **sf** Gold Coast (d. Studenikova 6–4 ret'd, Kandarr 6–4 6–4, Carlsson 6–2 6–2, lost Sugiyama 6–2 6–4), **sf** Hamburg (d. Schultz-McCarthy 6–2 6–1, Lugina 6–3 6–3, Langrova 6–1 4–6 6–1, lost Dragomir 6–4 6–0), **sf** Luxembourg (d. Schnyder 4–6 6–2 6–2, Habsudova 3–6 6–2 6–4, Nagyova 6–4 7–6, lost Paulus 6–3 6–4).

ALEXANDRA STEVENSON (USA)

Born San Diego, 15 December 1980, and lives there; RH; 6ft 1in; 157lb; career singles titles 0; 1997 prize money $11,960.

Coached by Pete Fischer, former coach of Sampras. Was advised to develop 1HB by former Wimbledon and US champ Ellsworth Vines. **1997:** Won US Open Jun doubles with Irvin.

KATARINA STUDENIKOVA (SVK)

Born Bratislava, 2 September 1972, and lives there; RH; 5ft 7in; 139lb; turned pro 1992; career singles titles 0; final 1997 WTA ranking 72; 1997 prize money $105,484.

Coached by Krta Tibor. **1990:** (630). **1991:** (312) Won Putigano on the satellite circuit. **1992:** (172) Reached qf Pattaya City on the main tour and won Ashkelon futures. **1993:** (76) A –, F 1, W 1, US –. Reached her 1st sf on the Kraft tour at Budapest, appeared in qf Jakarta and won Moulins Challenger. **1994:** (121) A 1, F 1, W 1, US 2. Reached qf Palermo and Hong Kong. **1995:** (72) A 1, F 1, W 1, US 4. Sf Prague was her best showing on the main tour, where she reached no other qf, although she won Sopot on the Futures circuit. A shoulder injury restricted progress and prevented her from working on her serve as she wished. **1996:** (36) A 2, F 1, W 4, US 1. She inflicted the upset of the year when she removed Seles 2r Wimbledon, where she was unseeded, and broke into the top 50. She reached sf Strasbourg (d. Paulus) and Karlovy Vary, plus qf Tokyo Japan Open, San Diego (d. Habsudova), Warsaw, Luxembourg and Moscow. **1997:** A 1, F 2, W 1, US 1. Qf Bol and Warsaw had been her best performances of the year until Oct., when, a qualifier at Luxembourg, she upset Po on her way to sf, where she took a set off Coetzer. **1997 HIGHLIGHTS – SINGLES: Australian Open 1r** (lost Perfetti 6–4 7–6), **French Open 2r** (d. Langrova 6–2 6–2, lost Schnyder 6–0 2–0 ret'd), **Wimbledon 1r** (lost Pratt 6–3 4–6 6–3), **US Open 1r** (lost Wagner 6–2 6–3); **sf** Luxembourg (d. Sugiyama 6–3 6–1, Po 6–4 6–2, Kruger 6–3 6–4, lost Coetzer 6–1 3–6 6–0).

AI SUGIYAMA (JPN)

Born Tokyo, 5 July 1975; lives Kanagawa; RH; 5ft 4in; 115lb; turned pro 1992; career singles titles 1; final 1997 WTA ranking 20 singles, 25 doubles; 1997 prize money $307,837.

Coached by Takaani Minowa. **1991:** (568) No. 2 in ITF Jun Rankings singles. **1992:** (180) Won Roanoke Futures. **1993:** (142) A –, F –, W 1, US –. **1994:** (72) A –, F –, W 1, US 1. Reached f both singles and doubles at Surabaya, but was forced to retire in singles and def. doubles with heat exhaustion. She also reached sf Osaka and qf Tokyo Nicherei (d. Sawamatsu). **1995:** (46) A 1, F 4, W 1, US 2. R/u Oakland (d. Spirlea and Garrison-Jackson), upset Sukova at French Open, where she was unseeded, and surprised Coetzer at San Diego, as well as reaching qf Zagreb. Played 2 doubles f with Nagatsuka, winning Hobart. **1996:** (32) A 3, F 1, W 4, US 2. She reached sf Tokyo Japan Open and qf Hobart, as well as scoring some big upsets across the year. At Wimbledon, where she was unseeded, she removed Huber before extending M. J. Fernandez to 3s, upset Wiesner at Auckland, Novotna at LIPC and Hingis at Olympics. In doubles she won Tokyo Japan Open with Date and joined with Nagatsuka to beat Graf/Huber as JPN d. GER in qf Fed Cup. **1997:** A 2, F 2, W 1, US 2. Won her 1st ever singles title on the main tour at Tokyo Japan Open and was r/u Gold Coast and Moscow (d. Schultz-McCarthy and Sanchez Vicario), as well as reaching qf Eastbourne. In doubles she won Tokyo Nicherei with Seles and r/u Strasbourg with Likhovtseva. **1997 HIGHLIGHTS – SINGLES: Australian Open 2r** (d. Cristea 7–6 6–4, lost Po 6–0 4–6 6–2), **French Open 2r** (d. Wagner 5–7 6–4 6–1, lost Sanchez Vicario [seed 6] 6–3 6–1), **Wimbledon 1r** (lost Basuki 6–3 6–0), **US Open 2r** (d. Grossman 6–7 7–5 6–2, lost Habsudova 5–7 6–3 7–5); **won** Tokyo Japan Open (d. Helgeson-Nielsen 6–3 7–5, Tu 6–2 6–2, Morariu 7–6 6–2, Po 5–7 6–4 6–1, Frazier 4–6 6–4 6–4); **r/u** Gold Coast (d. Miyagi 5–7 6–1 6–1, Grande 6–7 6–2 6–3, Appelmans 6–2 3–6 7–6, Sidot 6–2 6–4, lost Likhovtseva 3–6 7–6 6–3), **r/u** Moscow (d. Zvereva 6–4 7–6, Schultz-McCarthy 6–4 7–5, Sanchez Vicario 6–1 7–6, Van Roost 6–2 4–6 6–3, lost Novotna 6–3 6–4). **1997 HIGHLIGHTS – DOUBLES:** (with Seles) **won** Tokyo Nicherei (d. Halard-Decugis/Rubin 6–1 6–0); (with Likhovtseva) **r/u** Strasbourg (lost Sukova/Zvereva 6–1 6–1).

HELENA SUKOVA (CZE)

Born Prague, 23 February 1965; lives Monte Carlo, Monaco; RH; 6ft 2in; 150lb; turned pro 1983; career singles titles 10; final 1997 WTA ranking 80 singles, 10 doubles; 1997 prize money $362,457 ($6,308,521).

Coached by Jaromir Jirik. Daughter of 1962 Wimbledon finalist, the late Vera Sukova, and Cyril Suk. Brother Cyril, plays on the men's tour. **1981:** (74) A 3, F –, W –, US –. Beat A. Smith and Potter to reach last 16 Australian Open at age 16. **1982:** (24) A 1, F 2, W 1, US 1. Qf Swiss Open, r/u US CC and Avon Futures Champs. **1983:** (17) A 3, F 4, W 1, US 3. Sf Sydney. **1984:** (7) A r/u, F 1, W 4, US qf. Upset Navratilova on the way to f Australian Open and won Brisbane. **1985:** (9) A qf, F 2, W qf, US qf. R/u VS Champs and Eastbourne. Voted WTA Most Improved Player. **1986:** (5) F sf, W qf, US r/u. Won Canadian Open and Hilversum and r/u US Open (d. Evert-Lloyd first time in 15 career meetings). **1987:** (7) A 4, F 4, W qf, US sf. Won Eastbourne (d. Evert and Navratilova back-to-back) and New Jersey in singles and Wimbledon doubles with Kohde-Kilsch. Qualified for VS Champs in singles and doubles. **1988:** (8) A qf, F qf, W qf, US 4. In singles r/u Sydney, Pan Pacific Open and Berlin. In doubles r/u French Open with Kohde-Kilsch, won Olympic silver medal with Novotna, took 4 titles and reached 7 other f with various partners. Qualified for VS Champs in singles and doubles, reaching sf in both and beating Navratilova in qf singles. **1989:** (8) A r/u, F 2, W 4, US qf. At Brisbane she won her 1st title for 18 months, following with an upset of Navratilova at Australian Open, where she was again a finalist. Reached 5 more sf to qualify for VS Champs, where she reached qf. Tore cartilage in right knee at Eastbourne, which kept her out for 2 months, although she played Wimbledon with knee taped and won doubles there with Novotna. Appeared in 7 other doubles f, winning 4. **1990:** (14) A sf, F –, W 4, US 4. Extended Graf to 3s at Australian Open and was r/u Indian Wells, Birmingham and Brighton. Out for most of CC season undergoing treatment for Achilles tendon problems, missing French Open singles and playing doubles there only at the request of her partner Novotna, with whom she won 8 of her 10 titles. They captured Australian Open, French Open and Wimbledon, but missed a GS in doubles when they lost US Open f to G. Fernandez/Navratilova. Qualified for VS Champs in both singles and doubles, but lost 1r in both. **1991:** (17) A 3, F 2, W 1, US 3. In singles won Brisbane and reached sf VS Chicago (d. Capriati) and Filderstadt (d. M. J. Fernandez), but failed to pass 3r in GS. Qualified for VS Champs in singles and doubles (with Sanchez Vicario) but was forced to retire v M. J. Fernandez 1r singles. In women's doubles won 3 titles from 6 f with 4 different partners, and in mixed doubles won French Open with her brother, Cyril. **1992:** (12) A 3, F –, W 3, US 4. Won Osaka and Indianapolis, reached sf Montreal and Leipzig, and played 4 more qf. She had slipped so far down the singles rankings that she was unseeded at Wimbledon, although by year's end she had recovered some ground, despite her 1r loss to Capriati at VS Champs. With 4 different partners she won 9 doubles titles, including Australian Open, VS Champs and 4 others with Sanchez Vicario. R/u US Open mixed with Nijssen. **1993:** (17) A –, F –, W qf, US r/u. At US Open she swept past Navratilova and Sanchez Vicario to play her 4th GS final, but again failed to take that elusive 1st GS singles title. However, she won both women's doubles (with Sanchez Vicario) and mixed (with Woodbridge), becoming the first woman in the Open era to reach f of all 3 events at US Open (and 6th in all GS). In singles she also reached sf Indian Wells and 4 more qf, including Wimbledon (upsetting Sanchez Vicario), and in doubles she won a total of 8 women's titles with 6 different partners. Qualified for VS Champs in both singles and doubles, losing 1r singles to Sanchez Vicario, with whom she reached sf doubles. **1994:** (22) A 3, F 3, W 4, US –. She won no singles title, but was r/u Brighton (on her return from an absence with a broken toe) and reached sf VS Florida (d. Sabatini) and Zurich (d. Navratilova). She played 3 women's doubles f, without winning a title, but won Wimbledon mixed and was r/u Australian Open with Woodbridge. **1995:** (29) A 2, F 1, W 2, US 2. Out of action Feb. to May with a back injury. On her return she upset Sabatini on the way to sf Italian Open, but otherwise her best performances were qf Toronto (d. Sanchez Vicario), Brighton and Oakland, plus an upset of Zvereva at Zurich. Won Oakland and Philadelphia doubles with McNeil to qualify for WTA Champs. **1996:** (27) A 3, F 1, W 2, US 3. In singles she was r/u Rosmalen (d. Majoli) and reached sf Linz and Leipzig (d. Habsudova and Sanchez Vicario). In women's doubles, she played 11 f with 7 different partners, winning Wimbledon and Zurich with Hingis, Karlovy Vary with Habsudova and won an Olympic silver medal with Novotna. She completed her doubles success at Wimbledon by taking the mixed with her brother, Cyril Suk. **1997:** A 1, F 2, W 4, US 1. Upset Martinez at Wimbledon, where she was unseeded, and retained her mixed doubles title with brother, Cyril. In women's doubles, reached 6 f with 4 different partners, winning Strasbourg with Zvereva and Luxembourg with Neiland, with whom she qualified for Chase Champs. There they upset G. Fernandez/Zvereva, in Fernandez's last tourn before retirement, but lost sf to Davenport/Novotna. **1997 HIGHLIGHTS – SINGLES: Australian Open 1r** (lost Appelmans [seed 16] 6–2 6–2), **French Open 2r** (d. Dopfer 6–3 6–4, lost Babel 4–6 6–4 12–10), **Wimbledon last 16** [unseeded] (d. Siddall 7–6 6–1, Wang 6–0 6–3, Martinez [seed 10] 6–4 6–2, lost Kournikova 2–6 6–2 6–3), **US Open 1r** (lost Chladkova 6–1 1–6 6–1). **1997 HIGHLIGHTS – DOUBLES:** (with Neiland unless stated) (with Zvereva) **won** Strasbourg (d. Likhovtseva/Sugiyama 6–1 6–1), **won** Luxembourg (d. Babel/Courtois 6–2 6–4); (with McNeil) **shared** Eastbourne (with Arendt/Bollegraf; final cancelled), **r/u** Los Angeles (lost Basuki/Vis 7–6 6–3), (with Basuki) **r/u** Leipzig (lost Hingis/Novotna 6–2 6–2), **r/u** Zurich (lost Hingis/Sanchez Vicario 4–6 6–4 6–1). **MIXED DOUBLES:** (with Suk) **won Wimbledon** (d. Olhovskiy/Neiland 4–6 6–3 6–4). **CAREER HIGHLIGHTS – SINGLES: Australian Open – r/u 1984** (d. Kohde-Kilsch, Shriver, Navratilova 1–6 6–3 7–5, lost Evert-Lloyd 6–7 6–1 6–3), **r/u 1989** (d. Richardson, Ludloff, O'Neil, Tanvier 7–5 6–4, Navratilova 6–2 3–6 9–7, Cordwell 7–6 4–6 6–2, lost Graf 6–4 6–4), **sf 1990** (d. Morton, Medvedeva, Loosemore 6–3 4–6 6–3, Date 6–4 6–3, K. Maleeva 6–4 6–3, lost Graf 6–3 3–6 6–4); **US Open – r/u 1986** (d. Drescher, Gomer, Bonder, Garrison 6–4 2–6 6–4, Turnbull 6–4 6–0, Evert-Lloyd 6–2 6–4, lost Navratilova 6–3 6–2), **r/u 1993** (d. Bollegraf 6–4 3–6 7–6, Medvedeva 6–3 6–4,

Habsudova 3–6 6–2 6–4, Navratilova 7–5 6–4, K. Maleeva 6–4 6–7 6–3, Sanchez Vicario 6–7 7–5 6–2, lost Graf 6–3 6–3), **sf 1987** (d. Hobbs, Kohde-Kilsch 6–1 6–3, lost Navratilova 6–2 6–2), **qf 1984** (d. K. Jordan, lost Navratilova), **qf 1989** (d. Langrova, Magers 6–2 6–7 6–2, A. Minter 1–6 6–2 6–1, Savchenko 4–6 6–1 6–2, lost Graf 6–1 6–1); **VS Champs – r/u 1985–86** (lost Navratilova 6–3 7–5 6–4), **sf 1986** (lost Graf 7–6 3–6 6–1); **Wimbledon – qf 1986** (d. Parnell, Betzner, A. Minter, R. White 6–3 6–0, lost Evert-Lloyd 7–6 4–6 6–4), **qf 1993** (d. Baudone 6–0 7–6, Farina 6–4 6–2, Brioukhovets 6–7 6–3 6–3, Sanchez Vicario 6–3 6–4, lost Martinez 6–1 6–4). **CAREER HIGHLIGHTS – DOUBLES:** (with Kohde-Kilsch unless stated) **Australian Open** – (with Novotna) **won 1990** (d. Fendick/M. J. Fernandez 7–6 7–6), (with Novotna) **won 1992** (d. M. J. Fernandez/Garrison 7–6 7–5), **r/u 1984** (lost Navratilova/Shriver 6–3 6–4), **r/u 1985** (lost Navratilova/ Shriver 6–3 6–4); **French Open** – (with Novotna) **won 1990** (d. Savchenko/Zvereva 6–4 7–5), **r/u 1985** (lost Navratilova/Shriver 4–6 6–2 6–2), **r/u 1988** (lost Navratilova/Shriver 6–2 7–5); **Wimbledon** – **won 1987** (d. Nagelsen/Smylie 7–5 7–5), (with Novotna) **won 1989** (d. Savchenko/Zvereva 6–1 6–2), (with Novotna) **won 1990** (d. K. Jordan/Smylie 6–2 7–6), (with Hingis) **won 1996** (d. McGrath/ Neiland 5–7 7–5 6–1); **US Open** – **won 1985** (d. Navratilova/Shriver 6–7 6–2 6–3), (with Sanchez Vicario) **won 1993** (d. Coetzer/Gorrochategui 6–4 6–2); **VS Champs –** (with Sanchez Vicario) **won 1992** (d. Novotna/Savchenko-Neiland 7–6 6–1), **r/u 1984–85** (lost Navratilova/ Shriver 6–7 6–4 7–6), **r/u 1985–86** (lost Mandlikova/Turnbull 6–4 6–7 6–3), **r/u 1986** (lost Navratilova/ Shriver 7–6 6–3), **r/u 1987** (lost Navratilova/Shriver 6–1 6–1); **Olympics** – (with Novotna) **silver medal 1988** (lost Shriver/Garrison 4–6 6–2 10–8), (with Novotna) **silver medal 1996** (lost G./ M. J. Fernandez 7–6 6–4). **MIXED DOUBLES:** (with Woodbridge unless stated) **French Open** – (with Suk) **won 1991** (d. Haarhuis/Vis 3–6 6–4 6–1); **Wimbledon – won 1994** (d. Middleton/McNeil 3–6 7–5 6–3), (with Suk) **won 1996** (d. Woodforde/Neiland 1–6 6–3 6–2), (with Suk) **won 1997**; **US Open** – **won 1993** (d. Woodforde/ Navratilova 6–3 7–6).

TAMARINE TANASUGARN (THA)

Born Los Angeles, USA, 24 May 1977; lives Bangkok; RH; 2HB; 5ft 5in; 140lb; turned pro 1994; career singles titles 0; final 1997 WTA ranking 46; 1997 prize money $151,238.

Coached by father, Virachai Tanasugarn. Ranked No. 1 in her country. **1992:** (654). **1993:** (494). **1994:** (249). **1995:** (209) R/u Wimbledon Jun to Olsza. **1996:** (79) Upset Wild on the way to her 1st main tour sf at Beijing, then crowned her year with r/u Pattaya. On the satellite circuits,won 2 titles from 4 f in 4 weeks in Australia and singles and doubles at Saga. **1997:** A 3, F 2, W 3, US 3. She reached sf Auckland, won Surbiton Futures and upset Dragomir at Toronto. **1997 HIGHLIGHTS – SINGLES: Australian Open 3r** (d. Makarova 6–3 1–6 6–4, Taylor 6–4 6–3, lost Davenport [seed 7] 6–1 6–0), **French Open 2r** (d. Courtois 7–6 6–4, lost Raymond 6–1 6–1), **Wimbledon 3r** (d. Richterova 6–3 6–1, Sawamatsu 6–2 6–2, lost M. J. Fernandez [seed 11] 6–2 6–4), **US Open 3r** (d. Rubin 6–4 6–0, Vento 6–4 6–3, lost Kruger 6–7 7–5 6–4); **won** Surbiton Futures (d. Olsza 5–7 7–6 5–0 ret'd); **sf** Auckland (d. Fusai 6–2 6–1, Golarsa 6–2 6–3, Cacic 3–6 6–4 6–4, lost Maruska 3–6 6–3 6–3).

PATRICIA TARABINI (ARG)

Born La Plata, 6 August 1968; lives Tandil; RH; 5ft 5in; 135lb; turned pro 1986; career singles titles 0; final 1997 WTA ranking – 17 doubles; 1997 prize money $131,630.

Coached by Jorge Todero. **1981:** Won Nat Jun Champs. **1983:** Beat Sabatini in Argentine Nat. **1984:** R/u Orange Bowl 16s. **1985:** (305) In Jun singles r/u Orange Bowl; in Jun doubles with Perez-Roldan won French Open and Orange Bowl and r/u US Open, to finish ranked No. 1 in ITF Jun doubles rankings and No. 3 singles. **1986:** (125) F 2, W –, US –. Won French Open Jun, Orange Bowl and took Argentine Nat Jun for 4th straight year. In the senior game reached sf Bregenz and won 2 titles on the Italian satellite circuit. **1987:** (69) A –, F 1, W 1, US 3. Sf Berlin, qf Argentine Open and Athens. **1988:** (34) A –, F 2, W –, US –. Upset Man. Maleeva *en route* to sf Tampa and reached qf at Houston and Nice. Underwent ankle surgery, following an injury suffered at Aix-en-Provence, and was out for last 5 months of year. **1989:** (75) A –, F 1, W –, US 3. In singles reached f Strasbourg and Guaruja plus sf Estoril; in doubles with Cecchini won Arcachon, Athens and Paris Open. **1990:** (55) A –, F 3, W –, US 1. R/u Clarins and sf Estoril; reached 4 doubles f with various partners, winning 2 titles. **1991:** (116) Won Bayonne doubles with Tauziat. **1992:** (97) A 1, F 1, W 1, US –. Qf Sao Paulo and San Marino in singles and won Clarins doubles with Cecchini. Fractured her right ankle practising at Houston in April. **1993:** (60) A 1, F 2, W 1, US 1. In singles she reached sf Palermo and Prague and upset Maleeva-Fragniere *en route* to qf VS Houston. From 3 doubles f she won Prague with Gorrochategui and San Marino with Cecchini. **1994:** (104) A 2, F 1, W 2, US 1. Qf Barcelona (d. Tauziat) was her best showing in singles, and in doubles she won Styria with Cecchini. **1995:** (324) A 2, F 1, W –, US –. Played 2 doubles f with Martinez to qualify for WTA Champs. **1996:** A –, F –, W –, US –. Won a 1st GS title at French Open mixed with Frana, unseeded. **1997:** A –, F –, W –, US –. Although she appeared in no doubles f, she qualified for Chase Champs with Martinez. **CAREER HIGHLIGHTS – MIXED DOUBLES:** (with Frana) **French Open – won 1996** (d. L. Jensen/Arendt 6–2 6–2).

NATHALIE TAUZIAT (FRA)

Born Bangui, Central African Republic, 17 October 1967; lives Bayonne; RH; 5ft 5in; 120lb; career singles titles 4; final 1997 WTA ranking 11 singles, 13 doubles; 1997 prize money $600,642 ($3,014,864).

Coached by Regis DeCamaret. **1984:** (296) A –, F 1, W 1, US –. **1985:** (112) A –, F 3, W –, US –. Upset Casale at French Open and played Fed Cup. **1986:** (67) F 2, W 2, US –. Qf Hilversum. **1987:** (25) A –, F 4, W 2, US 2. Sf

Strasbourg, San Diego and Zurich and d. Rinaldi to reach qf LIPC. **1988:** (27) A –, F 4, W 2, US 2. R/u Nice, upset Zvereva and K. Maleeva *en route* to f Mahwah. In doubles with Demongeot upset Kohde-Kilsch/Sukova to win both Berlin and Zurich and qualified for VS Champs. **1989:** (25) A –, F 1, W 1, US 3. Sf Italian Open (d. Man. Maleeva) and San Diego. **1990:** (18) A –, F 4, W 4, US 4. Won her 1st primary circuit title at Bayonne; r/u Wichita and reached sf LIPC, Birmingham and Canadian Open (d. Maleeva-Fragniere) to qualify for VS Champs, where she fell 1r to M. J. Fernandez. **1991:** (13) A –, F qf, W 4, US 1. She scored some major upsets in reaching f Zurich (d. Sabatini), sf VS Palm Springs, VS Florida (d. M. J. Fernandez), Barcelona (d. Navratilova), San Diego and Bayonne and was close to beating Capriati at VS Champs, eventually losing their 1r match in 3s tb. Reached 3 doubles f, winning Bayonne with Tarabini. **1992:** (14) A –, F 4, W qf, US 2. R/u San Antonio and Bayonne and reached 9 more qf, including Wimbledon. Qualified for VS Champs, but lost 1r to Seles. **1993:** (18) A 4, F 3, W 4, US 4. Won Quebec City in Nov., having earlier appeared in sf Schenectady and Filderstadt plus 8 more qf, upsetting Maleeva-Fragniere at Tokyo Pan Pacific. Qualified for VS Champs but fell 1r again – to Navratilova. **1994:** (35) A 1, F 2, W 3, US 2. Although she did not progress beyond sf, she reached that stage at Birmingham, Schenectady and Quebec City, plus qf Italian Open and Brighton (d. Huber), and upset Martinez 1r Philadelphia. From 3 doubles f she won Quebec City with Reinach and Los Angeles with Halard, with whom she qualified for VS Champs. **1995:** (27) A –, F 3, W 3, US 3. Upset Zvereva on her way to the title at Eastbourne, surprised M. Maleeva at French Open and Pierce at Wimbledon and reached qf Barcelona. In doubles she won Linz with McGrath. **1996:** (30) A –, F 2, W 3, US 2. Confirming her liking for grass, she was r/u Birmingham, reached sf Eastbourne and upset M. Maleeva at Wimbledon. Otherwise she could not pass qf, although she reached that stage at Indian Wells (d. M. J. Fernandez), Italian Open, Berlin, Strasbourg and San Diego. In doubles she played 6 f with 4 different partners, winning Leipzig and Luxembourg with Boogert. **1997:** A –, F 3, W qf, US 1. She excelled at Birmingham again, winning the title. Her 2nd f of year came at Zurich and she was r/u again at Chicago, where she upset Novotna and Majoli back-to-back and took the doubles. Her only other sf was a big one, as she upset Coetzer and Majoli to reach that stage at Chase Champs, where she extended Pierce to 3s. She also reached qf Linz, Paris Open, Indian Wells, Eastbourne (d. M. J. Fernandez), Los Angeles and Wimbledon, where she was unseeded. She enjoyed a lucky escape in last 16 there, trailing 4–5 15–40 on Testud's serve in 3s when rain interrupted play: on the resumption 75 minutes later, she took 10 points in a row and finally won 10–12 fs. A member of the winning FRA Fed Cup team, she d. Sawamatsu 7–5 4–6 17–15 in that competition, playing the longest singles set and equalling the longest rubber (Baldovonis d. Connor 6–4 11–13 11–9 in 1974). She played 6 doubles f with 3 different partners, winning Linz and Chicago with Fusai. She qualified for Chase Champs in both singles and doubles, joining with Fusai to upset Hingis/Sanchez Vicario in ss and extend Davenport/Novotna to 3s in f. **1997 HIGHLIGHTS – SINGLES: French Open 3r** (d. Simpson 6–3 6–2, V. Williams 5–7 6–3 7–5, lost Seles [seed 3] 6–0 6–1), **Wimbledon qf** [unseeded] (d. Miyagi 6–3 6–4, Guse 6–0 6–3, Wiesner 3–6 6–3 6–2, Testud 4–6 7–5 12–10, lost Sanchez Vicario [seed 8] 6–2 7–5), **US Open 1r** (lost Habsudova 7–5 7–6); **won** Birmingham (d. Brandi 6–1 6–4, Barabanschikova 7–5 6–1, Zvereva 6–1 2–6 6–2, Basuki 2–6 6–2 6–2); **r/u** Zurich (d. Po 6–3 5–7 7–5, Van Roost 6–3 6–7 7–6, Appelmans 4–6 6–1 7–5, Raymond 6–3 7–5, lost Davenport 7–6 7–5), **r/u** Chicago (d. Dragomir 6–3 5–7 6–2, Appelmans 6–1 6–2, Novotna 7–5 6–3, Majoli 6–2 6–3, lost Davenport 6–0 7–6); **sf** Chase Champs (d. Coetzer 6–3 6–3, Majoli 7–6 7–6, lost Pierce 6–2 5–7 6–4). **1997 HIGHLIGHTS – DOUBLES:** (with Fusai unless stated) **won** Linz (d. Milicharova/Vildova 4–6 6–3 6–1), **won** Chicago (d. Davenport/Seles 6–3 6–2); (with Raymond) **r/u** Indian Wells (lost Davenport/Zvereva 6–3 6–2), (with Wild) **r/u** Birmingham (lost Adams/Neiland 6–2 6–3), **r/u** Atlanta (lost Arendt/Bollegraf 6–7 6–3 6–2), **r/u** Quebec City (lost Raymond/Stubbs 6–4 5–7 7–5), **r/u** Chase Champs (lost Davenport/Novotna 6–7 6–3 6–2). **CAREER HIGHLIGHTS – SINGLES: French Open** – **qf 1991** (d. Etchemendy 6–3 6–1, Guerree 6–2 6–1, Jagerman 6–4 6–0, Sawamatsu 7–5 2–6 12–10, lost Graf [seed 2] 6–3 6–2); **Wimbledon** – **qf 1992** (d. Schultz 6–4 6–0, Medvedeva 7–5 2–6 6–3, Provis 4–6 7–5 6–3, Frazier 6–0 6–3, lost Seles [seed 1] 6–1 6–3), **qf 1997.**

SANDRINE TESTUD (FRA)

Born Lyon, 3 April 1972, and lives there; RH; 5ft 9½in; 150lb; career singles titles 1; final 1997 WTA ranking 13; 1997 prize money $417,753 ($1,019,870).

Fiance Vittorio Magnelli. **1989:** (279) Won Nat Jun 18s and in the senior game won her 1st Futures title at Limoges. **1990:** (185) A –, F 1, W –, US –. Won Futures titles at Eastbourne, Caltagirone and Swindon. **1991:** (118) A –, F 1, W –, US –. Reached sf Bol, plus qf Albuquerque and St Petersburg. **1992:** (108) A 2, F 2, W 1, US 2. Qf Strasbourg. **1993:** (98) A 1, F 1, W 1, US 1. Upset McNeil on her way to sf Strasbourg and Strnadova to reach qf Pattaya City. **1994:** (81) A 4, F 1, W 1, US 2. Upset Sukova at Australian Open, where she was unseeded, but reached no qf on the main tour. **1995:** (41) A 3, F 2, W 2, US 3. Broke into the top 50 after appearances in sf Strasbourg (d. M. J. Fernandez) and San Diego (d. Zvereva), plus qf Puerto Rico (d. Halard) and Quebec City. **1996:** (39) A 1, F 3, W 2, US 4. Her best performances were sf Beijing and qf San Diego (d. Sugiyama). **1997:** A 2, F 3, W 4, US qf. She won her 1st career singles title at Palermo and upset Habsudova and Majoli on her way to f Atlanta, unseeded. She played no other sf, but moved into top 15 with qf US Open (unseeded, d. Majoli), Hannover (d. Schultz-McCarthy), Indian Wells (d. Raymond), LIPC (d. Sanchez Vicario), Strasbourg, San Diego (d. Sanchez Vicario again) and Moscow, and upset Davenport at Berlin. Having upset Seles 3r Wimbledon, again unseeded, she suffered a cruel reverse v Tauziat in her next match: 5–4 and 40–15 up in 3s, when rain interrupted play for 75 minutes, she dropped the next 10 points, going on to lose the set 10–12. Won her 2 crucial singles matches in Fed Cup f as FRA d. NED. Qualified for Chase Champs 1st time and extended Spirlea to 3s 1r. **1997 HIGHLIGHTS – SINGLES: Australian Open 2r** (d.

Wagner 6–3 6–1, lost Rubin [seed 15] 6–2 6–1), **French Open 3r** (d. Park 6–0 6–4, Cristea 6–0 6–4, lost Pierce [seed 10] 6–1 6–3), **Wimbledon last 16** [unseeded] (d. Schnitzer 6–3 6–0, Morariu 6–7 6–3 6–1, Seles [seed 2] 0–6 6–4 8–6, lost Tauziat 4–6 7–5 12–10), **US Open qf** [unseeded] (d. Sanchez Lorenzo 6–3 6–3, Majoli [seed 4] 6–4 2–6 6–1, Wagner 6–1 6–3, Habsudova 6–3 4–6 7–6, lost V. Williams 7–5 7–5); **won** Palermo (d. Kschwendt 6–2 6–2, Garrone 1–6 6–4 6–2, Gagliardi 6–7 6–2 6–3, Schett 0–6 6–3 7–6, Makarova 7–5 6–3); **r/u** Atlanta (d. Habsudova 6–3 6–1, Rubin 6–4 6–1, Seles def., Majoli 7–5 6–3, lost Davenport 6–4 6–1). **CAREER HIGHLIGHTS – SINGLES: US Open – qf 1997**.

DOMINIQUE VAN ROOST (BEL)

Born Verviers, 3 May 1973; lives Leuven; RH; 5ft 7in; 122lb; turned pro 1991; career singles titles 3; final 1997 WTA ranking 18; 1997 prize money $274,010.

Coached by Alfonso Gonzalez. Married in 1995; maiden name Monami. **1989:** (695). **1990:** (272) Won 5 consec. Futures titles on the European circuit. **1991:** (129) A –, F –, W –, US 1. Upset Golarsa at Linz. **1992:** (101) A 4, F 1, W 1, US 2. Surprised Sukova at Australian Open, where she was unseeded, and reached qf Linz and Bayonne. **1993:** (59) A 2, F 1, W 1, US 2. In singles she reached her 1st tour f at Montpellier and appeared in qf Palermo and Sapporo (d. Wang). From 3 doubles f she won Kitzbuhel with Li. **1994:** (133) A 1, F 1, W 3, US 1. In a quieter year she reached only qf Taipei and took a set off Novotna at Wimbledon. **1995:** (43) A –, F 2, W 2, US 2. Returned to the top 100 with r/u showing at Quebec City, where she upset Gorrochategui and Coetzer, and won both singles and doubles at Southampton Futures. **1996:** (46) A 1, F 1, W 3, US 1. Won her 1st singles title on the main tour at Cardiff and reached qf Rosmalen (d. Appelmans). On the Futures circuit, she won Limoges. **1997:** A qf, F 3, W 1, US 1. Her best year yet saw her breaking into top 20 by end of year. She began it in style with an upset of Wild on her way to the title at Hobart, where she was r/u doubles with Rittner, and finished it with a flourish at Pattaya, where she was r/u both singles and doubles (with Labat). Unseeded at Australian Open, she upset Sanchez Vicario and Rubin, before being forced to retire qf with an abdominal injury. She added the title at Surabaya, r/u Quebec City (d. Raymond), sf Moscow (d. Huber and Spirlea) and reached qf Cardiff, Birmingham, Rosmalen and Atlanta (d. Dragomir). **1997 HIGHLIGHTS – SINGLES: Australian Open qf** [unseeded] (d. Fulco-Villella 6–0 6–3, Yoshida 4–6 7–5 6–3, Sanchez Vicario [seed 2] 1–6 6–4 8–6, Rubin [seed 15] 7–5 6–4, lost M. J. Fernandez [seed 14] 7–5 4–0 ret'd), **French Open 3r** (d. Rittner 3–0 ret'd, Gagliardi 6–2 6–0, lost Sanchez Vicario [seed 6] 6–0 6–3), **Wimbledon 1r** (lost Pierce [seed 9] 6–3 6–4), **US Open 1r** (lost Schnyder 6–2 6–2); **won** Hobart (d. Wild 6–1 6–2, De Ville 6–3 6–0, Cenkova 6–0 1–0 ret'd, Endo 6–3 6–4, Werdel-Witmeyer 6–3 6–3), **won** Surabaya (d. Prakusya 6–4 6–4, Saeki 7–6 6–3, Randriantefy 6–0 6–2, McQuillan 6–2 7–5, Nemeckova 6–1 6–3); **r/u** Quebec City (d. Callens 6–4 6–2, A. Miller 6–1 7–5, Watanabe 6–1 6–2, Raymond 6–2 3–6 6–1, lost Schultz-McCarthy), **r/u** Pattaya (d. Van Lottum 6–4 6–0, Sangaram 6–0 6–1, Courtois 6–2 6–1, Barabanschikova 6–3 6–2, lost Nagyova 7–5 6–7 7–5); **sf** Moscow (d. Huber 5–7 6–4 6–3, Sukova 6–2 7–6, Spirlea 6–2 6–4, lost Sugiyama 6–2 4–6 6–3). **1997 HIGHLIGHTS – DOUBLES:** (with Rittner) **r/u** Hobart (lost Kijimuta/Miyagi 6–3 6–1), (with Labat) **r/u** Pattaya (lost Kunce/Morariu 6–3 6–4). **CAREER HIGHLIGHTS – SINGLES: Australian Open – qf 1997.**

MARIA ALEJANDRA VENTO (VEN)

Born Caracas, 24 May 1974; lives there and Miami, Fla.; RH; 2HB; 5ft 6in; 130lb; turned pro 1994; career singles titles 0; final 1997 WTA ranking 48; 1997 prize money $94,209.

Coached by George Paris. **1988:** (530). **1989:** (412) Won Guadalajara Futures. **1990:** (414) Won Aguascalientes Futures and joined VEN Fed Cup squad. **1991:** (515). **1992:** (549) A –, F –, W –, US 1. **1993:** (207) A –, F –, W –, US –. Won 4 Futures titles in USA, including 3 in consec. tourns. **1994:** (165) A –, F –, W –, US –. **1995:** (87) A –, F –, W 1, US 1. Reached her 1st qf on the main tour at Pattaya and won Brasilia Futures. **1996:** (170) A 1, F –, W –, US –. **1997:** A –, F –, W 4, US 2. She upset Wang on her way to sf Surabaya, Tauziat to reach qf Quebec City, and Maleeva *en route* to last 16 Wimbledon, after qualifying. On the Futures circuit she won Peachtree. **1997 HIGHLIGHTS – SINGLES: Wimbledon last 16** [unseeded] (d. Ellwood 7–5 6–1, Glass 2–1 ret'd, Maleeva 6–2 7–6, lost Chladkova 6–1 6–3), **US Open 2r** (d. Glass 1–6 7–6 6–2, lost Tanasugarn 6–4 6–3); **won** Peachtree Futures (d. Jeyaseelan 6–4 6–0); **sf** Surabaya (d. Wang 6–4 3–6 6–4, Dechy 6–3 7–5, Pitkowski 6–3 6–2, lost Nemeckova 6–4 6–3).

CAROLINE VIS (NED)

Born Vlaardingen, 4 March 1970, and lives there; RH; 5ft 11in; 158lb; turned pro 1989; career singles titles 0; final 1997 WTA ranking 11 doubles; 1997 prize money $153,819.

Coached by Auke Dykstra. **1989:** (253). **1990:** (209) Upset Savchenko at VS Nashville and r/u doubles there with Schultz. Joined her country's Fed Cup squad. **1991:** (417) R/u French Open mixed doubles with Haarhuis and in women's doubles reached f VS Nashville with Basuki. **1992:** (333) Won Waregem doubles with Bollegraf. **1993:** (208) Won Budapest doubles with Gorrochategui and r/u Prague with Golarsa. **1994:** (117) A –, F 1, W 1, US –. Upset Pierce *en route* to qf Paris Open and reached 3 doubles f with different partners. **1995:** (206) A 1, F –, W –, US –. In doubles played 3 f with different partners. **1996:** (313) A –, F –, W –, US –. Although she reached no doubles f, she was a regular in qf with various partners, qualifying for Chase Champs with Basuki. **1997:** In doubles won Los Angeles and Toronto back-to-back in Aug. with Basuki and qualified for Chase Champs. **1997 HIGHLIGHTS – DOUBLES:** (with Basuki) **won** Los Angeles (d. Neiland/Sukova 7–6 6–3), **won** Toronto (d. Arendt/Bollegraf 3–6 7–5 6–4); **r/u** Moscow (lost Sanchez Vicario/Zvereva 5–3 ret'd).

SHI-TING WANG (TPE)

Born Taiwan, 19 October 1973, and lives there; RH; 2HB; 5ft 7½in; 128lb; turned pro 1991; career singles titles 6; final 1997 WTA ranking 67; 1997 prize money $124,080.

Coached by her father, Wen-Chih Wang. Ranked No. 1 in Taipei. **1989:** Won French Open Jun doubles with Pratt. **1991:** (185) Won 5 titles on the Challenger circuit, including 4 in Taipei. **1992:** (55) A –, F 1, W –, US 1. Upset Huber in reaching her 1st senior tour sf at Indianapolis, appeared in qf Pattaya City and Taipei and upset Basuki at Tokyo Suntory. **1993:** (30) A 2, F –, W –, US 2. Won her 1st title on the main tour at Hong Kong, following 3 weeks later with Taipei. Upset Halard on her way to sf Brisbane and reached qf Osaka. **1994:** (42) A 2, F 3, W –, US 3. She finished the year in style when she retained her title at Taipei, having earlier appeared in sf Brisbane and Jakarta and qf Schenectady. **1995:** (44) A 1, F 3, W –, US –. Won Surabaya and was r/u Beijing in both singles and doubles, as well as reaching qf Jakarta. **1996:** (35) A 2, F 2, W –, US 2. Won Surabaya and Beijing back-to-back in Oct., having begun the year with an upset of Wiesner on her way to sf Hobart and reached qf Tokyo Nicherei, where she was r/u doubles with Park. **1997:** A 3, F 2, W 2, US –. Her best performances were qf Hobart, Tokyo Japan Open and Jakarta, where she also won the Futures title. **1997 HIGHLIGHTS – SINGLES: Australian Open 3r** (d. Wild 6–3 6–1, Watanabe 7–5 6–3 lost Habsudova [seed 9] 6–3 7–6), **French Open 2r** (d. De Ville 6–3 7–5, lost Paulus [seed 16] 6–2 6–2), **Wimbledon 2r** (d. McNeil 6–1 2–6 7–5, lost Sukova 6–0 6–3); **won** Jakarta Futures (d. Aizenberg 6–1 6–4).

MARLENE WEINGARTNER (GER)

Born Heidelberg, 30 January 1980, and lives there; RH; 5ft 7in; 122lb; career singles titles 0; final 1997 WTA ranking 131; 1997 prize money $38,664.

Coached by Sevei Dian. **1994:** European Under-14 champ. **1995:** (224) R/u French Open Jun to Cocheteux. **1997:** R/u Australian Open Jun to Lucic.

VENUS WILLIAMS (USA)

Born Lynwood, Cal., 17 June 1980; lives Palm Beach Gardens, Fla; RH; 2HB; 5ft 11in; 137lb; turned pro 1994; career singles titles 0; final 1997 WTA ranking 22; 1997 prize money $466,863.

Coached by her father, Richard, and Nick Bollettieri. Younger sister Serena has also made her debut on the tour. **1995:** (206) Qf Oakland (d. Frazier) and joined US Fed Cup squad. **1996:** (206) Upset Wild at Los Angeles. **1997:** A –, F 2, W 1, US r/u. She produced an extraordinary performance to reach f US Open, upsetting Huber and Spirlea (saving 2 mps in 3s tb) along the way to become the 1st unseeded women's finalist there since Darlene Hard in 1958. Until then her best performance had been at Indian Wells, where she qualified, upset Majoli and was 4–1 and 6–5 up in 3s qf v Davenport before losing their tb. After US Open, she failed to qualify at Filderstadt, but reached qf Zurich (as a qualifier) the next week and followed with the same stage Moscow. **1997 HIGHLIGHTS – SINGLES: French Open 2r** (d. Sawamatsu 6–2 6–7 7–5, lost Tauziat 5–7 6–3 7–5), **Wimbledon 1r** (lost Grzybowska 4–6 6–2 6–4), **r/u US Open** [unseeded] (d. Neiland 5–7 6–0 6–1, Leon-Garcia 6–0 6–1, Huber [seed 8] 6–3 6–4, Kruger 6–2 6–3, Testud 7–5 7–5, Spirlea [seed 11] 7–6 4–6 7–6, lost Hingis [seed 1] 6–0 6–4). **CAREER HIGHLIGHTS – SINGLES: US Open – r/u 1997.**

JASMIN WOHR (GER)

Born Tubingen, 21 August 1980; lives Balingen; RH; 2HB; 5ft 9in; 137lb; career singles titles 0; final 1997 WTA ranking 260; 1997 prize money $8,647.

Coached by Edgar Giffenig. **1994:** Led GER to victory in NTT World Jun Finals. **1996:** In GER team r/u World Youth Cup. **1997:** Won Australian Open Jun doubles with Lucic.

YUKA YOSHIDA (JPN)

Born Tettori-pref., 1 April 1976; lives Yokohama; RH; 2HB; 5ft 3in; 113lb; turned pro 1994; career singles titles 0; final 1997 WTA ranking 69; 1997 prize money $107,720.

Coached by Ms Yonezawa. **1993:** (346) R/u US Open Jun singles to Bentivoglio. **1994:** (208). **1995:** (202) A 1, F –, W –, US –. Won Tokyo Japan Open doubles with Saeki. **1996:** (126) Reached her 1st tour sf at Surabaya and upset Wang *en route* to qf Pattaya, where she won the doubles with Saeki. **1997:** A 2, F 2, W 2, US 2. Her best performance came at Jakarta, where she reached her 1st singles f on the main tour and was also r/u doubles with Nemeckova. **1997 HIGHLIGHTS – SINGLES: Australian Open 2r** (d. Adams 7–5 6–3, lost Van Roost 4–6 7–5 6–3), **French Open 2r** (d. McQuillan 6–2 6–4, lost Po 6–3 6–0), **Wimbledon 2r** (d. Hiraki 6–2 6–3, lost Martinez [seed 10 6–0 6–0), **US Open 2r** (d. Brandi 6–7 6–1 6–4, lost Schnyder 4–6 6–2 6–4); **r/u** Jakarta (d. Vaidyanathan 6–3 6–2, Chi 7–6 6–3, Wang 6–4 3–2 ret'd, Dechaume-Balleret 3–6 7–6 6–1, lost Sawamatsu 6–3 6–2). **1997 HIGHLIGHTS – DOUBLES:** (with Nemeckova) **r/u** Jakarta (lost Guse/Radford 6–4 5–7 7–5).

NATASHA ZVEREVA (BRS)

Born Minsk, 16 April 1971, and lives there; RH; 2HB; 5ft 8in; 138lb; turned pro 1988; career singles titles 3; final 1997 WTA ranking 25 singles, 1 doubles; 1997 prize money $746,643 ($6,082,686).

Named Natalia, but prefers to be called Natasha. She is advised by her father, Marat Zverev, but has no formal coach as she finds it hard to cope with anyone telling her what to do, and hires a local hitting partner at each tournament. **1985:** Won Bethesda on USTA circuit and World Jun Champs. **1986:** (92) In singles won Soviet Nat Champs (d. Savchenko), won Wimbledon Jun singles, USTA Bethesda, and was r/u to Rinaldi at VS Arkansas after qualifying, becoming at 15 years 7 months the youngest player to reach f of VS Series event. In doubles won French Open Jun and r/u Wimbledon Jun with Meskhi. **1987:** (19) A –, F 3, W 4, US 3. Futures Jun Champ; won Nat Champ, Jun singles at French Open, Wimbledon and US Open and Jun doubles at French Open and Wimbledon with Medvedeva. Did not compete in Australian Open Jun. At Wimbledon she beat McNeil and extended Sabatini to 3s; won Taranto on Italian satellite and reached f Arkansas and Chicago in consecutive weeks. **1988:** (7) A –, F r/u, W 4, US 1. Played her best tennis to upset Navratilova last 16 French Open, but disappointed in her 1st GS f there, being totally outclassed 6–0 6–0 in 32 minutes by Graf. Reached qf Olympics. In doubles with Savchenko r/u Wimbledon and won 2 titles. At VS Champs reached qf in singles and r/u in doubles. Voted WTA Newcomer of the Year. **1989:** (27) A –, F 1, W 3, US 4. Was less successful in singles, winning no title, although she reached f FC Cup (d. Navratilova) and Moscow plus 3 more sf. However, in doubles with Savchenko she won French Open, was r/u Wimbledon and VS Champs and reached 7 other f, winning 4. **1990:** (12) A 2, F 4, W qf, US 2. Won 1st senior singles title at Brisbane (upset Sukova qf), following with Sydney the next week. In doubles with Savchenko r/u French Open and won 3 titles; in mixed with Pugh won Australian Open and r/u US Open. Qualified for VS Champs in singles and doubles, losing 1r singles to Sanchez Vicario and 1r doubles to Adams/McNeil. **1991:** (21) A 4, F 2, W 2, US 4. In singles r/u Birmingham, sf FC Cup and reached last 16 Australian Open and US Open. In doubles GS won Wimbledon and r/u French Open with Savchenko and teamed with Shriver 1st time to win US Open. She also won VS Florida, Berlin, Eastbourne, Toronto and Los Angeles with Savchenko, Brighton with Shriver and FC Cup with Kohde-Kilsch, as well as reaching 4 more f with various partners, qualifying for VS Champs with Savchenko. In mixed doubles, r/u Wimbledon with Pugh. **1992:** (23) A 2, F qf, W qf, US 3. Unseeded in all the major tourns, she always made her mark. At French Open she upset Appelmans to reach qf, where she took a set off Graf; she reached the same stage at Wimbledon, upsetting Martinez and Garrison; at US Open she extended Sabatini to 3s and at Olympics she upset Novotna on her way to last 16. She also upset Navratilova at FC Cup, reaching qf there as well as at Italian Open, Oakland and Philadelphia. Yet it was in doubles where she really excelled, reaching 13 f, from which she won French Open, Wimbledon, US Open plus 2 others with G. Fernandez, 2 with Sanchez Vicario, 1 with Savchenko-Neiland and 1 with Sukova. In addition she won an Olympic bronze medal with Meskhi and qualified for VS Champs with G. Fernandez, losing sf to Novotna/Savchenko-Neiland. **1993:** (19) A 3, F 4, W qf, US qf. In singles she had passed no qf all year until Oct., when she stunned Navratilova on her way to f Filderstadt. Otherwise, again unseeded in all GS, her best performances came at Wimbledon, where she reached qf (d. K. Maleeva), at US Open, where she retired at same stage v Sanchez Vicario, and French Open, where she reached last 16 (d. Coetzer). In doubles with G. Fernandez, with whom she had never been beaten in GS f, won Australian Open, French Open and Wimbledon, extending to 6 their run of GS titles, 2nd only to Navratilova/Shriver's record 8 in the Open era. However, the string was broken at US Open, where, with Zvereva suffering from flu, they lost sf to Sanchez Vicario/Sukova. They won 7 other titles together, being r/u twice, and were voted WTA Doubles Team of Year. Qualified for VS Champs in both singles, in which she lost to Graf 1r, and doubles, which she and Fernandez won. **1994:** (10) A 1, F 4, W 1, US –. At Chicago she won both singles and doubles for only her 3rd singles title and her 1st since 1990. In singles she also reached f LIPC (d. Novotna and took a set off Graf), FC Cup (d. Pierce) and Zurich, as well as appearing in sf Eastbourne and Philadelphia. After qualifying for VS Champs in both singles and doubles again, she fell 1r singles to Martinez, but retained the doubles title with G. Fernandez. They excelled again as a partnership through the year: at Australian Open they won 7th of 8 consec. GS doubles tourns, following with French Open and Wimbledon, but again they missed the chance of a GS when they unexpectedly lost to K. Maleeva/White in sf US Open. In all they won a total of 11 titles from 13 f. **1995:** (14) A qf, F 1, W 3, US 4. In singles she reached f Indian Wells (d. Sanchez Vicario), sf FC Cup, Berlin and Eastbourne, and played qf Australian Open, LIPC, Manhattan Beach and Filderstadt. Her doubles partnership with G. Fernandez continued to flourish as they played all GS f, winning French and US Opens, and took 7 titles from 12 f. In mixed, she won Australian Open with Leach. Qualifying for VS Champs in both singles and doubles, she upset Sanchez Vicario and Sabatini (for the 1st time in 9 meetings) to reach sf singles and was r/u doubles with G. Fernandez, with whom she was voted Doubles Team of the Year. **1996:** (53) A 1, F 3, W 2, US 3. She withdrew from Indian Wells with a stress fracture of the ribcage (right side) and was out for 14 weeks. She went into French Open having played (and lost) only 3 matches all year and her only qf showing in singles was at Luxembourg in Oct. In doubles she won US Open and was r/u French Open with G. Fernandez, also taking Tokyo Toray with her and Los Angeles with Davenport. Qualified for Chase Champs with G. Fernandez, but lost sf to Davenport/M. J. Fernandez. **1997:** A 3, F 4, W 1, US 3. Reached sf Eastbourne (d. Majoli and extended Novotna to 7–5 3s) and qf Strasbourg (d. Davenport), Birmingham, San Diego (d. Spirlea), Los Angeles and Tokyo Nicherei. She also upset Habsudova at LIPC, Schultz-McCarthy at French Open (unseeded), and Martinez at Filderstadt, where she extended Hingis to 3s. She continued to excel in doubles and finished the year at the top of the rankings after appearing in 11 f, including all 4 GS – of which she won Australian Open with Hingis, French Open and Wimbledon with G. Fernandez, with whom she was also r/u US Open. They qualified together for Chase Champs, but there, in Fernandez's last tourn before retiring, they disappointingly lost 1r to Neiland/Sukova. Zvereva had also won 2 titles each with Davenport and Sanchez Vicario and 1 with Sukova. **1997 HIGHLIGHTS – SINGLES: Australian Open 3r** (d. Feber 7–6 6–1, Probst 7–6 6–3, lost Huber 7–5 6–0), **French Open last 16** [unseeded] (d. Tu 6–3 3–6 6–4, Lamarre 6–4 7–5, Schultz-McCarthy [seed 14] 7–6 6–4, lost Sanchez Vicario [seed 6] 6–4 6–2), **Wimbledon 1r** (lost Likhovtseva 6–2 6–2), **US Open 3r** (d. Zrubakova 6–1 7–5, Sawamatsu 6–4 3–6 6–3, lost Pierce [seed 9] 7–6 6–1); **sf** Eastbourne (d. Frazier 7–6 6–0, Majoli 6–2 7–5, Tauziat 6–4 5–7 6–4, lost Novotna 6–7 6–0 7–5). **1997 HIGHLIGHTS – DOUBLES:** (with G. Fernandez unless stated) (with Hingis) **won Australian Open** (d. Davenport/Raymond 6–2 6–2), **won French Open** (d. M. J. Fernandez/Raymond 6–2 6–3), **won Wimbledon** (d. Arendt/Bollegraf 7–6 6–4), **r/u US Open** (lost Davenport/Novotna 6–3 6–4); (with Davenport) **won** Tokyo Pan Pacific (d. G. Fernandez/Hingis 6–4 6–3), (with Davenport) **won** Indian Wells (d. Raymond/Tauziat 6–3 6–2), (with Sanchez Vicario) **won** LIPC (d. Appelmans/Oremans 6–2 6–3) (with Sukova) **won** Strasbourg (d. Likhovtseva/Sugiyama 6–1 6–1), (with Sanchez Vicario) **won** Moscow (d. Basuki/Vis 5–3 ret'd); (with Davenport) **r/u** Sydney (lost G. Fernandez/Sanchez Vicario 6–3 6–1), **r/u** Berlin (lost Davenport/Novotna 6–2 3–6 6–2). **CAREER HIGHLIGHTS – SINGLES: French Open** – **r/u 1988** (d. Golarsa, Field, Gurney, Navratilova 6–3 7–6, Sukova 6–2 6–3, Provis 6–3 6–7 7–5, lost Graf 6–0 6–0), **qf 1992** [unseeded] (d. Kohde-Kilsch, Appelmans 6–1 7–6, Mag. Maleeva, Hack, lost Graf 6–3 6–7 6–3); **Australian Open** – **qf 1995** (d. Fusai 6–4 6–0, Farina 6–4 6–2, Wiesner 4–6 7–6 6–4, Nagatsuka 3–6 6–3 6–1, lost Pierce 6–1 6–4); **Wimbledon** – **qf 1990** (d. Harper, G. Fernandez, Magers 2–6 6–2 6–4, Schultz 6–2 6–2, lost Sabatini 6–2 2–6 8–6), **qf 1992** [unseeded] (d. Herreman, Martinez [seed 8] 6–3 5–7 6–4, McNeil, Garrison 6–2 3–6 6–1, lost Graf 6–3 6–1), **qf 1993** [unseeded] (d. K. Maleeva 7–5 4–6 6–3, Strnadova 6–3 6–2, Appelmans 6–3 6–4, Garrison-Jackson 7–5 6–2, lost Navratilova 6–3 6–1); **US Open** – **qf 1993** [unseeded] (d. Smylie 6–3 6–2, Raymond 6–4 6–1, Garrison-Jackson 6–4 6–3, Gaidano 6–0 6–2, lost Sanchez Vicario 3–0 ret'd). **CAREER HIGHLIGHTS – DOUBLES:** (with G. Fernandez unless stated) **Australian Open** – **won 1993** (d. Shriver/Smylie 6–4 6–3), **won 1994** (d. Fendick/McGrath 6–3 4–6 6–4), (with Hingis) **won 1997, r/u 1995** (lost Novotna/Sanchez Vicario 6–3 6–7 6–4); **French Open** – (with Savchenko-Neiland) **won 1989** (d. Graf/Sabatini 6–4 6–4), **won 1992** (d. Martinez/Sanchez Vicario 6–3 6–2), **won 1993** (d. Neiland/Novotna 6–3 7–5), **won 1994** (d. Davenport/Raymond 6–2 6–2), **won 1995** (d. Novotna/Sanchez Vicario 6–7 6–4 7–5), (with Savchenko-Neiland) **r/u 1990** (lost Novotna/Sukova 6–4 7–5), (with Savchenko-Neiland) **r/u 1991** (lost G. Fernandez/Novotna 6–4 6–0), **r/u 1996** (lost Davenport/M. J. Fernandez 6–2 6–1), **won 1997**; **Wimbledon** – (with Savchenko-Neiland) **won 1991** (d. G. Fernandez/Novotna 6–4 3–6 6–4), **won 1992** (d. Novotna/Savchenko-Neiland 6–4 6–1), **won 1993** (d. Neiland/ Novotna 6–4 6–7 6–4), **won 1994** (d. Novotna/Sanchez Vicario 6–4 6–1), (with Savchenko-Neiland) **r/u 1988** (lost Graf/Sabatini 6–3 1–6 12–10), (with Savchenko-Neiland) **r/u 1989** (lost Novotna/Sukova 6–1 6–2), **r/u 1995** (lost Novotna/Sanchez Vicario 5–7 7–5 6–4), **won 1997**; **US Open** – (with Shriver) **won 1991** (d. Savchenko/Novotna 6–4 4–6 7–6), **won 1992** (d. Novotna/ Savchenko-Neiland 7–6 6–1), **won 1995** (d. Schultz/McCarthy 7–5 6–3), **won 1996** (d. Novotna/Sanchez Vicario 1–6 6–1 6–4), **won 1997**; **VS Champs – won 1993** (d. Neiland/Novotna 6–3 7–5), **won 1994** (d. Novotna/Sanchez Vicario 6–3 6–7 6–3), (with Savchenko-Neiland) **r/u 1988** (lost Navratilova/Shriver 6–3 6–4), (with Savchenko-Neiland) **r/u 1989** (lost Navratilova/Shriver 6–3 6–2). **MIXED DOUBLES: Australian Open** – (with Pugh) **won 1990** (d. R. Leach/Garrison 4–6 6–2 6–3), (with Leach) **won 1995** (d. Suk/G. Fernandez 7–6 6–7 6–4).

Only once did the game's greatest pre-war champions meet. At the Carlton Club, Cannes in 1926, Suzanne Lenglen of France (left), at the end of her dazzling career, narrowly beat the 20-year-old American Helen Wills, already the US champion and gold medallist at the Paris Olympics, who would be totally dominant in the next decade. (Wimbledon Museum)

All-Time Greats

David Gray and John Barrett

DAPHNE JESSIE **AKHURST** (Australia)
Born 22/4/03. Died 10/1/33. Became Mrs.R.S.Cozens (1930). The first of Australia's great women champions, she won five Australian singles titles (***1925/26/28/29/30***), five doubles titles with four different partners – S.Lance (***1924***), R.Harper (***1925***), Esna Boyd (***1928***) and L.M. Bickerton (***1929/31***), plus four mixed with three partners – J.Willard (***1924/25***), Jean Borotra (***1928***) and E.F. Moon (***1929***). She first travelled to Europe in ***1925*** and got to the quarter-finals at Wimbledon. Three years later she returned and reached the semi-finals after being a quarter-finalist in Paris, results which earned her an unofficial world ranking of No.3 that year. JB

WILMER LAWSON **ALLISON** (USA)
Born 8/12/04. Died 20/4/77. One of the greatest and most spectacular of American doubles specialists, he also gained some notable singles successes. Possessing a fierce smash, a serve with the 'kick of a Texas mustang', considerable power on the volley, and a fine backhand drive, he found an ideal doubles partner in John Van Ryn. They won at Wimbledon in ***1929–30*** and were runners-up in ***1935***. They took the US title in ***1931*** and ***1935*** and reached the final in ***1930/32/34/36***. His singles form was less consistent, but on his day could play brilliantly. He defeated Perry to win the US title in ***1935***, and in ***1930***, after beating Cochet, he was runner-up to Tilden at Wimbledon. Between ***1929–35*** he played in 45 D Cup rubbers, winning 18 out of 29 singles and 14 of his 16 doubles.

JOSEPH ASBOTH (Hungary)
Born 18/9/17. A stylish right-hander whose victory in the ***1947*** French singles, when he beat Petra, Tom Brown and Sturgess, was Hungary's most important tennis success before their victory in the Saab King's Cup in 1976; 7 times nat champ; 6 times winner of the Hungarian int title; he played 1st at Wimbledon in ***1939*** and impressed those who saw him against Austin in 1r. Lost to Bromwich in the ***1948*** sfs. From ***1938–57*** he played 41 D Cup rubbers in 16 ties, winning 18 of his 30 singles and 6 of 11 doubles.

ARTHUR ROBERT **ASHE** (USA)
Born 10/7/43. Died 13/2/93. A cool, thoughtful, dogged competitor, he was the first black American to win the Wimbledon men's singles title and, in ***1968***, playing as an amateur, he became the first US Open champion. Always happier on fast courts, he tried hard to succeed on clay but endured regular disappointments in Paris and never progressed further than the semi-finals (***1971***) in Rome. He was a semi-finalist at Wimbledon ***1968–69*** before surprising Connors in the ***1975*** final. He defeated Okker to win the US title in ***1968*** but in ***1972*** lost to Nastase after leading by two sets to one and 4–2 in the final. He won Australian singles ***1970*** and the WCT title ***1975***. Refused a visa to South Africa in ***1970***, he broke through apartheid laws to play in Johannesburg ***1973***, losing to Connors in the final and winning the doubles with Okker. After missing most of the ***1977*** season, he regained his place among the leaders of the circuit in ***1978*** and reached match-point against McEnroe in the Masters final. Between ***1963–78***, he appeared in 18 D Cup ties, winning 27 out of 32 singles and one of two doubles. US D Cup captain ***1980–85***, following his retirement from active play owing to a heart condition that had necessitated triple by-pass surgery. Started Arthur Ashe Foundation for the defeat of Aids, the sickness that claimed his life following a transfusion of contaminated blood during his heart operations.

CILLY AUSSEM (Germany)
Born 4/1/09. Died 22/3/63. Later the Contessa della Corta Brae (1936). The first German to win the women's singles at Wimbledon. Her strokes were not strong but she was a model of steadiness and persistence. 'Quite small and more of a girl in appearance with round brown eyes and a cherub face', wrote Helen Wills. 'Her agility on court and the distance that she covers in spite of her shortness are really astonishing.' ***1931*** – when the Californian did not compete – was

her best year. She beat Betty Nuthall in the French f and then defeated Hilde Krahwinkel in Wimbledon's only all-German final. That was a disappointing match, because both women were handicapped by blistered feet. Her victory compensated for an unlucky failure in ***1930***. Then she slipped and sprained an ankle at 4–4 in the fs of her sf against Elizabeth Ryan and had to be carried from the court.

HENRY WILFRED ('**BUNNY**') **AUSTIN** (Great Britain)
Born 26/8/06. Bunny Austin's Wimbledon record was remarkable (and unlucky), but his most important contribution to British tennis was in the D Cup. The possessor of elegant groundstrokes, which compensated for a lack of power in his serving and smashing, he played many of the crucial singles, alongside Perry, in Britain's successful campaigns in the ***1930s***. A former Cambridge Univ captain, he played in 24 ties between ***1929–37***, winning 36 of his 48 rubbers, all singles. He won 8 rubbers out of 12 and 5 out of 8 'live' rubbers in his 6 Challenge Rounds. At Wimbledon he failed only once to reach the qf or go further between ***1929–39***. R/u to Vines ***1932*** and Budge ***1938***, in sf ***1929*** and ***1936/37***, and r/u to Henkel in ***1937*** French singles.

TRACY ANN **AUSTIN** (USA)
Born 12/12/62. Now Mrs. Scott Holt (married on 17th April 1993). An infant prodigy with 25 national age group titles to her name from the 12s to 18s, her meteoric rise under the coaching of Robert Lansdorp inspired a whole generation of teenage wonders. The youngest member of a keen tennis playing family, whose sister Pam and three brothers, Jeff, John and Doug were all tournament players, Tracy defeated Chris Evert for the US Open title in ***1979*** to become, at 16 years 9 months, the youngest ever champion there. The following year her relentless baseline driving, single-handed on the forehand, two-handed on the backhand, plus her excellent court coverage, earned her the No.1 ranking on the WTA computer, ending the four year reign of Evert and Martina Navratilova. In ***1981*** she won a second US Open title at the expense of Navratilova and, with 29 titles to her name, seemed destined to rule the game. But a series of back and neck injuries curtailed her appearances in ***1983*** and she retired from the game in February ***1984***, the victim of physical burn-out. She returned to the Tour in doubles during ***1988*** and had just started to play singles again in ***1989*** when she broke a leg in a motor accident, an injury that required surgery. This delayed her return until ***1993*** when she competed in a few tournaments and played Team Tennis for Raleigh Edge. JB

WILFRED BADDELEY (Great Britain)
Born 11/1/1872. Died 24/1/1929. Youngest winner – at 19 years, 5 months and 23 days – of Wimbledon singles in ***1891*** until Becker in ***1985***. Also won singles in ***1892/95***, and doubles (with twin brother Herbert) ***1891/94/95/96***.

MARCEL BERNARD (France)
Born 18/ 5/14. Died 28/4/94. Shrewd and stylish, a canny left-hander with considerable touch, he is one of only two French players to have won in Paris since the days of the 'Musketeers' (the other is Noah, ***1983***); demonstrated his promise early, reaching the French singles sf and, with Boussus, the doubles in ***1932***, still in sufficient form to be chosen for the French D Cup team in ***1956***. In ***1946*** he won 5 set matches against Petra in the sf and Drobny in the final to take the French title; in sf on 3 other occasions; won the doubles with Borotra (***1936***) and with Petra (***1946***) and the mixed with Lollette Payot (***1935***) and Billie Yorke (***1936***). Between ***1935–56*** he played 42 D Cup rubbers in 25 ties (singles 13–8, doubles 16–5) and he also served as President of the French Tennis Federation.

PAULINE MAY **BETZ** (USA)
Born 6/8/19. Now Mrs Addie (1949). An agile, athletic competitor, who might have gained many more titles if the war had not interrupted international competition. She was ranked eighth in the US in ***1939*** and was the most successful player in wartime competitions there, winning the national title from ***1942–44***. She won Wimbledon at a cost of only 20 games in ***1946***, defeating Louise Brough 6–2 6–4 in the final. She and Miss Hart were runners-up to Miss Brough and Miss Osborne in the doubles and, if she was disappointed in Paris, where Miss Osborne beat her 1–6 8–6 7–5 in the final, after saving two match-points with drop-shots at 5–6 in the second set, she asserted her supremacy again at Forest Hills by defeating Doris Hart 11–9 6–3 in the final. Soon afterwards she turned professional.

BLANCHE BINGLEY (Great Britain)
Born 3/11/1863. Died 6/8/1946. Became Mrs Hillyard (1887). One of the determined pioneers of women's tennis. She competed in the first women's tournament at Wimbledon in ***1884*** and lost to Maud Watson, the eventual champion, in sfs. The following year Miss Watson defeated her in f, but she avenged those failures by beating the champion in the Challenge Round in ***1886***. That was the first of her six victories. Further successes followed in ***1889/94/97/99*** and ***1900***. Only Lottie Dod, who retired in ***1893***, troubled her until Mrs Sterry ended her supremacy in ***1901***. Like many early players, her game was founded on a powerful forehand and strict command of length. A reluctant volleyer who invariably ran round her backhand, she was so quick and so fit that she was difficult to outmanoeuvre. She wore white gloves to give her a better grip and her follow-through on the forehand was said to have been 'so complete that her left shoulder was often a mass of bruises from the impact of the racket'. She married Commander G. W. Hillyard, secretary of the All England Club from ***1907–24***; altogether she competed in the Championships 24 times.

PENELOPE **DORA** HARVEY **BOOTHBY** (Great Britain)
Born 2/8/1881. Died 22/2/1970. Became Mrs Geen (1914). One of the group of players from the county of Middlesex who dominated the early years of women's tennis at Wimbledon. In ***1909*** she won one of the most exciting of the pre-***1914*** f, defeating Miss A. M. Morton 6–4 4–6 8–6 'Few closer or more interesting struggles have ever been witnessed on the famous old court', wrote G. W. Hillyard. She lost the most dismal contest in the history of the Championships to Mrs Lambert Chambers, who beat her 6–0 6–0, in the ***1911*** Challenge Round. Mrs Lambert Chambers had beaten her by the same score at the Beckenham tournament two weeks earlier and had allowed her only four games in the Challenge Round in ***1910***. Somewhat fortunately she and Mrs McNair became Wimbledon's first women's doubles champions in 1913. They were down 2–6 2–4 to Mrs Lambert Chambers and Mrs Sterry in the final when Mrs Sterry fell and retired with a torn tendon. She and Mrs McNair were also semi-finalists in 1922.

BJORN RUNE **BORG** (Sweden)
Born 6/6/56. One of the coolest match players the game has ever known, he matured early, winning his first important title, the ***1974*** Italian Open, shortly before his 18th birthday and the first of his six French Championships just after it. With fierce topspin on both his forehand and his double-handed backhand, a powerful serve and speedy court coverage plus an indomitable will to win, he was virtually invincible on European clay between ***1974–81*** adding the French Open in ***1975/78/79/80/81*** and a second Italian title in ***1978*** as well as the US Pro Championship on US clay in ***1974/75/76***. Never an instinctive volleyer, he confounded those observers who thought his game was unsuited to grass by setting a modern record at Wimbledon where he won five successive titles between ***1976–80***. Only William Renshaw, in the days of the Challenge Round, won more (***1881–86***). He learned to win indoors, taking the WCT title in ***1976*** and the Masters twice (***1979/80***) and leading Sweden to their first D Cup success, a 3–2 victory over Czechoslovakia in Stockholm in ***1975***. But he never solved the problems of the high, fast bounce and positive foothold of US hard courts. Four times he was beaten in the US Open final, twice by Connors (***1976/78***) and twice by McEnroe (***1980/81***), the last three being on asphalt at Flushing Meadow. By the autumn of ***1981*** he felt burnt out and virtually retired from the mainstream, playing only exhibitions and special events. Although he attempted two comebacks, in ***1982/84***, he could no longer make the total commitment and turned to other interests. Seven years later he again attempted a return but fell in his first match to Jordi Arrese in Monte Carlo and competed no more in ***1991***. His legacy to Swedish tennis is immeasurable for he sparked the flame that has burned so brightly ever since through Wilander, Sundstrom, Jarryd, Nystrom and Edberg. His style of errorless, counter-attacking topspin inspired a whole generation of players around the world. JB

JEAN ROBERT **BOROTRA** (France)
Born 13/8/1898. Died 17/7/94. A brilliantly agile volleyer and a shrewd player. One of the 'Four Musketeers' who won the D Cup for France from ***1927–32***. Enthusiastic and popular, he continued to play competitive lawn tennis long past his 90th year. He represented France in every International Club match against Britain from the first in ***1929*** to his 116th and last in ***1993***. Won Wimbledon singles ***1924/26*** and doubles (with R. Lacoste) ***1925*** and (with J. Brugnon) ***1932/33***. French singles ***1924/31***, and the doubles 6 times – (with Lacoste) ***1924/25/29***, (with

Brugnon) ***1928/34***, (with Bernard) ***1936***. Won Australian singles and doubles (with Brugnon) ***1928***. Had long and spectacular covered court record, winning French singles title 12 times, British 11, and US 4. Played 54 D Cup rubbers ***1922–47***, winning 19 of 31 singles and 17 of 23 doubles rubbers in 32 ties.

JOHN EDWARD **BROMWICH** (Australia)
Born 14/11/18. A gracefully unorthodox player whose career might have been even more successful if it had not been interrupted by World War II. Ambidextrous but using both hands on the forehand, he used a very light, softly strung racket to control the ball with great subtlety. He won the Australian singles in ***1939*** and regained the title from Quist in ***1946***. Those were his only major singles victories, although he was agonisingly close to success in f of ***1948*** Wimbledon when he lost to Falkenburg after leading 5–2 in the fs and holding three match-points. But it was in doubles, mostly with Quist or Sedgman, that he earned most honours. He won at Wimbledon in ***1948*** (with Sedgman) ***1950*** (with Quist), took the US title three times, and he and Quist ruled in Australia from ***1938–40*** and ***1946–50***. Won the Wimbledon mixed with Louise Brough, ***1947/48***, and played in 51 D Cup rubbers between ***1937–50***, winning 19 of his 30 singles and 20 of his 21 doubles in 23 ties.

NORMAN EVERARD **BROOKES** (Australia)
Born 14/11/1877. Died 28/9/1968. The first overseas winner of men's singles at Wimbledon. Left-handed and a notable volleyer, he lost to H. L. Doherty in Challenge Round on first visit to Wimbledon 1905. Won singles and doubles (with A. F. Wilding) ***1907*** and ***1914*** and Australian singles in ***1911*** and doubles in ***1924*** with J. O. Anderson. With Wilding won the D Cup for Australasia in ***1907***. Between ***1905–20*** he played 39 rubbers and was 6 times a member of a side which won the Challenge Round. Returned to Wimbledon in ***1924*** at 46 and reached the 4r. Nicknamed 'The Wizard' he received the French Legion of Honour for his services as a captain in the British Army in World War One, and in ***1939*** he was knighted.

ALTHEA **LOUISE BROUGH** (USA)
Born 11/3/23. Now Mrs Clapp (1958). An aggressive server and volleyer, she played a major part in establishing American domination of women's tennis immediately after World War II. Won Wimbledon singles ***1948/49/50*** and again in ***1955*** after the retirement of Maureen Connolly (who beat her in ***1952*** and ***1954*** f), She also won US in ***1947***, and Australian, ***1950***. She and Margaret Osborne du Pont formed a redoubtable doubles partnership, winning 5 times at Wimbledon (***1946/48/49/50/54***) and 3 times in Paris, (***1946/47/49***) and holding the US title 12 times from ***1942–50*** and ***1955–57***. She was mixed doubles champ at Wimbledon with Tom Brown (***1946***), Bromwich (***1947/48***) and Sturgess (***1950***) and took all 3 titles in ***1948*** and ***1950***. She played 22 W Cup rubbers between ***1946–57*** and was never beaten.

JACQUES ('**TOTO**') **BRUGNON** (France)
Born 11/5/1895. Died 20/3/1978. The doubles specialist of the 'Four Musketeers', he gained most of his early success with Cochet and then formed a partnership with Borotra, which was still capable of reaching the ***1939*** French f, when he was 44 and Borotra 40, and coming three times within a point of the title. He and Borotra returned to Wimbledon and reached the 3r in ***1948***. Won Wimbledon doubles with Cochet (***1926/28***) and Borotra (***1932/33***). Between ***1927–34*** won French doubles 3 times with Cochet (***1927/30/32***) and twice with Borotra (***1928/34***). Also Australian doubles with Borotra (***1928***). Reached singles sf at Wimbledon, ***1926***. Played 31 D Cup doubles (winning 22) and 6 singles (winning 4) in 31 ties ***1921–34***.

JOHN DONALD ('**DON**') **BUDGE** (USA)
Born 13/6/15. The first player to bring off the Grand Slam of the 4 historic singles titles in one year – ***1938*** – after which he immediately turned professional. A relentless competitor with a majestic backhand he won all 3 titles at Wimbledon in ***1937*** and ***1938***, the doubles with G. Mako and mixed with Alice Marble. Won US singles ***1937/38*** and doubles with Mako ***1936/38***. plus French and Australian singles ***1938*** and won 19 out of 21 singles and 6 out of 8 doubles rubbers in 11 D Cup ties from ***1935*** to ***1938***.

MARIA ESTHER ANDION **BUENO** (Brazil)
Born 11/10/39. The most gracefully artistic of post-war women's champions. For nearly a decade her rivalry with Margaret Court provided the principal excitement of the women's

game, but at the end she was plagued by injury. Won Wimbledon singles ***1959/60/64***, and doubles (with Althea Gibson) ***1958***, (with Darlene Hard) ***1960/63***, (with Billie Jean King) ***1965***, and (with Nancy Gunter) ***1966***. US singles ***1959/63/64/66*** and doubles (with Darlene Hard) ***1960/62***, (with Nancy Gunter) ***1966***, and (with Margaret Court) ***1968***. French doubles (with Darlene Hard) ***1960***. Australian doubles (with Christine Truman) ***1960***. Italian singles, ***1958/61/65***.

DOROTHEA KATHERINE **CHAMBERS** (Great Britain)
Born 3/9/1878. Died 7/1/1960. Nee Douglass. Married Robert Lambert Chambers in 1907. The most successful British woman player before 1914, she won Wimbledon singles 7 times and lost dramatically to Suzanne Lenglen in 1919 Challenge Round after holding 2 match-points. Played in 1926 W Cup – 23 years after first success at Wimbledon. The daughter of an Ealing vicar, she became a coach in 1928. Won Wimbledon singles ***1903/04/06/10/11/13/14*** and reached f of ladies' doubles in ***1913***, its first year.

HENRI JEAN **COCHET** (France)
Born 14/12/01. Died 1/4/87. The great instinctive genius of lawn tennis, swift and imagin-ative, a master of the volley and half-volley, whose play could rise to dizzy heights and sometimes slip to unexpected disaster. Won Wimbledon singles ***1927/29*** and doubles (with J. Brugnon) ***1926/28***. US singles ***1928***. French singles ***1922/26/28/30/32*** and doubles (with Brugnon) ***1927/30/32***. With the other 'Musketeers', he played successfully in 6 Challenge Rounds. Between ***1922*** and ***1933***, when he turned professional, he won 34 of 42 D Cup singles rubbers and 10 out of 16 doubles from 26 ties. After the war reinstated as an amateur.

MAUREEN ('LITTLE MO') CATHERINE **CONNOLLY** (USA)
Born 17/9/34. Died 21/6/69. Became Mrs. Norman Brinker (1955). The most determined and concentrated of post-war women's champions she hit her groundstrokes with remorseless accuracy. Won US singles in ***1951*** at the age of 16 and thereafter lost only 4 matches – 2 to Doris Hart, one to Shirley Fry, and another to Beverley Fleitz – before she broke her leg in a riding accident in ***1954*** and retired. She was never beaten in singles at Wimbledon, winning ***1952/53/54***. She won US singles ***1951/52/53*** French singles ***1953/54*** and (with Mrs H. C. Hopman) doubles ***1954***. Australian singles and doubles (with Julie Sampson) ***1953*** Italian singles ***1954***. She won all 9 of her W Cup rubbers and in ***1953*** she was the first woman to bring off the Grand Slam of the 4 major singles titles in the same year.

JAMES ('**JIMMY**') SCOTT **CONNORS** (USA)
Born 2/9/52. One of the most durable of champions and a natural entertainer, he grew up in Bellville, Illinois where his mother Gloria, herself a fine player, and his grandmother, instilled the never-say-die attitude that was to make him one of the most competitive players of all time. Moving to California as a teenager, he was guided by the two Pancho's – Gonzales and Segura – and in ***1971*** won the NCAA Championships as a freshman at UCLA. A year later in Jacksonville, shrewdly guided by his manager Bill Riordan, he won his first professional title. Seventeen years later, in Tel Aviv, he won his last. It was his 109th tournament success – a record for men. Altogether he had spent 268 weeks as the world's No.1 ranked player (second only to Lendl's 270). His 160 consecutive weeks at the top from 29/7/74 to 23/8/77 is a world record. An aggressive left-hander with a lethal double-handed backhand, he was a natural 'street fighter', whose early vulgarity (which diminished with age), was ignored by his fans and forgiven by those who recognised his extraordinary ability as a fearless match player. The first Grand Slam title he won was the ***1973*** Wimbledon doubles, with Ilie Nastase, who also partnered him to victory in the ***1975*** US Open doubles. His service returns and passing shots were among the greatest ever seen and brought him one Australian (***1974***), two Wimbledon (***1974***,***1982***) and five US Open (***1974***,***1976***,***1978***,***1982***,***1983***) singles titles. He is the only man to have won the US title on all three surfaces – grass, clay and hard courts. His failure to win a major international title on clay was the only blemish on an otherwise brilliant career. JB

ASHLEY JOHN **COOPER** (Australia)
Born 15/9/36. A strong and determined competitor who maintained Australia's command of the international game after Hoad and Rosewall turned professional. After being overwhelmed by Hoad in the ***1957*** f at Wimbledon, he returned to beat Fraser in a stern test of endurance in

1958. He was US champion **1958** and won Australian ***1957–58***. His doubles victories included Australia ***1958***, France ***1957–58*** and US **1958**. He played singles when Australia successfully defended the D Cup in ***1957*** and in ***1958*** when Australia lost to the USA in Brisbane, winning one rubber in each match. He beat Seixas and lost to Mackay ***1957*** and beat Mackay and lost to Olmedo ***1958***.

CHARLOTTE REINAGLE **COOPER** (Great Britain)
Born 22/9/1870. Died 10/10/1966. Became Mrs Sterry (1901). One of the first successful women volleyers, she won at Wimbledon ***1895/96/98/1901/08***. Overshadowed at first by Mrs Hillyard – her first three victories were gained in years when the older player did not compete – she defeated her at last in ***1901***, the year of her marriage, after losing to Mrs Hillyard in four previous matches at the Championships. In ***1902*** she lost in the famous re-played Challenge Round to Muriel Robb (they stopped at 4–6 13–11 on the first evening, then began again and Miss Robb won 7–5 6–1) and then regained the title in ***1908*** after beating Mrs Lambert Chambers in the quarter-finals. She reached the All-Comers' final in ***1912*** and took Mrs McNair to 9–7 in the third set of a qf in ***1913***. Her attacking spirit delighted her contemporaries. 'Her smiling good temper and sportsmanship made her as popular a player as ever went on to the Centre Court', wrote Burrow. 'She had a constitution like the proverbial ostrich. She never knew what it was to be tired and was never sick or sorry', said Hillyard.

THELMA DOROTHY **COYNE** (Australia)
Born 14/10/18 Became Mrs.M.N. Long (30/1/41). A great all-rounder whose career coincided with that of Nancy Bolton who became a great friend and rival. She first reached the Australian final in ***1940*** where Bolton beat her, as she did again in ***1951***. The following year (***1952***) she won the first of two Australian titles (the other was in ***1954***). Ten of her twelve Australian doubles titles were won with Bolton (***1936/37/38/39/40/47/48/49/51/52***) and the other two with Mary Hawton (***1956/58***). Her four mixed titles were won with George Worthington (***1951/52/55***) and Rex Hartwig (***1954***). Her lone success outside Australia came in ***1956*** when she combined with Chile's Luis Ayala to win the French mixed title. JB

JOHN ('**JACK**') HERBERT **CRAWFORD** (Australia)
Born 22/3/08. Died 10/9/91. Classic stylist, he beat H. E. Vines in ***1933*** in one of the greatest of all Wimbledon f. Won Wimbledon doubles (with A. K. Quist) ***1935***. French singles ***1933*** and doubles (with Quist) ***1935***, Australian singles ***1931/33*** and doubles (with H. C. Hopman) ***1929/30***, (with E. F. Moon) ***1932***, and (with V. B. McGrath) ***1935***. Won 36 out of 58 D Cup rubbers (23–16 singles, 13–5 doubles) between ***1928–37***.

DWIGHT FILLEY **DAVIS** (USA)
Born 5/7/1879. Died 28/11/1945. The donor of the D Cup, the trophy at stake in the International Team Championship. A Harvard undergraduate, he played against the British Isles in the first two matches of that competition, winning a single and partnering Holcombe Ward successfully in the doubles in ***1900*** and, with H. Ward again, losing to the Dohertys in the doubles in ***1902***. A left-hander, he won the US doubles with H. Ward from ***1899–1901***, retiring undefeated, and also the All-Comers' final at Wimbledon with Ward in ***1901***, only to fall to the Dohertys in the Challenge Round. He was President of the US LTA in ***1923***, US Secretary of War ***1925–29*** and later Governor-General of the Philippines.

MAXIME ('**MAX**') OMER **DECUGIS** (France)
Born 24/9/1882. Died 6/9/1978. The first great French player. He spent his schooldays in England and won his first tournaments there. Short, quick, and wiry, he was an aggressive competitor, whom Laurie Doherty described as 'the most promising young player in the world'. He dominated French tennis from ***1903***, when he won in Paris for the first time, to the outbreak of World War I, winning the singles ***1903/04/07/09/12/14***, and the doubles from ***1902–14*** and again in ***1920*** when the Champs were resumed. He was still playing well enough to reach the singles final in ***1923*** when he was 41. By that time the age of the 'Musketeers' was dawning. Although he competed regularly at Wimbledon, he never progressed beyond the singles sf (***1911/12***) but, with Gobert, he gained France's first title by winning the doubles in ***1911***.

CHARLOTTE ('**LOTTIE**') **DOD** (Great Britain)
Born 24/9/1871. Died 27/6/1960. The first lawn tennis prodigy. Won the first of 5 Wimbledon titles in ***1887*** from a field of 5 challengers at the age of 15 years and 10 months. When she retired, she became an international golfer and hockey player. Nicknamed the 'Little Wonder', she won Wimbledon singles ***1887/88/91/92/93*** in years when there were never more than 9 players in the All-Comers' draw.

HUGH **LAURENCE DOHERTY** (Great Britain)
Born London, 8/10/1875. Died 21/8/1919. Learnt game with elder brother, Reginald Frank ('Reggie'), at Westminster School. Played for Cambridge Univ against Oxford in ***1896–98*** and developed into one of the most spectacular, aggressive, stylish, and successful of British players. 'Laurie' Doherty was celebrated for smashing and volleying, and for speed about the court. With his brother, formed one of the greatest doubles partnerships in the history of the game. Won All-Comers' singles at Wimbledon, ***1898***, and singles champ ***1902–06***. Doubles champ (with R. F. Doherty) ***1897–1901***, ***1903–05***. First overseas player to win US singles, ***1903***, and doubles, ***1902/03***. In 5 D Cup Challenge Rounds, ***1902–06***, he was never beaten, winning 7 singles rubbers and 5 doubles.

REGINALD FRANK **DOHERTY** (Great Britain)
Born London, 14/10/1872. Died 29/12/1910. The senior partner of the great Doherty combination and the most notable stylist of early lawn tennis. Contemporary observers called his backhand, produced with back swing, full follow-through and remarkable touch, 'a model of perfection'. Was Wimbledon singles champ ***1897–1900*** and doubles champ ***1897–1901*** and ***1903–05***. Reached the doubles Challenge Round at Wimbledon for first time with H. A. Nisbet in ***1896***. Thereafter he and his brother, H. L. Doherty, were beaten only by S. H. Smith and F. L. Riseley at Wimbledon. They lost to this pair in ***1902***, then beat them in the next three Challenge Rounds before falling to them again in ***1906***. The Dohertys won the US doubles in ***1902/03***. Won South African singles and doubles ***1909***.

JAROSLAV DROBNY (Great Britain)
Born 12/10/21. Exiled himself from Czechoslovakia in ***1949***, became Egyptian subject in ***1950*** and a naturalised Briton in ***1960***. One of the great post-war clay court competitors with tremendous left-hand serve and smash, and delicate touch, he played in some of Wimbledon's most dramatic and emotional matches and eventually won the singles in ***1954*** at the age of 33. In ***1946*** he beat Kramer, the favourite in 4 r and lost to Geoff Brown (AUS) in sf; he lost to Schroeder in the ***1949*** f; in ***1950*** he let a two-set lead slip against Sedgman; Mottram surprised him in **1951**; he fell to Sedgman again in the ***1952*** f; and in ***1953*** he never recovered from beating Patty 8–6 16–18 3–6 8–6 12–10 in Wimbledon's second longest singles. The following year, when his chance seemed to be slipping away, he beat Rosewall, then 19, in f. He won in Paris in ***1951/52*** (after another series of dramatic failures), Italy ***1950/51/53*** and Germany ***1950***. Between ***1946–49*** he won 37 of his 43 D Cup rubbers in 15 ties, (24–4 singles, 13–2 doubles).

FRANCOISE DURR (France)
Born 25/12/42. Now Mrs Browning (1975). The outstanding French woman player of the 1960s and 1970s. Shrewd and unorthodox, particularly in her serve and on the backhand, she excelled in doubles. She gained her major singles successes in ***1967*** when she won the French and German titles and reached the US semi-finals, but in doubles won a host of titles with a variety of partners, including five successive French victories – with Gail Sheriff (later Mrs Chanfreau and now Mrs Lovera) ***1967*** and ***1970/71***, and with Ann Jones, ***1968/69***. Won US doubles ***1972*** with Betty Stove, and Italian and South African titles ***1969*** with Jones. She failed, however, in six Wimbledon doubles finals between ***1965–75***. Won Wimbledon mixed doubles with Tony Roche ***1976*** and the French with Jean-Claude Barclay in ***1968/71/73***.

STEFAN **EDBERG** (Sweden)
Born 19 January 1966 in Vastervik, Sweden. One of the greatest of modern serve-and-volley players, he broke the Swedish double-handed mould created by Bjorn Borg when his first coach, Percy Rosberg (who had also coached Borg) advised him to change to a single-handed stroke because of his natural volleying ability. It was sound advice. In ***1983***, at the end of an outstanding junior career, he won the junior Grand Slam, the only time the feat has been achieved since

the four major tournaments became Championship events in ***1975***. (Butch Buchholz had won all four in ***1958*** when they were invitation tournaments). Major honours soon followed. Revelling in the fast conditions of Australian grass he won the last two Opens played at Kooyong in December ***1985*** and January ***1987*** (no Championship was held in 1996 to accommodate a return to the traditional January date). A year later (***1988***) he won the first of his two Wimbledon titles, beating his great rival Boris Becker in the final, a success he would repeat in ***1990*** after losing to the German in the ***1989*** final. On 13th August ***1990*** he became the No.1 player in the world, a position he would hold for a total of 66 weeks in three spells until finally displaced by Jim Courier on 5 October ***1992***. In ***1991*** he won the first of two US Opens with a blistering display of attacking tennis against Courier that Edberg himself believed was his best ever performance. His second US win in ***1992***, against Pete Sampras, was his last major success in a career that brought him 41 titles altogether from the 77 singles finals he contested and 18 doubles titles from 29 finals. His three Grand Slam doubles success came ten years apart - the first two (with Jarryd) were in ***1987*** at the Australian and US Opens, the last (with Korda) at the ***1997*** Australian Open in his farewell year. His only major disappointment was the loss to Chang in the French Open final of ***1989***. In Davis Cup he was a member of Sweden's successful teams in ***1984***, ***1985*** and ***1994*** winning 35 of his 50 singles rubbers and 12 of his 20 doubles rubbers in 35 ties between ***1983*** and ***1997***. At the Olympic Games he won the ***1984*** demonstration event in Los Angeles and won bronze medals in singles and doubles at the Seoul Games in ***1988***. In Barcelona(***1992***) he carried the Swedish flag in the opening ceremony. In a long and distinguished career that earned him prize money alone totalling $20.6 million, he was respected as much for his impeccable manners and his chivalry in victory and defeat as for his beautiful backhand, fluid court coverage and wonderfully quick reflexes. It was no surprise when his peers named the annual ATP Tour Sportsmanship Award after him. JB

MARK RONALD **EDMONDSON** (Australia)
Born 28/6/54. On two golden afternoons on the fast grass at Kooyong, this burly battler from Gosford, NSW. beat first Ken Rosewall, then defending champion John Newcombe, to capture the ***1976*** Australian Championships. Between ***1980*** and ***1984*** he won the Australian doubles title four times with three different partners (***1980***, ***1981*** with Warwick, ***1983*** with McNamee, ***1984*** with Stewart). Warwick was again his partner when he won the ***1985*** French doubles, his only other Grand Slam success. JB

ROY STANLEY **EMERSON** (Australia)
Born 3/11/36. A remarkable athlete, lean, keen, and 'trained to the last ounce', who led Australia's international challenge for five years after Laver turned professional in ***1962***. A Queenslander, his 28 Grand Slam titles (12 singles, 16 doubles) are a record for men. The only man to win singles and doubles at all four major championships, he won Wimbledon singles ***1964/65*** but injury in ***1966*** spoilt his chance of equalling Perry's record of three successive titles. Won the doubles with Fraser ***1959/61***, US singles ***1961/64*** and doubles ***1959/60*** (with Fraser) and ***1965/66*** (with Stolle), Australian singles ***1961*** and ***1963/64/65/66/67*** and doubles ***1962*** (with Fraser), ***1966*** (with Stolle) and ***1969*** (with Laver). On clay courts won the French singles ***1963/67***, Italian ***1959/61/66*** and German ***1967*** and his most interesting doubles achievement was to take the French title from ***1960–65*** with five different partners, Fraser ***1960/62***, Laver ***1961***, Santana ***1963***, Fletcher ***1964***, and Stolle ***1965***. He won 34 of his 38 D Cup rubbers (21–2 singles, 13–2 doubles) in 18 ties and played in 9 successive Challenge Rounds between ***1959–67***.

CHRISTINE ('**CHRIS**') MARIE **EVERT** (USA)
Born Fort Lauderdale, Fl., 21/12/54. Now Mrs Andy Mill (married 30 July 1988). Coached by father Jimmy in Fort Lauderdale to become the most consistent back–court player of her generation: she won at least one Grand Slam singles title every year from ***1974*** to ***1986*** during which period her friendly rivalry with Martina Navratilova dominated the women's game. When she and Jimmy Connors (who were engaged at the time) won the two Wimbledon singles titles in ***1974*** with their double-handed backhands they legitimised the stroke and set a fashion that became a world trend. Her metronomic consistency, unshakeable concentration and fearless resolve to go for her shots were legendary and earned her more professional titles (157) than any other player, male or female, during the Open era until Martina Navratilova passed that total in ***1992***, plus a fortune in prize money ($8,896,195). She competed for 19 consecutive years at the US Open and reached 9 finals, 8 semi-finals and was twice beaten in the quarter-finals,

including her last year ***1989*** when she won her 101st match at these Championships, a record. As a sixteen-year-old, in ***1971***, she reached the first of four consecutive semi-finals on grass at Forest Hills. In ***1975/76/77*** she won the title there on US clay and repeated that success on hard courts at Flushing Meadow in ***1978/80/82***, by which time her first husband, John Lloyd (married 17 April 1979, divorced April 1987) had helped her to become a much better volleyer. In 13 challenges in Paris between ***1973*** and ***1988*** she won seven of the nine finals she contested (***1974/75/ 79/80/83/85/86***) and only in her last year failed to reach the semi-final, losing in the third round to Arantxa Sanchez Vicario. She competed at Wimbledon every year from ***1972–89*** and only in ***1983*** (when she was ill and lost to Kathy Jordan) did she fail to reach the semi-finals. She was the champion 3 times (***1974/76/81***), a finalist 7 times (***1973/78/79/80/82/84/85***) and a semi-finalist 7 times (***1972/75/77/86/87/88/89***). She competed in the Australian Open six times between ***1974–88***, winning the title in ***1982*** and ***1984*** and reaching the final in ***1974/81/85/88***. Her 18 Grand Slam singles titles place her equal fourth with Martina Navratilova behind Margaret Court (26), Steffi Graf (22) and Helen Wills Moody (19) on the list of great champions. Her streak of 125 consecutive wins on clay courts ***August 1973–May 1979*** is an all-time record and her prodigious achievement in reaching the semi-finals or better at 52 of her last 56 Grand Slams is unlikely ever to be equalled. She represented the United States eight times in the Fed Cup and won all but two of her 42 singles rubbers and 16 of 18 doubles rubbers in 42 ties between ***1977–89***. She was unbeaten in 26 W Cup singles rubbers and won 8 of the 12 doubles rubbers she contested in 13 ties between ***1971– 85***. JB

ROBERT ('**BOB**') **FALKENBURG** (USA)
Born 29/1/26. Won the US Junior Championship in ***1943–44*** and came to Europe in ***1947*** with the reputation of possessing the fastest service in the US. He won at Queen's Club, but lost to Pails in qf at Wimbledon and then won the doubles with Kramer, defeating Mottram and Sidwell in f. The following year ***1948*** he won one of Wimbledon's most dramatic f, defeating Bromwich 7–5 0–6 6–2 3–6 7–5 after saving three match-points as 3–5 in 5s. He was born in New York, learnt most of his tennis in Los Angeles and moved to Brazil, for whom he played in the D Cup on a residential qualification.

NEALE ANDREW **FRASER** (Australia)
Born 3/10/33. A consistently aggressive left-hander, with a plain, direct serve-and-volley game, he was trained by Harry Hopman, winning 18 of 21 D Cup rubbers (11–1 singles, 7–2 doubles) in 11 ties between ***1958*** and ***1963***, and later captained the Australian team which recaptured the trophy at Cleveland in ***1973*** and at Melbourne in ***1978/83***. Fraser started his Wimbledon career in the qualifying competition and ended by winning the singles in ***1960*** after a remarkable escape in the qf. when Butch Buchholz, who had held 5 match-points against him, retired with cramp. He won the doubles with Emerson ***1959/61*** and mixed with du Pont in ***1962*** – the year in which he and his brother, John, a Melbourne doctor, both reached the singles sf. Neither got through to the f. He won the US singles ***1959/60*** and doubles in ***1957*** (with Cooper) and ***1959/60*** (with Emerson), the French doubles in ***1958*** (with Cooper) and ***1960/62*** (with Emerson) and Australian doubles, in ***1957*** (with Hoad), ***1958*** (with Cooper) and ***1962*** (with Emerson).

SHIRLEY JUNE **FRY** (USA)
Born 30/6/27. Now Mrs Irvin (1957). A persistent competitor, whose most notable performances were in doubles. She was first ranked in the top ten in the US in ***1944***, but she did not gain her two major singles successes until ***1956*** when she won both Wimbledon and Forest Hills. Until then she had always been thwarted by fellow-Americans. She won the Wimbledon doubles from ***1951–53*** with Doris Hart, losing only four games in capturing the title in ***1953*** and beat Helen Fletcher and Jean Quertier 6–0 6–0 in sf and Julie Sampson and Maureen Connolly by the same score in f. They won the US title ***1951–54***. Her other successes included the Wimbledon mixed, with Seixas, ***1956***, the Australian singles and doubles, with Althea Gibson, ***1957***, and the French singles, ***1951***, and doubles, with Hart, ***1950–53***. She played in six W Cup contests, winning 10 rubbers and losing twice.

VITAS KEVIN **GERULAITIS** (USA)
Born 26/7/54. Died 18/9/94. Ranked among the world's top ten from ***1977–1982*** when he won 27 titles from 55 finals, this popular American, the son of Lithuanian immigrants, reached three Grand Slam finals on three different surfaces, thanks to a fine all-court game that lacked only a

really decisive winning weapon. He won the Australian Open (***1977***), lost to John McEnroe in the US Open final (***1979***), and to his great friend Bjorn Borg in the French final (***1980***). Borg had also beaten him in the Wimbledon semi-final of ***1977***. This five set match of brilliant rallies contained few losers and was one of the greatest Centre Court battles of modern times. Two years earlier he had won the doubles at Wimbledon (***1975***) with Sandy Mayer, unseeded. He also reached two Masters finals. In ***1979*** Borg was simply too good for him but in ***1981*** he won the first two sets against Ivan Lendl and held a match point in the third but lost in five. He first represented the United States in the Davis Cup in ***1977*** and won 11 of the 14 rubbers he played, all in singles, in 7 ties. After retiring from the mainstream at the end of ***1985*** he played a lot of golf, became an excellent colour commentator on television, and played the guitar alongside John McEnroe to raise funds to help underprivileged kids in the New York area. In ***1994***, still a lively 40-year-old, he had started competing again on the seniors tour. Tragically, he died of carbon monoxide poisoning while watching TV at the poolside home of a friend in Southampton, Long Island, where the heater proved to be faulty. JB

ALTHEA GIBSON (USA)
Born 25/8/27. Became Mrs W A Darben (1965) and Mrs S Llewellyn (1983). The first black player to dominate international lawn tennis, relying on fierce serving and considerable strength and reach. Won Wimbledon singles ***1957/58*** and (doubles (with Angela Buxton) ***1957*** and (with Maria Bueno) ***/58***. US singles ***1957/58***. French singles and doubles (with Angela Buxton) ***1956***. Australian doubles (with Shirley Fry) ***1957***. Italian singles ***1956***. W Cup ***1957/58***, turned professional ***1958*** and for a brief spell competed on the women's golf tour.

ANDRE HENRI **GOBERT** (France)
Born 30/9/1890. Died 6/12/1951. Wallis Myers described him as 'perhaps the greatest indoor player of all time'. With Decugis, he gained France's first Wimbledon title by defeating the holders, Ritchie and Wilding, in ***1911***. Although they were beaten by Dixon and Roper Barrett the following year, the brilliant Gobert's compensation was a place in the All-Comers' singles f in which he lost to the experienced A. W. Gore. He won the French covered court title from ***1911–13*** and again in ***1920*** and the British covered court event in ***1911–12*** and again from ***1920–22***. He first played in the D Cup in ***1912*** and won 2 of his 7 singles and one of his 3 doubles rubbers in 5 ties He also won two Olympic gold medals in ***1912***.

RICHARD ALONZO ('**PANCHO**') **GONZALES** (USA)
Born 9/5/28. Died 3/7/95. A dramatic and spectacular competitor, who was undoubtedly the best player in the world for most of the 1950s. He turned pro in ***1949*** after winning the US singles in ***1948/49***, taking the US Clay Court title ***1948/49***, the US indoor title ***1949***, and winning the doubles in Paris and at Wimbledon – in his only amateur appearances there – in ***1949*** with Parker. Thereafter he played his brilliant, angry tennis away from the main arenas of the game until, at last, open competition was allowed. By then he was 40, but he played one last great match for the Wimbledon crowd. In ***1969*** he beat Pasarell 22–24 1–6 16–14 6–3 11–9 in 5hr 12min – the longest singles seen at Wimbledon. His only D Cup appearance was in the ***1949*** Challenge Round v. Australia when he beat both Sedgman and Sidwell as the USA retained the trophy.

EVONNE FAY **GOOLAGONG** (Australia)
Born 31/7/51. Now Mrs Roger Cawley (married in 1975). One of the most naturally gifted of champions, she was the first of her Aborigine race to excel at the game. Suddenly in ***1971*** at the age of 19, 3 years before her coach Vic Edwards had forecast she would, she swept through both the French Championships and Wimbledon on a cloud of inspiration to win her first major titles. Although she reached the Wimbledon final again the following year and twice more, in ***1975*** and ***1976***, it was not until ***1980*** that she won again – four years after the birth of her daughter, Kelly. This was the first win by a mother since Dorothea Lambert Chambers's success in ***1914***. The nine-year gap between her championships was also the greatest since Bill Tilden's wins in ***1921*** and ***1930***. She was always more at home on faster surfaces where her beautifully instinctive volleying paid handsome dividends and she won her native Australian Open on that surface four times – ***1974/75/76/78***. She was always a competent player on clay but tended to be rather erratic as her famous 'walkabouts' led to extravagant errors. Nevertheless, besides the French Open in ***1971*** she also won the Italian title

in ***1973***. The other highlights of her singles career were the victories in the South African Championships (***1972***) and the Virginia Slims Champs (***1974/76***). She was a good doubles player and won once at Wimbledon (***1974***), four times in Melbourne (***1971/74/75/ 76***) and twice in Johannesburg (***1971/72***). In seven years of Fed Cup duty for Australia from ***1971–82*** she won 33 of the 38 rubbers she contested in 24 ties. JB

ARTHUR WILLIAM CHARLES (WENTWORTH) **GORE** (Great Britain)
Born 2/1/1868. Died 1/12/1928. Wimbledon's oldest champ and probably the most persistent and industrious competitor in the history of the Champs. He played there for the first time in ***1888*** and although the Dohertys, Brookes, and Wilding were among his contemporaries, won the singles 3 times ***1901*** and ***1908/09*** and, at the age of 44 years and 6 months, won the right to challenge Wilding for the title in ***1912***. That was his seventh appearance in the Challenge Round in 13 years. He was almost entirely a forehand player, hitting the ball flat with the racket in a dead line with his outstretched arm. His lightness of foot enabled him to protect his backhand which was no more than a safe push. He competed at every Wimbledon between ***1888–1927*** and captained the first British D Cup team at Boston in ***1900***, reaching sf at the US Champs on that trip.

KAREN JANICE **HANTZE** (USA)
Born 11/12/42. Now Mrs Susman (1961). One of the new generation of aggressive Californians who arrived on the international scene at the start of the 1960s, she won the doubles at Wimbledon with the 17-year-old Billie Jean Moffitt in ***1961*** and then defeated Vera Sukova in the ***1962*** singles final. Marriage and motherhood restricted her tennis, but she won US doubles (again with Moffitt) ***1964***. She played W Cup ***1960–62*** and ***1965***, winning six of her nine matches, and Fed Cup ***1965***, when she played only in doubles and won all 4 rubbers.

DARLENE RUTH **HARD** (USA)
Born 6/1/36. An energetic volleyer, a shrewd tactician, and one of the best doubles players of her generation, she won the US singles in ***1960/61*** and the French singles ***1960***, but she failed in both her Wimbledon finals, losing to Althea Gibson in ***1957*** and Maria Bueno ***1960***. She won the Wimbledon doubles, with Gibson (***1957***), Jeanne Arth (***1959***), and twice with Bueno (***1960/63***) and the mixed in ***1957*** (with Rose), ***1959–60*** (with Laver). She won the US doubles six times – with Arth (***1958/59***), Bueno (***1960/62***), Turner (***1961***) and Durr (***1969***) and the French doubles three times – with Fleitz (***1955***), Bloomer (***1957***) and Buero (***1960***). Perhaps her most surprising American success came in ***1969***, some years after she had retired from regular competition, when she and Francoise Durr defeated Margaret Court and Virginia Wade 0–6 6–3 6–4 in f.

DORIS JANE **HART** (USA)
Born 20/6/25. In spite of childhood illness which impeded her movement, she became one of the subtlest and most graceful of post-war competitors. Won Wimbledon singles ***1951***, doubles (with Pat Todd) ***1947*** and (with Shirley Fry) ***1951/52/53***. US singles ***1954/55*** and doubles (with Shirley Fry) ***1951/52/53/54***. French singles ***1950/52*** and doubles (with Pat Todd) ***1948*** and (with Shirley Fry) ***1950/51/53***. Australian singles ***1949*** and doubles (with Louise Brough) ***1950***. Italian singles ***1951/53*** and South African singles ***1952***. Also won many mixed titles, notably with E. V. Seixas at Wimbledon ***1953/54/55***. Turned professional ***1955***.

ADRIANNE ('**ANN**') SHIRLEY **HAYDON** (Great Britain)
Born 17/10/38. Married Philip (Pip) Jones in 1962. A shrewd, persistent left-hander, who reached sf at Wimbledon 7 times in 10 years, she captured the title at last in ***1969*** after beating Margaret Court in sf and Billie Jean King, to whom she had been r/u in ***1967***, in f. She achieved international fame as a table tennis player, but decided to concentrate on lawn tennis after being r/u in three events in the ***1957*** World Table Tennis Champs. She won the French title in ***1961/66***, Rome in ***1966*** and was twice r/u at Forest Hills ***1961/67***. She took the French doubles (with Francoise Durr) in ***1968/69*** and won the Wimbledon mixed with Stolle in ***1969***. Her W Cup record – 15 successful rubbers out of 32 in 12 matches – is another remarkable illustration of her tenacity and consistency.

ROBERT ('**BOB**') ANTHONY JOHN **HEWITT** (South Africa)
Born in Sydney, Australia, 12/1/40. He moved to South Africa in the early ***1960s*** and started to represent that country when his residential qualification matured in ***1967***. A big brooding vol-

cano of a man, he had a deceptively fine touch and became one of the greatest right-court returners of the serve of modern times. He enjoyed two careers – first with fellow-Australian Fred Stolle and then with South Africa's Frew McMillan. With Stolle he won Wimbledon twice (***1962/64***) the Australian Championship twice (***1963/64***) and the Italian twice (***1963/64***) and with McMillan he added three more Wimbledon crowns (***1967/72/78***), two German (***1967/70***), one French (***1972***), one US (***1977***), one Masters (***1977***) and one WCT (***1974***) title as well as the Italian in ***1967*** and four at home in South Africa (***1967/70/72/74***). He registered four major mixed doubles successes with three different partners, winning in Australia with Jan Lehane in ***1961***, in Paris with Billie Jean King in ***1970*** and twice at Wimbledon with his pupil, Greer Stevens, in ***1977/79***. He represented South Africa in D Cup ***1967–74*** and was a member of the successful team of ***1974*** that won by default from India. JB

LEWIS ('**LEW**') ALAN **HOAD** (Australia)
Born 23/11/34. Died 3/7/94. Capable of generating fierce power with great ease, he was one of the 'boy wonders' Harry Hopman produced to beat the US in the ***1953*** D Cup final. The other was Rosewall, 21 days Hoad's senior, who was to thwart his attempt on the Grand Slam in ***1956*** by beating him at Forest Hills. That year Hoad had won the Australian and French titles, and had beaten Rosewall at Wimbledon. In ***1957*** he defeated Ashley Cooper in one of the most devastating Wimbledon f ever and then turned professional, but constant back trouble spoilt his pro career and also ended his attempt to return to the circuit when the game was opened to the pros. He won the Wimbledon doubles with Rosewall (***1953/56***) and Hartwig (***1955***), the US doubles (***1956***) and the French doubles (***1953***) both with Rosewall, and the Australian doubles with Rosewall (***1953/56***) and Fraser (***1957***). He won 17 rubbers out of 21 in 9 D. Cup duties between ***1953–56*** (10–2 singles, 7–2 doubles).

HENRY ('**HARRY**') CHRISTIAN **HOPMAN** (Australia)
Small in stature, he was a giant as Australia's Davis Cup captain, winning 16 Challenge Rounds between ***1939*** and ***1967*** and motivating some of the finest talent that has ever emerged from any country. The list of his teams reads like a who's who of post war tennis legends and includes Sedgman, McGregor, Hoad, Rosewall, Rose, Hartwig, Emerson, Stolle, Cooper, Anderson, Newcombe, Roche and Alexander. A fine player himself, especially in men's doubles and mixed, he reached three successive Australian singles finals (***1930/31/32***), losing the last two to Jack Crawford, his partner in winning the doubles in ***1929/30***. His four mixed wins, all achieved with his wife Nell (nee Hall, they married in March 1934) came in ***1930/36/37/39***. His own Davis Cup playing record was modest. He took part in 8 ties between ***1928*** and ***1939***, winning 4 of his 9 singles and four of seven doubles. JB

HAZEL VIRGINIA **HOTCHKISS** (USA)
Born 20/12/1886. Died 5/12/1974. Became Mrs G. W. Wightman (1912). One of the most remarkable and enthusiastic competitors that the game has known. She was the donor of the W Cup and a considerable influence in American tennis for more than 60 years. She gained the first of her four US singles titles (***1909/10/11/19***) in ***1909*** and won the US indoor doubles for the 10th (***1919/21/24 /27/28/29/30/31/33/43***) and last time in ***1943***. A remarkable volleyer with great speed about the court, she and Helen Wills were never beaten in doubles. They won the Wimbledon doubles in ***1924*** and the US doubles in ***1924/28***. Her four other US doubles wins came with E. E. Rotch (***1909/10***) and E. Sears (***1911/15***). She captained the first US W Cup team in ***1923*** and between ***1923–31*** won 3 doubles rubbers in 5 matches.

HELEN HULL **JACOBS** (USA)
Born 6/8/08. A tenacious competitor, notable for duels with fellow-Californian, Helen Wills Moody, 5 times a Wimbledon finalist between ***1929–39*** but won only in ***1936***. Won US singles ***1932/33/34/35*** and doubles (with Sarah Palfrey Fabyan) ***1930/34/35*** and mixed with George Lott ***1934***. Also won Italian singles ***1934***.

WILLIAM M. **JOHNSTON** (USA)
Born 2/11/1894. Died 1/5/1946. 'Little Bill', a Californian, small in physique but a brilliant volleyer and the possessor of a formidable topspin forehand, was 'Big Bill' Tilden's principal rival at home in the first half of the ***1920s***. He defeated McLoughlin to win the US singles in ***1915***, the first year at Forest Hills, lost to Williams in the ***1916*** final and then regained the title by beating Tilden in straight sets in ***1919***. Tilden gained his revenge the following year and, although

Johnston reached the final five times between ***1920*** and ***1925***, Tilden always frustrated him. He beat Hunter in the ***1923*** Wimbledon final, losing only one set in the tournament. He won the US doubles with Griffin ***1915/16*** and ***1920*** and played in eight D Cup challenge rounds, winning 18 of his 21 D Cup rubbers (14–3 singles, 4–0 doubles) in 10 ties from ***1920–1927***.

BILLIE JEAN MOFFITT **KING** (USA)
Born 22/11/43. Perhaps the most important single figure in the history of women's tennis, as player, stateswoman, innovator and entrepreneur (usually with lawyer husband Larry King, whom she married in ***1965***), she has worked tirelessly to gain recognition and respect for the women's game. One of the founders of the women's pro tour in ***1970***, twice President of the Women's Tennis Association, and the prime mover behind Team Tennis, she has been involved in most aspects of the game. As a player her natural exuberance and bubbling personality suited her attacking serve-and-volley game and made her a fearsome opponent. She will best be remembered for her 'Battle of the Sexes' against Bobby Riggs at the Houston Astrodome on 20 September, ***1973*** where the world's largest-ever crowd of 30,492 and some 50 million more around the world on TV, saw her win 6–4 6–3 6–3. In ***1979*** she achieved her 20th Wimbledon title to pass the record she had shared with fellow-Californian Elizabeth Ryan who, ironically, had died on the eve of that unique achievement. Her unparalleled record comprises 6 singles – ***1966/67/68/72/73/75***; 10 women's doubles between ***1961*** and ***1979*** – with Hantze-Susman (***1961/62***) Bueno (***1965***), Casals (***1967/68/70/71/73***), Stove (***1972***) and Navratilova (***1979***); 4 mixed doubles with Owen Davidson (***1967/71/ 73/74***). She first played at Wimbledon in ***1961*** and won the doubles with Karen Hantze. At her last appearance in ***1983*** she was competing for the 22nd year (she had not entered in ***1981***) and reached the mixed doubles final with Steve Denton when she played her 265th and last match at Wimbledon. It was also her 29th final and, as they lost to John Lloyd and Wendy Turnbull 7–5 in the final set, she was losing at that stage for only the 9th time. She was almost as successful in her own US Championships where she won 13 titles, 4 in singles – ***1967/71/72/74***, five in doubles – with Susman (***1964***), Casals (***1967/74***) and Navratilova (***1978/80***) and four in mixed – with Davidson (***1967/71/73***) and Phil Dent (***1976***) and, in addition she became the only woman to win US National titles on all four surfaces – grass, clay, hard and indoor – a feat she repeated in doubles – with Rosie Casals. She won the French Open singles and doubles with Stove in ***1972*** and the mixed – with Davidson (***1967***) and Hewitt (***1970***) and was successful in singles and mixed at the Australian Open in ***1968*** (with Crealy), the first year of open tennis. Her 39 Grand Slam titles put her third behind Margaret Court who won 62 and Navratilova who won 56. She was also the singles and doubles champion of Italy (***1970***) and of Germany (***1971***) and won the South African title 3 times ***1966/67/69***). With 21 winning rubbers from 26 played in 9 W Cup matches between ***1961–78***, plus 52 wins from 58 rubbers (26–3 singles, 26–1 doubles) in 6 years of Fed Cup play from ***1963–79*** she contributed hugely to American dominance in those team competitions. JB

JAN KODES (Czechoslovakia)
Born 1/3/46. A dogged, industrious player with great strength and determination. He won his first major victories on clay, winning the French singles ***1970/71*** and reaching the Italian final ***1970/71/72***, but he won the Wimbledon singles in the boycott year of ***1973*** and was runner-up in the US Champs ***1971/73***. Having served his apprenticeship in European junior team competitions (he was on a winning Galea Cup team), he first represented Czechoslovakia in D Cup in ***1966***, took them to the final in ***1975*** and was a member of their winning team in ***1980***. Altogether, in 39 ties over 15 years he won 39 of his 59 singles and 21 of his 36 doubles rubbers.

HILDE KRAHWINKEL (West Germany)
Born 26/3/08. Died 7/3/81. Became Mrs Sperling (1933). A tall German, later Danish by marriage, whose dogged ability to retrieve from the back of the court turned her matches into long tests of endurance. She won the German indoor title in ***1929*** and then, emerging rapidly as an international player, lost to Cilly Aussem in the only all-German women's f at Wimbledon in ***1931***. She reached the final again in ***1936***, losing 6–2 4–6 7–5 to Helen Jacobs, and altogether she was in qf (or better) 8 times. She won the French singles ***1935–37***, defeating Mrs Mathieu in each of the three f, the Italian title ***1935*** and she was German singles champ ***1933/35/37/39***. (There was no competition in 1936.) Her last important victory was in the Scandinavian indoor final in ***1950***.

JOHN ('**JACK**') ALBERT **KRAMER** (USA)
Born 1/8/21. A methodical and powerful exponent of the serve-and-volley game. Played for the US in the last pre-war D Cup Challenge Round against Australia and returned to the competition in **1946** and **1947** as USA regained, then retained the trophy v Australia. His brief D Cup record produced 7 wins from 9 rubbers (6–0 singles 1–2 doubles) in 4 ties. Won Wimbledon singles title in ***1947*** after losing dramatically to the then unknown Jaroslav Drobny in **1946**. Won doubles ***1946*** (with T. Brown) and ***1947*** (with Falkenburg). Won US singles ***1946/47*** and doubles ***1940/41/47*** (with Schroeder) and ***1943*** (with Parker). Turned pro ***1947*** and then controlled pro tennis for 15 years. He was the first executive director of ATP Sept. 1972–April 1975.

JOHAN KRIEK(USA)
Born 5/4/58. This speedy South African shot to prominence at the end of ***1981*** by winning the Australian Open after saving a match point in his semi-final against McNamee. In April that year he had already given notice of his improvement by reaching the WCT final in Dallas where McEnroe had beaten him. In ***1982***, now an American citizen, he retained his Australian title by beating the same opponent as in the previous year's final, the tall American with the cannonball serve, Steve Denton. JB

JEAN **RENE LACOSTE** (France)
Born 2/7/04. Died 12/10/96. In spite of ill health, he became the best groundstroke player and most astute tactician of pre-war lawn tennis. Won Wimbledon singles ***1925/28*** and doubles (with J. Borotra) ***1925***. Won US singles ***1926/27***, French singles ***1925/27/29*** and French doubles (with Borotra) ***1924/25/29***. Won 40 of his 51 D Cup rubbers in 26 ties between ***1923–28*** (32–8 singles, 8–3 doubles) and won the crucial rubbers of the ***1927*** challenge round which brought France the trophy for the first time, when he beat Tilden and Johnston in the singles. Retiring from the mainstream in ***1929*** he built up his Chemise Lacoste clothing business until it became one of the world's best known brands with its crocodile emblem.

WILLIAM ('**BILL**') AUGUSTUS **LARNED** (USA)
Born 30/12/1872. Committed suicide on 16/12/1926. Coming late to tennis, Larned won the first of his seven US Championships in ***1901*** at the age of 28 with his heavy groundstrokes, hit with considerable topspin on the forehand. He added the titles of ***1902/07/08/09/10/11*** and was 38 when he won for the last time, making him the oldest male champion. Ranked in the US Top Ten 19 times, he was the US No.1 eight times, a total second only to Tilden's 10. He played in 8 D Cup ties from ***1902***, winning 9 of his 14 singles. JB

ARTHUR ('**ART**') DAVID ('TAPPY') **LARSEN** (USA)
Born 6/4/25. A graceful, elegant left-hander with exquisite touch and some notable eccentricities, he was famous for his dressing-room superstitions, his physical twitches and his rituals on court. He was known as Tappy because he would have a lucky number for the day and would always tap the baseline, the umpire's chair – even his own toe – with his racket the required number of times before continuing. He won US singles ***1950***, US Clay Courts ***1952*** and US Indoor ***1953***. A motor-cycle accident in which he suffered severe head injuries ended his career in ***1957***.

RODNEY ('**ROD**') GEORGE **LAVER** (Australia)
Born 9/8/38. Arguably the greatest of all male champions, he became the first player to achieve the Grand Slam twice and the master of the old professional circuit, with Rosewall as his great rival, in its last days. A left-hander, red-haired like Budge, with a spectacularly aggressive style, he brought off the slam of the four major singles titles, as an amateur, in ***1962*** and then, as a professional, in ***1969***. Disciplined, unassuming, quick and light in movement, he could produce sudden bombardments of shots, heavy with spin, which totally disconcerted his opponents. Born at Rockhampton, Queensland, 'Rocket' was a perfect nickname for the first tennis millionaire. If he had not turned professional in **1963**, he would have won many more of the traditional titles. As it was, he won the singles at Wimbledon ***1961/62*** and ***1968/69***, the doubles with Emerson ***1971*** and the mixed, with Darlene Hard, ***1959/60***. He took the US singles and French singles ***1962*** and ***1969***, also winning the French doubles with Emerson and the mixed with Hard in ***1961***. His Australian singles victories came in ***1960/62/69***, with doubles ***1959/61*** (Mark) and ***1969*** (Emerson). He was Italian singles champion ***1962*** and ***1971***, German champion ***1961/62*** and a

member of the undefeated D Cup team from ***1959–62***. He returned to D Cup in ***1973***, collecting three more rubbers in Australia's 5–0 victory over the US in the final at Cleveland. Altogether, he won 20 of his 24 rubbers in 11 ties between ***1959–73***, (16–4 singles, 4–0 doubles).

IVAN LENDL (USA)
Born 7/3/60. Grew up in Ostrava, Czechoslovakia, but went to live in Greenwich, Connecticut in ***1984*** and became an American citizen on 7th July **1992**. This 6'2" 175lb right-hander was blessed with a fine physique and abundant talent, based on a lethal match-winning forehand, a reliable backhand that he would develop into a second winning weapon, and a heavy serve – plus superb fitness and deep concentration. He was nurtured from an early age by his lawyer father Jiri, himself a ranked player, and by his mother Olga, a former Czech No.3. The Orange Bowl 18's champion in ***1977***, Lendl became the first ITF World Junior Champion in ***1978*** after winning the Wimbledon, French and Italian junior titles. Turning pro the same year, he made rapid strides in the men's game and in ***1980*** won the first six of the 94 singles titles he would amass before his retirement at the end of ***1994***, successes that earned him $21,262,417 in prize money alone. (Only Jimmy Connors, with 109 titles, has won more tournaments in modern times though Tilden won 138 titles in the ***1920's***.) During those 15 years he reached 19 Grand Slam singles finals, winning 8 of them. After failing once in Paris (***1981***), twice in New York (**1982/83**) and once in Melbourne (***1983***) some observers wrote him off, saying he did not have the belief of a true champion. Over the next seven years, guided by his Australian coach, Tony Roche, he proved his critics spectacularly wrong by claiming the French Open three times (***1984/86/87***), the US Open three times (***1985/86/87***), and the Australian Open twice (***1989/90***) as well as The Masters five times (***1981/82/85/86/87***) from a record nine consective appearances in the final between ***1980*** and ***1988***. At Wimbledon he was unlucky to face inspired opponents in two consecutive finals; in ***1986*** 18-year-old Boris Becker successfully defended his title and in ***1987*** Pat Cash proved irresistible. Lendl first headed the world rankings on 28th February ***1983*** and altogether occupied the No.1 spot for a record 270 weeks, a span that inluded 157 consecutive weeks between **9/9/*85*** and ***12/9/88***. In a relatively short Davis Cup career (***1978–1985***) Lendl won 22 of the 37 rubbers he contested, including 18 of his 29 singles matches. JB

SUZANNE RACHEL FLORE **LENGLEN** (France)
Born 24/5/1899. Died 4/7/1938. The most exciting, and successful of women players. She survived 2 match-points to win at Wimbledon in ***1919*** against Mrs Lambert Chambers and thereafter lost only in a controversial match to Molla Mallory (US) in ***1921*** US Champs until her retirement in ***1926***. Quarrelled with the Wimbledon referee in ***1926*** and turned pro. Won Wimbledon singles and doubles (with Elizabeth Ryan) ***1919/20/21/22/23/25***. French singles and doubles (with various partners) ***1920/21/22/23***, while the Championships were closed to foreigners, and again in ***1925*** and ***1926*** (doubles with D. Vlasto) when they became international.

JOHN PATRICK **McENROE** (USA)
Born 16/2/59. A left-hander with immense talent and exquisite touch, he caused a sensation at Wimbledon in ***1977*** by reaching the semi-final from the qualifying competition, thus winning a record eight matches. He was to be the centre of many other sensations throughout a turbulent career during which his perfectionist attitude made it impossible for him to accept the incompetence (as he saw it) of court officials, many of whom were subjected to a torrent of intimidating verbal abuse. Fined for his behaviour on several occasions, he was finally defaulted at the Australian Open in ***1990*** during his fourth round match against Michael Pernfors. In between these outbursts he could produce tennis of a sublime quality. His deceptive serve, delivered from a closed stance, was difficult to read and there has never been a better close volleyer. His ability to take his service returns and passing shots early and project them to unlikely angles made him a very difficult opponent. His singles successes included four US Open titles (***1979,1980,1981,1984***) and three at Wimbledon (***1981,1983,1984***) where his two heroic battles against Bjorn Borg in the ***1980*** and ***1981*** finals reached epic proportions. Among his 77 career titles the three Masters successes (***1979***, ***1983,1984***) and five WCT victories (***1979,1981,1983,1984,1989***) were outstanding. He was never successful in Paris, where Lendl beat him in the ***1984*** final, or in Australia, where he lost to Wilander in the ***1983*** semi-final. His lightning fast reflexes and an instinctive positional sense made him an outstanding doubles player, arguably the best there has ever been. The ***1977*** French Open mixed, won with Mary Carillo, his neighbour from Douglaston, N.Y., was his first Grand Slam success. At Wimbledon

he won four times with Peter Fleming (***1979,1981,1983,1984***) and once with Michael Stich (***1992***). At the US Open Fleming helped him to three titles (***1979,1981,1983***) His seven consecutive Masters wins with Fleming (***1978–1984***) constitute a record that, surely, will never be broken. Always proud to represent his country, he had an outstanding D Cup record for the United States. In 12 years from ***1978*** he won 41 of his 49 singles rubbers and 18 of his 20 doubles rubbers in 30 ties. JB

KENNETH ('**KEN**') BRUCE **McGREGOR** (Australia)
Born 2/6/29. Tall, athletic and a natural competitor, this modest South Australian possessed one of the biggest serves in post war tennis. He at last became the Australian champion in ***1952*** by beating in the final his great friend and doubles partner, Frank Sedgman, who had thwarted him in the ***1950*** final. In between McGregor had lost the ***1951*** final to America's Dick Savitt who would also win their Wimbledon final six months later. With his height of 6'3", his long reach, his fast reactions and his fine touch on the volley, McGregor excelled in doubles. His short partnership with Sedgman was particularly fruitful. Together they became the Australian, French and Wimbledon champions in ***1951*** and ***1952***, and the US champions in ***1951***. Thus, in ***1951*** they became the first pair (and so far the only pair) to win the Grand Slam of men's doubles. With Margaret DuPont he also won the US mixed doubles of ***1950*** and in three years of Davis Cup play (***1950–1952***) he won four of his seven singles rubbers and both doubles rubbers in 5 ties, three of them Challenge Rounds. In ***1953*** he was lost to the amateur game when he and Sedgman signed professional forms for Jack Kramer. JB

KATHLEEN ('**KITTY**') **McKANE** (Great Britain)
Born 7/5/1896. Died 19/6/92. Became Mrs Godfree (**1926**). A fine match-player with a quick, aggressive game, she achieved the notable distinction of winning the Wimbledon singles twice – even though she was a contemporary of Suzanne Lenglen and Helen Wills. In Lenglen's absence, she beat the Californian (a feat which no other player achieved in the next 14 years at Wimbledon) in the ***1924*** final after trailing by a set and 1–4, and in ***1926*** she regained the title after being within a point of 1–4 in the third set against Lili d'Alvarez. She won the Wimbledon mixed (with Gilbert) in ***1924*** and in ***1926*** (with her husband, Leslie Godfree, the only married couple ever to do so). She was r/u to Miss Wills at Forest Hills in **1925** after beating Elizabeth Ryan and Molla Mallory, and she won the US doubles in ***1923*** (with Mrs Covell) ***1927*** (with Miss Harvey). She won 7 rubbers out of 17 in 7 W Cup matches between ***1923–34***.

CHARLES ('**CHUCK**') ROBERT **McKINLEY** (USA)
Born 5/1/41. Died 11/8/86. An energetic and athletic match-player, who won the Wimbledon singles title in ***1963*** without meeting another seeded player in the course of the tournament. He was runner-up to Laver in ***1961***, a disappointing competitor in ***1962*** but in ***1963*** bounced back to take the title. In the US Championships he never progressed further than the semi-finals, failing three times at that stage, but, with Ralston, he won the doubles in ***1961*** and ***1963–64***. Played in 16 D Cup ties between ***1960–65*** and won 29 of his 38 rubbers (16–6 singles, 13–3 doubles).

MAURICE EVANS **McLOUGHLIN** (USA)
Born 18/11/1890. Died 10/12/1957. 'The Californian Comet' was the first notable exponent of the cannonball service. Fiercely effective with volley and smash, he was US champ in***1912–13*** and his appearance at Wimbledon was, as a contemporary remarked, a sign of the way the modern game was developing. His spectacular style had considerable appeal. When he met Wilding for the title in ***1913***, there was such an indecent crush round the barriers of the Centre Court that, to avoid serious injury, several ladies had to be lifted over by policemen into the security of the arena. Wilding beat him 8–6 6–3 10–8, but McLoughlin had the consolation of winning 2 rubbers in the American capture of the D Cup from Britain at Wimbledon. In the ***1914*** D Cup Challenge Round at Forest Hills he beat both Brookes and Wilding, but Australasia took the trophy. He did not play after the war. His aggressive style was said to have burnt him out.

FREW DONALD **McMILLAN** (South Africa)
Born in Springs, a small Transvaal town, 20/5/42. A gifted and unusual doubles player who invariably wore a peaked white cloth cap and held the racket with two hands on both sides to produce just the right blend of disguise, finesse and power. His partnership with expatriate Australian Bob Hewitt was particularly fruitful and they became one of the three greatest pairs

of the post-Second World War years. Together they won their native South African title four times (***1967/70/72/74***) and succeeded at Wimbledon three times (***1967/72/78***). They won once each the French (***1972***), the US (***1977***), the Masters (***1977***) played in Jan '78), the WCT (***1974***) and the Italian (***1967***) titles and won the German twice (***1967/70***). But it was in mixed doubles that he won his first and last major championships. In ***1966*** he partnered Annette Van Zyl to the French title and in ***1981*** he captured the Wimbledon mixed for the second time with Betty Stove, with whom he had been successful in ***1978*** – the same year they won a second US Open together (***1977/ 78***). He played D Cup from ***1965–76*** and was a member of the only team ever to win the famous trophy by default – from India in ***1974***. In 28 ties he played 30 rubbers, winning both singles and 23 of his 28 doubles. JB

HANA MANDLIKOVA (Australia)
Born 19/2/62. Became Mrs J. Sadlek (1986). This Czech-born right-hander, who helped her country win the Federation Cup in ***1985***, became an Australian citizen on 1 January ***1988***. A talented athlete who won four Grand Slam singles titles and might have won more had her career not coincided with two truly outstanding champions – Evert and Navratilova. She first shot to prominence in Australia where, on the grass of Kooyong which ideally suited her natural serve-and-volley game, she won the ***1980*** title aged 18. When she took the ***1981*** French Open and 4 weeks later reached the Wimbledon final it seemed she might dislodge Evert and Navratilova from their dominant positions atop the world rankings. It was not to be. Another final round appearance, this time at the US Open of ***1981***, flattered to deceive. But in ***1985*** she did annexe that title and the following year reached the Wimbledon final for the second time. Sadly this was not the breakthrough to the summit all her supporters had hoped for. Her fourth Grand Slam success came in Melbourne in ***1987***, the last time the Australian Open was played on grass. Her lone Grand Slam doubles success came at the ***1989*** US Open in partnership with Navratilova. JB

ALICE MARBLE (USA)
Born 28/9/13. Died 13/12/90. The first brilliant server and volleyer in women's tennis whose career was interrupted by ill health and the war. Won Wimbledon singles ***1939*** and doubles (with Sarah Palfrey Fabyan) ***1938/39***. Won US singles ***1936/38/39/40*** and doubles (with Sarah Palfrey Fabyan) ***1937/38/39/40***. Turned pro ***1941***.

SIMONE MATHIEU (France)
Born 31/1/08. Died 7/1/80. Née Passemard, had married Rene Mathieu in Oct. 1925, before her tennis career had begun. A formidable clay court player, she succeeded Lenglen as the leader of the women's game in France. She was junior champ – as a married woman – at 18, and 3 years later reached the French f, losing 6–3 6–4 to Wills. She was r/u again in ***1933/36/37*** before she won at last in ***1938***, defeating Landry, and then retained her title ***1939*** against Jedrzejowska. She won the French doubles 6 times, twice with Ryan, (***1933/34***) three times with Yorke (***1936/37/38***) and once with Jedrzejowska (***1939***), and the Wimbledon doubles twice with Ryan (***1933/34***) and once with Yorke (***1937***.) Her soundness from the baseline carried her 4 times to the singles sf (***1930/31/32/34***).

FLORENCE **ANGELA** MARGARET **MORTIMER** (Great Britain)
Born 21/4/32. Now Mrs Barrett (1967). Britain's first post-war Wimbledon singles champ. Coached by Arthur Roberts at Torquay, she used an armoury of firmly controlled groundstrokes most effectively and considerable determination enabled her to overcome a certain frailty of physique. Her first notable success was the capture of the French title in ***1955*** – the first British victory in Paris since Peggy Scriven won in ***1934*** – and in the same year she won the Wimbledon doubles (with Anne Shilcock). She won the Australian title in ***1958***, after travelling there to recover from illness, and 6 months later was r/u to Althea Gibson at Wimbledon. She won the title in ***1961*** by beating Christine Truman in the first all–British f of the modern Wimbledon. She won 5 rubbers out of 16 in 6 W Cup matches and became W Cup captain ***1964–70*** and Fed Cup captain ***1967–70***.

ILLIE NASTASE (Romania)
Born 19/7/46. One of the most gifted shot-makers and fluid movers in the game's history, he was the first to be ranked No 1 on the ATP computer (***23/08/1973***) and was in top 10 ***1973–77***, but despite his 57 singles and 51 doubles titles, he never quite fulfilled his enormous potential.

His two Grand Slam titles were won on different surfaces – on grass in New York in ***1972*** and on clay in Paris the following year. He could also play beautifully indoors as his four Masters titles in ***1971/72/73/75*** testify. Sadly for his many admirers, a childlike and sometimes mischievous streak was his undoing on many occasions, particularly towards the end of his playing days when he fell foul of authority for his behaviour. Throughout his career the showman in him struggled constantly with the athlete so that there was often a lack of steel about his match play. This failing, and an inability to put the ball away with his somewhat lightweight volleys, cost him two chances to win the Wimbledon title – in ***1972*** when Smith beat him and in***1976*** when Borg won the first of his five titles. His lightning reflexes made him an excellent doubles player and he won major titles in Paris (***1970***) and Rome (***1970/72***) with fellow Romanian, Ion Tiriac, at Wimbledon (***1973***) with Connors and in New York (***1975***) also with Connors. He also won two mixed titles at Wimbledon with Rosie Casals (***1970/72***). His biggest disappointment was his failure to lead Romania to victory in the ***1972*** D Cup final against the Americans on clay in Bucharest where his loss to Smith in the opening rubber proved decisive. JB

MARTINA NAVRATILOVA (USA)
Born 18/10/56. Arguably the greatest of all women players, this Czech-born left-hander grew up in Prague but defected to the USA in ***1975*** and became an American citizen on 21st July ***1981***. With her defection she turned professional and embarked upon two decades of conquest that brought her a total of 56 Grand Slam titles (18 singles, 31 doubles, 7 mixed) between ***1975*** and ***1995***. Navratilova's attacking serve-and-volley game was ideally suited to the fast grass of Wimbledon where she reached 12 singles finals and won a record 9 times (***1978/79/82/83/84/85/86/87/90***). She also won 7 of her 9 doubles finals there (***1976*** with Chris Evert, ***1979*** with Billie Jean King, ***1981/82/83/84/86*** with Pam Shriver) and 3 of her 4 mixed finals (***1985*** with Paul McNamee, ***1993*** with Mark Woodforde and ***1995*** with Jonathan Stark) giving her a total of 19 Wimbledon titles, one short of Mrs. King's record of 20 which she had helped the American achieve in ***1979***. This glittering Grand Slam career had begun with a victory over Evonne Cawley at the ***1975*** Australian Open where she won twice more in singles (***1983/84***) from 6 appearances in the final. She won eight Australian doubles titles (***1980*** with Betsy Nagelsen,***1982/83/84/85/87/88/89*** with Shriver), but none in mixed. Slow red clay was the most difficult surface for her and despite appearing in 6 finals at the French Open she was successful only twice (***1982/84***). However, she won all 7 of her French doubles finals (***1975*** with Evert, ***1982*** with Ann Smith, ***1984/85/86/87/88*** with Shriver) and both mixed finals (***1971*** with Ivan Molina, ***1985*** with Heinz Gunthardt). At the US Open she was in 8 singles finals, winning 4 (***1983/84/86/87***), in 11 doubles finals, winning 9 (***1977*** with Betty Stove, ***1978/80*** with King, ***1983/84/86/87*** with Shriver, ***1989*** with Hana Mandlikova and ***1990*** with Gigi Fernandez), and in 4 mixed finals, winning 2 (***1985*** with Gunthardt, ***1987*** with Emilio Sanchez). Despite this formidable record she never won a calendar-year Grand Slam, though her victory at the French Open in **1984** meant that she held all four major titles at the same time, a feat that earned her a $1 million prize from the ITF. Her 167 singles and 165 doubles titles are a record for men and women as was her winning streak of 74 matches achieved in **1984** between January 16th and December 6th. For a total of 332 weeks she was ranked No.1 in the world and by training intensively and adopting the Haas diet she set new standards of strenght and fitness which others have tried to follow. With career prize money of $20,283,727 Navrartilova won more from her sport than any other female athlete and has been very generous in suporting charities and other deserving causes. Her endorsement income, though considerable, would undoubtedly have been higher had she not made public several lesbian relationships. JB

JOHN DAVID **NEWCOMBE** (Australia)
Born 23/5/44. The supreme exponent of the simple, rugged style in modern tennis. Splendidly confident and with great strength of personality, Newcombe relied upon a heavy service, forceful volleying and solid, powerful groundstrokes. His best singles successes were on grass – Wimbledon ***1967/70/71***, US Championships ***1967/73***, and Australia ***1973/75*** – but he also won, by doggedness and determination, the German (***1968***) and Italian (***1969***) titles. He and Roche formed one of the most successful of modern doubles partnerships, winning Wimbledon in ***1965***, ***1968–70***, and ***1974***. When Roche was injured in ***1966***, Fletcher replaced him at short notice and he and Newcombe won the title. He won the US doubles with Roche ***1967***, with Taylor ***1971***, and with Davidson ***1973***, the French twice with Roche (***1967/69***) and once with Okker (***1973***) and the Australian four times with Roche (***1965/67/71/76***) and once

with Anderson (***1973***). In ***1981***, aged 37, he and Stolle (42) took McEnroe/Fleming to 5s tie-break in US Open sf. He first played in the D Cup in ***1963*** when, aged 19, he became the youngest player to compete in a Challenge Round, and finally against Italy in Rome, ***1976***. Perhaps his best performance was in ***1973*** when he and Laver inflicted a 5–0 defeat upon the United States at Cleveland. In 15 ties he won 25 of his 34 rubbers (16–7 singles, 9–2 doubles).

YANNICK NOAH (France)
Born 16/5/60. The son of an African father who had met Yannick's mother when playing soccer for Sedan, he was discovered as a ten-year-old by Arthur Ashe on a goodwill tour in the Cameroons. Sent to the French Federation's training school in Nice, he was coached by Patrice Beust and then sent on to the FFT's school in Paris. A tall athletic figure with a tremendous serve, he was at his best on clay and although he could volley well he preferred to play aggressively from the baseline. He won his first professional title in ***1979*** in Nancy and eventually fulfilled all expectations by winning the French Open in ***1983***, the first Frenchman to do so since Marcel Bernard in ***1946***. The fairy tale had come true. In ***1984*** he teamed with fellow Frenchman, Henri Leconte, to win the French Open doubles title. After leading France to the final of the Davis Cup in ***1982***, when France had lost to the USA 4–1 in Grenoble, he became Davis Cup captain in ***1991*** and was the architect of a famous 3–1 revenge win against the Americans in Lyon, the first French success since ***1932***. JB

BETTY MAY **NUTHALL** (Great Britain)
Born 23/5/11. Died 8/11/83. Became Mrs Shoemaker. An aggressive and attractive competitor, with a remarkable record as a junior, she never progressed beyond qf at Wimbledon but gained her most impressive victories abroad. At 16, after beating Molla Mallory, No. 6 seed, at Wimbledon in ***1927***, she astonished the tennis world by reaching f at F Hills, where Helen Wills beat her 6–1 6–4. In ***1930*** she became the first British player to win that title with 6–4 6–1 victory over Mrs Harper. She won the US doubles ***1930/31/33*** with three different partners – Palfrey, Whittingstall and James and mixed ***1928/29/31*** with Lott and the French doubles ***1931*** with Whittingstall and mixed ***1931/32*** with Spence and Perry. Her only British success in a nat singles event was the capture of the HC title in ***1927***. She won the HC doubles ***1926/28/31/32*** and the mixed in ***1927***. She played in 8 W Cup matches between ***1927–39***, winning 6 rubbers and losing 7.

ALEJANDRO ('**ALEX**') RODRIGUEZ **OLMEDO** (USA)
Born 24/3/36. The son of a groundsman in Peru, this superb natural athlete rose like a comet in ***1958*** to win the D Cup for America in Brisbane almost single-handed. Selected by the captain, Perry T. Jones, Olmedo had rewarded him with two singles wins and a share with Ham Richardson in the doubles win that had sealed the victory. Success in the ***1959*** Australian Championships confirmed the quality of his play as he beat Neale Fraser in four sets. Six months later 'The Chief', as he was popularly known, won the ***1959*** Wimbledon from Rod Laver for the loss of only two sets, with one of the most competent displays of power tennis seen since the war. After taking part in the unsuccessful defence of the D Cup where he lost to Fraser but beat Laver again, he reached the final of the US Championships but failed once more against Fraser. Immediately he turned professional. JB

MANUEL ('**MANOLO**') **ORANTES** (Spain)
Born 6/2/49. A consumate artist on European clay with exquisite touch and gentle, generous manner, he quickly became an international favourite. A left-hander who, after leading Spain to two Galea Cup victories in ***1968/69***, won his first two important titles in ***1972*** – the German and Italian Opens. His best year was ***1975*** for, besides winning a second German title, the Canadian Open and the first of his two US Clay Court crowns (he won the second in ***1977***), he was triumphant on the clay at Forest Hills to win the US Open. After recovering miraculously to defeat Vilas in a night-time semi-final, having trailed one set to two and 0–5 in the fourth, he was back on court 15 hours later to thrash Jimmy Connors 6–4 6–3 6–3 in a near-perfect display of the clay-court art. In ***1976*** he won the Spanish Open and at the year's end won the Masters in Houston against Fibak with another brave recovery, coming back from one set to two and 1–4. He played in the losing Spanish team in the D Cup challenge round of ***1967*** in Brisbane but led his country to victory in the World Team Cup in Dusseldorf 11 years later. JB

MARGARET EVELYN **OSBORNE** (USA)
Born 4/3/18. Now Mrs du Pont (1947). One of the finest of American doubles players and a formidably successful competitor in singles. With her splendidly consistent serving and her strength and skill at the net, she did much to set the pattern for the period of American supremacy in women's tennis, which began in 1946. Won Wimbledon singles in ***1947*** Forest Hills ***1948/49/50*** and Paris in ***1946/49***. She and Louise Brough won the Wimbledon doubles in ***1946/48/49/50/54***. They ruled the US doubles from ***1942–50*** and ***1955–57***, and held the French title ***1946/47/49***. She won the Wimbledon mixed with Neale Fraser in ***1962*** – 15 years after her first singles victory, at the age of 44 years 125 days, to become Wimbledon's oldest champion of either sex in any event.

SARAH HAMMOND **PALFREY** (USA)
Born 18/9/12. Died 27/2/96 became Mrs J. A. Danzig (1951) formerly Mrs M. Fabyan (1934), and Mrs E. T. Cooke (1940). A fine volleyor with a sweeping backhand and a notable doubles player, she partnered Alice Marble to victory at Wimbledon in ***1938/39*** and won the US doubles title 9 times with a variety of partners – Betty Nuthall (***1930***), Helen Jacobs (***1932/34/35***), Alice Marble (***1937/38/39/40***) and Margaret Osborne (***1941***). She won the US singles in ***1941/45*** and was r/u to Helen Jacobs in***1934/35***. She was the US mixed champion on 4 occasions with Perry (***1932***), Maier (***1935***), Budge (***1937***) and Kramer (***1941***). She played in 10 W Cup matches and won 14 rubbers out of 21.

ADRIANO PANATTA (Italy)
Born 9/7/50. Without doubt, ***1976*** was the *annus mirabilis* of Panatta's career. Until then he had always been dashing and stylish, but had never made full use of his talent. In ***1976***, however, he lived dangerously and survived brilliantly. In Rome he became the first home player to win in Italy for 15 years after frustrating Warwick no fewer than 11 times at m-p in the first round. In Paris, against Hutka, he again faced a first-round m-p and again went on to take the championship. Four months later, when Italy won D Cup for the first time, Panatta played a major role in their victory. Paris, Rome and D Cup – this was Panatta's year! He was also the leading player in the Italian teams which reached the ***1977/79/80*** D Cup finals. He reached the French sf in ***1973/75*** and was runner-up in Rome ***1978*** and Hamburg ***1972***.

FRANK ANDREW **PARKER** (USA)
Born 31/1/16. Shrewd, persistent, and accurate in spite of a certain lightness of shot, he shared with Trabert the distinction, rare for an American, of winning the French title twice. At his best on slow courts, he was ranked in the first 10 in the US for 17 consecutive years between ***1933***, the year of the first of his 5 US Clay Court victories, and ***1949*** when he turned pro. His victories in Paris were in ***1948/49***, and in ***1949*** he won the doubles in Paris and Wimbledon with Gonzales. He won the US singles in ***1944/45*** as an Army sergeant and the doubles with Kramer in ***1943***. He played in the D Cup challenge round against Britain in ***1937*** when the US regained the trophy after 10 years and in the ***1939*** and ***1948*** challenge rounds. In 7 ties between ***1932*** and ***1948***, won 12 of 14 singles rubbers.

GERALD LEIGHTON **PATTERSON** (Australia)
Born 17/12/1895. Died 13/6/1967. Formidably aggressive with a cannonball service modelled on McLoughlin's, he was the dominating player when international competition was resumed in 1919. After being r/u to O'Hara Wood in the ***1914*** Australian singles, he became Wimbledon's first post-war champ by defeating Brookes in ***1919***. He lost his Wimbledon title to Tilden in ***1920*** but regained it against Lycett in ***1922***. R/u doubles in***1922*** (O'Hara Wood) and ***1928*** (Hawkes) and won the mixed with Suzanne Lenglen in***1920***. He won the Australian singles in his fourth final in ***1927***. Between ***1919–28*** he played 46 D Cup rubbers for Australia and Australasia, winning 21 out of his 31 singles and 11 of his 15 doubles in 16 ties. He was a nephew of Dame Nellie Melba and was the first man to win the Wimbledon singles by playing through when the Challenge Round was abolished there in ***1922***.

JOHN EDWARD ('**BUDGE**') **PATTY** (USA)
Born 11/2/24. An American who lived in Paris and developed his game there, 'Budge' Patty, with his elegant, effective forehand volley, was one of the great post-war stylists. ***1950*** – when he won both the Wimbledon and French singles – was the peak of his career, but his rivalry

with Drobny captured the public's imagination. The most notable of their long and dramatic matches was in the third round at Wimbledon in ***1953***. After 4 hours 20 minutes Patty lost 8–6 16–18 3–6 8–6 12–10 after holding 6 m-ps. He had beaten the Czech at Wimbledon in ***1947*** and 3 years later by 6–1 6–2 3–6 5–7 7–5 in his French f. The last of their meetings was in ***1954***. Drobny, on his way to the title, won a 4-set sf. Patty won his last title there in ***1957*** when he and Mulloy, then aged 43, beat Hoad and Fraser to take the men's doubles. He won the Italian singles ***1954***, and the German singles ***1953/54*** and doubles ***1953/54/55***.

FREDERICK ('**FRED**') JOHN **PERRY** (Great Britain)
Born 18/5/09. Died 2/2/95. A US citizen. The most successful modern British player, and the first man to win all four Grand Slam titles, a feat achieved only by three others – Budge, Emerson and Laver. He was an aggressive competitor with boundless self-confidence and a remarkable running forehand. Won Wimbledon singles ***1934/35/36*** – the first player since A. F. Wilding (***1910–13***) to take the title 3 years in succession – and mixed (with Dorothy Round) ***1935/36***. US singles ***1933/34/36***. French singles ***1935*** and doubles (with G. P. Hughes) ***1933***. Australian singles ***1934*** and doubles (with Hughes) ***1934***. The world no 1 ***1934–36***, he won 45 out of 52 D Cup rubbers, (34–4 singles, 11–3 doubles) between ***1931–36*** leading Britain to victory in ***1933/34/35/36***. Turned pro in ***1936*** and toured with Vines and Tilden, winning US Pro Champ ***1938/41***. Then founded a sports clothing business and became journalist and broadcaster for BBC Radio.

YVON FRANCOIS MARIE **PETRA** (France)
Born 8/3/16 in Indo–China. Died 12/9/84. Wimbledon's first post-war men's singles champion. Reached mixed f at Wimbledon ***1937*** with Simone Mathieu and won French doubles ***1938*** with Destremau, defeating Budge and Mako in f. Between ***1942***, when he was released from a prisoner-of-war camp, and ***1945***, he consolidated his reputation as France's most aggressive competitor in wartime domestic competitions. At Wimbledon, ***1946***, his strength, flair and, notably, the consistency of his heavy serving gained this formidably built player an unexpected title. Drobny beat Kramer, the favourite, in 4r. Petra disposed of Pails, the other expected finalist, in qf and then won 5s matches against Tom Brown and Geoff Brown. That was the peak of his career. Marcel Bernard beat him in the French sf – played in July that year – and his consolation was a doubles victory, partnered by Bernard, over Morea and Segura in f. Patty beat him easily on the second day at Forest Hills and in ***1947*** he lost to Tom Brown in qf at Wimbledon.

NICOLA PIETRANGELI (Italy)
Born 11/9/33. A master of the European clay court style, he was born in Tunis (of a French father and Russian mother) and between ***1954–72*** played in 163 D Cup rubbers for Italy, more than anyone in history. Won most rubbers (120), played most singles (109) and won most (78), played most doubles (54) and won most (42), and played in most ties (66). Appeared in the ***1960/61*** Challenge Rounds against Australia, but won only one 'dead' singles. Won French singles ***1959/60*** and doubles (with Sirola), Italian singles ***1957/61***, and German singles ***1960***. Reached sf at Wimbledon, ***1960***, and doubles final (with Sirola) ***1956***.

DR JOSHUA PIM (Ireland)
Born 20/5/1869. Died 15/4/1942. A robust, adventurous competitor, regarded by contemporary critics as one of the great geniuses of early tennis. 'When Pim was at his best he was virtually unplayable,' wrote Wallis Myers. 'It is scarcely exaggerating to say that he could hit a coin placed anywhere on the court.' He reached sf at Wimbledon ***1890***, losing to Hamilton, who became Wimbledon's first Irish champ, then lost in ***1891*** to Wilfred Baddeley in the All-Comers' f and again in ***1892*** Challenge Round. He gained his revenge, however, by beating Baddeley in the ***1893/94*** finals. Pim won the Irish title for the 3rd and last time in ***1895*** but then played little first-class tennis until he was controversially picked for the D Cup match against USA at New York in ***1902***. He was preferred to Laurie Doherty, lost both his singles badly and the British Isles were beaten 3–2. 'Although still very good, Pim had no more than a shadow of his former skill, but alas a great deal more than the shadow of his former weight,' wrote Commander Hillyard.

ADRIAN KARL **QUIST** (Australia)
Born 23/1/13. Died 17/11/91. A shrewd, graceful doubles player, whose wins at Wimbledon were separated by a 15 year gap. Won with J. H. Crawford in ***1935*** and, when almost a veteran,

with J. E. Bromwich ***1950***. Held Australian title from ***1936–50***, winning twice with D. P. Turnbull (***1936/37***) and 8 times with Bromwich (***1938/39/40/46/47/48/49/50***). Won US doubles (with Bromwich) ***1939***, French doubles (with J. H. Crawford) ***1935***, and Australian singles ***1936/40/48***. Won 42 out of 56 D Cup rubbers in 28 ties between ***1933–48*** (24–10 singles, 19–3 doubles)

WILLIAM CHARLES **RENSHAW** (Great Britain)
Born 3/1/1861. Died 12/8/1904. The first great champion. Learnt on asphalt at school at Cheltenham with twin brother, Ernest, a more graceful but less determined competitor. They were the first spectacular players and their skill – particularly in volleying and smashing – brought crowds to Wimbledon and contributed considerably to the development of lawn tennis as a spectator sport. 'Willie' Renshaw was singles champ at Wimbledon from ***1881–86*** and in ***1889*** and his seven titles remain a record for men. He held the doubles, with Ernest, in ***1884/85/86/88/89***. Ernest won the singles title in ***1888*** and was beaten by William in the challenge rounds of ***1882*** and ***1883***.

NANCY ANN **RICHEY** (USA)
Born 23/8/42. Later Mrs Gunter (1970). A Texan, famous for her shorts and peaked cap, she was, like her brother, George Clifford Richey, a tenacious baseliner, impressive on clay. Her determination occasionally brought unexpected success on grass. She reached the ***1969*** US final, losing 6–2 6–2 to Margaret Court. She won in Australia ***1967***, beating Lesley Turner, another clay-court specialist, in the final. At Wimbledon she reached qf seven times in nine years ***1964–72*** but was semi-finalist only in ***1968***. She won Wimbledon doubles with Maria Bueno ***1966***. On clay she won French singles ***1968***, beating Ann Jones to avenge a defeat in the ***1966*** final, but the best evidence of her quality was her record in US Clay Courts. She won Indianapolis from ***1963–68*** and even as late as ***1975*** led Chris Evert 7–5 5–0 in the semi-finals there, twice reaching m-p before retiring with cramp at 2–4 in the final set. She played W Cup from ***1962–68*** and three years of Fed Cup between ***1964–69*** winning 15 of her 17 rubbers (10–1 singles, 5–1 doubles).

ROBERT ('**BOBBY**') LARIMORE **RIGGS** (USA)
Born 25/2/18. Died 25/10/95. A shrewd, confident match–player, with remarkable versatility of shot, he won all 3 titles on his first appearance at Wimbledon in ***1939***. He also won Forest Hills in ***1939***, but lost to McNeill in the French f. He turned pro in ***1941*** and later became a notable competitor in veterans' events, but his greatest fame came at the age of 55. Profiting from the Women's Lib controversy, he challenged and beat Margaret Court 6–2 6–1 in a singles match in Ramona, Cal, and then lost to Billie Jean King 6–4 6–3 6–3, before a record television audience of almost 50 million and 30,492 paying spectators at the Houston Astrodome in September ***1973***.

ANTHONY ('**TONY**') DALTON **ROCHE** (Australia)
Born 17/5/45. Strong, rugged and a fine volleyer, he was the left-hander in one of Wimbledon's most successful doubles partnerships. He won the doubles with John Newcombe in ***1965***, from ***1968–70*** (the first hat-trick of titles since the Dohertys ***1903–5***) and in ***1974***. Other doubles victories with Newcombe included US ***1967***, French ***1967/69***, Australia ***1965/67/71/76*** (he also won in ***1977*** with Ashe) and Italy ***1965/71***. He also won Wimbledon mixed doubles with Francoise Durr ***1976***. He did not achieve as much as expected in singles, partly because of injury. The extraordinary operation on his left elbow, performed without knife or anaesthetic in the Philippines by a faith healer, received worldwide publicity. He never reached an Australian final in spite of numerous attempts, but was runner-up to Laver at Wimbledon in ***1968*** and lost two US Open finals: ***1969*** when Laver beat him to complete the Grand Slam and ***1970*** to Rosewall. His most successful year was ***1966*** when he won French and Italian titles. Played Davis Cup ***1964–78*** but did not play singles in a final until he beat Panatta in the opening match ***1977***. His record in 12 ties was 7–3 in singles and 7–2 in doubles.

KENNETH ('**KEN**') ROBERT **ROSEWALL** (Australia)
Born 2/11/34. For a quarter of a century Rosewall's grace and easy, economical style delighted the connoisseurs and the only regret about his long and distinguished career is that, in spite of four finals over a period of 20 years, he never won the Wimbledon singles title. He began in the 1950's as a Hopman prodigy and it was not until the end of ***1979*** that he retired from Grand Prix tennis. In ***1953***, aged 18, he won the Australian and French singles and, with Hoad, the

French and Wimbledon doubles. In ***1954*** he lost to Drobny in the Wimbledon final. Hoad beat him in the ***1956*** Wimbledon final, but Rosewall avenged that defeat in the US final, frustrating Hoad in the last leg of his attempt on the Grand Slam. Turning professional in ***1957***, he took over the leadership of the professional circuit from Gonzales until Laver's arrival in ***1963***. Rosewall's skills endured. In ***1968*** he won the first open tournament at Bournemouth and then recaptured some of his former titles. He regained the French singles and doubles (with Stolle) in ***1968***. In ***1970*** – 14 years after his first success and aged 35 – he won the US title again and reached his fourth final at Forest Hills in ***1974***. The gap between his Australian successes was even wider. After his victories in ***1953/55***, he won again in ***1971/72***. But Wimbledon always eluded him. Newcombe beat him in ***1970***, his third final, and Connors overwhelmed him in the ***1974*** final. In the D Cup he won 19 of his 22 rubbers in 11 ties between ***1953*** and ***1956*** (17–2 singles, 2–1 doubles).

DOROTHY EDITH **ROUND** (Great Britain)
Born 13/7/09. Died 12/11/82. Became Mrs D. L. Little (1937). Determined and efficient, possessing a fine forehand drive and shrewd drop-shot, she was one of the two British women's singles champs at Wimbledon between the wars. She gained her first notable victory there against Lili d'Alvarez in ***1931***, was r/u to Helen Wills Moody in ***1933***, then beat Helen Jacobs to win the title in ***1934*** and regained it against Jadwiga Jedrzejowska in ***1937***. She won the Australian singles in ***1935*** and the Wimbledon mixed in ***1934*** (with Miki) and ***1935/36*** (with Perry). She won 4 of her 13 W Cup rubbers between ***1931–36***.

ELIZABETH MONTAGUE **RYAN** (USA)
Born 5/2/1892. Died 6/7/1979. Suzanne Lenglen's doubles partner and the winner of 19 Wimbledon titles. A determined competitor with a cunningly chopped forehand and a great appetite for match-play, she was regarded by contemporaries as 'the best player never to win a great singles Championship'. With a variety of playing partners, she was victorious in the Wimbledon doubles 12 times – ***1914*** with Morton, ***1919/20/21/22/23/25*** with Lenghen, ***1926*** with Browne, ***1927/30*** with Wills Moody, ***1933/34*** with Matthieu. She won 7 mixed titles ***1919/21/23*** with Lycett, ***1927*** with Hunter, ***1928*** with Spence, ***1930*** with Crawford, ***1932*** with Maier. She also won US doubles in ***1926*** with Goss and the French doubles ***1930/32*** with Moody, ***1933/34*** with Matthieu.

GABRIELA **SABATINI** (Argentina)
Born on 16 May 1970 in Buenos Aires, Argentina. One of the most glamorous players ever to reach the heights 'Gaby' first appeared on the scene as an outstanding junior, inspired to take up the game by the example of Argentina's great men's champion Guillermo Vilas whose backhand she copied. The youngest player ever to win the Orange Bowl 18's when she took the ***1983*** event at the age of 13 years 7 months, she was the No.1 junior on the ITF rankings in ***1994*** and No.1 in Argentina and South America from ***1985-1989***. The youngest semi-finalist (at the time) in the ***1985*** French Open she never did better in Paris during the next 10 consecutive challenges. It was at the ***1990*** US Open that her considerable talent finally came to full flower when she upset the reigning champion and world No.1 Steffi Graf with a brilliant display of all-court tennis. She never reached those heights again and could look back on the ***1988*** US final and the ***1991*** Wimbledon final (when she twice served for the match against Graf) as the other highlights of her 43 Grand Slam appearances. Her ***1988*** doubles win at Wimbledon (with Graf) was her only major doubles success. Elsewhere her ***1987*** and ***1994*** Virginia Slims Championship wins were the best of her 27 career successes that earned her a total of $8.7 million. Her silver medal at the Seoul Olympics in ***1988*** brough her great personal satisfaction. In ***1992*** a rose was named after her and a Gaby Doll was marketed in her name. Towards the end of her career she developed her talent as a singer to make several recordings. JB

MANUEL ('**MANOLO**') **SANTANA** (Spain)
Born 10/5/38. Learnt the game as a ballboy in Madrid and, after a period in which he was the most admired clay court player in Europe, won US singles ***1965***, and Wimbledon singles ***1966***. Possesed a remarkable forehand and great delicacy of touch. Won French singles ***1961/ 64***, defeating Pietrangeli in both finals, and doubles (with Emerson) ***1963***, and South African singles ***1967***. The most successful Spanish player in history, he won 92 D Cup rubbers out of 120 in 46 ties between ***1958–73*** (69–17 singles, 23–11 doubles).

RICHARD ('**DICK**') **SAVITT** (USA)
Born 4/3/27. His talent was discovered in the classic fashion by a complete stranger who saw him playing in a public park, and after a modest junior career he became a powerful exponent of the serve-and-volley game. Concentrating on tennis after a basketball injury in ***1949***, he rose rapidly on the US ranking list, moving up from 16th to 6th after reaching sf at Forest Hills, ***1950***, with victories over Seixas and Bromwich. His remarkable year was ***1951***. He won both the Australian and Wimbledon titles, defeating McGregor in both finals. This was his first trip to Europe and he never achieved the same kind of success again, although he played some memorable matches, notably sf against Rosewall at Forest Hills, ***1956***, and a vain defence of his US indoor title in a three-hour f in ***1959***. He was a member of the US D Cup team in ***1951***, but was not chosen to play in the Challenge Round against Australia.

FREDERICK ('**TED**') RUDOLPH **SCHROEDER** (USA)
Born 20/7/21. A powerful Californian whose aggressive serve-and-volley game brought him much success on fast surfaces. The US National Junior Champion in ***1939***, he won the NCAA Championships from Stanford in ***1942*** and the same year won the US Championships, defeating Frank Parker in the final. In ***1949*** he reached the final again but lost in five sets to Pancho Gonzales. Earlier that same year, on his only visit to Wimbledon he had won the singles in heroic fashion after surviving four five-set matches. In the first round he had beaten his doubles partner, Gardnar Mulloy, 7–5 in the fifth (later they reached the doubles final and lost to Gonzales and Parker). In the quarter-finals he had been m-p down to Frank Sedgman and, despite being foot-faulted on his first serve, had followed in his second serve to hit a winning volley and finally won 9–7 in the final set. In all he played 291 games. Only two champions played more – Boris Becker (292) in ***1985*** and Ashley Cooper (322) in ***1958***. In doubles he won the US Championships with Jack Kramer in ***1940/41/47*** and the mixed with Louise Brough in ***1942***. A distinguished member of the US D Cup team between ***1946–51***, he played in six Challenge Rounds, winning eight of his 11 singles and one of his four doubles. Played in 8 ties, winning 13 of 19 rubbers (11–3 singles, 2–3 doubles). JB

RICHARD (**DICK**) DUDLEY **SEARS** (USA)
Born 16/10/1861 Died 8/4/1943. The first US Champion in ***1881*** while he was still a 19-year-old student at Harvard, this great Boston athlete was the youngest winner until the slightly younger Oliver Campbell won in ***1890*** aged 19 and a half. (They were both older than Pete Sampras who became the youngest ever winner in ***1990*** aged 19 years, 28 days). Sears retained his title for the next six years, playing through in ***1882/83*** and winning the newly introduced Challenge Round in ***1884/85/86/87***. He also won six doubles titles, five with James Dwight (***1882/83/84/96/97***) and one with Joseph Clark (***1885***). JB

FRANCIS ('**FRANK**') ARTHUR **SEDGMAN** (Australia)
Born 29/10/27. A superb volleyer who seemed to glide about the court, he was Australia's first post-war Wimbledon singles champ and, with Ken McGregor, he achieved the Grand Slam of the 4 major doubles titles in ***1951***. Won Wimbledon singles ***1952*** and doubles (with J. E. Bromwich) ***1948*** and (with McGregor) ***1951/52***. US singles ***1951/52*** and doubles (with Bromwich) ***1950*** and (with McGregor) ***1951***. French doubles (with McGregor) ***1951/52***. Australian singles ***1949/50*** (with McGregor) doubles ***1951/52***. Italian singles and doubles (with McGregor) ***1952***. Won 25 D Cup rubbers out of 28 in 10 ties between ***1949–52***(16–3 singles, 9–0 doubles). Turned pro in ***1953***.

FRANCISCO ('**PANCHO**') **SEGURA** (Ecuador)
Born 20/6/21. An unorthodox showman who made his reputation in his pro years – he achieved little as an amateur. Won the NCAA singles ***1943/44/45***, the only triple winner this century, plus the US Clay Court title in ***1944*** and the US Indoor in ***1946***, but made little mark at Wimbledon, losing to Tom Brown and to Drobny in his two singles appearances. He turned pro in ***1947*** and immediately became one of the great entertainers of the pro game, winning the US Pro title ***1950/51/52***. With his double-fisted forehand, his deadly lobs, his scuttling speed about the court, and his beaming smile, he was a most popular competitor for 20 years. If he did not win as many titles as he deserved, he was always capable of testing players of the quality of Kramer, Rosewall, and Gonzales.

ELIAS VICTOR ('**VIC**') **SEIXAS** (USA)
Born 30/8/23. A doggedly successful American competitor. Won Wimbledon singles ***1953*** and mixed 3 times with Doris Hart (***1953/54/55***) and once with Shirley Fry (***1956***). US singles ***1954*** and doubles (with M. G. Rose) ***1952*** and (with M. A. Trabert) ***1954***. French doubles (with Trabert) ***1954/55***. Played in 7 successive D Cup Challenge Rounds and won 38 out of 55 rubbers in 19 ties between ***1951–57*** (24–12 singles, 14–5 doubles).

MARGARET SMITH (Australia)
Born 16/7/42. Now Mrs Court (1967). In ***1970*** she became the second woman to achieve the Grand Slam of the major singles championships, having brought off a unique mixed doubles slam with Fletcher in ***1963***. A powerful athlete, superbly fit, with a heavy service, great stamina and a formidable reach on the volley, she won a record number of 62 GS titles – and would have won more if she had not been afflicted by occasional and often inexplicable losses of confidence. Her major singles successes were Wimbledon ***1963/65/70***, US Championships ***1962/65/69/70/73***, French Championships ***1962/64/69/70/73***, and Australian Championships ***1960–66***, ***1969–71*** and ***1973***. She was also three times the holder of the Italian (***1962/63/64***), German (***1964/65/66***) and South African (***1968/70/71***) titles. In addition, she won the doubles at Wimbledon twice, with Turner (***1964***) and Tegart (***1969***) and the mixed five times, with Fletcher (***1963/65/66/68***) and Riessen (***1975***). She took the US doubles five times – with Ebbern (***1963***), Bueno (***1968***) Dalton (***1970***) and Wade (***1973/75***), and the mixed on eight occasions with Mark (***1961***), Stolle (***1962/65***), Fletcher (***1963***), Newcombe (***1964***) and Riessen (***1969/70/72***). She won the French four times in doubles with Turner (***1964/65***), Tegart (***1966***) and Wade (***1973***) and mixed with Fletcher (***1963/64/65***) and Riessen (***1969***), and she held eight Australian doubles with Reitano (***1961***), Ebbern (***1962/63***), Turner (***1965***), Dalton (***1969/70***), Goolagong (***1971***) and Wade (***1973***) and two mixed titles with Fletcher (***1963/64***). She toured successfully, with the help of her husband, Barry, with two children, but retired in ***1977*** when she found that she was expecting a third baby.

STANLEY ('**STAN**') ROGER **SMITH** (USA)
Born 14/12/46. The very epitome of the All-American boy with his tall straight-backed figure, his fair hair and his clean-cut good looks, he became a national hero in ***1972***, as well as the world's No.1 player, when he won a magnificent Wimbledon final against Nastase and then beat the Rumanian again in the opening rubber of the D Cup final on unfriendly clay in Bucharest to launch the United States towards an improbable victory against the odds. Earlier, in ***1969***, he had won the US Nationals and the following year had beaten Laver and Rosewall to capture the first-ever Masters which, that year, was a round-robin competition. When he won the US Open in ***1971*** on the grass of Forest Hills he was perfecting the serve-and-volley technique that made him such an awkward opponent. Although his groundstrokes were never his strength, he used them intelligently to secure the few breaks of serve that were necessary as he blanketed the net to secure his own service games. His doubles partnership with Lutz was one of the best American pairings there has ever been. They are the only pair to have won US National titles on all four surfaces – grass, clay, hard and indoor. Four times they won the US Open – ***1968/74/78/ 80*** and in ***1977*** they were successful both in South Africa and the US Pro at Boston. In D Cup they are the only American pair to have won three Challenge Round rubbers and two in the Final Round. Overall his D Cup record is 35 wins and 7 losses in 24 ties between ***1968–79*** (15–4 singles, 20–3 doubles). JB

FREDERICK ('**FRED**') SYDNEY **STOLLE** (Australia)
Born 8/10/38. Former Sydney bank clerk, regarded primarily as doubles specialist, who by diligence and determination became one of the most successful singles players of the 1960s. Powerful serving and volleying, added to dogged consistency in return of service on the backhand, compensated for his lack of mobility and flexibility. Shared with Von Cramm the unlucky distinction of losing in 3 successive Wimbledon singles f, falling to McKinley (***1963***) and Emerson (***1964/65***). Was also r/u to Lundquist in ***1964*** Italian f, but won French singles ***1965*** and US and German titles ***1966***. Established himself first as a doubles player with Hewitt. They won Australia ***1963/64***, Wimbledon ***1962/64*** and Italy ***1963/64***. With Emerson, who had dominated him in singles, won French and US doubles ***1965*** and Australia, Italy and US ***1966***. In ***1981***, aged 42, he and Newcombe (37) took McEnroe/ Fleming to 5s tie-break in US Open sf. Became contract professional ***1967*** and reached Wimbledon doubles f with Rosewall ***1968***, and won mixed doubles

there with Ann Jones in ***1969***. Between ***1964–66*** he won 13 out of his 16 D Cup rubbers in 6 ties (10–2 singles, 3–1 doubles). Coached NY Sets to victory in World Team Tennis competition ***1976***.

ERIC WILLIAM **STURGESS** (South Africa)
Born 10/5/20. South Africa's most successful singles competitor and their nat champ on no fewer than 11 occasions, beginning a sequence of victories in ***1939/40*** and continuing in ***1946***, ***1948–54***, and ***1957***. Outside Johannesburg his major achievement was the capture of the German singles ***1952;*** r/u in Paris ***1947/51*** and lost to Gonzales in ***1948*** US f. Twice he was in Wimbledon sf, but in spite of speed, steadiness, and elegance, he lacked the weight of shot to win in the highest class and his second service was vulnerable. He won the French doubles with Fannin ***1947*** and a number of mixed titles, notably Wimbledon ***1949*** (with Sheila Summers) and ***1950*** (with Louise Brough), and F Hills ***1949*** (with Brough).

MAY GODFREY **SUTTON** (USA)
Born in Plymouth, England, 25/9/1886. Died 4/10/1975. Became Mrs T.C. Bundy (1912). In ***1905*** the first overseas player to win a Wimbledon title. The seventh and youngest child of a British naval officer, Captain A. de G. Sutton, she learnt tennis on asphalt courts after her family moved to California in ***1893***. She was forceful and vigorous with a disconcerting top-spin forehand. F. R. Burrow commented: 'She took a deep breath before every stroke and then hit the ball with all her force to the accompaniment of a very audible expiration.' After winning the US singles and doubles in ***1904*** she went, aged 18, to Wimbledon ***1905*** and defeated the holder, Miss Douglass, in the Challenge Round. Miss Douglass regained the title the following year, but then lost a third battle with the Californian in ***1907***. After winning the US Clay Court singles ***1912***, Miss Sutton married Thomas Bundy, 3 times a US doubles champ. She played doubles in the ***1925*** W Cup and in ***1929*** returned to Wimbledon at 42 to defeat Eileen Bennett, seeded 4, and reach the qf. She was still playing 44 years later. Her daughter Dorothy represented the US 3 times in the W Cup and won the Australian singles ***1938***, and a nephew, John Doeg, was US champ in ***1930***.

WILLIAM ('**BILLY**') FRANKLIN **TALBERT** (USA)
Born 4/9/18. An expert in the practice, technique and strategy of doubles. The best right-court player of his generation, his most important victories were gained with Mulloy, with whom he won the US doubles ***1942/45/46/48***, and a total of 84 out of 90 tournaments in ten years. With a variety of partners, he won US Clay Court doubles ***1942/44/45/46*** and the US Indoor Doubles ***1949/50/51/52/54***. Abroad, with the young Trabert, also from Cincinnati, he won French and Italian doubles ***1950***. He was runner-up to Parker in US singles ***1944/45*** and US Indoor champion ***1948/51***. He won nine of his ten D Cup rubbers ***1946–53***, in 8 ties, (2–0 singles, 7–1 doubles) and from ***1953–57*** he captained the US D Cup team. Later became Tournament Director of the US Open. All this was achieved despite the disability of diabetes.

WILLIAM ('**BILL**') TATEM **TILDEN** (USA)
Born 10/2/1893. Died 5/6/1953. For many critics the greatest player and student of match-strategy in the history of the game who was world No 1 ***1920–25*** and US No 1 ten years in a row ***1920–29***, a record. Tall, with a long reach and a long stride, great strength and versatility of shot, and a powerful sense of drama, Tilden did not win a major title until he was 27. Then won Wimbledon singles ***1920/21/30***, and doubles (with F. T. Hunter) ***1927***, and US singles ***1920/21/22/23/24/25/29***, and doubles (with Richards) ***1918/21/22***, (with Norton) ***1923***, (with Hunter) ***1927***. Was imprisoned for homosexual activities in ***1951***, and died in tragic circumstances two years later, penniless and with few remaining friends. Was first Italian champ in ***1930*** and played D Cup from ***1920–30*** winning 34 rubbers out of 41 and 21 out of 28 in Challenge Rounds. Between ***1920–26*** won 13 successive Challenge Round singles. His final record from 17 ties was 25–5 in singles and 9–2 in doubles. Turned pro in ***1931*** after winning 138 of the 192 tournaments he had contested as an amateur.

MARION ANTHONY ('**TONY**') **TRABERT** (USA)
Born 16/8/30. Won Wimbledon singles ***1955*** and US singles ***1953/55*** without losing a set. Won French singles ***1954/55*** and doubles victories included US in ***1954*** (with E. V. Seixas), French ***1950*** (with W. F. Talbert) and ***1954/55*** (with Seixas) and Italian ***1950*** (with Talbert). Won 27 out of 35 D Cup rubbers in 14 ties between ***1951–55*** (16–5 singles, 11–3 doubles). Served a term as US captain in the ***1970s***. Turned pro in ***1955***.

CHRISTINE CLARA **TRUMAN** (Great Britain)
Born 16/2/41. Now Mrs G. T. Janes (1967). Britain's most popular post-war player. She possessed a powerful forehand, a disconcerting ability to hit her way out of crises, a remarkable capacity for unorthodox volleying, and a temperament and court manners that made her a model for every schoolgirl in the country. She was always regarded as a potential Wimbledon champ and reached sf at the age of 16 at her first Wimbledon, where she lost to Althea Gibson, the eventual winner. Afterwards came a series of spectacular failures until she reached the ***1961*** f, only to fall to Angela Mortimer. Her best performances were a victory over Miss Gibson in the ***1958*** W Cup match, which helped to give Britain the trophy for the first time since the war, and the capture of the French and Italian singles titles in ***1959***. Won ***1960*** Australian doubles with Maria Bueno. She and her sister, Nell, formed an aggressively effective – and sometimes erratic – doubles partnership. She won 10 rubbers out of 25 in 11 W Cup matches.

LESLEY ROSEMARY **TURNER** (Australia)
Born 16/8/42. Now Mrs W. W. Bowrey (1968). Clever, strong and persistent, she gained her principal successes on European clay courts. In ***1961*** on her first European tour she lost to Maria Bueno in the Italian final and was runner-up again ***1962/64*** before winning the title ***1967/68***. She won the French singles ***1963***, defeating Ann Jones, and ***1965***, beating Margaret Court, and was runner-up ***1962/67***. She reached the Australian final ***1964/67***. In doubles, with Margaret Court, she won Wimbledon ***1964***, Paris ***1964/65*** and Australia ***1965***. Also took the Australian doubles title, with Judy Tegart, ***1964/67*** and the US doubles, with Darlene Hard, ***1961***. Won Wimbledon mixed doubles with Fred Stolle ***1961/64***.

JOHN ('**JOHNNY**') WILLIAM **VAN RYN** (USA)
Born 30/6/05. Formed one of the most famous of all doubles partnerships with Wilmer Allison. Pat Hughes described their combination as 'a perfect blending of styles...Van Ryn dipped the ball over from the right court and his partner stepped in at the psychological moment for the final volley'. George Lott thought that their deep personal friendship and knowledge of each other's movements and reactions played an important part in their success. With Allison, Van Ryn succeeded at Wimbledon in ***1929–30*** and took the US title in ***1931/35***. He won Paris and Wimbledon with Lott in ***1931***. In the ***1929*** D Cup Challenge Round he and Allison beat Cochet and Borotra and in the ***1932*** match they defeated Cochet and Brugnon. He was a member of the US team from ***1928–36*** and won 32 of his 44 rubbers in 24 ties. (18–10 singles, 14–2 doubles).

GUILLERMO VILAS (Argentina)
Born 17/8/52. For a man who had learned his tennis on the slow red clay of Buenos Aires it is remarkable that his first major success should have been to win the ***1974*** Masters title on grass at Kooyong Stadium, Melbourne. This was the only time the tournament was played on grass and his wins over Newcombe, Borg and Nastase were as brilliant as they were unexpected. He proved that this had been no fluke by winning the Australian Open twice, in ***1978*** and ***1979***. A powerfully built left-hander with heavily topped groundstrokes, he specialised in wearing down the opposition, which he did successfully in ***1977*** both at the French Open and the US Open, which for the third and last time was being played on American clay courts. That year he claimed 15 titles altogether. Coached and managed shrewdly by Ion Tiriac, he won 61 of the 103 finals he contested in a long career and in the ***1977/78*** seasons he won 46 consecutive singles matches, a record in the open era. JB

HENRY **ELLSWORTH VINES** (USA)
Born 28/9/11. Died 17/3/94. The possessor of a fine forehand and one of the fastest services of all time. Defeated Bunny Austin in ***1932*** 6–4 6–2 6–0 in one of the shortest Wimbledon f and lost title next year in a classic f against Jack Crawford. Won US singles ***1931/32*** and Australian doubles ***1933*** with Gledhill. Played D Cup ***1932/33***, winning 13 rubbers out of 16, all singles, in 8 ties. Turned pro ***1934***.

BARON **GOTTFRIED** ALEXANDER MAXIMILIAN WALTER KURT **VON CRAMM** (Germany)
Born 7/7/09. Died in car accident in Egypt 9/11/76. An elegant stylist and Germany's most successful player. Won French singles ***1934/36*** and doubles (with H. Henkel) ***1937***, and German singles ***1932/33/34/35/48/49*** and doubles ***1948/49/53/55***. Like F. S. Stolle, he was losing sin-

gles finalist at Wimbledon for 3 successive years – ***1935–37***. Won Wimbledon mixed (with Hilda Krahwinkel) **1933** and US doubles (with Henkel) ***1937***. Won 82 D Cup rubbers out of 102 (58–10 singles, 24–9 doubles) in 37 ties between ***1932–53***.

SARAH **VIRGINIA WADE** (Great Britain)
Born 10/7/45. A spectacular and dramatic competitor, at her 16th attempt she finally achieved her ambition of winning the women's singles at Wimbledon in the Centenary year of ***1977***. Until then her career had been an extravagant mixture of bitter disappointments, many of the worst endured at Wimbledon, and dazzling successes. Her first major success was gained at US Open ***1968*** when she defeated Billie Jean King 6–4 6–2 in the final. She won the Australian title, beating Evonne Goolagong in ***1972*** and gained her only major clay-court success in ***1971***, when she defeated Helga Masthoff in the Italian final. Her best doubles victories – France ***1973***, US ***1973/75***, Australia ***1975*** and Italy ***1968*** – were won with Margaret Court, but she also succeeded in Rome ***1971*** with Mrs Masthoff and ***1973*** with Olga Morozova. She also holds the record for the most appearances of any player of any nation in both Fed Cup (100 rubbers in 57 ties) and the W Cup (56 rubbers in 20 ties).

MATS ARNE OLOF **WILANDER** (Sweden)
Born 22/8/64. When he won the French Open junior title in 1981, little did anyone suspect that twelve months later, aged 17 years 9 months and 6 days, and unseeded, he would become the youngest ever French Open Champion (***1982***). (He would remain the youngest man to win a Grand Slam singles crown until Boris Becker won Wimbledon in 1985, aged 17 years 7 months. Then Michael Chang lowered the record to 17 years 3 months when he dramatically won the French Open in 1989). His relentless topspin driving, single-handed on the forehand, double-handed on the backhand, plus intense concentration and speedy court coverage (all so reminiscent of his great Swedish predecessor Bjorn Borg), brought him two more successes in Paris (***1985,1988***). It was a mark of his all-round ability that he should have been able to win the Australian Open on grass in ***1983*** with back-to-back wins against McEnroe and Lendl. The following year (***1984***) he won a second Australian title on grass and then won for a third time in ***1988*** when the Championship was played for the first time at the new National Tennis Centre at Flinders Park. When, later in ***1988***, he ended Lendl's streak of 157 consecutive weeks at No.1 to win the US Open title, he became the first man since Connors in ***1974*** to hold three of the four Grand Slam titles in the same year. That win also lifted him to the No.1 world ranking, a position he would hold for 20 weeks. Already in ***1985*** his second French win had given him a fourth Grand Slam title before his 21st birthday – the only man ever to achieve that feat. Altogether he won 33 singles and 7 doubles titles and went on competing spasmodically up to the end of ***1996***. A member of Sweden's successful Davis Cup teams in ***1984*** (d.USA 4–1), ***1985*** (d. W.Germany 3–2) and ***1987*** (d. India 5–0), he won 36 of his 50 singles rubbers and 7 of his 9 doubles rubbers in 26 ties spanning ten years from 1981. JB

ANTHONY FREDERICK **WILDING** (New Zealand)
Born 31/10/1883. Killed in action in Belgium 9/5/1915. Coached by his father, a notable cricketer, he won the champ of Canterbury, New Zealand, at the age of 17 and went to Cambridge Univ for which he played ***1904–05***. The Aus singles champion ***1906–09*** and ***1906*** doubles winner (with Heath), he became one of the great heroes of Edwardian tennis, winning the singles champ at Wimbledon ***1910/11/12/13***. Won doubles (with N. E. Brookes) in ***1907/14*** and (with M. J. G. Ritchie) ***1908/10***. He won 21 of the 30 D Cup rubbers which he played in 11 ties for Australasia between ***1905–14*** (15–6 singles, 6–3 doubles).

HELEN NEWINGTON **WILLS** (USA)
Born 6/10/05. Died 1/1/98. Became Mrs F. S. Moody (1929), later Mrs A. Roark (1939). Lenglen's successor as ruler of Wimbledon. A relentless baseliner, she won the singles 8 times in 9 attempts, losing only to Kitty McKane in 1924. Between ***1927–32*** she won all the major singles champs, except Australia, without losing a set. Won Wimbledon singles ***1927/28/29/30/32/33/35/38*** and doubles (with Hazel Wightman) ***1924*** and (with Elizabeth Ryan) ***1927/30***. US singles ***1923/24/25/27/28/29/31***, and doubles (with Mrs J. B. Jessup) ***1922***, (with Hazel Wightman) ***1924/28***, and (with Mary K. Browne) ***1925***. French singles ***1928/29/30/32*** and doubles (with Elizabeth Ryan) ***1930/31/32***.

SIDNEY BURR BEARDSLEE **WOOD** (USA)
Born 1/11/11. A nephew of the late Julian Myrick, a former President of the US LTA and the prime mover in ***1913*** in the development of Forest Hills as the national centre of tennis in the US, he made his first appearance at Wimbledon, aged 15, in ***1927***, playing Lacoste on the Centre Court. In ***1931***, aged 19 years and 243 days, he became Wimbledon's second youngest champion at the time. He won by default. Frank Shields fell in 4s of his sf against Borotra and damaged an ankle. Shields won, but was not fit enough to play in f. A shrewd strategist and a graceful stroke-maker, Wood was r/u to Allison at Forest Hills in ***1935*** but lost 6–2 6–2 6–3 in one of the tournament's most disappointing finals. He played in 7 Davis Cup ties, winning 8 out of his 14 rubbers (5–6 singles, 3–0 doubles) between ***1931*** and ***1934***.

NANCYE MEREDITH **WYNNE** (Australia)
Born 10/6/17. Became Mrs.G.F. Bolton (1940). The most successful of Australian champions until the arrival of Margaret Court, Nancy Wynne Bolton's career spanned the years of the Second World War. She won the Australian singles six times (***1937/40/46/47/48/51***) and the doubles on ten occasions, all with her great friend, Thelma Coyne Long (***1936/37/38/39/40/ 47/48/49/ 51/52***), plus four mixed with Colin Long (***1940/46/47/48***). In 1938 she became the first Australian to reach the final of the US Championships, losing to Alice Marble. In ***1947*** she was a quarter-finalist at Wimbledon and a semi-finalist in New York, performances that earned her a world ranking of No.4. JB

The game has lost the two great American rivals of the 1920s and 1930s – Helen Wills (above) and Helen Jacobs, who won only one of her 11 meetings against 'Little Miss Poker Face', a controversial retirement at the US Championships in 1933 when Wills was in danger of defeat, trailing 0–3 in the final set. (Wimbledon Museum)

Obituaries

PAT HUGHES, who died on 8 May 1997 at the age of 94, had been a member of the four successful British Davis Cup teams between 1933 and 1936, playing a valuable role as the doubles expert. Between 1929 and 1936 he competed in 21 Davis Cup ties winning both singles rubbers he contested and 13 of the 20 doubles rubbers for which he was selected. In 1933 and 1934 he won the French and Australian doubles titles with Fred Perry and in 1936 he took the Wimbledon title with Raymond Tuckey. Underestimated as a singles player, Hughes did have one major success in 1931 when he beat Henri Cochet to win the Italian Championships in Milan. Born in Sutton Coldfield on 21 December 1902, Hughes represented Essex in county matches. From 1927 until his retirement in 1968 he was employed by the Dunlop Sports Co. and was instrumental in making the Dunlop Maxply the most popular racket among international players of the immediate post Second World War years.

BASIL HUTCHINS, who died on 23 March 1997, aged 70, after a short illness, was a member of the committee of the All England Club from 1974 until 1994 when he became a Vice-President. Born on 1 September 1926 he was educated at St Bartholomew's Grammar School and St Catharine's College, Cambridge. At the tail end of World War Two he joined the Royal Air Force and following his demobilisation in 1948 he joined the family group of petroleum companies based in Newbury, eventually becoming chairman. From 1953–66 he represented Berkshire of which county he would later become President. An all round sportsman, he competed in The Championships between 1955 and 1959 having played rugby for Cambridge University XV Club and for Newbury, of which club he served a period as captain. He was also a life member of the Squash Rackets Association and of the British Olympic Association. A keen student of tennis history and an able administrator, he particularly enjoyed his role as Chairman of the Wimbledon Lawn Tennis Museum, a post he filled from 1985 until his death. He had also been consulted by his friends at the Rugby Football Union when that organization decided to build a Museum.

HELEN JACOBS, who died on 2 June 1997 at the age of 88, was one of America's greatest champions whose personal rivalry with the 'other' Helen, Helen Wills Moody, was one of the central themes of international tennis in the 1930s. Curiously both played at the Berkeley Club in California and even had the same coach. But the parallels went further. Both won the national junior title twice, both attended the University of California and Jacobs would eventually live in the Wills former family home. Born on 6 August 1908 in Globe, Arizona, Jacobs was a fine natural athlete whose dogged determination and skill at the net concealed a frail forehand that she learned to play with slice for safety. In 1927 she made her Wightman Cup debut and altogether contested 30 rubbers in 12 ties, winning 14 of her 22 singles matches and five of her eight doubles. She won four US Championships in a row from 1932 to 193 5 and carried off the doubles title three times (1930, '34 and '35) – all with Sarah Palfrey – and the mixed once, with George Lott in 1934. At Wimbledon she was less successful, winning only one of the five finals she contested. That was in 1936, exactly one year after she had failed on the only match point she ever held against Wills Moody in the 11 matches they played. However, Jacobs did gain a win against her arch-rival in the 1933 US final when Wills, trailing 0–3 in the final set, informed the umpire that her painful back made it impossible for her to continue. Ranked among the world's top10 for 12 years in a row from 1928, she was No. 1 in 1936. At home she was the US No. 1 four years in a row between 1932 and 1935 and a member of the national top ten 13 times in the years between 1927 and 1941.

DR AXEL MEYER-WOLDEN, who died on 18 August in Munich aged 56 after a long battle against cancer, was a man of many talents. A Munich lawyer, he represented many famous sportsmen and musicians, including Placido Domingo who was present to sing at the inaugural Compaq Grand Slam Cup, launched by Meyer-Woelden in 1990.

Two years later, recognising the opportunities that were materialising in televised sport, especially soccer in Germany, he founded his company, ISPR, which bought the marketing and television rights of the German Bundesliga for DM700m.

For the last three years of his life he acted as Boris Becker's agent and was instrumental in establishing the Mercedes-Benz Squad of young players with Becker as its manager.

HELEN WILLS MOODY, who died on 1 January 1988 at the age of 92 in a convalescent home in Carmel, California, was one of the game's greatest-ever champions. Without ever travelling to Australia, she won 19 Grand Slam singles titles – a total surpassed only by Steffi Graf (21) and Margaret Court (24), whose records contain respectively 4 and 11 Australian championships.

Remembered both for the eye shade she made famous and for her ice-cool temperament, between 1923 and 1938, this relentless baseliner claimed the US National title seven times, won four French titles and was the Wimbledon champion eight times, a record which stood until Martina Navratilova won there for the ninth time in 1990.

The daughter of Clarence Wills, a prominent Californian surgeon who bought a house overlooking the Berkeley Club in San Francisco, Helen watched the famous home and overseas players who competed there annually in the Pacific Coast Championships. Finding her father's racket in a cupboard the teenager decided to give the game a try. It was immediately apparent that she possessed abundant natural talent, a fact that was confirmed when she won the Californian junior title at the first attempt. A year later she became the national junior champion, a prelude to the capture of her first US Championship at Forest Hills in 1923 when she was 17.

Helen lived in an age when well educated young ladies, even sporting champions, were expected to develop other talents. During her years at the University of California Helen showed a keen interest in art and would later hold exhibitions of her work. She also became well known as a writer, contributing pieces on travel and tennis for American newspapers and publishing three books, one a novel.

In 1923 Helen was invited by Hazel Wightman to take part in the first Wightman Cup match, an annual contest between American and British women. Although she beat Kitty Godfree on that occasion it was the British No.1 who, the following year, inflicted the only defeat Helen ever suffered at Wimbledon (despite trailing by a set and 1–4).

During her best years Helen was virtually invincible. Between 1927 and 1932 she won 13 French, Wimbledon and US titles without dropping a set and won the gold medal at the Paris Olympics in 1924. Her iron concentration and lack of outward emotion, which earned her the title 'Little Miss Poker Face', concealed a perfectionism that was at the heart of her success.

Her great rivalry with 'the other Helen', Helen Jacobs, a fellow Californian and fellow member at Berkeley, had two poignant moments. In 1933, returning to the US Championships after a year's gap she defaulted to Jacobs in the final while trailing 0–3 in the final set. It was the only loss to her rival in 11 meetings. Two years later at Wimbledon, again after a year away, she played Jacobs for the third time in the final. Jacobs, playing her heart out, held a match point but misjudged an easy smash in the wind and lost 8–6.

In 1929 Helen married Freddie Moody, an American whom she had first met in 1926 during her visit to Cannes for the famous match at the Carlton Hotel against Suzanne Lenglen. In the only meeting between the two great stars of the inter-war years Suzanne won twice. After the umpire had called 'Game, set and match to Miss Lenglen, 6–3 7–5' a linesman rushed to the chair to explain that the call of 'out' on match point had not been his. Someone in the crowd had been responsible. To the amazement of all the match was resumed with Suzanne serving at 6–5 40–30. She lost that point and the game. It took a tiring Suzanne two more games to finish the match.

Drifting apart, Helen and Freddie were divorced in 1937 and two years later Helen married Aidan Roark. In her later years she became something of a recluse, living quietly in Carmel and refusing the many invitations she received from tennis organisations around the world to attend various functions.

Maiden Names and Married Names

MAIDEN NAME	MARRIED NAME(S)
Adamson, Nellie	Landry, Mme. P.H.
Akhurst, Daphne S.	Cozens, Mrs. R.S.
Alvarez, Elia (Lili) M.	Valdene, Countess, J. de G.
Andrus, Dorothy B.	Burke, Mrs. W.A.
Arnold, Mimi	Wheeler, Mrs. J.H.
Aussem, Cilly	Brae, Countess F. M. Della Corte
Austin, Joan W.	Lycett, Mrs. R.
	Chiesman, Mrs. F.R.
	Jepson, Mrs. D.S.
	Baker, Mrs. D.A.
Austin, Tracy A.	Holt, Mrs. S.
Austin, Edith L.	Greville, Mrs. T.G.P.
Baker, Beverley	Beckett, Mrs. S.
	Fleitz, Mrs. J.G.
Balleret, Alexia	Dechaume, Mrs. A.
Barclay, Joyce S.	Williams, Mrs. G.M.
	Hume, Mrs. I.
Bennett, Eileen V.	Fearnley Whittingstall, Mrs. E.O.
	Marsh, Mrs. M.M.
	Akroyd, Mrs. G.
	Forslind, Mrs. C.V.
Betz, Pauline M.	Addie, Mrs. R.R.
Bevis, Mary R.	Hawton, Mrs. K.E.
Bingley, Blanche	Hillyard, Mrs. G.W.
Bjurstedt, A. Margrethe(Molla)	Mallory, Mrs. F.I.
Bloomer, Shirley J.	Brasher, Mrs. C.W.
Boothby, P. Dora	Geen, Mrs. A.C.
Boucher, Edith M.	Hannam, Mrs. F.J.
Boulle, Michelle	Rodriguez, Mrs. P.H.
Bowder, Irene E.	Peacock, Mrs. G.E.
Boyd, Esna	Robertson, Mrs. A.
Broquedis, M. Marguerite	Billout, Mme. J.
	Bordes, Mme. P.R.M.
Brough, A. Louise	Clapp, Mrs. A.T.
Brown, Nina B.	Hamilton, Mrs. E.R.
Browne, Mary K.	Kenneth-Smith, Mrs. K.
Buding, Edda	Duechting, Mrs. E.
Bundy, Dorothy (Dodo) M.	Cheney, Mrs. A.C.
Buxton, Angela	Silk, Mrs. D.W.
Caldwell, Carole A.	Graebner, Mrs. C.E.
Canning, M. Patricia	Todd, Mrs. R.B.
Carter, Mary M.	Reitano, Mrs. S.J.
Cherneva, Svetlana	Parkhomenko, Mrs. S.
Coghlan, Lorraine G.	Robinson, Mrs. J.D.G.
	Green, Mrs. G.S.
Colyer, Evelyn L.	Munro, Mrs. H.A.
Connolly, Maureen C.	Brinker, Mrs. N.
Connor, Judith N.	Chaloner Mrs. J.D.
Cooper, Charlotte R.	Sterry, Mrs. A.
Cox, Marjorie	Crawford, Mrs. J.H.
Coyne, Thelma D.	Long, Mrs. M.N.

MAIDEN NAME	MARRIED NAME(S)
Cross, Edith A.	Jensen, Mrs. C.J.
Daniell, Agnes K.R.	Tuckey, Mrs. C.O.
Delhees, Petra	Jauch, Mrs. P.
Douglass, Dorothea K.	Chambers, Mrs. R.Lambert
Durr, Frankie	Browning, Mrs. B.J.
Eastlake-Smith, G.	Lamplough, Mrs. G.
Ebbern, Robin	Vincenzi, Mrs. E.J.
Eisel, Mary Ann	Curtis, Mrs. P.W.
Evert, Chris M.	Lloyd, Mrs. J.M.
	Evert Lloyd, Mrs. C.
	Mill, Mrs. A.R.
Floyd, Donna	Fales, Mrs. H.G.
Forbes, Jean R.	Drysdale, Mrs. E.C.
Fromholtz, Diane L.	Balestrat, Mrs. C.M.
Fry, Joan C.	Lakeman, Mrs. T.A.
Fry, Shirley J.	Irvin, Mrs. K.E.
Gannon, Joy	Mottram, Mrs. A.J.
Garrison, Zina L.	Jackson, Mrs. W.
Gibson, Althea	Darben, Mrs. W.A.
	Llewellyn, Mrs. S.
Gillou, Kate	Fenwick, Mme. F.
Goldsack, Elsie A.	Pitman, Mrs. J.B.
	Rowbottom, Mrs. G.F.
	Furlonge, Lady G.W.
Goolagong, Evonne F.	Cawley, Mrs. R.A.
Gourlay, Helen	Cawley, Mrs. R.L.
Groenman, Trudy	Walhof, Mrs. T.
Hall, Eleanor (Nell) M.	Hopman, Mrs. H.C.
Hanks, Carol	Aucamp, Mrs. D.C.
Hantze, Karen J.	Susman, Mrs. J.R.
Hard, Darlene R.	Waggoner, Mrs. R.
Hart, Mary M.	McIlquham, Mrs. C.G.
Haydon, Adrianne (Ann) S.	Jones, Mrs. P.F.
Head, Dorothy	Knode, Mrs. D.P.
Heeley, G.Mary	Cartwright, Mrs. D.F.
Heine, E.A.L.(Bobbie)	Miller, Mrs. J.H.K.
	Davie, Mrs. W.R.
Hogan, Patti. St.A.	Fordyce, Mrs. I.M.
Holcroft, Phoebe C.	Watson, Mrs. M.R.
	Blakstad, Mrs. W.L.
Hood, Emily	Westacott, Mrs.V.
Hotchkiss, Hazel V.	Wightman, Mrs. G.W.
Howkins, Phyllis, L.	Covell, Mrs. B.C.
Hy, Patricia	Boulais, Mrs. P.
Jackson, Helen	Atkins, Mrs. H.
James, Winifred (Freda) A.	Hammersley, Mrs. S.H.
Jedrzejowska, Jadwiga	Gallert, Mrs. A.
Jung, Sylvia	Lafaurie, Mrs. R.
	Henrotin, Mrs. C.F.
	Welton, Mrs. S.
Kiyomura, Ann K.	Hayashi, Mrs. D.
Krahwinkel, Hilde	Sperling, Mrs. S.
Lance, Sylvia	Harper, Mrs. R.
Lehane, Janice (Jan) P.	O'Neill, Mrs. J.J

MAIDEN NAME	MARRIED NAME(S)
Lidderdale, Kathleen E.	Bridge, Mrs. A.V.
Lofdahl, Ingrid A.R.F.	Bentzer, Mrs. J.A.
Lyle, Nancy	Glover, Mrs. P.F.
MacLennan, Frances V.M.	Taylor, Mrs. R.
Mandlikova, Hana	Sadlek, Mrs. J.
May, Kathryn (Kathy)	Teacher, Mrs. B.D. Paben, Mrs. D.
McCune, Anna V.	Harper, Mrs. L.A.
McInnes, Coral	Buttsworth, Mrs. C.
McKane, Margaret	Stocks, Mrs. A.D.
McKane, Kathleen (Kitty)	Godfree, Mrs. L.A.
Melville, Kerry A.	Reid, Mrs. G.E.
Metaxa, Doris E.	Howard, Mrs. P.D.
Moffitt, Billie Jean	King, Mrs. L.W.
Moran, Gertrude A.	Corbally, Mrs. T.J. Hand, Mrs. E.J. Simpson, Mrs. F.M.
Morozova, Olga V.	Rubanov, Mrs. V.B.
Mortimer, F. Angela M.	Barrett, Mrs. J.E.
Morton, Agnes M.	Stewart, Lady H.H.
Mudford, Phyllis E.	King, Mrs. M.R.
Muller, E.Fay	Robinson, Mrs. A.A.
Mutch, Margaret (Mal)	Molesworth, Mrs. M.
Nagelsen, H. Elizabeth (Betsy)	McCormack, Mrs. M.H.
Nelson, Vicki L.	Dunbar, Mrs. K.
Neumannova, M.	Pinterova, Mrs. M.
Newberry, Janet S.	Wright Mrs. F.I.
Nicholl, Jean	Bostock, Mrs. E.W.A.
Niessen, Helga	Masthoff, Frau H.
Osborne, Margaret E.	duPont, Mrs. W.
Palfrey, Sarah H.	Fabyan, Mrs. M. Cooke, Mrs. E.T. Danzig, Mrs. J.A.
Passemard, Simone	Mathieu, Mme. R.
Peiachov, Paulina	Peled, Mrs. E.
Piercey, Sheila A.	Summers, Mrs. R.A.
Prosen, Carol A.	Kalogeropoulos, Mrs. N.
Provis, Nicole A.L.	Bradtke, Mrs. M.R.
Puzejova, Vera	Sukova, Mrs. C.
Quertier, Jean	Rinkel, Mrs. I.
Ramsey, Winifred G.	Beamish, Mrs. A.E.
Reyes, Rosa (Rosie) M.	Darmon, Mrs. P.
Reynolds, Sandra	Price, Mrs. L.E.G.
Richey, Nancy A.	Gunter, Mrs. K.S.
Ridley, Joan C.	O'Meara, Mrs. D.J.P.
Rosenquest, Charlotte (Betty)	Pratt, Mrs. E.C.S.
Round, Dorothy E.	Little, Mrs. D.L.
Rush, Gretchen A.	Magers, Mrs. S.W.
Russell, JoAnne C.	Longdon, Mrs. G.
Sampson, Julia, A.	Haywood, Mrs. D.A.
Saunders, Margaret A.	Michell, Mrs. L.R.C.
Savchenko, Larisa I.	Neiland, Mrs. A.
Sawamatsu, Kazuko	Yoshida, Mrs. M.
Sayers, Elizabeth M.	Smylie, Mrs. P.D.
Schildknecht, Helge	Orth, Frau L.
Schofield, Barbara	Davidson, Mrs. G.
Schuurman, Renee	Haygarth, Mrs. P.
Seeney, Daphne G.	Fancutt, Mrs. T.T.
Shaw, Winnie M.	Wooldridge, Mrs. K.
Shepherd, Dorothy C.	Barron, Mrs. W.P.
Sheriff, Carol	Zeeman, Mrs. C.E.
Sheriff, Gail V.	Chanfreau, Mrs. J.B. Lovera, Mrs. J.J.
Shilcock, J. Anne	Spann, Mrs. J.K.
Sigart, Josane	Mme. J. de Meulemeester
Simpson, Alice M.	Pickering, Mrs. W.H.
Slocock, Winifred M.	McNair, Mrs. R.J.
Smith, Margaret	Court, Mrs. B.M.
Squire, Mabel B.	Parton, Mrs. E.G. Mavrogordato, Mrs. T.M.
St.George, Floris	Conway, Mrs. J.R.
Staley, Jennifer	Hoad, Mrs. L.A.
Stammers, Katherine (Kay) E.	Menzies, Mrs. M. Bullitt, Mrs. T.W.
Stevens, Greer R.	Leo-Smith, Mrs. K.
Sutton, May G.	Bundy, Mrs. T.C.
Tegart, Judy A.M.	Dalton, Mrs. D.E.
Thomson, Ethel W.	Larcombe, Mrs. D.T.R.
Tomanova, Renata	Roth, Mrs. W.R.
Truman, Christine C.	Janes, Mrs. G.T.
Turner, Lesley R.	Bowrey, Mrs. W.W.
Varner, Margaret	Bloss, Mrs. W.G.
Walkden, Pat M.	Pretorius, Mrs. Q.C.
Walsh, Sharon A .	Pete, Mrs. M.H.
Ward, Patricia E.	Hales, Mrs. R.
Watanabe, Tina B.	Mochizuki, Mrs. H.A.
Wills, Helen N.	Moody, Mrs. F.S. Roark, Mrs. A.
Wynne, Nancye M.	Bolton, Mrs. G.F.
Zyl, Annette, M. van	Plooy, Mrs. J. du

Championship Rolls

Note: The maiden names of married ladies appearing below can be found on pp 425–426.

AUSTRALIAN CHAMPIONSHIPS

1. Title: Held as the Australasian Championships from 1905 to 1926. In 1927 became the Australian Championships to coincide with the opening of the Kooyong Stadium in Melbourne. **2. Status:** The Championships became open in 1969. **3. Venues:** Since 1905 there have been 84 Championships held in the following cities (there were two Championships in 1977 (Jan and Dec) and from then until 1985 the event was staged in December. In 1986 there was no Championship so that the Jan date could be resumed in 1987): **MELBOURNE (40):** 1905, '14, '24, '27, 30, '33, '35, '39, '48, '50, '53, '57, '61, '65, '68, 1972–present (1927–1987 at Kooyong; since 1988 at the National Tennis Centre, Flinders Park). **SYDNEY (17):** 1908, '19, '22, '25, '28, '31, '34, '37, '40, '47, '51, '54, '58, '62, '66, '70, '71. **ADELAIDE (14):** 1910, '20, '26, '29, '32, '36, '38, '46, '49, '52, '55, '59, '63, '67. **BRISBANE (8):** 1907, '11, '15, '23, '56, '60, '64, '69. **PERTH (3):** 1909, '13, '21. **CHRISTCHURCH, NZL (1):** 1906. **HASTINGS, NZL (1):** 1912. **4. Surface:** Grass 1905–87; Rebound Ace (hard) 1988–present. **5.** Note: The asterisk symbol * denotes best of three sets only.

MEN'S SINGLES

	CHAMPION	*RUNNER-UP*	*SCORE*				
1905	R. W. Heath	A. H. Curtis	4–6	6–3	6–4	6–4	
1906	A. F. Wilding	F. M. B. Fisher	6–0	6–4	6–4		
1907	H. M. Rice	H. A. Parker	6–3	6–4	6–4		
1908	F. B. Alexander	A. W. Dunlop	3–6	3–6	6–0	6–2	6–3
1909	A. F. Wilding	E. F. Parker	6–1	7–5	6–2		
1910	R. W. Heath	H. M. Rice	6–4	6–3	6–2		
1911	N. E. Brookes	H. M. Rice	6–1	6–2	6–3		
1912	J. C. Parke	A. E. Beamish	3–6	6–3	1–6	6–1	7–5
1913	E. F. Parker	H. A. Parker	2–6	6–1	6–3	6–2	
1914	A. O'Hara Wood	G. L. Patterson	6–4	6–3	5–7	6–1	
1915	F. G. Lowe	H. M. Rice	4–6	6–1	6–1	6–4	
1916–18		*Not held*					
1919	A. R. F. Kingscote	E. O. Pockley	6–4	6–0	6–3		
1920	P. O'Hara Wood	R. V. Thomas	6–3	4–6	6–8	6–1	6–3
1921	R. H. Gemmell	A. Hedeman	7–5	6–1	6–4		
1922	J. O. Anderson	G. L. Patterson	6–0	3–6	3–6	6–3	6–2
1923	P. O'Hara Wood	C. B. St John	6–1	6–1	6–3		
1924	J. O. Anderson	R. E. Schlesinger	6–3	6–4	3–6	5–7	6–3
1925	J. O. Anderson	G. L. Patterson	11–9	2–6	6–2	6–3	
1926	J. B. Hawkes	J. Willard	6–1	6–3	6–1		
1927	G. L. Patterson	J. B. Hawkes	3–6	6–4	3–6	18–16	6–3
1928	J. Borotra	R. O. Cummings	6–4	6–1	4–6	5–7	6–3
1929	J. C. Gregory	R. E. Schlesinger	6–2	6–2	5–7	7–5	
1930	E. F. Moon	H. C. Hopman	6–3	6–1	6–3		
1931	J. H. Crawford	H. C. Hopman	6–4	6–2	2–6	6–1	
1932	J. H. Crawford	H. C. Hopman	4–6	6–3	3–6	6–3	6–1
1933	J. H. Crawford	K. Gledhill	2–6	7–5	6–3	6–2	
1934	F. J. Perry	J. H. Crawford	6–3	7–5	6–1		
1935	J. H. Crawford	F. J. Perry	2–6	6–4	6–4	6–4	
1936	A. K. Quist	J. H. Crawford	6–2	6–3	4–6	3–6	9–7
1937	V. B. McGrath	J. E. Bromwich	6–3	1–6	6–0	2–6	6–1
1938	J. D. Budge	J. E. Bromwich	6–4	6–2	6–1		
1939	J. E. Bromwich	A. K. Quist	6–4	6–1	6–3		
1940	A. K. Quist	J. H. Crawford	6–3	6–1	6–2		
1941–45		*Not held*					
1946	J. E. Bromwich	D. Pails	5–7	6–3	7–5	3–6	6–2
1947	D. Pails	J. E. Bromwich	4–6	6–4	3–6	7–5	8–6
1948	A. K. Quist	J. E. Bromwich	6–4	3–6	6–3	2–6	6–3

Year	Champion	Runner-up	Score					FIRST PRIZE (Aus $)
1949	F. A. Sedgman	J. E. Bromwich	6–3	6–2	6–2			
1950	F. A. Sedgman	K. B. McGregor	6–3	6–4	4–6	6–1		
1951	R. Savitt	K. B. McGregor	6–3	2–6	6–3	6–1		
1952	K. B. McGregor	F. A. Sedgman	7–5	12–10	2–6	6–2		
1953	K. R. Rosewall	M. G. Rose	6–0	6–3	6–4			
1954	M. G. Rose	R. N. Hartwig	6–2	0–6	6–4	6–2		
1955	K. R. Rosewall	L. A. Hoad	9–7	6–4	6–4			
1956	L. A. Hoad	K. R. Rosewall	6–4	3–6	6–4	7–5		
1957	A. J. Cooper	N. A. Fraser	6–3	9–11	6–4	6–2		
1958	A. J. Cooper	M. J. Anderson	7–5	6–3	6–4			
1959	A. Olmedo	N. A. Fraser	6–1	6–2	3–6	6–3		
1960	R. G. Laver	N. A. Fraser	5–7	3–6	6–3	8–6	8–6	
1961	R. S. Emerson	R. G. Laver	1–6	6–3	7–5	6–4		
1962	R. G. Laver	R. S. Emerson	8–6	0–6	6–4	6–4		
1963	R. S. Emerson	K. N. Fletcher	6–3	6–3	6–1			
1964	R. S. Emerson	F. S. Stolle	6–3	6–4	6–2			
1965	R. S. Emerson	F. S. Stolle	7–9	2–6	6–4	7–5	6–1	
1966	R. S. Emerson	A. R. Ashe	6–4	6–8	6–2	6–3		
1967	R. S. Emerson	A. R. Ashe	6–4	6–1	6–4			
1968	W. W. Bowrey	J. M. Gisbert	7–5	2–6	9–7	6–4		
1969	R. G. Laver	A. Gimeno	6–3	6–4	7–5			5,000
1970	A. R. Ashe	R. D. Crealy	6–4	9–7	6–2			3,800
1971	K. R. Rosewall	A. R. Ashe	6–1	7–5	6–3			10,000
1972	K. R. Rosewall	M. J. Anderson	7–6	6–3	7–5			2,240
1973	J. D. Newcombe	O. Parun	6–3	6–7	7–5	6–1		8,750
1974	J. S. Connors	P. Dent	7–6	6–4	4–6	6–3		9,750
1975	J. D. Newcombe	J. S. Connors	7–5	3–6	6–4	7–6		12,489
1976	M. Edmondson	J. D. Newcombe	6–7	6–3	7–6	6–1		32,000
1977	(Jan) R. Tanner	G. Vilas	6–3	6–3	6–3			32,000
1977	(Dec) V. Gerulaitis	J. M. Lloyd	6–3	7–6	5–7	3–6	6–2	28,000
1978	(Dec) G. Vilas	J. Marks	6–4	6–4	3–6	6–3		41,000
1979	(Dec) G. Vilas	J. Sadri	7–6	6–3	6–2			50,000
1980	(Dec) B. Teacher	K. Warwick	7–5	7–6	6–3			65,000
1981	(Dec) J. Kriek	S. Denton	6–2	7–6	6–7	6–4		65,000
1982	(Dec) J. Kriek	S. Denton	6–3	6–3	6–2			70,000
1983	(Dec) M. Wilander	I. Lendl	6–1	6–4	6–4			77,500
1984	(Dec) M. Wilander	K. Curren	6–7	6–4	7–6	6–2		100,000
1985	(Dec) S. Edberg	M. Wilander	6–4	6–3	6–3			100,000
1986	*Not held*							
1987	(Jan) S. Edberg	P. Cash	6–3	6–4	3–6	5–7	6–3	103,875
1988	M. Wilander	P. Cash	6–3	6–7	3–6	6–1	8–6	104,997
1989	I. Lendl	M. Mecir	6–2	6–2	6–2			140,000
1990	I. Lendl	S. Edberg	4–6	7–6	5–2	ret'd		200,000
1991	B. Becker	I. Lendl	1–6	6–4	6–4	6–4		246,400
1992	J. Courier	S. Edberg	6–3	3–6	6–4	6–2		274,909
1993	J. Courier	S. Edberg	6–2	6–1	2–6	7–5		410,000
1994	P. Sampras	T. Martin	7–6	6–4	6–4			460,000
1995	A. Agassi	P. Sampras	4–6	6–1	7–6	6–4		480,000
1996	B. Becker	M. Chang	6–2	6–4	2–6	6–2		562,000
1997	P. Sampras	C. Moya	6–2	6–3	6–3			585,000

WOMEN'S SINGLES

	CHAMPION	*RUNNER-UP*	*SCORE*		
1922	Mrs M. Molesworth	Miss E. F. Boyd	6–3	10–8	
1923	Mrs M. Molesworth	Miss E. F. Boyd	6–1	7–5	
1924	Miss S. Lance	Miss E. F. Boyd	6–3	3–6	8–6
1925	Miss D. S. Akhurst	Miss E. F. Boyd	1–6	8–6	6–4
1926	Miss D. S. Akhurst	Miss E. F. Boyd	6–1	6–3	
1927	Miss E. F. Boyd	Mrs S. Harper	5–7	6–1	6–2
1928	Miss D. S. Akhurst	Miss E. F. Boyd	7–5	6–2	
1929	Miss D. S. Akhurst	Miss L. M. Bickerton	6–1	5–7	6–2
1930	Miss D. S. Akhurst	Mrs S. Harper	10–8	2–6	7–5
1931	Mrs C. Buttsworth	Mrs J. H. Crawford	1–6	6–3	6–4
1932	Mrs C. Buttsworth	Miss K. Le Mesurier	9–7	6–4	
1933	Miss J. Hartigan	Mrs C. Buttsworth	6–4	6–3	

							FIRST PRIZE (Aus $)
1934	Miss J. Hartigan	Mrs M. Molesworth	6–1	6–4			
1935	Miss D. E. Round	Miss N. M. Lyle	1–6	6–1	6–3		
1936	Miss J. Hartigan	Miss N. M. Wynne	6–4	6–4			
1937	Miss N. M. Wynne	Mrs V. Westacott	6–3	5–7	6–4		
1938	Miss D. M. Bundy	Miss D. Stevenson	6–3	6–2			
1939	Mrs V. Westacott	Mrs H. C. Hopman	6–1	6–2			
1940	Mrs G. F. Bolton	Miss T. D. Coyne	5–7	6–4	6–0		
1941–45		*Not held*					
1946	Mrs G.F. Bolton	Miss J. Fitch	6–4	6–4			
1947	Mrs G.F. Bolton	Mrs H. C. Hopman	6–3	6–2			
1948	Mrs G.F. Bolton	Miss M. Toomey	6–3	6–1			
1949	Miss D. J. Hart	Mrs G.F. Bolton	6–3	6–4			
1950	Miss A. L. Brough	Miss D. J. Hart	6–4	3–6	6–4		
1951	Mrs G.F. Bolton	Mrs M. N. Long	6–1	7–5			
1952	Mrs M. N. Long	Miss H. Angwin	6–2	6–3			
1953	Miss M. Connolly	Miss J. Sampson	6–3	6–2			
1954	Mrs M. N. Long	Miss J. Staley	6–3	6–4			
1955	Miss B. Penrose	Mrs M. N. Long	6–4	6–3			
1956	Miss M. Carter	Mrs M. N. Long	3–6	6–2	9–7		
1957	Miss S. J. Fry	Miss A. Gibson	6–3	6–4			
1958	Miss A. Mortimer	Miss L. Coghlan	6–3	6–4			
1959	Mrs S. J. Reitano	Miss R. Schuurman	6–2	6–3			
1960	Miss M. Smith	Miss J. Lehane	7–5	6–2			
1961	Miss M. Smith	Miss J. Lehane	6–1	6–4			
1962	Miss M. Smith	Miss J. Lehane	6–0	6–2			
1963	Miss M. Smith	Miss J. Lehane	6–2	6–2			
1964	Miss M. Smith	Miss L. R. Turner	6–3	6–2			
1965	Miss M. Smith	Miss M. E. Bueno	5–7	6–4	5–2	ret'd	
1966	Miss M. Smith	Miss N. Richey	w.o.				
1967	Miss N. Richey	Miss L. R. Turner	6–1	6–4			
1968	Mrs L. W. King	Mrs B. M. Court	6–1	6–2			
1969	Mrs B. M. Court	Mrs L. W. King	6–4	6–1			2,000
1970	Mrs B. M. Court	Miss K. Melville	6–1	6–3			700
1971	Mrs B. M. Court	Miss E. Goolagong	2–6	7–6	7–5		1,800
1972	Miss S. V. Wade	Miss E. Goolagong	6–4	6–4			1,200
1973	Mrs B. M. Court	Miss E. Goolagong	6–4	7–5			5,700
1974	Miss E. Goolagong	Miss C. M. Evert	7–6	4–6	6–0		9,000
1975	Miss E. Goolagong	Miss M. Navratilova	6–3	6–2			8,115
1976	Mrs R. A. Cawley	Miss R. Tomanova	6–2	6–2			12,000
1977	(Jan) Mrs G. Reid	Miss D. Fromholtz	7–5	6–2			12,000
1977	(Dec) Mrs R. A. Cawley	Mrs R. L. Cawley	6–3	6–0			9,000
1978	(Dec) Miss C. O'Neil	Miss B. Nagelsen	6–3	7–6			6,000
1979	(Dec) Miss B. Jordan	Miss S. Walsh	6–3	6–3			10,000
1980	(Dec) Miss H. Mandlikova	Miss W. M. Turnbull	6–0	7–5			32,000
1981	(Dec) Miss M. Navratilova	Mrs J. M. Lloyd	6–7	6–4	7–5		34,000
1982	(Dec) Mrs J. M. Lloyd	Miss M. Navratilova	6–3	2–6	6–3		40,000
1983	(Dec) Miss M. Navratilova	Miss K. Jordan	6–2	7–6			5,000
1984	(Dec) Mrs J. M. Lloyd	Miss H. Sukova	6–7	6–1	6–3		100,000
1985	(Dec) Miss M. Navratilova	Mrs J. M. Lloyd	6–2	4–6	6–2		100,000
1986		*Not held*					
1987	(Jan) Miss H. Mandlikova	Miss M. Navratilova	7–5	7–6			115,000
1988	Miss S. Graf	Miss C. Evert	6–1	7–6			115,000
1989	Miss S. Graf	Miss H. Sukova	6–4	6–4			135,000
1990	Miss S. Graf	Miss M. J. Fernandez	6–3	6–4			190,000
1991	Miss M. Seles	Miss J. Novotna	5–7	6–3	6–1		246,400
1992	Miss M. Seles	Miss M. J. Fernandez	6–2	6–3			274,909
1993	Miss M. Seles	Miss S. Graf	4–6	6–3	6–2		410,000
1994	Miss S. Graf	Miss A. Sanchez Vic.	6–0	6–2			460,000
1995	Miss M. Pierce	Miss A. Sanchez Vic	6–3	6–2			480,000
1996	Miss M. Seles	Miss A. Huber	6–4	6–1			510,000
1997	Miss M. Hingis	Miss M. Pierce	6–2	6–2			542,000

MEN'S DOUBLES

	CHAMPIONS	*RUNNERS-UP*	*SCORE*				
1905	R. Lycett/T. Tachell	E. T. Barnard/B. Spence	11–9	8–6	1–6	4–6	6–1
1906	R. W. Heath/A. F. Wilding	C. C. Cox/H. A. Parker	6–2	6–4	6–2		
1907	W. A. Gregg/H. A. Parker	H. M. Rice/G. W. Wright	6–2	3–6	6–3	6–2	
1908	F. B. Alexander/A. W. Dunlop	G. G. Sharpe/A. F. Wilding	6–3	6–2	6–1		
1909	J. P. Keane/E. F. Parker	C. Crooks/A. F. Wilding	1–6	6–1	6–1	9–7	
1910	A. Campbell/H. M. Rice	R. W. Heath/J. L. O'Dea	6–3	6–3	6–2		
1911	H. W. Heath/R. Lycett	J. J. Addison/N. E. Brookes	6–2	7–5	6–0		
1912	C. P. Dixon/J. C. Parke	A. E. Beamish/F. G. Lowe	6–4	6–4	6–2		
1913	A. H. Hedemann/E. F. Parker	H. Parker/R. Taylor	8–6	4–6	6–4	6–4	
1914	A. Campbell/G. L. Patterson	R. W. Heath/A. O'Hara Wood	7–5	3–6	6–3	6–3	
1915	H. M. Rice/C. V. Todd	F. G. Lowe/C. St John	8–6	6–4	7–9	6–3	
1916–1918		*Not held*					
1919	P. O'Hara Wood/R. V. Thomas	J. O. Anderson/A. H. Lowe	7–5	6–1	7–9	3–6	6–3
1920	P. O'Hara Wood/R. V. Thomas	H. Rice/R. Taylor	6–1	6–0	7–5		
1921	S. H. Eaton/R. H. Gemmell	E. Stokes/N. Brearley	7–5	6–3	6–3		
1922	J. B. Hawkes/G. L. Patterson	J. O. Anderson/N. Peach	8–10	6–0	6–0	7–5	
1923	P. O'Hara Wood/C. B. St John	H. Rice/J. Bullough	6–4	6–3	3–6	6–0	
1924	J. O. Anderson/N. E. Brookes	P. O'Hara Wood/G. L. Patterson	6–2	6–4	6–3		
1925	P. O'Hara Wood/G. L. Patterson	J. O. Anderson/F. Kalms	6–4	8–6	7–5		
1926	J. B. Hawkes/G. L. Patterson	J. O. Anderson/P. O'Hara Wood	6–1	6–4	6–2		
1927	J. B. Hawkes/G. L. Patterson	I. McInnes/P. O'Hara Wood	8–6	6–2	6–1		
1928	J. Borotra/J. Brugnon	E. F. Moon/J. Willard	6–2	4–6	6–4	6–4	
1929	J. H. Crawford/H. C. Hopman	R. O. Cummings/E. F. Moon	6–1	6–8	4–6	6–1	6–3
1930	J. H. Crawford/H. C. Hopman	J. Fitchett/J. B. Hawkes	8–6	6–1	2–6	6–3	
1931	C. Donohoe/R. Dunlop	J. H. Crawford/H. O. Hopman	8–6	6–2	5–7	7–9	6–4
1932	J. H. Crawford/E. F. Moon	H. C. Hopman/G. L. Patterson	4–6	6–4	12–10	6–3	
1933	K. Gledhill/H. E. Vines	J. H. Crawford/E. F. Moon	6–4	10–8	6–2		
1934	G. P. Hughes/F. J. Perry	A. K. Quist/D. P. Turnbull	6–8	6–3	6–4	3–6	6–3
1935	J. H. Crawford/V. B. McGrath	G. P. Hughes/F. J. Perry	6–4	8–6	6–2		
1936	A. K. Quist/D. P. Turnbull	J. H. Crawford/V. B. McGrath	6–8	6–2	6–1	3–6	6–2
1937	A. K. Quist/D. P. Turnbull	J. E. Bromwich/J. E. Harper	6–2	9–7	1–6	6–8	6–4
1938	J. E. Bromwich/A. K. Quist	H. Henkel/G. Von Cramm	7–5	6–4	6–0		
1939	J. E. Bromwich/A. K. Quist	C. F. Long/D. P. Turnbull	6–4	7–5	6–2		
1940	J. E. Bromwich/A. K. Quist	J. H. Crawford/V. B. McGrath	6–3	7–5	6–1		
1941–1945		*Not held*					
1946	J. E. Bromwich/A. K. Quist	M. Newcombe/L. A. Schwartz	6–3	6–1	9–7		
1947	J. E. Bromwich/A. K. Quist	F. A. Sedgman/G. Worthington	6–1	6–3	6–1		
1948	J. E. Bromwich/A. K. Quist	C. Long/F. A. Sedgman	1–6	6–8	9–7	6–3	8–6
1949	J. E. Bromwich/A. K. Quist	G. Brown/O. W. Sidwell	1–6	7–5	6–2	6–3	
1950	J. E. Bromwich/A. K. Quist	J. Drobny/E. W. Sturgess	6–3	5–7	4–6	6–3	8–6
1951	K. B. McGregor/F. A. Sedgman	J. E. Bromwich/A. K. Quist	11–9	2–6	6–3	4–6	6–3
1952	K. B. McGregor/F. A. Sedgman	D. Candy/M. G. Rose	6–4	7–5	6–3		
1953	L. A. Hoad/K. R. Rosewall	D. Candy/M. G. Rose	9–11	6–4	10–8	6–4	
1954	R. N. Hartwig/M. G. Rose	N. A. Fraser/C. Wilderspin	6–3	6–4	6–2		
1955	E. V. Seixas/M. A. Trabert	L. A. Hoad/K. R. Rosewall	6–4	6–2	2–6	3–6	6–1
1956	L. A. Hoad/K. R. Rosewall	D. Candy/M. G. Rose	10–8	13–11	6–4		
1957	N. A. Fraser/L. A. Hoad	M. J. Anderson/A. J. Cooper	6–3	8–6	6–4		
1958	A. J. Cooper/N. A. Fraser	R. S. Emerson/R. Mark	7–5	6–8	3–6	6–3	7–5
1959	R. G. Laver/R. Mark	D. Candy/R. N. Howe	9–7	6–4	6–2		
1960	R. G. Laver/R. Mark	R. S. Emerson/N. A. Fraser	1–6	6–2	6–4	6–4	
1961	R. G. Laver/R. Mark	R. S. Emerson/M. F. Mulligan	6–3	7–5	3–6	9–11	6–2
1962	R. S. Emerson/N. A. Fraser	R. A. J. Hewitt/F. S. Stolle	4–6	4–6	6–1	6–4	11–9
1963	R. A. J. Hewitt/F. S. Stolle	K. N. Fletcher/J. D. Newcombe	6–2	3–6	6–3	3–6	6–3
1964	R. A. J. Hewitt/F. S. Stolle	R. S. Emerson/K. N. Fletcher	6–4	7–5	3–6	4–6	14–12
1965	J. D. Newcombe/A. D. Roche	R. S. Emerson/F. S. Stolle	3–6	4–6	13–11	6–3	6–4
1966	R. S. Emerson/F. S. Stolle	J. D. Newcombe/A. D. Roche	7–9	6–3	6–8	14–12	12–10
1967	J. D. Newcombe/A. D. Roche	W. W. Bowrey/O. K. Davidson	3–6	6–3	7–5	6–8	8–6
1968	R. D. Crealy/A. J. Stone	T. Addison/R. Keldie	10–8	6–4	6–3		PRIZE
1969	R. S. Emerson/R. G. Laver	K. R. Rosewall/F. S. Stolle	6–4	6–4	*		*(Aus$)*
1970	R. C. Lutz/S. R. Smith	J. G. Alexander/P. Dent	8–6	6–3	6–4		500
1971	J. D. Newcombe/A. D. Roche	T. S. Okker/M. C. Riessen	6–2	7–6			
1972	O. K. Davidson/K. R. Rosewall	R. Case/G. Masters	3–6	7–6	6–3		600
1973	M. J. Anderson/J. D. Newcombe	J. G. Alexander/P. Dent	6–3	6–4	7–6		
1974	R. Case/G. Masters	S. Ball/R. Giltinan	6–7	6–3	6–4		

1975	J. G. Alexander/P. Dent	R. Carmichael/A. J. Stone	6–3	7–6			
1976	J. D. Newcombe/A. D. Roche	R. Case/G. Masters	7–6	6–4			
1977	A. R. Ashe/A. D. Roche	C. Pasarell/E. Van Dillen	6–4	6–4			
1977	(Dec) R. O. Ruffels/A. J. Stone	J. G. Alexander/P. Dent	7–6	7–6			
1978	(Dec) W. Fibak/K. Warwick	P. Kronk/C. Letcher	7–6	7–5			
1979	(Dec) P. McNamara/P. McNamee	P. Kronk/C. Letcher	7–6	6–2			
1980	(Dec) M. R. Edmondson/K. Warwick	P. McNamara/P. McNamee	7–5	6–4			
1981	(Dec) M. R. Edmondson/K. Warwick	H. Pfister/J. Sadri	6–3	6–7	6–3		24,000
1982	(Dec) J. G. Alexander/J. Fitzgerald	A. Andrews/J. Sadri	6–4	7–6			28,000
1983	(Dec) M. Edmondson/P. McNamee	S. Denton/S. E. Stewart	6–3	7–6			30,000
1984	(Dec) M. Edmondson/S. E. Stewart	J. Nystrom/M. Wilander	6–2	6–2	7–5		38,700
1985	(Dec) P. Annacone/C. Van Rensburg	M. R. Edmondson/K. Warwick	3–6	7–6	6–4	6–4	34,193
1986		*Not held*					
1987	(Jan) S. Edberg/A. Jarryd	P. Doohan/L. Warder	6–4	6–4	7–6		35,518
1988	R. Leach/J. Pugh	M. J. Bates/P. Lundgren	6–3	6–2	6–3		36,400
1989	R. Leach/J. Pugh	D. Cahill/M. Kratzmann	6–4	6–4	6–4		48,533
1990	P. Aldrich/D. Visser	G. Connell/G. Michibata	6–4	4–6	6–1	6–4	125,000
1991	S. Davis/D. Pate	P. McEnroe/D. Wheaton	6–7	7–6	6–3	7–5	125,000
1992	T. Woodbridge/M. Woodforde	K. Jones/R. Leach	6–4	6–3	6–4		147,500
1993	D. Visser/L Warder	J. Fitzgerald/A. Jarryd	6–4	6–3	6–4		168,000
1994	J. Eltingh/P. Haarhuis	B. Black/J. Stark	6–7	6–3	6–4	6–3	190,000
1995	J. Palmer/R. Reneberg	M. Knowles/D. Nestor	6–3	3–6	6–3	6–2	200,000
1996	S. Edberg/P. Korda	S. Lareau/A. O'Brien	7–5	7–5	4–6	6–1	234,000
1997	T. Woodbridge/M. Woodforde	S. Lareau/A. O'Brien	4–6	7–5	7–5	6–3	244,000

WOMEN'S DOUBLES

	CHAMPIONS	*RUNNERS-UP*	*SCORE*		
1922	E. F. Boyd/M. Mountain	St George/H. S. Utz	3–6	6–4	7–5
1923	E. F. Boyd/S. Lance	M. Molesworth/H. Turner	6–1	6–4	
1924	D. S. Akhurst/S. Lance	K. Le Mesurier/M. O'Hara Wood	7–5	6–2	
1925	D. S. Akhurst/R. Harper	E. F. Boyd/K. Le Mesurier	6–4	6–3	
1926	E. F. Boyd/M. O'Hara Wood	D. S. Akhurst/M. Cox	6–3	6–8	8–6
1927	L. M. Bickerton/M. O'Hara Wood	E. F. Boyd/R. Harper	6–3	6–3	
1928	D. S. Akhurst/E. F. Boyd	K. Le Mesurier/D. Weston	6–3	6–1	
1929	D. S. Akhurst/L. M. Bickerton	R. Harper/M. O'Hara Wood	6–2	4–6	6–2
1930	E. Hood/M. Molesworth	M. Cox/R. Harper	6–3	0–6	7–5
1931	L. M. Bickerton/R. S. Cozens	A. Lloyd/H. S. Utz	6–2	6–4	
1932	C. Buttsworth/J. H. Crawford	K. Le Mesurier/D. Weston	6–2	6–2	
1933	M. Molesworth/V. Westacott	J. Hartigan/J. Van Ryn	6–3	6–3	
1934	M. Molesworth/V. Westacott	J. Hartigan/U. Valkenborg	6–8	6–4	6–4
1935	E. M. Dearman/N. M. Lyle	L. M. Bickerton/H. C. Hopman	6–3	6–4	
1936	T. D. Coyne/N. M. Wynne	M. Blick/K. Woodward	6–2	6–4	
1937	T. D. Coyne/N. M. Wynne	H. C. Hopman/V. Westacott	6–2	6–2	
1938	T. D. Coyne/N. M. Wynne	D. M. Bundy/D. E. Workman	9–7	6–4	
1939	T. D. Coyne/N. M. Wynne	M. Hardcastle/V. Westacott	7–5	6–4	
1940	T. D. Coyne/G.F. Bolton	J. Hartigan/E. Niemeyer	7–5	6–2	
1941–1945		*Not held*			
1946	M. Bevis/J. Fitch	G. F. Bolton/M. N. Long	9–7	6–4	
1947	G.F. Bolton/M. N. Long	M. Bevis/J. Fitch	6–3	6–3	
1948	G.F. Bolton/M. N. Long	M. Bevis/N. Jones	6–3	6–3	
1949	G.F. Bolton/M. N. Long	D. Hart/M. Toomey	6–0	6–1	
1950	L. Brough/D.J. Hart	G. F. Bolton/M. N. Long	6–3	2–6	6–3
1951	G.F. Bolton/M. N. Long	J. Fitch/M. Hawton	6–2	6–1	
1952	G.F. Bolton/M. N. Long	R. Baker/M. Hawton	6–1	6–1	
1953	M. Connolly/J. Sampson	M. Hawton/B. Penrose	6–4	6–2	
1954	M. Hawton/B. Penrose	H. Redick–Smith/J. Wipplinger	6–3	8–6	
1955	M. Hawton/B. Penrose	H. C. Hopman/A. Thiele	7–5	6–1	
1956	M. Hawton/M. N. Long	M. Carter/B. Penrose	6–3	5–7	9–7
1957	S. J. Fry/A. Gibson	M. Hawton/F. Muller	6–2	6–1	
1958	M. Hawton/M. N. Long	L. Coghlan/A. Mortimer	7–5	6–8	6–2
1959	S. Reynolds/R. Schuurman	L. Coghlan/M. Reitano	7–5	6–4	
1960	M. E. Bueno/C. Truman	L. Robinson/M. Smith	6–2	5–7	6–2
1961	M. Reitano/M. Smith	M. Hawton/J. Lehane	6–4	3–6	7–5
1962	R. Ebbern/M. Smith	D. R. Hard/M. Reintano	6–4	6–4	
1963	R. Ebbern/M. Smith	J. Lehane/L. R. Turner	6–1	6–3	
1964	J. A. M. Tegart/L. R. Turner	R. Ebbern/M. Smith	6–4	6–4	

1965	M. Smith/L. R. Turner	R. Ebbern/B. J. Moffitt	1–6	6–2	6–3	
1966	C. Graebner/N. Richey	M. Smith/L. R. Turner	6–4	7–5		
1967	J. A. M. Tegart/L. R. Turner	L. Robinson/E. Terras	6–0	6–2		FIRST
1968	K. Krantzcke/K. Melville	J. A. M. Tegart/L. R. Turner	6–4	3–6	6–2	PRIZE
1969	B. M. Court/J. A. M. Tegart	R. Casals/L. W. King	6–4	6–4		*(Aus $)*
1970	B. M. Court/D. Dalton	K. Krantzcke/K. Melville	6–3	6–1		120
1971	B. M. Court/E. F. Goolagong	J. Emmerson/L. Hunt	6–0	6–0		
1972	H. Gourlay/K. Harris	P. Coleman/K. Krantzcke	6–0	6–4		500
1973	B. M. Court/S. V. Wade	K. Harris/K. Melville	6–4	6–4		
1974	E. F. Goolagong/M. Michel	K. Harris/K. Melville	7–5	6–3		
1975	E. F. Goolagong/M. Michel	B. M. Court/O. Morozova	7–6	7–6		
1976	R. A. Cawley/H. Gourlay	W. W. Bowrey/R. Tomanova	8–1 (one set)			
1977	D. Fromholtz/H. Gourlay	B. Nagelsen/G. E. Reid	5–7	6–1	7–5	
1977	(Dec) R. A. Cawley/R. L. Cawley div'd	with M. Guerrant/G. E. Reid				
1978	(Dec) B. Nagelsen/R. Tomanova	N. Sato/P. Whytcross	7–5	6–2		
1979	(Dec) D. D. Chaloner/D. R. Evers	L. Harrison/M. Mesker	6–2	1–6	6–0	
1980	(Dec) B. Nagelsen/M. Navratilova	A. Kiyomura/C. Reynolds	6–4	6–4		
1981	(Dec) K. Jordan/A. E. Smith	M. Navratilova/P. H. Shriver	6–2	7–5		13,000
1982	(Dec) M. Navratilova/P. H. Shriver	C. Kohde/E. Pfaff	6–4	6–2		16,000
1983	(Dec) M. Navratilova/P. H. Shriver	A. E. Hobbs/W. M. Turnbull	6–4	6–7	6–2	30,000
1984	(Dec) M. Navratilova/P. H. Shriver	C. Kohde-Kilsch/H. Sukova	6–3	6–4		39,900
1985	(Dec) M. Navratilova/P. H. Shriver	C. Kohde-Kilsch/H. Sukova	6–3	6–4		40,000
1986		*Not held*				
1987	(Jan) M. Navratilova/P. H. Shriver	Z. Garrison/L. McNeil	6–1	6–0		40,000
1988	M. Navratilova/P. H. Shriver	C. Evert/W. M. Turnbull	6–0	7–5		35,000
1989	M. Navratilova/P. H. Shriver	P. Fendick/J. Hetherington	3–6	6–3	6–2	40,000
1990	J. Novotna/H. Sukova	P. Fendick/M. J. Fernandez	7–6	7–6		125,000
1991	P. Fendick/M. J. Fernandez	G. Fernandez/J. Novotna	7–6	6–1		125,000
1992	A. Sanchez Vic/H. Sukova	G. Fernandez/Z. Garrison	6–4	7–6		147,500
1993	G. Fernandez/N Zvereva	P. Shriver/E. Smylie	6–4	6–3		168,000
1994	G. Fernandez/N. Zvereva	P. Fendick/M. McGrath	6–3	4–6	6–4	190,000
1995	J. Novotna/A. Sanchez Vicario	G. Fernandez/N. Zvereva	6–3	6–7	6–4	200,000
1996	S. Rubin/A. Sanchez Vicario	L. Davenport/M. J. Fernandez	7–5	2–6	6–4	212,000
1997	M. Hingis/N. Zvereva	L. Davenport/L. Raymond	6–2	6–2		225,000

MIXED DOUBLES

	CHAMPIONS	*RUNNERS-UP*	*SCORE*		
1922	J. B. Hawkes/Miss E. F. Boyd	H. S. Utz/Mrs Utz	6–1	6–1	
1923	H. M. Rice/Miss S. Lance	C. St John/Miss M. Molesworth	2–6	6–4	6–4
1924	J. Willard/Miss D. S. Akhurst	G. M. Hone/Miss E. F. Boyd	6–3	6–4	
1925	J. Willard/Miss D. S. Akhurst	R. E. Schlesinger/Mrs R. Harper	6–4	6–4	
1926	J. B. Hawkes/Miss E. F. Boyd	J. Willard/Miss D. S. Akhurst	6–2	6–4	
1927	J. B. Hawkes/Miss E. F. Boyd	J. Willard/Miss Y. Anthony	6–1	6–3	
1928	J. Borotra/Miss D. S. Akhurst	J. B. Hawkes/Miss E. F. Boyd	w.o		
1929	E. F. Moon/Miss D. S. Akhurst	J. H. Crawford/Miss M. Cox	6–0	7–5	
1930	H. C. Hopman/Miss N. Hall	J. H. Crawford/Miss M. Cox	11–9	3–6	6–3
1931	J. H. Crawford/Mrs Crawford	A. Willard/Mrs V. Westacott	7–5	6–4	
1932	J. H. Crawford/Mrs Crawford	J. Satoh/Mrs P. O'Hara Wood	6–8	8–6	6–3
1933	J. H. Crawford/Mrs Crawford	H. E. Vines/Mrs J. Van Ryn	3–6	7–5	13–11
1934	E. F. Moon/Miss J. Hartigan	R. Dunlop/Mrs V. Westacott	6–3	6–4	
1935	C. Boussus/Miss L. Bickerton	V. G. Kirby/Mrs Bond	1–6	6–3	6–3
1936	H. C. Hopman/Mrs Hopman	A. A. Kay/Miss M. Blick	6–2	6–0	
1937	H. C. Hopman/Mrs Hopman	D. P. Turnbull/Miss D. Stevenson	3–6	6–3	6–2
1938	J. E. Bromwich/Miss J. Wilson	C. Long/Miss N. Wynne	6–3	6–2	
1939	H. C. Hopman/Mrs Hopman	J. E. Bromwich/Miss J. Wilson	6–8	6–2	6–3
1940	C. Long/Mrs G. F. Bolton	H. C. Hopman/Mrs Hopman	7–5	2–6	6–4
1941–1945		*Not held*			
1946	C. Long/Mrs G. F. Bolton	J. Bromwich/Miss J. Fitch	6–0	6–4	
1947	C. Long/Mrs G. F. Bolton	J. E. Bromwich/Miss J. Fitch	6–3	6–3	
1948	C. Long/Mrs G. F. Bolton	O. W. Sidwell/Mrs M. N. Long	7–5	4–6	8–6
1949	F. A. Sedgman/Miss D. J. Hart	J. E. Bromwich/Miss J. Fitch	6–1	5–7	12–10
1950	F. A. Sedgman/Miss D. J. Hart	E. W. Sturgess/Miss J. Fitch	8–6	6–4	
1951	G. A. Worthington/Mrs M. N. Long	J. May/Miss C. Proctor	6–4	3–6	6–2
1952	G. A. Worthington/Mrs M. N. Long	T. Warhurst/Mrs A. R. Thiele	9–7	7–5	
1953	R. N. Hartwig/Miss J. Sampson	H. Richardson/Miss M. Connolly	6–4	6–3	
1954	R. N. Hartwig/Mrs M. N. Long	J. E. Bromwich/Miss B. Penrose	4–6	6–1	6–2

Carlos Moya of Spain – who started the year brilliantly by reaching the final of the Australian Open unseeded – ignited the competitive fires among his contemporaries, five of whom finished in the top twenty in the world rankings for 1997. (Stephen Wake)

						PRIZE MONEY *(Aus$)*
1955	G. A. Worthington/Mrs M. N. Long	L. A. Hoad/Miss J. Staley	6–2	6–1		
1956	N. A. Fraser/Miss B. Penrose	R. S. Emerson/Mrs M. Hawton	6–2	6–4		
1957	M. J. Anderson/Miss F. Muller	W. A. Knight/Miss J. Langley	7–5	3–6	6–1	
1958	R. N. Howe/Mrs M. Hawton	A. Newman/Miss A. Mortimer	9–11	6–1	6–2	
1959	R. Mark/Miss S. Reynolds	R. G. Laver/Miss R. Schuurman	4–6	13–11	6–2	
1960	T. Fancutt/Miss J. Lehane	R. Mark/Mrs M. Reitano	6–2	7–5		
1961	R. A. J. Hewitt/Miss J. Lehane	J. Pearce/Mrs M. Reitano	9–7	6–2		
1962	F. S. Stolle/Miss L. R. Turner	R. Taylor/Miss D. R. Hard	6–3	9–7		
1963	K. N. Fletcher/Miss M. Smith	F. S. Stolle/Miss L. R. Turner	7–5	5–7	6–4	
1964	K. N. Fletcher/Miss M. Smith	M. J. Sangster/Miss J. Lehane	6–3	6–2		
1965	J. D. Newcombe/Miss M. Smith div'd with O. K. Davidson/Miss R. Ebbern					
1966	A. D. Roche/Miss J. A. Tegart	W. W. Bowrey/Miss R. Ebbern	6–1	6–3		
1967	O. K. Davidson/Miss L. R. Turner	A. D. Roche/Miss J. A. M. Tegart	9–7	6–4		
1968	R. D. Crealy/Mrs L. W. King	A. J. Stone/Mrs B. M. Court	w.o.			
1969	M. C. Riessen/Mrs B. M. Court div'd with F. S. Stolle/Mrs P. F. Jones					
1969–1986		*Not held*				
1987	S. E. Stewart/Miss Z. Garrison	A. Castle/Miss A. E. Hobbs	3–6	7–6	6–3	13,954
1988	J. Pugh/Miss J. Novotna	Tim Gullikson/Miss M. Navratilova	5–7	6–2	6–4	13,954
1989	J. Pugh/Miss J. Novotna	S. Stewart/Miss Z. Garrison	6–3	6–4		18,140
1990	J. Pugh/Miss N. Zvereva	R. Leach/Miss Z. Garrison	4–6	6–2	6–3	40,000
1991	J. Bates/Miss J. Durie	S. Davis/Miss R. White	2–6	6–4	6–4	40,000
1992	M. Woodforde/Miss N. Provis	T. Woodbridge/Miss A. Sanchez	6–3	4–6	11–9	62,600
1993	T. Woodbridge/Miss A. Sanchez Vic	R. Leach/Miss Z. Garrison Jackson	7–5	6–4		71,400
1994	A. Olhovskiy/Mrs L. Neiland	T. Woodbridge/Miss H. Sukova	7–5	6–7	6–2	80,000
1995	R. Leach/Miss N. Zvereva	C. Suk/Miss G. Fernandez	7–6	6–7	6–4	83,000
1996	M. Woodforde/Mrs L. Neiland	L. Jensen/Miss N. Arendt	4–6	7–5	6–0	88,000
1997	R. Leach/Miss M. Bollegraf	J. de Jager/Mrs L. Neiland	6–3	6–7	7–5	92,000

FRENCH CHAMPIONSHIPS

1. Venue and conditions of entry: From 1891 to 1924 the Championships, restricted to members of French clubs, were played at the Stade Francais ground at the Faisanderie in St. Cloud Park. They included the title 'World Clay Court Championship' between 1912 and 1924 when the title was abolished. International from 1925, the Championships were played for three years alternately at the Racing Club at Croix-Catelan in Paris and the Stade Francais at the Faisanderie. Since 1928 the Championships have been played continuously at the Stade Roland Garros, Porte D'Auteuil, Paris. **2. Status:** The Championships became 'Open' in 1968. **3. Surface:** Red clay (Terre Battu).

MEN'S SINGLES

1891	H. Briggs
1892	J. Schopfer
1893	L. Riboulet
1894–96	A. Vacherot
1897–1900	P. Ayme
1901	A. Vacherot
1902	M. Vacherot
1903–04	M. Decugis
1905–06	M. Germot
1907–09	M. Decugis
1910	M. Germot
1911	A. H. Gobert
1912–14	M. Decugis
1915–19	*Not held*
1920	A. H. Gobert
1921	J. Samazeuilh
1922	H. Cochet
1923	P. Blanchy
1924	J. Borotra

	CHAMPION	*RUNNER-UP*	*SCORE*	FIRST PRIZE *(in French francs)*
1925	R. Lacoste	J. Borotra	7–5 6–1 6–4	
1926	H. Cochet	R. Lacoste	6–2 6–4 6–3	
1927	R. Lacoste	W. T. Tilden	6–4 4–6 5–7 6–3 11–9	
1928	H. Cochet	R. Lacoste	5–7 6–3 6–1 6–3	
1929	R. Lacoste	J. Borotra	6–3 2–6 6–0 2–6 8–6	
1930	H. Cochet	W. T. Tilden	3–6 8–6 6–3 6–1	
1931	J. Borotra	C. Boussus	2–6 6–4 7–5 6–4	
1932	H. Cochet	G. de Stefani	6–0 6–4 4–6 6–3	
1933	J. H. Crawford	H. Cochet	8–6 6–1 6–3	
1934	G. von Cramm	J. H. Crawford	6–4 7–9 3–6 7–5 6–3	
1935	F. J. Perry	G. von Cramm	6–3 3–6 6–1 6–3	
1936	G. von Cramm	F. J. Perry	6–0 2–6 6–2 2–6 6–0	
1937	H. Henkel	H. W. Austin	6–1 6–4 6–3	
1938	J. D. Budge	R. Menzel	6–3 6–2 6–4	
1939	W. D. McNeill	R. L. Riggs	7–5 6–0 6–3	
1940–45		*Not held*		
1946	M. Bernard	J. Drobny	3–6 2–6 6–1 6–4 6–3	
1947	J. Asboth	E. W. Sturgess	8–6 7–5 6–4	
1948	F. A. Parker	J. Drobny	6–4 7–5 5–7 8–6	
1949	F. A. Parker	J. E. Patty	6–3 1–6 6–1 6–4	
1950	J. E. Patty	J. Drobny	6–1 6–2 3–6 5–7 7–5	
1951	J. Drobny	E. W. Sturgess	6–3 6–3 6–3	
1952	J. Drobny	F. A. Sedgman	6–2 6–0 3–6 6–4	
1953	K. R. Rosewall	E. V. Seixas	6–3 6–4 1–6 6–2	
1954	M. A. Trabert	A. Larsen	6–4 7–5 6–1	
1955	M. A. Trabert	S. Davidson	2–6 6–1 6–4 6–2	
1956	L. A. Hoad	S. Davidson	6–4 8–6 6–3	
1957	S. Davidson	H. Flam	6–3 6–4 6–4	
1958	M. G. Rose	L. Ayala	6–3 6–4 6–4	
1959	N. Pietrangeli	I. C. Vermaak	3–6 6–3 6–4 6–1	
1960	N. Pietrangeli	L. Ayala	3–6 6–3 6–4 4–6 6–3	
1961	M. Santana	N. Pietrangeli	4–6 6–1 3–6 6–0 6–2	
1962	R. G. Laver	R. S. Emerson	3–6 2–6 6–3 9–7 6–2	
1963	R. S. Emerson	P. Darmon	3–6 6–1 6–4 6–4	
1964	M. Santana	N. Pietrangeli	6–3 6–1 4–6 7–5	
1965	F. S. Stolle	A. D. Roche	3–6 6–0 6–2 6–3	
1966	A. D. Roche	I. Gulyas	6–1 6–4 7–5	
1967	R. S. Emerson	A. D. Roche	6–1 6–4 2–6 6–2	
1968	K. R. Rosewall	R. G. Laver	6–3 6–1 2–6 6–2	15,000
1969	R. G. Laver	K. R. Rosewall	6–4 6–3 6–4	35,000
1970	J. Kodes	Z. Franulovic	6–2 6–4 6–0	56,000
1971	J. Kodes	I. Nastase	8–6 6–2 2–6 7–5	48,000
1972	A. Gimeno	P. Proisy	4–6 6–3 6–1 6–1	48,000
1973	I. Nastase	N. Pilic	6–3 6–3 6–0	70,000

1974	B. Borg	M. Orantes	2–6	6–7	6–0	6–1	6–1	120,000
1975	B. Borg	G. Vilas	6–2	6–3	6–4			120,000
1976	A. Panatta	H. Solomon	6–1	6–4	4–6	7–6		130,000
1977	G. Vilas	B. E. Gottfried	6–0	6–3	6–0			190,000
1978	B. Borg	G. Vilas	6–1	6–1	6–3			210,000
1979	B. Borg	V. Pecci	6–3	6–1	6–7	6–4		208,200
1980	B. Borg	V. Gerulaitis	6–4	6–1	6–2			221,000
1981	B. Borg	I. Lendl	6–1	4–6	6–2	3–6	6–1	250,000
1982	M. Wilander	G. Vilas	1–6	7–6	6–0	6–4		400,000
1983	Y. Noah	M. Wilander	6–2	7–5	7–6			500,000
1984	I. Lendl	J. P. McEnroe	3–6	2–6	6–4	7–5	7–5	1,058,600
1985	M. Wilander	I. Lendl	3–6	6–4	6–2	6–2		1,338,200
1986	I. Lendl	M. Pernfors	6–3	6–2	6–4			1,397,250
1987	I. Lendl	M. Wilander	7–5	6–2	3–6	7–6		1,303,800
1988	M. Wilander	H. Leconte	7–5	6–2	6–1			1,500,240
1989	M. Chang	S. Edberg	6–1	3–6	4–6	6–4	6–2	1,791,390
1990	A. Gomez	A. Agassi	6–3	2–6	6–4	6–4		2,226,100
1991	J. Courier	A. Agassi	3–6	6–4	2–6	6–1	6–4	2,448,000
1992	J. Courier	P. Korda	7–5	6–2	6–1			2,680,000
1993	S. Bruguera	J. Courier	6–4	2–6	6–2	3–6	6–3	2,680,000
1994	S. Bruguera	A. Berasategui	6–3	7–5	2–6	6–1		3,160,000
1995	T. Muster	M. Chang	7–5	6–2	6–4			3,320,000
1996	Y. Kafelnikov	M. Stitch	7–6	7–5	7–6			3,542,000
1997	G. Kuerten	S. Bruguera	6–3	6–4	6–2			3,668,000

WOMEN'S SINGLES

1897–99	Mlle F. Masson	1906	Mme F. Fenwick	1915–19	*Not held*
1900	Mlle Y. Prevost	1907	Mme de Kermel	1920–23	Mlle S. Lenglen
1901	Mme P. Girod	1908	Mme F. Fenwick	1924	Mlle D. Vlasto
1902–03	Mlle F. Masson	1909–12	Mlle J. Matthey		
1904–05	Mlle K. Gillou	1913–14	Mlle M. Broquedis		

	CHAMPION	*RUNNER-UP*	*SCORE*		
1925	Mlle S. Lenglen	Miss K. McKane	6–1	6–2	
1926	Mlle S. Lenglen	Miss M. K. Browne	6–1	6–0	
1927	Mlle K. Bouman	Mrs G. Peacock	6–2	6–4	
1928	Miss H. N. Wills	Miss E. Bennett	6–1	6–2	
1929	Miss H. N. Wills	Mme R. Mathieu	6–3	6–4	
1930	Mrs F. S. Moody	Miss H. H. Jacobs	6–2	6–1	
1931	Frl C. Aussem	Miss B. Nuthall	8–6	6–1	
1932	Mrs F. S. Moody	Mme R. Mathieu	7–5	6–1	
1933	Miss M. C. Scriven	Mme R. Mathieu	6–2	4–6	6–4
1934	Miss M. C. Scriven	Miss H. H. Jacobs	7–5	4–6	6–1
1935	Mrs H. Sperling	Mme R. Mathieu	6–2	6–1	
1936	Mrs H. Sperling	Mme R. Mathieu	6–3	6–4	
1937	Mrs H. Sperling	Mme R. Mathieu	6–2	6–4	
1938	Mme R. Mathieu	Mme N. Landry	6–0	6–3	
1939	Mme R. Mathieu	Miss J. Jedrzejowska	6–3	8–6	
1940–45		*Not held*			
1946	Miss M. E. Osborne	Miss P. M. Betz	1–6	8–6	7–5
1947	Mrs P. C. Todd	Miss D. J. Hart	6–3	3–6	6–4
1948	Mme N. Landry	Miss S. J. Fry	6–2	0–6	6–0
1949	Mrs W. du Pont	Mme N. Adamson	7–5	6–2	
1950	Miss D. J. Hart	Mrs P. C. Todd	6–4	4–6	6–2
1951	Miss S. J. Fry	Miss D. J. Hart	6–3	3–6	6–3
1952	Miss D. J. Hart	Miss S. J. Fry	6–4	6–4	
1953	Miss M. Connolly	Miss D. J. Hart	6–2	6–4	
1954	Miss M. Connolly	Mme G. Bucaille	6–4	6–1	
1955	Miss A. Mortimer	Mrs D. P. Knode	2–6	7–5	10–8
1956	Miss A. Gibson	Miss A. Mortimer	6–0	12–10	
1957	Miss S. J. Bloomer	Mrs D. P. Knode	6–1	6–3	
1958	Mrs Z. Kormoczy	Miss S. J. Bloomer	6–4	1–6	6–2
1959	Miss C. C. Truman	Mrs Z. Kormoczy	6–4	7–5	
1960	Miss D. R. Hard	Miss Y. Ramirez	6–3	6–4	
1961	Miss A. S. Haydon	Miss Y. Ramirez	6–2	6–1	

						FIRST PRIZE (in French francs)
1962	Miss M. Smith	Miss L. R. Turner	6–3	3–6	7–5	
1963	Miss L. R. Turner	Mrs P. F. Jones	2–6	6–3	7–5	
1964	Miss M. Smith	Miss M. E. Bueno	5–7	6–1	6–2	
1965	Miss L. R. Turner	Miss M. Smith	6–3	6–4		
1966	Mrs P. F. Jones	Miss N. Richey	6–3	6–1		
1967	Mlle F. Durr	Miss L. R. Turner	4–6	6–3	6–4	
1968	Miss N. Richey	Mrs P. F. Jones	5–7	6–4	6–1	5,000
1969	Mrs B. M. Court	Mrs P. F. Jones	6–1	4–6	6–3	10,000
1970	Mrs B. M. Court	Miss H. Niessen	6–2	6–4		17,800
1971	Miss E. Goolagong	Miss H. Gourlay	6–3	7–5		13,500
1972	Mrs L. W. King	Miss E. Goolagong	6–3	6–3		13,500
1973	Mrs B. M. Court	Miss C. M. Evert	6–7	7–6	6–4	25,000
1974	Miss C. M. Evert	Mrs O. Morozova	6–1	6–2		40,000
1975	Miss C. M. Evert	Miss M. Navratilova	2–6	6–2	6–1	40,000
1976	Miss S. Barker	Miss R. Tomanova	6–2	0–6	6–2	30,000
1977	Miss M. Jausovec	Miss F. Mihai	6–2	6–7	6–1	35,000
1978	Miss V. Ruzici	Miss M. Jausovec	6–2	6–2		100,000
1979	Mrs J. M. Lloyd	Miss W. M. Turnbull	6–2	6–0		126,900
1980	Mrs J. M. Lloyd	Miss V. Ruzici	6–0	6–3		178,500
1981	Miss H. Mandlikova	Miss S. Hanika	6–2	6–4		200,000
1982	Miss M. Navratilova	Miss A. Jaeger	7–6	6–1		300,000
1983	Mrs J. M. Lloyd	Miss M. Jausovec	6–1	6–2		375,000
1984	Miss M. Navratilova	Mrs J. M. Lloyd	6–3	6–1		791,600
1985	Mrs J. M. Lloyd	Miss M. Navratilova	6–3	6–7	7–5	1,262,700
1986	Mrs J. M. Lloyd	Miss M. Navratilova	2–6	6–3	6–3	1,278,400
1987	Miss S. Graf	Miss M. Navratilova	6–4	4–6	8–6	1,178,840
1988	Miss S. Graf	Miss N. Zvereva	6–0	6–0		1,463,390
1989	Miss A. Sanchez	Miss S. Graf	7–6	3–6	7–5	1,593,175
1990	Miss M. Seles	Miss S. Graf	7–6	6–4		1,762,900
1991	Miss M. Seles	Miss A. Sanchez Vicario	6–3	6–4		2,237,000
1992	Miss M. Seles	Miss S. Graff	6–2	3–6	10–8	2,470,000
1993	Miss S. Graf	Miss M. J. Fernandez	4–6	6–2	6–4	2,470,000
1994	Miss A. Sanchez Vicario	Miss M. Pierce	6–4	6–4		2,930,000
1995	Miss S. Graf	Miss A. Sanchez Vicario	7–5	4–6	6–0	3,100,000
1996	Miss S. Graf	Miss A. Sanchez Vicario	6–3	6–7	10–8	3,224,000
1997	Miss I. Majoli	Miss M. Hingis	6–4	6–2		3,450,000

MEN'S DOUBLES

	CHAMPIONS	*RUNNERS-UP*	*SCORE*				
1925	J. Borotra/R. Lacoste	J. Brugnon/H. Cochet	7–5	4–6	6–3	2–6	6–3
1926	H. O. Kinsey/V. Richards	J. Brugnon/H. Cochet	6–4	6–1	4–6	6–4	
1927	J. Brugnon/H. Cochet	J. Borotra/R. Lacoste	2–6	6–2	6–0	1–6	6–4
1928	J. Borotra/J. Brugnon	R. de Buzelet/H. Cochet	6–4	3–6	6–2	3–6	6–4
1929	J. Borotra/R. Lacoste	J. Brugnon/H. Cochet	6–3	3–6	6–3	3–6	8–6
1930	J. Brugnon/H. Cochet	H. C. Hopman/J. Willard	6–3	9–7	6–3		
1931	G. M. Lott/J. Van Ryn	N. G. Farquharson/V. G. Kirby	6–4	6–3	6–4		
1932	J. Brugnon/H. Cochet	M. Bernard/C. Boussus	6–4	3–6	7–5	6–3	
1933	G. P. Hughes/F. J. Perry	V. B. McGrath/A. K. Quist	6–2	6–4	2–6	7–5	
1934	J. Borotra/J. Brugnon	J. H. Crawford/V. B. McGrath	11–9	6–3	2–6	4–6	9–7
1935	J. H. Crawford/A. K. Quist	V. B. McGrath/D. P. Turnbull	6–1	6–4	6–2		
1936	M. Bernard/J. Borotra	G. P. Hughes/C. R. D. Tuckey	6–2	3–6	9–7	6–1	
1937	G. Von Cramm/H. Henkel	N. G. Farquharson/V. G. Kirby	6–4	7–5	3–6	6–1	
1938	B. Destremau/Y. Petra	J. D. Budge/G. Mako	3–6	6–3	9–7	6–1	
1939	C. Harris/W. D. McNeil	J. Borotra/J. Brugnon	4–6	6–4	6–0	2–6	10–8
1940–1945		*Not held*					
1946	M. Bernard/Y. Petra	E. Morea/F. Segura	7–5	6–3	0–6	1–6	10–8
1947	E. Fannin/E. W. Sturgess	T. P. Brown/O. W. Sidwell	6–4	4–6	6–4	6–3	
1948	L. Bergelin/J. Drobny	H. C. Hopman/F. A. Sedgman	8–6	6–1	12–10		
1949	R. A. Gonzales/F. Parker	E. Fannin/E. W. Sturgess	6–3	8–6	5–7	6–3	
1950	W. F. Talbert/M. A. Trabert	J. Drobny/E. W. Sturgess	6–2	1–6	10–8	6–2	
1951	K. B. McGregor/F. A. Sedgman	G. Mulloy/R. Savitt	6–2	2–6	9–7	7–5	
1952	K. B. McGregor/F. A. Sedgman	G. Mulloy/R. Savitt	6–3	6–4	6–4		
1953	L. A. Hoad/K. R. Rosewall	M. G. Rose/C. Wilderspin	6–2	6–1	6–1		
1954	E. V. Seixas/M. A. Trabert	L. A. Hoad/K. R. Rosewall	6–4	6–2	6–1		
1955	E. V. Seixas/M. A. Trabert	N. Pietrangeli/O. Sirola	6–1	4–6	6–2	6–4	

Year	Champions	Runners-up						Prize
1956	D. W. Candy/R. M. Perry	A. J. Cooper/L. A. Hoad	7–5	6–3	6–3			
1957	M. J. Anderson/A. J. Cooper	D. W. Candy/M. G. Rose	6–3	6–0	6–3			
1958	A. J. Cooper/N. A. Fraser	R. N. Howe/A. Segal	3–6	8–6	6–3	7–5		
1959	N. Pietrangeli/O. Sirola	R. S. Emerson/N. A. Fraser	6–3	6–2	14–12			
1960	R. S. Emerson/N. A. Fraser	J. L. Arilla/A. Gimeno	6–2	8–10	7–5	6–4		
1961	R. S. Emerson/R. G. Laver	R. N. Howe/R. Mark	3–6	6–1	6–1	6–4		
1962	R. S. Emerson/N. A. Fraser	W. P. Bungert/C. Kuhnke	6–3	6–4	7–5			
1963	R. S. Emerson/M. Santana	G. L. Forbes/A. Segal	6–2	6–4	6–4			
1964	R. S. Emerson/K. N. Fletcher	J. D. Newcombe/A. D. Roche	7–5	6–3	3–6	7–5		
1965	R. S. Emerson/F. S. Stolle	K. N. Fletcher/R. A. J. Hewitt	6–8	6–3	8–6	6–2		
1966	C. E. Graebner/R. D. Ralston	I. Nastase/I. Tiriac	6–3	6–3	6–0			
1967	J. D. Newcombe/A. D. Roche	R. S. Emerson/K. N. Fletcher	6–3	9–7	12–10			
1968	K. R. Rosewall/F. S. Stolle	R. S. Emerson/R. G. Laver	6–3	6–4	6–3			
1969	J. D. Newcombe/A. D. Roche	R. S. Emerson/R. G. Laver	4–6	6–1	3–6	6–4	6–4	
1970	I. Nastase/I. Tiriac	A. R. Ashe/C. Pasarell	6–2	6–4	6–3			FF8,000
1971	A. R. Ashe/M. C. Riessen	T. W. Gorman/S. R. Smith	6–8	4–6	6–3	6–4	11–9	6,000
1972	R. A. J. Hewitt/F. D. McMillan	P. Cornejo/J. Fillol	6–3	8–6	3–6	6–1		10,000
1973	J. D. Newcombe/T. S. Okker	J. S. Connors/I. Nastase	6–1	3–6	6–3	5–7	6–4	24,000
1974	R. D. Crealy/O. Parun	R. C. Lutz/S. R. Smith	6–3	6–2	3–6	5–7	6–1	30,000
1975	B. E. Gottfried/R. Ramirez	J. G. Alexander/P. Dent	6–2	2–6	6–2	6–4		30,000
1976	F. McNair/S. E. Stewart	B. E. Gottfried/R. Ramirez	7–6	6–3	6–1			47,000
1977	B. E. Gottfried/R. Ramirez	W. Fibak/J. Kodes	7–6	4–6	6–3	6–4		76,000
1978	G. Mayer/H. Pfister	J. Higueras/M. Orantes	6–3	6–2	6–2			84,000
1979	A. A./G. Mayer	R. Case/P. Dent	6–4	6–4	6–4			83,280
1980	V. Amaya/H. Pfister	B. E. Gottfried/R. Ramirez	1–6	6–4	6–4	6–3		89,250
1981	H. Gunthardt/B. Taroczy	T. Moor/E. Teltscher	6–2	7–6	6–3			108,400
1982	S. E. Stewart/F. Taygan	H. Gildemeister/B. Prajoux	7–5	6–3	1–1	ret'd		160,400
1983	A. Jarryd/H. Simonsson	M. R. Edmondson/S. E. Stewart	7–6	6–4	6–2			262,970
1984	H. Leconte/Y. Noah	P. Slozil/T. Smid	6–4	2–6	3–6	6–3	6–2	423,380
1985	M. R. Edmondson/K. Warwick	S. Glickstein/H. Simonsson	6–3	6–4	6–7	6–3		535,400
1986	J. Fitzgerald/T. Smid	S. Edberg/A. Jarryd	6–3	4–6	6–3	6–7	14–12	558,900
1987	A. Jarryd/R. Seguso	G. Forget/Y. Noah	6–7	6–7	6–3	6–4	6–2	451,000
1988	A. Gomez/E. Sanchez	J. Fitzgerald/A. Jarryd	6–3	6–7	6–4	6–3		520,080
1989	J. Grabb/P. McEnroe	M. Bahrami/E. Winogradsky	6–4	2–6	6–4	7–6		621,024
1990	S. Casal/E. Sanchez	G. Ivanisevic/P. Korda	7–5	6–3				US$151,000
1991	J. Fitzgerald/A. Jarryd	R. Leach/J. Pugh	6–0	7–6				FF1,000,000
1992	J. Hlasek/M. Rosset	C. Adams/A. Olhovskiy	7–6	6–7	7–5			1,100,000
1993	L. Jensen/M. Jensen	M. K. Goellner/D. Prinosil	6–4	6–7	6–4			1,100,000
1994	B. Black/J. Stark	J. Apell/J. Bjorkman	6–4	7–6				1,200,000
1995	J. Eltingh/P. Haarhuis	N. Kulti/M. Larsson	6–7	6–4	6–1			1,364,000
1996	Y. Kafelnikov/D. Vacek	G. Forget/J. Hlasek	6–2	6–3				1,420,000
1997	Y. Kafelnikov/D. Vacek	T. Woodbridge/M. Woodforde	7–6	4–6	6–3			1,508,000

WOMEN'S DOUBLES

	CHAMPIONS	*RUNNERS-UP*	*SCORE*		
1925	S. Lenglen/D. Vlasto	E. Colyer/K. McKane	6–1	9–11	6–2
1926	S. Lenglen/D. Vlasto	E. Colyer/L. A. Godfree	6–1	6–1	
1927	E. L. Heine/G. Peacock	P. Saunders/P. H. Watson	6–2	6–1	
1928	E. Bennett/P. H. Watson	S. Deve/A. Lafaurie	6–0	6–2	
1929	L. de Alvarez/K. Bouman	E. L. Heine/A. Neave	7–5	6–3	
1930	F. S. Moody/E. Ryan	S. Barbier/S. Mathieu	6–3	6–1	
1931	B. Nuthall/E. F. Whittingstall	C. Aussem/E. Ryan	9–7	6–2	
1932	F. S. Moody/E. Ryan	B. Nuthall/E. F. Whittingstall	6–1	6–3	
1933	S. Mathieu/E. Ryan	S. Henrotin/C. Rosambert	6–1	6–3	
1934	S. Mathieu/E. Ryan	H. H. Jacobs/S. Palfrey	3–6	6–4	6–2
1935	M. C. Scriven/K. Stammers	N. Adamoff/H. Sperling	6–4	6–0	
1936	S. Mathieu/A. M. Yorke	S. Noel/J. Jedrzejowska	2–6	6–4	6–4
1937	S. Mathieu/A. M. Yorke	D. Andrus/S. Henrotin	3–6	6–2	6–2
1938	S. Mathieu/A. M. Yorke	A. Halff/N. Landry	6–3	6–3	
1939	J. Jedrzejowska/S. Mathieu	A. Florian/H. Kovac	7–5	7–5	
1940–1945		*Not held*			
1946	L. Brough/M. Osborne	P. Betz/D. Hart	6–4	0–6	6–1
1947	L. Brough/M. Osborne	D. Hart/P. C. Todd	7–5	6–2	
1948	D. Hart/P. C. Todd	S. Fry/M. A. Prentiss	6–4	6–2	
1949	L. Brough/W. du Pont	J. Gannon/B. Hilton	7–5	6–1	
1950	S. Fry/D. Hart	L. Brough/W. du Pont	1–6	7–5	6–2

1951	S. Fry/D. Hart	B. Bartlett/B. Scofield	10–8	6–3		
1952	S. Fry/D. Hart	H. Redick-Smith/J. Wipplinger	7–5	6–1		
1953	S. Fry/D. Hart	M. Connolly/J. Sampson	6–4	6–3		
1954	M. Connolly/N. Hopman	M. Galtier/S. Schmitt	7–5	4–6	6–0	
1955	B. Fleitz/D. R. Hard	S. J. Bloomer/P. Ward	7–5	6–8	13–11	
1956	A. Buxton/A. Gibson	D. R. Hard/D. Knode	6–8	8–6	6–1	
1957	S. J. Bloomer/D. R. Hard	Y. Ramirez/R. M. Reyes	7–5	4–6	7–5	
1958	Y. Ramirez/R. M. Reyes	M. K. Hawton/M. N. Long	6–4	7–5		
1959	S. Reynolds/R. Schuurman	Y. Ramirez/R. M. Reyes	2–6	6–0	6–1	
1960	M. E. Bueno/D. R. Hard	R. Hales/A. Haydon	6–2	7–5		
1961	S. Reynolds/R. Schuurman	M. E. Bueno/D. R. Hard	w.o.			
1962	S. Price/R. Schuurman	J. Bricka/M. Smith	6–4	6–4		
1963	P. F. Jones/R. Schuurman	R. A. Ebbern/M. Smith	7–5	6–4		
1964	M. Smith/L. R. Turner	N. Baylon/H. Schultze	6–3	6–1		
1965	M. Smith/L. R. Turner	F. Durr/J. Lieffrig	6–3	6–1		
1966	M. Smith/J. A. M. Tegart	J. Blackman/F. Toyne	4–6	6–1	6–1	
1967	F. Durr/G. Sheriff	A. M. Van Zyl/P. Walkden	6–2	6–2		
1968	F. Durr/P. F. Jones	R. Casals/L. W. King	7–5	4–6	6–4	
1969	F. Durr/P. F. Jones	M. Court/N. Richey	6–0	4–6	7–5	
1970	F. Durr/G. Chanfreau	R. Casals/L. W. King	6–1	3–6	6–3	FF6,000
1971	F. Durr/G. Chanfreau	H. Gourlay/K. Harris	6–4	6–1		4500
1972	L. W. King/B. Stove	W. Shaw/F. E. Truman	6–1	6–2		5,000
1973	M. Court/S. V. Wade	F. Durr/B. Stove	6–2	6–3		7,000
1974	C. Evert/O. Morozova	G. Chanfreau/K. Ebbinghaus	6–4	2–6	6–1	8,000
1975	C. Evert/M. Navratilova	J. Anthony/O. Morozova	6–3	6–2		8,000
1976	F. Bonicelli/G. Lovera	K. Harter/H. Masthoff	6–4	1–6	6–3	8,000
1977	R. Marsikova/P. Teeguarden	R. Fox/H. Gourlay	5–7	6–4	6–2	8,000
1978	M. Jausovec/V. Ruzici	N. Bowey/G. Lovera	5–7	6–4	8–6	20,000
1979	B. Stove/W. M. Turnbull	F. Durr/S. V. Wade	6–4	7–6		42,300
1980	K. Jordan/A. E. Smith	I. Madruga/I. Villagran	6–1	6–0		68,000
1981	R. Fairbank/T. Harford	C. Reynolds/P. Smith	6–1	6–3		80,000
1982	M. Navratilova/A. E. Smith	R. Casals/W. M. Turnbull	6–3	6–4		120,000
1983	R. Fairbank/C. Reynolds	K. Jordan/A. E. Smith	5–7	7–5	6–2	210,000
1984	M. Navratilova/P. H. Shriver	C. Kohde-Kilsch/H. Mandlikova	5–7	6–3	6–2	316,000
1985	M. Navratilova/P. H. Shriver	C. Kohde-Kilsch/H. Sukova	4–6	6–2	6–2	384,300
1986	M. Navratilova/A. Temesvari	S. Graf/G. Sabatini	6–1	6–2		398,200
1987	M. Navratilova/P. H. Shriver	S. Graf/G. Sabatini	6–2	6–1		365,300
1988	M. Navratilova/P. H. Shriver	C. Kohde-Kilsch/H. Sukova	6–2	7–5		453,230
1989	L. Savchenko/N. Zvereva	S. Graf/G. Sabatini	6–4	6–4		552,316
1990	J. Novotna/H. Sukova	L. Savchenko/N. Zvereva	6–4	7–5		US$103,080
1991	G. Fernandez/J. Novotna	L. Savchenko/N. Zvereva	6–4	6–0		FF786,500
1992	G. Fernandez/N. Zvereva	C. Martinez/A. Sanchez Vic.	6–3	6–2		865,000
1993	G. Fernandez/N. Zvereva	L. Neiland/J. Novotna	6–3	7–5		944,000
1994	G. Fernandez/N. Zvereva	L. Davenport/L. Raymond	6–2	6–2		1,020,000
1995	G. Fernandez/N. Zvereva	J. Novotna/A. Sanchez Vicario	6–7	6–4	7–5	1,070,000
1996	L. Davenport/M. J. Fernandez	G. Fernandez/N. Zvereva	6–2	6–1		1,112,800
1997	G. Fernandez/N. Zvereva	M. J. Fernandez/L. Raymond	3–6	6–4	6–1	1,182,400

MIXED DOUBLES

	CHAMPIONS	*RUNNERS-UP*	*SCORE*		
1925	J. Brugnon/Miss S. Lenglen	H. Cochet/Miss D. Vlasto	6–2	6–2	
1926	J. Brugnon/Miss S. Lenglen	J. Borotra/Mrs Le Besnerais	6–4	6–3	
1927	J. Borotra/Miss M. Broquedis	W. T. Tilden/Miss L. de Alvarez	6–4	2–6	6–2
1928	H. Cochet/Miss E. Bennett	F. T. Hunter/Miss H. Wills	3–6	6–3	6–3
1929	H. Cochet/Miss E. Bennett	F. T. Hunter/Miss H. Wills	6–3	6–2	
1930	W. T. Tilden/Miss C. Aussem	H. Cochet/Mrs F. Whittingstall	6–4	6–4	
1931	P. D. B. Spence/Miss B. Nuthall	H. W. Austin/Mrs D. C. Shepherd-Barron	6–3	5–7	6–3
1932	F. J. Perry/Miss B. Nuthall	S. B. Wood/Mrs F. S. Moody	6–4	6–2	
1933	J. H. Crawford/Miss M. C. Scriven	F. J. Perry/Miss B. Nuthall	6–2	6–3	
1934	J. Borotra/Miss C. Rosambert	A. K. Quist/Miss E. Ryan	6–2	6–4	
1935	M. Bernard/Miss L. Payot	A. M. Legeay/Mrs S. Henrotin	4–6	6–2	6–4
1936	M. Bernard/Miss A. M. Yorke	A. M. Legeay/Mrs S. Henrotin	7–5	6–8	6–3
1937	Y. Petra/Mrs S. Mathieu	R. Journu/Miss M. Horne	7–5	7–5	
1938	D. Mitic/Mrs S. Mathieu	C. Boussus/Miss N. Wynne	2–6	6–3	6–4
1939	E. T. Cooke/Mrs S. Fabyan	F. Kukuljevic/Mrs S. Mathieu	4–6	6–1	7–5
1940–1945		*Not held*			

1946	J. E. Patty/Miss P. M. Betz	T. P. Brown/Miss D. Bundy	7–5	9–7		
1947	E. W. Sturgess/Mrs S. P. Summers	C. Caralulis/Miss J. Jedrzejowska	6–0	6–0		
1948	J. Drobny/Mrs P. C. Todd	F. A. Sedgman/Miss D. Hart	6–3	3–6	6–3	
1949	E. W. Sturgess/Mrs S. P. Summers	G. D. Oakley/Miss J. Quertier	6–1	6–1		
1950	E. Morea/Miss B. Scofield	W. F. Talbert/Mrs P. C. Todd	w.o.			
1951	F. A. Sedgman/Miss D. Hart	M. G. Rose/Mrs M. N. Long	7–5	6–2		
1952	F. A. Sedgman/Miss D. Hart	E. W. Sturgess/Miss S. Fry	6–8	6–3	6–3	
1953	E. V. Seixas/Miss D. Hart	M. G. Rose/Miss M. Connolly	4–6	6–4	6–0	
1954	L. A. Hoad/Miss M. Connolly	R. N. Hartwig/Mrs J. Patorni	6–4	6–3		
1955	G. L. Forbes/Miss D. R. Hard	L. Ayala/Miss J. Staley	5–7	6–1	6–2	
1956	L. Ayala/Mrs M. N. Long	R. N. Howe/Miss D. R. Hard	4–6	6–4	6–1	
1957	J. Javorsky/Miss V. Puzejova	L. Ayala/Miss E. Buding	6–3	6–4		
1958	N. Pietrangeli/Miss S. J. Bloomer	R. N. Howe/Miss L. Coghlan	9–7	6–8	6–2	
1959	W. A. Knight/Miss R. Ramirez	R. G. Laver/Miss R. Schuurman	6–4	6–4		
1960	R. N. Howe/Miss M. Bueno	R. S. Emerson/Miss A. Haydon	1–6	6–1	6–2	
1961	R. G. Laver/Miss D. R. Hard	J. Javorsky/Miss V. Puzejova	6–0	2–6	6–3	
1962	R. N. Howe/Miss R. Schuurman	F. S. Stolle/Miss L. R. Turner	3–6	6–4	6–4	
1963	K. N. Fletcher/Miss M. Smith	F. S. Stolle/Miss L. R. Turner	6–1	6–2		
1964	K. N. Fletcher/Miss M. Smith	F. S. Stolle/Miss L. R. Turner	6–3	6–4		
1965	K. N. Fletcher/Miss M. Smith	J. D. Newcombe/Miss M. Bueno	6–4	6–4		
1966	F. D. McMillan/Miss A. M. Van Zyl	C. Graebner/Mrs P. F. Jones	1–6	6–3	6–2	
1967	O. K. Davidson/Mrs L. W. King	I. Tiriac/Mrs P. F. Jones	6–3	6–1		
1968	J. C. Barclay/Miss F. Durr	O. K. Davidson/Mrs L. W. King	6–1	6–4		*Prize Mon*
1969	M. C. Riessen/Mrs. B. M. Court	J. C. Barclay/Miss F. Durr	7–5	6–4		*(FF per team)*
1970	R. A. J. Hewitt/Mrs L. W. King	J. C. Barclay/Miss F. Durr	3–6	6–3	6–2	FF6,000
1971	J. C. Barclay/Miss F. Durr	T. Lejus/Miss W. Shaw	6–2	6–4		4,500
1972	K. Warwick/Miss E. F. Goolagong	J. C. Barclay/Miss F. Durr	6–2	6–4		5,000
1973	J. C. Barclay/Miss F. Durr	P. Dominguez/Miss B. Stove	6–1	6–4		6,000
1974	I. Molina/Miss M. Navratilova	M. Lara/Mrs R. M. Darmon	6–3	6–3		8,000
1975	T. Koch/Miss F. Bonicelli	J. Fillol/Miss P. Teeguarden	6–4	7–6		8,000
1976	K. Warwick/Miss I. Kloss	C. Dowdeswell/Miss L. Boshoff	5–7	7–6	6–2	8,000
1977	J. P. McEnroe/Miss M. Carillo	I. Molina/Miss F. Mihai	7–6	6–3		8,000
1978	P. Slozil/Miss R. Tomanova	P. Dominguez/Miss V. Ruzici	7–6	ret'd		10,000
1979	R. A. J. Hewitt/Miss W. M. Turnbull	I. Tiriac/Miss V. Ruzici	6–3	2–6	6–3	6,000
1980	W. Martin/Miss A. E. Smith	S. Birner/Miss R. Tomanova	2–6	6–4	8–6	11,000
1981	J. Arias/Miss A. Jaeger	F. D. McNair/Miss B. Stove	7–6	6–4		11,000
1982	J. M. Lloyd/Miss W. M. Turnbull	C. Motta/Miss C. Monteiro	6–2	7–6		13,200
1983	E. Teltscher/Miss B. Jordan	C. Strode/Miss L. Allen	6–2	6–3		20,000
1984	R. L. Stockton/Miss A. E. Smith	L. Warder/Miss A. Minter	6–2	6–4		32,000
1985	H. P. Gunthardt/Miss M. Navratilova	F. Gonzalez/Miss P. Smith	2–6	6–3	6–2	46,000
1986	K. Flach/Miss. K. Jordan	M. R. Edmondson/Miss. R. Fairbank	3–6	7–6	6–3	83,000
1987	E. Sanchez/Miss P. H. Shriver	S. E. Stewart/Miss L. McNeil	6–3	7–6		86,000
1988	J. Lozano/Miss L. McNeil	M. Schapers/Miss B. Schultz	7–5	6–2		120,000
1989	T. Nijssen/Miss M. Bollegraf	H. de la Pena/Miss A. Sanchez Vicario	6–3	6–7	6–2	135,000
1990	J. Lozano/Miss A. Sanchez Vicario	D. Visser/Miss N. Provis	7–6	7–6		US$30,000
1991	C. Suk/Miss H. Sukova	P. Haarhuis/Miss C. Vis	3–6	6–4	6–1	FF220,000
1992	T. Woodbridge/Miss A. Sanchez Vic.	B. Shelton/Miss L. McNeil	6–2	6–3		242,000
1993	A. Olhovskiy/Miss E. Maniokova	D. Visser/Miss E. Reinach	6–2	4–6	6–4	264,000
1994	M. Oosting/Miss K. Boogert	A. Olhovskiy/Mrs L. Neiland	7–5	3–6	7–5	285,000
1995	M. Woodforde/Mrs L. Neiland	J. de Jager/Miss J. Hetherington	7–6	7–6		300,000
1996	J. Frana/Miss P. Tarabini	L. Jensen/Miss N. Arendt	6–2	6–2		312,000
1997	M. Bhupathi/Miss R. Hiraki	P. Galbraith/Miss L. Raymond	6–4	6–1		330,000

THE CHAMPIONSHIPS – WIMBLEDON

1. Venue: From 1877–1921 The Championships were played at the Worple Road ground. Since 1922 they have been played at the present ground in Church Road. **2. Title:** For the years 1913, 1914, and 1919–23 inclusive, these records include the 'World's Championship on Grass' granted to the LTA by the ILTF. This title was then abolished. **3. Challenge Round:** Prior to 1922 the holder did not compete in the Championship but met the winner of the All-Comers singles in the Challenge Round. The Challenge Round was abolished in 1922 and the holder subsequently played through. **4. Seeding:** 'Modified seeding' was introduced in 1924. 'Full seeding', as we know it today, was first practised in 1927. **5. Status:** The Championships became 'open' in 1968. (There was a tie-break at 8-all in the years 1971–78. Thereafter the tie-break was played at 6-all.) **6. Surface:** Alone of the four Grand Slams, The Championships have always been played on grass courts. **7.** In the years marked with an asterisk*, the holder(s) did not defend the title.

MEN'S SINGLES

	CHAMPIONS	*RUNNER-UP*	*SCORE*				
1877	S. W. Gore	W. C. Marshall	6–1	6–2	6–4		
1878	P. F. Hadow	S. W. Gore	7–5	6–1	9–7		
1879*	J. T. Hartley	V. St L. Goold	6–2	6–4	6–2		
1880	J. T. Hartley	H. F. Lawford	6–3	6–2	2–6	6–3	
1881	W. Renshaw	J. T. Hartley	6–0	6–1	6–1		
1882	W. Renshaw	E. Renshaw	6–1	2–6	4–6	6–2	6–2
1883	W. Renshaw	E. Renshaw	2–6	6–3	6–3	4–6	6–3
1884	W. Renshaw	H. F. Lawford	6–0	6–4	9–7		
1885	W. Renshaw	H. F. Lawford	7–5	6–2	4–6	7–5	
1886	W. Renshaw	H. F. Lawford	6–0	5–7	6–3	6–4	
1887*	H. F. Lawford	E. Renshaw	1–6	6–3	3–6	6–4	6–4
1888	E. Renshaw	H. F. Lawford	6–3	7–5	6–0		
1889	W. Renshaw	E. Renshaw	6–4	6–1	3–6	6–0	
1890	W. J. Hamilton	W. Renshaw	6–8	6–2	3–6	6–1	6–1
1891*	W. Baddeley	J. Pim	6–4	1–6	7–5	6–0	
1892	W. Baddeley	J. Pim	4–6	6–3	6–3	6–2	
1893	J. Pim	W. Baddeley	3–6	6–1	6–3	6–2	
1894	J. Pim	W. Baddeley	10–8	6–2	8–6		
1895*	W. Baddeley	W. V. Eaves	4–6	2–6	8–6	6–2	6–3
1896	H. S. Mahony	W. Baddeley	6–2	6–8	5–7	8–6	6–3
1897	R. F. Doherty	H. S. Mahony	6–4	6–4	6–3		
1898	R. F. Doherty	H. L. Doherty	6–3	6–3	2–6	5–7	6–1
1899	R. F. Doherty	A. W. Gore	1–6	4–6	6–3	6–3	6–3
1900	R. F. Doherty	S. H. Smith	6–8	6–3	6–1	6–2	
1901	A. W. Gore	R. F. Doherty	4–6	7–5	6–4	6–4	
1902	H. L. Doherty	A. W. Gore	6–4	6–3	3–6	6–0	
1903	H. L. Doherty	F. L. Riseley	7–5	6–3	6–0		
1904	H. L. Doherty	F. L. Riseley	6–1	7–5	8–6		
1905	H. L. Doherty	N. E. Brookes	8–6	6–2	6–4		
1906	H. L. Doherty	F. L. Riseley	6–4	4–6	6–2	6–3	
1907*	N. E. Brookes	A. W. Gore	6–4	6–2	6–2		
1908*	A. W. Gore	H. Roper Barrett	6–3	6–2	4–6	3–6	6–4
1909	A. W. Gore	M. J. G. Ritchie	6–8	1–6	6–2	6–2	6–2
1910	A. F. Wilding	A. W. Gore	6–4	7–5	4–6	6–2	
1911	A. F. Wilding	H. Roper Barrett	6–4	4–6	2–6	6–2	ret'd
1912	A. F. Wilding	A. W. Gore	6–4	6–4	4–6	6–4	
1913	A. F. Wilding	M. E. McLoughlin	8–6	6–3	10–8		
1914	N. E. Brookes	A. F. Wilding	6–4	6–4	7–5		
1915–18		*Not held*					
1919	G. L. Patterson	N. E. Brookes	6–3	7–5	6–2		
1920	W. T. Tilden	G. L. Patterson	2–6	6–2	6–3	6–4	
1921	W. T. Tilden	B. I. C. Norton	4–6	2–6	6–1	6–0	7–5
1922*	G. L. Patterson	R. Lycett	6–3	6–4	6–2		
1923*	W. M. Johnston	F. T. Hunter	6–0	6–3	6–1		
1924	J. Borotra	R. Lacoste	6–1	3–6	6–1	3–6	6–4
1925	R. Lacoste	J. Borotra	6–3	6–3	4–6	8–6	
1926	J. Borotra	H. Kinsey	8–6	6–1	6–3		
1927	H. Cochet	J. Borotra	4–6	4–6	6–3	6–4	7–5
1928	R. Lacoste	H. Cochet	6–1	4–6	6–4	6–2	

Year	Winner	Runner-up						FIRST PRIZE (£)
1929	H. Cochet	J. Borotra	6–4	6–3	6–4			
1930	W. T. Tilden	W. L. Allison	6–3	9–7	6–4			
1931*	S. B. Wood	F. X. Shields	w.o.					
1932	H. E. Vines	H. W. Austin	6–4	6–2	6–0			
1933	J. H. Crawford	H. E. Vines	4–6	11–9	6–2	2–6	6–4	
1934	F. J. Perry	J. H. Crawford	6–3	6–0	7–5			
1935	F. J. Perry	G. von Cramm	6–2	6–4	6–4			
1936	F. J. Perry	G. von Cramm	6–1	6–1	6–0			
1937*	J. D. Budge	G. von Cramm	6–3	6–4	6–2			
1938	J. D. Budge	H. W. Austin	6–1	6–0	6–3			
1939*	R. L. Riggs	E. T. Cooke	2–6	8–6	3–6	6–3	6–2	
1940–45		*Not held*						
1946	Y. Petr	G.Brown	6–2	6–4	7–9	5–7	6–4	
1947	J. Kramer	T.Brown	6–1	6–3	6–2			
1948	B. Falkenburg	J. Bromwich	7–5	0–6	6–2	3–6	7–5	
1949	T. Schroeder	J. Drobny	3–6	6–0	6–3	4–6	6–4	
1950	B. Patty	F. A.Sedgman	6–1	8–10	6–2	6–3		
1951	D. Savitt	K. B. McGregor	6–4	6–4	6–4			
1952	F. A. Sedgman	J. Drobny	4–6	6–2	6–3	6–2		
1953	*V.* Seixas	K. Nielsen	9–7	6–3	6–4			
1954	J. Drobny	K. Rosewall	13–11	4–6	6–2	9–7.		
1955	T. Trabert	K. Nielsen	6–3	7–5	6–1			
1956*	L. A. Hoad	K. R. Rosewall	6–2	4–6	7–5	6–4		
1957	L. A. Hoad	A. J. Cooper	6–2	6–1	6–2			
1958*	A. J. Cooper	N. A. Fraser	3–6	6–3	6–4	13–11		
1959*	A. Olmedo	R. G. Laver	6–4	6–3	6–4			
1960*	N. A. Fraser	R. G. Laver	6–4	3–6	9–7	7–5		
1961	R. G. Laver	C. R. McKinley	6–3	6–1	6–4			
1962	R. G. Laver	M. F. Mulligan	6–2	6–2	6–1			
1963*	C. R. McKinley	F. S. Stolle	9–7	6–1	6–4			
1964	R. S. Emerson	F. S. Stolle	6–1	12–10	4–6	6–3		
1965	R. S. Emerson	F. S. Stolle	6–2	6–4	6–4			
1966	M. Santana	R. D. Ralston	6–4	11–9		6–4		
1967	J. D. Newcombe	W. P. Bungert	6–3	6–1	6–1			
1968	R. G. Laver	A. D. Roche	6–3	6–4	6–2			2,000
1969	R. G. Laver	J. D. Newcombe	6–4	5–7	6–4	6–4		3,000
1970	J. D. Newcombe	K. R. Rosewall	5–7	6–3	6–2	3–6	6–1	3,000
1971	J. D. Newcombe	S. R. Smith	6–3	5–7	2–6	6–4	6–4	3,750
1972*	S. R. Smith	I. Nastase	4–6	6–3	6–3	4–6	7–5	5,000
1973*	J. Kodes	A. Metreveli	6–1	9–8	6–3			5,000
1974	J. S. Connors	K. R. Rosewall	6–1	6–1	6–4			10,000
1975	A. R. Ashe	J. S. Connors	6–1	6–1	5–7	6–4		10,000
1976	B. Borg	I. Nastase	6–4	6–2	9–7			12,500
1977	B. Borg	J. S. Connors	3–6	6–2	6–1	5–7	6–4	15,000
1978	B. Borg	J. S. Connors	6–2	6–2	6–3			19,000
1979	B. Borg	R. Tanner	6–7	6–1	3–6	6–3	6–4	20,000
1980	B. Borg	J. P. McEnroe	1–6	7–5	6–3	6–7	8–6	20,000
1981	J. P. McEnroe	B. Borg	4–6	7–6	7–6	6–4		21,600
1982	J. S. Connors	J. P. McEnroe	3–6	6–3	6–7	7–6	6–4	41,667
1983	J. P. McEnroe	C. J. Lewis	6–2	6–2	6–2			66,600
1984	J. P. McEnroe	J. S. Connors	6–1	6–1	6–2			100,000
1985	B. Becker	K. Curren	6–3	6–7	7–6	6–4		130,000
1986	B. Becker	I. Lendl	6–4	6–3	7–5			140,000
1987	P. Cash	I. Lendl	7–6	6–2	7–5			155,000
1988	S. Edberg	B. Becker	4–6	7–6	6–4	6–2		165,000
1989	B. Becker	S. Edberg	6–0	7–6	6–4			190,000
1990	S. Edberg	B. Becker	6–2	6–2	3–6	3–6	6–4	230,000
1991	M. Stich	B. Becker	6–4	7–6	6–4			240,000
1992	A. Agassi	G. Ivanisevic	6–7	6–4	6–4	1–6	6–4	265,000
1993	P. Sampras	J. Courier	7–6	7–6	3–6	6–3		305,000
1994	P. Sampras	G. Ivanisevic	7–6	7–6	6–0			345,000
1995	P. Sampras	B. Becker	6–7	6–2	6–4	6–2		365,000
1996	R. Krajicek	M. Washington	6–3	6–4	6–3			392,500
1997	P. Sampras	C. Pioline	6–4	6–2	6–4			415,000

WOMEN'S SINGLES

	CHAMPION	*RUNNER-UP*	*SCORE*		
1884	Miss M. Watson	Miss L. Watson	6–8	6–3	6–3
1885	Miss M. Watson	Miss B. Bingley	6–1	7–5	
1886	Miss B. Bingley	Miss M. Watson	6–3	6–3	
1887	Miss C. Dod	Miss B. Bingley	6–2	6–0	
1888	Miss C. Dod	Mrs G. W. Hillyard	6–3	6–3	
1889*	Mrs G. W. Hillyard	Miss H. Rice	4–6	8–6	6–4
1890*	Miss H. Rice	Miss M. Jacks	6–4	6–1	
1891*	Miss C. Dod	Mrs G. W. Hillyard	6–2	6–1	
1892	Miss C. Dod	Mrs G. W. Hillyard	6–1	6–1	
1893	Miss C. Dod	Mrs G. W. Hillyard	6–8	6–1	6–4
1894*	Mrs G. W. Hillyard	Miss L. Austin	6–1	6–1	
1895*	Miss C. Cooper	Miss H. Jackson	7–5	8–6	
1896	Miss C. Cooper	Mrs W. H. Pickering	6–2	6–3	
1897	Mrs G. W. Hillyard	Miss C. Cooper	5–7	7–5	6–2
1898*	Miss C. Cooper	Miss L. Martin	6–4	6–4	
1899	Mrs G. W. Hillyard	Miss C. Cooper	6–2	6–3	
1900	Mrs G. W. Hillyard	Miss C. Cooper	4–6	6–4	6–4
1901	Mrs A. Sterry	Mrs G. W. Hillyard	6–2	6–2	
1902	Miss M. E. Robb	Mrs A. Sterry	7–5	6–1	
1903*	Miss D. K. Douglass	Miss E. W. Thomson	4–6	6–4	6–2
1904	Miss D. K. Douglass	Mrs A. Sterry	6–0	6–3	
1905	Miss M. Sutton	Miss D. K. Douglass	6–3	6–4	
1906	Miss D. K. Douglass	Miss M. Sutton	6–3	9–7	
1907	Miss M. Sutton	Mrs R. Lamb. Chambers	6–1	6–4	
1908*	Mrs A. Sterry	Miss A. M. Morton	6–4	6–4	
1909*	Miss D. P. Boothby	Miss A. M. Morton	6–4	4–6	8–6
1910	Mrs R. Lambert Chambers	Miss D. P. Boothby	6–2	6–2	
1911	Mrs R. Lambert Chambers	Miss D. P. Boothby	6–0	6–0	
1912*	Mrs D. R. Larcombe	Mrs A. Sterry	6–3	6–1	
1913*	Mrs R. Lambert Chambers	Mrs R. J. McNair	6–0	6–4	
1914	Mrs R. Lambert Chambers	Mrs D. R. Larcombe	7–5	6–4	
1915–18		*Not held*			
1919	Mlle S. Lenglen	Mrs R. Lamb. Chambers	10–8	4–6	9–7
1920	Mlle S. Lenglen	Mrs R. Lamb. Chambers	6–3	6–0	
1921	Mlle S. Lenglen	Miss E. Ryan	6–2	6–0	
1922	Mlle S. Lenglen	Mrs F. Mallory	6–2	6–0	
1923	Mlle S. Lenglen	Miss K. McKane	6–2	6–2	
1924	Miss K. McKane	Miss H. N. Wills	4–6	6–4	6–4
1925	Mlle S. Lenglen	Miss J. Fry	6–2	6–0	
1926	Mrs L. A. Godfree	Sta E. de Alvarez	6–2	4–6	6–3
1927	Miss H. N. Wills	Sta E. de Alvarez	6–2	6–4	
1928	Miss H. N. Wills	Sta E. de Alvarez	6–2	6–3	
1929	Miss H. N. Wills	Miss H. H. Jacobs	6–1	6–2	
1930	Mrs F. S. Moody	Miss E. Ryan	6–2	6–2	
1931*	Frl C. Aussem	Frl H. Krahwinkel	6–2	7–5	
1932*	Mrs F. S. Moody	Miss H. H. Jacobs	6–3	6–1	
1933	Mrs F. S. Moody	Miss D. E. Round	6–4	6–8	6–3
1934*	Miss D. E. Round	Miss H. H. Jacobs	6–2	5–7	6–3
1935	Mrs F. S. Moody	Miss H. H. Jacobs	6–3	3–6	7–5
1936*	Miss H. H. Jacobs	Mrs S. Sperling	6–2	4–6	7–5
1937	Miss D. E. Round	Miss J. Jedrzejowska	6–2	2–6	7–5
1938*	Mrs F. S. Moody	Miss H. H. Jacobs	6–4	6–0	
1939*	Miss A. Marble	Miss K. E. Stammers	6–2	6–0	
1940–45		*Not held*			
1946*	Miss P. M. Betz	Miss A. L. Brough	6–2	6–4	
1947*	Miss M. E. Osborne	Miss D. J. Hart	6–2	6–4	
1948	Miss A. L. Brough	Miss D. J. Hart	6–3	8–6	
1949	Miss A. L. Brough	Mrs W. du Pont	10–8	1–6	10–8
1950	Miss A. L. Brough	Mrs W. du Pont	6–1	3–6	6–1
1951	Miss D. J. Hart	Miss S. J. Fry	6–1	6–0	
1952	Miss M. Connolly	Miss A. L. Brough	6–4	6–3	
1953	Miss M. Connolly	Miss D. J. Hart	8–6	7–5	
1954	Miss M. Connolly	Miss A. L. Brough	6–2	7–5	
1955*	Miss A. L. Brough	Mrs J. G. Fleitz	7–5	8–6	

						FIRST PRIZE (£)
1956	Miss S. J. Fry	Miss A. Buxton	6–3	6–1		
1957*	Miss A. Gibson	Miss D. R. Hard	6–3	6–2		
1958	Miss A. Gibson	Miss A. Mortimer	8–6	6–2		
1959*	Miss M. E. Bueno	Miss D. R. Hard	6–4	6–3		
1960	Miss M. E. Bueno	Miss S. Reynolds	8–6	6–0		
1961*	Miss A. Mortimer	Miss C. C. Truman	4–6	6–4	7–5	
1962	Mrs J. R. Susman	Mrs V. Sukova	6–4	6–4		
1963*	Miss M. Smith	Miss B. J. Moffitt	6–3	6–4		
1964	Miss M. E. Bueno	Miss M. Smith	6–4	7–9	6–3	
1965	Miss M. Smith	Miss M. E. Bueno	6–4	7–5		
1966	Mrs L. W. King	Miss M. E. Bueno	6–3	3–6	6–1	
1967	Mrs L. W. King	Mrs P. F. Jones	6–3	6–4		
1968	Mrs L. W. King	Miss J. A. M. Tegart	9–7	7–5		750
1969	Mrs P. F. Jones	Mrs L. W. King	3–6	6–3	6–2	1,500
1970*	Mrs B. M. Court	Mrs L. W. King	14–12	11–9		1,500
1971	Miss E. F. Goolagong	Mrs B. M. Court	6–4	6–1		1,800
1972	Mrs L. W. King	Miss E. Goolagong	6–3	6–3		2,400
1973	Mrs L. W. King	Miss C. M. Evert	6–0	7–5		3,000
1974	Miss C. M. Evert	Mrs O. Morozova	6–0	6–4		7,000
1975	Mrs L. W. King	Mrs R. A. Cawley	6–0	6–1		7,000
1976*	Miss C. M. Evert	Mrs R. A. Cawley	6–3	4–6	8–6	10,000
1977	Miss S. V. Wade	Miss B. F. Stove	4–6	6–3	6–1	13,500
1978	Miss M. Navratilova	Miss C. M. Evert	2–6	6–4	7–5	17,100
1979	Miss M. Navratilova	Mrs J. M. Lloyd	6–4	6–4		18,000
1980	Mrs R. A. Cawley	Mrs J. M. Lloyd	6–1	7–6		18,000
1981	Mrs J. M. Lloyd	Miss H. Mandlikova	6–2	6–2		19,440
1982	Miss M. Navratilova	Mrs J. M. Lloyd	6–1	3–6	6–2	37,500
1983	Miss M. Navratilova	Miss A. Jaeger	6–0	6–3		60,000
1984	Miss M. Navratilova	Mrs J. M. Lloyd	7–6	6–2		90,000
1985	Miss M. Navratilova	Mrs J. M. Lloyd	4–6	6–3	6–2	117,000
1986	Miss M. Navratilova	Miss H. Mandlikova	7–6	6–3		126,000
1987	Miss M. Navratilova	Miss S. Graf	7–5	6–3		139,500
1988	Miss S. Graf	Miss M. Navratilova	5–7	6–2	6–1	148,500
1989	Miss S. Graf	Miss M. Navratilova	6–2	6–7	6–1	171,000
1990	Miss M. Navratilova	Miss Z. Garrison	6–4	6–1		207,000
1991	Miss S. Graf	Miss G. Sabatini	6–4	3–6	8–6	216,000
1992	Miss S.Graf	Miss M. Seles	6–2	6–1		240,000
1993	Miss S. Graf	Miss J. Novotna	7–6	1–6	6–4	275,000
1994	Miss C. Martinez	Miss M. Navratilova	6–4	3–6	6–3	310,000
1995	Miss S. Graf	Miss A. Sanchez Vicario	4–6	6–1	7–5	328,000
1996	Miss S. Graf	Miss A. Sanchez Vicario	6–3	7–5		353,000
1997	Miss M. Hingis	Miss J. Novotna	2–6	6–3	6–3	373,000

MEN'S DOUBLES

	CHAMPIONS	*RUNNERS-UP*	*SCORE*				
1884	E./W. Renshaw	E. W. Lewis/E. L. Williams	6–3	6–1	1–6	6–4	
1885	E./W. Renshaw	C. E. Farrer/A. J. Stanley	6–3	6–3	10–8		
1886	E./W. Renshaw	C. E. Farrer/A. J. Stanley	6–3	6–3	4–6	7–5	
1887*	P. B-Lyon/W. W. Wilberforce	E. Barratt-Smith/J. H. Crispe	7–5	6–3	6–2		
1888	E./W. Renshaw	P. B-Lyon/W. W. Wilberforce	2–6	1–6	6–3	6–4	6–3
1889	E./W. Renshaw	G. W. Hillyard/E. W. Lewis	6–4	6–4	3–6	0–6	6–1
1890*	J. Pim/F. O. Stoker	G. W. Hillyard/E. W. Lewis	6–0	7–5	6–4		
1891	H./W. Baddeley	J. Pim/F. O. Stoker	6–1	6–3	1–6	6–2	
1892	H. S. Barlow/E. W. Lewis	H./W. Baddeley	4–6	6–2	8–6	6–4	
1893	J. Pim/F. O. Stoker	H. S. Barlow/E. W. Lewis	4–6	6–3	6–1	2–6	6–0
1894*	H./W. Baddeley	H. S. Barlow/C. H. Martin	5–7	7–5	4–6	6–3	8–6
1895	H./W. Baddeley	W. V. Eaves/E. W. Lewis	8–6	5–7	6–4	6–3	
1896	H./W. Baddeley	R. F. Doherty/H. A. Nisbet	1–6	3–6	6–4	6–2	6–1
1897	H. L./R. F. Doherty	H./W. Baddeley	6–4	4–6	8–6	6–4	
1898	H. L./R. F. Doherty	C. Hobart/H. A. Nisbet	6–4	6–4	6–2		
1899	H. L./R. F. Doherty	C. Hobart/H. A. Nisbet	7–5	6–0	6–2		
1900	H. L./R. F. Doherty	H. A. Nisbet/H. Roper Barrett	9–7	7–5	4–6	3–6	6–3
1901	H. L./R. F. Doherty	D. F. Davis/H. Ward	4–6	6–2	6–3	9–7	
1902	F. L. Riseley/S. H. Smith	H. L./R. F. Doherty	4–6	8–6	6–3	4–6	11–9
1903	H. L./R. F. Doherty	F. L. Riseley/S. H. Smith	6–4	6–4	6–4		
1904	H. L./R. F. Doherty	F. L. Riseley/S. H. Smith	6–3	6–4	6–3		

1905	H. L./R. F. Doherty	F. L. Riseley/S. H. Smith	6–2	6–4	6–8	6–3		
1906	F. L. Riseley/S. H. Smith	H. L./R. F. Doherty	6–8	6–4	5–7	6–3	6–3	
1907*	N. E. Brookes/A. F. Wilding	K. Behr/B. C. Wright	6–4	6–4	6–2			
1908*	M. J. G. Ritchie/A. F. Wilding	A. W. Gore/H. Roper Barrett	6–1	6–2	1–6	1–6	9–7	
1909*	A. W. Gore/H. Roper Barrett	S. N. Doust/H. A. Parker	6–2	6–1	6–4			
1910	M. J. G. Ritchie/A. F. Wilding	A. W. Gore/H. Roper Barrett	6–1	6–1	6–2			
1911	M. Decugis/A. H. Gobert	M. J. G. Ritchie/A. F. Wilding	9–7	5–7	6–3	2–6	6–2	
1912	C. P. Dixon/H. Roper Barrett	M. Decugis/A. H. Gobert	3–6	6–3	6–4	7–5		
1913	C. P. Dixon/H. Roper Barrett	H. Kleinschroth/F. W. Rahe	6–2	6–4	4–6	6–2		
1914	N. E. Brookes/A. F. Wilding	C. P. Dixon/H. Roper Barrett	6–1	6–1	5–7	8–6		
1915–1918		*Not held*						
1919*	P. O'Hara Wood/R. V. Thomas	R. W. Heath/R. Lycett	6–4	6–2	4–6	6–2		
1920*	C. S. Garland/R. N. Williams	A. R. F. Kingscote/J. C. Parke	4–6	6–4	7–5	6–2		
1921*	R. Lycett/M. Woosnam	A. H./F. G. Lowe	6–3	6–0	7–5			
1922	J. O. Anderson/R. Lycett	P. O'Hara Wood/G.L. Patterson	3–6	7–9	6–4	6–3	11–9	
1923	L. A. Godfree/R. Lycett	E. Flaquer/Count M. de Gomar	6–3	6–4	3–6	6–3		
1924	F. T. Hunter/V. Richards	W. M. Washburn/R. N. Williams	6–3	3–6	8–10	8–6	6–3	
1925	J. Borotra/R. Lacoste	R. Casey/J. Hennessey	6–4	11–9	4–6	1–6	6–3	
1926	J. Brugnon/H. Cochet	H. Kinsey/V. Richards	7–5	4–6	6–3	6–2		
1927	F. T. Hunter/W. T. Tilden	J. Brugnon/H. Cochet	1–6	4–6	8–6	6–3	6–4	
1928	J. Brugnon/H. Cochet	J. B. Hawkes/G. L. Patterson	13–11	6–4	6–4			
1929	W. L. Allison/J. Van Ryn	I. G. Collins/J. C. Gregory	6–4	5–7	6–3	10–12	6–4	
1930	W. L. Allison/J. Van Ryn	J. H. Doeg/G. M. Lott	6–3	6–3	6–2			
1931	G. M. Lott/J. Van Ryn	J. Brugnon/H. Cochet	6–2	10–8	9–11	3–6	6–3	
1932	J. Borotra/J. Brugnon	G. P. Hughes/F. J. Perry	6–0	4–6	3–6	7–5	7–5	
1933	J. Borotra/J. Brugnon	R. Nunoi/J. Satoh	4–6	6–3	6–3	7–5		
1934	G. M. Lott/L. R. Stoefen	J. Borotra/J. Brugnon	6–2	6–3	6–4			
1935	J. H. Crawford/A. K Quist	W. L. Allison/J. Van Ryn	6–3	5–7	6–2	5–7	7–5	
1936	G. P. Hughes/C. R. D. Tuckey	C. E. Hare/F. H. D. Wilde	6–4	3–6	7–9	6–1	5–4	
1937	J. D. Budge/G. Mako	G. P. Hughes/C. R. D. Tuckey	6–0	6–4	6–8	6–1		
1938	J. D. Budge/G. Mako	H. Henkel/G. von Metaxa	6–4	3–6	6–3	8–6		
1939	E. T. Cooke/R. L. Riggs	C. E. Hare/F. H. D. Wilde	6–3	3–6	6–3	9–7		
1940–1945		*Not held*						
1946	T. Brown/J. A. Kramer	G. E. Brown/D. Pails	6–4	6–4	6–2			
1947	R. Falkenburg/J. A. Kramer	A. J. Mottram/O. W. Sidwell	8–6	6–3	6–3			
1948	J. E. Bromwich/F. A. Sedgman	T. Brown/G. Mulloy	5–7	7–5	7–5	9–7		
1949	R. A. Gonzales/F. A. Parker	G. Mulloy/F. R. Schroeder	6–4	6–4	6–2			
1950	J. E. Bromwich/A. K. Quist	G. E. Brown/O. W. Sidwell	7–5	3–6	6–3	3–6	6–2	
1951	K. B. McGregor/F. A. Sedgman	J. Drobny/E. W. Sturgess	3–6	6–2	6–3	3–6	6–3	
1952	K. B. McGregor/F. A. Sedgman	E. V. Seixas/E. W. Sturgess	6–3	7–5	6–4			
1953	L. A. Hoad/K. R. Rosewall	R. N. Hartwig/M. G. Rose	6–4	7–5	4–6	7–5		
1954	R. N. Hartwig/M. G. Rose	E. V. Seixas/M. A. Trabert	6–4	6–4	3–6	6–4		
1955	R. N. Hartwig/L. A. Hoad	N. A. Fraser/K. R. Rosewall	7–5	6–4	6–3			
1956	L. A. Hoad/K. R. Rosewall	N. Pietrangeli/O. Sirola	7–5	6–2	6–1			
1957	G. Mulloy/J. E. Patty	N. A. Fraser/L. A. Hoad	8–10	6–4	6–4	6–4		
1958	S. Davidson/U. Schmidt	A. J. Cooper/N. A. Fraser	6–4	6–4	8–6			
1959	R. Emerson/N. A. Fraser	R. Laver/R. Mark	8–6	6–3	14–16	9–7		
1960	R. H. Osuna/R. D. Ralston	M. G. Davies/R. K. Wilson	7–5	6–3	10–8			
1961	R. Emerson/N. A. Fraser	R. A. J. Hewitt/F. S. Stolle	6–4	6–8	6–4	6–8	8–6	
1962	R. A. J. Hewitt/F. S. Stolle	B. Jovanovic/N. Pilic	6–2	5–7	6–2	6–4		
1963	R. H. Osuna/A. Palafox	J. C. Barclay/P. Darmon	4–6	6–2	6–2	6–2		
1964	R. A. J. Hewitt/F. S. Stolle	R. Emerson/K. N. Fletcher	7–5	11–9	6–4			FIRST
1965	J. D. Newcombe/A. D. Roche	K. N. Fletcher/R. A. J. Hewitt	7–5	6–3	6–4			PRIZE
1966	K. N. Fletcher/J. D. Newcombe	W. W. Bowrey/O. K. Davidson	6–3	6–4	3–6	6–3		*(£ per*
1967	R. A. J. Hewitt/F. D. McMillan	R. Emerson/K. N. Fletcher	6–2	6–3	6–4			*team)*
1968	J. D. Newcombe/A. D. Roche	K. R. Rosewall/F. S. Stolle	3–6	8–6	5–7	14–12	6–3	800
1969	J. D. Newcombe/A. D. Roche	T. S. Okker/M. C. Riessen	7–5	11–9	6–3			1,000
1970	J. D. Newcombe/A. D. Roche	K. R. Rosewall/F. S. Stolle	10–8	6–3	6–1			1,000
1971	R. Emerson/R. Laver	A. R. Ashe/R. D. Ralston	4–6	9–7	6–8	6–4	6–4	750
1972	R. A. J. Hewitt/F. D. McMillan	S. R. Smith/E. Van Dillen	6–2	6–2	9–7			1,000
1973	J. S. Connors/I. Nastase	J. R. Cooper/N. A. Fraser	3–6	6–3	6–4	8–9	6–1	1,000
1974	J. D. Newcombe/A. D. Roche	R. C. Lutz/S. R. Smith	8–6	6–4	6–4			2,000
1975	V. Gerulaitis/A. Mayer	C. Dowdeswell/A. J. Stone	7–5	8–6	6–4			2,000
1976	B. E. Gottfried/R. Ramirez	R. L. Case/G. Masters	3–6	6–3	8–6	2–6	7–5	3,000
1977	R. L. Case/G. Masters	J. G. Alexander/P. C. Dent	6–3	6–4	3–6	8–9	6–4	6,000
1978	R. A. J. Hewitt/F. D. McMillan	P. Fleming/J. P. McEnroe	6–1	6–4	6–2			7,500

1979	P. Fleming/J. P. McEnroe	B. E. Gottfried/R. Ramirez	4–6	6–4	6–2	6–2		8,000
1980	P. McNamara/P. McNamee	R. C. Lutz/S. R. Smith	7–6	6–3	6–7	6–4		8,400
1981	P. Fleming/J. P. McEnroe	R. C. Lutz/S. R. Smith	6–4	6–4	6–4			9,070
1982	P. McNamara/P. McNamee	P. Fleming/J. P. McEnroe	6–3	6–2				16,666
1983	P. Fleming/J. P. McEnroe	T. E./T. R. Gullikson	6–4	6–3	6–4			26,628
1984	P. Fleming/J. P. McEnroe	P. Cash/P. McNamee	6–2	5–7	6–2	3–6	6–3	40,000
1985	H. P. Gunthardt/B. Taroczy	P. Cash/J. Fitzgerald	6–4	6–3	4–6	6–3		47,500
1986	J. Nystrom/M. Wilander	G. Donnelly/P. Fleming	7–6	6–3	6–3			48,500
1987	K. Flach/R. Seguso	S. Casal/E. Sanchez	3–6	6–7	7–6	6–1	6–4	53,730
1988	K. Flach/R. Seguso	J. Fitzgerald/A. Jarryd	6–4	2–6	6–4	7–6		57,200
1989	J. B. Fitzgerald/A. Jarryd	R. Leach/J. Pugh	3–6	7–6	6–4	7–6		65,870
1990	R. Leach/J. Pugh	P. Aldrich/D. Visser	7–6	7–6	7–6			94,230
1991	J. B. Fitzgerald/A. Jarryd	J. Franai/L. Lavalle	6–3	6–4	6–7	6–1		98,330
1992	J. P. McEnroe/M. Stich	J. Grabb/R. Reneberg	5–7	7–6	3–6	7–6	19–17	108,570
1993	T. Woodbridge/M. Woodforde	G. Connell/P. Galbraith	7–5	6–3	7–6			124,960
1994	T. Woodbridge/M. Woodforde	G. Connell/P. Galbraith	7–6	6–3	6–1			141,350
1995	T. Woodbridge/M. Woodforde	R. Leach/S. Melville	7–5	7–6	7–6			149,450
1996	T. Woodbridge/M. Woodforde	B. Black/G. Connell	4–6	6–1	6–3	6–2		160,810
1997	T. Woodbridge/M. Woodforde	J. Eltingh/P. Haarhuis	7–6	7–6	5–7	6–3		170,030

WOMEN'S DOUBLES

	CHAMPIONS	*RUNNERS-UP*	*SCORE*		
1913	R. J. McNair/P. D. H. Boothby	A. Sterry/R. Lambert Chambers	4–6	2–4	ret'd
1914	A. M. Morton/E. Ryan	F. J. Hannam/D. R. Larcombe	6–1	6–3	
1915–1918		*Not held*			
1919	S. Lenglen/E. Ryan	R. Lambert Chambers/D. R. Larcombe	4–6	7–5	6–3
1920	S. Lenglen/E. Ryan	R. Lambert Chambers/D. R. Larcombe	6–4	6–0	
1921	S. Lenglen/E. Ryan	A. E. Beamish/G. E. Peacock	6–1	6–2	
1922	S. Lenglen/E. Ryan	K. McKane/A. D. Stocks	6–0	6–4	
1923	S. Lenglen/E. Ryan	J. Austin/E. L. Colyer	6–3	6–1	
1924	G. Wightman/H. N. Wills	B. C. Covell/K. McKane	6–4	6–4	
1925	S. Lenglen/E. Ryan	A. V. Bridge/C. G. McIlquham	6–2	6–2	
1926	M. K. Browne/E. Ryan	L. A. Godfree/E. L. Colyer	6–1	6–1	
1927	H. N. Wills/E. Ryan	E. L. Heine/G. Peacock	6–3	6–2	
1928	P. Saunders/M. Watson	E. Bennett/E. H. Harvey	6–2	6–3	
1929	L. R. C. Michell/M. Watson	B. C. Covell/W. P. Shepherd-Barron	6–4	8–6	
1930	F. S. Moody/E. Ryan	E. Cross/S. Palfrey	6–2	9–7	
1931	W. P. Shepherd–Barron/P. E. Mudford	D. Metaxa/J. Sigart	3–6	6–3	6–4
1932	D. Metaxa/J. Sigart	H. H. Jacobs/E. Ryan	6–4	6–3	
1933	R. Mathieu/E. Ryan	W. A. James/A. M. Yorke	6–2	9–11	6–4
1934	R. Mathieu/E. Ryan	D. B. Andrus/S. Henrotin	6–3	6–3	
1935	F. James/K. E. Stammers	R. Mathieu/S. Sperling	6–1	6–4	
1936	F. James/K. E. Stammers	M. Fabyan/H. H. Jacobs	6–2	6–1	
1937	S. Mathieu/A. M. Yorke	M. R. King/J. B. Pittman	6–3	6–3	
1938	M. Fabyan/A. Marble	R. Mathieu/A. M. Yorke	6–2	6–3	
1939	M. Fabyan/A. Marble	H. H. Jacobs/A. M. Yorke	6–1	6–0	
1940–1945		*Not held*			
1946	A. L. Brough/M. E. Osborne	P. M. Betz/D. J. Hart	6–3	2–6	6–3
1947	D. J. Hart/R. B. Todd	A. L. Brough/M. E. Osborne	3–6	6–4	7–5
1948	A. L. Brough/W. du Pont	D. J. Hart/R. B. Todd	6–3	3–6	6–3
1949	A. L. Brough/W. du Pont	G. Moran/R. B. Todd	8–6	7–5	
1950	A. L. Brough/W. du Pont	S. J. Fry/D. J. Hart	6–4	5–7	6–1
1951	S. J. Fry/D. J. Hart	A. L. Brough/W. du Pont	6–3	13–11	
1952	S. J. Fry/D. J. Hart	A. L. Brough/M. Connolly	8–6	6–3	
1953	S. J. Fry/D. J. Hart	M. Connolly/J. Sampson	6–0	6–0	
1954	A. L. Brough/W. du Pont	S. J. Fry/D. J. Hart	4–6	9–7	6–3
1955	A. Mortimer/J. A. Shilcock	S. J. Bloomer/P. E. Ward	7–5	6–1	
1956	A. Buxton/A. Gibson	F. Muller/D. G. Seeney	6–1	8–6	
1957	A. Gibson/D. R. Hard	K. Hawton/M. N. Long	6–1	6–2	
1958	M. E. Bueno/A. Gibson	W. du Pont/M. Varner	6–3	7–5	
1959	J. Arth/D. R. Hard	J. G. Fleitz/C. C. Truman	2–6	6–2	6–3
1960	M. E. Bueno/D. R. Hard	S. Reynolds/R. Schuurman	6–4	6–0	
1961	K. Hantz/B. J. Moffitt	J. Lehane/M. Smith	6–3	6–4	
1962	B. J. Moffitt/J. R. Susman	L. E. G. Price/R. Schuurman	5–7	6–3	7–5
1963	M. E. Bueno/D. R. Hard	R. A. Ebbern/M. Smith	8–6	9–7	
1964	M. Smith/L. R. Turner	B. J. Moffitt/J. R. Susman	7–5	6–2	

						PRIZE (£ per team)
1965	M. E. Bueno/B. J. Moffitt	F. Durr/J. Lieffrig	6–2	7–5		
1966	M. E. Bueno/N. Richey	M. Smith/J. A. M. Tegart	6–3	4–6	6–4	
1967	R. Casals/L. W. King	M. E. Bueno/N. Richey	9–11	6–4	6–2	
1968	R. Casals/L. W. King	F. Durr/P. F. Jones	3–6	6–4	7–5	500
1969	B. M. Court/J. A. M. Tegart	P. S. A. Hogan/M. Michel	9–7	6–2		600
1970	R. Casals/L. W. King	F. Durr/S. V. Wade	6–2	6–3		600
1971	R. Casals/L. W. King	B. M. Court/E. Goolagong	6–3	6–2		450
1972	L. W. King/B. Stove	D. E. Dalton/F. Durr	6–2	4–6	6–3	600
1973	R. Casals/L. W. King	F. Durr/B. Stove	6–1	4–6	7–5	600
1974	E. F. Goolagong/M. Michel	H. F. Gourlay/K. M. Krantzcke	2–6	6–4	6–3	1,200
1975	A. Kiyomura/K. Sawamatsu	F. Durr/B. Stove	7–5	1–6	7–5	1,200
1976	C. Evert/M. Navratilova	L. W. King/B. Stove	6–1	3–6	7–5	2,400
1977	R. L. Cawley/J. C. Russell	M. Navratilova/B. Stove	6–3	6–3		5,200
1978	G. E. Reid/W. Turnbull	M. Jausovec/V. Ruzici	4–6	9–8	6–3	6,500
1979	L. W. King/M. Navratilova	B. Stove/W. M. Turnbull	5–7	6–3	6–2	6,930
1980	K. Jordan/A. E. Smith	R. Casals/W. M. Turnbull	4–6	7–5	6–1	7,276
1981	M. Navratilova/P. H. Shriver	K. Jordan/A. E. Smith	6–3	7–6		7,854
1982	M. Navratilova/P. H. Shriver	K. Jordan/A. E. Smith	6–4	6–1		14,450
1983	M. Navratilova/P. H. Shriver	R. Casals/W. M. Turnbull	6–2	6–2		23,100
1984	M. Navratilova/P. H. Shriver	K. Jordan/A. E. Smith	6–3	6–4		34,700
1985	K. Jordan/P. D. Smylie	M. Navratilova/P. H. Shriver	5–7	6–3	6–4	41,100
1986	M. Navratilova/P. H. Shriver	H. Mandlikova/W. M. Turnbull	6–1	6–3		42,060
1987	C. Kohde-Kilsch/H. Sukova	B. Nagelsen/P. D. Smylie	7–5	7–5		46,500
1988	S. Graf/G. Sabatini	L. Savchenko/N. Zvereva	6–3	1–6	12–10	49,500
1989	J. Novotna/H. Sukova	L. Savchenko/N. Zvereva	6–1	6–2		56,970
1990	J. Novotna/H. Sukova	K. Jordan/P. D. Smylie	6–3	6–4		81,510
1991	L. Savchenko/N. Zvereva	G. Fernandez/J. Novotna	6–4	3–6	6–4	85,060
1992	G. Fernandez/N. Zvereva	J. Novotna/L. Savchenko-Neiland	6–4	6–1		93,920
1993	G. Fernandez/N. Zvereva	L. Neiland/J. Novotna	6–4	6–7	6–4	108,100
1994	G. Fernandez/N. Zvereva	J. Novotna/A. Sanchez Vicario	6–4	6–1		122,200
1995	J. Novotna/A. Sanchez Vicario	G. Fernandez/N. Zvereva	5–7	7–5	6–4	129,300
1996	M.Hingis/H. Sukova	M. J. McGrath/L. Neiland	5–7	7–5	6–1	139,040
1997	G. Fernandez/N. Zvereva	N. Arendt/M. Bollegraf	6–1	6–2		147,010

MIXED DOUBLES

	CHAMPIONS	*RUNNERS-UP*	*SCORE*		
1913	H. Crisp/Mrs C. O. Tuckey	J. C. Parke/Mrs D. R. Larcombe	3–6	5–3	ret'd
1914	J. C. Parke/Mrs D. R. Larcombe	A. F. Wilding/Mlle M. Broquedis	4–6	6–4	6–2
1915–1918		*Not held*			
1919	R. Lycett/Miss E. Ryan	A. D. Prebble/Mrs R. Lamb. Chambers	6–0	6–0	
1920	G. L. Patterson/Mlle S. Lenglen	R. Lycett/Miss E. Ryan	7–5	6–3	
1921	R. Lycett/Miss E. Ryan	M. Woosnam/Miss P. L. Howkins	6–3	6–1	
1922	P. O'Hara Wood/Mlle S. Lenglen	R. Lycett/Miss E. Ryan	6–4	6–3	
1923	R. Lycett/Miss E. Ryan	L. S. Deane/Mrs W. P. Shep.–Barron	6–4	7–5	
1924	J. B. Gilbert/Miss K. McKane	L. A. Godfree/Mrs W. P. Shep.d–Barron	6–3	3–6	6–3
1925	J. Borotra/Mlle S. Lenglen	V. L. de Morpurgo/Miss E. Ryan	6–3	6–3	
1926	L. A./Mrs Godfree	H. Kinsey/Miss M. K. Browne	6–3	6–4	
1927	F. T. Hunter/Miss E. Ryan	L. A./Mrs Godfree	8–6	6–0	
1928	P. D. B. Spence/Miss E. Ryan	J. H. Crawford/Miss D. S. Akhurst	7–5	6–4	
1929	F. T. Hunter/Miss H. N. Wills	I. G. Collins/Miss J. Fry	6–1	6–4	
1930	J. H. Crawford/Miss E. Ryan	D. Prenn/Frl H. Krahwinkel	6–1	6–3	
1931	G. M. Lott/Mrs L. A. Harper	I. G. Collins/Miss J. C. Ridley	6–3	1–6	6–1
1932	E. Maier/Miss E. Ryan	H. C. Hopman/Mlle J. Sigart	7–5	6–2	
1933	G. von Cramm/Frl H. Krahwinkel	N. G. Farquharson/Miss M. Heeley	7–5	8–6	
1934	R. Miki/Miss D. E. Round	H. W. Austin/Mrs W. P. Shep.–Barron	3–6	6–4	6–0
1935	F. J. Perry/Miss D. E. Round	H. C./Mrs Hopman	7–5	4–6	6–2
1936	F. J. Perry/Miss D. E. Round	J. D. Budge/Mrs M. Fabyan	7–9	7–5	6–4
1937	J. D. Budge/Miss A. Marble	Y. Petra/Mme R. Mathieu	6–4	6–1	
1938	J. D. Budge/Miss A. Marble	H. Henkel/Mrs M. Fabyan	6–1	6–4	
1939	R. L. Riggs/Miss A. Marble	F. H. D. Wilde/Miss N. B. Brown	9–7	6–1	
1940–1945		*Not held*			
1946	T. Brown/Miss A. L. Brough	G. E. Brown/Miss D. Bundy	6–4	6–4	
1947	J. E. Bromwich/Miss A. L. Brough	C. F. Long/Mrs N. M. Bolton	1–6	6–4	6–2
1948	J. E. Bromwich/Miss A. L. Brough	F. A. Sedgman/Miss D. J. Hart	6–2	3–6	6–3
1949	E. W. Sturgess/Mrs R. A. Summers	J. E. Bromwich/Miss A. L. Brough	9–7	9–11	7–5
1950	E. W. Sturgess/Miss A. L. Brough	G. E. Brown/Mrs R.B. Todd	11–9	1–6	6–4

						FIRST PRIZE (£ per team)
1951	F. A. Sedgman/Miss D. J. Hart	M. G. Rose/Mrs G. F. Bolton	7–5	6–2		
1952	F. A. Sedgman/Miss D. J. Hart	E. Morea/Mrs M. N. Long	4–6	6–3	6–4	
1953	E. V. Seixas/Miss D. J. Hart	E. Morea/Miss S. J. Fry	9–7	7–5		
1954	E. V. Seixas/Miss D. J. Hart	K. R. Rosewall/Mrs W. du Pont	5–7	6–4	6–3	
1955	E. V. Seixas/Miss D. J. Hart	E. Morea/Miss A. L. Brough	8–6	2–6	6–3	
1956	E. V. Seixas/Miss S. J. Fry	G. Mulloy/Miss A. Gibson	2–6	6–2	7–5	
1957	M. G. Rose/Miss D. R. Hard	N. A. Fraser/Miss A. Gibson	6–4	7–5		
1958	R. N. Howe/Miss L. Coghlan	K. Nielsen/Miss A. Gibson	6–3	13–11		
1959	R. Laver/Miss D. R. Hard	N. A. Fraser/Miss M. E. Bueno	6–4	6–3		
1960	R. Laver/Miss D. R. Hard	R. N. Howe/Miss M. E. Bueno	13–11	3–6	8–6	
1961	F. S. Stolle/Miss L. R. Turner	R. N. Howe/Miss E. Buding	11–9	6–2		
1962	N. A. Fraser/Mrs W. du Pont	R. D. Ralston/Miss A. S. Haydon	2–6	6–3	13–11	
1963	K. N. Fletcher/Miss M. Smith	R. A. J. Hewitt/Miss D. R. Hard	11–9	6–4		
1964	F. S. Stolle/Miss L. R. Turner	K. N. Fletcher/Miss M. Smith	6–4	6–4		
1965	K. N. Fletcher/Miss M. Smith	A. D. Roche/Miss J. A. M. Tegart	12–10	6–3		
1966	K. N. Fletcher/Miss M. Smith	R. D. Ralston/Mrs L. W. King	4–6	6–3	6–3	
1967	O. K. Davidson/Mrs L. W. King	K. N. Fletcher/Miss M. E. Bueno	7–5	6–2		
1968	K. N. Fletcher/Mrs B. M. Court	A. Metreveli/Miss O. Morozova	6–1	14–12		450
1969	F. S. Stolle/Mrs P. F. Jones	A. D. Roche/Miss J. A. M. Tegart	6–2	6–3		500
1970	I. Nastase/Miss R. Casals	A. Metreveli/Miss O. Morozova	6–3	4–6	9–7	500
1971	O. K. Davidson/Mrs L. W. King	M. C. Rieseen/Mrs B. M. Court	3–6	6–2	15–13	375
1972	I. Nastase/Miss R. Casals	K. Warwick/Miss E. Goolagong	6–4	6–4		500
1973	O. K. Davidson/Mrs L. W. King	R. C. Ramirez/Miss J. Newberry	6–3	6–2		500
1974	O. K. Davidson/Mrs L. W. King	M. J. Farrell/Miss L. J. Charles	6–3	9–7		1,000
1975	M. C. Riessen/Mrs B. M. Court	A. J. Stone/Miss B. Stove	6–4	7–5		1,000
1976	A. D. Roche/Miss F. Durr	R. L. Stockton/Miss R. Casals	6–3	2–6	7–5	2,000
1977	R. A. J. Hewitt/Miss G. R. Stevens	F. D. McMillan/Miss B. Stove	3–6	7–5	6–4	3,000
1978	F. D. McMillan/Miss B. Stove	R. O. Ruffels/Mrs L. W. King	6–2	6–2		4,000
1979	R. A. J. Hewitt/Miss G. R. Stevens	F. D. McMillan/Miss B. Stove	7–5	7–6		4,200
1980	J. R. Austin/Miss T. Austin	M. R. Edmondson/Miss D. L. Fromholtz	4–6	7–6	6–3	4,420
1981	F. D. McMillan/Miss B. Stove	J. R. Austin/Miss T. Austin	4–6	7–6	6–3	4,770
1982	K. Curren/Miss A. E. Smith	J. M. Lloyd/Miss W. M. Turnbull	2–6	6–3	7–5	6,750
1983	J. M. Lloyd/Miss W. M. Turnbull	S. Denton/Mrs L. W. King	6–7	7–6	7–5	12,000
1984	J. M. Lloyd/Miss W. M. Turnbull	S. Denton/Miss K. Jordan	6–3	6–3		18,000
1985	P. McNamee/Miss M. Navratilova	J. Fitzgerald/Mrs P. D. Smylie	7–5	4–6	6–2	23,400
1986	K. Flach/Miss K. Jordan	H. P. Gunthardt/Miss M. Navratilova	6–3	7–6		25,200
1987	M. J. Bates/Miss J. M. Durie	D. Cahill/Miss N. Provis	7–6	6–3		27,900
1988	S. E. Stewart/Miss Z. Garrison	K. Jones/Mrs S. W. Magers	6–1	7–6		29,700
1989	J. Pugh/Miss J. Novotna	M. Kratzmann/Miss J. Byrne	6–4	5–7	6–4	34,200
1990	R. Leach/Miss Z. Garrison	J. Fitzgerald/Mrs P. D. Smylie	7–5	6–2		40,000
1991	J. B. Fitzgerald/Mrs P. D. Smylie	J. Pugh/Miss N. Zvereva	7–6	6–2		41,720
1992	C. Suk/Mrs L. Savchenko Neiland	J. Eltingh/Miss M. Oremans	7–6	6–2		46,070
1993	M. Woodforde/Miss M. Navratilova	T. Nijssen/Miss M. Bollegraf	6–3	6–4		53,020
1994	T. Woodbridge/Miss H. Sukova	T. Middleton/Miss L. McNeil	3–6	7–5	6–3	60,000
1995	J. Stark/Miss M. Navratilova	C. Suk/Miss G. Fernandez	6–4	6–4		63,500
1996	C. Suk/Miss H. Sukova	M. Woodforde/Miss L. Neiland	1–6	6–3	6–2	68,280
1997	C. Suk/Miss H. Sukova	A. Olhovskiy/Mrs L. Neiland	4–6	6–2	6–3	72,200

US CHAMPIONSHIPS

1. Challenge Round: A Challenge Round was introduced in the men's singles in 1884 and discontinued following the 1911 Championship. It was introduced in the women's singles in 1888 and discontinued following the 1919 Championship. In men's doubles it was instituted in 1881 and abolished in 1918, restored in 1919 and finally abolished in 1920. In the years marked with an asterisk (*) the holder did not defend his/her title so the winner of the All-Comers Singles became the champion. From 1891–1901 inclusive (but not in 1893) the women's singles final was contested over five sets. **2. The War Years:** In 1917 a National Patriotic Tournament was held in all five events. The winners were not recognised as National Champions. During World War II (1942–45) all five National Championships were staged together at the West Side Tennis Club, Forest Hills, N.Y. **3. Last Amateur Events:** During the first two years of Open Tennis (1968–69) a National Amateur Championship was held for all five events at the Longwood Cricket Club, Boston, as well as an Open Championship at Forest Hills, New York (although there was no open mixed in 1968). Thereafter the Amateur event was discontinued. **4. Dress:** The 'predominantly white' clothing rule was last enforced at the 1971 Championships. **5. Prize Money:** Equal prize money for men and women was introduced in 1973. **6. Surfaces:** 1881–1974 Grass; 1975–77 American clay (Har-Tru); 1978–present Hard courts (DecoTurf II). **7. Venues:** *Men's singles:* 1881–1914 The Casino, Newport, RI. 1915–20 West Side Tennis Club, Forest Hills, NY. 1921–23 Germantown Cricket Club, Philadelphia, PA. 1924–77 West Side Tennis Club, Forest Hills, NY. 1978–present National Tennis Center, Flushing Meadows, NY. *Women's singles:* 1887–1920 Philadelphia Cricket Club, PA. 1921–77 West Side Tennis Club, Forest Hills, NY. 1978–present National Tennis Center, Flushing Meadows, NY. *Men's doubles:* 1881–1914 The Casino, Newport, RI. 1915–16 West Side Tennis Club, Forest Hills, NY. 1917–33 Longwood Cricket Club, Boston, MA. 1934 Germantown Cricket Club, Philadelphia, PA. 1935–41 Longwood Cricket Club, Boston, MA. 1942–45 West Side Tennis Club, Forest Hills, NY. 1946–69 Longwood Cricket Club, Boston, MA (1968–69 Amateur). 1968–77 West Side Tennis Club, Forest Hills, NY. 1978–present National Tennis Center, Flushing Meadows, NY. *Women's doubles:* 1887–1920 Philadelphia Cricket Club, PA (1887,1888 non-Championship). 1921–34 West Side Tennis Club, Forest Hills, NY. 1935–41 Longwood Cricket Club, Boston, MA. 1942–45 West Side Tennis Club, Forest Hills, NY. 1946–69 Longwood Cricket Club, Boston, MA (1968–69 Amateur). 1968–77 West Side Tennis Club, Forest Hills, NY. 1978– present National Tennis Center, Flushing Meadows, NY. *Mixed doubles:* 1892–1920 Philadelphia Cricket Club, PA. 1921–34 Longwood Cricket Club, Boston, MA. 1935–66 West Side Tennis Club, Forest Hills, NY. 1967–69 Longwood Cricket Club, Boston, MA. 1969–77 West Side Tennis Club, Forest Hills, NY (not held 1968). 1978–present National Tennis Center, Flushing Meadows, NY.

MEN'S SINGLES

	CHAMPION	*RUNNER-UP*	*SCORE*				
1881	R. D. Sears	W. E. Glyn	6–0	6–3	6–2		
1882	R. D. Sears	C. M. Clark	6–1	6–4	6–0		
1883	R. D. Sears	J. Dwight	6–2	6–0	9–7		
1884	R. D. Sears	H. A. Taylor	6–0	1–6	6–0	6–2	
1885	R. D. Sears	G. M. Brinley	6–3	4–6	6–0	6–3	
1886	R. D. Sears	R. L. Beeckman	4–6	6–1	6–3	6–4	
1887	R. D. Sears	H. W. Slocum	6–1	6–3	6–2		
1888*	H. W. Slocum	H. A. Taylor	6–4	6–1	6–0		
1889	H. W. Slocum	Q. A. Shaw	6–3	6–1	4–6	6–2	
1890	O. S. Campbell	H. W. Slocum	6–2	4–6	6–3	6–1	
1891	O. S. Campbell	C. Hobart	2–6	7–5	7–9	6–1	6–2
1892	O. S. Campbell	F. H. Hovey	7–5	3–6	6–3	7–5	
1893*	R. D. Wrenn	F. H. Hovey	6–4	3–6	6–4	6–4	
1894	R. D. Wrenn	M. F. Goodbody	6–8	6–1	6–4	6–4	
1895	F. H. Hovey	R. D. Wrenn	6–3	6–2	6–4		
1896	R. D. Wrenn	F. H. Hovey	7–5	3–6	6–0	1–6	6–1
1897	R. D. Wrenn	W. V. Eaves	4–6	8–6	6–3	2–6	6–2
1898*	M. D. Whitman	D. F. Davis	3–6	6–2	6–2	6–1	
1899	M. D. Whitman	J. P. Paret	6–1	6–2	3–6	7–5	
1900	M. D. Whitman	W. A. Larned	6–4	1–6	6–2	6–2	
1901*	W. A. Larned	B. C. Wright	6–2	6–8	6–4	6–4	
1902	W. A. Larned	R. F. Doherty	4–6	6–2	6–4	8–6	
1903	H. L. Doherty	W. A. Larned	6–0	6–3	10–8		
1904*	H. Ward	W. J. Clothier	10–8	6–4	9–7		
1905	B. C. Wright	H. Ward	6–2	6–1	11–9		
1906	W. J. Clothier	B. C. Wright	6–3	6–0	6–4		
1907*	W. A. Larned	R. LeRoy	6–2	6–2	6–4		
1908	W. A. Larned	B. C. Wright	6–1	6–2	8–6		
1909	W. A. Larned	W. J. Clothier	6–1	6–2	5–7	1–6	6–1
1910	W. A. Larned	T. C. Bundy	6–1	5–7	6–0	6–8	6–1
1911	W. A. Larned	M. E. McLoughlin	6–4	6–4	6–2		
1912	M. E. McLoughlin	W. F. Johnson	3–6	2–6	6–2	6–4	6–2
1913	M. E. McLoughlin	R. N. Williams	6–4	5–7	6–3	6–1	
1914	R. N. Williams	M. E. McLoughlin	6–3	8–6	10–8		
1915	W. M. Johnston	M. E. McLoughlin	1–6	6–0	7–5	10–8	

								PRIZE MONEY (US$)
1916	R. N. Williams	W. M. Johnston	4–6	6–4	0–6	6–2	6–4	
1917	R. L. Murray	N. W. Niles	5–7	8–6	6–3	6–3		
1918	R. L. Murray	W. T. Tilden	6–3	6–1	7–5			
1919	W. M. Johnston	W. T. Tilden	6–4	6–4	6–3			
1920	W. T. Tilden	W. M. Johnston	6–1	1–6	7–5	5–7	6–3	
1921	W. T. Tilden	W. M. Johnson	6–1	6–3	6–1			
1922	W. T. Tilden	W. M. Johnston	4–6	3–6	6–2	6–3	6–4	
1923	W. T. Tilden	W. M. Johnston	6–4	6–1	6–4			
1924	W. T. Tilden	W. M. Johnston	6–1	9–7	6–2			
1925	W. T. Tilden	W. M. Johnston	4–6	11–9	6–3	4–6	6–3	
1926	R. Lacoste	J. Borotra	6–4	6–0	6–4			
1927	R. Lacoste	W. T. Tilden	11–9	6–3	11–9			
1928	H. Cochet	F. T. Hunter	4–6	6–4	3–6	7–5	6–3	
1929	W. T. Tilden	F. T. Hunter	3–6	6–3	4–6	6–2	6–4	
1930	J. H. Doeg	F. X. Shields	10–8	1–6	6–4	16–14		
1931	H. E. Vines	G. M. Lott	7–9	6–3	9–7	7–5		
1932	H. E. Vines	H. Cochet	6–4	6–4	6–4			
1933	F. J. Perry	J. H. Crawford	6–3	11–13	4–6	6–0	6–1	
1934	F. J. Perry	W. L. Allison	6–4	6–3	1–6	8–6		
1935	W. L. Allison	S. B. Wood	6–2	6–2	6–3			
1936	F. J. Perry	J. D. Budge	2–6	6–2	8–6	1–6	10–8	
1937	J. D. Budge	C. Von Cramm	6–1	7–9	6–1	3–6	6–1	
1938	J. D. Budge	G. Mako	6–3	6–8	6–2	6–1		
1939	R. L. Riggs	S. W. van Horn	6–4	6–2	6–4			
1940	W. D. McNeill	R. L. Riggs	4–6	6–8	6–3	6–3	7–5	
1941	R. L. Riggs	F. Kovacs	5–7	6–1	6–3	6–3		
1942	F. R. Schroeder	F. A. Parker	8–6	7–5	3–6	4–6	6–2	
1943	J. R. Hunt	J. A. Kramer	6–3	6–8	10–8	6–0		
1944	F. A. Parker	W. F. Talbert	6–4	3–6	6–3	6–3		
1945	F. A. Parker	W. F. Talbert	14–12	6–1	6–2			
1946	J. A. Kramer	T. P. Brown	9–7	6–3	6–0			
1947	J. A. Kramer	F. A. Parker	4–6	2–6	6–1	6–0	6–3	
1948	R. A. Gonzales	E. W. Sturgess	6–2	6–3	14–12			
1949	R. A. Gonzales	F. R. Schroeder	16–18	2–6	6–1	6–2	6–4	
1950	A. Larsen	H. Flam	6–3	4–6	5–7	6–4	6–3	
1951	F. A. Sedgman	E. V. Seixas	6–4	6–1	6–1			
1952	F. A. Sedgman	G. Mulloy	6–1	6–2	6–3			
1953	M. A. Trabert	E. V. Seixas	6–3	6–2	6–3			
1954	E. V. Seixas	R. N. Hartwig	3–6	6–2	6–4	6–4		
1955	M. A. Trabert	K. R. Rosewall	9–7	6–3	6–3			
1956	K. R. Rosewall	L. A. Hoad	4–6	6–2	6–3	6–3		
1957	M. J. Anderson	A. J. Cooper	10–8	7–5	6–4			
1958	A. J. Cooper	M. J. Anderson	6–2	3–6	4–6	10–8	8–6	
1959	N. A. Fraser	A. Olmedo	6–3	5–7	6–2	6–4		
1960	N. A. Fraser	R. G. Laver	6–4	6–4	9–7			
1961	R. S. Emerson	R. G. Laver	7–5	6–3	6–2			
1962	R. G. Laver	R. S. Emerson	6–2	6–4	5–7	6–4		
1963	R. H. Osuna	F. Froehling	7–5	6–4	6–2			
1964	R. S. Emerson	F. S. Stolle	6–4	6–2	6–4			
1965	M. Santana	E. C. Drysdale	6–2	7–9	7–5	6–1		
1966	F. S. Stolle	J. D. Newcombe	4–6	12–10	6–3	6–4		
1967	J. D. Newcombe	C. Graebner	6–4	6–4	8–6			
1968#	A. R. Ashe	R. C. Lutz	4–6	6–3	8–10	6–0	6–4	
1969#	S. R. Smith	R. C. Lutz	9–7	6–3	6–1			
1968	A. R. Ashe	T. S. Okker	14–12	5–7	6–3	3–6	6–3	14,000
1969	R. G. Laver	A. D. Roche	7–9	6–1	6–2	6–2		16,000
1970	K. R. Rosewall	A. D. Roche	2–6	6–4	7–6	6–3		20,000
1971	S. R. Smith	J. Kodes	3–6	6–3	6–2	7–6		15,000
1972	I. Nastase	A. R. Ashe	3–6	6–3	6–7	6–4	6–3	25,000
1973	J. D. Newcombe	J. Kodes	6–4	1–6	4–6	6–2	6–2	25,000
1974	J. S. Connors	K. R. Rosewall	6–1	6–0	6–1			22,500
1975	M. Orantes	J. S. Connors	6–4	6–3	6–3			25,000
1976	J. S. Connors	B. Borg	6–4	3–6	7–6	6–4		30,000
1977	G. Vilas	J. S. Connors	2–6	6–3	7–5	6–0		33,000
1978	J. S. Connors	B. Borg	6–4	6–2	6–2			38,000
1979	J. P. McEnroe	V. Gerulaitis	7–5	6–3	6–3			39,000

1980	J. P. McEnroe	B. Borg	7–6	6–1	6–7	5–7	6–4	46,000
1981	J. P. McEnroe	B. Borg	4–6	6–2	6–4	6–3		60,000
1982	J. S. Connors	I. Lendl	6–3	6–2	4–6	6–4		90,000
1983	J. S. Connors	I. Lendl	6–3	6–7	7–5	6–0		120,000
1984	J. P. McEnroe	I. Lendl	6–3	6–4	6–1			160,000
1985	I. Lendl	J. P. McEnroe	7–6	6–3	6–4			187,500
1986	I. Lendl	M. Mecir	6–4	6–2	6–0			210,000
1987	I. Lendl	M. Wilander	6–7	6–0	7–6	6–4		250,000
1988	M. Wilander	I. Lendl	6–4	4–6	6–3	5–7	6–4	275,000
1989	B. Becker	I. Lendl	7–6	1–6	6–3	7–6		300,000
1990	P. Sampras	A. Agassi	6–4	6–3	6–2			350,000
1991	S. Edberg	J. Courier	6–2	6–4	6–0			400,000
1992	S. Edberg	P. Sampras	3–6	6–4	7–6	6–2		500,000
1993	P. Sampras	C. Pioline	6–4	6–4	6–3			535,000
1994	A. Agassi	M. Stich	6–1	7–6	7–5			550,000
1995	P. Sampras	A. Agassi	6–4	6–3	4–6	7–5		575,000
1996	P. Sampras	M. Chang	6–1	6–4	7–6			600,000
1997	P. Rafter	G. Rusedski	6–3	6–2	4–6	7–5		650,000

WOMEN'S SINGLES

	CHAMPION	*RUNNER-UP*	*SCORE*				
1887	Miss E. Hansell	Miss L. Knight	6–1	6–0			
1888	Miss B. L. Townsend	Miss E. Hansell	6–3	6–5			
1889	Miss B. L. Townsend	Miss L. D. Voorhees	7–5	6–2			
1890	Miss E. C. Roosevelt	Miss B. L. Townsend	6–2	6–2			
1891	Miss M. E. Cahill	Miss E. C. Roosevelt	6–4	6–1	4–6	6–3	
1892	Miss M. E. Cahill	Miss E. H. Moore	5–7	6–3	6–4	4–6	6–2
1893*	Miss A. Terry	Miss A. L. Schultz	6–1	6–3			
1894	Miss H. Hellwig	Miss A. Terry	7–5	3–6	6–0	3–6	6–3
1895	Miss J. Atkinson	Miss H. Hellwig	6–4	6–2	6–1		
1896	Miss E. H. Moore	Miss J. Atkinson	6–4	4–6	6–2	6–2	
1897	Miss J. Atkinson	Miss E. H. Moore	6–3	6–3	4–6	3–6	6–3
1898	Miss J. Atkinson	Miss M. Jones	6–3	5–7	6–4	2–6	7–5
1899*	Miss M. Jones	Miss M. Banks	6–1	6–1	7–5		
1900*	Miss M. McAteer	Miss E. Parker	6–2	6–2	6–0		
1901	Miss E. H. Moore	Miss M. McAteer	6–4	3–6	7–5	2–6	6–2
1902	Miss M. Jones	Miss E. H. Moore	6–1	1–0	ret'd		
1903	Miss E. H. Moore	Miss M. Jones	7–5	8–6			
1904	Miss M. G. Sutton	Miss E. H. Moore	6–1	6–2			
1905*	Miss E. H. Moore	Miss H. Homans	6–4	5–7	6–1		
1906*	Miss H. Homans	Mrs M. Barger-Wallach	6–4	6–3			
1907*	Miss Evelyn Sears	Miss C. Neely	6–3	6–2			
1908	Mrs M. Barger-Wallach	Miss Evelyn Sears	6–3	1–6	6–3		
1909	Miss H. Hotchkiss	Mrs M. Barger-Wallach	6–0	6–1			
1910	Miss H. Hotchkiss	Miss L. Hammond	6–4	6–2			
1911	Miss H. Hotchkiss	Miss F. Sutton	8–10	6–1	9–7		
1912*	Miss M. K. Browne	Miss Eleanora Sears	6–4	6–2			
1913	Miss M. K. Browne	Miss D. Green	6–2	7–5			
1914	Miss M. K. Browne	Miss M. Wagner	6–2	1–6	6–1		
1915*	Miss M. Bjurstedt	Mrs G. W. Wightman	4–6	6–2	6–0		
1916	Miss M. Bjurstedt	Mrs L. H. Raymond	6–0	6–1			
1917	Miss M. Bjurstedt	Miss M. Vanderhoef	4–6	6–0	6–2		
1918	Miss M. Bjurstedt	Miss E. E. Goss	6–4	6–3			
1919	Mrs G. W. Wightman	Miss M. Zinderstein	6–1	6–2			
1920	Mrs F. Mallory	Miss M. Zinderstein	6–3	6–1			
1921	Mrs F. Mallory	Miss M. K. Browne	4–6	6–4	6–2		
1922	Mrs F. Mallory	Miss H. N. Wills	6–3	6–1			
1923	Miss H. N. Wills	Mrs F. Mallory	6–2	6–1			
1924	Miss H. N. Wills	Mrs F. Mallory	6–1	6–3			
1925	Miss H. N. Wills	Miss K. McKane	3–6	6–0	6–2		
1926	Mrs F. Mallory	Miss E. Ryan	4–6	6–4	9–7		
1927	Miss H. N. Wills	Miss B. Nuthall	6–1	6–4			
1928	Miss H. N. Wills	Miss H. H. Jacobs	6–2	6–1			
1929	Miss H. N. Wills	Mrs P. H. Watson	6–4	6–2			
1930	Miss B. Nuthall	Mrs L. A. Harper	6–1	6–4			
1931	Mrs F. S. Moody	Mrs F. Whittingstall	6–4	6–1			

							FIRST PRIZE (US$)
1932	Miss H. H. Jacobs	Miss C. A. Babcock	6–2	6–2			
1933	Miss H. H. Jacobs	Mrs F. S. Moody	8–6	3–6	3–0	ret'd	
1934	Miss H. H. Jacobs	Miss S. Palfrey	6–1	6–4			
1935	Miss H. H. Jacobs	Mrs S. P. Fabyan	6–2	6–4			
1936	Miss A. Marble	Miss H. H. Jacobs	4–6	6–3	6–2		
1937	Miss A. Lizana	Miss J. Jedrzejowksa	6–4	6–2			
1938	Miss A. Marble	Miss N. Wynne	6–0	6–3			
1939	Miss A. Marble	Miss H. H. Jacobs	6–0	8–10	6–4		
1940	Miss A. Marble	Miss H. H. Jacobs	6–2	6–3			
1941	Mrs E. T. Cooke	Miss P. M. Betz	7–5	6–2			
1942	Miss P. M. Betz	Miss A. L. Brough	4–6	6–1	6–4		
1943	Miss P. M. Betz	Miss A. L. Brough	6–3	5–7	6–3		
1944	Miss P. M. Betz	Miss M. E. Osborne	6–3	8–6			
1945	Mrs E. T. Cooke	Miss P. M. Betz	3–6	8–6	6–4		
1946	Miss P. M. Betz	Miss P. C. Canning	11–9	6–3			
1947	Miss A. L. Brough	Miss M. E. Osborne	8–6	4–6	6–1		
1948	Mrs W. D. du Pont	Miss A. L. Brough	4–6	6–4	15–13		
1949	Mrs W. D. du Pont	Miss D. J. Hart	6–3	6–1			
1950	Mrs W. D. du Pont	Miss D. J. Hart	6–4	6–3			
1951	Miss M. Connolly	Miss S. J. Fry	6–3	1–6	6–4		
1952	Miss M. Connolly	Miss D. J. Hart	6–3	7–5			
1953	Miss M. Connolly	Miss D. J. Hart	6–2	6–4			
1954	Miss D. J. Hart	Miss A. L. Brough	6–8	6–1	8–6		
1955	Miss D. J. Hart	Miss P. E. Ward	6–4	6–2			
1956	Miss S. J. Fry	Miss A. Gibson	6–3	6–4			
1957	Miss A. Gibson	Miss A. L. Brough	6–3	6–2			
1958	Miss A. Gibson	Miss D. R. Hard	3–6	6–1	6–2		
1959	Miss M. E. Bueno	Miss C. C. Truman	6–1	6–4			
1960	Miss D. R. Hard	Miss M. E. Bueno	6–4	10–12	6–4		
1961	Miss D. R. Hard	Miss A. S. Haydon	6–3	6–4			
1962	Miss M. Smith	Miss D. R. Hard	9–7	6–4			
1963	Miss M. E. Bueno	Miss M. Smith	7–5	6–4			
1964	Miss M. E. Bueno	Mrs C. Graebner	6–1	6–0			
1965	Miss M. Smith	Miss B. J. Moffitt	8–6	7–5			
1966	Miss M. E. Bueno	Miss N. Richey	6–3	6–1			
1967	Mrs L. W. King	Mrs P. F. Jones	11–9	6–4			
1968#	Mrs B. M. Court	Miss M. E. Bueno	6–2	6–2			
1969#	Mrs B. M. Court	Miss S. V. Wade	4–6	6–3	6–0		
1968	Miss S. V. Wade	Mrs L. W. King	6–4	6–2			6,000
1969	Mrs B. M. Court	Miss N. Richey	6–2	6–2			6,000
1970	Mrs B. M. Court	Miss R. Casals	6–2	2–6	6–1		7,500
1971	Mrs L. W. King	Miss R. Casals	6–4	7–6			5,000
1972	Mrs L. W. King	Miss K. Melville	6–3	7–5			10,000
1973	Mrs B. M. Court	Miss E. Goolagong	7–6	5–7	6–2		25,000
1974	Mrs L. W. King	Miss E. Goolagong	3–6	6–3	7–5		22,500
1975	Miss C. M. Evert	Mrs R. A. Cawley	5–7	6–4	6–2		25,000
1976	Miss C. M. Evert	Mrs R. A. Cawley	6–3	6–0			30,000
1977	Miss C. M. Evert	Miss W. Turnbull	7–6	6–2			33,000
1978	Miss C. M. Evert	Miss P. Shriver	7–5	6–4			38,000
1979	Miss T. A. Austin	Miss C. M. Evert	6–4	6–3			39,000
1980	Mrs J. M. Lloyd	Miss H. Mandlikova	5–7	6–1	6–1		46,000
1981	Miss T. A. Austin	Miss M. Navratilova	1–6	7–6	7–6		60,000
1982	Mrs J. M. Lloyd	Miss H. Mandlikova	6–3	6–1			90,000
1983	Miss M. Navratilova	Mrs J. M. Lloyd	6–1	6–3			120,000
1984	Miss M. Navratilova	Mrs J. M. Lloyd	4–6	6–4	6–4		160,000
1985	Miss H. Mandlikova	Miss M. Navratilova	7–6	1–6	7–6		187,500
1986	Miss M. Navratilova	Miss H. Sukova	6–3	6–2			210,000
1987	Miss M. Navratilova	Miss S. Graf	7–6	6–1			250,000
1988	Miss S. Graf	Miss G. Sabatini	6–3	3–6	6–1		275,000
1989	Miss S. Graf	Miss M. Navratilova	3–6	7–5	6–1		300,000
1990	Miss G. Sabatini	Miss S. Graf	6–2	7–6			350,000
1991	Miss M. Seles	Miss M. Navratilova	7–6	6–1			400,000
1992	Miss M. Seles	Miss A. Sanchez Vicario	6–3	6–3			500,000
1993	Miss S. Graf	Miss H. Sukova	6–3	6–3			535,000
1994	Miss A. Sanchez Vicario	Miss S. Graf	1–6	7–6	6–4		550,000
1995	Miss S. Graf	Miss M. Seles	7–6	0–6	6–3		575,000

1996	Miss S. Graf	Miss M. Seles	7–5	6–4	600,000
1997	Miss M. Hingis	Miss V. Williams	6–0	6–4	650,000

MEN'S DOUBLES

	CHAMPIONS	*RUNNERS-UP*	*SCORE*				
1881	C. M. Clark/F. W. Taylor	A. Van Rensselaer/A.E. Newbold	6–5	6–4	6–5		
1882	J. Dwight/R. D. Sears	W. Nightingale/G. M. Smith	6–2	6–4	6–4		
1883	J. Dwight/R. D. Sears	A. Van Rensselaer/A.E. Newbold	6–0	6–2	6–2		
1884	J. Dwight/R. D. Sears	A. Van Rensselaer/W. V. R. Berry	6–4	6–1	8–10	6–4	
1885	J. S. Clark/R. D. Sears	W. P. Knapp/H. W. Slocum	6–3	6–0	6–2		
1886	J. Dwight/R. D. Sears	G. M. Brinley/H. A. Taylor	7–5	5–7	7–5	6–4	
1887	J. Dwight/R. D. Sears	H. W. Slocum/H. A. Taylor	6–4	3–6	2–6	6–3	6–3
1888	O. S. Campbell/V. G. Hall	C. Hobart/E. P. MacMullen		6–4	6–2	6–4	
1889	H. W. Slocum/H. A. Taylor	O. S. Campbell/V. G. Hall	6–1	6–3	6–2		
1890	V. G. Hall/C. Hobart	C. W. Carver/J. A. Ryerson	6–3	4–6	6–2	2–6	6–3
1891	O. S. Campbell/R. P. Huntington	V. G. Hall/C. Hobart	6–3	6–4	8–6		
1892	O. S. Campbell/R. P. Huntington	V. G. Hall/E. L. Hall	6–4	6–2	4–6	6–3	
1893	C. Hobart/F. H. Hovey	O. S. Campbell/R. P. Huntington	6–3	6–4	4–6	6–2	
1894	C. Hobart/F. H. Hovey	C. B. Neel/S. R. Neel	6–3	8–6	6–1		
1895	M. G. Chace/R. D. Wrenn	C. Hobart/F. H. Hovey	7–5	6–1	8–6		
1896*	C. B./S. R. Neel	M. G. Chace/R. D. Wrenn	6–3	1–6	6–1	3–6	6–1
1897	L. E. Ware/G. P. Sheldon	H. S. Mahony/H. A. Nisbet	11–13	6–2	9–7	1–6	6–1
1898	L. E. Ware/G. P. Sheldon	D. F. Davis/H. Ward	1–6	7–5	6–4	4–6	7–5
1899	D. F. Davis/H. Ward	L. E. Ware/G. P. Sheldon	6–4	6–4	6–3		
1900	D. F. Davis/H. Ward	F. B. Alexander/R. D. Little	6–4	9–7	12–10		
1901	D. F. Davis/H. Ward	L. E. Ware/B. C. Wright	6–3	9–7	6–1		
1902	H. L./R. F. Doherty	D. F. Davis/H. Ward	11–9	12–10	6–4		
1903	H. L./R. F. Doherty	L. Collins/L. H. Waldner	7–5	6–3	6–3		
1904*	H. Ward/B. C. Wright	K. Collins/R. D. Little	1–6	6–2	3–6	6–4	6–1
1905	H. Ward/B. C. Wright	F. B. Alexander/H. H. Hackett	6–3	6–1	6–2		
1906	H. Ward/B. C. Wright	F. B. Alexander/H. H. Hackett	6–3	3–6	6–3	6–3	
1907*	F. B. Alexander/B. C. Wright	W. J. Clothier/W. A. Larned	6–3	6–1	6–4		
1908	F. B. Alexander/H. H. Hackett	R. D. Little/B. C. Wright	6–1	7–5	6–2		
1909	F. B. Alexander/H. H. Hackett	G. J. Janes/M. E. McLoughlin	6–4	6–1	6–0		
1910	F. B. Alexander/H. H. Hackett	T. C. Bundy/T. W. Hendrick	6–1	8–6	6–3		
1911	R. D. Little/G. F. Touchard	F. B. Alexander/H. H. Hackett	7–5	13–15	6–2	6–4	
1912	T. C. Bundy/M. E. McLoughlin	R. D. Little/G. F. Touchard	3–6	6–2	6–1	7–5	
1913	T. C. Bundy/M. E. McLoughlin	C. J. Griffin/J. R. Strachan	6–4	7–5	6–1		
1914	T. C. Bundy/M. E. McLoughlin	G. M. Church/D. Mathey	6–4	6–2	6–4		
1915	C. J. Griffin/W. M. Johnston	T. C. Bundy/M. E. McLoughlin	6–2	3–6	4–6	6–3	6–3
1916	C. J. Griffin/W. M. Johnston	W. Dawson/M. E. McLoughlin	6–4	6–3	5–7	6–3	
1917	F. B. Alexander/ H. A. Throckmorton	H. C. Johnson/I. C. Wright	11–9	6–4	6–4		
1918	V. Richards/W. T. Tilden	F. B. Alexander/B. C. Wright	6–3	6–4	3–6	2–6	6–2
1919	N. E. Brookes/G. L. Patterson	V. Richards/W. T. Tilden	8–6	6–3	4–6	6–2	
1920	C. J. Griffin/W. M. Johnston	W. F. Davis/R. Roberts	6–2	6–2	6–3		
1921	V. Richards/W. T. Tilden	W. M. Washburn/R. N. Williams	13–11	12–10	6–1		
1922	V. Richards/W. T. Tilden	P. O'Hara Wood/G. L. Patterson	4–6	6–1	6–3	6–4	
1923	B. I. C. Norton/W. T. Tilden	W. M. Washburn/R. N. Williams	3–6	6–2	6–3	5–7	6–2
1924	H. O./R. G. Kinsey	P. O'Hara Wood/G. L. Patterson	7–5	5–7	7–9	6–3	6–4
1925	V. Richards/R. N. Williams	J. B. Hawkes/G. L. Patterson	6–2	8–10	6–4	11–9	
1926	V. Richards/R. N. Williams	A. H. Chapin/W. T. Tilden	6–4	6–8	11–9	6–3	
1927	F. T. Hunter/W. T. Tilden	W. M. Washburn/R. N. Williams	10–8	6–3	6–3		
1928	J. F. Hennessey/G. M. Lott	J. B. Hawkes/G. L. Patterson	6–2	6–1	6–2		
1929	J. H. Doeg/G. M. Lott	R. B. Bell/L. N. White	10–8	16–14	6–1		
1930	J. H. Doeg/G. M. Lott	W. L. Allison/J. Van Ryn	8–6	6–3	3–6	13–15	6–4
1931	W. L. Allison/J. Van Ryn	R. B. Bell/G. S. Mangin	6–4	6–3	6–2		
1932	K. Gledhill/H. E. Vines	W. L. Allison/J. Van Ryn	6–4	6–3	6–2		
1933	G. M. Lott/L. R. Stoefen	F. A. Parker/F. X. Shields	11–13	9–7	9–7	6–3	
1934	G. M. Lott/L. R. Stoefen	W. L. Allison/J. Van Ryn	6–4	9–7	3–6	6–4	
1935	W. L. Allison/J. Van Ryn	J. D. Budge/G. Mako	6–2	6–3	2–6	3–6	6–1
1936	J. D. Budge/G. Mako	W. L. Allison/J. Van Ryn	6–4	6–2	6–4		
1937	G. Von Cramm/H. Henkel	J. D. Budge/G. Mako	6–4	7–5	6–4		
1938	J. D. Budge/G. Mako	J. E. Bromwich/A. K. Quist	6–3	6–2	6–1		
1939	J. E. Bromwich/A. K. Quist	J. H. Crawford/H. C. Hopman	8–6	6–1	6–4		
1940	J. A. Kramer/F. R. Schroeder	G. Mulloy/H. J. Prussoff	6–4	8–6	9–7		

1941	J. A. Kramer/F. R. Schroeder	G. Mulloy/W. Sabin	9–7	6–4	6–2			
1942	G. Mulloy/W. F. Talbert	F. R. Schroeder/S. B. Wood	9–7	7–5	6–1			
1943	J. A. Kramer/F. A. Parker	D. Freeman/W. F. Talbert	6–2	6–4	6–4			
1944	R. Falkenburg/W. D. McNeill	F. Segura/W. F. Talbert	7–5	6–4	3–6	6–1		
1945	G. Mulloy/W. F. Talbert	R. Falkenburg/J. Tuero	12–10	8–10	12–10	6–2		
1946	G. Mulloy/W. F. Talbert	G. Guernsey/W. D. McNeill	3–6	6–4	2–6	6–3	20–18	
1947	J. A. Kramer/F. R. Schroeder	W. F. Talbert/O. W. Sidwell	6–4	7–5	6–3			
1948	G. Mulloy/W. F. Talbert	F. A. Parker/F. R. Schroeder	1–6	9–7	6–3	3–6	9–7	
1949	J. Bromwich/O. W. Sidwell	F. A. Sedgman/G. Worthington	6–4	6–0	6–1			
1950	J. Bromwich/F. A. Sedgman	G. Mulloy/W. F. Talbert	7–5	8–6	3–6	6–1		
1951	K. B. McGregor/F. A. Sedgman	D. Candy/M. G. Rose	10–8	6–4	4–6	7–5		
1952	M. G. Rose/E. V. Seixas	K. B. McGregor/F. A. Sedgman	3–6	10–8	10–8	6–8	8–6	
1953	R. N. Hartwig/M. G. Rose	G. Mulloy/W. F. Talbert	6–4	4–6	6–2	6–4		
1954	E. V. Seixas/M. A. Trabert	L. A. Hoad/K. R. Rosewall	3–6	6–4	8–6	6–3		
1955	K. Kamo/A. Miyagi	G. Moss/W. Quillian	6–3	6–3	3–6	1–6	6–4	
1956	L. A. Hoad/K. R. Rosewall	H. Richardson/E. V. Seixas	6–2	6–2	3–6	6–4		
1957	A. J. Cooper/N. A. Fraser	G. Mulloy/J. E. Patty	4–6	6–3	9–7	6–3		
1958	A. Olmedo/H. Richardson	S. Giammalva/B. McKay	3–6	6–3	6–4	6–4		
1959	R. S. Emerson/N. A. Fraser	E. Buchholz/A. Olmedo	3–6	6–3	5–7	6–4	7–5	
1960	R. S. Emerson/N. A. Fraser	R. G. Laver/R. Mark	9–7	6–2	6–4			
1961	C. McKinley/R. D. Ralston	A. Palafox/R. H. Osuna	6–3	6–4	2–6	13–11		
1962	A. Palafox/R. H. Osuna	C. McKinley/R. D. Ralston	6–4	10–12	1–6	9–7	6–3	
1963	C. McKinley/R. D. Ralston	A. Palafox/R. H. Osuna	9–7	4–6	5–7	6–3	11–9	
1964	C. McKinley/R. D. Ralston	G. Stilwell/M. Sangster	6–3	6–2	6–4			
1965	R. S. Emerson/F. S. Stolle	F. Froehling/C. Pasarell	6–4	10–12	7–5	6–3		
1966	R. S. Emerson/F. S. Stolle	C. Graebner/R. D. Ralston	6–4	6–4	6–4			
1967	J. D. Newcombe/A. D. Roche	O. K. Davidson/W. W. Bowrey	6–8	9–7	6–3	6–3		
1968#	R. C. Lutz/S. R. Smith	R. A. J. Hewitt/R. J. Moore	6–4	6–4	9–7			
1969#	R. D. Crealy/A. Stone	W. W. Bowrey/C. Pasarell	9–11	6–3	7–5			
1968	R. C. Lutz/S. R. Smith	A. R. Ashe/A. Gimeno	11–9	6–1	7–5			*FIRST*
1969	K. R. Rosewall/F. S. Stolle	C. Pasarell/R. D. Ralston	2–6	7–5	13–11	6–3		*PRIZE*
1970	P. Barthes/N. Pilic	R. S. Emerson/R. G. Laver	6–3	7–6	4–6	7–6		*(US$)*
1971	J. D. Newcombe/R. Taylor	S. R. Smith/E. van Dillen	6–7	6–3	7–6	4–6	7–6	2,000
1972	E. C. Drysdale/R. Taylor	O. K. Davidson/J. D. Newcombe	6–4	7–6	6–3			
1973	O. K. Davidson/J. D. Newcombe	R. G. Laver/K. R. Rosewall	7–5	2–6	7–5	7–5		4,000
1974	R. C. Lutz/S. R. Smith	P. Cornejo/J. Fillol	6–3	6–3				4,500
1975	J. S. Connors/I. Nastase	T. S. Okker/M. C. Riessen	6–4	7–6				4,500
1976	T. S. Okker/M. C. Riessen	P. Kronk/C. Letcher	6–4	6–4				10,000
1977	R. A. J. Hewitt/F. D. McMillan	B. E. Gottfried/R. Ramirez	6–4	6–0				13,125
1978	R. C. Lutz/S. R. Smith	M. C. Riessen/S. E. Stewart	1–6	7–5	6–3			15,500
1979	P. Fleming/J. P. McEnroe	R. C. Lutz/S. R. Smith	6–2	6–4				15,750
1980	R. C. Lutz/S. R. Smith	P. Fleming/J. P. McEnroe	7–6	3–6	6–1	3–6	6–3	18,500
1981	P. Fleming/J. P. McEnroe	H. Gunthardt/P. McNamara	w.o.					26,400
1982	K. Curren/S. Denton	V. Amaya/H. Pfister	6–2	6–7	5–7	6–2	6–4	36,000
1983	P. Fleming/J. P. McEnroe	F. Buehning/V. Winitsky	6–3	6–4	6–2			48,000
1984	J. Fitzgerald/T. Smid	S. Edberg/A. Jarryd	7–6	6–3	6–3			64,000
1985	K. Flach/R. Seguso	H. Leconte/Y. Noah	6–7	7–6	7–6	6–0		65,000
1986	A. Gomez/S. Zivojinovic	J. Nystrom/M. Wilander	4–6	6–3	6–3	4–6	6–3	72,800
1987	S. Edberg/A. Jarryd	K. Flach/R. Seguso	7–6	6–2	4–6	5–7	7–6	87,000
1988	S. Casal/E. Sanchez	R. Leach/J. Pugh	w.o.					95,000
1989	J. P. McEnroe/M. Woodforde	K. Flach/R. Seguso	6–4	4–6	6–3	6–3		104,000
1990	P. Aldrich/D. Visser	P. Annacone/D. Wheaton	6–2	7–6	6–2			142,800
1991	J. B. Fitzgerald/A. Jarryd	S. Davis/D. Pate	6–3	3–6	6–3	6–3		163,500
1992	J. Grabb/R. Reneberg	K. Jones/R. Leach	3–6	7–6	6–3	6–3		184,000
1993	K. Flach/R. Leach	M. Damm/K. Novacek	6–7	6–4	6–2			200,000
1994	J. Eltingh/P. Haarhuis	T. Woodbridge/M. Woodforde	6–3	7–6				200,000
1995	T. Woodbridge/M. Woodforde	A. O'Brien/S. Stolle	6–3	6–3				210,000
1996	T. Woodbridge/M. Woodforde	J. Eltingh/P. Haarhuis	4–6	7–6	7–6			240,000
1997	Y. Kafelnikov/D. Vacek	J. Bjorkman/N. Kulti	7–6	6–3				300,000

#US Amateur Championships

WOMEN'S DOUBLES

	CHAMPIONS	*RUNNERS-UP*	*SCORE*		
1887†	E. F. Hansell/L. Knight	L. Allderdice/Church	6–0	6–4	
1888†	E. C. Roosevelt/G. W. Roosevelt	A. K. Robinson/V. Ward	3–6	6–3	6–4
1889	M. Ballard/B. L. Townsend	M. Wright/L. Knight	6–0	6–2	

1890	E. C. Roosevelt/G. W. Roosevelt	B. L. Townsend/M. Ballard	6–1	6–2			
1891	M. E. Cahill/Mrs W. F. Morgan	E. C. Roosevelt/G. W. Roosevelt	2–6	8–6	6–4		
1892	M. E. Cahill/A. M. McKinlay	Mrs A. H. Harris/A. R. Williams	6–1	6–3			
1893	H. Butler/A. M. Terry	A. L. Schultz/Stone	6–4	6–3			
1894	J. P. Atkinson/H. R. Hellwig	A. R. Williams/A. C. Wistar	6–4	8–6	6–2		
1895	J. P. Atkinson/H. R. Hellwig	E. H. Moore/A. R. Williams	6–2	6–2	12–10		
1896	J. P. Atkinson/E. H. Moore	A. R. Williams/A. C. Wistar	6–4	7–5			
1897	J. P. Atkinson/K. Atkinson	F. Edwards/E. J. Rastall	6–2	6–1	6–1		
1898	J. P. Atkinson/K. Atkinson	C. B. Neely/M. Wimer	6–1	2–6	4–6	6–1	6–2
1899	J. W. Craven/M. McAteer	M. Banks/E. J. Rastall		6–1	6–1	7–5	
1900	H. Champlin/E. Parker	M. McAteer/M. Wimer		9–7	6–2	6–2	
1901	J. P. Atkinson/M. McAteer	M. Jones/E. H. Moore		w.o.			
1902	J. P. Atkinson/M. Jones	M. Banks/N. Closterman		6–2	7–5		
1903	E. H. Moore/C. B. Neely	M. Jones/M. Hall		6–4	6–1	6–1	
1904	M. Hall/M. G. Sutton	E. H. Moore/C. B. Neely		3–6	6–3	6–3	
1905	H. Homans/C. B. Neely	V. Maule/M. F. Oberteuffer		6–0	6–1		
1906	Mrs L. S. Coe/Mrs D. S. Platt	C. Boldt/H. Homans		6–4	6–4		
1907	C. B. Neely/M. Wimer	E. Wildey/N. Wildey		6–1	2–6	6–4	
1908	M. Curtis/Evelyn Sears	C. B. Neely/M. Steever		6–3	5–7	9–7	
1909	H. V. Hotchkiss/E. E. Rotch	D. Green/L. Moyes		6–1	6–1		
1910	H. V. Hotchkiss/E. E. Rotch	A. Browning/E. Wildey		6–4	6–4		
1911	H. V. Hotchkiss/Eleanora Sears	D. Green/F. Sutton		6–4	4–6	6–2	
1912	M. K. Browne/D. Green	Mrs M. Barger-Wallach/Mrs F. Schmitz		6–2	5–7	6–0	
1913	M. K. Browne/ Mrs R. H. Williams	D. Green/E. Wildey		12–10	2–6	6–3	
1914	M. K. Browne/ Mrs R. H. Williams	Mrs E. Raymond/E. Wildey		8–6	6–2		
1915	Eleanora Sears/ Mrs G. W. Wightman	Mrs G. L. Chapman/Mrs M. McLean		10–8	6–2		
1916	M. Bjurstedt/Eleanora Sears	Mrs E. Raymond/E. Wildey		4–6	6–2	10–8	
1917	M. Bjurstedt/Eleanora Sears	Mrs R. LeRoy/P. Walsh		6–2	6–4		
1918	E. E. Goss/M. Zinderstein	M. Bjurstedt/Mrs J. Rogge		7–5	8–6		
1919	E. E. Goss/M. Zinderstein	E. Sears/Mrs G. W. Wightman		10–8	9–7		
1920	E. E. Goss/M. Zinderstein	H. Baker/E. Tennant		13–11	4–6	6–3	
1921	M. K. Browne/ Mrs R. H. Williams	H. Gilleaudeau/Mrs L. G. Morris		6–3	6–2		
1922	Mrs J. B. Jessup/H. N. Wills	Mrs F. I. Mallory/E. Sigourney		6–4	7–9	6–3	
1923	Mrs B. C. Covell/K. McKane	E. E. Goss/Mrs G. W. Wightman		2–6	6–2	6–1	
1924	Mrs G. W. Wightman/ H. N. Wills	E. E. Goss/Mrs J. B. Jessup		6–4	6–3		
1925	M. K. Browne/H. N. Wills	Mrs T. C. Bundy/E. Ryan		6–4	6–3		
1926	E. E. Goss/E. Ryan	M. K. Browne/Mrs A. H. Chapin		3–6	6–4	12–10	
1927	Mrs L. A. Godfree/E. H. Harvey	J. Fry/B. Nuthall		6–1	4–6	6–4	
1928	Mrs G. W. Wightman/H. N. Wills	E. Cross/Mrs L. A. Harper		6–2	6–2		
1929	Mrs L. R. C. Michell/ Mrs P. H. Watson	Mrs B. C. Covell/ Mrs D. C. Shepherd-Barron		2–6	6–3	6–4	
1930	B. Nuthall/S. Palfrey	E. Cross/Mrs L. A. Harper		3–6	6–3	7–5	
1931	B. Nuthall/ Mrs E. F. Whittingstall	H. H. Jacobs/D. E. Round		6–2	6–4		
1932	H. H. Jacobs/S. Palfrey	A. Marble/Mrs M. Painter		8–6	6–1		
1933	F. James/B. Nuthall	Mrs F. S. Moody/E. Ryan		w.o.			
1934	H. H. Jacobs/S. Palfrey	Mrs D. B. Andrus/C. A. Babcock		4–6	6–3	6–4	
1935	H. H. Jacobs/Mrs M. Fabyan	Mrs D. B. Andrus/C. A. Babcock		6–4	6–2		
1936	C. A. Babcock/Mrs J. Van Ryn	H. H. Jacobs/Mrs M. Fabyan		9–7	2–6	6–4	
1937	Mrs M. Fabyan/A. Marble	C. A. Babcock/Mrs J. Van Ryn		7–5	6–4		
1938	Mrs M. Fabyan/A. Marble	J. Jedrzejowska/Mrs R. Mathieu		6–8	6–4	6–3	
1939	Mrs M. Fabyan/A. Marble	Mrs S. H. Hammersley/K. E. Stammers		7–5	8–6		
1940	Mrs M. Fabyan/A. Marble	D. M. Bundy/Mrs J. Van Ryn		6–4	6–3		
1941	Mrs E. T. Cooke/M. E. Osborne	D. M. Bundy/D. J. Hart		3–6	6–1	6–4	
1942	A. L. Brough/M. E. Osborne	P. M. Betz/D. J. Hart		6–7	7–5	6–0	
1943	A. L. Brough/M. E. Osborne	P. M. Betz/D. J. Hart		6–1	6–3		
1944	A. L. Brough/M. E. Osborne	P. M. Betz/D. J. Hart		4–6	6–4	6–3	
1945	A. L. Brough/M. E. Osborne	P. M. Betz/D. J. Hart		6–4	6–4		
1946	A. L. Brough/M. E. Osborne	Mrs P. C. Todd/Mrs M. A. Prentiss		6–1	6–3		
1947	A. L. Brough/M. E. Osborne	Mrs P. C. Todd/D. J. Hart		5–7	6–3	7–5	
1948	A. L. Brough/Mrs W. D. du Pont	Mrs P. C. Todd/D. J. Hart		6–4	8–10	6–1	

1949	A. L. Brough/Mrs W. D. du Pont	S. J. Fry/D. J. Hart	6–4	10–8	
1950	A. L. Brough/Mrs W. D. du Pont	S. J. Fry/D. J. Hart	6–2	6–3	
1951	S. J. Fry/D. J. Hart	N. Chaffee/Mrs P. C. Todd	6–4	6–2	
1952	S. J. Fry/D. J. Hart	A. L. Brough/M. Connolly	10–8	6–4	
1953	S. J. Fry/D. J. Hart	A. L. Brough/Mrs W. D. du Pont	6–2	7–9	9–7
1954	S. J. Fry/D. J. Hart	A. L. Brough/Mrs W. D. du Pont	6–4	6–4	
1955	A. L. Brough/Mrs W. D. du Pont	S. J. Fry/D. J. Hart	6–3	1–6	6–3
1956	A. L. Brough/Mrs W. D. du Pont	Mrs B. R. Pratt/S. J. Fry	6–3	6–0	
1957	A. L. Brough/Mrs W. D. du Pont	A. Gibson/D. R. Hard	6–2	7–5	
1958	J. M. Arth/D. R. Hard	A. Gibson/M. E. Bueno	2–6	6–3	6–4
1959	J. M. Arth/D. R. Hard	S. Moore/M. E. Bueno	6–2	6–3	
1960	M. E. Bueno/D. R. Hard	D. M. Catt/A. A. Haydon	6–1	6–1	
1961	D. R. Hard/L. Turner	E. Buding/Y. Ramirez	6–4	5–7	6–0
1962	M. E. Bueno/D. R. Hard	Mrs R. Susman/B. J. Moffitt	4–6	6–3	6–2
1963	R. Ebbern/M. Smith	M. E. Bueno/D. R. Hard	4–6	10–8	6–3
1964	Mrs R. Susman/B. J. Moffitt	M. Smith/L. Turner	3–6	6–2	6–4
1965	N. Richey/Mrs C. Graebner	Mrs R. Susman/B. J. Moffitt	6–4	6–4	
1966	M. E. Bueno/N. Richey	R. Casals/Mrs L. W. King	6–3	6–4	
1967	R. Casals/Mrs L. W. King	M. A. Eisel/Mrs D. Fales	4–6	6–3	6–4
1968#	M. E. Bueno/M. Smith	S. V. Wade/Mrs G. M. Williams	6–3	7–5	
1969#	Mrs B. M. Court/S. V. Wade	Mrs P. W. Curtis/V. Ziegenfuss	6–1	6–3	
1968	M. E. Bueno/Mrs B. M. Court	R. Casals/Mrs L. W. King	4–6	9–7	8–6
1969	F. Durr/D. R. Hard	Mrs B. M. Court/S. V. Wade	0–6	6–4	6–4
1970	Mrs B. M. Court/Mrs D. Dalton	R. Casals/S. V. Wade	6–3	6–4	
1971	R. Casals/Mrs D. Dalton	Mrs J. B. Chanfreau/F. Durr	6–3	6–3	
1972	F. Durr/B. Stove	Mrs B. M. Court/S. V. Wade	6–3	1–6	6–3
1973	Mrs B. M. Court/S. V. Wade	R. Casals/Mrs L. W. King	3–6	6–3	7–5
1974	R. Casals/Mrs L. W. King	F. Durr/B. Stove	7–6	6–7	6–4
1975	Mrs B. M. Court/S. V. Wade	R. Casals/Mrs L. W. King	7–5	2–6	7–5
1976	L. Boshoff/I. Kloss	O. Morozova/S. V. Wade	6–1	6–4	
1977	M. Navratilova/B. Stove	R. Richards/B. Stuart	6–1	7–6	
1978	Mrs L. W. King/M. Navratilova	Mrs G. E. Reid/W. M. Turnbull	7–6	6–4	
1979	B. Stove/W. M. Turnbull	Mrs L. W. King/M. Navratilova	7–5	6–3	
1980	Mrs L. W. King/M. Navratilova	P. H. Shriver/B. Stove	7–6	7–5	
1981	K. Jordan/A. E. Smith	R. Casals/W. M. Turnbull	6–3	6–3	
1982	R. Casals/W. M. Turnbull	B. Potter/S. A. Walsh	6–4	6–4	
1983	M. Navratilova/P. H. Shriver	R. Fairbank/C. Reynolds	6–7	6–1	6–3
1984	M. Navratilova/P. H. Shriver	A. E. Hobbs/W. M. Turnbull	6–2	6–4	
1985	C. Kohde-Kilsch/H. Sukova	M. Navratilova/P. H. Shriver	6–7	6–2	6–3
1986	M. Navratilova/P. H. Shriver	H. Mandlikova/W. M. Turnbull	6–4	3–6	6–3
1987	M. Navratilova/P. H. Shriver	K. Jordan/Mrs P. Smylie	5–7	6–4	6–2
1988	G. Fernandez/R. White	J. Hetherington/P. Fendick	6–4	6–1	
1989	H. Mandlikova/M. Navratilova	M. J. Fernandez/P. H. Shriver	5–7	6–4	6–4
1990	G. Fernandez/M. Navratilova	J. Novotna/H. Sukova	6–2	6–4	
1991	P. H. Shriver/N. Zvereva	J. Novotna/L. Savchenko	6–4	4–6	7–6
1992	G. Fernandez/N. Zvereva	J. Novotna/L. Savchenko Neiland	7–6	6–1	
1993	A. Sanchez Vicario/H. Sukova	A. Coetzer/I. Gorrochategui	6–4	6–2	
1994	J. Novotna/A. Sanchez Vicario	K. Maleeva/R. White	6–3	6–3	
1995	G. Fernandez/N. Zvereva	B. Schultz-McCarthy/R. Stubbs	7–5	6–3	
1996	G. Fernandez/N. Zvereva	J. Novotna/A. Sanchez Vicario	1–6	6–1	6–4
1997	L. Davenport/J. Novotna	G Fernandez/N. Zvereva	3–6	7–6	6–2

#US Amateur Championships

†Not recognised as an official championship

MIXED DOUBLES

	CHAMPIONS	RUNNERS-UP	SCORE			
1887†	J. S. Clark/Miss L. Stokes	E. D. Faries/Miss L. Knight	7–5	6–4		
1888†	J. S. Clark/Miss M. Wright	P. Johnson/Miss A. Robinson	1–6	6–5	6–4	6–3
1889†	A. E. Wright/Miss G. W. Roosevelt	C. T. Lee/Miss B. L. Townsend	6–1	6–3	3–6	6–3
1890†	R. Beach/Miss M. E. Cahill	C. T. Lee/Miss B. L. Townsend	6–2	3–6	6–2	
1891†	M. R. Wright/Miss M. E. Cahill	C. T. Lee/Miss G. W. Roosevelt	6–4	6–0	6–5	
1892	C. Hobart/Miss M. E. Cahill	R. Beach/Miss E. H. Moore	6–1	6–3		
1893	C. Hobart/Miss E. C. Roosevelt	R. N. Willson/Miss E. Bankson	6–1	4–6	10–8	6–1
1894	E. P. Fischer/Miss J. P. Atkinson	G. Remak/Mrs McFadden	8–6	6–2	6–1	
1895	E. P. Fischer/Miss J. P. Atkinson	M. Fielding/Miss A. R. Williams	4–6	6–3	6–2	
1896	E. P. Fischer/Miss J. P. Atkinson	M. Fielding/Miss A. R. Williams	6–2	6–3	6–3	

1897	D. L. Magruder/Miss L. Henson	R. A. Griffin/Miss M. Banks	6–4	6–3	7–5
1898	E. P. Fischer/Miss C. B. Neely	J. A. Hill/Miss H. Chapman	6–2	6–4	8–6
1899	A. L. Hoskins/Miss E. J. Rastall	J. P. Gardner/Miss J. W. Craven	6–4	6–0	ret'd
1900	A. Codman/Miss M. J. Hunnewell	G. Atkinson/Miss T. Shaw	11–9	6–3	6–1
1901	R. D. Little/Miss M. Jones	C. Stevens/Miss M. McAteer	6–4	6–4	7–5
1902	W. C. Grant/Miss E. H. Moore	A. L. Hoskins/Miss E. J. Rastall	6–2	6–1	
1903	H. F. Allen/Miss H. Chapman	W. H. Rowland/Miss C. B. Neely	6–4	7–5	
1904	W. C. Grant/Miss E. H. Moore	F. B. Dallas/Miss M. Sutton	6–2	6–1	
1905	C. Hobart/Mrs Hobart	E. B. Dewhurst/Miss E. H. Moore	6–2	6–4	
1906	E. B. Dewhurst/Miss S. Coffin	J. B. Johnson/Miss M. Johnson	6–3	7–5	
1907	W. F. Johnson/Miss M. Sayres	H. M. Tilden/Miss N. Wildey	6–1	7–5	
1908	N. W. Niles/Miss E. E. Rotch	R. D. Little/Miss L. Hammond	6–4	4–6	6–4
1909	W. F. Johnson/Miss H. V. Hotchkiss	R. D. Little/Miss L. Hammond	6–2	6–0	
1910	J. R. Carpenter/Miss H. V. Hotchkiss	H. M. Tilden/Miss E. Wildey	6–2	6–2	
1911	W. F. Johnson/Miss H. V. Hotchkiss	H. M. Tilden/Miss E. Wildey	6–4	6–4	
1912	R. N. Williams/Miss M. K. Browne	W. J. Clothier/Miss Evelyn Sears	6–4	2–6	11–9
1913	W. T. Tilden/Miss M. K. Browne	C. S. Rogers/Miss D. Green	7–5	7–5	
1914	W. T. Tilden/Miss M. K. Browne	J. R. Rowland/Miss M. Myers	6–1	6–4	
1915	H. C. Johnson/Mrs G. W. Wightman	I. C. Wright/Miss M. Bjurstedt	6–0	6–1	
1916	W. E. Davis/Miss Evelyn Sears	W. T. Tilden/Miss F. A. Ballin	6–4	7–5	
1917	I. C. Wright/Miss M. Bjurstedt	W. T. Tilden/Miss F. A. Ballin	10–12	6–1	6–3
1918	I. C. Wright/Mrs G. W. Wightman	F. B. Alexander/Miss M. Bjurstedt	6–2	6–4	
1919	V. Richards/Miss M. Zinderstein	W. T. Tilden/Miss F. A. Ballin	2–6	11–9	6–2
1920	W. F. Johnson/Mrs G. W. Wightman	C. Biddle/Mrs F. I. Mallory	6–4	6–3	
1921	W. M. Johnston/Miss M. K. Browne	W. T. Tilden/Miss F. I. Mallory	3–6	6–4	6–3
1922	W. T. Tilden/Mrs F. I. Mallory	H. Kinsey/Miss H. N. Wills	6–4	6–3	
1923	W. T. Tilden/Mrs F. I. Mallory	J. B. Hawkes/Miss K. McKane	6–3	2–6	10–8
1924	V. Richards/Miss H. N. Wills	W. T. Tilden/Mrs F. I. Mallory	6–8	7–5	6–0
1925	J. B. Hawkes/Miss K. McKane	V. Richards/Miss E. H. Harvey	6–2	6–4	
1926	J. Borotra/Miss E. Ryan	R. Lacoste/Mrs G. W. Wightman	6–4	7–5	
1927	H. Cochet/Miss E. Bennett	R. Lacoste/Mrs G. W. Wightman	2–6	6–0	6–2
1928	J. B. Hawkes/Miss H. N. Wills	G. Moon/Miss E. Cross	6–3	6–3	
1929	G. M. Lott/Miss B. Nuthall	H. W. Austin/Mrs B. C. Lovell	6–3	6–3	
1930	W. L. Allison/Miss E. Cross	F. X. Shields/Miss M. Morrill	6–4	6–4	
1931	G. M. Lott/Miss B. Nuthall	W. L. Allison/Mrs L. A. Harper	6–3	6–3	
1932	F. J. Perry/Miss S. Palfrey	H. E. Vines/Miss H. H. Jacobs	6–3	7–5	
1933	H. E. Vines/Miss E. Ryan	G. M. Lott/Miss S. Palfrey	11–9	6–1	
1934	G. M. Lott/Miss H. H. Jacobs	L. R. Stoefen/Miss E. Ryan	4–6	13–11	6–2
1935	E. Maier/Mrs M. Fabyan	R. Menzel/Miss K. E. Stammers	6–3	3–6	6–4
1936	G. Mako/Miss A. Marble	J. D. Budge/Mrs M. Fabyan	6–3	6–2	
1937	J. D. Budge/Mrs M. Fabyan	Y. Petra/Mme S. Henrotin	6–2	8–10	6–0
1938	J. D. Budge/Miss A. Marble	J. E. Bromwich/Miss T. D. Coyne	6–1	6–2	
1939	H. C. Hopman/Miss A. Marble	E. T. Cooke/Mrs M. Fabyan	9–7	6–1	
1940	R. L. Riggs/Miss A. Marble	J. A. Kramer/Miss D. M. Bundy	9–7	6–1	
1941	J. A. Kramer/Mrs E. T. Cooke	R. L. Riggs/Miss P. M. Betz	4–6	6–4	6–4
1942	F. R. Schroeder/Miss A. L. Brough	A. D. Russell/Mrs P. C. Todd	3–6	6–1	6–4
1943	W. F. Talbert/Miss M. E. Osborne	F. Segura/Miss P. M. Betz	10–8	6–4	
1944	W. F. Talbert/Miss M. E. Osborne	W. D. McNeill/Miss D. M. Bundy	6–2	6–3	
1945	W. F. Talbert/Miss M. E. Osborne	R. Falkenburg/Miss D. J. Hart	6–4	6–4	
1946	W. F. Talbert/Miss M. E. Osborne	R. Kimbrell/Miss A. L. Brough	6–3	6–4	
1947	J. Bromwich/Miss A. L. Brough	F. Segura/Miss G. Morgan	6–3	6–1	
1948	T. P. Brown/Miss A. L. Brough	W. F. Talbert/Mrs W. D. du Pont	6–4	6–4	
1949	E. W. Sturgess/Miss A. L. Brough	W. F. Talbert/Mrs W. D. du Pont	4–6	6–3	7–5
1950	K. B. McGregor/Mrs W. D. du Pont	F. A. Sedgman/Miss D. J. Hart	6–4	3–6	6–3
1951	F. A. Sedgman/Miss D. J. Hart	M. G. Rose/Miss S. J. Fry	6–3	6–2	
1952	F. A. Sedgman/Miss D. J. Hart	L. A. Hoad/Mrs T. C. Long	6–3	7–5	
1953	E. V. Seixas/Miss D. J. Hart	R. N. Hartwig/Miss J. A. Sampson	6–2	4–6	6–4
1954	E. V. Seixas/Miss D. J. Hart	K. R. Rosewall/Mrs W. D. du Pont	4–6	6–1	6–1
1955	E. V. Seixas/Miss D. J. Hart	G. Mulloy/Miss S. J. Fry	7–5	5–7	6–2
1956	K. R. Rosewall/Mrs W. D. du Pont	L. A. Hoad/Miss D. R. Hard	9–7	6–1	
1957	K. Nielsen/Miss A. Gibson	R. N. Howe/Miss D. R. Hard	6–3	9–7	
1958	N. A. Fraser/Mrs W. D. du Pont	A. Olmedo/Miss M. E. Bueno	6–3	3–6	9–7
1959	N. A. Fraser/Mrs W. D. du Pont	R. Mark/Miss J. Hopps	7–5	13–15	6–2
1960	N. A. Fraser/Mrs W. D. du Pont	A. Palafox/Miss M. E. Bueno	6–3	6–2	
1961	R. Mark/Miss M. Smith	R. D. Ralston/Miss D. R. Hard		w.o.	
1962	F. S. Stolle/Miss M. Smith	F. Froehling/Miss L. Turner	7–5	6–2	

In their retirement year Gigi Fernandez and Natasha Zvereva won at the French Open and Wimbledon but had a disappointing finale when they lost in the final of the US Open to Lindsay Davenport and Jana Novotna. (Michael Cole)

Year	Winners	Runners-up				
1963	K. Fletcher/Miss M. Smith	E. Rubinoff/Miss J. Tegart	3–6	8–6	6–2	
1964	J. D. Newcombe/Miss M. Smith	E. Rubinoff/Miss J. Tegart	10–8	4–6	6–3	
1965	F. S. Stolle/Miss M. Smith	F. Froehling/Miss J. Tegart	5–2	6–2		
1966	O. K. Davidson/Mrs D. Fales	E. Rubinoff/Miss C. A. Aucamp	6–1	6–3		
1967	O. K. Davidson/Mrs L. W. King	S. R. Smith/Miss R. Casals	6–3	6–2		
1968#	P. W. Curtis/Miss M. A. Eisel	R. N. Perry/Miss T. A. Fretz	6–4	7–5		
1969#	P. Sullivan/Miss P. S. A. Hogan	T. Addison/Miss K. Pigeon	6–4	2–6	12–10	
1968		*Not held*				
1969	M. C. Riessen/Mrs B. M. Court	R. D. Ralston/Miss F. Durr	7–5	6–3		
1970	M. C. Riessen/Mrs B. M. Court	F. D. McMillan/Mrs D. Dalton	6–4	6–4		
1971	O. K. Davidson/Mrs L. W. King	R. R. Maud/Miss B. Stove	6–3	7–5		
1972	M. C. Riessen/Mrs B. M. Court	I. Nastase/Miss R. Casals	6–3	7–5		
1973	O. K. Davidson/Mrs L. W. King	M. C. Riessen/Miss B. M. Court	6–3	3–6	7–6	
1974	G. Masters/Miss P. Teeguarden	J. S. Connors/Miss C. M. Evert	6–1	7–6		
1975	R. L. Stockton/Miss R. Casals	F. S. Stolle/Mrs L. W. King	6–3	7–6		
1976	P. Dent/Mrs L. W. King	F. D. McMillan/Miss B. Stove	3–6	6–2	7–5	
1977	F. D. McMillan/Miss B. Stove	V. Gerulaitis/Mrs L. W. King	6–2	3–6	6–3	
1978	F. D. McMillan/Miss B. Stove	R. O. Ruffels/Mrs L. W. King	6–3	7–6		
1979	R. A. J. Hewitt/Miss G. Stevens	F. D. McMillan/Miss B. Stove	6–3	7–5		
1980	M. C. Riessen/Miss W. M. Turnbull	F. D. McMillan/Miss B. Stove	7–5	6–2		
1981	K. Curren/Miss A. E. Smith	S. Denton/Miss J. Russell	6–4	7–6		
1982	K. Curren/Miss A. E. Smith	F. Taygan/Miss B. Potter	6–7	7–6	7–6	
1983	J. Fitzgerald/Miss E. Sayers	F. Taygan/Miss B. Potter	3–6	6–3	6–4	
1984	Tom Gullikson/Miss M. Maleeva	J. Fitzgerald/Miss E. Sayers	2–6	7–5	6–4	
1985	H. Gunthardt/Miss M. Navratilova	J. Fitzgerald/Mrs P. Smylie	6–3	6–4		
1986	S. Casal/Miss R. Reggi	P. Fleming/Miss M. Navratilova	6–4	6–4		
1987	E. Sanchez/Miss M. Navratilova	P. Annacone/Miss B. Nagelsen	6–4	6–7	7–6	
1988	J. Pugh/Miss J. Novotna	P. McEnroe/Mrs P. Smylie	7–5	6–3		
1989	S. Cannon/Miss R. White	R. Leach/Miss M. McGrath	3–6	6–2	7–5	
1990	T. Woodbridge/Mrs P. Smylie	J. Pugh/Miss N. Zvereva	6–4	6–2		
1991	T. Nijssen/Miss M. Bollegraf	E. Sanchez/Miss A. Sanchez Vicario	6–2	7–6		
1992	M. Woodforde/Miss N. Provis	T. Nijssen/Miss H. Sukova	4–6	6–3	6–3	
1993	T. Woodbridge/Miss H. Sukova	M. Woodforde/Miss M. Navratilova	6–3	7–6		
1994	P. Galbraith/Miss E. Reinach	T. Woodbridge/Miss J. Novotna	6–2	6–4		*FIRST*
1995	M. Lucena/Miss M. McGrath	C. Suk/Miss G. Fernandez	6–4	6–4		*PRIZE*
1996	P. Galbraith/Miss L. Raymond	R. Leach/Miss M. Bollegraf	7–6	7–6		*(US$)*
1997	R. Leach/Miss M. Bollegraf	P. Albano/Miss M. Paz	3–6	7–5	7–6	100,000

#US Amateur Championships

†Not recognised as an official championship

GRAND SLAM CUP

A knockout competition launched in 1990 and held in Munich in December, for the 16 men who have amassed the most points in the four Grand Slam Championships of Australia, France, Great Britain and the USA. The competition, administered by the Grand Slam Committee (the four Chairmen) and an Administrator, is promoted by an independent German company and offers prize money of $6 million. A further $2 million goes annually to the Grand Slam Development Fund, administered by the ITF.

	WINNER	*RUNNER-UP*	*SCORE*					*FIRST PRIZE*
1990	P. Sampras	B. Gilbert	6–3	6–4	6–2			$2,000,000
1991	D. Wheaton	M. Chang	7–5	6–2	6–4			$2,000,000
1992	M. Stich	M. Chang	6–2	6–3	6–2			$2,000,000
1993	P. Korda	M. Stich	2–6	6–4	7–6	2–6	11–9	$1,625,000
1994	M. Larsson	P. Sampras	7–6	4–6	7–6	6–4		$1,625,000
1995	G. Ivanisevic	T. Martin	7–6	6–3	6–4			$1,625,000
1996	B. Becker	G. Ivanisevic	6–3	6–4	6–4			$1,875,000
1997	P. Sampras	P. Rafter	6–2	6–4	7–5			$2,000,000

GRAND SLAMS

The Grand Slam denotes holding the four championship titles of Australia, France, Wimbledon and the United States in the same year (shown in bold below). The list also includes consecutive wins, not in the same year.

MEN'S SINGLES

J. D. Budge: Wimbledon, US 1937, **Australia, France, Wimbledon, US 1938**
R. G. Laver: **Australia, France, Wimbledon, US 1962**
R. G. Laver: **Australia, France, Wimbledon, US 1969**

WOMEN'S SINGLES

Miss M. Connolly: Wimbledon, US 1952, **Australia, France, Wimbledon, US 1953**
Mrs B. M. Court: US 1969, **Australia, France, Wimbledon, US 1970,** Australia 1971
Miss M. Navratilova: Wimbledon, US, Australia 1983, France, Wimbledon, US 1984
Miss S. Graf: **Australia, France, Wimbledon, US 1988,** Australia 1989, France, Wimbledon, US 1993, Australia 1994

MEN'S DOUBLES

F. A. Sedgman: (With J. E. Bromwich) US 1950, **(with K. McGregor) Australia, France, Wimbledon, US 1951**, Australia, France, Wimbledon 1952
K. McGregor: **(With F. A. Sedgman) Australia, France, Wimbledon, US 1951**, Australia, France, Wimbledon 1952

WOMEN'S DOUBLES

Miss A. L. Brough: (with Mrs W. du Pont) France, Wimbledon, US 1949, (with Miss D. J. Hart) Australia 1950
Miss M. E. Bueno: **(with Miss C. C. Truman) Australia 1960, (with Miss D. R. Hard) France, Wimbledon, US 1960**
Miss M. Navratilova/Miss P. H. Shriver: Wimbledon, US, Australia 1983, France, Wimbledon, US, Australia 1984, France 1985; *Wimbledon, US 1986, Australia, France 1987
Miss G. Fernandez/Miss N. Zvereva: France, Wimbledon, US 1992, Australia, France, Wimbledon 1993
** Miss Navratilova also won France 1986 with Miss A. Temesvari.*

MIXED DOUBLES

Miss M. Smith: (With F. S. Stolle) US 1962, **(with K. N. Fletcher) Australia, France, Wimbledon, US 1963**, Australia, France 1964
K. N. Fletcher: **(With Miss M. Smith) Australia, France, Wimbledon, US 1963**, Australia, France 1964
O. K. Davidson: (With Mrs D. Fales) US 1966, **(with Miss L. R. Turner) Australia 1967, (with Mrs L. W. King) France, Wimbledon, US 1967**
Mrs L. W. King: (With O. K. Davidson) France, Wimbledon, US 1967, (with R. D. Crealy) Australia 1968

JUNIOR SINGLES

E. H. Buchholz: **Australia, France, Wimbledon, US 1958** (*Note:* The US event was not then conducted as an international event and entries at all four were by nomination of national associations.)
S. Edberg: **France, Wimbledon, US, Australia 1983** (*Note:* All Championship events.)

OPEN ERA GRAND SLAM WINNERS

See pp 126–127.

DAVIS CUP

The International Men's Team Championship of the World was initiated in 1900 when the British Isles, then comprising Great Britain and Ireland, challenged the United States for the trophy presented by Dwight F. Davis. The competition was enlarged in 1904 when Belgium and France took part. Each tie has comprised two players engaged in reverse singles plus a doubles match with the best of five sets throughout. In 1989 the tie-break was introduced for all sets except the fifth, in all matches.

From 1900 to 1971 the Champion Nation stood out until challenged by the winner of a knock-out competition between the challenging nations and had the choice of venue. Thereafter the Champion Nation played through. The format was changed in 1981, when the competition became sponsored by NEC and prize money was introduced. The Champion Nation became the winner of the World Group of the 16 strongest nations. Other nations competed in zonal groups, with eight earning the right to play against the eight first round losers in the World Group for places alongside the first round winners of the World Group in the following year's competition. A Zonal Group Three, in which nations from each geographic region play one another on a round-robin basis during one week at one venue to decide promotion to Zonal Group Two, was introduced in 1992. Entries passed the 100 mark for the 1993 competition when 101 nations entered. By 1996 the total had risen to 124.

CHALLENGE ROUNDS (in playing order)

1900 USA (Capt. Dwight Davis) **d. British Isles** (Capt. Arthur Gore) **3–0**, *Boston:* M. D. Whitman d. A. W. Gore 6–1 6–3 6–2; D. F. Davis d. E. D. Black 4–6 6–2 6–4 6–4; Davis/H. Ward d. Black/H. Roper Barrett 6–4 6–4 6–4; Davis div'd with Gore 9–7 9–9.

1901 Not held

1902 USA (Capt: Malcolm Whitman) **d. British Isles** (Capt: William Collins) **3–2**, *Brooklyn, New York:* W. A. Larned lost to R. F. Doherty 6–2 6–3 3–6 4–6 4–6; M. D. Whitman d. J. Pim 6–1 6–1 1–6 6–0; Larned d. Pim 6–3 6–2 6–3; Whitman d. R. F. Doherty 6–1 7–5 6–4; D. F. Davis/H. Ward lost to R. F./H. L. Doherty 6–3 8–10 3–6 4–6.

1903 British Isles (Capt: William Collins) **d. USA** (Capt: William Larned) **4–1**, *Boston:* H. L. Doherty d. R. D. Wrenn 6–0 6–3 6–4; R. F. Doherty lost to W. A. Larnedret'd; R. F./H. L. Doherty d. R. D./G. L. Wrenn 7–5 9–7 2–6 6–3; H. L. Doherty d. Larned 6–3 6–8 6–0 2–6 7–5; R. F. Doherty d. R. D. Wrenn 6–4 3–6 6–3 6–8 6–4.

1904 British Isles (Capt: William Collins) **d. Belgium** (Capt: Paul de Borman) **5–0**, *Wimbledon:* H. L. Doherty d. P. de Borman 6–4 6–1 6–1; F. L. Riseley d. W.Lemaire 6–1 6–4 6–2; R. F./H. L. Doherty d. de Borman/Lemaire 6–0 6–1 6–3; H. L. Doherty w.o. Lemaire; Riseley d. de Borman 4–6 6–2 8–6 7–5.

1905 British Isles (Capt: William Collins) **d. USA** (Capt: Paul Dashiel) **5–0**, *Wimbledon:* H. L. Doherty d. H. Ward 7–9 4–6 6–1 6–2 6–0; S. H. Smith d. W. A. Larned 6–4 6–4 5–7 6–4; R. F./H. L. Doherty d. Ward/B. Wright 8–10 6–2 6–2 4–6 8–6; Smith d. W. J. Clothier 4–6 6–1 6–4 6–3; H. L. Doherty d. Larned 6–4 2–6 6–8 6–4 6–2.

1906 British Isles (Capt: William Collins) **d. USA** (Capt: Beals Wright) **5–0**, *Wimbledon:* S. H. Smith d. R. D. Little 6–4 6–4 6–1; H. L. Doherty d. H. Ward 6–2 8–6 6–3; R. F./H. L. Doherty d. Little/Ward 3–6 11–9 9–7 6–1; Smith d. Ward 6–1 6–0 6–4; H. L. Doherty d. Little 3–6 6–3 6–8 6–1 6–3.

1907 Australasia (Capt: Norman Brookes) **d. British Isles** (Capt: Alfred Hickson) **3–2**, *Wimbledon:* N. E. Brookes d. A. W. Gore 7–5 6–1 7–5; A. F. Wilding d. H. Roper Barrett 1–6 6–4 6–3 7–5; Brookes/Wilding lost to Gore/Roper Barrett 6–3 6–4 5–7 2–6 11–13; Wilding lost to Gore 6–3 3–6 5–7 2–6; Brookes d. Roper Barrett 6–2 6–0 6–3.

1908 Australasia (Capt: Norman Brookes) **d. USA** (Capt: Beals Wright) **3–2**, *Melbourne:* N. E. Brookes d. F. B. Alexander 5–7 9–7 6–2 4–6 6–3; A. F. Wilding lost to B. Wright 6–3 5–7 3–6 1–6; Brookes/Wilding d. Alexander/Wright 6–4 6–2 5–7 1–6 6–4; Brookes lost to Wright 6–0 6–3 5–7 2–6 10–12; Wilding d. Alexander 6–3 6–4 6–1.

1909 Australasia (Capt: Norman Brookes) **d. USA** (Capt: Maurice McLoughlin) **5–0**, *Sydney:* N. E. Brookes d. M. E. McLoughlin 6–2 6–2 6–4; A. F. Wilding d. M. H. Long 6–2 7–5 6–1; Brookes/Wilding d. Long/McLoughlin 12–10 9–7 6–3; Brookes d. Long 6–4 7–5 8–6; Wilding d. McLoughlin 3–6 8–6 6–2 6–3.

1910 Not held

1911 Australasia (Capt: Norman Brookes) **d. USA** (Capt: William Larned) **5–0**, *Christchurch, NZ:* N. E. Brookes d. B. Wright 6–4 2–6 6–3 6–3; R. W. Heath d. W. A. Larned 2–6 6–1 7–5 6–2; Brookes/A. W. Dunlop d. Wright/M. E. McLoughlin 6–4 5–7 7–5 6–4; Brookes d. McLoughlin 6–4 3–6 4–6 6–3 6–4; Heath w.o. Wright.

1912 British Isles (Capt: Charles Dixon) **d. Australasia** (Capt: Norman Brookes) **3–2**, *Melbourne:* J. C. Parke d. N. E. Brookes 8–6 6–3 5–7 6–2; C. P. Dixon d. R. W. Heath 5–7 6–4 6–4 6–4; A. E. Beamish/Parke lost Brookes/A. W. Dunlop 4–6 1–6 5–7; Dixon lost to Brookes 2–6 4–6 4–6; Parke d. Heath 6–2 6–4 6–4.

1913 USA (Capt: Harold Hackett) **d. British Isles** (Capt: Roger McNair) **3–2**, *Wimbledon:* M. E. McLoughlin lost to J. C. Parke 10–8 5–7 4–6 6–1 5–7; R. N. Williams d. C. P. Dixon 8–6 3–6 6–2 1–6 7–5; H. Hackett/McLoughlin d. Dixon/H. Roper Barrett 5–7 6–1 2–6 7–5 6–4; McLoughlin d. Dixon 8–6 6–3 6–2; Williams lost to Parke 2–6 7–5 7–5 4–6 2–6.

1914 Australasia (Capt: Norman Brookes) **d. USA** (Capt: Maurice McLoughlin) **3–2**, *Forest Hills, NY:* A. F. Wilding d. R. N. Williams 7–5 6–2 6–3; N. E. Brookes lost to M. E. McLoughlin 15–17 3–6 3–6; Brookes/Wilding d. T. C. Bundy/McLoughlin 6–3 8–6 9–7; Brookes d. Williams 6–1 6–2 8–10 6–3; Wilding lost to McLoughlin 2–6 3–6 6–2 2–6.

1915–18 Not held

1919 Australasia (Capt: Norman Brookes) **d. British Isles** (Capt: Algernon Kingscote) **4–1**, *Sydney:* G. L. Patterson d. A. H. Lowe 6–4 6–3 2–6 6–3; J. O. Anderson lost to A. R. F. Kingscote 5–7 2–6 4–6; N. E. Brookes/Patterson d. A. E. Beamish/Kingscote 6–0 6–0 6–2; Patterson d. Kingscote 6–4 6–4 8–6; Anderson d. Lowe 6–4 5–7 6–3 4–6 12–10.
1920 USA (Capt: Sam Hardy) **d. Australasia** (Capt: Norman Brookes) **5–0**, *Auckland:* W. T. Tilden d. N. E. Brookes 10–8 6–4 1–6 6–4; W. M. Johnston d. G. L. Patterson 6–3 6–1 6–1; Johnston/Tilden d. Brookes/Patterson 4–6 6–4 6–0 6–4; Johnston d. Brookes 5–7 7–5 6–3 6–3; Tilden d. Patterson 5–7 6–2 6–3 6–3.
1921 USA (Capt: Norris Williams) **d. Japan** (Capt: Ichiya Kumagae) **5–0**, *Forest Hills, NY:* W. M. Johnston d. I. Kumagae 6–2 6–4 6–2; W. T. Tilden d. Z. Schimidzu 5–7 4–6 7–5 6–2 6–1; W. Washburn/R. N. Williams d. Kumagae/Shimidzu 6–2 7–5 4–6 7–5; Tilden d. Kumagae; 9–7 6–4 6–1; Johnston d. Shimidzu 6–3 5–7 6–2 6–4.
1922 USA (Capt: Norris Williams) **d. Australasia** (Capt: James Anderson) **4–1**, *Forest Hills, NY:* W. T. Tilden d. G. L. Patterson 7–5 10–8 6–0; W. M. Johnston d. J. O. Anderson 6–1 6–2 6–3; V. Richards/Tilden lost to P. O'Hara Wood/Patterson 4–6 0–6 3–6; Johnston d. Patterson 6–2 6–2 6–1; Tilden d. Anderson 6–4 5–7 3–6 6–4 6–2.
1923 USA (Capt: Norris Williams) **d. Australia** (Capt: Garald Patterson) **4–1**, *Forest Hills, NY:* W. M. Johnston lost to J. O. Anderson 6–4 2–6 6–2 5–7 2–6; W. T. Tilden d. J. B. Hawkes 6–4 6–2 6–1; Tilden/R. N. Williams d. Anderson/Hawkes 17–15 11–13 2–6 6–3 6–2; Johnston d. Hawkes 6–0 6–2 6–1; Tilden d. Anderson 6–2 6–3 1–6 7–5.
1924 USA (Capt: Norris Williams) **d. Australia** (Capt: Gerald Patterson) **5–0**, *Philadelphia:* W. T. Tilden d. G. L. Patterson 6–4 6–2 6–3; V. Richards d. P. O'Hara Wood 6–3 6–2 6–4; W. M. Johnston/Tilden d. O'Hara Wood/Patterson 5–7 6–3 6–4 6–1; Tilden d. O'Hara Wood 6–2 6–1 6–1; Richards d. Patterson 6–3 7–5 6–4.
1925 USA (Capt: Norris Williams) **d. France** (Capt: Max Decugis) **5–0**, *Philadelphia:* W. T. Tilden d. J. Borotra 4–6 6–0 2–6 9–7 6–4; W. M. Johnston d. R. Lacoste 6–1 6–1 6–8 6–3; V. Richards/R. N. Williams d. Borotra/Lacoste 6–4 6–4 6–3; Tilden d. Lacoste 3–6 10–12 8–6 7–5 6–2; Johnston d. Borotra 6–1 6–4 6–0.
1926 USA (Capt: Norris Williams) **d. France** (Capt: Pierre Gillou) **4–1**, *Philadelphia:* W. M. Johnston d. R. Lacoste 6–0 6–4 0–6 6–0; W. T. Tilden d. J. Borotra 6–2 6–3 6–3; V. Richards/R. N. Williams d. J. Brugnon/H. Cochet 6–4 6–4 6–2; Johnston d. Borotra 8–6 6–4 9–7; Tilden lost to Lacoste 6–4 4–6 6–8 6–8.
1927 France (Capt: Pierre Gillou) **d. USA** (Capt: Charles Garland) **3–2**, *Philadelphia:* R. Lacoste d. W. M. Johnston 6–3 6–2 6–2; H. Cochet lost to W. T. Tilden 4–6 6–2 2–6 6–8; J. Borotra/J. Brugnon lost to F. Hunter/Tilden 6–3 3–6 3–6 6–4 0–6; Lacoste d. Tilden 6–4 4–6 6–3 6–3; Cochet d. Johnston 6–4 4–6 6–2 6–4.
1928 France (Capt: Pierre Gillou) **d. USA** (Capt: Joseph Wear) **4–1**, *Paris:* R. Lacoste lost to W. T. Tilden 6–1 4–6 4–6 6–2 3–6; H. Cochet d. J. Hennessey 5–7 9–7 6–3 6–0; J. Borotra/Cochet d. F. Hunter/Tilden 6–4 6–8 7–5 4–6 6–2; Lacoste d. Hennessey 4–6 6–1 7–5 6–3; Cochet d. Tilden 9–7 8–6 6–4.
1929 France (Capt: Pierre Gillou) **d. USA** (Capt: Fitz-Eugene Dixon) **3–2**, *Paris:* H. Cochet d. W. T. Tilden 6–3 6–1 6–2; J. Borotra d. G. M. Lott 6–1 3–6 6–4 7–5; Borotra/Cochet lost to W. Allison/J. Van Ryn 1–6 6–8 4–6; Cochet d. Lott 6–1 3–6 6–0 6–3; Borotra lost to Tilden 6–4 1–6 4–6 5–7.
1930 France (Capt: Pierre Gillou) **d. USA** (Capt: Fitz-Eugene Dixon) **4–1**, *Paris:* J. Borotra lost to W. T. Tilden 6–2 5–7 4–6 5–7; H. Cochet d. G. M. Lott 6–4 6–2 6–2; J. Brugnon/Cochet d. W. Allison/J. Van Ryn 6–3 7–5 1–6 6–2; Borotra d. Lott 5–7 6–3 2–6 6–2 8–6; Cochet d. Tilden 4–6 6–3 6–1 7–5.
1931 France (Capt: Rene Lacoste) **d. Great Britain** (Capt: Herbert Barrett) **3–2**, *Paris:* H. Cochet d. H. W. Austin 3–6 11–9 6–2 6–4; J. Borotra lost to F. J. Perry 6–4 8–10 0–6 6–4 4–6; J. Brugnon/Cochet d. G. P Hughes/C. H. Kingsley 6–1 5–7 6–3 8–6; Cochet d. Perry 6–4 1–6 9–7 6–3; Borotra lost to Austin 5–7 3–6 6–3 5–7.
1932 France (Capt: Rene Lacoste) **d. USA** (Capt: Bernon Prentice) **3–2**, *Paris:* H. Cochet d. W. Allison 5–7 7–5 3–6 7–5 6–2; J. Borotra d. H. E. Vines 6–4 6–2 2–6 6–4; J. Brugnon/Cochet lost to Allison/J. Van Ryn 3–6 13–11 5–7 6–4 4–6; Borotra d. Allison 1–6 3–6 6–4 6–2 7–5; Cochet lost to Vines 6–4 6–0 5–7 6–8 2–6.
1933 Great Britain (Capt: Herbert Barrett) **d. France** (Capt: Rere Lacoste) **3–2**, *Paris:* H. W. Austin d. A. Merlin 6–3 6–4 6–0; F. J. Perry d. H. Cochet 8–10 6–4 8–6 3–6 6–1; G. P. Hughes/H. G. N. Lee lost to J. Borotra/J. Brugnon 3–6 6–8 2–6; Austin lost to Cochet 7–5 4–6 6–4 4–6 4–6; Perry d. Merlin 4–6 8–6 6–2 7–5.
1934 Great Britain (Capt: Herbert Barrett) **d. USA** (Capt: Norris Williams) **4–1**, *Wimbledon:* F. J. Perry d. S. B. Wood 6–1 4–6 5–7 6–0 6–3; H. W. Austin d. F. X. Shields 6–4 6–4 6–1; G. P. Hughes/H. G. N. Lee lost to G. M. Lott/L. Stoefen 5–7 0–6 6–4 7–9; Perry d. Shields 6–4 4–6 6–2 15–13; Austin d. Wood 6–4 6–0 6–8 6–3.
1935 Great Britain (Capt: Herbert Barrett) **d. USA** (Capt: Joseph Wear) **5–0**, *Wimbledon:* F. J. Perry d. J. D. Budge 6–0 6–8 6–3 6–4; H. W. Austin d. W. Allison 6–2 2–6 4–6 6–3 7–5; G. P. Hughes/C. R. D. Tuckey d. Allison/J. Van Ryn 6–2 1–6 6–8 6–3 6–3; Perry d. Allison 4–6 6–4 7–5 6–3; Austin d. Budge 6–2 6–4 6–8 7–5.
1936 Great Britain (Capt: Herbert Barrett) **d. Australia** (Capt: Cliff Sproule) **3–2**, *Wimbledon:* H. W. Austin d. J. H. Crawford 4–6 6–3 6–1 6–1; F. J. Perry d. A. K. Quist 6–1 4–6 7–5 6–2; G. P. Hughes/C. R. D. Tuckey lost to Crawford/Quist 4–6 6–2 5–7 8–10; Austin lost to Quist 4–6 6–3 5–7 2–6; Perry d. Crawford 6–2 6–3 6–3.
1937 USA (Capt: Walter Pate) **d. Great Britain** (Capt: Herbert Barrett) **4–1**, *Wimbledon:* F. A. Parker lost to H. W. Austin 3–6 2–6 5–7; J. D. Budge d. C. E. Hare 15–13 6–1 6–2; Budge/G. Mako d. C. R. D. Tuckey/F. H. D. Wilde 6–3 7–5 7–9 12–10; Parker d. Hare 6–2 6–4 6–2; Budge d. Austin 8–6 3–6 6–4 6–3.
1938 USA (Capt: Walter Pate) **d. Australia** (Capt: Harry Hopman) **3–2**, *Philadelphia:* R. L. Riggs d. A. K. Quist 4–6 6–0 8–6 6–1; J. D. Budge d. J. E. Bromwich 6–2 6–3 4–6 7–5; Budge/G. Mako lost to Bromwich/Quist 6–0 3–6 4–6 2–6; Budge d. Quist 8–6 6–1 6–2; Riggs lost to Bromwich 4–6 6–4 0–6 2–6.
1939 Australia (Capt: Harry Hopman) **d. USA** (Capt: Walter Pate) **3–2**, *Philadelphia:* J. E. Bromwich lost to R. L. Riggs 4–6 0–6 5–7; A. K. Quist lost to F. A. Parker 3–6 6–2 4–6 6–1 5–7; Bromwich/Quist d. J. R. Hunt/J. Kramer 5–7 6–2 7–5 6–2; Quist d. Riggs 6–1 6–4 3–6 3–6 6–4; Bromwich d. Parker 6–0 6–3 6–1.
1940–45 Not held
1946 USA (Capt: Walter Pate) **d. Australia** (Capt: Gerald Patterson) **5–0**, *Melbourne:* F. R. Schroeder d. J. E. Bromwich 3–6 6–1 6–2 0–6 6–3; J. Kramer d. D. Pails 8–6 6–2 9–7; Kramer/Schroeder d. Bromwich/A. K. Quist 6–2 7–5 6–4; Kramer d. Bromwich 8–6 6–4 6–2 6–4; G Mulloy d. Pails 6–3 6–3 6–4.

1947 USA (Capt: Alrick Man) **d. Australia** (Capt: Roy Cowling) **4–1**, *Forest Hills, NY:* J. Kramer d. D. Pails 6–2 6–1 6–2; F. R. Schroeder d. J. E. Bromwich 6–4 5–7 6–3 6–3; Kramer/Schroeder lost to Bromwich/C. F. Long 4–6 6–2 2–6 4–6; Schroeder d. Pails 6–3 8–6 4–6 9–11 10–8; Kramer d. Bromwich 6–3 6–2 6–2.
1948 USA (Capt: Alrick Man) **d. Australia** (Capt: Adrian Quist) **5–0**, *Forest Hills, NY:* F. A. Parker d. O. W. Sidwell 6–4 6–4 6–4; F. R. Schroeder d. A. K. Quist 6–3 4–6 6–0 6–0; G. Mulloy/W. F. Talbert d. C. F. Long/Sidwell 8–6 9–7 2–6 7–5; Parker d. Quist 6–2 6–2 6–3; Schroeder d. Sidwell 6–2 6–1 6–1.
1949 USA (Capt: Alrick Man) **d. Australia** (Capt: John Bromwich) **4–1**, *Forest Hills, NY:* F. R. Schroeder d. O. W. Sidwell 6–1 5–7 4–6 6–2 6–3; R. A. Gonzales d. F. A. Sedgman 8–6 6–4 9–7; G. Mulloy/W. F. Talbert lost to J. E. Bromwich/Sidwell 6–3 6–4 8–10 7–9 7–9; Schroeder d. Sedgman 6–4 6–3 6–3; Gonzales d. Sidwell 6–1 6–3 6–3.
1950 Australia (Capt: Harry Hopman) **d. USA** (Capt: Alrick Man) **4–1**, *Forest Hills, NY:* F. A. Sedgman d. T. Brown 6–0 8–6 9–7; K. McGregor d. F. R. Schroeder 13–11 6–3 6–4; J. E. Bromwich/Sedgman d. G. Mulloy/Schroeder 4–6 6–4 6–2 4–6 6–4; Sedgman d. Schroeder 6–2 6–2 6–2; McGregor lost to Brown 11–9 10–8 9–11 1–6 4–6.
1951 Australia (Capt: Harry Hopman) **d. USA** (Capt: Frank Shields) **3–2**, *Sydney:* M. G. Rose lost to E. V. Seixas 3–6 4–6 7–9; F. A. Sedgman d. F. R. Schroeder 6–4 6–3 4–6 6–4; K. McGregor/Sedgman d. Schroeder/M. A. Trabert 6–2 9–7 6–3; Rose lost to Schroeder 4–6 11–13 5–7; Sedgman d. Seixas 6–4 6–2 6–2.
1952 Australia (Capt: Harry Hopman) **d. USA** (Capt: Vic Seixas) **4–1**, *Adelaide:* F. A. Sedgman d. E. V. Seixas 6–3 6–4 6–3; K. McGregor d. M. A. Trabert 11–9 6–4 6–1; McGregor/Sedgman d. Seixas/Trabert 6–3 6–4 1–6 6–3; Sedgman d. Trabert 7–5 6–4 10–8; McGregor lost to Seixas 3–6 6–8 8–6 3–6.
1953 Australia (Capt: Harry Hopman) **d. USA** (Capt: Bill Talbert) **3–2**, *Melbourne:* L. A. Hoad d. E. V. Seixas 6–4 6–2 6–3; K. R. Rosewall lost to M. A. Trabert 3–6 4–6 4–6; R. Hartwig/Hoad lost to Seixas/Trabert 2–6 4–6 4–6; Hoad d. Trabert 13–11 6–3 2–6 3–6 7–5; Rosewall d. Seixas 6–2 2–6 6–3 6–4.
1954 USA (Capt: Bill Talbert) **d. Australia** (Capt: Harry Hopman) **3–2**, *Sydney:* M. A. Trabert d. L. A. Hoad 6–4 2–6 12–10 6–3; E. V. Seixas d. K. R. Rosewall 8–6 6–8 6–4 6–3; Seixas/Trabert d. Hoad/Rosewall 6–2 4–6 6–2 10–8; Trabert lost to Rosewall 7–9 5–7 3–6; Seixas lost to R. Hartwig 6–4 3–6 2–6 3–6.
1955 Australia (Capt: Harry Hopman) **d. USA** (Capt: Bill Talbert) **5–0**, *Forest Hills, NY:* K. R. Rosewall d. E. V. Seixas 6–3 10–8 4–6 6–2; L. A. Hoad d. M. A. Trabert 4–6 6–3 6–3 8–6; R. Hartwig/Hoad d. Seixas/Trabert 12–14 6–4 6–3 3–6 7–5; Rosewall d. H. Richardson 6–4 3–6 6–1 6–4; Hoad d. Seixas 7–9 6–1 6–4 6–4.
1956 Australia (Capt: Harry Hopman) **d. USA** (Capt: Bill Talbert) **5–0**, *Adelaide:* L. A. Hoad d. H. Flam 6–2 6–3 6–3; K. R. Rosewall d. E. V. Seixas 6–2 7–5 6–3; Hoad/Rosewall d. S. Giammalva/Seixas 1–6 6–1 7–5 6–4; Hoad d. Seixas 6–2 7–5 6–3; Rosewall d. Giammalva 4–6 6–1 8–6 7–5.
1957 Australia (Capt: Harry Hopman) **d. USA** (Capt: Bill Talbert) **3–2**, *Melbourne:* A. J. Cooper d. E. V. Seixas 3–6 7–5 6–1 1–6 6–3; M. J. Anderson d. B. MacKay 6–3 7–5 3–6 47–9 6–3; Anderson/M. G. Rose d. MacKay/Seixas 6–4 6–4 8–6; Cooper lost to MacKay 4–6 6–1 6–4 4–6 3–6; Anderson lost to Seixas 3–6 6–4 3–6 6–0 11–13.
1958 USA (Capt: Perry Jones) **d. Australia** (Capt: Harry Hopman) **3–2**, *Brisbane:* A. Olmedo d. M. J. Anderson 8–6 2–6 9–7 8–6; B. MacKay lost to A. J. Cooper 6–4 3–6 2–6 4–6; Olmedo/H. Richardson d. Anderson/N. A. Fraser 10–12 3–6 16–14 6–3 7–5; Olmedo d. Cooper 6–3 4–6 6–4 8–6; MacKay lost to Anderson 5–7 11–13 9–11.
1959 Australia (Capt: Harry Hopman) **d. USA** (Capt: Perry Jones) **3–2**, *Forest Hills, NY:* N. A. Fraser d. A. Olmedo 8–6 6–8 6–4 8–6; R. G. Laver lost to B. MacKay 5–7 4–6 1–6; R. S. Emerson/Fraser d. E. Buchholz/Olmedo 7–5 7–5 6–4; Laver lost to Olmedo 7–9 6–4 8–10 10–12; Fraser d. MacKay 8–6 3–6 6–2 6–4.
1960 Australia (Capt: Harry Hopman) **d. Italy** (Capt: Vanni Canapele) **4–1**, *Sydney:* N. A. Fraser d. O. Sirola 4–6 6–3 6–3 6–3; R. G. Laver d. N. Pietrangeli 8–6 6–4 6–3; R. S. Emerson/Fraser d. Pietrangeli/Sirola 10–8 5–7 6–3 6–4; Laver d. Sirola 9–7 6–2 6–3; Fraser lost to Pietrangeli 9–11 3–6 6–1 2–6.
1961 Australia (Capt: Harry Hopman) **d. Italy** (Capt: Vanni Canapele) **5–0**, *Melbourne:* R. S. Emerson d. N. Pietrangeli 8–6 6–4 6–0; R. G. Laver d. O. Sirola 6–1 6–4 6–3; Emerson/N. A. Fraser d. Pietrangeli/Sirola 6–2 6–3 6–4; Emerson d. Sirola 6–2 6–3 4–6 6–2; Laver d. Pietrangeli 6–3 3–6 4–6 6–3 8–6.
1962 Australia (Capt: Harry Hopman) **d. Mexico** (Capt: Franciso Contreras) **5–0**, *Brisbane:* N. A. Fraser d. A. Palafox 7–9 6–3 6–4 11–9; R. G. Laver d. R. H. Osuna 6–2 6–1 7–5; R. S. Emerson/Laver d. Osuna/Palafox 7–5 6–2 6–4; Fraser d. Osuna 3–6 11–9 6–1 3–6 6–4; Laver d. Palafox 6–1 4–6 6–4 8–6.
1963 USA (Capt: Robert Kelleher) **d. Australia** (Capt: Harry Hopman) **3–2**, *Adelaide:* R. D. Ralston d. J. D. Newcombe 6–4 6–1 3–6 4–6 7–5; C. R. McKinley lost to R. S. Emerson 3–6 6–3 5–7 5–7; McKinley/Ralston d. Emerson/N. A. Fraser 6–3 4–6 11–9 11–9; Ralston lost to Emerson 2–6 3–6 6–3 2–6; McKinley d. Newcombe 10–12 6–2 9–7 6–2.
1964 Australia (Capt: Harry Hopman) **d. USA** (Capt: Vic Seixas) **3–2**, *Cleveland, Ohio:* F. S. Stolle lost to C. R. McKinley 1–6 7–9 6–4 2–6; R. S. Emerson d. R. D. Ralston 6–3 6–1 6–3; Emerson/Stolle lost to McKinley/Ralston 4–6 6–4 6–4 3–6 4–6; Stolle d. Ralston 7–5 6–3 3–6 9–11 6–4; Emerson d. McKinley 3–6 6–2 6–4 6–4.
1965 Australia (Capt: Harry Hopman) **d. Spain** (Capt: Jaime Bartroli) **4–1**, *Sydney:* F. S. Stolle d. M. Santana 10–12 3–6 6–1 6–4 7–5; R. S. Emerson d. J. Gisbert 6–3 6–2 6–2; J. D. Newcombe/A. D. Roche d. J. L. Arilla/Santana 6–3 4–6 7–5 6–2; Emerson lost to Santana 6–2 3–6 4–6 13–15; Stolle d. Gisbert 6–2 6–4 8–6.
1966 Australia (Capt: Harry Hopman) **d. India** (Capt: Raj Khanna) **4–1**, *Melbourne:* F. S. Stolle d. R. Krishnan 6–3 6–2 6–4; R. S. Emerson d. J. Mukerjea 7–5 6–4 6–2; J. D. Newcombe/A. D. Roche lost to Krishnan/Mukerjea 6–4 5–7 4–6 4–6; Emerson d. Krishnan 6–0 6–2 10–8; Stolle d. Mukerjea 7–5 6–8 6–3 5–7 6–3.
1967 Australia (Capt: Harry Hopman) **d. Spain** (Capt: Jaime Bartroli) **4–1**, *Brisbane:* R. S. Emerson d. M. Santana 6–4 6–1 6–1; J. D. Newcombe d. M. Orantes 6–3 6–3 6–2; Newcombe/A. D. Roche d. Orantes/Santana 6–4 6–4 6–4; Newcombe lost to Santana 5–7 4–6 2–6; Emerson d. Orantes 6–1 6–1 2–6 6–4.
1968 USA (Capt: Donald Dell) **d. Australia** (Capt: Harry Hopman) **4–1**, *Adelaide:* C. Graebner d. W. W. Bowrey 8–10 6–4 8–6 3–6 6–1; A. R. Ashe d. R. O. Ruffels 6–8 7–5 6–3 6–3; R. C. Lutz/S. R. Smith d. J. G. Alexander/Ruffels 6–4 6–4 6–2; Graebner d. Ruffels 3–6 8–6 2–6 6–3 6–1; Ashe lost to Bowrey 6–2 3–6 9–11 6–8.

1969 USA (Capt: Donald Dell) **d. Romania** (Capt: Georgy Cobzucs) **5–0**, *Cleveland, Ohio:* A. R. Ashe d. I. Nastase 6–2 15–13 7–5; S. R. Smith d. I. Tiriac 6–8 6–3 5–7 6–4 6–4; R. C. Lutz/Smith d. Nastase/Tiriac 8–6 6–1 11–9; Smith d. Nastase 4–6 4–6 6–4 6–1 11–9; Ashe d. Tiriac 6–3 8–6 3–6 4–0 ret'd.
1970 USA (Capt: Edward Turville) **d. West Germany** (Capt: Ferdinand Henkel) **5–0**, *Cleveland, Ohio:* A. R. Ashe d. W. Bungert 6–2 10–8 6–2; C. Richey d. C. Kuhnke 6–3 6–4 6–2; R. C. Lutz/S. R. Smith d. Bungert/Kuhnke 6–3 7–5 6–4; Richey d. Bungert 6–4 6–4 7–5; Ashe d. Kuhnke 6–8 10–12 9–7 13–11 6–4.
1971 USA (Capt: Edward Turville) **d. Romania** (Capt: Stefan Georgescu) **3–2**, *Charlotte, NC:* S. R. Smith d. I. Nastase 7–5 6–3 6–1; F. A. Froehling d. I. Tiriac 3–6 1–6 6–1 6–3 8–6; Smith/E. Van Dillen lost to Nastase/Tiriac 5–7 4–6 8–6; Smith d. Tiriac 8–6 6–3 6–0; Froehling lost to Nastase 3–6 1–6 6–1 4–6.
Challenge Round abolished

FINAL ROUND SCORES

1972 USA (Capt: Dennis Ralston) **d. Romania** (Capt: Stefan Georgescu) **3–2**, *Bucharest:* S. R. Smith d. I. Nastase 11–9 6–2 6–3; T. Gorman lost to I. Tiriac 6–4 6–2 4–6 3–6 2–6; Smith/E. Van Dillen d. Nastase/Tiriac 6–2 6–0 6–3; Smith d. Tiriac 4–6 6–2 6–4 2–6 6–0; Gorman lost to Nastase 1–6 2–6 7–5 8–10.
1973 Australia (Capt: Neale Fraser) **d. USA** (Capt: Dennis Ralston) **5–0**, *Cleveland, Ohio (indoors):* J. D. Newcombe d. S. R. Smith 6–1 3–6 6–3 3–6 6–4; R. G. Laver d. T. Gorman 8–10 8–6 6–8 6–3 6–1; Laver/Newcombe d. Smith/E. Van Dillen 6–1 6–2 6–4; Newcombe d. Gorman 6–2 6–1 6–3; Laver d. Smith 6–3 6–4 3–6 6–2.
1974 South Africa w.o. India
1975 Sweden (Capt: Lennart Bergelin) **d. Czechoslovakia** (Capt: Antonin Bolardt) **3–2**, *Stockholm (indoors):* O. Bengtson lost to J. Kodes 4–6 6–2 5–7 4–6; B. Borg d. J. Hrebec 6–1 6–3 6–0; Bengtson/Borg d. Kodes/V. Zednik 6–4 6–4 6–4; Borg d. Kodes 6–4 6–2 6–2; Bengtson lost to Hrebec 6–1 3–6 1–6 4–6.
1976 Italy (Capt: Nicola Pietrangeli) **d. Chile** (Capt: Luis Ayala) **4–1**, *Santiago:* C. Barazzutti d. J. Fillol 7–5 4–6 7–5 6–1; A. Panatta d. P. Cornejo 6–3 6–1 6–3; P. Bertolucci/Panatta d. Cornejo/Fillol 3–6 6–2 9–7 6–3; Panatta d. Fillol 8–6 6–4 3–6 10–8; A. Zugarelli lost to B. Prajoux 4–6 4–6 2–6.
1977 Australia (Capt: Neale Fraser) **d. Italy** (Capt: Nicola Pietrangeli) **3–1**, *Sydney:* A. D. Roche d. A. Panatta 6–3 6–4 6–4; J. G. Alexander d. C. Barazzutti 6–2 8–6 4–6 6–2; Alexander/P. Dent lost to P. Bertolucci/Panatta 4–6 4–6 5–7; Alexander d. Panatta 6–4 4–6 2–6 8–6 11–9; Roche div'd with Barazzutti 12–12.
1978 USA (Capt: Tony Trabert) **d. Great Britain** (Capt: Paul Hutchins) **4–1**, *Palm Springs, California:* J. P. McEnroe d. J. M. Lloyd 6–1 6–2 6–2; B. E. Gottfried lost to C. J. Mottram 6–4 6–2 8–10 4–6 3–6; R. C. Lutz/S. R. Smith d. M. Cox/D. A. Lloyd 6–2 6–2 6–3; McEnroe d. Mottram 6–2 6–2 6–1; Gottfried d. J. M. Lloyd 6–1 6–2 6–4.
1979 USA (Capt: Tony Trabert) **d. Italy** (Capt: Vittorio Crotta) **5–0**, *San Francisco (indoors):* V. Gerulaitis d. C. Barazzutti 6–3 3–2 ret'd; J. P. McEnroe d. A. Panatta 6–2 6–3 6–4; R. C. Lutz/S. R. Smith d. P. Bertolucci/Panatta 6–4 12–10 6–2; McEnroe d. A. Zugarelli 6–4 6–3 6–1; Gerulaitis d. Panatta 6–1 6–3 6–3.
1980 Czechoslovakia (Capt: Antonin Bolardt) **d. Italy** (Capt: Vittorio Crotta) **4–1**, *Prague (indoors):* T. Smid d. A. Panatta 3–6 3–6 6–3 6–4 6–4; I. Lendl d. C. Barazzutti 4–6 6–1 6–1 6–2; Lendl/Smid d. P. Bertolucci/Panatta 3–6 6–3 3–6 6–3 6–4; Smid lost to Barazzutti 6–3 3–6 2–6; Lendl d. G. Ocleppo 6–3 6–3.
1981 USA (Capt: Arthur Ashe) **d. Argentina** (Capt: Carlos Junquet) **3–1**, *Cincinnati (indoors):* J. P. McEnroe d. G. Vilas 6–3 6–2 6–2; R. Tanner lost to J. L. Clerc 5–7 3–6 6–8; P. Fleming/McEnroe d. Clerc/Vilas 6–3 4–6 6–4 4–6 11–9; McEnroe d. Clerc 7–5 5–7 6–3 3–6 6–3; Tanner div'd with Vilas 11–10.
1982 USA (Capt: Arthur Ashe) **d. France** (Capt: Jean-Paul Loth) **4–1**, *Grenoble (indoors):* J. P. McEnroe d. Y. Noah 12–10 1–6 3–6 6–2 6–3; G. Mayer d. H. Leconte 6–2 6–2 7–9 6–4; P. Fleming/McEnroe d. Leconte/Noah 6–3 6–4 9–7; Mayer lost to Noah 1–6 0–6; McEnroe d. Leconte 6–2 6–3.
1983 Australia (Capt: Neale Fraser) **d. Sweden** (Capt: Hans Olsson) **3–2**, *Melbourne:* P. Cash lost to M. Wilander 3–6 6–4 7–9 3–6; J. Fitzgerald d. J. Nystrom 6–4 6–2 4–6 6–4; M. R. Edmondson/P. McNamee d. A. Jarryd/H. Simonsson 6–4 6–4 6–2; Cash d. Nystrom 6–4 6–1 6–1; Fitzgerald lost to Wilander 8–6 0–6 1–6.
1984 Sweden (Capt: Hans Olsson) **d. USA** (Capt: Arthur Ashe) **4–1**, *Gothenburg:* M. Wilander d. J. S. Connors 6–1 6–3 6–3; H. Sundstrom d. J. P. McEnroe 13–11 6–4 6–3; S. Edberg/A. Jarryd d. P. Fleming/McEnroe 7–5 5–7 6–2 7–5; Wilander lost to McEnroe 3–6 7–6 3–6; Sundstrom d. J. Arias 3–6 8–6 6–3.
1985 Sweden (Capt: Hans Olsson) **d. West Germany** (Capt: Wilhelm Bungert) **3–2**, *Munich:* M. Wilander d. M. Westphal 6–3 6–4 10–8; S. Edberg lost to B. Becker 3–6 6–3 5–7 6–8; Wilander/J. Nystrom d. Becker/A. Maurer 6–4 6–2 6–1; Wilander lost to Becker 3–6 6–2 3–6 3–6; Edberg d. Westphal 3–6 7–5 6–4 6–3.
1986 Australia (Capt: Neale Fraser) **d. Sweden** (Capt: Hans Olsson) **3–2**, *Melbourne:* P. Cash d. S. Edberg 13–11 13–11 6–4; P. McNamee lost to M. Pernfors 3–6 1–6 3–6; Cash/J. Fitzgerald d. Edberg/A. Jarryd 6–3 6–4 4–6 6–1; Cash d. Pernfors 2–6 4–6 6–3 6–4 6–3; McNamee lost to Edberg 8–10 4–6.
1987 Sweden (Capt: Hans Olsson) **d. India** (Capt: Vijay Amritraj) **5–0**, *Gothenburg:* M. Wilander d. R. Krishnan 6–4 6–1 6–3; A. Jarryd d. V. Amritraj 6–3 6–3 6–1; Wilander/J. Nystrom d. An./V. Amritraj 6–3 3–6 6–1 6–2; Jarryd d. Krishnan 6–4 6–3; Wilander d. V. Amritraj 6–2 6–0.
1988 West Germany (Capt: Niki Pilic) **d. Sweden** (Capt: Hans Olsson) **4–1**, *Gothenburg:* C.–U. Steeb d. M. Wilander 8–10 1–6 6–2 6–4 8–6; B. Becker d. S. Edberg 6–3 6–1 6–4; Becker/E. Jelen d. Edberg/A. Jarryd 3–6 2–6 7–5 6–3 6–2; Steeb lost to Edberg 4–6 6–8; P. Kuhnen w.o. K. Carlsson.
1989 West Germany (Capt: Niki Pilic) **d. Sweden** (Capt: John Anders Sjogren) **3–2**, *Stuttgart:* C.–U. Steeb lost to M. Wilander 7–5 6–7 7–6 2–6 3–6; B. Becker d. S. Edberg 6–2 6–2 6–4; Becker/E. Jelen d. A. Jarryd/J. Gunnarsson 7–6 6–4 3–6 6–7 6–4; Becker d. Wilander 6–2 6–0 6–2; Steeb lost to Edberg 2–6 4–6.
1990 USA (Capt: Tom Gorman) **d. Australia** (Capt: Neale Fraser) **3–2**, *St Petersburg:* A. Agassi d. R. Fromberg 4–6 6–4 4–6 6–2 6–4; M. Chang d. D. Cahill 6–2 7–6 6–0; R. Leach/J. Pugh d. P. Cash/J. Fitzgerald 6–4 6–2 3–6 7–6; Agassi lost to Cahill 4–6 6–4 ret.; Chang lost to Fromberg 5–7 6–2 3–6.

1991 France (Capt: Yannick Noah) **d. USA** (Capt: Tom Gorman) **3–1**, *Lyon:* G. Forget lost to A. Agassi 7–6 2–6 1–6 2–6; H. Leconte d. P. Sampras 6–4 7–5 6–4; Forget/Leconte d. K. Flach/R. Seguso 6–1 6–4 4–6 6–2; Forget d. Sampras 7–6 3–6 6–3 6–4; Leconte v Agassi not played.
1992 USA (Capt: Tom Gorman) **d. Switzerland** (Capt: Dmitri Sturdza) **3–1**, *Fort Worth:* A. Agassi d. J. Hlasek 6–1 6–2 6–2; J. Courier lost to M. Rosset 3–6 7–6 6–3 4–6 4–6; J. McEnroe/P. Sampras d. Rosset/Hlasek 6–7 6–7 7–5 6–1 6–2; Courier d. Hlasek 6–3 3–6 6–3 6–4; Agassi v Rossi not played.
1993 Germany (Capt: Niki Pilic) **d. Australia** (Capt: Neale Fraser) **4–1**, *Dusseldorf:* M. Stich d. J. Stoltenberg 6–7 6–3 6–1 4–6 6–3; R. Fromberg d. M.-K. Goellner 3–6 5–7 7–6 6–2 9–7; P. Kuhnen/Stich d. T. Woodbridge/M. Woodforde 7–6 4–6 6–3 7–6; Stich d. Fromberg 6–4 6–2 6–2; Goellner d. Stoltenberg 6–1 6–7 7–6.
1994 Sweden (Capt: John Anders Sjogren) **d. Russia** (Capt: Vadim Borisov) **4–1**, *Moscow:* S. Edberg d. A. Volkov 6–4 6–2 6–7 0–6 8–6; M. Larsson d. Y. Kafelnikov 6–0 6–2 3–6 2–6 6–3; J. Apell/J. Bjorkman d. Y. Kafelnikov/A. Olhovskiy 6–7 6–2 6–3 1–6 8–6; Edberg lost to Kafelnikov 6–4 4–6 0–6; Larsson d. Volkov 7–6 6–4.
1995 USA (Capt: Tom Gullikson) **d. Russia** (Capt: Anatoli Lepeshin) **3–2**, *Moscow:* P. Sampras d. A. Chesnokov 3–6 6–4 6–3 6–7 6–4; Y. Kafelnikov d. J. Courier 7–6 7–5 6–3; T. Martin/P. Sampras d. Y. Kafelnikov/A. Olhovskiy 7–5 6–4 6–3; P. Sampras d. Y. Kafelnikov 6–2 6–4 7–6; A. Chesnokov d. J. Courier 6–7 7–5 6–0.
1996 France (Capt: Yannick Noah) **d. Sweden** (Capt: Carl Axel-Hageskog) **3–2**, *Malmo SWE:* C. Pioline d. S. Edberg 6–3 6–4 6–3; T. Enqvist d. A. Boetsch 6–4 6–3 7–6(2); G. Forget/G. Raoux d. J. Bjorkman/N. Kulti 6–3 1–6 6–3 6–3; T. Enqvist d. C. Pioline 3–6 6–7(8) 6–4 6–4 9–7; A. Boetsch d. N. Kulti 7–6(2) 2–6 4–6 7–6(5) 10–8.
1997 Sweden (Capt: Carl-Axel Hageskog) **d. USA** (Capt: Tom Gullikson) **5–0**, *Gothenburg:* J. Bjorkman (SWE) d. M. Chang (USA) 7–5 1–6 6–3 6–3; M. Larsson (SWE) d. P. Sampras (USA) 3–6 7–6(1) 2–1 ret; J. Bjorkman/N. Kulti (SWE) d. T. Martin/J. Stark (USA) 6–4 6–4 6–4; J. Bjorkman (SWE) d. J. Stark (USA) 6–1 6–1; M. Larsson (SWE) d. M. Chang (USA) 7–6(4) 6–7(6) 6–4.

QUALIFIERS FOR WORLD GROUP 1998

Belgium	Germany	Russia	Switzerland
Brazil	India	Slovak Republic	Zimbabwe

FED CUP

Launched in 1963 to celebrate the 50th anniversary of the International Tennis Federation, the Federation Cup (as it was known until 1994) was played annually at one site as a week-long knock-out competition. Each tie comprised two singles rubbers and one doubles. A qualifying competition was introduced in 1992 to accommodate growing numbers. By 1994 there were 73 entries and it was decided to relaunch the competition in 1995 as the Fed Cup, to be played as a season-long home and away zonal competition with the eight top teams contesting the World Group. The final is played in the country of one of the finalists, towards the end of the year. Ties consist of five rubbers, two reverse singles and the doubles. Sponsored first by Colgate (1976–80), then by NEC (1981–94) it has been supported since 1996 by KB (Komereni Banka), one of the largest banks in the Czech Republic.

FINAL ROUNDS

1963 USA (Capt: William Kellog) **d. Australia** (Capt: Nell Hopman) **2–1**, *Queen's Club, London, 18–21 June:* D. R. Hard lost to M. Smith 3–6 0–6; B. J. Moffitt d. L. R. Turner 5–7 6–0 6–3; Hard/Moffitt d. Smith/Turner 3–6 13–11 6–3.
1964 Australia (Capt: Brian Tobin) **d. USA** (Capt: Madge Vosters) **2–1**, *Germanstown Cricket Club, Philadelphia, 2–5 September:* M. Smith d. B. J. Moffitt 6–2 6–3; L. R. Turner d. N. Richey 7–5 6–1; Smith/Turner lost to Moffitt/Mrs J. R. Susman 6–4 5–7 1–6.
1965 Australia (Capt: Margaret Smith) **d. USA** (Capt: Billie Jean Moffitt) **2–1**, *Kooyong Stadium, Melbourne, 12–18 January:* L. R. Turner d. Mrs C. Graebner 6–3 2–6 6–3; M. Smith d. B. J. Moffitt 6–4 8–6; Smith/J. M. Tegart lost to Graebner/Moffitt 5–7 6–4 4–6.
1966 USA (Capt: Ros Greenwood) **d. West Germany** (Capt: Edda Buding) **3–0**, *Turin, 11–15 May:* J. M. Heldman d. H. Niessen 4–6 7–5 6–1; Mrs L. W. King d. E. Buding 6–3 3–6 6–1; Mrs C. Graebner/Mrs King d. Buding/H. Schultse 6–4 6–2.
1967 USA (Capt: Donna Fales) **d. Great Britain** (Capt: Angela Mortimer Barrett) **2–0**, *Rot-Weiss Club, Berlin, 7–11 June:* R. Casals d. S. V. Wade 9–7 8–6; Mrs L. W. King d. Mrs P. F. Jones 6–3 6–4; Casals/Mrs King div'd with Mrs Jones/Wade 6–8 9–7.
1968 Australia (Capt: Margaret Court) **d. Netherlands** (Capt: Jenny Ridderhof) **3–0**, *Stade Roland Garros, Paris, 23–26 May:* K. A. Melville d. M. Jansen 4–6 7–5 6–3; Mrs B. M. Court d. A. Suurbeck 6–1 6–3; Court/Melville d. Suurbeck/L. Venneboer 6–3 6–8 7–5.
1969 USA (Capt: Donna Fales) **d. Australia** (Capt: Wayne Reid) **2–1**, *Athens, 19–25 May:* N. Richey d. K. A. Melville 6–4 6–3; J. M. Heldman lost to Mrs B. M. Court 1–6 6–8; J. Bartkowicz/Richey d. Court/J. M. Tegart 6–4 6–4.
1970 Australia (Capt: Alf Chave) **d. West Germany** (Capt: Edward Dorrenberg) **3–0**, *Freiburg, Germany, 19–24 May:* K. M. Krantzcke d. Mrs H. Hoesl 6–2 6–3; Mrs D. E. Dalton d. H. Niessen 4–6 6–3 6–3; Dalton/Krantzcke d. Hoesl/Niessen 6–2 7–5.

Nathalie Tauziat, a winner at Birmingham, was also a member of the successful French Fed Cup team and won the longest single set played in that competition when she defeated Naoko Sawamatsu 7–5 4–6 17–15. (Michael Cole)

1971 Australia (Capt: Margaret Court) **d. Great Britain** (Capt: Ann Haydon Jones) **3–0**, *Perth, Australia, 26–29 December 1970:* Mrs B. M. Court d. Mrs P. F. Jones 6–8 6–3 6–2; E. F. Goolagong d. S. V. Wade 6–4 6–1; Court/L. Hunt d. W. M. Shaw/Wade 6–4 6–4.

1972 South Africa (Capt: Dr. Jackie Du Toit) **d. Great Britain** (Capt: Virginia Wade) **2–1**, *Ellis Park, Johannesburg, 19–26 March:* Mrs Q. C. Pretorius lost to S. V. Wade 3–6 2–6; B. Kirk d. W. M. Shaw 4–6 7–5 6–0; Kirk/Pretorius d. Wade/Mrs G. M. Williams 6–1 7–5.

1973 Australia (Capt: Vic Edwards) **d. South Africa** (Capt: Dr. Jackie Du Toit) **3–0**, *Bad Homburg, Germany, 30 April–6 May:* E. F. Goolagong d. Mrs Q. C. Pretorius 6–0 6–2; P. Coleman d. B. Kirk 10–8 6–0; Goolagong/J. Young d. Kirk/Pretorius 6–1 6–2.

1974 Australia (Capt: Vic Edwards) **d. USA** (Capt: Donna Fales) **2–1**, *Naples, 13–19 May:* E. F. Goolagong d. J. M. Heldman 6–1 7–5; D. L. Fromholtz lost to C. M. Evert 6–2 5–7 3–6; Goolagong/J. Young d. Heldman/S. A. Walsh 7–5 8–6.

1975 Czechoslovakia (Capt: Vera Sukova) **d. Australia** (Capt: Vic Edwards) **3–0**, *Aix-en-Provence, 6–11 May:* M. Navratilova* d. E. F. Goolagong 6–3 6–4; R. Tomanova d. H Gourlay 6–4 6–2; Navratilova/Tomanova d. D. L. Fromholtz/Gourlay 6–3 6–1.

1976 USA (Capt: Billie Jean King) **d. Australia** (Capt: Neale Fraser) **2–1**, *Spectrum Stadium, Philadelphia, 22–29 August:* R. Casals lost to Mrs G. Reid 6–1 3–6 5–7; Mrs L. W. King d. Mrs E. Cawley 7–6 6–4; Casals/King d. Cawley/Reid 7–5 6–3.

1977 USA (Capt: Vicky Berner) **d. Australia** (Capt: Neale Fraser) **2–1**, *Devonshire Park, Eastbourne, 13–18 June:* Mrs L. W. King d. D. L. Fromholtz 6–1 2–6 6–2; C. M. Evert d. Mrs G. Reid 7–5 6–3; Casals/Evert lost to Reid/W. M. Turnbull 3–6 3–6.

1978 USA (Capt: Vicky Berner) **d. Australia** (Capt: Neale Fraser) **2–1**, *Kooyong Stadium, Melbourne, 27 November–3 December:* T. A. Austin lost to Mrs G. Reid 3–6 3–6; C. M. Evert d. W. M. Turnbull 3–6 6–1 6–1; Evert/Mrs L. W. King d. Reid/Turnbull 4–6 6–1 6–4.

1979 USA (Capt: Vicky Berner) **d. Australia** (Capt: Neale Fraser) **3–0**, *Madrid, 30 April–6 May:* T. A. Austin d. Mrs G. Reid 6–3 6–0; Mrs J. M. Lloyd d. D. L. Fromholtz 2–6 6–3 8–6; R. Casals/Mrs L. W. King d. Reid/W. M. Turnbull 3–6 6–3 8–6.

1980 USA (Capt: Vicky Berner) **d. Australia** (Capt: Mary Hawton) **3–0**, *Rot-Weiss Club, Berlin, 19–25 May:* Mrs J. M. Lloyd d. D. L. Fromholtz 4–6 6–1 6–1; T. A. Austin d. W. M. Turnbull 6–2 6–3; R. Casals/K. Jordan d. Fromholtz/S. Leo 2–6 6–4 6–4.

1981 USA (Capt: Mrs J. M. Lloyd) **d. Great Britain** (Capt: Sue Mappin) **3–0**, *Tokyo, 9–15 November:* A. Jaeger d. S. V. Wade 6–3 6–1; Mrs J. M. Lloyd d. S. Barker 6–2 6–1; R. Casals/K. Jordan d. J. M. Durie/Wade 6–4 7–5.

1982 USA (Capt: Mrs J. M. Lloyd) **d. West Germany** (Capt: Klaus Hofsass) **3–0**, *Santa Clara, California, 19–25 July:* Mrs J. M. Lloyd d. C. Kohde 2–6 6–1 6–3; M. Navratilova d. B. Bunge 6–4 6–4; Lloyd/Navratilova d. Bunge/Kohde 3–6 6–1 6–2.

1983 Czechoslovakia (Capt: Jan Kukal) **d. West Germany** (Capt: Klaus Hofsass) **2–1**, *Zurich, 18–24 July:* H. Sukova d. C. Kohde 6–4 2–6 6–2; H. Mandlikova d. B. Bunge 6–2 3–0 ret'd; I. Budarova/M. Skuherska lost to E. Pfaff/Kohde 6–3 2–6 1–6.

1984 Czechoslovakia (Capt: Jan Kukal) **d. Australia** (Capt: Judy Dalton) **2–1**, *Sao Paulo, 15–22 July:* H. Sukova lost to A. Minter 5–7 5–7; H. Mandlikova d. E. Sayers 6–1 6–0; Mandlikova/Sukova d. W. Turnbull/Sayers 6–2 6–2.

1985 Czechoslovakia (Capt: Jiri Medonos) **d. USA** (Capt: Tom Gorman) **2–1**, *Nagoya, 7–13 October:* H. Sukova d. E. Burgin 6–3 6–7 6–4; H. Mandlikova d. K. Jordan 7–5 6–1; A. Holikova/R. Marsikova lost to Burgin/Jordan 2–6 3–6.

1986 USA (Capt: Marty Riessen) **d. Czechoslovakia** (Capt: Jiri Medonos) **3–0**, *Prague, 21–27 July:* Mrs J. M. Lloyd d. H. Sukova 7–5 7–6; M. Navratilova d. H. Mandlikova 7–5 6–1; Navratilova/P. H. Shriver d. Mandlikova/Sukova 6–4 6–2.

1987 West Germany (Capt: Klaus Hofsass) **d. USA** (Capt: Marty Riessen) **2–1**, *Vancouver, 27 July–2 August:* C. Kohde-Kilsch lost to P. H. Shriver 0–6 6–7; S. Graf d. C. M. Evert 6–2 6–1; Kohde-Kilsch/Graf d. Evert/Shriver 1–6 7–5 6–4.

1988 Czechoslovakia (Capt: Jiri Medonos) **d. USSR** (Capt: Olga Morozova) **2–1**, *Melbourne, 7–11 December:* R. Zrubakova d. L. Savchenko 6–1 7–6; H. Sukova d. Zvereva 6–3 6–4; J. Novotna/J. Pospisilova lost to Savchenko/Zvereva 6–7 5–7.

1989 USA (Capt: Marty Riessen) **d. Spain** (Capt: Juan Alvarino) **3–0**, *Tokyo, 1–8 October:* C. Evert d. C. Martinez 6–3 6–2; M. Navratilova d. A. Sanchez 0–6 6–3 6–4; Z. Garrison/P. H. Shriver d. Martinez/Sanchez 7–5 6–1.

1990 USA (Capt: Marty Riessen) **d. USSR** (Capt: Olga Morozova) **2–1**, *Atlanta, 22–29 July:* J. Capriati d. L. Meskhi 7–6 6–2; Z. Garrison lost to N. Zvereva 6–4 3–6 3–6; Z. Garrison/G. Fernandez d. N. Zvereva/L. Savchenko 6–4 6–3.

1991 Spain (Capt: Juan Alvarino) **d. USA** (Capt: Marty Riessen) **2–1**, *Nottingham, 22–28 July:* C. Martinez lost to J. Capriati 6–4 6–7 1–6; A. Sanchez d. M. J. Fernandez 6–3 6–4; Martinez/Sanchez d. G. Fernandez/Z. Garrison 3–6 6–1 6–1.

1992 Germany (Capt: Klaus Hofsass) **d. Spain** (Capt: Juan Alvarino) **2–1**, *Frankfurt, 13–19 July:* A. Huber d. C. Martinez 6–3 6–7 6–1; S. Graff d. A. Sanchez-Vic. 6–4 6–2; A. Huber/B. Rittner lost to A. Sanchez–Vic./C. Martinez 1–6 2–6.

1993 Spain (Capt: Miguel Margets) **d. Austrialia** (Capt: Wendy Turnbull) **3–0**, *Frankfurt, 19–25 July:* C. Martinez d. M. Jaggard-Lai 6–0 6–2; A. Sanchez Vicario d. N. Provis 6–2 6–3; Martinez/Sanchez Vicario d. E.. Smylie/R. Stubbs 3–6 6–1 6–3.

1994 Spain (Capt: Miguel Margets) **d. USA** (Capt: Marty Riessen) **3–0**, *Frankfurt, 18–25 July:* C. Martinez d. M. J. Fernandez 6–2 6–2; A. Sanchez Vicario d. L. Davenport 6–2 6–1; Martinez/Sanchez Vicario d. G. Fernandez/M. J. Fernandez 6–3 6–4.

1995 Spain (Capt: Miguel Margets) **d. USA** (Capt: Billie Jean King) **3–2**, *Valencia, 25–26 November:* C. Martinez d. C.

Rubin 7–5 6–3; A. Sanchez Vicario d. M. J. Fernandez 6–3 6–2; C. Martinez d. M. J. Fernandez 6–3 6–4; A. Sanchez Vicario lost to C. Rubin 6–1 4–6 4–6; V. Ruano/M. A. Sanchez lost to L. Davenport/G. Fernandez 3–6 6–7.
1996 USA (Capt: Billie Jean King) **d. Spain** (Capt: Miguel Margets) **5–0**, *Atlantic City, 28–29 September:* M. Seles d. C. Martinez 6–2 6–4; L. Davenport d. A. Sanchez Vicario 7–5 6–1; M. Seles d. A. Sanchez Vicario 3–6 6–3 6–1; L. Davenport d. G. Leon Garcia 7–5 6–2; M. J. Fernandez/L. Wild d. G. Leon Garcia/V. Ruano-Pascual 6–1 6–4.
1997 France (Capt: Yannick Noah) **d. Netherlands** (Capt: Fred Hemmes) **4–1**, *Den Bosch, 4–5 October:* S. Testud d. B. Schultz-McCarthy 6–4 4–6 6–3; M. Pierce d. M. Oremans 6–4 6–1; B. Schultz-McCarthy d. M. Pierce 4–6 6–3 6–4; S. Testud d. M. Oremans 0–6 6–3 6–3; A. Fusai/N. Tauziat d. M. Bollegraf/C. Vis 6–3 6–4.
** M. Navratilova became a US citizen in 1981.*

OLYMPIC MEDAL WINNERS

1896 Athens
Men's singles: Gold – J Boland (IRL), Silver – D Kasdaglis (GRE). Men's Doubles: Gold – J Boland(IRL) and F Traun (AUT); Silver – D Kasdaglis and D Petrokokkinos (GRE).
1900 Paris
Men's singles: Gold – L Doherty (GBR), Silver – H Mahony (IRL), Bronze – R Doherty (GBR) and A Norris (GBR). Men's doubles: Gold – L and R Doherty (GBR), Silver – M Decugis (FRA) and S de Garmendia (USA), Bronze – A Prevost and G de la Chapelle (FRA); H Mahony (IRL) and A Norris (GBR). Women's singles: Gold – C Cooper (GBR), Silver – H Prevost (FRA), Bronze – M Jones (USA) and H Rosenbaumova (TCH). Mixed doubles: Gold – R Doherty and C Cooper (GBR), Silver – H Mahony (IRL) and H Prevost (FRA), Bronze – A Warden (GBR) and H Rosenbaumova (TCH); L Doherty (GBR) and M Jones (USA).
1904 St Louis
Men's singles: Gold – B Wright (USA), Silver – L LeRoy (USA). Men's doubles: Gold – E Leonard and B Wright (USA), Silver – A Bell and R LeRoy (USA).
1908 London
(Indoors at Queen's Club) Men's singles: Gold – A Gore (GBR), Silver – G Caridia (GBR), Bronze -M Ritchie (GBR). Men's doubles: Gold – A Gore and H Roper Barrett (GBR) SIlver – G Caridia and G Simond (GBR), Bronze – W Bostrom and G Setterwall (SWE). Women's singles: Gold – G Eastlake Smith (GBR), Silver – A Greene (GBR), Bronze Mrs M Adlerstrahle (SWE). (Outdoors at Wimbledon) Men's singles: Gold – M Ritchie (GBR), Silver – O Froitzheim (GER), Bronze – W Eaves (GBR). Men's doubles: Gold – R Doherty and G Hillyard (GBR), Silver – M Ritchie and J Parke (GBR), Bronze – C Cazalet and C Dixon (GBR). Women's singles: Gold – Mrs R Lambert Chambers (GBR), Silver – D Boothby (GBR), Bronze – Mrs R Winch (GBR).
1912 Stockholm
(Indoors) Men's singles: Gold – A Gobert (FRA), Silver – C Dixon (GBR), Bronze -A Wilding (NZL). Men's Doubles: Gold – M Germot and A Gobert (FRA), Silver – C Kempe and G Setterwall (SWE), Bronze – A Beamish and C Dixon (GBR). Women's singles: Gold – Mrs F Hannam (GBR), Silver – S Castenschoild (DEN), Bronze – Mrs E Parton (GBR). Mixed Doubles; Gold – C Dixon and Mrs Hannam (GBR), Silver – H Roper Barrett and F Aitchison (GBR), Bronze – G Setterwall and Mrs H Fick (SWE). (Outdoors). Men's singles: Gold – C Winslow (RSA), Silver – H Kitson (RSA), Bronze – O Kreuzer (GER). Men's doubles: Gold – H Kitson and C Winslow (RSA), Silver – F Pipes and A Zborzil (AUT), Bronze – A Canet and M Meny (FRA). Women's singles: Gold – M Broquedis (FRA), Silver – D Koring (GER), Bronze – M Bjorstedt (NOR). Mixed doubles: Gold – H Schomburgk and D Koring (GER), Silver – G Setterwall and Mrs H Fick (SWE), Bronze – A Canet and M Broquedis (FRA).
1920 Antwerp
Men's singles: Gold – L Raymond (RSA), Silver – I Kumagae (JPN), Bronze – C Winslow (RSA). Men's Doubles: Gold – O Turnbull and M Woosnam (GBR), Silver – S Kashio and Kumagae (JPN), Bronze – P Albarran and M Decugis (FRA). Women's singles: Gold – S Lenglen (FRA) , Silver – E Holman (GBR), Bronze – K McKane (GBR). Women's doubles: Gold – Mrs R McNAir and K McKane (GBR), Silver -MRs A Beamish and E Holman (GBR), Bronze – S Lenglen and E d'Ayen (FRA). Mixed doubles; Gold – M Decugis and S Lenglen (FRA), M Woosnam and K McKane (GBR), Bronze – M Zemla and M Skrobkova (TCH).
1924 Paris
Men's singles: Gold – V Richards (USA), Silver – H Cochet (FRA), Bronze – H de Morpurgo (ITA). Men's doubles: Gold – F Hunter and V Richards (USA), Silver – J Brugnon and H Cochet (FRA), Bronze – J Borotra and H Lacoste (FRA). Women's singles: Gold – H Wills (USA), Silver – J Vlasto (FRA), Bronze -K McKane (GBR). Women's doubles: Gold – Mrs H Wightman and H Wills (USA), Silver – Mrs E Covell and K McKane (GBR), Bronze – Mrs D Shepherd-Barron and E Colyer (GBR). Mixed doubles: Gold – R Williams and Mrs H Wightman (USA), Silver -V Richards and Mrs M Jessup (USA), Bronze – H Timmer and C Bouman (HOL).
1968 Mexico City (Demonstration Sport)
Men's singles: Gold – M Santana(ESP), Silver – M Orantes (ESP), Bronze – H Fitzgibbon (USA). Men's doubles: Gold – R Osuna and V Zarazua (MEX), Silver – J Gisbert and M Santana (ESP), Bronze – P Darmon(FRA) and J Loyo-Mayo (MEX). Women's singles: Gold – H Neissen (GER), Silver – J Bartkowicz (USA), Bronze – J Heldman (USA). Women's doubles: E Buding and H Neissen (GER), Silver – Mrs R Darmon (FRA) and J Heldman (USA), Bronze – J Bartkowicz and V Ziegenfuss (USA). Mixed doubles: Gold – H Fitzgibbon and J Heldman (USA), Silver – J Fassbender and H Neissen (GER), Bronze – J Osborne and J Bartkowicz (USA).
1984 Los Angeles (Demonstration Sport) *6–11 August*. Held at the Los Angeles Tennis Center, UCLA, on hard courts. Men's singles: Gold – S Edberg (SWE), Silver – F Maciel (MEX), Bronze – P Cane (ITA) and J Arias (USA). Women's singles: Gold – S Graf (GER), Silver – S Goles (YUG), Bronze -C Tanvier (FRA) and R Reggi (ITA).

1988 Seoul *20 September–1 October.* Held at Olympic Park Tennis Centre on hard courts
Men's singles: Gold – M Mecir (TCH), Silver – T Mayotte (USA), Bronze – S Edberg (SWE) and B Gilbert (USA). Men's doubles: Gold – K Flach and R Seguso (USA), Silver – S Casal and E Sanchez (ESP), Bronze – S Edberg and A Jarryd (SWE) and M Mecir and M Srejber (TCH). Women's singles: Gold – S Graf (GER), Silver – G Sabatini (ARG), Bronze – Z Garrison (USA) and M Maleeva (BUL). Women's doubles: Gold – P Shriver and Z Garrison (USA), Silver – J Novotna and H Sukova (TCH), Bronze – W Turnbull and E Smylie (AUS) and S Graf and C Kohde-Kilsch (GER).
1992 Barcelona *28 July–8 August.* Held at Vall D'Hebron Tennis Centre on red clay.
Men's singles: Gold – M Rosset (SUI), Silver – J Arrese (ESP), Bronze – G Ivanisevic (CRO) and A Cherkasov (CIS). Men's doubles: Gold – B Becker and M Stich (GER), Silver – W Ferreira and P Norval (RSA), Bronze – G Ivanisevic and G Prpic (CRO) and J Frana and C Miniussi (ARG). Women's singles: Gold – J Capriati (USA), Silver – S Graf (GER), Bronze – M J Fernandez (USA) and A Sanchez Vicario (ESP). Women's doubles: Gold – M J Fernandez and G Fernandez (USA), Silver – C Martinez and A Sanchez Vicario (ESP), Bronze – R McQuillan and N Provis (AUS) and L Meskhi and N Zvereva (CIS).
1996 Atlanta *23 July–3 August.* Held at Stone Mountain Park Tennis Center on hard courts.
Men's singles: Gold – A. Agassi (USA), Silver – S. Bruguera (ESP), Bronze – L. Paes (IND). Men's doubles: Gold – T. Woodbridge and M. Woodforde (AUS), Silver – N. Broad and T. Henman (GBR), Bronze – M. Goellner and D. Prinosil (GER). Women's singles: Gold – L. Davenport (USA), Silver – A. Sanchez Vicario (ESP), Bronze – J. Novotna (CZE). Women's doubles: Gold – G. Fernandez and M. J. Fernandez (USA), Silver – J. Novotna and H. Sukova (CZE), Bronze – C. Martinez and A. Sanchez Vicario (ESP).

WIGHTMAN CUP

Women's annual team contest between USA and Great Britain, for a silver trophy presented by Mrs Hazel Hotchkiss Wightman in 1923, each match comprising five singles and two doubles, with reverse singles played between the two top players. Discontinued in 1989.
Summary: USA 51 wins; Great Britain 10 wins. (Note: Full match results can be found in previous issues of *World of Tennis* up to 1996.)

EUROPEAN CUP – MEN

Formerly King's Cup. International Men's Team Championship on Indoor Courts. It was staged on a knock-out basis 1936–38, on a league basis, 1952–74, with ties home and away 1976–83. From 1984 the ties in each division were held concurrently at one venue. The Challenge Round system was used in the two opening years, with 1937 the only Challenge Round.

FINALS

1936 France d. Sweden 4–1, Stockholm: J. Borotra d. K. Schroder 2–6 6–2 6–1 6–3, d. C. Ostberg 6–1 6–3 7–5; B. Destremau d. Schroder 3–6 7–5 6–2 6–4, d. Ostberg 6–2 6–2 6–4; C. Boussus/J. Brugnon lost to Ostberg/ Schroder 2–6 6–3 4–6 6–3 4–6.
1937 France d. Sweden 5–0, *Paris:* B. Destremau d. K. Schroder 8–6 1–6 2–6 11–9 8–6, d. N. Rohlsson 1–6 1–6 6–3 6–1 6–0; Y. Petra d. Rohlsson 6–1 6–4 6–2, d. Schroder 6–3 3–6 6–3 6–4; H. Bolelli/J. Lesueur d. Schroder/H. Wallen 10–8 6–4 6–4.
1938 Germany d. Denmark 5–0, *Hamburg:* R. Menzel d. H. Plougmann 6–3 6–2 8–6; H. Henkel d. I. Gerdes 6–4 6–0 6–3, d. Plougmann 6–2 6–1 6–3; R. Redl d. Gerdes 6–3 6–3 6–2; Henkel/Menzel d. Gerdes/Plougmann 6–0 6–4 6–2.
1939–51 Not held
1952 Denmark d. Sweden 3–2, *Stockholm:* K. Nielsen lost to S. Davidson 3–6 7–9 4–6; T. Ulrich d. T. Johansson 7–5 0–6 6–4 6–2; Nielsen/Ulrich d. Davidson/Johansson 6–2 2–6 4–6 8–6 7–5; Nielsen d. Johansson 6–3 6–4 6–1; Ulrich lost to Davidson 6–4 4–6 1–6 6–1 2–6.
1953 Denmark d. Sweden 3–2, *Copenhagen:* T. Ulrich d. S. Davidson 14–12 11–9 1–6 11–9; J. Ulrich lost to T. Johansson 0–6 2–6 7–9; J. Ulrich/T. Ulrich d. Davidson/N. Rohlsson 6–4 6–4 4–6 3–6 6–3; J. Ulrich lost to Davidson 3–6 4–6 0–6; T. Ulrich d. Johansson 6–3 2–6 6–4 5–7 6–3.
1954 Denmark d. Italy 3–2, *Milan:* T. Ulrich d. G. Merlo 7–5 2–6 9–7 9–7; K. Nielsen lost to O. Sirola 5–7 6–8 8–6 6–2 3–6; Nielsen/Ulrich d. N. Pietrangeli/Sirola 2–6 2–6 11–9 6–1 12–10; Nielsen lost to Pietrangeli 5–7 6–3 9–7 3–6 5–7; Ulrich d. Sirola 7–5 10–8 6–4.
1955 Sweden d. Denmark 4–1, *Copenhagen:* S. Davidson d. J. Ulrich 7–5 12–10 6–1; U. Schmidt lost to K. Nielsen 3–6 2–6 6–4 4–6; Davidson/T. Johansson d. Nielsen/J. Ulrich 11–9 6–3 14–12; Davidson d. Nielsen 8–10 6–2 7–9 12–10 7–5; Schmidt d. J. Ulrich 7–9 3–6 6–0 8–6 6–3.
1956 Sweden d. France 4–1, *Paris:* S. Davidson lost to P. Darmon 7–9 6–2 5–7 6–8; U. Schmidt d. R. Haillet 6–1 /6–2 6–4; Davidson/Schmidt d. Darmon/P. Remy 8–6 3–6 6–1 6–4; Davidson d. Haillet 6–2 2–6 6–4 6–1; Schmidt d. Darmon 6–1 10–8 6–3.
1957 Sweden d. Denmark 3–2, *Copenhagen:* J. E. Lundqvist d. K. Nielsen 4–6 6–3 10–8 6–4; U. Schmidt lost to T. Ulrich 4–6 7–9 2–6; Lundqvist/Schmidt d. J. Ulrich/T. Ulrich 6–3 5–7 6–0 6–3; Lundqvist d. T. Ulrich 7–5 6–1 6–2; Schmidt lost to Nielsen 6–4 4–6 2–6 5–7.
1958 Sweden d. Denmark 3–2, *Stockholm:* B. Folke lost to J. Ulrich 11–13 3–6 4–6; S. Davidson d. K. Nielsen 6–0 6–1 6–4; Davidson/T. Johansson d. Nielsen/J. Ulrich 10–8 1–6 6–3 6–8 6–3; Folke lost to Nielsen 4–6 3–6 3–6; Davidson d. J. Ulrich 6–4 6–3 1–6 6–1.

1959 Denmark won, *Stockholm:* Denmark d. Italy 2–1, lost to Sweden 2–1, d. France 2–1 (12–11 sets); Sweden lost to France 2–1, d. Denmark 2–1, d. Italy 2–1 (10–10 sets); Italy lost to Denmark 2–1, d. France 2–1, lost to Sweden 2–1 (11–11 sets); France d. Sweden 2–1, lost to Italy 2–1, lost to France 2–1 (10–11 sets). Danish team: K. Nielsen and J. Ulrich.
1960 Denmark d. West Germany 3–0, *Paris:* J. Leschly d. B. Nitsche 6–4 8–6; J. Ulrich d. P. Scholl 6–2 6–3; Leschly/J. Ulrich d. Nitsche/Scholl 6–8 6–2 6–0.
1961 Sweden d. Denmark 2–1, *Cologne:* U. Schmidt d. J. Leschly 6–4 6–2; J. E. Lundqvist d. J. Ulrich 6–3 6–1; Lundqvist/Schmidt lost to Leschly/J. Ulrich 5–7 6–4 5–7.
1962 Denmark d. Italy 3–0, *Copenhagen:* J. Leschly d. G. Merlo 6–3 8–6; J. Ulrich d. N. Pietrangeli 6–4 6–2; Leschly/J. Ulrich d. Pietrangeli/O. Sirola 9–7 7–5.
1963 Yugoslavia d. Denmark 3–0, *Belgrade:* Yugoslav team: B. Jovanovic and N. Pilic.
1964 Great Britain d. Sweden 3–0, *Stockholm:* M. J. Sangster d. J. E. Lundquist 13–15 10–8 12–10; R. Taylor d. B. Holmstrom 6–3 9–7; Sangster/R. K. Wilson d. Holmstrom/L. Olander 4–6 12–10 6–4.
1965 Great Britain d. Denmark 2–1, *Torquay:* R. K. Wilson lost to J. Leschly 1–6 4–6; M. Cox d. C. Hedelund 6–4 6–3; A. R. Mills/Wilson d. Leschly/Hedelund 3–6 6–2 6–4 12–10.
1966 Great Britain d. Italy 3–0, *Milan:* R. Taylor d. N. Pietrangeli 6–4 6–4; M. J. Sangster d. G. Maioli 7–9 6–4 11–9; Sangster/R. K. Wilson d. D. di Maso/Maioli 6–4 6–1.
1967 Great Britain d. Sweden 2–1, *Stockholm:* R. Taylor d. O. Bengtson 2–6 6–3 9–7; R. K. Wilson d. M. Carlstein 8–6 6–2; M. Cox/Taylor lost to Bengtson/B. Homstrom 4–6 7–9.
1968 Sweden d. Netherlands 2–1, *Bratislava:* O. Bengtson lost to T. S. Okker 12–14 4–6; M. Carlstein d. J. Hordjik 6–4 6–3; Bengtson/Carlstein d. N. Fleury/Okker 1–6 4–6 7–5 6–3 6–4.
1969 Czechoslovakia d. Sweden 2–1, *Cologne:* V. Zednik d. H. Zahr 6–4, 7–5; J. Kukal d. O. Bengtson 6–1 5–7 11–9; Kukal/Zednik lost to Bengtson/H. Nerell 4–6 4–6.
1970 France d. Denmark 2–1, *Copenhagen:* J. B. Chanfreau d. J. Ulrich 6–3 8–6; G. Goven lost to J. Leschly 1–6 3–6; Chanfreau/Goven d. Ulrich/Leschly 2–6 6–4 7–5.
1971 Italy d. Spain 2–1, *Ancona:* A. Panatta lost to M. Orantes 2–6 3–6; N. Pietrangeli d. J. Gisbert 7–9 8–6 6–4; Panatta/Pietrangeli d. Gisbert/Orantes 4–6 8–6 6–3 6–4.
1972 Spain d. Hungary 3–0, *Madrid:* A. Gimeno d. S. Baranyi 10–8 6–2; J. Gisbert d. B. Taroczy 6–1 7–9 6–3; J. Herrera/A. Munoz d. R. Machan/Taroczy 6–4 3–6 7–5.
1973 Sweden d. Italy 2–1, *Hanover:* L. Johansson d. A. Zugarelli 6–4 6–3; B. Borg d. A. Panatta 4–6 6–2 8–6; Borg/Johansson lost to P. Bertolucci/Zugarelli 6–3 5–7 4–6.
1974 Italy d. Sweden 3–0, *Ancona:* A. Panatta d. R. Norberg 6–3 6–4; A. Zugarelli d. T. Svensson 6–3 6–4; P. Bertolucci/A. Panatta d. B. Andersson/Norberg 6–2 6–4.
1975 Not held
1976 Hungary 11 wins, Great Britain 10 wins (played entirely as round robin, each tie home and away). Hungarian team: P. Szoke, B. Taroczy. British team: M. Cox, J. M. Lloyd, C. J. Mottram, R. Taylor.
1977 Sweden d. West Germany 5–1, *Berlin:* R. Norberg d. U. Marten 6–2 4–6 6–4; K. Johansson d. K. Meiler 6–4 6–4; O. Bengtson/Norberg d. P. Elter/Meiler 6–2 6–2. *Linkoping:* Norberg d. U. Pinner 7–6 6–2; Johansson d. Meiler 6–7 6–2 6–3; Bengtson/Norberg lost to Elter/Marten 6–3 4–6 4–6.
1978 Sweden d. Hungary 3–3 (9–7 sets), *Uppsala:* T. Svensson d. P. Szoke 6–2 6–4; O. Bengtson lost to B. Taroczy 6–7 6–7; Bengtson/Svensson lost to Szoke/Taroczy 6–7 4–6; *Debrecen:* Svensson d. Szoke 6–2 6–2; Bengtson d. Taroczy 6–4 7–6; Bengtson/Svensson lost to Szoke/Taroczy 3–6 6–3 3–6.
1979 Czechoslovakia d. Hungary 4–2, *Pecs:* I. Lendl lost to J. Benyik 6–7 7–5 6–7; T. Smid d. B. Taroczy 5–7 6–3 6–4; P. Slozil/T. Smid d. P. Szoke/Taroczy 6–4 6–4; *Chrudin:* Lendl lost to Benyik 6–4 2–6 0–6; Smid d. Szoke 6–3 3–6 6–2; Slozil/Smid d. Benyik/Szoke 6–4 6–2.
1980 Czechoslovakia d. Hungary 5–1, *Chrudin:* T. Smid d. R. Machan 6–4 6–2; I. Lendl d. B. Taroczy 6–2 6–1; Smid/P. Slozil d. P. Szoke/Machan 6–4 7–5; *Debreden:* Smid d. J. Benyik 6–2 3–6 6–2; Lendl d. Machan 6–0 6–2; Smid/Slozil lost to Machan/Szoke 6–3 3–6 2–6.
1981 West Germany d. USSR 3–3 (9–7 sets), *Moscow,* **2–1**, *and Hamburg,* **1–2.**
1982 West Germany d. Czechoslovakia 2–1, Dortmund: K. Eberhard lost to J. Navratil 4–6 1–6; U. Pinnder d. P. Slozilp 6–4 6–4; C. Zipf/H. D. Beutel d. Navratil/Slozil 6–3 6–4.
1983 West Germany d. Czechoslovakia 2–1, *Uppsala:* H. J. Schwaier lost to L. Pimek 6–4 2–6 3–6; M. Westphal d. J. Navratil 3–6 6–2 6–3; E. Jelen/W. Popp d. Navratil/Piimek 6–1 1–6 7–6.
1984 Czechoslovakia d. Sweden 2–1, *Essen:* M. Mecir d. J. Gunnarsson 7–6 6–4; L. Pimek lost to J. Nystrom 3–6 5–7; Pimek/J. Navratil d. Gunnarsson/Nystrom 3–6 6–2 6–4.
1985 Sweden d. Switzerland 3–0, *Essen:* T. Hogstedt d. R. Stadler 6–3 6–2; J. Gunnarsson d. J. Hlasek 7–5 4–6 6–2; S. Simonsson d. Hlasek/Stadler 6–3 3–6 6–3.
1986 Switzerland d. Czechoslovakia 2–1, *Queen's Club, London:* R. Stadler d. M. Vajda 6–4 7–5; J. Hlasek lost L. Pimek 7–5 3–6 5–7; Hlasek/Stadler d. Pimek/P. Korda 6–2 6–3.
1987 Switzerland d. Great Britain 2–1, *Hanover:* R. Stadler lost to M. J. Bates 6–7 2–6; J. Hlasek d. A. Castle 6–3 6–7 6–2; Hlasek/Stadler d. Bates/Castle 3–6 7–5 6–0.
1988 Czechoslovakia d. Netherlands 2–0, *Zurich:* P. Korda d. M. Oosting 6–3 7–6; doubles not played.
1989 Czechoslovakia d. West Germany 2–1, *Ostrava:* P. Korda lost to C.-U. Steeb 3–6 3–6; M. Srejber d. E. Jelen 7–5 6–3; Srejber/Korda d. P. Kuhnen/Jelen 7–6 7–6.
1990 Germany d. USSR 2–1, *Metz:* U. Riglewski lost to D. Poliakov 7–5 3–6 2–6; M. Stich d. A. Cherkasov 6–3 7–6; Stich/Riglewski d. A. Olhovskiy/V. Gabrichidze 6–3 7–6.
1991 Czechoslovakia d. Netherlands 2–1, *Lengnau:* D. Rikl lost to T. Kempers 6–3 5–7 1–6; M. Damm d. F. Wibier 6–4 6–1; Damm/T. Zdrazila d. Kempers/Wibier 6–3 6–3.

1992 Sweden d. Germany 2–1, *Trieste:* N. Kulti d. M. Goellner 6–4 7–6; T. Enqvist lost to M. Naewie 3–6 4–6; M. Tillstrom/N. Kulti d. M. Naewie/M. Goellner 4–6 6–3 7–6
1993 Sweden d. Germany 2–0, *Trieste:* J. Bjorkman d. J. Renzenbrink 6–1 6–3; N. Kulti d. D. Prinosil 6–4 6–4 (doubles not played).
1994 Italy d. Sweden 2–1, *Trieste:* O. Camporese d. M. Norman 6–2 6–2; C. Caratti lost to T. Johansson 4–6 1–6; Camporese/C. Brandi d. Flyght/Johansson 6–4 6–2.
1995 Italy d. Czech Republic 2–0, *Reggio Calabria:* O. Camporese d. D. Miketa 6–2 6–4; C. Caratti d. Novak 6–7(5–7) 6–4 6–0. Doubles not played.
1996 Sweden d. Italy 2–1, *Reggio Calabria:* G. Galimberti d. T. Johansson 2–6 6–3 6–3; N. Timfjord d. M. Navarra 6–2 6–4; M. Rentröm/N. Timfjord d. M. Navarra/M. Martelli 6–7 6–4 6–1.
1997 Great Britain d. Netherlands 2–1, *Reggio Calabria:* M. Verkerk (NED) d. M. Lee (GBR) 4–6 7–6(5) 6–2; D. Sapsford (GBR) d. P. Wessels (NED) 7–6(4) 6–4; D. Sapsford/M. Lee (GBR) d. T. Kempes/P. Wessels (NED) 6–3 7–5.

EUROPEAN CUP – WOMEN

A team competition for women launched in 1986 to commemorate the 50th anniversary of the European Cup for men (which had originally been the King's Cup). Ties consist of two singles rubbers and one doubles rubber.

FINALS

1986 Sweden d. W. Germany 2–0 *Eindhoven 27–30 November:* C. Carlsson(SWE) d. A. Betzner (GER) 6–0 6–3; C. Lindqvist (SWE) d. S. Meier (GER) 6–2 7–6. Doubles not played.
1987 France d. Netherlands 2–0 *Lomma-Bjarred 26–29 November:* P. Paradis (FRA) d. M. Mesker (NED) 3–6 7–5 6–2; J. Halard (FRA) d. M. Bollegraf (NED) 6–2 6–4. Doubles not played.
1988 France d. Netherlands 2–1 *Nantes 7–13 November:* K. Quentrec (FRA) d. M. Bollegraf (NED) 6–3 6–4; C. Suire (FRA) d. H. Schultz (NED) 6–2 6–1; Bollegraf/C. Vis (NED) d. Suire/C. Tanvier (FRA) 6–4 4 6–7–6.
1989 USSR d. Great Britain 2–1 *Nantes 23–26 November:* J. Durie (GBR) d. N. Zvereva (URS) 7–6 6–4; L. Meskhi d. C. Wood 6–3 6–1; L. Savchenko/Zvereva (URS) d. Durie/A. Hobbs (GBR) 6–2 6–2.
1990 USSR d. Great Britain 2–1 *Nantes 29 November – 2 December:* Brioukhovets (URS) d. M. Javer (GBR) 7–5 6–3; N. Medvedeva (URS) d. J. Durie 6–3 6–3; Durie/C. Wood (GBR) d. Brioukhovets/ Medvedeva (URS) 7–6 ret.
1991 Netherlands d. Italy 2–0 *Nantes 28 November – 1 December:* M. Oremans d. K. Piccolini 6–4 6–2; S. Rottier (NED) d. L. Ferrando (ITA) 6–1 3–6 7–5. Doubles not played.
1992 Great Britain d. Netherlands 2–1 *Prague, 26–29 November:* C. Wood (GBR) lost to M. Kiene 2–6 3–6; J. Durie (GBR) d. N. Muns Jagerman 7–6 6–4; Durie/Wood d. Kiene/M. Oremans 6–3 6–2.
1993 Germany d. Netherlands 2–0 *Sheffield, 24–28 November:* C. Porwick (GER) d. K. Boogert (NED) 7–5 6–3; B. Rittner (GER) d. S. Rottier (NED) 7–5 6–2. Doubles not played.
1994 Italy d. Germany 2–1 *Aachen, 23–27 November:* M. Babel (GER) d. L. Golarsa (ITA) 6–4 6–2; S. Cecchini (ITA) d. B. Rittner (GER) 6–2 6–4; Cecchini/Golarsa (ITA) d. Rittner/C. Singer (GER) 7–6 6–4.
1995 Belgium d. Netherlands 2–1 *Aachen, 29 November–1 December:* M. Oremans (BEL) d. D. Monami (NED) 6–2 5–7 6–4; S. Appelmans (NED) d. K. Boogert (BEL) 5–7 6–1 6–1; Oremans/C. Vis (BEL) d. Appelmans/ L.Courtois (NED) 6–2 6–4.
1996 Germany d. Netherlands 2–0, *Aachen:* M. Weingartner d. C. Vis 6–0 3–6 6–1; B. Rittner d. M. Oremans 7–5 6–7 6–2; Doubles not played.
1997 Spain d. Italy 2–1, *Barcelona:* G. Leon (ESP) d. F. Perfetti (ITA) 6–4 7–6(3); F. Lubiani (ITA) d. V. Ruano-Pascual (ESP) 4–6 6–4 7–6(6); G. Leon/V. Ruano-Pascual (ESP) d. G. Casoni/F. Perfetti (ITA) 6–2 6–2.

WORLD TEAM CUP

Eight-nation men's team event, qualification by individual ATP rating. Formerly Nations Cup.

FINALS

Played at Kingston, Jamaica
1975 USA d. Great Britain 2–1: R. Tanner (USA) d. R. Taylor (GBR) 6–3 2–6 6–4; A. R. Ashe (USA) lost to C. J. Mottram (GBR) 5–7 7–5 1–6; Ashe/Tanner d. Mottram/Taylor 6–1 1–6 6–4.
***1976–77* Not held**
Played at Dusseldorf
1978 Spain d. Australia 2–1: J. Higueras (ESP) d. J. D. Newcombe (AUS) 6–2 6–3; M. Orantes (ESP) d. P. Dent (AUS) 6–3 6–4; Higueras/ Orantes lost to Dent/Newcombe 6–7 4–6.
1979 Australia d. Italy 2–1: J. G. Alexander (AUS) d. C. Barazzutti (ITA) 6–2 6–0; P. Dent (AUS) lost to A. Panatta (ITA) 3–6 3–6; Alexander/Dent d. P. Bertolucci/Panatta 6–3 7–6.
1980 Argentina d. Italy 3–0: G. Vilas (ARG) d. C. Barazzutti (ITA) 6–3 6–2; J. L. Clerc (ARG) d. A. Panatta (ITA) 7–6 6–3; Clerc/Vilas d. P. A Bertolucci/Panatta 6–2 6–3.
1981 Czechoslovakia d. Australia 2–1: I. Lendl (TCH) lost to P. McNamara (AUS) 3–6 4–6; T. Smid (TCH) d. P. McNamee (AUS) 6–4 7–6; Lendl/Smid d. McNamara/McNamee 6–4 6–3.
1982 USA d. Australia 2–1: G. Mayer (USA) d. K. Warwick (AUS) 7–6 6–2; E. Teltscher (USA) d. P. McNamara (AUS) 6–4 7–6; Mayer/S. E. Stewart lost to M. R. Edmondson/McNamara 1–6 1–6.

1983 Spain d. Australia 2–1: J. Higueras (ESP) d. M. R. Edmondson (AUS) 6–2 6–4; M. Orantes (ESP) d. P. Cash (AUS) 6–3 6–2; A. Gimenez/Higueras lost to Cash/Edmondson 5–7 6–4 1–6.
1984 USA d. Czechoslovakia 2–1: J. P. McEnroe (USA) d. I. Lendl (TCH) 6–3 6–2; J. Arias (USA) lost to T. Smid (TCH) 6–4 6–7 4–6; P. Fleming/McEnroe d. Lendl/Smid 6–1 6–2.
1985 USA d. Czechoslovakia 2–1: J. P. McEnroe (USA) lost to I. Lendl (TCH) 7–6 6–7 3–6; J. S. Connors (USA) d. M. Mecir (TCH) 6–3 3–6 7–5; K. Flach/R. Seguso (USA) d. Lendl/T. Smid 6–3 7–6
1986 France d. Sweden 2–1: H. Leconte (FRA) d. A. Jarryd (SWE) 6–3 3–6 6–1; T. Tulasne (FRA) lost to M. Wilander (SWE) 1–6 4–6; G. Forget/Leconte d. Jarryd/Wilander 6–3 2–6 6–2.
1987 Czechoslovakia d. USA 2–1: M. Mecir (TCH) d. J. P. McEnroe (USA) 7–5 2–6 2–1 disqual.; M. Srejber (TCH) lost to B. Gilbert (USA) 4–6 7–5 4–6; Mecir/T. Smid d. Gilbert/R. Seguso 6–3 6–1.
1988 Sweden d. USA 2–1: S. Edberg (SWE) d. T. Mayotte (USA) 6–4 6–2; K. Carlsson (SWE) d. A. Krickstein (USA) 6–4 6–3; Edberg/A. Jarryd lost to K. Flach/R. Seguso (USA) 7–6 3–6 6–7.
1989 West Germany d. Argentina 2–1: B. Becker (GER) d. G. Perez Roldan (ARG) 6–0 2–6 6–2; C.-U. Steeb (GER) lost to M. Jaite (ARG) 4–6 3–6; Becker/E. Jelen d. J. Frana/G. Luna 6–4 7–5.
1990 Yugoslavia d. USA 2–1: G. Prpic (YUG) d. B. Gilbert (USA) 6–4 6–4; G. Ivanisevic (YUG) d. J. Courier (USA) 3–6 7–5 6–1; Prpic/S. Zivojinovic lost to K. Flach/R. Seguso (USA) 5–7 6–7.
1991 Sweden d. Yugoslavia 2–1: M. Gustafsson (SWE) d. G. Prpic (YUG) 6–2 3–6 6–4; S. Edberg (SWE) d G. Ivanisevic (YUG) 6–4 7–5; Edberg/Gustafsson lost to Prpic/S. Zivojinovic 6–3 3–6 4–6.
1992 Spain d. Czechoslovakia 3–0: E. Sanchez (ESP) d. P. Korda (TCH) 3–6 6–2 7–6; S. Brugera (ESP) d. K. Novacek (TCH) 6–2 6–4; S. Casal/E. Sanchez d. K. Novacek/C. Suk 1–6 6–4 6–3.
1993 USA d. Germany 3–0: P. Sampras (USA) d. M. Stich (GER) 6–4 6–2; M. Chang (USA) d. C.-U. Steeb (GER) 6–3 7–6; P. McEnroe/R. Reneberg (USA) d. P. Kuhnen/M. Stich 6–4 6–3.
1994 Germany d. Spain 2–1: M. Stich (GER) d. S. Bruguera (ESP) 2–6 6–4 6–3; C. Costa (ESP) d. B. Karbacher (GER) 6–2 6–4 6–0; P. Kuhnen/Stich (GER) d. T. Carbonnel/Costa (ESP) 7–5 4–6 6–4.
1995 Sweden d. Croatia 2–1: M. Larsson (SWE) lost to G. Ivanisevic (CRO) 4–6 4–6; S. Edberg (SWE) d. S. Hirszon (CRO) 6–1 6–4; J. Bjorkman/S. Edberg (SWE) d. S. Hirszon/G. Ivanisevic (CRO) 4–6 6–3 6–3.
1996 Switzerland d. Czech Republic 2–1: J. Hlasek (SUI) lost to P. Korda (CZE) 3–6 4–6; M. Rosset (SUI) d. B. Ulihrach (CZE) 7–6 6–2; Hlasek/Rosset (SUI) d. Korda/D. Vacek (CZE) 6–3 6–4
1997 Spain d. Australia 3–0: F. Mantilla (ESP) d. M. Woodforde (AUS) 7–5 6–2; A. Costa (ESP) d. M. Philippoussis (AUS) 3–6 7–6(3) 7–6(7); T. Carbonell/F.Roig (ESP) d. T. Woodbridge/M. Woodforde (AUS) 6–3 7–5.

MEN'S GRAND PRIX (1970–1989)

A points-linked circuit of men's tournaments with a bonus pool distributed to the points leaders at the end of the year and a Masters tournament where field varied in size. Full details available in *World of Tennis 1996*, and previous issues.

ATP TOUR CHAMPIONSHIP

A season-ending tournament for the top eight men on the ATP Tour ranking list, played in two round-robin groups of four players each and knock-out semi-finals and final.

SINGLES

	VENUE	*WINNER*	*RUNNER-UP*	*SCORE*					*FIRST PRIZE*
1990	Frankfurt	A. Agassi	S. Edberg	5–7	7–6	7–5	6–2		$950,000
1991	Frankfurt	P. Sampras	J. Courier	3–6	7–6	6–3	6–4		$1,020,000
1992	Frankfurt	B. Becker	J. Courier	6–4	6–3	7–5			$1,020,000
1993	Frankfurt	M. Stich	P. Sampras	7–6	2–6	7–6	6–2		$1,240,000
1994	Frankfurt	P. Sampras	B. Becker	4–6	6–3	7–5	6–4		$1,235,000
1995	Frankfurt	B. Becker	M. Chang	7–6	6–0	7–6			$1,225,000
1996	Hanover	P. Sampras	B. Becker	3–6	7–6	7–6	6–7	6–4	$1,340,000
1997	Hanover	P. Sampras	Y. Kafelnikov	6–3	6–2	6–2			$1,340,000

DOUBLES

	VENUE	*WINNER*	*RUNNER-UP*	*SCORE*					*FIRST PRIZE*
1990	Sanctuary Cove	G. Forget/J. Hlasek	S. Casal/E. Sanchez	6–4	7–6	5–7	6–4		$225,000
1991	Johannesburg	J. Fitzgerald/A. Jarryd	K. Flach/R. Seguso	6–4	6–4	2–6	6–4		$325,000
1992	Johannesburg	T. Woodbridge/M. Woodforde	J. Fitzgerald/A. Jarryd	6–2	7–6	5–7	3–6	6–3	$325,000
1993	Johannesburg	J. Eltingh/P. Haarhuis	T. Woodbridge/ M. Woodforde	7–6	7–6	6–4			$365,000
1994	Jakarta	J. Apell/J. Bjorkman	T. Woodbridge/ M. Woodforde	6–4	4–6	4–6	7–6	7–6	$275,000
1995	Eindhoven	G. Connell/P.Galbraith	J. Eltingh/P. Haarhuis	7–6	7–6	3–6	7–6		$225,000
1996	Hartford	T. Woodbridge/M. Woodforde	S. Lareau/A. O'Brien	6–4	5–7	6–2	7–6		$165,000
1997	Hartford	R. Leach/J. Stark	M. Bhupathi/L. Paes	6–3	6–4	7–6			$145,000

WOMEN'S INTERNATIONAL SERIES CHAMPIONSHIPS

(1974–78 Virginia Slims, 1979–82 Avon, 1983–94 Virginia Slims, 1995 Corel, 1996 Chase) Best of 3 sets 1977–1982, best of 5 sets 1983–present.

SINGLES

	VENUE	*WINNER*	*RUNNER-UP*	*SCORE*	*FIRST PRIZE*
1977	Palm Springs	Miss C. M. Evert	Mrs L. W. King	6–2 6–2	$75,000
1978	Palm Springs	Miss C. M. Evert	Miss M. Navratilova	6–3 6–3	$75,000
1979*	Landover, Maryland	Miss M. Navratilova	Miss T. A. Austin	6–2 6–1	$75,000
1980*	Palm Springs	Miss T. A. Austin	Miss A. Jaeger	6–2 6–2	$75,000
1981	East Rutherford, NJ	Miss T. A. Austin	Miss M. Navratilova	2–6 6–4 6–2	$75,000
1982	East Rutherford, NJ	Miss M. Navratilova	Mrs J. M. Lloyd	4–6 6–1 6–2	$75,000
1983*	Madison Sq. Gdn, NY	Miss M. Navratilova	Mrs J. M. Lloyd	6–3 7–5 6–1	$125,000
1984*	Madison Sq. Gdn, NY	Miss M. Navratilova	Miss H. Sukova	6–3 7–5 6–4	$125,000
1985*	Madison Sq. Gdn, NY	Miss M. Navratilova	Miss H. Mandlikova	6–2 6–0 3–6 6–1	$125,000
1986	Madison Sq. Gdn, NY	Miss M. Navratilova	Miss S. Graf	7–6 6–3 6–2	$125,000
1987	Madison Sq. Gdn, NY	Miss S. Graf	Miss G. Sabatini	4–6 6–4 6–0 6–4	$125,000
1988	Madison Sq. Gdn, NY	Miss G. Sabatini	Miss P. H. Shriver	7–5 6–2 6–2	$125,000
1989	Madison Sq. Gdn, NY	Miss S. Graf	Miss M. Navratilova	6–4 7–5 2–6 6–2	$125,000
1990	Madison Sq. Gdn, NY	Miss M. Seles	Miss G. Sabatini	6–4 5–7 3–6 6–4 6–2	$250,000
1991	Madison Sq. Gdn, NY	Miss M. Seles	Miss M. Navratilova	6–4 3–6 7–5 6–0	$250,000
1992	Madison Sq. Gdn, NY	Miss M. Seles	Miss M. Navratilova	7–5 6–3 6–1	$250,000
1993	Madison Sq. Gdn, NY	Miss S. Graf	Miss A. Sanchez Vic.	6–1 6–4 3–6 6–1	$250,000
1994	Madison Sq. Gdn, NY	Miss G. Sabatini	Miss L. Davenport	6–3 6–2 6–4	$250,000
1995	Madison Sq. Gdn, NY	Miss S. Graf	Miss A. Huber	6–1 2–6 6–1 4–6 6–3	$500,000
1996	Madison Sq. Gdn, NY	Miss S. Graf	Miss M. Hingis	6–3 4–6 6–0 4–6 6–0	$500,000
1997	Madison Sq. Gdn, NY	Miss J. Novotna	Miss M. Pierce	7–6 6–2 6–3	$500,000

**Played in the following year*

DOUBLES

	WINNERS	*RUNNERS-UP*	*SCORE*
1977	Miss F. Durr/Miss S. V. Wade	Mrs H. Gourlay Cawley/Miss J. Russell	6–1 4–6 6–4
1978	Mrs L. W. King/Miss M. Navratilova	Mrs G. E. Reid/Miss W. M. Turnbull	6–3 6–4
1979*	Mrs L. W. King/Miss M. Navratilova	Miss R. Casals/Mrs J. M. Lloyd	6–4 6–3
1980*	Miss R. Casals/Miss W. M. Turnbull	Miss C. Reynolds/Miss P. Smith	6–3 4–6 7–6
1991	Miss M. Navratilova/Miss P. H. Shriver	Miss R. Casals/Miss W. M. Turnbull	6–3 6–4
1982	Miss M. Navratilova/Miss P. H. Shriver	Miss C. Reynolds/Miss P. Smith	6–4 7–5
1983*	Miss M. Navratilova/Miss P. H. Shriver	Miss J. M. Durie/Miss A. Kiyomura	6–3 6–1
1984*	Miss M. Navratilova/Miss P. H. Shriver	Miss C. Kohde-Kilsch/Miss H. Sukova	6–7 6–4 7–6
1985*	Miss H. Mandlikova/Miss W. M. Turnbull	Miss C. Kohde-Kilsch/Miss H. Sukova	6–4 6–7 6–3
1986	Miss M. Navratilova/Miss P. H. Shriver	Miss C. Kohde-Kilsch/Miss H. Sukova	7–6 6–3
1987	Miss M. Navratilova/Miss P. H. Shriver	Miss C. Kohde-Kilsch/Miss H. Sukova	6–1 6–1
1988	Miss M. Navratilova/Miss P. H. Shriver	Miss L. Savchenko/Miss N. Zvereva	6–3 6–4
1989	Miss M. Navratilova/Miss P. H. Shriver	Miss L. Savchenko/Miss N. Zvereva	6–3 6–2
1990	Miss K. Jordan/Mrs P. Smylie	Miss M. Paz/Miss A. Sanchez Vicario	7–6 6–4
1991	Miss M. Navratilova/Miss P. H. Shriver	Miss G. Fernandez/Miss J. Novotna	4–6 7–5 6–4
1992	Miss A. Sanchez Vic./Miss H. Sukova	Miss J. Novotna/Mrs L. Savchenko-Neil.	7–6 6–1
1993	Miss G. Fernandez/Miss N. Zvereva	Miss L. Neiland/J. Novotna	6–3 7–6
1994	Miss G. Fernandez/Miss N. Zvereva	Miss J. Novotna/Miss A. Sanchez Vicario	6–3 6–7 6–3
1995	Miss J, Novotna/Miss A. Sanchez Vicario	Miss G. Fernandez/Miss N. Zvereva	6–2 6–1
1996	Miss L. Davenport/Miss M. J. Fernandez	Miss J. Novotna/Miss A. Sanchez Vicario	6–2 6–3
1997	Miss L. Davenport/Miss J. Novotna	Miss A. Fusai/Miss N. Tauziat	6–7 6–3 6–2

** Played in the following year.*

WORLD CHAMPIONSHIP TENNIS

An independent circuit organised by Lamar Hunt's Dallas-based World Championship Tennis Inc which pre-dated the Grand Prix. The eight-man playoff staged annually in Dallas for the points leaders on the circuit set the standard for professionally promoted tennis tournaments. Begun in 1971, the circuit ended with the 1989 World Championship of Tennis. A doubles event was added in 1973 and continued until 1985. From 1986 the doubles event was incorporated into the Masters Doubles. Final round results and prize money can be found in *World of Tennis 1996* and previous issues.

HOPMAN CUP

A mixed team event which takes place annually at the Burswood Resort, Perth, Western Australia. Each tie consists of a men's singles, a ladies' singles and a mixed doubles. Held annually in January. In 1997 became the ITF's official Mixed Teams Championship.

1989 Czechoslovakia d. Australia 2–0: H.Sukova (TCH) d H.Mandlikova (AUS) 6–4 6–3; M.Mecir/Mandlikova (TCH) d P.Cash/Mandlikova (AUS) 6–2 6–4
1990 Spain d. USA 2–1: A.Sanchez Vicario (ESP) d P.Shriver (USA) 6–3 6–3; E.Sanchez (ESP) d P.McEnroe (USA) 5–7 7–5 7–5; McEnroe/Shriver (USA) d Sanchez/Sanchez Vicario (ESP) 6–3 6–2
1991 Yugoslavia d. USA 3–0: M.Seles (YUG) d Z.Garrison (USA) 6–1 6–1; G.Prpic (YUG) d D.Wheaton (USA) 4–6 6–3 7–5; Prpic/Seles (YUG) d Wheaton/Garrison 8–3 (pro set)
1992 Switzerland d. Czechoslovakia 2–1: M.Maleeva-Fragniere (SUI) d H.Sukova (TCH) 6–2 6–4; J.Hlasek (SUI) d K.Novacek (TCH) 6–4 6–4; Novacek/Sukova (TCH) d Hlasek/Maleeva-Fragniere (SUI) 8–4 (pro set)
1993 Germany d. Spain 3–0: S.Graf (GER) d A.Sanchez Vicario (ESP) 6–4 6–3; M.Stich (GER) d E.Sanchez (ESP) 7–5 6–4; Doubles conceded
1994 Czech Republic d. Germany 2–1: J.Novotna (CZE) d A.Huber (GER) 1–6 6–4 6–3; P.Korda (CZE) d B.Karbacher (GER) 6–3 6–3; Karbacher/Huber (GER) d Korda/Novotna (CZE) 8-3 (pro set)
1995 Germany d. Ukraine 3–0: A.Huber (GER) d N.Medvedeva (UKR) 6–4 3–6 6–4; B.Becker (GER) d A.Medvedev (UKR) 6–3 6–7 6–3; Becker/Huber (GER) wo Medvedev/Medvedeva (UKR) (Medvedev injured)
1996 Croatia d Switzerland 2–1: M.Hingis (SUI) d I.Majoli (CRO) 6–3 6–0; G.Ivanisevic (CRO) d M.Rosset (SUI) 7–6 7–5 ; Ivanisevic/Majoli d Rosset/Hingis (SUI) 3–6 7–6 5–5 ret (Rosset injured)
1997 USA d. South Africa 2–1: C. Rubin (USA) d. A. Coetzer (RSA) 7–5 6–2; W. Ferreira (RSA) d. J. Gimelstob (USA) 6–4 7–6; Gimelstob/Rubin (USA) d. Ferreira/Coetzer (RSA) 3–6 6–2 7–5.

ITF VETERAN WORLD CHAMPIONSHIPS

1981 Sao Paulo, Brazil, 21–26 September

MEN			WOMEN		
45 Singles	Sven Davidson	(SWE)	40 Singles	Estrella de Molina	(ARG)
45 Doubles	Sven Davidson	(SWE)	40 Doubles	Nancy Reed	(USA)
	Hugh Stewart	(USA)		M A Plante	(USA)
55 Singles	Straight Clark	(USA)	50 Singles	Amelia Cury	(BRA)
55 Doubles	Straight Clark	(USA)			
	Torsten Johansson	(SWE)			

1982 Pörtschach, Austria, 7–13 June

45 Singles	Istvan Gulyas	(HUN)	40 Singles	Renate Drisaldi	(GER)
45 Doubles	Jason Morton	(USA)	40 Doubles	Charleen Hillebrand	(USA)
	Jim Nelson	(USA)		Nancy Reed	(USA)
55 Singles	Robert McCarthy	(AUS)	50 Singles	Eva Sluytermann	(GER)
55 Doubles	Adi Hussmuller	(GER)	50 Doubles	Eva Sluytermann	(GER)
	Laci Legenstein	(AUT)		I Burmester	(GER)
60 Singles	Torsten Johansson	(SWE)			
60 Doubles	Torsten Johansson	(SWE)			
	Albert Ritzenberg	(USA)			
65 Singles	Fritz Klein	(USA)			
65 Doubles	Fritz Klein	(USA)			
	Jean Becker	(FRA)			

1983 Bahia, Brazil, 7–13 August

45 Singles	Istvan Gulyas	(HUN)	40 Singles	Helga Masthoff	(GER)
45 Doubles	Klaus Fuhrmann	(GER)	40 Doubles	Helga Masthoff	(GER)
	Folker Seemann	(GER)		Heide Orth	(GER)
55 Singles	Robert McCarthy	(AUS)	50 Singles	Ines de Pla	(ARG)
55 Doubles	Laci Legenstein	(AUT)	50 Doubles	Gladys Barbosa	(ARG)
	Adi Hussmuller	(GER)		Julia Borzone	(ARG)
65 Singles	Ricardo San Martin	(CHI)			
65 Doubles	Federico Barboza	(ARG)			
	Hector Hugo Pizani	(ARG)			

1984 Cervia, Italy, 23 May–3 June

35 Singles	Jurgen Fassbender	(GER)	40 Singles	Helga Masthoff	(GER)
35 Doubles	Gene Malin	(USA)	40 Doubles	Helga Masthoff	(GER)
	Armistead Neely	(USA)		Heide Orth	(GER)
45 Singles	Istvan Gulyas	(HUN)	50 Singles	Clelia Mazzoleni	(ITA)

45 Doubles	Klaus Fuhrmann	(GER)	50 Doubles	Hana Brabenec	(CAN)
	Folker Seemann	(GER)		Pam Wearne	(AUS)
55 Singles	Giuseppe Merlo	(ITA)			
55 Doubles	Jason Morton	(USA)			
	Hugh Stewart	(USA)			
65 Singles	Gardnar Mulloy	(USA)			
65 Doubles	Gardnar Mulloy	(USA)			
	Fritz Klein	(USA)			

1985 Melbourne, Australia, 25–31 March

35 Singles	Jurgen Fassbender	(GER)	40 Singles	Heide Orth	(GER)
35 Doubles	Jurgen Fassbender	(GER)	40 Doubles	Heide Orth	(GER)
	Federico Gadoni	(ITA)		Judy Dalton	(AUS)
45 Singles	Ian Barclay	(AUS)	50 Singles	Ilse Michael	(GER)
45 Doubles	Robert Duesler	(USA)	50 Doubles	Ann Fotheringham	(AUS)
	Jim Nelson	(USA)		Helen Polkinghorne	(AUS)
55 Singles	Hugh Stewart	(USA)			
55 Doubles	Hugh Stewart	(USA)			
	Jason Morton	(USA)			
65 Singles	Jim Gilchrist	(AUS)			
65 Doubles	Fritz Klein	(USA)			
	Albert Ritzenberg	(USA)			

1986 Pörtschach, Austria, 16–22 June

35 Singles	Robert Machan	(HUN)	40 Singles	Helga Masthoff	(GER)
35 Doubles	Jurgen Fassbender	(GER)	40 Doubles	Helga Masthoff	(GER)
	Hans-Joachim Plotz	(GER)		Heide Orth	(GER)
45 Singles	Jorge Lemann	(BRA)	50 Singles	Shirley Brasher	(GBR)
45 Doubles	Jorge Lemann	(BRA)	50 Doubles	Shirley Brasher	(GBR)
	Ivo Ribeiro	(BRA)		Lorna Cawthorn	(GBR)
55 Singles	Lorne Main	(CAN)			
55 Doubles	Bob Howe	(AUS)			
	Russell Seymour	(USA)			
65 Singles	Torsten Johansson	(SWE)			
65 Doubles	Gardnar Mulloy	(USA)			
	Verne Hughes	(USA)			

1987 Garmisch-Partenkirchen, Germany, 15–21 June

35 Singles	Robert Machan	(HUN)	40 Singles	Marie Pinterova	(HUN)
35 Doubles	Robert Machan	(HUN)	40 Doubles	Marie Pinterova	(HUN)
	Jurgen Fassbender	(GER)		Gail Lovera	(FRA)
45 Singles	Giorgio Rohrich	(ITA)	50 Singles	Shirley Brasher	(GBR)
45 Doubles	Hans Gradischnig	(AUT)	50 Doubles	Shirley Brasher	(GBR)
	Peter Pokorny	(AUT)		Lorna Cawthorn	(GBR)
55 Singles	Istvan Gulyas	(HUN)	60 Singles	Dorothy Cheney	(USA)
55 Doubles	Istvan Gulyas	(HUN)	60 Doubles	Dorothy Cheney	(USA)
	Hugh Stewart	(USA)		Cortez Murdock	(USA)
60 Singles	Bob Howe	(AUS)			
60 Doubles	Andreas Stolpa	(GER)			
	Laci Legenstein	(AUT)			
65 Singles	Alex Swetka	(USA)			
65 Doubles	Bernhard Kempa	(GER)			
	Walter Kessler	(GER)			
70 Singles	Fritz Klein	(USA)			
70 Doubles	Gardnar Mulloy	(USA)			
	Verne Hughes	(USA)			

1988 Huntington Beach, California, USA 21–8 August

35 Singles	Alvin Gardiner	(USA)	40 Singles	Marie Pinterova	(HUN)
35 Doubles	Lajos Levai	(GER)	40 Doubles	Rosie Darmon	(FRA)
	Robert Machan	(HUN)		Gail Lovera	(FRA)
45 Singles	Keith Diepraam	(USA)	50 Singles	Dorothy Matthiessen	(USA)
45 Doubles	Friedhelm Krauss	(GER)	50 Doubles	Dorothy Matthiessen	(USA)
	Gunter Krauss	(GER)		Jane Crofford	(USA)
55 Singles	Istvan Gulyas	(HUN)	60 Singles	Virginia Glass	(USA)
55 Doubles	Sven Davidson	(SWE)	60 Doubles	Dorothy Cheney	(USA)
	Hugh Stewart	(USA)		Cortez Murdock	(USA)

60 Singles	Robert McCarthy	(AUS)
60 Doubles	Robert McCarthy	(AUS)
	Bob Howe	(AUS)
65 Singles	Tom Brown	(USA)
65 Doubles	Lee Hammel	(USA)
	Bob Sherman	(USA)
70 Singles	Fritz Klein	(USA)
70 Doubles	Glen Hippenstiel	(USA)
	Geoff Young	(USA)

1989 Vina del Mar, Chile, 22–29 October

35 Singles	Alvaro Fillol	(CHI)
35 Doubles	Robert Machan	(HUN)
	Lajos levai	(GER)
45 Singles	Harold Elschenbroich	(GER)
45 Doubles	Bodo Nitsche	(GER)
	Gunter Krauss	(GER)
55 Singles	Istvan Gulyas	(HUN)
55 Doubles	Chuck de Voe	(USA)
	John Powless	(USA)
60 Singles	Robert McCarthy	(AUS)
60 Doubles	Robert McCarthy	(AUS)
	Bob Howe	(AUS)
65 Singles	Armando Vieira	(BRA)
65 Doubles	Armando Vieira	(BRA)
	Sergio Verrati	(FRA)
70 Singles	Albert Ritzenberg	(USA)
70 Doubles	Albert Ritzenberg	(USA)
	Fritz Klein	(USA)

40 Singles	Marie Pinterova	(HUN)
40 Doubles	Marie Pinterova	(HUN)
	Heide Orth	(GER)
50 Singles	Ilse Michael	(GER)
50 Doubles	Nancy Reed	(USA)
	Barbel Allendorf	(GER)
60 Singles	Betty Pratt	(USA)
60 Doubles	Dorothy Cheney	(USA)
	Cortez Murdock	(USA)

1990 Umag, Yugoslavia, 26 May–3 June

35 Singles	Robert Machan	(HUN)
35 Doubles	Robert Machan	(HUN)
	Lajos Levai	(GER)
45 Singles	Harald Elschenbroich	(GER)
45 Doubles	Dick Johnson	(USA)
	Jiim Parker	(USA)
55 Singles	Istvan Gulyas	(HUN)
55 Doubles	Ken Sinclair	(CAN)
	Lorne Main	(CAN)
60 Singles	Sven Davidson	(SWE)
60 Doubles	Sven Davidson	(SWE)
	Hugh Stewart	(USA)
65 Singles	Robert McCarthy	(AUS)
65 Doubles	Oskar Jirkovsky	(AUT)
	Josef Karlhofer	(AUT)
70 Singles	William Parsons	(USA)
70 Doubles	Alex Swetka	(USA)
	Albert Ritzenberg	(USA)

40 Singles	Marie Pinterova	(HUN)
40 Doubles	Barbara Mueller	(USA)
	Louise Cash	(USA)
50 Singles	Margit Schultze	(ESP)
50 Doubles	Kay Schiavinato	(AUS)
	Jan Blackshaw	(AUS)
60 Singles	Louise Owen	(USA)
60 Doubles	Lurline Stock	(AUS)
	Dulcie Young	(AUS)

1991 Perth, Australia, 17–23 May

35 Singles	Paul Torre	(FRA)
35 Doubles	Yustedjo Traik	(INA)
	Atet Wijono	(INA)
45 Singles	Don McCormick	(CAN)
45 Doubles	Bruce Burns	(AUS)
	John Weaver	(AUS)
55 Singles	Peter Froelich	(AUS)
55 Doubles	Gordon Davis	(USA)
	Herman Ahlers	(USA)
60 Singles	Lorne Main	(CAN)
60 Doubles	Frank Sedgman	(AUS)
	Clive Wilderspin	(AUS)
65 Singles	Robert McCarthy	(AUS)
65 Doubles	Robert McCarthy	(AUS)
	Bob Howe	(AUS)

40 Singles	Carol Bailey	(USA)
40 Doubles	Carol Bailey	(USA)
	Barbara Mueller	(USA)
50 Singles	Charleen Hillebrand	(USA)
50 Doubles	Betty Whitelaw	(AUS)
	Jan Blackshaw	(AUS)
55 Singles	Carol Wood	(USA)
55 Doubles	Carol Wood	(USA)
	Margaret Kohler	(USA)
60 Singles	Betty Pratt	(USA)
60 Doubles	Ruth Illingworth	(GBR)
	Ann Williams	(GBR)

70 Singles	Robert Sherman	(USA)
70 Doubles	Verne Hughes	(USA)
	Merwin Miller	(USA)

1992 Palermo, Sicily, 17–23 May

35 Singles	Ferrante Rocchi-Landir	(ITA)
35 Doubles	Paul French	(GBR)
	Stanislav Birner	(CZE)
45 Singles	Rolf Staguhn	(GER)
45 Doubles	Gary Penberthy	(AUS)
	Bens de Jell	(NED)
50 Singles	Jorge Lemann	(BRA)
50 Doubles	Gerhard Schelch	(AUT)
	Peter Fuchs	(AUT)
55 Singles	Klaus Fuhrmann	(GER)
55 Doubles	Hugh Stewart	(USA)
	Les Dodson	(USA)
60 Singles	Werner Mertins	(GER)
60 Doubles	Ken Sinclair	(CAN)
	Lorne Main	(CAN)
65 Singles	Robert McCarthy	(AUS)
65 Doubles	Robert McCarthy	(AUS)
	Bob Howe	(AUS)
70 Singles	Robert Sherman	(USA)
70 Doubles	Robert Sherman	(USA)
	Mario Isidori	(ITA)
75 Singles	Gaetano Longo	(ITA)
75 Doubles	Tiverio de Grad	(ROM)
	Georg Hunger	(GER)

35 Singles	Sally Freeman	(GBR)
35 Doubles	Luisa Figueroa	(ARG)
	Oliveira Villani	(BRA)
40 Singles	Marilyn Rasmussen	(AUS)
40 Doubles	Marilyn Rasmussen	(AUS)
	Lesley Charles	(GBR)
45 Singles	Marie Pinterova	(HUN)
45 Doubles	Marie Pinterova	(HUN)
	Shirley Brasher	(GBR)
50 Singles	Charleen Hillebrand	(USA)
50 Doubles	Charleen Hillebrand	(USA)
	Jacqueline Boothman	(GBR)
55 Singles	Nancy Reed	(USA)
55 Doubles	Nancy Reed	(USA)
	Belmar Gunderson	(USA)
60 Singles	Beverley Rae	(AUS)
60 Doubles	Beverley Rae	(AUS)
	Astri Hobson	(AUS)

1993 Barcelona, Spain, 4–11 April

35 Singles	Fernando Luna	(ESP)
35 Doubles	Steven Packham	(AUS)
	Tony Luttrell	(AUS)
45 Singles	Robert Machan	(HUN)
45 Doubles	Robert Machan	(HUN)
	Miodrag Mijuca	(GER)
50 Singles	Jorge Lemann	(BRA)
50 Doubles	James Parker	(USA)
	Ken Robinson	(USA)
55 Singles	King Van Nostrand	(USA)
55 Doubles	King Van Nostrand	(USA)
	Juan Manuel Couder	(ESP)
60 Singles	Lorne Main	(CAN)
60 Doubles	Lorne Main	(CAN)
	Ken Sinclair	(CAN)
65 Singles	Jason Morton	(USA)
65 Doubles	Laci Legenstein	(AUT)
	Hugh Stewart	(USA)
70 Singles	Tom Brown	(USA)
70 Doubles	Tom Brown	(USA)
	Buck Archer	(USA)
75 Singles	Gordon Henley	(AUS)
75 Doubles	Albert Ritzenberg	(USA)
	Mirek Kizlink	(GBR)

35 Singles	Jutta Fahlbusch	(GER)
35 Doubles	Jutta Fahlbusch	(GER)
	Dagmar Anwar	(GER)
40 Singles	Maria Geyer	(AUT)
40 Doubles	Elizabeth Craig	(AUS)
	Carol Campling	(AUS)
45 Singles	Marie Pinterova	(HUN)
45 Doubles	Marie Pinterova	(HUN)
	Tuija Hannuakainen	(FIN)
50 Singles	Cathie Anderson	(USA)
50 Doubles	Brigitte Hoffman	(GER)
	Siegrun Fuhrmann	(GER)
55 Singles	Roberta Beltrame	(ITA)
55 Doubles	Belmar Gunderson	(USA)
	Nancy Reed	(USA)
60 Singles	Nancy Reed	(USA)
60 Doubles	Marta Pombo	(ESP)
	Ana Maria Estalella	(ESP)
65 Singles	Betty Pratt	(USA)
65 Doubles	Betty Pratt	(USA)
	Betty Cookson	(USA)

1994 (Group A) Buenos Aires, Argentina, 30 October–6 November

35 Singles	Jose Luis Clerc	(ARG)
35 Doubles	Jose Luis Clerc	(ARG)
	Victor Pecci	(PAR)
45 Singles	Jairo Velasco	(ESP)
45 Doubles	Jairo Velasco	(ESP)
	Thomaz Koch	(BRA)
50 Singles	James Parker	(USA)
50 Doubles	James Parker	(USA)
	Ken Robinson	(USA)

35 Singles	Jutta Fahlbusch	(GER)
35 Doubles	Marcela de Gregorio	(ARG)
	Beatriz Villaverde	(ARG)
45 Singles	Renata Vojtischek	(GER)
45 Doubles	Tina Karwasky	(USA)
	Susan Stone	(CAN)
50 Singles	Louise Cash	(USA)
50 Doubles	Carol Campling	(AUS)
	Elizabeth Craig	(AUS)

1994 (Group B) Los Gatos, California, USA 22–29 May

55 Singles	Gil Howard	(USA)	50 Singles	Petro Kruger	(RSA)
55 Doubles	Klaus Fuhrmann	(GER)	50 Doubles	Ellen Bryant	(USA)
	Leslie Dodson	(USA)		Barbara Mueller	(USA)
60 Singles	King Van Nostrand	(USA)	55 Singles	Rosie Darmon	(FRA)
60 Doubles	Russell Seymour	(USA)	55 Doubles	Dorothy Matthiessen	(USA)
	Whitney Reed	(USA)		Lynn Little	(USA)
65 Singles	Jason Morton	(USA)	60 Singles	Ilse Michael	(GER)
65 Doubles	Jason Morton	(USA)	60 Doubles	Nancy Reed	(USA)
	William Davis	(USA)		Belmar Gunderson	(USA)
70 Singles	Oskar Jirkovsky	(AUT)	65 Singles	Louise Owen	(USA)
70 Doubles	Francis Bushmann	(USA)	65 Doubles	Louise Owen	(USA)
	Vincent Fotre	(USA)		Liz Harper	(USA)
75 Singles	Alex Swetka	(USA)			
75 Doubles	Dan Walker	(USA)			
	Verne Hughes	(USA)			

1995 (Group A), Bad Neuenahr, Germany, 6–13 August

MEN			WOMEN		
35 Singles	Thibaut Kuentz	(FRA)	35 Singles	Regina Marsikova	(CZE)
35 Doubles	Thibaut Kuentz	(FRA)			
	Stephan Medem	(GER)			
45 Singles	Robert Machan	(HUN)	40 Singles	Renata Vojtishek	(GER)
45 Doubles	Armistead Neely	(USA)	40 Doubles	Renata Vojtishek	(GER)
	Larry Turville	(USA)		Tina Karwasky	(USA)
50 Singles	Giorgio Rohrich	(ITA)	45 Singles	Marie Pinterova	(HUN)
50 Doubles	Jody Rush	(USA)	45 Doubles	Elizabeth Craig-Allan	(AUS)
	Richard Johnson	(USA)		Carol Campling	(AUS)

1995 (Group B), Nottingham, England, 21–28 May

55 Singles	Len Saputo	(USA)	50 Singles	Charleen Hillebrand	(USA)
55 Doubles	Leslie Dodson	(USA)	50 Doubles	Elly Keocke	(NED)
	Klaus Fuhrmann	(GER)		Jacqueline Boothman	(GBR)
60 Singles	James Nelson	(USA)	55 Singles	Renate Mayer-Zdralek	(GER)
60 Doubles	James Nelson	(USA)	55 Doubles	Carol Wood	(USA)
	Leonard Lindborg	(USA)		Sinclair Bill	(USA)
65 Singles	Lorne Main	(CAN)	60 Singles	Jennifer Hoad	(ESP)
65 Doubles	Lorne Main	(CAN)	60 Doubles	Rita Lauder	(GBR)
	Ken Sinclair	(CAN)		Ruth Illingworth	(GBR)
70 Singles	Oskar Jirkovsky	(AUT)	65 Singles	Betty Pratt	(USA)
70 Doubles	Brian Hurley	(AUS)	65 Doubles	Louise Owen	(USA)
	Neale Hook	(AUS)		Elaine Mason	(USA)
75 Singles	Robert Sherman	(USA)			
75 Doubles	Mirek Kizlink	(GBR)			
	Antony Starling	(GBR)			

1996 (Group A) Velden, Austria 15–22 September 1996

35 Singles	Greg Neuhart	(USA)	35 Singles	Regina Marsikova	(CZE)
35 Doubles	Greg Neuhart	(USA)	35 Doubles	Regina Marsikova	(CZE)
	Mike Fedderly	(USA)		Jutta Fahlbusch	(GER)
40 Singles	Julio Goes	(BRA)	40 Singles	Renata Vojtischek	(GER)
40 Doubles	Julio Goes	(BRA)	40 Doubles	Renata Vojtischek	(GER)
	Harry Ufer	(BRA)		Tina Karwasky	(USA)
45 Singles	Jairo Velasco	(ESP)	45 Singles	Marie Pinterova	(HUN)
45 Doubles	Jairo Velasco	(ESP)	45 Doubles	Marie Pinterova	(HUN)
	Robert Machan	(HUN)		Heide Orth	(GER)
50 Singles	Peter Pokorny	(AUT)	50 Singles	Eva Szabo	(HUN)
50 Doubles	Ted Hoehn	(USA)	50 Doubles	Carol Campling	(AUS)
	Richard Johnson	(USA)		Elizabeth Craig-Allan	(AUS)

1996 (Group B), Vienna, Austria 26 May–2 June 1996

55 Singles	Giorgio Rohrich	(ITA)	55 Singles	Charleen Hillebrand	(USA)
55 Doubles	Peter Pokorny	(AUT)	55 Doubles	Dorothy Matthiessen	(USA)
	Hans Gradischnig	(AUT)		Sinclair Bill	(USA)
60 Singles	King Van Nostrand	(USA)	60 Singles	Ilse Michael	(GER)
60 Doubles	Jim Nelson	(USA)	60 Doubles	Inge Weber	(CAN)

	Bob Duesler	(USA)		Nancy Reed	(USA)
65 Singles	Lorne Main	(CAN)	65 Singles	Ines de Pla	(ARG)
65 Doubles	Lorne Main	(CAN)	65 Doubles	Ruth Illingworth	(GBR)
	Ken Sinclair	(CAN)		Rita Lauder	(GBR)
70 Singles	Fred Kovaleski	(USA)	70 Singles	Betty Pratt	(USA)
70 Doubles	Fred Kovaleski	(USA)	70 Doubles	Betty Pratt	(USA)
	Bob Howe	(AUS)		Elaine Mason	(USA)
75 Singles	Robert Sherman	(USA)			
75 Doubles	Merwin Miller	(USA)			
	Verne Hughes	(USA)			
80 Singles	Dan Miller	(USA)			
80 Doubles	Dan Miller	(USA)			
	Irving Converse	(USA)			

1997 (Group A) Johannesburg, South Africa 21–28 September 1997

35 Singles	Greg Neuhart	(USA)	35 Singles	Tracy Houk	(USA)
35 Doubles	Chris Loock	(RSA)	35 Doubles	Alexi Beggs	(USA)
	Kobus Visagie	(RSA)		Vikki Beggs	(USA)
40 Singles	Pierre Godfroid	(BEL)	40 Singles	Renata Vojtischek	(GER)
40 Doubles	Pierre Godfroid	(BEL)	40 Doubles	Sherri Bronson	(USA)
	Bruce Osborne	(AUS)		Helle Viragh	(USA)
45 Singles	Frank Puncec	(RSA)	45 Singles	Rita Theron	(RSA)
45 Doubles	Max Bates	(AUS)	45 Doubles	Kerry Ballard	(AUS)
	Andrew Rae	(AUS)		Wendy Gilchrist	(AUS)
50 Singles	Jairo Velasco	(ESP)	50 Singles	Marie Pinterova	(HUN)
50 Doubles	Jairo Velasco	(ESP)	50 Doubles	Elizabeth Craig-Allan	(AUS)
	Luis Flor	(ESP)		Carol Campling	(AUS)

1997 (Group B) Newcastle, New South Wales 14–20 April 1997

55 Singles	Bob Howes	(AUS)	55 Singles	Heide Orth	(GER)
55 Doubles	Maurice Broom	(AUS)	55 Doubles	Lyn Wayte	(AUS)
	Max Senior	(AUS)		Margaret Wayte	(AUS)
60 Singles	Klaus Fuhrmann	(GER)	60 Singles	Judith Dalton	(AUS)
60 Doubles	Robert Duesler	(USA)	60 Doubles	Lorice Forbes	(AUS)
	Jim Nelson	(USA)		Peg Hoysted	(AUS)
65 Singles	Russell Seymour	(USA)	65 Singles	Beverley Rae	(AUS)
65 Doubles	William Davis	(USA)	65 Doubles	Ruth Illingworth	(GBR)
	Chuck de Voe	(USA)		Rita Lauder	(GBR)
70 Singles	Laci Legenstein	(AUT)	70 Singles	Twinx Rogers	(RSA)
70 Doubles	Laci Legenstein	(AUT)	70 Doubles	Deedy Krebs	(USA)
	Fred Kovaleski	(USA)		Elaine Mason	(USA)
75 Singles	Robert Sherman	(USA)			
75 Doubles	Robert Sherman	(USA)			
	Ellis Williamson	(USA)			
80 Singles	Alex Swetka	(USA)			
80 Doubles	Alex Swetka	(USA)			
	Gordon Henley	(AUS)			

ITALIA CUP

International Men's Team Competition for 35 year age group.

	VENUE	*WINNERS*	*RUNNERS-UP*	*FINAL SCORE*
1982	Cervia (ITA)	Italy	USA	2–1
1983	Cervia (ITA)	West Germany	USA	2–1
1984	Brand (AUT)	West Germany	France	2–1
1985	Reggio Calabria (ITA)	USA	Italy	2–0
1986	Bagnoles de l'Orne (FRA)	West Germany	USA	3–0
1987	Grado (ITA)	USA	Austria	2–1
1988	Bol (YUG)	West Germany	USA	3–0
1989	Mainz (FRG)	West Germany	USA	3–0
1990	Glasgow (GBR)	Spain	Australia	2–1
1991	Melbourne (AUS)	Australia	Spain	3–0
1992	Ancona, (ITA)	Italy	France	2–1
1993	Barcelona (ESP)	Spain	France	3–0
1994	Rosario, Argentina (ARG)	Germany	USA	2–1

1995	Dormagen (GER)	Germany	USA	2–1
1996	Rome (ITA)	USA	Italy	2–1
1997	Johannesburg (RSA)	USA	Great Britain	2–1

DUBLER CUP

International Men's Team Competition for 45 year age group.

FINALS

	VENUE	*WINNERS*	*RUNNERS-UP*	*FINAL SCORE*
1958	Monte Carlo (FRA)	Italy	West Germany	3–1
1959	Bad Ischl (AUT)	Switzerland	Italy	4–1
1960	Bad Gastain (AUT)	Italy	Switzerland	5–0
1961	Ancona (ITA)	Italy	Austria	4–1
1962	Merano (ITA)	Italy	France	3–2
1963	Merano (FRA)	Italy	Belgium	4–1
1964	Merano (FRA)	Italy	West Germany	5–0
	VENUE	*WINNERS*	*RUNNERS-UP*	*FINAL SCORE*
1965	Merano (FRA)	Italy	Sweden	3–0
1966	Florence (ITA)	Sweden	Italy	4–1
1967	Avesta (SWE)	France	Sweden	3–2
1968	Paris (FRA)	USA	France	5–0
1969	St Louis (USA)	USA	Sweden	4–1
1970	Cleveland (USA)	USA	Sweden	4–1
1971	La Costa (USA)	USA	Sweden	3–2
1972	Le Touquet (FRA)	USA	France	4–1
1973	London (GBR)	Australia	USA	3–1
1974	New York (USA)	USA	Australia	3–2
1975	London (GBR)	Australia	USA	5–0
1976	Alassio (ITA)	Italy	Canada	3–2
1977	Barcelona (ESP)	USA	France	4–1
1978	Le Touquet (FRA)	USA	Australia	4–1
1979	Vienna (AUT)	Austria	USA	3–2
1980	Cervia (ITA)	Sweden	Austria	2–1
1981	Buenos Aires (ARG)	USA	Great Britain	2–1
1982	Athens (GRE)	USA	Great Britain	2–1
1983	New York (USA)	USA	West Germany	2–1
1984	Bastad (SWE)	West Germany	USA	3–0
1985	Perth (AUS)	West Germany	Australia	2–1
1986	Berlin (GER)	West Germany	Switzerland	3–0
1987	Portschach (AUT)	Italy	Austria	2–1
1988	Huntington Beach (USA)	USA	West Germany	3–0
1989	Montevideo (URU)	USA	West Germany	2–1
1990	Bol (YUG)	Germany	USA	2–1
1991	Sydney (AUS)	USA	Germany	3–0
1992	Portschach (AUT)	Germany	Spain	2–1
1993	Barcelona (ESP)	Spain	France	2–1
1994	Santiago (CHI)	USA	Chile	2–1
1995	Saarbrucken (GER)	USA	Germany	2–1
1996	Velden (AUT)	USA	Australia	3–0
1997	Pretoria (RSA)	Austria	South Africa	2–1

** From 1958 to 1979 the early rounds were played zonally*

FRED PERRY CUP

International Men's Team Competition for 50 year age group.

	VENUE	*WINNERS*	*RUNNERS-UP*	*FINAL SCORE*
1991	Bournemouth (GBR)	Germany	Great Britain	3–0
1992	Berlin (GER)	Germany	USA	3–0
1993	Royan (FRA)	Germany	USA	2–1
1994	Buenos Aires (ARG)	France	USA	2–1
1995	Luchow (GER)	France	Germany	2–1
1996	Pörtschach (AUT)	Germany	Austria	2–1
1997	Sun City (RSA)	Spain	Germany	2–1

AUSTRIA CUP

International Men's Team Competition for 55 year age group.

	VENUE	*WINNERS*	*RUNNERS-UP*	*FINAL SCORE*
1977	Baden (AUT)	Great Britain	Austria	2–1
1978	Brand (AUT)	USA	Sweden	2–1
1979	Brand (AUT)	USA	Sweden	3–0
1980	Brand (AUT)	USA	Sweden	2–1
1981	Portschach (AUT)	USA	Sweden	3–0
1982	Cervia (ITA)	Australia	USA	2–1
1983	New York (USA)	Australia	USA	2–1
1984	Pörtschach (AUT)	USA	Australia	2–1
1985	Perth (AUS)	Australia	USA	3–0
1986	Pörtschach (AUT)	Australia	Canada	2–1
1987	Umag (YUG)	Canada	Australia	3–0
1988	Huntington Beach (USA)	Canada	West Germany	3–0
1989	Buenos Aires (ARG)	Canada	USA	2–1
1990	Pörtschach (AUT)	Canada	USA	3–0
	VENUE	*WINNERS*	*RUNNERS-UP*	*FINAL SCORE*
1991	Sydney (AUS)	USA	Australia	3–0
1992	Monte Carlo (FRA)	Germany	USA	3–0
1993	Murcia (ESP)	USA	Australia	3–0
1994	Carmel Valley (USA)	Australia	USA	2–1
1995	Dublin (IRL)	Germany	Austria	2–1
1996	Pörtschach (AUT)	Austria	USA	2–1
1997	Canberra (AUS)	Austria	Germany	2–1

GOTTFRIED VON CRAMM CUP

International Men's Team Competition for 60 year age group.

	VENUE	*WINNERS*	*RUNNERS-UP*	*FINAL SCORE*
1989	Kempten (GER)	Australia	New Zealand	3–0
1990	Ontario (CAN)	USA	Austria	2–1
1991	Adelaide (AUS)	USA	New Zealand	2–1
1992	Bournemouth (GBR)	Canada	USA	2–1
1993	Aix les Bains (FRA)	USA	France	3–0
1994	Burlingame (USA)	USA	Germany	3–0
1995	Pörtschach (AUT)	USA	Germany	3–0
1996	Velden (AUT)	USA	France	3–0
1997	Hamilton (NZL)	USA	Australia	3–0

BRITANNIA CUP

International Men's Team Competition for 65 year age group.

	VENUE	*WINNERS*	*RUNNERS-UP*	*FINAL SCORE*
1979	London (GBR)	USA	Great Britain	3–0
1980	Frinton-on-Sea (GBR)	USA	Sweden	3–0
1981	London (GBR)	USA	Sweden	3–0
1982	New York (USA)	USA	Canada	3–0
1983	Pörtschach (AUT)	USA	Australia	3–0
1984	Pörtschach (AUT)	USA	Australia	3–0
1985	Pörtschach (AUT)	USA	Australia	3–0
1986	Bournemouth (GBR)	USA	Norway	3–0
1987	Bastad (SWE)	USA	Sweden	2–1
1988	Huntington Beach (USA)	USA	France	3–0
1989	Umag (CRO)	USA	France	3–0
1990	Bournemouth (GBR)	USA	Australia	2–1
1991	Canberra (AUS)	Austria	Australia	2–1
1992	Seefeld (AUT)	Australia	Austria	2–1
1993	Le Touquet (FRA)	USA	Italy	2–1
1994	Portola Valley (USA)	USA	Austria	2–1
1995	Glasgow (GBR)	USA	Canada	2–1
1996	Villach (AUT)	USA	Canada	2–1
1997	Hamilton (NZL)	USA	Canada	2–1

CRAWFORD CUP

International Men's Team Competition for 70 year age group.

	VENUE	*WINNERS*	*RUNNERS-UP*	*FINAL SCORE*
1983	Brand (AUT)	USA	Sweden	3–0
1984	Helsinki (FIN)	USA	Great Britain	3–0
1985	Brand (AUT)	USA	Australia	3–0
1986	Seefeld (AUT)	USA	France	3–0
1987	Pörtschach (AUT)	USA	Great Britain	3–0
1988	Keszthely (HUN)	USA	Great Britain	3–0
1989	Bol (YUG)	USA	Brazil	3–0
1990	Brand (AUT)	USA	Brazil	3–0
1991	Canberra (AUS)	Germany	USA	2–1
1992	Le Touquet (FRA)	USA	Germany	3–0
1993	Menorca (ESP)	USA	France	3–0
1994	Oakland (USA)	Australia	France	2–1
	VENUE	*WINNERS*	*RUNNERS-UP*	*FINAL SCORE*
1995	Aix-les-Bains (FRA)	USA	Australia	2–1
1996	Seeboden (AUT)	Austria	USA	2–1
1997	Adelaide (AUS)	Austria	USA	2–1

BITSY GRANT CUP

International Men's Team Competition for 75 year age group.

	VENUE	*WINNERS*	*RUNNERS-UP*	*FINAL SCORE*
1994	Mill Valley (USA)	USA	Mexico	3–0
1995	Bournemouth (GBR)	USA	Sweeden	3–0
1996	Bad Waltersdorf (AUT)	USA	Germany	3–0
1997	Hobart, Tasmania (AUS)	USA	Australia	3–0

GARDNAR MULLOY CUP

International Men's Team Competition for 80 year age group.

	VENUE	*WINNERS*	*RUNNERS-UP*	*FINAL SCORE*
1996	Seefeld (AUT)	USA	Mexico	Round Robin
1997	Melbourne (AUS)	USA	Australia	Round Robin

YOUNG CUP

International Women's Team Competition for 40 year age group.

	VENUE	*WINNERS*	*RUNNERS-UP*	*FINAL SCORE*
1977	Malmo (SWE)	Argentina	Germany	3–0
1978	Ancona (ITA)	Italy	Germany	3–0
1979	Cannes (FRA)	West Germany	USA	3–0
1980	Bad Wiessee (GER)	West Germany	Italy	3–0
1981	Bad Wiessee (GER)	France	Italy	2–1
1982	Brand (AUT)	France	Italy	3–0
1983	Cervia (ITA)	West Germany	France	2–1
1984	Cervia (ITA)	USA	France	3–0
1985	Pörtschach (AUT)	West Germany	France	3–0
1986	Brand (AUT)	West Germany	USA	2–1
1987	Venice (ITA)	France	USA	2–1
1988	Bagnoles de l'Orne (FRA)	Great Britain	West Germany	3–0
1989	Pörtschach (AUT)	France	West Germany	3–0
1990	Keszthely (HUN)	France	USA	3–0
1991	Brisbane (AUS)	Australia	Germany	2–1
1992	Macahide (IRE)	Great Britain	Australia	2–1
1993	Bournemouth (GBR)	USA	Great Britain	2–1
1994	Montivideo (URU)	USA	Germany	2–1
1995	Dortmund (GER)	USA	Germany	2–1
1996	Bad Hofgastein (AUT)	USA	Germany	2–1
1997	Pretoria (RSA)	USA	Germany	3–0

MARGARET COURT CUP

International Women's Team Competition for 45 year age group.

	VENUE	*WINNERS*	*RUNNERS-UP*	*FINAL SCORE*
1994	Perth (AUS)	France	USA	2–1
1995	Gladbeck (GER)	USA	Australia	3–0
1996	Seeboden (AUT)	USA	South Africa	2–1
1997	Pretoria (RSA)	USA	France	3–0

MARIA ESTHER BUENO CUP

International Women's Team Competition for 50 year age group.

	VENUE	*WINNERS*	*RUNNERS-UP*	*FINAL SCORE*
1983	Pörtschach (AUT)	Great Britain	USA	2–1
1984	Le Touquet (FRA)	USA	France	3–0
1985	Bremen (GER)	USA	Great Britain	3–0
1986	Brand (AUT)	USA	Great Britain	2–1
1987	Helsinki (FIN)	USA	Great Britain	2–1
	VENUE	*WINNERS*	*RUNNERS-UP*	*FINAL SCORE*
1988	Bahia (BRA)	USA	Canada	2–1
1989	Bournemouth (GBR)	USA	Great Britain	2–1
1990	Barcelona (ESP)	Australia	Spain	2–1
1991	Perth (AUS)	USA	France	3–0
1992	Bagnoles de L'Orne (FRA)	USA	France	2–1
1993	Barcelona (ESP)	USA	Germany	2–1
1994	San Francisco (USA)	USA	Germany	3–0
1995	Velden (AUT)	Netherlands	USA	2–1
1996	St. Kanzian (AUT)	Australia	Germany	2–1
1997	Pretoria (RSA)	Australia	Germany	2–1

MAUREEN CONNOLLY CUP

International Women's Team Competition for 55 year age group.

	VENUE	*WINNERS*	*RUNNERS-UP*	*FINAL SCORE*
1992	Tyler (USA)	Australia	Great Britain	2–1
1993	Corsica (FRA)	USA	France	3–0
1994	Carmel (USA)	USA	France	2–1
1995	Le Touquet (FRA)	France	South Africa	2–1
1996	Eugendorf (AUT)	France	USA	2–1
1997	Canberra (AUS)	USA	France	3–0

ALICE MARBLE CUP

International Women's Team Competition for 60 year age group.

	VENUE	*WINNERS*	*RUNNERS-UP*	*FINAL SCORE*
1988	Pörtschach (AUT)	USA	West Germany	3–0
1989	Brand (AUT)	USA	West Germany	2–1
1990	Paderborn (GER)	USA	Germany	2–1
1991	Perth (AUS)	USA	Great Britain	3–0
1992	Keszthely (HUN)	Great Britain	USA	2–1
1993	Pörtschach (AUT)	USA	Great Britain	2–1
1994	Carmel Valley (USA)	USA	Great Britain	2–1
1995	Worthing (GBR)	USA	Spain	2–1
1996	Bad Hofgastein (AUT)	USA	Spain	3–0
1997	Adelaide (AUS)	USA	Canada	3–0

KITTY GODFREE CUP

International Women's Team Competition for 65 year age group.

	VENUE	*WINNERS*	*RUNNERS-UP*	*FINAL SCORE*
1995	Bournemouth (GBR)	USA	Canada	2–1
1996	Brand (AUT)	Great Britain	USA	2–1
1997	Melbourne (AUS)	Great Britain	USA	2–1

AUSTRALIAN INTERNATIONAL JUNIOR CHAMPIONSHIPS

BOYS' SINGLES

1946	F. A. Sedgman	1956	R. Mark	1965	G. Goven (FRA)
1947	D. Candy	1957	R. G. Laver	1966	K. Coombes
1948	K. B. McGregor	1958	M. Mulligan	1967	B. Fairlie (NZL)
1949	C. Wilderspin	1959	E. Buchholz (USA)	1968	P. Dent
1950	K. R. Rosewall	1960	W. Coghlan	1969	A. McDonald
1951	L. Hoad	1961	J. D. Newcombe	1970	J. Alexander
1952	K. Rosewall	1962	J. D. Newcombe	1971	C. Letcher
1953	W. Gilmour	1963	J. D. Newcombe	1972	P. Kronk
1954	W. A. Knight (GBR)	1964	A. Roche	1973	P. McNamee
1955	G. Moss				

	WINNER	*RUNNER-UP*	*SCORE*
1974	H. Brittain (AUS)		
1975	B. Drewett (AUS)		
1976	R. Kelly (AUS)	J. Dilouie (USA)	6–2 6–4
1977	(Jan.) B. Drewett (AUS)	T. Wilkison (USA)	6–4 7–6
1977	(Dec.) R. Kelly (AUS)		
1978	P. Serrett (AUS)	C. Johnstone (AUS)	6–4 6–3

	WINNER	*RUNNER-UP*	*SCORE*
1979	G. Whitecross (AUS)	C. Miller (AUS)	6–4 6–3
1980	C. Miller (AUS)	W. Masur (AUS)	7–6 6–2
1981	J. Windahl (SWE)	P. Cash (AUS)	6–4 6–4
1982	M. Kratzman (AUS)	S. Youl (AUS)	6–3 7–5
1983	S. Edberg (SWE)	S. Youl (AUS)	6–4 6–4
1984	M. Kratzman (AUS)	P. Flyn (AUS)	6–4 6–1
1985	S. Barr (AUS)	S. Furlong (AUS)	7–6 6–7 6–3
1986	*Not held*		
1987	J. Stoltenberg (AUS)	T. Woodbridge (AUS)	6–2 7–6
1988	J. Anderson (AUS)	A. Florent (AUS)	7–5 7–6
1989	N. Kulti (SWE)	T. Woodbridge (AUS)	6–2 6–0
1990	D. Dier (GER)	L. Paes (IND)	6–4 7–6
1991	T. Enqvist (SWE)	S. Gleeson (AUS)	7–6 6–7 6–1
1992	G. Doyle (AUS)	B. Dunn (USA)	6–2 6–0
1993	J. Baily (GBR)	S. Downs (NZL)	6–3 6–2
1994	B. Ellwood (AUS)	A. Illie (AUS)	5–7 6–3 6–3
1995	N. Kiefer (GER)	J-M Lee (KOR)	6–4 6–4
1996	B. Rehnqvist (SWE)	M. Hellstrom (SWE)	2–6 6–2 7–5
1997	D. Elsner (GER)	W. Whitehouse (RSA)	7–6 6–2

GIRLS' SINGLES

1946	S. Grant	1956	L. Coghlan	1965	K. Melville
1947	J. Tuckfield	1957	M. Rayson	1966	K. Krantzcke
1948	B. Penrose	1958	J. Lehane	1967	A. Kenny
1949	J. Warnock	1959	J. Lehane	1968	L. Hunt
1950	B. McIntyre	1960	L. Turner	1969	L. Hunt
1951	M. Carter	1961	R. Ebbern	1970	E. Goolagong
1952	M. Carter	1962	R. Ebbern	1971	P. Coleman
1953	J. Staley	1963	R. Ebbern	1972	P. Coleman
1954	E. Orton	1964	K. Dening	1973	C. O'Neill
1955	E. Orton				

	WINNER	*RUNNER-UP*	*SCORE*
1974	J. Walker (AUS)		
1975	S. Barker (GBR)	C. O'Neill (AUS)	6–2 7–6
1976	S. Saliba (AUS)	J. Fenwick (AUS)	2–6 6–3 6–4
1977	(Jan.) P. Bailey (AUS)	A. Tobin (AUS)	6–2 6–3
1977	(Dec.) A. Tobin (AUS)	L. Harrison (AUS)	6–1 6–2
1978	E. Little (AUS)	S. Leo (AUS)	6–1 6–2
1979	A. Minter (AUS)	S. Leo (AUS)	6–4 6–3
1980	A. Minter (AUS)	E. Sayers (AUS)	6–4 6–2
1981	A. Minter (AUS)	C. Vanier (FRA)	6–4 6–2
1982	A. Brown (GBR)	P. Paradis (FRA)	6–3 6–4
1983	A. Brown (GBR)	B. Randall (AUS)	7–6 6–3

1984	A. Croft (GBR)	H. Dahlstrom (SWE)	6–0	6–1	
1985	J. Byrne (AUS)	L. Field (AUS)	6–1	6–3	
1986	*Not held*				
1987	M. Jaggard (AUS)	N. Provis (AUS)	6–2	6–4	
1988	J. Faull (AUS)	E. Derly (FRA)	6–4	6–4	
1989	K. Kessaris (USA)	A. Farley (USA)	6–1	6–2	
1990	M. Maleeva (BUL)	L. Stacey (AUS)	7–5	6–7	6–1
1991	N. Pratt (AUS)	K. Godridge (AUS)	6–4	6–3	
1992	J. Limmer (AUS)	L. Davenport (USA)	7–5	6–2	
1993	H. Rusch (GER)	A. Glass (GER)	6–1	6–2	
1994	T. Musgrave (AUS)	B. Schett (AUT)	4–6	6–4	6–2
1995	S. Drake-Brockman (AUS)	A. Elwood (AUS)	6–3	4–6	7–5
1996	M. Grzybowska (POL)	N. Dechy (FRA)	6–1	4–6	6–1
1997	M. Lucic (CRO)	M.Weingartner (GER)	6–2	6–2	

BOYS' DOUBLES

	WINNERS	*RUNNERS-UP*	*SCORE*		
1983	J. Harty (AUS)/D. Tyson (AUS)	A. Lane (AUS)/D. Cahill (AUS)	3–6	6–4	6–3
1984	M. Kratzman (AUS)/M. Baroch (AUS)	B. Custer (AUS)/D. Macpherson (AUS)	6–2	5–7	7–5
1985	B. Custer (AUS)/D. Macpherson (AUS)	C. Suk (TCH)/P. Korda (TCH)	7–5	6–2	
1986	*Not held*				
	WINNERS	*RUNNERS-UP*	*SCORE*		
1987	J. Stoltenberg (AUS)/T. Woodbridge (AUS)	S. Barr (AUS)/D. Roe (AUS)	6–2	6–4	
1988	J. Stoltenberg (AUS)/T. Woodbridge (AUS)	J. Anderson (AUS)/R. Fromberg (AUS)	6–3	6–2	
1989	J. Anderson (AUS)/T. Woodbridge (AUS)	J. Morgan (AUS)/A. Kratzmann (AUS)	6–4	6–2	
1990	R. Petterson (SWE)/M. Renstroem (SWE)	R.Janecek (CAN)/E.Munoz de Cote (MEX)	4–6	7–6	6–1
1991	G. Doyle (AUS)/J. Eagle (AUS)	J. Holmes (AUS)/P. Kilderry (AUS)	7–6	6–4	
1992	G. Doyle (AUS)/B. Sceney (AUS)	L. Carrington (USA)/J. Thompson (USA)	6–4	6–4	
1993	L. Rehmann (GER)/C. Tambue (GER)	S. Humphries (USA)/J. Jackson (USA)	6–7	7–5	6–2
1994	B. Ellwood (AUS)/M. Philippoussis (AUS)	J. Delgado (GBR)/R. Kukal (SVK)	4–6	6–2	6–1
1995	L. Borgeois (AUS)/J.-M. Lee (KOR)	N. Kiefer (GER)/U. Seetzen (GER)	6–2	6–1	
1996	D. Bracciali (ITA)/J.-Robichaud (CAN)	M. Lee (GBR)/ J. Trotman (GBR)	6–2	6–4	
1997	D. Sherwood (GBR)/J. Trotman (GBR)	J. Van Der Westhuizen (RSA)/ W. Whitehouse (RSA)	7–6	6–3	

GIRLS' DOUBLES

	WINNERS	RUNNERS-UP	SCORE		
1983	B. Randall (AUS)/K. Staunton (AUS)	J. Byrne (AUS)/J. Thompson (AUS)	3–6	6–3	6–3
1984	L. Field (AUS)/L. Savchenko (URS)	M. Parun (NZL)/J. Masters (AUS)	7–6	6–2	
1985	J. Byrne (AUS)/J. Thompson (AUS)	A. Scott (AUS)/S. McCann (AUS)	6–0	6–3	
1986	*Not held*				
1987	N. Provis (AUS)/A. Devries (BEL)	D. Jones (AUS)/G. Dwyer (AUS)	6–3	6–1	
1988	R. McQuillan (AUS)/J. Faull (AUS)	R. Stubbs (AUS)/K. McDonald (AUS)	6–1	7–5	
1989	A. Strnadova (TCH)/E. Sviglerova (TCH)	N. Pratt (AUS)/A. Woolcock (AUS)	6–2	6–0	
1990	L. Zaltz (ISR)/R. Mayer (ISR)	J. Hodder (AUS)/N. Pratt (AUS)	6–4	6–4	
1991	K. Habsudova (TCH/B. Rittner (GER)	J. Limmer (AUS)/A. Woolcock (AUS)	6–2	6–0	
1992	L. Davenport (USA)/N. London (USA)	M. Avotins (AUS)/J. Limmer (AUS)	6–2	7–5	
1993	J. Manta (SUI)/L. Richterova (TCH)	A. Carlsson (SWE)/C. Cristea (ROM)	6–3	6–2	
1994	C. Morariu (USA)/L. Varmuzov (CZE)	Y. Basting(NED)/A. Scheider(GER)	7–5	2–6	7–5
1995	C. Morariu (USA)/L. Varmuzov (CZE)	S. Obata(JPN)/N. Urabe (JPN)	6–1	6–2	
1996	M. Pastikova (CZE)/J. Schonfeldova (CZE)	O. Barabanschikova (BLR)/M. Lucic (CRO)	6–1	6–3	
1997	M. Lucic (CRO)/J. Wohr (GER)	Y-J. Cho (KOR)/S. Hisamatsu (JPN)	6–2	6–2	

FRENCH INTERNATIONAL JUNIOR CHAMPIONSHIPS

BOYS' SINGLES

	WINNER	*RUNNER-UP*	*SCORE*		
1974	C. Casa (FRA)	U. Marten (GER)	2–6	6–1	6–4
1975	C. Roger–Vasselin (FRA)	P. Elter (GER)	6–1	6–2	
1976	H. Gunthardt (SUI)	J. L. Clerc (ARG)	4–6	7–6	6–4
1977	J. P. McEnroe (USA)	R. Kelly (AUS)	6–1	6–1	
1978	I. Lendl (TCH)	P. Hjertquist (SWE)	7–6	6–4	
1979	R. Krishnan (IND)	B. Testerman (USA)	2–6	6–1	6–0
1980	H. Leconte (FRA)	A. Tous (ESP)	7–6	6–3	
1981	M. Wilander (SWE)	J. Brown (USA)	7–5	6–1	
1982	T. Benhabiles (FRA)	L. Courteau (FRA)	7–6	6–2	

1983	S. Edberg (SWE)	F. Fevrier (FRA)	6–4	7–6	
1984	K. Carlsson (SWE)	M. Kratzman (AUS)	6–3	6–3	
1985	J. Yzaga (PER)	T. Muster (AUT)	2–6	6–3	6–0
1986	G. Perez Roldan (ARG)	S. Grenier (FRA)	4–6	6–3	6–2
1987	G. Perez Roldan (ARG)	J. Stoltenberg (AUS)	6–3	3–6	6–1
1988	N. Pereira (VEN)	M. Larsson (SWE)	7–6	6–3	
1989	F. Santoro (FRA)	J. Palmer (USA)	6–3	3–6	9–7
1990	A. Gaudenzi (ITA)	T. Enqvist (SWE)	2–6	7–6	6–4
1991	A. Medvedev (URS)	T. Enqvist (SWE)	6–4	7–6	
1992	A. Pavel (ROM)	M. Navarra (ITA)	7–6	6–3	
1993	R. Carretero (ESP)	A. Costa (ESP)	6–0	7–6	
1994	J. Diaz (ESP)	G. Galimberti (ITA)	6–3	7–6	
1995	M. Zabaleta (ARG)	M. Puerta (ARG)	6–2	6–3	
1996	A. Martin (ESP)	B. Rehnqvist (SWE)	6–3	7–6	
1997	D. Elsner (GER)	L. Horna (PER)	6–4	6–4	

GIRLS' SINGLES

	WINNER	*RUNNER-UP*	*SCORE*		
1974	M. Simionescu (ROM)	S. Barker (GBR)	6–3	6–3	
1975	R. Marsikova (TCH)	L. Mottram (GBR)	6–3	5–7	6–2
1976	M. Tyler (GBR)	M. Zoni (ITA)	6–1	6–3	
1977	A. E. Smith (USA)	H. Strachanova (TCH)	6–3	7–6	
	WINNER	*RUNNER-UP*	*SCORE*		
1978	H. Mandlikova (TCH)	M. Rothschild (FRG)	6–1	6–1	
1979	L. Sandin (SWE)	M. L. Piatek (USA)	6–3	6–1	
1980	K. Horvath (USA)	K. Henry (USA)	6–2	6–2	
1981	B. Gadusek (USA)	H. Sukova (TCH)	6–7	6–1	6–4
1982	M. Maleeva (BUL)	P. Barg (USA)	7–5	6–2	
1983	P. Paradis (FRA)	D. Spence (USA)	7–6	6–3	
1984	G. Sabatini (ARG)	K. Maleeva (BUL)	6–3	5–7	6–3
1985	L. Garrone (ITA)	D. Van Rensburg (RSA)	6–1	6–3	
1986	P. Tarabini (ARG)	N. Provis (AUS)	6–3	6–3	
1987	N. Zvereva (URS)	J. Pospisilova(TCH)	6–1	6–0	
1988	J. Halard (FRA)	A. Farley (USA)	6–2	4–6	7–5
1989	J. Capriati (USA)	E. Sviglerova (TCH)	6–4	6–0	
1990	M. Maleeva (BUL)	T. Ignatieva (URS)	6–2	6–3	
1991	A. Smashnova (ISR)	I. Gorrochategui (ARG)	2–6	7–5	6–1
1992	R. De Los Rios (PAR)	P. Suarez (ARG)	6–4	6–0	
1993	M. Hingis(SUI)	L. Courtois (BEL)	7–5	7–5	
1994	M. Hingis (SUI)	S. Jeyaseelan (CAN)	6–3	6–1	
1995	A. Cocheteux (FRA)	M. Weingartner (GER)	7–5	6–4	
1996	A. Mauresmo (FRA)	M. Shaughnessy (USA)	6–0	6–4	
1997	J. Henin (BER)	C. Black (ZIM)	4–6	6–4	6–4

BOYS' DOUBLES

	WINNERS	*RUNNERS-UP*	*SCORE*		
1983	M. Kratzman (AUS)/S. Youl (AUS)	A. Chesnokov (URS)/A. Olhovskiy (URS)	6–2	6–3	
1985	P. Korda (TCH)/C. Suk (TCH)	V. Godrichidze (URS)/V. Volkov (URS)	4–6	6–0	7–5
1986	F. Davin (ARG)/G. Perez-Roldan (ARG)	T. Carbonell (ESP)/J. Sanchez (ESP)	7–5	5–7	6–3
1987	J. Courier (USA)/J. Stark (USA)	F. Davin (ARG)/G. Perez-Roldan (ARG)	6–7	6–4	6–3
1988	J. Stoltenberg (AUS)/T. Woodbridge (AUS)	C. Caratti (ITA)/G. Ivanisevic (YUG)	7–6	7–5	
1989	J. Anderson (AUS)/T. Woodbridge (AUS)	L. Herrera (MEX)/M. Knowles (BAH)	6–3	4–6	6–2
1990	S. La Reau (CAN)/P. Le Blanc (CAN)	C. Marsh (RSA)/M. Ondruska (RSA)	7–6	6–7	9–7
1991	T. Enqvist (SWE)/M. Martinelle (SWE)	J. Knowle (AUT)/J. Unterberger (AUT)	6–1	6–3	
1992	E. Abaroa (MEX)/G. Doyle (AUS)	Y. Kafelnikov (CIS)/A. Radulescu (ROM)	7–6	6–3	
1993	S. Downs (NZL)/J. Greenhalgh (NZL)	N. Godwin (RSA)/G. Williams (RSA)	6–1	6–1	
1994	G. Kuerten (BRA)/N. Lapentti (ECU)	M. Boye (FRA)/N. Escude (FRA)	6–2	6–4	
1995	R. Sluiter (NED)/P. Wessels (NED)	J. Gimelstob (USA)/R. Wolters (USA)	7–6	7–5	
1996	S. Grosjean (FRA)/O. Mutis (FRA)	J. Brandt (GER)/D. Elsner (GER)	6–2	6–3	
1997	J. De Armas (VEN)/L. Horna (PER)	A. di Pasquale (FRA)/J. Jeanpierre (FRA)	6–4	2–6	7–5

GIRLS' DOUBLES

	WINNERS	*RUNNERS-UP*	*SCORE*		
1983	C. Anderholm (SWE)/H. Olsson (SWE)	K./M. Maleeva (BUL)	6–4	6–1	
1985	M Perez-Roldan (ARG)/P. Tarabini (ARG)	A. Holikova (TCH)/R. Zrubakova (TCH)	6–3	5–7	6–4
1986	L. Meskhi (URS)/N. Zvereva (URS)	J. Novotna (TCH)/R. Rajchrtova (TCH)	1–6	6–3	6–0
1987	N. Medvedeva (URS)/N. Zvereva (URS)	M. Jaggard (AUS)/N. Provis (AUS)	6–3	6–3	

1988	A. Dechaume (FRA)/E. Derly (FRA)	J. Halard (FRA)/M. Laval (FRA)	6–4	3–6	6–3
1989	N. Pratt (AUS)/S.-T. Wang (TPE)	C. Caverzasio (ITA)/S. Farina (ITA)	7–5	3–6	8–6
1990	R. Dragomir (ROM)/I. Spirlea (ROM)	T. Ignatieva (URS)/I. Soukhova (URS)	6–3	6–1	
1991	E. Bes (ESP)/I. Gorrochategui (ARG)	Z. Malkova (TCH)/E. Martincova (TCH)	6–1	6–3	
1992	L. Courtois (BEL)/N. Feber (BEL)	L. Davenport (USA)/C. Rubin (USA)	6–1	5–7	6–4
1993	L. Courtois (BEL)/N. Feber (BEL)	L. Bitter (NED)/M. Koutstaal (NED)	6–4	7–6	
1994	M. Hingis (SUI)/M. Nedelkova (SVK)	L. Cenkova (CZE)/L. Richterova (CZE)	6–3	6–2	
1995	C. Morariu (USA)/L. Varmuzova (CZE)	A. Canepa (ITA)/G. Casoni (ITA)	7–6	7–5	
1996	A. Canepa (ITA)/G. Casoni (ITA)	A. Kournikova (RUS)/L. Varmuzova (CZE)	6–2	5–7	7–5
1997	C. Black (ZIM)/I. Selyutina (KAZ)	M. Matevzic (SLO)/K. Srebotnik (SLO)	6–0	5–7	7–5

WIMBLEDON INTERNATIONAL JUNIOR CHAMPIONSHIPS

The event originated as an invitation tournament, boys' singles in 1947 and girls' singles in 1948. It became a Championship event in 1975.

BOYS' SINGLES

1947 K. Nielsen (DEN)
1948 S. Stockenberg (SWE)
1949 S. Stockenberg (SWE)
1950 J. A. T. Horn (GBR)
1951 J. Kupferburger (RSA)
1952 R. K. Wilson (GBR)
1953 W. A. Knight (GBR)
1954 R. Krishnan (IND)
1955 M. P. Hann (GBR)
1956 R. Holmberg (USA)
1957 J. I. Tattersall (GBR)
1958 E. Buchholz (USA)
1959 T. Lejus (URS)
1960 A. R. Mandelstam (RSA)
1961 C. E. Graebner (USA)
1962 S. Matthews (GBR)
1963 N. Kalogeropoulous (GRE)
1964 I. El Shafei (EGY)
1965 V. Korotkov (URS)
1966 V. Korotkov (URS)
1967 M. Orantes (ESP)
1968 J. G. Alexander (AUS)
1969 B. Bertram (RSA)
1970 B. Bertram (RSA)
1971 R. Kreiss (USA)
1972 B. Borg (SWE)
1973 W. Martin (USA)
1974 W. Martin (USA)

	WINNER	*RUNNER-UP*	*SCORE*		
1975	C. J. Lewis (NZL)	R. Ycaza (ECU)	6–1	6–4	
1976	H. Gunthardt (SUI)	P. Elter (FRG)	6–4	7–5	
1977	V. Winitsky (USA)	E. Teltscher (USA)	6–1	1–6	8–6
1978	I. Lendl (TCH)	J. Turpin (USA)	6–3	6–4	
1979	R. Krishnan (IND)	D. Siegler (USA)	6–3	6–4	
1980	T. Tulasne (FRA)	H. D. Beutel (FRG)	6–4	3–6	6–4
1981	M. Anger (USA)	P. Cash (AUS)	7–6	7–5	
1982	P. Cash (AUS)	H. Sundstrom (SWE)	6–4	6–7	6–3
1983	S. Edberg (SWE)	J. Frawley (AUS)	6–3	7–6	
1984	M. Kratzman (AUS)	S. Kruger (RSA)	6–4	4–6	6–3
1985	L. Lavalle (MEX)	E. Velez (MEX)	6–4	6–4	
1986	E. Velez (MEX)	J. Sanchez (ESP)	6–3	7–5	
1987	D. Nargiso (ITA)	J. Stoltenberg (AUS)	7–6	6–4	
1988	N. Pereira (VEN)	G. Raoux (FRA)	7–6	6–2	
1989	N. Kulti (SWE)	T. Woodbridge (AUS)	6–4	6–3	
1990	L. Paes (IND)	M. Ondruska (RSA)	7–6	6–2	
1991	T. Enqvist (SWE)	M. Joyce (USA)	6–4	6–3	
1992	D. Skoch (TCH)	B. Dunn (USA)	6–4	6–3	
1993	R. Sabau (ROM)	J. Szymanski (VEN)	6–1	6–3	
1994	S. Humphries (USA)	M. Philippoussis (AUS)	7–6	3–6	6–4
1995	O. Mutis (FRA)	N. Kiefer (GER)	6–2	6–2	
1996	V. Voltchkov (BLR)	I. Ljubicic (CRO)	3–6	6–2	6–3
1997	W. Whitehouse (RSA)	D. Elsner (GER)	6–3	7–6	

GIRLS' SINGLES

1948 O. Miskova (TCH)
1949 C. Mercelis (BEL)
1950 L. Cornell (GBR)
1951 L. Cornell (GBR)
1952 ten Bosch (HOL)
1953 D. Kilian (RSA)
1954 V. A. Pitt (GBR)
1955 S. M. Armstrong (GBR)
1956 A. S. Haydon (GBR)
1957 M. Arnold (USA)
1958 S. M. Moore (USA)
1959 J. Cross (RSA)
1960 K. Hantze (USA)
1961 G. Baksheeva (URS)
1962 G. Baksheeva (URS)
1963 D. M. Salfati (RSA)
1964 P. Barkowicz (USA)
1965 O. Morozova (URS)
1966 B. Lindstrom (FIN)
1967 J. Salome (HOL)
1968 K. Pigeon (USA)
1969 K. Sawamatsu (JPN)
1970 S. Walsh (USA)
1971 M. Kroschina (URS)
1972 I. Kloss (RSA)
1973 A. Kiyomura (USA)
1974 M. Jausovec (YUG)

	WINNER	*RUNNER-UP*	*SCORE*		
1975	N. Y. Chmyreva (URS)	R. Marsikova (TCH)	6–4	6–3	
1976	N. Y. Chmyreva (URS)	M. Kruger (RSA)	6–3	2–6	6–1

1977	L. Antonoplis (USA)	Mareen Louie (USA)	6–5	6–1	
1978	T. A. Austin (USA)	H. Mandlikova (TCH)	6–0	3–6	6–4
1979	M. L. Piatek (USA)	A. Moulton (USA)	6–1	6–3	
1980	D. Freeman (AUS)	S. Leo (AUS)	7–6	7–5	
1981	Z. Garrison (USA)	R. Uys (RSA)	6–4	3–6	6–0
1982	C. Tanvier (FRA)	H. Sukova (TCH)	6–2	7–5	
1983	P. Paradis (FRA)	P. Hy (HKG)	6–2	6–1	
1984	A. N. Croft (GBR)	E. Reinach (RSA)	3–6	6–3	6–2
1985	A. Holikova (TCH)	J. Byrne (AUS)	7–5	6–1	
1986	N. Zvereva (URS)	L. Meskhi (URS)	2–6	6–2	9–7
1987	N. Zvereva (URS)	J. Halard (FRA)	6–4	6–4	
1988	B. Schultz (HOL)	E. Derly (FRA)	7–6	6–1	
1989	A. Strnadova (TCH)	M. McGrath (USA)	6–2	6–3	
1990	A. Strnadova (TCH)	K. Sharpe (AUS)	6–2	6–4	
1991	B. Rittner (GER)	E. Makarova (URS)	6–7	6–2	6–3
1992	C. Rubin (USA)	L. Courtois (BEL)	6–2	7–5	
1993	N. Feber (BEL)	R. Grande (ITA)	7–6	1–6	6–2
1994	M. Hingis (SUI)	M-R. Jeon (KOR)	7–5	6–4	
1995	A. Olsza (POL)	T. Tanasugarn (THA)	7–5	7–6	
1996	A. Mauresmo (FRA)	M. Serna (ESP)	4–6	6–3	6–4
1997	C. Black (ZIM)	A. Rippner (USA)	6–3	7–5	

BOYS' DOUBLES

	WINNERS	*RUNNERS-UP*	*SCORE*		
1982	P. Cash (AUS)/J. Frawley (AUS)	R. Leach (USA)/J. Ross (USA)	6–3	6–2	
1983	M. Kratzman (AUS)/S. Youl (AUS)	M. Nastase (ROM)/O. Rahnasto (FIN)	6–4	6–4	
1984	R. Brown (USA)/R. Weiss (USA)	M. Kratzman (AUS)/J. Svensson (SWE)	1–6	6–4	11–9
1985	A. Moreno (MEX)/J. Yzaga (PER)	P. Korda (TCH)/C. Suk (TCH)	7–6	6–4	
1986	T. Carbonell (ESP)/P. Korda (TCH)	S. Barr (AUS)/H. Karrasch (CAN)	6–1	6–1	
1987	J. Stoltenberg (AUS)/T. Woodbridge (AUS)	D. Nargiso (ITA)/E. Rossi (ITA)	6–3	7–6	
1988	J. Stoltenberg (AUS)/T. Woodbridge (AUS)	D. Rikl (TCH)/T. Zdrazila (TCH)	6–4	1–6	7–6
1989	J. Palmer (USA)/J. Stark (USA)	J.-L. De Jager (RSA)/W. Ferreira (RSA)	7–6	7–6	
1990	S. Lareau (CAN)/S. LeBlanc (CAN)	C. Marsh (RSA)/M. Ondruska (RSA)	7–6	4–6	6–3
1991	K. Alami (MAR)/G. Rusedski (CAN)	J-L. De Jager (RSA)/A. Medvedev (URS)	1–6	7–6	6–4
1992	S. Baldas (AUS)/S. Draper (AUS)	M. Bhupathi (IND)/N. Kirtane (IND)	6–1	4–6	9–7
1993	S. Downs (NZL)/J. Greenhalgh (NZL)	N. Godwin (RSA)/G. Williams (RSA)	6–7	7–6	
1994	B. Ellwood (AUS)/M. Philippoussis (AUS)	V. Platenik(SVK)/R. Schlachter (BRA)	6–2	6–4	
1995	M. Lee (GBR)/G. Trotman (GBR)	A. Hernandez (MEX)/M. Puerta (ARG)	7–6	6–4	
1996	D. Bracciali (ITA)/J. Robichaud (CAN)	D. Roberts (RSA)/W. Whitehouse (RSA)	6–2	6–4	
1997	L. Horna (PER)/N. Massu (CHI)	J. Van Der Westhuizen (RSA)/ W. Whitehouse (RSA)	6–4	6–2	

GIRLS' DOUBLES

	WINNERS	*RUNNERS-UP*	*SCORE*		
1982	B. Herr (USA)/P. Barg (USA)	B. S. Gerken (USA)/G. Rush (USA)	6–1	6–4	
1983	P. Fendick (USA)/P. Hy (HKG)	C. Anderholm (SWE)/H. Olsson (SWE)	6–1	7–5	
1984	C. Kuhlman (USA)/S. Rehe (USA)	V. Milvidskaya (URS)/L. Savchenko (URS)	6–3	5–7	6–4
1985	L. Field (AUS)/J. Thompson (AUS)	E. Reinach (SAF)/J. Richardson (NZL)	6–1	6–2	
1986	M. Jaggard (AUS)/L. O'Neill (AUS)	L. Meskhi (URS)/N. Zvereva (URS)	7–6	6–4	
1987	N. Medvedeva (URS)/N. Zvereva (URS)	I. S. Kim (KOR)/P. M. Modena (HKG)	2–6	7–5	6–0
1988	J. Faull (AUS)/R. McQuillan (AUS)	A. Dechaume (FRA)/E. Derly (FRA)	4–6	6–2	6–3
1989	J. Capriati (USA)/M. McGrath (USA)	A. Strnadova (TCH)/E. Sviglerova (TCH)	6–4	6–2	
1990	K. Habsudova (TCH)/A. Strnadova (TCH)	N. Pratt (AUS)/K. Sharpe (AUS)	6–2	6–4	
1991	C. Barclay (AUS)/L. Zaltz (ISR)	J. Limmer (AUS)/A. Woolcock (AUS)	6–4	6–4	
1992	P. Nelson (USA)/J. Steven (USA)	M. Avotins (AUS)/L. McShea (AUS)	2–6	6–4	6–3
1993	L. Courtois (BEL)/N. Feber (BEL)	H. Mochizuki (JPN)/Y. Yoshida (JPN)	6–3	6–4	
1994	E. De Villiers (RSA)/E. Jelfs (GBR)	C. Morariu (USA)/L. Varmuzova (CZE)	6–3	6–4	
1995	C. Black (ZIM)/A. Olsza (POL)	T. Musgrave (AUS)/J. Richardson (AUS)	6–0	7–6	
1996	O. Barabanschikova (BLR)/A. Mauresmo (FRA)	L. Osterloh (USA)/ S. Reeves (USA)	5–7	6–3	6–1
1997	C. Black (ZIM)/I. Selyutina (KAZ)	M. Matevzic (SLO)/K. Srebotnik (SLO)	3–6	7–5	6–3

US INTERNATIONAL JUNIOR CHAMPIONSHIPS

BOYS' SINGLES

	WINNER	*RUNNER-UP*	*SCORE*	
1974	W. Martin (USA)	F. Taygan (USA)	6–4	6–2
1975	H. Schonfield (USA)	C. J. Lewis (NZL)	6–4	6–3

1976	Y. Ycaza (ECU)	J. L. Clerc (ARG)	6–4	5–7	6–0
1977	V. Winitsky (USA)	E. Teltscher (USA)	6–4	6–4	
1978	P. Hjertquist (SWE)	S. Simonsson (SWE)	7–6	1–6	7–6
1979	S. Davis (USA)	J. Gunnarsson (SWE)	6–3	6–1	
1980	M. Falberg (USA)	E. Korita (USA)	6–0	6–2	
1981	T. Hogstedt (SWE)	H. Schwaier (FRG)	7–5	6–3	
1982	P. Cash (AUS)	G. Forget (FRA)	6–3	6–3	
1983	S. Edberg (SWE)	S. Youl (AUS)	6–2	6–4	
1984	M. Kratzman (AUS)	B. Becker (FRG)	6–3	7–6	
1985	T. Trigueiro (USA)	J. Blake (USA)	6–2	6–3	
1986	J. Sanchez (ESP)	F. Davin (ARG)	6–2	6–2	
1987	D. Wheaton (USA)	A. Cherkasov (URS)	7–5	6–0	
1988	N. Pereira (VEN)	N. Kulti (SWE)	6–1	6–2	
1989	J. Stark (USA)	N. Kulti (SWE)	6–4	6–1	
1990	A. Gaudenzi (ITA)	M. Tillstroem (SWE)	6–2	4–6	7–6
1991	L. Paes (IND)	K. Alami (MAR)	6–4	6–4	
1992	B. Dunn (USA)	N. Behr (ISR)	7–5	6–2	
1993	M. Rios (CHI)	S. Downs (NZL)	7–6	6–3	
1994	S. Schalken (NED)	M. Tahiri (MAR)	6–2	7–6	
1995	N. Kiefer (GER)	U. Seetzen (GER)	6–3	6–4	
1996	D. Elsner (GER)	M. Hipfl (AUT)	6–3	6–2	
1997	A. di Pasquale (FRA)	W. Whitehouse (RSA)	6–7	6–4	6–1

GIRLS' SINGLES

	WINNER	*RUNNER-UP*	*SCORE*		
1974	I. Kloss (RSA)	M. Jausovec (YUG)	6–4	6–3	
1975	N. T. Chmyreva (URS)	G. Stevens (RSA)	6–7	6–2	6–2
1976	M. Kruger (RSA)	L. Romanov (ROM)	6–3	7–5	
1977	C. Casabianca (ARG)	L. Antonoplis (USA)	6–3	2–6	6–2
1978	L. Siegel (USA)	I. Madruga (ARG)	6–4	6–4	
1979	A. Moulton (USA)	M. L. Piatek (USA)	7–6	7–6	
1980	S. Mascarin (USA)	K. Keil (USA)	6–3	6–4	
1981	Z. Garrison (USA)	K. Gompert (USA)	6–0	6–3	
1982	B. Herr (USA)	G. Rush (USA)	6–3	6–1	
1983	E. Minter (AUS)	M. Werdel (USA)	6–3	7–5	
1984	K. Maleeva (BUL)	N. Sodupe (USA)	6–1	6–2	
1985	L. Garrone (ITA)	A. Holikova (TCH)	6–2	7–6	
1986	E. Hakami (USA)	S. Stafford (USA)	6–2	6–1	
1987	N. Zvereva (URS)	S. Birch (USA)	6–0	6–3	
1988	C. Cunningham (USA)	R. McQuillan (AUS)	6–3	6–1	
1989	J. Capriati (USA)	R. McQuillan (AUS)	6–2	6–3	
1990	M. Maleeva (BUL)	N. Van Lottum (FRA)	7–5	6–2	
1991	K. Habsudova (TCH)	A. Mall (USA)	6–1	6–3	
1992	L. Davenport (USA)	J. Steven (USA)	6–2	6–2	
1993	M. F. Bentivoglio (ITA)	Y. Yoshida (JPN)	7–6	6–4	
1994	M. Tu (USA)	M. Hingis (SUI)	6–2	6–4	
1995	T. Snyder (USA)	A. Ellwood (AUS)	6–4	4–6	6–2
1996	M. Lucic (CRO)	M. Weingartner (GER)	6–2	6–1	
1997	C. Black (ZIM)	K. Chevalier (FRA)	6–7	6–1	6–3

BOYS' DOUBLES

	WINNERS	*RUNNERS-UP*	*SCORE*		
1982	J. Canter (USA)/M. Kures (USA)	P. Cash (AUS)/J. Frawley (AUS)	7–6	6–3	
1983	M. Kratzman (AUS)/S. Youl (AUS)	P. McEnroe (USA)/B. Pearce (USA)	6–1	7–6	
1984	L. Lavelle (MEX)/M. Nastase (ROM)	J. Ycaza (PER)/A. Moreno (MEX)	7–6	1–6	6–1
1985	J. Blake (USA)/D. Yates (USA)	P. Flynn (USA)/D. McPherson (USA)	3–6	6–3	6–4
1986	T. Carbonell (ESP)/J. Sanchez (ESP)	J. Tarango (USA)/D. Wheaton (USA)	6–4	1–6	6–1
1987	G. Ivanisevic (YUG)/D. Nargiso (ITA)	Z. Ali (IND)/B. Steven (NZL)	3–6	6–4	6–3
1988	J. Stark (USA)/J. Yoncey (USA)	M. Boscatta (ITA)/S. Pescosolido (ITA)	7–6	7–5	
1989	W. Ferreira (RSA)/G. Stafford (RSA)	M. Damm (TCH)/J. Kodes (TCH)	6–3	6–4	
1990	M. Renstroem (SWE)/M. Tillstroem (SWE)	S. LeBlanc (CAN)/G. Rusedski (CAN)	6–7	6–3	6–4
1991	K. Alami (MAR)/J–L. De Jager (RSA)	M. Joyce (USA)/V. Spadea (USA)	6–4	6–7	6–1
1992	J. Jackson (USA)/E. Taino (USA)	M. Rios (CHI)/G. Silberstein (CHI)	6–3	6–7	6–4
1993	N. Godwin (RSA)/G. Williams (RSA)	B. Ellwood (AUS)/J. Sekulov (AUS)	6–3	6–3	
1994	B. Ellwood (AUS)/N. Lapentti (ECU)	P. Goldstein (USA)/S. Humphries (USA)	6–2	6–0	
1995	J-M. Lee (KOR)/J. Robichaud (CAN)	R. Sluiter (NED)/P. Wessels (NED)	7–6	6–2	

1996	B. Bryan (USA)/M. Bryan (USA)	D. Bracciali (ITA)/J. Robichaud (CAN)	5–7	6–3	6–4
1997	F. Gonzalez (CHI)/N. Massu (CHI)	J-R. Lisnard (FRA)/M. Llodra (FRA)	6–4	6–4	

GIRLS' DOUBLES

	WINNERS	*RUNNERS-UP*	*SCORE*		
1982	P. Barg (USA)/B. Herr (USA)	A. Hulbert (AUS)/B. Randall (AUS)	1–6	7–5	7–6
1983	A. Hulbert (AUS)/B. Randall (AUS)	N. Riva (URS)/L. Savchenko (URS)	6–4	6–2	
1984	G. Sabatini (ARG)/M. Paz (ARG)	S. MacGregor (USA)/S. London (USA)	6–4	3–6	6–2
1985	R. Zrubakova (TCH)/A. Holikova (TCH)	P. Tarabini (ARG)/M. Perez Roldan (ARG)	6–4	2–6	7–5
1986	R. Zrubakova (TCH)/J. Novotna (TCH)	E. Brioukhovets (URS)/L. Meskhi (URS)	6–4	6–2	
1987	M. McGrath (USA)/K. Po (USA)	Il-Soon Kim (KOR)/Shi-Ting Wang (TPE)	6–4	7–5	
1988	M. McGrath (USA)/K. Po (USA)	K. Caverzasio (ITA)/L. Lapi (ITA)	6–3	6–1	
1989	J. Capriati (USA)/M. McGrath (USA)	J. Faull (AUS)/R. McQuillan (AUS)	6–0	6–3	
1990	K. Godridge (AUS)/K. Sharpe (AUS)	E. deLone (USA)/L. Raymond (USA)	4–6	7–5	6–2
1991	K. Godridge (AUS)/N. Pratt (AUS)	A. Carlsson (SWE)/C. Cristea (ROM)	7–6	7–5	
1992	L. Davenport (USA)/N. London (USA)	K. Schlukebit (USA)/J. Steven (USA)	7–5	6–7	6–4
1993	N. London (USA)/J. Steven (USA)	H. Mochizuki (JPN)/Y. Yoshida (JPN)	6–3	6–4	
1994	S. de Beer (RSA)/C. Reuter (NED)	N. De Villiers (RSA) /E. Jelfs (GBR)	4–6	6–4	6–2
1995	C. Morariu (USA)/L. Varmuzova (CZE)	A. Kournikova (RUS)/A. Olsza (POL)	6–3	6–3	
1996	S. de Beer (RSA)/J. Steck (RSA)	P. Rampre (SLO)/K. Srebotnik (SLO)	6–4	6–3	
1997	M. Irvin (USA)/A. Stevenson (USA)	C. Black (ZIM)/I. Selyutina (KAZ)	6–2	7–6	

ITALIAN INTERNATIONAL JUNIOR CHAMPIONSHIPS

The event originated as an Under-21 Invitational tournament for boys and girls singles in 1959. It became a Championship event in 1976.

BOYS' SINGLES

	WINNER	*RUNNER–UP*	*SCORE*		
1976	H. Gunthardt (SUI)	F. Luna (ESP)	6–4	6–1	
1977	Y. Noah (FRA)	R. Venter (ESP)	6–4	6–2	
1978	I. Lendl (TCH)	P. Hjertquist (SWE)	2–6	6–2	6–0
1979	H. Simonsson (SWE)	B. Testerman (USA)	6–0	6–3	
1980	T. Tulasne (FRA)	H. Leconte (FRA)	6–2	6–3	
1981	B. Zivojinovic (YUG)	L. Bottazzi (ITA)	7–6	2–6	6–3
1982	G. Forget (FRA)	M. Zampieri (ITA)	6–3	6–4	
1983	M. Fioroni (ITA)	K. Novacek (TCH)	5–7	6–1	6–3
1984	L. Jensen (USA)	B. Oresar (YUG)	6–4	6–4	
1985	A. Padovani (ITA)	C. Pistolesi (ITA)	6–2	6–1	
1986	F. Davin (ARG)	G. Perez-Roldan (ARG)	6–4	4–6	6–0
1987	J. Courier (USA)	A. Aramburu (PER)	7–6	1–6	6–3
1988	G. Ivanisevic (YUG)	F. Fontang (FRA)	6–3	6–2	
1989	S. Pescosolido (ITA)	F. Santoro (FRA)	6–1	6–0	
1990	I. Baron (USA)	O. Fernandez (MEX)	7–5	6–1	
1991	G. Doyle (AUS)	K. Carlsen (DEN)	1–6	6–3	9–7
1992	Y. Kafelnikov (CIS)	D. Skoch (TCH)	7–6	6–4	
1993	J. Szymanski (VEN)	R. Sabau (ROM)	6–3	6–4	
1994	F. Browne (ARG)	G. Galimberti (ITA)	6–3	6–2	
1995	M. Zabaleta (ARG)	M. Lee (GBR)	6–4	6–2	
1996	O. Mutis (FRA)	D. Sciortino (ITA)	6–1	6–3	
1997	F. Allgauer (ITA)	L. Horna (PER)	6–3	6–4	

GIRLS' SINGLES

	WINNER	*RUNNER–UP*	*SCORE*		
1977	H. Strachanova (CZE)	C. Casabianca (ARG)	7–6	6–0	
1978	H. Mandlikova (TCH)	I. Madruga (ARG)	7–6	6–3	
1979	M. L. Piatek (USA)	L. Sandin (SWE)	6–3	3–6	6–3
1980	S. Mascarin (USA)	K. Horvath (USA)	6–4	6–3	
1981	A. Minter (USA)	E. Sayers (AUS)	1–6	6–2	6–3
1982	G. Rush (USA)	B. Herr (USA)	6–7	7–6	6–4
1983	S. Goles (YUG)	A.M. Cecchini (ITA)	6–3	6–4	
1984	G. Sabatini (ARG)	S. Schilder (HOL)	7–6	6–1	
1985	P. Tarabini (ARG)	L. Golarsa (ITA)	6–0	6–1	
1986	B. Fulco (ARG)	P. Tarabini (ARG)	7–6	6–2	
1987	N. Zvereva (URS)	C. Martinez (ESP)	6–3	6–2	

1988	C. Tessi (ARG)	F. Labat (ARG)	3–6	7–6	6–3
1989	F. Labat (ARG)	M. Anderson (RSA)	6–2	6–2	
1990	S. Farina (ITA)	N. Baudone (ITA)	6–1	6–2	
1991	Z. Malkova (TCH)	E. Makarova (URS)	6–2	6–1	
1992	R. De Los Rios (PAR)	N. Feber (BEL)	6–1	7–5	
1993	N. Louarssabichvili (GEO)	J. Lee (USA)	6–4	6–7	7–5
1994	T. Panova (RUS)	S. Ventura (ITA)	1–6	6–3	6–0
1995	A. Kournikova (RUS)	C. Reuter (NED)	6–2	6–0	
1996	O. Barabanschikova (BLR)	S. Drake-Brockman (AUS)	2–6	7–5	6–2
1997	K. Srebotnik (SLO)	T. Pisnik (SLO)	6–1	6–2	

BOYS' DOUBLES

	WINNER	*RUNNER–UP*	*SCORE*		
1993	N. London (USA)/J. Steven (USA)	H. Mochizuki (JPN)/Y. Yoshida (JPN)	6–3	6–4	
1976	F. Van Oertzen (BRA)/C.Sacomandi (BRA)	C. Motta (BRA)/H. Roverano (BRA)	6–3	6–2	
1980	S. Giammalva (USA)/M. Anger (USA)	W. Masur (AUS)/C. Miller (AUS)	7–6	6–0	
1981	E. Korita (USA)/J.Brown (USA)	R. Bengston (CAN)/M. Perkins (CAN)	6–2	6–4	
1982	F. Maciel (MEX)/F.Perez (MEX)	M. Kures (USA)/R. Leach (USA)	6–3	7–5	
1983	S. Edberg (SWE)/J.Svensson (SWE)	F. Garcia (ESP)/E. Sanchez (ESP)	6–2	6–3	
1984	A. Moreno (MEX)/J.Yzaga (PER)	A. Antonitsch (AUT)/H. Skoff (AUT)	6–7	7–6	6–4
1985	F. Errard (FRA)/P. Lacombrade (FRA)	G. Saacks (RSA)/D. Shapiro (RSA)	7–6	4–6	6–4
1986	F. Davin (ARG)/G. Perez-Roldan (ARG)	A. Mancini (ARG)/N. Pereira (URU)	6–2	6–2	
1987	G. Carbonari (ARG)/J.L. Noriega (PER)	L. Bale (RSA)/D. Naikin (RSA)	2–6	6–3	6–4
1988	S. Hirszon (YUG)/G. Ivanisevic (YUG)	M. Boscatto (ITA)/F. Pisilli (ITA)	6–3	6–4	
1989	M. Bascatto (ITA)/ S. Pescosolido (ITA)	W. Ferreira (RSA)/ G. Stafford (RSA)	7–5	6–4	
1990	W. Bulls (USA)/ B. MacPhie (USA)	J. De Jager (RSA)/ J. De Beer (RSA)	7–6	5–7	6–4
1991	G. Doyle (AUS)/ J. Eagle (AUS)	S. Sargsian (URS)/D. Tomachevitch (URS)	6–1	6–1	
1992	M. Bertolini (ITA)/ M. Navarra (ITA)	Y. Kafelnikov (CIS)/ A. Radulescu (ROM)	6–4	4–6	6–4
1993	T. Johansson (SWE)/M. Norman (SWE)	B. Ellwood (AUS)/ J. Sekulov (AUS)	7–6	6–3	
1994	B. Ellwood (AUS)/M. Philippoussis (AUS)	A. Hernandez (MEX)/ G. Venegas MEX)	6–2	6–3	
1995	G. Canas (ARG)/ M. Garcia (ARG)	S. Grosjean (FRA)/Y. Romero (VEN)	6–2	7–6	
1996	M. Lee (GBR)/J. Trotman (GBR)	A. Krasevec (SLO)/G. Krusic (SLO)	7–6	2–6	6–1
1997	J. Van Der Westhuizen (RSA)/ W. Whitehouse (RSA)	F. Gonzalez (CHI)/N. Massu (CHI)	2–0	ret.	

GIRLS' DOUBLES

	WINNER	*RUNNER–UP*	*SCORE*		
1980	B. Moulds (RSA)/ R. Uys (RSA)	K. Horvath (USA)/ P. Murgo (ITA)	4–6	6–2	6–4
1981	H. Sukova (TCH)/ M. Maleeva (BUL)	M. Linstrom (SWE)/ C. Lindquist (SWE)	3–6	6–4	6–4
1982	B. Gerken (USA)/ B. Herr (USA)	B. Randall (AUS)/ E. Minter (AUS)	6–3	6–4	
1983	P. Fendick (USA)/ J. Fuchs (USA)	B. Bowes (USA)/ A. Hubert (USA)	6–4	6–4	
1984	D. Ketelaar (HOL)/ S. Schilder (HOL)	M. Paz (ARG)/ G. Sabatini (ARG)	5–7	6–4	6–2
1985	P. Tarabini (ARG)/M. Perez-Roldan (ARG)	J. Novotna (TCH)/ R. Rajchrtova (TCH)	6–4	6–4	
1986	A. Dechaume (FRA)/S. Niox Chateau (FRA)	E. Derly (FRA)/ F. Martin (FRA)	6–2	6–4	
1987	N. Medvedeva (URS)/ N. Zvereva (URS)	P. Miller (URU)/ C. Tessi (ARG)	7–5	6–1	
1988	D. Graham (USA)/ A. Grossman (USA)	C. Cunningham (USA)/ A. Farley (USA)	6–2	7–5	
1989	R. Bobkova (TCH)/ A. Strnadova (TCH)	N. Baudone (ITA)/ S. Farina (ITA)	5–7	6–4	6–4
1990	T. Ignatieva (URS)/ I. Sukhova (URS)	C. Barclay (AUS)/ J. Stacey (AUS)	5–7	6–2	9–7
1991	B. Martincova (TCH)/ I. Horvat (YUG)	I. Gorrochategui (ARG)/ R. Grande (ITA)	6–3	6–4	
1992	N. Feber (BEL)/ L. Courtois (BEL)	M. Avotins (AUS)/ L. McShea (AUS)	6–4	5–7	6–3
1993	C. Moros (USA)/ S. Nickitas (USA)	M. D. Campana (CHI)/ B. Castro (CHI)	7–5	7–5	
1994	M. Nedelkova (SVK)/ M. Hasanova (SVK)	K. Mesa (COL)/ C. Giraldo (COL)	1–6	6–3	6–4
1995	A. Canepa (ITA)/ G. Casoni (ITA)	O. Barabanschikova (BLR)/L. Varmuzova (CZE)	6–4	5–7	6–3
1996	A. Canepa (ITA)/G. Casoni (ITA)	S. Drake-Brockman (AUS)/A. Kournikova (RUS)	5–7	6–4	6–3
1997	T. Hergold (SLO)/T. Pisnik (SLO)	S. Bajin (CAN)/I. Visic (CRO)	6–1	6–2	

NEC WORLD YOUTH CUP

International Team Championship for boys and girls aged 16 and under. Early rounds played zonally.

BOYS' FINALS

1985 Australia d. USA 2–1, *Kobe Japan:* R. Fromberg lost to F. Montana 2–6 2–6, S. Barr d. J. A. Falbo 6–4 6–4; Barr/J. Stoltenberg d. Montana/Falbo 4–6 6–7 7–5.

1986 Australia d. USA 2–1, *Tokyo, Japan:* J. Stoltenberg d. J. Courier 6–2 6–4; R. Fromberg lost to M. Chang 4–6 4–6; Stoltenberg/T. Woodbridge d. Courier/Kass 7–6 6–2.

1987 Australia d. Netherlands 3–0, *Freiburg, West Germany:* T. Woodbridge d. P. Dogger 7–5 3–6 6–2; J. Anderson d. F. Wibier 6–0 6–1; J. Morgan/Woodbridge d. Dogger/Wibier 6–3 6–2.
1988 Czechoslovakia d. USA 2–1, *Perth, Australia:* J. Kodes d. J. Leach 7–6 6–2; M. Damm d. B. MacPhie 6–2 6–7 6–4; Damm/L. Hovorka lost to W. Bull/Leach 4–6 4–6.
1989 West Germany d. Czechoslovakia 2–1, *Asuncion, Paraguay:* S. Gessner lost to L. Thomas 5–7 5–7; G. Paul d. P. Gazda 6–4 6–4; Paul/D. Prinosil d. Gazda/Thomas 7–5 6–1.
1990 USSR d. Australia 2–1, *Rotterdam, Netherlands:* D. Thomashevitch d. T. Vasiliadis 6–3 6–2; A. Medvedev lost to G. Doyle 6–2 4–6 5–7; E. Kafelnikov/Medvedev d. Doyle/B. Sceney 7–6 6–3.
1991 Spain d. Czechoslovakia 2–1, *Barcelona, Spain:* G. Corrales d. D. Skock 7–5 7–5; A. Costa lost to F. Kascak 4–6 5–7; Corrales /Costa d. Kascak/Skock 6–4 6–2.
1992 France d. Germany 2–1, *Barcelona, Spain:* M. Boye d. A. Nickel 7–5 0–6 6–3; N. Escude lost to R. Nicklish 2–6, 6–3, 3–6; Boye/Escude d. Nickel/Nicklish 6–7 6–0 6–3.
1993 France d. New Zealand 2–1, *Wellington, New Zealand:* O. Mutis lost to T. Susnjak 1–6 6–1 3–6; J-F Bachelot d. S. Clark 4–6 6–4 6–4; Mutis/J. Potron d. Clark/N. Nielsen 6–3 6–4.
1994 Netherlands d. Austria 2–1, *Tucson, Arizona:* P. Wessels lost to C. Trimmel 6–4 3–6 5–7; R. Sluiter d. M. Hipfl 7–6 6–1; Sluiter/Wessels d. Hipfl/Trimmel 6–3 6–4.
1995 Germany d. Czech Republic 3–0, *Essen, Germany:* T. Messmer d. P. Kralert 6–3 7–5; D. Elsner d. M. Tabara 6–3 6–4; D. Elsner/T. Zivnicek d. P. Kralert/P. Riha 6–7(4) 6–4 6–4.
1996 France d. Australia 2–1, *Zurich, Switzerland:* J. Haehnel d. N. Healey 6–4 6–2; J. Jeanpierre d. L. Hewitt 6–3 7–5; J. Haehnel/O. Patience lost to N. Healey/L. Hewitt 5–7 6–4 6–7(5).
1997 Czech Republic d. Venezuela 2–0, *Vancouver, Canada:* J. Levinsky d. E. Nastari 6–0 6–2; L. Chramosta d. J. De Armas 7–6(2) 6–2.

GIRLS' FINALS

1985 Czechoslovakia d. Australia 3–0, *Kobe, Japan:* J. Pospisilova d. S. McCann 6–4 6–4; R. Zrubakova d. N. Provis 7–6 7–5; Pospisilova/Zrubakova d. Provis/W. Frazer 7–5 6–4.
1986 Belgium d. Czechoslovakia 2–1, *Tokyo, Japan:* A. Devries d. R. Zrubakova 6–3 6–4; S. Wasserman d. P. Langrova 6–4 7–5; Devries/C. Neuprez lost to Langrova/Zrubakova 4–6 2–6.
1987 Australia d. USSR 2–1, *Freiburg, West Germany:* J. Faull lost to N. Medvedeva 6–4 2–6 2–6; R. McQuillan d. E. Brioukhovets 3–6 6–2 6–3; Faull/McQuillan d. Brioukhovets/Medvedeva 6–3 6–1.
1988 Australia d. Argentina 3–0, *Perth, Australia:* K. A. Guse d. F. Haumuller 7–6 6–4; L. Guse d. C. Tessi 7–6 1–6 6–2; K. A. Guse/K. Sharpe d. I. Gorrachategui/Tessi 6–0 6–2.
1989 West Germany d. Czechoslovakia 2–1, *Asuncion, Paraguay:* M. Skulj–Zivec d. K. Matouskova 6–0 7–5; A. Huber d. K. Habsudova 6–0 6–3; K. Duell/Skulj–Zivec lost to Habsudova/P. Kucova 3–6 0–6.
1990 Netherlands d. USSR 2–1, *Rotterdam, Netherlands:* P. Kamstra d. I. Soukhova 6–1 7–6; L. Niemantsverdriet lost to T. Ignatieva 0–6 6–1 4–6; Kamstra/Niemantsverdriet d. Ignatieva/Soukhova 6–3 4–6 6–1.
1991 Germany d. Paraguay 2–1, *Barcelona, Spain:* H. Rusch lost to L. Schaerer 6–7 3–6; M. Kochta d. R de los Rios 6–3 6–1; K. Freye/Kochta d. de los Rios/Schaerer 5–7 6–3 6–3.
1992 Belgium d. Argentina 3–0, *Barcelona, Spain:* L. Courtois d. L. Montalvo 6–1 6–3; N. Feber d. L. Reynares 1–6 6–4 6–1; Courtois/S. Deville d. M. Oliva/Montalvo 1–6 7–5 6–4.
1993 Australia d. USA 2–1, *Wellington, New Zealand:* S. Drake-Brockman d. S. Nickitas 6–2 5–7 6–2; A. Ellwood d. A. Basica 6–2 6–1; Ellwood/J. Richardson lost to C. Maros/Nickitas 6–2 5–7 0–6.
1994 South Africa d. France 3–0, *Tucson, Arizona:* J. Steck d. A. Cocheteux 7–5 6–3; S. De Beer d. A. Castera 6–4 6–3; doubles not played.
1995 France d. Germany 2–1, *Essen, Germany:* K. Jagieniak lost to S. Kovacic 4–6 3–6; A. Mauresmo d. S. Klosel 6–0 6–3; K. Chevalier/A. Mauresmo d. C. Christian/S.-Kovacic 6–3 7–5.
1996 Slovenia d. Germany 2–1, *Zurich, Switzerland:* K. Srebotnik d. S. Kovacic 6–1 6–3; P. Rampre lost to J. Wohr 2–6 1–6; P. Rampre/K. Srebotnik d. S. Kovacic/J. Wohr 6–1 6–4.
1997 Russia d. France 2–0, *Vancouver, Canada:* A. Myskina d. S. Schoeffel 6–3 2–6 8–6; E. Dementieva d. S. Rizzi 6–2 4–6 6–4.

WORLD JUNIOR TENNIS COMPETITION

International Team Championship for boys and girls aged 14 and under, known as NTT World Junior Tennis 1991–96.

BOYS' FINALS

1991 Spain d. Italy 2–1, *Yamanakako, Japan:* A. Martin d. C. Zoppi 6–2 7–6; J-A. Saiz d. P. Tabini 6–2 6–1; Martin/J-M. Vincente lost to A. Ciceroni/Tabini 7–5 4–6 6–8.
1992 Austria d. USA 2–1, *Yamanakako, Japan:* K. Trimmel d. C. Brill 4–6 6–2 6–2; M. Hipfl d. G. Adams 6–4 6–0; Trimmel/Hipfl lost to Abrams/R. Bryan 6–1 6–2.
1993 France d. Slovenia 2–1, *Yamanakako, Japan:* J-R. Lisnard d. A. Krasevec 7–6 6–3; A. di Pasquale d. M. Gregoric 6–1 6–1; A. di Pasquale/V. Lavergne lost to P. Kralert/J. Krejci 2–6 6–2 6–7.
1994 Italy d. Belgium 2–1, *Yamanakako, Japan:* N. Frocassi lost to O. Rochus 6–7 6–3 3–6; F. Luzzi d. X. Malisse 6–3 7–6; Frocassi/Luzzi d. Malisse/Rochus 6–4 1–6 6–3.

1995 Great Britain d. Germany 3–0, *Yamanakako, Japan:* M. Hilton d. P. Hammer 6–3 4–6 6–4; S. Dickson d. B. Bachert 7–5 6–2; S. Dickson/A. Mackin d. B. Bachert/R. Neurohr 7–5 6–1.
1996 Argentina d. Sweden 3–0, *Nagoya, Japan:* G. Coria d. F. Prpic 6–1 6–1; D. Nalbandian d. J. Johansson 6–3 6–3; G. Coria/A. Pastorino d. J. Johansson/F. Prpic 6–1 6–3.
1997 South Africa d. Czech Republic 2–1, *Nagoya, Japan:* A. Anderson d. M. Kokta 7–5 6–4; D. Stegmann d. J. Masik 6–3 6–0; A. Anderson/R. Blair lost to D. Karol/J. Masik 1–6 0–6.

GIRLS' FINALS
1991 Czechoslovakia d. Australia 3–0, *Yamanakako, Japan:* L. Cenkova d. A. Ellwood 7–5 6–2; A. Havrlkova d. A. Venkatesan 6–1 6–2; Cenkova/Havrlkova d. Ellwood/E. Knox 6–2 7–6.
1992 USA d. Australia 3–0, *Yamanakako, Japan:* M. Tu d. A. Ellwood 6–4 6–4; A. Basica d. R. Reid 6–3 6–7 6–4; Basica/A. Augustus d. Reid/S. Drake-Brockman 6–2 7–5.
1993 Germany d. USA 2–1, *Yamanakako, Japan:* C. Christian lost to S. Halsell 0–6 3–6; S. Klosel d. K. Gates 6–4 7–6; C. Christian/S. Klosel d. K. Gates/S. Halsell 3–6 6–3 7–5.
1994 Germany d. Czech Republic 2–1, *Yamanakako, Japan:* J. Wohr d. J. Schonfeldova 7–5 6–0; S. Kovacic d. M. Pastikova 6–2 7–5; S. Lozel/Wohr lost to Pastikova/Schonfeldova 4–6 1–6.
1995 Slovenia d. Hungary 2–1, *Yamanakako, Japan:* T. Pisnik d. S. Szegedi 7–6(5) 6–3; K. Srebotnik lost to Z. Gubacsi 6–4 3–6 4–6; T. Pisnik/K. Srebotnik d. Z. Gubacsi/I. Szalai 6–3 6–3.
1996 Slovak Republic d. Great Britain 3–0, Nagoya, Japan: S. Hrozenska d. S. Gregg 6–1 6–2; K. Basternakova d. H. Collin 6–3 6–1; S. Hrozenska/Z. Kucova d. H. Collin/H. Reesby 6–4 6–2.
1997 Russia d. Slovak Republic 2–1, *Nagoya, Japan:* L. Krasnoroutskaia d. D. Hantuchova 6–2 6–4; E. Bovina d. M. Babakova 6–4 6–1; G. Fokina/L. Krasnoroutskaia lost to D. Hantuchova/L. Kurhajcova 2–6 6–2 2–6.

ORANGE BOWL

International 18 and Under Championship played in Miami each December. There are also events for players aged 16 and under, and 14 and under.

BOYS' SINGLES

	WINNER	*RUNNER-UP*	*SCORE*				
1974	W. Martin (USA)	T. Smid (TCH)	6–7	4–6	6–2	6–1	7–6
1975	F. Luna (ESP)	B. E. Gottfried (USA)	6–4	6–4			
1976	J. P. McEnroe (USA)	E. Teltscher (USA)	7–5	6–1			
1977	I. Lendl (TCH)	Y. Noah (FRA)	4–6	7–6	6–3		
1978	G. Urpi (ESP)	S. van der Merwe (SAF)	6–3	6–1			
1979	R. Viver (ECU)	P. Arraya (PER)	7–6	6–4			
1980	J. Nystrom (SWE)	C. Castqtellan (ARG)	7–5	7–6			
1981	R. Arguello (ARG)	R. Joaquim (BRA)	6–2	6–1			
1982	G. Forget (FRA)	J. Bardou (ESP)	7–5	2–6	6–1		
1983	K. Carlsson (SWE)	E. Sanchez (ESP)	6–2	6–4			
1984	R. Brown (USA)	J. Berger (USA)	6–3	6–3			
1985	C. Pistolesi (ITA)	B. Oresar (YUG)	6–2	6–0			
1986	J. Sanchez (ESP)	A. Parker (USA)	6–3	6–4			
1987	J. Courier (USA)	A. Cherkasov (URS)	6–3	6–2			
1988	M. Rosset (SUI)	S. Pescosolido (ITA)	7–6	3–6	6–1		
1989	F. Meligeni (ARG)	G. Lopez (ESP)	7–6	7–6			
1990	A. Medvedev (URS)	O. Fernandez (MEX)	6–4	2–6	6–2		
1991	M. Charpentier (ARG)	K. Alami (MAR)	6–4	6–3			
1992	V. Spadea (USA)	G. Etlis(ARG)	7–6	6–3			
1993	A. Costa (ESP)	R. Carretero (ESP)	6–3	6–4			
1994	N. Lapentti (ECU)	G. Kuerten (BRA)	6–3	7–6			
1995	M. Zabaleta (ARG)	T. Haas (GER)	6–2	3–6	6–1		
1996	A. Martin (ESP)	A. di Pasquale (FRA)	6–0	6–1			
1997	N. Massu (CHI)	R. Rake (USA)	6–1	6–7	6–3		

GIRLS' SINGLES

	WINNER	*RUNNER-UP*	*SCORE*		
1974	L. Epstein (USA)	C. Penn (USA)	6–1	6–2	
1975	L. Epstein (USA)	S. McInerny (USA)	6–2	6–1	
1976	M. Kruger (SAF)	A. .E. Smith (USA)	2–6	6–3	6–4
1977	A. E. Smith (USA)	H. Strachonova (TCH)	7–6	7–5	
1978	A. Jaeger (USA)	R. Fairbank (SAF)	6–1	6–3	
1979	K. Horvath (USA)	P. Murgo (ITA)	7–5	6–0	
1980	S. Mascarin (USA)	R. Sasak (YUG)	6–3	3–6	6–4
1981	P. Barg (USA)	H. Fukarkova (TCH)	6–2	6–3	

1982	C. Bassett (CAN)	M. Maleeva (BUL)	6–4	ret'd	
1983	D. Spence (USA)	A. Cecchini (ITA)	2–6	7–5	6–4
1984	G. Sabatini (ARG)	K. Maleeva (BUL)	6–1	6–3	
1985	M. J. Fernandez (USA)	P. Tarabini (ARG)	7–5	6–1	
1986	P. Tarabini (ARG)	B. Fulco (ARG)	6–2	6–2	
1987	N. Zvereva (URS)	L. Lapi (ITA)	6–2	6–0	
1988	C. Cunningham (USA)	L. Lapi (ITA)	6–0	6–1	
1989	L. Spadea (USA)	S. Albinus (DEN)	6–0	6–3	
1990	P. Perez (ESP)	S. Ramon (ESP)	6–1	7–6	
1991	E. Likhovtseva (URS)	M-J. Gaidono (ARG)	7–6	6–1	
1992	B. Mulej (SLO)	R. De Los Rios (PAR)	7–5	7–5	
1993	A. Montolio (ESP)	S. Jeyaseelan (CAN)	6–7	6–1	6–1
1994	M. Ramon (ESP)	A. Kournikova (RUS)	7–5	6–4	
1995	A. Kournikova (RUS)	S. Nacuk (YUG)	6–3	6–2	
1996	A. Alcazar (ESP)	K. Srebotnik (SLO)	6–3	6–0	
1997	T. Pisnik (SLO)	G. Volekova (SVK)	6–2	6–0	

VASCO VALERIO CUP

International Team Championship for boys aged 18 and under. Played zonally with the final stages in Lesa, Italy. Administered by the European Tennis Association.

FINALS

1970 Sweden d. France 4–1: L. Johansson d. F. Caujolle 10–8 6–3; T. Svensson d. E. Naegelen 6–4 6–0; R. Norbeg lost to E. Deblicker 4–6 0–6; M. Stig d. A. Collinot 6–3 6–1; Johansson/Stig d. Deblicker/Naegelen 6–3 6–3.
1971 Italy d. West Germany 4–0: M. Consolini d. U. Pinner 6–2 1–0 ret'd; N. Gasparini d. R. Gehring 6–1 3–6 6–0; C. Borea d. A. Hongsag 3–6 6–4 6–3; C. Barazzutti v L. Jelitto 5–1 abandoned; Barazzutti/Gasparini d. Gehring/Jelitto 6–4 6–4.
1972 Czechoslovakia d. USSR 3–2: I. Hora lost to V. Borisov 6–4 7–9 5–7; P. Slozil d. A. Machavez 6–2 2–6 6–4; Slozil/J. Granat d. A. Bogomolov/Borisov 6–3 7–5; T. Smid lost to K. Pugaev 3–6 8–6 4–6; Granat d. Bogomolov 6–3 6–4.
1973 Czechoslovakia d. USSR 4–1: A. Jankowski lost to V. Borisov 6–4 2–3 ret'd; P. Slozil d. A. Machavez 6–3 5–7 6–4: J. Granat d. K. Pugaev 3–6 6–4 6–3; T. Smid d. V. Katsnelson 6–4 6–4; Jankowski/Slozil d. Borisov/Pugaev 6–8 10–8 6–3.
1974 Spain d. Italy 3–2: L. Fargas d. A. Meneschincheri 6–1 6–1; A. Capitan /M. Mir lost to A. Marchetti/A. Vattuone 6–3 4–6 3–6; M. Mir lost to G. Ocleppo 4–6 2–6; A. Torralbo d. Vattuone 9–11 6–4 6–3; Capitan d. G. Marchetti 8–6 3–6 6–3.
1975 Italy d. USSR 3–2: G. Ocleppo d. S. Baranov 7–5 6–5 ret'd; A. Spiga d. S. Molodoikov 6–4 6–8 6–0; A. Merlone d. V. Gruzman 6–2 0–6 6–3; A. Meneschincheri lost to S. Elerdashvili 9–11 4–6; Ocleppo/Merlone lost to Baranov/ Gruzman 5–7 4–6.
1976 West Germany d. France 4–1: P. Elter d. P. Portes 6–3 6–2; W. Popp lost to Y. Noah 3–6 0–6; J. Henn d. J. Kuentz 6–2 6–2; A. Maurer d. G. Geniau 6–4 6–3; Elter/Popp d. G. Moretton/Noah 6–3 3–6 6–3.
1977 Italy d. Rumania 5–0: G. Rinaldini d. E. Pana 6–1 6–1; M. Rivaroli d. L. Mancas 6–2 6–4; N. Canessa d. A. Dirzu 6–3 2–6 6–4; P. Parrini d. F. Segarceanu 6–1 6–0; Canessa/Parrini d. Dirzu/Segarceanu 7–5 6–2.
1978 Sweden d. Italy 3–2: M. Wennberg d. F. Moscino 6–2 6–2; P. Hjertquist/S. Simonsson d. M. Alciati/C. Panatta 6–1 6–3; Hjertquist d. M. Ferrari 6–1 6–3; Simonsson lost to Alciati 4–6 1–6; A. Jarryd lost to Panatta 0–6 1–6.
1979 Sweden d. West Germany 4–1: S. Simonsson d. H. D. Beutel 6–4 6–0; T. Svensson d. C. Zipf 2–6 6–4 6–4; A. Jarryd d. K. Vogel 6–2 7–5; J. Gunnarsson d. A. Schulz 7–5 6–4; Simonsson/Svensson lost to Beutel/Zipf 3–6 6–2 6–8.
1980 Spain d. France 4–1: J. Aguilera d. T. Pham 6–4 1–6 6–3; A. Tous/S. Casal d. J. Potier/J. M. Piacentile 6–2 3–6 6–4; Tous lost to Potier 1–6 6–7; R. Mensua d. P. Kuchna 6–4 6–1; Casal d. Miacentile 6–1 6–1.
1981 Sweden d. Italy 3–2: H. Sundstrom d. S. Ercoli 6–4 6–2; J. Nystrom/M. Tideman lost to L. Botazzi/F. Cancellotti 6–1 3–6 4–6; Nystrom d. Botazzi 6–3 6–2; T. Hogstedt lost to Cancellotti 4–6 1–6; Tideman d. S. Colombo 6–2 7–6.
1982 Italy d. Spain 3–2: S. Ercoli lost to M. Jaite 2–6 6–7; M. Fiorini d. D. de Miguel 6–2 7–5; P. Cane d. E. Sanchez 6–1 3–6 6–4; M. Zampieri lost to J. Bardou 4–6 4–6; Cane/Fioroni d. Bardou/Jaite 4–6 6–3 8–6.
1983 Sweden d. Spain 4–1: J. Svensson d. G. R. Fernando 4–6 6–4 7–5; J./K. Carlsson d. D. de Miguel/J. Bardou 6–2 1–6 6–2; J. Carlsson lost to Bardou 4–6 2–6; K. Carlsson d. E. Sanchez 3–6 6–0 6–1; P. Lundgren d. L. F. Garcia 6–3 6–4.
1984 Italy d. France 3–1: F. Ricci d. G. Tournant 6–4 3–6 7–5; N. Devide d. P. Gardarein 6–3 6–4; I. Cappelloni d. O. Cayla 7–5 7–6; Gardarein/Winogradski d. Devide/Pistolesi 5–7 6–4 6–4.
1985 Italy d. Sweden 3–2: A. Baldoni lost to D. Engel 2–6 1–6; C. Pistolesi/S. Mezzadri d. C. Allgaardh/T. Nydahll 6–4 6–4; Pistolesi d. Allgaardh 6–3 6–4; U. Colombini d. C. Bergstrom 7–6 6–2; O. Camporese lost to U. Stenlund 0–6 3–6.
1986 Italy d. Spain 3–2: E. Rossi lost to J. Sanchez 6–7 4–6; O. Camporese lost to T. Carbonell 3–6 4–6; U. Pigato d. F. Anda 6–1 6–3; A. Baldoni d. F. Roig 7–5 6–4; Camporese/Rossi d. Carbonell/Sanchez 3–6 6–3 6–4.
1987 Czechoslovakia d. West Germany 2–0: D. Rikl d. C. Arriens 6–1 6–1; T. Zdrazila d. S. Nensel 6–1 4–6 6–2.
1988 Sweden d. Israel 3–0: N. Kulti d. R. Weidenfeld 7–6 6–2; L. Jonsson d. B. Merenstein 6–2 6–1; Kulti/M. Larsson d. Merenstein/O. Weinberg 6–3 3–6 6–4.
1989 Sweden d. West Germany 3–0: O. Kristiansson d. A. Kloodt 6–2 6–3; R. PettersAoson d. R. Leissler 6–2 6–1; D. Geivald/Kristiansson d. Kloodt/Leissler 6–7 6–1 6–2.

1990 Sweden d. USSR 2–1: M. Renstroem d. A. Rybalko 6–3 7–6; O. Ogorodov lost to R. Petterson 6–3 6–7 0–6; Renstroem/M. Tillstroem d. Ogordov/Rybalko 6–2 6–1
1991 Spain d. Germany 2–0: A. Berasategui d. S. Gessner 6–4 6–2; A. Corretja d. G. Paul 6–2 3–6 6–0.
1992 Spain d. Italy 2–0: A. Corretja d. M. Navarra 6–3 6–1; J. Gisbert d. M. Bertolini 6–1 7–6 (doubles not played).
1993 Spain d. Germany 3–0: R. Carretero d. C. Vinck 6–4 6–4; A. Costa d. L. Rehmann 6–3 6–3; G. Corrales/Costa d. Rehmann/Tambue 7–6 7–5.
1994 Spain d. France 2–1: C. Moya d. M. Huard 6–1 6–0; J. Diaz lost to N. Escude 6–3 6–7 2–6; C. Moya/F. Vicente d. J. F. Bachelot/N. Escude 7–5 6–2.
1995 Czech Republic d. Sweden 2–1: J. Vanek d. N. Timfjord 6–4 6–3; M. Tabara d. F. Jonsson 7–5 6–4; O. Fukarek/J. Vanek lost to F. Jonsson/N. Timfjord 6–7 6–3 3–6.
1996 France d. Czech Republic 2–1: S. Grosjean lost to J. Vanek 5–7 4–6; O. Mutis d. M. Tabara 7–6(6) 6–2; S. Grosjean/O. Mutis d. R. Stepanek/J. Vanek 6–0 6–4.
1997 France d. Czech Republic 3–0: J. Jeanpierre d. P. Kralert 6–3 6–2; A. di Pasquale d. M. Tabara 6–2 6–0; A. di Pasquale/J. Jeanpierre d. P. Kralert/M. Stepanek 6–3 7–6.

JEAN BOROTRA CUP

International Team Championship for boys aged 16 and under; originally the Jean Becker Cup. Finals played in Le Touquet. Administered by the European Tennis Association.

FINALS

1972 Spain d. France 4–1: M. Mir d. Ph. Gruthchet 6–3 6–2; F. Riba d. C. Freyss 6–2 1–6 6–4; A. Capitan d. R. Brunet 6–3 7–5; Masana/Mir lost to Frantz/Grutchet 6–4 6–7 3–6; Capitan/Riba d. Brunet/Freyss 7–5 3–6 9–7.
1973 Italy d. West Germany 3–2: M. Attolini lost to K. Eberhardt 1–6 1–6; G. Sileo d. P. Elter 7–5 6–4; M. Spiga d. U. Wellerdieck 6–2 7–5; Attolini/Sileo lost to Eberhardt/Elter 0–6 5–7; Mazzocchi/Spiga d. Liebthal/WellerAdieck 6–3 6–2.
1974 West Germany d. Italy 4–1: Buchbinder d. G. Rinaldi 6–2 6–2; P. Elter d. Risi 6–0 6–1; A. Maurer d. Gardi 6–7 7–5 6–1; Buchbinder/W. Popp lost to Gardi/Rinaldi 6–2 6–7 8–10; Elter/Maurer d. Risi/M. Rivarolli 6–0 6–3.
1975 Czechoslovakia d. Italy 3–2: M. Lacek d. G. Rinaldini 7–5 6–1; I. Lendl d. A. Ciardi 6–1 6–3; J. Kucera d. P. Parreni 6–4 6–4; Lacek/Kucera lost to Parreni/A. Rivaroli 4–6 4–6; Lendl/A. Vantuch lost to Ciardi/Rinaldini 6–1 4–6 3–6.
1976 Sweden d. Czechoslovakia 3–2: P. Hjertquist lost to I. Lendl 6–0 3–6 4–6; S. Simonsson d. A. Vikopa 6–3 6–0; H. Johansson d. T. Pitra 6–3 6–2; Simonsson/A. Fritzner lost to Lendl/J. Kerezek 6–4 3–6 1–6; Hjertquist/Johansson d. Pitra/J. Vikopal 6–3 6–2.
1977 Italy d. Sweden 3–2: A. Costa d. A. Jarryd 7–5 6–2; A. Giacomini lost to S. Simonsson 1–6 1–6; A. Moscino d. S. Svensson 6–4 6–4; Giacomini/A. Odling lost to Simonsson/Jarryd 3–6 4–6; Costa/Moscino d. Svensson/M. Wennberg 6–2 6–4.
1978 Sweden d. France 3–2: S. Svensson d. T. Tulasne 6–4 6–2; H. Simonsson lost to J. Potier 6–3 2–6 7–9 disqualified; J. Gunnarsson d. T. Pham 6–2 5–7 6–2; M. Wilander lost to J. L. Cotard 2–6 7–5 4–6; Svensson/ Simonsson d. Cotard/J. M. Piacentile 6–3 6–1.
1979 Sweden d. France 4–1: J. Windahll lost to T. Tulasne 2–6 1–6; M. Wilander d. H. Leconte 6–2 1–6 6–3; T. Hogstedt d. P. Kuchna 6–2 6–1; J. Sjogren d. J. M. Piacentile 6–1 6–1; Hogstedt/Wilander d. Leconte/Piacentile 3–6 6–3 6–4.
1980 Sweden d. Czechoslovakia 3–0: M. Wilander d. M. Mecir 3–6 6–1 6–1; A. Mansson d. K. Novacek 6–3 6–3; H. Sundstrom/Wilander d. Mecir/B. Stankovic 6–3 3–0 ret'd.
1981 France d. Sweden 3–2: T. Benhabiles d. S. Edberg 6–4 6–4; F. Hamonet d. J. B. Svensson 6–0 6–2; T. Chamsion lost to P. Svensson 3–6 6–2 0–6; O. Cayla lost to A. Henricsson 6–1 4–6 3–6; Hamonet/G. Forget d. Edberg/P. Svensson 6–4 1–6 6–2.
1982 Sweden d. Spain 4–1: J. Svensson d. J. Maso 6–2 6–2; S. Edberg d. F. Garcia 6–4 6–4; P. Svensson d. J. Oltra 6–2 6–1; J. Carlsson lost to S. Castello 5–7 1–6; Edberg/P. Svensson d. Garcia/Oltra 6–2 6–1.
1983 Sweden d. USSR 3–2: D. Engel d. V. Gabritchidze 7–5 6–1; K. Carlsson d. A. Volkov 6–2 6–4; C. Allgaardh d. A. Tchernetsky 7–5 6–3; C. Bergstrom lost to I. Metreveli 6–0 6–7 3–6; Carlsson/Allgaardh d. Volkov/Metreveli 6–3 6–7 6–3.
1984 Italy d. Sweden 4–1: P. Chinellato lost to T. Nydhal 4–6 6–4 3–6; O. Camporese d. H. Holm 6–4 6–0; A. Baldoni d. A. Rosen 6–4 6–0; S. Sorensen d. N. Utgren 6–2 6–4; Baldoni/E. Rossi d. T. Nydal/P. Henricsson 7–6 1–6 6–3.
1985 Sweden d. France 3–2: P. Henricsson lost to A. Boetsch 3–6 2–6; P. Wennberg d. P. Ventura 6–2 6–2; N. Utgren d. S. Blanquie 6–1 6–2; M. Zeile d. C. Sebastiani 6–1 6–3; Henricsson/Utgren lost to Boetsch/R. Pedros 2–6 6–3 4–6.
1986 Italy d. Netherlands 3–2: F. Mordegan lost to P. Dogger 5–7 6–3 1–6; D. Nargiso lost to J. Eltingh 5–7 2–6; C. Caratti d. J. Siemerink 7–5 6–0; R. Furlan d. R. Heethius 7–5 5–7 7–5; Caratti/Nargiso d. Eltingh/Siemerink 4–6 7–5 6–3.
1987 Austria d. Italy 3–2: T. Buchmayer d. F. Pisilli 6–3 6–1; O. Fuchs lost to S. Pescosolido 4–6 1–6; H. Priller d. M. Ardinghi 6–3 6–4; G. Bohm lost to M. Boscatto 6–2 1–6 6–8; Buchmayer/Priller d. Boscatto/Pescosolido 1–6 6–4 6–4.
1988 Sweden d. Czechoslovakia 3–2: J. Alven d. M. Damm 6–1 6–4; R. Pettersson d. J. Kodes 2–6 7–5 6–3; J. Sunnemark lost to L. Hovorka 6–3 0–6 3–6; M. Renstroem d. P. Gazda 6–1 2–6 6–2; Alven/Pettersson lost to Damm/Horkova 0–6 6–3 6–7.
1989 Czechoslovakia d. West Germany 4–1: P. Gazda d. A. Kriebel 7–5 6–3; R. Hanak d. D. Prinosil 6–0 6–4; L. Thomas d. J. Weinzierl 6–2 6–4; B. Galik d. M. Kohlmann 6–4 6–2; Gazda/Thomas lost to M. Kuckenbecker/ Prinosil 6–4 3–6 4–6.
1990 France d. Spain 3–2: N. Kischkewitz d. J. Gisbert 6–4 6–2; P. Lasserre d. A. Corretja 6–4 6–3; J. Hanquez lost to J.

Martinez 7–6 5–7 2–6; O. Tauma d. G. Corrales 3–6 6–4 6–0; Kischkewitz/Tauma lost to Corretja/Gisbert 3–6 2–6.
1991 Spain d. Czechoslovakia 4–1: A. Costa d. F. Kascak 6–4 6–2; G. Corrales d. P. Pala 6–7 6–1 6–3; R. Carretero d. D. Skoch 5–7 7–6 7–5; J. Balcells lost to D. Miketa 5–7 6–1 1–6; Corrales/Costa d. Kascak/Pala 6–1 6–4.
1992 France d. Sweden 2–1: N. Escude d. M. Norman 2–6 6–4 6–4; M. Huard lost to A. Stenman 5–7 5-7; Esude/Huard d. Norman/M. Sjoquist 6–2 6–2.
1993 France d. Sweden 2–1: J-F Bachelot lost to F. Jonsson 1–6 6–3 12–14; J. Potron d. N. Timfjord 6–2 6–2; O. Mutis/Potron d. Jonsson/Timfjord 4–6 6–1 6–0.
1994 Spain d. Netherlands 3–0: O. Serrano d. P. Wessels 6–4 1–6 6–3; A. Martin d. R. Sluiter 6–3 6–3; A. Gordon/O. Serrano d. R. Sluiter/P. Wessels 3–6 6–4 14–13.
1995 Germany d. France 2–1: T. Zivnicek d. N. Tourte 6–2 6–2; D. Elsner d. A. di Pasquale 6–2 0–6 6–2; D. Elsner/T. Messmer lost to A. di Pasquale/N. Tourte 2–6 2–6.
1996 Belgium d. Russia 2–1: O. Rochus lost to A. Derepasko 6–2 3–6 4–6; X. Malisse d. M. Safin 6–4 6–1; X. Malisse/O. Rochus d. A. Derepasko/K. Ivanov-Smolenski 7–5 6–1.
1997 Spain d. Italy 2–1: T. Robredo lost to F. Volandri 3–6 3–6; F. Lopez d. U. Vico 6–3 4–6 7–5; F. Lopez/T. Robredo d. U. Vico/F. Volandri 4–6 6–1 6–1.

DEL SOL CUP

International Team Championship for boys aged 14 and under. Played in zones with finals in Barcelona. Administered by the European Tennis Association.

FINALS

1979 Italy d. France 3–2: M. Fioroni d. M. Cartier 6–0 6–2; G. Possani d. G. Forget 6–7 7–5 6–3; A. Paris lost to T. Benhabiles 0–6 5–7; L. Baglioni lost to F. Hamonet 0–6 0–6; Possani/Paris d. Benhabiles/Hamonet 6–1 6–4.
1980 Sweden d. Italy 4–1: P. Svensson d. R. Salemme 6–4 7–6; S. Edberg d. F. Ricci 7–5 6–3; R. Lofquist d. F. Filippi 6–3 6–4; J. Svensson lost to P. Poggioli 4–6 2–6; Edberg/P. Svensson d. Filippi/A. Vacca 6–4 6–1.
1981 Sweden d. Israel 3–2: T. Johansson lost to A. Naor 2–6 6–7; C. Allgaardh lost to G. Blom 4–6 6–2 4–6; K. Carlsson d. R. Weinberg 6–0 6–0; C. Bergstrom d. M. Osherov 2–6 7–5 7–5; Allgaardh/Carlsson d. Blom/ Osherov 6–2 6–1.
1982 Sweden d. West Germany 4–1: H. Kolm d. U. Kraft 6–1 6–0; K. Carlsson d. O. Sachau 6–0 6–0; P. Ekstrand lost to I. Kroll 0–6 2–6; T. Nydahl d. C. Guhl 6–0 1–6 6–1; Carlsson/Nydahl d. Guhl/Kraft 6–1 6–4.
1983 Sweden d. West Germany 3–2: U. Persson d. H. Stang 6–2 6–2; P. Henricsson d. P. Pfleger 6–4 6–1; U. Eriksson lost to U. Kraft 7–6 3–6 2–6; P. Wennberg lost to L. Orzessek 2–6 3–6; Henricsson/M. Urgren d. Kraft/Orzessek 6–2 6–3.
1984 West Germany d. Spain 4–1: S. Scheider d. F. Alfonso 6–3 4–6 7–5; F. Loddenkemper/A. Thoms d. J. Olivert/S. Bruguera 6–3 6–2; Loddenkemper d. Olivert 7–6 7–6; D. Richter d. A. Martinez 6–1 7–5; A. Thoms lost to Bruguera 3–6 6–2 4–6.
1985 Austria d. Italy 5–0: G. Bohm d. F. Casa 6–4 6–2; T. Buchmayer/O. Fuchs d. S. Pescosolido/F. Pisilli 6–2 6–3; Buchmayer d. Pescosolido 6–3 4–6 6–4; Fuchs d. Pisilli 6–3 7–6; H. Prilled d. M. Ardinghi 6–2 6–1.
1986 Sweden d. Yugoslavia 4–1: J. Alven d. S. Hirszon 6–3 6–4; R. Pettersson lost to B. Trupy 2–6 3–6; M. Ekstrand d. A. Tonejc 3–6 6–4 6–3; J. Henriksson d. S. Ban 6–4 7–6; Alven/Pettersson d. Hirszon/Trupej 6–2 6–4.
1987 West Germany d. Austria 4–1: J. Weinzierl lost to R. Wawra 3–6 2–6; G. Paul d. N. Patzak 6–0 6–1; S. Petraschek d. J. Knowle 3–6 6–2 6–2; A. Kriebel d. H. Kugler 6–2 6–3; Paul/Petraschek d. Knowle/Wawra 4–6 6–2 6–2.
1988 West Germany d. Spain 3–2: M. Kohlman d. A. Corretja 6–2 6–1; T. Ruhle lost to A. Bragado 0–6 3–6; J. Schors d. J. Martinez 6–2 6–4; G. Hecht lost to J. Velasco 6–0 5–7 1–6; Kohlman/M. Nacke d. Bragado/Corretja 7–6 7–6.
1989 France d. Sweden 4–1: N. Bertsch d. T.A Johansson 7–5 7–6; A. De Cret d. K. Bergh 6–4 6–2; S. Martinez d. P. Salasca 6–2 6–3; M. Dallay d. D. Winberg 7–5 6–4; Bertsch/De Cret lost to Johansson/Salasca 6–4 3–6 1–6 7–6 7–6.
1990 France d. Spain 5–0: M. Boye d. A. Pastor 7–6 3–6 6–4; N. Maurier d. J. Diaz 7–6 6–4; J. Van Lottum d. A. Gandarias 1–6 6–2 6–2; K. Dous d. E. Xapelli 6–4 6–1; Boye/Maurier d. Diaz/Pastor 6–2 6–2.
1991 Spain d. USSR 5–0: J–A. Saiz d. I. Pridankine 7–6 6–1; F. Vincente d. J. Michejev 7–6 6–7 6–4; J. Vincente d. A. Gonopolskij 6–0 6–4; A. Martin d. A. Stoljarov 6–7 6–3 8–6; Martin/J. Vincente d. Pridankine/Stoljarov 7–6 6–3.
1992 Germany d. France 3–1: T. Haas lost to O. Mutis 4–6 4-6; J.-R. Brandt d. J.-R. Lisnard 7–5 6–1; J.-P. Wenner d. J. Barras 6–3 7–6; Brandt/Haas d. M.-O. Baron/Mutis 6–4 6–3.
1993 France d. Italy 4–1: K. Fernandez d. D. Bramanti 7–6 7–5; A di Pasquale d. F. Allgauer 7–5 6–3; V. Lavergne lost to A. Capodimonte 6–4 3–6 2–6; J-R Lisnard d. D. Sciortino 6–3 6–1; di Pasquale/Lisnard d. Capodimonte/ Sciortino 6–3 4–6 7–5.
1994 France d. Italy 3–2: N. Senelle d. M. Aprile 6–4 6–3; J. Haenelt d. N. Frocassi 6–4 6–3; A. Rafidison lost to F. Luzzi 3–6 1–6; J. Jeanpierre d. M. Armadroy 6–1 6–1; N. Devilder/J. Jeanpierre lost to N. Frocassi/Luzzi 5–7 2–6.
1995 Great Britain d. Spain 3–2: A. Mackin d. I. Navarro 6–3 6–7(2) 7–5; N. Greenhouse lost to M. Marco w/o; M. Hilton d. F. Lopez 2–6 6–4 6–1; S. Dickson d. T. Robredo 6–1 6–0; S. Dickson/M. Hilton lost to F. Lopez/T. Robredo 5–7 6–4 5–7.
1996 France d. Croatia 4–1: D. Voravoncsa d. V. Sirola 6–0 6–1; P. Capdeville d. M. Ancic 2–6 6–0 6–2; N. Mahut lost to M. Radic 2–6 7–5 3–6; P-H. Mathieu d. R. Karanusic 6–2 6–0; P. Capdeville/P-H. Mathieu d. R. Karanusic/M. Radic 6–3 6–0.
1997 France d. Czech Republic 5–0: N. Beuque d. D. Novak 6–0 7–5; C. Roche d. D. Karol 6–3 6–1; J-M. Ali-Cayol d. M. Kokta 6–2 6–1; J. Maigret d. J. Masik 7–5 6–0; J-M. Ali-Cayol/C. Roche d. D. Karol/J. Masik 7–5 7–6(8).

GALEA CUP AND ANNIE SOISBAULT CUP (Discontinued in 1990)

International Team Championship for men and women respectively aged 20 and under. Full results of final rounds can be found in *World of Tennis 1996* and earlier editions.

HM QUEEN SOFIA CUP

International Team Championship for girls aged 18 and under. Played zonally with the final stages in Spain. Administered by the European Tennis Association.

FINALS

1972 Rumania d. West Germany 3–2: F. Mihai d. A. Spiedel 6–4 7–5; V. Ruzici/M. Simionescu d. B. Portcheller/B. Kasler 8–6 6–1; Ruzici d. Portcheller 2–6 6–0 6–1; Simionescu lost to Kasler 4–6 3–6; M. Neuweiller lost to K. Pohmann 4–6 3–6.

1973 Great Britain d. Spain 4–1: B. L. Thompson d. G. Nogues 6–4 6–4; L. J. Mottram d. J. Mateo 6–3 12–10; S. Barker d. J. Alvarez 7–5 6–0; Barker/Mottram d. Mateo/C. Chillida 6–2 6–2; J. Potterton lost to Chillida 3–6 0–6.

1974 Czechoslovakia d. France 4–1: L. Plchova d. M. Cozaux 6–4 6–1; Y. Brzakova lost to B. Simon 6–8 6–2 4–6; H. Strachonova d. C. Gimmig 6–3 6–0; R. Marsikova d. F. Thibault 8–4 6–4; Brzakova/A. Kulankova d. Thibault/A. Duguy 9–7 4–6 6–4.

1975 Great Britain d. Czechoslovakia 4–1: M. Tyler d. A. Kulhankova 6–1 3–6 6–3; C. Harrison d. J. Kopekova 6–3 6–3; L. J. Mottram d. H. Strachonova 2–6 11–9 6–3; J. Cottrell lost to K. Skronska 1–6 1–6; A. Cooper/Cottrell d. Skronska/Kulhankova 1–6 6–4 6–4.

1976 Great Britain d. Switzerland 3–1: J. M. Durie d. C. Jolissaint 4–6 6–3 6–4; A. Cooper lost to M. Simmen 6–4 0–6 4–6; C. Harrison d. A. Ruegg 6–4 6–7 6–2; M. Tyler d. P. Delhees 6–2 6–2.

1977 Czechoslovakia d. Sweden 5–0: H. Mandlikova d. M. Wiedel 6–2 6–2; I. Budarova d. H. Brywe 6–1 6–1; Mandlikova/Budarova d. A. C. Mansson/A. Nilsson 6–1 6–3; M. Skuherska d. Nilsson 6–0 6–4; H. Strachonova d. Mansson 6–3 7–5.

1978 Czechoslovakia d. Sweden 5–0: M. Skuherska d. L. Jacobson 6–3 6–2; H. Mandlikova d. H. Brywe 6–1 6–1; I. Budarova/Mandlikova d. Jacobson/L. Sandin 6–3 6–1; I. Petru d. A. Nilsson 6–1 6–2; Budarova d. Sandin 6–3 5–7 7–5.

1979 Czechoslovakia d. Switzerland 3–1: I. Bendlova d. P. Frey 6–1 6–1; M. Skuherska/I. Petru lost to C. Jolissaint/I. Villiger 3–6 4–6; Skuherska d. Villiger 3–6 6–1 6–1; I. Novakova d. Jolissaint 6–7 6–3 6–3; Petru v C. Pasquale 5–7 abandoned.

1980 Switzerland d. USSR 3–2: K. Stampfli d. J. Kashevarova 6–3 6–3; I. Villiger/L. Drescher lost to O. Zaitseva/S. Cherneva 4–6 5–7; Villiger d. Zaitseva 6–2 7–5; C. Pasquale lost to Cherneva 4–6 7–5 7–9; Drescher d. J. Salnikova 7–6 6–4.

1981 Sweden d. Czechoslovakia 3–2: B. Bjort d. P. Dutkova 6–2 6–3; M. Lindstrom/C. Lindqvist d. H. Sukova/M. Pazderova 6–3 6–3; C. Jexell lost to Pazderova 6–3 2–6 0–6; Lindqvist d. N. Piskackova 6–2 6–2; Lindstrom lost to Sukova 6–7 3–6.

1982 Italy d. Czechoslovakia 4–1: R. Reggi d. I. Petru 6–3 6–4; N. Virgintino lost to H. Fukarkova 7–5 2–6 3–6; A. Cecchini d. P. Dutkova 7–6 7–6; F. Bonsignori d. A. Souckova 6–3 6–0; Reggi/Virgintino d. Petru/Fukarkova 7–5 4–6 6–2.

1983 Italy d. Czechoslovakia 4–1: L. Ferrando d. A. Souckova 6–0 6–3; B. Romano/N. Virgintino d. A. Holikova/Souckova 6–3 6–7 6–3; A. M. Cecchini d. O. Votavova 6–7 6–3 6–1; Virgintino d. P. Tesarova 6–3 6–1; S. Dalla Valle lost to Holikova 5–7 3–6.

1984 Sweden d. Czechoslovakia 3–2: H. Dahlstrom d. O. Votavova 6–3 6–3; A. Karlsson d. A. Holikova 6–3 6–0; A. Souckova d. M. Lundquist 7–5 7–5; K. Karlsson d. P. Tesarova 6–1 6–2; Votavova/Holikova d. Lundquist/Olsson 6–4 6–2.

1985 Italy d. Sweden 4–1: L. Lapi lost to C. Dahlman 0–6 1–6; L. Garrone/L. Golarsa d. A. K. Ollson/M. Lundquist 6–1 6–3; Garrone d. H. Dahlstrom 6–2 6–7 6–2; C. Nozzoli d. Ollson 6–4 6–4; Golarsa d. Lundquist 6–2 6–0.

1986 Czechoslovakia d. Sweden 5–0: R. Rajchrtova d. C. Dahlstrom 6–4 6–0; R. Zbrubakova d. J. Jonerup 6–3 6–3; J. Novotna d. M. Stradlund 6–4 6–2; D. Krajcovicova d. M. Ekstrand 6–3 7–5; Novotna/Rajchrtova d. M. Nilsson/Stradlund 6–0 6–1.

1987 France d. Czechoslovakia 3–0: A. Dechaume d. R. Zrubakova 6–4 6–3; E. Derly d. P. Langrova 7–5 6–1; Dechaume/S. Niox–Chateau d. Langrova/Zrubakova 6–7 6–4 6–3.

1988 Spain d. USSR 2–1: A. Sanchez d. N. Medvedeva 3–6 6–2 6–3; C. Martinez d. E. Brioukhovets 6–2 6–2; Martinez/Sanchez lost to Brioukhovets/Medvedeva 6–7 0–4 ret'd.

1989 Spain d. Czechoslovakia 3–0: A. Sanchez d. A. Strnadova 6–1 6–3; N. Avila d. J. Dubcova 6–3 6–0; S. Ramon/Sanchez d. K. Balnova/Strnadova 6–4 7–5.

1990 Spain d. France 2–1: P. Perez d. A. Zugasti 6–4 6–0; S. Ramon lost to A. Fusai 6–3 4–6 1–6; Perez/Ramon d. Fusai/Zugasti 7–5 6–2.

1991 Spain d. Sweden 3–0: E. Botini d. A. Carlsson 5–7 6–2 6–4; E. Bes d. M. Vallin 6–2 6–1; Botini/C. Torrens d. Vallin/Carlsson 4–6 7–6 6–2.

1992 Germany d. Spain 2–1: P. Begerow d. E. Bottini 6–2 7–5; K. Freye lost to C. Torrens 2–6 3–6; Freye/S. Wachtershauser d. Bottini/E.Jimenez 2–6 7–5 6–2.

1993 France d. Italy 3–0: S. Pitkowski d. P. Tampieri 6–0 6–0; A. Olivier d. A. Serra-Zanetti 0–6 6–2 6–1; Olivier/C. Toyre d. Serra-Zanetti/Tampieri 8–3.

1994 Italy d. Spain 2–1: F. Lubiani d. M. Ramon 6–4 6–3; A. Serrazanetti lost to M. A. Sanchez 5–7 6–4 1–6; F. Lubiani/A. Serezzanetti d. M. Ramon/M .A. Sanchez 6–0 6–4.
1995 Italy d. Czech Republic 2–1: G. Casoni lost to P. Plackova 3–6 6–4 4–6; A. Canepa d. S. Kleinova 6–2 7–6(2); A. Canepa/G. Casoni d. S. Kleinova/J. Ondrouchova 6–0 6–2.
1996 Slovak Republic d. Spain 2–1: L. Cervanova d. A. Alcazar 7–5 6–4; Z. Valekova lost to M-L. Serna 0–6 1–6; L. Cervanova/Z. Valekova d. A. Alcazar/M-L. Serna 1–6 6–3 10–8.
1997 France d. Czech Republic 2–1: A. Mauresmo d. M. Pastikova 6–3 6–3; N. Dechy d. J. Schonfeldova 6–3 6–4; France defaulted in doubles.

HELVETIE CUP

International Team Championship for girls aged 16 and under. Played zonally with final stages at Leysin, Switzerland.

FINALS
1977 Italy d. Switzerland 3–2: P. Cigognani lost to C. Jolissaint 0–6 3–6; B. Rossi d. I. Villiger 6–3 6–7 8–6; M. Calabria d. K. Stampfli 6–1 6–2; P. Murgo d. C. Pasquale 6–3 6–3; Rossi/Murgo lost to Jolissaint/Villiger 4–6 3–6.
1978 Bulgaria d. West Germany 5–0: M. Condova d. C. Kohde 1–6 6–3 6–1; A. Veltcheva d. Haas 6–3 5–7 6–4; I. Chichkova d. Hammig 6–3 6–0; I. Christova d. Wilmsmeyer 3–6 7–6 6–3; Condova/Veltcheva d. Kohde/Haas 3–6 6–2 6–2.
1979 Sweden d. France 5–0: C. Lindqvist d. I. Vernhes 6–7 6–3 6–0; B. Bjork d. C. Vanier 4–6 6–3 6–3; A. Flodin d. S. Gardette 6–0 6–1; H. Olsson/K. Marivall d. M. Callejo/Vanier 6–3 6–3; Olsson d. Calleja 6–2 6–1.
1980 Sweden d. West Germany 3–2: C. Anderholm d. M. Schropp 6–1 6–2; H. Olsson lost to K. Reuter 5–7 4–6; M. Schultz d. P. Keppeler 6–4 6–4; N. Nielson d. M. Reinhard 6–7 6–3 6–2; Olsson/Schultz lost to Reuter/Reinhard 6–1 4–6 5–7.
1981 Sweden d. Italy 3–2: A. Bjork lost to F. Sollenti 2–6 6–7; H. Olsson/C. Anderholm d. R. Reggi/F. Virgintino 0–6 6–2 6–1; Olsson d. A. M. Cecchini 6–4 7–5; Anderholm d. Reggi 6–3 3–6 6–4; I. Sjogreen lost to Virgintino 0–6 0–6.
1982 USSR d. France 3–2: I. Fishkina d. I. Demongeot 6–1 6–2; L. Savchenko/V. Milvidskaya lost to P. Paradis/N. Phan-Thanh 4–6 7–5 4–6; N. Bykova lost to Paradis 1–6 2–6; Savchenko d. Phan-Thanh 6–2 6–3; Mildvidskaya d. N. Herreman 6–1 6–4.
1983 USSR d. Sweden 3–2: A. Kuzmina d. A. K. Olsson 6–3 1–6 6–3; V. Milvidskaya d. H. Dahlmstrom 3–6 6–2 6–4; I. Fischkina lost to M. Lundquist 4–6 4–6; I. Fateeva lost to E. Helmersson 2–6 3–6; Fishkina/Mildvidskaya d. Dahlstrom/Lundquist 6–4 7–5.
1984 Czechoslovakia d. West Germany 4–1: R. Wlona lost to M. Gartner 7–6 3–6 4–6; J. Novotna/R. Rajchrotova d. S. Meier/R. Weiser 6–0 7–6; Novotna d. Meier 7–5 6–2; Rajchrotova d. Weiser 6–3 4–6 6–1; P. Sedkackova d. S. Hack 6–4 4–6 6–2.
1985 West Germany d. Sweden 4–1: M. Schurhoff d. M. Ekstrand 6–2 4–6 6–4; M. Gartner/S. Hack lost to M. Strandlund/M. Nilsson 3–6 3–6; Gartner/J. Jonerup 7–6 6–2; Hack d. Strandlund 6–1 6–1; W. Probst d. M. Nilsson 6–1 6–1.
1986 Switzerland d. Czechoslovakia 3–1 (one rubber not played)**:** E. Zardo d. M. Frimmelova 6–4 6–2; M. Strebel d. L. Laskova 7–5 6–1; S. Jaquet v. P. Langrova not played; M. Plocher d. E. Sviglerova 6–4 6–2; Jacquet/Plocher lost to Frimmelova/Langrova 6–0 1–6 5–7.
1987 Netherlands d. Switzerland 3–2: N. Van Dierendonck lost to S. Jacquet 6–7 3–6; B. Sonneveld lost to M. Plocher 6–2 3–6 4–6; Y. Grubben d. G. Villiger 7–5 7–6; E. Haslinghuis d. S. Bregnard 6–1 6–0; Sonneveld/Van Dierendonck d. Jacquet/Plocher 7–5 6–3..
1988 West Germany d. Czechoslovakia 3–2: V. Martinek d. K. Balnova 6–3 6–0; K. Duell lost to A. Strnadova 2–6 3–6; M. Skulj-Zivec d. H. Vildova 7–5 6–1; A. Popp lost to R. Bobkova 4–6 6–1 5–7; C. Hofmann/Martinek d. Balnova/Strnadova 7–5 7–5.
1989 Czechoslovakia d. USSR 3–2: R. Bobkova d. S. Komleva 6–2 6–1; K. Habsudova d. E. Makarova 7–6 6–0; K. Matouskova lost to M. Chirikova 3–6 6–3 5–7; K. Kroupova lost to T. Ignatieva 2–6 2–6; Bobkova/Matouskova d. Chirikova/Komleva 4–6 6–0 8–6.
1990 USSR d. West Germany 3–2: T. Ignatieva d. K. Freye 6–4 4–6 6–3; I. Soukhova d. S. Wachterhauser 7–5 6–2; V. Vitels lost to M. Babel 4–6 0–3 ret.; G. Beleni lost to P. Begerow 3–6 3–6; Ignatieva/Soukhova d. Babel/J. Dobberstein 6–4 6–4.
1991 Czechoslovakia d. Spain 4–1: Z. Malkova d. E. Jiminez 6–4 6–0; E. Martincova lost to M. Cruells 3–6 6–7; E. Hostacova d. A. Ortuno 6–3 7–5; M. Hautova d. A. Montolio 4–6 6–3 6–1; Malkova/Martincova d. Cruells/ Jiminez 6–3 6–1.
1992 Belgium d. Germany 2–1: N. Feber d. A. Glass 6–3 6–2; L. Courtois lost to H. Rusch 6–3 6–7 3–6; Courtoios/Feber d. Glass/C. Muller 6-7 6–3 6–0.
1993 Czech/Slovak Republic d. Netherlands 2–1: L. Cenkova d. C. Reimering 6–3 6–3; A. Havrlikova lost to Y. Basting 3–6 6–1 2–6; Cenkova/L. Richterova d. Basting/D. Haak 6–3 7–5.
1994 France d. Czech Republic 2–1: A. Cocheteaux d. D. Chadkova 6–2 6–3; A. Castera d. S. Kleinova 7–5 1–6 6–0; A. Cocheteaux/I. Taesch lost to D. Chadkova/S. Kleinova 1–6 6–0 2–6.
1995 Czech Republic d. Germany 2–1: J. Lubasova lost to M. Frohlich 6–7(6) 3–6; D. Chladkova d. C. Christian 6–2 7–6(3); D. Chladkova/J. Lubasova d. C. Christian/M. Frohlich 6–2 6–4.

1996 Slovenia d. France 2–1: K. Srebotnik d. K. Chevalier 2–6 7–5 6–2; P. Rampre d. E. le Bescond 6–4 4–6 6–0; M. Matevzic/P. Rampre lost to K. Chevalier/E. le Bescond 6–4 1–6 4–6.
1997 Slovenia d. Spain 2–1: T. Hojnik lost to M. Marrero 3–6 7–6(5) 4–6; T. Pisnik d. L. Dominguez 6–2 6–0; T. Hergold/T. Pisnik d. L. Dominguez/M. Marrero 7–6(4) 6–3.

EUROPA CUP

International Team Championship for girls aged 14 and under. Administered by the European Tennis Association.

FINALS
1981 West Germany d. France 3–2, *Winterslag, Belgium:* I. Cueto d. J. Clerin 6–3 2–6 6–1; R. Wieser lost to E. Folcher 1–6 6–3 1–6; S. Graf d. M. Phan-Thanh 7–5 6–3; S. Luidinant d. E. Grousseau 6–2 6–2; Graf/Wieser lost to Folcher/Grousseau 6–4 2–6 1–6.
1982 Sweden d. West Germany 3–2, *Mons, Belgium:* C. Dahlman d. S. Meier 7–5 7–5; H. Dahlstrom d. B. Herget 6–0 6–4; E. Helmersson lost to I. Cueto 3–6 7–6 0–6; I. Mattiasson lost to E. Walliser 5–7 2–6; Dahlstrom/Helmersson d. Cueto/Walliser 6–2 6–2.
1983 West Germany d. France 3–2, *Lee-on-Solent, Hampshire:* N. Vassen d. S. N. Chateau 4–6 6–3 6–2; W. Probst d. M. C. Rolet 7–5 5–7 ret'd; S. Hack lost to C. Bourdais 6–3 2–6 0–6; M. Gartner d. A. Dechaume 6–4 4–6 7–5; Gartner/Vassen lost to Bourdais/Dechaume 3–6 1–6.
1984 France d. Sweden 4–1: S. Dussault lost to R. Narbe 0–6 6–4 3–6; A. Dechaume/E. Derly d. M. Ekstrand/H. Johnsson 6–3 6–3; Dechaume d. Ekstrand 7–5 6–2; Derly d. Salsgard 6–4 3–6 6–1; M. Laval d. Johnsson 6–4 6–4.
1985 USSR d. Italy 3–2: N. Zvereva d. A. Dell'Orso 6–2 4–6 6–4; T. Tchernysova lost to F. Romano 3–6 2–6; E. Brihovec lost to S. Favini w.o.; A. Blumberga d. G. Boscheiro 6–3 4–6 6–4; Zvereva/Tchernysova d. Boscheiro/Dell'Orso 6–4 6–3.
1986 Netherlands d. Italy 3–2: Y. Grubben lost to Boscheiro 5–7 4–6; N. Van Lottum d. Favini 6–2 6–1; E. Markestein d. Migliori 6–4 6–4; E. Haslinghuis lost to Bertelloni 2–6 2–6; Grubben/Van Lottum d. Boscheiro/Migliori 6–2 6–2.
1987 Czechoslovakia d. Austria 3–2: P. Kucova lost to U. Priller 3–6 0–6; R. Bobkova d. D. Bidmon 6–2 6–4; P. Markova lost to N. Dobrovits 4–6 1–6; K. Matouskova d. S. Suchan 1–6 6–0 10–8; Bobkova/Kucova d. Dobrovits/Priller 6–4 4–6 7–5.
1988 Hungary d. West Germany 3–2: A. Foeldenyi d. A. Huber 6–0 3–6 8–6; B. Bathory lost to K. Denn–Samuel 0–6 3–6; M. Zsoldos d. P. Kemper 6–1 4–6 6–4; K. Kocsis lost to M. Kochta 6–4 1–6 1–6; Foeldenyi/Zsoldos d. Denn–Samuel/Huber 4–6 7–6 6–3.
1989 Czechoslovakia d. Italy 5–0: E. Martiucova d. R. Grande 7–6 6–3; I. Malkova d. G. Pizzichini 6–2 7–5; O. Hostakova d. S. Pifferi 5–7 6–1 7–5; M. Hautova d. A. Serra-Zanetti 6–0 6–2; Malkova/Martiucova d. Grande/Pifferi 6–1 6–4.
1990 Czechoslovakia d. Yugoslavia 3–2: S. Radevicova lost to I. Majoli 2–6 6–4 1–6; Z. Rebekova lost to T. Doric 5–7 4–6; A. Havrlikova d. S. Milas 6–1 6–2; A. Gersi d. D. Karadz 7–6 6–0; Havrlikova/Redevicova d. Doric/Majoli 6–3 7–5.
1991 Germany d. Czechoslovakia 5–0: M. Vladulescu d. A. Havrlikova 6–0 6–3; N. Raidt d. R. Surova 7–6 6–2; S. Schmidle d. K. Bakalarova 6–0 6–4; A. Barna d. R. Pelikanova 6–2 6–4; Barna/T. Karsten d. L. Cenkova/Havrlikova 6–2 6–1.
1992 Czechoslovakia d. France 3–2: L. Varmuzova d. I. Taesch 4–6 6–43 6–4; H. Nagyova lost to A. Castera 3–6 2–6; S. Kleinova lost to E. Curutchet 3–6 6–3 2–6; J. Ondrouchova d. G. Goultefard 6–2 6–2; Kleinova/Ondrouchova d. Castera/Curutchet 3–6 7–5 6–4.
1993 Czech/Slovak Republic d. Germany 3–2: J. Lubasova lost to S. Kovacic 3–6 3–6; D. Chladkova d. M. Weingartner 6–4 6–3; L. Faltynkova lost to M. Frohlich 5–7 3–6; L. Varmuzova d. S. Klosel 6–1 4–6 6–2; Chladkova/Faltynkova d. E. Brunn/Klosel 5–7 6–2 8–6.
1994 Germany d. Czech Republic 3–2: D. Wallenhorst d. D. Luzarova 6–4 6–0; J. Wohr lost to B. Stejsjkalova w/o; S. Losel lost to J. Schonfeldova 7–6 1–6 2–6; S. Kovacic d. M. Pastikova 6–2 6–2; L. Fritz/S. Kovacic d. M. Pastikova/J. Schonfeldova 3–6 6–1 6–1.
1995 Slovenia d. Slovak Republic 4–1: T. Hojnik lost to E. Fislova 2–6 2–6; T. Hergold d. K. Basternakova 1–0 ret; T. Pisnik d. V. Stoklasova 5–7 6–0 10–8; K. Srebotnik d. G. Volekova 6–3 6–1; T. Pisnik/K. Srebotnik d. V. Stoklasova/G. Volekova 2–6 6–1 6–3.
1996 Belgium d. Slovak Republic 3–1: E. Clijsters lost to D. Hantuchova 7–5 1–6 2–6; K. Clijsters d. Z. Kucova; J. Henin d. K. Basternakova 6–3 6–2; K. Clijsters/J. Henin d. S. Hrozenska/K. Basternakova 1–6 7–5 7–5.
1997 Slovak Republic d. Russia 4–1: M. Kunova d. G. Fokina 7–5 6–3; L. Kurhajcova d. I. Murashkintceva 6–1 7–6(4); D. Hantuchova d. L. Krasnoroutskaia 6–3 6–1; M. Babakova lost to E. Bovina 2–6 6–4 4–6; M. Babakova/D. Hantuchova d. E. Bovina/L. Krasnoroutskaia 7–6(3) 6–4.

Do you recognise these four champions from the 1985 ITF Sport Goofy Trophy, played at the Disney headquarters in Orlando, Florida? They are (left to right) Michael Chang (Boys' 14), Natasha Zvereva (Girls' 14), Monica Seles (Girls' 12) and Tommy Ho (Boys' 12) (ITF)

The International Tennis Federation

Regional Reports • Wheelchair Tennis
ITF Junior Tennis • ITF Veteran Tennis
National Association Addresses

Germany's Daniel Elsner, the 1996 US Open junior champion, won the first two junior Grand Slams of 1997 in Australia and France before losing in the Wimbledon final and was pipped at the post for the No. 1 world junior ranking by Arnaud di Pasquale of France. (Stephen Wake)

The International Tennis Federation

Palliser Road, Barons Court, London W14 9EN
Telephone: 44 171 381 8060 Fax: 44 171 381 3989
Web site http://www.itftennis.com

President: Brian Tobin.

Honorary Life President: Philippe Chatrier.

Vice Presidents: Heinz Grimm, Eiichi Kawatei, Eduardo Moline O'Connor.

Honorary Life Vice-Presidents: Allan Heyman, Pablo Llorens.

Honorary Life Counsellors: Paolo Angeli, Jim Cochrane, Robert A Cookson, Hunter L Delatour, J Howard Frazer, J Randolph Gregson, Gordon Jorgensen, R K Khanna, Stan Malless, David Markin, Enrique Morea, Radmilo Nikolic, Geoff Paish, Alvaro Peña, Francesco Ricci Bitti, William H Woods.

Trustees: Hunter L Delatour, David Jude, Pablo Llorens.

Committee of Management: Brian Tobin, Christian Bimes, Ismail El Shafei, Fathi Farah, Jan Francke, Heinz Grimm, Eiichi Kawatei, Ian King, Julia Levering, Juan Margets, Harry Marmion, Eduardo Moline O'Connor, Geoff Pollard.

Honorary Treasurer: David Jude.

Auditors: Messrs Ernst & Young, London.

Legal Counsel: UK - Townleys, Wedlake Bell.

Committees: Davis Cup, Fed Cup, Finance, Women's Circuit, Junior Competitions, Olympic, Rules of the ITF, Rules of Tennis, Wheelchair, Veterans.

Commissions: Coaches, Media, Medical, Technical.

GRAND SLAM COMMITTEE

Australian Open: Geoff Pollard; ***French Open:*** Christian Bimes;
Wimbledon: John Curry; ***US Open:*** Harry Marmion.
Grand Slam Committee Administrator: William Babcock.

WTA TOUR BOARD OF DIRECTORS

ITF Representatives: Ingrid Bentzer, Brian Tobin (Alternate: Heinz Grimm).

SATELLITES JOINT COMMITTEE

ITF Representatives: William Babcock, Juan Duran, Ismail El Shafei, Heinz Grimm, Eiichi Kawatei.

CHALLENGERS JOINT COMMITTEE

ITF Representatives: William Babcock, Ismail El Shafei, Heinz Grimm, Eiichi Kawatei.

SECRETARIAT

General Manager/Director of Development: Doug MacCurdy

Directors: William Babcock, Men's Professional Tournaments/Grand Slam Administrator/Officials; Malcolm Bool, Finance; Thomas Hallberg, Davis Cup Competition/World Youth Cup/World Junior Tennis/Rules of Tennis; Sally Holdsworth, Administration and Personnel; Deborah Jevans, Fed Cup/Medical (and Olympic Games Administrator); Christopher Stokes, Marketing.

Managers: Ingrid Bentzer, Women's Circuit; Andrew Coe, Technical; Ellen de Lange, Wheelchair; Tony Gathercole, Veterans; Alun James, Communications; Jan Menneken, Head of Television; Dave Miley, Development; Jackie Nesbitt, Junior Competitions; Ian Takats, Information Technology.

Administrators: Frances Cason, Finance; Josette Cohen, Development; Johanna Dickin, Sponsorship; Stefan Fransson, Officiating; Charles Langhorne, Sponsorship Sales; Sarah Orr, Men's Professional Tournaments; Tessa Radcliffe, AGM/Rules of the ITF; Alison Sowersby, Fed Cup/Olympics/Medical; Barbara Travers, Communications; John Treleven, Computer Rankings.

Regional Reports

Asian Tennis Federation 'ATF'

No matter which way you look at it, Asian tennis continues to flourish like never before. Take the performance of India's Mahesh Bhupathi and Rika Hiraki of Japan in the mixed doubles at Roland Garros for example, where they needed only 58 minutes to clinch the final from right under the noses of the top seeds.

Or perhaps you may prefer to reflect on Asia's top doubles team, and the claimants of the number four slot on the ATP's world team rankings, the venerable duo of Leander Paes and Mahesh Bhupathi. Not only did they reach the final of this year's US Open, they then went on to take the winner's trophy at the China Open in Beijing, and the Heineken Open in Singapore, raising their tally of doubles titles to nine for 1997. They also ensured that India retained its place in the World Group of the Davis Cup by NEC when they defeated Chile 3–2 at home in New Delhi.

Indonesia's Yayuk Basuki continues to impress as well by making her way into the top 20 in the WTA rankings, earning a nomination for the Doubles Team of the Year Award in the 1997 Corel WTA Tour end of season awards. She has made her way through to a number of finals including the DFS Classic in Edgbaston, England. Rika Hiraki and Ai Sugiyama have also been nominated for the Karen Krantzcke Sportmanship Award, an award Basuki actually won herself last year.

Then there are the five gold medals that were won by Asians at the World Student Games in Palmero, Italy during September. Korea took gold in the men's singles, doubles and mixed doubles whilst Chinese Taipei took gold in the women's singles and doubles. Proof indeed, that Asian tennis is riding high at the moment.

To ensure that this favourable situation continues the ATF, in liaison with the AITA, decided to add a new men's team event to the calendar. Restricted to the eight strongest teams in the region, the inaugural event took place in India during the 3–8 November and was a resounding success thanks to the strong teams that were selected.

It is our intention to close the gap that currently exists between our male and female players, and this initiative is only one of many ways that we propose to do just that over the course of the next 24 months.

Work is also underway to introduce an Asian Hopman Cup in 1998, with the winners going on to play in the qualifying round of the Hyundai Hopman Cup in Perth, Australia. However, we have not lost sight of our junior programmes either and intend to have a 16 & Under and a 14 & Under junior circuit fully functional next year.

The ITF Travelling Academy will continue again in 1998, and next year's Asian Coaches Workshop will be held in Thailand. The work of the Development Officer for Central Asia, Suresh Menon, will also continue unabated. Suresh has made a very significant contribution to our developing countries during the last 12 months, and thanks to him and the staunch support of the ITF, we are already starting to see results.

We remain fully aware however, that much work remains to be done before we can rest on our laurels, which is why we have already identified a number of areas upon which we intend to improve next year. Amongst these is the standard of our officiating which is hindered somewhat by the level of English that is spoken by a number of our officials.

The infrastructure in Asia also continues to grow in line with our ideals, with Vietnam and China spearheading our efforts by recently building three new tennis stadia. Bhutan, Myanmar and Nepal also intend to build new tennis courts during the course of 1998, which gives further indication of just how far we have come as a regional association in such a short space of time.

Furthermore, 1997 saw our membership increase to a total of 40 countries thanks to the addition of Yemen and Laos to the family. Palestine has applied to become a member, too, and its application will be put forward for approval at the 1998 AGM which will be held in Hong Kong next April.

No doubt about it, we do have a busy time ahead, but we are ready for the challenges that now await us. After all, the ATF is fully committed to keeping Asian tennis at the forefront.

Oceania Tennis Federation 'OFT'

The third Oceania Tennis Federation (OFT) General Meeting was held in Melbourne, Australia in January 1997 with all nations being represented, including observers from New Caledonia and Tahiti. We were especially privileged to have Brian Tobin, ITF President, and Eiichi Kawatei, Asian Tennis Federation President as our guests. The support from our international body and our neighbouring region assists us in the establishment and co-ordination of our various development programmes.

The new Executive Committee (see below) was elected, with special contributions from Robert Aisi (Papua New Guinea) and Evelyne Jacobe (Vanuatu), who did not seek re-election.

The OTF Executive Committee (1997–99) comprises:

President	Geoff Pollard (Australia)
Vice President	Ian Wells (New Zealand)
Joint Secretaries-General	Mike Daws (Australia) and
	Pat O'Rourke (New Zealand)

Committee members (representing the widest possible cross-section of member nations), Paras Naidu (Fiji), Perelini Perelini (American Samoa), Jeff Race (Northern Mariana Islands) and Waikaremoana So'onalole (Samoa), observer – Dan O'Connell (ITF Development Officer – Pacific Oceania).

The membership of the OTF has now increased to 18 nations at the end of 1997, with the recent additions of Palau, the venue of the 1998 Micronesian Games, and Norfolk Island, the venue for the 2001 South Pacific Mini Games. This leaves Niue, Pitcairn Island, Tokelau and Tuvalu as the only remaining unaffiliated nations/territories within the region. We will be encouraging them all to join us over the next 12 months. We will also continue to work closely with the French territories, New Caledonia and Tahiti, in helping to develop further tennis within the region.

At the General Meeting, the new OTF Development Plan (1997–2000) was approved. By virtue of the Australia South Pacific 2000 programme, the Australian Government is assisting the OTF in attaining a major goal of the Development Plan which is to have a Pacific Oceania tennis player, male and female compete in the Sydney 2000 Olympic Games.

We have been successful in obtaining ASP High Performance Athlete grants for our region's top players to help provide them with competitive opportunities at Challenger/Satellite Circuits held in Australia/New Zealand.

The highlight for 1997 was the promotion of Pacific Oceania's Davis Cup team to Group II for 1998. The team of Motuliki Kailahi (Tonga), Lency Tenai (Solomon Islands), Lawrence Tere (Papua New Guinea), Sanjeev Tikaram (Fiji) and Naga Reddy (Non-playing Captain, Fiji) did the region proud at the Asia/Oceania Group III event in Doha, Qatar in March.

The team finished top of its round robin group, and won its semi-final against Kuwait to earn promotion as one of the top two nations in Group III. It faces a difficult first round away Group II tie against Pakistan in April 1998.

A special mention must be made of Naga Reddy's outstanding leadership during his two year tenure as Davis Cup Captain. He has travelled and guided the team through two tours of New Zealand, maintained a strong sense of discipline within the team at all times and developed a high level of team morale. Naga deserves as much praise as the players for the promotion to Group II.

There was sad news for all of Oceania in August when Davis Cup player, Motuliki Kailahi was tragically killed in a car accident in Tonga. Our sincere condolences go to Motuliki's family and to members of the Tongan Tennis Association.

The continued improvement of our Fed Cup team also gave cause for celebration. The team comprising Tagifano ('Dengue') So'onalole (Samoa), Vera Tere (Papua New Guinea), Adriana Thaggard (Fiji), Simone Wichman (Cook Islands) and Malcolm Kajer (Non-playing Captain, Cook Islands) achieved their best result ever at the Fed Cup Asia/Oceania Regional Qualifying Group II event held in Wellington, New Zealand. Finishing second in our round robin group, the team lost in the semi-finals to Uzbekistan in a cliff hanger. Dengue was the star of the team, winning all of her singles matches against quality opposition. Next year, the Fed Cup team is keen to emulate the men by earning promotion in the 1998 competition.

The Pacific Oceania Closed Championships were played in Nadi and Lautoka, Fiji in January and included women for the first time. The name change from Davis Cup qualifying tournament reflects its appeal as an elite and development tournament for the region. Despite consistent rain, the organisers from the Fiji Tennis Association worked wonders to complete the event. The men's competition was won by Lency Tenai with Motuliki Kailahi as runner-up. Simone Wichman defeated Vera Tera to take the women's title.

Due to the increasing number of activities undertaken by the OTF in recent years, the Executive Committee has appointed Paras Naidu, Secretary of the Fiji Tennis Association (FTA) as its first part-time OTF administrator.

While Paras will also have responsibilities to the ITF for the co-ordination of the Pacific Oceania Junior Circuit and Fiji's mini tennis programme and to FTA for secretarial duties, he will manage the ANZ programme throughout the region, in association with Dan O'Connell (ITF), and will take care of our Davis Cup and Fed Cup campaigns. The Joint Secretaries-General will continue to act as the main liaison point with the ITF and will look after the OTF finances.

The ITF Pacific Oceania Regional Training Centre is soon to begin construction in Lautoka, Fiji following a memorable ceremony in October 1997. It will become the home of the FTA and the regional home of the OTF. The new centre will also serve as a base for our Pacific Oceania Davis Cup and Fed Cup teams, and will host a variety of international events. However, most importantly, it will be a training centre for our regional scholarship holders.

Great news for the region came with ANZ Bank's announcement that its sponsorship of the Pacific Tennis Development Programme would be extended to the end of 1999. The number of countries involved with the Programme has increased from nine in 1996 to 13 in 1997. The Programme commences in the schools through the teaching of mini tennis, followed by educating the teachers. It now includes ANZ Stars Competitions for those keen to develop their tennis further and coaching scholarships for competition winners.

The OTF also acknowledges the invaluable financial support from the ITF and ONOC.

The ITF supports Pacific Oceania Junior Circuit, the scholarship programme, senior and junior tours, the mini tennis programme and the camps programme (in 1997 held in Vanuatu, Kiribati, Fiji and Samoa/American Samoa) and allocates various facility and equipment grants. In addition, it provides the salary for our hard working Development Officer, Dan O'Connell.

ONOC funded, through Olympic Solidarity, courses in 1997 in Vanuatu, Tonga, Fiji, Cook Islands and Papua New Guinea, and the regional programme jointly with the ITF.

The standard of tennis in the Oceania region continues to improve as more competitive and coaching opportunities become available. In its short five year history, a tremendous amount has been achieved, but much more needs to be done. As the OTF's motto says 'Let's do it as a team!'

European Tennis Association 'ETA'

During 1997 the European Tennis Association (ETA) worked closely with the ITF to expand its activities and to look after its 48 member nations.

Nineteen-ninety-seven saw the introduction of the European Champion Clubs Cup for women. The ETA has been organising a similar event successfully for the men for several years and this combined with the development of women's tennis within Europe, confirmed the need to introduce a women's tournament. The first event was held in Estoril, Portugal and was won by TC Slavia Pravnik (Slovak Republic). The European Champion Clubs Cup for men was played in Rennes, France and AS Patton Rennes 35 successfully defended their 1996 title. Both European Club Championships were extremely well attended and, as a result, the ETA has managed to obtain contracts with the organisers for several years.

The European Women's and Men's Team Championships, traditionally played the last week of November and the first week of December respectively, continue to fufil an important function for the ETA member nations. These competitions offer excellent opportunities to give additional, international team competition experience to top players, as well as a first experience to juniors who may be considered for Fed Cup or Davis Cup teams by their National Associations.

Once again there was an increase in the activities and participation of the junior programmes with more teams competing in The European Junior Indoor Team Championships and the European Junior Team Championships. The European Junior Team Championships increased in value acting as European qualifying rounds to the ITF World Junior Tennis Event, ITF 14 & Under, the ITF World Youth Cup 16 & Under and the newly introduced 18 & Under World Championships. The European Junior Individual Championships (age categories 18 & Under/16 & Under/14 & Under) are undoubtedly the flagship events in the junior game producing some of the best junior tennis in the world.

The ETA Junior Circuit for the 16 & Under and 14 & Under again saw an increase in the number of tournaments in 1997. Since 1996 this circuit also has an end of season Junior Masters and for the second successive year it was held in Prato, Italy with the top eight ETA junior ranked players invited to participate.

Veterans' tennis activities in Europe saw further growth and improvements during 1997 now that the ETA Veterans Circuit is well established and the ETA Veterans Ranking is up and running. As a result of the worldwide boom in Veterans tennis, this area of the game continues to expand in Europe with the introduction of additional European Veteran Club Championships.

Working closely with the ITF, the ETA has continued to execute the 1996–2000 Development Programme for European nations. The appointment of an ITF/ETA Junior/Development Administrator is considered an important step forward. It will give an additional dimension to the development activities that the ETA performs on behalf of the ITF and will allow for improved co-operation and control of programmes such as the parent-receiver scheme, mini tennis, school tennis, training and education programmes etc. The support in this area coming from the ITF Grand Slam Development Fund is of immense value and has benefited many European nations. The ETA Development Committee organised the ETA General Secretaries' Meeting in Sliema, Malta and the European Coaches Symposium in Makarska, Croatia.

Together with the ITF, the ETA has continued to organise schools for officials and to consolidate the levels of support provided by the ITF Grand Slam Development Fund.

Throughout 1997 the ETA has handled the administration for the European Women's Tournaments which form part of the ITF Women's Circuit, processing entries and withdrawals for over 120 tournaments in the ETA office in Basle.

During 1998, the ETA and ITF will work together to organise a European Tournament Conference. This Conference, to be held in mid March in Bergen, Norway, will focus on the entry level professional events and will deal with matters such as the officiating, marketing and promotion of these tournaments. Throughout next year, the ETA will continue its work arranging ETA official events and ETA official meetings and promoting the growth of the game.

South American Confederation of Tennis 'COSAT'

The regional institution of South American tennis was founded on 20 October, 1947 and this year it celebrated 50 years of successful involvement in tennis, thanks largely to the support of the presidency and the following people: Alfredo Archondo – Chile (1947–1968), Horacio Billock – Argentina (1981–1982), Alberto Plaza – Venezuela (1982–1986), Carlos Rymer – Uruguay (1986–1990), Nicolas Macchiavello – Ecuador (1990–1992) Eugenio Saller – Brazil (1992–1994) and Vicente Calderon – Bolivia (1994–2000).

At the 1997 ITF AGM official dinner, ITF President Brian Tobin presented a beautiful tray to the COSAT President to commemorate COSAT's 50th anniversary.

This year, the COSAT 97 Junior Circuit has expanded greatly and now offers ten weeks of competition in ten South American countries and attracts an average of 250 players (boys and girls at each level) of whom 70% are from South America.

In 1997, ITF President Brian Tobin and General Manager of the ITF Doug MacCurdy visited the Permanent Secretary of COSAT in La Paz and also took the opportunity to visit Argentina, Brazil, Bolivia, Chile, Paraguay and Uruguay. During their visit, they witnessed the success of the schools' tennis programme at first hand and learned of the recent achievements of the 14–16-year-old COSAT teams.

In the men's professional satellites, 13 tournaments took place with prize money of US$25,000, resulting in 54 continuous weeks of competition. In the women's events, 15 tournaments were held with prize money of US$10,000 while four offered US$25,000, demonstrating the continual improvement in quality and importance of the women's tournaments.

Six Level One tennis coaches' courses have taken place with 110 receiving coaches' badges. In addition, ITF referee courses have been held, including two at Level One and one at Level Two. Next year, we anticipate carrying out similar courses with the addition of one at Level Three.

In 1997, the South American Veterans women's and men's events (35–70 age categories) took place with 240 players participating in Asuncion, Paraguay. The competition was such a success that COSAT has promised to hold this on an annual basis.

During 1998, we plan to consolidate on our progress over the last 50 years, further developing South American tennis in all areas.

Review of Wheelchair Tennis

Ellen de Lange

Nineteen-ninety-seven will be remembered as the most significant in the 20-year history of wheelchair tennis. The merger between the International Wheelchair Tennis Federation (IWTF) and the International Tennis Federation (ITF) was agreed and commences on 1 January 1998.

The continued support of NEC enabled the IWTF to provide a full programme of activities including the NEC Wheelchair Tennis Tour and NEC Wheelchair Tennis Masters. Invacare Corporation provided a substantial backing for the Action World Team Cup and a number of camps for juniors and novice players around the world.

An increased number and quality of tournaments on the NEC Wheelchair Tennis Tour provided wheelchair tennis players with a variety of opportunities at all levels. From the start of the season, the competition was fierce and the challenge for ranking points would determine the World Champions at the end of the year. With tournaments in more than 30 of the 50 nations of the IWTF, the growth of the NEC Wheelchair Tennis Tour continued.

At the ITF World Champions Dinner, held during Roland Garros in Paris, the 1996 World Champions, Ricky Molier and Chantal Vandierendonck, both from the Netherlands were presented with their awards alongside their able bodied peers.

Once again in conjunction with the Dutch Open, the IWTF organised an international junior camp which attracted 32 players and 14 coaches from 10 different countries. Some of the most promising and talented athletes were taught by top coaches.

In July, a record 32 men's and 15 women's teams participated in the Action World Team Cup, organised in Nottingham, England. The event was officially opened by the Duchess of Gloucester who saw the USA team of Stephen Welch, Scott Douglas, Chip Parmelly win the title defeating France 3–0 in the final. Defending champions Australia overcame Great Britain to take third place. In the women's final the Dutch team of Chantal Vandierendonck, Maaike Smit, Esther Vergeer and Sonja Peters recorded their 11th victory in the event with a 3–0 win over the surprise team of the competition, Belgium. Japan were third, 2–1 winners over France.

The Annual General Meeting of the IWTF, held during the Action World Team Cup, confirmed the integration of wheelchair tennis into the ITF, to formalise a relationship that began in 1991. The IWTF member nations agreed that the future of wheelchair tennis would be secured in this new era. The formation of the International Wheelchair Tennis Association (IWTA) will replace the IWTF, and act as an advisory body to the ITF Wheelchair Tennis Committee. The President and Vice President of the IWTA will have seats on the ITF Wheelchair Tennis Committee.

After four years as President of the IWTF, Frenchman Pierre Fusade retired and Martin McElhatton of Great Britain was elected, with Sweden's Stig Ericson becoming Vice President.

A development tour of South America by Ellen de Lange included several clinics and exhibitions in Argentina, Brazil, Chile and Peru. This resulted in various new programmes being established and two international tournaments placed on the NEC Wheelchair Tennis Tour for 1998.

A new video, *No Brakes*, featuring some of the world's top players was produced to provide a much needed resource material for coaching wheelchair tennis. A new ranking for quads was introduced this year to provide a stimulus for growth in this section of wheelchair tennis and a video on quad tennis was made to support the ever popular game.

The year concluded with the NEC Wheelchair Tennis Masters in Eindhoven, the Netherlands for the world's top eight men and women players. The event is fast becoming the most prestigious in the game and two exciting finals brought the season to a fitting end. Kai Schrameyer, from Germany won his first major title this year defeating 1996 Champion, Stephen Welch, USA 4–6 7–5 6–0. In the all-Dutch women's final, Paralympic Champion, Maaike Smit defeated Monique Kalkman 6–3 4–6 7–5 in another thrilling match.

Wheelchair tennis has many challenges ahead, and dedicated support from grass roots to international level will be essential to ensure that our sport grows from strength to strength.

The two NEC Wheelchair Masters champions for 1997 were Maaike Smit of the Netherlands (above) and *Germany's Kai Schrameyer* (left).

The 1996 Paralympic Champion, David Hall of Australia (right) won last year's US Open title with something to spare. (ITF)

NEC INTERNATIONAL WHEELCHAIR TENNIS RANKINGS (As at 25 November 1997)

Men's Singles

1	MOLIER, Ricky	NED	3880
2	HALL, David	AUS	3602
3	WELCH, Stephen	USA	3067
4	GIAMMARTINI, Laurent	FRA	2945
5	SCHRAMEYER, Kai	GER	2571
6	PARMELLY, Chip	USA	1968
7	SARTOV, Eyal	ISR	1468
8	LEGNER, Martin	AUT	1455
9	GREER, John	USA	1296
10	MISTRY, Jayant	GBR	1195
11	SAIDA, Satoshi	JPN	1145
12	HINSON, Lee	USA	918
13	LARSSON, Niclas	SWE	905
14	LACHMAN, Daniel	USA	901
15	KEEMAN, Carl	NZL	886
16	KRUSZELNICKI, Tadeusz	POL	860
17	HOSHI, Yoshiteru	JPN	858
18	TURNER, Chip	USA	745
19	HAGLUND, Johan	SWE	744
20	HATT, Simon	GBR	740

Women's Singles

1	VANDIERENDONCK, Chantal	NED	3150
2	SMIT, Maaike	NED	2938
3	DI TORO, Daniela	AUS	2463
4	KALKMAN, Monique	NED	1851
5	ROLLISON, Patricia	USA	1595
6	OLSON, Nancy	USA	1544
7	MCMORRAN, Janet	GBR	1481
8	CLARK, Sharon	USA	1414
9	AMERYCKX, Brigitte	BEL	1326
10	MARX, Oristelle	FRA	1276
11	CHOKYU, Yuka	CAN	1163
12	WALRAVEN, Sharon	NED	1014
13	HEGI, Eveline	SUI	964
14	VERGEER, Esther	NED	892
15	LEWELLEN, Hope	USA	806
16	SALTZBURG, Nicole	USA	742
17	PETERS, Sonja	NED	654
18	OHMAE, Chiyoko	JPN	641
19	O'NEILL, Mary Ann	USA	528
20	COURTIER, Jacque	NZL	528

ITF WHEELCHAIR TENNIS WORLD CHAMPIONS

Men

1991	Randy Snow	USA
1992	Laurent Giammartini	FRA
1993	Kai Schrameyer	GER
1994	Laurent Giammartini	FRA
1995	David Hall	AUS
1996	Ricky Molier	NED
1997	Ricky Molier	NED

Women

1991	Chantal Vandierendonck	NED
1992	Monique Kalkman	NED
1993	Monique Kalkman	NED
1994	Monique Kalkman	NED
1995	Monique Kalkman	NED
1996	Chantal Vandierendonck	NED
1997	Chantal Vandierendonck	NED

NEC INTERNATIONAL WHEELCHAIR TENNIS TOUR 1997

Date	*Tournament*	*Grade*	*Singles*	*Doubles*
23–27 Jan	Sydney Summer Open	CS3	D. Hall d. L. Giammartini 6–4 6–4	D. Hall/M. Connell d. J. Greer/L. Giammartini 7–5 6–7 6–1
			D. di Toro d. Y. Chokyu 6–2 6–3	Y. Chokyu/E. Hegi d. D. di Toro/R. Hinson 6–4 6–7 6–2
29 Jan–1 Feb	Ford Australian Open	CS2	D. Hall d. L. Giammartini 7–5 6–1	M. Connell/L. Giammartini d. D. Hall/C. Tresch 6–0 6–2
			D. di Toro d. J. Courtier 6–0 6–0	D. di Toro/R. Hinson d. J. Courtier/S. Twelftree 6–2 6–3
4–7 Feb	New Zealand Open	CS4	C. Keeman d. J. Greer 7–6 6–4	J. Greer/C. Keeman d. G. Barnes/J. Luyten 6–1 6–2
			Y. Chokyu d. E. Hegi 4–6 6–2 6–2	E. Hegi/Y. Chokyu d. J. Courtier/R. Hinson 7–6 6–4
26–30 Mar	Lipton Champs	CS2	D. Hall d. R. Molier 0–6 6–1 7–5	L. Giammartini/R. Molier d. D. Hall/D. Lachman 6–2 0–6 7–5
			D. di Toro d. N. Olson 6–2 6–2	C. Vandierendonck/D. di Toro d. N. Olson/E. de Lange 6–4 6–1
3–6 Apr	Florida Open	CS1	D. Hall d. R. Molier 4–6 6–4 6–2	R. Molier/E. Sartov d. J. Greer/C. Parmelly 2–6 6–3 6–1
			M. Smit d. C. Vandierendonck 7–5 6–2	H. Lewellen/M. Smit d. Y. Chokyu/H. Simard 3–6 6–3 7–6
9–13 Apr	Clay Court Champs	CS3	J. Mistry d. L. Hinson 6–1 6–2	S. Hatt/J. Mistry d. J. Ward/S. Wood 6–1 6–2
			B. Ameryckx d. S. Walraven 6–4 6–3	
17–20 Apr	Lichtenberg Buick-Mazda Champs	CS3	S. Welch d. S. Hatt 6–1 6–1	
			N. Saltzburg d. J. McMorran 3–6 7–6 6–3	
26–29 Apr	Kobe Open	CS3	J. Greer d. S. Saida 7–6 6–3	J. Greer/C. Turner d. S. Saida/A. Ikeda 7–5 5–7 6–2
			K. Kitamoto d. P. Rollison 6–4 6–3	P. Rollison/H. Lewellen d. K. Kitamoto/C. Omae 6–7 6–0 6–1
29 Apr–4 May	Spanish Open	CS3	L. Giammartini d. M. Legner 6–2 6–4	M. Legner/K. Schrameyer d. L. Giammartini/R. Molier w/o
			O. Marx d. S. Walraven 6–2 7–5	E. Hegi/A. Racineux d. F. Birra/O. Marx 1–6 7–6 7–5
8–11 May	USTA National Outdoor Champs	CS1	R. Molier d. D. Hall 6–7 6–4 6–4	D. Lachman/C. Parmelly d. S. Douglas/J. Mistry 6–4 7–5
			C. Vandierendonck d. N. Olson 6–3 7–6	D. di Toro/C. Vandierendonck d. H. Lewellen/P. Rollison 6–1 6–4
13–17 May	Slovakia Open	CS4	M. Legner d. S. Bitterauf 6–1 6–4	C. Keeman/M. Legner d. T. Nijhoff/L. Shevchick 6–4 5–7 6–2
14–18 May	Lakeshore Foundation World Challenge	CS3	D. Hall d. S. Welch 7–5 6–1	S. Douglas/S. Welch d. D. Lachman/C. Parmelly 5–7 6–2 6–0
			D. di Toro d. P. Rollison 6–1 6–0	
21–25 May	Japan Open	CS1	L. Giammartini d. D. Hall 7–6 7–6	L. Giammartini/D. Hall d. N. Larsson/J. Haglund 6–1 6–2
			C. Vandierendonck d. J. McMorran 6–4 5–7	C. Vandierendonck/Y. Chokyu d. K. Kitamoto/C. Omae 6–4 6–2
21–25 May	Czech Open	CS4	R. Molier d. M. Legner 6–3 6–1	C. Keeman/M. Legner d. T. Nijhoff/R. Molier 6–4 6–3
29 May–1 Jun	Polish Open	CS4	R. Molier d. M. Legner 6–3 5–7 6–2	R. Molier/A. Dikkeschey d. M. Legner/C. Keeman 6–4 6–7 6–4
5–8 Jun	Thai Open	CS3	C. Omae d. S. Walraven 6–1 6–1	
12–15 Jun	Farwest Regional Champs	CS2	C. Parmelly d. M. Foulks 6–0 7–5	D. Lachman/C. Parmelly d. M. Foulks/M. Pruitt 7–5 6–4
			P. Rollison d. S. Clark 6–2 6–0	Y. Chokyu/H. Simard d. J. Dryden/P. Rollison 6–2 6–4
12–15 Jun	Swedish Colours Open	CS4	A. Westman d. J. Haglund 7–6 5–7 6–4	N. Larsson/J. Haglund d. M. Kallberg/A. Westman 6–0 6–1
			M. Ruth d. C. Johansson 6–3 6–1	
17–22 Jun	Québec Challenge	CS4	L. Giammartini d. R. Molier 6–4 6–1	
20–22 Jun	San Diego/Hendrickson Open	CS4	D. Bolton d. D. Vann 6–3 7–6	
			S. Clark d. K. Korb 6–4 6–3	
2–6 Jul	French Open	CS1	R. Molier d. L. Giammartini 0–6 6–1 6–1	R. Molier/S. Welch d. L. Giammartini/Y. Albespy 0–6 6–2 6–2
			M. Smit d. C. Vandierendonck 6–1 5–7 7–5	H. Lewellen/M. Smit d. B. Ameryckx/C. Seyen 6–3 6–4

Date	Tournament	Grade	Singles	Doubles
8–13 Jul	Dutch Open	CS2	S. Welch d. D. Hall 7–5 7–6	R. Molier/S. Welch d. L. Giammartini/Y. Albespy w/o
			C. Vandierendonck d. M. Smit 6–3 6–4	M. Kalkman/E. Vergeer d. O. Marx/C. Vandierendonck 0–6 6–4 ret
15–20 Jul	Belgian Open	CS2	S. Welch d. R. Molier 6–3 6–2	L. Giammartini/R. Molier d. M. Legner/C. Parmelly 7–6 6–4 S
			M. Smit d. E. Vergeer 6–3 6–0	Peters/E. Vergeer d. N. Olson/P. Rollison 4–6 6–4 6–3
21–26 Jul	British Open	SS	R. Molier d. L. Giammartini 6–0 2–6 7–5	S. Douglas/S. Welch d. D. Johnson/D. Hall 6–2 6–4
			C. Vandierendonck d. O. Marx 6–4 7–6	M. Kalkman/E. Vergeer d. M. Smit/H. Lewellen 6–3 6–3
31 Jul–3 Aug	Japan Cup	CS3	S. Saida d. J. Greer 5–7 7–5 6–4	J. Greer/T. Ambler d. Y. Omori/S. Saida 7–6 3–6 6–3
			N. Kawashima d. C. Imaizumi 6–0 6–0	R. Sakamoto/N. Kawashima d. K. Mori/M. Fukazawa 6–2 6–2
5–10 Aug	Austrian Open	CS2	R. Molier d. S. Welch 6–3 6–2	M. Legner/J. Mistry d. C. Parmelly/R. Weisang 6–7 6–2 6–2
			J. McMorran d. C. Vandierendonck 6–3 6–4	
13–17 Aug	German Open	CS3	S. Welch d. K. Schrameyer 1–6 6–1 6–3	M. Legner/K. Schrameyer d. C. Keeman/T. Kruszelnicki 6–2 6–4
			R. Isecke d. C. Otterbach 6–0 6–1	B. Ameryckx/C. Seyen d. I. van Keulen/A. Maas 7–5 6–4
18–24 Aug	Swiss Open	CS2	C. Vandierendonck d. M. Smit 6–4 5–7 6–2	K. Schrameyer/M. Legner d. S. Welch/L. Giammartini 6–4 6–4
			R. Molier d. S. Welch 1–6 7–6 6–2	C. Vandierendonck/M. Smit d. E. Vergeer/M. Kalkman 6–4 3–6 6–4
2–7 Sep	Citta di Livorno	CS4	L. Giammartini d. M. Legner 6–3 6–1	Keeman/M. Legner d. L. Giammartini/C. Rigolo 6–2 6–0
			B. Ameryckx d. A. Broadway 6–3 6–3	
4–7 Sep	Southwest Reg Champs	CS2	S. Welch d. C. Parmelly 6–0 6–1	S. Welch/S. Douglas d. C. Parmelly/D. Lachman 4–6 6–4 6–1
			M. Kalkman d. P. Rollison 6–3 6–3	Y. Chokyu/L. Seideman d. H. Lewellen/S. Clark 4–6 6–4 7–5
12–14 Jul	Santa Rosa Champs	CS3	S. Welch d. M. Haynes 6–1 6–0	S. Welch/W. Leavitt d. J. Ward/M. Pruitt 6–2 6–0
19–21 Sep	USPTR/Roho Champs	CS4	S. Welch d. S. Douglas 6–1 4–6 6–4	S. Welch/S. Douglas d. D. Lachman/M. Thompson 6–0 6–2
23–28 Sep	Radl Cup	CS3	L. Giammartini d. R. Molier 7–6 4–6 7–6	R. Molier/L. Giammartini d. M. Legner/J. Mistry 6–7 6–4 3–0 ret
			M. Smit d. J. McMorran 6–0 6–1	
3–5 Oct	Tahoe Donner Champs	CS4	E. Sartov d. D. Johnson 6–2 6–3	M. Foulks/E. Sartov d. P. Johnson/M. Pruitt 6–3 6–3
			P. Rollison d. H. Lewellen 2–6 6–4 6–2	S. Clark/H. Lewellen d. J. Courtier/R. Hinson 6–0 6–4
7–10 Oct	Newport Beach	CS4	C. Parmelly d. R. Molier 7–5 4–6 6–4	D. Hall/D. Johnson d. J. Mistry/B. Dockerill 3–6 6–2 6–2
13–19 Oct	US Open	SS	D. Hall d. K. Schrameyer 6–2 3–6 6–4	S. Welch/S. Douglas d. D. Lachman/C. Parmelly 6–1 4–6 6–3
			D. di Toro d. S. Clark 6–1 6–2	D. di Toro/C. Vandierendonck d. H. Lewellen/M. Smit 6–2 6–1
18–23 Nov	NEC Masters	CS1	K. Schrameyer d. S. Welch 4–6 7–5 6–0	
			M. Smit d. M. Kalkman 6–3 4–6 7–5	

(Above, left to right) Arnaud di Pasquale of France, Christian Bimes, President of the French Federation and Cara Black of Zimbabwe, a finalist in Paris and the junior champion at Wimbledon and the US Open. (Stephen Wake)
(Below) Westley *Whitehouse of South Africa, winner of the junior title at Wimbledon, ended the year ranked No.3 in the world.* (Ron Angle)

Review of the Junior Game

Jackie Nesbitt

Junior tennis in 1997 has enjoyed one of its most successful periods. Ensuring a good turn out of players on the ITF Junior Circuit has never been a problem, but the very best participants have not always been present, even for the most prestigious of junior tournaments.

Usually the best place for 18 & Under juniors is in the junior game, where players have the time to develop both physically and mentally for the considerable pressures of the professional circuits. However, many talented juniors have understandably looked more and more to the lower level professional circuits.

This is because the junior game has been without a link to the professional game. As a result, the value of the ITF Junior Circuit as a training ground for future professionals has become lost on many. At least among the women, this attitude is changing.

As a result of discussions between the ITF Women's Committee and the COREL WTA TOUR, a small but significant breakthrough occurred at the beginning of the year with the introduction of the Junior Exempt Project. This scheme awarded the top ten girls singles players from 1996 direct main draw positions in ITF Women's Circuit tournaments ranging from $25,000 to $75,000 prize-money level. At last players could see a benefit in playing junior tournaments and could be suitably rewarded for good performances. Having introduced the project the obvious questions arose – would the impact of the project be felt by the players and would they justify their rewards?

World champion, Amelie Mauresmo took up an exempt position at a $50,000 tournament in Greece and defeated Spain's Eva Bes 6–0 6–0 in the final. Mirjana Lucic, went one better and polished off all opponents to win a $75,000 tournament in Croatia and several other players produced performances that proved them worthy of their places. How nice it was too to listen to the press conference given by France's Kildine Chevalier, this year's US Open runner-up, who stated that her aim for the rest of the year was to gain a top ten finish and qualify for the Exempt Project.

Kildine failed to make the top ten, but may yet benefit from wild cards made available by her Federation. One who could not rely on this option was Slovenia's Katarina Srebotnik. Although Katarina was unable to capture the Orange Bowl title, which was essential if she was to become world champion, her disappointment was tempered by the prospect of playing in events that would previously been out of reach.

Let us hope that those in charge of the men's game can be persuaded to establish a link with the junior game in the not too distant future.

Who then were the players helping to make 1997 such a fine year for junior tennis? The rivalry in the boys section between Arnaud di Pasquale, Westley Whitehouse and Daniel Elsner ensured that those lucky enough to see the junior finals at the major tournaments were wonderfully entertained.

Germany's Elsner, who only just missed out on becoming the 1996 boys' singles world champion, was in determined form early in the year, taking the Australian Open title with victory over South Africa's Westley Whitehouse. A limited schedule, clearly designed to target only the major tournaments, meant no reappearance until the French Open where Elsner despatched local favourite di Pasquale in the semi-finals and Peru's Luis Horna in the final for his second Grand Slam title. Seemingly unstoppable, Elsner's gamble looked like paying off, but a third major title and the all important bonus points were destined to remain just out of reach.

Di Pasquale took some time to get over his disappointment in Paris, missing Wimbledon where the title went to Whitehouse, finally victorious over Elsner following a thrilling final. This unexpected win by the South African keep the title race open and badly dented the aura of invincibility built up by Elsner. Di Pasquale, always a committed team player and ably backed by Julien Jeanpierre, claimed the prestigious European Team Championships for France and followed this by becoming the European Individual Champion.

Elsner's confidence received another blow just prior to the US Open when he was surprisingly defeated by Olivier Levant at the Canadian Championships. Di Pasquale took that title and when Whitehouse defeated Elsner in the semi-finals at Flushing Meadows, the French player seized his opportunity and moved to the top of the rankings with a fine win over Whitehouse.

Had di Pasquale not journeyed to Japan and collected a second Group A title, the two other title contenders might have revised their plans and committed to the end of year US circuit. Win he did, however, and Whitehouse for one was left too far behind on points to make up ground. It was particularly gratifying for his Federation and for the ITF that di Pasquale agreed to be pressed into action once more. Teaming with Jeanpierre and Levant, he led France to success in the Sunshine Cup, a team competition which has existed for 40 years, but which was organised for the first time by the ITF, in conjunction with the USTA.

A French player was therefore once again to thwart Elsner who finished second in the rankings, ahead of Whitehouse and Horna. Nicolas Massu, who had occupied 2nd spot in the rankings for the first half of the year, managed a last gasp victory at the Orange Bowl to move ahead of the unfortunate Jeanpierre into fifth position.

For most of the year it appeared that the battle for the girls' singles world crown would be a two-horse race between Katerina Srebotnik of Slovenia and Zimbabwe's Cara Black. True, the remarkable German 15-year-old Mirjana Lucic captured the first Grand Slam title in Australia, but that was to be her parting gesture to junior tennis as she progressed to the professional tour where she was destined to make quite an impact.

Slovenia had another talented prospect on their hands in the shape of Tina Pisnik, who, with Srebotnik, were expected to feature highly in the girls rankings. Srebotnik was generally accepted to be the stronger of the two and duly defeated Pisnik in the final of the Italian Open and again at the World Super Junior Championships in Japan, to claim two Group A titles.

Her poor performances at the Grand Slams, however, proved to be her undoing. Despite winning the ITF Connolly Continental Cup in tandem with Pisnik, Srebotnik still needed victory at the Orange Bowl to clinch the world title. The draw which pitched her against Croatia's Jelena Kostanic was unfortunate, but nevertheless the world no. 2 should have been up to the task. An opening round defeat spelt two fold disaster. Not only did it cost her a chance of becoming world champion, but it also opened the field for Pisnik who captured the title, moved ahead of her compatriot in the rankings and also claimed a better position under the Junior Exempt Project.

Pisnik's late run certainly moved her up into second place in the rankings, but it was not enough to make her world champion. That title was claimed by Zimbabwe's Cara Black. A member of the ITF Women's Team funded by the Grand Slam Development Fund, it initially seemed that Cara might be overshadowed by her team mate, Kazakhstan's Irina Selyutina. Two fairly comprehensive singles defeats at the hands of Irina on the South American circuit early on did not bode well, but Cara finally made a significant breakthrough against her doubles partner at the Astrid Bowl.

Her confidence boosted, Cara launched into a tremendous run at the major tournaments. Despite losing the final of the French Open in three sets to Justine Henin, Cara bounced back impressively to claim both the Wimbledon and US Open titles and pole position in the rankings. Not content with her singles exploits, Cara combined with Irina to form a devastating doubles partnership that saw them crowned joint world champions having collected a total of ten titles, including the French Open and Wimbledon.

Only at the US Open where they lost in the final to Melissa Irvin and Alexandra Stevenson were they found wanting. Cara and Irina could, however, be forgiven the loss nearing the end of an extremely busy year. Also competing in selected ITF Women's Circuit tournaments, they reached a respectable joint WTA doubles ranking inside the top 200 and apparently aim to make an assault on the top 100 rankings in 1998. So near yet so far once again for Srebotnik who claimed third place to match her singles ranking.

Final mention goes to Chile's Nicolas Massu, who captured seven doubles titles on his way to becoming boys' doubles world champion for the year. Six of the seven, including the US Open, were won in partnership with compatriot Fernando Gonzalez, but a seventh major victory at Wimbledon was collected with Luis Horna and this was responsible for relegating the unfortunate Gonzalez to second place, one ahead of Horna.

ITF JUNIOR WORLD RANKINGS 1997 – POINTS EXPLANATION

The ITF Junior World Ranking is a world-wide points-linked circuit of 154 tournaments, 6 continental championships and 4 team competitions in 91 countries, under the management of the International Tennis Federation. There are ten separate points categories covering the three types of events. There is no limit to the number of tournaments in which a player may compete each year. The best six results from tournaments (Groups A and 1–5), continental championships (Groups B1–B3) and team competitions (Group C) count towards a players' ranking. To qualify for a final year-end ranking a player must have competed in at least six events, including at least three Group A tournaments and at least three outside his or her own country.

Tournaments & Regional Championships

Singles

	A	1	2	3	4	5	B1	B2	B3
Winner	250	120	80	60	40	30	180	100	80
Runner-up	180	100	65	50	30	20	120	80	50
Semi-Finalists	120	75	50	30	20	10	80	60	30
Quarter-Finalists *	80	50	30	20	10	5	60	40	15
Losers in last 16 **	50	30	15	10	5	–	30	25	5
Losers in last 32 ***	30	20	–	–	–	–	20	10	–

* only if 16 or more players in draw (excluding withdrawals)
** only if 32 or more players in draw (excluding withdrawals)
*** only if 64 or more players in draw (excluding withdrawals)

Doubles (Each Player)

	A	1	2	3	4	5	B1	B2	B3
Winners	180	100	65	50	30	20	120	80	50
Runners-up	120	75	50	30	20	10	80	60	30
Semi-Finalists *	80	50	30	20	10	5	60	40	15
Quarter-Finalists **	50	30	15	10	5	–	30	25	5
Losers in last 16 ***	30	20	–	–	–	–	20	10	–

* only if 8 or more pairs in draw (excluding withdrawals)
** only if 16 or more pairs in draw (excluding withdrawals)
*** only if 32 or more pairs in draw (excluding withdrawals)

POINTS TABLE (Group C – Team Competition)

	No. 1 Singles Player Win	No. 2 Singles Player Win	Doubles Win Each Player
Final	100	80	80
Semi-Final	80	60	60
Quarter-Final	60	40	40

POINTS TABLE (Group A Super Series Bonus Points)

	Singles	Doubles
Winner of 3 or more Group A events	150	150

ITF JUNIOR WORLD RANKING RESULTS 1997

DATE	TOURNAMENT	GROUP	BOYS' SINGLES FINAL	GIRLS' SINGLES FINAL
22–28 Dec	Casablanca Cup, Mexico	1	N. Massu (CHI) d. A. Ram (ISR) 7–5 6–4	K. Srebotnik (SLO) d. R. Teperberg (ISR) 1–6 7–5 6–3
27–31 Dec	Adejumo, Nigeria	5	R. Jegede (NGR) d. K. Ibrahim (NGR) 6–4 6–3	A. Mohammed (GHA) d. P. Osedumme (NGR) 6–3 7–6
30 Dec–5 Jan	Coffee Bowl, Costa Rica	1	N. Massu (CHI) d. B. Vahaly (USA) 6–2 6–1	M. Matevzic (SLO) d. J. Lehnhoff (USA) 6–2 6–7 7–5
1–7 Jan	Salk Indoor, Sweden	4	J. Christensen (SWE) d. J. Adaktusson (SWE) 6–4 7–5	F. Engblom (SWE) d. E. Dyrberg (DEN) 2–6 7–6 6–3
2–6 Jan	Lome, Togo	5	R. Jegede (NGR) d. K. Ibrahim (NGR) 6–3 7–5	A. Mohammed (GHA) d. P. Osedumme (NGR) 6–3 6–4
3–8 Jan	Victoria, Australia	2	W. Whitehouse (RSA) d. K.Ziv (ISR) 4–6 7–6 7–5	B. Stewart (AUS) d. E. Dominikovic (AUS) 6–0 5–7 6–2
6–12 Jan	Caracas, Venezuela	A	J. Jeanpierre (FRA) d. L. Horna (PER) 6–7 6–1 6–2	M. Middleton (USA) d. J. Lehnhoff (USA) 6–1 2–6 6–2
8–11 Jan	Vasteras, Sweden	4	J. Adaktusson (SWE) d. T. Berendijas (SLO) 6–4 6–3	E. Dyrberg (DEN) d. M. Wolfbrandt (SWE) 6–3 6–3
8–12 Jan	Winneba, Ghana	5	R. Jegede (NGR) d. C. Anyidoho (GHA) 3–6 6–1 6–4	A. Mohammed (GHA) d. A. Berthe (SEN) 6–1 6–4
13–18 Jan	Australian Hardcourts, Victoria	1	D. Elsner (GER) d. K. Ziv (ISR) 6–2 6–1	M. Lucic (CRO) d. J. Wohr (GER) 6–2 6–7 6–0
13–19 Jan	Pony Malta, Colombia	1	A. Dulko (ARG) d. F. Gonzalez (CHI) 6–3 3–6 6–2	C. Castano (COL) d. G. Volekova (SVK) 6–1 6–3
20–26 Jan	Australian Open	A	D. Elsner (GER) d. W. Whitehouse (RSA) 7–6 6–2	M. Lucic (CRO) d. M. Weingartner (GER) 6–2 6–2
20–26 Jan	N. Macchiavello, Ecuador	2	A. Dulko (ARG) d. J-I. Chela (ARG) 6–2 6–4	O. Rejniak (POL) d. C. Castano (COL) 6–2 2–6 6–4
27 Jan–1 Feb	Colombo, Sri Lanka	4	D. Udomchoke (THA) d. M. Mahadevan (IND) 6–7 6–3 6–2	L. Herbert (GBR) d. O. Wongkamalasai (THA) 6–4 6–3
27 Jan–2 Feb	Inka Bowl, Peru	3	L. Horna (PER) d. A. Simoni (BRA) 6–1 6–1	O. Rejniak (POL) d. P. Palencia (MEX) 6–3 6–4
28 Jan–2 Feb	Slovak Indoor, Bratislava	3	J. Adaktusson (SWE) d. M. Grolmus (SVK) 6–0 6–4	S. Petrutiu (ROM) d. T. Pisnik (SLO) 2–6 6–4 6–4
3–8 Feb	New Delhi, India	5	H. Mankad (IND) d. D. Fassoulas (GRE) 6–4 6–1	U. Khan (IND) d. L. Herbert (GBR) 6–3 2–6 6–1
3–9 Feb	Czech Indoor, Prerov	2	R. Vik (CZE) d. M. Grolmus (SVK) 4–6 6–4 7–6	J. Schonfeldova (CZE) d. Z. Ondraskova (CZE) 6–1 6–2
4–9 Feb	Condor de Plata, Bolivia	3	S. Roitman (ARG) d. J. Ilowski (POL) 6–4 4–6 7–5	B. Colosio (BRA) d. O. Rejniak (POL) 6–4 6–2
10–16 Feb	Milo Cup, Chile	2	N. Massu (CHI) d. F. Gonzalez (CHI) 6–1 6–2	C. Tiene (BRA) d. V. Voletic (YUG) 6–2 6–0
10–17 Feb	Yamunagar, India	5	A. Fasching (AUT) d. M. Mahadevan (IND) 6–1 6–1	U. Khan (IND) d. K. Patel (IND) 6–2 6–4
12–16 Feb	Bavarian Indoor, Germany	2	B. Vaci (HUN) d. S. Aickele (GER) 4–6 6–4 7–6	S. Bammer (AUT) d. M. Iversen (DEN) 6–4 6–2
17–23 Feb	Argentina Cup, Mar del Plata	2	J-I. Chela (ARG) d. D. Perez (ARG) 6–3 6–2	I. Seliyutina (KAZ) d. B. Mouhtassine (MAR) 7–5 6–4
17–23 Feb	Dhaka, Bangladesh	4	D. Udomchoke (THA) d. M. Mahadevan (IND) 6–4 6–4	J-H. Kim (KOR) d. S. Viratprasert (THA) 4–6 6–1 6–3
19–23 Feb	British Indoor	3	X. Malisse (BEL) d. T. Messmer (GER) 3–6 6–3 6–4	H. Collin (GBR) d. A. Myskina (RUS) 6–4 6–3
24 Feb–1 Mch	Uruguay Bowl, Montevideo	2	O. Levant (FRA) d. J. De Armas (VEN) 7–5 6–1	I. Seliyutina (KAZ) d. C. Black (ZIM) 6–3 6–3
3–9 Mch	Asuncion Bowl, Paraguay	1	N. Massu (CHI) d. R. Rake (USA) 1–6 7–5 6–1	M. Middleton (USA) d. C. Black (ZIM) 6–3 7–5
4–9 Mch	Kuala Lumpur, Malaysia	4	T. Berendijas (SLO) d. F. Widhiyanto (INA) 6–2 6–2	M. Iversen (DEN) d. E. Dyrberg (DEN) 7–6 6–4
10–14 Mch	Torneo Taca, El Salvador	5	C. Vargas (PAN) d. M. Hanlin (GBR) 7–6 2–6 7–5	Z. Reyes (MEX) d. D. Reynolds (MEX) 2–6 6–3 6–2
10–16 Mch	Banana Bowl, Brazil	1	L. Horna (PER) d. F. Gonzalez (CHI) 6–3 6–2	S. Taylor (USA) d. V. Dag (ARG) 7–6 6–3
10–16 Mch	Singapore	3	T. Terachi (JPN) d. W-J. Cheng (TPE) 6–3 6–2	M. Iversen (DEN) d. N. Horikawa (JPN) 6–0 6–1
17–20 Mch	Sth American Closed, Brazil	B2	L. Horna (PER) d. N. Massu (CHI) 6–4 6–4	C. Castano (COL) d. J. Cortez (BRA) 6–3 7–5
17–21 Mch	Costa Rican Bowl, San Jose	5	A. Barragan (MEX) d. I. Ogrinc (SLO) 6–2 6–4	A. Broderick (JAM) d. L. Lopez (MEX) 6–4 6–4
17–22 Mch	Bandar Seri Begawan, Brunei	4	J. Melzer (AUT) d. P. Joubert (RSA) 7–5 6–2	J-H. Kim (KOR) d. L-Y. Tan (MAS) 6–3 4–6 6–3
24–29 Mch	Dakar, Senegal	5	V. Sanon (CIV) d. M. Belbacha (MAR) 3–6 6–2 7–6	N. Grandin (RSA) d. B. Mouhtassine (MAR) 6–3 6–1
24–30 Mch	Panama	5	J. Hernandez (MEX) d. C. Haid (AUT) 6–1 6–2	K. Koukalova (CZE) d. A. Cardoso (POR) 6–4 7–5
25–30 Mch	Pascuas Bowl, Paraguay	4	M. Badaracco (ARG) d. E. Massa (ARG) 6–3 3–6 6–3	R. Fonda (PAR) d. S. Damario (ARG) 7–6 6–0
25–30 Mch	Jakarta, Indonesia	3	F. Widhiyanto (INA) d. D. Grgic (CRO) 3–6 6–3 6–4	W. Prakusya (INA) d. V. Koksova (CZE) 6–7 6–4 7–5

DATE	TOURNAMENT	GROUP	BOYS' SINGLES FINAL	GIRLS' SINGLES FINAL
26–31 Mch	Florence, Italy	2	A. Derepasko (RUS) d. I. Ancic (CRO) 6–1 6–2	T. Pisnik (SLO) d. K. Chevalier (FRA) 6–2 6–4
30 Mch–5 Apr	Namangan, Uzbekistan	5	M. Belski (BLR) d. J. Cariov (LTU) 6–1 6–7 6–3	Li. Biktyakova (UZB) d. Lu. Biktyakova (UZB) 4–6 6–1 6–4
31 Mch–5 Apr	Ste Marie, Martinique	5	M. Porry (FRA) d. S. Sanford (FRA) 4–6 6–4 6–4	N. Etienne (HAI) d. B. Burlet (FRA) 6–2 6–4
31 Mch–6 Apr	Mali Milk Cup, Thailand	3	W. Whitehouse (RSA) d. F. Widhiyanto (INA) 6–3 6–3	M. Niroj (THA) d. D. Poglitsch (AUT) 6–2 6–4
31 Mch–6 Apr	African Closed, Senegal	B3	V. Sanon (CIV) d. M. Belbacha (MAR) 6–3 6–0	B. Mouhtassine (MAR) d. L. Van Rooyen (RSA) 4–6 6–3 7–5
31 Mch–6 Apr	Moscow, Russia	5	I. Kunitcin (RUS) d. T. Zabrocki (POL) 4–6 6–0 6–1	E. Dementieva (RUS) d. N. Ostrovskaja (BLR) 6–1 6–2
6–12 Apr	Taskent, Uzbekistan	5	I. Kunitcin (RUS) d. M. Belski (BLR) 3–6 6–4 6–3	L. Skavronskaya (RUS) d. E. Voropaeva (RUS) 6–4 2–6 7–6
7–12 Apr	St Michael, Barbados	5	M. Hanlin (GBR) d. R. Steckley (CAN) 3–6 6–4 6–3	N. Rencken (RSA) d. B. Burlet (FRA) 6–2 0–6 6–2
8–13 Apr	Manila, Philippines	2	L. Hewitt (AUS) d. W. Whitehouse (RSA) 6–4 6–3	M. Fernandez (PHI) d. S. Bajin (CAN) 6–1 6–3
14–20 Apr	Sochi, Russia	4	M. Belski (BLR) d. J. Plugarev (MDA) 6–4 7–6	E. Bovina (RUS) d. M. Samoilenko (RUS) 6–4 6–1
15–19 Apr	Bat Yam, Israel	4	D. Mc Gregor (RSA) d. B. Borella (DEN) 1–6 6–1 6–1	R. Teperberg (ISR) d. N. Petrova (RUS) 6–1 7–6
15–20 Apr	Japan Open, Tokyo	1	W. Whitehouse (RSA) d. R. Vik (CZE) 7–6 7–6	S. Taylor (USA) d. M. Inoue (JPN) 6–0 6–3
20–25 Apr	Beer Sheva, Israel	4	K. Ziv (ISR) d. N. Mc Donald (RSA) 6–4 7–5	R. Teperberg (ISR) d. I. Tulyaganova (UZB) 6–1 6–3
21–27 Apr	Beaulieu Sur Mer, France	4	J-C. Ferrero (ESP) d. D. Grgic (CRO) 6–1 6–0	C. Pin (FRA) d. D. Mendiburu (FRA) 6–4 6–2
21–27 Apr	Quebec, Canada	5	C-A. Sevigny (CAN) d. A. Niculescu (ROM) 6–7 7–6 6–2	G. Houle (CAN) d. L. Lopez (MEX) 6–1 7–5
22–27 Apr	Asian Closed, Japan	B2	S-H. Lee (KOR) d. W-J. Cheng (TPE) 7–5 3–6 7–6	A. Morigami (JPN) d. S. Hisamatsu (JPN) 6–3 0–6 7–5
28 Apr–2 May	Seoul, Korea	4	S-H. Lee (KOR) d. C-H. Lee (KOR) 6–0 6–4	E-Y. Ha (KOR) d. J-Y. Choi (KOR) 6–2 4–6 6–2
28 Apr–3 May	Slovakia Cup, Bratislava	2	F. Babej (SVK) d. M. Grolmus (SVK) 1–6 6–4 7–6	A. Sebova (SVK) d. G. Volekova (SVK) 6–0 6–4
28 Apr–4 May	Salsomaggiore, Italy	2	M. Llodra (FRA) d. D. Bramanti (ITA) 6–4 3–6 6–4	Z. Gubacsi (HUN) d. F. Schiavone (ITA) 6–2 7–6
5–11 May	Prato, Italy	2	R. Federer (SUI) d. L. Kutanjac (CRO) 6–4 6–0	Z. Gubacsi (HUN) d. L. Kalavaria (USA) 6–3 6–3
5–11 May	Taiwan, Taipei	3	W-J. Cheng (TPE) d. S. Bourke (AUS) 7–5 4–6 6–4	A, Morigami (JPN) d. Y-A. Chen (TPE) 6–3 6–0
12–18 May	Santa Croce, Italy	1	X. Malisse (BEL) d. L. Horna (PER) 7–5 2–6 6–3	I. Seliyutina (KAZ) d. M. Pastikova (CZE) 6–4 4–6 7–6
14–18 May	Raiffeisen Spring Bowl, Austria	3	P. Mullner (AUT) d. Z. Papp (HUN) 6–3 6–1	S. Hrozenska (SVK) d. V. Stoklasova (SVK) 6–3 6–3
19–24 May	Italian Open, Milan	A	F. Allgauer (ITA) d. L. Horna (PER) 6–3 6–3	K. Srebotnik (SLO) d. T. Pisnik (SLO) 6–1 6–2
26–31 May	Astrid Bowl, Belgium	1	N. Massu (CHI) d. X. Malisse (BEL) 6–2 6–2	C. Black (ZIM) d. I. Seliyutina (KAZ) 6–4 7–5
1–8 Jne	French Open	A	D. Elsner (GER) d. L. Horna (PER) 6–4 6–4	J. Henin (BEL) d. C. Black (ZIM) 4–6 6–4 6–4
3–7 Jne	Villach, Austria	4	J. Gorisek (SLO) d. T. Hajek (CZE) 6–4 4–6 6–4	P. Navratilova (CZE) d. R. Sottova (CZE) 6–2 6–1
3–8 Jne	Ontario, Canada	5	R. Steckley (CAN) d. B. Veress (HUN) 6–2 6–0	I. Khelifi (CAN) d. J. Musgrove (CAN) 1–6 6–4 7–6
10–14 Jne	Eravis Epitok Cup, Hungary	4	V. Koczan (HUN) d. B. Borella (DEN) 6–4 6–2	J. Schruff (GER) d. M. Czink (HUN) 6–3 6–0
10–15 Jne	Luxembourg	4	A. Qureshi (PAK) d. T. Job (GER) 6–3 7–6	G. Seliounina (BLR) d. D. Caporusso (FRA) 3–6 6–0 16–14
11–15 Jne	Umag, Croatia	3	D. Grgic (CRO) d. A. Kracman (SLO) 6–4 6–1	J. Kostanic (CRO) d. R. Sottova (CZE) 6–4 6–1
17–22 Jne	East Molesey, England	2	W. Whitehouse (RSA) d. W-J. Cheng (TPE) 6–3 6–4	E. Dominikovic (AUS) d. B. Stewart (AUS) 6–4 6–2
24–28 Jne	Rungsted Kyst, Denmark	3	V. Sanon (CIV) d. M. Kullenberg (SWE) 6–3 6–4	J. Kostanic (CRO) d. D. Penic (CRO) 4–6 7–5 7–5
24–29 Jne	Roehampton, England	1	J. Jeanpierre (FRA) d. L. Hewitt (AUS) 6–4 6–2	A. Rippner (USA) d. Y-J. Cho (KOR) 7–6 6–4
24–29 Jne	Donetsk Cup, Ukraine	5	O. Tereshchuk (UKR) d. E. Tanik (TUR) 6–3 6–1	T. Kovalchuk (UKR) d. O. Teplinskaia (UKR) 6–0 3–6 6–0
28 Jne–6 Jly	Wimbledon	A	W. Whitehouse (RSA) d. D. Elsner (GER) 6–3 7–6	C. Black (ZIM) d. A. Rippner (USA) 6–3 7–5
30 Jne–6 Jly	Curacao, Netherlands Antilles	5	J-J. Rojer (AHO) d. M. Gallardo (MEX) 6–4 6–1	M-L. Fernandez (MEX) d. K. Richards (JAM) 6–3 6–2
30 Jne–6 Jly	Meditarranee 2000, Morocco	5	B. Messaoudi (MAR) d. J. Chafai (MAR) 6–1 6–3	M. Weirich (RSA) d. M. Haddad (MAR) 6–0 6–1
1–5 Jly	Castricum, Netherlands	3	E. Prodon (FRA) d. J-C. Faurel (FRA) 6–2 6–2	J. Kostanic (CRO) d. S. Hrozenska (SVK) 4–6 6–3 6–2
7–12 Jly	Darwin, Australia	5	D. Burden (AUS) d. M. Fitzgerald (AUS) 6–3 6–1	A. Molik (AUS) d. K. Pinchbeck (AUS) 6–0 6–1

DATE	TOURNAMENT	GROUP	BOYS' SINGLES FINAL	GIRLS' SINGLES FINAL
7–12 Jly	Aruba, Netherlands Antilles	5	J. Haro (MEX) d. C-D. Lee (KOR) 6–3 6–2	J. Balbuena (USA) d. L. Porras (PAN) 6–4 6–3
7–13 Jly	Tunis, Tunisia	5	E. Tanik (TUR) d. D. Milojcic (SLO) 7–6 6–1	M. Weirich (RSA) d. A. Cardoso (POR) 6–0 6–3
8–13 Jly	German Open, Essen	1	L. Uebel (GER) d. T. Zivnicek (GER) 6–1 7–6	T. Pisnik (SLO) d. Z. Ondraskova (CZE) 7–6 6–3
14–19 Jly	Winchester, England	5	S. Rhodes (GBR) d. B. Scollo (GBR) 6–4 6–7 6–4	I. Tulyaganova (UZB) d. R. Faurfelt (DEN) 6–2 6–4
14–20 Jly	Marsa, Malta	5	R. De Voest (RSA) d. D. Coetzee (RSA) 7–5 6–1	M. Weirich (RSA) d. S. Bozicnik (SLO) 6–1 6–1
14–20 Jly	Copa Merengue, Dominican Rep.	5	A. Sierra (MEX) d. A. Barragan (MEX) 7–6 6–1	D. Reynolds (MEX) d. M-L. Fernandez (MEX) 4–6 6–2 6–2
15–20 Jly	Davos, Switzerland	2	V. Sanon (CIV) d. I. Labadze (GEO) 4–6 6–4 7–6	J. Kostanic (CRO) d. R. Sottova (CZE) 6–3 6–1
18–20 Jly	European Team Championships	C	France d. Czech Republic 3–0	France d. Czech Republic 2–1
21–25 Jly	Vancouver, Canada	5	E. Dmytruk (CAN) d. D. Devriendt (CAN) 6–2 6–4	J. Buczkowska (CAN) d. J. Wojas (CAN) 6–4 6–2
21–26 Jly	Montego Bay, Jamaica	5	P. Gordon (JAM) d. J. Smith (JAM) 6–1 6–1	Z. Reyes (MEX) d. A. Broderick (JAM) 7–6 6–4
21–27 Jly	European Closed, Switzerland	B1	A. Di Pasquale (FRA) d. P. Kralert (CZE) 4–6 6–4 6–4	B. Schwartz (AUT) d. E. Dyrberg (DEN) 6–3 6–4
23–27 Jly	Plzen, Czech Republic	3	L. Zovko (CRO) d. P. Snobel (CZE) 6–4 6–4	V. Raimrova (CZE) d. V. Koksova (CZE) 6–2 2–6 6–3
23–27 Jly	Johannesburg, South Africa	5	J. Van der Westhuizen (RSA) d. C. Swart (RSA) 6–3 6–3	N. Rencken (RSA) d. M. Van Schalkwyk (RSA) 6–3 6–1
28 Jly–2 Aug	JITIC, Carb. & C. Am. Clsd.	B3	J. Smith (JAM) d. R. Echagaray (MEX) 6–0 7–6	P. Palencia (MEX) d. D. Reynolds (MEX) 6–7 6–2 6–2
28 Jly–3 Aug	Porto, Portugal	5	J-C. Ferrero (ESP) d. V. Ferreira (POR) 6–0 6–1	M. Mesa (COL) d. C. Seal (GBR) 6–3 6–1
29 Jly–2 Aug	Pretoria, South Africa	4	C. Swart (RSA) d. J. Masson (RSA) 6–2 6–3	N. Rencken (RSA) d. A. Mojzis (RSA) 7–5 6–4
29 Jly–2 Aug	K Swiss, Ireland	5	C-M. Straka (GER) d. D-J. Mullins (IRL) 6–4 6–1	A. Srndovic (SWE) d. C. Coombs (GBR) 7–6 6–4
30 Jly–3 Aug	Leciva Czech Junior Open, Czech Rep	3	T. Jecminek (CZE) d. A. Kedryuk (KAZ) 7–6 6–2	A. Plackova (CZE) d. A. Masarykova (SVK) 6–2 6–4
1–10 Aug	USTA Boys' Closed, Michigan	1	R. Rake (USA) d. J. Blake (USA) 6–0 4–6 6–4 6–4	—
3–10 Aug	USTA Girls' Closed, California	1	—	J. Trail (USA) d. W. Laiho (USA) 6–3 7–5
4–9 Aug	Gaborone, Botswana	5	J. Auckland (GBR) d. C. Anyidoho (GHA) 4–6 7–6 6–2	A. Mojzis (RSA) d. N. Van der Merwe (RSA) 6–1 6–2
4–9 Aug	Copa Mundo Maya, Guatemala	5	J. Garcia (DOM) d. A. Sierra (MEX) 6–4 4–6 6–3	Z. Reyes (MEX) d. P. Castillejos (MEX) 6–1 6–2
4–9 Aug	St Lucia, West Indies	5	J-J. Rojer (AHO) d. P. Gordon (JAM) 6–1 6–2	D. Reynolds (MEX) d. K. Richards (JAM) 3–6 6–2 6–3
4–10 Aug	Arab Championships, Egypt	5	J. Chafai (MAR) d. I-H. Fathi (Mar) 6–3 6–4	N. Petrova (RUS) d. M. Addou (MAR) 6–1 6–1
5–9 Aug	Leiria, Portugal	5	J. Lido (ESP) d. F. Aldi (ITA) 7–5 6–4	K. Thomas (GBR) d. J. Garcia (COL) 6–2 6–0
6–10 Aug	Domzale, Slovenia	4	S. Wernhart (AUT) d. P. Hubener (GER) 7–5 7–6	D. Hantuchova (SVK) d. K. Basternakova (SVK) 6–3 6–1
11–16 Aug	Taca Bowl, El Salvador	4	L. Magdincev (MKD) d. J. Garcia (DOM) 6–2 6–1	Z. Reyes (MEX) d. P. Castillejos (MEX) 6–2 6–0
11–16 Aug	Limbe, Malawi	5	G. Chidzikwe (ZIM) d. M. Mamoun (EGY) 6–1 6–4	A. Mojzis (RSA) d. N. Kockott (RSA) 6–1 6–2
11–16 Aug	Trinidad, West Indies	5	J-J. Rojer (AHO) d. P. Gordon (JAM) 6–4 6–3	J-K. Wong (USA) d. K. Richards (JAM) 6–4 6–3
11–16 Aug	Tehran, Iran	5	E. Kalantaryan (ARM) d. A. Shahgholi (IRI)	—
11–17 Aug	USTA Grass Court, Philadelphia	3	P. Handoyo (INA) d. R. Kendrick (USA) 7–5 6–2	J. Dokic (AUS) d. A. Molik (AUS) 3–6 6–3 7–6
11–17 Aug	Cairo, Egypt	5	J. Chafai (MAR) d. A. Mc Dade (RSA) 6–3 6–3	N. Petrova (RUS) d. I. Weirich (RSA) 6–1 6–0
12–17 Aug	Pancevo, Yugoslavia	5	I. Kunitcin (RUS) d. M. Lacic (YUG) 6–3 3–6 6–4	D. Jovanovic (YUG) d. S. Hegedis (YUG) 6–2 7–6
13–16 Aug	Wels, Austria	4	V. Mazarakis (GRE) d. S. Wernhart (AUT) 6–2 6–1	J. Schruff (GER) d. B. Pirker (AUT) 6–2 6–0
18–23 Aug	Harare, Zimbabwe	5	G. Chidzikwe (ZIM) d. J. Igbinovia (NGR) 6–1 6–1	A. Mojzis (RSA) d. A. Rafolomanantsiatosik (MAD) 6–7 6–3 6–1
18–23 Aug	Coast Maya World Cup, Mexico	5	R. Echagaray (MEX) d. V. Romero (MEX) 7–5 6–4	P. Palencia (MEX) d. D. Reynolds (MEX) 6–4 6–0
18–24 Aug	USTA Hard Court, Maryland	3	V. Sanon (CIV) d. D. Martin (USA) 6–7 6–3 6–2	W. Laiho (USA) d. L. Kalavaria (USA) 7–5 6–4
18–24 Aug	Giza, Egypt	5	M. Polessnig (AUT) d. J. Chafai (MAR) 6–3 6–2	N. Petrova (RUS) d. S. Ben Youcef (ALG) 6–1 6–1

DATE	*TOURNAMENT*	*GROUP*	*BOYS' SINGLES FINAL*	*GIRLS' SINGLES FINAL*
20–24 Aug	Mera Cup, Poland	5	K. Lewandowicz (POL) d. T. Wawrzyniak (POL) 6–3 6–4	K. Kolodynskaia (BLR) d. A. Plackova (CZE) 4–6 6–3 6–3
25–30 Aug	Damascus, Syria	5	M. Polessnig (AUT) d. M. Dounaev (RUS) 6–3 6–2	S. Ben Naser (ALG) d. N. Bruckner (AUT) 6–3 6–1
25–31 Aug	Canadian Open, Quebec	1	A. Di Pasquale (FRA) d. K. Ziv (ISR) 6–2 6–1	J. Kostanic (CRO) d. E. Dominikovic (AUS) 6–3 6–2
26–30 Aug	BB Cup, Hungary	4	V. Mazarakis (GRE) d. A. Kracman (SLO) 7–5 2–0 RET	E. Fislova (SVK) d. P. Novotnikova (CZE) 6–2 6–1
27–31 Aug	Corfu, Greece	5	A. Mackin (GBR) d. L. Alexiou (GRE) 6–1 6–7 6–2	M. Horvath (HUN) d. D. Kastamoniti (GRE) 6–2 6–1
31 Aug–7 Spt	US Open	A	A. Di Pasquale (FRA) d. W. Whitehouse (RSA) 6–7 6–4 6–1	C. Black (ZIM) d. K. Chevalier (FRA) 6–7 6–1 6–3
1–7 Spt	Beirut, Lebanon	5	J. Chafai (MAR) d. B. Becker (GER) 6–4 2–6 6–1	E. Shahab (EGY) d. N. El Sawaf (EGY) 4–6 6–4 7–6
1–7 Spt	Bucharest, Romania	5	J. Cariov (LTU) d. T-D. Craciun (ROM) 6–1 6–7 7–6	I. Gaspar (ROM) d. B. Berecz (HUN) 6–2 6–2
3–7 Spt	Agrinio, Greece	5	J. Auckland (GBR) d. B. Fulcher (GBR) 6–7 6–3 6–4	H. Farr (GBR) d. A. Barnes (GBR) 6–2 6–2
5–9 Spt	South Pacific Closed, Fiji	B3	J. Rovo (VAN) d. A. Godinet (ASA) 6–2 6–2	D. Godinet (ASA) d. A. Reddy (FIJ) 6–3 6–1
8–14 Spt	Aphrodite Cup, Cyprus	5	O. Tereshchuk (UKR) d. M. Moussa (EGY) 7–6 6–1	L. Kurhajcova (SVK) d. T. Nemeth (HUN) 6–4 3–6 6–3
9–14 Spt	Pelican Bowl, Bulgaria	5	A. Ioujnyi (RUS) d. J. Cariov (LTU) 7–6 6–4	P. Novotnikova (CZE) d. E. Jarichko (BLR) 7–6 6–4
10–14 Spt	Sugar Bowl, USA	2	W-J. Cheng (TPE) d. V. Sanon (CIV) 6–3 6–4	H. Collin (GBR) d. S. Hrozenska (SVK) 1–0 RET
15–20 Spt	Clermont-Ferrand, France	5	O. Ramos (FRA) d. F. Vatin (FRA) 7–6 6–3	O. Sanchez(FRA) d. F. Vieillegrosjean (FRA) 6–4 6–4
15–21 Spt	Port Washington, USA	3	D. Sherwood (GBR) d. S. Dickson (GBR) 7–5 6–7 7–5	K. Krishnamurthy (CAN) d. H. Vieira (ANG) 6–3 6–2
24–28 Spt	Frankfurt, Germany	3	J-C. Faurel (FRA) d. P. Hammer (GER) 6–4 6–4	D. Buschhuter (GER) d. Z. Kucova (SVK) 4–6 6–3 7–5
26–29 Spt	Santiago, Chile	5	D. Perez (ARG) d. S. Uriarte (ARG) 6–4 6–4	C. Seal (GBR) d. J. Smith (GBR) 6–3 6–2
30 Spt–5 Oct	Tao Yuan, Chinese Taipei	5	W-J. Cheng (TPE) d. Y-Y. Lee (KOR) 6–4 6–1	Y-A. Chen (TPE) d. I-T. Wang (TPE) 2–6 6–3 6–1
2–6 Oct	Salomon Melnick, Chile	5	C. Gonzalez (CHI) d. A. Loyola (CHI) 6–2 6–4	A. Artayeta (ARG) d. M. Strussova (SVK) 6–2 7–5
6–11 Oct	Bahia Cup, Brazil	3	J-I. Chela (ARG) d. F. Cardinali (ARG) 6–3 6–0	I. Selyutina (KAZ) d. C. Black (ZIM) 6–3 7–6
6–12 Oct	New Territories, Hong Kong	2	W-J. Cheng (TPE) d. I. Kunitcin (RUS) 6–3 6–4	V. Razzano (FRA) d. L. Baker (NZL) 6–1 6–2
13–19 Oct	Osaka, Japan	A	A. Di Pasquale (FRA) d. R. Vik (CZE) 6–3 6–2	K. Srebotnik (SLO) d. T. Pisnik (SLO) 1–6 6–1 6–0
13–19 Oct	Gerdau-Cooper Cup, Brazil	3	A. Simoni (BRA) d. S. Roitman (ARG) 6–3 6–0	C. Black (ZIM) d. I. Selyutina (KAZ) 6–3 6–3
14–19 Oct	Doha, Qatar	5	B. Behles (GER) d. A. Kedryuk (KAZ) 3–6 6–2 6–3	—
20–26 Oct	Samutprakarn,Thailand	3	D. Udomchoke (THA) d. A-U-H. Qureshi (PAK) 6–3 7–6	R. Hudson (NZL) d. L. Baker (NZL) 6–4 6–2
20–26 Oct	Hawalli, Kuwait	5	A. Kedryuk (KAZ) d. D. Britzen (GER) 6–1 6–2	—
5–9 Nov	Guangzhou, China	4	N. Yan (CHN) d. S. Boretti (NOR) 7–6 6–3	W-N. Liu (CHN) d. Y. Yu (CHN) 6–4 6–4
10–15 Nov	Bandar Seri Begawan, Brunei	4	S. Boretti (NOR) d. K-Y. Yang (KOR) 6–4 7–5	A-N. Lee (KOR) d. S-M. Im (KOR) 6–1 6–1
24–29 Nov	Islamabad, Pakistan	5	A. Kedriouk (KAZ) d. N. Greenhouse (GBR) 6–4 6–2	A. Velts (KAZ) d. L. Naquashbandi (GBR) 3–6 6–2 6–1
1–6 Dec	Yucatan Cup, Mexico	2	J. De Armas (VEN) d. V. Romero (MEX) 6–4 6–2	C. Black (ZIM) d. Z. Gubacsi (HUN) 6–2 6–1
1–6 Dec	Nairobi, Kenya	5	J. Masson (RSA) d. M. Mamoun (EGY) 6–3 6–4	N. Grandin (RSA) d. N. Kockott (RSA) 6–0 6–1
1–7 Dec	Tats Open, Finland	5	T. Vilen (FIN) d. C. Hansen (SWE) 6–3 2–6 6–3	G. Fattakhitdinova (RUS) d. D. Bedanova (CZE) 6–0 6–7
7–5				
2–6 Dec	Kuala Lumpur, Malaysia	3	W. Wong (HKG) d. Y-M. Si (MAS) 6–4 6–7 6–3	K-P. Tong (HKG) d. R. Tezuka (JPN) 6–0 6–3
8–13 Dec	Dar Es Salaam	5	M. Mamoun (EGY) d. J. Masson (RSA) 6–3 6–3	N. Grandin (RSA) d. N. Kockott (RSA) 6–1 6–3
8–13 Dec	Chandigarh, India	5	V. Kannan (IND) d. H-T. Kim (KOR) 6–3 6–3	A-N. Lee (KOR) d. U. Khan (IND) 6–1 6–2
8–14 Dec	Eddie Herr, USA	1	X. Malisse (BEL) d. P. Handoyo (INA) 6–2 6–1	Z. Gubasci (HUN) d. K. Srebotnik (SLO) 6–4 6–1
15–20 Dec	ITF Sunshine Cup, USA	C	France d. Germany 2–1	—
15–20 Dec	ITF Connolly Continental Cup, USA	C	—	Slovenia d. Russia 2–1
21–28 Dec	Orange Bowl, USA	A	N. Massu d. R. Rake (USA) 6–1 6–2	T. Pisnik d. G. Volekova (SVK) 6–2 6–0

Like her two older brothers Byron and Wayne, Cara Black, the world's No. 1 junior, has proved herself a winner. (Stephen Wake)

ITF JUNIOR WORLD RANKINGS 1997

Only those players who qualified for a year-end ranking are listed. The minimum requirements for this were having played six events, three of which were outside their own country and three of which were Group A status.

BOYS' SINGLES

1	Arnaud di Pasquale	FRA
2	Daniel Elsner	GER
3	Westley Whitehouse	RSA
4	Luis Horna	PER
5	Nicolas Massu	CHI
6	Julien Jeanpierre	FRA
7	Rodolfo Rake	USA
8	Robin Vik	CZE
9	Kobi Ziv	ISR
10	Xavier Malisse	BEL
11	Olivier Rochus	BEL
12	Fernando Gonzalez	CHI
13	Wei-Jen Cheng	TPE
14	Florian Allgauer	ITA
15	Valentin Sanon	CIV
16	Jean-Rene Lisnard	FRA
17	Lleyton Hewitt	AUS
18	Brian Vahaly	USA
19	Andy Ram	ISR
20	Olivier Levant	FRA

GIRLS' SINGLES

1	Cara Black	ZIM
2	Tina Pisnik	SLO
3	Katarina Srebotnik	SLO
4	Melissa Middleton	USA
5	Gabriela Volekova	SVK
6	Justine Henin	BEL
7	Irina Selyutina	KAZ
8	Zsofia Gubacsi	HUN
9	Jessica Lehnhoff	USA
10	Jelena Kostanic	CRO
11	Catalina Castano	COL
12	Kildine Chevalier	FRA
13	Evie Dominikovic	AUS
14	Sarah Taylor	USA
15	Bryanne Stewart	AUS
16	Akiko Morigami	JPN
17	Andrea Sebova	SVK
18	Nikola Hubnerova	CZE
19	Jitka Schonfeldova	CZE
20	Elena Dementieva	RUS

BOYS' DOUBLES

1	Nicolas Massu	CHI
2	Fernando Gonzalez	CHI
3	Luis Horna	PER
4	Jaco Van Der Westhuizen	RSA
5	David Sherwood	GBR
6	Jose De Armas	VEN
7	Julien Jeanpierre	FRA
8	Westley Whitehouse	RSA
9	Jerome Haehnel	FRA
10	Jean-Rene Lisnard	FRA
11	Jaroslav Levinsky	CZE
12	Lovro Zovko	CRO
13	Lleyton Hewitt	AUS
14	Peter Handoyo	INA
15	Simon Dickson	GBR
16	Arnaud di Pasquale	FRA
17	Marwan Ziwar	EGY
18	Nathan Healey	AUS
19	Olivier Levant	FRA
20	Robin Vik	CZE

GIRLS' DOUBLES

1=	Cara Black	ZIM
1=	Irina Selyutina	KAZ
3	Katarina Srebotnik	SLO
4	Marissa Irvin	USA
5	Tina Pisnik	SLO
6	Gabriela Volekova	SVK
7	Maja Matevzic	SLO
8	Ivana Visic	CRO
9	Andrea Sebova	SVK
10	Bruna Colosio	BRA
11	Zsofia Gubacsi	HUN
12	Kildine Chevalier	FRA
13	Silvia Urickova	SVK
14	Tina Hergold	SLO
15	Elena Dementieva	RUS
16	Jasmin Wohr	GER
17	Paola Palencia	MEX
18	Jelena Kostanic	CRO
19	Cristina Popescu	CAN
20	Anastasia Myskina	RUS

(Left) *Frank Puncec of South Africa, the Men's 45 Singles World Champion.* (ITF)

(Below) *Led by Gardnar Mulloy himself (second from left) the United States retained the Cup named after the former US Davis Cup player and US national doubles champion.* (ITF)

ITF Veterans Tennis

Tony Gathercole

It can never be said that the Veterans Game is stationary, either in the number of events played, numbers of players taking part or in the venues that host the ITF Veteran Team Competitions and World Championships. This does not imply that the venues themselves are on the move, more that the selected sites are different each year and situated in all four corners of the globe. This year was termed 'travel year' by many countries who journeyed to South Africa, Australia and New Zealand.

The year began in April with Team Competitions being held in Canberra, Adelaide, Melbourne, Hobart and Hamilton, followed by the World Championships in Newcastle, New South Wales. The entries for these events were not affected by the distance. Ninety-eight teams from twenty-five countries competed in the nine Team Competitions. There were one hundred and forty-four local Australians (including our oldest competitor, 86-year-old Arthur Matthews) among a total of three hundred and ninety-seven competitors for the ten singles and ten doubles World Championships' events.

This was the first time New Zealand had hosted an ITF Veteran event, but they have sent representative teams to compete in other countries on many occasions. The Von Cramm and Britannia Cups were treated to some remarkable Maori hospitality at the Waikato Tennis Club in Hamilton.

Memorial Drive Tennis Club, Adelaide hosted the Alice Marble and Crawford Cups, which commenced the day after the Davis Cup tie between Australia and the Czech Republic. Co-ordination with Tennis Australia enabled the 20 teams to march onto centre court during the interval between the reverse singles in the tie, in front of 4,000 spectators, the largest crowd that has seen a gathering of ITF Veterans.

Australian hospitality has always been a feature welcomed by overseas teams and this year was no exception; reports from all teams indicated a good time was had by all. Our Australian hosts were so delighted not to have to travel abroad again this year, that they are already endeavouring to entice everyone back 'down-under' sooner rather than later.

In an effort to provide some social intercourse, two Team Competitions were scheduled at one venue wherever possible, if the court facilities allowed. This proved to be very popular and it is hoped to continue this formula in the future.

The United States' teams continued to produce impressive performances, retaining the Von Cramm (Men's 60) and Britannia (Men's 65) Cups in Hamilton; the Bitsy Grant Cup (Men's 75) in Hobart; the Gardnar Mulloy Cup (Men's 80) in Melbourne; and the Alice Marble Cup (Women's 60) in Adelaide. The Americans also defeated the French team, holders of the Maureen Connolly Cup (Women's 55) for the past two years, in Canberra.

The Austrian quartet of Peter Pokorny, Hans Gradischnig, Laci Legenstein and Oskar Jirkovsky retained both the Austria (Men's 55) and Crawford (Men's 70) Cups respectively. Great Britain were successful in defence of the Kitty Godfree Cup (Women's 65) for the second year in succession.

The World Championships held on the artificial grass courts of District Park, Newcastle, New South Wales, attracted many former Davis Cup players including Gardnar Mulloy (USA); Laci Legenstein (AUT); Lorne Main (CAN); Mabrouk Mohammed-Ali (EGY) and John Barry (NZL), with Federation Cups players Rosie Darmon (FRA) and Heide Orth (GER), together with former champion Judy Dalton (AUS) – Wimbledon singles finalist in 1968

The Veterans Tennis Association of Australia were delighted when Judy Dalton won the Women's 60, Beverley Rae the Women's 65 and Bob Howes the Men's 55. The remaining singles results were evenly distributed – Russell Seymour the Men's 65, Robert Sherman the Men's 75 and Alex Swetka the Men's 80 for the USA; Heide Orth and Klaus Fuhrmann were successful in the Women's 55 and Men's 60 respectively for Germany. Twinx Rogers won the Women's 70 for South Africa, while Laci Legenstein won his first World Championships' Singles, the Men's 70, for Austria. The event was a huge success and tournament director, Barry Plucknett and his team are to be congratulated on their hard work.

Since the readmission of South Africa to international tennis, Martin Gering, Chairman of their Veterans Tennis Association, together with Jean Hubert, Lorna Krog and their organising committees, had been enthusiastically preparing for the younger age group events (35-50 years) which were held in their country for the first time.

The six Team Competitions produced a total of eighty-seven entries from twenty-five countries with venues again hosting two events where possible. The Dubler (Men's 45) and Young (Women's 40) Cups were held at the Groenkloof Stadium, Pretoria; while the Margaret Court (Women's 45) and Maria Esther Bueno (Women's 50) Cups were held at Pretoria University. The Italia Cup (Men's 35) was held at the famous Wanderers' Club in Johannesburg and the Fred Perry Cup (Men's 50) was held in the spectacular surroundings of the Sun City complex.

These events also attracted many former top players including US Open quarter-finalist Jairo Velasco of Spain and former Wimbledon mixed doubles champion Jeremy Bates of Great Britain. The women's entry included Renata Vojtischek (née Tomanova-Roth) representing Germany, who reached the finals of the Australian and French Opens in 1976. The year before, she had teamed up with Martina Navratilova to bring Czechoslovakia its first Federation Cup trophy. Other outstanding players included France's Gail Lovera who reached four Grand Slam quarter-finals, her compatriot Brigitte Simon-Glinel, French Open semi-finalist in 1978, and Trudy Groenman of the Netherlands.

The honours for these events were more evenly distributed than the Group B events. For the second year running Australia retained the Maria Esther Bueno Cup, together with the Dubler Cup after a break of 22 years and Spain were victorious in the Fred Perry Cup for the first time since its inception. The USA retained the Margaret Court and Young Cups and only just managed to retain the Italia Cup, after being two match points down to a very strong Latvian team in the deciding doubles match in the semi-final. Great Britain also pushed them to a deciding doubles in the final, after Jeremy Bates, playing for the first time for Great Britain, had defeated World Champion, Greg Neuhart 6–2 6–4 in the Number 1 Singles spot.

The World Championships at the Wanderers' Club in Johannesburg, also producing some exciting tennis of a very high standard, with 281 players in total competing in eight singles and eight doubles events.

Despite a strong international entry, the South Africans emerged as one of the most successful contingents with two singles titles (Frank Puncec winning the Men's 45 and Rita Theron the Women's 40), a doubles title and several other finalists in both singles and doubles. Considering it was the first time South Africa had emerged with more than a single title, this was an impressive performance indeed. Only the United States, with two singles titles and two doubles titles were more successful than the host nation.

The Australians certainly dominated this year's World Championships' doubles events, with victory in the Women's 45, 50, 55 and 60 as well as the Men's 45 and 55 events. Carol Campling and Elizabeth Craig-Allan are to be congratulated on retaining their fifth doubles title in succession. Bruce Osborne, playing with Pierre Godfroid (BEL), also won the Men's 40, while Gordon Henley, paired with Alex Swetka (USA), won the Men's 80 competition.

Women's 40 Singles World Champion, Barbara Vojtischek of Germany. (ITF)

ITF VETERAN WORLD RANKINGS 1997 (As at 5 January 1998)

MEN

35 AGE GROUP

1	Greg Neuhart (USA)	540
2	Brett Edwards (AUS)	510
3=	Alain Moracchini (FRA)	420
3=	Gerado Sueyro (ARG)	420
5	Pedro Rebolledo (CHI)	400
6	Mike Tammen (USA)	390
7	Alejandro Cerundolo (ARG)	360
8	Kobus Visagie (RSA)	304
9	Nicholas Reimer (ARG)	300
10	Pierre Godfroid (BEL)	295

40 AGE GROUP

1	Pierre Godfroid (BEL)	460
2	Julio Goes (BRA)	450
3=	Enrique Grimolizzi (ARG)	420
3=	Bruce Osborne (AUS)	420
5=	John Austin (USA)	400
5=	Givaldo Barbosa (BRA)	400
5=	Mark Vines (USA)	400
8	Graham Rhodes (RSA)	340
9=	Jeff Davis (USA)	300
9=	Matt Wooldridge (USA)	300

45 AGE GROUP

1	Frank Puncec (RSA)	640
2=	Max Bates (AUS)	480
2=	Lubomir Petrov (BUL)	480
2=	Andrew Rae (AUS)	480
5=	Julio Lavagno (ARG)	400
5=	Pavel Sevcik (GER)	400
7	Marco Botteri (ITA)	360
8	Frank Briscoe (RSA)	326
9	Alfonso Pereira (BRA)	324
10	Wesley Jackson (USA)	320

50 AGE GROUP

1	Jairo Velasco (ESP)	575
2	Michael Mijuca (GER)	510
3	Peter Peczely (HUN)	480
4=	Rene Bortolani (SUI)	400
4=	John Chalder (AUS)	400
4=	Brian Cheney (USA)	400
4=	Benns de Jel (NED)	400
4=	Julian Ganzabal (ARG)	400
4=	Daniel Harms (ARG)	400
10=	David Bohannon (USA)	360
10=	Hannes Futterknecht (AUT)	360
10=	Richard Johnson (USA)	360
10=	Klaus Kuhlmey (GER)	360

55 AGE GROUP

1	Robert Howes (AUS)	540
2	Peter Pokorny (AUT)	520
3	Max Senior (AUS)	510
4=	Roberto Aubone (ARG)	480
4=	Jaime Pinto-Bravo (CHI)	480
6	Bernd Reinholz (GER)	450
7=	Rob Cadwallader (USA)	420
7=	Bodo Nitsche (GER)	420
9	Iouri Khokhlov (RUS)	400
10=	Leland Housman (USA)	360
10=	Stasys Labanauskas (LTU)	360
10=	Mervin Watson (CAN)	360

60 AGE GROUP

1	Klaus Fuhrmann (GER)	600
2	Robert Duesler (USA)	510
3	Juan Cruder (ARG)	420
4	Les Dodson (USA)	400
5	Ollie Smith (AUS)	370
6=	Peter Froelich (AUS)	360
6=	Ricardo Narcio (MEX)	360
6=	Jim Perley (USA)	360
9=	Yves Doncieux (FRA)	340
9=	James Nelson (USA)	340

65 AGE GROUP

1	Russell Seymour (USA)	600
2	Lorne Main (CAN)	510
3=	Hans Jell (AUT)	480
3=	Heino Krampe (GER)	480
5=	Eduardo Polledo (ARG)	420
5=	Ernesto Rios (ARG)	420
7	Fernand Brun (FRA)	400
8	John O'Brien (AUS)	384
9	Rene Marik (CZE)	360
10=	Alan Bailey (AUS)	340
10=	Hans Walter Ovenhausen (GER)	340

70 AGE GROUP

1	Laci Legenstein (AUT)	600
2	Fred Kovaleski (USA)	510
3	Adalbert Hussmuller (GER)	480
4=	Andres Funes (ARG)	420
4=	Oskar Jirkovsky (AUT)	420
4=	Rudolf Kowelka (AUT)	420
4=	Laszlo Lenart (HUN)	420
8	Harward Hillier (AUS)	400
9	Lionel Matton (FRA)	360
10	Jack Dunn (USA)	320

75 AGE GROUP

1	Robert Sherman (USA)	600
2	Neville Halligan (AUS)	510
3=	Jose Heighes (PER)	480
3=	Bernhard Kempa (GER)	480
5=	Cees Marre (NED)	420
5=	Mischa Stachowitsch (AUT)	420
7	Ellis Williamson (USA)	346
8	Tom Brown (USA)	340
9=	James O'Connor (USA)	336
9=	Andreas Stolpa (GER)	336

80 AGE GROUP

1	Alex Swetka (USA)	600
2	Gordon Henley (AUS)	510
3=	Friedrich Klein (USA)	420
3=	Dan Miller (USA)	420
5=	Irving Converse (USA)	324
5=	Reg Smith (GBR)	324
7=	Georg Hunger (GER)	300
7=	Gardnar Mulloy (USA)	300
7=	William Parsons (USA)	300
10=	Claude de Montgolfier (FRA)	216
10=	Bernhard Flakus (GER)	216
10=	Robert Mann (BEL)	216

WOMEN

35 AGE GROUP

1	Tracy Houk (USA)	600
2	Francesca Ciardi (ITA)	480
3	Amanda Chaplin (AUS)	420
4	Laura Fernandez Thomas (ARG)	360
5	Alet Vorster (RSA)	345
6	Patricia Medrado (BRA)	320
7=	Helena Abreu (BRA)	300
7=	Susanne Turi (HUN)	300
9	Ellie Compton (USA)	280
10	Teresa Stochel (POL)	235

40 AGE GROUP

1	Renata Vojtischek (GER)	600
2	Gabriela Leinen (GER)	480
3=	Eugenvjc Birukova (ITA)	420
3=	Gloria Moreno Quintana (ARG)	420
5	Elizabeth Villani (BRA)	384
6	Lynette Vermaak (RSA)	378
7	Ann Etheridge (USA)	370
8	Rosangela Fritelli (BRA)	360
9	Tina Karwasky (USA)	340
10	Roswitha Woltsche (AUT)	336

45 AGE GROUP

1	Rita Theron (RSA)	520
2	Danuta Szwaj (GER)	480
3	Tina Karwasky (USA)	465
4=	Isabella Enz (SUI)	420
4=	Wendy Gilchrist (AUS)	420
6	Kerry Young (USA)	408
7	Emma Swanepoel (RSA)	390
8=	Radomila Martinicova (CZE)	360
8=	Lilian Pelz-Petow (USA)	360
10	Leyla Musalem (CHI)	340

50 AGE GROUP

1	Marie Pinterova (HUN)	600
2	Trish Faulkner (USA)	510
3	Heide Orth (GER)	480
4	Elizabeth Craig-Allan (AUS)	465
5	Renate Schroder (GER)	450
6=	Ana Maria Arias (CHI)	420
6=	Marta Galli (ARG)	420
6=	Mariana Karolyi (HUN)	420
9	Carol Campling (AUS)	324
10	Marietjie Viljoen (RSA)	304

55 AGE GROUP

1	Heide Orth (GER)	600
2	Charleen Hillebrand (USA)	510
3	Renate Mayer-Zdralek (GER)	480
4	Dawn Martin (AUS)	384
5=	Cathie Anderson (USA)	360
5=	Renate Niesler (GER)	360
5=	Ana Maria Piotti (ARG)	360
5=	Suella Steel (USA)	360
9	Elsa Colistro (URU)	340
10=	Lynne Nette (AUS)	300
10=	Susana Perez (ARG)	300

60 AGE GROUP

1	Elisabeth Perusch (AUT)	480
2=	Judy Dalton (AUS)	465
2=	Dorothy Matthiessen (USA)	465
4	Francisca Gaspar (ARG)	420
5	Margaret Robinson (AUS)	390
6	Brigitte Jung (GER)	384
7=	Ilse Michael (GER)	360
7=	Nancy Reed (USA)	360
7=	Annemarie Theyson (GER)	360
10=	Marielle Gallay (FRA)	340
10=	Jaqueline Lecaillon (FRA)	340

65 AGE GROUP

1	Beverley Rae (AUS)	535
2	Rita Lauder (GBR)	490
3=	Magdalena Jauch (GER)	480
3=	Clelia Mazzoleni (ITA)	480
5	Louise Owen (USA)	384
6	Monique Kyburz (SUI)	360
7	Lee Burling (USA)	346
8	Mary Boswell (USA)	340
9=	Louise Russ (USA)	300
9=	Erika Steinle (GER)	300

70 AGE GROUP

1	Kathe Sorge (GER)	510
2	Eva Zilakova (CZE)	480
3	Elaine Mason (USA)	420
4=	Reni Portscheller (GER)	360
4=	Pinuccia Russo (ITA)	360
6	Ingeborg Haas (GER)	340
7=	Doris Clark (USA)	300
7=	Dorothy Knode (USA)	300
7=	Maximiliane Marczewski (GER)	300
10	Jutta Apel (GER)	240

National Associations and Voting Rights

Abbreviations

T = Telephone Number **FAX** = Telecopier Number

The date given in parenthesis denotes the foundation date of the National Tennis Association where known.

Members with voting rights (131)

ALGERIA – ALG (1962) **(Votes 1)**

Fédération Algérienne de Tennis
Centre des Fédérations Sportives
Cité Olympique B P 88 El Biar Algers 16030
T (213) 2 92 29 **FAX** (213) 2 92 46 13
Pres: Dr Mohamed Bouabdallah
Sec: Miss Naciba Seddik

ANDORRA – AND (1986) **(Votes 1)**

Federación Andorrana de Tenis Sant Antoni
C/Verge del Pilar 5 3er Desp. no. 10
Andorra la Vella
T (376) 861381 **FAX** (376) 868381
Pres: Mr Antoni Ricart **Sec:** Mr Joan Grau

ANTIGUA – ANT (1982) **(Votes 1)**

The Antigua and Barbuda Tennis Association
PO Box 2758 St John's Antigua
T (1-809) 461 3708 (Pres)/462 8341 (Sec)
FAX (1-809) 462 4811
Pres: Mr John Maginley **Sec:** Mr Elijah Amstrong

ARGENTINA – ARG (1921) **(Votes 7)**

Asociación Argentina de Tenis
Avda San Juan 1307 1148 Buenos Aires
T (54) 1 304 2256/2470/2477/2483
FAX (54) 1 305 0296
Pres: Mr Enrique Morea
Sec: Mr Roberto Fernandaz

ARMENIA – ARM (1940) **(Votes 1)**

Armenian Tennis Association
Tennis School of Armenia Yerevan 375082
T (3742) 565665/345995
FAX (3742) 151721/151069
Pres: Mr Hrachik Israelian **Sec:** Mr Hajk Kirakossian

AUSTRALIA – AUS (1904) **(Votes 12)**

Tennis Australia Private Bag 6060 Richmond South
3121 Victoria
T (61) 3 9286 1177 **FAX** (61) 3 9650 2743
Pres: Mr Geoff Pollard
Tennis Operations Mgr: Mr Mike Daws
Tennis Mgr: Barry McMillan

AUSTRIA – AUT (1902) **(Votes 5)**

Osterreichischer Tennisverband
Haekelstrasse 33 1235 Vienna
T (43 1) 865 4506/1235 **FAX** (43 1) 865 9806
Pres: Dr Ernst Wolner **Sec:** Mr Peter Nader

AZERBAIJAN – AZE (1956) **(Votes 1)**

Azerbaijan Tennis Federation Flat 46
44/46 B Madjedov Str Baku 370002
T (994) 12 395172 **FAX** (994) 12 394023
Pres: Mr Nazim Ibragimov
Sec: Mr Djavanshir Ibragimov

BAHAMAS – BAH (1961) **(Votes 1)**

The Bahamas Lawn Tennis Association
PO Box N-10169 Nassau
T (1 242) 363 2930 (Pres)/363 2930 (Sec)
FAX (1 242) 327 0808
E-MAIL reb@bahamas.net.bs
or capkit@100jamz.com (Pres)
Pres: Mr Kit Spencer **Sec:** Mr R E Barnes

BAHRAIN – BRN (1981) **(Votes 1)**

Bahrain Lawn Tennis Federation
P O Box 26985 Bahrain
T (973) 687236 **FAX** (973) 781 533
Pres: Shaikh Ahmed Al Kalifa
Sec: Dr Mohammad Saleh Abdul Latif

BANGLADESH – BAN (1972) **(Votes 1)**

Bangladesh Tennis Federation Tennis
Complex Ramna Green Dhaka 1000
T (880) 2 506650/866688 (Sec)
FAX (880) 2 966 2711
Pres: Mr Syed A F Chowdhury
Sec: Mr Masud H Jamaly

BARBADOS – BAR (1948) **(Votes 1)**

Barbados Lawn Tennis Association
PO Box 615c Bridgetown
T (1-246) 426 6215 (Pres) 428 6453 (Sec)
FAX (1-246) 429 4854/427 8317
E-MAIL symmonds@ndl.net
Pres: Mr Raymond Ford **Sec:** Mrs Jean Date

BELARUS – BLR (1990) (Votes 1)

Tennis Association of the Republic of Belarus
Masherov Avenue 63 Minsk 220035
T (375) 172 271735/269271/269374
FAX (375) 172 279823
Pres: Mr Seimon Kagan **Sec** Mr Georgi Matsuk

BELGIUM – BEL (1902) (Votes 5)

Fédération Royale Belge de Tennis
Galerie de la Porte Louise 203 (8 sème étage)
1050 Brussels
T (32) 2 513 29 27
FAX (32) 2 513 79 50
Pres: Mr Pierre de Keghel
Secs: Mr Walter Goethals and Mr Franz Lemaire

BENIN – BEN (1963) (Votes 1)

Fédération Beninoise de Lawn Tennis
BP 2709 Cotonou I
T (229) 315153/312149
FAX (229) 311252
Pres: Mr Edgar-Yves Monnou
Sec: Mr Mohamed Bio Tchane

BERMUDA – BER (1994) (Votes 1)

Bermuda Lawn Tennis Association
PO Box HM 341 Hamilton HMBX
T (1441) 296 0834
FAX (1441) 295 3056
Pres: Mr David Lambert
Administrator: Mr Joseph Morley
Sec: Ms Airlie Arton

BOLIVIA – BOL (1937) (Votes 1)

Federación Boliviana de Tenis
Calle René Moreno 685 Casilla No 1041 Santa Cruz
T (591) 336 8625 **FAX** (591) 336 8625
Pres: Mr Edmundo Rodriguez
Sec: Mr Johnny Grinstein

BOSNIA/HERZEGOVINA – BIH (1950) (Votes 1)

Tennis Association of Bosnia and Herzegovina
c/o President St Marsala Tita 7/1 71 000 Sarajevo
c/o Secretary St Slavka Micica 9 75000 Tuzla
T (387) 71663514/75251439
FAX (387) 75251439/75282565
Pres: Mr Tarik Kupusovic
Sec Gen: Mr Haris Barucija

BOTSWANA – BOT (1994) (Votes 1)

Botswana Tennis Association
PO Box 1174 Gabarone
T/FAX (267) 373193
Pres: Mr Khaulani Fichani
Sec: Miss Gaobolae Seleka

BRAZIL – BRA (1956) (Votes 7)

Confederacao Brasileira de Tenis
Av Paulista Nr. 326 – 2° – cj 26/27
01310 – 902 Sao Paulo
T (55) 11 283 1788
FAX (55) 11 283 0768
Pres: Mr Nelson Nastas
Sec: Mr Carlos Alberto Martelotte

BRUNEI DARUSSALAM – BRU (1967) (Votes 1)

Brunei Darussalam Lawn Tennis Association
PO Box 859 Pejabat Pos Gadong
Bandar Seri Bagawan 3018
T/FAX (673) 2 381205
Pres: Mr Abdu Bakar Abdul Rahman
Sec: Mr Tom Butcher

BULGARIA – BUL (1930) (Votes 1)

Bulgarian Tennis Federation
bul. Vasil Levski 75 Sofia 1040
T (359) 2 963 1310 **FAX** (359) 2 981 5728/3377
Pres: Mr Krassimir Angarski
Sec: Mr Chavdar Ganev

CAMEROON – CMR (1966) (Votes 1)

Fédération Camerounaise de Lawn Tennis
BP 13001 Douala
T (237) 370790/370795 **FAX** (237) 376218
Pres: Mr Gilbert Kadji
Sec: Mr Victor Momha

CANADA – CAN (1920) (Votes 7)

Tennis Canada 3111 Steeles Avenue West
Downsview Ontario M3J 3H2 Canada
T (1) 416 665 9777 **FAX** (1) 416 665 9017
Pres: Mr Robert H Moffatt
Exec Sec: Mrs Kim Ali

CHILE – CHI (1920) (Votes 5)

Federación de Tenis de Chile Avda. José Joaquín
Prieto No 4040 Paradero 7 Gran Avenida Santiago
T (56) 2 554 0068/0154/0224/0319
FAX (56) 2 554 1078
Pres: Mr Carlos Herrera Arredondo
Sec: Mr Guillermo Toral Bustamante

CHINA, P R of – CHN (1953) (Votes 1)

Tennis Association of the People's Rep. of China
9 Tiyuguan Road Beijing 100061
T/FAX (86) 10 6711 4096/5858
Pres: Mr Lu Zhengchao **Sec:** Mr Zhang Xiaoning

CHINESE TAIPEI – TPE (1973) (Votes 3)

Chinese Taipei Tennis Ass Room 1108
11th Floor 20 Chu Lun St Taipei
T (886) 2 772 0298 **FAX** (886) 2 771 1696
Pres: Mr P Y Young
Sec General: Mr Samuel Mu

COLOMBIA – COL (1932) (Votes 5)

Federación Colombiana de Tenis
Calle 19 No. 3–10 Ofic Edificio B Barichara
402 Bogota
T (571) 282 3084/282 7294/283 0618
FAX (571) 341 5643/283 2461
Pres: Dr Ricardo Mejia Pelaez
Sec: Mr Arturo Rojas

CONGO – CGO (1962) (Votes 1)

Fédération Congolaise de Lawn Tennis BP 550
Brazzaville
T (242) 821965 **FAX** (242) 825656
Pres: Mr Germain Ickonga Akindou
Sec: Mr Antoine Ouabonzi

COSTA RICA – CRC (1960) (Votes 1)

Federación Costarricense de Tenis
PO Box 326-1005 Barrio Mexico San José
T (506) 256 5563/3869 **FAX** (506) 256 2182
Pres: Dr Rafael Porras Madrigal
Sec: Ana Lorena Vega

COTE D'IVOIRE – CIV (1969) (Votes 1)

Fédération Ivoirienne de Tennis
01 BP V 273 Abidjan 01
T (225) 441354/440050 **FAX** (225) 447434
Pres: Mr Jean-Claude Delafosse
Gen Sec: Mr Gadjro

CROATIA – CRO (1922) (Votes 5)

Croatian Tennis Association
HR – 10 000 Zagreb Gundulieeva 3
T (385) 1 481 1968 **FAX** (385) 1 481 1256
Pres: Mr Suad Rizvanbegovic
Gen Sec: Mr Dubravko Lipnjak

CUBA – CUB (1925) (Votes 1)

Federación Cubana de Tenis de Campo
Calle 13 NR 601 Esq AC Vedado Habana 4
T (53) 7 972121/973011
FAX (53) 7 335310/331914/330945
Pres: Mr Rolando Martinez Perez
Sec: Mr M O Rodriguez

CYPRUS – CYP (1951) (Votes 1)

Cyprus Tennis Federation
Ionos Str 20 PO Box 3931 Nicosia
T (357) 2 366822/450875 **FAX** (357) 2 458016
Pres: Mr Philios Christodoulou
Sec: Mr Demetris Metaxas

CZECH REPUBLIC – CZE (1906) (Votes 7)

Czech Tennis Association
Ostrov Stvanice 38 170 00 Prague 7
C Sportsvaz, Prague
T (420 2) 2 231 1270 (Pres) 481 0238 (Sec)
FAX (420 2) 248 10276 (Pres) 248 10301 (Sec)
Pres: Mr Jan Kodes **Gen Sec:** Mr Karel Papousek

DENMARK – DEN (1920) (Votes 5)

Dansk Tennis Forbund Idraettens Hus
Broendby Stadion 20 DK- 2605 Broendby
T (45) 43 262660 **FAX** (45) 43 262670
Pres: Mr Peter Schak Larsen
Gen Sec: Mr Niels Persson

DJIBOUTI – DJI (1978) (Votes 1)

Fédération Djiboutienne de Tennis
Rue Pierre-Pascal B P 728 Djibouti
T (253) 352536 **FAX** (253) 351363/353363
Pres: Mr Houmed Houssein
Gen Sec: Mr Bourhan Daoud

DOMINICAN REPUBLIC – DOM (1929) (Votes 1)

Federación Dominicana de Tenis
Club Deportivo Naco Calle Central Ens Naco
Santo Domingo
T (1-809) 549 5031/567 1055
FAX (1-809) 565 0835 (Pres)/549 5131.
Pres: Mr Gonzalo Mejia **Sec:** Mr J Ravelo

ECUADOR – ECU (1967) (Votes 3)

Federación Ecuatoriana de Tenis
Oficio Multi Parqueo Piso 7 Junín
214 y Pedro Carbo Guayaquil
T (593) 4 518 599/597/604
FAX (593) 513 995/514 046 (Pres)
Pres: Mr Jamie Guzmán Maspons
Sec: Mrs Nuria Guzmán de Ferretti

EGYPT – EGY (1920) (Votes 5)

Egyptian Tennis Federation
13 Kasr el Nil Street Cairo
T (20) 2 5747697/5740973
FAX (20) 2 5753235
Pres: Mr Mohammed Halawa
Vice Pres: Mr Mohammed El Sokary

EL SALVADOR – ESA (1949) (Votes 1)

Federación Salvadoreña de Tenis
Apartado Postal (01) 110 San Salvador
T (503) 278 7832/8069 or 226 3832 (Pres)
FAX (503) 278 8087/225 6366
Pres: Mr Enrique Molins Rubio
Sec: Mr Jose Martinez

ESTONIA – EST (1932) (Votes 1)

Estonian Tennis Association
Herne Street 38 EE0001 Tallinn
T/FAX (37 2) 641 0404
Pres: Mr Jaak Ulman **Sec:** Mr Mati Kuum
Ass Dir: Mr Tonu Ottoson

ETHIOPIA – ETH (1972) (Votes 1)

Ethiopian Tennis Federation
Attn: Mr Teklemariam Zemichael,
PO Box 31902 Addis Ababa
T (251)1 513007/516324
FAX (251) 1 514144
Pres: Col. Mohammed Abduslam
Sec: Mr Teklemairam Zemicail

FINLAND – FIN (1911) (Votes 3)

Suomen Tennisliitto Varikkotie 4 SF-00900 Helsinki
T (358) 9 338122/338023 (Sec)
FAX (358) 9 331105
Pres: Mr Jukka Roiha **Sec:** Mr Eero Kiuttu

FRANCE – FRA (1920) (Votes 12)

Fédération Française de Tennis
Stade Roland Garros 2 Avenue Gordon Bennett
75016 Paris
T (33) 1 47 43 48 00
FAX (33) 1 47 43 04 94
and (33) 1 47 43 40 37 (Pres)
Pres: Mr Christian Bîmes **Sec:** Mr Jacques Dürr

GEORGIA – GEO (1992) (Votes 1)

Georgian Tennis Federation
K Marjanishvili St 29 Tbilisi
T (995 32) 952 781/953 800
FAX (995 32) 952 781/953 892
Pres: Mr Merab Adeishvili
Vice Pres: Mr Emzar Zenaishvili
Sec: Mr Zurab Katsharava

GERMANY – GER (1902) (Votes 12)

Deutscher Tennis Bund eV
Hallerstrasse 89 20149 Hamburg
T (49) 40 411780 **FAX** (49) 40 411 78 222
Pres: Dr Claus Stauder
Exec Dir: Mr Günter Sanders

GHANA – GHA (1909) (Votes 1)

Ghana Tennis Association
PO Box T-95 Sports Stadium Post Office Accra
T (233) 21 667267/303502
FAX (233) 21 667267
Pres: Mr Stanley-Owusu
Gen Sec: Mr George Billings Awuakye

GREAT BRITAIN – GBR (1888) (Votes 12)

Lawn Tennis Association The Queen's Club
West Kensington London, W14 9EG
T (44) 71 381 7000 **FAX** (44) 71 381 5965
Pres: Mr Geoffrey Cass
Chief Exec: Mr John Crowther
Sec: Mr John C U James

GREECE – GRE (1938) (Votes 3)

Hellenic Tennis Federation Athens Tennis Complex
Olympic Stadium
37 Kifissias St 15123 Maroussi Athens
T (30) 1 6852511/512/513 **FAX** (30) 1 6831865
Pres: Mr Spyros Zannias **Sec:** Mr Panagiotis Kontos

GUATEMALA – GUA (1948) (Votes 1)

Federación Nacionale de Tenis de Guatemala
Section 1551
PO Box 02-5339 Miami FL 33102-5339
T/FAX (502) 331 0261
Pres: Mr Julio Henkle **Sec:** Mr Manuel Lucero

HAITI – HAI (1950) (Votes 1)

Fédération Haïtienne de Tennis
PO Box 1442 Port-au-Prince
T (509) 4 50703/51461/51462
FAX (509) 4 51451/51461
E-MAIL abhardware@compa.net
Pres: Mr Michel Dominique **Sec:** Ms Josette Nazon

HONDURAS – HON (1989) (Votes 1)

Federación Hondureña de Tenis
PO Box 30152 Toncontin Comayaguela MDC
T (504) 39 68 90/32 11 47 **FAX** (504) 39 68 87
Vice Pres: Mr Humberto Rodriguez
Sec: Mr Rodulio Perdomo

HONG KONG – HKG (1909) (Votes 1)

Hong Kong Tennis Association Ltd
Room 1021 Sports House 1 Stadium Bath
So Kon Po Causeway Bay
T (852) 2 504 8266 **FAX** (852) 2 894 8704
Pres: Dr Philip Kwok **Sec:** Mr Herman Hu

HUNGARY – HUN (1907) (Votes 5)

Magyar Tenisz Szovetseg
Dozsa Gyorgy ut I-3 H-1143 Budapest
T (36) 1 252 6687/183 2114
FAX (36) 1 251 0107
Pres: Dr Janos Berenyi **Sec:** Mr Péter Sándor

ICELAND – ISL (1987) (Votes 1)

Icelandic Tennis Association
Ithrotamidstoedinni i Laugardal 104 Reykjavik
T (354) 5 813377
FAX (354) 5 888848
Pres: Mr Stefan Eggertsson
Sec: Mr Hjalmar Aoalsteinsson

INDIA – IND (1920) (Votes 9)

All India Tennis Association DLTA Tennis Complex
Africa Avenue New Delhi 110 029
T (91) 11 617 9062/617 9084
FAX (91) 11 617 3159
Pres: Mr Raj Khanna **Gen Sec:** Mr R D Desai

INDONESIA – INA (1935) (Votes 5)

Indonesian Tennis Association
Gelora Senayan Tennis Stadium Jakarta 10270
T (62) 21 5710298/5707203
FAX (62) 21 5700l57
Pres: Mr Sarwono Kusumaatmadja
Gen Sec: Mr Zainal Abidin

IRAN – IRI (1937) (Votes 3)

Tennis Federation of Islamic Republic of Iran
PO Box 15815-1881 Tehran
T/FAX (98) 21 8844731
Pres: Mr Seyed Lankarani
Sec: Mr Hamid Reza Shayesteh Zad

IRAQ – IRQ (1959) (Votes 1)

Iraqi Tennis Federation
PO Box 8200 Saliheya Baghdad
T (964) 1 7748261 **FAX:** (964) 1 7728424
Pres: Mr Sabah Al-Faysal
Sec: Mr Manhal J Kubba

IRELAND – IRL (1895) (Votes 3)

Tennis Ireland Argyle Square Donnybrook Dublin 4
T (353) 1 6681841
FAX (353) 1 6683411
Pres: Mr Ciaran O'Donovan
Sec: Mr Frank Goodman

ISRAEL – ISR (1946) (Votes 3)

Israel Tennis Association Hashmonaim Tower
100 Hashmoniam St Tel Aviv
T (972) 3 562 7564/5
FAX (972) 3 562 8276
Chairman: Mr David Harnik
Sec: Mr Yair Engel

ITALY – ITA (1910) (Votes 9)

Federazione Italiana Tennis Viale Tiziano 70
00196 Rome
T (39) 6 3685 8106/8402/8218
FAX (39) 6 3685 8166
Pres: Mr Paolo Galgani **Sec:** Mr Claudio Santini

JAMAICA – JAM (Votes 1)

Jamaica Lawn Tennis Association
2A Piccadilly Road PO Box 175 Kingston 5
T (1-809) 929 5878
FAX (1-809) 927 9436 (Pres)
Pres: Mr Ken Morgan **Sec:** Ms Joycelin Morgan

JAPAN – JPN (1922) **(Votes 9)**

Japan Tennis Association c/o Kishi Memorial Hall
1-1-1 Jinnan Shibuya-ku Tokyo 150
T (81) 3 3481 2321 **FAX** (81) 3 3467 5192
Pres: Mr Kiichiro Nakamuta
Sec: Mr Shin-Ichi Shimizu

JORDAN – JOR (1980) **(Votes 1)**

Jordan Tennis Federation PO Box 961046 Amman
T/FAX (962) 6 682 796
Pres: Mr Abdullah Al-Khalil **Sec:** Mr Ziad Al-Turk

KAZAKHSTAN – KZK (1991) **(Votes 1)**

Tennis Federation of the Republic of Kazakhstan
Central Sports Club of the Army
480051 Almaty, Republic of Kazakhstan
T (7 3272) 64 04 69/64 16 21
FAX (7 3272) 64 04 69/47 89 71
Pres Mr Pavel Novikov **Sec:** Mr Valery Kovalev

KENYA – KEN (1922) **(Votes 1)**

Kenya Lawn Tennis Association
PO Box 43l84 Nairobi
T (254) 2 558905/543049
FAX (254) 2 725672
Pres: Mr James Kenani
Gen Sec: Mr Patrick Gichira

KOREA, REPUBLIC OF – KOR (1945) **(Votes 5)**

Korea Tennis Association
Room 108 Olympic Gym No 2 88-2 Oryun-dong
Songpa-gu Seoul 138-678
T (82) 2 420 4285/6
FAX (82) 2 420 4284
Pres: Mr Doo-Hwan Kim
Sec: Mr Yeoung-Moo Huh

KUWAIT – KUW (1967) **(Votes 1)**

Kuwait Tennis Federation
PO Box 1462 Hawalli 32015
T (965) 539 7260/539 7261
FAX (965) 539 0617
Pres: Sheik Ahmed Al-Sabah
Sec: Mr Abdul-Ridha Ghareeb

LATVIA – LAT (1928) **(Votes 1)**

Latvian Tennis Union Oskara Kalpaka pr. 16
LV 2010 Jurmala
T (371) 2 752121 **FAX** (371) 789 2750
Pres: Mr Ivars Godmanis **Sec:** Mr Janis Pliens

LEBANON – LIB (1945) **(Votes 1)**

Fédération Libanaise de Tennis PO Box Il-261 Beirut
T (961) 1 425 872/873/530/157
(attn: Mr E A Yazbeck)
FAX (961) 426 233 or via New York (212) 478 2119
Pres: Mr Riad Haddad **Sec:** Mr Nohad V Schoucair

LIECHTENSTEIN – LIE (1968) **(Votes 1)**

Liechtensteiner Tennisverband
Heiligkreuz 28 9490 Vaduz
T (41) 75 392 1188/232 9531
FAX (41) 75 392 1192
Pres: Mr Joseph Schweiger
Sec: Mr Werner Schächle

LITHUANIA – LTU **(Votes 1)**

Lithuanian Tennis Union
Sausio 13 str 2 2050 Vilnius
T (3702) 659229 or (Pres) 70 52 80
FAX (3702) 26 93 41
Pres: Mr Vytautas Lapinskas
Sec: Mr Romas Kachanauskas

LUXEMBOURG – LUX (1946) **(Votes 1)**

Fédération Luxembourgeoise de Tennis
Boîte Postale 134 L 4002 Esch-sur-Alzette
T (352) 57 44 70 **FAX** (352) 57 44 73
Pres: Mr Paul Hemlinger **Gen Sec:** Mr Erny Betzen

FORMER YUGOSLAV REPUBLIC OF MACEDONIA – MKD (1993) **(Votes 1)**

FYR Macedonian Tennis Association
91000 Skopje Gradski Park 88
T (389 91) 117 271/116 387/117 394
FAX (389 91) 116 146/117 435/127 172
Pres: Mr George Gurkovic
Sec: Miss Marija Gavrilovska

MADAGASCAR – MAD (1979) **(Votes 1)**

Fédération Malagasy de Tennis
BP 8410-101 Tsaralalana Antananarivo
T (261) 20 22 351 62 **FAX** (261) 20 22 338 06
Pres: Mr Serge Ramiandrasoa
Sec: Dr Serge Andriamampandry

MALAYSIA – MAS (1921) **(Votes 1)**

Lawn Tennis Association of Malaysia
c/o National Tennis Centre Jalan Duta
50480 Kuala Lumpur Malaysia
T (60) 3 651 2377/8050
FAX (60) 3 651 8070
Pres: Mr Abdul Ghafar Baba
All correspondence to be sent to:
Mr Akbar Baba

MALTA – MLT (1966) **(Votes 1)**

Malta Tennis Federation PO Box 50
Sliema Post Office Sliema
T (356) 312945 (Pres)/330363 (Sec)
FAX (356) 331259 (Pres)/345330 (Sec)
E-MAIL mtfinfo@keyworld.net
Pres: Dr L Farrugia Sacco
Gen Sec: Mr Michael J Borg Cardona

MEXICO – MEX (1952) **(Votes 7)**

Federación Mexicana de Tenis
Miguel Angel de Quevedo 953
Mexico City 04330 DF
T (52) 5 689 9733
FAX (52) 5 689 6307/549 1956
E-MAIL fmtoptan@mail.internet.com.mx
WEB SITE http://www.internet.com.mx/fmt
Pres: Mr Alejando Hernandez
Sec: Mr Manuel Moctezumam

MOLDOVA – MDA (1953) **(Votes 1)**

Tennis Federation of the Republic of Moldova
202 Bulevardul Stefan Cel Mare Chisinau 2050
T/FAX (3732) 638 888
Pres: Mr Grigorii Kushnir **Sec:** Mr Slavian Gutu

MONACO – MON (1927) **(Votes 1)**

Fédération Monegasque de Lawn Tennis
27 Boulevard de Belgique 98000 Monaco
T (377 93) 25 55 74 **FAX** (377 93) 30 54 82
Pres: Mrs Elisabeth de Massy **Sec:** Mr Bernard Noat

MOROCCO – MAR (1957) **(Votes 3)**

Fédération Royale Marocaine de Tennis
Parc de la Ligue Arabe B P 15794 Casablanca
T (212) 2 981266/981262 **FAX** (212) 2 981 265
Pres: Mr Mohamed M'Jid
Sec: Mr Hachem Kacimi My

NETHERLANDS – NED (1899) **(Votes 9)**

Koninklijke Nederlandse Lawn Tennis Bond
PO Box 107 1200 AC Hilversum
T (31) 35 62 64 100 **FAX** (31) 35 62 40 760
Pres: Mr Ruurd de Boer **Sec:** Mr Tames Kokke

NETHERLANDS ANTILLES – AHO (1941) **(Votes 1)**

Netherlands Antilles Tennis Association
Louise de Colignylaan 18 PO Box 3571 Curacao
T (599) 9 7373192/8681774
FAX (599) 9 7369100/8681774
Pres: Mr Maximo Rufino Paula
Sec: Mr Hilberto Thomas

NEW ZEALAND – NZL (1886) **(Votes 7)**

New Zealand Tennis Inc PO Box 11-541
Manners Street Wellington
T (64) 4 4731115 **FAX** (64) 4 4712152
Chairman: Mr Ian D Wells
Sec: Mrs Christine Burr

NIGERIA – NGR (1927) **(Votes 3)**

Nigeria Tennis Federation
National Stadium Surulere PO Box 145 Lagos
T (234) 1 264 6443/4 **FAX** (234) 1 264 6444
or 1 960165 (Pres)
Chairman: Mr Chuka Momah
Sec: Mrs Hauwa-Kulu Akinyemi

NORWAY – NOR (1909) **(Votes 3)**

Norges Tennisforbund Haslevangen 33
PO Box 287 0511 Oslo
T (47) 2 265 7550 **FAX** (47) 2 264 6409
Pres: Mr Jarl Whist
Sec: Mr Jon-Erik Ross

OMAN – OMA (1986) **(Votes 1)**

Oman Tennis Association PO Box 2226 Ruwi
Postal Code 112 Sultanate of Oman
T (968) 751402 **FAX** (968) 751394
Pres: Mr Rashad Mohammed Al Zubair
Vice Pres: Mr Abdulla Mohammed Al Saeedi
Sec: Mr Mohamed Salim Khawwar

PAKISTAN – PAK (1947) **(Votes 3)**

Pakistan Tennis Federation
39-A Jinnah Stadium Pakistan Sports Complex
Kashmir Highway Islamabad
T (92) 51 921 2846/920 2410/13 ext 727
FAX (92) 51 921 2846
Pres: Mr Anwar Saifullah Khan
Sec: Mr Mohammad Ali Akbar

PANAMA, REPUBLIC OF – PAN **(Votes 1)**

Federación Panameña de Tenis
Apartado 6-4965 El Dorado
T (507) 232 5120 **FAX** (507) 232 6841
Pres: Mrs Norma Maduro
Vice Pres: Mrs Yolanda Varela
Sec: Mr Rogelio Valenzuela

PARAGUAY – PAR (1920) **(Votes 3)**

Asociación Paraguaya de Tenis Casilla de Correo 26
Av Colon 1054 1st Floor Asunción
T (595) 21 503 921 **FAX** (595) 21 503 721
Pres: Mr Miguel Carrizosa
Sec: Mrs Esther Tami

PERU – PER (1930) **(Votes 3)**

Federación de Tenis del Peru
Cercado Campo de Marte s/n
Casilla Nro 11-0488 Lima 11
T (51) 14 249979 **FAX** (51) 14 320201
Pres: Ing. Alfredo Acuña
Sec: Sr. Julio Chang

PHILIPPINES – PHI (1946) **(Votes 3)**

All correspondence to be addressed to:
Mr Nilo Natividad (Coordinator)
Philippine Tennis Association
Rizal Memorial Sports Complex
Pablo Ocampo Sr. Street Manila
T (63) 2 525 6415/6434/2016 **FAX** (63) 2 522 0229
Pres: Col Salvador H Andrada
Sec: Mr Romeo Magat

POLAND – POL (1921) **(Votes 3)**

Polski Zwiazek Tenisowy
ul. Marszalkowska 2 3rd Floor 00 – 581 Warsaw
T (48) 22 621 8101/22 229 2621
FAX (48) 22 621 8001
Pres: Mr Jacek Durski **Sec:** Ms Regina Sokolowska
Address all correspondence to Mr Wojclech Radomski

PORTUGAL – POR (1925) **(Votes 3)**

Federaçao Portuguesa de Tenis
Estadio Nacional Apartado 210
2796 Linda-a-Velha Codex Portugal
T (351) 1 4151356/4151394
FAX (351) 1 414 1520
Pres: Dr Paulo Andrade
Sec: Mr José Costa

PUERTO RICO – PUR (1959) **(Votes 1)**

Puerto Rico Tennis Association PO Box 40456
Minillas Sta Santurce PR 00940
T (1 787) 724 7782 **FAX** (1 787) 724 7990
Pres: Mr Carlos Garcia Rullán
Sec: Dr Jaime Ariza

QATAR – QAT (1984) **(Votes 1)**

Qatar Tennis and Squash Federation
PO Box 4959 Doha
T (974) 409666/409612/832991
FAX (974) 832990
Pres: Mr Ali Hussein Al Fardan
Sec: Mr Mohammad Ismail Moh'd Noor

ROMANIA – ROM (1929) (Votes 1)

Federatia Romana de Tennis
Str Vasile Conta 16 70139 Bucharest
T (40) 1 2117824 **FAX** (40) 1 2107599
Pres: Mr Ilie Nastase **Sec:** Prof Lucian Vasiliu

RUSSIA – RUS (1975) (Votes 5)

All Russia Tennis Association Lutzhnetskaya nab 8
119871 Moscow
T (7) 095 201 1095/1249
FAX (7) 095 201 0362
Pres: Mr Yaroslav Kalagursky
Vice Pres: Mr Alexander Kalivod

ST LUCIA – (LCA) (Votes 1)

St Lucia Lawn Tennis Association
PO Box 126 Castries Saint Lucia West Indies
T (785) 450 0106/9277/0551
FAX (785) 450 9277/0281
Pres: Mr John Easter
Sec: Ms Jane Duboulay

SAN MARINO – SMR (1956) (Votes 1)

Federazione Sammarinese Tennis
Casella Postale no 2 Dogana 47031
Republic of San Marino
T (378) 990578 **FAX** (378) 990584
or 901817 (Pres)
Pres: Mr Remo Raimondi
Sec: Mr Christian Forcellini

SAUDI ARABIA – KSA (1956) (Votes 1)

Saudi Arabian Tennis Federation
PO Box 29454 Riyadh 11457
T (966) 1 482 0188 **FAX** (966) 1 482 2829
Pres: Mr Abdulaziz S Kridis
Sec: Mr Mohamed Al Sheikh

SENEGAL – SEN (1960) (Votes 1)

Fédération Sénégalaise de Tennis
Tennis Club de Dakar BP 510 Dakar
T/FAX (221) 820 3269
Pres: Mr Diagna N'diaye
Sec: Mr Jean Jacques Ntab

SINGAPORE – SIN (1928) (Votes 1)

Singapore Lawn Tennis Association
93 Hougang Ave 4 Hougang Sports Hall
Singapore 538832
T (65) 386 9492 **FAX** (65) 386 9489
Pres: Mr Andy Choi
Hon Sec: Mr S. Uthrapathy

SLOVAKIA – SVK (1968) (Votes 3)

Slovak Tennis Association Junacka 6
832 80 Bratislava Slovak Republic
T (421) 7 5049197/5049262/5049134 (Sec)
FAX (421) 7 5049533/5049524
Pres: Mr Peter Malovec **Sec:** Mr Lubomir Palenik

SLOVENIA – SLO (1946) (Votes 1)

Slovene Tennis Association Vurnikova 2/VI
61000 Ljubljana Slovenia
T (386) 61 133 7170
FAX (386) 61 133 4281/62 227 362
Pres: Mr Goran Ivkovic **Sec:** Mr Fredi Reicher

SOUTH AFRICA – RSA (1991) (Votes 9)

South African Tennis Association PO Box 15978
Doornfontein Johannesburg 2028
T (27) 11 402 3616 **FAX** (27) 11 402 0242
Pres: Mr Terry Rosenberg
Chairman: Mr Gordon Forbes
Vice Chairman: Mr Stan Gumede
Gen Manager: Mr Hardie Botha

SPAIN – ESP (1901) (Votes 9)

Real Federación Española de Tenis
Avda Diagonal 618 3 D 08021 Barcelona
T (34) 3 2005355/2010844/2005878/2015586
FAX (34) 3 2021279
Pres: Mr Agustin Pujol Niubo
Sec: Mr Tomas Garcia Balmaseda

SRI LANKA – SRI (1915) (Votes 1)

Sri Lanka Tennis Association
45 Sir Marcus Fernando Mawatha Colombo 7
T (94) 1 686174 **FAX** (94) 1 580721/502561
E-MAIL naro@sri.lanka.net
Pres: Mr N M Udeshi **Sec:** Mr N A Bandaranaike

SUDAN – SUD (1956) (Votes 1)

Sudan Lawn Tennis Association
PO Box 3792 Khartoum
T (249) 11 70081/781818
Chairman: Mr Hassab El Rosoul
Sec: Mr Nour Eldine Elsadig

SWEDEN – SWE (1906) (Votes 9)

The Swedish Tennis Association PO Box 27915
S-115 94 Stockholm Sweden
T (46) 8 667 9770 **FAX** (46) 8 664 6606
Pres: Mr Jan Francke
Gen Sec: Mr Anders Wetterberg

SWITZERLAND – SUI (1896) (Votes 7)

Swiss Tennis Solothurnstrasse 112
Postfach 2501 Biel-Bienne
T (41) 32 344 0707 **FAX** (41) 32 344 0700
Pres:: Mrs Christine Ungricht
Managing Dir: Mr Geri Staudenmann

SYRIAN ARAB REPUBLIC – SYR (1953) (Votes 1)

Syrian Arab Tennis Federation PO Box 967, 421
Baramke Damascus
T (963) 11 212 5026/34/52 **FAX** (963) 11 212 3346
Pres: Mr Ahmad Hamod **Sec:** Mr Fayez Masalkhi

TAJIKISTAN – TJK (1992) (Votes 1)

National Tennis Federation of the Republic of
Tajikistan Tennis Palace a/b 308 Dushanbe 734001
T (7 3772) 360962 **FAX** (7 3772) 360606/217815
Pres: Mr Amircul Azimov
Sec: Mr Ludmila Layshenko

THAILAND – THA (1927) (Votes 1)

The Lawn Tennis Association of Thailand
Sport Authority of Thailand
Hua Mark Bangkok 10204
T (66) 2 319 0484/308 2020
FAX (66) 2 319 5868/308 2990
Pres: Gen Akaradej Sasiprapha
Sec: Mr Pichai Pantrakul

TOGO – TOG (1955) (Votes 1)

Fédération Togolaise de Tennis B P 12720 Lome
T (228) 274353 (Pres)/215181 (Sec)
FAX (228) 220272 (Pres) 222397 (Sec)
Pres: Mr Kouassi Luc Dofontien
Sec: Mr Koffi Galokpo

TRINIDAD AND TOBAGO – TRI (1951) (Votes 1)

The Tennis Association of Trinidad and Tobago
21 Taylor Street Woodbrook Port of Spain Trinidad
T (839) 625 3939 (Sec)/658 0672 (Pres)
FAX (839) 625 3939
Pres: Mr Earle James **Sec:** Ms Sadie Robarts

TUNISIA – TUN (1954) (Votes 1)

Fédération Tunisienne de Tennis
BP 350 El Menzah 1004 Tunis
T (216) 1 844144/798844 **FAX** (216) 1 798844
Pres: Mr Moncef Belkhodja
Sec: Mr Jaleledinne Ayari

TURKEY – TUR (1923) (Votes 3)

Turkiye Tenis Federasyonu Ulus Is Hani Ankara
T (90) 312 310 7345 **FAX** (90) 312 311 2554
Pres: Mr Sadi Toker **Sec:** Mr Yenner Dogru

UGANDA – UGA (1948) (Votes 1)

Uganda Tennis Association
PO No 9825 Kampala
T (256) 41 258 183/258 174
FAX (256) 41 258188/236333
Chairman: Prof Fredrick F Ssempebwa
Sec: Mr Gideon M Karyoko

UKRAINE – UKR (1946) (Votes 1)

Ukrainian National Lawn Tennis Federation
"A/C B-2" P O Box 252001 Kiev
T (38) 044 224 8782/221 6745
FAX (38) 044 224 8782/290 4062/220 1294
Pres: Mr German Benyaminov
Sec: Mr Volodimir Gerashchenko

UNITED ARAB EMIRATES – UAE (1982) (Votes 1)

United Arab Emirates Tennis Association
PO Box 22466 Dubai
T (971) 4 690393 **FAX** (971) 4 669390
Pres: Sheikh Hasher Al-Maktoum
Sec: Mr Nasser Madani

UNITED STATES OF AMERICA – USA (1881) (Votes 12)

United States Tennis Association
70 West Red Oak Lane White Plains
New York NY 10604
T (1) 914 696 7000 **FAX** (1) 914 696 7167
Pres: Dr Harry Marmion
First Vice Pres: Mrs Julia Levering
Sec: Mr Michael Kohlhoff

US VIRGIN ISLANDS – ISV (1973)

Virgin Islands Tennis Association
PO Box 306715 St Thomas USVI 00803-6715
T (1-809) 776 1010
FAX (1-809) 775 2185
Pres: Mr Wilburt Callender
Sec: Mr Delores Stephen Rivas

URUGUAY – URU (1915) (Votes 3)

Asociacion Uruguaya de Tenis Galicia l392
CP 11.200 Montevideo
T (598) 2 901 5020/902 9391
FAX (598) 2 902 9391/1809
Pres: Sr Gilberto Saenz
Sec: Sr Elbio Arias

UZBEKISTAN – UZB (1992) (Votes 1)

Tennis Association of Republic of Uzbekistan
17B Togolok Moldo Street 720033 Bishkek
T (733 12) 21 47 56/21 88 74
FAX (733 12) 21 47 56/22 09 83
Pres: Mr Karimov Shavkat
Sec: Mr Samuk Abidov

VENEZUELA – VEN (1927) (Votes 3)

Federacion Venezolana de Tenis
Calle 'A' Santa Rosa de Lima Apartado 70539
Caracas 1070-A
T (58) 2 979 7095/2421/6523/8011
FAX (58) 2 979 2694/7462
E-MAIL fevtnis@ibmnet
Pres: Mr Fermin Perez
Sec: Mr Jose Amador Diaz

YUGOSLAVIA – YUG (1922) (Votes 3)

Tenis Savez Yugoslavije
Aleksandra Stambolishkog 26 11000 Beograd
T/FAX (381) 11 667540
Pres: Mr Radoman Bozovic
Vice Pres: Mr Zvonko Nikezic
Gen Sec: Mr Milan Smiljanic

ZAMBIA – ZAM (1975) (Votes 1)

Zambia Lawn Tennis Association
c/o Ndola Tennis Association
PO Box 70436 Ndola
T/FAX (260) 1 650 193
Pres: Mr Henry Musenge
Sec: Mr Mike Kamungu

ZIMBABWE – ZIM (1904) (Votes 1)

Tennis Association of Zimbabwe
PO Box No A575 Avondale Harare
T (263) 4 224079 (Sec – mornings only)
(263) 4 667691/665938/9 (Pres)
FAX (263) 4 224079 (Pres)
Pres: Mr Paul Chingoka
Sec: Mrs Gladys Mutyiri

Associate Members without voting rights (65)

AFGHANISTAN – AFG

Afghan Lawn Tennis Association
c/o Mr Muhammad Khalil
House No. 400 Street No. 89 Sector G-9/4
Islamabad Pakistan
T (92) 51 260987
FAX (92) 51 299756/264916
Pres: Mr Homayun Parvanta
Sec: Mr Muhammad Khalil

ALBANIA – ALB

Federata Shqiptare e Tenisit
Karttogarfike sh.a. Rruga "Siri Kodra" Tirana
T/FAX (355) 4225925
Pres: Mr Perlat Voshtina **Sec:** Mr Ilir Reci

AMERICAN SAMOA – ASA (1985)

American Samoa Tennis Ass PO Box PPB Pago Pago
American Samoa 96799
T (684) 644 5251 **FAX** (684) 644 5005
Pres: Mr Perelini Perelini
Sec: Dr Jerome Amoa

ANGOLA – ANG (1983)

Federaçao Angolana de Ténis Cidadeia Desportive
PO Box 3677 Luanda
T (244) 2 350961/337884
FAX (244) 2 332388/350961
Pres: Mr Luis da Rosa Lopes
Sec: Mr Costantino Miguel da Costa

ARUBA – ARU (1954)

Aruba Lawn Tennis Bond Fergusonstraat nr 40-A
PO Box 1151 Oranjestad Aruba
Netherlands Antilles
T (297) 8 59310 **FAX** (297) 8 34570
Pres: Mr Lucas (Arie) Rasmijn
Sec: Ms Barbara Kroonenberg
Treasurer: Ms Aisha Anthony

BELIZE – BIZ (1910)

Belize Tennis Association
PO Box 365 Belize City
T (501) 2 77070 **FAX** (501) 2 75593
Pres: Mr Edward Nabil Musa
Sec: Mr Clement Usher

BHUTAN – BHU (1976)

Bhutan Tennis Federation P O Box 103 Thimphu
T (975) 2 22138 **FAX** (975) 2 23937
Pres: Mr Dasho Passang Dorji
Sec: Mr Jigme Wangmo

BRITISH VIRGIN ISLANDS – IVB (1983)

British Virgin Islands Tennis Association
PO Box 948 Road Town Tortola
T (1-809) 494 3650/494 3854(VP)/494 2526(Pres)
FAX (1-809) 494 5671/494 4245(VP)
Pres: Mr Lloyd Black
First Vice Pres: Mr Alfonso Warner
Gen Sec: Mr Clive Gumbs

BURKINA FASO – BUR (1970)

Fédération Burkinabe de Tennis
01 B P 6457 Ouagadougou 01
T (226) 31 27 33/31 33 40 **FAX** (226) 31 10 29
Pres: Mr Zambo Martin Zongo
Sec: Mr Andre Batiana

BURUNDI – BDI (1993)

Fédération de Tennis du Burundi
PO Box 2221 Bujumbura
T (257) 227214/224890
FAX (257) 220900/228559
Pres: Mr Tharcisse Rufyikiri
Sec: Mrs Dominique Niyonizigiye

CAMBODIA – CAM

The Tennis Federation of Cambodia
PO Box 101 Phnom Penh
T/FAX (855) 233 62578
Pres: Mr Cham Prasidh
Vice Pres: Mr Om Radsady
Sec: Mme Chan Sarin

CAPE VERDE – CPV (1986)

Federacao Cabo-Verdiana de Tenis
Ministerio da Informacao Cultura e Desportos
Rua 5 de Julho Praia
T (238) 613309 **FAX** (238) 611362
Pres: Mr Antero Barros **Sec:** Mr Antonio Ferreira

CAYMAN ISLANDS – CAY (1973)

Tennis Federation of the Cayman Islands
PO Box 219 GT Grand Cayman Cayman Islands
British West Indies
T (1-809) 949 7000 **FAX** (1-809) 949 8154
Pres: Mr Chris Johnson
Sec: Mr John Smith

CENTRAL AFRICAN REPUBLIC – CAF (1990)

Fédération Centrafricaine de Tennis BP 804 Bangui
République Centrafricaine (RCA)
T (236) 61 18 05/61 18 10 **FAX** (236) 61 56 60
Pres: Mr I Kamach **Sec:** Ms Jean Ombi

COMORES – COM (1985)

Fédération Comorienne de Tennis
BP 701 Moroni Comores
T (269) 73 21 13/73 26 48
FAX (269) 73 18 01/73 31 66
Pres: Mr Ali Youssouf Ali
Sec: Mr Youssouf Ahamada

CONGO, DEMOCRATIC REPUBLIC OF THE – ZAI (1984)

Fédération Congolaise Démocratique de Lawn
Tennis BP 20750 Kin 15 Kinshasa
President's Mail:
17 Chaussée de la Hulpe
Boite No 3 1170 Brussels Belgium
T (243) 881 0013 or via New York (212) 376 9291
FAX via New York (212) 376 9291
Pres: Mr Kanyama Mishindu
Sec: Mr Eleko Botuna Bo'osisa

COOK ISLANDS – COK (1947)

Tennis Cook Islands P O Box 72 Rarotonga
T (682) 22327 (Pres) 28722 (Sec)
FAX (682) 23602 (Pres) 22469 (Sec)
Pres: Mrs June Baudinet **Sec:** Ms Elizabeth Ponga

DOMINICA – DMA (1960)

Dominica Lawn Tennis Association
c/o Thomas Dorsett PO Box 1593 Roseau
Commonwealth of Dominica West Indies
T (1-809) 448 2681 **FAX** (1-809) 448 5397
Pres: Mr Kenny Alleyne **Sec:** Ms Lucia Stedman

EQUATORIAL GUINEA – GEQ (1992)

Equatorial Guinea Tennis Federation
PO Box 980 BN Malabo Equatorial Guinea
T (240) 9 2866 **FAX** (240) 9 3313
Pres: Mr Enrique Mercader Costa
Sec: Mr Francisco Sibita

FIJI – FIJ (1934)

Fiji Tennis Association c/o Mr Paras Naidu
PO Box 3664 Lautoka
T (679) 315988/300280 **FAX** (679) 302409
Pres: Mr Cliff Benson **Sec:** Mr Paras Naidu

GABON – GAB (1988)

Fédération Gabonaise de Tennis
PO Box 4241 Libreville
T (241) 724707/767004(Sec)/778971(Pres)
FAX (241) 70 31 90
Pres: Mr Samuel Minko Mi Ndong
Sec: Mr Jean-Bernard Romporouet

GAMBIA – GAM (1938)

Gambia Tennis Association PMB 664 Sere-Kunda
T (220) 495834 **FAX** (220) 496270
Pres: Mr Charles Thomas
Sec: Mr Geoffrey M Renner

GRENADA – GRN (1973)

Grenada Lawn Tennis Association
PO Box 514 St George's
T (1-809) 440 3343/0801 (Pres)
FAX (1-809) 440 3010
Pres: Mr Ken Aberdeen **Sec:** Mr Wayne Murray

GUAM – GUM (1973)

Tennis Association of Guam
PO Box 21809 GMF Guam 96921
T/FAX (67l) 475 4662
Pres: Mr Torgun Smith **Sec:** Mr Rick Ninete

GUINEE CONAKRY – GUI (1980)

Fédération Guinéenne de Tennis BP 4897
T (224) 444019/445041 **FAX** (224) 411926
Pres: Mme Magass-Malado Diallo
Sec: Mr Baba Bayo

GUYANA – GUY (1933)

Guyana Lawn Tennis Association
PO Box 10205 Georgetown
T (592) 2 66704 (Pres)(592) 2 58221 (Sec)
FAX (592) 2 68940/57362
Pres: Mr Wilfred A Lee
Sec: Mr Lionel Kandasammy

KIRIBATI – (1979)

Kiribati Tennis Association
PO Box 325 Bikenibeu Tarawa
T (686) 28071 **FAX** (686) 28202
Pres: Mr Peter Itibita

KOREA, DEMOCRATIC PEOPLE'S REPUBLIC – PRK (1945)

Tennis Association of the Democratic People's Rep of Korea
Munsin-Dong Dongdaewon Dist Pyongyang
T (82) 62386/63998/73198/22386/23998
FAX (850) 2381 4403
Pres: Mr Kim Ju Yong **Sec:** Mr Li Won Gun

KYRGYZSTAN – KGZ (1992)

Kyrgyzstan Tennis Federation
17B Togolok Moldo Street 720033 Bishkek
T (733 12) 214756/218874
FAX (733 12) 214756/220983
Pres: Mr Nikolai Tanaev **Sec:** Mr Valentin Akinishin

LESOTHO – LES (1920)

Lesotho Lawn Tennis Association
PO Box 156 Maseru 100
T c/o (266) 317340/314281 **FAX** c/o (266) 310047
Pres: Mr P M Morolong
Sec: Mr Clement M Nots'i

LIBERIA – LBR (1987)

Liberia Tennis Association
PO Box 1742 1000 Monrovia
T (231) 226639 **FAX** (231) 226101
Pres: Mr S Wogah Snyder **Vice Pres:** Mr Mohammed Nanou **Sec:** Mr Jeffery Harmon

LIBYA – LBA

Libyan Amateur Tennis Federation
Physical Education Faculty Al-Fatah University
PO Box 13118 Tripoli Jamahiriya
T (218) 21 441274 **FAX** (218) 21 4441424
Pres: Mrs Amal Abdulla Tumi
Sec: Mr Almonder Omran Altunsi

MALAWI – MAW (1966)

Lawn Tennis Association of Malawi
PO Box 1417 Blantyre
T (265) 623670/620144 (Pres) 622959 (Sec)
FAX (265) 620549
Chairman: Mr Hugh C King **Sec:** Mrs Joan Fenton

MALDIVES – MDV (1983)

Tennis Association of the Maldives
PO Box 20175 Male Republic of Maldives
T (960) 317018 **FAX** (960) 310325
Chairman: Mr Ahmed Aslam
Sec: Mr Abdul Rasheed

MALI – MLI (1963)

Fédération Malienne de Tennis
via Ministère des Relations Extérieures Koulouba
T (223) 226740 (Sec) 226329 (VP)
FAX (223) 225226 (Sec)/225085/224250 (VP)
Pres: Mr Siaka Sangaré
Vice Pres: Mme Bah Youmahané
Sec: Mr Amedine Traore